THE
HEBREW SCRIPTURES

Don't say I never gave you anything !!

J.S.

TH[...]
HEBREW S[...]

Rick,

Thank you for being such an important part of my journey. I pray this helps you love the OT even more

Blessings

Joshua Stewart

McGahan

MᴄGᴀʜᴀɴ Pᴜʙʟɪsʜɪɴɢ Hᴏᴜsᴇ | Lʏɴᴄʜʙᴜʀɢ, Tᴇɴɴᴇssᴇᴇ
www.mphbooks.com
Requests for information should be sent to:
info@mphbooks.com

ISBN 978-1-951252-14-4 (Hardcover)
ISBN 978-1-951252-15-1 (EPUB)

Lɪʙʀᴀʀʏ ᴏғ Cᴏɴɢʀᴇss Cᴏɴᴛʀᴏʟ Nᴜᴍʙᴇʀ: 2021944935

Contents

Contributors

General Editor

Joshua E. Stewart, PhD, Associate Professor of Old Testament and Hebrew, Luther Rice College and Seminary, Lithonia, Georgia

Associate Editors

Jeffrey G. Audirsch, PhD, Associate Professor of Biblical Studies, Leavell College, New Orleans, Louisiana

A. Lauren Brown, MDiv, Independent Scholar, Atlanta, Georgia

Authors

Joel Barker, PhD, Professor of Biblical Studies, Heritage College and Seminary, Cambridge, Ontario, Canada

Cory Barnes, PhD, Associate Professor of Old Testament and Hebrew, New Orleans Baptist Theological Seminary, New Orleans, Louisiana

Walter E. Brown, PhD, Adjunct Instructor in Christian Studies, Bryan College; Retired Professor of Old Testament and Hebrew, Bridge City, Louisiana

David Casas, PhD, Assistant Professor of Old Testament Literature, Luther Rice College and Seminary, Lithonia, Georgia

Robert Cole, PhD, Independent Scholar, Retired, North Carolina

R. Dennis Cole, PhD, Professor of Old Testament and Archaeology occupying the McFarland Chair of Archaeology, New Orleans Baptist Theological Seminary, New Orleans, Louisiana

Nancy L. deClaissé-Walford, PhD, Carolyn Ward Professor of Old Testament and Biblical Languages, Mercer University, Atlanta, Georgia

Stephen Dempster, PhD, Professor of Religious Studies, Crandall University, Moncton, New Brunswick, Canada

Jason S. DeRouchie, PhD, Research Professor of Old Testament and Biblical Theology, Midwestern Baptist Theological Seminary, Kansas City, Missouri

Archie W. England, PhD, Professor of Old Testament and Hebrew occupying the J. Wash Watts Chair of Old Testament and Hebrew, New Orleans Baptist Theological Seminary, New Orleans, Louisiana

David Firth, PhD, Tutor in Old Testament, Trinity College Bristol, Bristol, England

Jill Firth, PhD, Lecturer in Hebrew and Old Testament, Ridley College, Parkville, Australia

John Goldingay, PhD, Senior Professor of Old Testament and David Allan Hubbard Professor Emeritus of Old Testament, Fuller Theological Seminary, Pasadena, California

Ralph Hawkins, PhD, Associate Professor of Religious Studies, Averett University, Danville, Virginia

John Hobbins, MA, Lecturer in Hebrew, Davnant Institute; Pastor of Youth and Family Ministries, Zion Lutheran Church, Oshkosh, Wisconsin.

Casey Hough, PhD, Assistant Professor of Biblical Interpretation, Luther Rice College and Seminary, Lithonia, Georgia

David M. Howard, Jr., PhD, Professor of Old Testament, Bethlehem College and Seminary, Minneapolis, Minnesota; Emeritus Professor of Old Testament, Bethel Seminary

Benjamin Johnson, PhD, Associate Professor of Biblical Studies, LeTourneau University, Longview, Texas

Andrew King, PhD, Assistant Professor of Biblical Studies, Midwestern Baptist Theological Seminary, Kansas City, Missouri

Ron Lindo, Jr., PhD, Independent Scholar, Sherwood, Arkansas

Tremper Longman III, PhD, Distinguished Scholar of Biblical Studies, Westmont College, Santa Barbara, California

Russell Meek, PhD, Visiting Professor of Old Testament, William Tennent School of Theology, Littleton, Colorado

Jean P. Musavuli, MA, Lecturer of Bible and Theology, Christian Bilingual University of the Congo, Beni, Nord-Kivu, Democratic Republic of the Congo

William R. Osborne, PhD, Associate Professor of Biblical and Theological Studies, College of the Ozarks, Point Lookout, Missouri

Richard A. Purcell, PhD, Visiting Assistant Professor of Religion, Florida Southern College, Lakeland, Florida

Andrea Robinson, PhD, Independent Scholar, Associate Pastor, Building Church, Madison, Alabama

Jillian Ross, PhD, Associate Professor of Biblical Studies, Liberty University, Lynchburg, Virginia

Ryan Stokes, PhD, Associate Professor of Religion, Carson-Newman University, Jefferson City, Tennessee

Beth Stovell, PhD, Associate Professor of Old Testament, Ambrose University, Calgary, Alberta, Canada

Brent Strawn, PhD, Professor of Old Testament, Professor of Law, Duke University Divinity School, Durham, North Carolina

Myrto Theocharous, PhD, Professor of Old Testament, Greek Bible College, Athens, Greece

Preface to *The Hebrew Scriptures*

What you hold in your hand, or as a digital file, is a Bible project that is unique. *The Hebrew Scriptures* is a new way for Christians to rediscover the beauty of the Old Testament (OT). The format and presentation found within is our attempt to make the Hebrew canon accessible for the English reader. Every aspect of this volume is meant to offer a profound reading experience focusing on the literary artistry which shapes the theological message of the parts and the whole of the OT.

One of the unique features of this volume is the presentation of the text of the OT. Here we present the text differently from modern English translations. Each page consists of a single column without the hindrance of verse numbers, although we use line numbers as a means of locating specific passages. By doing this, we believe that readers will more easily recognize the literary nature of these sacred texts, and thereby see how they are shaped in such a way that their theological nature is illuminated.

This volume follows a canonical ordering of the OT books that most Christians are unfamiliar with. Herein the OT books are ordered according to the long-standing traditional Hebrew order, common in Judaism, called the Law (*Torah*), the Prophets (*Nevi'im*), and the Writings (*Ketuvim*). In a sense, we can say that by reading the OT in this order you will come nearer to reading the Scriptures of Jesus (Luke 24:44). This ordering connects the parts to the whole in a manner that follows the development of thought(s) throughout the different periods of Israel's journey. We also believe that the Hebrew order connects the OT with the New Testament (NT) in a different way than the modern English order. We do not say in a better way, rather in a different way.

The thirty-nine introductions (four major introductions and thirty-five introductions to the books) are written by OT scholars from across the globe and Christian theological traditions. Each introduction focuses on matters such as the literary shape, theological content, movement and direction of the writer, and the arrangement of the section and book within the specific canonical tradition of the Hebrew Scriptures (HS). Each contributor provides a list of resources that are beneficial for further study of each section or book of the OT. McGahan Publishing House licensed the biblical text of the CSB translation for this project, but the scholarly views expressed in the introductions are those of the contributors and do not necessarily reflect the opinions or doctrinal positions of Lifeway Christian Resources.

Since we use line numbers instead of verse numbers, a brief tutorial related to the procedure we used for references will be helpful. Traditionally one would see Gen 1:2 as a means of referencing the second verse of chapter one of the book of Genesis. However, based on the format of this volume the reference would be Gen 1.2–3 since the traditional verse reference is on both line 2 and line 3 of the first chapter of Genesis. Note the style in which a single period is used instead of the traditional colon. We understand that this will take a little time to get used to, but we believe it is necessary as you attempt to read the text in a more traditional manner (similar to every other work of literature you read). Additionally, we have decided to use the Hebrew name for God (i.e., "Yahweh") throughout the various introductions. The exception to this is within the Torah when the Hebrew uses *Elohim*; "God" is used in these cases.

For years, we have taught the OT based on its traditional Hebraic order and have longed for an English translation that does just that, so here you have it. We believe strongly that reading the HS in this order and in this presentation will facilitate a profound reading and will draw you into the journey of the Israelites as they came to learn the nature of Yahweh. We hope that you will come to a better understanding of how this strange and wonderful literature in its own unique way helps us to better know and understand God. We believe that the difficulties of the OT may be a little easier to understand as you revisit these texts and allow the introductions to function as your personal tour guide. Our purpose is to serve a broad audience, from laypeople to students and ministers; we believe this project will also be helpful to professors and scholars. We pray that through this volume you will come to better know and love the triune God.

Jeffrey G. Audirsch
A. Lauren Brown
Joshua E. Stewart

February 27, 2022
Transfiguration Sunday
Psalm 99
Luke 9:28–36

Introduction to the *Hebrew Scriptures* & Canon

Stephen Dempster

One of the little-known facts about the Bible for the average Protestant Christian is that there is quite a difference between the Old Testament read in the Church on a Sunday morning and the Bible read in the Synagogue on a Saturday morning.[1] While the two Scriptures contain exactly the same content, the books are divided differently (39 in the Church and 24 in the Synagogue). The Jewish division reduces the number by combining books to achieve the smaller number. Thus, the eight books of 1–2 Samuel (Samuel Corpus), 1–2 Kings (Kings Corpus), 1–2 Chronicles (Chronicles Corpus), and Ezra and Nehemiah become 4 books in the Hebrew Scriptures (HS) and the twelve minor prophets (Hosea–Malachi) become one book—the Book of the Twelve. This is simply a matter of cutting up the same pie into larger slices but it testifies to the original Hebrew enumeration since the division of books into two scrolls was necessitated by the use of vowels in later Greek translations which considerably utilized more scroll space than the earlier Hebrew consonantal text.

Another important difference is that the slices of the pie are arranged differently. The Christian OT has a quadripartite structure: the Law, the Historical Books, the Poetic Books, and the Prophetic Books while the HS has a tripartite structure from whence it gets its name, the TaNaK, which is an acronym for its three divisions: **Torah** (Law), **Nevi'im** (Prophets) and **Ketuvim** (Writings).[2] The two canons differ in other ways as books from the second division of the Christian Bible—Ruth, Chronicles, Ezra, Nehemiah, and Esther—are found in the third division of the HS, as are all the poetic books as well as two prophetic books, Daniel and Lamentations.

Which of these orders is the oldest and was more likely the Bible of Jesus? The Jewish list is more likely since it is easier to explain the derivation of the four-part Christian order from the tripartite Jewish order than vice versa. Moreover, in early Christian lists of the books of the OT, the books of the canon are virtually identical to those in the HS. The major difference is that of sequence with the prophets weighted towards the end in the OT of the Christian Scriptures. The order in which Malachi closes the canon as in our present English Bibles is not attested in any list until the end of the 4th century AD.

The tripartite order in Jewish Bibles is a consistent feature from the earliest of times. It is probably found in the prologue to Ben Sira where it occurs three times (Prologue, Lines: 1, 9, 24). In the literature of Second Temple Judaism and the New Testament, the collection of inspired writings,

---

1. There are minor differences with the Roman Catholic and Eastern Orthodox Bibles in that in the former there are 7 additional books with some additions to other books, (e.g. Esther and Daniel) and in the latter there are 2 additional books to the Catholic Bible.

2. The four-part structure of the Christian Bible is the same for Catholicism and Eastern Orthodoxy.

is termed variously, "The Scriptures (Mark 12:24)," "The Law and the Prophets (Matt 5:17)" or "Moses and the Prophets" (Luke 16:29). But once in the New Testament the collection is labelled "The Law of Moses, The Prophets and the Psalms" (Luke 24:44). The Psalter was a large book near the beginning of the Writings and was probably understood as representative of the entire division. There may be similar evidence in Qumran for a collection entitled, "the Law, the Prophets and David" (4QMMT 10). Within Judaism, roughly around the 2nd century AD, there is no doubt about a tripartite structure of the Hebrew Scriptures. There is even a Rabbinic list which specifies the exact order of the twenty-four books, which concludes with the Chronicles Corpus.[3]

Even Jewish lists that reduce the number of books to twenty-two probably arrive at that figure for aesthetic and theological reasons as the number matches the letters of the Hebrew alphabet.[4] Thus the canon provides the basics for theological literacy. In this order Ruth is combined with Judges and Lamentations with Jeremiah but the tripartite nature is not changed.[5] Jesus may allude to the entire canon of Scripture when he refers to the future judgment of the Jewish nation bringing down the condemnation of all the innocent blood shed from the death of Abel, the first martyr in the canon, to the death of Zechariah, the last martyr (Luke 11:49–51). This would mean all the martyrs from Genesis to Chronicles, the entire sweep of Israel's Scriptures, since the Zechariah mentioned is probably the Zechariah in 2 Chr 24.[6]

The different arrangements provide a type of interpretive lens for understanding the content. Sequence is crucial for understanding as readers understand words and sentences in a certain context, paragraphs in a deliberate arrangement, and entire books in a sequence as well. For the Protestant canon, one cannot but note that the main divisions are based on genre (law, history, poetry, and prophecy), and there is a general chronological orientation: the text starts in the past in the Law, continues in that mode through the historical books in chronological order, shifts to the present with the more timeless poetic books, and then launches into the future with the prophetic books. One could diagram the movement using an arrow whose feathered base begins in the past and whose shaft moves through the past and the present with its tip pointing to the future. The Hebrew sequence suggests that the Torah is a nucleus surrounded by the expanding circles of the Prophets and the Writings. One sees more of an ethical focus rather than an eschatological one with the Torah being

---

3. See the *baraita* in *Baba Bathra* 14b. A *baraita* is a saying of the Rabbis, dating from the first or early second century AD that was not included in the Mishna, which was compiled around 200 AD. The order in this *baraita* assumes the five books of the Torah and then provides the orders for the second two divisions: Prophets (Joshua, Judges, Samuel, Kings, Jeremiah, Ezekiel, Isaiah, the Twelve [minor prophets]); Writings (Ruth, Psalms, Job, Proverbs, Ecclesiastes, Song of Songs, Lamentations, Daniel, Esther, Ezra-Nehemiah, Chronicles). In other Jewish literature of the second century AD there are three more references to the tripartite structure: *Jerusalem Hagigah* 77b, *Sanhedrin* 90b, *Vayyiqra Rabbah* 16:4.

4. Josephus, *Against Apion*.

5. See e.g., Jerome where he describes the two different lists in terms of one tripartite structure (*Helmeted Preface to Reigns*).

6. The last prophet martyred chronologically in the Bible was Uriah (Jer 26:38–44), slain nearly 200 years later than Zechariah (2 Chr 24:36–41).

a hermeneutical hub. Jesus reinforces this with his narrower hermeneutical center of the double commandment taken from the Torah: the love of Yahweh and neighbor (Deut 6.6–7; Lev 19.23–24; Matt 22:39–40). This may be the reason why the Torah often reigns supreme in Jewish contexts, and is central for the task of repairing the world through obedience to the divine commands, while for Christians the Kingdom of God announced by the Prophets is the perfect segue for the transition to the NT.

This difference between ethics and eschatology, however, should not be overemphasized in the canonical structures. The Hebrew order, which begins with Genesis and ends with Chronicles, is organized in a way that points both to its ultimate authority as Scripture and the consequent importance of internalizing it and reflecting on it while waiting for a new revelation in the future.[7] Each of the major divisions begins with a focus on the divine word. In Gen 1 the divine word creates light and establishes the rhythm of the day and night. At or near the beginning of the second and third divisions there is the injunction to meditate on the Torah day and night and experience life and blessing (Josh 1.11–13; Ps 1.5–10). Thus, the HS stress the fundamental importance of making Yahweh's word a part of one's vision and action and one's very being.[8] The Scriptures are not just normative; they are to be transformative.

A definite eschatological component is often overlooked, even what might be considered a messianic hermeneutic. The first book, Genesis, which begins with the creation of Adam, is organized in the form of genealogies leading to the blessing of a descendant from the tribe of Judah, to whom will be the obedience of the nations (Gen 49.21–37). This is resoundingly echoed in the last book, Chronicles, which begins with the genealogy of Adam, leading up to the history of David and his line from the tribe of Judah. This evokes images from the previous story line of a Davidic ruler who will rule the world with peace and justice on the basis of the Davidic covenant. Also at the end of the first book, Joseph predicts that God will surely *visit* the Israelites in Egypt and *bring them up* out of the land (Gen 50.34–37). At the end of the last book, Cyrus announces that Yahweh has *visited* him (appointed) to enable the exiles *to go up* from Babylon to return to Jerusalem to rebuild the temple (2 Chr 36.40–45). Thus, the first book ends with a note of an anticipated exodus from Egypt and the last one ends with a similar note of exodus from Babylon. The question is left open. From which of these exiles will be the Davidic descendant to lead this new and greater exodus and rebuild the temple?

At the end of each major division in the HS, there is a pointer to the future as well. With the death of Moses at the end of Deuteronomy, it is clear that not only has the Torah been completed but that many prophets have come and gone since that time. None, however, has measured up to the stature of Moses (Deut 34.13–14). This suggests that there is the expectation of some such figure (see Deut

---

7. There were other Hebrew orders which arose, and these mainly have to do with the orders of the Writings. In the earliest complete Hebrew codex which dates to a period many centuries later (1000 AD), the Bible ends with Ezra-Nehemiah and not Chronicles. Later medieval manuscripts contain other orders but many have Chronicles at the end.

8. See the importance of the fundamental command in Judaism, the Shema: Deut 6.7–12.

18.16–17). At the end of the Prophets, in which no such prophetic figure has arisen, there is a focus on the Torah of Moses (Mal 4.7–8 [Heb 3:22]) and the future coming of Elijah (Mal 4.8–10 [Heb 3:23–24]). With the coordination of Moses and Elijah, not only is there the dual complement of the Law and the Prophets, there is the continuing look to the future for a fuller revelation of a Moses-like prophetic figure. Finally, at the end of the Writings, there is a reference to all three canonical divisions. Reference to the Babylonian exile of 70 years is also a reference to the Torah with its prediction of such judgment as a relief for Sabbath violation (Lev 23), and a reference to the Prophets as well as the length of that judgment is specified by Jeremiah (Jer 25.13–24). This reference also clearly evokes the Writings in Daniel where the titular character seeks out the meaning of Jeremiah's oracle on the judgment's length of time. Daniel is told in no uncertain terms that the seventy years is symbolic for a much larger period of time: seventy times seven! The end of this period will mark the inauguration of the Kingdom of God by a Messiah (Dan 9.1–4, 44–74). Thus, this early arrangement of the Hebrew Scriptures closes with the end of the 70 years of exile which has set the eschatological clock ticking. Israel is in exile, meditating on the Torah day and night, waiting for the dawning of the messianic age.

When the NT begins, it commences with a new Genesis, and a long genealogy from Abraham to David, from David to the exile, and from the exile to the Messiah, Jesus of Nazareth (Matt 1:1–17). The long wait is over.[9]

Suggested Resources

Beckwith, Roger T. *The Old Testament of the New Testament Church*. Grand Rapids: Eerdmans, 1985.

Dempster, Stephen G. "Canons on the Left and Canons on the Right: Finding a Resolution inthe Canon Debate." *Journal of the Evangelical Theological Society* 52 (2009): 47–77.

Gallagher, Edmond, and John Meade. *The Biblical Canon Lists from Early Christianity: Text and Analysis*. Oxford: Oxford University Press, 2017.

Leiman, Sid Z. *The Canonization of Hebrew Scripture: The Talmudic and Midrashic Evidence*. New Haven: Connecticut Academy of Arts and Sciences, 1976.

Lim, Timothy. *The Formation of the Jewish Canon*. New Haven: Yale University Press, 2013.

---

9. In later times there were many other Hebrew orders for the Writings, and some of these were clearly liturgical as the five books of the *megillot* (Ruth, Songs, Lamentations, Ecclesiastes, Esther) were combined for reading on five important festivals. In the earliest complete manuscript of the Hebrew Bible which dates from 1000 AD, the Writings begin with Chronicles and end with Ezra-Nehemiah, but it is again a liturgical order. The present Christian order became fixed with the invention of the printing press.

The Torah
(Law)

Introduction to the Torah

John Goldingay

The Torah, the Jewish name for the first five books of the Bible, comprises the first half of a narrative running from Genesis to Kings, dealing with the background to Israel's story and then the story of their beginnings. The dominant human figure in the story is Moses, who is born in the second chapter of Exodus and dies in the last chapter of Deuteronomy. But he is not as prominent in the story as Yahweh, Israel's God, who creates the world, makes plans for its future, confronts the Israelites' Egyptian overlords, gets the Israelites out of Egypt, seals a covenant with them at Mount Sinai, accompanies them towards Canaan, and reseals the covenant with them on the edge of Canaan. The Torah's framework is thus a story. The Hebrew word *torah* means instruction, and the Torah is as long as it is because it is dominated by instructions from Yahweh and Moses to the Israelites about their life.

A key characteristic of the Torah, then, is the combination of story and instruction. On one hand, the origin and basis of Yahweh's relationship with Israel lies in the action he took in creating the world, making promises to Israel's ancestors, getting the Israelites out of Egypt, and accompanying them to Canaan. On the other hand, that relationship also finds expression in his having expectations of the life Israel will live in serving him and in being faithful to one another. Israel's commitment to meeting those expectations is integral to the relationship continuing. To put the point in later theological terms, Yahweh's grace and Israel's works are both essential to the relationship. Yahweh's grace had to come first, but Israel's action had to follow.

The Torah is thus a story before it is a book of instructions about behavior. The Gospels follow its pattern. In both cases, the reason relates to a facet of Israelite faith and of Christian faith. The Torah is the beginning of a vast narrative, a metanarrative, in two senses. In origin the word narrative means a story and a metanarrative is a big overall story, the story of everything. So the Torah begins the scriptural narrative that starts with creation and takes readers through things going wrong, Yahweh's making promises to Israel's ancestors that relate to the fulfillment of his original plan, and the beginning of the promises' fulfillment. It thus envisions Israel living its life in the context of this metanarrative. Israel needs to keep reading its story in order to know how to fit into it. The Torah also suggests a metanarrative in the looser sense of a worldview, an understanding of Yahweh, the world, human beings, Israel, work, family, and so on. Here too its purpose is to enable people to live in light of a true understanding of these realities. The stories it tells thus focus on what Yahweh was doing despite, as much as through, the actions of people. The stories do not usually give people examples to follow or avoid, but illustrations of how people are and of how Yahweh relates to them.

The word *torah* was translated into European languages with words meaning "law," which is misleading. The Torah is not legalistic. It is more like a rule for life, a set of commitments that people accept as part of their relationship with Yahweh. This rule then covers a wide range of areas of life: worship, family life, marriage, sexual relations, farming, neighborly relations, war, the support of pastors, dealing with homicide, the treatment of aliens, and many others. The nature of many of these instructions shows that they are a code of law for implementation in a court. Another characteristic with this implication is that they make execution the penalty for a wide range of acts such as adultery, rebellion against parents, worshiping other gods, acting as a medium, and falsely claiming to be a virgin when getting married. Subsequent Scriptures suggest that Israel did not take these penalties literally. To say that something deserves death is a way of saying how serious a wrong it is, not to say what should actually be done to punish it. In this respect the Torah works the same way as the law books of other Middle Eastern peoples. None are designed to function like a Euro-American law book. But like a lawbook and like the stories, the Torah focuses much of the time on wrongdoing. It illustrates a point that Jesus will make, that much of it is written "for your hardness of heart." The Torah is an exposition of ideals written into creation, but also an attempt to get some order into the moral and religious turmoil of human life as it is. Jesus notes that this aim explains the relatively low level of demand it often places on people.

The Torah gives no direct information on who wrote it or when. To call it "the Torah of Moses" need not imply that Moses was its author. One of its characteristics is to cover the same ground more than once, so that (for instance): Exod 21 gives instructions for dealing with the problem of people getting into economic difficulties and having to become someone else's farmhands for a while, Lev 25 gives another, different set of instructions for dealing with the problem, and Deut 15 gives another set, and all are set in the Torah in the time before Israel is in the land and engaged in farming. The Torah also includes four sets of instructions for the annual pilgrimage festivals to be celebrated in Canaan (Exod 23; Exod 34; Lev 23; Deut 16), before they will be engaged in such a pilgrimage even once. Three times Moses instructs people not to cook a baby goat in its mother's milk (Exod 23; Exod 34; Deut 14).

It would seem odd for Yahweh to give Israel these different sets of instructions before they were even in the land of Canaan. More likely Yahweh took Israel through a process along the following lines. In connection with the beginnings of his life with them, he gave them a set of basic instructions that would suit their early years in Canaan. In due course the growth of the nation, the institution of central government, the building of the temple, and the development of urbanization necessitated instructions to fit the new situations. The Holy Spirit then guided priests, prophets, and other thinkers in developing new versions of the instructions to match the new contexts. They would also cover new issues that had not arisen earlier; for instance, Deut 13 and 18 give instructions about how to distinguish between prophets who truly speak for Yahweh and prophets who do not. The instructions in Exod 19–24 and 32–34 fit the earlier stage of Israel's story, while Leviticus and Deuteronomy fit the time between the establishment of Jerusalem as Israel's capital and the building of the temple (about 1000 BC and just after), and the destruction of Jerusalem and the temple (587 BC). The usual scholarly view is they belong later rather than earlier in that time period, and their finalizing to a time after 587 BC. Referring to the entire Torah as coming from Moses could recognize him as the fountainhead of this process, acknowledge it as the kind of thing he would say in a later context, and declare that it has his authority.

Similar considerations arise in connection with the story of Israel. Genesis gives two accounts of creation, of the reasons for the flood, of Yahweh making a covenant with Abraham, of the naming of Beersheba and of Bethel, and so on. And sometimes the stories speak in terms that suggest a later time than Moses or David: for instance, they refer to "Ur of the Chaldeans," who were in Ur later, but not in that earlier time. Further, one can construct two sets of stories out of the doublings, so that they comprise two versions of the story as a whole. So, it looks as if there was more than one version of Israel's story, as there will be several versions of Jesus's story in the Gospels. The usual scholarly view is that the form of the stories as we know them belongs later rather than earlier in the time between David and the fall of Jerusalem and that they reached the form in which we know them sometime after 587 BC. Ezra's bringing the Torah scroll from Babylon (Ezra 7) may then mark its having been completed there. Another way in which the Gospels will correspond to the Torah is that the differences between versions of the stories show that the stories aim to do more than give a purely factual account of the events they relate to. They often tell a story in a way that shows its significance for people who will be hearing it in later contexts. They are thus more like a movie "based on fact" than like the news that purports to give people the bare facts. Part of the Holy Spirit's inspiration of the stories, then, is to show how they are significant for people in their living context.

The five books constitute a continuous narrative, and the divisions between them are in part made for convenience. In other words, each book is only semi-complete on its own. One could compare it with a series of a television drama. It looks as if one consideration in making the divisions was a desire to make the five books reasonably similar in length. If one sets aside that consideration, then the Torah outlines as follows.

Outline

1. Yahweh creates the world and blesses it (Gen 1–11)

2. Yahweh makes promises to Israel's ancestors and begins to fulfil them (Gen 12–50)

3. Through Moses, Yahweh gets the Israelites out from Egypt and leads them to Mount Sinai (Exod 1–18)

4. Through Moses, Yahweh gives the Israelites instructions at Mount Sinai, and they build a sanctuary (Exod 19.1–Num 10.14)

5. Through Moses, Yahweh leads the Israelites to the edge of Canaan (Num 10.15–36.23)

6. On Yahweh's behalf, Moses gives a final set of instructions to Israel and dies (Deut 1–34)

Suggested Resources

Briggs, Richard S., and Joel N. Lohr, eds. *A Theological Introduction to the Pentateuch*. Grand Rapids: Baker Academic, 2012.

Fretheim, Terence E. *The Pentateuch*. Nashville: Abingdon, 1996.

Goldingay, John. *An Introduction to the Old Testament*. Downers Grove, IL: InterVarsity Press, 2015.

Kaminsky, Joel S., and Joel N. Lohr. *The Torah*. Oxford: Oneworld, 2011.

Wenham, Gordon J. *Exploring the Old Testament: A Guide to the Pentateuch*. Downers Grove, IL: InterVarsity Press, 2003.

Introduction to Genesis

John Hobbins

The title "Genesis" comes from the Greek translation of *geneseōs*, which means "generations/origins," found in Gen 2.5. The Hebrew name of the book, *Bereshith*, means "in the beginning" and is derived from the first word in the HS as well as the book itself.

The book consists of a chain of narratives organized by the theme of generations. The complexity of the book, both cosmologically and historically, is traced back to protological agents and events. Although written as a narrative, the book contains vivid, terse dialogues fraught with world-changing consequences.

Genesis begins with the creation of the cosmos, its manifold destabilization by human and angelic initiative, and its restabilization by sovereign divine choice (Gen 1–11). Yahweh elects one family, that of Abraham, and perseveres in that election over four generations through cycles of conflict, betrayal, and reconciliation (Gen 12–50).

In Gen 1–3, the creator God sets events in motion, but his purposes are often thwarted and his commands contravened. The provision of a habitat (i.e., Eden) is given, taken away, and re-promised (Gen 1–3; 6–9; 12–50). Throughout the narrative, the gift of continuation is repeatedly threatened but never withdrawn (Gen 3; 4; 22–50).

The God of Genesis is filled with solicitude for everything he creates. He fashions a woman for the first man and brings her to him (2.30–31). The couple forfeit their inheritance in paradise but before they depart, he makes them garments of skin and clothes them (3.50–51). Yahweh mitigates the punishment he foreordained should they not listen; rather than end their lives then and there, Yahweh chooses to exile them (3.52–53). Soon after, Cain kills his brother Abel, but Yahweh does not have him killed in return; Cain is compelled to wander instead (4.21–22).

The narrative transitions when Yahweh gives Abram the divine imperative to leave everything and head for an unfamiliar destination (12.1–5). The first patriarch is commanded to "walk in my presence and be blameless" (17.1–2) and he is given the promise of a place of one's own and a continuation in his posterity (Gen 12–13; 15–17; 22)—the imperatives and promises are of more than historical interest. The imperatives remain in force down to the day in which the text's readers accept them for themselves.

The book's emphasis on cosmology, the divine-human relationship, family, and society is fraught with truth claims of the highest order. The promises to Noah (Gen 9) and Abraham (Gen 17) remain Yahweh's to keep. The promise that in Abraham all the nations will be blessed is given along with the command to go to "the land that I will show you" (12.1–27). The struggle between Yahweh and humanity is taken to extreme lengths in several places: the failed intercession of Abraham on behalf of Sodom and Gomorrah (Gen 18–19); the test of Abraham in which he must offer up the life of his son (Gen 22); and Jacob's one-on-one combat with a divine being (Gen 32).

Vendettas and chicanery are commonplace: Cain kills Abel (Gen 4); Noah curses part of his posterity (Gen 9); Abram and Sarai banish Hagar and Ishmael (Gen 21); Jacob tricks his brother Esau and his father Isaac; Laban tricks Jacob (Gen 25–32); and Jacob's elder sons rid themselves of favored Joseph by selling him into slavery (Gen 37–50). The narrative contains complex, flawed personalities of the first order, among them Abraham, Isaac, and Jacob. Strong, contentious women play key roles, among them Sarah (Gen 21) and Tamar (Gen 38).

The narrative high points include Yahweh's provision of an heir, Isaac, to Abraham and Sarah (Gen 21). Additionally, Yahweh provides a substitute sacrifice in lieu of Isaac (Gen 22) and Jacob reconciles his relationship with Esau (Gen 33). Similarly, Joseph reconciles his relationship with his brothers (Gen 45).

Everyone has their own agenda in the book of Genesis. Yahweh plays off one human agenda against another; in the process, the first is made last and the last is made first, and healing takes the place of brokenness. The narrative is generative and paves the way for all that follows in the continuation of the Primary History, from Exodus to the Kings Corpus and beyond.

Outline

1. A primeval history (1.1–11.32)
    a. The two creation accounts (1.1–2.37)
    b. The fall of Adam and Eve (3.1–56)
    c. Cain and Abel and the genealogy of Adam to Noah (4.1–5.27)
    d. The mighty flood and Yahweh's provision through Noah and his descendants (6.1–10.34)
    e. The Tower of Babel narrative (11.1–32)

2. A cycle of narratives centered around the forefathers and foremothers of Israel: Abraham and Sarah, Isaac and Rebekah, and Jacob, Leah, and Rachel (12.1–36.92)
    a. The Abraham and Sarah narrative (12.1–23.26; 25.1–41)
    b. The Isaanic narrative (24.1–104; 26.1–27.90)
    c. The Jacob and Esau narrative (28.1–36.92)

3. The Joseph story (37.1–50.38)
    a. Joseph's dream and subsequent misfortune (37.1–59)
    b. The interruption of the Judah narrative (38.1–51)
    c. Joseph in Egypt (39.1–50.38)

Suggested Resources

Atkinson, David. *The Message of Genesis 1–11*. The Bible Speaks Today Series. Downers Grove, IL: InterVarsity Press, 1990.

Baldwin, Joyce G. *The Message of Genesis 12–50*. The Bible Speaks Today Series. Downers Grove, IL: InterVarsity Press, 1986.

Kidner, Derek. *Genesis: An Introduction and Commentary*. Tyndale Old Testament Commentaries. London: Tyndale Press, 1976.

Sarna, Nahum M. *Genesis*. Jewish Publication Society Torah Commentary. Philadelphia: Jewish Publication Society, 1989.

Von Rad, Gerhard. *Genesis*. Old Testament Library. Rev. ed. London: SCM. 1963.

Walton, John. *Genesis*. NIV Application Commentary. Grand Rapids: Zondervan, 2001.

Westermann, Claus. *Genesis 1–11*. Continental Commentary. Minneapolis: Fortress, 1994.

————. *Genesis 12–36*. Continental Commentary. Minneapolis: Fortress, 1995.

————. *Genesis 37–50*. Continental Commentary. Minneapolis: Augsburg Fortress, 1986.

Genesis

I In the beginning God created the heavens and the earth.

Now the earth was formless and empty, darkness covered the surface of the watery depths, and the Spirit of God was hovering over the surface of the waters. Then God said, "Let there be light," and there was light. God saw that the light was good, and God separated the light from the darkness. God called the light "day," and the darkness he called "night." There was an evening, and there was a morning: one day.

Then God said, "Let there be an expanse between the waters, separating water from water." So God made the expanse and separated the water under the expanse from the water above the expanse. And it was so. God called the expanse "sky." Evening came and then morning: the
10 second day.

Then God said, "Let the water under the sky be gathered into one place, and let the dry land appear." And it was so. God called the dry land "earth," and the gathering of the water he called "seas." And God saw that it was good. Then God said, "Let the earth produce vegetation: seed-bearing plants and fruit trees on the earth bearing fruit with seed in it according to their kinds." And it was so. The earth produced vegetation: seed-bearing plants according to their kinds and trees bearing fruit with seed in it according to their kinds. And God saw that it was good. Evening came and then morning: the third day.

Then God said, "Let there be lights in the expanse of the sky to separate the day from the night. They will serve as signs for seasons and for days and years. They will be lights in the expanse of the
20 sky to provide light on the earth." And it was so. God made the two great lights—the greater light to rule over the day and the lesser light to rule over the night—as well as the stars. God placed them in the expanse of the sky to provide light on the earth, to rule the day and the night, and to separate light from darkness. And God saw that it was good. Evening came and then morning: the fourth day.

Then God said, "Let the water swarm with living creatures, and let birds fly above the earth across the expanse of the sky." So God created the large sea-creatures and every living creature that moves and swarms in the water, according to their kinds. He also created every winged creature according to its kind. And God saw that it was good. God blessed them: "Be fruitful, multiply, and fill the waters of the seas, and let the birds multiply on the earth." Evening came and then morning: the fifth day.

30 Then God said, "Let the earth produce living creatures according to their kinds: livestock, creatures that crawl, and the wildlife of the earth according to their kinds." And it was so. So God made the wildlife of the earth according to their kinds, the livestock according to their

kinds, and all the creatures that crawl on the ground according to their kinds. And God saw that it was good.

Then God said, "Let us make man in our image, according to our likeness. They will rule the fish of the sea, the birds of the sky, the livestock, the whole earth, and the creatures that crawl on the earth."

> So God created man in his own image;
> he created him in the image of God;
> 40   he created them male and female.

God blessed them, and God said to them, "Be fruitful, multiply, fill the earth, and subdue it. Rule the fish of the sea, the birds of the sky, and every creature that crawls on the earth." God also said, "Look, I have given you every seed-bearing plant on the surface of the entire earth and every tree whose fruit contains seed. This will be food for you, for all the wildlife of the earth, for every bird of the sky, and for every creature that crawls on the earth—everything having the breath of life in it—I have given every green plant for food." And it was so. God saw all that he had made, and it was very good indeed. Evening came and then morning: the sixth day.

2 So the heavens and the earth and everything in them were completed. On the seventh day God had completed his work that he had done, and he rested on the seventh day from all his work that he had done. God blessed the seventh day and declared it holy, for on it he rested from all his work of creation.

These are the records of the heavens and the earth, concerning their creation. At the time that the Lord God made the earth and the heavens, no shrub of the field had yet grown on the land, and no plant of the field had yet sprouted, for the Lord God had not made it rain on the land, and there was no man to work the ground. But mist would come up from the earth and water all the ground. Then the Lord God formed the man out of the dust from the ground and breathed the
10 breath of life into his nostrils, and the man became a living being.

The Lord God planted a garden in Eden, in the east, and there he placed the man he had formed. The Lord God caused to grow out of the ground every tree pleasing in appearance and good for food, including the tree of life in the middle of the garden, as well as the tree of the knowledge of good and evil.

A river went out from Eden to water the garden. From there it divided and became the source of four rivers. The name of the first is Pishon, which flows through the entire land of Havilah, where there is gold. Gold from that land is pure; bdellium and onyx are also there. The name of the second river is Gihon, which flows through the entire land of Cush. The name of the third river is Tigris, which runs east of Assyria. And the fourth river is the Euphrates.

20   The Lord God took the man and placed him in the garden of Eden to work it and watch over it. And the Lord God commanded the man, "You are free to eat from any tree of the garden, but you must not eat from the tree of the knowledge of good and evil, for on the day you eat from it, you will certainly die." Then the Lord God said, "It is not good for the man to be alone. I will make a helper corresponding to him." The Lord God formed out of the ground every wild animal and every bird of the sky, and brought each to the man to see what he would call it. And whatever the man called a living creature, that was its name. The man gave names to all the livestock, to the birds of the sky, and to every wild animal; but for the man no helper was found corresponding to him. So the Lord God caused a deep sleep to come over the man, and he slept. God took one of his ribs and closed the flesh at that place.

30   Then the Lord God made the rib he had taken from the man into a woman and brought her to the man. And the man said:

> This one, at last, is bone of my bone
> and flesh of my flesh;
> this one will be called "woman,"
> for she was taken from man.

This is why a man leaves his father and mother and bonds with his wife, and they become one flesh. Both the man and his wife were naked, yet felt no shame.

3 Now the serpent was the most cunning of all the wild animals that the Lord God had made. He said to the woman, "Did God really say, 'You can't eat from any tree in the garden'?"

    The woman said to the serpent, "We may eat the fruit from the trees in the garden. But about the fruit of the tree in the middle of the garden, God said, 'You must not eat it or touch it, or you will die.'"

    "No! You will certainly not die," the serpent said to the woman. "In fact, God knows that when you eat it your eyes will be opened and you will be like God, knowing good and evil." The woman saw that the tree was good for food and delightful to look at, and that it was desirable for obtaining wisdom. So she took some of its fruit and ate it; she also gave some

10 to her husband, who was with her, and he ate it. Then the eyes of both of them were opened, and they knew they were naked; so they sewed fig leaves together and made coverings for themselves.

    Then the man and his wife heard the sound of the Lord God walking in the garden at the time of the evening breeze, and they hid from the Lord God among the trees of the garden. So the Lord God called out to the man and said to him, "Where are you?"

    And he said, "I heard you in the garden, and I was afraid because I was naked, so I hid."

Then he asked, "Who told you that you were naked? Did you eat from the tree that I commanded you not to eat from?"

The man replied, "The woman you gave to be with me—she gave me some fruit from the tree, and I ate."

So the LORD God asked the woman, "What have you done?"

And the woman said, "The serpent deceived me, and I ate."

So the LORD God said to the serpent:

> Because you have done this,
> you are cursed more than any livestock
> and more than any wild animal.
> You will move on your belly
> and eat dust all the days of your life.
> I will put hostility between you and the woman,
> and between your offspring and her offspring.
> He will strike your head,
> and you will strike his heel.

He said to the woman:

> I will intensify your labor pains;
> you will bear children with painful effort.
> Your desire will be for your husband,
> yet he will rule over you.

And he said to the man, "Because you listened to your wife and ate from the tree about which I commanded you, 'Do not eat from it':

> The ground is cursed because of you.
> You will eat from it by means of painful labor
> all the days of your life.
> It will produce thorns and thistles for you,
> and you will eat the plants of the field.
> You will eat bread by the sweat of your brow
> until you return to the ground,
> since you were taken from it.
> For you are dust,
> and you will return to dust."

50   The man named his wife Eve because she was the mother of all the living. The LORD God made clothing from skins for the man and his wife, and he clothed them.

    The LORD God said, "Since the man has become like one of us, knowing good and evil, he must not reach out, take from the tree of life, eat, and live forever." So the LORD God sent him away from the garden of Eden to work the ground from which he was taken. He drove the man out and stationed the cherubim and the flaming, whirling sword east of the garden of Eden to guard the way to the tree of life.

4   The man was intimate with his wife Eve, and she conceived and gave birth to Cain. She said, "I have had a male child with the LORD's help." She also gave birth to his brother Abel. Now Abel became a shepherd of flocks, but Cain worked the ground. In the course of time Cain presented some of the land's produce as an offering to the LORD. And Abel also presented an offering—some of the firstborn of his flock and their fat portions. The LORD had regard for Abel and his offering, but he did not have regard for Cain and his offering. Cain was furious, and he looked despondent.

    Then the LORD said to Cain, "Why are you furious? And why do you look despondent? If you do what is right, won't you be accepted? But if you do not do what is right, sin is crouching at the door. Its desire is for you, but you must rule over it."

10   Cain said to his brother Abel, "Let's go out to the field." And while they were in the field, Cain attacked his brother Abel and killed him.

    Then the LORD said to Cain, "Where is your brother Abel?"

    "I don't know," he replied. "Am I my brother's guardian?"

    Then he said, "What have you done? Your brother's blood cries out to me from the ground! So now you are cursed, alienated from the ground that opened its mouth to receive your brother's blood you have shed. If you work the ground, it will never again give you its yield. You will be a restless wanderer on the earth."

    But Cain answered the LORD, "My punishment is too great to bear! Since you are banishing me today from the face of the earth, and I must hide from your presence and become a restless

20 wanderer on the earth, whoever finds me will kill me."

    Then the LORD replied to him, "In that case, whoever kills Cain will suffer vengeance seven times over." And he placed a mark on Cain so that whoever found him would not kill him. Then Cain went out from the LORD's presence and lived in the land of Nod, east of Eden.

    Cain was intimate with his wife, and she conceived and gave birth to Enoch. Then Cain became the builder of a city, and he named the city Enoch after his son. Irad was born to Enoch, Irad fathered Mehujael, Mehujael fathered Methushael, and Methushael fathered Lamech. Lamech took two wives for himself, one named Adah and the other named Zillah. Adah bore Jabal; he was the first of the nomadic herdsmen. His brother was named Jubal; he was the first of all who play the lyre and the flute. Zillah bore Tubal-cain, who made all kinds of bronze and iron tools. Tubal-cain's sister was Naamah.

30   Lamech said to his wives:

> Adah and Zillah, hear my voice;
> wives of Lamech, pay attention to my words.
> For I killed a man for wounding me,
> a young man for striking me.
> If Cain is to be avenged seven times over,
> then for Lamech it will be seventy-seven times!

Adam was intimate with his wife again, and she gave birth to a son and named him Seth, for she said, "God has given me another offspring in place of Abel, since Cain killed him." A son was
10 born to Seth also, and he named him Enosh. At that time people began to call on the name of the Lord.

5 This is the document containing the family records of Adam. On the day that God created man, he made him in the likeness of God; he created them male and female. When they were created, he blessed them and called them mankind.

Adam was 130 years old when he fathered a son in his likeness, according to his image, and named him Seth. Adam lived 800 years after he fathered Seth, and he fathered other sons and daughters. So Adam's life lasted 930 years; then he died.

Seth was 105 years old when he fathered Enosh. Seth lived 807 years after he fathered Enosh, and he fathered other sons and daughters. So Seth's life lasted 912 years; then he died.

Enosh was 90 years old when he fathered Kenan. Enosh lived 815 years after he fathered
10 Kenan, and he fathered other sons and daughters. So Enosh's life lasted 905 years; then he died.

Kenan was 70 years old when he fathered Mahalalel. Kenan lived 840 years after he fathered Mahalalel, and he fathered other sons and daughters. So Kenan's life lasted 910 years; then he died.

Mahalalel was 65 years old when he fathered Jared. Mahalalel lived 830 years after he fathered Jared, and he fathered other sons and daughters. So Mahalalel's life lasted 895 years; then he died.

Jared was 162 years old when he fathered Enoch. Jared lived 800 years after he fathered Enoch, and he fathered other sons and daughters. So Jared's life lasted 962 years; then he died.

Enoch was 65 years old when he fathered Methuselah. And after he fathered Methuselah, Enoch walked with God 300 years and fathered other sons and daughters. So Enoch's life lasted 365 years. Enoch walked with God; then he was not there because God took him.

20 Methuselah was 187 years old when he fathered Lamech. Methuselah lived 782 years after he fathered Lamech, and he fathered other sons and daughters. So Methuselah's life lasted 969 years; then he died.

Lamech was 182 years old when he fathered a son. And he named him Noah, saying, "This one will bring us relief from the agonizing labor of our hands, caused by the ground the Lord has cursed." Lamech lived 595 years after he fathered Noah, and he fathered other sons and daughters. So Lamech's life lasted 777 years; then he died.

Noah was 500 years old, and he fathered Shem, Ham, and Japheth.

6 When mankind began to multiply on the earth and daughters were born to them, the sons of God saw that the daughters of mankind were beautiful, and they took any they chose as wives for themselves. And the LORD said, "My Spirit will not remain with mankind forever, because they are corrupt. Their days will be 120 years." The Nephilim were on the earth both in those days and afterward, when the sons of God came to the daughters of mankind, who bore children to them. They were the powerful men of old, the famous men.

When the LORD saw that human wickedness was widespread on the earth and that every inclination of the human mind was nothing but evil all the time, the LORD regretted that he had made man on the earth, and he was deeply grieved. Then the LORD said, "I will wipe mankind,
10 whom I created, off the face of the earth, together with the animals, creatures that crawl, and birds of the sky—for I regret that I made them." Noah, however, found favor with the LORD.

These are the family records of Noah. Noah was a righteous man, blameless among his contemporaries; Noah walked with God. And Noah fathered three sons: Shem, Ham, and Japheth.
Now the earth was corrupt in God's sight, and the earth was filled with wickedness. God saw how corrupt the earth was, for every creature had corrupted its way on the earth. Then God said to Noah, "I have decided to put an end to every creature, for the earth is filled with wickedness because of them; therefore I am going to destroy them along with the earth.

"Make yourself an ark of gopher wood. Make rooms in the ark, and cover it with pitch inside and outside. This is how you are to make it: The ark will be 450 feet long, 75 feet wide, and
20 45 feet high. You are to make a roof, finishing the sides of the ark to within eighteen inches of the roof. You are to put a door in the side of the ark. Make it with lower, middle, and upper decks.

"Understand that I am bringing a flood—floodwaters on the earth to destroy every creature under heaven with the breath of life in it. Everything on earth will perish. But I will establish my covenant with you, and you will enter the ark with your sons, your wife, and your sons' wives. You are also to bring into the ark two of all the living creatures, male and female, to keep them alive with you. Two of everything—from the birds according to their kinds, from the livestock according to their kinds, and from the animals that crawl on the ground according to their kinds—will come to you so that you can keep them alive. Take with you every kind of food that
30 is eaten; gather it as food for you and for them." And Noah did this. He did everything that God had commanded him.

7 Then the LORD said to Noah, "Enter the ark, you and all your household, for I have seen that you alone are righteous before me in this generation. You are to take with you seven pairs, a male and its female, of all the clean animals, and two of the animals that are not clean, a male and its female, and seven pairs, male and female, of the birds of the sky—in order to keep offspring alive throughout the earth. Seven days from now I will make it rain on the earth forty days and forty nights, and every living thing I have made I will wipe off the face of the earth." And Noah did everything that the LORD commanded him.

Noah was six hundred years old when the flood came and water covered the earth. So Noah, his sons, his wife, and his sons' wives entered the ark because of the floodwaters. From the animals
10 that are clean, and from the animals that are not clean, and from the birds and every creature that crawls on the ground, two of each, male and female, came to Noah and entered the ark, just as God had commanded him. Seven days later the floodwaters came on the earth.

In the six hundredth year of Noah's life, in the second month, on the seventeenth day of the month, on that day all the sources of the vast watery depths burst open, the floodgates of the sky were opened, and the rain fell on the earth forty days and forty nights. On that same day Noah and his three sons, Shem, Ham, and Japheth, entered the ark, along with Noah's wife and his three sons' wives. They entered it with all the wildlife according to their kinds, all livestock according to their kinds, all the creatures that crawl on the earth according to their kinds, every flying creature—all the birds and every winged creature—according to their kinds. Two of every creature that has the
20 breath of life in it came to Noah and entered the ark. Those that entered, male and female of every creature, entered just as God had commanded him. Then the LORD shut him in.

The flood continued for forty days on the earth; the water increased and lifted up the ark so that it rose above the earth. The water surged and increased greatly on the earth, and the ark floated on the surface of the water. Then the water surged even higher on the earth, and all the high mountains under the whole sky were covered. The mountains were covered as the water surged above them more than twenty feet. Every creature perished—those that crawl on the earth, birds, livestock, wildlife, and those that swarm on the earth, as well as all mankind. Everything with the breath of the spirit of life in its nostrils—everything on dry land died. He wiped out every living thing that was on the face of the earth, from mankind to livestock, to creatures that crawl, to the birds of the sky, and they were wiped off the earth. Only Noah was left, and those that were with him in the ark. And the water surged on the earth 150 days.

8 God remembered Noah, as well as all the wildlife and all the livestock that were with him in the ark. God caused a wind to pass over the earth, and the water began to subside. The sources of the watery depths and the floodgates of the sky were closed, and the rain from the sky stopped. The water steadily receded from the earth, and by the end of 150 days the water had decreased significantly. The ark came to rest in the seventh month, on the seventeenth day of the month, on the mountains of Ararat.

The water continued to recede until the tenth month; in the tenth month, on the first day of the month, the tops of the mountains were visible. After forty days Noah opened the window of the ark that he had made, and he sent out a raven. It went back and forth until the water had dried up from the earth. Then he sent out a dove to see whether the water on the earth's surface had gone down, but the dove found no resting place for its foot. It returned to him in the ark because water covered the surface of the whole earth. He reached out and brought it into the ark to himself. So Noah waited seven more days and sent out the dove from the ark again. When the dove came to him at evening, there was a plucked olive leaf in its beak. So Noah knew that the water on the earth's surface had gone down. After he had waited another seven days, he sent out the dove, but it did not return to him again. In the six hundred first year, in the first month, on the first day of the month, the water that had covered the earth was dried up. Then Noah removed the ark's cover and saw that the surface of the ground was drying. By the twenty-seventh day of the second month, the earth was dry.

Then God spoke to Noah, "Come out of the ark, you, your wife, your sons, and your sons' wives with you. Bring out all the living creatures that are with you—birds, livestock, those that crawl on the earth—and they will spread over the earth and be fruitful and multiply on the earth." So Noah, along with his sons, his wife, and his sons' wives, came out. All the animals, all the creatures that crawl, and all the flying creatures—everything that moves on the earth—came out of the ark by their families.

Then Noah built an altar to the LORD. He took some of every kind of clean animal and every kind of clean bird and offered burnt offerings on the altar. When the LORD smelled the pleasing aroma, he said to himself, "I will never again curse the ground because of human beings, even though the inclination of the human heart is evil from youth onward. And I will never again strike down every living thing as I have done.

> As long as the earth endures,
> seedtime and harvest, cold and heat,
> summer and winter, and day and night
> will not cease."

9 God blessed Noah and his sons and said to them, "Be fruitful and multiply and fill the earth. The fear and terror of you will be in every living creature on the earth, every bird of the sky, every creature that crawls on the ground, and all the fish of the sea. They are placed under your authority. Every creature that lives and moves will be food for you; as I gave the green plants, I have given you everything. However, you must not eat meat with its lifeblood in it. And I will require a penalty for your lifeblood; I will require it from any animal and from any human; if someone murders a fellow human, I will require that person's life.

> Whoever sheds human blood,
> by humans his blood will be shed,
> for God made humans in his image.

But you, be fruitful and multiply; spread out over the earth and multiply on it."

Then God said to Noah and his sons with him, "Understand that I am establishing my covenant with you and your descendants after you, and with every living creature that is with you—birds, livestock, and all wildlife of the earth that are with you—all the animals of the earth that came out of the ark. I establish my covenant with you that never again will every creature be wiped out by floodwaters; there will never again be a flood to destroy the earth."

And God said, "This is the sign of the covenant I am making between me and you and every living creature with you, a covenant for all future generations: I have placed my bow in the clouds, and it will be a sign of the covenant between me and the earth. Whenever I form clouds over the earth and the bow appears in the clouds, I will remember my covenant between me and you and all the living creatures: water will never again become a flood to destroy every creature. The bow will be in the clouds, and I will look at it and remember the permanent covenant between God and all the living creatures on earth." God said to Noah, "This is the sign of the covenant that I have established between me and every creature on earth."

Noah's sons who came out of the ark were Shem, Ham, and Japheth. Ham was the father of Canaan. These three were Noah's sons, and from them the whole earth was populated.

Noah, as a man of the soil, began by planting a vineyard. He drank some of the wine, became drunk, and uncovered himself inside his tent. Ham, the father of Canaan, saw his father naked and told his two brothers outside. Then Shem and Japheth took a cloak and placed it over both their shoulders, and walking backward, they covered their father's nakedness. Their faces were turned away, and they did not see their father naked.

When Noah awoke from his drinking and learned what his youngest son had done to him, he said:

> Canaan is cursed.
> He will be the lowest of slaves to his brothers.

He also said:

> Blessed be the LORD, the God of Shem;
> Let Canaan be Shem's slave.
> Let God extend Japheth;
> let Japheth dwell in the tents of Shem;
> let Canaan be Shem's slave.

Now Noah lived 350 years after the flood. So Noah's life lasted 950 years; then he died.

10 These are the family records of Noah's sons, Shem, Ham, and Japheth. They also had sons after the flood.

Japheth's sons: Gomer, Magog, Madai, Javan, Tubal, Meshech, and Tiras. Gomer's sons: Ashkenaz, Riphath, and Togarmah. And Javan's sons: Elishah, Tarshish, Kittim, and Dodanim. From these descendants, the peoples of the coasts and islands spread out into their lands according to their clans in their nations, each with its own language.

Ham's sons: Cush, Mizraim, Put, and Canaan. Cush's sons: Seba, Havilah, Sabtah, Raamah, and Sabteca. And Raamah's sons: Sheba and Dedan.

Cush fathered Nimrod, who began to be powerful in the land. He was a powerful hunter in
10 the sight of the LORD. That is why it is said, "Like Nimrod, a powerful hunter in the sight of the LORD." His kingdom started with Babylon, Erech, Accad, and Calneh, in the land of Shinar. From that land he went to Assyria and built Nineveh, Rehoboth-ir, Calah, and Resen, between Nineveh and the great city Calah.

Mizraim fathered the people of Lud, Anam, Lehab, Naphtuh, Pathrus, Casluh (the Philistines came from them), and Caphtor.

Canaan fathered Sidon his firstborn and Heth, as well as the Jebusites, the Amorites, the Girgashites, the Hivites, the Arkites, the Sinites, the Arvadites, the Zemarites, and the Hamathites. Afterward the Canaanite clans scattered. The Canaanite border went from Sidon going toward Gerar as far as Gaza, and going toward Sodom, Gomorrah, Admah, and Zeboiim as
20 far as Lasha.

These are Ham's sons by their clans, according to their languages, in their lands and their nations.

And Shem, Japheth's older brother, also had sons. Shem was the father of all the sons of Eber. Shem's sons were Elam, Asshur, Arpachshad, Lud, and Aram.

Aram's sons: Uz, Hul, Gether, and Mash.

Arpachshad fathered Shelah, and Shelah fathered Eber. Eber had two sons. One was named Peleg, for during his days the earth was divided; his brother was named Joktan. And Joktan fathered Almodad, Sheleph, Hazarmaveth, Jerah, Hadoram, Uzal, Diklah, Obal, Abimael, Sheba, Ophir, Havilah, and Jobab. All these were Joktan's sons. Their settlements extended from Mesha
30 to Sephar, the eastern hill country.

These are Shem's sons by their clans, according to their languages, in their lands and their nations.

These are the clans of Noah's sons, according to their family records, in their nations. The nations on earth spread out from these after the flood.

11 The whole earth had the same language and vocabulary. As people migrated from the east, they found a valley in the land of Shinar and settled there. They said to each other, "Come, let's make oven-fired bricks." (They used brick for stone and asphalt for mortar.) And they said, "Come, let's build ourselves a city and a tower with its top in the sky. Let's make a name for ourselves; otherwise, we will be scattered throughout the earth."

Then the LORD came down to look over the city and the tower that the humans were building. The LORD said, "If they have begun to do this as one people all having the same language, then nothing they plan to do will be impossible for them. Come, let's go down there and confuse their language so that they will not understand one another's speech." So from there the LORD scattered them throughout the earth, and they stopped building the city. Therefore it is called Babylon, for there the LORD confused the language of the whole earth, and from there the LORD scattered them throughout the earth.

These are the family records of Shem. Shem lived 100 years and fathered Arpachshad two years after the flood. After he fathered Arpachshad, Shem lived 500 years and fathered other sons and daughters. Arpachshad lived 35 years and fathered Shelah. After he fathered Shelah, Arpachshad lived 403 years and fathered other sons and daughters. Shelah lived 30 years and fathered Eber. After he fathered Eber, Shelah lived 403 years and fathered other sons and daughters. Eber lived 34 years and fathered Peleg. After he fathered Peleg, Eber lived 430 years and fathered other sons and daughters. Peleg lived 30 years and fathered Reu. After he fathered Reu, Peleg lived 209 years and fathered other sons and daughters. Reu lived 32 years and fathered Serug. After he fathered Serug, Reu lived 207 years and fathered other sons and daughters. Serug lived 30 years and fathered Nahor. After he fathered Nahor, Serug lived 200 years and fathered other sons and daughters. Nahor lived 29 years and fathered Terah. After he fathered Terah, Nahor lived 119 years and fathered other sons and daughters. Terah lived 70 years and fathered Abram, Nahor, and Haran.

These are the family records of Terah. Terah fathered Abram, Nahor, and Haran, and Haran fathered Lot. Haran died in his native land, in Ur of the Chaldeans, during his father Terah's lifetime. Abram and Nahor took wives: Abram's wife was named Sarai, and Nahor's wife was named Milcah. She was the daughter of Haran, the father of both Milcah and Iscah. Sarai was unable to conceive; she did not have a child.

Terah took his son Abram, his grandson Lot (Haran's son), and his daughter-in-law Sarai, his son Abram's wife, and they set out together from Ur of the Chaldeans to go to the land of Canaan. But when they came to Haran, they settled there. Terah lived 205 years and died in Haran.

12 The LORD said to Abram:

> Go from your land,
> your relatives,
> and your father's house
> to the land that I will show you.
> I will make you into a great nation,

> I will bless you,
> I will make your name great,
> and you will be a blessing.
> I will bless those who bless you,
> I will curse anyone who treats you with contempt,
> and all the peoples on earth
> will be blessed through you.

So Abram went, as the LORD had told him, and Lot went with him. Abram was seventy-five years old when he left Haran. He took his wife, Sarai, his nephew Lot, all the possessions they had accumulated, and the people they had acquired in Haran, and they set out for the land of Canaan. When they came to the land of Canaan, Abram passed through the land to the site of Shechem, at the oak of Moreh. (At that time the Canaanites were in the land.) The LORD appeared to Abram and said, "To your offspring I will give this land." So he built an altar there to the LORD who had appeared to him. From there he moved on to the hill country east of Bethel and pitched his tent, with Bethel on the west and Ai on the east. He built an altar to the LORD there, and he called on the name of the LORD. Then Abram journeyed by stages to the Negev.

There was a famine in the land, so Abram went down to Egypt to stay there for a while because the famine in the land was severe. When he was about to enter Egypt, he said to his wife, Sarai, "Look, I know what a beautiful woman you are. When the Egyptians see you, they will say, 'This is his wife.' They will kill me but let you live. Please say you're my sister so it will go well for me because of you, and my life will be spared on your account." When Abram entered Egypt, the Egyptians saw that the woman was very beautiful. Pharaoh's officials saw her and praised her to Pharaoh, so the woman was taken to Pharaoh's household. He treated Abram well because of her, and Abram acquired flocks and herds, male and female donkeys, male and female slaves, and camels.

But the LORD struck Pharaoh and his household with severe plagues because of Abram's wife, Sarai. So Pharaoh sent for Abram and said, "What have you done to me? Why didn't you tell me she was your wife? Why did you say, 'She's my sister,' so that I took her as my wife? Now, here is your wife. Take her and go!" Then Pharaoh gave his men orders about him, and they sent him away with his wife and all he had.

13 Abram went up from Egypt to the Negev—he, his wife, and all he had, and Lot with him. Abram was very rich in livestock, silver, and gold. He went by stages from the Negev to Bethel, to the place between Bethel and Ai where his tent had formerly been, to the site where he had built the altar. And Abram called on the name of the LORD there.

Now Lot, who was traveling with Abram, also had flocks, herds, and tents. But the land was unable to support them as long as they stayed together, for they had so many possessions that they could not stay together, and there was quarreling between the herdsmen of Abram's livestock and the herdsmen of Lot's livestock. (At that time the Canaanites and the Perizzites were living in the land.)

10 So Abram said to Lot, "Please, let's not have quarreling between you and me, or between your herdsmen and my herdsmen, since we are relatives. Isn't the whole land before you? Separate from me: if you go to the left, I will go to the right; if you go to the right, I will go to the left."

Lot looked out and saw that the entire plain of the Jordan as far as Zoar was well watered everywhere like the LORD's garden and the land of Egypt. (This was before the Lord destroyed Sodom and Gomorrah.) So Lot chose the entire plain of the Jordan for himself. Then Lot journeyed eastward, and they separated from each other. Abram lived in the land of Canaan, but Lot lived in the cities on the plain and set up his tent near Sodom. (Now the men of Sodom were evil, sinning immensely against the Lord.)

After Lot had separated from him, the LORD said to Abram, "Look from the place where you 20 are. Look north and south, east and west, for I will give you and your offspring forever all the land that you see. I will make your offspring like the dust of the earth, so that if anyone could count the dust of the earth, then your offspring could be counted. Get up and walk around the land, through its length and width, for I will give it to you."

So Abram moved his tent and went to live near the oaks of Mamre at Hebron, where he built an altar to the LORD.

14 In those days King Amraphel of Shinar, King Arioch of Ellasar, King Chedorlaomer of Elam, and King Tidal of Goiim waged war against King Bera of Sodom, King Birsha of Gomorrah, King Shinab of Admah, and King Shemeber of Zeboiim, as well as the king of Bela (that is, Zoar). All of these came as allies to the Siddim Valley (that is, the Dead Sea). They were subject to Chedorlaomer for twelve years, but in the thirteenth year they rebelled. In the fourteenth year Chedorlaomer and the kings who were with him came and defeated the Rephaim in Ashteroth-karnaim, the Zuzim in Ham, the Emim in Shaveh-kiriathaim, and the Horites in the mountains of Seir, as far as El-paran by the wilderness. Then they came back to invade En-mishpat (that is, Kadesh), and they defeated the whole territory of the Amalekites, as well as the Amorites who lived in Hazazon-tamar.

10 Then the king of Sodom, the king of Gomorrah, the king of Admah, the king of Zeboiim, and the king of Bela (that is, Zoar) went out and lined up for battle in the Siddim Valley against King Chedorlaomer of Elam, King Tidal of Goiim, King Amraphel of Shinar, and King Arioch of Ellasar—four kings against five. Now the Siddim Valley contained many asphalt pits, and as the kings of Sodom and Gomorrah fled, some fell into them, but the rest fled to the mountains. The four kings took all the goods of Sodom and Gomorrah and all their food and went on. They also took Abram's nephew Lot and his possessions, for he was living in Sodom, and they went on.

One of the survivors came and told Abram the Hebrew, who lived near the oaks belonging to Mamre the Amorite, the brother of Eshcol and the brother of Aner. They were bound by a treaty

with Abram. When Abram heard that his relative had been taken prisoner, he assembled his
20   318 trained men, born in his household, and they went in pursuit as far as Dan. And he and his
servants deployed against them by night, defeated them, and pursued them as far as Hobah to the
north of Damascus. He brought back all the goods and also his relative Lot and his goods, as well
as the women and the other people.

After Abram returned from defeating Chedorlaomer and the kings who were with him, the king of
Sodom went out to meet him in the Shaveh Valley (that is, the King's Valley). Melchizedek, king
of Salem, brought out bread and wine; he was a priest to God Most High. He blessed him and said:

> Abram is blessed by God Most High,
> Creator of heaven and earth,
> and blessed be God Most High
30   who has handed over your enemies to you.

And Abram gave him a tenth of everything.

Then the king of Sodom said to Abram, "Give me the people, but take the possessions for
yourself."

But Abram said to the king of Sodom, "I have raised my hand in an oath to the LORD, God
Most High, Creator of heaven and earth, that I will not take a thread or sandal strap or anything
that belongs to you, so you can never say, 'I made Abram rich.' I will take nothing except what
the servants have eaten. But as for the share of the men who came with me—Aner, Eshcol, and
Mamre—they can take their share."

15   After these events, the word of the LORD came to Abram in a vision:

> Do not be afraid, Abram.
> I am your shield;
> your reward will be very great.

But Abram said, "Lord GOD, what can you give me, since I am childless and the heir of my
house is Eliezer of Damascus?" Abram continued, "Look, you have given me no offspring, so a
slave born in my house will be my heir."

Now the word of the LORD came to him: "This one will not be your heir; instead, one who
comes from your own body will be your heir." He took him outside and said, "Look at the sky and
10   count the stars, if you are able to count them." Then he said to him, "Your offspring will be that
numerous."

Abram believed the LORD, and he credited it to him as righteousness.

He also said to him, "I am the LORD who brought you from Ur of the Chaldeans to give you
this land to possess."

But he said, "Lord GOD, how can I know that I will possess it?"

He said to him, "Bring me a three-year-old cow, a three-year-old female goat, a three-year-old ram, a turtledove, and a young pigeon."

So he brought all these to him, cut them in half, and laid the pieces opposite each other, but he did not cut the birds in half. Birds of prey came down on the carcasses, but Abram drove them away. As the sun was setting, a deep sleep came over Abram, and suddenly great terror and darkness descended on him.

Then the LORD said to Abram, "Know this for certain: Your offspring will be resident aliens for four hundred years in a land that does not belong to them and will be enslaved and oppressed. However, I will judge the nation they serve, and afterward they will go out with many possessions. But you will go to your ancestors in peace and be buried at a good old age. In the fourth generation they will return here, for the iniquity of the Amorites has not yet reached its full measure."

When the sun had set and it was dark, a smoking fire pot and a flaming torch appeared and passed between the divided animals. On that day the LORD made a covenant with Abram, saying, "I give this land to your offspring, from the Brook of Egypt to the great river, the Euphrates River: the land of the Kenites, Kenizzites, Kadmonites, Hethites, Perizzites, Rephaim, Amorites, Canaanites, Girgashites, and Jebusites."

16 Abram's wife, Sarai, had not borne any children for him, but she owned an Egyptian slave named Hagar. Sarai said to Abram, "Since the LORD has prevented me from bearing children, go to my slave; perhaps through her I can build a family." And Abram agreed to what Sarai said. So Abram's wife, Sarai, took Hagar, her Egyptian slave, and gave her to her husband, Abram, as a wife for him. This happened after Abram had lived in the land of Canaan ten years. He slept with Hagar, and she became pregnant. When she saw that she was pregnant, her mistress became contemptible to her. Then Sarai said to Abram, "You are responsible for my suffering! I put my slave in your arms, and when she saw that she was pregnant, I became contemptible to her. May the LORD judge between me and you."

Abram replied to Sarai, "Here, your slave is in your power; do whatever you want with her." Then Sarai mistreated her so much that she ran away from her.

The angel of the LORD found her by a spring in the wilderness, the spring on the way to Shur. He said, "Hagar, slave of Sarai, where have you come from and where are you going?"

She replied, "I'm running away from my mistress Sarai."

The angel of the LORD said to her, "Go back to your mistress and submit to her authority." The angel of the LORD said to her, "I will greatly multiply your offspring, and they will be too many to count."

The angel of the LORD said to her, "You have conceived and will have a son. You will name him Ishmael, for the LORD has heard your cry of affliction. This man will be like a wild donkey. His hand will be against everyone, and everyone's hand will be against him; he will settle near all his relatives."

So she named the LORD who spoke to her: "You are El-roi," for she said, "In this place, have I actually seen the one who sees me?" That is why the well is called Beer-lahai-roi. It is between Kadesh and Bered.

So Hagar gave birth to Abram's son, and Abram named his son (whom Hagar bore) Ishmael. Abram was eighty-six years old when Hagar bore Ishmael to him.

17 When Abram was ninety-nine years old, the LORD appeared to him, saying, "I am God Almighty. Live in my presence and be blameless. I will set up my covenant between me and you, and I will multiply you greatly."

Then Abram fell facedown and God spoke with him: "As for me, here is my covenant with you: You will become the father of many nations. Your name will no longer be Abram; your name will be Abraham, for I will make you the father of many nations. I will make you extremely fruitful and will make nations and kings come from you. I will confirm my covenant that is between me and you and your future offspring throughout their generations. It is a permanent covenant to be your God and the God of your offspring after you. And to you and your future offspring I will give the

10 land where you are residing—all the land of Canaan—as a permanent possession, and I will be their God."

God also said to Abraham, "As for you, you and your offspring after you throughout their generations are to keep my covenant. This is my covenant between me and you and your offspring after you, which you are to keep: Every one of your males must be circumcised. You must circumcise the flesh of your foreskin to serve as a sign of the covenant between me and you. Throughout your generations, every male among you is to be circumcised at eight days old—every male born in your household or purchased from any foreigner and not your offspring. Whether born in your household or purchased, he must be circumcised. My covenant will be marked in your flesh as a permanent covenant. If any male is not circumcised in the flesh of his foreskin, that

20 man will be cut off from his people; he has broken my covenant."

God said to Abraham, "As for your wife Sarai, do not call her Sarai, for Sarah will be her name. I will bless her; indeed, I will give you a son by her. I will bless her, and she will produce nations; kings of peoples will come from her."

Abraham fell facedown. Then he laughed and said to himself, "Can a child be born to a hundred-year-old man? Can Sarah, a ninety-year-old woman, give birth?" So Abraham said to God, "If only Ishmael were acceptable to you!"

But God said, "No. Your wife Sarah will bear you a son, and you will name him Isaac. I will confirm my covenant with him as a permanent covenant for his future offspring. As for Ishmael, I have heard you. I will certainly bless him; I will make him fruitful and will multiply him greatly.

30 He will father twelve tribal leaders, and I will make him into a great nation. But I will confirm my covenant with Isaac, whom Sarah will bear to you at this time next year." When he finished talking with him, God withdrew from Abraham.

So Abraham took his son Ishmael and those born in his household or purchased—every male among the members of Abraham's household—and he circumcised the flesh of their foreskin on that very day, just as God had said to him. Abraham was ninety-nine years old when the flesh of his foreskin was circumcised, and his son Ishmael was thirteen years old when the flesh of his foreskin was circumcised. On that very day Abraham and his son Ishmael were circumcised. And all the men of his household—whether born in his household or purchased from a foreigner—were circumcised with him.

18 The LORD appeared to Abraham at the oaks of Mamre while he was sitting at the entrance of his tent during the heat of the day. He looked up, and he saw three men standing near him. When he saw them, he ran from the entrance of the tent to meet them, bowed to the ground, and said, "My lord, if I have found favor with you, please do not go on past your servant. Let a little water be brought, that you may wash your feet and rest yourselves under the tree. I will bring a bit of bread so that you may strengthen yourselves. This is why you have passed your servant's way. Later, you can continue on."

"Yes," they replied, "do as you have said."

So Abraham hurried into the tent and said to Sarah, "Quick! Knead three measures of fine flour and make bread." Abraham ran to the herd and got a tender, choice calf. He gave it to a 10 young man, who hurried to prepare it. Then Abraham took curds and milk, as well as the calf that he had prepared, and set them before the men. He served them as they ate under the tree.

"Where is your wife Sarah?" they asked him.

"There, in the tent," he answered.

The LORD said, "I will certainly come back to you in about a year's time, and your wife Sarah will have a son!" Now Sarah was listening at the entrance of the tent behind him.

Abraham and Sarah were old and getting on in years. Sarah had passed the age of childbearing. So she laughed to herself: "After I am worn out and my lord is old, will I have delight?"

But the LORD asked Abraham, "Why did Sarah laugh, saying, 'Can I really have a baby when I'm old?' Is anything impossible for the LORD? At the appointed time I will come back to you, and 20 in about a year she will have a son."

Sarah denied it. "I did not laugh," she said, because she was afraid.

But he replied, "No, you did laugh."

The men got up from there and looked out over Sodom, and Abraham was walking with them to see them off. Then the LORD said, "Should I hide what I am about to do from Abraham? Abraham is to become a great and powerful nation, and all the nations of the earth will be blessed through him. For I have chosen him so that he will command his children and his house after him to keep the way of the LORD by doing what is right and just. This is how the LORD will fulfill to Abraham what he promised him." Then the LORD said, "The outcry against Sodom and

Gomorrah is immense, and their sin is extremely serious. I will go down to see if what they have done justifies the cry that has come up to me. If not, I will find out."

The men turned from there and went toward Sodom while Abraham remained standing before the Lord. Abraham stepped forward and said, "Will you really sweep away the righteous with the wicked? What if there are fifty righteous people in the city? Will you really sweep it away instead of sparing the place for the sake of the fifty righteous people who are in it? You could not possibly do such a thing: to kill the righteous with the wicked, treating the righteous and the wicked alike. You could not possibly do that! Won't the Judge of the whole earth do what is just?"

The Lord said, "If I find fifty righteous people in the city of Sodom, I will spare the whole place for their sake."

Then Abraham answered, "Since I have ventured to speak to my lord—even though I am dust and ashes—suppose the fifty righteous lack five. Will you destroy the whole city for lack of five?"

He replied, "I will not destroy it if I find forty-five there."

Then he spoke to him again, "Suppose forty are found there?"

He answered, "I will not do it on account of forty."

Then he said, "Let my lord not be angry, and I will speak further. Suppose thirty are found there?"

He answered, "I will not do it if I find thirty there."

Then he said, "Since I have ventured to speak to my lord, suppose twenty are found there?"

He replied, "I will not destroy it on account of twenty."

Then he said, "Let my lord not be angry, and I will speak one more time. Suppose ten are found there?"

He answered, "I will not destroy it on account of ten." When the Lord had finished speaking with Abraham, he departed, and Abraham returned to his place.

19 The two angels entered Sodom in the evening as Lot was sitting in Sodom's gateway. When Lot saw them, he got up to meet them. He bowed with his face to the ground and said, "My lords, turn aside to your servant's house, wash your feet, and spend the night. Then you can get up early and go on your way."

"No," they said. "We would rather spend the night in the square." But he urged them so strongly that they followed him and went into his house. He prepared a feast and baked unleavened bread for them, and they ate.

Before they went to bed, the men of the city of Sodom, both young and old, the whole population, surrounded the house. They called out to Lot and said, "Where are the men who came to you tonight? Send them out to us so we can have sex with them!"

10 Lot went out to them at the entrance and shut the door behind him. He said, "Don't do this evil, my brothers. Look, I've got two daughters who haven't been intimate with a man. I'll bring them out to you, and you can do whatever you want to them. However, don't do anything to these men, because they have come under the protection of my roof."

"Get out of the way!" they said, adding, "This one came here as an alien, but he's acting like a judge! Now we'll do more harm to you than to them." They put pressure on Lot and came up to break down the door. But the angels reached out, brought Lot into the house with them, and shut the door. They struck the men who were at the entrance of the house, both young and old, with blindness so that they were unable to find the entrance.

Then the angels said to Lot, "Do you have anyone else here: a son-in-law, your sons and 20 daughters, or anyone else in the city who belongs to you? Get them out of this place, for we are about to destroy this place because the outcry against its people is so great before the Lord, that the Lord has sent us to destroy it."

So Lot went out and spoke to his sons-in-law, who were going to marry his daughters. "Get up," he said. "Get out of this place, for the Lord is about to destroy the city!" But his sons-in-law thought he was joking.

At daybreak the angels urged Lot on: "Get up! Take your wife and your two daughters who are here, or you will be swept away in the punishment of the city." But he hesitated. Because of the Lord's compassion for him, the men grabbed his hand, his wife's hand, and the hands of his two daughters. They brought him out and left him outside the city.

30 As soon as the angels got them outside, one of them said, "Run for your lives! Don't look back and don't stop anywhere on the plain! Run to the mountains, or you will be swept away!"

But Lot said to them, "No, my lords—please. Your servant has indeed found favor with you, and you have shown me great kindness by saving my life. But I can't run to the mountains; the disaster will overtake me, and I will die. Look, this town is close enough for me to flee to. It is a small place. Please let me run to it—it's only a small place, isn't it?—so that I can survive."

And he said to him, "All right, I'll grant your request about this matter too and will not demolish the town you mentioned. Hurry up! Run to it, for I cannot do anything until you get there." Therefore the name of the city is Zoar.

The sun had risen over the land when Lot reached Zoar. Then out of the sky the Lord rained 40 on Sodom and Gomorrah burning sulfur from the Lord. He demolished these cities, the entire plain, all the inhabitants of the cities, and whatever grew on the ground. But Lot's wife looked back and became a pillar of salt.

Early in the morning Abraham went to the place where he had stood before the Lord. He looked down toward Sodom and Gomorrah and all the land of the plain, and he saw that smoke was going up from the land like the smoke of a furnace. So it was, when God destroyed the cities of the plain, he remembered Abraham and brought Lot out of the middle of the upheaval when he demolished the cities where Lot had lived.

Lot departed from Zoar and lived in the mountains along with his two daughters, because he was afraid to live in Zoar. Instead, he and his two daughters lived in a cave. Then the firstborn said to 50 the younger, "Our father is old, and there is no man in the land to sleep with us as is the custom of all the land. Come, let's get our father to drink wine so that we can sleep with him and preserve our father's line." So they got their father to drink wine that night, and the firstborn came and slept with her father; he did not know when she lay down or when she got up.

The next day the firstborn said to the younger, "Look, I slept with my father last night. Let's get him to drink wine again tonight so you can go sleep with him and we can preserve our father's line." That night they again got their father to drink wine, and the younger went and slept with him; he did not know when she lay down or when she got up.

So both of Lot's daughters became pregnant by their father. The firstborn gave birth to a son and named him Moab. He is the father of the Moabites of today. The younger also gave birth to a son, and she named him Ben-ammi. He is the father of the Ammonites of today.

20 From there Abraham traveled to the region of the Negev and settled between Kadesh and Shur. While he was staying in Gerar, Abraham said about his wife Sarah, "She is my sister." So King Abimelech of Gerar had Sarah brought to him.

But God came to Abimelech in a dream by night and said to him, "You are about to die because of the woman you have taken, for she is a married woman."

Now Abimelech had not approached her, so he said, "Lord, would you destroy a nation even though it is innocent? Didn't he himself say to me, 'She is my sister'? And she herself said, 'He is my brother.' I did this with a clear conscience and clean hands."

Then God said to him in the dream, "Yes, I know that you did this with a clear conscience. I have also kept you from sinning against me. Therefore I have not let you touch her. Now return the man's wife, for he is a prophet, and he will pray for you and you will live. But if you do not return her, know that you will certainly die, you and all who are yours."

Early in the morning Abimelech got up, called all his servants together, and personally told them all these things, and the men were terrified.

Then Abimelech called Abraham in and said to him, "What have you done to us? How did I sin against you that you have brought such enormous guilt on me and on my kingdom? You have done things to me that should never be done." Abimelech also asked Abraham, "What made you do this?"

Abraham replied, "I thought, 'There is absolutely no fear of God in this place. They will kill me because of my wife.' Besides, she really is my sister, the daughter of my father though not the daughter of my mother, and she became my wife. So when God had me wander from my father's house, I said to her: Show your loyalty to me wherever we go and say about me, 'He's my brother.'"

Then Abimelech took flocks and herds and male and female slaves, gave them to Abraham, and returned his wife Sarah to him. Abimelech said, "Look, my land is before you. Settle wherever you want." And he said to Sarah, "Look, I am giving your brother one thousand pieces of silver. It is a verification of your honor to all who are with you. You are fully vindicated."

Then Abraham prayed to God, and God healed Abimelech, his wife, and his female slaves so that they could bear children, for the Lord had completely closed all the wombs in Abimelech's household on account of Sarah, Abraham's wife.

21 The Lord came to Sarah as he had said, and the Lord did for Sarah what he had promised. Sarah became pregnant and bore a son to Abraham in his old age, at the appointed time God had told him. Abraham named his son who was born to him—the one Sarah bore to him—Isaac. When his son Isaac was eight days old, Abraham circumcised him, as God had commanded him. Abraham was a hundred years old when his son Isaac was born to him.

Sarah said, "God has made me laugh, and everyone who hears will laugh with me." She also said, "Who would have told Abraham that Sarah would nurse children? Yet I have borne a son for him in his old age."

The child grew and was weaned, and Abraham held a great feast on the day Isaac was weaned. But Sarah saw the son mocking—the one Hagar the Egyptian had borne to Abraham. So she said to Abraham, "Drive out this slave with her son, for the son of this slave will not be a coheir with my son Isaac!"

This was very distressing to Abraham because of his son. But God said to Abraham, "Do not be distressed about the boy and about your slave. Whatever Sarah says to you, listen to her, because your offspring will be traced through Isaac, and I will also make a nation of the slave's son because he is your offspring."

Early in the morning Abraham got up, took bread and a waterskin, put them on Hagar's shoulders, and sent her and the boy away. She left and wandered in the Wilderness of Beer-sheba. When the water in the skin was gone, she left the boy under one of the bushes and went and sat at a distance, about a bowshot away, for she said, "I can't bear to watch the boy die!" While she sat at a distance, she wept loudly.

God heard the boy crying, and the angel of God called to Hagar from heaven and said to her, "What's wrong, Hagar? Don't be afraid, for God has heard the boy crying from the place where he is. Get up, help the boy up, and grasp his hand, for I will make him a great nation." Then God opened her eyes, and she saw a well. So she went and filled the waterskin and gave the boy a drink. God was with the boy, and he grew; he settled in the wilderness and became an archer. He settled in the Wilderness of Paran, and his mother got a wife for him from the land of Egypt.

At that time Abimelech, accompanied by Phicol the commander of his army, said to Abraham, "God is with you in everything you do. Swear to me by God here and now, that you will not break an agreement with me or with my children and descendants. As I have been loyal to you, so you will be loyal to me and to the country where you are a resident alien."

And Abraham said, "I swear it." But Abraham complained to Abimelech because of the well that Abimelech's servants had seized.

Abimelech replied, "I don't know who did this thing. You didn't report anything to me, so I hadn't heard about it until today."

Abraham took flocks and herds and gave them to Abimelech, and the two of them made a covenant. Abraham separated seven ewe lambs from the flock. And Abimelech said to Abraham, "Why have you separated these seven ewe lambs?"

He replied, "You are to accept the seven ewe lambs from me so that this act will serve as my witness that I dug this well." Therefore that place was called Beer-sheba because it was there that the two of them swore an oath. After they had made a covenant at Beer-sheba, Abimelech and Phicol, the commander of his army, left and returned to the land of the Philistines.

Abraham planted a tamarisk tree in Beer-sheba, and there he called on the name of the Lord, the Everlasting God. And Abraham lived as an alien in the land of the Philistines for many days.

22

After these things God tested Abraham and said to him, "Abraham!"

"Here I am," he answered.

"Take your son," he said, "your only son Isaac, whom you love, go to the land of Moriah, and offer him there as a burnt offering on one of the mountains I will tell you about."

So Abraham got up early in the morning, saddled his donkey, and took with him two of his young men and his son Isaac. He split wood for a burnt offering and set out to go to the place God had told him about. On the third day Abraham looked up and saw the place in the distance. Then Abraham said to his young men, "Stay here with the donkey. The boy and I will go over there to worship; then we'll come back to you." Abraham took the wood for the burnt offering and laid it on his son Isaac. In his hand he took the fire and the knife, and the two of them walked on together.

Then Isaac spoke to his father Abraham and said, "My father."

And he replied, "Here I am, my son."

Isaac said, "The fire and the wood are here, but where is the lamb for the burnt offering?"

Abraham answered, "God himself will provide the lamb for the burnt offering, my son." Then the two of them walked on together.

When they arrived at the place that God had told him about, Abraham built the altar there and arranged the wood. He bound his son Isaac and placed him on the altar on top of the wood. Then Abraham reached out and took the knife to slaughter his son.

But the angel of the Lord called to him from heaven and said, "Abraham, Abraham!"

He replied, "Here I am."

Then he said, "Do not lay a hand on the boy or do anything to him. For now I know that you fear God, since you have not withheld your only son from me." Abraham looked up and saw a ram caught in the thicket by its horns. So Abraham went and took the ram and offered it as a burnt offering in place of his son. And Abraham named that place The Lord Will Provide, so today it is said, "It will be provided on the Lord's mountain."

Then the angel of the LORD called to Abraham a second time from heaven and said, "By myself I have sworn," this is the LORD's declaration: "Because you have done this thing and have not
30 withheld your only son, I will indeed bless you and make your offspring as numerous as the stars of the sky and the sand on the seashore. Your offspring will possess the city gates of their enemies. And all the nations of the earth will be blessed by your offspring because you have obeyed my command."

Abraham went back to his young men, and they got up and went together to Beer-sheba. And Abraham settled in Beer-sheba.

Now after these things Abraham was told, "Milcah also has borne sons to your brother Nahor: Uz his firstborn, his brother Buz, Kemuel the father of Aram, Chesed, Hazo, Pildash, Jidlaph, and Bethuel." And Bethuel fathered Rebekah. Milcah bore these eight to Nahor, Abraham's brother. His concubine, whose name was Reumah, also bore Tebah, Gaham, Tahash, and Maacah.

23 Now Sarah lived 127 years; these were all the years of her life. Sarah died in Kiriath-arba (that is, Hebron) in the land of Canaan, and Abraham went in to mourn for Sarah and to weep for her.

When Abraham got up from beside his dead wife, he spoke to the Hethites: "I am an alien residing among you. Give me burial property among you so that I can bury my dead."

The Hethites replied to Abraham, "Listen to us, my lord. You are a prince of God among us. Bury your dead in our finest burial place. None of us will withhold from you his burial place for burying your dead."

Then Abraham rose and bowed down to the Hethites, the people of the land. He said to them, "If you are willing for me to bury my dead, listen to me and ask Ephron son of Zohar on my behalf
10 to give me the cave of Machpelah that belongs to him; it is at the end of his field. Let him give it to me in your presence, for the full price, as burial property."

Ephron was sitting among the Hethites. So in the hearing of all the Hethites who came to the gate of his city, Ephron the Hethite answered Abraham: "No, my lord. Listen to me. I give you the field, and I give you the cave that is in it. I give it to you in the sight of my people. Bury your dead."

Abraham bowed down to the people of the land and said to Ephron in the hearing of the people of the land, "Listen to me, if you please. Let me pay the price of the field. Accept it from me, and let me bury my dead there."

Ephron answered Abraham and said to him, "My lord, listen to me. Land worth four hundred shekels of silver—what is that between you and me? Bury your dead." Abraham agreed with
20 Ephron, and Abraham weighed out to Ephron the silver that he had agreed to in the hearing of the Hethites: four hundred standard shekels of silver. So Ephron's field at Machpelah near Mamre—the field with its cave and all the trees anywhere within the boundaries of the field— became Abraham's possession in the sight of all the Hethites who came to the gate of his city. After this, Abraham buried his wife Sarah in the cave of the field at Machpelah near Mamre (that

is, Hebron) in the land of Canaan. The field with its cave passed from the Hethites to Abraham as burial property.

24 Abraham was now old, getting on in years, and the LORD had blessed him in everything. Abraham said to his servant, the elder of his household who managed all he owned, "Place your hand under my thigh, and I will have you swear by the LORD, God of heaven and God of earth, that you will not take a wife for my son from the daughters of the Canaanites among whom I live, but will go to my land and my family to take a wife for my son Isaac."

The servant said to him, "Suppose the woman is unwilling to follow me to this land? Should I have your son go back to the land you came from?"

Abraham answered him, "Make sure that you don't take my son back there. The LORD, the God of heaven, who took me from my father's house and from my native land, who spoke to me
10 and swore to me, 'I will give this land to your offspring'—he will send his angel before you, and you can take a wife for my son from there. If the woman is unwilling to follow you, then you are free from this oath to me, but don't let my son go back there." So the servant placed his hand under his master Abraham's thigh and swore an oath to him concerning this matter.

The servant took ten of his master's camels, and with all kinds of his master's goods in hand, he went to Aram-naharaim, to Nahor's town. At evening, the time when women went out to draw water, he made the camels kneel beside a well outside the town.

"LORD, God of my master Abraham," he prayed, "make this happen for me today, and show kindness to my master Abraham. I am standing here at the spring where the daughters of the men of the town are coming out to draw water. Let the girl to whom I say, 'Please lower your water jug
20 so that I may drink,' and who responds, 'Drink, and I'll water your camels also'—let her be the one you have appointed for your servant Isaac. By this I will know that you have shown kindness to my master."

Before he had finished speaking, there was Rebekah—daughter of Bethuel son of Milcah, the wife of Abraham's brother Nahor—coming with a jug on her shoulder. Now the girl was very beautiful, a virgin—no man had been intimate with her. She went down to the spring, filled her jug, and came up. Then the servant ran to meet her and said, "Please let me have a little water from your jug."

She replied, "Drink, my lord." She quickly lowered her jug to her hand and gave him a drink. When she had finished giving him a drink, she said, "I'll also draw water for your camels until they
30 have had enough to drink." She quickly emptied her jug into the trough and hurried to the well again to draw water. She drew water for all his camels while the man silently watched her to see whether or not the LORD had made his journey a success.

As the camels finished drinking, the man took a gold ring weighing half a shekel, and for her wrists two bracelets weighing ten shekels of gold. "Whose daughter are you?" he asked. "Please tell me, is there room in your father's house for us to spend the night?"

She answered him, "I am the daughter of Bethuel son of Milcah, whom she bore to Nahor." She also said to him, "We have plenty of straw and feed and a place to spend the night."

Then the man knelt low, worshiped the LORD, and said, "Blessed be the LORD, the God of my master Abraham, who has not withheld his kindness and faithfulness from my master. As for me, the LORD has led me on the journey to the house of my master's relatives."

The girl ran and told her mother's household about these things. Now Rebekah had a brother named Laban, and Laban ran out to the man at the spring. As soon as he had seen the ring and the bracelets on his sister's wrists, and when he had heard his sister Rebekah's words—"The man said this to me!"—he went to the man. He was standing there by the camels at the spring.

Laban said, "Come, you who are blessed by the LORD. Why are you standing out here? I have prepared the house and a place for the camels." So the man came to the house, and the camels were unloaded. Straw and feed were given to the camels, and water was brought to wash his feet and the feet of the men with him.

A meal was set before him, but he said, "I will not eat until I have said what I have to say."

So Laban said, "Please speak."

"I am Abraham's servant," he said. "The LORD has greatly blessed my master, and he has become rich. He has given him flocks and herds, silver and gold, male and female slaves, and camels and donkeys. Sarah, my master's wife, bore a son to my master in her old age, and he has given him everything he owns. My master put me under this oath: 'You will not take a wife for my son from the daughters of the Canaanites in whose land I live but will go to my father's family and to my clan to take a wife for my son.' But I said to my master, 'Suppose the woman will not come back with me?' He said to me, 'The LORD before whom I have walked will send his angel with you and make your journey a success, and you will take a wife for my son from my clan and from my father's family. Then you will be free from my oath if you go to my family and they do not give her to you—you will be free from my oath.'

"Today when I came to the spring, I prayed: LORD, God of my master Abraham, if only you will make my journey successful! I am standing here at a spring. Let the young woman who comes out to draw water, and I say to her, 'Please let me drink a little water from your jug,' and who responds to me, 'Drink, and I'll draw water for your camels also'—let her be the woman the LORD has appointed for my master's son.

"Before I had finished praying silently, there was Rebekah coming with her jug on her shoulder, and she went down to the spring and drew water. So I said to her, 'Please let me have a drink.' She quickly lowered her jug from her shoulder and said, 'Drink, and I'll water your camels also.' So I drank, and she also watered the camels. Then I asked her, 'Whose daughter are you?' She responded, 'The daughter of Bethuel son of Nahor, whom Milcah bore to him.' So I put the ring on her nose and the bracelets on her wrists. Then I knelt low, worshiped the LORD, and blessed the LORD, the God of my master Abraham, who guided me on the right way to take the granddaughter of my master's brother for his son. Now, if you are going to show kindness and faithfulness to my master, tell me; if not, tell me, and I will go elsewhere."

Laban and Bethuel answered, "This is from the LORD; we have no choice in the matter. Rebekah is here in front of you. Take her and go, and let her be a wife for your master's son, just as the LORD has spoken."

When Abraham's servant heard their words, he bowed to the ground before the LORD. Then he brought out objects of silver and gold, and garments, and gave them to Rebekah. He also gave precious gifts to her brother and her mother. Then he and the men with him ate and drank and spent the night.

When they got up in the morning, he said, "Send me to my master."

But her brother and mother said, "Let the girl stay with us for about ten days. Then she can go."

But he responded to them, "Do not delay me, since the LORD has made my journey a success. Send me away so that I may go to my master."

So they said, "Let's call the girl and ask her opinion."

They called Rebekah and said to her, "Will you go with this man?"

She replied, "I will go." So they sent away their sister Rebekah with the one who had nursed and raised her, and Abraham's servant and his men.

They blessed Rebekah, saying to her:

> Our sister, may you become
> thousands upon ten thousands.
> May your offspring possess
> the city gates of their enemies.

Then Rebekah and her female servants got up, mounted the camels, and followed the man. So the servant took Rebekah and left.

Now Isaac was returning from Beer-lahai-roi, for he was living in the Negev region. In the early evening Isaac went out to walk in the field, and looking up he saw camels coming. Rebekah looked up, and when she saw Isaac, she got down from her camel and asked the servant, "Who is that man in the field coming to meet us?"

The servant answered, "It is my master." So she took her veil and covered herself. Then the servant told Isaac everything he had done.

And Isaac brought her into the tent of his mother Sarah and took Rebekah to be his wife. Isaac loved her, and he was comforted after his mother's death.

25 Abraham had taken another wife, whose name was Keturah, and she bore him Zimran, Jokshan, Medan, Midian, Ishbak, and Shuah. Jokshan fathered Sheba and Dedan. Dedan's sons were the Asshurim, Letushim, and Leummim. And Midian's sons were Ephah, Epher, Hanoch, Abida, and Eldaah. All these were sons of Keturah. Abraham gave everything he owned to Isaac.

But Abraham gave gifts to the sons of his concubines, and while he was still alive he sent them eastward, away from his son Isaac, to the land of the East.

This is the length of Abraham's life: 175 years. He took his last breath and died at a good old age, old and contented, and he was gathered to his people. His sons Isaac and Ishmael buried him in the cave of Machpelah near Mamre, in the field of Ephron son of Zohar the Hethite. This was
10 the field that Abraham bought from the Hethites. Abraham was buried there with his wife Sarah. After Abraham's death, God blessed his son Isaac, who lived near Beer-lahai-roi.

These are the family records of Abraham's son Ishmael, whom Hagar the Egyptian, Sarah's slave, bore to Abraham. These are the names of Ishmael's sons; their names according to the family records are Nebaioth, Ishmael's firstborn, then Kedar, Adbeel, Mibsam, Mishma, Dumah, Massa, Hadad, Tema, Jetur, Naphish, and Kedemah. These are Ishmael's sons, and these are their names by their settlements and encampments: twelve leaders of their clans. This is the length of Ishmael's life: 137 years. He took his last breath and died, and was gathered to his people. And they settled from Havilah to Shur, which is opposite Egypt as you go toward Asshur. He stayed near all his relatives.

These are the family records of Isaac son of Abraham. Abraham fathered Isaac. Isaac was forty
20 years old when he took as his wife Rebekah daughter of Bethuel the Aramean from Paddan-aram and sister of Laban the Aramean. Isaac prayed to the LORD on behalf of his wife because she was childless. The LORD was receptive to his prayer, and his wife Rebekah conceived. But the children inside her struggled with each other, and she said, "Why is this happening to me?" So she went to inquire of the LORD. And the LORD said to her:

> Two nations are in your womb;
> two peoples will come from you and be separated.
> One people will be stronger than the other,
> and the older will serve the younger.

When her time came to give birth, there were indeed twins in her womb. The first one came
30 out red-looking, covered with hair like a fur coat, and they named him Esau. After this, his brother came out grasping Esau's heel with his hand. So he was named Jacob. Isaac was sixty years old when they were born.

When the boys grew up, Esau became an expert hunter, an outdoorsman, but Jacob was a quiet man who stayed at home. Isaac loved Esau because he had a taste for wild game, but Rebekah loved Jacob.
Once when Jacob was cooking a stew, Esau came in from the field exhausted. He said to Jacob, "Let me eat some of that red stuff, because I'm exhausted." That is why he was also named Edom.

Jacob replied, "First sell me your birthright."

"Look," said Esau, "I'm about to die, so what good is a birthright to me?"

Jacob said, "Swear to me first." So he swore to Jacob and sold his birthright to him. Then Jacob
40 gave bread and lentil stew to Esau; he ate, drank, got up, and went away. So Esau despised his
birthright.

26 There was another famine in the land in addition to the one that had occurred in Abraham's
time. And Isaac went to Abimelech, king of the Philistines, at Gerar. The LORD appeared to him
and said, "Do not go down to Egypt. Live in the land that I tell you about; stay in this land as an
alien, and I will be with you and bless you. For I will give all these lands to you and your offspring,
and I will confirm the oath that I swore to your father Abraham. I will make your offspring as
numerous as the stars of the sky, I will give your offspring all these lands, and all the nations of the
earth will be blessed by your offspring, because Abraham listened to me and kept my mandate, my
commands, my statutes, and my instructions." So Isaac settled in Gerar.

When the men of the place asked about his wife, he said, "She is my sister," for he was afraid to
10 say "my wife," thinking, "The men of the place will kill me on account of Rebekah, for she is a
beautiful woman." When Isaac had been there for some time, Abimelech king of the Philistines
looked down from the window and was surprised to see Isaac caressing his wife Rebekah.

Abimelech sent for Isaac and said, "So she is really your wife! How could you say, 'She is my
sister'?"

Isaac answered him, "Because I thought I might die on account of her."

Then Abimelech said, "What have you done to us? One of the people could easily have slept
with your wife, and you would have brought guilt on us." So Abimelech warned all the people,
"Whoever harms this man or his wife will certainly be put to death."

Isaac sowed seed in that land, and in that year he reaped a hundred times what was sown. The LORD
20 blessed him, and the man became rich and kept getting richer until he was very wealthy. He had
flocks of sheep, herds of cattle, and many slaves, and the Philistines were envious of him. Philistines
stopped up all the wells that his father's servants had dug in the days of his father Abraham, filling
them with dirt. And Abimelech said to Isaac, "Leave us, for you are much too powerful for us."

So Isaac left there, camped in the Gerar Valley, and lived there. Isaac reopened the wells
that had been dug in the days of his father Abraham and that the Philistines had stopped up
after Abraham died. He gave them the same names his father had given them. Then Isaac's
servants dug in the valley and found a well of spring water there. But the herdsmen of Gerar
quarreled with Isaac's herdsmen and said, "The water is ours!" So he named the well Esek
because they argued with him. Then they dug another well and quarreled over that one also,
30 so he named it Sitnah. He moved from there and dug another, and they did not quarrel over

it. He named it Rehoboth and said, "For now the LORD has made space for us, and we will be fruitful in the land."

From there he went up to Beer-sheba, and the LORD appeared to him that night and said, "I am the God of your father Abraham. Do not be afraid, for I am with you. I will bless you and multiply your offspring because of my servant Abraham."

So he built an altar there, called on the name of the LORD, and pitched his tent there. Isaac's servants also dug a well there.

Now Abimelech came to him from Gerar with Ahuzzath his adviser and Phicol the commander of his army. Isaac said to them, "Why have you come to me? You hated me and sent me away from you."

40 They replied, "We have clearly seen how the LORD has been with you. We think there should be an oath between two parties—between us and you. Let us make a covenant with you: You will not harm us, just as we have not harmed you but have done only what was good to you, sending you away in peace. You are now blessed by the LORD."

So he prepared a banquet for them, and they ate and drank. They got up early in the morning and swore an oath to each other. Isaac sent them on their way, and they left him in peace. On that same day Isaac's servants came to tell him about the well they had dug, saying to him, "We have found water!" He called it Sheba. Therefore the name of the city is still Beer-sheba today.

When Esau was forty years old, he took as his wives Judith daughter of Beeri the Hethite, and Basemath daughter of Elon the Hethite. They made life bitter for Isaac and Rebekah.

27 When Isaac was old and his eyes were so weak that he could not see, he called his older son Esau and said to him, "My son."

And he answered, "Here I am."

He said, "Look, I am old and do not know the day of my death. So now take your hunting gear, your quiver and bow, and go out in the field to hunt some game for me. Then make me a delicious meal that I love and bring it to me to eat, so that I can bless you before I die."

Now Rebekah was listening to what Isaac said to his son Esau. So while Esau went to the field to hunt some game to bring in, Rebekah said to her son Jacob, "Listen! I heard your father talking with your brother Esau. He said, 'Bring me game and make a delicious meal for me to eat so that I can 10 bless you in the LORD's presence before I die.' Now, my son, listen to me and do what I tell you. Go to the flock and bring me two choice young goats, and I will make them into a delicious meal for your father—the kind he loves. Then take it to your father to eat so that he may bless you before he dies."

Jacob answered Rebekah his mother, "Look, my brother Esau is a hairy man, but I am a man with smooth skin. Suppose my father touches me. Then I will be revealed to him as a deceiver and bring a curse rather than a blessing on myself."

His mother said to him, "Your curse be on me, my son. Just obey me and go get them for me."

So he went and got the goats and brought them to his mother, and his mother made the delicious food his father loved. Then Rebekah took the best clothes of her older son Esau, which were in the house, and had her younger son Jacob wear them. She put the skins of the young goats on his hands and the smooth part of his neck. Then she handed the delicious food and the bread she had made to her son Jacob.

When he came to his father, he said, "My father."

And he answered, "Here I am. Who are you, my son?"

Jacob replied to his father, "I am Esau, your firstborn. I have done as you told me. Please sit up and eat some of my game so that you may bless me."

But Isaac said to his son, "How did you ever find it so quickly, my son?"

He replied, "Because the LORD your God made it happen for me."

Then Isaac said to Jacob, "Please come closer so I can touch you, my son. Are you really my son Esau or not?"

So Jacob came closer to his father Isaac. When he touched him, he said, "The voice is the voice of Jacob, but the hands are the hands of Esau." He did not recognize him, because his hands were hairy like those of his brother Esau; so he blessed him. Again he asked, "Are you really my son Esau?"

And he replied, "I am."

Then he said, "Bring it closer to me, and let me eat some of my son's game so that I can bless you." Jacob brought it closer to him, and he ate; he brought him wine, and he drank.

Then his father Isaac said to him, "Please come closer and kiss me, my son." So he came closer and kissed him. When Isaac smelled his clothes, he blessed him and said:

> Ah, the smell of my son
> is like the smell of a field
> that the LORD has blessed.
> May God give to you—
> from the dew of the sky
> and from the richness of the land—
> an abundance of grain and new wine.
> May peoples serve you
> and nations bow in homage to you.
> Be master over your relatives;
> may your mother's sons bow in homage to you.
> Those who curse you will be cursed,
> and those who bless you will be blessed.

As soon as Isaac had finished blessing Jacob and Jacob had left the presence of his father Isaac, his brother Esau arrived from his hunting. He had also made some delicious food and brought it to his father. He said to his father, "Let my father get up and eat some of his son's game, so that you may bless me."

But his father Isaac said to him, "Who are you?"

He answered, "I am Esau your firstborn son."

Isaac began to tremble uncontrollably. "Who was it then," he said, "who hunted game and brought it to me? I ate it all before you came in, and I blessed him. Indeed, he will be 60 blessed!"

When Esau heard his father's words, he cried out with a loud and bitter cry and said to his father, "Bless me too, my father!"

But he replied, "Your brother came deceitfully and took your blessing."

So he said, "Isn't he rightly named Jacob? For he has cheated me twice now. He took my birthright, and look, now he has taken my blessing." Then he asked, "Haven't you saved a blessing for me?"

But Isaac answered Esau, "Look, I have made him a master over you, have given him all of his relatives as his servants, and have sustained him with grain and new wine. What then can I do for you, my son?"

70 Esau said to his father, "Do you have only one blessing, my father? Bless me too, my father!" And Esau wept loudly.

His father Isaac answered him,

> Look, your dwelling place will be
> away from the richness of the land,
> away from the dew of the sky above.
> You will live by your sword,
> and you will serve your brother.
> But when you rebel,
> you will break his yoke from your neck.

80 Esau held a grudge against Jacob because of the blessing his father had given him. And Esau determined in his heart, "The days of mourning for my father are approaching; then I will kill my brother Jacob."

When the words of her older son Esau were reported to Rebekah, she summoned her younger son Jacob and said to him, "Listen, your brother Esau is consoling himself by planning to kill you. So now, my son, listen to me. Flee at once to my brother Laban in Haran, and stay with him for a few days until your brother's anger subsides—until your brother's rage turns away from you and he forgets what you have done to him. Then I will send for you and bring you back from there. Why should I lose you both in one day?"

So Rebekah said to Isaac, "I'm sick of my life because of these Hethite girls. If Jacob marries
90 someone from around here, like these Hethite girls, what good is my life?"

28 So Isaac summoned Jacob, blessed him, and commanded him, "Do not marry a Canaanite girl.
Go at once to Paddan-aram, to the house of Bethuel, your mother's father. Marry one of the
daughters of Laban, your mother's brother. May God Almighty bless you and make you fruitful
and multiply you so that you become an assembly of peoples. May God give you and your
offspring the blessing of Abraham so that you may possess the land where you live as a foreigner,
the land God gave to Abraham." So Isaac sent Jacob to Paddan-aram, to Laban son of Bethuel the
Aramean, the brother of Rebekah, the mother of Jacob and Esau.

Esau noticed that Isaac blessed Jacob and sent him to Paddan-aram to get a wife there. When
he blessed him, Isaac commanded Jacob, "Do not marry a Canaanite girl." And Jacob listened to
10 his father and mother and went to Paddan-aram. Esau realized that his father Isaac disapproved
of the Canaanite women, so Esau went to Ishmael and married, in addition to his other wives,
Mahalath daughter of Ishmael, Abraham's son. She was the sister of Nebaioth.

Jacob left Beer-sheba and went toward Haran. He reached a certain place and spent the night there
because the sun had set. He took one of the stones from the place, put it there at his head, and lay
down in that place. And he dreamed: A stairway was set on the ground with its top reaching the sky,
and God's angels were going up and down on it. The LORD was standing there beside him, saying,
"I am the LORD, the God of your father Abraham and the God of Isaac. I will give you and your
offspring the land on which you are lying. Your offspring will be like the dust of the earth, and you will
spread out toward the west, the east, the north, and the south. All the peoples on earth will be blessed
20 through you and your offspring. Look, I am with you and will watch over you wherever you go. I will
bring you back to this land, for I will not leave you until I have done what I have promised you."

When Jacob awoke from his sleep, he said, "Surely the LORD is in this place, and I did not
know it." He was afraid and said, "What an awesome place this is! This is none other than the
house of God. This is the gate of heaven."

Early in the morning Jacob took the stone that was near his head and set it up as a marker.
He poured oil on top of it and named the place Bethel, though previously the city was named
Luz. Then Jacob made a vow: "If God will be with me and watch over me during this journey
I'm making, if he provides me with food to eat and clothing to wear, and if I return safely to my
father's family, then the LORD will be my God. This stone that I have set up as a marker will be
30 God's house, and I will give to you a tenth of all that you give me."

29 Jacob resumed his journey and went to the eastern country. He looked and saw a well in a field.
Three flocks of sheep were lying there beside it because the sheep were watered from this well.
But a large stone covered the opening of the well. The shepherds would roll the stone from the

opening of the well and water the sheep when all the flocks were gathered there. Then they would return the stone to its place over the well's opening.

Jacob asked the men at the well, "My brothers! Where are you from?"

"We're from Haran," they answered.

"Do you know Laban, Nahor's grandson?" Jacob asked them.

They answered, "We know him."

10 "Is he well?" Jacob asked.

"Yes," they said, "and here is his daughter Rachel, coming with his sheep."

Then Jacob said, "Look, it is still broad daylight. It's not time for the animals to be gathered. Water the flock, then go out and let them graze."

But they replied, "We can't until all the flocks have been gathered and the stone is rolled from the well's opening. Then we will water the sheep."

While he was still speaking with them, Rachel came with her father's sheep, for she was a shepherdess. As soon as Jacob saw his uncle Laban's daughter Rachel with his sheep, he went up and rolled the stone from the opening and watered his uncle Laban's sheep. Then Jacob kissed Rachel and wept loudly. He told Rachel that he was her father's relative, Rebekah's son. She ran

20 and told her father.

When Laban heard the news about his sister's son Jacob, he ran to meet him, hugged him, and kissed him. Then he took him to his house, and Jacob told him all that had happened.

Laban said to him, "Yes, you are my own flesh and blood."

After Jacob had stayed with him a month, Laban said to him, "Just because you're my relative, should you work for me for nothing? Tell me what your wages should be."

Now Laban had two daughters: the older was named Leah, and the younger was named Rachel. Leah had tender eyes, but Rachel was shapely and beautiful. Jacob loved Rachel, so he answered Laban, "I'll work for you seven years for your younger daughter Rachel."

Laban replied, "Better that I give her to you than to some other man. Stay with me." So Jacob

30 worked seven years for Rachel, and they seemed like only a few days to him because of his love for her.

Then Jacob said to Laban, "Since my time is complete, give me my wife, so I can sleep with her." So Laban invited all the men of the place and sponsored a feast. That evening, Laban took his daughter Leah and gave her to Jacob, and he slept with her. And Laban gave his slave Zilpah to his daughter Leah as her slave.

When morning came, there was Leah! So he said to Laban, "What have you done to me? Wasn't it for Rachel that I worked for you? Why have you deceived me?"

Laban answered, "It is not the custom in our country to give the younger daughter in marriage before the firstborn. Complete this week of wedding celebration, and we will also give you this

40 younger one in return for working yet another seven years for me."

And Jacob did just that. He finished the week of celebration, and Laban gave him his daughter Rachel as his wife. And Laban gave his slave Bilhah to his daughter Rachel as her slave. Jacob slept with Rachel also, and indeed, he loved Rachel more than Leah. And he worked for Laban another seven years.

When the LORD saw that Leah was neglected, he opened her womb; but Rachel was unable to conceive. Leah conceived, gave birth to a son, and named him Reuben, for she said, "The LORD has seen my affliction; surely my husband will love me now."

She conceived again, gave birth to a son, and said, "The LORD heard that I am neglected and has given me this son also." So she named him Simeon.

50 She conceived again, gave birth to a son, and said, "At last, my husband will become attached to me because I have borne three sons for him." Therefore he was named Levi.

And she conceived again, gave birth to a son, and said, "This time I will praise the LORD." Therefore she named him Judah. Then Leah stopped having children.

30 When Rachel saw that she was not bearing Jacob any children, she envied her sister. "Give me sons, or I will die!" she said to Jacob.

Jacob became angry with Rachel and said, "Am I in the place of God? He has withheld offspring from you!"

Then she said, "Here is my maid Bilhah. Go sleep with her, and she'll bear children for me so that through her I too can build a family." So Rachel gave her slave Bilhah to Jacob as a wife, and he slept with her. Bilhah conceived and bore Jacob a son. Rachel said, "God has vindicated me; yes, he has heard me and given me a son," so she named him Dan.

Rachel's slave Bilhah conceived again and bore Jacob a second son. Rachel said, "In my 10 wrestlings with God, I have wrestled with my sister and won," and she named him Naphtali.

When Leah saw that she had stopped having children, she took her slave Zilpah and gave her to Jacob as a wife. Leah's slave Zilpah bore Jacob a son. Then Leah said, "What good fortune!" and she named him Gad.

When Leah's slave Zilpah bore Jacob a second son, Leah said, "I am happy that the women call me happy," so she named him Asher.

Reuben went out during the wheat harvest and found some mandrakes in the field. When he brought them to his mother Leah, Rachel asked, "Please give me some of your son's mandrakes."

But Leah replied to her, "Isn't it enough that you have taken my husband? Now you also want to take my son's mandrakes?"

20 "Well then," Rachel said, "he can sleep with you tonight in exchange for your son's mandrakes."

When Jacob came in from the field that evening, Leah went out to meet him and said, "You must come with me, for I have hired you with my son's mandrakes." So Jacob slept with her that night.

God listened to Leah, and she conceived and bore Jacob a fifth son. Leah said, "God has rewarded me for giving my slave to my husband," and she named him Issachar.

Then Leah conceived again and bore Jacob a sixth son. "God has given me a good gift," Leah said. "This time my husband will honor me because I have borne six sons for him," and she named him Zebulun. Later, Leah bore a daughter and named her Dinah.

Then God remembered Rachel. He listened to her and opened her womb. She conceived and
30 bore a son, and she said, "God has taken away my disgrace." She named him Joseph and said, "May the LORD add another son to me."

After Rachel gave birth to Joseph, Jacob said to Laban, "Send me on my way so that I can return to my homeland. Give me my wives and my children that I have worked for, and let me go. You know how hard I have worked for you."

But Laban said to him, "If I have found favor with you, stay. I have learned by divination that the LORD has blessed me because of you." Then Laban said, "Name your wages, and I will pay them."

So Jacob said to him, "You know how I have served you and how your herds have fared with me. For you had very little before I came, but now your wealth has increased. The LORD has
40 blessed you because of me. And now, when will I also do something for my own family?"

Laban asked, "What should I give you?"

And Jacob said, "You don't need to give me anything. If you do this one thing for me, I will continue to shepherd and keep your flock. Let me go through all your sheep today and remove every sheep that is speckled or spotted, every dark-colored sheep among the lambs, and the spotted and speckled among the female goats. Such will be my wages. In the future when you come to check on my wages, my honesty will testify for me. If I have any female goats that are not speckled or spotted, or any lambs that are not black, they will be considered stolen."

"Good," said Laban. "Let it be as you have said."

That day Laban removed the streaked and spotted male goats and all the speckled and spotted
50 female goats—every one that had any white on it—and every dark-colored one among the lambs, and he placed his sons in charge of them. He put a three-day journey between himself and Jacob. Jacob, meanwhile, was shepherding the rest of Laban's flock.

Jacob then took branches of fresh poplar, almond, and plane wood, and peeled the bark, exposing white stripes on the branches. He set the peeled branches in the troughs in front of the sheep—in the water channels where the sheep came to drink. And the sheep bred when they came to drink. The flocks bred in front of the branches and bore streaked, speckled, and spotted young. Jacob separated the lambs and made the flocks face the streaked sheep and the completely dark sheep in Laban's flocks. Then he set his own stock apart and didn't put them with Laban's sheep.

Whenever the stronger of the flock were breeding, Jacob placed the branches in the troughs, in
60 full view of the flocks, and they would breed in front of the branches. As for the weaklings of the

flocks, he did not put out the branches. So it turned out that the weak sheep belonged to Laban and the stronger ones to Jacob. And the man became very rich. He had many flocks, female and male slaves, and camels and donkeys.

31 Now Jacob heard what Laban's sons were saying: "Jacob has taken all that was our father's and has built this wealth from what belonged to our father." And Jacob saw from Laban's face that his attitude toward him was not the same as before.

The Lord said to him, "Go back to the land of your ancestors and to your family, and I will be with you."

Jacob had Rachel and Leah called to the field where his flocks were. He said to them, "I can see from your father's face that his attitude toward me is not the same as before, but the God of my father has been with me. You know that with all my strength I have served your father and that he has cheated me and changed my wages ten times. But God has not let him harm me. If he
10 said, 'The spotted sheep will be your wages,' then all the sheep were born spotted. If he said, 'The streaked sheep will be your wages,' then all the sheep were born streaked. God has taken away your father's herds and given them to me.

"When the flocks were breeding, I saw in a dream that the streaked, spotted, and speckled males were mating with the females. In that dream the angel of God said to me, 'Jacob!' and I said, 'Here I am.' And he said, 'Look up and see: all the males that are mating with the flocks are streaked, spotted, and speckled, for I have seen all that Laban has been doing to you. I am the God of Bethel, where you poured oil on the stone marker and made a solemn vow to me. Get up, leave this land, and return to your native land.'"

Then Rachel and Leah answered him, "Do we have any portion or inheritance in our father's
20 family? Are we not regarded by him as outsiders? For he has sold us and has certainly spent our purchase price. In fact, all the wealth that God has taken away from our father belongs to us and to our children. So do whatever God has said to you."

So Jacob got up and put his children and wives on the camels. He took all the livestock and possessions he had acquired in Paddan-aram, and he drove his herds to go to the land of Canaan, to his father Isaac. When Laban had gone to shear his sheep, Rachel stole her father's household idols. And Jacob deceived Laban the Aramean, not telling him that he was fleeing. He fled with all his possessions, crossed the Euphrates, and headed for the hill country of Gilead.

On the third day Laban was told that Jacob had fled. So he took his relatives with him, pursued Jacob for seven days, and overtook him in the hill country of Gilead. But God came to Laban the
30 Aramean in a dream at night. "Watch yourself!" God warned him. "Don't say anything to Jacob, either good or bad."

When Laban overtook Jacob, Jacob had pitched his tent in the hill country, and Laban and his relatives also pitched their tents in the hill country of Gilead. Laban said to Jacob, "What have you done? You have deceived me and taken my daughters away like prisoners of war! Why did you secretly flee from me, deceive me, and not tell me? I would have sent you away with joy and singing, with tambourines and lyres, but you didn't even let me kiss my grandchildren and my daughters. You have acted foolishly. I could do you great harm, but last night the God of your father said to me, 'Watch yourself! Don't say anything to Jacob, either good or bad.' Now you have gone off because you long for your father's family—but why have you stolen my gods?"

40 Jacob answered, "I was afraid, for I thought you would take your daughters from me by force. If you find your gods with anyone here, he will not live! Before our relatives, point out anything that is yours and take it." Jacob did not know that Rachel had stolen the idols.

So Laban went into Jacob's tent, Leah's tent, and the tents of the two concubines, but he found nothing. When he left Leah's tent, he went into Rachel's tent. Now Rachel had taken Laban's household idols, put them in the saddlebag of the camel, and sat on them. Laban searched the whole tent but found nothing.

She said to her father, "Don't be angry, my lord, that I cannot stand up in your presence; I am having my period." So Laban searched, but could not find the household idols.

Then Jacob became incensed and brought charges against Laban. "What is my crime?" he said to 50 Laban. "What is my sin, that you have pursued me? You've searched all my possessions! Have you found anything of yours? Put it here before my relatives and yours, and let them decide between the two of us. I've been with you these twenty years. Your ewes and female goats have not miscarried, and I have not eaten the rams from your flock. I did not bring you any of the flock torn by wild beasts; I myself bore the loss. You demanded payment from me for what was stolen by day or by night. There I was—the heat consumed me by day and the frost by night, and sleep fled from my eyes. For twenty years in your household I served you—fourteen years for your two daughters and six years for your flocks—and you have changed my wages ten times! If the God of my father, the God of Abraham, the Fear of Isaac, had not been with me, certainly now you would have sent me off empty-handed. But God has seen my affliction and my hard work, and he issued his verdict last night."

60 Then Laban answered Jacob, "The daughters are my daughters; the children, my children; and the flocks, my flocks! Everything you see is mine! But what can I do today for these daughters of mine or for the children they have borne? Come now, let's make a covenant, you and I. Let it be a witness between the two of us."

So Jacob picked out a stone and set it up as a marker. Then Jacob said to his relatives, "Gather stones." And they took stones and made a mound, then ate there by the mound. Laban named the mound Jegar-sahadutha, but Jacob named it Galeed.

Then Laban said, "This mound is a witness between you and me today." Therefore the place was called Galeed and also Mizpah, for he said, "May the LORD watch between you and me when we are out of each other's sight. If you mistreat my daughters or take other wives, though no 70 one is with us, understand that God will be a witness between you and me." Laban also said to

52

Jacob, "Look at this mound and the marker I have set up between you and me. This mound is a witness and the marker is a witness that I will not pass beyond this mound to you, and you will not pass beyond this mound and this marker to do me harm. The God of Abraham, and the gods of Nahor—the gods of their father—will judge between us." And Jacob swore by the Fear of his father Isaac. Then Jacob offered a sacrifice on the mountain and invited his relatives to eat a meal. So they ate a meal and spent the night on the mountain. Laban got up early in the morning, kissed his grandchildren and daughters, and blessed them. Then Laban left to return home.

32 Jacob went on his way, and God's angels met him. When he saw them, Jacob said, "This is God's camp." So he called that place Mahanaim.

Jacob sent messengers ahead of him to his brother Esau in the land of Seir, the territory of Edom. He commanded them, "You are to say to my lord Esau, 'This is what your servant Jacob says. I have been staying with Laban and have been delayed until now. I have oxen, donkeys, flocks, and male and female slaves. I have sent this message to inform my lord, in order to seek your favor.'"

When the messengers returned to Jacob, they said, "We went to your brother Esau; he is coming to meet you—and he has four hundred men with him." Jacob was greatly afraid and
10 distressed; he divided the people with him into two camps, along with the flocks, herds, and camels. He thought, "If Esau comes to one camp and attacks it, the remaining one can escape."

Then Jacob said, "God of my father Abraham and God of my father Isaac, the LORD who said to me, 'Go back to your land and to your family, and I will cause you to prosper,' I am unworthy of all the kindness and faithfulness you have shown your servant. Indeed, I crossed over the Jordan with my staff, and now I have become two camps. Please rescue me from my brother Esau, for I am afraid of him; otherwise, he may come and attack me, the mothers, and their children. You have said, 'I will cause you to prosper, and I will make your offspring like the sand of the sea, too numerous to be counted.'"

He spent the night there and took part of what he had brought with him as a gift for his
20 brother Esau: two hundred female goats, twenty male goats, two hundred ewes, twenty rams, thirty milk camels with their young, forty cows, ten bulls, twenty female donkeys, and ten male donkeys. He entrusted them to his slaves as separate herds and said to them, "Go on ahead of me, and leave some distance between the herds."

And he told the first one, "When my brother Esau meets you and asks, 'Who do you belong to? Where are you going? And whose animals are these ahead of you?' then tell him, 'They belong to your servant Jacob. They are a gift sent to my lord Esau. And look, he is behind us.'"

He also told the second one, the third, and everyone who was walking behind the animals, "Say the same thing to Esau when you find him. You are also to say, 'Look, your servant Jacob is right behind us.'" For he thought, "I want to appease Esau with the gift that is going ahead of me. After
30 that, I can face him, and perhaps he will forgive me."

So the gift was sent on ahead of him while he remained in the camp that night. During the night Jacob got up and took his two wives, his two slave women, and his eleven sons, and crossed the ford of Jabbok. He took them and sent them across the stream, along with all his possessions.

Jacob was left alone, and a man wrestled with him until daybreak. When the man saw that he could not defeat him, he struck Jacob's hip socket as they wrestled and dislocated his hip. Then he said to Jacob, "Let me go, for it is daybreak."

But Jacob said, "I will not let you go unless you bless me."

"What is your name?" the man asked.

"Jacob," he replied.

40 "Your name will no longer be Jacob," he said. "It will be Israel because you have struggled with God and with men and have prevailed."

Then Jacob asked him, "Please tell me your name."

But he answered, "Why do you ask my name?" And he blessed him there.

Jacob then named the place Peniel, "For I have seen God face to face," he said, "yet my life has been spared." The sun shone on him as he passed by Penuel—limping because of his hip. That is why, still today, the Israelites don't eat the thigh muscle that is at the hip socket: because he struck Jacob's hip socket at the thigh muscle.

33 Now Jacob looked up and saw Esau coming toward him with four hundred men. So he divided the children among Leah, Rachel, and the two slave women. He put the slaves and their children first, Leah and her children next, and Rachel and Joseph last. He himself went on ahead and bowed to the ground seven times until he approached his brother.

But Esau ran to meet him, hugged him, threw his arms around him, and kissed him. Then they wept. When Esau looked up and saw the women and children, he asked, "Who are these with you?"

He answered, "The children God has graciously given your servant." Then the slaves and their children approached him and bowed down. Leah and her children also approached and bowed down, and then Joseph and Rachel approached and bowed down.

10 So Esau said, "What do you mean by this whole procession I met?"

"To find favor with you, my lord," he answered.

"I have enough, my brother," Esau replied. "Keep what you have."

But Jacob said, "No, please! If I have found favor with you, take this gift from me. For indeed, I have seen your face, and it is like seeing God's face, since you have accepted me. Please take my present that was brought to you, because God has been gracious to me and I have everything I need." So Jacob urged him until he accepted.

Then Esau said, "Let's move on, and I'll go ahead of you."

Jacob replied, "My lord knows that the children are weak, and I have nursing flocks and herds. If they are driven hard for one day, the whole herd will die. Let my lord go ahead of his servant. I

20 will continue on slowly, at a pace suited to the livestock and the children, until I come to my lord at Seir."

Esau said, "Let me leave some of my people with you."

But he replied, "Why do that? Please indulge me, my lord."

That day Esau started on his way back to Seir, but Jacob went to Succoth. He built a house for himself and shelters for his livestock; that is why the place was called Succoth.

After Jacob came from Paddan-aram, he arrived safely at Shechem in the land of Canaan and camped in front of the city. He purchased a section of the field where he had pitched his tent from the sons of Hamor, Shechem's father, for a hundred pieces of silver. And he set up an altar there and called it God, the God of Israel.

34 Leah's daughter Dinah, whom Leah bore to Jacob, went out to see some of the young women of the area. When Shechem—son of Hamor the Hivite, who was the region's chieftain—saw her, he took her and raped her. He became infatuated with Jacob's daughter Dinah. He loved the young girl and spoke tenderly to her. "Get me this girl as a wife," he told his father.

Jacob heard that Shechem had defiled his daughter Dinah, but since his sons were with his livestock in the field, he remained silent until they returned. Meanwhile, Shechem's father Hamor came to speak with Jacob. Jacob's sons returned from the field when they heard about the incident. They were deeply grieved and very angry, for Shechem had committed an outrage against Israel by raping Jacob's daughter, and such a thing should not be done.

10 Hamor said to Jacob's sons, "My son Shechem has his heart set on your daughter. Please give her to him as a wife. Intermarry with us; give your daughters to us, and take our daughters for yourselves. Live with us. The land is before you. Settle here, move about, and acquire property in it."

Then Shechem said to Dinah's father and brothers, "Grant me this favor, and I'll give you whatever you say. Demand of me a high compensation and gift; I'll give you whatever you ask me. Just give the girl to be my wife!"

But Jacob's sons answered Shechem and his father Hamor deceitfully because he had defiled their sister Dinah. "We cannot do this thing," they said to them. "Giving our sister to an uncircumcised man is a disgrace to us. We will agree with you only on this condition: if all your males are circumcised as we are. Then we will give you our daughters, take your daughters for

20 ourselves, live with you, and become one people. But if you will not listen to us and be circumcised, then we will take our daughter and go."

Their words seemed good to Hamor and his son Shechem. The young man did not delay doing this, because he was delighted with Jacob's daughter. Now he was the most important in all his father's family. So Hamor and his son Shechem went to the gate of their city and spoke to the men of their city.

"These men are peaceful toward us," they said. "Let them live in our land and move about in it, for indeed, the region is large enough for them. Let's take their daughters as our wives and give our daughters to them. But the men will agree to live with us and be one people only on this condition: if all our men are circumcised as they are. Won't their livestock, their possessions, and all their animals become ours? Only let's agree with them, and they will live with us."

All the men who had come to the city gates listened to Hamor and his son Shechem, and all those men were circumcised. On the third day, when they were still in pain, two of Jacob's sons, Simeon and Levi, Dinah's brothers, took their swords, went into the unsuspecting city, and killed every male. They killed Hamor and his son Shechem with their swords, took Dinah from Shechem's house, and went away. Jacob's sons came to the slaughter and plundered the city because their sister had been defiled. They took their flocks, herds, donkeys, and whatever was in the city and in the field. They captured all their possessions, dependents, and wives and plundered everything in the houses.

Then Jacob said to Simeon and Levi, "You have brought trouble on me, making me odious to the inhabitants of the land, the Canaanites and the Perizzites. We are few in number; if they unite against me and attack me, I and my household will be destroyed."

But they answered, "Should he treat our sister like a prostitute?"

35 God said to Jacob, "Get up! Go to Bethel and settle there. Build an altar there to the God who appeared to you when you fled from your brother Esau."

So Jacob said to his family and all who were with him, "Get rid of the foreign gods that are among you. Purify yourselves and change your clothes. We must get up and go to Bethel. I will build an altar there to the God who answered me in my day of distress. He has been with me everywhere I have gone."

Then they gave Jacob all their foreign gods and their earrings, and Jacob hid them under the oak near Shechem. When they set out, a terror from God came over the cities around them, and they did not pursue Jacob's sons. So Jacob and all who were with him came to Luz (that is, Bethel) in the land of Canaan. Jacob built an altar there and called the place El-bethel because it was there that God had revealed himself to him when he was fleeing from his brother.

Deborah, the one who had nursed and raised Rebekah, died and was buried under the oak south of Bethel. So Jacob named it Allon-bacuth.

God appeared to Jacob again after he returned from Paddan-aram, and he blessed him. God said to him, "Your name is Jacob; you will no longer be named Jacob, but your name will be Israel." So he named him Israel. God also said to him, "I am God Almighty. Be fruitful and multiply. A nation, indeed an assembly of nations, will come from you, and kings will descend from you. I will give to you the land that I gave to Abraham and Isaac. And I will give the land to your future descendants." Then God withdrew from him at the place where he had spoken to him.

Jacob set up a marker at the place where he had spoken to him—a stone marker. He poured a drink offering on it and poured oil on it. Jacob named the place where God had spoken with him Bethel.

They set out from Bethel. When they were still some distance from Ephrath, Rachel began to give birth, and her labor was difficult. During her difficult labor, the midwife said to her, "Don't be afraid, for you have another son." With her last breath—for she was dying—she named him Ben-oni, but his father called him Benjamin. So Rachel died and was buried on the way to Ephrath (that is, Bethlehem). Jacob set up a marker on her grave; it is the marker at Rachel's grave still today.

Israel set out again and pitched his tent beyond the Tower of Eder. While Israel was living in that region, Reuben went in and slept with his father's concubine Bilhah, and Israel heard about it.

Jacob had twelve sons:

30   Leah's sons were Reuben (Jacob's firstborn),
       Simeon, Levi, Judah,
       Issachar, and Zebulun.
       Rachel's sons were
       Joseph and Benjamin.
       The sons of Rachel's slave Bilhah
       were Dan and Naphtali.
       The sons of Leah's slave Zilpah
       were Gad and Asher.

These are the sons of Jacob, who were born to him in Paddan-aram.

40   Jacob came to his father Isaac at Mamre in Kiriath-arba (that is, Hebron), where Abraham and Isaac had stayed. Isaac lived 180 years. He took his last breath and died, and was gathered to his people, old and full of days. His sons Esau and Jacob buried him.

36   These are the family records of Esau (that is, Edom). Esau took his wives from the Canaanite women: Adah daughter of Elon the Hethite, Oholibamah daughter of Anah and granddaughter of Zibeon the Hivite, and Basemath daughter of Ishmael and sister of Nebaioth. Adah bore Eliphaz to Esau, Basemath bore Reuel, and Oholibamah bore Jeush, Jalam, and Korah. These were Esau's sons, who were born to him in the land of Canaan.

Esau took his wives, sons, daughters, and all the people of his household, as well as his herds, all his livestock, and all the property he had acquired in Canaan; he went to a land away from his brother Jacob. For their possessions were too many for them to live together, and because of their herds, the land where they stayed could not support them. So Esau (that is, Edom) lived in the mountains of Seir.

10   These are the family records of Esau, father of the Edomites in the mountains of Seir.

       These are the names of Esau's sons:
       Eliphaz son of Esau's wife Adah,
       and Reuel son of Esau's wife Basemath.
       The sons of Eliphaz were

Teman, Omar, Zepho, Gatam, and Kenaz.
Timna, a concubine of Esau's son Eliphaz,
bore Amalek to Eliphaz.
These are the sons of Esau's wife Adah.

These are Reuel's sons:
Nahath, Zerah, Shammah, and Mizzah.
These are the sons of Esau's wife Basemath.

These are the sons of Esau's wife Oholibamah
daughter of Anah and granddaughter of Zibeon:
She bore Jeush, Jalam, and Korah to Edom.

These are the chiefs among Esau's sons:
the sons of Eliphaz, Esau's firstborn:
chief Teman, chief Omar, chief Zepho, chief Kenaz,
chief Korah, chief Gatam, and chief Amalek.
These are the chiefs descended from Eliphaz
in the land of Edom.
These are the sons of Adah.

These are the sons of Reuel, Esau's son:
chief Nahath, chief Zerah, chief Shammah, and chief Mizzah.
These are the chiefs descended from Reuel
in the land of Edom.
These are the sons of Esau's wife Basemath.

These are the sons of Esau's wife Oholibamah:
chief Jeush, chief Jalam, and chief Korah.
These are the chiefs descended from Esau's wife Oholibamah
daughter of Anah.
These are the sons of Esau (that is, Edom),
and these are their chiefs.

These are the sons of Seir the Horite,
the inhabitants of the land:
Lotan, Shobal, Zibeon, Anah,
Dishon, Ezer, and Dishan.

These are the chiefs among the Horites,
the sons of Seir, in the land of Edom.
The sons of Lotan were Hori and Heman.
Timna was Lotan's sister.
These are Shobal's sons:
Alvan, Manahath, Ebal, Shepho, and Onam.
These are Zibeon's sons: Aiah and Anah.
This was the Anah who found the hot springs in the wilderness
while he was pasturing the donkeys of his father Zibeon.
These are the children of Anah:
Dishon and Oholibamah daughter of Anah.
These are Dishon's sons:
Hemdan, Eshban, Ithran, and Cheran.
These are Ezer's sons:
Bilhan, Zaavan, and Akan.
These are Dishan's sons: Uz and Aran.

These are the chiefs among the Horites:
chief Lotan, chief Shobal, chief Zibeon, chief Anah,
chief Dishon, chief Ezer, and chief Dishan.
These are the chiefs among the Horites,
clan by clan, in the land of Seir.

These are the kings who reigned in the land of Edom
before any king reigned over the Israelites:
Bela son of Beor reigned in Edom;
the name of his city was Dinhabah.
When Bela died, Jobab son of Zerah from Bozrah reigned in his place.
When Jobab died, Husham from the land of the Temanites reigned in his place.
When Husham died, Hadad son of Bedad reigned in his place.
He defeated Midian in the field of Moab;
the name of his city was Avith.
When Hadad died, Samlah from Masrekah reigned in his place.
When Samlah died, Shaul from Rehoboth on the Euphrates River reigned in his place.
When Shaul died, Baal-hanan son of Achbor reigned in his place.
When Baal-hanan son of Achbor died, Hadar reigned in his place.
His city was Pau, and his wife's name was Mehetabel
daughter of Matred daughter of Me-zahab.

These are the names of Esau's chiefs,
according to their families and their localities,
by their names:
chief Timna, chief Alvah, chief Jetheth,
chief Oholibamah, chief Elah, chief Pinon,
chief Kenaz, chief Teman, chief Mibzar,
chief Magdiel, and chief Iram.
90 These are Edom's chiefs,
according to their settlements in the land they possessed.
Esau was father of the Edomites.

37 Jacob lived in the land where his father had stayed, the land of Canaan. These are the family records of Jacob.

At seventeen years of age, Joseph tended sheep with his brothers. The young man was working with the sons of Bilhah and Zilpah, his father's wives, and he brought a bad report about them to their father.

Now Israel loved Joseph more than his other sons because Joseph was a son born to him in his old age, and he made a long-sleeved robe for him. When his brothers saw that their father loved him more than all his brothers, they hated him and could not bring themselves to speak peaceably to him.

10 Then Joseph had a dream. When he told it to his brothers, they hated him even more. He said to them, "Listen to this dream I had: There we were, binding sheaves of grain in the field. Suddenly my sheaf stood up, and your sheaves gathered around it and bowed down to my sheaf."

"Are you really going to reign over us?" his brothers asked him. "Are you really going to rule us?" So they hated him even more because of his dream and what he had said.

Then he had another dream and told it to his brothers. "Look," he said, "I had another dream, and this time the sun, moon, and eleven stars were bowing down to me."

He told his father and brothers, and his father rebuked him. "What kind of dream is this that you have had?" he said. "Am I and your mother and your brothers really going to come and bow down to the ground before you?" His brothers were jealous of him, but his father kept the matter
20 in mind.

His brothers had gone to pasture their father's flocks at Shechem. Israel said to Joseph, "Your brothers, you know, are pasturing the flocks at Shechem. Get ready. I'm sending you to them."

"I'm ready," Joseph replied.

Then Israel said to him, "Go and see how your brothers and the flocks are doing, and bring word back to me." So he sent him from the Hebron Valley, and he went to Shechem.

A man found him there, wandering in the field, and asked him, "What are you looking for?"

"I'm looking for my brothers," Joseph said. "Can you tell me where they are pasturing their flocks?"

"They've moved on from here," the man said. "I heard them say, 'Let's go to Dothan.'" So Joseph set out after his brothers and found them at Dothan.

30

They saw him in the distance, and before he had reached them, they plotted to kill him. They said to one another, "Oh, look, here comes that dream expert! So now, come on, let's kill him and throw him into one of the pits. We can say that a vicious animal ate him. Then we'll see what becomes of his dreams!"

When Reuben heard this, he tried to save him from them. He said, "Let's not take his life." Reuben also said to them, "Don't shed blood. Throw him into this pit in the wilderness, but don't lay a hand on him"—intending to rescue him from them and return him to his father.

When Joseph came to his brothers, they stripped off Joseph's robe, the long-sleeved robe that he had on. Then they took him and threw him into the pit. The pit was empty, without water.

40

They sat down to eat a meal, and when they looked up, there was a caravan of Ishmaelites coming from Gilead. Their camels were carrying aromatic gum, balsam, and resin, going down to Egypt.

Judah said to his brothers, "What do we gain if we kill our brother and cover up his blood? Come on, let's sell him to the Ishmaelites and not lay a hand on him, for he is our brother, our own flesh," and his brothers agreed. When Midianite traders passed by, his brothers pulled Joseph out of the pit and sold him for twenty pieces of silver to the Ishmaelites, who took Joseph to Egypt.

When Reuben returned to the pit and saw that Joseph was not there, he tore his clothes. He went back to his brothers and said, "The boy is gone! What am I going to do?" So they took Joseph's robe, slaughtered a male goat, and dipped the robe in its blood. They sent the long-sleeved robe to their father and said, "We found this. Examine it. Is it your son's robe or not?"

50

His father recognized it. "It is my son's robe," he said. "A vicious animal has devoured him. Joseph has been torn to pieces!" Then Jacob tore his clothes, put sackcloth around his waist, and mourned for his son many days. All his sons and daughters tried to comfort him, but he refused to be comforted. "No," he said. "I will go down to Sheol to my son, mourning." And his father wept for him.

Meanwhile, the Midianites sold Joseph in Egypt to Potiphar, an officer of Pharaoh and the captain of the guards.

38 At that time Judah left his brothers and settled near an Adullamite named Hirah. There Judah saw the daughter of a Canaanite named Shua; he took her as a wife and slept with her. She conceived and gave birth to a son, and he named him Er. She conceived again, gave birth to a son, and named him Onan. She gave birth to another son and named him Shelah. It was at Chezib that she gave birth to him.

Judah got a wife for Er, his firstborn, and her name was Tamar. Now Er, Judah's firstborn, was evil in the LORD's sight, and the LORD put him to death. Then Judah said to Onan, "Sleep with your brother's wife. Perform your duty as her brother-in-law and produce offspring for your brother." But Onan knew that the offspring would not be his, so whenever he slept with his brother's wife, he released his semen on the ground so that he would not produce offspring for his brother. What he did was evil in the LORD's sight, so he put him to death also.

Then Judah said to his daughter-in-law Tamar, "Remain a widow in your father's house until my son Shelah grows up." For he thought, "He might die too, like his brothers." So Tamar went to live in her father's house.

After a long time Judah's wife, the daughter of Shua, died. When Judah had finished mourning, he and his friend Hirah the Adullamite went up to Timnah to his sheepshearers. Tamar was told, "Your father-in-law is going up to Timnah to shear his sheep." So she took off her widow's clothes, veiled her face, covered herself, and sat at the entrance to Enaim, which is on the way to Timnah. For she saw that, though Shelah had grown up, she had not been given to him as a wife. When Judah saw her, he thought she was a prostitute, for she had covered her face.

He went over to her and said, "Come, let me sleep with you," for he did not know that she was his daughter-in-law.

She said, "What will you give me for sleeping with me?"

"I will send you a young goat from my flock," he replied.

But she said, "Only if you leave something with me until you send it."

"What should I give you?" he asked.

She answered, "Your signet ring, your cord, and the staff in your hand." So he gave them to her and slept with her, and she became pregnant by him. She got up and left, then removed her veil and put her widow's clothes back on.

When Judah sent the young goat by his friend the Adullamite in order to get back the items he had left with the woman, he could not find her. He asked the men of the place, "Where is the cult prostitute who was beside the road at Enaim?"

"There has been no cult prostitute here," they answered.

So the Adullamite returned to Judah, saying, "I couldn't find her, and besides, the men of the place said, 'There has been no cult prostitute here.'"

Judah replied, "Let her keep the items for herself; otherwise we will become a laughingstock. After all, I did send this young goat, but you couldn't find her."

About three months later Judah was told, "Your daughter-in-law, Tamar, has been acting like a prostitute, and now she is pregnant."

"Bring her out," Judah said, "and let her be burned to death!"

As she was being brought out, she sent her father-in-law this message: "I am pregnant by the man to whom these items belong." And she added, "Examine them. Whose signet ring, cord, and staff are these?"

Judah recognized them and said, "She is more in the right than I, since I did not give her to my son Shelah." And he did not know her intimately again.

When the time came for her to give birth, there were twins in her womb. As she was giving birth, one of them put out his hand, and the midwife took it and tied a scarlet thread around it, announcing, "This one came out first." But then he pulled his hand back, out came his brother, 50 and she said, "What a breakout you have made for yourself!" So he was named Perez. Then his brother, who had the scarlet thread tied to his hand, came out, and was named Zerah.

39 Now Joseph had been taken to Egypt. An Egyptian named Potiphar, an officer of Pharaoh and the captain of the guards, bought him from the Ishmaelites who had brought him there. The LORD was with Joseph, and he became a successful man, serving in the household of his Egyptian master. When his master saw that the LORD was with him and that the LORD made everything he did successful, Joseph found favor with his master and became his personal attendant. Potiphar also put him in charge of his household and placed all that he owned under his authority. From the time that he put him in charge of his household and of all that he owned, the LORD blessed the Egyptian's house because of Joseph. The LORD's blessing was on all that he owned, in his house and in his fields. He left all that he owned under Joseph's authority; he did not concern himself 10 with anything except the food he ate.

Now Joseph was well-built and handsome. After some time his master's wife looked longingly at Joseph and said, "Sleep with me."

But he refused. "Look," he said to his master's wife, "with me here my master does not concern himself with anything in his house, and he has put all that he owns under my authority. No one in this house is greater than I am. He has withheld nothing from me except you, because you are his wife. So how could I do this immense evil, and how could I sin against God?"

Although she spoke to Joseph day after day, he refused to go to bed with her. Now one day he went into the house to do his work, and none of the household servants were there. She grabbed him by his garment and said, "Sleep with me!" But leaving his garment in her hand, 20 he escaped and ran outside. When she saw that he had left his garment with her and had run outside, she called her household servants. "Look," she said to them, "my husband brought a Hebrew man to make fools of us. He came to me so he could sleep with me, and I screamed as loud as I could. When he heard me screaming for help, he left his garment beside me and ran outside."

She put Joseph's garment beside her until his master came home. Then she told him the same story: "The Hebrew slave you brought to us came to make a fool of me, but when I screamed for help, he left his garment beside me and ran outside."

When his master heard the story his wife told him—"These are the things your slave did to me"—he was furious and had him thrown into prison, where the king's prisoners were confined.
30 So Joseph was there in prison.

But the LORD was with Joseph and extended kindness to him. He granted him favor with the prison warden. The warden put all the prisoners who were in the prison under Joseph's authority, and he was responsible for everything that was done there. The warden did not bother with anything under Joseph's authority, because the LORD was with him, and the LORD made everything that he did successful.

40 After this, the king of Egypt's cupbearer and baker offended their master, the king of Egypt. Pharaoh was angry with his two officers, the chief cupbearer and the chief baker, and put them in custody in the house of the captain of the guards in the prison where Joseph was confined. The captain of the guards assigned Joseph to them as their personal attendant, and they were in custody for some time.

The king of Egypt's cupbearer and baker, who were confined in the prison, each had a dream. Both had a dream on the same night, and each dream had its own meaning. When Joseph came to them in the morning, he saw that they looked distraught. So he asked Pharaoh's officers who were in custody with him in his master's house, "Why do you look so sad today?"

"We had dreams," they said to him, "but there is no one to interpret them."

10 Then Joseph said to them, "Don't interpretations belong to God? Tell me your dreams."

So the chief cupbearer told his dream to Joseph: "In my dream there was a vine in front of me. On the vine were three branches. As soon as it budded, its blossoms came out and its clusters ripened into grapes. Pharaoh's cup was in my hand, and I took the grapes, squeezed them into Pharaoh's cup, and placed the cup in Pharaoh's hand."

"This is its interpretation," Joseph said to him. "The three branches are three days. In just three days Pharaoh will lift up your head and restore you to your position. You will put Pharaoh's cup in his hand the way you used to when you were his cupbearer. But when all goes well for you, remember that I was with you. Please show kindness to me by mentioning me to Pharaoh, and get me out of this prison. For I was kidnapped from the land of the Hebrews, and even here I have
20 done nothing that they should put me in the dungeon."

When the chief baker saw that the interpretation was positive, he said to Joseph, "I also had a dream. Three baskets of white bread were on my head. In the top basket were all sorts of baked goods for Pharaoh, but the birds were eating them out of the basket on my head."

"This is its interpretation," Joseph replied. "The three baskets are three days. In just three days Pharaoh will lift up your head—from off you—and hang you on a tree. Then the birds will eat the flesh from your body."

On the third day, which was Pharaoh's birthday, he gave a feast for all his servants. He elevated the chief cupbearer and the chief baker among his servants. Pharaoh restored the chief cupbearer

to his position as cupbearer, and he placed the cup in Pharaoh's hand. But Pharaoh hanged the
30 chief baker, just as Joseph had explained to them. Yet the chief cupbearer did not remember
Joseph; he forgot him.

41 At the end of two years Pharaoh had a dream: He was standing beside the Nile, when seven
healthy-looking, well-fed cows came up from the Nile and began to graze among the reeds. After
them, seven other cows, sickly and thin, came up from the Nile and stood beside those cows along
the bank of the Nile. The sickly, thin cows ate the healthy, well-fed cows. Then Pharaoh woke up.
He fell asleep and dreamed a second time: Seven heads of grain, plump and good, came up on one
stalk. After them, seven heads of grain, thin and scorched by the east wind, sprouted up. The thin
heads of grain swallowed up the seven plump, full ones. Then Pharaoh woke up, and it was only a
dream.

When morning came, he was troubled, so he summoned all the magicians of Egypt and all its
10 wise men. Pharaoh told them his dreams, but no one could interpret them for him.

Then the chief cupbearer said to Pharaoh, "Today I remember my faults. Pharaoh was angry
with his servants, and he put me and the chief baker in the custody of the captain of the guards.
He and I had dreams on the same night; each dream had its own meaning. Now a young Hebrew,
a slave of the captain of the guards, was with us there. We told him our dreams, he interpreted our
dreams for us, and each had its own interpretation. It turned out just the way he interpreted them
to us: I was restored to my position, and the other man was hanged."

Then Pharaoh sent for Joseph, and they quickly brought him from the dungeon. He shaved,
changed his clothes, and went to Pharaoh.

Pharaoh said to Joseph, "I have had a dream, and no one can interpret it. But I have heard it
20 said about you that you can hear a dream and interpret it."

"I am not able to," Joseph answered Pharaoh. "It is God who will give Pharaoh a favorable
answer."

So Pharaoh said to Joseph, "In my dream I was standing on the bank of the Nile, when seven
well-fed, healthy-looking cows came up from the Nile and grazed among the reeds. After them,
seven other cows—weak, very sickly, and thin—came up. I've never seen such sickly ones as these
in all the land of Egypt. Then the thin, sickly cows ate the first seven well-fed cows. When they
had devoured them, you could not tell that they had devoured them; their appearance was as bad
as it had been before. Then I woke up. In my dream I also saw seven heads of grain, full and good,
coming up on one stalk. After them, seven heads of grain—withered, thin, and scorched by the
east wind—sprouted up. The thin heads of grain swallowed the seven good ones. I told this to the
magicians, but no one can tell me what it means."

Then Joseph said to Pharaoh, "Pharaoh's dreams mean the same thing. God has revealed to
Pharaoh what he is about to do. The seven good cows are seven years, and the seven good heads
are seven years. The dreams mean the same thing. The seven thin, sickly cows that came up after

them are seven years, and the seven worthless heads of grain scorched by the east wind are seven years of famine.

"It is just as I told Pharaoh: God has shown Pharaoh what he is about to do. Seven years of great abundance are coming throughout the land of Egypt. After them, seven years of famine will take place, and all the abundance in the land of Egypt will be forgotten. The famine will devastate 40 the land. The abundance in the land will not be remembered because of the famine that follows it, for the famine will be very severe. Since the dream was given twice to Pharaoh, it means that the matter has been determined by God, and he will carry it out soon.

"So now, let Pharaoh look for a discerning and wise man and set him over the land of Egypt. Let Pharaoh do this: Let him appoint overseers over the land and take a fifth of the harvest of the land of Egypt during the seven years of abundance. Let them gather all the excess food during these good years that are coming. Under Pharaoh's authority, store the grain in the cities, so they may preserve it as food. The food will be a reserve for the land during the seven years of famine that will take place in the land of Egypt. Then the country will not be wiped out by the famine."

50 The proposal pleased Pharaoh and all his servants, and he said to them, "Can we find anyone like this, a man who has God's spirit in him?" So Pharaoh said to Joseph, "Since God has made all this known to you, there is no one as discerning and wise as you are. You will be over my house, and all my people will obey your commands. Only I, as king, will be greater than you." Pharaoh also said to Joseph, "See, I am placing you over all the land of Egypt." Pharaoh removed his signet ring from his hand and put it on Joseph's hand, clothed him with fine linen garments, and placed a gold chain around his neck. He had Joseph ride in his second chariot, and servants called out before him, "Make way!" So he placed him over all the land of Egypt. Pharaoh said to Joseph, "I am Pharaoh and no one will be able to raise his hand or foot in all the land of Egypt without your permission." Pharaoh gave Joseph the name Zaphenath-paneah and gave him a wife, Asenath 60 daughter of Potiphera, priest at On. And Joseph went throughout the land of Egypt.

Joseph was thirty years old when he entered the service of Pharaoh king of Egypt. Joseph left Pharaoh's presence and traveled throughout the land of Egypt.

During the seven years of abundance the land produced outstanding harvests. Joseph gathered all the excess food in the land of Egypt during the seven years and put it in the cities. He put the food in every city from the fields around it. So Joseph stored up grain in such abundance—like the sand of the sea—that he stopped measuring it because it was beyond measure.

Two sons were born to Joseph before the years of famine arrived. Asenath daughter of Potiphera, priest at On, bore them to him. Joseph named the firstborn Manasseh and said, "God has made me forget all my hardship and my whole family." And the second son he named Ephraim 70 and said, "God has made me fruitful in the land of my affliction."

Then the seven years of abundance in the land of Egypt came to an end, and the seven years of famine began, just as Joseph had said. There was famine in every land, but in the whole land of Egypt there was food. When the whole land of Egypt was stricken with famine, the people cried out to Pharaoh for food. Pharaoh told all Egypt, "Go to Joseph and do whatever he tells you." Now the famine had spread across the whole region, so Joseph opened all the storehouses and sold grain to the Egyptians, for the famine was severe in the land of Egypt. Every land came to Joseph in Egypt to buy grain, for the famine was severe in every land.

42 When Jacob learned that there was grain in Egypt, he said to his sons, "Why do you keep looking at each other? Listen," he went on, "I have heard there is grain in Egypt. Go down there and buy some for us so that we will live and not die." So ten of Joseph's brothers went down to buy grain from Egypt. But Jacob did not send Joseph's brother Benjamin with his brothers, for he thought, "Something might happen to him."

The sons of Israel were among those who came to buy grain, for the famine was in the land of Canaan. Joseph was in charge of the country; he sold grain to all its people. His brothers came and bowed down before him with their faces to the ground. When Joseph saw his brothers, he recognized them, but he treated them like strangers and spoke harshly to them.

10 "Where do you come from?" he asked.

"From the land of Canaan to buy food," they replied.

Although Joseph recognized his brothers, they did not recognize him. Joseph remembered his dreams about them and said to them, "You are spies. You have come to see the weakness of the land."

"No, my lord. Your servants have come to buy food," they said. "We are all sons of one man. We are honest; your servants are not spies."

"No," he said to them. "You have come to see the weakness of the land."

But they replied, "We, your servants, were twelve brothers, the sons of one man in the land of Canaan. The youngest is now with our father, and one is no longer living."

Then Joseph said to them, "I have spoken: 'You are spies!' This is how you will be tested: As 20 surely as Pharaoh lives, you will not leave this place unless your youngest brother comes here. Send one from among you to get your brother. The rest of you will be imprisoned so that your words can be tested to see if they are true. If they are not, then as surely as Pharaoh lives, you are spies!" So Joseph imprisoned them together for three days.

On the third day Joseph said to them, "I fear God—do this and you will live. If you are honest, let one of you be confined to the guardhouse, while the rest of you go and take grain to relieve the hunger of your households. Bring your youngest brother to me so that your words can be confirmed; then you won't die." And they consented to this.

Then they said to each other, "Obviously, we are being punished for what we did to our brother. We saw his deep distress when he pleaded with us, but we would not listen. That is why 30 this trouble has come to us."

But Reuben replied, "Didn't I tell you not to harm the boy? But you wouldn't listen. Now we must account for his blood!"

They did not realize that Joseph understood them, since there was an interpreter between them. He turned away from them and wept. When he turned back and spoke to them, he took Simeon from them and had him bound before their eyes. Joseph then gave orders to fill their containers with grain, return each man's silver to his sack, and give them provisions for their journey. This order was carried out. They loaded the grain on their donkeys and left there.

At the place where they lodged for the night, one of them opened his sack to get feed for his donkey, and he saw his silver there at the top of his bag. He said to his brothers, "My silver has 40 been returned! It's here in my bag." Their hearts sank. Trembling, they turned to one another and said, "What has God done to us?"

When they reached their father Jacob in the land of Canaan, they told him all that had happened to them: "The man who is the lord of the country spoke harshly to us and accused us of spying on the country. But we told him, 'We are honest and not spies. We were twelve brothers, sons of the same father. One is no longer living, and the youngest is now with our father in the land of Canaan.' The man who is the lord of the country said to us, 'This is how I will know if you are honest: Leave one brother with me, take food to relieve the hunger of your households, and go. Bring back your youngest brother to me, and I will know that you are not spies but honest men. I will then give your brother back to you, and you can trade in the country.'"

50 As they began emptying their sacks, there in each man's sack was his bag of silver! When they and their father saw their bags of silver, they were afraid.

Their father Jacob said to them, "It's me that you make childless. Joseph is gone, and Simeon is gone. Now you want to take Benjamin. Everything happens to me!"

Then Reuben said to his father, "You can kill my two sons if I don't bring him back to you. Put him in my care, and I will return him to you."

But Jacob answered, "My son will not go down with you, for his brother is dead and he alone is left. If anything happens to him on your journey, you will bring my gray hairs down to Sheol in sorrow."

43 Now the famine in the land was severe. When they had used up the grain they had brought back from Egypt, their father said to them, "Go back and buy us a little food."

But Judah said to him, "The man specifically warned us, 'You will not see me again unless your brother is with you.' If you will send our brother with us, we will go down and buy food for you. But if you will not send him, we will not go, for the man said to us, 'You will not see me again unless your brother is with you.'"

"Why have you caused me so much trouble?" Israel asked. "Why did you tell the man that you had another brother?"

They answered, "The man kept asking about us and our family: 'Is your father still alive? Do
10 you have another brother?' And we answered him accordingly. How could we know that he would
say, 'Bring your brother here'?"

Then Judah said to his father Israel, "Send the boy with me. We will be on our way so that we
may live and not die—neither we, nor you, nor our dependents. I will be responsible for him. You
can hold me personally accountable! If I do not bring him back to you and set him before you, I
will be guilty before you forever. If we had not delayed, we could have come back twice by now."

Then their father Israel said to them, "If it must be so, then do this: Put some of the best
products of the land in your packs and take them down to the man as a gift—a little balsam and
a little honey, aromatic gum and resin, pistachios and almonds. Take twice as much silver with
you. Return the silver that was returned to you in the top of your bags. Perhaps it was a mistake.
20 Take your brother also, and go back at once to the man. May God Almighty cause the man to be
merciful to you so that he will release your other brother and Benjamin to you. As for me, if I am
deprived of my sons, then I am deprived."

The men took this gift, double the amount of silver, and Benjamin. They immediately went down
to Egypt and stood before Joseph.

When Joseph saw Benjamin with them, he said to his steward, "Take the men to my house.
Slaughter an animal and prepare it, for they will eat with me at noon." The man did as Joseph had
said and brought them to Joseph's house.

But the men were afraid because they were taken to Joseph's house. They said, "We have
been brought here because of the silver that was returned in our bags the first time. They intend
30 to overpower us, seize us, make us slaves, and take our donkeys." So they approached Joseph's
steward and spoke to him at the doorway of the house.

They said, "My lord, we really did come down here the first time only to buy food. When we
came to the place where we lodged for the night and opened our bags of grain, each one's silver was
at the top of his bag! It was the full amount of our silver, and we have brought it back with us. We
have brought additional silver with us to buy food. We don't know who put our silver in the bags."

Then the steward said, "May you be well. Don't be afraid. Your God and the God of your
father must have put treasure in your bags. I received your silver." Then he brought Simeon out to
them. The steward brought the men into Joseph's house, gave them water to wash their feet, and
got feed for their donkeys. Since the men had heard that they were going to eat a meal there, they
40 prepared their gift for Joseph's arrival at noon. When Joseph came home, they brought him the
gift they had carried into the house, and they bowed to the ground before him.

He asked if they were well, and he said, "How is your elderly father that you told me about? Is
he still alive?"

They answered, "Your servant our father is well. He is still alive." And they knelt low and paid
homage to him.

When he looked up and saw his brother Benjamin, his mother's son, he asked, "Is this your youngest brother that you told me about?" Then he said, "May God be gracious to you, my son." Joseph hurried out because he was overcome with emotion for his brother, and he was about to weep. He went into an inner room and wept there. Then he washed his face and came out. 50 Regaining his composure, he said, "Serve the meal."

They served him by himself, his brothers by themselves, and the Egyptians who were eating with him by themselves, because Egyptians could not eat with Hebrews, since that is detestable to them. They were seated before him in order by age, from the firstborn to the youngest. The men looked at each other in astonishment. Portions were served to them from Joseph's table, and Benjamin's portion was five times larger than any of theirs. They drank and became drunk with Joseph.

44 Joseph commanded his steward, "Fill the men's bags with as much food as they can carry, and put each one's silver at the top of his bag. Put my cup, the silver one, at the top of the youngest one's bag, along with the silver for his grain." So he did as Joseph told him.

At morning light, the men were sent off with their donkeys. They had not gone very far from the city when Joseph said to his steward, "Get up. Pursue the men, and when you overtake them, say to them, 'Why have you repaid evil for good? Isn't this the cup that my master drinks from and uses for divination? What you have done is wrong!'"

When he overtook them, he said these words to them. They said to him, "Why does my lord say these things? Your servants could not possibly do such a thing. We even brought back to you 10 from the land of Canaan the silver we found at the top of our bags. How could we steal silver or gold from your master's house? If it is found with one of us, your servants, he must die, and the rest of us will become my lord's slaves."

The steward replied, "What you have said is right, but only the one who is found to have it will be my slave, and the rest of you will be blameless."

So each one quickly lowered his sack to the ground and opened it. The steward searched, beginning with the oldest and ending with the youngest, and the cup was found in Benjamin's sack. Then they tore their clothes, and each one loaded his donkey and returned to the city.

When Judah and his brothers reached Joseph's house, he was still there. They fell to the ground before him. "What have you done?" Joseph said to them. "Didn't you know that a man like 20 me could uncover the truth by divination?"

"What can we say to my lord?" Judah replied. "How can we plead? How can we justify ourselves? God has exposed your servants' iniquity. We are now my lord's slaves—both we and the one in whose possession the cup was found."

Then Joseph said, "I swear that I will not do this. The man in whose possession the cup was found will be my slave. The rest of you can go in peace to your father."

But Judah approached him and said, "My lord, please let your servant speak personally to my lord. Do not be angry with your servant, for you are like Pharaoh. My lord asked his servants, 'Do you have a father or a brother?' and we answered my lord, 'We have an elderly father and a younger brother, the child of his old age. The boy's brother is dead. He is the only one of his mother's sons left, and his

30 father loves him.' Then you said to your servants, 'Bring him to me so that I can see him.' But we said to my lord, 'The boy cannot leave his father. If he were to leave, his father would die.' Then you said to your servants, 'If your younger brother does not come down with you, you will not see me again.'

"This is what happened when we went back to your servant my father: We reported to him the words of my lord. But our father said, 'Go again, and buy us a little food.' We told him, 'We cannot go down unless our younger brother goes with us. If our younger brother isn't with us, we cannot see the man.' Your servant my father said to us, 'You know that my wife bore me two sons. One is gone from me—I said he must have been torn to pieces—and I have never seen him again. If you also take this one from me and anything happens to him, you will bring my gray hairs down to Sheol in sorrow.'

40 "So if I come to your servant my father and the boy is not with us—his life is wrapped up with the boy's life—when he sees that the boy is not with us, he will die. Then your servants will have brought the gray hairs of your servant our father down to Sheol in sorrow. Your servant became accountable to my father for the boy, saying, 'If I do not return him to you, I will always bear the guilt for sinning against you, my father.' Now please let your servant remain here as my lord's slave, in place of the boy. Let him go back with his brothers. For how can I go back to my father without the boy? I could not bear to see the grief that would overwhelm my father."

45 Joseph could no longer keep his composure in front of all his attendants, so he called out, "Send everyone away from me!" No one was with him when he revealed his identity to his brothers. But he wept so loudly that the Egyptians heard it, and also Pharaoh's household heard it. Joseph said to his brothers, "I am Joseph! Is my father still living?" But they could not answer him because they were terrified in his presence.

Then Joseph said to his brothers, "Please, come near me," and they came near. "I am Joseph, your brother," he said, "the one you sold into Egypt. And now don't be grieved or angry with yourselves for selling me here, because God sent me ahead of you to preserve life. For the famine has been in the land these two years, and there will be five more years without plowing or

10 harvesting. God sent me ahead of you to establish you as a remnant within the land and to keep you alive by a great deliverance. Therefore it was not you who sent me here, but God. He has made me a father to Pharaoh, lord of his entire household, and ruler over all the land of Egypt.

"Return quickly to my father and say to him, 'This is what your son Joseph says: "God has made me lord of all Egypt. Come down to me without delay. You can settle in the land of Goshen and be near me—you, your children, and your grandchildren, your flocks, your herds, and all you have. There I will sustain you, for there will be five more years of famine. Otherwise, you, your household, and everything you have will become destitute."' Look! Your eyes and the eyes of my brother Benjamin can see that I'm the one speaking to you. Tell my father about all my glory in Egypt and about all you have seen. And bring my father here quickly."

20 Then Joseph threw his arms around his brother Benjamin and wept, and Benjamin wept on his shoulder. Joseph kissed each of his brothers as he wept, and afterward his brothers talked with him.

When the news reached Pharaoh's palace, "Joseph's brothers have come," Pharaoh and his servants were pleased. Pharaoh said to Joseph, "Tell your brothers, 'Do this: Load your animals and go on back to the land of Canaan. Get your father and your families, and come back to me. I will give you the best of the land of Egypt, and you can eat from the richness of the land.' You are also commanded to tell them, 'Do this: Take wagons from the land of Egypt for your dependents and your wives and bring your father here. Do not be concerned about your belongings, for the best of all the land of Egypt is yours.'"

30 The sons of Israel did this. Joseph gave them wagons as Pharaoh had commanded, and he gave them provisions for the journey. He gave each of the brothers changes of clothes, but he gave Benjamin three hundred pieces of silver and five changes of clothes. He sent his father the following: ten donkeys carrying the best products of Egypt and ten female donkeys carrying grain, food, and provisions for his father on the journey. So Joseph sent his brothers on their way, and as they were leaving, he said to them, "Don't argue on the way."

So they went up from Egypt and came to their father Jacob in the land of Canaan. They said, "Joseph is still alive, and he is ruler over all the land of Egypt!" Jacob was stunned, for he did not believe them. But when they told Jacob all that Joseph had said to them, and when he saw the wagons that Joseph had sent to transport him, the spirit of their father Jacob revived.

Then Israel said, "Enough! My son Joseph is still alive. I will go to see him before I die."

46 Israel set out with all that he had and came to Beer-sheba, and he offered sacrifices to the God of his father Isaac. That night God spoke to Israel in a vision: "Jacob, Jacob!" he said.

And Jacob replied, "Here I am."

God said, "I am God, the God of your father. Do not be afraid to go down to Egypt, for I will make you into a great nation there. I will go down with you to Egypt, and I will also bring you back. Joseph will close your eyes when you die."

Jacob left Beer-sheba. The sons of Israel took their father Jacob in the wagons Pharaoh had sent to carry him, along with their dependents and their wives. They also took their cattle and possessions they had acquired in the land of Canaan. Then Jacob and all his offspring with

10 him came to Egypt. His sons and grandsons, his daughters and granddaughters, indeed all his offspring, he brought with him to Egypt.

These are the names of the sons of Israel who came to Egypt—Jacob and his sons:

Jacob's firstborn: Reuben.

Reuben's sons: Hanoch, Pallu, Hezron, and Carmi.

Simeon's sons: Jemuel, Jamin, Ohad, Jachin, Zohar, and Shaul, the son of a Canaanite woman.

Levi's sons: Gershon, Kohath, and Merari.

Judah's sons: Er, Onan, Shelah, Perez, and Zerah; but Er and Onan died in the land of Canaan.

The sons of Perez were Hezron and Hamul.

Issachar's sons: Tola, Puvah, Jashub, and Shimron.

Zebulun's sons: Sered, Elon, and Jahleel.

These were Leah's sons born to Jacob in Paddan-aram, as well as his daughter Dinah. The total number of persons: thirty-three.

Gad's sons: Ziphion, Haggi, Shuni, Ezbon, Eri, Arodi, and Areli.

Asher's sons: Imnah, Ishvah, Ishvi, Beriah, and their sister Serah.

Beriah's sons were Heber and Malchiel.

These were the sons of Zilpah—whom Laban gave to his daughter Leah—that she bore to Jacob: sixteen persons.

The sons of Jacob's wife Rachel: Joseph and Benjamin.

Manasseh and Ephraim were born to Joseph in the land of Egypt. They were born to him by Asenath daughter of Potiphera, a priest at On.

Benjamin's sons: Bela, Becher, Ashbel, Gera, Naaman, Ehi, Rosh, Muppim, Huppim, and Ard.

These were Rachel's sons who were born to Jacob: fourteen persons.

Dan's son: Hushim.

Naphtali's sons: Jahzeel, Guni, Jezer, and Shillem.

These were the sons of Bilhah, whom Laban gave to his daughter Rachel. She bore to Jacob: seven persons.

The total number of persons belonging to Jacob—his direct descendants, not including the wives of Jacob's sons—who came to Egypt: sixty-six.

And Joseph's sons who were born to him in Egypt: two persons.

All those of Jacob's household who came to Egypt: seventy persons.

Now Jacob had sent Judah ahead of him to Joseph to prepare for his arrival at Goshen. When they came to the land of Goshen, Joseph hitched the horses to his chariot and went up to Goshen to meet his father Israel. Joseph presented himself to him, threw his arms around him, and wept for a long time.

Then Israel said to Joseph, "I'm ready to die now because I have seen your face and you are still alive!"

Joseph said to his brothers and to his father's family, "I will go up and inform Pharaoh, telling
50 him, 'My brothers and my father's family, who were in the land of Canaan, have come to me. The
men are shepherds; they also raise livestock. They have brought their flocks and herds and all
that they have.' When Pharaoh addresses you and asks, 'What is your occupation?' you are to say,
'Your servants, both we and our ancestors, have raised livestock from our youth until now.' Then
you will be allowed to settle in the land of Goshen, since all shepherds are detestable to Egyptians."

47 So Joseph went and informed Pharaoh: "My father and my brothers, with their flocks and herds
and all that they own, have come from the land of Canaan and are now in the land of Goshen."

He took five of his brothers and presented them to Pharaoh. And Pharaoh asked his brothers,
"What is your occupation?"

They said to Pharaoh, "Your servants, both we and our ancestors, are shepherds." And they
said to Pharaoh, "We have come to stay in the land for a while because there is no grazing land
for your servants' sheep, since the famine in the land of Canaan has been severe. So now, please let
your servants settle in the land of Goshen."

10 Then Pharaoh said to Joseph, "Now that your father and brothers have come to you, the land
of Egypt is open before you; settle your father and brothers in the best part of the land. They can
live in the land of Goshen. If you know of any capable men among them, put them in charge of my
livestock."

Joseph then brought his father Jacob and presented him to Pharaoh, and Jacob blessed
Pharaoh. Pharaoh said to Jacob, "How many years have you lived?"

Jacob said to Pharaoh, "My pilgrimage has lasted 130 years. My years have been few and hard,
and they have not reached the years of my ancestors during their pilgrimages." So Jacob blessed
Pharaoh and departed from Pharaoh's presence.

Then Joseph settled his father and brothers in the land of Egypt and gave them property in the
20 best part of the land, the land of Rameses, as Pharaoh had commanded. And Joseph provided his
father, his brothers, and all his father's family with food for their dependents.

But there was no food in the entire region, for the famine was very severe. The land of Egypt and
the land of Canaan were exhausted by the famine. Joseph collected all the silver to be found in
the land of Egypt and the land of Canaan in exchange for the grain they were purchasing, and he
brought the silver to Pharaoh's palace. When the silver from the land of Egypt and the land of
Canaan was gone, all the Egyptians came to Joseph and said, "Give us food. Why should we die
here in front of you? The silver is gone!"

But Joseph said, "Give me your livestock. Since the silver is gone, I will give you food in
exchange for your livestock." So they brought their livestock to Joseph, and he gave them food in
30 exchange for the horses, the flocks of sheep, the herds of cattle, and the donkeys. That year he
provided them with food in exchange for all their livestock.

When that year was over, they came the next year and said to him, "We cannot hide from our lord that the silver is gone and that all our livestock belongs to our lord. There is nothing left for our lord except our bodies and our land. Why should we die here in front of you—both us and our land? Buy us and our land in exchange for food. Then we with our land will become Pharaoh's slaves. Give us seed so that we can live and not die, and so that the land won't become desolate."

In this way, Joseph acquired all the land in Egypt for Pharaoh, because every Egyptian sold his field since the famine was so severe for them. The land became Pharaoh's, and Joseph made the people servants from one end of Egypt to the other. The only land he did not acquire belonged to 40 the priests, for they had an allowance from Pharaoh. They ate from their allowance that Pharaoh gave them; therefore they did not sell their land.

Joseph said to the people, "Understand today that I have acquired you and your land for Pharaoh. Here is seed for you. Sow it in the land. At harvest, you are to give a fifth of it to Pharaoh, and four-fifths will be yours as seed for the field and as food for yourselves, your households, and your dependents."

"You have saved our lives," they said. "We have found favor with our lord and will be Pharaoh's slaves." So Joseph made it a law, still in effect today in the land of Egypt, that a fifth of the produce belongs to Pharaoh. Only the priests' land does not belong to Pharaoh.

Israel settled in the land of Egypt, in the region of Goshen. They acquired property in it and 50 became fruitful and very numerous. Now Jacob lived in the land of Egypt 17 years, and his life span was 147 years. When the time approached for him to die, he called his son Joseph and said to him, "If I have found favor with you, put your hand under my thigh and promise me that you will deal with me in kindness and faithfulness. Do not bury me in Egypt. When I rest with my ancestors, carry me away from Egypt and bury me in their burial place."

Joseph answered, "I will do what you have asked."

And Jacob said, "Swear to me." So Joseph swore to him. Then Israel bowed in thanks at the head of his bed.

48 Some time after this, Joseph was told, "Your father is weaker." So he set out with his two sons, Manasseh and Ephraim. When Jacob was told, "Your son Joseph has come to you," Israel summoned his strength and sat up in bed.

Jacob said to Joseph, "God Almighty appeared to me at Luz in the land of Canaan and blessed me. He said to me, 'I will make you fruitful and numerous; I will make many nations come from you, and I will give this land as a permanent possession to your future descendants.' Your two sons born to you in the land of Egypt before I came to you in Egypt are now mine. Ephraim and Manasseh belong to me just as Reuben and Simeon do. Children born to you after them will be yours and will be recorded under the names of their brothers with regard to their inheritance. 10 When I was returning from Paddan, to my sorrow Rachel died along the way, some distance from Ephrath in the land of Canaan. I buried her there along the way to Ephrath" (that is, Bethlehem).

When Israel saw Joseph's sons, he said, "Who are these?"

And Joseph said to his father, "They are my sons God has given me here."

So Israel said, "Bring them to me and I will bless them." Now his eyesight was poor because of old age; he could hardly see. Joseph brought them to him, and he kissed and embraced them. Israel said to Joseph, "I never expected to see your face again, but now God has even let me see your offspring." Then Joseph took them from his father's knees and bowed with his face to the ground.

20 Then Joseph took them both—with his right hand Ephraim toward Israel's left, and with his left hand Manasseh toward Israel's right—and brought them to Israel. But Israel stretched out his right hand and put it on the head of Ephraim, the younger, and crossing his hands, put his left on Manasseh's head, although Manasseh was the firstborn. Then he blessed Joseph and said:

> The God before whom my fathers Abraham and Isaac walked,
>   the God who has been my shepherd all my life to this day,
>   the angel who has redeemed me from all harm—
>   may he bless these boys.
>   And may they be called by my name
>   and the names of my fathers Abraham and Isaac,
30   and may they grow to be numerous within the land.

When Joseph saw that his father had placed his right hand on Ephraim's head, he thought it was a mistake and took his father's hand to move it from Ephraim's head to Manasseh's. Joseph said to his father, "Not that way, my father! This one is the firstborn. Put your right hand on his head."

But his father refused and said, "I know, my son, I know! He too will become a tribe, and he too will be great; nevertheless, his younger brother will be greater than he, and his offspring will become a populous nation." So he blessed them that day, putting Ephraim before Manasseh when he said, "The nation Israel will invoke blessings by you, saying, 'May God make you like Ephraim and Manasseh.'"

40 Israel said to Joseph, "Look, I am about to die, but God will be with you and will bring you back to the land of your fathers. Over and above what I am giving your brothers, I am giving you the one mountain slope that I took from the Amorites with my sword and bow."

49 Then Jacob called his sons and said, "Gather around, and I will tell you what will happen to you in the days to come.

Come together and listen, sons of Jacob;
listen to your father Israel:

Reuben, you are my firstborn,
my strength and the firstfruits of my virility,
excelling in prominence, excelling in power.
Turbulent as water, you will not excel,
because you got into your father's bed
and you defiled it—he got into my bed.

Simeon and Levi are brothers;
their knives are vicious weapons.
May I never enter their council;
may I never join their assembly.
For in their anger they kill men,
and on a whim they hamstring oxen.
Their anger is cursed, for it is strong,
and their fury, for it is cruel!
I will disperse them throughout Jacob
and scatter them throughout Israel.

Judah, your brothers will praise you.
Your hand will be on the necks of your enemies;
your father's sons will bow down to you.
Judah is a young lion—
my son, you return from the kill.
He crouches; he lies down like a lion
or a lioness—who dares to rouse him?
The scepter will not depart from Judah
or the staff from between his feet
until he whose right it is comes
and the obedience of the peoples belongs to him.
He ties his donkey to a vine,
and the colt of his donkey to the choice vine.
He washes his clothes in wine
and his robes in the blood of grapes.
His eyes are darker than wine,
and his teeth are whiter than milk.

Zebulun will live by the seashore
and will be a harbor for ships,
40   and his territory will be next to Sidon.

Issachar is a strong donkey
lying down between the saddlebags.
He saw that his resting place was good
and that the land was pleasant,
so he leaned his shoulder to bear a load
and became a forced laborer.

Dan will judge his people
as one of the tribes of Israel.
Dan will be a snake by the road,
50   a viper beside the path,
that bites the horse's heels
so that its rider falls backward.

I wait for your salvation, LORD.

Gad will be attacked by raiders,
but he will attack their heels.

Asher's food will be rich,
and he will produce royal delicacies.

Naphtali is a doe set free
that bears beautiful fawns.

60   Joseph is a fruitful vine,
a fruitful vine beside a spring;
its branches climb over the wall.
The archers attacked him,
shot at him, and were hostile toward him.
Yet his bow remained steady,
and his strong arms were made agile
by the hands of the Mighty One of Jacob,

by the name of the Shepherd, the Rock of Israel,
by the God of your father who helps you,
70 and by the Almighty who blesses you
with blessings of the heavens above,
blessings of the deep that lies below,
and blessings of the breasts and the womb.
The blessings of your father excel
the blessings of my ancestors
and the bounty of the ancient hills.
May they rest on the head of Joseph,
on the brow of the prince of his brothers.

Benjamin is a wolf; he tears his prey.
80 In the morning he devours the prey,
and in the evening he divides the plunder."

These are the tribes of Israel, twelve in all, and this is what their father said to them. He blessed them, and he blessed each one with a suitable blessing.

Then he commanded them, "I am about to be gathered to my people. Bury me with my ancestors in the cave in the field of Ephron the Hethite. The cave is in the field of Machpelah near Mamre, in the land of Canaan. This is the field Abraham purchased from Ephron the Hethite as burial property. Abraham and his wife Sarah are buried there, Isaac and his wife Rebekah are buried there, and I buried Leah there. The field and the cave in it were purchased from the Hethites." When Jacob had finished giving charges to his sons, he drew his feet into the bed, took his last 90 breath, and was gathered to his people.

50 Then Joseph, leaning over his father's face, wept and kissed him. He commanded his servants who were physicians to embalm his father. So they embalmed Israel. They took forty days to complete this, for embalming takes that long, and the Egyptians mourned for him seventy days.

When the days of mourning were over, Joseph said to Pharaoh's household, "If I have found favor with you, please tell Pharaoh that my father made me take an oath, saying, 'I am about to die. You must bury me there in the tomb that I made for myself in the land of Canaan.' Now let me go and bury my father. Then I will return."

So Pharaoh said, "Go and bury your father in keeping with your oath."

Then Joseph went to bury his father, and all Pharaoh's servants, the elders of his household, 10 and all the elders of the land of Egypt went with him, along with all Joseph's family, his brothers, and his father's family. Only their dependents, their flocks, and their herds were left in the land of

Goshen. Horses and chariots went up with him; it was a very impressive procession. When they reached the threshing floor of Atad, which is across the Jordan, they lamented and wept loudly, and Joseph mourned seven days for his father. When the Canaanite inhabitants of the land saw the mourning at the threshing floor of Atad, they said, "This is a solemn mourning on the part of the Egyptians." Therefore the place is named Abel-mizraim. It is across the Jordan.

So Jacob's sons did for him what he had commanded them. They carried him to the land of Canaan and buried him in the cave at Machpelah in the field near Mamre, which Abraham had purchased as burial property from Ephron the Hethite. After Joseph buried his father, he returned to Egypt with his brothers and all who had gone with him to bury his father.

When Joseph's brothers saw that their father was dead, they said to one another, "If Joseph is holding a grudge against us, he will certainly repay us for all the suffering we caused him."

So they sent this message to Joseph, "Before he died your father gave a command: 'Say this to Joseph: Please forgive your brothers' transgression and their sin—the suffering they caused you.' Therefore, please forgive the transgression of the servants of the God of your father." Joseph wept when their message came to him. His brothers also came to him, bowed down before him, and said, "We are your slaves!"

But Joseph said to them, "Don't be afraid. Am I in the place of God? You planned evil against me; God planned it for good to bring about the present result—the survival of many people. Therefore don't be afraid. I will take care of you and your children." And he comforted them and spoke kindly to them.

Joseph and his father's family remained in Egypt. Joseph lived 110 years. He saw Ephraim's sons to the third generation; the sons of Manasseh's son Machir were recognized by Joseph.

Joseph said to his brothers, "I am about to die, but God will certainly come to your aid and bring you up from this land to the land he swore to give to Abraham, Isaac, and Jacob." So Joseph made the sons of Israel take an oath: "When God comes to your aid, you are to carry my bones up from here."

Joseph died at the age of 110. They embalmed him and placed him in a coffin in Egypt.

Introduction to Exodus

Brent Strawn

The name "Exodus" comes into English from the Greek title of the book, *Exodos Aigyptou*, which means "the departure from Egypt." The Hebrew name of the book, *Shemot*, means "names" and is drawn from the first significant word in Exod 1.1. In truth, Exodus contains more names than just those of the sons of Jacob listed in 1.3–5. *Moses* is obviously one very important name (and person) who comes on the biblical scene in Exod 2. Even more significant is the fact that Exodus has much to say about the divine name *Yhwh* (usually vocalized as "Yahweh," but traditionally translated as "the LORD"), which is revealed and discussed in several places in the book (see especially 3.25–28; 6.3–13; 15.10–11, 76–79; 20.2–3, 6–10; 29.63–65; 31.12–14; 34.9–13).

Indeed, in some ways, Exodus could be seen as an extended book-length explanation of who God is and what the divine name *Yhwh* means. Although that name is also found in Genesis, it is said to be revealed in special if not initial ways in Exodus (twice, in fact: 3.25–28; 6.3–4). It is initially related to the verb "to be" (Hebrew *hāyāh*) in the act of self-naming God shares with Moses: "I AM WHO I AM" (3:14). But what does this designation mean? If it is meant to be revelatory it is a revelation that remains enigmatic, concealing as much as it reveals. Even the translation is uncertain; it could also be translated "I WILL BE WHO I WILL BE." This latter rendering leaves things quite open-ended, with the book of Exodus filling out the divine profile as it goes, starting already with how God *will be with* Moses (3.21–22). In Moses' first exchange with Pharaoh, the Egyptian king asks "Who is the LORD?" (5.3–4). Although Pharaoh does not yet know the Lord, he will become intimately—even painfully—acquainted with Israel's God before the book is half done. It is not without a good bit of irony, therefore, that the "book of names" leaves the seemingly all-powerful Egyptian monarch entirely *unnamed*.

Also unnamed is the author or authors who wrote Exodus. While tradition ascribes the Torah to Moses, the same is true of David and the Psalms, and Solomon and the wisdom literature found in the biblical books of Proverbs, Song of Songs, and Ecclesiastes. In each case, we know from various pieces of data that Moses, David, and Solomon are best understood as "patron saints" of the literature with which they are associated. In no case are these three individuals responsible for the entirety of the material that is now linked to them in the HS, even though some of it may well go back to their times. Rather than being the work of just one hand, Exodus, no less than other books in the HS, is the end result of a long and complex set of processes to which many hands contributed. This lends even more credibility to the book which now comes to us as a weighty collection of authoritative, time-tested, valued, and validated traditions.

Exodus is arguably the most important book of the HS, recounting, as it does, the fundamental saving act of Yahweh in the HS: delivering Israel from Egypt. The exodus event dominates the narrative history and memory of Israel in the Torah, and references to it appear also in the Psalms (e.g., Pss 78, 105, 114, 135), the prophets (e.g., Isa 43.56–81; 48.72–83; 51.40–54; 52.46–53), and beyond (e.g., Josh 24.30–33; Judg 2.1–3; 1 Sam 8.9–11). In this way, the *exodus event* becomes a rather large and widely-attested *exodus tradition*. The writings of the NT, too, draw heavily from the book of Exodus and the exodus tradition. Indeed, the Four Gospels' presentation of Passion Week depends directly and extensively upon the book of Exodus (e.g., Passover, see Exod 12), making Yahweh's work in the exodus the fundamental redemptive divine act in all of Scripture. As but one example, in Luke's account of the transfiguration, what Jesus, Moses, and Elijah discuss is his "departure," in Greek, his *exodos*, "which he was about to accomplish in Jerusalem" (Luke 9:31).

Outline
1. Out of Pharaoh's Empire (1.1–18.43)
    a. Prelude to Deliverance (1.1–2.41)
    b. The Deliverer Called (3.1–4.43)
    c. Prelude to Conflict (4.44–7.9)
    d. Yahweh vs. Pharaoh (7.10–13.25)
    e. Flight and Freedom (13.26–18.43)

2. Into Yahweh's Covenant (19.1–40.45)
    a. At the Mountain (19.1–25)
    b. The Tabernacle Commanded (25.1–31.22)
    c. The Covenant Endangered (32.1–34.61)
    d. The Tabernacle Constructed (35.1–40.45)

Suggested Resources
Brueggemann, Walter. "The Book of Exodus: Introduction, Commentary, and Reflections." Pages 675–981 in vol. 1 of *The New Interpreter's Bible*. Nashville: Abingdon, 1994.

Childs, Brevard S. *The Book of Exodus*. Old Testament Library. Louisville: Westminster, 1974.

Fretheim, Terence E. *Exodus*. Interpretation. Louisville: Westminster John Knox, 1991.

Houtman, Cornelis. *Exodus*. Historical Commentary on the Old Testament. 4 vols. Leuven: Peeters, 1993–2002.

Janzen, J. Gerald. *Exodus*. Westminster Bible Companion. Louisville: Westminster John Knox, 1997.

Propp, William H. C. *Exodus*. Anchor Bible Commentary. 2 vols. New York: Doubleday, 1999–2006.

Exodus

I These are the names of the sons of Israel who came to Egypt with Jacob; each came with his family:

> Reuben, Simeon, Levi, and Judah;
> Issachar, Zebulun, and Benjamin;
> Dan and Naphtali; Gad and Asher.

The total number of Jacob's descendants was seventy; Joseph was already in Egypt.

Joseph and all his brothers and all that generation eventually died. But the Israelites were fruitful, increased rapidly, multiplied, and became extremely numerous so that the land was filled with them.

A new king, who did not know about Joseph, came to power in Egypt. He said to his people, "Look, the Israelite people are more numerous and powerful than we are. Come, let's deal shrewdly with them; otherwise they will multiply further, and when war breaks out, they will join our enemies, fight against us, and leave the country." So the Egyptians assigned taskmasters over the Israelites to oppress them with forced labor. They built Pithom and Rameses as supply cities for Pharaoh. But the more they oppressed them, the more they multiplied and spread so that the Egyptians came to dread the Israelites. They worked the Israelites ruthlessly and made their lives bitter with difficult labor in brick and mortar and in all kinds of fieldwork. They ruthlessly imposed all this work on them.

The king of Egypt said to the Hebrew midwives—the first, whose name was Shiphrah, and the second, whose name was Puah—"When you help the Hebrew women give birth, observe them as they deliver. If the child is a son, kill him, but if it's a daughter, she may live." The midwives, however, feared God and did not do as the king of Egypt had told them; they let the boys live. So the king of Egypt summoned the midwives and asked them, "Why have you done this and let the boys live?"

The midwives said to Pharaoh, "The Hebrew women are not like the Egyptian women, for they are vigorous and give birth before the midwife can get to them."

So God was good to the midwives, and the people multiplied and became very numerous. Since the midwives feared God, he gave them families. Pharaoh then commanded all his people, "You must throw every son born to the Hebrews into the Nile, but let every daughter live."

2 Now a man from the family of Levi married a Levite woman. The woman became pregnant and gave birth to a son; when she saw that he was beautiful, she hid him for three months. But when she could no longer hide him, she got a papyrus basket for him and coated it with asphalt and pitch. She placed the child in it and set it among the reeds by the bank of the Nile. Then his sister stood at a distance in order to see what would happen to him.

Pharaoh's daughter went down to bathe at the Nile while her servant girls walked along the riverbank. She saw the basket among the reeds, sent her slave girl, took it, opened it, and saw him, the child—and there he was, a little boy, crying. She felt sorry for him and said, "This is one of the Hebrew boys."

10 Then his sister said to Pharaoh's daughter, "Should I go and call a Hebrew woman who is nursing to nurse the boy for you?"

"Go," Pharaoh's daughter told her. So the girl went and called the boy's mother. Then Pharaoh's daughter said to her, "Take this child and nurse him for me, and I will pay your wages." So the woman took the boy and nursed him. When the child grew older, she brought him to Pharaoh's daughter, and he became her son. She named him Moses, "Because," she said, "I drew him out of the water."

Years later, after Moses had grown up, he went out to his own people and observed their forced labor. He saw an Egyptian striking a Hebrew, one of his people. Looking all around and seeing no one, he struck the Egyptian dead and hid him in the sand. The next day he went 20 out and saw two Hebrews fighting. He asked the one in the wrong, "Why are you attacking your neighbor?"

"Who made you a commander and judge over us?" the man replied. "Are you planning to kill me as you killed the Egyptian?"

Then Moses became afraid and thought, "What I did is certainly known."

When Pharaoh heard about this, he tried to kill Moses. But Moses fled from Pharaoh and went to live in the land of Midian, and sat down by a well.

Now the priest of Midian had seven daughters. They came to draw water and filled the troughs to water their father's flock. Then some shepherds arrived and drove them away, but Moses came to their rescue and watered their flock. When they returned to their father Reuel, he asked, "Why 30 have you come back so quickly today?"

They answered, "An Egyptian rescued us from the shepherds. He even drew water for us and watered the flock."

"So where is he?" he asked his daughters. "Why then did you leave the man behind? Invite him to eat dinner."

Moses agreed to stay with the man, and he gave his daughter Zipporah to Moses in marriage. She gave birth to a son whom he named Gershom, for he said, "I have been a resident alien in a foreign land."

After a long time, the king of Egypt died. The Israelites groaned because of their difficult labor, they cried out, and their cry for help because of the difficult labor ascended to God. God heard
40 their groaning, and God remembered his covenant with Abraham, with Isaac, and with Jacob. God saw the Israelites, and God knew.

3 Meanwhile, Moses was shepherding the flock of his father-in-law Jethro, the priest of Midian. He led the flock to the far side of the wilderness and came to Horeb, the mountain of God. Then the angel of the LORD appeared to him in a flame of fire within a bush. As Moses looked, he saw that the bush was on fire but was not consumed. So Moses thought, "I must go over and look at this remarkable sight. Why isn't the bush burning up?"

When the LORD saw that he had gone over to look, God called out to him from the bush, "Moses, Moses!"

"Here I am," he answered.

"Do not come closer," he said. "Remove the sandals from your feet, for the place where you are
10 standing is holy ground." Then he continued, "I am the God of your father, the God of Abraham, the God of Isaac, and the God of Jacob." Moses hid his face because he was afraid to look at God.

Then the LORD said, "I have observed the misery of my people in Egypt, and have heard them crying out because of their oppressors. I know about their sufferings, and I have come down to rescue them from the power of the Egyptians and to bring them from that land to a good and spacious land, a land flowing with milk and honey—the territory of the Canaanites, Hethites, Amorites, Perizzites, Hivites, and Jebusites. So because the Israelites' cry for help has come to me, and I have also seen the way the Egyptians are oppressing them, therefore, go. I am sending you to Pharaoh so that you may lead my people, the Israelites, out of Egypt."

But Moses asked God, "Who am I that I should go to Pharaoh and that I should bring the
20 Israelites out of Egypt?"

He answered, "I will certainly be with you, and this will be the sign to you that I am the one who sent you: when you bring the people out of Egypt, you will all worship God at this mountain."

Then Moses asked God, "If I go to the Israelites and say to them, 'The God of your ancestors has sent me to you,' and they ask me, 'What is his name?' what should I tell them?"

God replied to Moses, "I AM WHO I AM. This is what you are to say to the Israelites: I AM has sent me to you." God also said to Moses, "Say this to the Israelites: The LORD, the God of your ancestors, the God of Abraham, the God of Isaac, and the God of Jacob, has sent me to you. This is my name forever; this is how I am to be remembered in every generation.

"Go and assemble the elders of Israel and say to them: The LORD, the God of your ancestors,
30 the God of Abraham, Isaac, and Jacob, has appeared to me and said: I have paid close attention to you and to what has been done to you in Egypt. And I have promised you that I will bring you up from the misery of Egypt to the land of the Canaanites, Hethites, Amorites, Perizzites, Hivites, and Jebusites—a land flowing with milk and honey. They will listen to what you say. Then you,

along with the elders of Israel, must go to the king of Egypt and say to him: The Lord, the God of the Hebrews, has met with us. Now please let us go on a three-day trip into the wilderness so that we may sacrifice to the Lord our God.

"However, I know that the king of Egypt will not allow you to go, even under force from a strong hand. But when I stretch out my hand and strike Egypt with all my miracles that I will perform in it, after that, he will let you go. And I will give these people such favor with the Egyptians that when you go, you will not go empty-handed. Each woman will ask her neighbor and any woman staying in her house for silver and gold jewelry, and clothing, and you will put them on your sons and daughters. So you will plunder the Egyptians."

4 Moses answered, "What if they won't believe me and will not obey me but say, 'The Lord did not appear to you'?"

The Lord asked him, "What is that in your hand?"

"A staff," he replied.

"Throw it on the ground," he said. So Moses threw it on the ground, it became a snake, and he ran from it. The Lord told Moses, "Stretch out your hand and grab it by the tail." So he stretched out his hand and caught it, and it became a staff in his hand. "This will take place," he continued, "so that they will believe that the Lord, the God of their ancestors, the God of Abraham, the God of Isaac, and the God of Jacob, has appeared to you."

In addition the Lord said to him, "Put your hand inside your cloak." So he put his hand inside his cloak, and when he took it out, his hand was diseased, resembling snow. "Put your hand back inside your cloak," he said. So he put his hand back inside his cloak, and when he took it out, it had again become like the rest of his skin. "If they will not believe you and will not respond to the evidence of the first sign, they may believe the evidence of the second sign. And if they don't believe even these two signs or listen to what you say, take some water from the Nile and pour it on the dry ground. The water you take from the Nile will become blood on the ground."

But Moses replied to the Lord, "Please, Lord, I have never been eloquent—either in the past or recently or since you have been speaking to your servant—because my mouth and my tongue are sluggish."

The Lord said to him, "Who placed a mouth on humans? Who makes a person mute or deaf, seeing or blind? Is it not I, the Lord? Now go! I will help you speak and I will teach you what to say."

Moses said, "Please, Lord, send someone else."

Then the Lord's anger burned against Moses, and he said, "Isn't Aaron the Levite your brother? I know that he can speak well. And also, he is on his way now to meet you. He will rejoice when he sees you. You will speak with him and tell him what to say. I will help both you and him to speak and will teach you both what to do. He will speak to the people for you. He will serve as a mouth for you, and you will serve as God to him. And take this staff in your hand that you will perform the signs with."

Then Moses went back to his father-in-law, Jethro, and said to him, "Please let me return to my
30 relatives in Egypt and see if they are still living."

Jethro said to Moses, "Go in peace."

Now in Midian the LORD told Moses, "Return to Egypt, for all the men who wanted to kill you
are dead." So Moses took his wife and sons, put them on a donkey, and returned to the land of
Egypt. And Moses took God's staff in his hand.

The LORD instructed Moses, "When you go back to Egypt, make sure you do before Pharaoh
all the wonders that I have put within your power. But I will harden his heart so that he won't let
the people go. And you will say to Pharaoh: This is what the LORD says: Israel is my firstborn son.
I told you: Let my son go so that he may worship me, but you refused to let him go. Look, I am
about to kill your firstborn son!"

40 On the trip, at an overnight campsite, it happened that the LORD confronted him and intended
to put him to death. So Zipporah took a flint, cut off her son's foreskin, threw it at Moses's feet,
and said, "You are a bridegroom of blood to me!" So he let him alone. At that time she said, "You
are a bridegroom of blood," referring to the circumcision.

Now the LORD had said to Aaron, "Go and meet Moses in the wilderness." So he went and met
him at the mountain of God and kissed him. Moses told Aaron everything the LORD had sent him
to say, and about all the signs he had commanded him to do. Then Moses and Aaron went and
assembled all the elders of the Israelites. Aaron repeated everything the LORD had said to Moses
and performed the signs before the people. The people believed, and when they heard that the
LORD had paid attention to them and that he had seen their misery, they knelt low and worshiped.

5 Later, Moses and Aaron went in and said to Pharaoh, "This is what the LORD, the God of Israel,
says: Let my people go, so that they may hold a festival for me in the wilderness."

But Pharaoh responded, "Who is the LORD that I should obey him by letting Israel go? I don't
know the LORD, and besides, I will not let Israel go."

They answered, "The God of the Hebrews has met with us. Please let us go on a three-day trip
into the wilderness so that we may sacrifice to the LORD our God, or else he may strike us with
plague or sword."

The king of Egypt said to them, "Moses and Aaron, why are you causing the people to neglect
their work? Get to your labor!" Pharaoh also said, "Look, the people of the land are so numerous,
10 and you would stop them from their labor."

That day Pharaoh commanded the overseers of the people as well as their foremen, "Don't
continue to supply the people with straw for making bricks, as before. They must go and gather
straw for themselves. But require the same quota of bricks from them as they were making before;

do not reduce it. For they are slackers—that is why they are crying out, 'Let us go and sacrifice to our God.' Impose heavier work on the men. Then they will be occupied with it and not pay attention to deceptive words."

So the overseers and foremen of the people went out and said to them, "This is what Pharaoh says: 'I am not giving you straw. Go get straw yourselves wherever you can find it, but there will be no reduction at all in your workload.'" So the people scattered throughout the land of Egypt to gather stubble for straw. The overseers insisted, "Finish your assigned work each day, just as you did when straw was provided." Then the Israelite foremen, whom Pharaoh's slave drivers had set over the people, were beaten and asked, "Why haven't you finished making your prescribed number of bricks yesterday or today, as you did before?"

So the Israelite foremen went in and cried for help to Pharaoh: "Why are you treating your servants this way? No straw has been given to your servants, yet they say to us, 'Make bricks!' Look, your servants are being beaten, but it is your own people who are at fault."

But he said, "You are slackers. Slackers! That is why you are saying, 'Let us go sacrifice to the LORD.' Now get to work. No straw will be given to you, but you must produce the same quantity of bricks."

The Israelite foremen saw that they were in trouble when they were told, "You cannot reduce your daily quota of bricks." When they left Pharaoh, they confronted Moses and Aaron, who stood waiting to meet them.

"May the LORD take note of you and judge," they said to them, "because you have made us reek to Pharaoh and his officials—putting a sword in their hand to kill us!"

So Moses went back to the LORD and asked, "Lord, why have you caused trouble for this people? And why did you ever send me? Ever since I went in to Pharaoh to speak in your name he has caused trouble for this people, and you haven't rescued your people at all."

6 But the LORD replied to Moses, "Now you will see what I will do to Pharaoh: because of a strong hand he will let them go, and because of a strong hand he will drive them from his land."

Then God spoke to Moses, telling him, "I am the LORD. I appeared to Abraham, Isaac, and Jacob as God Almighty, but I was not known to them by my name 'the LORD.' I also established my covenant with them to give them the land of Canaan, the land they lived in as aliens. Furthermore, I have heard the groaning of the Israelites, whom the Egyptians are forcing to work as slaves, and I have remembered my covenant.

"Therefore tell the Israelites: I am the LORD, and I will bring you out from the forced labor of the Egyptians and rescue you from slavery to them. I will redeem you with an outstretched arm and great acts of judgment. I will take you as my people, and I will be your God. You will know that I am the LORD your God, who brought you out from the forced labor of the Egyptians. I will bring you to the land that I swore to give to Abraham, Isaac, and Jacob, and I will give it to you as a possession. I am the Lord." Moses told this to the Israelites, but they did not listen to him because of their broken spirit and hard labor.

Then the Lord spoke to Moses, "Go and tell Pharaoh king of Egypt to let the Israelites go from his land."

But Moses said in the Lord's presence, "If the Israelites will not listen to me, then how will Pharaoh listen to me, since I am such a poor speaker?" Then the Lord spoke to Moses and Aaron and gave them commands concerning both the Israelites and Pharaoh king of Egypt to bring the Israelites out of the land of Egypt.

These are the heads of their fathers' families:
    The sons of Reuben, the firstborn of Israel:
    Hanoch and Pallu, Hezron and Carmi.
    These are the clans of Reuben.

    The sons of Simeon:
    Jemuel, Jamin, Ohad, Jachin,
    Zohar, and Shaul, the son of a Canaanite woman.
    These are the clans of Simeon.

    These are the names of the sons of Levi
    according to their family records;
    Gershon, Kohath, and Merari.
    Levi lived 137 years.
    The sons of Gershon:
    Libni and Shimei, by their clans.
    The sons of Kohath:
    Amram, Izhar, Hebron, and Uzziel.
    Kohath lived 133 years.
    The sons of Merari:
    Mahli and Mushi.
    These are the clans of the Levites
    according to their family records.

    Amram married his father's sister Jochebed,
    and she bore him Aaron and Moses.
    Amram lived 137 years.
    The sons of Izhar:
    Korah, Nepheg, and Zichri.

The sons of Uzziel:
Mishael, Elzaphan, and Sithri.
Aaron married Elisheba,
daughter of Amminadab and sister of Nahshon.
She bore him Nadab and Abihu, Eleazar and Ithamar.
The sons of Korah:
Assir, Elkanah, and Abiasaph.
These are the clans of the Korahites.
Aaron's son Eleazar married
one of the daughters of Putiel,
and she bore him Phinehas.
These are the heads of the Levite families by their clans.

It was this Aaron and Moses whom the LORD told, "Bring the Israelites out of the land of Egypt according to their military divisions." Moses and Aaron were the ones who spoke to Pharaoh king of Egypt in order to bring the Israelites out of Egypt.

On the day the LORD spoke to Moses in the land of Egypt, he said to him, "I am the LORD; tell Pharaoh king of Egypt everything I am telling you."

But Moses replied in the LORD's presence, "Since I am such a poor speaker, how will Pharaoh listen to me?"

7 The LORD answered Moses, "See, I have made you like God to Pharaoh, and Aaron your brother will be your prophet. You must say whatever I command you; then Aaron your brother must declare it to Pharaoh so that he will let the Israelites go from his land. But I will harden Pharaoh's heart and multiply my signs and wonders in the land of Egypt. Pharaoh will not listen to you, but I will put my hand into Egypt and bring the military divisions of my people the Israelites out of the land of Egypt by great acts of judgment. The Egyptians will know that I am the LORD when I stretch out my hand against Egypt and bring out the Israelites from among them."

So Moses and Aaron did this; they did just as the LORD commanded them. Moses was eighty years old and Aaron eighty-three when they spoke to Pharaoh.

The LORD said to Moses and Aaron, "When Pharaoh tells you, 'Perform a miracle,' tell Aaron, 'Take your staff and throw it down before Pharaoh. It will become a serpent.'" So Moses and Aaron went in to Pharaoh and did just as the LORD had commanded. Aaron threw down his staff before Pharaoh and his officials, and it became a serpent. But then Pharaoh called the wise men and sorcerers—the magicians of Egypt, and they also did the same thing by their occult practices. Each one threw down his staff, and it became a serpent. But Aaron's staff swallowed their staffs. However, Pharaoh's heart was hard, and he did not listen to them, as the LORD had said.

Then the LORD said to Moses, "Pharaoh's heart is hard: He refuses to let the people go. Go to Pharaoh in the morning. When you see him walking out to the water, stand ready to meet him by the bank of the Nile. Take in your hand the staff that turned into a snake. Tell him: The LORD, the God of the Hebrews, has sent me to tell you: Let my people go, so that they may worship me in the wilderness. But so far you have not listened. This is what the LORD says: Here is how you will know that I am the LORD. Watch. I am about to strike the water in the Nile with the staff in my hand, and it will turn to blood. The fish in the Nile will die, the river will stink, and the Egyptians will be unable to drink water from it."

So the LORD said to Moses, "Tell Aaron: Take your staff and stretch out your hand over the waters of Egypt—over their rivers, canals, ponds, and all their water reservoirs—and they will become blood. There will be blood throughout the land of Egypt, even in wooden and stone containers."

Moses and Aaron did just as the LORD had commanded; in the sight of Pharaoh and his officials, he raised the staff and struck the water in the Nile, and all the water in the Nile was turned to blood. The fish in the Nile died, and the river smelled so bad the Egyptians could not drink water from it. There was blood throughout the land of Egypt.

But the magicians of Egypt did the same thing by their occult practices. So Pharaoh's heart was hard, and he would not listen to them, as the LORD had said. Pharaoh turned around, went into his palace, and didn't take even this to heart. All the Egyptians dug around the Nile for water to drink because they could not drink the water from the river. Seven days passed after the LORD struck the Nile.

8 Then the LORD said to Moses, "Go in to Pharaoh and tell him: This is what the LORD says: Let my people go, so that they may worship me. But if you refuse to let them go, then I will plague all your territory with frogs. The Nile will swarm with frogs; they will come up and go into your palace, into your bedroom and on your bed, into the houses of your officials and your people, and into your ovens and kneading bowls. The frogs will come up on you, your people, and all your officials."

The LORD then said to Moses, "Tell Aaron: Stretch out your hand with your staff over the rivers, canals, and ponds, and cause the frogs to come up onto the land of Egypt." When Aaron stretched out his hand over the waters of Egypt, the frogs came up and covered the land of Egypt. But the magicians did the same thing by their occult practices and brought frogs up onto the land of Egypt.

Pharaoh summoned Moses and Aaron and said, "Appeal to the LORD to remove the frogs from me and my people. Then I will let the people go and they can sacrifice to the LORD."

Moses said to Pharaoh, "You may have the honor of choosing. When should I appeal on behalf of you, your officials, and your people, that the frogs be taken away from you and your houses, and remain only in the Nile?"

"Tomorrow," he answered.

Moses replied, "As you have said, so that you may know there is no one like the LORD our God, the frogs will go away from you, your houses, your officials, and your people. The frogs will remain only in the Nile." After Moses and Aaron went out from Pharaoh, Moses cried out to the LORD for help concerning the frogs that he had brought against Pharaoh. The LORD did as Moses had 20 said: the frogs in the houses, courtyards, and fields died. They piled them in countless heaps, and there was a terrible odor in the land. But when Pharaoh saw there was relief, he hardened his heart and would not listen to them, as the LORD had said.

Then the LORD said to Moses, "Tell Aaron: Stretch out your staff and strike the dust of the land, and it will become gnats throughout the land of Egypt." And they did this. Aaron stretched out his hand with his staff, and when he struck the dust of the land, gnats were on people and animals. All the dust of the land became gnats throughout the land of Egypt. The magicians tried to produce gnats using their occult practices, but they could not. The gnats remained on people and animals.

"This is the finger of God," the magicians said to Pharaoh. But Pharaoh's heart was hard, and he would not listen to them, as the LORD had said.

30 The LORD said to Moses, "Get up early in the morning and present yourself to Pharaoh when you see him going out to the water. Tell him: This is what the LORD says: Let my people go, so that they may worship me. But if you will not let my people go, then I will send swarms of flies against you, your officials, your people, and your houses. The Egyptians' houses will swarm with flies, and so will the land where they live. But on that day I will give special treatment to the land of Goshen, where my people are living; no flies will be there. This way you will know that I, the LORD, am in the land. I will make a distinction between my people and your people. This sign will take place tomorrow."

And the LORD did this. Thick swarms of flies went into Pharaoh's palace and his officials' houses. Throughout Egypt the land was ruined because of the swarms of flies. Then Pharaoh summoned Moses and Aaron and said, "Go sacrifice to your God within the country."

40 But Moses said, "It would not be right to do that, because what we will sacrifice to the LORD our God is detestable to the Egyptians. If we sacrifice what the Egyptians detest in front of them, won't they stone us? We must go a distance of three days into the wilderness and sacrifice to the LORD our God as he instructs us."

Pharaoh responded, "I will let you go and sacrifice to the LORD your God in the wilderness, but don't go very far. Make an appeal for me."

"As soon as I leave you," Moses said, "I will appeal to the LORD, and tomorrow the swarms of flies will depart from Pharaoh, his officials, and his people. But Pharaoh must not act deceptively again by refusing to let the people go and sacrifice to the LORD." Then Moses left Pharaoh's presence and appealed to the LORD. The LORD did as Moses had said: He removed the swarms of 50 flies from Pharaoh, his officials, and his people; not one was left. But Pharaoh hardened his heart this time also and did not let the people go.

9 Then the LORD said to Moses, "Go in to Pharaoh and say to him: This is what the LORD, the God of the Hebrews, says: Let my people go, so that they may worship me. But if you refuse to let them go and keep holding them, then the LORD's hand will bring a severe plague against your livestock in the field—the horses, donkeys, camels, herds, and flocks. But the LORD will make a distinction between the livestock of Israel and the livestock of Egypt, so that nothing of all that the Israelites own will die." And the LORD set a time, saying, "Tomorrow the LORD will do this thing in the land." The LORD did this the next day. All the Egyptian livestock died, but none among the Israelite livestock died. Pharaoh sent messengers who saw that not a single one of the Israelite livestock was dead. But Pharaoh's heart was hard, and he did not let the people go.

10 Then the LORD said to Moses and Aaron, "Take handfuls of furnace soot, and Moses is to throw it toward heaven in the sight of Pharaoh. It will become fine dust over the entire land of Egypt. It will become festering boils on people and animals throughout the land of Egypt." So they took furnace soot and stood before Pharaoh. Moses threw it toward heaven, and it became festering boils on people and animals. The magicians could not stand before Moses because of the boils, for the boils were on the magicians as well as on all the Egyptians. But the LORD hardened Pharaoh's heart and he did not listen to them, as the LORD had told Moses.

Then the LORD said to Moses, "Get up early in the morning and present yourself to Pharaoh. Tell him: This is what the LORD, the God of the Hebrews says: Let my people go, so that they may worship me. For this time I am about to send all my plagues against you, your officials, and 20 your people. Then you will know there is no one like me on the whole earth. By now I could have stretched out my hand and struck you and your people with a plague, and you would have been obliterated from the earth. However, I have let you live for this purpose: to show you my power and to make my name known on the whole earth. You are still acting arrogantly against my people by not letting them go. Tomorrow at this time I will rain down the worst hail that has ever occurred in Egypt from the day it was founded until now. Therefore give orders to bring your livestock and all that you have in the field into shelters. Every person and animal that is in the field and not brought inside will die when the hail falls on them." Those among Pharaoh's officials who feared the word of the LORD made their servants and livestock flee to shelters, but those who didn't take to heart the LORD's word left their servants and livestock in the field. 30 Then the LORD said to Moses, "Stretch out your hand toward heaven and let there be hail throughout the land of Egypt—on people and animals and every plant of the field in the land of Egypt." So Moses stretched out his staff toward heaven, and the LORD sent thunder and hail. Lightning struck the land, and the LORD rained hail on the land of Egypt. The hail, with lightning flashing through it, was so severe that nothing like it had occurred in the land of Egypt since it had become a nation. Throughout the land of Egypt, the hail struck down everything in the field, both people and animals. The hail beat down every plant of the field and shattered every tree in the field. The only place it didn't hail was in the land of Goshen, where the Israelites were.

Pharaoh sent for Moses and Aaron. "I have sinned this time," he said to them. "The LORD is the righteous one, and I and my people are the guilty ones. Make an appeal to the LORD. There has been enough of God's thunder and hail. I will let you go; you don't need to stay any longer."

Moses said to him, "When I have left the city, I will spread out my hands to the LORD. The thunder will cease, and there will be no more hail, so that you may know the earth belongs to the LORD. But as for you and your officials, I know that you still do not fear the LORD God."

The flax and the barley were destroyed because the barley was ripe and the flax was budding, but the wheat and the spelt were not destroyed since they are later crops.

Moses left Pharaoh and the city, and spread out his hands to the LORD. Then the thunder and hail ceased, and rain no longer poured down on the land. When Pharaoh saw that the rain, hail, and thunder had ceased, he sinned again and hardened his heart, he and his officials. So Pharaoh's heart was hard, and he did not let the Israelites go, as the LORD had said through Moses.

10 Then the LORD said to Moses, "Go to Pharaoh, for I have hardened his heart and the hearts of his officials so that I may do these miraculous signs of mine among them, and so that you may tell your son and grandson how severely I dealt with the Egyptians and performed miraculous signs among them, and you will know that I am the LORD."

So Moses and Aaron went in to Pharaoh and told him, "This is what the LORD, the God of the Hebrews, says: How long will you refuse to humble yourself before me? Let my people go, that they may worship me. But if you refuse to let my people go, then tomorrow I will bring locusts into your territory. They will cover the surface of the land so that no one will be able to see the land. They will eat the remainder left to you that escaped the hail; they will eat every tree you have growing in the fields. They will fill your houses, all your officials' houses, and the houses of all the Egyptians—something your fathers and grandfathers never saw since the time they occupied the land until today." Then he turned and left Pharaoh's presence.

Pharaoh's officials asked him, "How long must this man be a snare to us? Let the men go, so that they may worship the LORD their God. Don't you realize yet that Egypt is devastated?"

So Moses and Aaron were brought back to Pharaoh. "Go, worship the LORD your God," Pharaoh said. "But exactly who will be going?"

Moses replied, "We will go with our young and with our old; we will go with our sons and with our daughters, with our flocks and with our herds because we must hold the LORD's festival."

He said to them, "The Lord would have to be with you if I would ever let you and your families go! Look out—you're heading for trouble. No, go—just able-bodied men—worship the LORD, since that's what you want." And they were driven from Pharaoh's presence.

The LORD then said to Moses, "Stretch out your hand over the land of Egypt, and the locusts will come up over it and eat every plant in the land, everything that the hail left." So Moses stretched out his staff over the land of Egypt, and the LORD sent an east wind over the land all that day and through the night. By morning the east wind had brought in the locusts. The locusts went up over the entire land of Egypt and settled on the whole territory of Egypt. Never before had there been such a large number of locusts, and there never will be again. They covered the surface of the whole land so that the land was black, and they consumed all the plants on the ground and all the fruit on the trees that the hail had left. Nothing green was left on the trees or the plants in the field throughout the land of Egypt.

30

Pharaoh urgently sent for Moses and Aaron and said, "I have sinned against the LORD your God and against you. Please forgive my sin once more and make an appeal to the LORD your God, so that he will just take this death away from me." Moses left Pharaoh's presence and appealed to the LORD. Then the LORD changed the wind to a strong west wind, and it carried off the locusts and blew them into the Red Sea. Not a single locust was left in all the territory of Egypt. But the LORD hardened Pharaoh's heart, and he did not let the Israelites go.

Then the LORD said to Moses, "Stretch out your hand toward heaven, and there will be darkness over the land of Egypt, a darkness that can be felt." So Moses stretched out his hand toward heaven, and there was thick darkness throughout the land of Egypt for three days. One person could not see another, and for three days they did not move from where they were. Yet all the Israelites had light where they lived.

40

Pharaoh summoned Moses and said, "Go, worship the LORD. Even your families may go with you; only your flocks and herds must stay behind."

Moses responded, "You must also let us have sacrifices and burnt offerings to prepare for the LORD our God. Even our livestock must go with us; not a hoof will be left behind because we will take some of them to worship the LORD our God. We will not know what we will use to worship the LORD until we get there."

But the LORD hardened Pharaoh's heart, and he was unwilling to let them go. Pharaoh said to him, "Leave me! Make sure you never see my face again, for on the day you see my face, you will die."

"As you have said," Moses replied, "I will never see your face again."

11 The LORD said to Moses, "I will bring one more plague on Pharaoh and on Egypt. After that, he will let you go from here. When he lets you go, he will drive you out of here. Now announce to the people that both men and women should ask their neighbors for silver and gold items." The LORD gave the people favor with the Egyptians. In addition, Moses himself was very highly regarded in the land of Egypt by Pharaoh's officials and the people.

So Moses said, "This is what the LORD says: About midnight I will go throughout Egypt, and every firstborn male in the land of Egypt will die, from the firstborn of Pharaoh who sits on his throne to the firstborn of the servant girl who is at the grindstones, as well as every firstborn of the

livestock. Then there will be a great cry of anguish through all the land of Egypt such as never was
before or ever will be again. But against all the Israelites, whether people or animals, not even a
dog will snarl, so that you may know that the LORD makes a distinction between Egypt and Israel.
All these officials of yours will come down to me and bow before me, saying: Get out, you and all
the people who follow you. After that, I will get out." And he went out from Pharaoh's presence
fiercely angry.

The LORD said to Moses, "Pharaoh will not listen to you, so that my wonders may be
multiplied in the land of Egypt." Moses and Aaron did all these wonders before Pharaoh, but the
LORD hardened Pharaoh's heart, and he would not let the Israelites go out of his land.

12 The LORD said to Moses and Aaron in the land of Egypt, "This month is to be the beginning of
months for you; it is the first month of your year. Tell the whole community of Israel that on the
tenth day of this month they must each select an animal of the flock according to their fathers'
families, one animal per family. If the household is too small for a whole animal, that person and
the neighbor nearest his house are to select one based on the combined number of people; you
should apportion the animal according to what each will eat. You must have an unblemished
animal, a year-old male; you may take it from either the sheep or the goats. You are to keep it
until the fourteenth day of this month; then the whole assembly of the community of Israel
will slaughter the animals at twilight. They must take some of the blood and put it on the two
doorposts and the lintel of the houses where they eat them. They are to eat the meat that night;
they should eat it, roasted over the fire along with unleavened bread and bitter herbs. Do not eat
any of it raw or cooked in boiling water, but only roasted over fire—its head as well as its legs and
inner organs. You must not leave any of it until morning; any part of it left until morning you must
burn. Here is how you must eat it: You must be dressed for travel, your sandals on your feet, and
your staff in your hand. You are to eat it in a hurry; it is the LORD's Passover.

"I will pass through the land of Egypt on that night and strike every firstborn male in the land
of Egypt, both people and animals. I am the LORD; I will execute judgments against all the gods of
Egypt. The blood on the houses where you are staying will be a distinguishing mark for you; when
I see the blood, I will pass over you. No plague will be among you to destroy you when I strike the
land of Egypt.

"This day is to be a memorial for you, and you must celebrate it as a festival to the LORD. You
are to celebrate it throughout your generations as a permanent statute. You must eat unleavened
bread for seven days. On the first day you must remove yeast from your houses. Whoever eats
what is leavened from the first day through the seventh day must be cut off from Israel. You are to
hold a sacred assembly on the first day and another sacred assembly on the seventh day. No work
may be done on those days except for preparing what people need to eat—you may do only that.

"You are to observe the Festival of Unleavened Bread because on this very day I brought
your military divisions out of the land of Egypt. You must observe this day throughout your

generations as a permanent statute. You are to eat unleavened bread in the first month, from
the evening of the fourteenth day of the month until the evening of the twenty-first day. Yeast
must not be found in your houses for seven days. If anyone eats something leavened, that person,
whether a resident alien or native of the land, must be cut off from the community of Israel. Do
not eat anything leavened; eat unleavened bread in all your homes."

Then Moses summoned all the elders of Israel and said to them, "Go, select an animal from the
flock according to your families, and slaughter the Passover animal. Take a cluster of hyssop, dip it
in the blood that is in the basin, and brush the lintel and the two doorposts with some of the blood
in the basin. None of you may go out the door of his house until morning. When the LORD passes
through to strike Egypt and sees the blood on the lintel and the two doorposts, he will pass over
the door and not let the destroyer enter your houses to strike you.

"Keep this command permanently as a statute for you and your descendants. When you enter
the land that the LORD will give you as he promised, you are to observe this ceremony. When
your children ask you, 'What does this ceremony mean to you?' you are to reply, 'It is the Passover
sacrifice to the LORD, for he passed over the houses of the Israelites in Egypt when he struck the
Egyptians, and he spared our homes.'" So the people knelt low and worshiped. Then the Israelites
went and did this; they did just as the LORD had commanded Moses and Aaron.

Now at midnight the LORD struck every firstborn male in the land of Egypt, from the firstborn
of Pharaoh who sat on his throne to the firstborn of the prisoner who was in the dungeon, and
every firstborn of the livestock. During the night Pharaoh got up, he along with all his officials
and all the Egyptians, and there was a loud wailing throughout Egypt because there wasn't a house
without someone dead. He summoned Moses and Aaron during the night and said, "Get out
immediately from among my people, both you and the Israelites, and go, worship the LORD as you
have said. Take even your flocks and your herds as you asked and leave, and also bless me."

Now the Egyptians pressured the people in order to send them quickly out of the country, for
they said, "We're all going to die!" So the people took their dough before it was leavened, with
their kneading bowls wrapped up in their clothes on their shoulders.

The Israelites acted on Moses's word and asked the Egyptians for silver and gold items and for
clothing. And the LORD gave the people such favor with the Egyptians that they gave them what
they requested. In this way they plundered the Egyptians.

The Israelites traveled from Rameses to Succoth, about six hundred thousand able-bodied men
on foot, besides their families. A mixed crowd also went up with them, along with a huge number
of livestock, both flocks and herds. The people baked the dough they had brought out of Egypt
into unleavened loaves, since it had no yeast; for when they were driven out of Egypt, they could
not delay and had not prepared provisions for themselves.

The time that the Israelites lived in Egypt was 430 years. At the end of 430 years, on that same
day, all the LORD's military divisions went out from the land of Egypt. It was a night of vigil in

honor of the LORD, because he would bring them out of the land of Egypt. This same night is in honor of the LORD, a night vigil for all the Israelites throughout their generations.

The LORD said to Moses and Aaron, "This is the statute of the Passover: no foreigner may eat it. But any slave a man has purchased may eat it, after you have circumcised him. A temporary resident or hired worker may not eat the Passover. It is to be eaten in one house. You may not take any of the meat outside the house, and you may not break any of its bones. The whole community of Israel must celebrate it. If an alien resides among you and wants to observe the LORD's Passover, every male in his household must be circumcised, and then he may participate; he will become like a native of the land. But no uncircumcised person may eat it. The same law will apply to both the native and the alien who resides among you."

Then all the Israelites did this; they did just as the LORD had commanded Moses and Aaron. On that same day the LORD brought the Israelites out of the land of Egypt according to their military divisions.

13 The LORD spoke to Moses: "Consecrate every firstborn male to me, the firstborn from every womb among the Israelites, both man and domestic animal; it is mine."

Then Moses said to the people, "Remember this day when you came out of Egypt, out of the place of slavery, for the LORD brought you out of here by the strength of his hand. Nothing leavened may be eaten. Today, in the month of Abib, you are going out. When the LORD brings you into the land of the Canaanites, Hethites, Amorites, Hivites, and Jebusites, which he swore to your ancestors that he would give you, a land flowing with milk and honey, you must carry out this ceremony in this month. For seven days you must eat unleavened bread, and on the seventh day there is to be a festival to the LORD. Unleavened bread is to be eaten for those seven days. Nothing leavened may be found among you, and no yeast may be found among you in all your territory. On that day explain to your son, 'This is because of what the LORD did for me when I came out of Egypt.' Let it serve as a sign for you on your hand and as a reminder on your forehead, so that the LORD's instruction may be in your mouth; for the LORD brought you out of Egypt with a strong hand. Keep this statute at its appointed time from year to year.

"When the LORD brings you into the land of the Canaanites, as he swore to you and your ancestors, and gives it to you, you are to present to the LORD every firstborn male of the womb. All firstborn offspring of the livestock you own that are males will be the LORD's. You must redeem every firstborn of a donkey with a flock animal, but if you do not redeem it, break its neck. However, you must redeem every firstborn among your sons.

"In the future, when your son asks you, 'What does this mean?' say to him, 'By the strength of his hand the LORD brought us out of Egypt, out of the place of slavery. When Pharaoh stubbornly refused to let us go, the LORD killed every firstborn male in the land of Egypt, both the firstborn of humans and the firstborn of livestock. That is why I sacrifice to the LORD all the firstborn of the womb that are males, but I redeem all the firstborn of my sons.' So let it be a sign on your hand and a symbol on your forehead, for the LORD brought us out of Egypt by the strength of his hand."

When Pharaoh let the people go, God did not lead them along the road to the land of the Philistines, even though it was nearby; for God said, "The people will change their minds and return to Egypt if they face war." So he led the people around toward the Red Sea along the road of the wilderness. And the Israelites left the land of Egypt in battle formation.

30 Moses took the bones of Joseph with him, because Joseph had made the Israelites swear a solemn oath, saying, "God will certainly come to your aid; then you must take my bones with you from this place."

They set out from Succoth and camped at Etham on the edge of the wilderness. The LORD went ahead of them in a pillar of cloud to lead them on their way during the day and in a pillar of fire to give them light at night, so that they could travel day or night. The pillar of cloud by day and the pillar of fire by night never left its place in front of the people.

14 Then the LORD spoke to Moses: "Tell the Israelites to turn back and camp in front of Pi-hahiroth, between Migdol and the sea; you must camp in front of Baal-zephon, facing it by the sea. Pharaoh will say of the Israelites: They are wandering around the land in confusion; the wilderness has boxed them in. I will harden Pharaoh's heart so that he will pursue them. Then I will receive glory by means of Pharaoh and all his army, and the Egyptians will know that I am the LORD." So the Israelites did this.

When the king of Egypt was told that the people had fled, Pharaoh and his officials changed their minds about the people and said, "What have we done? We have released Israel from serving us." So he got his chariot ready and took his troops with him; he took six hundred of the best chariots and all the rest of the chariots of Egypt, with officers in each one. The LORD hardened the

10 heart of Pharaoh king of Egypt, and he pursued the Israelites, who were going out defiantly. The Egyptians—all Pharaoh's horses and chariots, his horsemen, and his army—chased after them and caught up with them as they camped by the sea beside Pi-hahiroth, in front of Baal-zephon.

As Pharaoh approached, the Israelites looked up and there were the Egyptians coming after them! The Israelites were terrified and cried out to the LORD for help. They said to Moses, "Is it because there are no graves in Egypt that you have taken us away to die in the wilderness? What have you done to us by bringing us out of Egypt? Isn't this what we told you in Egypt: Leave us alone so that we may serve the Egyptians? It would have been better for us to serve the Egyptians than to die in the wilderness."

But Moses said to the people, "Don't be afraid. Stand firm and see the LORD's salvation that he

20 will accomplish for you today; for the Egyptians you see today, you will never see again. The LORD will fight for you, and you must be quiet."

The LORD said to Moses, "Why are you crying out to me? Tell the Israelites to break camp. As for you, lift up your staff, stretch out your hand over the sea, and divide it so that the Israelites can go through the sea on dry ground. As for me, I am going to harden the hearts of the Egyptians so that they will go in after them, and I will receive glory by means of Pharaoh, all his army, and his chariots and horsemen. The Egyptians will know that I am the LORD when I receive glory through Pharaoh, his chariots, and his horsemen."

Then the angel of God, who was going in front of the Israelite forces, moved and went behind them. The pillar of cloud moved from in front of them and stood behind them. It came between the Egyptian and Israelite forces. There was cloud and darkness, it lit up the night, and neither group came near the other all night long.

Then Moses stretched out his hand over the sea. The LORD drove the sea back with a powerful east wind all that night and turned the sea into dry land. So the waters were divided, and the Israelites went through the sea on dry ground, with the waters like a wall to them on their right and their left.

The Egyptians set out in pursuit—all Pharaoh's horses, his chariots, and his horsemen—and went into the sea after them. During the morning watch, the LORD looked down at the Egyptian forces from the pillar of fire and cloud, and threw the Egyptian forces into confusion. He caused their chariot wheels to swerve and made them drive with difficulty. "Let's get away from Israel," the Egyptians said, "because the LORD is fighting for them against Egypt!"

Then the LORD said to Moses, "Stretch out your hand over the sea so that the water may come back on the Egyptians, on their chariots and horsemen." So Moses stretched out his hand over the sea, and at daybreak the sea returned to its normal depth. While the Egyptians were trying to escape from it, the LORD threw them into the sea. The water came back and covered the chariots and horsemen, plus the entire army of Pharaoh that had gone after them into the sea. Not even one of them survived.

But the Israelites had walked through the sea on dry ground, with the waters like a wall to them on their right and their left. That day the LORD saved Israel from the power of the Egyptians, and Israel saw the Egyptians dead on the seashore. When Israel saw the great power that the LORD used against the Egyptians, the people feared the LORD and believed in him and in his servant Moses.

15 Then Moses and the Israelites sang this song to the LORD. They said:

> I will sing to the LORD,
>   for he is highly exalted;
> he has thrown the horse
>   and its rider into the sea.
> The LORD is my strength and my song;
>   he has become my salvation.

This is my God, and I will praise him,
my father's God, and I will exalt him.
10   The LORD is a warrior;
the LORD is his name.

He threw Pharaoh's chariots
and his army into the sea;
the elite of his officers
were drowned in the Red Sea.
The floods covered them;
they sank to the depths like a stone.
LORD, your right hand is glorious in power.
LORD, your right hand shattered the enemy.
20   You overthrew your adversaries
by your great majesty.
You unleashed your burning wrath;
it consumed them like stubble.
The water heaped up at the blast from your nostrils;
the currents stood firm like a dam.
The watery depths congealed in the heart of the sea.
The enemy said:
"I will pursue, I will overtake,
I will divide the spoil.
30   My desire will be gratified at their expense.
I will draw my sword;
my hand will destroy them."
But you blew with your breath,
and the sea covered them.
They sank like lead
in the mighty waters.

LORD, who is like you among the gods?
Who is like you, glorious in holiness,
revered with praises, performing wonders?
40   You stretched out your right hand,
and the earth swallowed them.
With your faithful love,
you will lead the people

you have redeemed;
you will guide them to your holy dwelling
with your strength.

When the peoples hear, they will shudder;
anguish will seize the inhabitants of Philistia.
Then the chiefs of Edom will be terrified;
50   trembling will seize the leaders of Moab;
all the inhabitants of Canaan will panic;
terror and dread will fall on them.
They will be as still as a stone
because of your powerful arm
until your people pass by, Lord,
until the people whom you purchased pass by.

You will bring them in and plant them
on the mountain of your possession;
Lord, you have prepared the place
60   for your dwelling;
Lord, your hands have established the sanctuary.
The Lord will reign forever and ever!

When Pharaoh's horses with his chariots and horsemen went into the sea, the Lord brought
the water of the sea back over them. But the Israelites walked through the sea on dry ground.
Then the prophetess Miriam, Aaron's sister, took a tambourine in her hand, and all the women
came out following her with tambourines and dancing. Miriam sang to them:
Sing to the Lord,
for he is highly exalted;
he has thrown the horse
70   and its rider into the sea.

Then Moses led Israel on from the Red Sea, and they went out to the Wilderness of Shur. They
journeyed for three days in the wilderness without finding water. They came to Marah, but they
could not drink the water at Marah because it was bitter—that is why it was named Marah. The
people grumbled to Moses, "What are we going to drink?" So he cried out to the Lord, and the
Lord showed him a tree. When he threw it into the water, the water became drinkable.
    The Lord made a statute and ordinance for them at Marah, and he tested them there. He said,
"If you will carefully obey the Lord your God, do what is right in his sight, pay attention to his

commands, and keep all his statutes, I will not inflict any illnesses on you that I inflicted on the Egyptians. For I am the LORD who heals you."

80 Then they came to Elim, where there were twelve springs and seventy date palms, and they camped there by the water.

16 The entire Israelite community departed from Elim and came to the Wilderness of Sin, which is between Elim and Sinai, on the fifteenth day of the second month after they had left the land of Egypt. The entire Israelite community grumbled against Moses and Aaron in the wilderness. The Israelites said to them, "If only we had died by the LORD's hand in the land of Egypt, when we sat by pots of meat and ate all the bread we wanted. Instead, you brought us into this wilderness to make this whole assembly die of hunger!"

Then the LORD said to Moses, "I am going to rain bread from heaven for you. The people are to go out each day and gather enough for that day. This way I will test them to see whether or not they will follow my instructions. On the sixth day, when they prepare what they bring in, it will be 10 twice as much as they gather on other days."

So Moses and Aaron said to all the Israelites, "This evening you will know that it was the LORD who brought you out of the land of Egypt, and in the morning you will see the LORD's glory because he has heard your complaints about him. For who are we that you complain about us?" Moses continued, "The LORD will give you meat to eat this evening and all the bread you want in the morning, for he has heard the complaints that you are raising against him. Who are we? Your complaints are not against us but against the LORD."

Then Moses told Aaron, "Say to the entire Israelite community, 'Come before the LORD, for he has heard your complaints.'" As Aaron was speaking to the entire Israelite community, they turned toward the wilderness, and there in a cloud the LORD's glory appeared.

20 The LORD spoke to Moses, "I have heard the complaints of the Israelites. Tell them: At twilight you will eat meat, and in the morning you will eat bread until you are full. Then you will know that I am the LORD your God."

So at evening quail came and covered the camp. In the morning there was a layer of dew all around the camp. When the layer of dew evaporated, there were fine flakes on the desert surface, as fine as frost on the ground. When the Israelites saw it, they asked one another, "What is it?" because they didn't know what it was.

Moses told them, "It is the bread the LORD has given you to eat. This is what the LORD has commanded: 'Gather as much of it as each person needs to eat. You may take two quarts per individual, according to the number of people each of you has in his tent.'"

30 So the Israelites did this. Some gathered a lot, some a little. When they measured it by quarts, the person who gathered a lot had no surplus, and the person who gathered a little had no shortage. Each gathered as much as he needed to eat. Moses said to them, "No one is to let any of it remain until morning." But they didn't listen to Moses; some people

left part of it until morning, and it bred worms and stank. Therefore Moses was angry with them.

They gathered it every morning. Each gathered as much as he needed to eat, but when the sun grew hot, it melted. On the sixth day they gathered twice as much food, four quarts apiece, and all the leaders of the community came and reported this to Moses. He told them, "This is what the LORD has said: 'Tomorrow is a day of complete rest, a holy Sabbath to the LORD. Bake what you want to bake, and boil what you want to boil, and set aside everything left over to be kept until morning.'"

So they set it aside until morning as Moses commanded, and it didn't stink or have maggots in it. "Eat it today," Moses said, "because today is a Sabbath to the LORD. Today you won't find any in the field. For six days you will gather it, but on the seventh day, the Sabbath, there will be none."

Yet on the seventh day some of the people went out to gather, but they did not find any. Then the LORD said to Moses, "How long will you refuse to keep my commands and instructions? Understand that the LORD has given you the Sabbath; therefore on the sixth day he will give you two days' worth of bread. Each of you stay where you are; no one is to leave his place on the seventh day." So the people rested on the seventh day.

The house of Israel named the substance manna. It resembled coriander seed, was white, and tasted like wafers made with honey. Moses said, "This is what the LORD has commanded: 'Two quarts of it are to be preserved throughout your generations, so that they may see the bread I fed you in the wilderness when I brought you out of the land of Egypt.'"

Moses told Aaron, "Take a container and put two quarts of manna in it. Then place it before the LORD to be preserved throughout your generations." As the LORD commanded Moses, Aaron placed it before the testimony to be preserved.

The Israelites ate manna for forty years, until they came to an inhabited land. They ate manna until they reached the border of the land of Canaan. (They used a measure called an omer, which held two quarts.)

17 The entire Israelite community left the Wilderness of Sin, moving from one place to the next according to the LORD's command. They camped at Rephidim, but there was no water for the people to drink. So the people complained to Moses, "Give us water to drink."

"Why are you complaining to me?" Moses replied to them. "Why are you testing the LORD?"

But the people thirsted there for water and grumbled against Moses. They said, "Why did you ever bring us up from Egypt to kill us and our children and our livestock with thirst?"

Then Moses cried out to the LORD, "What should I do with these people? In a little while they will stone me!"

The LORD answered Moses, "Go on ahead of the people and take some of the elders of Israel with you. Take the staff you struck the Nile with in your hand and go. I am going to stand there in front of you on the rock at Horeb; when you hit the rock, water will come out of it and the people will drink." Moses did this in the sight of the elders of Israel. He named the place Massah and Meribah because the Israelites complained, and because they tested the LORD, saying, "Is the LORD among us or not?"

At Rephidim, Amalek came and fought against Israel. Moses said to Joshua, "Select some men for us and go fight against Amalek. Tomorrow I will stand on the hilltop with God's staff in my hand." Joshua did as Moses had told him, and fought against Amalek, while Moses, Aaron, and Hur went up to the top of the hill. While Moses held up his hand, Israel prevailed, but whenever he put his hand down, Amalek prevailed. When Moses's hands grew heavy, they took a stone and

20 put it under him, and he sat down on it. Then Aaron and Hur supported his hands, one on one side and one on the other so that his hands remained steady until the sun went down. So Joshua defeated Amalek and his army with the sword.

The LORD then said to Moses, "Write this down on a scroll as a reminder and recite it to Joshua: I will completely blot out the memory of Amalek under heaven."

And Moses built an altar and named it, "The LORD Is My Banner." He said, "Indeed, my hand is lifted up toward the LORD's throne. The LORD will be at war with Amalek from generation to generation."

18 Moses's father-in-law, Jethro, the priest of Midian, heard about everything that God had done for Moses and for God's people Israel when the LORD brought Israel out of Egypt.

Now Jethro, Moses's father-in-law, had taken in Zipporah, Moses's wife, after he had sent her back, along with her two sons, one of whom was named Gershom (because Moses had said, "I have been a resident alien in a foreign land") and the other Eliezer (because he had said, "The God of my father was my helper and rescued me from Pharaoh's sword").

Moses's father-in-law, Jethro, along with Moses's wife and sons, came to him in the wilderness where he was camped at the mountain of God. He sent word to Moses, "I, your father-in-law Jethro, am coming to you with your wife and her two sons."

10 So Moses went out to meet his father-in-law, bowed down, and then kissed him. They asked each other how they had been and went into the tent. Moses recounted to his father-in-law all that the LORD had done to Pharaoh and the Egyptians for Israel's sake, all the hardships that confronted them on the way, and how the LORD rescued them.

Jethro rejoiced over all the good things the LORD had done for Israel when he rescued them from the power of the Egyptians. "Blessed be the LORD," Jethro exclaimed, "who rescued you from the power of Egypt and from the power of Pharaoh. He has rescued the people from under the power of Egypt! Now I know that the LORD is greater than all gods, because he did wonders when the Egyptians acted arrogantly against Israel."

Then Jethro, Moses's father-in-law, brought a burnt offering and sacrifices to God, and Aaron

20 came with all the elders of Israel to eat a meal with Moses's father-in-law in God's presence.

The next day Moses sat down to judge the people, and they stood around Moses from morning until evening. When Moses's father-in-law saw everything he was doing for them he asked, "What is this you're doing for the people? Why are you alone sitting as judge, while all the people stand around you from morning until evening?"

Moses replied to his father-in-law, "Because the people come to me to inquire of God. Whenever they have a dispute, it comes to me, and I make a decision between one man and another. I teach them God's statutes and laws."

"What you're doing is not good," Moses's father-in-law said to him. "You will certainly wear out both yourself and these people who are with you, because the task is too heavy for you. You
30 can't do it alone. Now listen to me; I will give you some advice, and God be with you. You be the one to represent the people before God and bring their cases to him. Instruct them about the statutes and laws, and teach them the way to live and what they must do. But you should select from all the people able men, God-fearing, trustworthy, and hating dishonest profit. Place them over the people as commanders of thousands, hundreds, fifties, and tens. They should judge the people at all times. Then they can bring you every major case but judge every minor case themselves. In this way you will lighten your load, and they will bear it with you. If you do this, and God so directs you, you will be able to endure, and also all these people will be able to go home satisfied."

Moses listened to his father-in-law and did everything he said. So Moses chose able men from
40 all Israel and made them leaders over the people as commanders of thousands, hundreds, fifties, and tens. They judged the people at all times; they would bring the hard cases to Moses, but they would judge every minor case themselves.

Moses let his father-in-law go, and he journeyed to his own land.

19 In the third month from the very day the Israelites left the land of Egypt, they came to the Sinai Wilderness. They traveled from Rephidim, came to the Sinai Wilderness, and camped in the wilderness. Israel camped there in front of the mountain.

Moses went up the mountain to God, and the LORD called to him from the mountain: "This is what you must say to the house of Jacob and explain to the Israelites: 'You have seen what I did to the Egyptians and how I carried you on eagles' wings and brought you to myself. Now if you will carefully listen to me and keep my covenant, you will be my own possession out of all the peoples, although the whole earth is mine, and you will be my kingdom of priests and my holy nation.' These are the words that you are to say to the Israelites."

10 After Moses came back, he summoned the elders of the people and set before them all these words that the LORD had commanded him. Then all the people responded together, "We will do all that the LORD has spoken." So Moses brought the people's words back to the LORD.

The LORD said to Moses, "I am going to come to you in a dense cloud, so that the people will hear when I speak with you and will always believe you." Moses reported the people's words to the

LORD, and the LORD told Moses, "Go to the people and consecrate them today and tomorrow. They must wash their clothes and be prepared by the third day, for on the third day the LORD will come down on Mount Sinai in the sight of all the people. Put boundaries for the people all around the mountain and say: Be careful that you don't go up on the mountain or touch its base. Anyone who touches the mountain must be put to death. No hand may touch him; instead he will be
20 stoned or shot with arrows and not live, whether animal or human. When the ram's horn sounds a long blast, they may go up the mountain."

Then Moses came down from the mountain to the people and consecrated them, and they washed their clothes. He said to the people, "Be prepared by the third day. Do not have sexual relations with women."

On the third day, when morning came, there was thunder and lightning, a thick cloud on the mountain, and a very loud blast from a ram's horn, so that all the people in the camp shuddered. Then Moses brought the people out of the camp to meet God, and they stood at the foot of the mountain. Mount Sinai was completely enveloped in smoke because the LORD came down on it in fire. Its smoke went up like the smoke of a furnace, and the whole mountain shook violently. As
30 the sound of the ram's horn grew louder and louder, Moses spoke and God answered him in the thunder.

The LORD came down on Mount Sinai at the top of the mountain. Then the LORD summoned Moses to the top of the mountain, and he went up. The LORD directed Moses, "Go down and warn the people not to break through to see the LORD; otherwise many of them will die. Even the priests who come near the LORD must consecrate themselves, or the LORD will break out in anger against them."

Moses responded to the LORD, "The people cannot come up Mount Sinai, since you warned us: Put a boundary around the mountain and consecrate it." And the LORD replied to him, "Go down and come back with Aaron. But the priests and the people must not break through to come
40 up to the LORD, or he will break out in anger against them." So Moses went down to the people and told them.

20 Then God spoke all these words:

I am the LORD your God, who brought you out of the land of Egypt, out of the place of slavery.

Do not have other gods besides me.

Do not make an idol for yourself, whether in the shape of anything in the heavens above or on the earth below or in the waters under the earth. Do not bow in worship to them, and do not serve them; for I, the LORD your God, am a jealous God, bringing the consequences of the fathers' iniquity on the children to the third and fourth generations of those who hate me, but showing faithful love to a thousand generations of those who
10 love me and keep my commands.

107

Do not misuse the name of the LORD your God, because the LORD will not leave anyone unpunished who misuses his name.

Remember the Sabbath day, to keep it holy: You are to labor six days and do all your work, but the seventh day is a Sabbath to the LORD your God. You must not do any work—you, your son or daughter, your male or female servant, your livestock, or the resident alien who is within your city gates. For the LORD made the heavens and the earth, the sea, and everything in them in six days; then he rested on the seventh day. Therefore the LORD blessed the Sabbath day and declared it holy.

Honor your father and your mother so that you may have a long life in the land that the LORD your God is giving you.

Do not murder.

Do not commit adultery.

Do not steal.

Do not give false testimony against your neighbor.

Do not covet your neighbor's house. Do not covet your neighbor's wife, his male or female servant, his ox or donkey, or anything that belongs to your neighbor.

All the people witnessed the thunder and lightning, the sound of the ram's horn, and the mountain surrounded by smoke. When the people saw it they trembled and stood at a distance. "You speak to us, and we will listen," they said to Moses, "but don't let God speak to us, or we will die."

Moses responded to the people, "Don't be afraid, for God has come to test you, so that you will fear him and will not sin." And the people remained standing at a distance as Moses approached the total darkness where God was.

Then the LORD told Moses, "This is what you are to say to the Israelites: You have seen that I have spoken to you from heaven. Do not make gods of silver to rival me; do not make gods of gold for yourselves.

"Make an earthen altar for me, and sacrifice on it your burnt offerings and fellowship offerings, your flocks and herds. I will come to you and bless you in every place where I cause my name to be remembered. If you make a stone altar for me, do not build it out of cut stones. If you use your chisel on it, you will defile it. Do not go up to my altar on steps, so that your nakedness is not exposed on it.

21   "These are the ordinances that you are to set before them:

"When you buy a Hebrew slave, he is to serve for six years; then in the seventh he is to leave as a free man without paying anything. If he arrives alone, he is to leave alone; if he arrives with a wife, his wife is to leave with him. If his master gives him a wife and she bears him sons or daughters, the wife and her children belong to her master, and the man must leave alone.

"But if the slave declares, 'I love my master, my wife, and my children; I do not want to leave as a free man,' his master is to bring him to the judges and then bring him to the door or doorpost. His master will pierce his ear with an awl, and he will serve his master for life.

10 "When a man sells his daughter as a concubine, she is not to leave as the male slaves do. If she is displeasing to her master, who chose her for himself, then he must let her be redeemed. He has no right to sell her to foreigners because he has acted treacherously toward her. Or if he chooses her for his son, he must deal with her according to the customary treatment of daughters. If he takes an additional wife, he must not reduce the food, clothing, or marital rights of the first wife. And if he does not do these three things for her, she may leave free of charge, without any payment.

"Whoever strikes a person so that he dies must be put to death. But if he did not intend any harm, and yet God allowed it to happen, I will appoint a place for you where he may flee. If a person schemes and willfully acts against his neighbor to murder him, you must take him from my altar to be put to death.

"Whoever strikes his father or his mother must be put to death.

"Whoever kidnaps a person must be put to death, whether he sells him or the person is found 20 in his possession.

"Whoever curses his father or his mother must be put to death.

"When men quarrel and one strikes the other with a stone or his fist, and the injured man does not die but is confined to bed, if he can later get up and walk around outside leaning on his staff, then the one who struck him will be exempt from punishment. Nevertheless, he must pay for his lost work time and provide for his complete recovery.

"When a man strikes his male or female slave with a rod, and the slave dies under his abuse, the owner must be punished. However, if the slave can stand up after a day or two, the owner should not be punished because he is his owner's property.

"When men get in a fight and hit a pregnant woman so that her children are born prematurely 30 but there is no injury, the one who hit her must be fined as the woman's husband demands from him, and he must pay according to judicial assessment. If there is an injury, then you must give life for life, eye for eye, tooth for tooth, hand for hand, foot for foot, burn for burn, bruise for bruise, wound for wound.

"When a man strikes the eye of his male or female slave and destroys it, he must let the slave go free in compensation for his eye. If he knocks out the tooth of his male or female slave, he must let the slave go free in compensation for his tooth.

"When an ox gores a man or a woman to death, the ox must be stoned, and its meat may not be eaten, but the ox's owner is innocent. However, if the ox was in the habit of goring, and its owner has been warned yet does not restrain it, and it kills a man or a woman, the ox must 40 be stoned, and its owner must also be put to death. If instead a ransom is demanded of him, he can pay a redemption price for his life in the full amount demanded from him. If it gores a son or a daughter, he is to be dealt with according to this same law. If the ox gores a male or female slave, he must give thirty shekels of silver to the slave's master, and the ox must be stoned.

"When a man uncovers a pit or digs a pit, and does not cover it, and an ox or a donkey falls into it, the owner of the pit must give compensation; he must pay to its owner, but the dead animal will become his.

"When a man's ox injures his neighbor's ox and it dies, they must sell the live ox and divide its proceeds; they must also divide the dead animal. If, however, it is known that the ox was in the
50 habit of goring, yet its owner has not restrained it, he must compensate fully, ox for ox; the dead animal will become his.

22 "When a man steals an ox or a sheep and butchers it or sells it, he must repay five cattle for the ox or four sheep for the sheep. If a thief is caught in the act of breaking in, and he is beaten to death, no one is guilty of bloodshed. But if this happens after sunrise, the householder is guilty of bloodshed. A thief must make full restitution. If he is unable, he is to be sold because of his theft. If what was stolen—whether ox, donkey, or sheep—is actually found alive in his possession, he must repay double.

"When a man lets a field or vineyard be grazed in, and then allows his animals to go and graze in someone else's field, he must repay with the best of his own field or vineyard.

"When a fire gets out of control, spreads to thornbushes, and consumes stacks of cut grain, standing grain, or a field, the one who started the fire must make full restitution for what was
10 burned.

"When a man gives his neighbor valuables or goods to keep, but they are stolen from that person's house, the thief, if caught, must repay double. If the thief is not caught, the owner of the house must present himself to the judges to determine whether or not he has taken his neighbor's property. In any case of wrongdoing involving an ox, a donkey, a sheep, a garment, or anything else lost, and someone claims, 'That's mine,' the case between the two parties is to come before the judges. The one the judges condemn must repay double to his neighbor.

"When a man gives his neighbor a donkey, an ox, a sheep, or any other animal to care for, but it dies, is injured, or is stolen, while no one is watching, there must be an oath before the LORD between the two of them to determine whether or not he has taken his neighbor's property. Its
20 owner must accept the oath, and the other man does not have to make restitution. But if, in fact, the animal was stolen from his custody, he must make restitution to its owner. If it was actually torn apart by a wild animal, he is to bring it as evidence; he does not have to make restitution for the torn carcass.

"When a man borrows an animal from his neighbor, and it is injured or dies while its owner is not there with it, the man must make full restitution. If its owner is there with it, the man does not have to make restitution. If it was rented, the loss is covered by its rental price.

"If a man seduces a virgin who is not engaged, and he sleeps with her, he must certainly pay the bridal price for her to be his wife. If her father absolutely refuses to give her to him, he must pay an amount in silver equal to the bridal price for virgins.

30 "Do not allow a sorceress to live.

"Whoever has sexual intercourse with an animal must be put to death.

"Whoever sacrifices to any gods, except the LORD alone, is to be set apart for destruction.

"You must not exploit a resident alien or oppress him, since you were resident aliens in the land of Egypt.

"You must not mistreat any widow or fatherless child. If you do mistreat them, they will no doubt cry to me, and I will certainly hear their cry. My anger will burn, and I will kill you with the sword; then your wives will be widows and your children fatherless.

"If you lend silver to my people, to the poor person among you, you must not be like a creditor to him; you must not charge him interest.

40 "If you ever take your neighbor's cloak as collateral, return it to him before sunset. For it is his only covering; it is the clothing for his body. What will he sleep in? And if he cries out to me, I will listen because I am gracious.

"You must not blaspheme God or curse a leader among your people.

"You must not hold back offerings from your harvest or your vats. Give me the firstborn of your sons. Do the same with your cattle and your flock. Let them stay with their mothers for seven days, but on the eighth day you are to give them to me.

"Be my holy people. You must not eat the meat of a mauled animal found in the field; throw it to the dogs.

23 "You must not spread a false report. Do not join the wicked to be a malicious witness.

"You must not follow a crowd in wrongdoing. Do not testify in a lawsuit and go along with a crowd to pervert justice. Do not show favoritism to a poor person in his lawsuit.

"If you come across your enemy's stray ox or donkey, you must return it to him.

"If you see the donkey of someone who hates you lying helpless under its load, and you want to refrain from helping it, you must help with it.

"You must not deny justice to a poor person among you in his lawsuit. Stay far away from a false accusation. Do not kill the innocent and the just, because I will not justify the guilty. You must not take a bribe, for a bribe blinds the clear-sighted and corrupts the words of the righteous.

10 You must not oppress a resident alien; you yourselves know how it feels to be a resident alien because you were resident aliens in the land of Egypt.

"Sow your land for six years and gather its produce. But during the seventh year you are to let it rest and leave it uncultivated, so that the poor among your people may eat from it and the wild animals may consume what they leave. Do the same with your vineyard and your olive grove.

"Do your work for six days but rest on the seventh day so that your ox and your donkey may rest, and the son of your female slave as well as the resident alien may be refreshed.

"Pay strict attention to everything I have said to you. You must not invoke the names of other gods; they must not be heard on your lips.

"Celebrate a festival in my honor three times a year. Observe the Festival of Unleavened Bread.
20 As I commanded you, you are to eat unleavened bread for seven days at the appointed time in the month of Abib, because you came out of Egypt in that month. No one is to appear before me empty-handed. Also observe the Festival of Harvest with the firstfruits of your produce from what you sow in the field, and observe the Festival of Ingathering at the end of the year, when you gather your produce from the field. Three times a year all your males are to appear before the Lord God.

"You must not offer the blood of my sacrifices with anything leavened. The fat of my festival offering must not remain until morning.

"Bring the best of the firstfruits of your land to the house of the Lord your God.

"You must not boil a young goat in its mother's milk.

"I am going to send an angel before you to protect you on the way and bring you to the place I have
30 prepared. Be attentive to him and listen to him. Do not defy him, because he will not forgive your acts of rebellion, for my name is in him. But if you will carefully obey him and do everything I say, then I will be an enemy to your enemies and a foe to your foes. For my angel will go before you and bring you to the land of the Amorites, Hethites, Perizzites, Canaanites, Hivites, and Jebusites, and I will wipe them out. Do not bow in worship to their gods, and do not serve them. Do not imitate their practices. Instead, demolish them and smash their sacred pillars to pieces. Serve the Lord your God, and he will bless your bread and your water. I will remove illnesses from you. No woman will miscarry or be childless in your land. I will give you the full number of your days.

"I will cause the people ahead of you to feel terror and will throw into confusion all the nations
39 you come to. I will make all your enemies turn their backs to you in retreat. I will send hornets in front of you, and they will drive the Hivites, Canaanites, and Hethites away from you. I will not drive them out ahead of you in a single year; otherwise, the land would become desolate, and wild animals would multiply against you. I will drive them out little by little ahead of you until you have become numerous and take possession of the land. I will set your borders from the Red Sea to the Mediterranean Sea, and from the wilderness to the Euphrates River. For I will place the inhabitants of the land under your control, and you will drive them out ahead of you. You must not make a covenant with them or their gods. They must not remain in your land, or else they will make you sin against me. If you serve their gods, it will be a snare for you."

24 Then he said to Moses, "Go up to the LORD, you and Aaron, Nadab, and Abihu, and seventy of Israel's elders, and bow in worship at a distance. Moses alone is to approach the LORD, but the others are not to approach, and the people are not to go up with him."

Moses came and told the people all the commands of the LORD and all the ordinances. Then all the people responded with a single voice, "We will do everything that the LORD has commanded." And Moses wrote down all the words of the LORD. He rose early the next morning and set up an altar and twelve pillars for the twelve tribes of Israel at the base of the mountain. Then he sent out young Israelite men, and they offered burnt offerings and sacrificed bulls as fellowship offerings to the LORD. Moses took half the blood and set it in basins; the other half of the blood he splattered 10 on the altar. He then took the covenant scroll and read it aloud to the people. They responded, "We will do and obey all that the LORD has commanded."

Moses took the blood, splattered it on the people, and said, "This is the blood of the covenant that the LORD has made with you concerning all these words."

Then Moses went up with Aaron, Nadab, and Abihu, and seventy of Israel's elders, and they saw the God of Israel. Beneath his feet was something like a pavement made of lapis lazuli, as clear as the sky itself. God did not harm the Israelite nobles; they saw him, and they ate and drank.

The LORD said to Moses, "Come up to me on the mountain and stay there so that I may give you the stone tablets with the law and commandments I have written for their instruction."

So Moses arose with his assistant Joshua and went up the mountain of God. He told the 20 elders, "Wait here for us until we return to you. Aaron and Hur are here with you. Whoever has a dispute should go to them." When Moses went up the mountain, the cloud covered it. The glory of the LORD settled on Mount Sinai, and the cloud covered it for six days. On the seventh day he called to Moses from the cloud. The appearance of the LORD's glory to the Israelites was like a consuming fire on the mountaintop. Moses entered the cloud as he went up the mountain, and he remained on the mountain forty days and forty nights.

25 The LORD spoke to Moses: "Tell the Israelites to take an offering for me. You are to take my offering from everyone who is willing to give. This is the offering you are to receive from them: gold, silver, and bronze; blue, purple, and scarlet yarn; fine linen and goat hair; ram skins dyed red and fine leather; acacia wood; oil for the light; spices for the anointing oil and for the fragrant incense; and onyx along with other gemstones for mounting on the ephod and breastpiece.

"They are to make a sanctuary for me so that I may dwell among them. You must make it according to all that I show you—the pattern of the tabernacle as well as the pattern of all its furnishings.

"They are to make an ark of acacia wood, forty-five inches long, twenty-seven inches wide, and 10 twenty-seven inches high. Overlay it with pure gold; overlay it both inside and out. Also make a gold molding all around it. Cast four gold rings for it and place them on its four feet, two rings on

one side and two rings on the other side. Make poles of acacia wood and overlay them with gold. Insert the poles into the rings on the sides of the ark in order to carry the ark with them. The poles are to remain in the rings of the ark; they must not be removed from it. Put the tablets of the testimony that I will give you into the ark. Make a mercy seat of pure gold, forty-five inches long and twenty-seven inches wide. Make two cherubim of gold; make them of hammered work at the two ends of the mercy seat. Make one cherub at one end and one cherub at the other end. At its two ends, make the cherubim of one piece with the mercy seat. The cherubim are to have wings spread out above, covering the mercy seat with their wings, and are to face one another. The faces
20 of the cherubim should be toward the mercy seat. Set the mercy seat on top of the ark and put the tablets of the testimony that I will give you into the ark. I will meet with you there above the mercy seat, between the two cherubim that are over the ark of the testimony; I will speak with you from there about all that I command you regarding the Israelites.

"You are to construct a table of acacia wood, thirty-six inches long, eighteen inches wide, and twenty-seven inches high. Overlay it with pure gold and make a gold molding all around it. Make a three-inch frame all around it and make a gold molding for it all around its frame. Make four gold rings for it, and attach the rings to the four corners at its four legs. The rings should be next to the frame as holders for the poles to carry the table. Make the poles of acacia wood and overlay them with gold, and the table can be carried by them. You are also to make its plates and cups, as well as
30 its pitchers and bowls for pouring drink offerings. Make them out of pure gold. Put the Bread of the Presence on the table before me at all times.

"You are to make a lampstand out of pure, hammered gold. It is to be made of one piece: its base and shaft, its ornamental cups, and its buds and petals. Six branches are to extend from its sides, three branches of the lampstand from one side and three branches of the lampstand from the other side. There are to be three cups shaped like almond blossoms, each with a bud and petals, on one branch, and three cups shaped like almond blossoms, each with a bud and petals, on the next branch. It is to be this way for the six branches that extend from the lampstand. There are to be four cups shaped like almond blossoms on the lampstand shaft along with its buds and petals. For the six branches that extend from the lampstand, a bud must be under the first pair
40 of branches from it, a bud under the second pair of branches from it, and a bud under the third pair of branches from it. Their buds and branches are to be of one piece. All of it is to be a single hammered piece of pure gold.
"Make its seven lamps, and set them up so that they illuminate the area in front of it. Its snuffers and firepans must be of pure gold. The lampstand with all these utensils is to be made from seventy-five pounds of pure gold. Be careful to make them according to the pattern you have been shown on the mountain.

26 "You are to construct the tabernacle itself with ten curtains. You must make them of finely spun linen, and blue, purple, and scarlet yarn, with a design of cherubim worked into them. Each curtain should be forty-two feet long and six feet wide; all the curtains are to have the same measurements. Five of the curtains should be joined together, and the other five curtains joined together. Make loops of blue yarn on the edge of the last curtain in the first set, and do the same on the edge of the outermost curtain in the second set. Make fifty loops on the one curtain and make fifty loops on the edge of the curtain in the second set, so that the loops line up together. Also make fifty gold clasps and join the curtains together with the clasps, so that the tabernacle may be a single unit.

10 "You are to make curtains of goat hair for a tent over the tabernacle; make eleven of these curtains. Each curtain should be forty-five feet long and six feet wide. All eleven curtains are to have the same measurements. Join five of the curtains by themselves, and the other six curtains by themselves. Then fold the sixth curtain double at the front of the tent. Make fifty loops on the edge of one curtain, the outermost in the first set, and make fifty loops on the edge of the corresponding curtain of the second set. Make fifty bronze clasps; put the clasps through the loops and join the tent together so that it is a single unit. As for the flap that remains from the tent curtains, the leftover half curtain is to hang over the back of the tabernacle. What remains along the length of the tent curtains—a half yard on one side and a half yard on the other side—should hang over the sides of the tabernacle on either side to cover it. Make a covering for the tent from 20 ram skins dyed red and a covering of fine leather on top of that.

"You are to make upright supports of acacia wood for the tabernacle. Each support is to be fifteen feet long and twenty-seven inches wide. Each support will have two tenons for joining. Do the same for all the supports of the tabernacle. Make the supports for the tabernacle as follows: twenty supports for the south side, and make forty silver bases under the twenty supports, two bases under the first support for its two tenons, and two bases under the next support for its two tenons; twenty supports for the second side of the tabernacle, the north side, along with their forty silver bases, two bases under the first support and two bases under each support; and make six supports for the west side of the tabernacle. Make two additional supports for the two back corners of the tabernacle. They are to be paired at the bottom, and joined together at the top in 30 a single ring. So it should be for both of them; they will serve as the two corners. There are to be eight supports with their silver bases: sixteen bases; two bases under the first support and two bases under each support.

"You are to make five crossbars of acacia wood for the supports on one side of the tabernacle, five crossbars for the supports on the other side of the tabernacle, and five crossbars for the supports on the back side of the tabernacle on the west. The central crossbar is to run through the middle of the supports from one end to the other. Then overlay the supports with gold, and make their rings of gold as the holders for the crossbars. Also overlay the crossbars with gold. You are to set up the tabernacle according to the plan for it that you have been shown on the mountain.

"You are to make a curtain of blue, purple, and scarlet yarn, and finely spun linen with a design
40 of cherubim worked into it. Hang it on four gold-plated pillars of acacia wood that have gold
hooks and that stand on four silver bases. Hang the curtain under the clasps and bring the ark
of the testimony there behind the curtain, so the curtain will make a separation for you between
the holy place and the most holy place. Put the mercy seat on the ark of the testimony in the
most holy place. Place the table outside the curtain and the lampstand on the south side of the
tabernacle, opposite the table; put the table on the north side.

"For the entrance to the tent you are to make a screen embroidered with blue, purple, and
scarlet yarn, and finely spun linen. Make five pillars of acacia wood for the screen and overlay them
with gold; their hooks are to be gold, and you are to cast five bronze bases for them.

27 "You are to construct the altar of acacia wood. The altar must be square, 7 ½ feet long, and 7 ½
feet wide; it must be 4 ½ feet high. Make horns for it on its four corners; the horns are to be of one
piece. Overlay it with bronze. Make its pots for removing ashes, and its shovels, basins, meat forks,
and firepans; make all its utensils of bronze. Construct a grate for it of bronze mesh, and make
four bronze rings on the mesh at its four corners. Set it below, under the altar's ledge, so that the
mesh comes halfway up the altar. Then make poles for the altar, poles of acacia wood, and overlay
them with bronze. The poles are to be inserted into the rings so that the poles are on two sides of
the altar when it is carried. Construct the altar with boards so that it is hollow. They are to make
it just as it was shown to you on the mountain.

10 "You are to make the courtyard for the tabernacle. Make hangings for the south side of the courtyard
out of finely spun linen, 150 feet long on that side including twenty posts and twenty bronze bases,
with silver hooks and silver bands for the posts. And so make hangings 150 feet long for the north
side, including twenty posts and their twenty bronze bases, with silver hooks and silver bands for
the posts. For the width of the courtyard, make hangings 75 feet long for the west side, including
their ten posts and their ten bases. And for the width of the courtyard on the east side toward the
sunrise, 75 feet, make hangings 22 ½ feet long for one side of the gate, including their three posts and
their three bases. And make hangings 22 ½ feet long for the other side, including their three posts
and their three bases. The gate of the courtyard is to have a 30-foot screen embroidered with blue,
purple, and scarlet yarn, and finely spun linen. It is to have four posts and their four bases.

20 "All the posts around the courtyard are to be banded with silver and have silver hooks and bronze
bases. The courtyard is to be 150 feet long, 75 feet wide at each end, and 7 ½ feet high, all of it made
of finely spun linen. The bases of the posts are to be bronze. All the utensils of the tabernacle for
every use and all its tent pegs as well as all the tent pegs of the courtyard are to be made of bronze.

"You are to command the Israelites to bring you pure oil from crushed olives for the light, in order
to keep the lamp burning regularly. In the tent of meeting outside the curtain that is in front of the

testimony, Aaron and his sons are to tend the lamp from evening until morning before the Lord. This is to be a permanent statute for the Israelites throughout their generations.

28 "Have your brother Aaron, with his sons, come to you from the Israelites to serve me as priest— Aaron, his sons Nadab and Abihu, Eleazar and Ithamar. Make holy garments for your brother Aaron, for glory and beauty. You are to instruct all the skilled artisans, whom I have filled with a spirit of wisdom, to make Aaron's garments for consecrating him to serve me as priest. These are the garments that they must make: a breastpiece, an ephod, a robe, a specially woven tunic, a turban, and a sash. They are to make holy garments for your brother Aaron and his sons so that they may serve me as priests. They should use gold; blue, purple, and scarlet yarn; and fine linen.

"They are to make the ephod of finely spun linen embroidered with gold, and with blue, purple, and scarlet yarn. It must have two shoulder pieces attached to its two edges so that it can be joined
10 together. The artistically woven waistband that is on the ephod must be of one piece, according to the same workmanship of gold, of blue, purple, and scarlet yarn, and of finely spun linen.
    "Take two onyx stones and engrave on them the names of Israel's sons: six of their names on the first stone and the remaining six names on the second stone, in the order of their birth. Engrave the two stones with the names of Israel's sons as a gem cutter engraves a seal. Mount them, surrounded with gold filigree settings. Fasten both stones on the shoulder pieces of the ephod as memorial stones for the Israelites. Aaron will carry their names on his two shoulders before the Lord as a reminder. Fashion gold filigree settings and two chains of pure gold; you will make them of braided cord work, and attach the cord chains to the settings.

"You are to make an embroidered breastpiece for making decisions. Make it with the same
20 workmanship as the ephod; make it of gold, of blue, purple, and scarlet yarn, and of finely spun linen. It must be square and folded double, nine inches long and nine inches wide. Place a setting of gemstones on it, four rows of stones:
        The first row should be
        a row of carnelian, topaz, and emerald;
        the second row,
        a turquoise, a lapis lazuli, and a diamond;
        the third row,
        a jacinth, an agate, and an amethyst;
        and the fourth row,
30   a beryl, an onyx, and a jasper.
They should be adorned with gold filigree in their settings. The twelve stones are to correspond to the names of Israel's sons. Each stone must be engraved like a seal, with one of the names of the twelve tribes.

"You are to make braided chains of pure gold cord work for the breastpiece. Fashion two gold rings for the breastpiece and attach them to its two corners. Then attach the two gold cords to the two gold rings at the corners of the breastpiece. Attach the other ends of the two cords to the two filigree settings, and in this way attach them to the ephod's shoulder pieces in the front. Make two other gold rings and put them at the two other corners of the breastpiece on the edge that is next to the inner border of the ephod. Make two more gold rings and attach them to the bottom of the ephod's two shoulder pieces on its front, close to its seam, and above the ephod's woven waistband. The artisans are to tie the breastpiece from its rings to the rings of the ephod with a cord of blue yarn, so that the breastpiece is above the ephod's waistband and does not come loose from the ephod.

"Whenever he enters the sanctuary, Aaron is to carry the names of Israel's sons over his heart on the breastpiece for decisions, as a continual reminder before the LORD. Place the Urim and Thummim in the breastpiece for decisions, so that they will also be over Aaron's heart whenever he comes before the LORD. Aaron will continually carry the means of decisions for the Israelites over his heart before the LORD.

"You are to make the robe of the ephod entirely of blue yarn. There should be an opening at its top in the center of it. Around the opening, there should be a woven collar with an opening like that of body armor so that it does not tear. Make pomegranates of blue, purple, and scarlet yarn on its lower hem and all around it. Put gold bells between them all the way around, so that gold bells and pomegranates alternate around the lower hem of the robe. The robe will be worn by Aaron whenever he ministers, and its sound will be heard when he enters the sanctuary before the LORD and when he exits, so that he does not die.

"You are to make a pure gold medallion and engrave it, like the engraving of a seal: HOLY TO THE LORD. Fasten it to a cord of blue yarn so it can be placed on the turban; the medallion is to be on the front of the turban. It will be on Aaron's forehead so that Aaron may bear the guilt connected with the holy offerings that the Israelites consecrate as all their holy gifts. It is always to be on his forehead, so that they may find acceptance with the LORD.

"You are to weave the tunic from fine linen, make a turban of fine linen, and make an embroidered sash. Make tunics, sashes, and headbands for Aaron's sons to give them glory and beauty. Put these on your brother Aaron and his sons; then anoint, ordain, and consecrate them, so that they may serve me as priests. Make them linen undergarments to cover their naked bodies; they must extend from the waist to the thighs. These must be worn by Aaron and his sons whenever they enter the tent of meeting or approach the altar to minister in the sanctuary area, so that they do not incur guilt and die. This is to be a permanent statute for Aaron and for his future descendants.

29 "This is what you are to do for them to consecrate them to serve me as priests. Take a young bull and two unblemished rams, with unleavened bread, unleavened cakes mixed with oil, and unleavened wafers coated with oil. Make them out of fine wheat flour, put them in a basket, and bring them in the basket, along with the bull and two rams. Bring Aaron and his sons to the entrance to the tent of meeting and wash them with water. Then take the garments and clothe Aaron with the tunic, the robe for the ephod, the ephod itself, and the breastpiece; fasten the ephod on him with its woven waistband. Put the turban on his head and place the holy diadem on the turban. Take the anointing oil, pour it on his head, and anoint him. You must also bring his sons and clothe them with tunics. Tie the sashes on Aaron and his sons and fasten headbands on them. The priesthood is to be theirs by a permanent statute. This is the way you will ordain Aaron and his sons.

"You are to bring the bull to the front of the tent of meeting, and Aaron and his sons must lay their hands on the bull's head. Slaughter the bull before the LORD at the entrance to the tent of meeting. Take some of the bull's blood and apply it to the horns of the altar with your finger; then pour out all the rest of the blood at the base of the altar. Take all the fat that covers the entrails, the fatty lobe of the liver, and the two kidneys with the fat on them, and burn them on the altar. But burn the bull's flesh, its hide, and its waste outside the camp; it is a sin offering.

"Take one ram, and Aaron and his sons are to lay their hands on the ram's head. You are to slaughter the ram, take its blood, and splatter it on all sides of the altar. Cut the ram into pieces. Wash its entrails and legs, and place them with its head and its pieces on the altar. Then burn the whole ram on the altar; it is a burnt offering to the LORD. It is a pleasing aroma, a food offering to the LORD.

"You are to take the second ram, and Aaron and his sons must lay their hands on the ram's head. Slaughter the ram, take some of its blood, and put it on Aaron's right earlobe, on his sons' right earlobes, on the thumbs of their right hands, and on the big toes of their right feet. Splatter the remaining blood on all sides of the altar. Take some of the blood that is on the altar and some of the anointing oil, and sprinkle them on Aaron and his garments, as well as on his sons and their garments. So he and his garments will be holy, as well as his sons and their garments.

"Take the fat from the ram, the fat tail, the fat covering the entrails, the fatty lobe of the liver, the two kidneys and the fat on them, and the right thigh (since this is a ram for ordination); take one loaf of bread, one cake of bread made with oil, and one wafer from the basket of unleavened bread that is before the LORD; and put all of them in the hands of Aaron and his sons and present them as a presentation offering before the LORD. Take them from their hands and burn them on the altar on top of the burnt offering, as a pleasing aroma before the LORD; it is a food offering to the LORD.

"Take the breast from the ram of Aaron's ordination and present it as a presentation offering before the LORD; it is to be your portion. Consecrate for Aaron and his sons the breast of the presentation offering that is presented and the thigh of the contribution that is lifted up from the ram of ordination. This will belong to Aaron and his sons as a regular portion from the Israelites, for it is a contribution. It will be the Israelites' contribution from their fellowship sacrifices, their

40 contribution to the LORD.

"The holy garments that belong to Aaron are to belong to his sons after him, so that they can be anointed and ordained in them. Any priest who is one of his sons and who succeeds him and enters the tent of meeting to minister in the sanctuary must wear them for seven days.

"You are to take the ram of ordination and boil its flesh in a holy place. Aaron and his sons are to eat the meat of the ram and the bread that is in the basket at the entrance to the tent of meeting. They must eat those things by which atonement was made at the time of their ordination and consecration. An unauthorized person must not eat them, for these things are holy. If any of the meat of ordination or any of the bread is left until morning, burn what is left over. It must not be eaten because it is holy.

50 "This is what you are to do for Aaron and his sons based on all I have commanded you. Take seven days to ordain them. Sacrifice a bull as a sin offering each day for atonement. Purify the altar when you make atonement for it, and anoint it in order to consecrate it. For seven days you must make atonement for the altar and consecrate it. The altar will be especially holy. Whatever touches the altar will be consecrated.

"This is what you are to offer regularly on the altar every day: two year-old lambs. In the morning offer one lamb, and at twilight offer the other lamb. With the first lamb offer two quarts of fine flour mixed with one quart of oil from crushed olives, and a drink offering of one quart of wine. You are to offer the second lamb at twilight. Offer a grain offering and a drink offering with it, like the one in the morning, as a pleasing aroma, a food offering to the LORD. This will be a

60 regular burnt offering throughout your generations at the entrance to the tent of meeting before the LORD, where I will meet you to speak with you. I will also meet with the Israelites there, and that place will be consecrated by my glory. I will consecrate the tent of meeting and the altar; I will also consecrate Aaron and his sons to serve me as priests. I will dwell among the Israelites and be their God. And they will know that I am the LORD their God, who brought them out of the land of Egypt, so that I might dwell among them. I am the LORD their God.

30 "You are to make an altar for the burning of incense; make it of acacia wood. It must be square, eighteen inches long and eighteen inches wide; it must be thirty-six inches high. Its horns must be of one piece with it. Overlay its top, all around its sides, and its horns with pure gold; make a gold molding all around it. Make two gold rings for it under the molding on two of its sides; put these on opposite sides of it to be holders for the poles to carry it with. Make the poles of acacia wood and overlay them with gold.

"You are to place the altar in front of the curtain by the ark of the testimony—in front of the mercy seat that is over the testimony—where I will meet with you. Aaron must burn fragrant incense on it; he must burn it every morning when he tends the lamps. When Aaron sets up

10 the lamps at twilight, he must burn incense. There is to be an incense offering before the LORD

throughout your generations. You must not offer unauthorized incense on it, or a burnt or grain offering; you are not to pour a drink offering on it.

"Once a year Aaron is to perform the atonement ceremony for the altar. Throughout your generations he is to perform the atonement ceremony for it once a year, with the blood of the sin offering for atonement on the horns. The altar is especially holy to the LORD."

The LORD spoke to Moses: "When you take a census of the Israelites to register them, each of the men must pay a ransom for his life to the LORD as they are registered. Then no plague will come on them as they are registered. Everyone who is registered must pay half a shekel according to the sanctuary shekel (twenty gerahs to the shekel). This half shekel is a contribution to the LORD. Each man who is registered, twenty years old or more, must give this contribution to the LORD. The wealthy may not give more and the poor may not give less than half a shekel when giving the contribution to the LORD to atone for your lives. Take the atonement price from the Israelites and use it for the service of the tent of meeting. It will serve as a reminder for the Israelites before the LORD to atone for your lives."

The LORD spoke to Moses: "Make a bronze basin for washing and a bronze stand for it. Set it between the tent of meeting and the altar, and put water in it. Aaron and his sons must wash their hands and feet from the basin. Whenever they enter the tent of meeting or approach the altar to minister by burning a food offering to the LORD, they must wash with water so that they will not die. They must wash their hands and feet so that they will not die; this is to be a permanent statute for them, for Aaron and his descendants throughout their generations."

The LORD spoke to Moses: "Take for yourself the finest spices: 12 ½ pounds of liquid myrrh, half as much (6 ¼ pounds) of fragrant cinnamon, 6 ¼ pounds of fragrant cane, 12 ½ pounds of cassia (by the sanctuary shekel), and a gallon of olive oil. Prepare from these a holy anointing oil, a scented blend, the work of a perfumer; it will be holy anointing oil.

"With it you are to anoint the tent of meeting, the ark of the testimony, the table with all its utensils, the lampstand with its utensils, the altar of incense, the altar of burnt offering with all its utensils, and the basin with its stand. Consecrate them and they will be especially holy. Whatever touches them will be consecrated. Anoint Aaron and his sons and consecrate them to serve me as priests.

"Tell the Israelites: This will be my holy anointing oil throughout your generations. It must not be used for ordinary anointing on a person's body, and you must not make anything like it using its formula. It is holy, and it must be holy to you. Anyone who blends something like it or puts some of it on an unauthorized person must be cut off from his people."

The LORD said to Moses, "Take fragrant spices: stacte, onycha, and galbanum; the spices and pure frankincense are to be in equal measures. Prepare expertly blended incense from these; it is to be seasoned with salt, pure and holy. Grind some of it into a fine powder and put some in front of the testimony in the tent of meeting, where I will meet with you. It must be especially holy to you. As for the incense you are making, you must not make any for yourselves using its formula. It is to be regarded by you as holy—belonging to the Lord. Anyone who makes something like it to smell its fragrance must be cut off from his people."

31 The Lord also spoke to Moses: "Look, I have appointed by name Bezalel son of Uri, son of Hur, of the tribe of Judah. I have filled him with God's Spirit, with wisdom, understanding, and ability in every craft to design artistic works in gold, silver, and bronze, to cut gemstones for mounting, and to carve wood for work in every craft. I have also selected Oholiab son of Ahisamach, of the tribe of Dan, to be with him. I have put wisdom in the heart of every skilled artisan in order to make all that I have commanded you: the tent of meeting, the ark of the testimony, the mercy seat that is on top of it, and all the other furnishings of the tent—the table with its utensils, the pure gold lampstand with all its utensils, the altar of incense, the altar of burnt offering with all its utensils, the basin with its stand—the specially woven garments, both the holy garments for the

10 priest Aaron and the garments for his sons to serve as priests, the anointing oil, and the fragrant incense for the sanctuary. They must make them according to all that I have commanded you."

The Lord said to Moses, "Tell the Israelites: You must observe my Sabbaths, for it is a sign between me and you throughout your generations, so that you will know that I am the Lord who consecrates you. Observe the Sabbath, for it is holy to you. Whoever profanes it must be put to death. If anyone does work on it, that person must be cut off from his people. Work may be done for six days, but on the seventh day there must be a Sabbath of complete rest, holy to the Lord. Anyone who does work on the Sabbath day must be put to death. The Israelites must observe the Sabbath, celebrating it throughout their generations as a permanent covenant. It is a sign forever between me and the Israelites, for in six days the Lord made the heavens and the earth, but on the

20 seventh day he rested and was refreshed."

When he finished speaking with Moses on Mount Sinai, he gave him the two tablets of the testimony, stone tablets inscribed by the finger of God.

32 When the people saw that Moses delayed in coming down from the mountain, they gathered around Aaron and said to him, "Come, make gods for us who will go before us because this Moses, the man who brought us up from the land of Egypt—we don't know what has happened to him!"

Aaron replied to them, "Take off the gold rings that are on the ears of your wives, your sons, and your daughters and bring them to me." So all the people took off the gold rings that were on their ears and brought them to Aaron. He took the gold from them, fashioned it with an engraving tool, and made it into an image of a calf.

Then they said, "Israel, these are your gods, who brought you up from the land of Egypt!"

When Aaron saw this, he built an altar in front of it and made an announcement: "There will be a festival to the LORD tomorrow." Early the next morning they arose, offered burnt offerings, and presented fellowship offerings. The people sat down to eat and drink, and got up to party.

The LORD spoke to Moses: "Go down at once! For your people you brought up from the land of Egypt have acted corruptly. They have quickly turned from the way I commanded them; they have made for themselves an image of a calf. They have bowed down to it, sacrificed to it, and said, 'Israel, these are your gods, who brought you up from the land of Egypt.'" The LORD also said to Moses, "I have seen this people, and they are indeed a stiff-necked people. Now leave me alone, so that my anger can burn against them and I can destroy them. Then I will make you into a great nation."

But Moses sought the favor of the LORD his God: "LORD, why does your anger burn against your people you brought out of the land of Egypt with great power and a strong hand? Why should the Egyptians say, 'He brought them out with an evil intent to kill them in the mountains and eliminate them from the face of the earth'? Turn from your fierce anger and relent concerning this disaster planned for your people. Remember your servants Abraham, Isaac, and Israel—you swore to them by yourself and declared, 'I will make your offspring as numerous as the stars of the sky and will give your offspring all this land that I have promised, and they will inherit it forever.'" So the LORD relented concerning the disaster he had said he would bring on his people.

Then Moses turned and went down the mountain with the two tablets of the testimony in his hands. They were inscribed on both sides—inscribed front and back. The tablets were the work of God, and the writing was God's writing, engraved on the tablets.

When Joshua heard the sound of the people as they shouted, he said to Moses, "There is a sound of war in the camp."

But Moses replied,

> It's not the sound of a victory cry
> and not the sound of a cry of defeat;
> I hear the sound of singing!

As he approached the camp and saw the calf and the dancing, Moses became enraged and threw the tablets out of his hands, smashing them at the base of the mountain. He took the calf they had made, burned it up, and ground it to powder. He scattered the powder over the surface of the water and forced the Israelites to drink the water.

Then Moses asked Aaron, "What did these people do to you that you have led them into such a grave sin?"

"Don't be enraged, my lord," Aaron replied. "You yourself know that the people are intent on evil. They said to me, 'Make gods for us who will go before us because this Moses, the man who brought us up from the land of Egypt—we don't know what has happened to him!' So I said to them, 'Whoever has gold, take it off,' and they gave it to me. When I threw it into the fire, out came this calf!"

Moses saw that the people were out of control, for Aaron had let them get out of control, making them a laughingstock to their enemies. And Moses stood at the camp's entrance and said, "Whoever is for the LORD, come to me." And all the Levites gathered around him. He told them, "This is what the LORD, the God of Israel, says, 'Every man fasten his sword to his side; go back and forth through the camp from entrance to entrance, and each of you kill his brother, his friend, and his neighbor.'" The Levites did as Moses commanded, and about three thousand men fell dead that day among the people. Afterward Moses said, "Today you have been dedicated to the LORD, since each man went against his son and his brother. Therefore you have brought a blessing on yourselves today."

The following day Moses said to the people, "You have committed a grave sin. Now I will go up to the LORD; perhaps I will be able to atone for your sin."

So Moses returned to the LORD and said, "Oh, these people have committed a grave sin; they have made a god of gold for themselves. Now if you would only forgive their sin. But if not, please erase me from the book you have written."

The LORD replied to Moses, "Whoever has sinned against me I will erase from my book. Now go, lead the people to the place I told you about; see, my angel will go before you. But on the day I settle accounts, I will hold them accountable for their sin." And the LORD inflicted a plague on the people for what they did with the calf Aaron had made.

33 The LORD spoke to Moses: "Go up from here, you and the people you brought up from the land of Egypt, to the land I promised to Abraham, Isaac, and Jacob, saying: I will give it to your offspring. I will send an angel ahead of you and will drive out the Canaanites, Amorites, Hethites, Perizzites, Hivites, and Jebusites. Go up to a land flowing with milk and honey. But I will not go up with you because you are a stiff-necked people; otherwise, I might destroy you on the way." When the people heard this bad news, they mourned and didn't put on their jewelry.

For the LORD said to Moses, "Tell the Israelites: You are a stiff-necked people. If I went up with you for a single moment, I would destroy you. Now take off your jewelry, and I will decide what to do with you." So the Israelites remained stripped of their jewelry from Mount Horeb onward.

Now Moses took a tent and pitched it outside the camp, at a distance from the camp; he called it the tent of meeting. Anyone who wanted to consult the LORD would go to the tent of meeting that was outside the camp. Whenever Moses went out to the tent, all the people would stand up, each one at the door of his tent, and they would watch Moses until he entered the tent. When Moses entered the tent, the pillar of cloud would come down and remain at the entrance to the tent, and the LORD would speak with Moses. As all the people saw the pillar of cloud remaining at the entrance to the tent, they would stand up, then bow in worship, each one at the door of his tent. The LORD would speak with Moses face to face, just as a man speaks with his friend, then Moses would return to the camp. His assistant, the young man Joshua son of Nun, would not leave the inside of the tent.

20 Moses said to the Lord, "Look, you have told me, 'Lead this people up,' but you have not let me know whom you will send with me. You said, 'I know you by name, and you have also found favor with me.' Now if I have indeed found favor with you, please teach me your ways, and I will know you, so that I may find favor with you. Now consider that this nation is your people."

And he replied, "My presence will go with you, and I will give you rest."

"If your presence does not go," Moses responded to him, "don't make us go up from here. How will it be known that I and your people have found favor with you unless you go with us? I and your people will be distinguished by this from all the other people on the face of the earth."

The Lord answered Moses, "I will do this very thing you have asked, for you have found favor with me, and I know you by name."

30 Then Moses said, "Please, let me see your glory."

He said, "I will cause all my goodness to pass in front of you, and I will proclaim the name 'the Lord' before you. I will be gracious to whom I will be gracious, and I will have compassion on whom I will have compassion." But he added, "You cannot see my face, for humans cannot see me and live." The Lord said, "Here is a place near me. You are to stand on the rock, and when my glory passes by, I will put you in the crevice of the rock and cover you with my hand until I have passed by. Then I will take my hand away, and you will see my back, but my face will not be seen."

34 The Lord said to Moses, "Cut two stone tablets like the first ones, and I will write on them the words that were on the first tablets, which you broke. Be prepared by morning. Come up Mount Sinai in the morning and stand before me on the mountaintop. No one may go up with you; in fact, no one should be seen anywhere on the mountain. Even the flocks and herds are not to graze in front of that mountain."

Moses cut two stone tablets like the first ones. He got up early in the morning, and taking the two stone tablets in his hand, he climbed Mount Sinai, just as the Lord had commanded him.

The Lord came down in a cloud, stood with him there, and proclaimed his name, "the Lord." The Lord passed in front of him and proclaimed:

10 The Lord—the Lord is a compassionate and gracious God, slow to anger and abounding in faithful love and truth, maintaining faithful love to a thousand generations, forgiving iniquity, rebellion, and sin. But he will not leave the guilty unpunished, bringing the consequences of the fathers' iniquity on the children and grandchildren to the third and fourth generation.

Moses immediately knelt low on the ground and worshiped. Then he said, "My Lord, if I have indeed found favor with you, my Lord, please go with us (even though this is a stiff-necked people), forgive our iniquity and our sin, and accept us as your own possession."

And the Lord responded, "Look, I am making a covenant. In the presence of all your people I will perform wonders that have never been done in the whole earth or in any nation. All the people you live among will see the Lord's work, for what I am doing with you is awe-inspiring. Observe what I command you today. I am going to drive out before you the Amorites, Canaanites, Hethites, Perizzites, Hivites, and Jebusites. Be careful not to make a treaty with the inhabitants of the land that you are going to enter; otherwise, they will become a snare among you. Instead, you must tear down their altars, smash their sacred pillars, and chop down their Asherah poles. Because the Lord is jealous for his reputation, you are never to bow down to another god. He is a jealous God.

"Do not make a treaty with the inhabitants of the land, or else when they prostitute themselves with their gods and sacrifice to their gods, they will invite you, and you will eat their sacrifices. Then you will take some of their daughters as brides for your sons. Their daughters will prostitute themselves with their gods and cause your sons to prostitute themselves with their gods.

"Do not make cast images of gods for yourselves.

"Observe the Festival of Unleavened Bread. You are to eat unleavened bread for seven days at the appointed time in the month of Abib, as I commanded you, for you came out of Egypt in the month of Abib.

"The firstborn male from every womb belongs to me, including all your male livestock, the firstborn of cattle or sheep. You may redeem the firstborn of a donkey with a sheep, but if you do not redeem it, break its neck. You must redeem all the firstborn of your sons. No one is to appear before me empty-handed.

"You are to labor six days but you must rest on the seventh day; you must even rest during plowing and harvesting times.

"Observe the Festival of Weeks with the firstfruits of the wheat harvest, and the Festival of Ingathering at the turn of the agricultural year. Three times a year all your males are to appear before the Lord God, the God of Israel. For I will drive out nations before you and enlarge your territory. No one will covet your land when you go up three times a year to appear before the Lord your God.

"Do not present the blood for my sacrifice with anything leavened. The sacrifice of the Passover Festival must not remain until morning.

"Bring the best firstfruits of your land to the house of the Lord your God.

"You must not boil a young goat in its mother's milk."

The Lord also said to Moses, "Write down these words, for I have made a covenant with you and with Israel based on these words."

Moses was there with the Lord forty days and forty nights; he did not eat food or drink water. He wrote the Ten Commandments, the words of the covenant, on the tablets.

As Moses descended from Mount Sinai—with the two tablets of the testimony in his hands as he descended the mountain—he did not realize that the skin of his face shone as a result of his speaking with the LORD. When Aaron and all the Israelites saw Moses, the skin of his face shone! They were afraid to come near him. But Moses called out to them, so Aaron and all the leaders of the community returned to him, and Moses spoke to them. Afterward all the Israelites came near, and he commanded them to do everything the LORD had told him on Mount Sinai. When Moses had finished speaking with them, he put a veil over his face. But whenever Moses went before the LORD to speak with him, he would remove the veil until he came out. After he came out, he would tell the Israelites what he had been commanded, and the Israelites would see that Moses's face was radiant. Then Moses would put the veil over his face again until he went to speak with the LORD.

35 Moses assembled the entire Israelite community and said to them, "These are the things that the LORD has commanded you to do: For six days work is to be done, but on the seventh day you are to have a holy day, a Sabbath of complete rest to the LORD. Anyone who does work on it must be executed. Do not light a fire in any of your homes on the Sabbath day."

Then Moses said to the entire Israelite community, "This is what the LORD has commanded: Take up an offering among you for the LORD. Let everyone whose heart is willing bring this as the LORD's offering: gold, silver, and bronze; blue, purple, and scarlet yarn; fine linen and goat hair; ram skins dyed red and fine leather; acacia wood; oil for the light; spices for the anointing oil and for the fragrant incense; and onyx with gemstones to mount on the ephod and breastpiece.

"Let all the skilled artisans among you come and make everything that the LORD has commanded: the tabernacle—its tent and covering, its clasps and supports, its crossbars, its pillars and bases; the ark with its poles, the mercy seat, and the curtain for the screen; the table with its poles, all its utensils, and the Bread of the Presence; the lampstand for light with its utensils and lamps as well as the oil for the light; the altar of incense with its poles; the anointing oil and the fragrant incense; the entryway screen for the entrance to the tabernacle; the altar of burnt offering with its bronze grate, its poles, and all its utensils; the basin with its stand; the hangings of the courtyard, its posts and bases, and the screen for the gate of the courtyard; the tent pegs for the tabernacle and the tent pegs for the courtyard, along with their ropes; and the specially woven garments for ministering in the sanctuary—the holy garments for the priest Aaron and the garments for his sons to serve as priests."

Then the entire Israelite community left Moses's presence. Everyone whose heart was moved and whose spirit prompted him came and brought an offering to the LORD for the work on the tent of meeting, for all its services, and for the holy garments. Both men and women came; all who had willing hearts brought brooches, earrings, rings, necklaces, and all kinds of gold jewelry—everyone who presented a presentation offering of gold to the LORD. Everyone who possessed blue, purple, or scarlet yarn, fine linen or goat hair, ram skins dyed red or fine leather, brought them. Everyone making an offering of silver or bronze brought it as a contribution to the LORD. Everyone who possessed acacia wood useful for any task in the work brought it. Every skilled

woman spun yarn with her hands and brought it: blue, purple, and scarlet yarn, and fine linen.
30 And all the women whose hearts were moved spun the goat hair by virtue of their skill. The leaders brought onyx and gemstones to mount on the ephod and breastpiece, as well as the spice and oil for the light, for the anointing oil, and for the fragrant incense. So the Israelites brought a freewill offering to the Lord, all the men and women whose hearts prompted them to bring something for all the work that the Lord, through Moses, had commanded to be done.

Moses then said to the Israelites, "Look, the Lord has appointed by name Bezalel son of Uri, son of Hur, of the tribe of Judah. He has filled him with God's Spirit, with wisdom, understanding, and ability in every kind of craft to design artistic works in gold, silver, and bronze, to cut gemstones for mounting, and to carve wood for work in every kind of artistic craft. He has also given both him and Oholiab son of Ahisamach, of the tribe of Dan, the ability to teach others. He
40 has filled them with skill to do all the work of a gem cutter; a designer; an embroiderer in blue,
36 purple, and scarlet yarn and fine linen; and a weaver. They can do every kind of craft and design artistic designs. Bezalel, Oholiab, and all the skilled people are to work based on everything the Lord has commanded. The Lord has given them wisdom and understanding to know how to do all the work of constructing the sanctuary."

So Moses summoned Bezalel, Oholiab, and every skilled person in whose heart the Lord had placed wisdom, all whose hearts moved them, to come to the work and do it. They took from Moses's presence all the contributions that the Israelites had brought for the task of making the sanctuary. Meanwhile, the people continued to bring freewill offerings morning after morning.

Then all the artisans who were doing all the work for the sanctuary came one by one from the
10 work they were doing and said to Moses, "The people are bringing more than is needed for the construction of the work the Lord commanded to be done."

After Moses gave an order, they sent a proclamation throughout the camp: "Let no man or woman make anything else as an offering for the sanctuary." So the people stopped. The materials were sufficient for them to do all the work. There was more than enough.

All the skilled artisans among those doing the work made the tabernacle with ten curtains. Bezalel made them of finely spun linen, as well as blue, purple, and scarlet yarn, with a design of cherubim worked into them. Each curtain was forty-two feet long and six feet wide; all the curtains had the same measurements. He joined five of the curtains to each other, and the other five curtains he joined to each other. He made loops of blue yarn on the edge of the last curtain in the first set and did the same
20 on the edge of the outermost curtain in the second set. He made fifty loops on the one curtain and fifty loops on the edge of the curtain in the second set, so that the loops lined up with each other. He also made fifty gold clasps and joined the curtains to each other, so that the tabernacle became a single unit.

He made curtains of goat hair for a tent over the tabernacle; he made eleven of them. Each curtain was forty-five feet long and six feet wide. All eleven curtains had the same measurements.

He joined five of the curtains together, and the other six together. He made fifty loops on the edge of the outermost curtain in the first set and fifty loops on the edge of the corresponding curtain in the second set. He made fifty bronze clasps to join the tent together as a single unit. He also made a covering for the tent from ram skins dyed red and a covering of fine leather on top of it.

He made upright supports of acacia wood for the tabernacle. Each support was fifteen feet long and twenty-seven inches wide. Each support had two tenons for joining one to another. He did the same for all the supports of the tabernacle. He made supports for the tabernacle as follows: He made twenty for the south side, and he made forty silver bases to put under the twenty supports, two bases under the first support for its two tenons, and two bases under each of the following supports for their two tenons. For the second side of the tabernacle, the north side, he made twenty supports, with their forty silver bases, two bases under the first support and two bases under each of the following ones. And for the back of the tabernacle, on the west side, he made six supports. He also made two additional supports for the two back corners of the tabernacle. They were paired at the bottom and joined together at the top in a single ring. This is what he did with both of them for the two corners. So there were eight supports with their sixteen silver bases, two bases under each one.

He made five crossbars of acacia wood for the supports on one side of the tabernacle, five crossbars for the supports on the other side of the tabernacle, and five crossbars for those at the back of the tabernacle on the west. He made the central crossbar run through the middle of the supports from one end to the other. He overlaid them with gold and made their rings out of gold as holders for the crossbars. He also overlaid the crossbars with gold.

Then he made the curtain with blue, purple, and scarlet yarn, and finely spun linen. He made it with a design of cherubim worked into it. He made four pillars of acacia wood for it and overlaid them with gold; their hooks were of gold. And he cast four silver bases for the pillars.

He made a screen embroidered with blue, purple, and scarlet yarn, and finely spun linen for the entrance to the tent, together with its five pillars and their hooks. He overlaid the tops of the pillars and their bands with gold, but their five bases were bronze.

37 Bezalel made the ark of acacia wood, forty-five inches long, twenty-seven inches wide, and twenty-seven inches high. He overlaid it with pure gold inside and out and made a gold molding all around it. He cast four gold rings for it, for its four feet, two rings on one side and two rings on the other side. He made poles of acacia wood and overlaid them with gold. He inserted the poles into the rings on the sides of the ark for carrying the ark.

He made a mercy seat of pure gold, forty-five inches long and twenty-seven inches wide. He made two cherubim of gold; he made them of hammered work at the two ends of the mercy seat, one cherub at one end and one cherub at the other end. At each end, he made a cherub of one piece with the mercy seat. They had wings spread out. They faced each other and covered the mercy seat with their wings. The faces of the cherubim were looking toward the mercy seat.

He constructed the table of acacia wood, thirty-six inches long, eighteen inches wide, and twenty-seven inches high. He overlaid it with pure gold and made a gold molding all around it. He made a three-inch frame all around it and made a gold molding all around its frame. He cast four gold rings for it and attached the rings to the four corners at its four legs. The rings were next to the frame as holders for the poles to carry the table. He made the poles for carrying the table from acacia wood and overlaid them with gold. He also made the utensils that would be on the table out of pure gold: its plates and cups, as well as its bowls and pitchers for pouring drink offerings.

Then he made the lampstand out of pure hammered gold. He made it all of one piece: its base and shaft, its ornamental cups, and its buds and petals. Six branches extended from its sides, three 20 branches of the lampstand from one side and three branches of the lampstand from the other side. There were three cups shaped like almond blossoms, each with a bud and petals, on one branch, and three cups shaped like almond blossoms, each with a bud and petals, on the next branch. It was this way for the six branches that extended from the lampstand. There were four cups shaped like almond blossoms on the lampstand shaft along with its buds and petals. For the six branches that extended from it, a bud was under the first pair of branches from it, a bud under the second pair of branches from it, and a bud under the third pair of branches from it. Their buds and branches were of one piece with it. All of it was a single hammered piece of pure gold. He also made its seven lamps, snuffers, and firepans of pure gold. He made it and all its utensils of seventy-five pounds of pure gold.

30 He made the altar of incense out of acacia wood. It was square, eighteen inches long and eighteen inches wide; it was thirty-six inches high. Its horns were of one piece with it. He overlaid it, its top, all around its sides, and its horns with pure gold. Then he made a gold molding all around it. He made two gold rings for it under the molding on two of its sides; he put these on opposite sides of it to be holders for the poles to carry it with. He made the poles of acacia wood and overlaid them with gold.

He also made the holy anointing oil and the pure, fragrant, and expertly blended incense.

38 Bezalel constructed the altar of burnt offering from acacia wood. It was square, 7 ½ feet long and 7 ½ feet wide, and was 4 ½ feet high. He made horns for it on its four corners; the horns were of one piece with it. Then he overlaid it with bronze.

He made all the altar's utensils: the pots, shovels, basins, meat forks, and firepans; he made all its utensils of bronze. He constructed for the altar a grate of bronze mesh under its ledge, halfway up from the bottom. He cast four rings at the four corners of the bronze grate as holders for the poles. He made the poles of acacia wood and overlaid them with bronze. Then he inserted the poles into the rings on the sides of the altar in order to carry it with them. He constructed the altar with boards so that it was hollow.

10 He made the bronze basin and its stand from the bronze mirrors of the women who served at the entrance to the tent of meeting.

Then he made the courtyard. The hangings on the south side of the courtyard were of finely spun linen, 150 feet long, including their twenty posts and their twenty bronze bases, with silver hooks and silver bands for the posts. The hangings on the north side were also 150 feet long, including their twenty posts and twenty bronze bases. The hooks and bands of the posts were silver. The hangings on the west side were 75 feet long, including their ten posts and their ten bases, with silver hooks and silver bands for the posts. And for the east side toward the sunrise, 75 feet long, the hangings on one side of the gate were 22 ½ feet, including their three posts and their three bases. It was the same for the other side of the courtyard gate. The hangings were 22 ½ feet, including their

20 three posts and their three bases. All the hangings around the courtyard were of finely spun linen. The bases for the posts were bronze; the hooks and bands of the posts were silver; and the plating for the tops of the posts was silver. All the posts of the courtyard were banded with silver.

The screen for the gate of the courtyard was made of finely spun linen, expertly embroidered with blue, purple, and scarlet yarn. It was 30 feet long, and like the hangings of the courtyard, 7 ½ feet high. It had four posts with their four bronze bases. Their hooks were silver, and their top plating and their bands were silver. All the tent pegs for the tabernacle and for the surrounding courtyard were bronze.

This is the inventory for the tabernacle, the tabernacle of the testimony, that was recorded at Moses's command. It was the work of the Levites under the direction of Ithamar son of Aaron

30 the priest. Bezalel son of Uri, son of Hur, of the tribe of Judah, made everything that the LORD commanded Moses. With him was Oholiab son of Ahisamach, of the tribe of Dan, a gem cutter, a designer, and an embroiderer with blue, purple, and scarlet yarn, and fine linen.

All the gold of the presentation offering that was used for the project in all the work on the sanctuary, was 2,193 pounds, according to the sanctuary shekel. The silver from those of the community who were registered was 7,544 pounds, according to the sanctuary shekel—one-fifth of an ounce per man, that is, half a shekel according to the sanctuary shekel, from everyone twenty years old or more who had crossed over to the registered group, 603,550 men. There were 7,500 pounds of silver used to cast the bases of the sanctuary and the bases of the curtain—one hundred bases from 7,500 pounds, 75 pounds for each base. With the remaining 44 pounds he made the

40 hooks for the posts, overlaid their tops, and supplied bands for them.

The bronze of the presentation offering totaled 5,310 pounds. He made with it the bases for the entrance to the tent of meeting, the bronze altar and its bronze grate, all the utensils for the altar, the bases for the surrounding courtyard, the bases for the gate of the courtyard, all the tent pegs for the tabernacle, and all the tent pegs for the surrounding courtyard.

39 They made specially woven garments for ministry in the sanctuary, and the holy garments for Aaron from the blue, purple, and scarlet yarn, just as the Lord had commanded Moses.

Bezalel made the ephod of gold, of blue, purple, and scarlet yarn, and of finely spun linen. They hammered out thin sheets of gold, and he cut threads from them to interweave with the blue, purple, and scarlet yarn, and the fine linen in a skillful design. They made shoulder pieces for attaching it; it was joined together at its two edges. The artistically woven waistband that was on the ephod was of one piece with the ephod, according to the same workmanship of gold, of blue, purple, and scarlet yarn, and of finely spun linen, just as the Lord had commanded Moses.

10 Then they mounted the onyx stones surrounded with gold filigree settings, engraved with the names of Israel's sons as a gem cutter engraves a seal. He fastened them on the shoulder pieces of the ephod as memorial stones for the Israelites, just as the Lord had commanded Moses.

He also made the embroidered breastpiece with the same workmanship as the ephod of gold, of blue, purple, and scarlet yarn, and of finely spun linen. They made the breastpiece square and folded double, nine inches long and nine inches wide. They mounted four rows of gemstones on it.

The first row was
a row of carnelian, topaz, and emerald;
the second row,
a turquoise, a lapis lazuli, and a diamond;
the third row,
20 a jacinth, an agate, and an amethyst;
and the fourth row,
a beryl, an onyx, and a jasper.

They were surrounded with gold filigree in their settings.

The twelve stones corresponded to the names of Israel's sons. Each stone was engraved like a seal with one of the names of the twelve tribes.

They made braided chains of pure gold cord for the breastpiece. They also fashioned two gold filigree settings and two gold rings and attached the two rings to its two corners. Then they attached the two gold cords to the two gold rings on the corners of the breastpiece. They attached the other ends of the two cords to the two filigree settings, and in this way they attached them 30 to the ephod's shoulder pieces in front. They made two other gold rings and put them at the two other corners of the breastpiece on the edge that is next to the inner border of the ephod. They made two more gold rings and attached them to the bottom of the ephod's two shoulder pieces on its front, close to its seam, above the ephod's woven waistband. Then they tied the breastpiece from its rings to the rings of the ephod with a cord of blue yarn, so that the breastpiece was above the ephod's waistband and did not come loose from the ephod. They did just as the Lord had commanded Moses.

They made the woven robe of the ephod entirely of blue yarn. There was an opening in the center of the robe like that of body armor with a collar around the opening so that it would not tear. They made pomegranates of finely spun blue, purple, and scarlet yarn on the lower hem of the robe.
40 They made bells of pure gold and attached the bells between the pomegranates, all around the hem of the robe between the pomegranates, a bell and a pomegranate alternating all around the lower hem of the robe to be worn for ministry. They made it just as the LORD had commanded Moses.

They made the tunics of fine woven linen for Aaron and his sons. They made the turban and the ornate headbands of fine linen, the linen undergarments of finely spun linen, and the sash of finely spun linen expertly embroidered with blue, purple, and scarlet yarn. They did just as the LORD had commanded Moses.

They made a medallion, the holy diadem, out of pure gold and wrote on it an inscription like the engraving on a seal: HOLY TO THE LORD. They attached a cord of blue yarn to it in order to mount it on the turban, just as the LORD had commanded Moses.

50 So all the work for the tabernacle, the tent of meeting, was finished. The Israelites did everything just as the LORD had commanded Moses. They brought the tabernacle to Moses: the tent with all its furnishings, its clasps, its supports, its crossbars, and its pillars and bases; the covering of ram skins dyed red and the covering of fine leather; the curtain for the screen; the ark of the testimony with its poles and the mercy seat; the table, all its utensils, and the Bread of the Presence; the pure gold lampstand, with its lamps arranged and all its utensils, as well as the oil for the light; the gold altar; the anointing oil; the fragrant incense; the screen for the entrance to the tent; the bronze altar with its bronze grate, its poles, and all its utensils; the basin with its stand; the hangings of the courtyard, its posts and bases, the screen for the gate of the courtyard, its ropes and tent pegs, and all the furnishings for the service of the tabernacle, the tent of meeting; and the specially woven garments for ministering in the sanctuary, the
60 holy garments for the priest Aaron and the garments for his sons to serve as priests. The Israelites had done all the work according to everything the LORD had commanded Moses. Moses inspected all the work they had accomplished. They had done just as the LORD commanded. Then Moses blessed them.

40

The LORD spoke to Moses: "You are to set up the tabernacle, the tent of meeting, on the first day of the first month. Put the ark of the testimony there and screen off the ark with the curtain. Then bring in the table and lay out its arrangement; also bring in the lampstand and set up its lamps. Place the gold altar for incense in front of the ark of the testimony. Put up the screen for the entrance to the tabernacle. Position the altar of burnt offering in front of the entrance to the tabernacle, the tent of meeting. Place the basin between the tent of meeting and the altar, and put water in it. Assemble the surrounding courtyard and hang the screen for the gate of the courtyard.

"Take the anointing oil and anoint the tabernacle and everything in it; consecrate it along with all its furnishings so that it will be holy. Anoint the altar of burnt offering and all its utensils; consecrate the altar so that it will be especially holy. Anoint the basin and its stand and consecrate it.

"Then bring Aaron and his sons to the entrance to the tent of meeting and wash them with water. Clothe Aaron with the holy garments, anoint him, and consecrate him, so that he can serve me as a priest. Have his sons come forward and clothe them in tunics. Anoint them just as you anointed their father, so that they may also serve me as priests. Their anointing will serve to inaugurate a permanent priesthood for them throughout their generations."

Moses did everything just as the LORD had commanded him. The tabernacle was set up in the first month of the second year, on the first day of the month. Moses set up the tabernacle: He laid its bases, positioned its supports, inserted its crossbars, and set up its pillars. Then he spread the tent over the tabernacle and put the covering of the tent on top of it, just as the LORD had commanded Moses.

Moses took the testimony and placed it in the ark, and attached the poles to the ark. He set the mercy seat on top of the ark. He brought the ark into the tabernacle, put up the curtain for the screen, and screened off the ark of the testimony, just as the LORD had commanded him.

Moses placed the table in the tent of meeting on the north side of the tabernacle, outside the curtain. He arranged the bread on it before the LORD, just as the LORD had commanded him. He put the lampstand in the tent of meeting opposite the table on the south side of the tabernacle and set up the lamps before the LORD, just as the LORD had commanded him.

Moses installed the gold altar in the tent of meeting, in front of the curtain, and burned fragrant incense on it, just as the LORD had commanded him. He put up the screen at the entrance to the tabernacle. He placed the altar of burnt offering at the entrance to the tabernacle, the tent of meeting, and offered the burnt offering and the grain offering on it, just as the LORD had commanded him.

He set the basin between the tent of meeting and the altar and put water in it for washing. Moses, Aaron, and his sons washed their hands and feet from it. They washed whenever they came to the tent of meeting and approached the altar, just as the LORD had commanded Moses.

Next Moses set up the surrounding courtyard for the tabernacle and the altar and hung a screen for the gate of the courtyard. So Moses finished the work.

The cloud covered the tent of meeting, and the glory of the LORD filled the tabernacle. Moses was unable to enter the tent of meeting because the cloud rested on it, and the glory of the LORD filled the tabernacle.

The Israelites set out whenever the cloud was taken up from the tabernacle throughout all the stages of their journey. If the cloud was not taken up, they did not set out until the day it was taken up. For the cloud of the LORD was over the tabernacle by day, and there was a fire inside the cloud by night, visible to the entire house of Israel throughout all the stages of their journey.

Introduction to Leviticus

Walter E. Brown

For many Bible readers Leviticus stands as a specter to be feared, an obstacle to be overcome, alien rules to be ignored, or a treasure field of symbols pointing to Jesus. Certainly, the book can be intimidating and studying it seriously can be difficult. Much of its content is foreign to modern readers, and some texts still remain a puzzle. But when readers take the challenge of Leviticus appropriately, they discover that this book is central to the Torah, crucial for understanding the HS as a whole and foundational to biblical theology. The title "Leviticus" comes into English from the Latin *Leviticus*, which is derived from the Greek term *Leuitikon*. Both the Latin and Greek titles highlight the book's connection to the tribe of Levi. The Hebrew name of the book, *Wayyiqra'*, means "and He called" and comes from the first word in Lev 1.1.

Leviticus develops the theme of the presence of Yahweh rooted in the creation materials (Lev 9.33–34; 10.2–3; 22.3–5 [lit. *Elohim*]). The living God chose not only to create human beings but also to live in fellowship with them, only to see them disregard that gift and rebel, resulting in their exclusion from that presence. But Yahweh, in mercy, continued to reach out to people in order to accomplish the purposes intended in creation.

That work led to the formation of a special people, the Israelites, who were to be Yahweh's representatives among all people. And Yahweh intended not only to work through those special people to reach all the world, but he desired to accomplish that purpose by being with them, by living among them. And while the book of Exodus focuses on the creation of a place for Yahweh to dwell among the people, the book of Leviticus focuses on how that arrangement was to become a reality that the people could experience as a way of life. Consequently, *ritual law is not to be seen as threat and burden but as invitation and opportunity*. The living God would reside in the center of the Israelite community, providing for them ongoing relationship and fellowship.

The book highlights the holiness of Yahweh (Lev 11.67–70; 19.1–2; 20.9–10, 39–40; 22.1–2, 43–45). Again, the book of Exodus records the revelation of the nature of Yahweh as holy, along with the people's initial fear of him, based on that awesome quality (Exod 19.25–41; 20.27–32). But while distance from holy God was wise at Mount Sinai, the bulk of Exodus shows that Yahweh intended to diminish that distance by living among the people in a structure they would build. The content of the book of Leviticus provides guidance to Israel aimed at ensuring that the holy God would continue to live among the people. In turn, the people were themselves to be holy as well, and the laws therein were aimed at helping the people reflect that holiness in all aspects of life and to provide a remedy when they failed to do so. Without Leviticus, our understanding of Yahweh as holy would be radically diminished.

Because of the difficulty of understanding the Levitical texts, and a misunderstanding of a few NT texts, some suggest that the sacrificial ritual was nothing more than shadow and symbol, having no substantive or lasting effect on and for those who followed that guidance. But the texts themselves are quite clear that those who offered sacrifice for sin as prescribed received forgiveness (Lev 4.29, 37–38, 45–47, 52–55; 5.19–21, 25–27, 31–38; 6.9–10). Holy God chose to be present among the Israelites, establishing a relationship and fellowship with them. Yahweh also provided *sacred ritual as the avenue through which the people could express that relationship to Yahweh and maintain their fellowship with him.* When we understand these truths, we are in the best position to appreciate the fact that Jesus Christ is the same God who came to be present in human form and who accomplished full and final forgiveness through his own self–sacrifice.

Outline
1. The Sacrifices: The Means through which the People Approach Holy Yahweh (Lev 1–7)
    a. The Burnt Offering (1.1–26)
    b. The Grain Offering (2.1–23)
    c. The Fellowship Offering (3.1–24)
    d. The Sin Offering (4.1–5.27)
    e. The Guilt Offering (5.28–6.10)
    f. Regulations for Priests Related to the Offerings (6.11–7.50)

2. The Priests: The Officiants Authorized to Superintend the Offering of the Sacrifices (Lev 8–10)

3. Laws of Clean and Unclean: Guidance for the Practical Use of Sacrificial Ritual in the Life of Holiness (Lev 11–15)

4. The Day of Atonement: An Annual, National Day of Reflection, Repentance, and Worship on which Sacrifice for National Sin is Offered and the Tabernacle is Purified (Lev 16)

5. Laws for Living: Guidance for Reflecting Yahweh's Holiness in the Variety of Life Experiences (Lev 17–27)
    a. Place of Animal Sacrifice (17.1–11)
    b. Blood Sacredness (17.12–27)
    c. Sexual Relations (18.1–39)
    d. Collection of Miscellaneous Laws (19.1–52)
    e. Consequences and Punishment for Violation of Laws (Lev 20.1–42)
    f. Regulations for Priests (21.1–22.45)
    g. Sabbath and Feast Observance (23.1–24.12)

h. A Case of Blasphemy; Just Penalties (24.13–29)

i. Sabbath Year, Jubilee, and Implications for Land and Slaves (25.1–76)

j. Blessings and Judgments (26.1–68)

k. Vows, Dedications, and Tithes (27.1–52)

Suggested Resources

Milgrom, Jacob. *Leviticus*. Anchor Bible Commentary. 3 vols. New York: Doubleday, 1991–2001.

Sklar, Jay. *Leviticus*. Tyndale Old Testament Commentaries. Downers Grove, IL: InterVarsity Press, 2014.

Sprinkle, Joe M. *Leviticus and Numbers*. Teach the Text Commentary Series. Grand Rapids: Baker Academic, 2015.

Wenham, Gordon J. *The Book of Leviticus*. New International Commentary on the Old Testament. Grand Rapids: Eerdmans, 1979.

Leviticus

1 Then the Lord summoned Moses and spoke to him from the tent of meeting: "Speak to the Israelites and tell them: When any of you brings an offering to the Lord from the livestock, you may bring your offering from the herd or the flock.

"If his offering is a burnt offering from the herd, he is to bring an unblemished male. He will bring it to the entrance to the tent of meeting so that he may be accepted by the Lord. He is to lay his hand on the head of the burnt offering so it can be accepted on his behalf to make atonement for him. He is to slaughter the bull before the Lord; Aaron's sons the priests are to present the blood and splatter it on all sides of the altar that is at the entrance to the tent of meeting. Then he is to skin the burnt offering and cut it into pieces. The sons of Aaron the priest will prepare a fire on the altar and arrange wood on the fire. Aaron's sons the priests are to arrange the pieces, the head, and the fat on top of the burning wood on the altar. The offerer is to wash its entrails and legs with water. Then the priest will burn all of it on the altar as a burnt offering, a food offering, a pleasing aroma to the Lord.

"But if his offering for a burnt offering is from the flock, from sheep or goats, he is to present an unblemished male. He will slaughter it on the north side of the altar before the Lord. Aaron's sons the priests will splatter its blood against the altar on all sides. He will cut the animal into pieces with its head and its fat, and the priest will arrange them on top of the burning wood on the altar. But he is to wash the entrails and legs with water. The priest will then present all of it and burn it on the altar; it is a burnt offering, a food offering, a pleasing aroma to the Lord.

"If his offering to the Lord is a burnt offering of birds, he is to present his offering from the turtledoves or young pigeons. Then the priest is to bring it to the altar, and will twist off its head and burn it on the altar; its blood should be drained at the side of the altar. He will remove its digestive tract, cutting off the tail feathers, and throw it on the east side of the altar at the place for ashes. He will tear it open by its wings without dividing the bird. Then the priest is to burn it on the altar on top of the burning wood. It is a burnt offering, a food offering, a pleasing aroma to the Lord.

2 "When anyone presents a grain offering as an offering to the Lord, it is to consist of fine flour. He is to pour olive oil on it, put frankincense on it, and bring it to Aaron's sons the priests. The priest will take a handful of fine flour and oil from it, along with all its frankincense, and will burn this memorial portion of it on the altar, a food offering, a pleasing aroma to the Lord. But the rest of the grain offering will belong to Aaron and his sons; it is the holiest part of the food offerings to the Lord.

"When you present a grain offering baked in an oven, it is to be made of fine flour, either unleavened cakes mixed with oil or unleavened wafers coated with oil. If your offering is a grain offering prepared on a griddle, it is to be unleavened bread made of fine flour mixed with oil. Break it into pieces and pour oil on it; it is a grain offering. If your offering is a grain offering prepared in a pan, it is to be made of fine flour with oil. When you bring to the LORD the grain offering made in any of these ways, it is to be presented to the priest, and he will take it to the altar. The priest will remove the memorial portion from the grain offering and burn it on the altar, a food offering, a pleasing aroma to the LORD. But the rest of the grain offering will belong to Aaron and his sons; it is the holiest part of the food offerings to the LORD.

"No grain offering that you present to the LORD is to be made with yeast, for you are not to burn any yeast or honey as a food offering to the LORD. You may present them to the LORD as an offering of firstfruits, but they are not to be offered on the altar as a pleasing aroma. You are to season each of your grain offerings with salt; you must not omit from your grain offering the salt of the covenant with your God. You are to present salt with each of your offerings.

"If you present a grain offering of firstfruits to the LORD, you are to present fresh heads of grain, crushed kernels, roasted on the fire, for your grain offering of firstfruits. You are to put oil and frankincense on it; it is a grain offering. The priest will then burn some of its crushed kernels and oil with all its frankincense as a food offering to the LORD.

3 "If his offering is a fellowship sacrifice, and he is presenting an animal from the herd, whether male or female, he is to present one without blemish before the LORD. He is to lay his hand on the head of his offering and slaughter it at the entrance to the tent of meeting. Then Aaron's sons the priests will splatter the blood on all sides of the altar. He will present part of the fellowship sacrifice as a food offering to the LORD: the fat surrounding the entrails, all the fat that is on the entrails, and the two kidneys with the fat on them at the loins; he will also remove the fatty lobe of the liver with the kidneys. Aaron's sons will burn it on the altar along with the burnt offering that is on the burning wood, a food offering, a pleasing aroma to the LORD.

"If his offering as a fellowship sacrifice to the LORD is from the flock, he is to present a male or female without blemish. If he is presenting a lamb for his offering, he is to present it before the LORD. He must lay his hand on the head of his offering, then slaughter it before the tent of meeting. Aaron's sons will splatter its blood on all sides of the altar. He will then present part of the fellowship sacrifice as a food offering to the LORD consisting of its fat and the entire fat tail, which he is to remove close to the backbone. He will also remove the fat surrounding the entrails, all the fat on the entrails, the two kidneys with the fat on them at the loins, and the fatty lobe of the liver above the kidneys. Then the priest will burn the food on the altar, as a food offering to the LORD.

"If his offering is a goat, he is to present it before the LORD. He must lay his hand on its head and slaughter it before the tent of meeting. Aaron's sons will splatter its blood on all sides of the altar. He will present part of his offering as a food offering to the LORD: the fat surrounding the

20 entrails, all the fat that is on the entrails, and the two kidneys with the fat on them at the loins; he will also remove the fatty lobe of the liver with the kidneys. Then the priest will burn the food on the altar, as a food offering for a pleasing aroma.

"All fat belongs to the LORD. This is a permanent statute throughout your generations, wherever you live: you must not eat any fat or any blood."

4 Then the LORD spoke to Moses: "Tell the Israelites: When someone sins unintentionally against any of the LORD's commands and does anything prohibited by them—

"If the anointed priest sins, bringing guilt on the people, he is to present to the LORD a young, unblemished bull as a sin offering for the sin he has committed. He is to bring the bull to the entrance to the tent of meeting before the LORD, lay his hand on the bull's head, and slaughter it before the LORD. The anointed priest will then take some of the bull's blood and bring it into the tent of meeting. The priest is to dip his finger in the blood and sprinkle some of it seven times before the LORD in front of the curtain of the sanctuary. The priest is to apply some of the blood to the horns of the altar of fragrant incense that is before the LORD in the tent of meeting. He

10 must pour out the rest of the bull's blood at the base of the altar of burnt offering that is at the entrance to the tent of meeting. He is to remove all the fat from the bull of the sin offering: the fat surrounding the entrails, all the fat that is on the entrails, and the two kidneys with the fat on them at the loins. He will also remove the fatty lobe of the liver with the kidneys, just as the fat is removed from the ox of the fellowship sacrifice. The priest is to burn them on the altar of burnt offering. But the hide of the bull and all its flesh, with its head and legs, and its entrails and waste—all the rest of the bull—he must bring to a ceremonially clean place outside the camp to the ash heap, and must burn it on a wood fire. It is to be burned at the ash heap.

"Now if the whole community of Israel errs, and the matter escapes the notice of the assembly, so that they violate any of the LORD's commands and incur guilt by doing what is prohibited, then the

20 assembly must present a young bull as a sin offering. They are to bring it before the tent of meeting when the sin they have committed in regard to the command becomes known. The elders of the community are to lay their hands on the bull's head before the LORD and it is to be slaughtered before the LORD. The anointed priest will bring some of the bull's blood into the tent of meeting. The priest is to dip his finger in the blood and sprinkle it seven times before the LORD in front of the curtain. He is to apply some of the blood to the horns of the altar that is before the LORD in the tent of meeting. He will pour out the rest of the blood at the base of the altar of burnt offering that is at the entrance to the tent of meeting. He is to remove all the fat from it and burn it on the altar. He is to offer this bull just as he did with the bull in the sin offering; he will offer it the same way. So the priest will make atonement on their behalf, and they will be forgiven. Then he will bring the bull

30 outside the camp and burn it just as he burned the first bull. It is the sin offering for the assembly.

"When a leader sins and unintentionally violates any of the commands of the LORD his God by doing what is prohibited, and incurs guilt, or someone informs him about the sin he has committed, he is to bring an unblemished male goat as his offering. He is to lay his hand on the head of the goat and slaughter it at the place where the burnt offering is slaughtered before the LORD. It is a sin offering. Then the priest is to take some of the blood from the sin offering with his finger and apply it to the horns of the altar of burnt offering. The rest of its blood he is to pour out at the base of the altar of burnt offering. He must burn all its fat on the altar, like the fat of the fellowship sacrifice. In this way the priest will make atonement on his behalf for that person's sin, and he will be forgiven.

40 "Now if any of the common people sins unintentionally by violating one of the LORD's commands, does what is prohibited, and incurs guilt, or if someone informs him about the sin he has committed, then he is to bring an unblemished female goat as his offering for the sin that he has committed. He is to lay his hand on the head of the sin offering and slaughter it at the place of the burnt offering. Then the priest is to take some of its blood with his finger and apply it to the horns of the altar of burnt offering. He is to pour out the rest of its blood at the base of the altar. He is to remove all its fat just as the fat is removed from the fellowship sacrifice. The priest is to burn it on the altar as a pleasing aroma to the LORD. In this way the priest will make atonement on his behalf, and he will be forgiven.

"Or if the offering that he brings as a sin offering is a lamb, he is to bring an unblemished female. He is to lay his hand on the head of the sin offering and slaughter it as a sin offering at the 50 place where the burnt offering is slaughtered. Then the priest is to take some of the blood of the sin offering with his finger and apply it to the horns of the altar of burnt offering. He is to pour out the rest of its blood at the base of the altar. He is to remove all its fat just as the fat of the lamb is removed from the fellowship sacrifice. The priest will burn it on the altar along with the food offerings to the LORD. In this way the priest will make atonement on his behalf for the sin he has committed, and he will be forgiven.

5 "When someone sins in any of these ways:
If he has seen, heard, or known about something he has witnessed, and did not respond to a public call to testify, he will bear his iniquity.
Or if someone touches anything unclean—a carcass of an unclean wild animal, or unclean livestock, or an unclean swarming creature—without being aware of it, he is unclean and incurs guilt.
Or if he touches human uncleanness—any uncleanness by which one can become defiled— without being aware of it, but later recognizes it, he incurs guilt.
Or if someone swears rashly to do what is good or evil—concerning anything a person may speak rashly in an oath—without being aware of it, but later recognizes it, he incurs guilt in 10 such an instance.

If someone incurs guilt in one of these cases, he is to confess he has committed that sin. He must bring his penalty for guilt for the sin he has committed to the LORD: a female lamb or goat from the flock as a sin offering. In this way the priest will make atonement on his behalf for his sin.

"But if he cannot afford an animal from the flock, then he may bring to the LORD two turtledoves or two young pigeons as penalty for guilt for his sin—one as a sin offering and the other as a burnt offering. He is to bring them to the priest, who will first present the one for the sin offering. He is to twist its head at the back of the neck without severing it. Then he will sprinkle some of the blood of the sin offering on the side of the altar, while the rest of the blood is to be drained out at the base of the altar; it is a sin offering. He will prepare the second bird as a burnt offering according to the regulation. In this way the priest will make atonement on his behalf for the sin he has committed, and he will be forgiven.

"But if he cannot afford two turtledoves or two young pigeons, he may bring two quarts of fine flour as an offering for his sin. He must not put olive oil or frankincense on it, for it is a sin offering. He is to bring it to the priest, who will take a handful from it as its memorial portion and burn it on the altar along with the food offerings to the LORD; it is a sin offering. In this way the priest will make atonement on his behalf concerning the sin he has committed in any of these cases, and he will be forgiven. The rest will belong to the priest, like the grain offering."

Then the LORD spoke to Moses: "If someone offends by sinning unintentionally in regard to any of the LORD's holy things, he must bring his penalty for guilt to the LORD: an unblemished ram from the flock (based on your assessment of its value in silver shekels, according to the sanctuary shekel) as a guilt offering. He is to make restitution for his sin regarding any holy thing, adding a fifth of its value to it, and give it to the priest. Then the priest will make atonement on his behalf with the ram of the guilt offering, and he will be forgiven.

"If someone sins and without knowing it violates any of the LORD's commands concerning anything prohibited, he is guilty, and he will bear his iniquity. He must bring an unblemished ram from the flock according to your assessment of its value as a guilt offering to the priest. Then the priest will make atonement on his behalf for the error he has committed unintentionally, and he will be forgiven. It is a guilt offering; he is indeed guilty before the LORD."

6 The LORD spoke to Moses: "When someone sins and offends the LORD by deceiving his neighbor in regard to a deposit, a security, or a robbery; or defrauds his neighbor; or finds something lost and lies about it; or swears falsely about any of the sinful things a person may do—once he has sinned and acknowledged his guilt—he must return what he stole or defrauded, or the deposit entrusted to him, or the lost item he found, or anything else about which he swore falsely. He will make full restitution for it and add a fifth of its value to it. He is to pay it to its owner on the day he acknowledges his guilt. Then he is to bring his guilt offering to the LORD: an unblemished ram from the flock according to your assessment of its value as a guilt offering to the priest. In this way the priest will make atonement on his behalf before the LORD, and he will be forgiven for anything he may have done to incur guilt."

The LORD spoke to Moses: "Command Aaron and his sons: This is the law of the burnt offering; the burnt offering itself must remain on the altar's hearth all night until morning, while the fire of the altar is kept burning on it. The priest is to put on his linen robe and linen undergarments. He is to remove the ashes of the burnt offering the fire has consumed on the altar, and place them beside the altar. Then he will take off his garments, put on other clothes, and bring the ashes outside the camp to a ceremonially clean place. The fire on the altar is to be kept burning; it must not go out. Every morning the priest will burn wood on the fire. He is to arrange the burnt offering on the fire and burn the fat portions from the fellowship offerings on it. Fire must be kept burning on the altar continually; it must not go out.

20 "Now this is the law of the grain offering: Aaron's sons will present it before the LORD in front of the altar. The priest is to remove a handful of fine flour and olive oil from the grain offering, with all the frankincense that is on the offering, and burn its memorial portion on the altar as a pleasing aroma to the LORD. Aaron and his sons may eat the rest of it. It is to be eaten in the form of unleavened bread in a holy place; they are to eat it in the courtyard of the tent of meeting. It must not be baked with yeast; I have assigned it as their portion from my food offerings. It is especially holy, like the sin offering and the guilt offering. Any male among Aaron's descendants may eat it. It is a permanent portion throughout your generations from the food offerings to the LORD. Anything that touches the offerings will become holy."

The LORD spoke to Moses: "This is the offering that Aaron and his sons are to present to the
30 LORD on the day that he is anointed: two quarts of fine flour as a regular grain offering, half of it in the morning and half in the evening. It is to be prepared with oil on a griddle; you are to bring it well-kneaded. You are to present it as a grain offering of baked pieces, a pleasing aroma to the LORD. The priest, who is one of Aaron's sons and will be anointed to take his place, is to prepare it. It must be completely burned as a permanent portion for the LORD. Every grain offering for a priest will be a whole burnt offering; it is not to be eaten."

The LORD spoke to Moses: "Tell Aaron and his sons: This is the law of the sin offering. The sin offering is most holy and must be slaughtered before the LORD at the place where the burnt offering is slaughtered. The priest who offers it as a sin offering will eat it. It is to be eaten in a holy place, in the courtyard of the tent of meeting. Anything that touches its flesh will become holy, and if any of its blood spatters on a garment, then you must wash that garment in a holy place.
40 A clay pot in which the sin offering is boiled is to be broken; if it is boiled in a bronze vessel, it is to be scoured and rinsed with water. Any male among the priests may eat it; it is especially holy. But no sin offering may be eaten if its blood has been brought into the tent of meeting to make atonement in the holy place; it must be burned.

7 "Now this is the law of the guilt offering; it is especially holy. The guilt offering is to be slaughtered at the place where the burnt offering is slaughtered, and the priest is to splatter its blood on all sides of the altar. The offerer is to present all the fat from it: the fat tail, the fat surrounding the entrails, and the two kidneys with the fat on them at the loins; he will also remove the fatty lobe of the liver with the kidneys. The priest will burn them on the altar as a food offering to the LORD; it is a guilt offering. Any male among the priests may eat it. It is to be eaten in a holy place; it is especially holy.

"The guilt offering is like the sin offering; the law is the same for both. It belongs to the priest who makes atonement with it. As for the priest who presents someone's burnt offering, the hide of the burnt offering he has presented belongs to him; it is the priest's. Any grain offering that is
10 baked in an oven or prepared in a pan or on a griddle belongs to the priest who presents it; it is his. But any grain offering, whether dry or mixed with oil, belongs equally to all of Aaron's sons.

"Now this is the law of the fellowship sacrifice that someone may present to the LORD: If he presents it for thanksgiving, in addition to the thanksgiving sacrifice, he is to present unleavened cakes mixed with olive oil, unleavened wafers coated with oil, and well-kneaded cakes of fine flour mixed with oil. He is to present as his offering cakes of leavened bread with his thanksgiving sacrifice of fellowship. From the cakes he is to present one portion of each offering as a contribution to the LORD. It will belong to the priest who splatters the blood of the fellowship offering; it is his. The meat of his thanksgiving sacrifice of fellowship must be eaten on the day he offers it; he may not leave any of it until morning.

"If the sacrifice he offers is a vow or a freewill offering, it is to be eaten on the day he presents
20 his sacrifice, and what is left over may be eaten on the next day. But what remains of the sacrificial meat by the third day must be burned. If any of the meat of his fellowship sacrifice is eaten on the third day, it will not be accepted. It will not be credited to the one who presents it; it is repulsive. The person who eats any of it will bear his iniquity.

"Meat that touches anything unclean must not be eaten; it is to be burned. Everyone who is clean may eat any other meat. But the one who eats meat from the LORD's fellowship sacrifice while he is unclean, that person must be cut off from his people. If someone touches anything unclean, whether human uncleanness, an unclean animal, or any unclean, abhorrent creature, and eats meat from the LORD's fellowship sacrifice, that person is to be cut off from his people."

The LORD spoke to Moses: "Tell the Israelites: You are not to eat any fat of an ox, a sheep, or a
30 goat. The fat of an animal that dies naturally or is mauled by wild beasts may be used for any other purpose, but you must not eat it. If anyone eats animal fat from a food offering presented to the LORD, the person who eats it is to be cut off from his people. Wherever you live, you must not eat the blood of any bird or animal. Whoever eats any blood is to be cut off from his people."

The LORD spoke to Moses: "Tell the Israelites: The one who presents a fellowship sacrifice to the LORD is to bring an offering to the LORD from his sacrifice. His own hands will bring the food offerings to the LORD. He will bring the fat together with the breast. The breast is to be presented as a presentation offering before the LORD. The priest is to burn the fat on the altar, but the breast belongs to Aaron and his sons. You are to give the right thigh to the priest as a contribution from your fellowship sacrifices. The son of Aaron who presents the blood of the fellowship offering

40 and the fat will have the right thigh as a portion. I have taken from the Israelites the breast of the presentation offering and the thigh of the contribution from their fellowship sacrifices, and have assigned them to the priest Aaron and to his sons as a permanent portion from the Israelites."

This is the portion from the food offerings to the LORD for Aaron and his sons since the day they were presented to serve the LORD as priests. The LORD commanded this to be given to them by the Israelites on the day he anointed them. It is a permanent portion throughout their generations.

This is the law for the burnt offering, the grain offering, the sin offering, the guilt offering, the ordination offering, and the fellowship sacrifice, which the LORD commanded Moses on Mount Sinai on the day he commanded the Israelites to present their offerings to the LORD in the Wilderness of Sinai.

8 The LORD spoke to Moses: "Take Aaron, his sons with him, the garments, the anointing oil, the bull of the sin offering, the two rams, and the basket of unleavened bread, and assemble the whole community at the entrance to the tent of meeting." So Moses did as the LORD commanded him, and the community assembled at the entrance to the tent of meeting. Moses said to them, "This is what the LORD has commanded to be done."

Then Moses presented Aaron and his sons and washed them with water. He put the tunic on Aaron, wrapped the sash around him, clothed him with the robe, and put the ephod on him. He put the woven band of the ephod around him and fastened it to him. Then he put the breastpiece on him and placed the Urim and Thummim into the breastpiece. He also put the turban on his

10 head and placed the gold medallion, the holy diadem, on the front of the turban, as the LORD had commanded Moses.

Then Moses took the anointing oil and anointed the tabernacle and everything in it to consecrate them. He sprinkled some of the oil on the altar seven times, anointing the altar with all its utensils, and the basin with its stand, to consecrate them. He poured some of the anointing oil on Aaron's head and anointed and consecrated him. Then Moses presented Aaron's sons, clothed them with tunics, wrapped sashes around them, and fastened headbands on them, as the LORD had commanded Moses.

Then he brought the bull near for the sin offering, and Aaron and his sons laid their hands on the head of the bull for the sin offering. Then Moses slaughtered it, took the blood, and applied it

20 with his finger to the horns of the altar on all sides, purifying the altar. He poured out the blood at the base of the altar and consecrated it so that atonement can be made on it. Moses took all the fat that was on the entrails, the fatty lobe of the liver, and the two kidneys with their fat, and he

burned them on the altar. He burned the bull with its hide, flesh, and waste outside the camp, as the LORD had commanded Moses.

Then he presented the ram for the burnt offering, and Aaron and his sons laid their hands on the head of the ram. Moses slaughtered it and splattered the blood on all sides of the altar. Moses cut the ram into pieces and burned the head, the pieces, and the fat, but he washed the entrails and legs with water. He then burned the entire ram on the altar. It was a burnt offering for a pleasing aroma, a food offering to the LORD as he had commanded Moses.

30 Next he presented the second ram, the ram of ordination, and Aaron and his sons laid their hands on the head of the ram. Moses slaughtered it, took some of its blood, and put it on Aaron's right earlobe, on the thumb of his right hand, and on the big toe of his right foot. Moses also presented Aaron's sons and put some of the blood on their right earlobes, on the thumbs of their right hands, and on the big toes of their right feet. Then Moses splattered the blood on all sides of the altar. He took the fat—the fat tail, all the fat that was on the entrails, the fatty lobe of the liver, and the two kidneys with their fat—as well as the right thigh. From the basket of unleavened bread that was before the LORD he took one cake of unleavened bread, one cake of bread made with oil, and one wafer, and placed them on the fat portions and the right thigh. He put all these in the hands of Aaron and his sons and presented them before the LORD as a presentation offering.

40 Then Moses took them from their hands and burned them on the altar with the burnt offering. This was an ordination offering for a pleasing aroma, a food offering to the LORD. He also took the breast and presented it before the LORD as a presentation offering; it was Moses's portion of the ordination ram as the LORD had commanded him.

Then Moses took some of the anointing oil and some of the blood that was on the altar and sprinkled them on Aaron and his garments, as well as on his sons and their garments. In this way he consecrated Aaron and his garments, as well as his sons and their garments.

Moses said to Aaron and his sons, "Boil the meat at the entrance to the tent of meeting and eat it there with the bread that is in the basket for the ordination offering as I commanded: Aaron and his sons are to eat it. Burn up what remains of the meat and bread. Do not go outside the entrance

50 to the tent of meeting for seven days, until the time your days of ordination are completed, because it will take seven days to ordain you. The LORD commanded what has been done today in order to make atonement for you. You must remain at the entrance to the tent of meeting day and night for seven days and keep the LORD's charge so that you will not die, for this is what I was commanded." So Aaron and his sons did everything the LORD had commanded through Moses.

9 On the eighth day Moses summoned Aaron, his sons, and the elders of Israel. He said to Aaron, "Take a young bull for a sin offering and a ram for a burnt offering, both without blemish, and present them before the LORD. And tell the Israelites: Take a male goat for a sin offering; a calf and a lamb, male yearlings without blemish, for a burnt offering; an ox and a ram for a fellowship offering to sacrifice before the LORD; and a grain offering mixed with oil. For today the LORD is going to appear to you."

They brought what Moses had commanded to the front of the tent of meeting, and the whole community came forward and stood before the LORD. Moses said, "This is what the LORD commanded you to do, that the glory of the LORD may appear to you." Then Moses said to Aaron, "Approach the altar and sacrifice your sin offering and your burnt offering; make atonement for yourself and the people. Sacrifice the people's offering and make atonement for them, as the LORD commanded."

So Aaron approached the altar and slaughtered the calf as a sin offering for himself. Aaron's sons brought the blood to him, and he dipped his finger in the blood and applied it to the horns of the altar. He poured out the blood at the base of the altar. He burned the fat, the kidneys, and the fatty lobe of the liver from the sin offering on the altar, as the LORD had commanded Moses. He burned the flesh and the hide outside the camp.

Then he slaughtered the burnt offering. Aaron's sons brought him the blood, and he splattered it on all sides of the altar. They brought him the burnt offering piece by piece, along with the head, and he burned them on the altar. He washed the entrails and the legs and burned them with the burnt offering on the altar.

Aaron presented the people's offering. He took the male goat for the people's sin offering, slaughtered it, and made a sin offering with it as he did before. He presented the burnt offering and sacrificed it according to the regulation. Next he presented the grain offering, took a handful of it, and burned it on the altar in addition to the morning burnt offering.

Finally, he slaughtered the ox and the ram as the people's fellowship sacrifice. Aaron's sons brought him the blood, and he splattered it on all sides of the altar. They also brought the fat portions from the ox and the ram—the fat tail, the fat surrounding the entrails, the kidneys, and the fatty lobe of the liver—and placed these on the breasts. Aaron burned the fat portions on the altar, but he presented the breasts and the right thigh as a presentation offering before the LORD, as Moses had commanded.

Aaron lifted up his hands toward the people and blessed them. He came down after sacrificing the sin offering, the burnt offering, and the fellowship offering. Moses and Aaron then entered the tent of meeting. When they came out, they blessed the people, and the glory of the LORD appeared to all the people. Fire came from the LORD and consumed the burnt offering and the fat portions on the altar. And when all the people saw it, they shouted and fell facedown.

10 Aaron's sons Nadab and Abihu each took his own firepan, put fire in it, placed incense on it, and presented unauthorized fire before the LORD, which he had not commanded them to do. Then fire came from the LORD and consumed them, and they died before the LORD. Moses said to Aaron, "This is what the LORD has spoken:

> I will demonstrate my holiness
>> to those who are near me,
> and I will reveal my glory
>> before all the people."

And Aaron remained silent.

10   Moses summoned Mishael and Elzaphan, sons of Aaron's uncle Uzziel, and said to them, "Come here and carry your relatives away from the front of the sanctuary to a place outside the camp." So they came forward and carried them in their tunics outside the camp, as Moses had said.

    Then Moses said to Aaron and his sons Eleazar and Ithamar, "Do not let your hair hang loose and do not tear your clothes, or else you will die, and the LORD will become angry with the whole community. However, your brothers, the whole house of Israel, may weep over the fire that the LORD caused. You must not go outside the entrance to the tent of meeting or you will die, for the LORD's anointing oil is on you." So they did as Moses said.

    The LORD spoke to Aaron: "You and your sons are not to drink wine or beer when you enter the tent of meeting, or else you will die; this is a permanent statute throughout your generations. You 20 must distinguish between the holy and the common, and the clean and the unclean, and teach the Israelites all the statutes that the LORD has given to them through Moses."

    Moses spoke to Aaron and his remaining sons, Eleazar and Ithamar: "Take the grain offering that is left over from the food offerings to the LORD, and eat it prepared without yeast beside the altar, because it is especially holy. You must eat it in a holy place because it is your portion and your sons' from the food offerings to the LORD, for this is what I was commanded. But you and your sons and your daughters may eat the breast of the presentation offering and the thigh of the contribution in any ceremonially clean place, because these portions have been assigned to you and your children from the Israelites' fellowship sacrifices. They are to bring the thigh of the contribution and the breast of the presentation offering, together with the food offerings of the fat 30 portions, to present as a presentation offering before the LORD. It will belong permanently to you and your children, as the LORD commanded."

    Then Moses inquired carefully about the male goat of the sin offering, but it had already been burned up. He was angry with Eleazar and Ithamar, Aaron's surviving sons, and asked, "Why didn't you eat the sin offering in the sanctuary area? For it is especially holy, and he has assigned it to you to take away the guilt of the community and make atonement for them before the LORD. Since its blood was not brought inside the sanctuary, you should have eaten it in the sanctuary area, as I commanded."

    But Aaron replied to Moses, "See, today they presented their sin offering and their burnt offering before the LORD. Since these things have happened to me, if I had eaten the sin offering 40 today, would it have been acceptable in the LORD's sight?" When Moses heard this, it was acceptable to him.

11   The LORD spoke to Moses and Aaron: "Tell the Israelites: You may eat all these kinds of land animals. You may eat any animal with divided hooves and that chews the cud. But among the ones that chew the cud or have divided hooves you are not to eat these:

camels, though they chew the cud,
do not have divided hooves—they are unclean for you;
hyraxes, though they chew the cud,
do not have hooves—they are unclean for you;
hares, though they chew the cud,
do not have hooves—they are unclean for you;
10   pigs, though they have divided hooves,
do not chew the cud—they are unclean for you.
Do not eat any of their meat or touch their carcasses—they are unclean for you.

"This is what you may eat from all that is in the water: You may eat everything in the water that has fins and scales, whether in the seas or streams. But these are to be abhorrent to you: everything in the seas or streams that does not have fins and scales among all the swarming things and other living creatures in the water. They are to remain abhorrent to you; you must not eat any of their meat, and you must abhor their carcasses. Everything in the water that does not have fins and scales will be abhorrent to you.

"You are to abhor these birds. They must not be eaten because they are abhorrent:
eagles, bearded vultures,
20   Egyptian vultures, kites,
any kind of falcon,
every kind of raven, ostriches,
short-eared owls, gulls,
any kind of hawk,
little owls, cormorants,
long-eared owls,
barn owls, eagle owls,
ospreys, storks,
any kind of heron,
30   hoopoes, and bats.

"All winged insects that walk on all fours are to be abhorrent to you. But you may eat these kinds of all the winged insects that walk on all fours: those that have jointed legs above their feet for hopping on the ground. You may eat these:
any kind of locust, katydid, cricket, and grasshopper.
All other winged insects that have four feet are to be abhorrent to you.

"These will make you unclean. Whoever touches their carcasses will be unclean until evening, and whoever carries any of their carcasses is to wash his clothes and will be unclean until evening. All animals that have hooves but do not have a divided hoof and do not chew the cud are unclean for you. Whoever touches them becomes unclean. All the four-footed animals that walk on their paws are unclean for you. Whoever touches their carcasses will be unclean until evening, and anyone who carries their carcasses is to wash his clothes and will be unclean until evening. They are unclean for you.

"These creatures that swarm on the ground are unclean for you:

> weasels, mice,
> any kind of large lizard,
> geckos, monitor lizards,
> common lizards, skinks,
> and chameleons.

These are unclean for you among all the swarming creatures. Whoever touches them when they are dead will be unclean until evening. When any one of them dies and falls on anything it becomes unclean—any item of wood, clothing, leather, sackcloth, or any implement used for work. It is to be rinsed with water and will remain unclean until evening; then it will be clean. If any of them falls into any clay pot, everything in it will become unclean; you are to break it. Any edible food coming into contact with that unclean water will become unclean, and any drinkable liquid in any container will become unclean. Anything one of their carcasses falls on will become unclean. If it is an oven or stove, it is to be smashed; it is unclean and will remain unclean for you. A spring or cistern containing water will remain clean, but someone who touches a carcass in it will become unclean. If one of their carcasses falls on any seed that is to be sown, it is clean; but if water has been put on the seed and one of their carcasses falls on it, it is unclean for you.

"If one of the animals that you use for food dies, anyone who touches its carcass will be unclean until evening. Anyone who eats some of its carcass is to wash his clothes and will be unclean until evening. Anyone who carries its carcass must wash his clothes and will be unclean until evening.

"All the creatures that swarm on the earth are abhorrent; they must not be eaten. Do not eat any of the creatures that swarm on the earth, anything that moves on its belly or walks on all fours or on many feet, for they are abhorrent. Do not become contaminated by any creature that swarms; do not become unclean or defiled by them. For I am the LORD your God, so you must consecrate yourselves and be holy because I am holy. Do not defile yourselves by any swarming creature that crawls on the ground. For I am the LORD, who brought you up from the land of Egypt to be your God, so you must be holy because I am holy.

"This is the law concerning animals, birds, all living creatures that move in the water, and all creatures that swarm on the ground, in order to distinguish between the unclean and the clean, between the animals that may be eaten and those that may not be eaten."

12 The LORD spoke to Moses: "Tell the Israelites: When a woman becomes pregnant and gives birth to a male child, she will be unclean seven days, as she is during the days of her menstrual impurity. The flesh of his foreskin must be circumcised on the eighth day. She will continue in purification from her bleeding for thirty-three days. She must not touch any holy thing or go into the sanctuary until completing her days of purification. But if she gives birth to a female child, she will be unclean for two weeks as she is during her menstrual impurity. She will continue in purification from her bleeding for sixty-six days.

"When her days of purification are complete, whether for a son or daughter, she is to bring to the priest at the entrance to the tent of meeting a year-old male lamb for a burnt offering, 10 and a young pigeon or a turtledove for a sin offering. He will present them before the LORD and make atonement on her behalf; she will be clean from her discharge of blood. This is the law for a woman giving birth, whether to a male or female. But if she doesn't have sufficient means for a sheep, she may take two turtledoves or two young pigeons, one for a burnt offering and the other for a sin offering. Then the priest will make atonement on her behalf, and she will be clean."

13 The LORD spoke to Moses and Aaron: "When a person has a swelling, scab, or spot on the skin of his body, and it may be a serious disease on the skin of his body, he is to be brought to the priest Aaron or to one of his sons, the priests. The priest will examine the sore on the skin of his body. If the hair in the sore has turned white and the sore appears to be deeper than the skin of his body, it is in fact a serious skin disease. After the priest examines him, he must pronounce him unclean. But if the spot on the skin of his body is white and does not appear to be deeper than the skin, and the hair in it has not turned white, the priest will quarantine the stricken person for seven days. The priest will then reexamine him on the seventh day. If he sees that the sore remains unchanged and has not spread on the skin, the priest will quarantine him for another seven days. The priest 10 will examine him again on the seventh day. If the sore has faded and has not spread on the skin, the priest is to pronounce him clean; it is a scab. The person is to wash his clothes and will become clean. But if the scab spreads further on his skin after he has presented himself to the priest for his cleansing, he is to present himself again to the priest. The priest will examine him, and if the scab has spread on the skin, then the priest must pronounce him unclean; he has a serious skin disease.

"When a case of serious skin disease may have developed on a person, he is to be brought to the priest. The priest will examine him. If there is a white swelling on the skin that has turned the hair white, and there is a patch of raw flesh in the swelling, it is a chronic serious disease on the skin of his body, and the priest must pronounce him unclean. He need not quarantine him, for he is unclean. But if the skin disease breaks out all over the skin so that it covers all the skin of the 20 stricken person from his head to his feet so far as the priest can see, the priest will look, and if the skin disease has covered his entire body, he is to pronounce the stricken person clean. Since he has turned totally white, he is clean. But whenever raw flesh appears on him, he will be unclean. When the priest examines the raw flesh, he must pronounce him unclean. Raw flesh is unclean; this is a serious skin disease. But if the raw flesh changes and turns white, he is to go to the priest. The priest will examine him, and if the sore has turned white, the priest must pronounce the stricken person clean; he is clean.

"When a boil appears on the skin of someone's body and it heals, and a white swelling or a reddish-white spot develops where the boil was, the person is to present himself to the priest. The priest will make an examination, and if the spot seems to be beneath the skin and the hair in it has turned white, the priest must pronounce him unclean; it is a case of serious skin disease that has broken out in the boil. But when the priest examines it, if there is no white hair in it, and it is not beneath the skin but is faded, the priest will quarantine him seven days. If it spreads further on the skin, the priest must pronounce him unclean; it is in fact a disease. But if the spot remains where it is and does not spread, it is only the scar from the boil. The priest is to pronounce him clean.

"When there is a burn on the skin of one's body produced by fire, and the patch made raw by the burn becomes reddish-white or white, the priest is to examine it. If the hair in the spot has turned white and the spot appears to be deeper than the skin, it is a serious skin disease that has broken out in the burn. The priest must pronounce him unclean; it is a serious skin disease. But when the priest examines it, if there is no white hair in the spot and it is not beneath the skin but is faded, the priest will quarantine him seven days. The priest will reexamine him on the seventh day. If it has spread further on the skin, the priest must pronounce him unclean; it is in fact a case of serious skin disease. But if the spot has remained where it was and has not spread on the skin but is faded, it is the swelling from the burn. The priest is to pronounce him clean, for it is only the scar from the burn.

"When a man or woman has a condition on the head or chin, the priest is to examine the condition. If it appears to be deeper than the skin, and the hair in it is yellow and sparse, the priest must pronounce the person unclean. It is a scaly outbreak, a serious skin disease of the head or chin. When the priest examines the scaly condition, if it does not appear to be deeper than the skin, and there is no black hair in it, the priest will quarantine the person with the scaly condition for seven days. The priest will reexamine the condition on the seventh day. If the scaly outbreak has not spread and there is no yellow hair in it and it does not appear to be deeper than the skin, the person is to shave himself but not shave the scaly area. Then the priest will quarantine the person who has the scaly outbreak for another seven days. The priest will examine the scaly outbreak on the seventh day, and if it has not spread on the skin and does not appear to be deeper than the skin, the priest is to pronounce the person clean. He is to wash his clothes, and he will be clean. But if the scaly outbreak spreads further on the skin after his cleansing, the priest is to examine the person. If the scaly outbreak has spread on the skin, the priest does not need to look for yellow hair; the person is unclean. But if as far as he can see, the scaly outbreak remains unchanged and black hair has grown in it, then it has healed; he is clean. The priest is to pronounce the person clean.

"When a man or a woman has white spots on the skin of the body, the priest is to make an examination. If the spots on the skin of the body are dull white, it is only a rash that has broken out on the skin; the person is clean.

"If a man loses the hair of his head, he is bald, but he is clean. Or if he loses the hair at his hairline, he is bald on his forehead, but he is clean. But if there is a reddish-white condition on the bald head or forehead, it is a serious skin disease breaking out on his head or forehead. The priest is to examine him, and if the swelling of the condition on his bald head or forehead is reddish-white, like the appearance of a serious skin disease on his body, the man is afflicted with a serious

70 skin disease; he is unclean. The priest must pronounce him unclean; the infection is on his head.

"The person who has a case of serious skin disease is to have his clothes torn and his hair hanging loose, and he must cover his mouth and cry out, 'Unclean, unclean!' He will remain unclean as long as he has the disease; he is unclean. He must live alone in a place outside the camp.

"If a fabric is contaminated with mildew—in wool or linen fabric, in the warp or weft of linen or wool, or in leather or anything made of leather—and if the contamination is green or red in the fabric, the leather, the warp, the weft, or any leather article, it is a mildew contamination and is to be shown to the priest. The priest is to examine the contamination and quarantine the contaminated fabric for seven days. The priest is to reexamine the contamination on the seventh day. If it has spread in the fabric, the warp, the weft, or the leather, regardless of how it is used, the

80 contamination is harmful mildew; it is unclean. He is to burn the fabric, the warp or weft in wool or linen, or any leather article, which is contaminated. Since it is harmful mildew it must be burned.

"When the priest examines it, if the contamination has not spread in the fabric, the warp or weft, or any leather article, the priest is to order whatever is contaminated to be washed and quarantined for another seven days. After it has been washed, the priest is to reexamine the contamination. If the appearance of the contaminated article has not changed, it is unclean. Even though the contamination has not spread, you must burn the fabric. It is a fungus on the front or back of the fabric.

"If the priest examines it, and the contamination has faded after it has been washed, he is to cut the contaminated section out of the fabric, the leather, or the warp or weft. But if it reappears

90 in the fabric, the warp or weft, or any leather article, it has broken out again. You must burn whatever is contaminated. But if the contamination disappears from the fabric, the warp or weft, or any leather article, which have been washed, it is to be washed again, and it will be clean.

"This is the law concerning a mildew contamination in wool or linen fabric, warp or weft, or any leather article, in order to pronounce it clean or unclean."

14 The LORD spoke to Moses: "This is the law concerning the person afflicted with a skin disease on the day of his cleansing. He is to be brought to the priest, who will go outside the camp and examine him. If the skin disease has disappeared from the afflicted person, the priest will order that two live clean birds, cedar wood, scarlet yarn, and hyssop be brought for the one who is to be cleansed. Then the priest will order that one of the birds be slaughtered over fresh water in a clay pot. He is to take the live bird together with the cedar wood, scarlet yarn, and hyssop, and dip them all into the blood of the bird that was slaughtered over the fresh water. He will then sprinkle the blood seven times on the one who is to be cleansed from the skin disease. He is to pronounce him clean and release the live bird over the open countryside. The one who is to be cleansed must wash his clothes, shave off all his

10 hair, and bathe with water; he is clean. Afterward he may enter the camp, but he must remain outside his tent for seven days. He is to shave off all his hair again on the seventh day: his head, his beard, his eyebrows, and the rest of his hair. He is to wash his clothes and bathe himself with water; he is clean.

"On the eighth day he must take two unblemished male lambs, an unblemished year-old ewe lamb, a grain offering of six quarts of fine flour mixed with olive oil, and one-third of a quart of olive oil. The priest who performs the cleansing will place the person who is to be cleansed, together with these offerings, before the LORD at the entrance to the tent of meeting. The priest is to take one male lamb and present it as a guilt offering, along with the one-third quart of olive oil, and he will present them as a presentation offering before the LORD. He is to slaughter the male lamb at the place in the sanctuary area where the sin offering and burnt offering are slaughtered, for like the

20 sin offering, the guilt offering belongs to the priest; it is especially holy. The priest is to take some of the blood from the guilt offering and put it on the lobe of the right ear of the one to be cleansed, on the thumb of his right hand, and on the big toe of his right foot. Then the priest will take some of the one-third quart of olive oil and pour it into his left palm. The priest will dip his right finger into the oil in his left palm and sprinkle some of the oil with his finger seven times before the LORD. From the oil remaining in his palm the priest will put some on the lobe of the right ear of the one to be cleansed, on the thumb of his right hand, and on the big toe of his right foot, on top of the blood of the guilt offering. What is left of the oil in the priest's palm he is to put on the head of the one to be cleansed. In this way the priest will make atonement for him before the LORD. The priest is to sacrifice the sin offering and make atonement for the one to be cleansed from his uncleanness.

30 Afterward he will slaughter the burnt offering. The priest is to offer the burnt offering and the grain offering on the altar. The priest will make atonement for him, and he will be clean.

"But if he is poor and cannot afford these, he is to take one male lamb for a guilt offering to be presented in order to make atonement for him, along with two quarts of fine flour mixed with olive oil for a grain offering, one-third of a quart of olive oil, and two turtledoves or two young pigeons, whatever he can afford, one to be a sin offering and the other a burnt offering. On the eighth day he is to bring these things for his cleansing to the priest at the entrance to the tent of meeting before the LORD. The priest will take the male lamb for the guilt offering and the one-third quart of olive oil, and present them as a presentation offering before the LORD. After he slaughters the male lamb for the guilt offering, the priest is to take some of the blood of the guilt

40 offering and put it on the right earlobe of the one to be cleansed, on the thumb of his right hand, and on the big toe of his right foot. Then the priest will pour some of the oil into his left palm.

With his right finger the priest will sprinkle some of the oil in his left palm seven times before the LORD. The priest will also put some of the oil in his palm on the right earlobe of the one to be cleansed, on the thumb of his right hand, and on the big toe of his right foot, on the same place as the blood of the guilt offering. What is left of the oil in the priest's palm he is to put on the head of the one to be cleansed to make atonement for him before the LORD. He is to then sacrifice one type of what he can afford, either the turtledoves or young pigeons, one as a sin offering and the other as a burnt offering, sacrificing what he can afford together with the grain offering. In this way the priest will make atonement before the LORD for the one to be cleansed. This is the law for someone who has a skin disease and cannot afford the cost of his cleansing."

50

The LORD spoke to Moses and Aaron: "When you enter the land of Canaan that I am giving you as a possession, and I place a mildew contamination in a house in the land you possess, the owner of the house is to come and tell the priest: Something like mildew contamination has appeared in my house. The priest must order them to clear the house before he enters to examine the contamination, so that nothing in the house becomes unclean. Afterward the priest will come to examine the house. He will examine it, and if the contamination in the walls of the house consists of green or red indentations that appear to be beneath the surface of the wall, the priest is to go outside the house to its doorway and quarantine the house for seven days. The priest is to return on the seventh day and examine it. If the contamination has spread on the walls of the house, the priest must order that the stones with the contamination be pulled out and thrown into an unclean place outside the city. He is to have the inside of the house completely scraped, and have the plaster that is scraped off dumped in an unclean place outside the city. Then they are to take different stones to replace the former ones and take additional plaster to replaster the house.

60

"If the contamination reappears in the house after the stones have been pulled out, and after the house has been scraped and replastered, the priest is to come and examine it. If the contamination has spread in the house, it is harmful mildew; the house is unclean. It must be torn down with its stones, its beams, and all its plaster, and taken outside the city to an unclean place. Whoever enters the house during any of the days the priest quarantines it will be unclean until evening. Whoever lies down in the house is to wash his clothes, and whoever eats in it is to wash his clothes.

70

"But when the priest comes and examines it, if the contamination has not spread in the house after it was replastered, he is to pronounce the house clean because the contamination has disappeared. He is to take two birds, cedar wood, scarlet yarn, and hyssop to purify the house, and he is to slaughter one of the birds over a clay pot containing fresh water. He will take the cedar wood, the hyssop, the scarlet yarn, and the live bird, dip them in the blood of the slaughtered bird and the fresh water, and sprinkle the house seven times. He will purify the house with the blood of the bird, the fresh water, the live bird, the cedar wood, the hyssop, and the scarlet yarn. Then he is to release the live bird into the open countryside outside the city. In this way he will make atonement for the house, and it will be clean.

"This is the law for any skin disease or mildew, for a scaly outbreak, for mildew in clothing or
80 on a house, and for a swelling, scab, or spot, to determine when something is unclean or clean.
This is the law regarding skin disease and mildew."

15 The LORD spoke to Moses and Aaron: "Speak to the Israelites and tell them: When any man has
a discharge from his member, he is unclean. This is uncleanness of his discharge: Whether his
member secretes the discharge or retains it, he is unclean. All the days that his member secretes
or retains anything because of his discharge, he is unclean. Any bed the man with the discharge
lies on will be unclean, and any furniture he sits on will be unclean. Anyone who touches his bed
is to wash his clothes and bathe with water, and he will remain unclean until evening. Whoever
sits on furniture that the man with the discharge was sitting on is to wash his clothes and bathe
with water, and he will remain unclean until evening. Whoever touches the body of the man with
a discharge is to wash his clothes and bathe with water, and he will remain unclean until evening.
10 If the man with the discharge spits on anyone who is clean, he is to wash his clothes and bathe
with water, and he will remain unclean until evening. Any saddle the man with the discharge rides
on will be unclean. Whoever touches anything that was under him will be unclean until evening,
and whoever carries such things is to wash his clothes and bathe with water, and he will remain
unclean until evening. If the man with the discharge touches anyone without first rinsing his
hands in water, the person who was touched is to wash his clothes and bathe with water, and he
will remain unclean until evening. Any clay pot that the man with the discharge touches must be
broken, while any wooden utensil is to be rinsed with water.

"When the man with the discharge has been cured of it, he is to count seven days for his
cleansing, wash his clothes, and bathe his body in fresh water; he will be clean. He must take two
20 turtledoves or two young pigeons on the eighth day, come before the LORD at the entrance to the
tent of meeting, and give them to the priest. The priest is to sacrifice them, one as a sin offering
and the other as a burnt offering. In this way the priest will make atonement for him before the
LORD because of his discharge.

"When a man has an emission of semen, he is to bathe himself completely with water, and he
will remain unclean until evening. Any clothing or leather on which there is an emission of semen
is to be washed with water, and it will remain unclean until evening. If a man sleeps with a woman
and has an emission of semen, both of them are to bathe with water, and they will remain unclean
until evening.

"When a woman has a discharge, and it consists of blood from her body, she will be unclean
30 because of her menstruation for seven days. Everyone who touches her will be unclean until
evening. Anything she lies on during her menstruation will become unclean, and anything she
sits on will become unclean. Everyone who touches her bed is to wash his clothes and bathe with
water, and he will remain unclean until evening. Everyone who touches any furniture she was
sitting on is to wash his clothes and bathe with water, and he will remain unclean until evening. If

discharge is on the bed or the furniture she was sitting on, when he touches it he will be unclean until evening. If a man sleeps with her, and blood from her menstruation gets on him, he will be unclean for seven days, and every bed he lies on will become unclean.

"When a woman has a discharge of her blood for many days, though it is not the time of her menstruation, or if she has a discharge beyond her period, she will be unclean all the days of her 40 unclean discharge, as she is during the days of her menstruation. Any bed she lies on during the days of her discharge will be like her bed during menstrual impurity; any furniture she sits on will be unclean as in her menstrual period. Everyone who touches them will be unclean; he must wash his clothes and bathe with water, and he will remain unclean until evening. When she is cured of her discharge, she is to count seven days, and after that she will be clean. On the eighth day she must take two turtledoves or two young pigeons and bring them to the priest at the entrance to the tent of meeting. The priest is to sacrifice one as a sin offering and the other as a burnt offering. In this way the priest will make atonement for her before the LORD because of her unclean discharge.

"You must keep the Israelites from their uncleanness, so that they do not die by defiling my tabernacle that is among them. This is the law for someone with a discharge: a man who has an 50 emission of semen, becoming unclean by it; a woman who is in her menstrual period; anyone who has a discharge, whether male or female; and a man who sleeps with a woman who is unclean."

16 The LORD spoke to Moses after the death of two of Aaron's sons when they approached the presence of the LORD and died. The LORD said to Moses, "Tell your brother Aaron that he may not come whenever he wants into the holy place behind the curtain in front of the mercy seat on the ark or else he will die, because I appear in the cloud above the mercy seat.

"Aaron is to enter the most holy place in this way: with a young bull for a sin offering and a ram for a burnt offering. He is to wear a holy linen tunic, and linen undergarments are to be on his body. He is to tie a linen sash around him and wrap his head with a linen turban. These are holy garments; he must bathe his body with water before he wears them. He is to take from the Israelite community two male goats for a sin offering and one ram for a burnt offering.

10 "Aaron will present the bull for his sin offering and make atonement for himself and his household. Next he will take the two goats and place them before the LORD at the entrance to the tent of meeting. After Aaron casts lots for the two goats, one lot for the LORD and the other for an uninhabitable place, he is to present the goat chosen by lot for the LORD and sacrifice it as a sin offering. But the goat chosen by lot for an uninhabitable place is to be presented alive before the LORD to make atonement with it by sending it into the wilderness for an uninhabitable place.

"When Aaron presents the bull for his sin offering and makes atonement for himself and his household, he will slaughter the bull for his sin offering. Then he is to take a firepan full of blazing coals from the altar before the LORD and two handfuls of finely ground fragrant incense, and bring them inside the curtain. He is to put the incense on the fire before the LORD, so that the cloud of 20 incense covers the mercy seat that is over the testimony, or else he will die. He is to take some of the bull's blood and sprinkle it with his finger against the east side of the mercy seat; then he will sprinkle some of the blood with his finger before the mercy seat seven times.

"When he slaughters the male goat for the people's sin offering and brings its blood inside the curtain, he will do the same with its blood as he did with the bull's blood: He is to sprinkle it against the mercy seat and in front of it. He will make atonement for the most holy place in this way for all their sins because of the Israelites' impurities and rebellious acts. He will do the same for the tent of meeting that remains among them, because it is surrounded by their impurities. No one may be in the tent of meeting from the time he enters to make atonement in the most holy place until he leaves after he has made atonement for himself, his household, and the whole assembly of Israel. Then he will go out to the altar that is before the LORD and make atonement for it. He is to take some of the bull's blood and some of the goat's blood and put it on the horns on all sides of the altar. He is to sprinkle some of the blood on it with his finger seven times to cleanse and set it apart from the Israelites' impurities.

"When he has finished making atonement for the most holy place, the tent of meeting, and the altar, he is to present the live male goat. Aaron will lay both his hands on the head of the live goat and confess over it all the Israelites' iniquities and rebellious acts—all their sins. He is to put them on the goat's head and send it away into the wilderness by the man appointed for the task. The goat will carry all their iniquities into a desolate land, and the man will release it there.

"Then Aaron is to enter the tent of meeting, take off the linen garments he wore when he entered the most holy place, and leave them there. He will bathe his body with water in a holy place and put on his clothes. Then he must go out and sacrifice his burnt offering and the people's burnt offering, he will make atonement for himself and for the people. He is to burn the fat of the sin offering on the altar. The man who released the goat for an uninhabitable place is to wash his clothes and bathe his body with water; afterward he may reenter the camp. The bull for the sin offering and the goat for the sin offering, whose blood was brought into the most holy place to make atonement, must be brought outside the camp and their hide, flesh, and waste burned. The one who burns them is to wash his clothes and bathe himself with water; afterward he may reenter the camp.

"This is to be a permanent statute for you: In the seventh month, on the tenth day of the month you are to practice self-denial and do no work, both the native and the alien who resides among you. Atonement will be made for you on this day to cleanse you, and you will be clean from all your sins before the LORD. It is a Sabbath of complete rest for you, and you must practice self-denial; it is a permanent statute. The priest who is anointed and ordained to serve as high priest in place of his father will make atonement. He will put on the linen garments, the holy garments, and make atonement for the most holy place. He will make atonement for the tent of meeting and the altar and will make atonement for the priests and all the people of the assembly. This is to be a permanent statute for you, to make atonement for the Israelites once a year because of all their sins." And all this was done as the LORD commanded Moses.

17 The LORD spoke to Moses: "Speak to Aaron, his sons, and all the Israelites and tell them: This is what the LORD has commanded: Anyone from the house of Israel who slaughters an ox, sheep, or goat in the camp, or slaughters it outside the camp, instead of bringing it to the entrance to the tent of meeting to present it as an offering to the LORD before his tabernacle—that person will be considered guilty. He has shed blood and is to be cut off from his people. This is so the Israelites will bring to the LORD the sacrifices they have been offering in the open country. They are to bring them to the priest at the entrance to the tent of meeting and offer them as fellowship sacrifices to the LORD. The priest will then splatter the blood on the LORD's altar at the entrance to the tent of meeting and burn the fat as a pleasing aroma to the LORD. They must no longer offer their

10 sacrifices to the goat-demons that they have prostituted themselves with. This will be a permanent statute for them throughout their generations.

"Say to them: Anyone from the house of Israel or from the aliens who reside among them who offers a burnt offering or a sacrifice but does not bring it to the entrance to the tent of meeting to sacrifice it to the LORD, that person is to be cut off from his people.

"Anyone from the house of Israel or from the aliens who reside among them who eats any blood, I will turn against that person who eats blood and cut him off from his people. For the life of a creature is in the blood, and I have appointed it to you to make atonement on the altar for your lives, since it is the lifeblood that makes atonement. Therefore I say to the Israelites: None of you and no alien who resides among you may eat blood.

20 "Any Israelite or alien residing among them, who hunts down a wild animal or bird that may be eaten must drain its blood and cover it with dirt. Since the life of every creature is its blood, I have told the Israelites: You are not to eat the blood of any creature, because the life of every creature is its blood; whoever eats it must be cut off.

"Every person, whether the native or the resident alien, who eats an animal that died a natural death or was mauled by wild beasts is to wash his clothes and bathe with water, and he will remain unclean until evening; then he will be clean. But if he does not wash his clothes and bathe himself, he will bear his iniquity."

18 The LORD spoke to Moses: "Speak to the Israelites and tell them: I am the LORD your God. Do not follow the practices of the land of Egypt, where you used to live, or follow the practices of the land of Canaan, where I am bringing you. You must not follow their customs. You are to practice my ordinances and you are to keep my statutes by following them; I am the LORD your God. Keep my statutes and ordinances; a person will live if he does them. I am the LORD.

"You are not to come near any close relative for sexual intercourse; I am the LORD. You are not to violate the intimacy that belongs to your father and mother. She is your mother; you must not have sexual intercourse with her. You are not to have sex with your father's wife; she is your father's family. You are not to have sexual intercourse with your sister, either your father's

10 daughter or your mother's, whether born at home or born elsewhere. You are not to have sex with her. You are not to have sexual intercourse with your son's daughter or your daughter's daughter, for they are your family. You are not to have sexual intercourse with your father's wife's daughter, who is adopted by your father; she is your sister. You are not to have sexual intercourse with your father's sister; she is your father's close relative. You are not to have sexual intercourse with your mother's sister, for she is your mother's close relative. You are not to violate the intimacy that belongs to your father's brother by approaching his wife to have sexual intercourse; she is your aunt. You are not to have sexual intercourse with your daughter-in-law. She is your son's wife; you are not to have sex with her. You are not to have sexual intercourse with your brother's wife; she is your brother's family. You are not to have sexual intercourse with a woman and her daughter. You

20 are not to marry her son's daughter or her daughter's daughter and have sex with her. They are close relatives; it is depraved. You are not to marry a woman as a rival to her sister and have sexual intercourse with her during her sister's lifetime.

"You are not to approach a woman during her menstrual impurity to have sexual intercourse with her. You are not to have sexual intercourse with your neighbor's wife, defiling yourself with her.

"You are not to sacrifice any of your children in the fire to Molech. Do not profane the name of your God; I am the LORD. You are not to sleep with a man as with a woman; it is detestable. You are not to have sexual intercourse with any animal, defiling yourself with it; a woman is not to present herself to an animal to mate with it; it is a perversion.

30 "Do not defile yourselves by any of these practices, for the nations I am driving out before you have defiled themselves by all these things. The land has become defiled, so I am punishing it for its iniquity, and the land will vomit out its inhabitants. But you are to keep my statutes and ordinances. You must not commit any of these detestable acts—not the native or the alien who resides among you. For the people who were in the land prior to you have committed all these detestable acts, and the land has become defiled. If you defile the land, it will vomit you out as it has vomited out the nations that were before you. Any person who does any of these detestable practices is to be cut off from his people. You must keep my instruction to not do any of the detestable customs that were practiced before you, so that you do not defile yourselves by them; I am the LORD your God."

19 The LORD spoke to Moses: "Speak to the entire Israelite community and tell them: Be holy because I, the LORD your God, am holy.

"Each of you is to respect his mother and father. You are to keep my Sabbaths; I am the LORD your God. Do not turn to worthless idols or make cast images of gods for yourselves; I am the LORD your God.

"When you offer a fellowship sacrifice to the LORD, sacrifice it so that you may be accepted. It is to be eaten on the day you sacrifice it or on the next day, but what remains on the third day must be burned. If any is eaten on the third day, it is a repulsive thing; it will not be accepted. Anyone who eats it will bear his iniquity, for he has profaned what is holy to the LORD. That person is to be cut off from his people.

"When you reap the harvest of your land, you are not to reap to the very edge of your field or gather the gleanings of your harvest. Do not strip your vineyard bare or gather its fallen grapes. Leave them for the poor and the resident alien; I am the LORD your God.

"Do not steal. Do not act deceptively or lie to one another. Do not swear falsely by my name, profaning the name of your God; I am the LORD.

"Do not oppress your neighbor or rob him. The wages due a hired worker must not remain with you until morning. Do not curse the deaf or put a stumbling block in front of the blind, but you are to fear your God; I am the LORD.

"Do not act unjustly when deciding a case. Do not be partial to the poor or give preference to the rich; judge your neighbor fairly. Do not go about spreading slander among your people; do not jeopardize your neighbor's life; I am the LORD.

"Do not harbor hatred against your brother. Rebuke your neighbor directly, and you will not incur guilt because of him. Do not take revenge or bear a grudge against members of your community, but love your neighbor as yourself; I am the LORD.

"You are to keep my statutes. Do not crossbreed two different kinds of your livestock, sow your fields with two kinds of seed, or put on a garment made of two kinds of material.

"If a man has sexual intercourse with a woman who is a slave designated for another man, but she has not been redeemed or given her freedom, there must be punishment. They are not to be put to death, because she had not been freed. However, he must bring a ram as his guilt offering to the LORD at the entrance to the tent of meeting. The priest will make atonement on his behalf before the LORD with the ram of the guilt offering for the sin he has committed, and he will be forgiven for the sin he committed.

"When you come into the land and plant any kind of tree for food, you are to consider the fruit forbidden. It will be forbidden to you for three years; it is not to be eaten. In the fourth year all its fruit is to be consecrated as a praise offering to the LORD. But in the fifth year you may eat its fruit. In this way its yield will increase for you; I am the LORD your God.

"You are not to eat anything with blood in it. You are not to practice divination or witchcraft. You are not to cut off the hair at the sides of your head or mar the edge of your beard. You are not to make gashes on your bodies for the dead or put tattoo marks on yourselves; I am the LORD.

"Do not debase your daughter by making her a prostitute, or the land will be prostituted and filled with depravity. Keep my Sabbaths and revere my sanctuary; I am the LORD.

"Do not turn to mediums or consult spiritists, or you will be defiled by them; I am the LORD your God.

"You are to rise in the presence of the elderly and honor the old. Fear your God; I am the LORD.

"When an alien resides with you in your land, you must not oppress him. You will regard the alien who resides with you as the native-born among you. You are to love him as yourself, for you were aliens in the land of Egypt; I am the LORD your God.

"Do not be unfair in measurements of length, weight, or volume. You are to have honest
50 balances, honest weights, an honest dry measure, and an honest liquid measure; I am the LORD your God, who brought you out of the land of Egypt. Keep all my statutes and all my ordinances and do them; I am the LORD."

20 The LORD spoke to Moses: "Say to the Israelites: Any Israelite or alien residing in Israel who gives any of his children to Molech must be put to death; the people of the country are to stone him. I will turn against that man and cut him off from his people, because he gave his offspring to Molech, defiling my sanctuary and profaning my holy name. But if the people of the country look the other way when that man gives any of his children to Molech, and do not put him to death, then I will turn against that man and his family, and cut off from their people both him and all who follow him in prostituting themselves with Molech.

"Whoever turns to mediums or spiritists and prostitutes himself with them, I will turn against that person and cut him off from his people. Consecrate yourselves and be holy, for I am the LORD
10 your God. Keep my statutes and do them; I am the LORD who sets you apart.

"If anyone curses his father or mother, he must be put to death. He has cursed his father or mother; his death is his own fault.

"If a man commits adultery with a married woman—if he commits adultery with his neighbor's wife—both the adulterer and the adulteress must be put to death. If a man sleeps with his father's wife, he has violated the intimacy that belongs to his father. Both of them must be put to death; their death is their own fault. If a man sleeps with his daughter-in-law, both of them must be put to death. They have acted perversely; their death is their own fault. If a man sleeps with a man as with a woman, they have both committed a detestable act. They must be put to death; their death is their own fault. If a man marries a woman and her mother, it is depraved. Both he and they
20 must be burned, so that there will be no depravity among you. If a man has sexual intercourse with an animal, he must be put to death; you are also to kill the animal. If a woman approaches any animal and mates with it, you are to kill the woman and the animal. They must be put to death; their death is their own fault. If a man marries his sister, whether his father's daughter or his mother's daughter, and they have sexual relations, it is a disgrace. They are to be cut off publicly from their people. He has had sexual intercourse with his sister; he will bear his iniquity. If a man sleeps with a menstruating woman and has sexual intercourse with her, he has exposed the source of her flow, and she has uncovered the source of her blood. Both of them are to be cut off from their people. You must not have sexual intercourse with your mother's sister or your father's sister, for it is exposing one's own blood relative; both people will bear their iniquity. If a man sleeps

163

30 with his aunt, he has violated the intimacy that belongs to his uncle; they will bear their guilt and die childless. If a man marries his brother's wife, it is impurity. He has violated the intimacy that belongs to his brother; they will be childless.

"You are to keep all my statutes and all my ordinances, and do them, so that the land where I am bringing you to live will not vomit you out. You must not follow the statutes of the nations I am driving out before you, for they did all these things, and I abhorred them. And I promised you: You will inherit their land, since I will give it to you to possess, a land flowing with milk and honey. I am the Lord your God who set you apart from the peoples. Therefore you are to distinguish the clean animal from the unclean one, and the unclean bird from the clean one. Do not become contaminated by any land animal, bird, or whatever crawls on the ground; I have set these apart as unclean for you. You are 40 to be holy to me because I, the Lord, am holy, and I have set you apart from the nations to be mine.

"A man or a woman who is a medium or a spiritist must be put to death. They are to be stoned; their death is their own fault."

21 The Lord said to Moses, "Speak to Aaron's sons, the priests, and tell them: A priest is not to make himself ceremonially unclean for a dead person among his relatives, except for his immediate family: his mother, father, son, daughter, or brother. He may make himself unclean for his unmarried virgin sister in his immediate family. He is not to make himself unclean for those related to him by marriage and so defile himself.

"Priests may not make bald spots on their heads, shave the edge of their beards, or make gashes on their bodies. They are to be holy to their God and not profane the name of their God. For they present the food offerings to the Lord, the food of their God, and they must be holy. They are not to marry a woman defiled by prostitution. They are not to marry one divorced by her husband, 10 for the priest is holy to his God. You are to consider him holy since he presents the food of your God. He will be holy to you because I, the Lord who sets you apart, am holy. If a priest's daughter defiles herself by promiscuity, she defiles her father; she must be burned to death.

"The priest who is highest among his brothers, who has had the anointing oil poured on his head and has been ordained to wear the clothes, must not dishevel his hair or tear his clothes. He must not go near any dead person or make himself unclean even for his father or mother. He must not leave the sanctuary or he will desecrate the sanctuary of his God, for the consecration of the anointing oil of his God is on him; I am the Lord.

"He is to marry a woman who is a virgin. He is not to marry a widow, a divorced woman, or one defiled by prostitution. He is to marry a virgin from his own people, so that he does not 20 corrupt his bloodline among his people, for I am the Lord who sets him apart."

The Lord spoke to Moses: "Tell Aaron: None of your descendants throughout your generations who has a physical defect is to come near to present the food of his God. No man who has any defect is to come near: no man who is blind, lame, facially disfigured, or deformed; no man who has a broken foot or hand, or who is a hunchback or a dwarf, or who has an eye defect, a festering rash, scabs, or a crushed testicle. No descendant of the priest Aaron who has a defect is to come near to present the food offerings to the LORD. He has a defect and is not to come near to present the food of his God. He may eat the food of his God from what is especially holy as well as from what is holy. But because he has a defect, he must not go near the curtain or approach the altar. He is not to desecrate my holy places, for I am the LORD who sets them apart." Moses said this to Aaron and his sons and to all the Israelites.

22 The LORD spoke to Moses: "Tell Aaron and his sons to deal respectfully with the holy offerings of the Israelites that they have consecrated to me, so they do not profane my holy name; I am the LORD. Say to them: If any man from any of your descendants throughout your generations is in a state of uncleanness yet approaches the holy offerings that the Israelites consecrate to the LORD, that person will be cut off from my presence; I am the LORD. No man of Aaron's descendants who has a skin disease or a discharge is to eat from the holy offerings until he is clean. Whoever touches anything made unclean by a dead person or by a man who has an emission of semen, or whoever touches any swarming creature that makes him unclean or any person who makes him unclean—whatever his uncleanness—the man who touches any of these will remain unclean until evening and is not to eat from the holy offerings unless he has bathed his body with water. When the sun has set, he will become clean, and then he may eat from the holy offerings, for that is his food. He must not eat an animal that died naturally or was mauled by wild beasts, making himself unclean by it; I am the LORD. They must keep my instruction, or they will be guilty and die because they profane it; I am the LORD who sets them apart.

"No one outside a priest's family is to eat the holy offering. A foreigner staying with a priest or a hired worker is not to eat the holy offering. But if a priest purchases someone with his own silver, that person may eat it, and those born in his house may eat his food. If the priest's daughter is married to a man outside a priest's family, she is not to eat from the holy contributions. But if the priest's daughter becomes widowed or divorced, has no children, and returns to her father's house as in her youth, she may share her father's food. But no outsider may share it. If anyone eats a holy offering in error, he is to add a fifth to its value and give the holy offering to the priest. The priests must not profane the holy offerings the Israelites give to the LORD by letting the people eat their holy offerings and having them bear the penalty of restitution. For I am the LORD who sets them apart."

The LORD spoke to Moses: "Speak to Aaron, his sons, and all the Israelites and tell them: Any man of the house of Israel or of the resident aliens in Israel who presents his offering—whether they present payment of vows or freewill gifts to the LORD as burnt offerings—must offer an unblemished male from the cattle, sheep, or goats in order for you to be accepted. You are not to present anything that has a defect, because it will not be accepted on your behalf.

"When a man presents a fellowship sacrifice to the Lord to fulfill a vow or as a freewill offering
30 from the herd or flock, it has to be unblemished to be acceptable; there must be no defect in it.
You are not to present any animal to the Lord that is blind, injured, maimed, or has a running
sore, festering rash, or scabs; you may not put any of them on the altar as a food offering to the
Lord. You may sacrifice as a freewill offering any animal from the herd or flock that has an
elongated or stunted limb, but it is not acceptable as a vow offering. You are not to present to the
Lord anything that has bruised, crushed, torn, or severed testicles; you must not sacrifice them in
your land. Neither you nor a foreigner are to present food to your God from any of these animals.
They will not be accepted for you because they are deformed and have a defect."

The Lord spoke to Moses: "When an ox, sheep, or goat is born, it is to remain with its mother
for seven days; from the eighth day on, it will be acceptable as an offering, a food offering to the
40 Lord. But you are not to slaughter an animal from the herd or flock on the same day as its young.
When you offer a thanksgiving sacrifice to the Lord, offer it so that you may be accepted. It is to
be eaten on the same day. Do not let any of it remain until morning; I am the Lord.

"You are to keep my commands and do them; I am the Lord. You must not profane my holy
name; I must be treated as holy among the Israelites. I am the Lord who sets you apart, the one
who brought you out of the land of Egypt to be your God; I am the Lord."

23 The Lord spoke to Moses: "Speak to the Israelites and tell them: These are my appointed times,
the times of the Lord that you will proclaim as sacred assemblies.

"Work may be done for six days, but on the seventh day there is to be a Sabbath of complete
rest, a sacred assembly. You are not to do any work; it is a Sabbath to the Lord wherever you live.

"These are the Lord's appointed times, the sacred assemblies you are to proclaim at their
appointed times. The Passover to the Lord comes in the first month, at twilight on the
fourteenth day of the month. The Festival of Unleavened Bread to the Lord is on the fifteenth
day of the same month. For seven days you must eat unleavened bread. On the first day you are
to hold a sacred assembly; you are not to do any daily work. You are to present a food offering to
10 the Lord for seven days. On the seventh day there will be a sacred assembly; do not do any daily
work."

The Lord spoke to Moses: "Speak to the Israelites and tell them: When you enter the land
I am giving you and reap its harvest, you are to bring the first sheaf of your harvest to the priest.
He will present the sheaf before the Lord so that you may be accepted; the priest is to present it
on the day after the Sabbath. On the day you present the sheaf, you are to offer a year-old male
lamb without blemish as a burnt offering to the Lord. Its grain offering is to be four quarts of fine
flour mixed with oil as a food offering to the Lord, a pleasing aroma, and its drink offering will be
one quart of wine. You must not eat bread, roasted grain, or any new grain until this very day, and
until you have brought the offering to your God. This is to be a permanent statute throughout
20 your generations wherever you live.

"You are to count seven complete weeks starting from the day after the Sabbath, the day you brought the sheaf of the presentation offering. You are to count fifty days until the day after the seventh Sabbath and then present an offering of new grain to the Lord. Bring two loaves of bread from your settlements as a presentation offering, each of them made from four quarts of fine flour, baked with yeast, as firstfruits to the Lord. You are to present with the bread seven unblemished male lambs a year old, one young bull, and two rams. They will be a burnt offering to the Lord, with their grain offerings and drink offerings, a food offering, a pleasing aroma to the Lord. You are also to prepare one male goat as a sin offering, and two male lambs a year old as a fellowship sacrifice. The priest will present the lambs with the bread of firstfruits as a presentation offering before the Lord; the bread and the two lambs will be holy to the Lord for the priest. On that same day you are to make a proclamation and hold a sacred assembly. You are not to do any daily work. This is to be a permanent statute wherever you live throughout your generations. When you reap the harvest of your land, you are not to reap all the way to the edge of your field or gather the gleanings of your harvest. Leave them for the poor and the resident alien; I am the Lord your God."

The Lord spoke to Moses: "Tell the Israelites: In the seventh month, on the first day of the month, you are to have a day of complete rest, commemoration, and trumpet blasts—a sacred assembly. You must not do any daily work, but you must present a food offering to the Lord."

The Lord again spoke to Moses: "The tenth day of this seventh month is the Day of Atonement. You are to hold a sacred assembly and practice self-denial; you are to present a food offering to the Lord. On this particular day you are not to do any work, for it is a Day of Atonement to make atonement for yourselves before the Lord your God. If any person does not practice self-denial on this particular day, he is to be cut off from his people. I will destroy among his people anyone who does any work on this same day. You are not to do any work. This is a permanent statute throughout your generations wherever you live. It will be a Sabbath of complete rest for you, and you must practice self-denial. You are to observe your Sabbath from the evening of the ninth day of the month until the following evening."

The Lord spoke to Moses: "Tell the Israelites: The Festival of Shelters to the Lord begins on the fifteenth day of this seventh month and continues for seven days. There is to be a sacred assembly on the first day; you are not to do any daily work. You are to present a food offering to the Lord for seven days. On the eighth day you are to hold a sacred assembly and present a food offering to the Lord. It is a solemn assembly; you are not to do any daily work.

"These are the Lord's appointed times that you are to proclaim as sacred assemblies for presenting food offerings to the Lord, burnt offerings and grain offerings, sacrifices and drink offerings, each on its designated day. These are in addition to the offerings for the Lord's Sabbaths, your gifts, all your vow offerings, and all your freewill offerings that you give to the Lord.

"You are to celebrate the Lord's festival on the fifteenth day of the seventh month for seven days after you have gathered the produce of the land. There will be complete rest on the first day and complete rest on the eighth day. On the first day you are to take the product of majestic

trees—palm fronds, boughs of leafy trees, and willows of the brook—and rejoice before the
60 LORD your God for seven days. You are to celebrate it as a festival to the LORD seven days each
year. This is a permanent statute for you throughout your generations; celebrate it in the seventh
month. You are to live in shelters for seven days. All the native-born of Israel must live in shelters,
so that your generations may know that I made the Israelites live in shelters when I brought them
out of the land of Egypt; I am the LORD your God." So Moses declared the LORD's appointed
times to the Israelites.

24 The LORD spoke to Moses: "Command the Israelites to bring you pure oil from crushed olives for
the light, in order to keep the lamp burning regularly. Aaron is to tend it continually from evening
until morning before the LORD outside the curtain of the testimony in the tent of meeting. This
is a permanent statute throughout your generations. He must continually tend the lamps on the
pure gold lampstand in the LORD's presence.

"Take fine flour and bake it into twelve loaves; each loaf is to be made with four quarts. Arrange
them in two rows, six to a row, on the pure gold table before the LORD. Place pure frankincense
near each row, so that it may serve as a memorial portion for the bread and a food offering to the
LORD. The bread is to be set out before the LORD every Sabbath day as a permanent covenant
10 obligation on the part of the Israelites. It belongs to Aaron and his sons, who are to eat it in a holy
place, for it is the holiest portion for him from the food offerings to the LORD; this is a permanent
rule."

Now the son of an Israelite mother and an Egyptian father was among the Israelites. A fight broke out
in the camp between the Israelite woman's son and an Israelite man. Her son cursed and blasphemed
the Name, and they brought him to Moses. (His mother's name was Shelomith, a daughter of Dibri
of the tribe of Dan.) They put him in custody until the LORD's decision could be made clear to them.

Then the LORD spoke to Moses: "Bring the one who has cursed to the outside of the camp and
have all who heard him lay their hands on his head; then have the whole community stone him.
And tell the Israelites: If anyone curses his God, he will bear the consequences of his sin. Whoever
20 blasphemes the name of the LORD must be put to death; the whole community is to stone him. If
he blasphemes the Name, he is to be put to death, whether the resident alien or the native.

"If a man kills anyone, he must be put to death. Whoever kills an animal is to make restitution
for it, life for life. If any man inflicts a permanent injury on his neighbor, whatever he has done is
to be done to him: fracture for fracture, eye for eye, tooth for tooth. Whatever injury he inflicted
on the person, the same is to be inflicted on him. Whoever kills an animal is to make restitution
for it, but whoever kills a person is to be put to death. You are to have the same law for the
resident alien and the native, because I am the LORD your God."

After Moses spoke to the Israelites, they brought the one who had cursed to the outside of the
camp and stoned him. So the Israelites did as the LORD had commanded Moses.

25 The LORD spoke to Moses on Mount Sinai: "Speak to the Israelites and tell them: When you enter the land I am giving you, the land will observe a Sabbath to the LORD. You may sow your field for six years, and you may prune your vineyard and gather its produce for six years. But there will be a Sabbath of complete rest for the land in the seventh year, a Sabbath to the LORD: you are not to sow your field or prune your vineyard. You are not to reap what grows by itself from your crop, or harvest the grapes of your untended vines. It is to be a year of complete rest for the land. Whatever the land produces during the Sabbath year can be food for you—for yourself, your male or female slave, and the hired worker or alien who resides with you. All of its growth may serve as food for your livestock and the wild animals in your land.

10 "You are to count seven sabbatical years, seven times seven years, so that the time period of the seven sabbatical years amounts to forty-nine. Then you are to sound a ram's horn loudly in the seventh month, on the tenth day of the month; you will sound it throughout your land on the Day of Atonement. You are to consecrate the fiftieth year and proclaim freedom in the land for all its inhabitants. It will be your Jubilee, when each of you is to return to his property and each of you to his clan. The fiftieth year will be your Jubilee; you are not to sow, reap what grows by itself, or harvest its untended vines. It is to be holy to you because it is the Jubilee; you may only eat its produce directly from the field.

"In this Year of Jubilee, each of you will return to his property. If you make a sale to your neighbor or a purchase from him, do not cheat one another. You are to make the purchase from your neighbor 20 based on the number of years since the last Jubilee. He is to sell to you based on the number of remaining harvest years. You are to increase its price in proportion to a greater amount of years, and decrease its price in proportion to a lesser amount of years, because what he is selling to you is a number of harvests. You are not to cheat one another, but fear your God, for I am the LORD your God.

"You are to keep my statutes and ordinances and carefully observe them, so that you may live securely in the land. Then the land will yield its fruit, so that you can eat, be satisfied, and live securely in the land. If you wonder, 'What will we eat in the seventh year if we don't sow or gather our produce?' I will appoint my blessing for you in the sixth year, so that it will produce a crop sufficient for three years. When you sow in the eighth year, you will be eating from the previous harvest. You will be eating this until the ninth year when its harvest comes in.

30 "The land is not to be permanently sold because it is mine, and you are only aliens and temporary residents on my land. You are to allow the redemption of any land you occupy. If your brother becomes destitute and sells part of his property, his nearest relative may come and redeem what his brother has sold. If a man has no family redeemer, but he prospers and obtains enough to redeem his land, he may calculate the years since its sale, repay the balance to the man he sold it to, and return to his property. But if he cannot obtain enough to repay him, what he sold will remain in the possession of its purchaser until the Year of Jubilee. It is to be released at the Jubilee, so that he may return to his property.

"If a man sells a residence in a walled city, his right of redemption will last until a year has passed after its sale; his right of redemption will last a year. If it is not redeemed by the end of a full year, then the house in the walled city is permanently transferred to its purchaser throughout

40 his generations. It is not to be released on the Jubilee. But houses in settlements that have no walls around them are to be classified as open fields. The right to redeem such houses stays in effect, and they are to be released at the Jubilee.

"Concerning the Levitical cities, the Levites always have the right to redeem houses in the cities they possess. Whatever property one of the Levites can redeem—a house sold in a city they possess—is to be released at the Jubilee, because the houses in the Levitical cities are their possession among the Israelites. The open pastureland around their cities may not be sold, for it is their permanent possession.

"If your brother becomes destitute and cannot sustain himself among you, you are to support him as an alien or temporary resident, so that he can continue to live among you. Do not profit

50 or take interest from him, but fear your God and let your brother live among you. You are not to lend him your silver with interest or sell him your food for profit. I am the LORD your God, who brought you out of the land of Egypt to give you the land of Canaan and to be your God.

"If your brother among you becomes destitute and sells himself to you, you must not force him to do slave labor. Let him stay with you as a hired worker or temporary resident; he may work for you until the Year of Jubilee. Then he and his children are to be released from you, and he may return to his clan and his ancestral property. They are not to be sold as slaves, because they are my servants that I brought out of the land of Egypt. You are not to rule over them harshly but fear your God. Your male and female slaves are to be from the nations around you; you may purchase male and female slaves. You may also purchase them from the aliens residing with you, or from

60 their families living among you—those born in your land. These may become your property. You may leave them to your sons after you to inherit as property; you can make them slaves for life. But concerning your brothers, the Israelites, you must not rule over one another harshly.

"If an alien or temporary resident living among you prospers, but your brother living near him becomes destitute and sells himself to the alien living among you, or to a member of the resident alien's clan, he has the right of redemption after he has been sold. One of his brothers may redeem him. His uncle or cousin may redeem him, or any of his close relatives from his clan may redeem him. If he prospers, he may redeem himself. The one who purchased him is to calculate the time from the year he sold himself to him until the Year of Jubilee. The price of his sale will be determined by the number of years. It will be set for him like the daily wages of a hired worker.

70 If many years are still left, he must pay his redemption price in proportion to them based on his purchase price. If only a few years remain until the Year of Jubilee, he will calculate and pay the price of his redemption in proportion to his remaining years. He will stay with him like a man hired year by year. A resident alien is not to rule over him harshly in your sight. If he is not redeemed in any of these ways, he and his children are to be released at the Year of Jubilee. For the Israelites are my servants. They are my servants that I brought out of the land of Egypt; I am the LORD your God.

26 "Do not make worthless idols for yourselves, set up a carved image or sacred pillar for yourselves, or place a sculpted stone in your land to bow down to it, for I am the LORD your God. Keep my Sabbaths and revere my sanctuary; I am the LORD.

"If you follow my statutes and faithfully observe my commands, I will give you rain at the right time, and the land will yield its produce, and the trees of the field will bear their fruit. Your threshing will continue until grape harvest, and the grape harvest will continue until sowing time; you will have plenty of food to eat and live securely in your land. I will give peace to the land, and you will lie down with nothing to frighten you. I will remove dangerous animals from the land, and no sword will pass through your land. You will pursue your enemies, and they will fall before you by the sword. Five of you will pursue a hundred, and a hundred of you will pursue ten thousand; your enemies will fall before you by the sword.

"I will turn to you, make you fruitful and multiply you, and confirm my covenant with you. You will eat the old grain of the previous year and will clear out the old to make room for the new. I will place my residence among you, and I will not reject you. I will walk among you and be your God, and you will be my people. I am the LORD your God, who brought you out of the land of Egypt, so that you would no longer be their slaves. I broke the bars of your yoke and enabled you to live in freedom.

"But if you do not obey me and observe all these commands—if you reject my statutes and despise my ordinances, and do not observe all my commands—and break my covenant, then I will do this to you: I will bring terror on you—wasting disease and fever that will cause your eyes to fail and your life to ebb away. You will sow your seed in vain because your enemies will eat it. I will turn against you, so that you will be defeated by your enemies. Those who hate you will rule over you, and you will flee even though no one is pursuing you.

"But if after these things you will not obey me, I will proceed to discipline you seven times for your sins. I will break down your strong pride. I will make your sky like iron and your land like bronze, and your strength will be used up for nothing. Your land will not yield its produce, and the trees of the land will not bear their fruit.

"If you act with hostility toward me and are unwilling to obey me, I will multiply your plagues seven times for your sins. I will send wild animals against you that will deprive you of your children, ravage your livestock, and reduce your numbers until your roads are deserted.

"If in spite of these things you do not accept my discipline, but act with hostility toward me, then I will act with hostility toward you; I also will strike you seven times for your sins. I will bring a sword against you to execute the vengeance of the covenant. Though you withdraw into your cities, I will send a pestilence among you, and you will be delivered into enemy hands. When I cut off your supply of bread, ten women will bake your bread in a single oven and ration out your bread by weight, so that you will eat but not be satisfied.

"And if in spite of this you do not obey me but act with hostility toward me, I will act with furious hostility toward you; I will also discipline you seven times for your sins. You will eat the flesh of your sons; you will eat the flesh of your daughters. I will destroy your high places, cut down your shrines, and heap your lifeless bodies on the lifeless bodies of your idols; I will reject you. I will reduce your cities to ruins and devastate your sanctuaries. I will not smell the pleasing aroma of your sacrifices. I also will devastate the land, so that your enemies who come to live there will be appalled by it. But I will scatter you among the nations, and I will draw a sword to chase after you. So your land will become desolate, and your cities will become ruins.

"Then the land will make up for its Sabbath years during the time it lies desolate, while you are in the land of your enemies. At that time the land will rest and make up for its Sabbaths. As long as it lies desolate, it will have the rest it did not have during your Sabbaths when you lived there.

"I will put anxiety in the hearts of those of you who survive in the lands of their enemies. The sound of a wind-driven leaf will put them to flight, and they will flee as one flees from a sword, and fall though no one is pursuing them. They will stumble over one another as if fleeing from a sword though no one is pursuing them. You will not be able to stand against your enemies. You will perish among the nations; the land of your enemies will devour you. Those who survive in the lands of your enemies will waste away because of their iniquity; they will also waste away because of their ancestors' iniquities along with theirs.

"But when they confess their iniquity and the iniquity of their ancestors—their unfaithfulness that they practiced against me, and how they acted with hostility toward me, and I acted with hostility toward them and brought them into the land of their enemies—and when their uncircumcised hearts are humbled and they make amends for their iniquity, then I will remember my covenant with Jacob. I will also remember my covenant with Isaac and my covenant with Abraham, and I will remember the land. For the land abandoned by them will make up for its Sabbaths by lying desolate without the people, while they make amends for their iniquity, because they rejected my ordinances and abhorred my statutes. Yet in spite of this, while they are in the land of their enemies, I will not reject or abhor them so as to destroy them and break my covenant with them, since I am the Lord their God. For their sake I will remember the covenant with their ancestors, whom I brought out of the land of Egypt in the sight of the nations to be their God; I am the Lord."

These are the statutes, ordinances, and laws the Lord established between himself and the Israelites through Moses on Mount Sinai.

27 The Lord spoke to Moses: "Speak to the Israelites and tell them: When someone makes a special vow to the Lord that involves the assessment of people, if the assessment concerns a male from twenty to sixty years old, your assessment is fifty silver shekels measured by the standard sanctuary shekel. If the person is a female, your assessment is thirty shekels. If the person is from five to twenty years old, your assessment for a male is twenty shekels and for a female ten shekels. If the person is from one month to five years old, your assessment for a male is five silver shekels, and for a female your assessment is three shekels of silver. If the person is sixty years or more, your assessment is fifteen shekels for a male and ten shekels for a female. But if one is too poor to pay the assessment, he is to present the person before the priest and the priest will set a value for him. The priest will set a value for him according to what the one making the vow can afford.

"If the vow involves one of the animals that may be brought as an offering to the LORD, any of these he gives to the LORD will be holy. He may not replace it or make a substitution for it, either good for bad, or bad for good. But if he does substitute one animal for another, both that animal and its substitute will be holy.

"If the vow involves any of the unclean animals that may not be brought as an offering to the LORD, the animal must be presented before the priest. The priest will set its value, whether high or low; the price will be set as the priest makes the assessment for you. If the one who brought it decides to redeem it, he must add a fifth to the assessed value.

"When a man consecrates his house as holy to the LORD, the priest will assess its value, whether high or low. The price will stand just as the priest assesses it. But if the one who consecrated his house redeems it, he must add a fifth to the assessed value, and it will be his.

"If a man consecrates to the LORD any part of a field that he possesses, your assessment of value will be proportional to the seed needed to sow it, at the rate of fifty silver shekels for every six bushels of barley seed. If he consecrates his field during the Year of Jubilee, the price will stand according to your assessment. But if he consecrates his field after the Jubilee, the priest will calculate the price for him in proportion to the years left until the next Year of Jubilee, so that your assessment will be reduced. If the one who consecrated the field decides to redeem it, he must add a fifth to the assessed value, and the field will transfer back to him. But if he does not redeem the field or if he has sold it to another man, it is no longer redeemable. When the field is released in the Jubilee, it will be holy to the LORD like a field permanently set apart; it becomes the priest's property.

"If a person consecrates to the LORD a field he has purchased that is not part of his inherited landholding, then the priest will calculate for him the amount of the assessment up to the Year of Jubilee, and the person will pay the assessed value on that day as a holy offering to the LORD. In the Year of Jubilee the field will return to the one he bought it from, the original owner. All your assessed values will be measured by the standard sanctuary shekel, twenty gerahs to the shekel.

"But no one can consecrate a firstborn of the livestock, whether an animal from the herd or flock, to the LORD, because a firstborn already belongs to the LORD. If it is one of the unclean livestock, it can be ransomed according to your assessment by adding a fifth of its value to it. If it is not redeemed, it can be sold according to your assessment.

"Nothing that a man permanently sets apart to the LORD from all he owns, whether a person, an animal, or his inherited landholding, can be sold or redeemed; everything set apart is especially holy to the LORD. No person who has been set apart for destruction is to be ransomed; he must be put to death.

"Every tenth of the land's produce, grain from the soil or fruit from the trees, belongs to the LORD; it is holy to the LORD. If a man decides to redeem any part of this tenth, he must add a fifth to its value. Every tenth animal from the herd or flock, which passes under the shepherd's rod, will be holy to the LORD. He is not to inspect whether it is good or bad, and he is not to make a substitution for it. But if he does make a substitution, both the animal and its substitute will be holy; they cannot be redeemed."

These are the commands the LORD gave Moses for the Israelites on Mount Sinai.

Introduction to Numbers

R. Dennis Cole

The message of the book of Numbers is about faithfulness—the portrayal of the faithfulness of Yahweh who desires faithful obedience from his people. But the book also portrays Yahweh as dealing justly with people who are often disobedient and unfaithful, resulting in severe judgment in some cases and yet longsuffering forgiveness in others. As a whole the book presents a challenge to the people of Yahweh to live holy and righteous lives according to his revealed word.

Numbers presents several recurrent Torah themes: (1) Yahweh's revelation to humankind through his word and his mighty acts; (2) Yahweh's work in history through the lives of the patriarchs and their descendants; (3) the birthing of the nation at Mount Sinai; (4) Yahweh's blessing through the gift of a productive land; and (5) the polar themes of inheritance and disinheritance, obedience and disobedience, and of unity and disunity. Numbers anticipates both the inheritance of the land under Joshua's leadership and the internal and external conflicts of Judges, Samuel, and Kings. Prophets such as Hosea and Jeremiah build upon the history and themes of this book, and the Psalmists regularly refer to incidents contained within.

The title "Numbers" derives from the two military censuses in chs. 1–2, and 26 and the Levite count in ch. 3. The Hebrew title, *B'midbar*, which means "In the Wilderness," describes the geographical setting of much of the book—from the Wilderness of Sinai to the semi-arid Plains of Moab, across the Jordan River from Jericho. After deliverance from bondage and oppression in Egypt, Israel would experience Yahweh's leadership and faithfulness in the wilderness regions of Sinai, Paran, Kadesh-barnea, and finally in the Transjordan. Throughout their journeys Yahweh provided for their needs and promised them a land of fullness and prosperity—"flowing with milk and honey." The challenge for the nation was making the decision to live faithfully to Yahweh's revelation and to receive her inheritance of the land promised to Abraham and the patriarchs in the past and their descendants in the present and future.

The outline of the book of Numbers reflects this challenging message of faithfulness. The book is primarily narrative with portions of case law interwoven into a vibrant literary fabric. The book consists of seven cycles of material in three parts. Parts one and two present the end of the generation that Yahweh delivered from bondage and affliction in the land of Egypt. The first part (chs. 1–10) depicts the tribes of Israel at Mount Sinai in harmonious relationship to Yahweh, symmetrically arranged around the tabernacle, the symbol of his presence. The military is numbered for battle, the duties of the Levites are outlined, and the Nazirite vow laws are presented. The Israelites celebrate the second Passover just prior to departure, heading toward the promised land where Yahweh promises good for his people (10.38–44).

After departing Mount Sinai, the place of harmony and celebration, the nation degenerates into discord and grumbling; their relationship to Yahweh changes radically. Part two (chs. 11–25) presents Israel in three rounds of rebellion: (1) from grumbling evil in 11.1 to rejecting the gift of the land (chs. 13–14), (2) the Korah rebellion challenging the Aaronic priesthood (chs. 16–17), and (3) Moses and Aaron striking the rock in an unholy manner (ch. 20) and the idolatry of Baal-peor (ch. 25). Each section contains messages of grace, redemption, and purification (chs. 15; 19; and 23–24). Yahweh's (lit. *Elohim*) promise of blessing upon his people is dramatically depicted in the Balaam account and oracles (chs. 22–24).

Part three (chs. 26–36) poses the question for Israel as they stand at the door of the promised land: Will she be faithful as described in part one or unfaithful to Yahweh as depicted in part two? A second military census of the new generation, new leadership under Joshua, new laws governing the land for the future, and a model for holy war is presented in the Midianite campaign (ch. 31). Thus the conclusion is: if the people would be faithful in the manner in which the holy and united Israelites are portrayed in Num 1–10 and drive out the idolatrous Canaanites from the land, then they will assume their inheritance with all of Yahweh's blessings (33.60–69). But if they unfaithfully fail in this quest, Yahweh will remove them from the land.

Outline

Book One: The End of the First Generation in the Wilderness (1.1–25.23)
1. The Faithfulness of Israel at Sinai (1.1–10.14)
   a. Military Census and Levite Responsibilities (1.1–6.45)
   b. Tabernacle Service and Preparation for Departure (7.1–10.14)
2. The Rebellious Generation in the Wilderness (10.15–25.23)
   a. Rebellion Cycle 1: Rejection of the Promised Land (10.15–15.54)
   b. Rebellion Cycle 2: Korah vs. Aaronic Priesthood (16.1–19.94)
   c. Rebellion Cycle 3: Moses, Aaron, & Baal-peor (20.1–25.23)

Book Two: The New Generation Prepares for Entering the Promised Land (Num 26.1–30.26)
3. Setting the Stage for the New Generation (26.1–36.23)
   a. Preparation of the New Generation of Israel (26.1–30.26)
   b. Preparation for War and Entry into the Promised Land (Num 31.1–36.23)

Suggested Resources

Ashley, Timothy R. *Numbers*. New International Commentary on the Old Testament. Grand Rapids: Eerdmans, 1993.

Cole, R. Dennis. *Numbers*. New American Commentary. Nashville: Broadman & Holman, 2000.

Gane, Roy. *Numbers*. NIV Application Commentary. Grand Rapids: Zondervan, 2004.

Milgrom, Jacob. *Numbers*. Jewish Publication Society Torah Commentary. Philadelphia: Jewish Publication Society, 2003.

Stubbs, David L. *Numbers*. Brazos Theological Commentary on the Bible. Grand Rapids: Brazos, 2020.

Wenham, Gordon J. *Numbers*. Tyndale Old Testament Commentaries. Downers Grove, IL: InterVarsity Press, 2008.

Numbers

1 The Lord spoke to Moses in the tent of meeting in the Wilderness of Sinai, on the first day of the second month of the second year after Israel's departure from the land of Egypt: "Take a census of the entire Israelite community by their clans and their ancestral families, counting the names of every male one by one. You and Aaron are to register those who are twenty years old or more by their military divisions—everyone who can serve in Israel's army. A man from each tribe is to be with you, each one the head of his ancestral family. These are the names of the men who are to assist you:

> Elizur son of Shedeur from Reuben;
> Shelumiel son of Zurishaddai from Simeon;
> Nahshon son of Amminadab from Judah;
> Nethanel son of Zuar from Issachar;
> Eliab son of Helon from Zebulun;
> from the sons of Joseph:
> Elishama son of Ammihud from Ephraim,
> Gamaliel son of Pedahzur from Manasseh;
> Abidan son of Gideoni from Benjamin;
> Ahiezer son of Ammishaddai from Dan;
> Pagiel son of Ochran from Asher;
> Eliasaph son of Deuel from Gad;
> Ahira son of Enan from Naphtali.

These are the men called from the community; they are leaders of their ancestral tribes, the heads of Israel's clans."

So Moses and Aaron took these men who had been designated by name, and they assembled the whole community on the first day of the second month. They recorded their ancestry by their clans and their ancestral families, counting one by one the names of those twenty years old or more, just as the Lord commanded Moses. He registered them in the Wilderness of Sinai:

The descendants of Reuben, the firstborn of Israel: according to their family records by their clans and their ancestral families, counting one by one the names of every male twenty years old or more, everyone who could serve in the army, those registered for the tribe of Reuben numbered 46,500.

The descendants of Simeon: according to their family records by their clans and their ancestral families, those registered counting one by one the names of every male twenty years old or more, everyone who could serve in the army, those registered for the tribe of Simeon numbered 59,300.

The descendants of Gad: according to their family records by their clans and their ancestral families, counting the names of those twenty years old or more, everyone who could serve in the army, those registered for the tribe of Gad numbered 45,650.

The descendants of Judah: according to their family records by their clans and their ancestral families, counting the names of those twenty years old or more, everyone who could serve in the army, those registered for the tribe of Judah numbered 74,600.

The descendants of Issachar: according to their family records by their clans and their ancestral families, counting the names of those twenty years old or more, everyone who could serve in the army, those registered for the tribe of Issachar numbered 54,400.

The descendants of Zebulun: according to their family records by their clans and their ancestral families, counting the names of those twenty years old or more, everyone who could serve in the army, those registered for the tribe of Zebulun numbered 57,400.

The descendants of Joseph:

The descendants of Ephraim: according to their family records by their clans and their ancestral families, counting the names of those twenty years old or more, everyone who could serve in the army, those registered for the tribe of Ephraim numbered 40,500.

The descendants of Manasseh: according to their family records by their clans and their ancestral families, counting the names of those twenty years old or more, everyone who could serve in the army, those registered for the tribe of Manasseh numbered 32,200.

The descendants of Benjamin: according to their family records by their clans and their ancestral families, counting the names of those twenty years old or more, everyone who could serve in the army, those registered for the tribe of Benjamin numbered 35,400.

The descendants of Dan: according to their family records by their clans and their ancestral families, counting the names of those twenty years old or more, everyone who could serve in the army, those registered for the tribe of Dan numbered 62,700.

60 The descendants of Asher: according to their family records by their clans and their ancestral families, counting the names of those twenty years old or more, everyone who could serve in the army, those registered for the tribe of Asher numbered 41,500.

The descendants of Naphtali: according to their family records by their clans and their ancestral families, counting the names of those twenty years old or more, everyone who could serve in the army, those registered for the tribe of Naphtali numbered 53,400.

These are the men Moses and Aaron registered, with the assistance of the twelve leaders of Israel; each represented his ancestral family. So all the Israelites twenty years old or more, everyone who could serve in Israel's army, were registered by their ancestral families. All those registered numbered 603,550.

70 But the Levites were not registered with them by their ancestral tribe. For the Lord had told Moses, "Do not register or take a census of the tribe of Levi with the other Israelites. Appoint the Levites over the tabernacle of the testimony, all its furnishings, and everything in it. They are to transport the tabernacle and all its articles, take care of it, and camp around it. Whenever the tabernacle is to move, the Levites are to take it down, and whenever it is to stop at a campsite, the Levites are to set it up. Any unauthorized person who comes near it is to be put to death.

"The Israelites are to camp by their military divisions, each man with his encampment and under his banner. The Levites are to camp around the tabernacle of the testimony and watch over it, so that no wrath will fall on the Israelite community." The Israelites did everything just as the Lord had commanded Moses.

2 The Lord spoke to Moses and Aaron: "The Israelites are to camp under their respective banners beside the flags of their ancestral families. They are to camp around the tent of meeting at a distance from it:

Judah's military divisions will camp on the east side toward the sunrise under their banner. The leader of the descendants of Judah is Nahshon son of Amminadab. His military division numbers 74,600. The tribe of Issachar will camp next to it. The leader of the Issacharites is Nethanel son of Zuar. His military division numbers 54,400. The tribe of Zebulun will be next. The leader of the Zebulunites is Eliab son of Helon. His military division numbers 57,400. The total number in their military divisions who belong to Judah's encampment is
10 186,400; they will move out first.

Reuben's military divisions will camp on the south side under their banner. The leader of the Reubenites is Elizur son of Shedeur. His military division numbers 46,500. The tribe of

Simeon will camp next to it. The leader of the Simeonites is Shelumiel son of Zurishaddai. His military division numbers 59,300. The tribe of Gad will be next. The leader of the Gadites is Eliasaph son of Deuel. His military division numbers 45,650. The total number in their military divisions who belong to Reuben's encampment is 151,450; they will move out second.

The tent of meeting is to move out with the Levites' camp, which is in the middle of the camps. They are to move out just as they camp, each in his place, with their banners.

Ephraim's military divisions will camp on the west side under their banner. The leader of the Ephraimites is Elishama son of Ammihud. His military division numbers 40,500. The tribe of Manasseh will be next to it. The leader of the Manassites is Gamaliel son of Pedahzur. His military division numbers 32,200. The tribe of Benjamin will be next. The leader of the Benjaminites is Abidan son of Gideoni. His military division numbers 35,400. The total in their military divisions who belong to Ephraim's encampment number 108,100; they will move out third.

Dan's military divisions will camp on the north side under their banner. The leader of the Danites is Ahiezer son of Ammishaddai. His military division numbers 62,700. The tribe of Asher will camp next to it. The leader of the Asherites is Pagiel son of Ochran. His military division numbers 41,500. The tribe of Naphtali will be next. The leader of the Naphtalites is Ahira son of Enan. His military division numbers 53,400. The total number who belong to Dan's encampment is 157,600; they are to move out last, with their banners."

These are the Israelites registered by their ancestral families. The total number in the camps by their military divisions is 603,550. But the Levites were not registered among the Israelites, just as the LORD had commanded Moses.

The Israelites did everything the LORD commanded Moses; they camped by their banners in this way and moved out the same way, each man by his clan and by his ancestral family.

3 These are the family records of Aaron and Moses at the time the LORD spoke with Moses on Mount Sinai. These are the names of Aaron's sons: Nadab, the firstborn, and Abihu, Eleazar, and Ithamar. These are the names of Aaron's sons, the anointed priests, who were ordained to serve as priests. But Nadab and Abihu died in the LORD's presence when they presented unauthorized fire before the LORD in the Wilderness of Sinai, and they had no sons. So Eleazar and Ithamar served as priests under the direction of Aaron their father.

The LORD spoke to Moses: "Bring the tribe of Levi near and present them to the priest Aaron to assist him. They are to perform duties for him and the entire community before the

tent of meeting by attending to the service of the tabernacle. They are to take care of all the
furnishings of the tent of meeting and perform duties for the Israelites by attending to the service
of the tabernacle. Assign the Levites to Aaron and his sons; they have been assigned exclusively
to him from the Israelites. You are to appoint Aaron and his sons to carry out their priestly
responsibilities, but any unauthorized person who comes near the sanctuary is to be put to death."

The Lord spoke to Moses: "See, I have taken the Levites from the Israelites in place of every
firstborn Israelite from the womb. The Levites belong to me, because every firstborn belongs to
me. At the time I struck down every firstborn in the land of Egypt, I consecrated every firstborn in
Israel to myself, both man and animal. They are mine; I am the Lord."

The Lord spoke to Moses in the Wilderness of Sinai: "Register the Levites by their ancestral
families and their clans. You are to register every male one month old or more." So Moses
registered them in obedience to the Lord as he had been commanded:

> These were Levi's sons by name: Gershon, Kohath, and Merari. These were the names of
> Gershon's sons by their clans: Libni and Shimei. Kohath's sons by their clans were Amram,
> Izhar, Hebron, and Uzziel. Merari's sons by their clans were Mahli and Mushi. These were the
> Levite clans by their ancestral families.

> The Libnite clan and the Shimeite clan came from Gershon; these were the Gershonite
> clans. Those registered, counting every male one month old or more, numbered 7,500.
> The Gershonite clans camped behind the tabernacle on the west side, and the leader of the
> Gershonite families was Eliasaph son of Lael. The Gershonites' duties at the tent of meeting
> involved the tabernacle, the tent, its covering, the screen for the entrance to the tent of meeting,
> the hangings of the courtyard, the screen for the entrance to the courtyard that surrounds the
> tabernacle and the altar, and the tent ropes—all the work relating to these.

> The Amramite clan, the Izharite clan, the Hebronite clan, and the Uzzielite clan came from
> Kohath; these were the Kohathites. Counting every male one month old or more, there were
> 8,600 responsible for the duties of the sanctuary. The clans of the Kohathites camped on the
> south side of the tabernacle, and the leader of the families of the Kohathite clans was Elizaphan
> son of Uzziel. Their duties involved the ark, the table, the lampstand, the altars, the sanctuary
> utensils that were used with these, and the screen—and all the work relating to them. The chief
> of the Levite leaders was Eleazar son of Aaron the priest; he had oversight of those responsible
> for the duties of the sanctuary.

> The Mahlite clan and the Mushite clan came from Merari; these were the Merarite clans.
> Those registered, counting every male one month old or more, numbered 6,200. The leader of

the families of the Merarite clans was Zuriel son of Abihail; they camped on the north side of the tabernacle. The assigned duties of Merari's descendants involved the tabernacle's supports, crossbars, pillars, bases, all its equipment, and all the work related to these, in addition to the posts of the surrounding courtyard with their bases, tent pegs, and ropes.

Moses, Aaron, and his sons, who performed the duties of the sanctuary as a service on behalf of the Israelites, camped in front of the tabernacle on the east, in front of the tent of meeting toward the sunrise. Any unauthorized person who came near it was to be put to death.

50 The total number of all the Levite males one month old or more that Moses and Aaron registered by their clans at the LORD's command was 22,000.

The LORD told Moses, "Register every firstborn male of the Israelites one month old or more, and list their names. You are to take the Levites for me—I am the LORD—in place of every firstborn among the Israelites, and the Levites' cattle in place of every firstborn among the Israelites' cattle." So Moses registered every firstborn among the Israelites, as the LORD commanded him. The total number of the firstborn males one month old or more listed by name was 22,273.

The LORD spoke to Moses again: "Take the Levites in place of every firstborn among the Israelites, and the Levites' cattle in place of their cattle. The Levites belong to me; I am the LORD. As the redemption price for the 273 firstborn Israelites who outnumber the Levites, collect five shekels for each person, according to the standard sanctuary shekel—twenty gerahs to the shekel. Give the

60 silver to Aaron and his sons as the redemption price for those who are in excess among the Israelites."

So Moses collected the redemption amount from those in excess of the ones redeemed by the Levites. He collected the silver from the firstborn Israelites: 1,365 shekels measured by the standard sanctuary shekel. He gave the redemption silver to Aaron and his sons in obedience to the LORD, just as the LORD commanded Moses.

4 The LORD spoke to Moses and Aaron: "Among the Levites, take a census of the Kohathites by their clans and their ancestral families, men from thirty years old to fifty years old—everyone who is qualified to do work at the tent of meeting.

"The service of the Kohathites at the tent of meeting concerns the most holy objects. Whenever the camp is about to move on, Aaron and his sons are to go in, take down the screening curtain, and cover the ark of the testimony with it. They are to place over this a covering made of fine leather, spread a solid blue cloth on top, and insert its poles.

"They are to spread a blue cloth over the table of the Presence and place the plates and cups on it, as well as the bowls and pitchers for the drink offering. The regular bread offering is to be on it.

10 They are to spread a scarlet cloth over them, cover them with a covering made of fine leather, and insert the poles in the table.

"They are to take a blue cloth and cover the lampstand used for light, with its lamps, snuffers, and firepans, as well as its jars of oil by which they service it. Then they are to place it with all its utensils inside a covering made of fine leather and put them on the carrying frame.

"They are to spread a blue cloth over the gold altar, cover it with a covering made of fine leather, and insert its poles. They are to take all the serving utensils they use in the sanctuary, place them in a blue cloth, cover them with a covering made of fine leather, and put them on a carrying frame.

"They are to remove the ashes from the bronze altar, spread a purple cloth over it, and place all the equipment on it that they use in serving: the firepans, meat forks, shovels, and basins—all the equipment of the altar. They are to spread a covering made of fine leather over it and insert its poles.

"Aaron and his sons are to finish covering the holy objects and all their equipment whenever the camp is to move on. The Kohathites will come and carry them, but they are not to touch the holy objects or they will die. These are the transportation duties of the Kohathites regarding the tent of meeting.

"Eleazar, son of Aaron the priest, has oversight of the lamp oil, the fragrant incense, the daily grain offering, and the anointing oil. He has oversight of the entire tabernacle and everything in it, the holy objects and their utensils."

Then the LORD spoke to Moses and Aaron: "Do not allow the Kohathite tribal clans to be wiped out from the Levites. Do this for them so that they may live and not die when they come near the most holy objects: Aaron and his sons are to go in and assign each man his task and transportation duty. The Kohathites are not to go in and look at the holy objects as they are covered or they will die."

The LORD spoke to Moses: "Take a census of the Gershonites also, by their ancestral families and their clans. Register men from thirty years old to fifty years old, everyone who is qualified to perform service, to do work at the tent of meeting. This is the service of the Gershonite clans regarding work and transportation duties: They are to transport the tabernacle curtains, the tent of meeting with its covering and the covering made of fine leather on top of it, the screen for the entrance to the tent of meeting, the hangings of the courtyard, the screen for the entrance at the gate of the courtyard that surrounds the tabernacle and the altar, along with their ropes and all the equipment for their service. They will carry out everything that needs to be done with these items.

"All the service of the Gershonites, all their transportation duties and all their other work, is to be done at the command of Aaron and his sons; you are to assign to them all that they are responsible to carry. This is the service of the Gershonite clans at the tent of meeting, and their duties will be under the direction of Ithamar son of Aaron the priest.

"As for the Merarites, you are to register them by their clans and their ancestral families. Register men from thirty years old to fifty years old, everyone who is qualified to do the work of the tent of meeting. This is what they are responsible to carry as the whole of their service at the tent of

meeting: the supports of the tabernacle, with its crossbars, pillars, and bases, the posts of the surrounding courtyard with their bases, tent pegs, and ropes, including all their equipment and all
50 the work related to them. You are to assign by name the items that they are responsible to carry. This is the service of the Merarite clans regarding all their work at the tent of meeting, under the direction of Ithamar son of Aaron the priest."

So Moses, Aaron, and the leaders of the community registered the Kohathites by their clans and their ancestral families, men from thirty years old to fifty years old, everyone who was qualified for work at the tent of meeting. The men registered by their clans numbered 2,750. These were the registered men of the Kohathite clans, everyone who could serve at the tent of meeting. Moses and Aaron registered them at the LORD's command through Moses.

The Gershonites were registered by their clans and their ancestral families, men from thirty years old to fifty years old, everyone who was qualified for work at the tent of meeting. The men
60 registered by their clans and their ancestral families numbered 2,630. These were the registered men of the Gershonite clans. At the LORD's command Moses and Aaron registered everyone who could serve at the tent of meeting.

The men of the Merarite clans were registered by their clans and their ancestral families, those from thirty years old to fifty years old, everyone who was qualified for work at the tent of meeting. The men registered by their clans numbered 3,200. These were the registered men of the Merarite clans; Moses and Aaron registered them at the LORD's command through Moses.

Moses, Aaron, and the leaders of Israel registered all the Levites by their clans and their ancestral families, from thirty years old to fifty years old, everyone who was qualified to do the work of serving at the tent of meeting and transporting it. Their registered men numbered 8,580. At the LORD's command they were registered under the direction of Moses, each one according to his work and transportation duty, and his assignment was as the LORD commanded Moses.

5   The LORD instructed Moses, "Command the Israelites to send away anyone from the camp who is afflicted with a skin disease, anyone who has a discharge, or anyone who is defiled because of a corpse. Send away both male or female; send them outside the camp, so that they will not defile their camps where I dwell among them." The Israelites did this, sending them outside the camp. The Israelites did as the LORD instructed Moses.

The LORD spoke to Moses: "Tell the Israelites: When a man or woman commits any sin against another, that person acts unfaithfully toward the LORD and is guilty. The person is to confess the sin he has committed. He is to pay full compensation, add a fifth of its value to it, and give it to the individual he has wronged. But if that individual has no relative to receive compensation, the
10 compensation goes to the LORD for the priest, along with the atonement ram by which the priest will make atonement for the guilty person. Every holy contribution the Israelites present to the

priest will be his. Each one's holy contribution is his to give; what each one gives to the priest will be his."

The LORD spoke to Moses: "Speak to the Israelites and tell them: If any man's wife goes astray, is unfaithful to him, and sleeps with another, but it is concealed from her husband, and she is undetected, even though she has defiled herself, since there is no witness against her, and she wasn't caught in the act; and if a feeling of jealousy comes over the husband and he becomes jealous because of his wife who has defiled herself—or if a feeling of jealousy comes over him and he becomes jealous of her though she has not defiled herself—then the man is to bring his wife to the priest. He is also to bring an offering
20 for her of two quarts of barley flour. He is not to pour oil over it or put frankincense on it because it is a grain offering of jealousy, a grain offering for remembrance to draw attention to guilt.

"The priest is to bring her forward and have her stand before the LORD. Then the priest is to take holy water in a clay bowl, take some of the dust from the tabernacle floor, and put it in the water. After the priest has the woman stand before the LORD, he is to let down her hair and place in her hands the grain offering for remembrance, which is the grain offering of jealousy. The priest is to hold the bitter water that brings a curse. The priest will require the woman to take an oath and will say to her, 'If no man has slept with you, if you have not gone astray and become defiled while under your husband's authority, be unaffected by this bitter water that brings a curse. But if you have gone astray while under your husband's authority, if you have defiled yourself and a man other than your husband has slept with you'—at this point the priest will make the woman take the
30 oath with the sworn curse, and he is to say to her—'May the LORD make you into an object of your people's cursing and swearing when he makes your womb shrivel and your belly swell. May this water that brings a curse enter your stomach, causing your belly to swell and your womb to shrivel.'

"And the woman will reply, 'Amen, Amen.'

"Then the priest is to write these curses on a scroll and wash them off into the bitter water. He will require the woman to drink the bitter water that brings a curse, and it will enter her to cause bitter suffering. The priest is to take the grain offering of jealousy from the woman, present the offering before the LORD, and bring it to the altar. The priest is to take a handful of the grain offering as a memorial portion and burn it on the altar. Afterward, he will require the woman to
40 drink the water.

"When he makes her drink the water, if she has defiled herself and been unfaithful to her husband, the water that brings a curse will enter her to cause bitter suffering; her belly will swell, and her womb will shrivel. She will become a curse among her people. But if the woman has not defiled herself and is pure, she will be unaffected and will be able to conceive children.

"This is the law regarding jealousy when a wife goes astray and defiles herself while under her husband's authority, or when a feeling of jealousy comes over a husband and he becomes jealous of his wife. He is to have the woman stand before the LORD, and the priest will carry out all these instructions for her. The husband will be free of guilt, but that woman will bear her iniquity."

6 The LORD instructed Moses, "Speak to the Israelites and tell them: When a man or woman makes a special vow, a Nazirite vow, to consecrate himself to the LORD, he is to abstain from wine and beer. He must not drink vinegar made from wine or from beer. He must not drink any grape juice or eat fresh grapes or raisins. He is not to eat anything produced by the grapevine, from seeds to skin, during the period of his consecration.

"You must not cut his hair throughout the time of his vow of consecration. He may be holy until the time is completed during which he consecrates himself to the LORD; he is to let the hair of his head grow long. He must not go near a dead body during the time he consecrates himself to the LORD. He is not to defile himself for his father or mother, or his brother or sister, when they
10 die, while the mark of consecration to his God is on his head. He is holy to the LORD during the time of consecration.

"If someone suddenly dies near him, defiling his consecrated head, he must shave his head on the day of his purification; he is to shave it on the seventh day. On the eighth day he is to bring two turtledoves or two young pigeons to the priest at the entrance to the tent of meeting. The priest is to offer one as a sin offering and the other as a burnt offering to make atonement on behalf of the Nazirite, since he incurred guilt because of the corpse. On that day he is to consecrate his head again. He is to rededicate his time of consecration to the LORD and to bring a year-old male lamb as a guilt offering. But do not count the initial period of consecration because it became defiled.

"This is the law of the Nazirite: On the day his time of consecration is completed, he is to
20 be brought to the entrance to the tent of meeting. He is to present an offering to the LORD of one unblemished year-old male lamb as a burnt offering, one unblemished year-old female lamb as a sin offering, one unblemished ram as a fellowship offering, along with their grain offerings and drink offerings, and a basket of unleavened cakes made from fine flour mixed with oil, and unleavened wafers coated with oil.

"The priest is to present these before the LORD and sacrifice the Nazirite's sin offering and burnt offering. He will also offer the ram as a fellowship sacrifice to the LORD, together with the basket of unleavened bread. Then the priest will offer the accompanying grain offering and drink offering.

"The Nazirite is to shave his consecrated head at the entrance to the tent of meeting, take the hair from his head, and put it on the fire under the fellowship sacrifice. The priest is to take the
30 boiled shoulder from the ram, one unleavened cake from the basket, and one unleavened wafer, and put them into the hands of the Nazirite after he has shaved his consecrated head. The priest is to present them as a presentation offering before the LORD. It is a holy portion for the priest, in addition to the breast of the presentation offering and the thigh of the contribution. After that, the Nazirite may drink wine.

"These are the instructions about the Nazirite who vows his offering to the LORD for his consecration, in addition to whatever else he can afford; he must fulfill whatever vow he makes in keeping with the instructions for his consecration."

The LORD spoke to Moses: "Tell Aaron and his sons, 'This is how you are to bless the Israelites. You should say to them,

40
> "May the LORD bless you and protect you;
> may the LORD make his face shine on you
> and be gracious to you;
> may the LORD look with favor on you
> and give you peace.'"

In this way they will pronounce my name over the Israelites, and I will bless them."

7 On the day Moses finished setting up the tabernacle, he anointed and consecrated it and all its furnishings, along with the altar and all its utensils. After he anointed and consecrated these things, the leaders of Israel, the heads of their ancestral families, presented an offering. They were the tribal leaders who supervised the registration. They brought as their offering before the LORD six covered carts and twelve oxen, a cart from every two leaders and an ox from each one, and presented them in front of the tabernacle.

The LORD said to Moses, "Accept these from them to be used in the work of the tent of meeting, and give this offering to the Levites, to each division according to their service."

So Moses took the carts and oxen and gave them to the Levites. He gave the Gershonites two
10 carts and four oxen corresponding to their service, and gave the Merarites four carts and eight oxen corresponding to their service, under the direction of Ithamar son of Aaron the priest. But he did not give any to the Kohathites, since their responsibility was service related to the holy objects carried on their shoulders.

The leaders also presented the dedication gift for the altar when it was anointed. The leaders presented their offerings in front of the altar. The LORD told Moses, "Each day have one leader present his offering for the dedication of the altar."

The one who presented his offering on the first day was Nahshon son of Amminadab from the tribe of Judah. His offering was one silver dish weighing 3 ¼ pounds and one silver basin weighing 1 ¾ pounds, measured by the standard sanctuary shekel, both of them full of fine
20 flour mixed with oil for a grain offering; one gold bowl weighing four ounces, full of incense; one young bull, one ram, and one male lamb a year old, for a burnt offering; one male goat for a sin offering; and two bulls, five rams, five male goats, and five male lambs a year old, for the fellowship sacrifice. This was the offering of Nahshon son of Amminadab.

On the second day Nethanel son of Zuar, leader of Issachar, presented an offering. As his offering, he presented one silver dish weighing 3 ¼ pounds and one silver basin weighing 1 ¾ pounds, measured by the standard sanctuary shekel, both of them full of fine flour mixed with oil for a grain offering; one gold bowl weighing four ounces, full of incense; one young bull, one ram, and one male lamb a year old, for a burnt offering; one male goat for a sin offering; and two bulls, five rams, five male goats, and five male lambs a year old, for the fellowship 30 sacrifice. This was the offering of Nethanel son of Zuar.

On the third day Eliab son of Helon, leader of the Zebulunites, presented an offering. His offering was one silver dish weighing 3 ¼ pounds and one silver basin weighing 1 ¾ pounds, measured by the standard sanctuary shekel, both of them full of fine flour mixed with oil for a grain offering; one gold bowl weighing four ounces, full of incense; one young bull, one ram, and one male lamb a year old, for a burnt offering; one male goat for a sin offering; and two bulls, five rams, five male goats, and five male lambs a year old, for the fellowship sacrifice. This was the offering of Eliab son of Helon.

On the fourth day Elizur son of Shedeur, leader of the Reubenites, presented an offering. His offering was one silver dish weighing 3 ¼ pounds and one silver basin weighing 1 ¾ pounds, 40 measured by the standard sanctuary shekel, both of them full of fine flour mixed with oil for a grain offering; one gold bowl weighing four ounces, full of incense; one young bull, one ram, and one male lamb a year old, for a burnt offering; one male goat for a sin offering; and two bulls, five rams, five male goats, and five male lambs a year old, for the fellowship sacrifice. This was the offering of Elizur son of Shedeur.

On the fifth day Shelumiel son of Zurishaddai, leader of the Simeonites, presented an offering. His offering was one silver dish weighing 3 ¼ pounds and one silver basin weighing 1 ¾ pounds, measured by the standard sanctuary shekel, both of them full of fine flour mixed with oil for a grain offering; one gold bowl weighing four ounces, full of incense; one young bull, one ram, and one male lamb a year old, for a burnt offering; one male goat for a sin offering; and 50 two bulls, five rams, five male goats, and five male lambs a year old, for the fellowship sacrifice. This was the offering of Shelumiel son of Zurishaddai.

On the sixth day Eliasaph son of Deuel, leader of the Gadites, presented an offering. His offering was one silver dish weighing 3 ¼ pounds and one silver basin weighing 1 ¾ pounds, measured by the standard sanctuary shekel, both of them full of fine flour mixed with oil for a grain offering; one gold bowl weighing four ounces full of incense; one young bull, one ram, and one male lamb a year old, for a burnt offering; one male goat for a sin offering; and two bulls, five rams, five male goats, and five male lambs a year old, for the fellowship sacrifice. This was the offering of Eliasaph son of Deuel.

On the seventh day Elishama son of Ammihud, leader of the Ephraimites, presented an 60 offering. His offering was one silver dish weighing 3 ¼ pounds and one silver basin weighing

1 ¾ pounds, measured by the standard sanctuary shekel, both of them full of fine flour mixed with oil for a grain offering; one gold bowl weighing four ounces, full of incense; one young bull, one ram, and one male lamb a year old, for a burnt offering; one male goat for a sin offering; and two bulls, five rams, five male goats, and five male lambs a year old, for the fellowship sacrifice. This was the offering of Elishama son of Ammihud.

On the eighth day Gamaliel son of Pedahzur, leader of the Manassites, presented an offering. His offering was one silver dish weighing 3 ¼ pounds and one silver basin weighing 1 ¾ pounds, measured by the standard sanctuary shekel, both of them full of fine flour mixed with oil for a grain offering; one gold bowl weighing four ounces, full of incense; one young bull, one ram, and one male lamb a year old, for a burnt offering; one male goat for a sin offering; and two bulls, five rams, five male goats, and five male lambs a year old, for the fellowship sacrifice. This was the offering of Gamaliel son of Pedahzur.

On the ninth day Abidan son of Gideoni, leader of the Benjaminites, presented an offering. His offering was one silver dish weighing 3 ¼ pounds and one silver basin weighing 1 ¾ pounds, measured by the standard sanctuary shekel, both of them full of fine flour mixed with oil for a grain offering; one gold bowl weighing four ounces, full of incense; one young bull, one ram, and one male lamb a year old, for a burnt offering; one male goat for a sin offering; and two bulls, five rams, five male goats, and five male lambs a year old, for the fellowship sacrifice. This was the offering of Abidan son of Gideoni.

On the tenth day Ahiezer son of Ammishaddai, leader of the Danites, presented an offering. His offering was one silver dish weighing 3 ¼ pounds and one silver basin weighing 1 ¾ pounds, measured by the standard sanctuary shekel, both of them full of fine flour mixed with oil for a grain offering; one gold bowl weighing four ounces, full of incense; one young bull, one ram, and one male lamb a year old, for a burnt offering; one male goat for a sin offering; and two bulls, five rams, five male goats, and five male lambs a year old, for the fellowship sacrifice. This was the offering of Ahiezer son of Ammishaddai.

On the eleventh day Pagiel son of Ochran, leader of the Asherites, presented an offering. His offering was one silver dish weighing 3 ¼ pounds and one silver basin weighing 1 ¾ pounds, measured by the standard sanctuary shekel, both of them full of fine flour mixed with oil for a grain offering; one gold bowl weighing four ounces, full of incense; one young bull, one ram, and one male lamb a year old, for a burnt offering; one male goat for a sin offering; and two bulls, five rams, five male goats, and five male lambs a year old, for the fellowship sacrifice. This was the offering of Pagiel son of Ochran.

On the twelfth day Ahira son of Enan, leader of the Naphtalites, presented an offering. His offering was one silver dish weighing 3 ¼ pounds and one silver basin weighing 1 ¾ pounds, measured by the standard sanctuary shekel, both of them full of fine flour mixed with oil for a grain offering; one gold bowl weighing four ounces, full of incense; one young bull, one ram, and one male lamb a year old, for a burnt offering; one male goat for a sin offering; and two bulls, five rams, five male goats, and five male lambs a year old, for the fellowship sacrifice. This was the offering of Ahira son of Enan.

This was the dedication gift from the leaders of Israel for the altar when it was anointed: twelve silver dishes, twelve silver basins, and twelve gold bowls. Each silver dish weighed 3 ¼ pounds, and each basin 1 ¾ pounds. The total weight of the silver articles was 60 pounds measured by the standard sanctuary shekel. The twelve gold bowls full of incense each weighed four ounces measured by the standard sanctuary shekel. The total weight of the gold bowls was 3 pounds. All the livestock for the burnt offering totaled twelve bulls, twelve rams, and twelve male lambs a year old, with their grain offerings, and twelve male goats for the sin offering. All the livestock for the fellowship sacrifice totaled twenty-four bulls, sixty rams, sixty male goats, and sixty male lambs a year old. This was the dedication gift for the altar after it was anointed.

When Moses entered the tent of meeting to speak with the LORD, he heard the voice speaking to him from above the mercy seat that was on the ark of the testimony, from between the two cherubim. He spoke to him that way.

8 The LORD spoke to Moses: "Speak to Aaron and tell him: When you set up the lamps, the seven lamps are to give light in front of the lampstand." So Aaron did this; he set up its lamps to give light in front of the lampstand just as the LORD had commanded Moses. This is the way the lampstand was made: it was a hammered work of gold, hammered from its base to its flower petals. The lampstand was made according to the pattern the LORD had shown Moses.

The LORD spoke to Moses: "Take the Levites from among the Israelites and ceremonially cleanse them. Do this to them for their purification: Sprinkle them with the purification water. Have them shave their entire bodies and wash their clothes, and so purify themselves.

"They are to take a young bull and its grain offering of fine flour mixed with oil, and you are to take a second young bull for a sin offering. Bring the Levites before the tent of meeting and assemble the entire Israelite community. Then present the Levites before the LORD, and have the Israelites lay their hands on them. Aaron is to present the Levites before the LORD as a presentation offering from the Israelites, so that they may perform the LORD's work. Next the Levites are to lay their hands on the heads of the bulls. Sacrifice one as a sin offering and the other as a burnt offering to the LORD, to make atonement for the Levites.

"You are to have the Levites stand before Aaron and his sons, and you are to present them before the LORD as a presentation offering. In this way you are to separate the Levites from the rest of the Israelites so that the Levites will belong to me. After that the Levites may come to serve at the tent of meeting, once you have ceremonially cleansed them and presented them as a presentation

20 offering. For they have been exclusively assigned to me from the Israelites. I have taken them for myself in place of all who come first from the womb, every Israelite firstborn. For every firstborn among the Israelites is mine, both man and animal. I consecrated them to myself on the day I struck down every firstborn in the land of Egypt. But I have taken the Levites in place of every firstborn among the Israelites. From the Israelites, I have given the Levites exclusively to Aaron and his sons to perform the work for the Israelites at the tent of meeting and to make atonement on their behalf, so that no plague will come against the Israelites when they approach the sanctuary."

Moses, Aaron, and the entire Israelite community did this to the Levites. The Israelites did everything to them the LORD commanded Moses regarding the Levites. The Levites purified themselves and washed their clothes; then Aaron presented them before the LORD as a

30 presentation offering. Aaron also made atonement for them to cleanse them ceremonially. After that, the Levites came to do their work at the tent of meeting in the presence of Aaron and his sons. So they did to them as the LORD had commanded Moses concerning the Levites.

The LORD spoke to Moses: "In regard to the Levites: From twenty-five years old or more, a man enters the service in the work at the tent of meeting. But at fifty years old he is to retire from his service in the work and no longer serve. He may assist his brothers to fulfill responsibilities at the tent of meeting, but he must not do the work. This is how you are to deal with the Levites regarding their duties."

9 In the first month of the second year after their departure from the land of Egypt, the LORD told Moses in the Wilderness of Sinai, "The Israelites are to observe the Passover at its appointed time. You must observe it at its appointed time on the fourteenth day of this month at twilight; you are to observe it according to all its statutes and ordinances." So Moses told the Israelites to observe the Passover, and they observed it in the first month on the fourteenth day at twilight in the Wilderness of Sinai. The Israelites did everything as the LORD had commanded Moses.

But there were some men who were unclean because of a human corpse, so they could not observe the Passover on that day. These men came before Moses and Aaron the same day and said to him, "We are unclean because of a human corpse. Why should we be excluded from presenting

10 the LORD's offering at its appointed time with the other Israelites?"

Moses replied to them, "Wait here until I hear what the LORD commands for you."

Then the LORD spoke to Moses: "Tell the Israelites: When any one of you or your descendants is unclean because of a corpse or is on a distant journey, he may still observe the Passover to the LORD. Such people are to observe it in the second month, on the fourteenth day at twilight. They are to eat the animal with unleavened bread and bitter herbs; they may not leave any of it until morning or break any of its bones. They must observe the Passover according to all its statutes.

"But the man who is ceremonially clean, is not on a journey, and yet fails to observe the Passover is to be cut off from his people, because he did not present the LORD's offering at its appointed time. That man will bear the consequences of his sin.

20 "If an alien resides with you and wants to observe the Passover to the LORD, he is to do it according to the Passover statute and its ordinances. You are to apply the same statute to both the resident alien and the native of the land."

On the day the tabernacle was set up, the cloud covered the tabernacle, the tent of the testimony, and it appeared like fire above the tabernacle from evening until morning. It remained that way continuously: the cloud would cover it, appearing like fire at night. Whenever the cloud was lifted up above the tent, the Israelites would set out; at the place where the cloud stopped, there the Israelites camped. At the LORD's command the Israelites set out, and at the LORD's command they camped. As long as the cloud stayed over the tabernacle, they camped.

30 Even when the cloud stayed over the tabernacle many days, the Israelites carried out the LORD's requirement and did not set out. Sometimes the cloud remained over the tabernacle for only a few days. They would camp at the LORD's command and set out at the LORD's command. Sometimes the cloud remained only from evening until morning; when the cloud lifted in the morning, they set out. Or if it remained a day and a night, they moved out when the cloud lifted. Whether it was two days, a month, or longer, the Israelites camped and did not set out as long as the cloud stayed over the tabernacle. But when it was lifted, they set out. They camped at the LORD's command, and they set out at the LORD's command. They carried out the LORD's requirement according to his command through Moses.

10 The LORD spoke to Moses: "Make two trumpets of hammered silver to summon the community and have the camps set out. When both are sounded in long blasts, the entire community is to gather before you at the entrance to the tent of meeting. However, if one is sounded, only the leaders, the heads of Israel's clans, are to gather before you.

"When you sound short blasts, the camps pitched on the east are to set out. When you sound short blasts a second time, the camps pitched on the south are to set out. Short blasts are to be sounded for them to set out. When calling the assembly together, you are to sound long blasts, not short ones. The sons of Aaron, the priests, are to sound the trumpets. Your use of these is a permanent statute throughout your generations.

10 "When you enter into battle in your land against an adversary who is attacking you, sound short blasts on the trumpets, and you will be remembered before the LORD your God and be saved from your enemies. You are to sound the trumpets over your burnt offerings and your fellowship sacrifices and on your joyous occasions, your appointed festivals, and the beginning of each of your months. They will serve as a reminder for you before your God: I am the LORD your God."

During the second year, in the second month on the twentieth day of the month, the cloud was lifted up above the tabernacle of the testimony. The Israelites traveled on from the Wilderness of Sinai, moving from one place to the next until the cloud stopped in the Wilderness of Paran. They set out for the first time according to the LORD's command through Moses.

The military divisions of the camp of Judah's descendants with their banner set out first, and Nahshon son of Amminadab was over their divisions. Nethanel son of Zuar was over the division of the tribe of Issachar's descendants, and Eliab son of Helon was over the division of the tribe of Zebulun's descendants. The tabernacle was then taken down, and the Gershonites and the Merarites set out, transporting the tabernacle.

The military divisions of the camp of Reuben with their banner set out, and Elizur son of Shedeur was over their divisions. Shelumiel son of Zurishaddai was over the division of the tribe of Simeon's descendants, and Eliasaph son of Deuel was over the division of the tribe of Gad's descendants. The Kohathites then set out, transporting the holy objects; the tabernacle was to be set up before their arrival.

Next the military divisions of the camp of Ephraim's descendants with their banner set out, and Elishama son of Ammihud was over their divisions. Gamaliel son of Pedahzur was over the division of the tribe of Manasseh's descendants, and Abidan son of Gideoni was over the division of the tribe of Benjamin's descendants.

The military divisions of the camp of Dan's descendants with their banner set out, serving as rear guard for all the camps, and Ahiezer son of Ammishaddai was over their divisions. Pagiel son of Ochran was over the division of the tribe of Asher's descendants, and Ahira son of Enan was over the division of the tribe of Naphtali's descendants. This was the order of march for the Israelites by their military divisions as they set out.

Moses said to Hobab, descendant of Reuel the Midianite and Moses's relative by marriage, "We're setting out for the place the LORD promised, 'I will give it to you.' Come with us, and we will treat you well, for the LORD has promised good things to Israel."

But he replied to him, "I don't want to go. Instead, I will go to my own land and my relatives."

"Please don't leave us," Moses said, "since you know where we should camp in the wilderness, and you can serve as our eyes. If you come with us, whatever good the LORD does for us we will do for you."

They set out from the mountain of the LORD on a three-day journey with the ark of the LORD's covenant traveling ahead of them for those three days to seek a resting place for them. Meanwhile, the cloud of the LORD was over them by day when they set out from the camp.

Whenever the ark set out, Moses would say:

Arise, LORD!
Let your enemies be scattered,
and those who hate you flee from your presence.

When it came to rest, he would say:
Return, Lord,
to the countless thousands of Israel.

11 Now the people began complaining openly before the Lord about hardship. When the Lord heard, his anger burned, and fire from the Lord blazed among them and consumed the outskirts of the camp. Then the people cried out to Moses, and he prayed to the Lord, and the fire died down. So that place was named Taberah, because the Lord's fire had blazed among them.

The riffraff among them had a strong craving for other food. The Israelites wept again and said, "Who will feed us meat? We remember the free fish we ate in Egypt, along with the cucumbers, melons, leeks, onions, and garlic. But now our appetite is gone; there's nothing to look at but this manna!"

The manna resembled coriander seed, and its appearance was like that of bdellium. The people walked around and gathered it. They ground it on a pair of grinding stones or crushed it in a
10   mortar, then boiled it in a cooking pot and shaped it into cakes. It tasted like a pastry cooked with the finest oil. When the dew fell on the camp at night, the manna would fall with it.

Moses heard the people, family after family, weeping at the entrance of their tents. The Lord was very angry; Moses was also provoked. So Moses asked the Lord, "Why have you brought such trouble on your servant? Why are you angry with me, and why do you burden me with all these people? Did I conceive all these people? Did I give them birth so you should tell me, 'Carry them at your breast, as a nursing mother carries a baby,' to the land that you swore to give their ancestors? Where can I get meat to give all these people? For they are weeping to me, 'Give us meat to eat!' I can't carry all these people by myself. They are too much for me. If you are going to treat me like this, please kill me right now if I have found favor with you, and don't let me see my
20   misery anymore."

The Lord answered Moses, "Bring me seventy men from Israel known to you as elders and officers of the people. Take them to the tent of meeting and have them stand there with you. Then I will come down and speak with you there. I will take some of the Spirit who is on you and put the Spirit on them. They will help you bear the burden of the people, so that you do not have to bear it by yourself.

"Tell the people: Consecrate yourselves in readiness for tomorrow, and you will eat meat because you wept in the Lord's hearing, 'Who will feed us meat? We were better off in Egypt.' The Lord will give you meat and you will eat. You will eat, not for one day, or two days, or five days, or ten days, or twenty days, but for a whole month—until it comes out of your nostrils and becomes nauseating to you—because you have rejected the Lord who is among you, and wept
30   before him, 'Why did we ever leave Egypt?'"

But Moses replied, "I'm in the middle of a people with six hundred thousand foot soldiers, yet you say, 'I will give them meat, and they will eat for a month.' If flocks and herds were slaughtered for them, would they have enough? Or if all the fish in the sea were caught for them, would they have enough?"

The LORD answered Moses, "Is the LORD's arm weak? Now you will see whether or not what I have promised will happen to you."

Moses went out and told the people the words of the LORD. He brought seventy men from the elders of the people and had them stand around the tent. Then the LORD descended in the cloud and spoke to him. He took some of the Spirit who was on Moses and placed the Spirit on the seventy elders. As the Spirit rested on them, they prophesied, but they never did it again. Two men had remained in the camp, one named Eldad and the other Medad; the Spirit rested on them—they were among those listed, but had not gone out to the tent—and they prophesied in the camp. A young man ran and reported to Moses, "Eldad and Medad are prophesying in the camp."

Joshua son of Nun, assistant to Moses since his youth, responded, "Moses, my lord, stop them!"

But Moses asked him, "Are you jealous on my account? If only all the LORD's people were prophets and the LORD would place his Spirit on them!" Then Moses returned to the camp along with the elders of Israel.

A wind sent by the LORD came up and blew quail in from the sea; it dropped them all around the camp. They were flying three feet off the ground for about a day's journey in every direction. The people were up all that day and night and all the next day gathering the quail—the one who took the least gathered sixty bushels—and they spread them out all around the camp.

While the meat was still between their teeth, before it was chewed, the LORD's anger burned against the people, and the LORD struck them with a very severe plague. So they named that place Kibroth-hattaavah, because there they buried the people who had craved the meat.

From Kibroth-hattaavah the people moved on to Hazeroth and remained there.

12 Miriam and Aaron criticized Moses because of the Cushite woman he married (for he had married a Cushite woman). They said, "Does the LORD speak only through Moses? Does he not also speak through us?" And the LORD heard it. Moses was a very humble man, more so than anyone on the face of the earth.

Suddenly the LORD said to Moses, Aaron, and Miriam, "You three come out to the tent of meeting." So the three of them went out. Then the LORD descended in a pillar of cloud, stood at the entrance to the tent, and summoned Aaron and Miriam. When the two of them came forward, he said:

"Listen to what I say:
If there is a prophet among you from the LORD,
I make myself known to him in a vision;
I speak with him in a dream.

> Not so with my servant Moses;
> he is faithful in all my household.
> I speak with him directly,
> openly, and not in riddles;
> he sees the form of the LORD.

So why were you not afraid to speak against my servant Moses?" The LORD's anger burned against them, and he left.

20 As the cloud moved away from the tent, Miriam's skin suddenly became diseased, resembling snow. When Aaron turned toward her, he saw that she was diseased and said to Moses, "My lord, please don't hold against us this sin we have so foolishly committed. Please don't let her be like a dead baby whose flesh is half eaten away when he comes out of his mother's womb."

Then Moses cried out to the LORD, "God, please heal her!"

The LORD answered Moses, "If her father had merely spit in her face, wouldn't she remain in disgrace for seven days? Let her be confined outside the camp for seven days; after that she may be brought back in." So Miriam was confined outside the camp for seven days, and the people did not move on until Miriam was brought back in. After that, the people set out from Hazeroth and camped in the Wilderness of Paran.

13 The LORD spoke to Moses: "Send men to scout out the land of Canaan I am giving to the Israelites. Send one man who is a leader among them from each of their ancestral tribes." Moses sent them from the Wilderness of Paran at the LORD's command. All the men were leaders in Israel. These were their names:

> Shammua son of Zaccur from the tribe of Reuben;
> Shaphat son of Hori from the tribe of Simeon;
> Caleb son of Jephunneh from the tribe of Judah;
> Igal son of Joseph from the tribe of Issachar;
> Hoshea son of Nun from the tribe of Ephraim;
10 Palti son of Raphu from the tribe of Benjamin;
> Gaddiel son of Sodi from the tribe of Zebulun;
> Gaddi son of Susi from the tribe of Manasseh (from the tribe of Joseph);
> Ammiel son of Gemalli from the tribe of Dan;
> Sethur son of Michael from the tribe of Asher;
> Nahbi son of Vophsi from the tribe of Naphtali;
> Geuel son of Machi from the tribe of Gad.

These were the names of the men Moses sent to scout out the land, and Moses renamed Hoshea son of Nun, Joshua.

20 When Moses sent them to scout out the land of Canaan, he told them, "Go up this way to the Negev, then go up into the hill country. See what the land is like, and whether the people who live there are strong or weak, few or many. Is the land they live in good or bad? Are the cities they live in encampments or fortifications? Is the land fertile or unproductive? Are there trees in it or not? Be courageous. Bring back some fruit from the land." It was the season for the first ripe grapes.

So they went up and scouted out the land from the Wilderness of Zin as far as Rehob near the entrance to Hamath. They went up through the Negev and came to Hebron, where Ahiman, Sheshai, and Talmai, the descendants of Anak, were living. Hebron was built seven years before Zoan in Egypt. When they came to Eshcol Valley, they cut down a branch with a single cluster of grapes, which was carried on a pole by two men. They also took some pomegranates and figs. That place was called Eshcol Valley because of the cluster of grapes the Israelites cut there. At the end 30 of forty days they returned from scouting out the land.

The men went back to Moses, Aaron, and the entire Israelite community in the Wilderness of Paran at Kadesh. They brought back a report for them and the whole community, and they showed them the fruit of the land. They reported to Moses, "We went into the land where you sent us. Indeed it is flowing with milk and honey, and here is some of its fruit. However, the people living in the land are strong, and the cities are large and fortified. We also saw the descendants of Anak there. The Amalekites are living in the land of the Negev; the Hethites, Jebusites, and Amorites live in the hill country; and the Canaanites live by the sea and along the Jordan."

Then Caleb quieted the people in the presence of Moses and said, "Let's go up now and take possession of the land because we can certainly conquer it!"

40 But the men who had gone up with him responded, "We can't attack the people because they are stronger than we are!" So they gave a negative report to the Israelites about the land they had scouted: "The land we passed through to explore is one that devours its inhabitants, and all the people we saw in it are men of great size. We even saw the Nephilim there—the descendants of Anak come from the Nephilim! To ourselves we seemed like grasshoppers, and we must have seemed the same to them."

14 Then the whole community broke into loud cries, and the people wept that night. All the Israelites complained about Moses and Aaron, and the whole community told them, "If only we had died in the land of Egypt, or if only we had died in this wilderness! Why is the LORD bringing us into this land to die by the sword? Our wives and children will become plunder. Wouldn't it be better for us to go back to Egypt?" So they said to one another, "Let's appoint a leader and go back to Egypt."

Then Moses and Aaron fell facedown in front of the whole assembly of the Israelite community. Joshua son of Nun and Caleb son of Jephunneh, who were among those who scouted out the land, tore their clothes and said to the entire Israelite community, "The land we passed through and explored is an extremely good land. If the LORD is pleased with us, he will bring us

10 into this land, a land flowing with milk and honey, and give it to us. Only don't rebel against the LORD, and don't be afraid of the people of the land, for we will devour them. Their protection has been removed from them, and the LORD is with us. Don't be afraid of them!"

While the whole community threatened to stone them, the glory of the LORD appeared to all the Israelites at the tent of meeting.

The LORD said to Moses, "How long will these people despise me? How long will they not trust in me despite all the signs I have performed among them? I will strike them with a plague and destroy them. Then I will make you into a greater and mightier nation than they are."

But Moses replied to the LORD, "The Egyptians will hear about it, for by your strength you brought up this people from them. They will tell it to the inhabitants of this land. They have 20 heard that you, LORD, are among these people, how you, LORD, are seen face to face, how your cloud stands over them, and how you go before them in a pillar of cloud by day and in a pillar of fire by night. If you kill this people with a single blow, the nations that have heard of your fame will declare, 'Since the LORD wasn't able to bring this people into the land he swore to give them, he has slaughtered them in the wilderness.'

"So now, may my Lord's power be magnified just as you have spoken: The LORD is slow to anger and abounding in faithful love, forgiving iniquity and rebellion. But he will not leave the guilty unpunished, bringing the consequences of the fathers' iniquity on the children to the third and fourth generation. Please pardon the iniquity of this people, in keeping with the greatness of your faithful love, just as you have forgiven them from Egypt until now."

30 The LORD responded, "I have pardoned them as you requested. Yet as I live and as the whole earth is filled with the LORD's glory, none of the men who have seen my glory and the signs I performed in Egypt and in the wilderness, and have tested me these ten times and did not obey me, will ever see the land I swore to give their ancestors. None of those who have despised me will see it. But since my servant Caleb has a different spirit and has remained loyal to me, I will bring him into the land where he has gone, and his descendants will inherit it. Since the Amalekites and Canaanites are living in the lowlands, turn back tomorrow and head for the wilderness in the direction of the Red Sea."

Then the LORD spoke to Moses and Aaron: "How long must I endure this evil community that keeps complaining about me? I have heard the Israelites' complaints that they make against me. Tell them: As I live—this is the LORD's declaration—I will do to you exactly as I heard you say. 40 Your corpses will fall in this wilderness—all of you who were registered in the census, the entire number of you twenty years old or more—because you have complained about me. I swear that none of you will enter the land I promised to settle you in, except Caleb son of Jephunneh and Joshua son of Nun. I will bring your children whom you said would become plunder into the land you rejected, and they will enjoy it. But as for you, your corpses will fall in this wilderness. Your children will be shepherds in the wilderness for forty years and bear the penalty for your acts of unfaithfulness until all your corpses lie scattered in the wilderness. You will bear the consequences

of your iniquities forty years based on the number of the forty days that you scouted the land, a year for each day. You will know my displeasure. I, the LORD, have spoken. I swear that I will do this to the entire evil community that has conspired against me. They will come to an end in the
50 wilderness, and there they will die."

So the men Moses sent to scout out the land, and who returned and incited the entire community to complain about him by spreading a negative report about the land—those men who spread the negative report about the land were struck down by the LORD. Only Joshua son of Nun and Caleb son of Jephunneh remained alive of those men who went to scout out the land.

When Moses reported these words to all the Israelites, the people were overcome with grief. They got up early the next morning and went up the ridge of the hill country, saying, "Let's go to the place the LORD promised, for we were wrong."

But Moses responded, "Why are you going against the LORD's command? It won't succeed. Don't go, because the LORD is not among you and you will be defeated by your enemies. The
60 Amalekites and Canaanites are right in front of you, and you will fall by the sword. The LORD won't be with you, since you have turned from following him."

But they dared to go up the ridge of the hill country, even though the ark of the LORD's covenant and Moses did not leave the camp. Then the Amalekites and Canaanites who lived in that part of the hill country came down, attacked them, and routed them as far as Hormah.

15 The LORD instructed Moses, "Speak to the Israelites and tell them: When you enter the land I am giving you to settle in, and you make a food offering to the LORD from the herd or flock— either a burnt offering or a sacrifice, to fulfill a vow, or as a freewill offering, or at your appointed festivals—to produce a pleasing aroma for the LORD, the one presenting his offering to the LORD is also to present a grain offering of two quarts of fine flour mixed with a quart of oil. Prepare a quart of wine as a drink offering with the burnt offering or sacrifice of each lamb.

"If you prepare a grain offering with a ram, it is to be four quarts of fine flour mixed with a third of a gallon of oil. Also present a third of a gallon of wine for a drink offering as a pleasing aroma to the LORD.

10 "If you prepare a young bull as a burnt offering or as a sacrifice, to fulfill a vow, or as a fellowship offering to the LORD, a grain offering of six quarts of fine flour mixed with two quarts of oil is to be presented with the bull. Also present two quarts of wine as a drink offering. It is a food offering, a pleasing aroma to the LORD. This is to be done for each ox, ram, lamb, or goat. This is how you are to prepare each of them, no matter how many.

"Every Israelite is to prepare these things in this way when he presents a food offering as a pleasing aroma to the LORD. When an alien resides with you or someone else is among you and wants to prepare a food offering as a pleasing aroma to the LORD, he is to do exactly as you do throughout your generations. The assembly is to have the same statute for both you and the resident alien as a

permanent statute throughout your generations. You and the alien will be alike before the LORD. The
same law and the same ordinance will apply to both you and the alien who resides with you."

The LORD instructed Moses, "Speak to the Israelites and tell them: After you enter the land
where I am bringing you, you are to offer a contribution to the LORD when you eat from the food
of the land. You are to offer a loaf from your first batch of dough as a contribution; offer it just like
a contribution from the threshing floor. Throughout your generations, you are to give the LORD a
contribution from the first batch of your dough.

"When you sin unintentionally and do not obey all these commands that the LORD spoke to
Moses—all that the LORD has commanded you through Moses, from the day the LORD issued
the commands and onward throughout your generations—and if it was done unintentionally
without the community's awareness, the entire community is to prepare one young bull for a burnt
offering as a pleasing aroma to the LORD, with its grain offering and drink offering according to
the regulation, and one male goat as a sin offering. The priest will then make atonement for the
entire Israelite community so that they may be forgiven, for the sin was unintentional. They are to
bring their offering, a food offering to the LORD, and their sin offering before the LORD for their
unintentional sin. The entire Israelite community and the alien who resides among them will be
forgiven, since it happened to all the people unintentionally.

"If one person sins unintentionally, he is to present a year-old female goat as a sin offering. The
priest will then make atonement before the LORD on behalf of the person who acts in error sinning
unintentionally, and when he makes atonement for him, he will be forgiven. You are to have the same
law for the person who acts in error, whether he is an Israelite or an alien who resides among you.

"But the person who acts defiantly, whether native or resident alien, blasphemes the LORD.
That person is to be cut off from his people. He will certainly be cut off, because he has despised
the LORD's word and broken his command; his guilt remains on him."

While the Israelites were in the wilderness, they found a man gathering wood on the Sabbath day.
Those who found him gathering wood brought him to Moses, Aaron, and the entire community.
They placed him in custody because it had not been decided what should be done to him. Then
the LORD told Moses, "The man is to be put to death. The entire community is to stone him
outside the camp." So the entire community brought him outside the camp and stoned him to
death, as the LORD had commanded Moses.

The LORD said to Moses, "Speak to the Israelites and tell them that throughout their generations they
are to make tassels for the corners of their garments, and put a blue cord on the tassel at each corner.
These will serve as tassels for you to look at, so that you may remember all the LORD's commands and
obey them and not prostitute yourselves by following your own heart and your own eyes. This way
you will remember and obey all my commands and be holy to your God. I am the LORD your God
who brought you out of the land of Egypt to be your God; I am the LORD your God."

16 Now Korah son of Izhar, son of Kohath, son of Levi, with Dathan and Abiram, sons of Eliab, and On son of Peleth, sons of Reuben, took two hundred fifty prominent Israelite men who were leaders of the community and representatives in the assembly, and they rebelled against Moses. They came together against Moses and Aaron and told them, "You have gone too far! Everyone in the entire community is holy, and the Lord is among them. Why then do you exalt yourselves above the Lord's assembly?"

When Moses heard this, he fell facedown. Then he said to Korah and all his followers, "Tomorrow morning the Lord will reveal who belongs to him, who is set apart, and the one he will let come near him. He will let the one he chooses come near him. Korah, you and all your followers are to do this: take firepans, and tomorrow place fire in them and put incense on them 10 before the Lord. Then the man the Lord chooses will be the one who is set apart. It is you Levites who have gone too far!"

Moses also told Korah, "Now listen, Levites! Isn't it enough for you that the God of Israel has separated you from the Israelite community to bring you near to himself, to perform the work at the Lord's tabernacle, and to stand before the community to minister to them? He has brought you near, and all your fellow Levites who are with you, but you are pursuing the priesthood as well. Therefore, it is you and all your followers who have conspired against the Lord! As for Aaron, who is he that you should complain about him?"

Moses sent for Dathan and Abiram, the sons of Eliab, but they said, "We will not come! Is it not enough that you brought us up from a land flowing with milk and honey to kill us in the 20 wilderness? Do you also have to appoint yourself as ruler over us? Furthermore, you didn't bring us to a land flowing with milk and honey or give us an inheritance of fields and vineyards. Will you gouge out the eyes of these men? We will not come!"

Then Moses became angry and said to the Lord, "Don't respect their offering. I have not taken one donkey from them or mistreated a single one of them." So Moses told Korah, "You and all your followers are to appear before the Lord tomorrow—you, they, and Aaron. Each of you is to take his firepan, place incense on it, and present his firepan before the Lord—250 firepans. You and Aaron are each to present your firepan also."

Each man took his firepan, placed fire in it, put incense on it, and stood at the entrance to the tent of meeting along with Moses and Aaron. After Korah assembled the whole community 30 against them at the entrance to the tent of meeting, the glory of the Lord appeared to the whole community. The Lord spoke to Moses and Aaron, "Separate yourselves from this community so I may consume them instantly."

But Moses and Aaron fell facedown and said, "God, God who gives breath to all, when one man sins, will you vent your wrath on the whole community?"

The Lord replied to Moses, "Tell the community: Get away from the dwellings of Korah, Dathan, and Abiram."

Moses got up and went to Dathan and Abiram, and the elders of Israel followed him. He warned the community, "Get away now from the tents of these wicked men. Don't touch anything

that belongs to them, or you will be swept away because of all their sins." So they got away from
the dwellings of Korah, Dathan, and Abiram. Meanwhile, Dathan and Abiram came out and
stood at the entrance of their tents with their wives, children, and infants.

Then Moses said, "This is how you will know that the LORD sent me to do all these things and
that it was not of my own will: If these men die naturally as all people would, and suffer the fate of
all, then the LORD has not sent me. But if the LORD brings about something unprecedented, and
the ground opens its mouth and swallows them along with all that belongs to them so that they go
down alive into Sheol, then you will know that these men have despised the LORD."

Just as he finished speaking all these words, the ground beneath them split open. The earth
opened its mouth and swallowed them and their households, all Korah's people, and all their
possessions. They went down alive into Sheol with all that belonged to them. The earth closed
over them, and they vanished from the assembly. At their cries, all the people of Israel who were
around them fled because they thought, "The earth may swallow us too!" Fire also came out from
the LORD and consumed the 250 men who were presenting the incense.

Then the LORD spoke to Moses: "Tell Eleazar son of Aaron the priest to remove the firepans
from the burning debris, because they are holy, and scatter the fire far away. As for the firepans of
those who sinned at the cost of their own lives, make them into hammered sheets as plating for the
altar, for they presented them before the LORD, and the firepans are holy. They will be a sign to
the Israelites."

So the priest Eleazar took the bronze firepans that those who were burned had presented, and
they were hammered into plating for the altar, just as the LORD commanded him through Moses.
It was to be a reminder for the Israelites that no unauthorized person outside the lineage of Aaron
should approach to offer incense before the LORD and become like Korah and his followers.

The next day the entire Israelite community complained about Moses and Aaron, saying,
"You have killed the LORD's people!" When the community assembled against them, Moses and
Aaron turned toward the tent of meeting, and suddenly the cloud covered it, and the LORD's glory
appeared.

Moses and Aaron went to the front of the tent of meeting, and the LORD said to Moses, "Get
away from this community so that I may consume them instantly." But they fell facedown.

Then Moses told Aaron, "Take your firepan, place fire from the altar in it, and add incense. Go
quickly to the community and make atonement for them, because wrath has come from the LORD;
the plague has begun." So Aaron took his firepan as Moses had ordered, ran into the middle of the
assembly, and saw that the plague had begun among the people. After he added incense, he made
atonement for the people. He stood between the dead and the living, and the plague was halted.
But those who died from the plague numbered 14,700, in addition to those who died because of
the Korah incident. Aaron then returned to Moses at the entrance to the tent of meeting, since the
plague had been halted.

17 The LORD instructed Moses, "Speak to the Israelites and take one staff from them for each ancestral tribe, twelve staffs from all the leaders of their tribes. Write each man's name on his staff. Write Aaron's name on Levi's staff, because there is to be one staff for the head of each tribe. Then place them in the tent of meeting in front of the testimony where I meet with you. The staff of the man I choose will sprout, and I will rid myself of the Israelites' complaints that they have been making about you."

So Moses spoke to the Israelites, and each of their leaders gave him a staff, one for each of the leaders of their tribes, twelve staffs in all. Aaron's staff was among them. Moses placed the staffs before the LORD in the tent of the testimony.

10 The next day Moses entered the tent of the testimony and saw that Aaron's staff, representing the house of Levi, had sprouted, formed buds, blossomed, and produced almonds! Moses then brought out all the staffs from the LORD's presence to all the Israelites. They saw them, and each man took his own staff. The LORD told Moses, "Put Aaron's staff back in front of the testimony to be kept as a sign for the rebels, so that you may put an end to their complaints before me, or else they will die." So Moses did as the LORD commanded him.

Then the Israelites declared to Moses, "Look, we're perishing! We're lost; we're all lost! Anyone who comes near the LORD's tabernacle will die. Will we all perish?"

18 The LORD said to Aaron, "You, your sons, and your ancestral family will be responsible for iniquity against the sanctuary. You and your sons will be responsible for iniquity involving your priesthood. But also bring your relatives with you from the tribe of Levi, your ancestral tribe, so they may join you and assist you and your sons in front of the tent of the testimony. They are to perform duties for you and for the whole tent. They must not come near the sanctuary equipment or the altar; otherwise, both they and you will die. They are to join you and guard the tent of meeting, doing all the work at the tent, but no unauthorized person may come near you.

"You are to guard the sanctuary and the altar so that wrath may not fall on the Israelites again. Look, I have selected your fellow Levites from the Israelites as a gift for you, assigned by the LORD
10 to work at the tent of meeting. But you and your sons will carry out your priestly responsibilities for everything concerning the altar and for what is inside the curtain, and you will do that work. I am giving you the work of the priesthood as a gift, but an unauthorized person who comes near the sanctuary will be put to death."

Then the LORD spoke to Aaron, "Look, I have put you in charge of the contributions brought to me. As for all the holy offerings of the Israelites, I have given them to you and your sons as a portion and a permanent statute. A portion of the holiest offerings kept from the fire will be yours; every one of their offerings that they give me, whether the grain offering, sin offering, or guilt offering will be most holy for you and your sons. You are to eat it as a most holy offering. Every male may eat it; it is to be holy to you.

20 "The contribution of their gifts also belongs to you. I have given all the Israelites' presentation offerings to you and to your sons and daughters as a permanent statute. Every ceremonially clean person in your house may eat it. I am giving you all the best of the fresh oil, new wine, and grain, which the Israelites give to the LORD as their firstfruits. The firstfruits of all that is in their land, which they bring to the LORD, belong to you. Every clean person in your house may eat them.

"Everything in Israel that is permanently dedicated to the LORD belongs to you. The firstborn of every living thing, human or animal, presented to the LORD belongs to you. But you must certainly redeem a human firstborn, and redeem the firstborn of an unclean animal. You will pay the redemption price for a month-old male according to your assessment: five shekels of silver by the standard sanctuary shekel, which is twenty gerahs.

30 "However, you must not redeem the firstborn of an ox, a sheep, or a goat; they are holy. You are to splatter their blood on the altar and burn their fat as a food offering for a pleasing aroma to the LORD. But their meat belongs to you. It belongs to you like the breast of the presentation offering and the right thigh.

"I give to you and to your sons and daughters all the holy contributions that the Israelites present to the LORD as a permanent statute. It is a permanent covenant of salt before the LORD for you as well as your offspring."

The LORD told Aaron, "You will not have an inheritance in their land; there will be no portion among them for you. I am your portion and your inheritance among the Israelites.

"Look, I have given the Levites every tenth in Israel as an inheritance in return for the work 40 they do, the work of the tent of meeting. The Israelites must never again come near the tent of meeting, or they will incur guilt and die. The Levites will do the work of the tent of meeting, and they will bear the consequences of their iniquity. The Levites will not receive an inheritance among the Israelites; this is a permanent statute throughout your generations. For I have given them the tenth that the Israelites present to the LORD as a contribution for their inheritance. That is why I told them that they would not receive an inheritance among the Israelites."

The LORD instructed Moses, "Speak to the Levites and tell them: When you receive from the Israelites the tenth that I have given you as your inheritance, you are to present part of it as an offering to the LORD—a tenth of the tenth. Your offering will be credited to you as if it were your grain from the threshing floor or the full harvest from the winepress. You are to present an 50 offering to the LORD from every tenth you receive from the Israelites. Give some of it to the priest Aaron as an offering to the LORD. You must present the entire offering due the LORD from all your gifts. The best part of the tenth is to be consecrated.

"Tell them further: Once you have presented the best part of the tenth, and it is credited to you Levites as the produce of the threshing floor or the winepress, then you and your household may eat it anywhere. It is your wage in return for your work at the tent of meeting. You will not incur guilt because of it once you have presented the best part of it, but you must not defile the Israelites' holy offerings, so that you will not die."

19 The LORD spoke to Moses and Aaron, "This is the legal statute that the LORD has commanded: Instruct the Israelites to bring you an unblemished red cow that has no defect and has never been yoked. Give it to the priest Eleazar, and he will have it brought outside the camp and slaughtered in his presence. The priest Eleazar is to take some of its blood with his finger and sprinkle it seven times toward the front of the tent of meeting. The cow is to be burned in his sight. Its hide, flesh, and blood are to be burned along with its waste. The priest is to take cedar wood, hyssop, and crimson yarn, and throw them onto the fire where the cow is burning. Then the priest must wash his clothes and bathe his body in water; after that he may enter the camp, but he will remain ceremonially unclean until evening. The one who burned the cow must also wash his clothes and bathe his body in water, and he will remain unclean until evening.

"A man who is clean is to gather up the cow's ashes and deposit them outside the camp in a ceremonially clean place. The ashes will be kept by the Israelite community for preparing the water to remove impurity; it is a sin offering. Then the one who gathers up the cow's ashes must wash his clothes, and he will remain unclean until evening. This is a permanent statute for the Israelites and for the alien who resides among them.

"The person who touches any human corpse will be unclean for seven days. He is to purify himself with the water on the third day and the seventh day; then he will be clean. But if he does not purify himself on the third and seventh days, he will not be clean. Anyone who touches a body of a person who has died, and does not purify himself, defiles the tabernacle of the LORD. That person will be cut off from Israel. He remains unclean because the water for impurity has not been sprinkled on him, and his uncleanness is still on him.

"This is the law when a person dies in a tent: everyone who enters the tent and everyone who is already in the tent will be unclean for seven days, and any open container without a lid tied on it is unclean. Anyone in the open field who touches a person who has been killed by the sword or has died, or who even touches a human bone, or a grave, will be unclean for seven days. For the purification of the unclean person, they are to take some of the ashes of the burnt sin offering, put them in a jar, and add fresh water to them. A person who is clean is to take hyssop, dip it in the water, and sprinkle the tent, all the furnishings, and the people who were there. He is also to sprinkle the one who touched a bone, a grave, a corpse, or a person who had been killed.

"The one who is clean is to sprinkle the unclean person on the third day and the seventh day. After he purifies the unclean person on the seventh day, the one being purified must wash his clothes and bathe in water, and he will be clean by evening. But a person who is unclean and does not purify himself, that person will be cut off from the assembly because he has defiled the sanctuary of the LORD. The water for impurity has not been sprinkled on him; he is unclean. This is a permanent statute for them. The person who sprinkles the water for impurity is to wash his clothes, and whoever touches the water for impurity will be unclean until evening. Anything the unclean person touches will become unclean, and anyone who touches it will be unclean until evening."

20 The entire Israelite community entered the Wilderness of Zin in the first month, and they settled in Kadesh. Miriam died and was buried there.

There was no water for the community, so they assembled against Moses and Aaron. The people quarreled with Moses and said, "If only we had perished when our brothers perished before the LORD. Why have you brought the LORD's assembly into this wilderness for us and our livestock to die here? Why have you led us up from Egypt to bring us to this evil place? It's not a place of grain, figs, vines, and pomegranates, and there is no water to drink!"

Then Moses and Aaron went from the presence of the assembly to the doorway of the tent of meeting. They fell facedown, and the glory of the LORD appeared to them. The LORD spoke to
10 Moses, "Take the staff and assemble the community. You and your brother Aaron are to speak to the rock while they watch, and it will yield its water. You will bring out water for them from the rock and provide drink for the community and their livestock."

So Moses took the staff from the LORD's presence just as he had commanded him. Moses and Aaron summoned the assembly in front of the rock, and Moses said to them, "Listen, you rebels! Must we bring water out of this rock for you?" Then Moses raised his hand and struck the rock twice with his staff, so that abundant water gushed out, and the community and their livestock drank.

But the LORD said to Moses and Aaron, "Because you did not trust me to demonstrate my holiness in the sight of the Israelites, you will not bring this assembly into the land I have given them." These are the Waters of Meribah, where the Israelites quarreled with the LORD, and he
20 demonstrated his holiness to them.

Moses sent messengers from Kadesh to the king of Edom, "This is what your brother Israel says, 'You know all the hardships that have overtaken us. Our ancestors went down to Egypt, and we lived in Egypt many years, but the Egyptians treated us and our ancestors badly. When we cried out to the LORD, he heard our plea, and sent an angel, and brought us out of Egypt. Now look, we are in Kadesh, a city on the border of your territory. Please let us travel through your land. We won't travel through any field or vineyard, or drink any well water. We will travel the King's Highway; we won't turn to the right or the left until we have traveled through your territory.'"

But Edom answered him, "You will not travel through our land, or we will come out and confront you with the sword."
30 "We will go on the main road," the Israelites replied to them, "and if we or our herds drink your water, we will pay its price. There will be no problem; only let us travel through on foot."

Yet Edom insisted, "You may not travel through." And they came out to confront them with a large force of heavily-armed people. Edom refused to allow Israel to travel through their territory, and Israel turned away from them.

After they set out from Kadesh, the entire Israelite community came to Mount Hor. The LORD said to Moses and Aaron at Mount Hor on the border of the land of Edom, "Aaron will be

gathered to his people; he will not enter the land I have given the Israelites, because you both rebelled against my command at the Waters of Meribah. Take Aaron and his son Eleazar and bring them up Mount Hor. Remove Aaron's garments and put them on his son Eleazar. Aaron
40 will be gathered to his people and die there."

So Moses did as the LORD commanded, and they climbed Mount Hor in the sight of the whole community. After Moses removed Aaron's garments and put them on his son Eleazar, Aaron died there on top of the mountain. Then Moses and Eleazar came down from the mountain. When the whole community saw that Aaron had passed away, the entire house of Israel mourned for him thirty days.

21 When the Canaanite king of Arad, who lived in the Negev, heard that Israel was coming on the Atharim road, he fought against Israel and captured some prisoners. Then Israel made a vow to the LORD, "If you will hand this people over to us, we will completely destroy their cities." The LORD listened to Israel's request and handed the Canaanites over to them, and Israel completely destroyed them and their cities. So they named the place Hormah.

Then they set out from Mount Hor by way of the Red Sea to bypass the land of Edom, but the people became impatient because of the journey. The people spoke against God and Moses: "Why have you led us up from Egypt to die in the wilderness? There is no bread or water, and we detest this wretched food!" Then the LORD sent poisonous snakes among the people, and they bit them
10 so that many Israelites died.

The people then came to Moses and said, "We have sinned by speaking against the LORD and against you. Intercede with the LORD so that he will take the snakes away from us." And Moses interceded for the people.

Then the LORD said to Moses, "Make a snake image and mount it on a pole. When anyone who is bitten looks at it, he will recover." So Moses made a bronze snake and mounted it on a pole. Whenever someone was bitten, and he looked at the bronze snake, he recovered.

The Israelites set out and camped at Oboth. They set out from Oboth and camped at Iye-abarim in the wilderness that borders Moab on the east. From there they went and camped at Zered Valley. They set out from there and camped on the other side of the Arnon River, in the
20 wilderness that extends from the Amorite border, because the Arnon was the Moabite border between Moab and the Amorites. Therefore it is stated in the Book of the LORD's Wars:

> Waheb in Suphah
> and the ravines of the Arnon,
> even the slopes of the ravines
> that extend to the site of Ar
> and lie along the border of Moab.

From there they went to Beer, the well the LORD told Moses about, "Gather the people so I may give them water." Then Israel sang this song:

> Spring up, well—sing to it!
> The princes dug the well;
> the nobles of the people hollowed it out
> with a scepter and with their staffs.

They went from the wilderness to Mattanah, from Mattanah to Nahaliel, from Nahaliel to Bamoth, from Bamoth to the valley in the territory of Moab near the Pisgah highlands that overlook the wasteland.

Israel sent messengers to say to King Sihon of the Amorites, "Let us travel through your land. We won't go into the fields or vineyards. We won't drink any well water. We will travel the King's Highway until we have traveled through your territory." But Sihon would not let Israel travel through his territory. Instead, he gathered his whole army and went out to confront Israel in the wilderness. When he came to Jahaz, he fought against Israel. Israel struck him with the sword and took possession of his land from the Arnon to the Jabbok, but only up to the Ammonite border, because it was fortified.

Israel took all the cities and lived in all these Amorite cities, including Heshbon and all its surrounding villages. Heshbon was the city of King Sihon of the Amorites, who had fought against the former king of Moab and had taken control of all his land as far as the Arnon. Therefore the poets say:

> Come to Heshbon, let it be rebuilt;
> let the city of Sihon be restored.
> For fire came out of Heshbon,
> a flame from the city of Sihon.
> It consumed Ar of Moab,
> the citizens of Arnon's heights.
> Woe to you, Moab!
> You have been destroyed, people of Chemosh!
> He gave up his sons as refugees,
> and his daughters into captivity
> to Sihon the Amorite king.
> We threw them down;
> Heshbon has been destroyed as far as Dibon.
> We caused desolation as far as Nophah,
> which reaches as far as Medeba.

So Israel lived in the Amorites' land. After Moses sent spies to Jazer, Israel captured its surrounding villages and drove out the Amorites who were there.

Then they turned and went up the road to Bashan, and King Og of Bashan came out against them with his whole army to do battle at Edrei. But the LORD said to Moses, "Do not fear him, for I have handed him over to you along with his whole army and his land. Do to him as you did to King Sihon of the Amorites, who lived in Heshbon." So they struck him, his sons, and his whole army until no one was left, and they took possession of his land.

22 The Israelites traveled on and camped in the plains of Moab near the Jordan across from Jericho. Now Balak son of Zippor saw all that Israel had done to the Amorites. Moab was terrified of the people because they were numerous, and Moab dreaded the Israelites. So the Moabites said to the elders of Midian, "This horde will devour everything around us like an ox eats up the green plants in the field."

Since Balak son of Zippor was Moab's king at that time, he sent messengers to Balaam son of Beor at Pethor, which is by the Euphrates in the land of his people. Balak said to him, "Look, a people has come out of Egypt; they cover the surface of the land and are living right across from me. Please come and put a curse on these people for me because they are more powerful than I am. I may be able to defeat them and drive them out of the land, for I know that those you bless are 10 blessed and those you curse are cursed."

The elders of Moab and Midian departed with fees for divination in hand. They came to Balaam and reported Balak's words to him. He said to them, "Spend the night here, and I will give you the answer the LORD tells me." So the officials of Moab stayed with Balaam.

Then God came to Balaam and asked, "Who are these men with you?"

Balaam replied to God, "Balak son of Zippor, king of Moab, sent this message to me: 'Look, a people has come out of Egypt, and they cover the surface of the land. Now come and put a curse on them for me. I may be able to fight against them and drive them away.'"

Then God said to Balaam, "You are not to go with them. You are not to curse this people, for they are blessed."

20 So Balaam got up the next morning and said to Balak's officials, "Go back to your land, because the LORD has refused to let me go with you."

The officials of Moab arose, returned to Balak, and reported, "Balaam refused to come with us."

Balak sent officials again who were more numerous and higher in rank than the others. They came to Balaam and said to him, "This is what Balak son of Zippor says: 'Let nothing keep you from coming to me, for I will greatly honor you and do whatever you ask me. So please come and put a curse on these people for me!'"

But Balaam responded to the servants of Balak, "If Balak were to give me his house full of silver and gold, I could not go against the command of the LORD my God to do anything small or great. Please stay here overnight as the others did, so that I may find out what else the LORD has to tell 30 me."

God came to Balaam at night and said to him, "Since these men have come to summon you, get up and go with them, but you must only do what I tell you." When he got up in the morning, Balaam saddled his donkey and went with the officials of Moab.

But God was incensed that Balaam was going, and the angel of the LORD took his stand on the path to oppose him. Balaam was riding his donkey, and his two servants were with him. When the donkey saw the angel of the LORD standing on the path with a drawn sword in his hand, she turned off the path and went into the field. So Balaam hit her to return her to the path. Then the angel of the LORD stood in a narrow passage between the vineyards, with a stone wall on either side. The donkey saw the angel of the LORD and pressed herself against the wall, squeezing

40 Balaam's foot against it. So he hit her once again. The angel of the LORD went ahead and stood in a narrow place where there was no room to turn to the right or the left. When the donkey saw the angel of the LORD, she crouched down under Balaam. So he became furious and beat the donkey with his stick.

Then the LORD opened the donkey's mouth, and she asked Balaam, "What have I done to you that you have beaten me these three times?"

Balaam answered the donkey, "You made me look like a fool. If I had a sword in my hand, I'd kill you now!"

But the donkey said, "Am I not the donkey you've ridden all your life until today? Have I ever treated you this way before?"

50 "No," he replied.

Then the LORD opened Balaam's eyes, and he saw the angel of the LORD standing in the path with a drawn sword in his hand. Balaam knelt low and bowed in worship on his face. The angel of the LORD asked him, "Why have you beaten your donkey these three times? Look, I came out to oppose you, because I consider what you are doing to be evil. The donkey saw me and turned away from me these three times. If she had not turned away from me, I would have killed you by now and let her live."

Balaam said to the angel of the LORD, "I have sinned, for I did not know that you were standing in the path to confront me. And now, if it is evil in your sight, I will go back."

Then the angel of the LORD said to Balaam, "Go with the men, but you are to say only what I

60 tell you." So Balaam went with Balak's officials.

When Balak heard that Balaam was coming, he went out to meet him at the Moabite city on the Arnon border at the edge of his territory. Balak asked Balaam, "Did I not send you an urgent summons? Why didn't you come to me? Am I really not able to reward you?"

Balaam said to him, "Look, I have come to you, but can I say anything I want? I must speak only the message God puts in my mouth." So Balaam went with Balak, and they came to Kiriath-huzoth. Balak sacrificed cattle, sheep, and goats and sent for Balaam and the officials who were with him.

In the morning, Balak took Balaam and brought him to Bamoth-baal. From there he saw the outskirts of the people's camp.

23 Then Balaam said to Balak, "Build me seven altars here and prepare seven bulls and seven rams for me." So Balak did as Balaam directed, and they offered a bull and a ram on each altar. Balaam said to Balak, "Stay here by your burnt offering while I am gone. Maybe the LORD will meet with me. I will tell you whatever he reveals to me." So he went to a barren hill.

God met with him and Balaam said to him, "I have arranged seven altars and offered a bull and a ram on each altar." Then the LORD put a message in Balaam's mouth and said, "Return to Balak and say what I tell you."

So he returned to Balak, who was standing there by his burnt offering with all the officials of Moab.

10 Balaam proclaimed his poem:

> Balak brought me from Aram;
> the king of Moab, from the eastern mountains:
> "Come, put a curse on Jacob for me;
> come, denounce Israel!"
> How can I curse someone God has not cursed?
> How can I denounce someone the LORD has not denounced?
> I see them from the top of rocky cliffs,
> and I watch them from the hills.
> There is a people living alone;
> 20   it does not consider itself among the nations.
> Who has counted the dust of Jacob
> or numbered even one-fourth of Israel?
> Let me die the death of the upright;
> let the end of my life be like theirs.

"What have you done to me?" Balak asked Balaam. "I brought you to curse my enemies, but look, you have only blessed them!"

He answered, "Shouldn't I say exactly what the LORD puts in my mouth?"

Then Balak said to him, "Please come with me to another place where you can see them. You will only see the outskirts of their camp; you won't see all of them. From there, put a curse on them for 30 me." So Balak took him to Lookout Field on top of Pisgah, built seven altars, and offered a bull and a ram on each altar.

Balaam said to Balak, "Stay here by your burnt offering while I seek the LORD over there."

The Lord met with Balaam and put a message in his mouth. Then he said, "Return to Balak and say what I tell you."

So he returned to Balak, who was standing there by his burnt offering with the officials of Moab. Balak asked him, "What did the Lord say?"

Balaam proclaimed his poem:

> Balak, get up and listen;
> son of Zippor, pay attention to what I say!

40
> God is not a man, that he might lie,
> or a son of man, that he might change his mind.
> Does he speak and not act,
> or promise and not fulfill?
> I have indeed received a command to bless;
> since he has blessed, I cannot change it.
> He considers no disaster for Jacob;
> he sees no trouble for Israel.
> The Lord their God is with them,
> and there is rejoicing over the King among them.

50
> God brought them out of Egypt;
> he is like the horns of a wild ox for them.
> There is no magic curse against Jacob
> and no divination against Israel.
> It will now be said about Jacob and Israel,
> "What great things God has done!"
> A people rise up like a lioness;
> they rouse themselves like a lion.
> They will not lie down until they devour the prey
> and drink the blood of the slain.

60
Then Balak told Balaam, "Don't curse them and don't bless them!"

But Balaam answered him, "Didn't I tell you: Whatever the Lord says, I must do?"

Again Balak said to Balaam, "Please come. I will take you to another place. Maybe it will be agreeable to God that you can put a curse on them for me there." So Balak took Balaam to the top of Peor, which overlooks the wasteland.

Balaam told Balak, "Build me seven altars here and prepare seven bulls and seven rams for me." So Balak did as Balaam said and offered a bull and a ram on each altar.

24 Since Balaam saw that it pleased the Lord to bless Israel, he did not go to seek omens as on previous occasions, but turned toward the wilderness. When Balaam looked up and saw Israel encamped tribe by tribe, the Spirit of God came on him, and he proclaimed his poem:

> The oracle of Balaam son of Beor,
> the oracle of the man whose eyes are opened,
> the oracle of one who hears the sayings of God,
> who sees a vision from the Almighty,
> who falls into a trance with his eyes uncovered:
> How beautiful are your tents, Jacob,
> your dwellings, Israel.
> They stretch out like river valleys,
> like gardens beside a stream,
> like aloes the Lord has planted,
> like cedars beside the water.
> Water will flow from his buckets,
> and his seed will be by abundant water.
> His king will be greater than Agag,
> and his kingdom will be exalted.
> God brought him out of Egypt;
> he is like the horns of a wild ox for them.
> He will feed on enemy nations
> and gnaw their bones;
> he will strike them with his arrows.
> He crouches, he lies down like a lion
> or a lioness—who dares to rouse him?
> Those who bless you will be blessed,
> and those who curse you will be cursed.

Then Balak became furious with Balaam, struck his hands together, and said to him, "I summoned you to put a curse on my enemies, but instead, you have blessed them these three times. Now go to your home! I said I would reward you richly, but look, the Lord has denied you a reward."

Balaam answered Balak, "Didn't I previously tell the messengers you sent me: If Balak were to give me his house full of silver and gold, I could not go against the Lord's command, to do anything good or bad of my own will? I will say whatever the Lord says. Now I am going back to my people, but first, let me warn you what these people will do to your people in the future."

Then he proclaimed his poem:

> The oracle of Balaam son of Beor,
> the oracle of the man whose eyes are opened;
> the oracle of one who hears the sayings of God
> and has knowledge from the Most High,
> who sees a vision from the Almighty,
> who falls into a trance with his eyes uncovered:
> I see him, but not now;
> I perceive him, but not near.
> A star will come from Jacob,
> and a scepter will arise from Israel.
> He will smash the forehead of Moab
> and strike down all the Shethites.
> Edom will become a possession;
> Seir will become a possession of its enemies,
> but Israel will be triumphant.
> One who comes from Jacob will rule;
> he will destroy the city's survivors.

Then Balaam saw Amalek and proclaimed his poem:

> Amalek was first among the nations,
> but his future is destruction.

Next he saw the Kenites and proclaimed his poem:

> Your dwelling place is enduring;
> your nest is set in the cliffs.
> Kain will be destroyed
> when Asshur takes you captive.

Once more he proclaimed his poem:

> Ah, who can live when God does this?
> Ships will come from the coast of Kittim;
> they will carry out raids against Asshur and Eber,
> but they too will come to destruction.

Balaam then arose and went back to his homeland, and Balak also went his way.

25 While Israel was staying in the Acacia Grove, the people began to prostitute themselves with the women of Moab. The women invited them to the sacrifices for their gods, and the people ate and bowed in worship to their gods. So Israel aligned itself with Baal of Peor, and the LORD's anger burned against Israel. The LORD said to Moses, "Take all the leaders of the people and execute them in broad daylight before the LORD so that his burning anger may turn away from Israel."

So Moses told Israel's judges, "Kill each of the men who aligned themselves with Baal of Peor."

An Israelite man came bringing a Midianite woman to his relatives in the sight of Moses and the whole Israelite community while they were weeping at the entrance to the tent of meeting. When Phinehas son of Eleazar, son of Aaron the priest, saw this, he got up from the assembly, took a spear in his hand, followed the Israelite man into the tent, and drove it through both the Israelite man and the woman—through her belly. Then the plague on the Israelites was stopped, but those who died in the plague numbered twenty-four thousand.

The LORD spoke to Moses, "Phinehas son of Eleazar, son of Aaron the priest, has turned back my wrath from the Israelites because he was zealous among them with my zeal, so that I did not destroy the Israelites in my zeal. Therefore declare: I grant him my covenant of peace. It will be a covenant of perpetual priesthood for him and his future descendants, because he was zealous for his God and made atonement for the Israelites."

The name of the slain Israelite man, who was struck dead with the Midianite woman, was Zimri son of Salu, the leader of a Simeonite family. The name of the slain Midianite woman was Cozbi, the daughter of Zur, a tribal head of a family in Midian.

The LORD told Moses, "Attack the Midianites and strike them dead. For they attacked you with the treachery that they used against you in the Peor incident. They did the same in the case involving their sister Cozbi, daughter of the Midianite leader who was killed the day the plague came at Peor."

26 After the plague, the LORD said to Moses and Eleazar son of Aaron the priest, "Take a census of the entire Israelite community by their ancestral families of those twenty years old or more who can serve in Israel's army."

So Moses and the priest Eleazar said to them in the plains of Moab by the Jordan across from Jericho, "Take a census of those twenty years old or more, as the LORD had commanded Moses and the Israelites who came out of the land of Egypt."

Reuben was the firstborn of Israel.
Reuben's descendants:
the Hanochite clan from Hanoch;
the Palluite clan from Pallu;
the Hezronite clan from Hezron;
the Carmite clan from Carmi.
These were the Reubenite clans,
and their registered men numbered 43,730.

The son of Pallu was Eliab.

The sons of Eliab were Nemuel, Dathan, and Abiram.

(It was Dathan and Abiram, chosen by the community, who fought against Moses and Aaron; they and Korah's followers fought against the Lord. The earth opened its mouth and swallowed them with Korah, when his followers died and the fire consumed 250 men. They serve as a warning sign. The sons of Korah, however, did not die.)

Simeon's descendants by their clans:

the Nemuelite clan from Nemuel;

the Jaminite clan from Jamin;

the Jachinite clan from Jachin;

the Zerahite clan from Zerah;

the Shaulite clan from Shaul.

These were the Simeonite clans, numbering 22,200 men.

Gad's descendants by their clans:

the Zephonite clan from Zephon;

the Haggite clan from Haggi;

the Shunite clan from Shuni;

the Oznite clan from Ozni;

the Erite clan from Eri;

the Arodite clan from Arod;

the Arelite clan from Areli.

These were the Gadite clans numbered by their registered men: 40,500.

Judah's sons included Er and Onan, but they died in the land of Canaan. Judah's descendants by their clans:

the Shelanite clan from Shelah;

the Perezite clan from Perez;

the Zerahite clan from Zerah.

The descendants of Perez:

the Hezronite clan from Hezron;

the Hamulite clan from Hamul.

These were Judah's clans numbered by their registered men: 76,500.

Issachar's descendants by their clans:

the Tolaite clan from Tola;

the Punite clan from Puvah;

the Jashubite clan from Jashub;
50   the Shimronite clan from Shimron.
These were Issachar's clans numbered by their registered men: 64,300.

Zebulun's descendants by their clans:
the Seredite clan from Sered;
the Elonite clan from Elon;
the Jahleelite clan from Jahleel.
These were the Zebulunite clans numbered by their registered men: 60,500.

Joseph's descendants by their clans from Manasseh and Ephraim:
Manasseh's descendants:
the Machirite clan from Machir.
60   Machir fathered Gilead;
the Gileadite clan from Gilead.
These were Gilead's descendants:
the Iezerite clan from Iezer;
the Helekite clan from Helek;
the Asrielite clan from Asriel;
the Shechemite clan from Shechem;
the Shemidaite clan from Shemida;
the Hepherite clan from Hepher;
Zelophehad son of Hepher had no sons—only daughters. The names of Zelophehad's
70   daughters were Mahlah, Noah, Hoglah, Milcah, and Tirzah.
These were Manasseh's clans, numbered by their registered men: 52,700.
These were Ephraim's descendants by their clans:
the Shuthelahite clan from Shuthelah;
the Becherite clan from Becher;
the Tahanite clan from Tahan.
These were Shuthelah's descendants:
the Eranite clan from Eran.
These were the Ephraimite clans numbered by their registered men: 32,500.
These were Joseph's descendants by their clans.

80   Benjamin's descendants by their clans:
the Belaite clan from Bela;
the Ashbelite clan from Ashbel;
the Ahiramite clan from Ahiram;

the Shuphamite clan from Shupham;
the Huphamite clan from Hupham.
Bela's descendants from Ard and Naaman:
the Ardite clan from Ard;
the Naamite clan from Naaman.
These were the Benjaminite clans numbered by their registered men: 45,600.

90 These were Dan's descendants by their clans:
the Shuhamite clan from Shuham.
These were the clans of Dan by their clans.
All the Shuhamite clans numbered by their registered men: 64,400.

Asher's descendants by their clans:
the Imnite clan from Imnah;
the Ishvite clan from Ishvi;
the Beriite clan from Beriah.
From Beriah's descendants:
the Heberite clan from Heber;
100 the Malchielite clan from Malchiel.
And the name of Asher's daughter was Serah.
These were the Asherite clans numbered by their registered men: 53,400.

Naphtali's descendants by their clans:
the Jahzeelite clan from Jahzeel;
the Gunite clan from Guni;
the Jezerite clan from Jezer;
the Shillemite clan from Shillem.
These were the Naphtali clans numbered by their registered men: 45,400.

These registered Israelite men numbered 601,730.

110 The LORD spoke to Moses, "The land is to be divided among them as an inheritance based
on the number of names. Increase the inheritance for a large tribe and decrease it for a small one.
Each is to be given its inheritance according to those who were registered in it. The land is to be
divided by lot; they will receive an inheritance according to the names of their ancestral tribes.
Each inheritance will be divided by lot among the larger and smaller tribes."
These were the Levites registered by their clans:
the Gershonite clan from Gershon;

the Kohathite clan from Kohath;
the Merarite clan from Merari.
These were the Levite family groups:
120   the Libnite clan,
the Hebronite clan,
the Mahlite clan,
the Mushite clan,
and the Korahite clan.

Kohath was the ancestor of Amram. The name of Amram's wife was Jochebed, a descendant of Levi, born to Levi in Egypt. She bore to Amram: Aaron, Moses, and their sister Miriam. Nadab, Abihu, Eleazar, and Ithamar were born to Aaron, but Nadab and Abihu died when they presented unauthorized fire before the LORD. Those registered were 23,000, every male one month old or more; they were not registered among the other Israelites, because no inheritance 130 was given to them among the Israelites.

These were the ones registered by Moses and the priest Eleazar when they registered the Israelites on the plains of Moab by the Jordan across from Jericho. But among them there was not one of those who had been registered by Moses and the priest Aaron when they registered the Israelites in the Wilderness of Sinai. For the LORD had said to them that they would all die in the wilderness. None of them was left except Caleb son of Jephunneh and Joshua son of Nun.

27 The daughters of Zelophehad approached; Zelophehad was the son of Hepher, son of Gilead, son of Machir, son of Manasseh from the clans of Manasseh, the son of Joseph. These were the names of his daughters: Mahlah, Noah, Hoglah, Milcah, and Tirzah. They stood before Moses, the priest Eleazar, the leaders, and the entire community at the entrance to the tent of meeting and said, "Our father died in the wilderness, but he was not among Korah's followers, who gathered together against the LORD. Instead, he died because of his own sin, and he had no sons. Why should the name of our father be taken away from his clan? Since he had no son, give us property among our father's brothers."

Moses brought their case before the LORD, and the LORD answered him, "What Zelophehad's daughters say is correct. You are to give them hereditary property among their father's brothers 10 and transfer their father's inheritance to them. Tell the Israelites: When a man dies without having a son, transfer his inheritance to his daughter. If he has no daughter, give his inheritance to his brothers. If he has no brothers, give his inheritance to his father's brothers. If his father has no brothers, give his inheritance to the nearest relative of his clan, and he will take possession of it. This is to be a statutory ordinance for the Israelites as the LORD commanded Moses."

Then the LORD said to Moses, "Go up this mountain of the Abarim range and see the land that I have given the Israelites. After you have seen it, you will also be gathered to your people, as Aaron your brother was. When the community quarreled in the Wilderness of Zin, both of you rebelled against my command to demonstrate my holiness in their sight at the waters." Those were the Waters of Meribah-kadesh in the Wilderness of Zin.

20 So Moses appealed to the LORD, "May the LORD, the God who gives breath to all, appoint a man over the community who will go out before them and come back in before them, and who will bring them out and bring them in, so that the LORD's community won't be like sheep without a shepherd."

The LORD replied to Moses, "Take Joshua son of Nun, a man who has the Spirit in him, and lay your hands on him. Have him stand before the priest Eleazar and the whole community, and commission him in their sight. Confer some of your authority on him so that the entire Israelite community will obey him. He will stand before the priest Eleazar who will consult the LORD for him with the decision of the Urim. He and all the Israelites with him, even the entire community, will go out and come back in at his command."

Moses did as the LORD commanded him. He took Joshua, had him stand before the priest 30 Eleazar and the entire community, laid his hands on him, and commissioned him, as the LORD had spoken through Moses.

28 The LORD spoke to Moses, "Command the Israelites and say to them: Be sure to present to me at its appointed time my offering and my food as my food offering, a pleasing aroma to me. And say to them: This is the food offering you are to present to the LORD:

"Each day present two unblemished year-old male lambs as a regular burnt offering. Offer one lamb in the morning and the other lamb at twilight, along with two quarts of fine flour for a grain offering mixed with a quart of olive oil from crushed olives. It is a regular burnt offering established at Mount Sinai for a pleasing aroma, a food offering to the LORD. The drink offering is to be a quart with each lamb. Pour out the offering of beer to the LORD in the sanctuary area. Offer the second lamb at twilight, along with the same kind of grain offering and drink offering as 10 in the morning. It is a food offering, a pleasing aroma to the LORD.

"On the Sabbath day present two unblemished year-old male lambs, four quarts of fine flour mixed with oil as a grain offering, and its drink offering. It is the burnt offering for every Sabbath, in addition to the regular burnt offering and its drink offering.

"At the beginning of each of your months present a burnt offering to the LORD: two young bulls, one ram, seven male lambs a year old—all unblemished—with six quarts of fine flour mixed with oil as a grain offering for each bull, four quarts of fine flour mixed with oil as a grain offering for the ram, and two quarts of fine flour mixed with oil as a grain offering for each lamb. It is a burnt offering, a pleasing aroma, a food offering to the LORD. Their drink offerings are to be two quarts of wine with each bull, one and a third quarts with the ram, and one quart with each male lamb. This

20 is the monthly burnt offering for all the months of the year. And one male goat is to be offered as a sin offering to the LORD, in addition to the regular burnt offering with its drink offering.

"The Passover to the LORD comes in the first month, on the fourteenth day of the month. On the fifteenth day of this month there will be a festival; unleavened bread is to be eaten for seven days. On the first day there is to be a sacred assembly; you are not to do any daily work. Present a food offering, a burnt offering to the LORD: two young bulls, one ram, and seven male lambs a year old. Your animals are to be unblemished. The grain offering with them is to be of fine flour mixed with oil; offer six quarts with each bull and four quarts with the ram. Offer two quarts with each of the seven lambs and one male goat for a sin offering to make atonement for yourselves. Offer these with the morning burnt offering that is part of the regular burnt offering. You are to offer the same food each day for seven days as a food 30 offering, a pleasing aroma to the LORD. It is to be offered with its drink offering and the regular burnt offering. On the seventh day you are to hold a sacred assembly; you are not to do any daily work.

"On the day of firstfruits, you are to hold a sacred assembly when you present an offering of new grain to the LORD at your Festival of Weeks; you are not to do any daily work. Present a burnt offering as a pleasing aroma to the LORD: two young bulls, one ram, and seven male lambs a year old, with their grain offering of fine flour mixed with oil, six quarts with each bull, four quarts with the ram, and two quarts with each of the seven lambs, and one male goat to make atonement for yourselves. Offer them with their drink offerings in addition to the regular burnt offering and its grain offering. Your animals are to be unblemished.

29 "You are to hold a sacred assembly in the seventh month, on the first day of the month, and you are not to do any daily work. This will be a day of trumpet blasts for you. Offer a burnt offering as a pleasing aroma to the LORD: one young bull, one ram, seven male lambs a year old—all unblemished—with their grain offering of fine flour mixed with oil, six quarts with the bull, four quarts with the ram, and two quarts with each of the seven male lambs. Also offer one male goat as a sin offering to make atonement for yourselves. These are in addition to the monthly and regular burnt offerings with their prescribed grain offerings and drink offerings. They are a pleasing aroma, a food offering to the LORD.

"You are to hold a sacred assembly on the tenth day of this seventh month and practice self-denial; do not do any work. Present a burnt offering to the LORD, a pleasing aroma: one young bull, one 10 ram, and seven male lambs a year old. All your animals are to be unblemished. Their grain offering is to be of fine flour mixed with oil, six quarts with the bull, four quarts with the ram, and two quarts with each of the seven lambs. Offer one male goat for a sin offering. The regular burnt offering with its grain offering and drink offerings are in addition to the sin offering of atonement.

"You are to hold a sacred assembly on the fifteenth day of the seventh month; you do not do any daily work. You are to celebrate a seven-day festival for the LORD. Present a burnt offering, a food offering, a pleasing aroma to the LORD: thirteen young bulls, two rams, and fourteen male lambs a year old. They are to be unblemished. Their grain offering is to be of fine flour mixed with oil, six quarts with each of the thirteen bulls, four quarts with each of the two rams, and two quarts with each of the fourteen lambs. Also offer one male goat as a sin offering. These are in addition to the regular burnt offering with its grain and drink offerings.

"On the second day present twelve young bulls, two rams, and fourteen male lambs a year old—all unblemished—with their grain and drink offerings for the bulls, rams, and lambs, in proportion to their number. Also offer one male goat as a sin offering. These are in addition to the regular burnt offering with its grain and drink and their drink offerings.

"On the third day present eleven bulls, two rams, fourteen male lambs a year old—all unblemished—with their grain and drink offerings for the bulls, rams, and lambs, in proportion to their number. Also offer one male goat as a sin offering. These are in addition to the regular burnt offering with its grain and drink offerings.

"On the fourth day present ten bulls, two rams, fourteen male lambs a year old—all unblemished—with their grain and drink offerings for the bulls, rams, and lambs, in proportion to their number. Also offer one male goat as a sin offering. These are in addition to the regular burnt offering with its grain and drink offerings.

"On the fifth day present nine bulls, two rams, fourteen male lambs a year old—all unblemished—with their grain and drink offerings for the bulls, rams, and lambs, in proportion to their number. Also offer one male goat as a sin offering. These are in addition to the regular burnt offering with its grain and drink offerings.

"On the sixth day present eight bulls, two rams, fourteen male lambs a year old—all unblemished—with their grain and drink offerings for the bulls, rams, and lambs, in proportion to their number. Also offer one male goat as a sin offering. These are in addition to the regular burnt offering with its grain and drink offerings.

"On the seventh day present seven bulls, two rams, and fourteen male lambs a year old—all unblemished—with their grain and drink offerings for the bulls, rams, and lambs, in proportion to their number. Also offer one male goat as a sin offering. These are in addition to the regular burnt offering with its grain and drink offerings.

"On the eighth day you are to hold a solemn assembly; you are not to do any daily work. Present a burnt offering, a food offering, a pleasing aroma to the LORD: one bull, one ram, seven male lambs a year old—all unblemished—with their grain and drink offerings for the bulls, rams, and lambs, in proportion to their number. Also offer one male goat as a sin offering. These are in addition to the regular burnt offering with its grain and drink offerings.

"Offer these to the LORD at your appointed times in addition to your vow and freewill offerings, whether burnt, grain, drink, or fellowship offerings." So Moses told the Israelites everything the LORD had commanded him.

30 Moses told the leaders of the Israelite tribes, "This is what the LORD has commanded: When a man makes a vow to the LORD or swears an oath to put himself under an obligation, he must not break his word; he must do whatever he has promised.

"When a woman in her father's house during her youth makes a vow to the LORD or puts herself under an obligation, and her father hears about her vow or the obligation she put herself under, and he says nothing to her, all her vows and every obligation she put herself under are binding. But if her father prohibits her on the day he hears about it, none of her vows and none of the obligations she put herself under are binding. The LORD will release her because her father has prohibited her.

10 "If a woman marries while her vows or the rash commitment she herself made are binding, and her husband hears about it and says nothing to her when he finds out, her vows are binding, and the obligations she put herself under are binding. But if her husband prohibits her when he hears about it, he will cancel her vow that is binding or the rash commitment she herself made, and the LORD will release her.

"Every vow a widow or divorced woman puts herself under is binding on her.

"If a woman in her husband's house has made a vow or put herself under an obligation with an oath, and her husband hears about it, says nothing to her, and does not prohibit her, all her vows are binding, and every obligation she put herself under is binding. But if her husband cancels them on the day he hears about it, nothing that came from her lips, whether her vows or her obligation, 20 is binding. Her husband has canceled them, and the LORD will release her. Her husband may confirm or cancel any vow or any sworn obligation to deny herself. If her husband says nothing at all to her from day to day, he confirms all her vows and obligations, which are binding. He has confirmed them because he said nothing to her when he heard about them. But if he cancels them after he hears about them, he will be responsible for her commitment."

These are the statutes that the LORD commanded Moses concerning the relationship between a man and his wife, or between a father and his daughter in his house during her youth.

31 The LORD spoke to Moses, "Execute vengeance for the Israelites against the Midianites. After that, you will be gathered to your people."

So Moses spoke to the people, "Equip some of your men for war. They will go against Midian to inflict the LORD's vengeance on them. Send one thousand men to war from each Israelite tribe." So one thousand were recruited from each Israelite tribe out of the thousands in Israel—twelve thousand equipped for war. Moses sent one thousand from each tribe to war. They went with Phinehas son of Eleazar the priest, in whose care were the holy objects and signal trumpets.

They waged war against Midian, as the LORD had commanded Moses, and killed every male. Along with the others slain by them, they killed the Midianite kings—Evi, Rekem, Zur, Hur, and 10 Reba, the five kings of Midian. They also killed Balaam son of Beor with the sword. The Israelites took the Midianite women and their dependents captive, and they plundered all their cattle, flocks, and property. Then they burned all the cities where the Midianites lived, as well as all their encampments, and took away all the spoils of war and the captives, both people and animals. They brought the prisoners, animals, and spoils of war to Moses, the priest Eleazar, and the Israelite community at the camp on the plains of Moab by the Jordan across from Jericho.

Moses, the priest Eleazar, and all the leaders of the community went to meet them outside the camp. But Moses became furious with the officers, the commanders of thousands and commanders of hundreds, who were returning from the military campaign. "Have you let every female live?" he asked them. "Yet they are the ones who, at Balaam's advice, incited the Israelites to unfaithfulness against the LORD in the Peor incident, so that the plague came against the LORD's community. So now, kill every male among the dependents and kill every woman who has gone to bed with a man, but keep alive for yourselves all the young females who have not gone to bed with a man.

"You are to remain outside the camp for seven days. All of you and your prisoners who have killed a person or touched the dead are to purify yourselves on the third day and the seventh day. Also purify everything: garments, leather goods, things made of goat hair, and every article of wood."

Then the priest Eleazar said to the soldiers who had gone to battle, "This is the legal statute the LORD commanded Moses: The gold, silver, bronze, iron, tin, and lead—everything that can withstand fire—you are to pass through fire, and it will be clean. It must still be purified with the purification water. Anything that cannot withstand fire, pass through the water. On the seventh day wash your clothes, and you will be clean. After that you may enter the camp."

The LORD told Moses, "You, the priest Eleazar, and the family heads of the community are to take a count of what was captured, people and animals. Then divide the captives between the troops who went out to war and the entire community. Set aside a tribute for the LORD from what belongs to the fighting men who went out to war: one out of every five hundred people, cattle, donkeys, sheep, and goats. Take the tribute from their half and give it to the priest Eleazar as a contribution to the LORD. From the Israelites' half, take one out of every fifty from the people, cattle, donkeys, sheep, and goats, all the livestock, and give them to the Levites who perform the duties of the LORD's tabernacle."

So Moses and the priest Eleazar did as the LORD commanded Moses. The captives remaining from the plunder the army had taken totaled:

> 675,000 sheep and goats,
> 72,000 cattle,
> 61,000 donkeys,
> and 32,000 people, all the females who had not gone to bed with a man.

The half portion for those who went out to war numbered:

> 337,500 sheep and goats,
> and the tribute to the LORD was 675
> from the sheep and goats;

from the 36,000 cattle,

50   the tribute to the LORD was 72;

from the 30,500 donkeys,

the tribute to the LORD was 61;

and from the 16,000 people,

the tribute to the LORD was 32 people.

Moses gave the tribute to the priest Eleazar as a contribution for the LORD, as the LORD had commanded Moses.

From the Israelites' half, which Moses separated from the men who fought, the community's half was:

337,500 sheep and goats,

60   36,000 cattle,

30,500 donkeys,

and 16,000 people.

Moses took one out of every fifty, selected from the people and the livestock of the Israelites' half. He gave them to the Levites who perform the duties of the LORD's tabernacle, as the LORD had commanded him.

The officers who were over the thousands of the army, the commanders of thousands and of hundreds, approached Moses and told him, "Your servants have taken a census of the fighting men under our command, and not one of us is missing. So we have presented to the LORD an offering of the gold articles each man found—armlets, bracelets, rings, earrings, and necklaces—to make

70 atonement for ourselves before the LORD."

Moses and the priest Eleazar received from them all the articles made out of gold. All the gold of the contribution they offered to the LORD, from the commanders of thousands and of hundreds, was 420 pounds. Each of the soldiers had taken plunder for himself. Moses and the priest Eleazar received the gold from the commanders of thousands and of hundreds and brought it into the tent of meeting as a memorial for the Israelites before the LORD.

32 The Reubenites and Gadites had a very large number of livestock. When they surveyed the lands of Jazer and Gilead, they saw that the region was a good one for livestock. So the Gadites and Reubenites came to Moses, the priest Eleazar, and the leaders of the community and said, "The territory of Ataroth, Dibon, Jazer, Nimrah, Heshbon, Elealeh, Sebam, Nebo, and Beon, which the LORD struck down before the community of Israel, is good land for livestock, and your servants own livestock." They said, "If we have found favor with you, let this land be given to your servants as a possession. Don't make us cross the Jordan."

But Moses asked the Gadites and Reubenites, "Should your brothers go to war while you stay here? Why are you discouraging the Israelites from crossing into the land the LORD has given

10 them? That's what your ancestors did when I sent them from Kadesh-barnea to see the land.

After they went up as far as Eshcol Valley and saw the land, they discouraged the Israelites from entering the land the Lord had given them. So the Lord's anger burned that day, and he swore an oath: 'Because they did not remain loyal to me, none of the men twenty years old or more who came up from Egypt will see the land I swore to give Abraham, Isaac, and Jacob—none except Caleb son of Jephunneh the Kenizzite and Joshua son of Nun, because they did remain loyal to the Lord.' The Lord's anger burned against Israel, and he made them wander in the wilderness forty years until the whole generation that had done what was evil in the Lord's sight was gone. And here you, a brood of sinners, stand in your ancestors' place adding even more to the Lord's burning anger against Israel. If you turn back from following him, he will once again leave this

20 people in the wilderness, and you will destroy all of them."

Then they approached him and said, "We want to build sheep pens here for our livestock and cities for our dependents. But we will arm ourselves and be ready to go ahead of the Israelites until we have brought them into their place. Meanwhile, our dependents will remain in the fortified cities because of the inhabitants of the land. We will not return to our homes until each of the Israelites has taken possession of his inheritance. Yet we will not have an inheritance with them across the Jordan and beyond, because our inheritance will be across the Jordan to the east."

Moses replied to them, "If you do this—if you arm yourselves for battle before the Lord, and every one of your armed men crosses the Jordan before the Lord until he has driven his enemies from his presence, and the land is subdued before the Lord—afterward you may return and be

30 free from obligation to the Lord and to Israel. And this land will belong to you as a possession before the Lord. But if you don't do this, you will certainly sin against the Lord; be sure your sin will catch up with you. Build cities for your dependents and pens for your flocks, but do what you have promised."

The Gadites and Reubenites answered Moses, "Your servants will do just as my lord commands. Our dependents, wives, livestock, and all our animals will remain here in the cities of Gilead, but your servants are equipped for war before the Lord and will go across to the battle as my lord orders."

So Moses gave orders about them to the priest Eleazar, Joshua son of Nun, and the family heads of the Israelite tribes. Moses told them, "If the Gadites and Reubenites cross the Jordan

40 with you, every man in battle formation before the Lord, and the land is subdued before you, you are to give them the land of Gilead as a possession. But if they don't go across with you in battle formation, they must accept land in Canaan with you."

The Gadites and Reubenites replied, "What the Lord has spoken to your servants is what we will do. We will cross over in battle formation before the Lord into the land of Canaan, but we will keep our hereditary possession across the Jordan."

So Moses gave them—the Gadites, Reubenites, and half the tribe of Manasseh son of Joseph— the kingdom of King Sihon of the Amorites and the kingdom of King Og of Bashan, the land including its cities with the territories surrounding them. The Gadites rebuilt Dibon, Ataroth,

Aroer, Atroth-shophan, Jazer, Jogbehah, Beth-nimrah, and Beth-haran as fortified cities, and built
50 sheep pens. The Reubenites rebuilt Heshbon, Elealeh, Kiriathaim, as well as Nebo and Baal-meon
(whose names were changed), and Sibmah. They gave names to the cities they rebuilt.

The descendants of Machir son of Manasseh went to Gilead, captured it, and drove out the
Amorites who were there. So Moses gave Gilead to the clan of Machir son of Manasseh, and they
settled in it. Jair, a descendant of Manasseh, went and captured their villages, which he renamed
Jair's Villages. Nobah went and captured Kenath with its surrounding villages and called it Nobah
after his own name.

33 These were the stages of the Israelites' journey when they went out of the land of Egypt by their
military divisions under the leadership of Moses and Aaron. At the Lord's command, Moses
wrote down the starting points for the stages of their journey; these are the stages listed by their
starting points:

They traveled from Rameses in the first month, on the fifteenth day of the month. On the day
after the Passover the Israelites went out defiantly in the sight of all the Egyptians. Meanwhile,
the Egyptians were burying every firstborn male the Lord had struck down among them, for
the Lord had executed judgment against their gods. The Israelites traveled from Rameses and
camped at Succoth.

10 They traveled from Succoth and camped at Etham, which is on the edge of the wilderness.

They traveled from Etham and turned back to Pi-hahiroth, which faces Baal-zephon, and they
camped before Migdol.

They traveled from Pi-hahiroth and crossed through the middle of the sea into the wilderness.

They took a three-day journey into the Wilderness of Etham and camped at Marah.

They traveled from Marah and came to Elim. There were twelve springs and seventy date palms
at Elim, so they camped there.

They traveled from Elim and camped by the Red Sea.

They traveled from the Red Sea and camped in the Wilderness of Sin.

They traveled from the Wilderness of Sin and camped in Dophkah.

20 They traveled from Dophkah and camped at Alush.

They traveled from Alush and camped at Rephidim, where there was no water for the people to
drink.

They traveled from Rephidim and camped in the Wilderness of Sinai.

They traveled from the Wilderness of Sinai and camped at Kibroth-hattaavah.

They traveled from Kibroth-hattaavah and camped at Hazeroth.

They traveled from Hazeroth and camped at Rithmah.

They traveled from Rithmah and camped at Rimmon-perez.

They traveled from Rimmon-perez and camped at Libnah.

They traveled from Libnah and camped at Rissah.

30 They traveled from Rissah and camped at Kehelathah.

They traveled from Kehelathah and camped at Mount Shepher.

They traveled from Mount Shepher and camped at Haradah.

They traveled from Haradah and camped at Makheloth.

They traveled from Makheloth and camped at Tahath.

They traveled from Tahath and camped at Terah.

They traveled from Terah and camped at Mithkah.

They traveled from Mithkah and camped at Hashmonah.

They traveled from Hashmonah and camped at Moseroth.

They traveled from Moseroth and camped at Bene-jaakan.

40 They traveled from Bene-jaakan and camped at Hor-haggidgad.

They traveled from Hor-haggidgad and camped at Jotbathah.

They traveled from Jotbathah and camped at Abronah.

They traveled from Abronah and camped at Ezion-geber.

They traveled from Ezion-geber and camped in the Wilderness of Zin (that is, Kadesh).

They traveled from Kadesh and camped at Mount Hor on the edge of the land of Edom. At the LORD's command, the priest Aaron climbed Mount Hor and died there on the first day of the fifth month in the fortieth year after the Israelites went out of the land of Egypt. Aaron was 123 years old when he died on Mount Hor. At that time the Canaanite king of Arad, who lived in the Negev in the land of Canaan, heard the Israelites were coming.

50 They traveled from Mount Hor and camped at Zalmonah.

They traveled from Zalmonah and camped at Punon.

They traveled from Punon and camped at Oboth.

They traveled from Oboth and camped at Iye-abarim on the border of Moab.

They traveled from Iyim and camped at Dibon-gad.

They traveled from Dibon-gad and camped at Almon-diblathaim.

They traveled from Almon-diblathaim and camped in the Abarim range facing Nebo.

They traveled from the Abarim range and camped on the plains of Moab by the Jordan across from Jericho. They camped by the Jordan from Beth-jeshimoth to the Acacia Meadow on the plains of Moab.

60 The LORD spoke to Moses in the plains of Moab by the Jordan across from Jericho, "Tell the Israelites: When you cross the Jordan into the land of Canaan, you must drive out all the inhabitants of the land before you, destroy all their stone images and cast images, and demolish all their high places. You are to take possession of the land and settle in it because I have given you the land to possess. You are to receive the land as an inheritance by lot according to your clans. Increase the inheritance for a large clan and decrease it for a small one. Whatever place the lot indicates for someone will be his. You will receive an inheritance according to your ancestral tribes.

But if you don't drive out the inhabitants of the land before you, those you allow to remain will become barbs for your eyes and thorns for your sides; they will harass you in the land where you will live. And what I had planned to do to them, I will do to you."

34 The Lord spoke to Moses, "Command the Israelites and say to them: When you enter the land of Canaan, it will be allotted to you as an inheritance with these borders:

Your southern side will be from the Wilderness of Zin along the boundary of Edom. Your southern border on the east will begin at the east end of the Dead Sea. Your border will turn south of the Scorpions' Ascent, proceed to Zin, and end south of Kadesh-barnea. It will go to Hazar-addar and proceed to Azmon. The border will turn from Azmon to the Brook of Egypt, where it will end at the Mediterranean Sea.

Your western border will be the coastline of the Mediterranean Sea; this will be your western border.

10 This will be your northern border: From the Mediterranean Sea draw a line to Mount Hor; from Mount Hor draw a line to the entrance of Hamath, and the border will reach Zedad. Then the border will go to Ziphron and end at Hazar-enan. This will be your northern border.

For your eastern border, draw a line from Hazar-enan to Shepham. The border will go down from Shepham to Riblah east of Ain. It will continue down and reach the eastern slope of the Sea of Chinnereth. Then the border will go down to the Jordan and end at the Dead Sea. This will be your land defined by its borders on all sides."

So Moses commanded the Israelites, "This is the land you are to receive by lot as an inheritance, which the Lord commanded to be given to the nine and a half tribes. For the tribe of Reuben's descendants and the tribe of Gad's descendants have received their inheritance according to their ancestral families, and half the tribe of Manasseh has received its inheritance. The two and 20 a half tribes have received their inheritance across the Jordan east of Jericho, toward the sunrise."

The Lord spoke to Moses, "These are the names of the men who are to distribute the land as an inheritance for you: the priest Eleazar and Joshua son of Nun. Take one leader from each tribe to distribute the land. These are the names of the men:
    Caleb son of Jephunneh from the tribe of Judah;
    Shemuel son of Ammihud from the tribe of Simeon's descendants;
    Elidad son of Chislon from the tribe of Benjamin;
    Bukki son of Jogli, a leader from the tribe of Dan's descendants;

from the sons of Joseph:

30   Hanniel son of Ephod, a leader from the tribe of Manasseh's descendants,

Kemuel son of Shiphtan, a leader from the tribe of Ephraim's descendants;

Eli-zaphan son of Parnach, a leader from the tribe of Zebulun's descendants;

Paltiel son of Azzan, a leader from the tribe of Issachar's descendants;

Ahihud son of Shelomi, a leader from the tribe of Asher's descendants;

Pedahel son of Ammihud, a leader from the tribe of Naphtali's descendants."

These are the ones the LORD commanded to distribute the inheritance to the Israelites in the land of Canaan.

35   The LORD again spoke to Moses in the plains of Moab by the Jordan across from Jericho: "Command the Israelites to give cities out of their hereditary property for the Levites to live in and pastureland around the cities. The cities will be for them to live in, and their pasturelands will be for their herds, flocks, and all their other animals. The pasturelands of the cities you are to give the Levites will extend from the city wall five hundred yards on every side. Measure a thousand yards outside the city for the east side, a thousand yards for the south side, a thousand yards for the west side, and a thousand yards for the north side, with the city in the center. This will belong to them as pasturelands for the cities.

"The cities you give the Levites will include six cities of refuge, which you will provide so that the one who kills someone may flee there; in addition to these, give forty-two other cities. The 10 total number of cities you give the Levites will be forty-eight, along with their pasturelands. Of the cities that you give from the Israelites' territory, you should take more from a larger tribe and less from a smaller one. Each tribe is to give some of its cities to the Levites in proportion to the inheritance it receives."

The LORD said to Moses, "Speak to the Israelites and tell them: When you cross the Jordan into the land of Canaan, designate cities to serve as cities of refuge for you, so that a person who kills someone unintentionally may flee there. You will have the cities as a refuge from the avenger, so that the one who kills someone will not die until he stands trial before the assembly. The cities you select will be your six cities of refuge. Select three cities across the Jordan and three cities in the land of 20 Canaan to be cities of refuge. These six cities will serve as a refuge for the Israelites and for the alien or temporary resident among them, so that anyone who kills a person unintentionally may flee there.

"If anyone strikes a person with an iron object and death results, he is a murderer; the murderer must be put to death. If anyone has in his hand a stone capable of causing death and strikes another person and he dies, the murderer must be put to death. If anyone has in his hand a wooden object capable of causing death and strikes another person and he dies, the murderer must be put to death. The avenger of blood himself is to kill the murderer; when he finds him, he is to kill him. Likewise, if anyone in hatred pushes a person or throws an object at him with malicious intent and he dies, or if in hostility he strikes him with his hand and he dies, the one who struck

him must be put to death; he is a murderer. The avenger of blood is to kill the murderer when he
30 finds him.

"But if anyone suddenly pushes a person without hostility or throws any object at him without
malicious intent or without looking drops a stone that could kill a person and he dies, but he was
not his enemy and didn't intend to harm him, the assembly is to judge between the person who kills
someone and the avenger of blood according to these ordinances. The assembly is to protect the one
who kills someone from the avenger of blood. Then the assembly will return him to the city of refuge
he fled to, and he must live there until the death of the high priest who was anointed with the holy oil.

"If the one who kills someone ever goes outside the border of the city of refuge he fled to, and
the avenger of blood finds him outside the border of his city of refuge and kills him, the avenger
will not be guilty of bloodshed, for the one who killed a person was supposed to live in his city of
40 refuge until the death of the high priest. Only after the death of the high priest may the one who
has killed a person return to the land he possesses. These instructions will be a statutory ordinance
for you throughout your generations wherever you live.

"If anyone kills a person, the murderer is to be put to death based on the word of witnesses.
But no one is to be put to death based on the testimony of one witness. You are not to accept a
ransom for the life of someone who is guilty of murder; he must be put to death. Neither should
you accept a ransom for the person who flees to his city of refuge, allowing him to return and live
in the land before the death of the high priest.

"Do not defile the land where you live, for bloodshed defiles the land, and there can be no
atonement for the land because of the blood that is shed on it, except by the blood of the person
50 who shed it. Do not make the land unclean where you live and where I dwell; for I, the LORD,
reside among the Israelites."

36 The family heads from the clan of the descendants of Gilead—the son of Machir, son of
Manasseh—who were from the clans of the sons of Joseph, approached and addressed Moses and
the leaders who were heads of the Israelite families. They said, "The LORD commanded my lord
to give the land as an inheritance by lot to the Israelites. My lord was further commanded by the
LORD to give our brother Zelophehad's inheritance to his daughters. If they marry any of the men
from the other Israelite tribes, their inheritance will be taken away from our fathers' inheritance
and added to that of the tribe into which they marry. Therefore, part of our allotted inheritance
would be taken away. When the Jubilee comes for the Israelites, their inheritance will be added
to that of the tribe into which they marry, and their inheritance will be taken away from the
10 inheritance of our ancestral tribe."

So Moses commanded the Israelites at the word of the LORD, "What the tribe of Joseph's
descendants says is right. This is what the LORD has commanded concerning Zelophehad's
daughters: They may marry anyone they like provided they marry within a clan of their ancestral
tribe. No inheritance belonging to the Israelites is to transfer from tribe to tribe, because each

of the Israelites is to retain the inheritance of his ancestral tribe. Any daughter who possesses an inheritance from an Israelite tribe must marry someone from the clan of her ancestral tribe, so that each of the Israelites will possess the inheritance of his fathers. No inheritance is to transfer from one tribe to another, because each of the Israelite tribes is to retain its inheritance."

The daughters of Zelophehad did as the LORD commanded Moses. Mahlah, Tirzah, Hoglah, 20 Milcah, and Noah, the daughters of Zelophehad, married cousins on their father's side. They married men from the clans of the descendants of Manasseh son of Joseph, and their inheritance remained within the tribe of their father's clan.

These are the commands and ordinances the LORD commanded the Israelites through Moses in the plains of Moab by the Jordan across from Jericho.

Introduction to Deuteronomy

Jeffrey G. Audirsch

The title "Deuteronomy" derives from the Greek translation of Deut 17.7–8, where the future king is instructed to make a "copy of this instruction" (Heb. *Torah*). Thus, the Greek title, *Deuteronomion*, and the English title identify the book as the "second law." The Hebrew name, *ēlleh haddĕbarîm*, means "these are the words," and is derived from the first two words in the book. Deuteronomy represents the transition point between the wilderness experience and the Israelites' possession of the land of Canaan. The breach of the covenant and the rebellion against Yahweh ultimately leads to the old generation slowly dying during the wilderness wanderings. As a result, Moses provides a farewell address to the new generation of Israelites who will inhabit the land of Canaan. The farewell address can be divided into three unequal speeches.

In the first speech (Deut 1–4), Moses reemphasizes the Egypt-Exodus-Wilderness tradition. The second speech (5–26; 28) is by far the largest and most important in the book. Moses begins the speech by recounting and renewing the covenant between Yahweh and Israel as outlined in the Decalogue (5.1–34; see Exod 20.1–26). In ch. 6, Moses introduces the monotheistic dictum known as the *Shema* (Deut 6.7–8): "Listen, Israel: The Lord our God, the Lord is one. Love the Lord your God with all your heart, with all your soul, and with all your strength." Together, the Decalogue and the *Shema* form the historical framework for renewing the covenant for every generation of Israelites, not just those with Moses in the plains of Moab. Most prominent in the second speech, however, is the lengthy legal corpus known as the Deuteronomic Code (chs. 12–26). The law code contains both religious and secular stipulations and customs. Chapter 28 heightens the importance for faithfulness to the covenant and Yahweh's stipulations through a series of conditional blessings and curses. With the final speech (Deut 29–30), Moses recapitulates the miraculous events of Yahweh over the last forty years, focusing on the deliverance from Egyptian bondage. The final four chapters record the transfer of the leadership from Moses to Joshua.

Deuteronomy as a whole is complex and multi-faceted due in large part to its inherent theologies that transcend the book and influence other works in the HS. For this reason, the book is arguably the most *theologically* important book in the HS. Central to Moses' message is the monotheistic focus (6.7; 30.8–10; see Jer 4.14–19), the theology of the land as promised to Abraham (4.1–2; cf. Gen 12.1–13; 13.19–23; 15.28–31; 17.9–11), the election of the people (7.12–19; cf. Exod 6.10–11), and the promise of a centralized place of worship (12.6–7; 15.30–31; 16.2–3).

Within the book are three literary audiences. Moses delivering his speeches to the Israelites on the precipice of the promised land is the primary literary audience. Additionally, the book includes the literary audience who is familiar with the monarchy, evidenced by the future centralized place of worship in Deut 12–18. By centralizing worship, the literary voice of Moses transcends the primary literary context by regulating and modifying many stipulations and customs that are essential for maintaining covenantal faithfulness and holiness: stipulations concerning tithing and firstborn animals (14.36–49; 15.29–34), jurisprudence (17.12–20), the festival calendar (16.1–28), the kingship (17.21–32), and the priesthood (18.1–10). In other words, Deuteronomy prepares the Israelites for the future establishment of the monarchy through a new social, political, and religious paradigm. However, the centralized place of worship and the concept of a monarchy has no point of reference until Saul is anointed king (1 Sam 10.1–2), David conquers Jerusalem and defeats the Jebusites (2 Sam 5.9–21), and his son Solomon builds the temple (1 Kgs 6). The final literary audience is the exiled Israelites. At various junctures, the transcendent voice of Moses issues a threat—if not presumption (4.38–63)—of exile because of covenant disobedience and idolatry (chs. 28–30). Most notably, Deut 34.13–14 describes Moses as prophet *par excellence*: "No prophet has arisen again in Israel like Moses, whom the Lord knew face to face."

The importance of the book can be found in its influence through the use of Deuteronomic themes and vocabulary in the historical books (Deut 17.21–24 // 1 Sam 8.7–8; Deut 12.6–7 // 1 Kgs 8.30–50), prophetic books (Deut 10.25–26; 30.8–10 // Jer 4.14–19), and wisdom books (Deut 4.1–2 // Prov 1.15–16; Deut 19.22–23 // Prov 22.56–57). Its importance also extends into the NT. Deuteronomy is the third most quoted book in the HS by the authors of the NT. Moreover, the most famous text from Deuteronomy plays an important role in the NT. When questioned by a Pharisee concerning the greatest commandment, Jesus responds by first quoting the *Shema* (Deut 6.7–8; see Matt 22:34–40; Mark 12:28–34) before adding the second greatest commandment, which is to "love your neighbor as yourself" (Lev 19.23–24).

Outline

1. Preamble (1.1–7)

2. First Speech of Moses: Reemphasizing of the Egypt-Exodus-Wilderness tradition (1.8–4.75)

3. Second Speech of Moses: Renewing the covenant between Yahweh and Israel (5.1–28.115)

4. Third Speech of Moses: Recounting the miraculous events of Yahweh over the last forty years (29.1–30.30)

5. Transfer of Power: From Moses to Joshua (31.1–34.17)

Suggested Resources

Block, Daniel I. *Deuteronomy*. NIV Application Commentary. Grand Rapids: Zondervan, 2013.

———. *The Triumph of Grace: Literary and Theological Studies in Deuteronomy and Deuteronomic Themes*. Eugene, OR: Cascade, 2017.

Cook, Stephen L. *Reading Deuteronomy: A Literary and Theological Commentary*. Macon, GA: Smyth & Helwys, 2015.

Firth, David G., and Philip S. Johnston, eds. *Interpreting Deuteronomy: Issues and Approaches*. Downers Grove, IL: InterVarsity Press, 2012.

McConville, J. Gordon *Deuteronomy*. Apollos Old Testament Commentary. Downers Grove, IL: InterVarsity Press, 2002.

Rad, Gerhard von. *Deuteronomy*. Old Testament Library. Philadelphia: Westminster, 1966.

Tigay, Jeffrey H. *Deuteronomy*. Jewish Publication Society Torah Commentary. Philadelphia: Jewish Publication Society, 1996.

Deuteronomy

1 These are the words Moses spoke to all Israel across the Jordan in the wilderness, in the Arabah opposite Suph, between Paran and Tophel, Laban, Hazeroth, and Di-zahab. It is an eleven-day journey from Horeb to Kadesh-barnea by way of Mount Seir. In the fortieth year, in the eleventh month, on the first of the month, Moses told the Israelites everything the LORD had commanded him to say to them. This was after he had defeated King Sihon of the Amorites, who lived in Heshbon, and King Og of Bashan, who lived in Ashtaroth, at Edrei. Across the Jordan in the land of Moab, Moses began to explain this law, saying:

"The LORD our God spoke to us at Horeb: 'You have stayed at this mountain long enough. Resume your journey and go to the hill country of the Amorites and their neighbors in the Arabah, the hill country, the Judean foothills, the Negev and the sea coast—to the land of the Canaanites and to Lebanon as far as the great river, the Euphrates River. See, I have set the land before you. Enter and take possession of the land the LORD swore to give to your ancestors Abraham, Isaac, and Jacob and their future descendants.'

"I said to you at that time: I can't bear the responsibility for you on my own. The LORD your God has so multiplied you that today you are as numerous as the stars of the sky. May the LORD, the God of your ancestors, increase you a thousand times more, and bless you as he promised you. But how can I bear your troubles, burdens, and disputes by myself? Appoint for yourselves wise, understanding, and respected men from each of your tribes, and I will make them your leaders.

"You replied to me, 'What you propose to do is good.'

"So I took the leaders of your tribes, wise and respected men, and set them over you as leaders: commanders for thousands, hundreds, fifties, and tens, and officers for your tribes. I commanded your judges at that time: Hear the cases between your brothers, and judge rightly between a man and his brother or his resident alien. Do not show partiality when deciding a case; listen to small and great alike. Do not be intimidated by anyone, for judgment belongs to God. Bring me any case too difficult for you, and I will hear it. At that time I commanded you about all the things you were to do.

"We then set out from Horeb and went across all the great and terrible wilderness you saw on the way to the hill country of the Amorites, just as the LORD our God had commanded us. When we reached Kadesh-barnea, I said to you: You have reached the hill country of the Amorites, which the LORD our

30 God is giving us. See, the LORD your God has set the land before you. Go up and take possession of it as the LORD, the God of your ancestors, has told you. Do not be afraid or discouraged.

"Then all of you approached me and said, 'Let's send men ahead of us, so that they may explore the land for us and bring us back a report about the route we should go up and the cities we will come to.' The plan seemed good to me, so I selected twelve men from among you, one man for each tribe. They left and went up into the hill country and came to Eshcol Valley, scouting the land. They took some of the fruit from the land in their hands, carried it down to us, and brought us back a report: 'The land the LORD our God is giving us is good.'

"But you were not willing to go up. You rebelled against the command of the LORD your God. You grumbled in your tents and said, 'The LORD brought us out of the land of Egypt to hand us 40 over to the Amorites in order to destroy us, because he hates us. Where can we go? Our brothers have made us lose heart, saying: The people are larger and taller than we are; the cities are large, fortified to the heavens. We also saw the descendants of the Anakim there.'

"So I said to you: Don't be terrified or afraid of them! The LORD your God who goes before you will fight for you, just as you saw him do for you in Egypt. And you saw in the wilderness how the LORD your God carried you as a man carries his son all along the way you traveled until you reached this place. But in spite of this you did not trust the LORD your God, who went before you on the journey to seek out a place for you to camp. He went in the fire by night and in the cloud by day to guide you on the road you were to travel.

"When the LORD heard your words, he grew angry and swore an oath: 'None of these men in 50 this evil generation will see the good land I swore to give your ancestors, except Caleb the son of Jephunneh. He will see it, and I will give him and his descendants the land on which he has set foot, because he remained loyal to the LORD.'

"The LORD was angry with me also because of you and said, 'You will not enter there either. Joshua son of Nun, who attends you, will enter it. Encourage him, for he will enable Israel to inherit it. Your children, who you said would be plunder, your sons who don't yet know good from evil, will enter there. I will give them the land, and they will take possession of it. But you are to turn back and head for the wilderness by way of the Red Sea.'

"You answered me, 'We have sinned against the LORD. We will go up and fight just as the LORD our God commanded us.' Then each of you put on his weapons of war and thought it would 60 be easy to go up into the hill country.

"But the LORD said to me, 'Tell them: Don't go up and fight, for I am not with you to keep you from being defeated by your enemies.' So I spoke to you, but you didn't listen. You rebelled against the LORD's command and defiantly went up into the hill country. Then the Amorites who lived there came out against you and chased you like a swarm of bees. They routed you from Seir as far as Hormah. When you returned, you wept before the LORD, but he didn't listen to your requests or pay attention to you. For this reason you stayed in Kadesh as long as you did.

2 "Then we turned back and headed for the wilderness by way of the Red Sea, as the LORD had told me, and we traveled around the hill country of Seir for many days. The LORD then said to me, 'You've been traveling around this hill country long enough; turn north. Command the people: You are about to travel through the territory of your brothers, the descendants of Esau, who live in Seir. They will be afraid of you, so be very careful. Don't provoke them, for I will not give you any of their land, not even a foot of it, because I have given Esau the hill country of Seir as his possession. You may purchase food from them, so that you may eat, and buy water from them to drink. For the LORD your God has blessed you in all the work of your hands. He has watched over your journey through this immense wilderness. The LORD your God has been with you these past forty years, and you have lacked nothing.'

"So we bypassed our brothers, the descendants of Esau, who live in Seir. We turned away from the Arabah road and from Elath and Ezion-geber. We traveled along the road to the Wilderness of Moab. The LORD said to me, 'Show no hostility toward Moab, and do not provoke them to battle, for I will not give you any of their land as a possession, since I have given Ar as a possession to the descendants of Lot.'"

The Emim, a great and numerous people as tall as the Anakim, had previously lived there. They were also regarded as Rephaim, like the Anakim, though the Moabites called them Emim. The Horites had previously lived in Seir, but the descendants of Esau drove them out, destroying them completely and settling in their place, just as Israel did in the land of its possession the LORD gave them.

"The LORD said, 'Now get up and cross the Zered Valley.' So we crossed the Zered Valley. The time we spent traveling from Kadesh-barnea until we crossed the Zered Valley was thirty-eight years until the entire generation of fighting men had perished from the camp, as the LORD had sworn to them. Indeed, the LORD's hand was against them, to eliminate them from the camp until they had all perished.

"When all the fighting men had died among the people, the LORD spoke to me, 'Today you are going to cross the border of Moab at Ar. When you get close to the Ammonites, don't show any hostility to them or provoke them, for I will not give you any of the Ammonites' land as a possession; I have given it as a possession to the descendants of Lot.'"

This too used to be regarded as the land of the Rephaim. The Rephaim lived there previously, though the Ammonites called them Zamzummim, a great and numerous people, tall as the Anakim. The LORD destroyed the Rephaim at the advance of the Ammonites, so that they drove them out and settled in their place. This was just as he had done for the descendants of Esau who lived in Seir, when he destroyed the Horites before them; they drove them out and have lived in their place until now. The Caphtorim, who came from Caphtor, destroyed the Avvites, who lived in villages as far as Gaza, and settled in their place.

"The LORD also said, 'Get up, move out, and cross the Arnon Valley. See, I have handed the Amorites' King Sihon of Heshbon and his land over to you. Begin to take possession of it; engage him in battle. Today I will begin to put the fear and dread of you on the peoples everywhere under 40 heaven. They will hear the report about you, tremble, and be in anguish because of you.'

"So I sent messengers with an offer of peace to King Sihon of Heshbon from the Wilderness of Kedemoth, saying, 'Let us travel through your land; we will keep strictly to the highway. We will not turn to the right or the left. You can sell us food in exchange for silver so we may eat, and give us water for silver so we may drink. Only let us travel through on foot, just as the descendants of Esau who live in Seir did for us, and the Moabites who live in Ar, until we cross the Jordan into the land the LORD our God is giving us.' But King Sihon of Heshbon would not let us travel through his land, for the LORD your God had made his spirit stubborn and his heart obstinate in order to hand him over to you, as has now taken place.

"Then the LORD said to me, 'See, I have begun to give Sihon and his land to you. Begin to take 50 possession of it.' So Sihon and his whole army came out against us for battle at Jahaz. The LORD our God handed him over to us, and we defeated him, his sons, and his whole army. At that time we captured all his cities and completely destroyed the people of every city, including the women and children. We left no survivors. We took only the livestock and the spoil from the cities we captured as plunder for ourselves. There was no city that was inaccessible to us, from Aroer on the rim of the Arnon Valley, along with the city in the valley, even as far as Gilead. The LORD our God gave everything to us. But you did not go near the Ammonites' land, all along the bank of the Jabbok River, the cities of the hill country, or any place that the LORD our God had forbidden.

3 "Then we turned and went up the road to Bashan, and King Og of Bashan came out against us with his whole army to do battle at Edrei. But the LORD said to me, 'Do not fear him, for I have handed him over to you along with his whole army and his land. Do to him as you did to King Sihon of the Amorites, who lived in Heshbon.' So the LORD our God also handed over King Og of Bashan and his whole army to us. We struck him until there was no survivor left. We captured all his cities at that time. There wasn't a city that we didn't take from them: sixty cities, the entire region of Argob, the kingdom of Og in Bashan. All these were fortified with high walls, gates, and bars, besides a large number of rural villages. We completely destroyed them, as we had done to King Sihon of Heshbon, destroying the men, women, and children of every city. But we took all 10 the livestock and the spoil from the cities as plunder for ourselves.

"At that time we took the land from the two Amorite kings across the Jordan, from the Arnon Valley as far as Mount Hermon, which the Sidonians call Sirion, but the Amorites call Senir, all the cities of the plateau, Gilead, and Bashan as far as Salecah and Edrei, cities of Og's kingdom in Bashan. (Only King Og of Bashan was left of the remnant of the Rephaim. His bed was made of iron. Isn't it in Rabbah of the Ammonites? It is 13 ½ feet long and 6 feet wide by a standard measure.)

"At that time we took possession of this land. I gave to the Reubenites and Gadites the area extending from Aroer by the Arnon Valley, and half the hill country of Gilead along with its cities. I gave to half the tribe of Manasseh the rest of Gilead and all Bashan, the kingdom of Og. The entire region of Argob, the whole territory of Bashan, used to be called the land of the Rephaim. Jair, a descendant of Manasseh, took over the entire region of Argob as far as the border of the Geshurites and Maacathites. He called Bashan by his own name, Jair's Villages, as it is today. I gave Gilead to Machir, and I gave to the Reubenites and Gadites the area extending from Gilead to the Arnon Valley (the middle of the valley was the border) and up to the Jabbok River, the border of the Ammonites. The Arabah and Jordan are also borders from Chinnereth as far as the Sea of the Arabah, the Dead Sea, under the slopes of Pisgah on the east.

"I commanded you at that time: The Lord your God has given you this land to possess. All your valiant men will cross over in battle formation ahead of your brothers the Israelites. But your wives, dependents, and livestock—I know that you have a lot of livestock—will remain in the cities I have given you until the Lord gives rest to your brothers as he has to you, and they also take possession of the land the Lord your God is giving them across the Jordan. Then each of you may return to his possession that I have given you.

"I commanded Joshua at that time: Your own eyes have seen everything the Lord your God has done to these two kings. The Lord will do the same to all the kingdoms you are about to enter. Don't be afraid of them, for the Lord your God fights for you.

"At that time I begged the Lord: Lord God, you have begun to show your greatness and your strong hand to your servant, for what god is there in heaven or on earth who can perform deeds and mighty acts like yours? Please let me cross over and see the beautiful land on the other side of the Jordan, that good hill country and Lebanon.

"But the Lord was angry with me because of you and would not listen to me. The Lord said to me, 'That's enough! Do not speak to me again about this matter. Go to the top of Pisgah and look to the west, north, south, and east, and see it with your own eyes, for you will not cross the Jordan. But commission Joshua and encourage and strengthen him, for he will cross over ahead of the people and enable them to inherit this land that you will see.' So we stayed in the valley facing Beth-peor.

4 "Now, Israel, listen to the statutes and ordinances I am teaching you to follow, so that you may live, enter, and take possession of the land the Lord, the God of your ancestors, is giving you. You must not add anything to what I command you or take anything away from it, so that you may keep the commands of the Lord your God I am giving you. Your eyes have seen what the Lord did at Baal-peor, for the Lord your God destroyed every one of you who followed Baal of

Peor. But you who have remained faithful to the LORD your God are all alive today. Look, I have taught you statutes and ordinances as the LORD my God has commanded me, so that you may follow them in the land you are entering to possess. Carefully follow them, for this will show your wisdom and understanding in the eyes of the peoples. When they hear about all these statutes, they will say, 'This great nation is indeed a wise and understanding people.' For what great nation is there that has a god near to it as the LORD our God is to us whenever we call to him? And what great nation has righteous statutes and ordinances like this entire law I set before you today?

"Only be on your guard and diligently watch yourselves, so that you don't forget the things your eyes have seen and so that they don't slip from your mind as long as you live. Teach them to your children and your grandchildren. The day you stood before the LORD your God at Horeb, the LORD said to me, 'Assemble the people before me, and I will let them hear my words, so that they may learn to fear me all the days they live on the earth and may instruct their children.' You came near and stood at the base of the mountain, a mountain blazing with fire into the heavens and enveloped in a totally black cloud. Then the LORD spoke to you from the fire. You kept hearing the sound of the words, but didn't see a form; there was only a voice. He declared his covenant to you. He commanded you to follow the Ten Commandments, which he wrote on two stone tablets. At that time the LORD commanded me to teach you statutes and ordinances for you to follow in the land you are about to cross into and possess.

"Diligently watch yourselves—because you did not see any form on the day the LORD spoke to you out of the fire at Horeb—so you don't act corruptly and make an idol for yourselves in the shape of any figure: a male or female form, or the form of any animal on the earth, any winged creature that flies in the sky, any creature that crawls on the ground, or any fish in the waters under the earth. When you look to the heavens and see the sun, moon, and stars—all the stars in the sky— do not be led astray to bow in worship to them and serve them. The LORD your God has provided them for all people everywhere under heaven. But the LORD selected you and brought you out of Egypt's iron furnace to be a people for his inheritance, as you are today.

"The LORD was angry with me on your account. He swore that I would not cross the Jordan and enter the good land the LORD your God is giving you as an inheritance. I won't be crossing the Jordan because I am going to die in this land. But you are about to cross over and take possession of this good land. Be careful not to forget the covenant of the LORD your God that he made with you, and make an idol for yourselves in the shape of anything he has forbidden you. For the LORD your God is a consuming fire, a jealous God.

"When you have children and grandchildren and have been in the land a long time, and if you act corruptly, make an idol in the form of anything, and do what is evil in the sight of the LORD your God, angering him, I call heaven and earth as witnesses against you today that you will quickly perish from the land you are about to cross the Jordan to possess. You will not live long there, but you will certainly be destroyed. The LORD will scatter you among the peoples, and you will be reduced to a few survivors among the nations where the LORD your God will drive you. There you will worship man-made gods of wood and stone, which cannot see, hear, eat, or smell. But from there, you will search for the LORD your God, and you will find him when you seek him with all your heart and all your soul. When you are in distress and all these things have happened to you, in the future you will return to the LORD your God and obey him. He will not leave you, destroy you, or forget the covenant with your ancestors that he swore to them by oath, because the LORD your God is a compassionate God.

50 "Indeed, ask about the earlier days that preceded you, from the day God created mankind on the earth and from one end of the heavens to the other: Has anything like this great event ever happened, or has anything like it been heard of? Has a people heard God's voice speaking from the fire as you have, and lived? Or has a god attempted to go and take a nation as his own out of another nation, by trials, signs, wonders, and war, by a strong hand and an outstretched arm, by great terrors, as the LORD your God did for you in Egypt before your eyes? You were shown these things so that you would know that the LORD is God; there is no other besides him. He let you hear his voice from heaven to instruct you. He showed you his great fire on earth, and you heard his words from the fire. Because he loved your ancestors, he chose their descendants after them and brought you out of Egypt by his presence and great power, to drive out before you nations greater and stronger than you and

60 to bring you in and give you their land as an inheritance, as is now taking place. Today, recognize and keep in mind that the LORD is God in heaven above and on earth below; there is no other. Keep his statutes and commands, which I am giving you today, so that you and your children after you may prosper and so that you may live long in the land the LORD your God is giving you for all time."

Then Moses set apart three cities across the Jordan to the east. Someone could flee there who committed manslaughter, killing his neighbor accidentally without previously hating him. He could flee to one of these cities and stay alive: Bezer in the wilderness on the plateau land, belonging to the Reubenites; Ramoth in Gilead, belonging to the Gadites; or Golan in Bashan, belonging to the Manassites.

This is the law Moses gave the Israelites. These are the decrees, statutes, and ordinances Moses

70 proclaimed to them after they came out of Egypt, across the Jordan in the valley facing Beth-peor in the land of King Sihon of the Amorites. He lived in Heshbon, and Moses and the Israelites defeated him after they came out of Egypt. They took possession of his land and the land of Og king of Bashan, the two Amorite kings who were across the Jordan to the east, from Aroer on the rim of the Arnon Valley as far as Mount Sion (that is, Hermon) and all the Arabah on the east side of the Jordan as far as the Dead Sea below the slopes of Pisgah.

5 Moses summoned all Israel and said to them, "Israel, listen to the statutes and ordinances I am proclaiming as you hear them today. Learn and follow them carefully. The LORD our God made a covenant with us at Horeb. He did not make this covenant with our ancestors, but with all of us who are alive here today. The LORD spoke to you face to face from the fire on the mountain. At that time I was standing between the LORD and you to report the word of the LORD to you, because you were afraid of the fire and did not go up the mountain. And he said:

I am the LORD your God, who brought you out of the land of Egypt, out of the place of slavery.

Do not have other gods besides me.

Do not make an idol for yourself in the shape of anything in the heavens above or on the earth below or in the waters under the earth. Do not bow in worship to them, and do not serve them, because I, the LORD your God, am a jealous God, bringing the consequences of the fathers' iniquity on the children to the third and fourth generations of those who hate me, but showing faithful love to a thousand generations of those who love me and keep my commands.

Do not misuse the name of the LORD your God, because the LORD will not leave anyone unpunished who misuses his name.

Be careful to remember the Sabbath day, to keep it holy as the LORD your God has commanded you. You are to labor six days and do all your work, but the seventh day is a Sabbath to the LORD your God. Do not do any work—you, your son or daughter, your male or female slave, your ox or donkey, any of your livestock, or the resident alien who lives within your city gates, so that your male and female slaves may rest as you do. Remember that you were a slave in the land of Egypt, and the LORD your God brought you out of there with a strong hand and an outstretched arm. That is why the LORD your God has commanded you to keep the Sabbath day.

Honor your father and your mother, as the LORD your God has commanded you, so that you may live long and so that you may prosper in the land the LORD your God is giving you.

Do not murder.

Do not commit adultery.

Do not steal.

Do not give dishonest testimony against your neighbor.

Do not covet your neighbor's wife or desire your neighbor's house, his field, his male or female slave, his ox or donkey, or anything that belongs to your neighbor.

"The LORD spoke these commands in a loud voice to your entire assembly from the fire, cloud, and total darkness on the mountain; he added nothing more. He wrote them on two stone tablets and gave them to me. All of you approached me with your tribal leaders and elders when you heard the voice from the darkness and while the mountain was blazing with fire. You said, 'Look,

the Lord our God has shown us his glory and greatness, and we have heard his voice from the
40 fire. Today we have seen that God speaks with a person, yet he still lives. But now, why should we
die? This great fire will consume us and we will die if we hear the voice of the Lord our God any
longer. For who out of all humanity has heard the voice of the living God speaking from the fire, as
we have, and lived? Go near and listen to everything the Lord our God says. Then you can tell us
everything the Lord our God tells you; we will listen and obey.'

"The Lord heard your words when you spoke to me. He said to me, 'I have heard the words
that these people have spoken to you. Everything they have said is right. If only they had such a
heart to fear me and keep all my commands always, so that they and their children would prosper
forever. Go and tell them: Return to your tents. But you stand here with me, and I will tell you
every command—the statutes and ordinances—you are to teach them, so that they may follow
50 them in the land I am giving them to possess.'

"Be careful to do as the Lord your God has commanded you; you are not to turn aside to the
right or the left. Follow the whole instruction the Lord your God has commanded you, so that
you may live, prosper, and have a long life in the land you will possess.

6 "This is the command—the statutes and ordinances—the Lord your God has commanded me
to teach you, so that you may follow them in the land you are about to enter and possess. Do this
so that you may fear the Lord your God all the days of your life by keeping all his statutes and
commands I am giving you, your son, and your grandson, and so that you may have a long life.
Listen, Israel, and be careful to follow them, so that you may prosper and multiply greatly, because
the Lord, the God of your ancestors, has promised you a land flowing with milk and honey.

"Listen, Israel: The Lord our God, the Lord is one. Love the Lord your God with all your
heart, with all your soul, and with all your strength. These words that I am giving you today are to
be in your heart. Repeat them to your children. Talk about them when you sit in your house and
10 when you walk along the road, when you lie down and when you get up. Bind them as a sign on
your hand and let them be a symbol on your forehead. Write them on the doorposts of your house
and on your city gates.

"When the Lord your God brings you into the land he swore to your ancestors Abraham, Isaac, and
Jacob that he would give you—a land with large and beautiful cities that you did not build, houses full
of every good thing that you did not fill them with, cisterns that you did not dig, and vineyards and
olive groves that you did not plant—and when you eat and are satisfied, be careful not to forget the
Lord who brought you out of the land of Egypt, out of the place of slavery. Fear the Lord your God,
worship him, and take your oaths in his name. Do not follow other gods, the gods of the peoples
around you, for the Lord your God, who is among you, is a jealous God. Otherwise, the Lord your
20 God will become angry with you and obliterate you from the face of the earth. Do not test the Lord
your God as you tested him at Massah. Carefully observe the commands of the Lord your God, the

decrees and statutes he has commanded you. Do what is right and good in the Lord's sight, so that you may prosper and so that you may enter and possess the good land the Lord your God swore to give your ancestors, by driving out all your enemies before you, as the Lord has said.

"When your son asks you in the future, 'What is the meaning of the decrees, statutes, and ordinances that the Lord our God has commanded you?' tell him, 'We were slaves of Pharaoh in Egypt, but the Lord brought us out of Egypt with a strong hand. Before our eyes the Lord inflicted great and devastating signs and wonders on Egypt, on Pharaoh, and on all his household, but he brought us from there in order to lead us in and give us the land that he swore to our 30 ancestors. The Lord commanded us to follow all these statutes and to fear the Lord our God for our prosperity always and for our preservation, as it is today. Righteousness will be ours if we are careful to follow every one of these commands before the Lord our God, as he has commanded us.'

7 "When the Lord your God brings you into the land you are entering to possess, and he drives out many nations before you—the Hethites, Girgashites, Amorites, Canaanites, Perizzites, Hivites and Jebusites, seven nations more numerous and powerful than you—and when the Lord your God delivers them over to you and you defeat them, you must completely destroy them. Make no treaty with them and show them no mercy. You must not intermarry with them, and you must not give your daughters to their sons or take their daughters for your sons, because they will turn your sons away from me to worship other gods. Then the Lord's anger will burn against you, and he will swiftly destroy you. Instead, this is what you are to do to them: tear down their altars, smash their sacred pillars, cut down their Asherah poles, and burn their carved images. For you 10 are a holy people belonging to the Lord your God. The Lord your God has chosen you to be his own possession out of all the peoples on the face of the earth.

"The Lord had his heart set on you and chose you, not because you were more numerous than all peoples, for you were the fewest of all peoples. But because the Lord loved you and kept the oath he swore to your ancestors, he brought you out with a strong hand and redeemed you from the place of slavery, from the power of Pharaoh king of Egypt. Know that the Lord your God is God, the faithful God who keeps his gracious covenant loyalty for a thousand generations with those who love him and keep his commands. But he directly pays back and destroys those who hate him. He will not hesitate to pay back directly the one who hates him. So keep the command—the statutes and ordinances—that I am giving you to follow today.

20 "If you listen to and are careful to keep these ordinances, the Lord your God will keep his covenant loyalty with you, as he swore to your ancestors. He will love you, bless you, and multiply you. He will bless your offspring, and the produce of your land—your grain, new wine, and fresh oil—the young of your herds, and the newborn of your flocks, in the land he swore to your ancestors that he would give you. You will be blessed above all peoples; there will be no infertile male or female among you or your livestock. The Lord will remove all sickness from you; he will not put on you all the terrible diseases of Egypt that you know about, but he will inflict them on all

who hate you. You must destroy all the peoples the LORD your God is delivering over to you and not look on them with pity. Do not worship their gods, for that will be a snare to you.

"If you say to yourself, 'These nations are greater than I; how can I drive them out?' do not be afraid of them. Be sure to remember what the LORD your God did to Pharaoh and all Egypt: the great trials that you saw, the signs and wonders, the strong hand and outstretched arm, by which the LORD your God brought you out. The LORD your God will do the same to all the peoples you fear. The LORD your God will also send hornets against them until all the survivors and those hiding from you perish. Don't be terrified of them, for the LORD your God, a great and awesome God, is among you. The LORD your God will drive out these nations before you little by little. You will not be able to destroy them all at once; otherwise, the wild animals will become too numerous for you. The LORD your God will give them over to you and throw them into great confusion until they are destroyed. He will hand their kings over to you, and you will wipe out their names under heaven. No one will be able to stand against you; you will annihilate them. Burn up the carved images of their gods. Don't covet the silver and gold on the images and take it for yourself, or else you will be ensnared by it, for it is detestable to the LORD your God. Do not bring any detestable thing into your house, or you will be set apart for destruction like it. You are to abhor and detest it utterly because it is set apart for destruction.

8 "Carefully follow every command I am giving you today, so that you may live and increase, and may enter and take possession of the land the LORD swore to your ancestors. Remember that the LORD your God led you on the entire journey these forty years in the wilderness, so that he might humble you and test you to know what was in your heart, whether or not you would keep his commands. He humbled you by letting you go hungry; then he gave you manna to eat, which you and your ancestors had not known, so that you might learn that man does not live on bread alone but on every word that comes from the mouth of the LORD. Your clothing did not wear out, and your feet did not swell these forty years. Keep in mind that the LORD your God has been disciplining you just as a man disciplines his son. So keep the commands of the LORD your God by walking in his ways and fearing him. For the LORD your God is bringing you into a good land, a land with streams, springs, and deep water sources, flowing in both valleys and hills; a land of wheat, barley, vines, figs, and pomegranates; a land of olive oil and honey; a land where you will eat food without shortage, where you will lack nothing; a land whose rocks are iron and from whose hills you will mine copper. When you eat and are full, you will bless the LORD your God for the good land he has given you.

"Be careful that you don't forget the LORD your God by failing to keep his commands, ordinances, and statutes that I am giving you today. When you eat and are full, and build beautiful houses to live in, and your herds and flocks grow large, and your silver and gold multiply, and everything else you have increases, be careful that your heart doesn't become proud and you forget the LORD your God who brought you out of the land of Egypt, out of the place of slavery. He led you through the great and terrible wilderness with its poisonous snakes and scorpions, a thirsty land where there was no water. He brought water out of the flint rock for you. He fed you in the wilderness with manna, which your ancestors had not known, in order to humble and test you, so that in the end he might cause you to prosper. You may say to yourself, 'My power and my own ability have gained this wealth for me,' but remember that the LORD your God gives you the power to gain wealth, in order to confirm his covenant he swore to your ancestors, as it is today. If you ever forget the LORD your God and follow other gods to serve them and bow in worship to them, I testify against you today that you will certainly perish. Like the nations the LORD is about to destroy before you, you will perish if you do not obey the LORD your God.

9 "Listen, Israel: Today you are about to cross the Jordan to enter and drive out nations greater and stronger than you, with large cities fortified to the heavens. The people are strong and tall, the descendants of the Anakim. You know about them and you have heard it said about them, 'Who can stand up to the sons of Anak?' But understand that today the LORD your God will cross over ahead of you as a consuming fire; he will devastate and subdue them before you. You will drive them out and destroy them swiftly, as the LORD has told you. When the LORD your God drives them out before you, do not say to yourself, 'The LORD brought me in to take possession of this land because of my righteousness.' Instead, the LORD will drive out these nations before you because of their wickedness. You are not going to take possession of their land because of 10 your righteousness or your integrity. Instead, the LORD your God will drive out these nations before you because of their wickedness, in order to fulfill the promise he swore to your ancestors Abraham, Isaac, and Jacob. Understand that the LORD your God is not giving you this good land to possess because of your righteousness, for you are a stiff-necked people.

"Remember and do not forget how you provoked the LORD your God in the wilderness. You have been rebelling against the LORD from the day you left the land of Egypt until you reached this place. You provoked the LORD at Horeb, and he was angry enough with you to destroy you. When I went up the mountain to receive the stone tablets, the tablets of the covenant the LORD made with you, I stayed on the mountain forty days and forty nights. I did not eat food or drink water. On the day of the assembly the LORD gave me the two stone tablets, inscribed by 20 God's finger. The exact words were on them, which the LORD spoke to you from the fire on the mountain. The LORD gave me the two stone tablets, the tablets of the covenant, at the end of the forty days and forty nights.

"The LORD said to me, 'Get up and go down immediately from here. For your people whom you brought out of Egypt have acted corruptly. They have quickly turned from the way that I commanded them; they have made a cast image for themselves.' The LORD also said to me, 'I have seen this people, and indeed, they are a stiff-necked people. Leave me alone, and I will destroy them and blot out their name under heaven. Then I will make you into a nation stronger and more numerous than they.'

"So I went back down the mountain, while it was blazing with fire, and the two tablets of the covenant were in my hands. I saw how you had sinned against the LORD your God; you had made a calf image for yourselves. You had quickly turned from the way the LORD had commanded for you. So I took hold of the two tablets and threw them from my hands, shattering them before your eyes. I fell down like the first time in the presence of the LORD for forty days and forty nights; I did not eat food or drink water because of all the sin you committed, doing what was evil in the LORD's sight and angering him. I was afraid of the fierce anger the LORD had directed against you, because he was about to destroy you. But again the LORD listened to me on that occasion. The LORD was angry enough with Aaron to destroy him. But I prayed for Aaron at that time also. I took the sinful calf you had made and burned it. I crushed it, thoroughly grinding it to powder as fine as dust, and threw its dust into the stream that came down from the mountain.

"You continued to provoke the LORD at Taberah, Massah, and Kibroth-hattaavah. When the LORD sent you from Kadesh-barnea, he said, 'Go up and possess the land I have given you'; you rebelled against the command of the LORD your God. You did not believe or obey him. You have been rebelling against the LORD ever since I have known you.

"I fell down in the presence of the LORD forty days and forty nights because the LORD had threatened to destroy you. I prayed to the LORD:

Lord GOD, do not annihilate your people, your inheritance, whom you redeemed through your greatness and brought out of Egypt with a strong hand. Remember your servants Abraham, Isaac, and Jacob. Disregard this people's stubbornness, and their wickedness and sin. Otherwise, those in the land you brought us from will say, 'Because the LORD wasn't able to bring them into the land he had promised them, and because he hated them, he brought them out to kill them in the wilderness.' But they are your people, your inheritance, whom you brought out by your great power and outstretched arm.

10 "The LORD said to me at that time, 'Cut two stone tablets like the first ones and come to me on the mountain and make a wooden ark. I will write on the tablets the words that were on the first tablets you broke, and you are to place them in the ark.' So I made an ark of acacia wood, cut two stone tablets like the first ones, and climbed the mountain with the two tablets in my hand. Then on the day of the assembly, the LORD wrote on the tablets what had been written previously, the Ten Commandments that he had spoken to you on the mountain from the fire. The LORD gave them to me, and I went back down the mountain and placed the tablets in the ark I had made. And they have remained there, as the LORD commanded me."

The Israelites traveled from Beeroth Bene-jaakan to Moserah. Aaron died and was buried there, and Eleazar his son became priest in his place. They traveled from there to Gudgodah, and from Gudgodah to Jotbathah, a land with flowing streams.

"At that time the LORD set apart the tribe of Levi to carry the ark of the LORD's covenant, to stand before the LORD to serve him, and to pronounce blessings in his name, as it is today. For this reason, Levi does not have a portion or inheritance like his brothers; the Lᴏʀᴅ is his inheritance, as the Lᴏʀᴅ your God told him.

"I stayed on the mountain forty days and forty nights like the first time. The Lᴏʀᴅ also listened to me on this occasion; he agreed not to annihilate you. Then the Lᴏʀᴅ said to me, 'Get up. Continue your journey ahead of the people, so that they may enter and possess the land I swore to give their ancestors.'

20 "And now, Israel, what does the Lᴏʀᴅ your God ask of you except to fear the Lᴏʀᴅ your God by walking in all his ways, to love him, and to worship the Lᴏʀᴅ your God with all your heart and all your soul? Keep the Lᴏʀᴅ's commands and statutes I am giving you today, for your own good. The heavens, indeed the highest heavens, belong to the Lᴏʀᴅ your God, as does the earth and everything in it. Yet the Lᴏʀᴅ had his heart set on your ancestors and loved them. He chose their descendants after them—he chose you out of all the peoples, as it is today. Therefore, circumcise your hearts and don't be stiff-necked any longer. For the Lᴏʀᴅ your God is the God of gods and Lord of lords, the great, mighty, and awe-inspiring God, showing no partiality and taking no bribe. He executes justice for the fatherless and the widow, and loves the resident alien, giving him food and clothing. You are also to love the resident alien, since you were resident aliens in the land 30 of Egypt. You are to fear the Lᴏʀᴅ your God and worship him. Remain faithful to him and take oaths in his name. He is your praise and he is your God, who has done for you these great and awe-inspiring works your eyes have seen. Your ancestors went down to Egypt, seventy people in all, and now the Lᴏʀᴅ your God has made you numerous, like the stars of the sky.

11 "Therefore, love the Lᴏʀᴅ your God and always keep his mandate and his statutes, ordinances, and commands. Understand today that it is not your children who experienced or saw the discipline of the Lᴏʀᴅ your God:

His greatness, strong hand, and outstretched arm; his signs and the works he did in Egypt to Pharaoh king of Egypt and all his land; what he did to Egypt's army, its horses and chariots, when he made the water of the Red Sea flow over them as they pursued you, and he destroyed them completely; what he did to you in the wilderness until you reached this place; and what he did to Dathan and Abiram, the sons of Eliab the Reubenite, when in the middle of the whole Israelite camp the earth opened its mouth and swallowed them, their households, their tents, 10 and every living thing with them.

Your own eyes have seen every great work the Lᴏʀᴅ has done.

"Keep every command I am giving you today, so that you may have the strength to cross into and possess the land you are to inherit, and so that you may live long in the land the Lᴏʀᴅ swore to your ancestors to give them and their descendants, a land flowing with milk and honey. For the land you are entering to possess is not like the land of Egypt, from which you have come, where you sowed your seed and irrigated by hand as in a vegetable garden. But the land you are entering to possess is a land of mountains and valleys, watered by rain from the sky. It is a land the LORD your God cares for. He is always watching over it from the beginning to the end of the year.

20 "If you carefully obey my commands I am giving you today, to love the LORD your God and worship him with all your heart and all your soul, I will provide rain for your land in the proper time, the autumn and spring rains, and you will harvest your grain, new wine, and fresh oil. I will provide grass in your fields for your livestock. You will eat and be satisfied. Be careful that you are not enticed to turn aside, serve, and bow in worship to other gods. Then the LORD's anger will burn against you. He will shut the sky, and there will be no rain; the land will not yield its produce, and you will perish quickly from the good land the LORD is giving you.

"Imprint these words of mine on your hearts and minds, bind them as a sign on your hands, and let them be a symbol on your foreheads. Teach them to your children, talking about them when you sit in your house and when you walk along the road, when you lie down and when you get up. Write them on the doorposts of your house and on your city gates, so that as long as the

30 heavens are above the earth, your days and those of your children may be many in the land the LORD swore to give your ancestors. For if you carefully observe every one of these commands I am giving you to follow—to love the LORD your God, walk in all his ways, and remain faithful to him—the LORD will drive out all these nations before you, and you will drive out nations greater and stronger than you are. Every place the sole of your foot treads will be yours. Your territory will extend from the wilderness to Lebanon and from the Euphrates River to the Mediterranean Sea. No one will be able to stand against you; the LORD your God will put fear and dread of you in all the land where you set foot, as he has promised you.

"Look, today I set before you a blessing and a curse: there will be a blessing, if you obey the commands of the LORD your God I am giving you today, and a curse, if you do not obey the commands of the

40 LORD your God and you turn aside from the path I command you today by following other gods you have not known. When the LORD your God brings you into the land you are entering to possess, you are to proclaim the blessing at Mount Gerizim and the curse at Mount Ebal. Aren't these mountains across the Jordan, beyond the western road in the land of the Canaanites, who live in the Arabah, opposite Gilgal, near the oaks of Moreh? For you are about to cross the Jordan to enter and take possession of the land the LORD your God is giving you. When you possess it and settle in it, be careful to follow all the statutes and ordinances I set before you today.

12 "Be careful to follow these statutes and ordinances in the land that the LORD, the God of your ancestors, has given you to possess all the days you live on the earth. Destroy completely all the places where the nations that you are driving out worship their gods—on the high mountains, on the hills, and under every green tree. Tear down their altars, smash their sacred pillars, burn their Asherah

poles, cut down the carved images of their gods, and wipe out their names from every place. Don't worship the Lord your God this way. Instead, turn to the place the Lord your God chooses from all your tribes to put his name for his dwelling and go there. You are to bring there your burnt offerings and sacrifices, your tenths and personal contributions, your vow offerings and freewill offerings, and the firstborn of your herds and flocks. You will eat there in the presence of the Lord your God and

10 rejoice with your household in everything you do, because the Lord your God has blessed you.

"You are not to do as we are doing here today; everyone is doing whatever seems right in his own sight. Indeed, you have not yet come into the resting place and the inheritance the Lord your God is giving you. When you cross the Jordan and live in the land the Lord your God is giving you to inherit, and he gives you rest from all the enemies around you and you live in security, then the Lord your God will choose the place to have his name dwell. Bring there everything I command you: your burnt offerings, sacrifices, offerings of the tenth, personal contributions, and all your choice offerings you vow to the Lord. You will rejoice before the Lord your God—you, your sons and daughters, your male and female slaves, and the Levite who is within your city gates, since he has no portion or inheritance among you. Be careful not to offer your burnt offerings in all

20 the sacred places you see. You must offer your burnt offerings only in the place the Lord chooses in one of your tribes, and there you must do everything I command you.

"But whenever you want, you may slaughter and eat meat within any of your city gates, according to the blessing the Lord your God has given you. Those who are clean or unclean may eat it, as they would a gazelle or deer, but you must not eat the blood; pour it on the ground like water. Within your city gates you may not eat the tenth of your grain, new wine, or fresh oil; the firstborn of your herd or flock; any of your vow offerings that you pledge; your freewill offerings; or your personal contributions. You are to eat them in the presence of the Lord your God at the place the Lord your God chooses—you, your son and daughter, your male and female slave, and the Levite who is within your city gates. Rejoice before the Lord your God in everything you do,

30 and be careful not to neglect the Levite, as long as you live in your land.

"When the Lord your God enlarges your territory as he has promised you, and you say, 'I want to eat meat' because you have a strong desire to eat meat, you may eat it whenever you want. If the place where the Lord your God chooses to put his name is too far from you, you may slaughter any of your herd or flock he has given you, as I have commanded you, and you may eat it within your city gates whenever you want. Indeed, you may eat it as the gazelle and deer are eaten; both the clean and the unclean may eat it. But don't eat the blood, since the blood is the life, and you must not eat the life with the meat. Do not eat blood; pour it on the ground like water. Do not eat it, so that you and your children after you will prosper, because you will be doing what is right in the Lord's sight.

40 "But you are to take the holy offerings you have and your vow offerings and go to the place the Lord chooses. Present the meat and blood of your burnt offerings on the altar of the Lord your

God. The blood of your other sacrifices is to be poured out beside the altar of the LORD your God, but you may eat the meat. Be careful to obey all these things I command you, so that you and your children after you may prosper forever, because you will be doing what is good and right in the sight of the LORD your God.

"When the LORD your God annihilates the nations before you, which you are entering to take possession of, and you drive them out and live in their land, be careful not to be ensnared by their ways after they have been destroyed before you. Do not inquire about their gods, asking, 'How did these nations worship their gods? I'll also do the same.' You must not do the same to the LORD

50 your God, because they practice every detestable act, which the LORD hates, for their gods. They even burn their sons and daughters in the fire to their gods. Be careful to do everything I command you; do not add anything to it or take anything away from it.

13 "If a prophet or someone who has dreams arises among you and proclaims a sign or wonder to you, and that sign or wonder he has promised you comes about, but he says, 'Let's follow other gods,' which you have not known, 'and let's worship them,' do not listen to that prophet's words or to that dreamer. For the LORD your God is testing you to know whether you love the LORD your God with all your heart and all your soul. You must follow the LORD your God and fear him. You must keep his commands and listen to him; you must worship him and remain faithful to him. That prophet or dreamer must be put to death, because he has urged rebellion against the LORD your God who brought you out of the land of Egypt and redeemed you from the place of slavery, to turn you from the way the LORD your God has commanded you to walk. You must purge the evil from you.

10 "If your brother, the son of your mother, or your son or daughter, or the wife you embrace, or your closest friend secretly entices you, saying, 'Let's go and worship other gods'—which neither you nor your ancestors have known, any of the gods of the peoples around you, near you or far from you, from one end of the earth to the other—do not yield to him or listen to him. Show him no pity, and do not spare him or shield him. Instead, you must kill him. Your hand is to be the first against him to put him to death, and then the hands of all the people. Stone him to death for trying to turn you away from the LORD your God who brought you out of the land of Egypt, out of the place of slavery. All Israel will hear and be afraid, and they will no longer do anything evil like this among you.

"If you hear it said about one of your cities the LORD your God is giving you to live in, that wicked men have sprung up among you, led the inhabitants of their city astray, and said, 'Let's

20 go and worship other gods,' which you have not known, you are to inquire, investigate, and interrogate thoroughly. If the report turns out to be true that this detestable act has been done among you, you must strike down the inhabitants of that city with the sword. Completely destroy everyone in it as well as its livestock with the sword. You are to gather all its spoil in the middle of the city square and completely burn the city and all its spoil for the LORD your God. The city is to remain a mound of ruins forever; it is not to be rebuilt. Nothing set apart for destruction is

to remain in your hand, so that the LORD will turn from his burning anger and grant you mercy, show you compassion, and multiply you as he swore to your ancestors. This will occur if you obey the LORD your God, keeping all his commands I am giving you today, doing what is right in the sight of the LORD your God.

14 "You are sons of the LORD your God; do not cut yourselves or make a bald spot on your head on behalf of the dead, for you are a holy people belonging to the LORD your God. The LORD has chosen you to be his own possession out of all the peoples on the face of the earth.

"You must not eat any detestable thing. These are the animals you may eat:

> oxen, sheep, goats,
> deer, gazelles, roe deer,
> wild goats, ibexes, antelopes,
> and mountain sheep.

You may eat any animal that has hooves divided in two and chews the cud. But among the ones
10 that chew the cud or have divided hooves, you are not to eat these:

> camels, hares, and hyraxes,
> though they chew the cud, they do not have hooves—
> they are unclean for you;
> and pigs, though they have hooves, they do not chew the cud—
> they are unclean for you.

Do not eat their meat or touch their carcasses.

"You may eat everything from the water that has fins and scales, but you may not eat anything that does not have fins and scales—it is unclean for you.

"You may eat every clean bird, but these are the ones you may not eat:
20

> eagles, bearded vultures,
> black vultures, the kites,
> any kind of falcon,
> every kind of raven, ostriches,
> short-eared owls, gulls,
> any kind of hawk,
> little owls, long-eared owls,
> barn owls, eagle owls,
> ospreys, cormorants, storks,
> any kind of heron,
30
> hoopoes, and bats.

All winged insects are unclean for you; they may not be eaten. But you may eat every clean flying creature.

"You are not to eat any carcass; you may give it to a resident alien within your city gates, and he may eat it, or you may sell it to a foreigner. For you are a holy people belonging to the Lord your God. Do not boil a young goat in its mother's milk.

"Each year you are to set aside a tenth of all the produce grown in your fields. You are to eat a tenth of your grain, new wine, and fresh oil, and the firstborn of your herd and flock, in the presence of the Lord your God at the place where he chooses to have his name dwell, so that you will always learn to fear the Lord your God. But if the distance is too great for you to carry it, 40 since the place where the Lord your God chooses to put his name is too far away from you and since the Lord your God has blessed you, then exchange it for silver, take the silver in your hand, and go to the place the Lord your God chooses. You may spend the silver on anything you want: cattle, sheep, goats, wine, beer, or anything you desire. You are to feast there in the presence of the Lord your God and rejoice with your family. Do not neglect the Levite within your city gates, since he has no portion or inheritance among you.

"At the end of every three years, bring a tenth of all your produce for that year and store it within your city gates. Then the Levite, who has no portion or inheritance among you, the resident alien, the fatherless, and the widow within your city gates may come, eat, and be satisfied. And the Lord your God will bless you in all the work of your hands that you do.

15 "At the end of every seven years you must cancel debts. This is how to cancel debt: Every creditor is to cancel what he has lent his neighbor. He is not to collect anything from his neighbor or brother, because the Lord's release of debts has been proclaimed. You may collect something from a foreigner, but you must forgive whatever your brother owes you.

"There will be no poor among you, however, because the Lord is certain to bless you in the land the Lord your God is giving you to possess as an inheritance—if only you obey the Lord your God and are careful to follow every one of these commands I am giving you today. When the Lord your God blesses you as he has promised you, you will lend to many nations but not borrow; you will rule many nations, but they will not rule you.

10 "If there is a poor person among you, one of your brothers within any of your city gates in the land the Lord your God is giving you, do not be hardhearted or tightfisted toward your poor brother. Instead, you are to open your hand to him and freely loan him enough for whatever need he has. Be careful that there isn't this wicked thought in your heart, 'The seventh year, the year of canceling debts, is near,' and you are stingy toward your poor brother and give him nothing. He will cry out to the Lord against you, and you will be guilty. Give to him, and don't have a stingy heart when you give, and because of this the Lord your God will bless you in all your work and in everything you do. For there will never cease to be poor people in the land; that is why I am commanding you, 'Open your hand willingly to your poor and needy brother in your land.'

"If your fellow Hebrew, a man or woman, is sold to you and serves you six years, you must set
20 him free in the seventh year. When you set him free, do not send him away empty-handed. Give
generously to him from your flock, your threshing floor, and your winepress. You are to give him
whatever the LORD your God has blessed you with. Remember that you were a slave in the land
of Egypt and the LORD your God redeemed you; that is why I am giving you this command today.
But if your slave says to you, 'I don't want to leave you,' because he loves you and your family, and
is well off with you, take an awl and pierce through his ear into the door, and he will become your
slave for life. Also treat your female slave the same way. Do not regard it as a hardship when you
set him free, because he worked for you six years—worth twice the wages of a hired worker. Then
the LORD your God will bless you in everything you do.

"Consecrate to the LORD your God every firstborn male produced by your herd and flock. You are
30 not to put the firstborn of your oxen to work or shear the firstborn of your flock. Each year you and
your family are to eat it before the LORD your God in the place the LORD chooses. But if there is
a defect in the animal, if it is lame or blind or has any serious defect, you may not sacrifice it to the
LORD your God. Eat it within your city gates; both the unclean person and the clean may eat it, as
though it were a gazelle or deer. But you must not eat its blood; pour it on the ground like water.

16 "Set aside the month of Abib and observe the Passover to the LORD your God, because the LORD your
God brought you out of Egypt by night in the month of Abib. Sacrifice to the LORD your God a Passover
animal from the herd or flock in the place where the LORD chooses to have his name dwell. Do not eat
leavened bread with it. For seven days you are to eat unleavened bread with it, the bread of hardship—
because you left the land of Egypt in a hurry—so that you may remember for the rest of your life the day
you left the land of Egypt. No yeast is to be found anywhere in your territory for seven days, and none of
the meat you sacrifice in the evening of the first day is to remain until morning. You are not to sacrifice
the Passover animal in any of the towns the LORD your God is giving you. Sacrifice the Passover animal
only at the place where the LORD your God chooses to have his name dwell. Do this in the evening as
10 the sun sets at the same time of day you departed from Egypt. You are to cook and eat it in the place the
LORD your God chooses, and you are to return to your tents in the morning. Eat unleavened bread for six
days. On the seventh day there is to be a solemn assembly to the LORD your God; do not do any work.

"You are to count seven weeks, counting the weeks from the time the sickle is first put to the standing
grain. You are to celebrate the Festival of Weeks to the LORD your God with a freewill offering that
you give in proportion to how the LORD your God has blessed you. Rejoice before the LORD your
God in the place where he chooses to have his name dwell—you, your son and daughter, your male
and female slave, the Levite within your city gates, as well as the resident alien, the fatherless, and the
widow among you. Remember that you were slaves in Egypt; carefully follow these statutes.

"You are to celebrate the Festival of Shelters for seven days when you have gathered in everything
20   from your threshing floor and winepress. Rejoice during your festival—you, your son and
daughter, your male and female slave, as well as the Levite, the resident alien, the fatherless, and
the widow within your city gates. You are to hold a seven-day festival for the LORD your God in
the place he chooses, because the LORD your God will bless you in all your produce and in all the
work of your hands, and you will have abundant joy.

    "All your males are to appear three times a year before the LORD your God in the place he
chooses: at the Festival of Unleavened Bread, the Festival of Weeks, and the Festival of Shelters.
No one is to appear before the LORD empty-handed. Everyone must appear with a gift suited to
his means, according to the blessing the LORD your God has given you.

"Appoint judges and officials for your tribes in all your towns the LORD your God is giving you. They
30   are to judge the people with righteous judgment. Do not deny justice or show partiality to anyone.
Do not accept a bribe, for it blinds the eyes of the wise and twists the words of the righteous. Pursue
justice and justice alone, so that you will live and possess the land the LORD your God is giving you.

"Do not set up an Asherah of any kind of wood next to the altar you will build for the LORD your
God, and do not set up a sacred pillar, the LORD your God hates them.

17   "Do not sacrifice to the LORD your God an ox or sheep with a defect or any serious flaw, for that is
detestable to the LORD your God.

"If a man or woman among you in one of your towns that the LORD your God will give you is
discovered doing evil in the sight of the LORD your God and violating his covenant and has gone
to serve other gods by bowing in worship to the sun, moon, or all the stars in the sky—which I
have forbidden—and if you are told or hear about it, then investigate it thoroughly. If the report
turns out to be true that this detestable act has been done in Israel, you are to bring out to your
city gates that man or woman who has done this evil thing and stone them to death. The one
condemned to die is to be executed on the testimony of two or three witnesses. No one is to be
10   executed on the testimony of a single witness. The witnesses' hands are to be the first in putting
him to death, and after that, the hands of all the people. You must purge the evil from you.

"If a case is too difficult for you—concerning bloodshed, lawsuits, or assaults—cases disputed at
your city gates, then go up to the place the LORD your God chooses. You are to go to the Levitical
priests and to the judge who presides at that time. Ask, and they will give you a verdict in the
case. You must abide by the verdict they give you at the place the LORD chooses. Be careful to do
exactly as they instruct you. You must abide by the instruction they give you and the verdict they

announce to you. Do not turn to the right or the left from the decision they declare to you. The person who acts arrogantly, refusing to listen either to the priest who stands there serving the LORD your God or to the judge, must die. You must purge the evil from Israel. Then all the people 20 will hear about it, be afraid, and no longer behave arrogantly.

"When you enter the land the LORD your God is giving you, take possession of it, live in it, and say, 'I will set a king over me like all the nations around me,' you are to appoint over you the king the LORD your God chooses. Appoint a king from your brothers. You are not to set a foreigner over you, or one who is not of your people. However, he must not acquire many horses for himself or send the people back to Egypt to acquire many horses, for the LORD has told you, 'You are never to go back that way again.' He must not acquire many wives for himself so that his heart won't go astray. He must not acquire very large amounts of silver and gold for himself. When he is seated on his royal throne, he is to write a copy of this instruction for himself on a scroll in the presence of the Levitical priests. It is to remain with him, and he is to read from it all the days of his life, so 30 that he may learn to fear the LORD his God, to observe all the words of this instruction, and to do these statutes. Then his heart will not be exalted above his countrymen, he will not turn from this command to the right or the left, and he and his sons will continue reigning many years in Israel.

18 "The Levitical priests, the whole tribe of Levi, will have no portion or inheritance with Israel. They will eat the LORD's food offerings; that is their inheritance. Although Levi has no inheritance among his brothers, the LORD is his inheritance, as he promised him. This is the priests' share from the people who offer a sacrifice, whether it is an ox, a sheep, or a goat; the priests are to be given the shoulder, jaws, and stomach. You are to give him the firstfruits of your grain, new wine, and fresh oil, and the first sheared wool of your flock. For the LORD your God has chosen him and his sons from all your tribes to stand and minister in his name from now on. When a Levite leaves one of your towns in Israel where he was staying and wants to go to the place the LORD chooses, he may serve in the name of the LORD his God like all his fellow Levites who minister there in the presence of the 10 LORD. They will eat equal portions besides what he has received from the sale of the family estate.

"When you enter the land the LORD your God is giving you, do not imitate the detestable customs of those nations. No one among you is to sacrifice his son or daughter in the fire, practice divination, tell fortunes, interpret omens, practice sorcery, cast spells, consult a medium or a spiritist, or inquire of the dead. Everyone who does these acts is detestable to the LORD, and the LORD your God is driving out the nations before you because of these detestable acts. You must be blameless before the LORD your God. Though these nations you are about to drive out listen to fortune-tellers and diviners, the LORD your God has not permitted you to do this.

"The LORD your God will raise up for you a prophet like me from among your own brothers. You must listen to him. This is what you requested from the LORD your God at Horeb on the day

20 of the assembly when you said, 'Let us not continue to hear the voice of the LORD our God or see this great fire any longer, so that we will not die!' Then the LORD said to me, 'They have spoken well. I will raise up for them a prophet like you from among their brothers. I will put my words in his mouth, and he will tell them everything I command him. I will hold accountable whoever does not listen to my words that he speaks in my name. But the prophet who presumes to speak a message in my name that I have not commanded him to speak, or who speaks in the name of other gods—that prophet must die.' You may say to yourself, 'How can we recognize a message the LORD has not spoken?' When a prophet speaks in the LORD's name, and the message does not come true or is not fulfilled, that is a message the LORD has not spoken. The prophet has spoken it presumptuously. Do not be afraid of him.

19 "When the LORD your God annihilates the nations whose land he is giving you, so that you drive them out and live in their cities and houses, you are to set apart three cities for yourselves within the land the LORD your God is giving you to possess. You are to determine the distances and divide the land the LORD your God is granting you as an inheritance into three regions, so that anyone who commits manslaughter can flee to these cities.

"Here is the law concerning a case of someone who kills a person and flees there to save his life, having killed his neighbor accidentally without previously hating him: If, for example, he goes into the forest with his neighbor to cut timber, and his hand swings the ax to chop down a tree, but the blade flies off the handle and strikes his neighbor so that he dies, that person may flee to one of these 10 cities and live. Otherwise, the avenger of blood in the heat of his anger might pursue the one who committed manslaughter, overtake him because the distance is great, and strike him dead. Yet he did not deserve to die, since he did not previously hate his neighbor. This is why I am commanding you to set apart three cities for yourselves. If the LORD your God enlarges your territory as he swore to your ancestors, and gives you all the land he promised to give them—provided you keep every one of these commands I am giving you today and follow them, loving the LORD your God and walking in his ways at all times—you are to add three more cities to these three. In this way, innocent blood will not be shed, and you will not become guilty of bloodshed in the land the LORD your God is giving you as an inheritance. But if someone hates his neighbor, lies in ambush for him, attacks him, and strikes him fatally, and flees to one of these cities, the elders of his city are to send for him, take him 20 from there, and hand him over to the avenger of blood and he will die. Do not look on him with pity but purge from Israel the guilt of shedding innocent blood, and you will prosper.

"Do not move your neighbor's boundary marker, established at the start in the inheritance you will receive in the land the LORD your God is giving you to possess.

"One witness cannot establish any iniquity or sin against a person, whatever that person has done. A fact must be established by the testimony of two or three witnesses.

"If a malicious witness testifies against someone accusing him of a crime, the two people in the dispute are to stand in the presence of the LORD before the priests and judges in authority at that time. The judges are to make a careful investigation, and if the witness turns out to be a liar who has falsely accused his brother, you must do to him as he intended to do to his brother. You must
30 purge the evil from you. Then everyone else will hear and be afraid, and they will never again do anything evil like this among you. Do not show pity: life for life, eye for eye, tooth for tooth, hand for hand, and foot for foot.

20 "When you go out to war against your enemies and see horses, chariots, and an army larger than yours, do not be afraid of them, for the LORD your God, who brought you out of the land of Egypt, is with you. When you are about to engage in battle, the priest is to come forward and address the army. He is to say to them, 'Listen, Israel: Today you are about to engage in battle with your enemies. Do not be cowardly. Do not be afraid, alarmed, or terrified because of them. For the LORD your God is the one who goes with you to fight for you against your enemies to give you victory.'

"The officers are to address the army, 'Has any man built a new house and not dedicated it? Let him leave and return home. Otherwise, he may die in battle and another man dedicate it. Has any man planted a vineyard and not begun to enjoy its fruit? Let him leave and return home. Otherwise
10 he may die in battle and another man enjoy its fruit. Has any man become engaged to a woman and not married her? Let him leave and return home. Otherwise he may die in battle and another man marry her.' The officers will continue to address the army and say, 'Is there any man who is afraid or cowardly? Let him leave and return home, so that his brothers won't lose heart as he did.' When the officers have finished addressing the army, they will appoint military commanders to lead it.

"When you approach a city to fight against it, make an offer of peace. If it accepts your offer of peace and opens its gates to you, all the people found in it will become forced laborers for you and serve you. However, if it does not make peace with you but wages war against you, lay siege to it. When the LORD your God hands it over to you, strike down all its males with the sword. But you may take the women, dependents, animals, and whatever else is in the city—all its spoil—as plunder. You
20 may enjoy the spoil of your enemies that the LORD your God has given you. This is how you are to treat all the cities that are far away from you and are not among the cities of these nations. However, you must not let any living thing survive among the cities of these people the LORD your God is giving you as an inheritance. You must completely destroy them—the Hethite, Amorite, Canaanite, Perizzite, Hivite, and Jebusite—as the LORD your God has commanded you, so that they won't teach you to do all the detestable acts they do for their gods, and you sin against the LORD your God.

"When you lay siege to a city for a long time, fighting against it in order to capture it, do not destroy its trees by putting an ax to them, because you can get food from them. Do not cut them down. Are trees of the field human, to come under siege by you? But you may destroy the trees that you know do not produce food. You may cut them down to build siege works against the city
30 that is waging war against you, until it falls.

"If a murder victim is found lying in a field in the land the LORD your God is giving you to possess, and it is not known who killed him, your elders and judges are to come out and measure the distance from the victim to the nearby cities. The elders of the city nearest to the victim are to get a young cow that has not been yoked or used for work. The elders of that city will bring the cow down to a continually flowing stream, to a place not tilled or sown, and they will break its neck there by the stream. Then the priests, the sons of Levi, will come forward, for the LORD your God has chosen them to serve him and pronounce blessings in his name, and they are to give a ruling in every dispute and case of assault. All the elders of the city nearest to the victim will wash their hands by the stream over the young cow whose neck has been broken. They will declare, 'Our hands did not shed this blood; our eyes did not see it. LORD, wipe away the guilt of your people Israel whom you redeemed, and do not hold the shedding of innocent blood against them.' Then the responsibility for bloodshed will be wiped away from them. You must purge from yourselves the guilt of shedding innocent blood, for you will be doing what is right in the LORD's sight.

"When you go to war against your enemies and the LORD your God hands them over to you and you take some of them prisoner, and if you see a beautiful woman among the captives, desire her, and want to take her as your wife, you are to bring her into your house. She is to shave her head, trim her nails, remove the clothes she was wearing when she was taken prisoner, live in your house, and mourn for her father and mother a full month. After that, you may have sexual relations with her and be her husband, and she will be your wife. Then if you are not satisfied with her, you are to let her go where she wants, but you must not sell her or treat her as merchandise, because you have humiliated her.

"If a man has two wives, one loved and the other neglected, and both the loved and the neglected bear him sons, and if the neglected wife has the firstborn son, when that man gives what he has to his sons as an inheritance, he is not to show favoritism to the son of the loved wife as his firstborn over the firstborn of the neglected wife. He must acknowledge the firstborn, the son of the neglected wife, by giving him two shares of his estate, for he is the firstfruits of his virility; he has the rights of the firstborn.

"If a man has a stubborn and rebellious son who does not obey his father or mother and doesn't listen to them even after they discipline him, his father and mother are to take hold of him and bring him to the elders of his city, to the gate of his hometown. They will say to the elders of his city, 'This son of ours is stubborn and rebellious; he doesn't obey us. He's a glutton and a drunkard.' Then all the men of his city will stone him to death. You must purge the evil from you, and all Israel will hear and be afraid.

"If anyone is found guilty of an offense deserving the death penalty and is executed, and you hang his body on a tree, you are not to leave his corpse on the tree overnight but are to bury him that day, for anyone hung on a tree is under God's curse. You must not defile the land the LORD your God is giving you as an inheritance.

22 "If you see your brother Israelite's ox or sheep straying, do not ignore it; make sure you return it to your brother. If your brother does not live near you or you don't know him, you are to bring the animal to your home to remain with you until your brother comes looking for it; then you can return it to him. Do the same for his donkey, his garment, or anything your brother has lost and you have found. You must not ignore it. If you see your brother's donkey or ox fallen down on the road, do not ignore it; help him lift it up.

"A woman is not to wear male clothing, and a man is not to put on a woman's garment, for everyone who does these things is detestable to the Lord your God.

10 "If you come across a bird's nest with chicks or eggs, either in a tree or on the ground along the road, and the mother is sitting on the chicks or eggs, do not take the mother along with the young. You may take the young for yourself, but be sure to let the mother go free, so that you may prosper and live long. If you build a new house, make a railing around your roof, so that you don't bring bloodguilt on your house if someone falls from it. Do not plant your vineyard with two types of seed; otherwise, the entire harvest, both the crop you plant and the produce of the vineyard, will be defiled. Do not plow with an ox and a donkey together. Do not wear clothes made of both wool and linen. Make tassels on the four corners of the outer garment you wear.

"If a man marries a woman, has sexual relations with her, and comes to hate her, and accuses her of shameful conduct, and gives her a bad name, saying, 'I married this woman and was intimate with her, but I didn't find any evidence of her virginity,' the young woman's father and mother will take 20 the evidence of her virginity and bring it to the city elders at the city gate. The young woman's father will say to the elders, 'I gave my daughter to this man as a wife, but he hates her. He has accused her of shameful conduct, saying, "I didn't find any evidence of your daughter's virginity," but here is the evidence of my daughter's virginity.' They will spread out the cloth before the city elders. Then the elders of that city will take the man and punish him. They will also fine him a hundred silver shekels and give them to the young woman's father, because that man gave an Israelite virgin a bad name. She will remain his wife; he cannot divorce her as long as he lives. But if this accusation is true and no evidence of the young woman's virginity is found, they will bring the woman to the door of her father's house, and the men of her city will stone her to death. For she has committed an outrage in Israel by being promiscuous while living in her father's house. You must purge the evil from you.

30 "If a man is discovered having sexual relations with another man's wife, both the man who had sex with the woman and the woman must die. You must purge the evil from Israel. If there is a young woman who is a virgin engaged to a man, and another man encounters her in the city and sleeps with her, take the two of them out to the gate of that city and stone them to death— the young woman because she did not cry out in the city and the man because he has violated his neighbor's fiancée. You must purge the evil from you. But if the man encounters an engaged woman in the open country, and he seizes and rapes her, only the man who raped her must die.

Do nothing to the young woman, because she is not guilty of an offense deserving death. This case is just like one in which a man attacks his neighbor and murders him. When he found her in the field, the engaged woman cried out, but there was no one to rescue her. If a man encounters
40 a young woman, a virgin who is not engaged, takes hold of her and rapes her, and they are discovered, the man who raped her is to give the young woman's father fifty silver shekels, and she will become his wife because he violated her. He cannot divorce her as long as he lives.

"A man is not to marry his father's wife; he must not violate his father's marriage bed.

23 "No man whose testicles have been crushed or whose penis has been cut off may enter the LORD's assembly. No one of illegitimate birth may enter the LORD's assembly; none of his descendants, even to the tenth generation, may enter the LORD's assembly. No Ammonite or Moabite may enter the LORD's assembly; none of their descendants, even to the tenth generation, may ever enter the LORD's assembly. This is because they did not meet you with food and water on the journey after you came out of Egypt, and because Balaam son of Beor from Pethor in Aram-naharaim was hired to curse you. Yet the LORD your God would not listen to Balaam, but he turned the curse into a blessing for you because the LORD your God loves you. Never pursue their welfare or prosperity as long as you live. Do not despise an Edomite, because he is your brother. Do not despise an Egyptian, because you were a resident alien in
10 his land. The children born to them in the third generation may enter the LORD's assembly.

"When you are encamped against your enemies, be careful to avoid anything offensive. If there is a man among you who is unclean because of a bodily emission during the night, he must go outside the camp; he may not come anywhere inside the camp. When evening approaches, he is to wash with water, and when the sun sets he may come inside the camp. You are to have a place outside the camp and go there to relieve yourself. You are to have a digging tool in your equipment; when you relieve yourself, dig a hole with it and cover up your excrement. For the LORD your God walks throughout your camp to protect you and deliver your enemies to you; so your encampments must be holy. He must not see anything indecent among you or he will turn away from you.

"Do not return a slave to his master when he has escaped from his master to you. Let him live
20 among you wherever he wants within your city gates. Do not mistreat him.

"No Israelite woman is to be a cult prostitute, and no Israelite man is to be a cult prostitute. Do not bring a female prostitute's wages or a male prostitute's earnings into the house of the LORD your God to fulfill any vow, because both are detestable to the LORD your God.

"Do not charge your brother interest on silver, food, or anything that can earn interest. You may charge a foreigner interest, but you must not charge your brother Israelite interest, so that the LORD your God may bless you in everything you do in the land you are entering to possess.

"If you make a vow to the LORD your God, do not be slow to keep it, because he will require it of you, and it will be counted against you as sin. But if you refrain from making a vow, it will not be
30 counted against you as sin. Be careful to do whatever comes from your lips, because you have freely vowed what you promised to the LORD your God.

"When you enter your neighbor's vineyard, you may eat as many grapes as you want until you are full, but do not put any in your container. When you enter your neighbor's standing grain, you may pluck heads of grain with your hand, but do not put a sickle to your neighbor's grain.

24 "If a man marries a woman, but she becomes displeasing to him because he finds something indecent about her, he may write her a divorce certificate, hand it to her, and send her away from his house. If after leaving his house she goes and becomes another man's wife, and the second man hates her, writes her a divorce certificate, hands it to her, and sends her away from his house or if he dies, the first husband who sent her away may not marry her again after she has been defiled, because that would be detestable to the LORD. You must not bring guilt on the land the LORD your God is giving you as an inheritance.

"When a man takes a bride, he must not go out with the army or be liable for any duty. He is free to stay at home for one year, so that he can bring joy to the wife he has married.

"Do not take a pair of grindstones or even the upper millstone as security for a debt, because that
10 is like taking a life as security.

"If a man is discovered kidnapping one of his Israelite brothers, whether he treats him as a slave or sells him, the kidnapper must die. You must purge the evil from you.

"Be careful with a person who has a case of serious skin disease, following carefully everything the Levitical priests instruct you to do. Be careful to do as I have commanded them. Remember what the LORD your God did to Miriam on the journey after you left Egypt.

"When you make a loan of any kind to your neighbor, do not enter his house to collect what he offers as security. Stand outside while the man you are making the loan to brings the security out to you. If he is a poor man, do not sleep with the garment he has given as security. Be sure to return it to him at sunset. Then he will sleep in it and bless you, and this will be counted as
20 righteousness to you before the LORD your God.

"Do not oppress a hired worker who is poor and needy, whether one of your Israelite brothers or one of the resident aliens in a town in your land. You are to pay him his wages each day before the sun sets, because he is poor and depends on them. Otherwise he will cry out to the LORD against you, and you will be held guilty.

"Fathers are not to be put to death for their children, and children are not to be put to death for their fathers; each person will be put to death for his own sin. Do not deny justice to a resident alien or fatherless child, and do not take a widow's garment as security. Remember that you were a slave in Egypt, and the LORD your God redeemed you from there. Therefore I am commanding you to do this.

30 "When you reap the harvest in your field, and you forget a sheaf in the field, do not go back to get it. It is to be left for the resident alien, the fatherless, and the widow, so that the LORD your God may bless you in all the work of your hands. When you knock down the fruit from your olive tree, do not go over the branches again. What remains will be for the resident alien, the fatherless, and the widow. When you gather the grapes of your vineyard, do not glean what is left. What remains will be for the resident alien, the fatherless, and the widow. Remember that you were a slave in the land of Egypt. Therefore I am commanding you to do this.

25 "If there is a dispute between men, they are to go to court, and the judges will hear their case. They will clear the innocent and condemn the guilty. If the guilty party deserves to be flogged, the judge will make him lie down and be flogged in his presence with the number of lashes appropriate for his crime. He may be flogged with forty lashes, but no more. Otherwise, if he is flogged with more lashes than these, your brother will be degraded in your sight.

"Do not muzzle an ox while it treads out grain.

"When brothers live on the same property and one of them dies without a son, the wife of the dead man may not marry a stranger outside the family. Her brother-in-law is to take her as his wife, have sexual relations with her, and perform the duty of a brother-in-law for her. The first 10 son she bears will carry on the name of the dead brother, so his name will not be blotted out from Israel. But if the man doesn't want to marry his sister-in-law, she is to go to the elders at the city gate and say, 'My brother-in-law refuses to preserve his brother's name in Israel. He isn't willing to perform the duty of a brother-in-law for me.' The elders of his city will summon him and speak with him. If he persists and says, 'I don't want to marry her,' then his sister-in-law will go up to him in the sight of the elders, remove his sandal from his foot, and spit in his face. Then she will declare, 'This is what is done to a man who will not build up his brother's house.' And his family name in Israel will be 'The house of the man whose sandal was removed.'

"If two men are fighting with each other, and the wife of one steps in to rescue her husband from the one striking him, and she puts out her hand and grabs his genitals, you are to cut off her 20 hand. Do not show pity.

"Do not have differing weights in your bag, one heavy and one light. Do not have differing dry measures in your house, a larger and a smaller. You must have a full and honest weight, a full and honest dry measure, so that you may live long in the land the LORD your God is giving you. For everyone who does such things and acts unfairly is detestable to the LORD your God.

"Remember what the Amalekites did to you on the journey after you left Egypt. They met you along the way and attacked all your stragglers from behind when you were tired and weary. They did not fear God. When the LORD your God gives you rest from all the enemies around you in the land the LORD your God is giving you to possess as an inheritance, blot out the memory of Amalek under heaven. Do not forget.

26 "When you enter the land the LORD your God is giving you as an inheritance, and you take possession of it and live in it, take some of the first of all the land's produce that you harvest from the land the LORD your God is giving you and put it in a basket. Then go to the place where the LORD your God chooses to have his name dwell. When you come before the priest who is serving at that time, say to him, 'Today I declare to the LORD your God that I have entered the land the LORD swore to our ancestors to give us.'

"Then the priest will take the basket from you and place it before the altar of the LORD your God. You are to respond by saying in the presence of the LORD your God:

My father was a wandering Aramean. He went down to Egypt with a few people and resided there as an alien. There he became a great, powerful, and populous nation. But the Egyptians mistreated and oppressed us, and forced us to do hard labor. So we called out to the LORD, the God of our ancestors, and the LORD heard our cry and saw our misery, hardship, and oppression. Then the LORD brought us out of Egypt with a strong hand and an outstretched arm, with terrifying power, and with signs and wonders. He led us to this place and gave us this land, a land flowing with milk and honey. I have now brought the first of the land's produce that you, LORD, have given me.

You will then place the container before the LORD your God and bow down to him. You, the Levites, and the resident aliens among you will rejoice in all the good things the LORD your God has given you and your household.

"When you have finished paying all the tenth of your produce in the third year, the year of the tenth, you are to give it to the Levites, resident aliens, fatherless children, and widows, so that they may eat in your towns and be satisfied. Then you will say in the presence of the LORD your God:

I have taken the consecrated portion out of my house; I have also given it to the Levites, resident aliens, fatherless children, and widows, according to all the commands you gave me. I have not violated or forgotten your commands. I have not eaten any of it while in mourning, or removed any of it while unclean, or offered any of it for the dead. I have obeyed the LORD my God; I have done all you commanded me. Look down from your holy dwelling, from heaven, and bless your people Israel and the land you have given us as you swore to our ancestors, a land flowing with milk and honey.

"The LORD your God is commanding you this day to follow these statutes and ordinances. Follow them carefully with all your heart and all your soul. Today you have affirmed that the LORD is your God and that you will walk in his ways, keep his statutes, commands, and ordinances, and obey him. And today the LORD has affirmed that you are his own possession as he promised you, that you are to keep all his commands, that he will elevate you to praise, fame, and glory above all the nations he has made, and that you will be a holy people to the LORD your God as he promised."

27 Moses and the elders of Israel commanded the people, "Keep every command I am giving you today. When you cross the Jordan into the land the LORD your God is giving you, set up large stones and cover them with plaster. Write all the words of this law on the stones after you cross to enter the land the LORD your God is giving you, a land flowing with milk and honey, as the LORD, the God of your ancestors, has promised you. When you have crossed the Jordan, you are to set up these stones on Mount Ebal, as I am commanding you today, and you are to cover them with plaster. Build an altar of stones there to the LORD your God—do not use any iron tool on them. Use uncut stones to build the altar of the LORD your God and offer burnt offerings to the LORD your God on it. There you are to sacrifice fellowship offerings, eat, and rejoice in the presence of the LORD your God. Write clearly all the words of this law on the plastered stones."

Moses and the Levitical priests spoke to all Israel, "Be silent, Israel, and listen! This day you have become the people of the LORD your God. Obey the LORD your God and follow his commands and statutes I am giving you today."

On that day Moses commanded the people, "When you have crossed the Jordan, these tribes will stand on Mount Gerizim to bless the people: Simeon, Levi, Judah, Issachar, Joseph, and Benjamin. And these tribes will stand on Mount Ebal to deliver the curse: Reuben, Gad, Asher, Zebulun, Dan, and Naphtali. The Levites will proclaim in a loud voice to every Israelite:

'The person who makes a carved idol or cast image, which is detestable to the LORD, the work of a craftsman, and sets it up in secret is cursed.'

And all the people will reply, 'Amen!'

'The one who dishonors his father or mother is cursed.'

And all the people will say, 'Amen!'

'The one who moves his neighbor's boundary marker is cursed.'

And all the people will say, 'Amen!'

'The one who leads a blind person astray on the road is cursed.'

And all the people will say, 'Amen!'

'The one who denies justice to a resident alien, a fatherless child, or a widow is cursed.'

And all the people will say, 'Amen!'

'The one who sleeps with his father's wife is cursed, for he has violated his father's marriage bed.'

And all the people will say, 'Amen!'

'The one who has sexual intercourse with any animal is cursed.'

And all the people will say, 'Amen!'

'The one who sleeps with his sister, whether his father's daughter or his mother's daughter is cursed.'

And all the people will say, 'Amen!'

'The one who sleeps with his mother-in-law is cursed.'

And all the people will say, 'Amen!'

'The one who secretly kills his neighbor is cursed.'

40 And all the people will say, 'Amen!'

'The one who accepts a bribe to kill an innocent person is cursed.'

And all the people will say, 'Amen!'

'Anyone who does not put the words of this law into practice is cursed.'

And all the people will say, 'Amen!'

28 "Now if you faithfully obey the LORD your God and are careful to follow all his commands I am giving you today, the LORD your God will put you far above all the nations of the earth. All these blessings will come and overtake you, because you obey the LORD your God:

> You will be blessed in the city
> and blessed in the country.
> Your offspring will be blessed,
> and your land's produce,
> and the offspring of your livestock,
> including the young of your herds
10 and the newborn of your flocks.
> Your basket and kneading bowl will be blessed.
> You will be blessed when you come in
> and blessed when you go out.

"The LORD will cause the enemies who rise up against you to be defeated before you. They will march out against you from one direction but flee from you in seven directions. The LORD will grant you a blessing on your barns and on everything you do; he will bless you in the land the LORD your God is giving you. The LORD will establish you as his holy people, as he swore to you, if you obey the commands of the LORD your God and walk in his ways. Then all the peoples of the earth will see that you bear the LORD's name, and they will stand in awe of you. The LORD
20 will make you prosper abundantly with offspring, the offspring of your livestock, and your land's produce in the land the LORD swore to your ancestors to give you. The LORD will open for you his abundant storehouse, the sky, to give your land rain in its season and to bless all the work of your

hands. You will lend to many nations, but you will not borrow. The LORD will make you the head and not the tail; you will only move upward and never downward if you listen to the LORD your God's commands I am giving you today and are careful to follow them. Do not turn aside to the right or the left from all the things I am commanding you today, and do not follow other gods to worship them.

"But if you do not obey the LORD your God by carefully following all his commands and statutes I am giving you today, all these curses will come and overtake you:

30   You will be cursed in the city
     and cursed in the country.
     Your basket and kneading bowl will be cursed.
     Your offspring will be cursed,
     and your land's produce,
     the young of your herds,
     and the newborn of your flocks.
     You will be cursed when you come in
     and cursed when you go out.

The LORD will send against you curses, confusion, and rebuke in everything you do until you
40 are destroyed and quickly perish, because of the wickedness of your actions in abandoning me. The LORD will make pestilence cling to you until he has exterminated you from the land you are entering to possess. The LORD will afflict you with wasting disease, fever, inflammation, burning heat, drought, blight, and mildew; these will pursue you until you perish. The sky above you will be bronze, and the earth beneath you iron. The LORD will turn the rain of your land into falling dust; it will descend on you from the sky until you are destroyed. The LORD will cause you to be defeated before your enemies. You will march out against them from one direction but flee from them in seven directions. You will be an object of horror to all the kingdoms of the earth. Your corpses will be food for all the birds of the sky and the wild animals of the earth, with no one to scare them away.

"The LORD will afflict you with the boils of Egypt, tumors, a festering rash, and scabies, from
50 which you cannot be cured. The LORD will afflict you with madness, blindness, and mental confusion, so that at noon you will grope as a blind person gropes in the dark. You will not be successful in anything you do. You will only be oppressed and robbed continually, and no one will help you. You will become engaged to a woman, but another man will rape her. You will build a house but not live in it. You will plant a vineyard but not enjoy its fruit. Your ox will be slaughtered before your eyes, but you will not eat any of it. Your donkey will be taken away from you and not returned to you. Your flock will be given to your enemies, and no one will help you. Your sons and daughters will be given to another people, while your eyes grow weary looking for them every day. But you will be powerless to do anything. A people you don't know will eat your land's produce and everything you have labored for. You will only be oppressed and crushed

60 continually. You will be driven mad by what you see. The LORD will afflict you with painful and incurable boils on your knees and thighs—from the sole of your foot to the top of your head.

"The LORD will bring you and your king that you have appointed to a nation neither you nor your ancestors have known, and there you will worship other gods, of wood and stone. You will become an object of horror, scorn, and ridicule among all the peoples where the LORD will drive you.

"You will sow much seed in the field but harvest little, because locusts will devour it. You will plant and cultivate vineyards but not drink the wine or gather the grapes, because worms will eat them. You will have olive trees throughout your territory but not moisten your skin with oil, because your olives will drop off. You will father sons and daughters, but they will not remain

70 yours, because they will be taken prisoner. Buzzing insects will take possession of all your trees and your land's produce. The resident alien among you will rise higher and higher above you, while you sink lower and lower. He will lend to you, but you won't lend to him. He will be the head, and you will be the tail.

"All these curses will come, pursue, and overtake you until you are destroyed, since you did not obey the LORD your God and keep the commands and statutes he gave you. These curses will be a sign and a wonder against you and your descendants forever. Because you didn't serve the LORD your God with joy and a cheerful heart, even though you had an abundance of everything, you will serve your enemies that the LORD will send against you, in famine, thirst, nakedness, and a lack of everything. He will place an iron yoke on your neck until he has destroyed you.

80 The LORD will bring a nation from far away, from the ends of the earth, to swoop down on you like an eagle, a nation whose language you won't understand, a ruthless nation, showing no respect for the old and not sparing the young. They will eat the offspring of your livestock and your land's produce until you are destroyed. They will leave you no grain, new wine, fresh oil, young of your herds, or newborn of your flocks until they cause you to perish. They will besiege you within all your city gates until your high and fortified walls, that you trust in, come down throughout your land. They will besiege you within all your city gates throughout the land the LORD your God has given you.

"You will eat your offspring, the flesh of your sons and daughters the LORD your God has given you during the siege and hardship your enemy imposes on you. The most sensitive and

90 refined man among you will look grudgingly at his brother, the wife he embraces, and the rest of his children, refusing to share with any of them his children's flesh that he will eat because he has nothing left during the siege and hardship your enemy imposes on you in all your towns. The most sensitive and refined woman among you, who would not venture to set the sole of her foot on the ground because of her refinement and sensitivity, will begrudge the husband she embraces, her son, and her daughter, the afterbirth that comes out from between her legs and the children she bears, because she will secretly eat them for lack of anything else during the siege and hardship your enemy imposes on you within your city gates.

"If you are not careful to obey all the words of this law, which are written in this scroll, by fearing this glorious and awe-inspiring name—the LORD, your God—he will bring wondrous
100 plagues on you and your descendants, severe and lasting plagues, and terrible and chronic sicknesses. He will afflict you again with all the diseases of Egypt, which you dreaded, and they will cling to you. The LORD will also afflict you with every sickness and plague not recorded in the book of this law, until you are destroyed. Though you were as numerous as the stars of the sky, you will be left with only a few people, because you did not obey the LORD your God. Just as the LORD was glad to cause you to prosper and to multiply you, so he will also be glad to cause you to perish and to destroy you. You will be ripped out of the land you are entering to possess. Then the LORD will scatter you among all peoples from one end of the earth to the other, and there you will worship other gods, of wood and stone, which neither you nor your ancestors have known. You will find no peace among those nations, and there will be no resting place for the sole of your
110 foot. There the LORD will give you a trembling heart, failing eyes, and a despondent spirit. Your life will hang in doubt before you. You will be in dread night and day, never certain of survival. In the morning you will say, 'If only it were evening!' and in the evening you will say, 'If only it were morning!'—because of the dread you will have in your heart and because of what you will see. The LORD will take you back in ships to Egypt by a route that I said you would never see again. There you will sell yourselves to your enemies as male and female slaves, but no one will buy you."

29 These are the words of the covenant that the LORD commanded Moses to make with the Israelites in the land of Moab, in addition to the covenant he had made with them at Horeb. Moses summoned all Israel and said to them, "You have seen with your own eyes everything the LORD did in Egypt to Pharaoh, to all his officials, and to his entire land. You saw with your own eyes the great trials and those great signs and wonders. Yet to this day the LORD has not given you a mind to understand, eyes to see, or ears to hear. I led you forty years in the wilderness; your clothes and the sandals on your feet did not wear out; you did not eat food or drink wine or beer—so that you might know that I am the LORD your God. When you reached this place, King Sihon of Heshbon and King Og of Bashan came out against us in battle, but we defeated them. We took their land and
10 gave it as an inheritance to the Reubenites, the Gadites, and half the tribe of Manasseh. Therefore, observe the words of this covenant and follow them, so that you will succeed in everything you do.

"All of you are standing today before the LORD your God—your leaders, tribes, elders, officials, all the men of Israel, your dependents, your wives, and the resident aliens in your camps who cut your wood and draw your water—so that you may enter into the covenant of the LORD your God, which he is making with you today, so that you may enter into his oath and so that he may establish you today as his people and he may be your God as he promised you and as he swore to your ancestors Abraham, Isaac, and Jacob. I am making this covenant and this oath not only with you, but also with those who are standing here with us today in the presence of the LORD our God and with those who are not here today.

20 "Indeed, you know how we lived in the land of Egypt and passed through the nations where you traveled. You saw their abhorrent images and idols made of wood, stone, silver, and gold, which were among them. Be sure there is no man, woman, clan, or tribe among you today whose heart turns away from the LORD our God to go and worship the gods of those nations. Be sure there is no root among you bearing poisonous and bitter fruit. When someone hears the words of this oath, he may consider himself exempt, thinking, 'I will have peace even though I follow my own stubborn heart.' This will lead to the destruction of the well-watered land as well as the dry land. The LORD will not be willing to forgive him. Instead, his anger and jealousy will burn against that person, and every curse written in this scroll will descend on him. The LORD will blot out his name under heaven, and single him out for harm from all the tribes of Israel, according to all the curses

30 of the covenant written in this book of the law.

"Future generations of your children who follow you and the foreigner who comes from a distant country will see the plagues of that land and the sicknesses the LORD has inflicted on it. All its soil will be a burning waste of sulfur and salt, unsown, producing nothing, with no plant growing on it, just like the fall of Sodom and Gomorrah, Admah and Zeboiim, which the LORD demolished in his fierce anger. All the nations will ask, 'Why has the LORD done this to this land? Why this intense outburst of anger?' Then people will answer, 'It is because they abandoned the covenant of the LORD, the God of their ancestors, which he had made with them when he brought them out of the land of Egypt. They began to serve other gods, bowing in worship to gods they had not known—gods that the LORD had not permitted them to worship. Therefore the LORD's

40 anger burned against this land, and he brought every curse written in this book on it. The LORD uprooted them from their land in his anger, rage, and intense wrath, and threw them into another land where they are today.' The hidden things belong to the LORD our God, but the revealed things belong to us and our children forever, so that we may follow all the words of this law.

30 "When all these things happen to you—the blessings and curses I have set before you—and you come to your senses while you are in all the nations where the LORD your God has driven you, and you and your children return to the LORD your God and obey him with all your heart and all your soul by doing everything I am commanding you today, then he will restore your fortunes, have compassion on you, and gather you again from all the peoples where the LORD your God has scattered you. Even if your exiles are at the farthest horizon, he will gather you and bring you back from there. The LORD your God will bring you into the land your ancestors possessed, and you will take possession of it. He will cause you to prosper and multiply you more than he did your ancestors. The LORD your God will circumcise your heart and the hearts of your descendants, and

10 you will love him with all your heart and all your soul so that you will live. The LORD your God will put all these curses on your enemies who hate and persecute you. Then you will again obey him and follow all his commands I am commanding you today. The LORD your God will make you prosper

abundantly in all the work of your hands, your offspring, the offspring of your livestock, and the produce of your land. Indeed, the LORD will again delight in your prosperity, as he delighted in that of your ancestors, when you obey the LORD your God by keeping his commands and statutes that are written in this book of the law and return to him with all your heart and all your soul.

"This command that I give you today is certainly not too difficult or beyond your reach. It is not in heaven so that you have to ask, 'Who will go up to heaven, get it for us, and proclaim it to us so that we may follow it?' And it is not across the sea so that you have to ask, 'Who will cross the sea, get it for us, and proclaim it to us so that we may follow it?' But the message is very near you, in your mouth and in your heart, so that you may follow it. See, today I have set before you life and prosperity, death and adversity. For I am commanding you today to love the LORD your God, to walk in his ways, and to keep his commands, statutes, and ordinances, so that you may live and multiply, and the LORD your God may bless you in the land you are entering to possess. But if your heart turns away and you do not listen and you are led astray to bow in worship to other gods and serve them, I tell you today that you will certainly perish and will not prolong your days in the land you are entering to possess across the Jordan. I call heaven and earth as witnesses against you today that I have set before you life and death, blessing and curse. Choose life so that you and your descendants may live, love the LORD your God, obey him, and remain faithful to him. For he is your life, and he will prolong your days as you live in the land the LORD swore to give to your ancestors Abraham, Isaac, and Jacob."

31 Then Moses continued to speak these words to all Israel, saying, "I am now 120 years old; I can no longer act as your leader. The LORD has told me, 'You will not cross the Jordan.' The LORD your God is the one who will cross ahead of you. He will destroy these nations before you, and you will drive them out. Joshua is the one who will cross ahead of you, as the LORD has said. The LORD will deal with them as he did Sihon and Og, the kings of the Amorites, and their land when he destroyed them. The LORD will deliver them over to you, and you must do to them exactly as I have commanded you. Be strong and courageous; don't be terrified or afraid of them. For the LORD your God is the one who will go with you; he will not leave you or abandon you."

Moses then summoned Joshua and said to him in the sight of all Israel, "Be strong and courageous, for you will go with this people into the land the LORD swore to give to their ancestors. You will enable them to take possession of it. The LORD is the one who will go before you. He will be with you; he will not leave you or abandon you. Do not be afraid or discouraged."

Moses wrote down this law and gave it to the priests, the sons of Levi, who carried the ark of the LORD's covenant, and to all the elders of Israel. Moses commanded them, "At the end of every seven years, at the appointed time in the year of debt cancellation, during the Festival of Shelters, when all Israel assembles in the presence of the LORD your God at the place he chooses, you are to read this law aloud before all Israel. Gather the people—men, women, dependents, and the resident aliens within your city gates—so that they may listen and learn to fear the LORD your

God and be careful to follow all the words of this law. Then their children who do not know the law will listen and learn to fear the LORD your God as long as you live in the land you are crossing the Jordan to possess."

The LORD said to Moses, "The time of your death is now approaching. Call Joshua and present yourselves at the tent of meeting so that I may commission him." When Moses and Joshua went and presented themselves at the tent of meeting, the LORD appeared at the tent in a pillar of cloud, and the cloud stood at the entrance to the tent.

The LORD said to Moses, "You are about to rest with your ancestors, and these people will soon prostitute themselves with the foreign gods of the land they are entering. They will abandon me and break the covenant I have made with them. My anger will burn against them on that day; I will abandon them and hide my face from them so that they will become easy prey. Many troubles and afflictions will come to them. On that day they will say, 'Haven't these troubles come to us because our God is no longer with us?' I will certainly hide my face on that day because of all the evil they have done by turning to other gods. Therefore write down this song for yourselves and teach it to the Israelites; have them sing it, so that this song may be a witness for me against the Israelites. When I bring them into the land I swore to give their ancestors, a land flowing with milk and honey, they will eat their fill and prosper. They will turn to other gods and worship them, despising me and breaking my covenant. And when many troubles and afflictions come to them, this song will testify against them, because their descendants will not have forgotten it. For I know what they are prone to do, even before I bring them into the land I swore to give them." So Moses wrote down this song on that day and taught it to the Israelites.

The LORD commissioned Joshua son of Nun, "Be strong and courageous, for you will bring the Israelites into the land I swore to them, and I will be with you."

When Moses had finished writing down on a scroll every single word of this law, he commanded the Levites who carried the ark of the LORD's covenant, "Take this book of the law and place it beside the ark of the covenant of the LORD your God so that it may remain there as a witness against you. For I know how rebellious and stiff-necked you are. If you are rebelling against the LORD now, while I am still alive, how much more will you rebel after I am dead! Assemble all your tribal elders and officers before me so that I may speak these words directly to them and call heaven and earth as witnesses against them. For I know that after my death you will become completely corrupt and turn from the path I have commanded you. Disaster will come to you in the future, because you will do what is evil in the LORD's sight, angering him with what your hands have made." Then Moses recited aloud every single word of this song to the entire assembly of Israel:

32   Pay attention, heavens, and I will speak;
                  listen, earth, to the words from my mouth.

Let my teaching fall like rain
and my word settle like dew,
like gentle rain on new grass
and showers on tender plants.
For I will proclaim the LORD's name.
Declare the greatness of our God!
The Rock—his work is perfect;
all his ways are just.
A faithful God, without bias,
he is righteous and true.

His people have acted corruptly toward him;
this is their defect—they are not his children
but a devious and crooked generation.
Is this how you repay the LORD,
you foolish and senseless people?
Isn't he your Father and Creator?
Didn't he make you and sustain you?
Remember the days of old;
consider the years of past generations.
Ask your father, and he will tell you,
your elders, and they will teach you.
When the Most High gave the nations their inheritance
and divided the human race,
he set the boundaries of the peoples
according to the number of the people of Israel.
But the LORD's portion is his people,
Jacob, his own inheritance.

He found him in a desolate land,
in a barren, howling wilderness;
he surrounded him, cared for him,
and protected him as the pupil of his eye.
He watches over his nest like an eagle
and hovers over his young;
he spreads his wings, catches him,
and carries him on his feathers.
The LORD alone led him,

with no help from a foreign god.
40 He made him ride on the heights of the land
and eat the produce of the field.
He nourished him with honey from the rock
and oil from flinty rock,
curds from the herd and milk from the flock,
with the fat of lambs,
rams from Bashan, and goats,
with the choicest grains of wheat;
you drank wine from the finest grapes.

Then Jeshurun became fat and rebelled—
50 you became fat, bloated, and gorged.
He abandoned the God who made him
and scorned the Rock of his salvation.
They provoked his jealousy with different gods;
they enraged him with detestable practices.
They sacrificed to demons, not God,
to gods they had not known,
new gods that had just arrived,
which your ancestors did not fear.
You ignored the Rock who gave you birth;
60 you forgot the God who gave birth to you.

When the LORD saw this, he despised them,
angered by his sons and daughters.
He said, "I will hide my face from them;
I will see what will become of them,
for they are a perverse generation—
unfaithful children.
They have provoked my jealousy
with what is not a god;
they have enraged me with their worthless idols.
70 So I will provoke their jealousy
with what is not a people;
I will enrage them with a foolish nation.
For fire has been kindled because of my anger
and burns to the depths of Sheol;

it devours the land and its produce,
and scorches the foundations of the mountains.

"I will pile disasters on them;
I will use up my arrows against them.
They will be weak from hunger,
ravaged by pestilence and bitter plague;
I will unleash on them wild beasts with fangs,
as well as venomous snakes that slither in the dust.
Outside, the sword will take their children,
and inside, there will be terror;
the young man and the young woman will be killed,
the infant and the gray-haired man.

"I would have said: I will cut them to pieces
and blot out the memory of them from mankind,
if I had not feared provocation from the enemy,
or feared that these foes might misunderstand
and say, 'Our own hand has prevailed;
it wasn't the Lord who did all this.'"

Israel is a nation lacking sense
with no understanding at all.
If only they were wise, they would comprehend this;
they would understand their fate.
How could one pursue a thousand,
or two put ten thousand to flight,
unless their Rock had sold them,
unless the Lord had given them up?
But their "rock" is not like our Rock,
as even our enemies concede.
For their vine is from the vine of Sodom
and from the fields of Gomorrah.
Their grapes are poisonous;
their clusters are bitter.
Their wine is serpents' venom,
the deadly poison of cobras.

"Is it not stored up with me,
110   sealed up in my vaults?
Vengeance and retribution belong to me.
In time their foot will slip,
for their day of disaster is near,
and their doom is coming quickly."
The Lord will indeed vindicate his people
and have compassion on his servants
when he sees that their strength is gone
and no one is left—slave or free.
He will say, "Where are their gods,
120   the 'rock' they found refuge in?
Who ate the fat of their sacrifices
and drank the wine of their drink offerings?
Let them rise up and help you;
let it be a shelter for you.
See now that I alone am he;
there is no God but me.
I bring death and I give life;
I wound and I heal.
No one can rescue anyone from my power.
130   I raise my hand to heaven and declare:
As surely as I live forever,
when I sharpen my flashing sword,
and my hand takes hold of judgment,
I will take vengeance on my adversaries
and repay those who hate me.
I will make my arrows drunk with blood
while my sword devours flesh—
the blood of the slain and the captives,
the heads of the enemy leaders."

140   Rejoice, you nations, concerning his people,
for he will avenge the blood of his servants.
He will take vengeance on his adversaries;
he will purify his land and his people.

Moses came with Joshua son of Nun and recited all the words of this song in the presence of the people. After Moses finished reciting all these words to all Israel, he said to them, "Take to heart all these words I am giving as a warning to you today, so that you may command your children to follow all the words of this law carefully. For they are not meaningless words to you but they are your life, and by them you will live long in the land you are crossing the Jordan to possess."

On that same day the LORD spoke to Moses, "Go up Mount Nebo in the Abarim range in the
150 land of Moab, across from Jericho, and view the land of Canaan I am giving the Israelites as a possession. Then you will die on the mountain that you go up, and you will be gathered to your people, just as your brother Aaron died on Mount Hor and was gathered to his people. For both of you broke faith with me among the Israelites at the Waters of Meribath-kadesh in the Wilderness of Zin by failing to treat me as holy in their presence. Although from a distance you will view the land that I am giving the Israelites, you will not go there."

33 This is the blessing that Moses, the man of God, gave the Israelites before his death. He said:

> The LORD came from Sinai
> and appeared to them from Seir;
> he shone on them from Mount Paran
> and came with ten thousand holy ones,
> with lightning from his right hand for them.
> Indeed he loves the people.
> All your holy ones are in your hand,
> and they assemble at your feet.
10 Each receives your words.
> Moses gave us instruction,
> a possession for the assembly of Jacob.
> So he became King in Jeshurun
> when the leaders of the people gathered
> with the tribes of Israel.

> Let Reuben live and not die
> though his people become few.

He said this about Judah:
> LORD, hear Judah's cry and bring him to his people.
20 He fights for his cause with his own hands,
> but may you be a help against his foes.

He said about Levi:
> Your Thummim and Urim belong to your faithful one;

you tested him at Massah
and contended with him at the Waters of Meribah.
He said about his father and mother,
"I do not regard them."
He disregarded his brothers
and didn't acknowledge his sons,
30   for they kept your word
and maintained your covenant.
They will teach your ordinances to Jacob
and your instruction to Israel;
they will set incense before you
and whole burnt offerings on your altar.
LORD, bless his possessions,
and accept the work of his hands.
Break the back of his adversaries and enemies,
so that they cannot rise again.
40 He said about Benjamin:
The LORD's beloved rests securely on him.
He shields him all day long,
and he rests on his shoulders.
He said about Joseph:
May his land be blessed by the LORD
with the dew of heaven's bounty
and the watery depths that lie beneath;
with the bountiful harvest from the sun
and the abundant yield of the seasons;
50   with the best products of the ancient mountains
and the bounty of the eternal hills;
with the choice gifts of the land
and everything in it;
and with the favor of him
who appeared in the burning bush.
May these rest on the head of Joseph,
on the brow of the prince of his brothers.
His firstborn bull has splendor,
and horns like those of a wild ox;
60   he gores all the peoples with them
to the ends of the earth.

Such are the ten thousands of Ephraim,
and such are the thousands of Manasseh.
He said about Zebulun:
Rejoice, Zebulun, in your journeys,
and Issachar, in your tents.
They summon the peoples to a mountain;
there they offer acceptable sacrifices.
For they draw from the wealth of the seas
70   and the hidden treasures of the sand.
He said about Gad:
The one who enlarges Gad's territory
will be blessed.
He lies down like a lion
and tears off an arm or even a head.
He chose the best part for himself,
because a ruler's portion was assigned there for him.
He came with the leaders of the people;
he carried out the LORD's justice
80   and his ordinances for Israel.
He said about Dan:
Dan is a young lion,
leaping out of Bashan.
He said about Naphtali:
Naphtali, enjoying approval,
full of the LORD's blessing,
take possession to the west and the south.
He said about Asher:
May Asher be the most blessed of the sons;
90   may he be the most favored among his brothers
and dip his foot in olive oil.
May the bolts of your gate be iron and bronze,
and your strength last as long as you live.

There is none like the God of Jeshurun,
who rides the heavens to your aid,
the clouds in his majesty.
The God of old is your dwelling place,
and underneath are the everlasting arms.

100   He drives out the enemy before you
and commands, "Destroy!"
So Israel dwells securely;
Jacob lives untroubled
in a land of grain and new wine;
even his skies drip with dew.
How happy you are, Israel!
Who is like you,
a people saved by the LORD?
He is the shield that protects you,
110   the sword you boast in.
Your enemies will cringe before you,
and you will tread on their backs.

34 Then Moses went up from the plains of Moab to Mount Nebo, to the top of Pisgah, which faces Jericho, and the LORD showed him all the land: Gilead as far as Dan, all of Naphtali, the land of Ephraim and Manasseh, all the land of Judah as far as the Mediterranean Sea, the Negev, and the plain in the Valley of Jericho, the City of Palms, as far as Zoar. The LORD then said to him, "This is the land I promised Abraham, Isaac, and Jacob, 'I will give it to your descendants.' I have let you see it with your own eyes, but you will not cross into it."

So Moses the servant of the LORD died there in the land of Moab, according to the LORD's word. He buried him in the valley in the land of Moab facing Beth-peor, and no one to this day knows where his grave is. Moses was one hundred twenty years old when he died; his eyes were 10 not weak, and his vitality had not left him. The Israelites wept for Moses in the plains of Moab thirty days. Then the days of weeping and mourning for Moses came to an end.

Joshua son of Nun was filled with the spirit of wisdom because Moses had laid his hands on him. So the Israelites obeyed him and did as the LORD had commanded Moses. No prophet has arisen again in Israel like Moses, whom the LORD knew face to face. He was unparalleled for all the signs and wonders the LORD sent him to do against the land of Egypt—to Pharaoh, to all his officials, and to all his land, and for all the mighty acts of power and terrifying deeds that Moses performed in the sight of all Israel.

The Nevi'im
(Prophets)

Introduction to the Prophets

Beth M. Stovell

The portion of the HS called "the Prophets" (in Hebrew *Nevi'im*) begins immediately after the Torah with Judges and closes with Malachi. In our English Bibles, the Prophets are divided into two groupings with the Writings (in Hebrew *Ketuvim*) in the middle. The Prophets prior to the Writings are known as the "Former Prophets" (Joshua, Judges, Samuel Corpus, Kings Corpus)[1] and the Prophets after the Writings are known as the "Latter Prophets" (Isaiah–Malachi). The Latter Prophets (Isaiah–Malachi) are further subdivided into the three Major Prophets (Isaiah, Jeremiah, and Ezekiel), and the twelve Minor Prophets (Hosea–Malachi). The twelve Minor Prophets are treated as a single book in the HS, the Book of the Twelve.

Unlike the order in our English Bibles, the Masoretic Text (MT) groups the Former and Latter Prophets together in one section collectively called "The Prophets" that follows the Torah and comes before the Writings. These differences between our typical English Bibles and the MT are due to our English Bibles generally following the four part canonical order of the Greek translation of the HS called the Septuagint (LXX). Torah, historical books, poetic books, and prophetic books. This difference is present on the macroscale with the placement of the Latter Prophets and also on the microscale with the organization of the Twelve. In the Twelve, the ordering of the first six books differs between the MT (Hosea, Joel, Amos, Obadiah, Jonah, Micah) and the LXX (Hosea, Amos, Micah, Joel, Obadiah, Jonah). In this case, English Bibles follow the MT for the order of the Twelve.

With such a wide diversity of books within the Prophets, it is unsurprising that this section covers a wide swath of Israelite history and their story as a people. Depending on how one dates the Canaanite conquest in Joshua, these books cover either from the 15th century or 13th century BC to the 6th century BC. The Former Prophets tell the story of the conquest (Joshua), the development of judges to rule the people and eventual request for a king (Judges), and the rise of a united monarchy and the division of that monarchy (Samuel, Kings). In the Latter Prophets, we hear the voices of the prophets who rose up and spoke to the kings and to the people at Yahweh's direction from the 8th century to the 6th century BC. These Latter Prophets cover the time prior to the Assyrian invasion, during the Assyrian invasion, through the Babylonian exile, and to the time of return to the land of Israel under Persian rule. Thus, the story of the Prophets takes us from Yahweh's giving the land to the people of Israel and placing an Israelite king on the throne, through the divisions and destruction

---

1. In our English Bibles, Ruth, which is part of the Writings, also comes after Judges because Ruth's story is set during the time of the Judges.

of the Israelite kingdom, their tumultuous history with powerful foreign empires who invaded and took their land, to the people's return to their land under foreign rule.

This complex and sweeping history shapes the themes running throughout the Prophets and how these books relate to the other two divisions of the HS, the Torah and the Writings. The earliest of the Prophets, Joshua, so closely follows the story of the Torah that some argue that Joshua must be read alongside the Torah in order to form a meaningful story arc. Where the Torah gives us a story of Yahweh's promise of a future land to Abraham and the story of how Yahweh led his people out of Egyptian slavery towards this promised land, Deuteronomy ends at the edge of the promised land with the people awaiting their full entry. Joshua picks up the Torah's story and demonstrates how Joshua's faithful leadership allows the people to finally enter and possess the land promised.

Judges complicates this history. The valour we witness in Joshua becomes dimmed by what we see in Judges: failure of Israel to complete the Canaanite conquest and rampant violence and apostasy. Judges gives us the haunting refrain: "there was no king in Israel; everyone did whatever seemed right to him" (Judg 17.9–10; 21.40) as the people turn away from Yahweh and give into their own destructive desires. When enemy forces threaten to destroy the people, they cry out to Yahweh. The Lord lifts up judges to respond to these recurring crises. While some of these judges show wisdom, strength, and bravery and temporarily create peace, the destructive cycle repeats across the book. The tension around power and authority in Israel erupts in 1 Sam 8 as the people insist on having a king "like all the other nations" who will govern them and fight their battles (1 Sam 8.24–25). Whereas Judges leans toward the need for a king, the people reject Samuel's warning about the troubles a king will bring as he speaks on behalf of Yahweh (1 Sam 8.13–23). The Samuel Corpus emphasizes Samuel's role as the first prophet after Moses, the high priest, and as the final judge. Samuel emphasizes Yahweh's kingship that the people have rejected. This picture of Yahweh as the great king is a key theological message in the Samuel Corpus that will echo throughout the rest of the Prophets. Nonetheless, the people are insistent, and the Lord gives them what they demand: a human king (1 Sam 8.26–27).

Thus begins the shift in our story from judges to kings. The complicated story of kingship and its impact on the people and the land become the dominant themes for the remainder of the Samuel and Kings Corpora. First Samuel 9–15 tells the story of Saul who is appointed king over Yahweh's people. While Saul seems like the perfect king initially, we witness his growing anger and eventual madness until the fall of his kingship in 1 Sam 31. In 1 Sam 16, David is anointed as the new king of Israel. However, the remainder of 1 Samuel tells how David's kingship eventually eclipses Saul's kingship, as David slowly gains the approval of others while winning battles against Israel's enemies. Second Samuel begins with David hearing of Saul's death and tells the story of David's reign. The king who began as a small shepherd boy becomes a man after Yahweh's own heart (1 Sam 13.27–29) and a successful warrior in battle. But he also becomes a murderer and an adulterer as he takes the married Bathsheba from her home and places her husband at the front lines of the battle, ensuring his death. David's choices lead to the ultimate unraveling of his house as David's sons turn against one another: one of David's sons, Amnon, violates his own sister, Tamar, and his son Absalom fosters a conspiracy against David (2 Sam 13–20). In 1 Kings, we transition from David's reign to the story of Solomon, David's son, as king. At first Solomon seems like he might be on a better path than his brothers. His life is characterized by wisdom and prosperity (1 Kgs 1–10), but Solomon has a love for foreign women and agrees to worship at the altars of their foreign gods (1 Kgs 11). This action causes Yahweh to raise Solomon's enemies against him to his ultimate demise (1 Kgs 11). Under Solomon's son Rehoboam and through his foolhardy choices, the once united kingdom splits into the Northern Kingdom of Israel and the Southern Kingdom of Judah. Rehoboam remains the king of Judah in the south while Jeroboam becomes the king of Israel in the north. At this point the Kings Corpus chronicles the northern and southern kings. The stories of these kings—both the good and the wicked—emphasize obedience, justice, and worship of Yahweh as the measures of success for good kings and disobedience, injustice, and worship of idols as the measure for destruction of wicked kings.

The Former Prophets tell these stories of Israel using an ancient form of writing used for chronicling history called historiography. The Latter Prophets overlap with the final portions of these stories and add to them through a prophetic style of writing. This prophetic genre joins narrative with poetry, descriptions of visions, and oracles from Yahweh about blessing and warning. Several of the prophets in the Latter Prophets overlap in their times with the kings described in the Kings Corpus. Second Kings tells the stories of the reigns of Uzziah (788–748 BC; 2 Kgs 15), Jotham (759–743 BC; 2 Kgs 15), Ahaz (743–727 BC; 2 Kgs 15), and Hezekiah (727–698/9 BC; 2 Kgs 18–20) in Judah and the reign of Jeroboam II (782–753 BC; 2 Kgs 14) in Israel. Amos, Isaiah, and Hosea prophesied under Uzziah, while Isaiah, Hosea, and Micah prophesied under Jotham to Hezekiah. Where the Kings Corpus describes the actions of these kings, the prophets describe in their poetry and oracles the impact of the kings' reigns on the people and the land and Yahweh's prophetic call to the kings and the people.

The Latter Prophets also draw us into an increasingly dark time in Israel's history with its own theological importance: the Babylonian exile. Because of the vast impact of this exilic experience, we often divide the Latter Prophets into prophets who are preexilic, exilic, and postexilic (after Israel's return to the land). Each of these prophetic stages has their own key themes and messages. Preexilic prophets warn of the upcoming invasions, first by the Assyrians and later by the Babylonians. The Assyrian invasion in 721 BC destroyed the Northern Kingdom and deeply impacted the Southern Kingdom, leaving it vulnerable to attack. The Babylonians conquered their enemies in a two fold method: destroy their buildings, particularly their temples, and then take the most powerful and influential among the remaining peoples to Babylon to assimilate them. We hear in the exilic prophets the way the people and Yahweh responded to this combination of traumatic violence and loss that the Southern Kingdom of Judah experienced at the hands of the Babylonians and the fear of losing their language, their history, and their identity as the powerful and influential leaders were taken to Babylon. The exilic prophets witness an outcry of lament among the Israelite people and Yahweh's call for the prophet to comfort his hurting people. This outcry is recorded not only in parts of Isaiah, Jeremiah, and Ezekiel and in parts of the Twelve, but also in portions of the Psalms and Lamentations. During the exile, the Israelite people questioned whether Yahweh was still listening to them, whether Yahweh's promises were still intact, and where Yahweh was present in their suffering. They also asked why this horrible event had happened to them. This leads the exilic prophets to often focus on the reason for the exile itself: Israel's turn away from Yahweh toward idols and Israel's injustice against their own people and against their neighbors. These two reasons violated the heart of Yahweh's law to love Yahweh and love one's neighbor. Thus, the exilic prophets focus extensively on proclaiming the need for the people to return to Yahweh so that Yahweh will return to them and to "act justly, love mercy, and walk humbly with their God" (Micah 6.28–32).

The theme of return continues into the postexilic period. When the Persians conquered the Babylonians and took over the land of Israel, they allowed for the return of the exiled Israelites to their homes. While many of the Israelite people physically returned to their land, they did not necessarily return to Yahweh in their hearts. The hopes they cultivated during the exile pictured in the exilic prophets—to return to their land, to return to Yahweh's law, to restore the temple, and to have a Davidic king again—were only partially fulfilled upon their return to the land. The postexilic prophets call for the people to return fully to Yahweh so that they can see these hopes fulfilled. They also turn from the hopes of a human king to focus more on Yahweh as the great king who will restore all things.

The Prophets—both the Former and the Latter—share with us the sweeping story of Israel's history from judges to kings to a divided monarchy to the loss of the exile and the eventual return to their land. They also share the words of Yahweh for his people and their leaders through the voice of the prophets as they are reminded to love Yahweh and love their neighbor, to remember Yahweh's law and to restore justice.

Suggested Resources

Dallaire, Hélène. "Joshua." P 815–1042 in vol. 3 of *The Expositor's Bible Commentary*. Rev. ed. Grand Rapids: Zondervan, 2012.

Firth, David G. *The Message of Joshua*. The Bible Speaks Today. Downers Grove, IL: InterVarsity Press, 2015.

Hess, Richard S. *Joshua: An Introduction and Commentary*. Tyndale Old Testament Commentaries. Downers Grove, IL: InterVarsity Press, 1996.

Howard, David M., Jr. *Joshua*. New American Commentary. Nashville: Broadman & Holman, 1998.

Lennox, Stephen J. *Joshua: A Commentary in the Wesleyan Tradition*. New Beacon Bible Commentary. Kansas City: Beacon Hill, 2015.

Introduction to Joshua

David M. Howard, Jr.

Most people who know anything about the book of Joshua think first (if not entirely) of its battles, typified by the old spiritual "Joshua Fit the Battle of Jericho." As with most stereotypes, there is some truth to this picture, but there are distortions as well. Certainly the book contains accounts of great victories and miracles by Yahweh on his people's behalf. He fought for them (10.34–35; 21.72–74; etc.), giving victory after victory, including cities, houses, cisterns, and vineyards that they had not built (Deut 6.13–16; Josh 24.22–24).

Beyond its battles, however, the book is far more interested in the land of Canaan, the possession of which is the goal of these conflicts. Yahweh had long ago promised to *give* this land to Abraham and his descendants as an *inheritance* (Gen 12.18–20), and he fulfilled his promises (Josh 21.71–75). The book begins with the careful preparations necessary before Israel embarked on its campaign to take this land (chs. 1–5). These campaigns were primarily spiritual in nature to them, emphasizing the point that, before Israel could inherit the land, it must stand in proper relationship with Yahweh, who was graciously *giving* the land.

Even in the taking of the land (chs. 6–12), spiritual concerns were paramount. At Jericho, the city was not taken directly, but only after a series of ritual marches around the city, as if the city itself were a sacrifice to Yahweh. Sin in the camp caused Israel's only defeat in the land. When the Israelites took the bulk of the land, it was Yahweh who went before them.

After these conflicts, the heart of the book comes when the long-promised inheritance was actually distributed among the tribes (chs. 13–21). Here, the contours of Yahweh's promises are fleshed out in the extensive details about each tribe's land. In these detailed listings, the message is crystal clear: Yahweh was true to his promises and he was equitably rewarding each of the tribes.

The book ends with Joshua's reflections about what Yahweh had done for his people and his exhortations about life ahead in the land (chs. 22–24). The book ends on a satisfying note, with the people settled in their lands and everything seemingly in order.

Joshua occupies a pivotal position in the HS. The book points backward to many passages in the Torah and shows the fulfillment of many promises there. In addition, it relates settling into the land after hundreds of years of anticipation. The book also points forward, as it stands at the head of the great collection of historical-narrative books known in the HS as the "Former Prophets" (Joshua, Judges, Samuel Corpus, and Kings Corpus). This collection begins in Joshua with the first years of life in the land, and it ends in 2 Kings with the tragic events of exile away from that land.

The book's central theme is summarized as *Yahweh gave the promised land of Canaan to his people Israel as an inheritance*. Note the absence of the words *battle* or *conquest*. These two concepts were simply a means toward a greater end, which was Yahweh's fulfillment of his promises. The horrific destructions of people in this book were for two purposes: (1) to allow Israel's fledgling sense of identity as a nation under Yahweh to take root without the temptations of debased Canaanite religious practices; and (2) to punish the Canaanites for their own terrible sins, which rose to levels far above any of their neighbors (Gen 15.25–26; Lev 18.30–32).

In Joshua, the future for Israel looks very bright. Yet, there are also hints of coming troubles (15.57–58; 16.15–16), which are revealed in Judges and the subsequent books. Thus, it is a very realistic book, glorifying Yahweh and showing his mercies on his people, but also warns of the dangers of rebellion and disobedience against him.

Outline

1. Preparations for Inheriting the Land (1.1–5.22)
    a. Instructions for Inheriting the Land (1.1–30)
    b. A Foreigner's Welcome (2.1–39)
    c. Crossing the Jordan (3.1–5.2)
    d. Ritual Preparations (5.3–27)

2. Taking the Land of Inheritance (6.1–12.49)
    a. The Destruction of Jericho (6.1–51)
    b. Covenant Disobedience (7.1–50)
    c. The Destruction of Ai (8.1–48)
    d. Covenant Affirmations (8.49–60)
    e. The Gibeonite Treaty Established (9.1–44)
    f. The Gibeonite Treaty Tested; Southern Campaign Begun (10.1–55)
    g. Southern Campaign Completed (10.56–82)
    h. Northern Campaign Begun (11.1–24)
    i. Northern Campaign Completed (11.25–39)
    j. List of Conquered Kings and Land (12.1–49)

3. Apportioning the Land of Inheritance (13.1–21.75)
    a. The Command to Distribute the Land (13.1–11)
    b. The Transjordan Distribution Recalled (13.12–49)
    c. The Cisjordan Distribution Introduced (14.1–7)
    d. Judah's Inheritance (14.8–15.58)
    e. Joseph's Inheritance (16.1–17.38)
    f. The Other Tribes' Inheritance (18.1–19.51)
    g. Joshua's Inheritance (19.52–54)
    h. The Cisjordan Distribution Concluded (19.55–57)

i. The Cities of Refuge (20.1–17)
j. The Levitical Cities (21.1–70)
k. All Promises Fulfilled (21.71–75)

4. Farewells in the Land of Inheritance (22.1–24.61)
   a. Joshua's Farewell to the Transjordan Tribes (22.1–14)
   b. A Crisis of Loyalties (22.15–66)
   c. Joshua's First Farewell to All Israel (23.1–28)
   d. Joshua's Second Farewell to All Israel (24.1–52)
   e. Conclusion: Burial Notices (24.53–61)

Suggested Resources

Dallaire, Hélène. "Joshua," pages 815–1042 in *The Expositor's Bible Commentary: Rev. ed.* Grand Rapids: Zondervan, 2012.

Firth, David G., *The Message of Joshua.* The Bible Speaks Today. Downers Grove: IVP Academic, 2015.

Hess, Richard S., *Joshua: An Introduction and Commentary.* Tyndale Old Testament Commentary 6. Downers Grove: InterVarsity, 1996.

Howard, David M., Jr., *Joshua.* New American Commentary 5. Nashville: Broadman & Holman Publishers, 1998.

Lennox, Stephen J., *Joshua: A Commentary in the Wesleyan Tradition.* New Beacon Bible Commentary. Kansas City: Beacon Hill, 2015.

Joshua

I After the death of Moses the Lord's servant, the Lord spoke to Joshua son of Nun, Moses's assistant: "Moses my servant is dead. Now you and all the people prepare to cross over the Jordan to the land I am giving the Israelites. I have given you every place where the sole of your foot treads, just as I promised Moses. Your territory will be from the wilderness and Lebanon to the great river, the Euphrates River—all the land of the Hittites—and west to the Mediterranean Sea. No one will be able to stand against you as long as you live. I will be with you, just as I was with Moses. I will not leave you or abandon you.

"Be strong and courageous, for you will distribute the land I swore to their ancestors to give them as an inheritance. Above all, be strong and very courageous to observe carefully the whole instruction my servant Moses commanded you. Do not turn from it to the right or the left, so that you will have success wherever you go. This book of instruction must not depart from your mouth; you are to meditate on it day and night so that you may carefully observe everything written in it. For then you will prosper and succeed in whatever you do. Haven't I commanded you: be strong and courageous? Do not be afraid or discouraged, for the Lord your God is with you wherever you go."

Then Joshua commanded the officers of the people, "Go through the camp and tell the people, 'Get provisions ready for yourselves, for within three days you will be crossing the Jordan to go in and take possession of the land the Lord your God is giving you to inherit.'"

Joshua said to the Reubenites, the Gadites, and half the tribe of Manasseh, "Remember what Moses the Lord's servant commanded you when he said, 'The Lord your God will give you rest, and he will give you this land.' Your wives, dependents, and livestock may remain in the land Moses gave you on this side of the Jordan. But your best soldiers must cross over in battle formation ahead of your brothers and help them until the Lord gives your brothers rest, as he has given you, and they too possess the land the Lord your God is giving them. You may then return to the land of your inheritance and take possession of what Moses the Lord's servant gave you on the east side of the Jordan."

They answered Joshua, "Everything you have commanded us we will do, and everywhere you send us we will go. We will obey you, just as we obeyed Moses in everything. Certainly the Lord your God will be with you, as he was with Moses. Anyone who rebels against your order and does not obey your words in all that you command him, will be put to death. Above all, be strong and courageous!"

2 Joshua son of Nun secretly sent two men as spies from the Acacia Grove, saying, "Go and scout the land, especially Jericho." So they left, and they came to the house of a prostitute named Rahab, and stayed there.

The king of Jericho was told, "Look, some of the Israelite men have come here tonight to investigate the land." Then the king of Jericho sent word to Rahab and said, "Bring out the men who came to you and entered your house, for they came to investigate the entire land."

But the woman had taken the two men and hidden them. So she said, "Yes, the men did come to me, but I didn't know where they were from. At nightfall, when the city gate was about to close, the men went out, and I don't know where they were going. Chase after them quickly, and you can catch up with them!" But she had taken them up to the roof and hidden them among the stalks of flax that she had arranged on the roof. The men pursued them along the road to the fords of the Jordan, and as soon as they left to pursue them, the city gate was shut.

Before the men fell asleep, she went up on the roof and said to them, "I know that the LORD has given you this land and that the terror of you has fallen on us, and everyone who lives in the land is panicking because of you. For we have heard how the LORD dried up the water of the Red Sea before you when you came out of Egypt, and what you did to Sihon and Og, the two Amorite kings you completely destroyed across the Jordan. When we heard this, we lost heart, and everyone's courage failed because of you, for the LORD your God is God in heaven above and on earth below. Now please swear to me by the LORD that you will also show kindness to my father's family, because I showed kindness to you. Give me a sure sign that you will spare the lives of my father, mother, brothers, sisters, and all who belong to them, and save us from death."

The men answered her, "We will give our lives for yours. If you don't report our mission, we will show kindness and faithfulness to you when the LORD gives us the land."

Then she let them down by a rope through the window, since she lived in a house that was built into the wall of the city. "Go to the hill country so that the men pursuing you won't find you," she said to them. "Hide there for three days until they return; afterward, go on your way."

The men said to her, "We will be free from this oath you made us swear, unless, when we enter the land, you tie this scarlet cord to the window through which you let us down. Bring your father, mother, brothers, and all your father's family into your house. If anyone goes out the doors of your house, his death will be his own fault, and we will be innocent. But if anyone with you in the house should be harmed, his death will be our fault. And if you report our mission, we are free from the oath you made us swear."

"Let it be as you say," she replied, and she sent them away. After they had gone, she tied the scarlet cord to the window.

So the two men went into the hill country and stayed there three days until the pursuers had returned. They searched all along the way, but did not find them. Then the men returned, came down from the hill country, and crossed the Jordan. They went to Joshua son of Nun and reported everything that had happened to them. They told Joshua, "The LORD has handed over the entire land to us. Everyone who lives in the land is also panicking because of us."

3 Joshua started early the next morning and left the Acacia Grove with all the Israelites. They went as far as the Jordan and stayed there before crossing. After three days the officers went through the camp and commanded the people, "When you see the ark of the covenant of the LORD your God carried by the Levitical priests, you are to break camp and follow it. But keep a distance of about a thousand yards between yourselves and the ark. Don't go near it, so that you can see the way to go, for you haven't traveled this way before."

Joshua told the people, "Consecrate yourselves, because the LORD will do wonders among you tomorrow." Then he said to the priests, "Carry the ark of the covenant and go on ahead of the people." So they carried the ark of the covenant and went ahead of them.

10 The LORD spoke to Joshua: "Today I will begin to exalt you in the sight of all Israel, so they will know that I will be with you just as I was with Moses. Command the priests carrying the ark of the covenant: When you reach the edge of the water, stand in the Jordan."

Then Joshua told the Israelites, "Come closer and listen to the words of the LORD your God." He said, "You will know that the living God is among you and that he will certainly dispossess before you the Canaanites, Hethites, Hivites, Perizzites, Girgashites, Amorites, and Jebusites when the ark of the covenant of the Lord of the whole earth goes ahead of you into the Jordan. Now choose twelve men from the tribes of Israel, one man for each tribe. When the feet of the priests who carry the ark of the LORD, the Lord of the whole earth, come to rest in the Jordan's water, its water will be cut off. The water flowing downstream will stand up in a mass."

20 When the people broke camp to cross the Jordan, the priests carried the ark of the covenant ahead of the people. Now the Jordan overflows its banks throughout the harvest season. But as soon as the priests carrying the ark reached the Jordan, their feet touched the water at its edge and the water flowing downstream stood still, rising up in a mass that extended as far as Adam, a city next to Zarethan. The water flowing downstream into the Sea of the Arabah—the Dead Sea— was completely cut off, and the people crossed opposite Jericho. The priests carrying the ark of the LORD's covenant stood firmly on dry ground in the middle of the Jordan, while all Israel crossed on dry ground until the entire nation had finished crossing the Jordan.

4 After the entire nation had finished crossing the Jordan, the LORD spoke to Joshua: "Choose twelve men from the people, one man for each tribe, and command them: Take twelve stones from this place in the middle of the Jordan where the priests are standing, carry them with you, and set them down at the place where you spend the night."

So Joshua summoned the twelve men he had selected from the Israelites, one man for each tribe, and said to them, "Go across to the ark of the LORD your God in the middle of the Jordan. Each of you lift a stone onto his shoulder, one for each of the Israelite tribes, so that this will be a sign among you. In the future, when your children ask you, 'What do these stones mean to you?' you should tell them, 'The water of the Jordan was cut off in front of the ark of the Lord's covenant. When it crossed the Jordan, the Jordan's water was cut off.' Therefore these stones will always be a memorial for the Israelites."

The Israelites did just as Joshua had commanded them. The twelve men took stones from the middle of the Jordan, one for each of the Israelite tribes, just as the Lord had told Joshua. They carried them to the camp and set them down there. Joshua also set up twelve stones in the middle of the Jordan where the priests who carried the ark of the covenant were standing. The stones are still there today.

The priests carrying the ark continued standing in the middle of the Jordan until everything was completed that the Lord had commanded Joshua to tell the people, in keeping with all that Moses had commanded Joshua. The people hurried across, and after everyone had finished crossing, the priests with the ark of the Lord crossed in the sight of the people. The Reubenites, Gadites, and half the tribe of Manasseh went in battle formation in front of the Israelites, as Moses had instructed them. About forty thousand equipped for war crossed to the plains of Jericho in the Lord's presence.

On that day the Lord exalted Joshua in the sight of all Israel, and they revered him throughout his life, as they had revered Moses. The Lord told Joshua, "Command the priests who carry the ark of the testimony to come up from the Jordan."

So Joshua commanded the priests, "Come up from the Jordan." When the priests carrying the ark of the Lord's covenant came up from the middle of the Jordan, and their feet stepped out on solid ground, the water of the Jordan resumed its course, flowing over all the banks as before.

The people came up from the Jordan on the tenth day of the first month, and camped at Gilgal on the eastern limits of Jericho. Then Joshua set up in Gilgal the twelve stones they had taken from the Jordan, and he said to the Israelites, "In the future, when your children ask their fathers, 'What is the meaning of these stones?' you should tell your children, 'Israel crossed the Jordan on dry ground.' For the Lord your God dried up the water of the Jordan before you until you had crossed over, just as the Lord your God did to the Red Sea, which he dried up before us until we had crossed over. This is so that all the peoples of the earth may know that the Lord's hand is strong, and so that you may always fear the Lord your God."

5 When all the Amorite kings across the Jordan to the west and all the Canaanite kings near the sea heard how the Lord had dried up the water of the Jordan before the Israelites until they had crossed over, they lost heart and their courage failed because of the Israelites.

At that time the Lord said to Joshua, "Make flint knives and circumcise the Israelite men again." So Joshua made flint knives and circumcised the Israelite men at Gibeath-haaraloth. This is the reason Joshua circumcised them: All the people who came out of Egypt who were males— all the men of war—had died in the wilderness along the way after they had come out of Egypt. Though all the people who came out were circumcised, none of the people born in the wilderness

along the way were circumcised after they had come out of Egypt. For the Israelites wandered in
the wilderness forty years until all the nation's men of war who came out of Egypt had died off
because they did not obey the LORD. So the LORD vowed never to let them see the land he had
sworn to their ancestors to give us, a land flowing with milk and honey. He raised up their sons
in their place; it was these Joshua circumcised. They were still uncircumcised, since they had not
been circumcised along the way. After the entire nation had been circumcised, they stayed where
they were in the camp until they recovered. The LORD then said to Joshua, "Today I have rolled
away the disgrace of Egypt from you." Therefore, that place is still called Gilgal today.

While the Israelites camped at Gilgal on the plains of Jericho, they observed the Passover on the
evening of the fourteenth day of the month. The day after Passover they ate unleavened bread and
roasted grain from the produce of the land. And the day after they ate from the produce of the
land, the manna ceased. Since there was no more manna for the Israelites, they ate from the crops
of the land of Canaan that year.

When Joshua was near Jericho, he looked up and saw a man standing in front of him with a drawn
sword in his hand. Joshua approached him and asked, "Are you for us or for our enemies?"

"Neither," he replied. "I have now come as commander of the LORD's army."

Then Joshua bowed with his face to the ground in homage and asked him, "What does my lord
want to say to his servant?"

The commander of the LORD's army said to Joshua, "Remove the sandals from your feet, for
the place where you are standing is holy." And Joshua did that.

6 Now Jericho was strongly fortified because of the Israelites—no one leaving or entering. The
LORD said to Joshua, "Look, I have handed Jericho, its king, and its best soldiers over to you.
March around the city with all the men of war, circling the city one time. Do this for six days.
Have seven priests carry seven ram's-horn trumpets in front of the ark. But on the seventh day,
march around the city seven times, while the priests blow the rams' horns. When there is a
prolonged blast of the horn and you hear its sound, have all the troops give a mighty shout. Then
the city wall will collapse, and the troops will advance, each man straight ahead."

So Joshua son of Nun summoned the priests and said to them, "Take up the ark of the covenant
and have seven priests carry seven rams' horns in front of the ark of the LORD." He said to the troops,
"Move forward, march around the city, and have the armed men go ahead of the ark of the LORD."

After Joshua had spoken to the troops, seven priests carrying seven rams' horns before the
LORD moved forward and blew the rams' horns; the ark of the LORD's covenant followed them.
While the rams' horns were blowing, the armed men went in front of the priests who blew the
rams' horns, and the rear guard went behind the ark. But Joshua had commanded the troops, "Do
not shout or let your voice be heard. Don't let one word come out of your mouth until the time I

say, 'Shout!' Then you are to shout." So the ark of the LORD was carried around the city, circling it once. They returned to the camp and spent the night there.

Joshua got up early the next morning. The priests took the ark of the LORD, and the seven priests carrying seven rams' horns marched in front of the ark of the LORD. While the rams' horns were
20 blowing, the armed men went in front of them, and the rear guard went behind the ark of the LORD. On the second day they marched around the city once and returned to the camp. They did this for six days.

Early on the seventh day, they started at dawn and marched around the city seven times in the same way. That was the only day they marched around the city seven times. After the seventh time, the priests blew the rams' horns, and Joshua said to the troops, "Shout! For the LORD has given you the city. But the city and everything in it are set apart to the LORD for destruction. Only Rahab the prostitute and everyone with her in the house will live, because she hid the messengers we sent. But keep yourselves from the things set apart, or you will be set apart for destruction. If you take any of those things, you will set apart the camp of Israel for destruction and make trouble for it. For all the silver and gold, and the articles of bronze and iron, are dedicated to the LORD and
30 must go into the LORD's treasury."

So the troops shouted, and the rams' horns sounded. When they heard the blast of the rams' horn, the troops gave a great shout, and the wall collapsed. The troops advanced into the city, each man straight ahead, and they captured the city. They completely destroyed everything in the city with the sword—every man and woman, both young and old, and every ox, sheep, and donkey.

Joshua said to the two men who had scouted the land, "Go to the prostitute's house and bring the woman out of there, and all who are with her, just as you swore to her." So the young men who had scouted went in and brought out Rahab and her father, mother, brothers, and all who belonged to her. They brought out her whole family and settled them outside the camp of Israel.

They burned the city and everything in it, but they put the silver and gold and the articles
40 of bronze and iron into the treasury of the LORD's house. However, Joshua spared Rahab the prostitute, her father's family, and all who belonged to her, because she hid the messengers Joshua had sent to spy on Jericho, and she still lives in Israel today.

At that time Joshua imposed this curse:

> The man who undertakes
> the rebuilding of this city, Jericho,
> is cursed before the LORD.
> He will lay its foundation
> at the cost of his firstborn;
> he will finish its gates
50 > at the cost of his youngest.

And the LORD was with Joshua, and his fame spread throughout the land.

7 The Israelites, however, were unfaithful regarding the things set apart for destruction. Achan son of Carmi, son of Zabdi, son of Zerah, of the tribe of Judah, took some of what was set apart, and the LORD's anger burned against the Israelites.

Joshua sent men from Jericho to Ai, which is near Beth-aven, east of Bethel, and told them, "Go up and scout the land." So the men went up and scouted Ai.

After returning to Joshua they reported to him, "Don't send all the people, but send about two thousand or three thousand men to attack Ai. Since the people of Ai are so few, don't wear out all our people there." So about three thousand men went up there, but they fled from the men of Ai. The men of Ai struck down about thirty-six of them and chased them from outside the city gate to the quarries, striking them down on the descent. As a result, the people lost heart.

Then Joshua tore his clothes and fell facedown to the ground before the ark of the LORD until evening, as did the elders of Israel; they all put dust on their heads. "Oh, Lord GOD," Joshua said, "why did you ever bring these people across the Jordan to hand us over to the Amorites for our destruction? If only we had been content to remain on the other side of the Jordan! What can I say, Lord, now that Israel has turned its back and run from its enemies? When the Canaanites and all who live in the land hear about this, they will surround us and wipe out our name from the earth. Then what will you do about your great name?"

The LORD then said to Joshua, "Stand up! Why have you fallen facedown? Israel has sinned. They have violated my covenant that I appointed for them. They have taken some of what was set apart. They have stolen, deceived, and put those things with their own belongings. This is why the Israelites cannot stand against their enemies. They will turn their backs and run from their enemies, because they have been set apart for destruction. I will no longer be with you unless you remove from among you what is set apart.

"Go and consecrate the people. Tell them to consecrate themselves for tomorrow, for this is what the LORD, the God of Israel, says: There are things that are set apart among you, Israel. You will not be able to stand against your enemies until you remove what is set apart. In the morning, present yourselves tribe by tribe. The tribe the LORD selects is to come forward clan by clan. The clan the LORD selects is to come forward family by family. The family the LORD selects is to come forward man by man. The one who is caught with the things set apart must be burned, along with everything he has, because he has violated the LORD's covenant and committed an outrage in Israel."

Joshua got up early the next morning. He had Israel come forward tribe by tribe, and the tribe of Judah was selected. He had the clans of Judah come forward, and the Zerahite clan was selected. He had the Zerahite clan come forward by heads of families, and Zabdi was selected. He then had Zabdi's family come forward man by man, and Achan son of Carmi, son of Zabdi, son of Zerah, of the tribe of Judah, was selected.

So Joshua said to Achan, "My son, give glory to the LORD, the God of Israel, and make a confession to him. I urge you, tell me what you have done. Don't hide anything from me."

Achan replied to Joshua, "It is true. I have sinned against the LORD, the God of Israel. This is what I did: When I saw among the spoils a beautiful cloak from Babylon, five pounds of silver,
40 and a bar of gold weighing a pound and a quarter, I coveted them and took them. You can see for yourself. They are concealed in the ground inside my tent, with the silver under the cloak." So Joshua sent messengers who ran to the tent, and there was the cloak, concealed in his tent, with the silver underneath. They took the things from inside the tent, brought them to Joshua and all the Israelites, and spread them out in the LORD's presence.

Then Joshua and all Israel with him took Achan son of Zerah, the silver, the cloak, and the bar of gold, his sons and daughters, his ox, donkey, and sheep, his tent, and all that he had, and brought them up to the Valley of Achor. Joshua said, "Why have you brought us trouble? Today the LORD will bring you trouble!" So all Israel stoned them to death. They burned their bodies, threw stones on them, and raised over him a large pile of rocks that remains still today. Then the
50 LORD turned from his burning anger. Therefore that place is called the Valley of Achor still today.

8 The LORD said to Joshua, "Do not be afraid or discouraged. Take all the troops with you and go attack Ai. Look, I have handed over to you the king of Ai, his people, city, and land. Treat Ai and its king as you did Jericho and its king, except that you may plunder its spoil and livestock for yourselves. Set an ambush behind the city."

So Joshua and all the troops set out to attack Ai. Joshua selected thirty thousand of his best soldiers and sent them out at night. He commanded them, "Pay attention. Lie in ambush behind the city, not too far from it, and all of you be ready. Then I and all the people who are with me will approach the city. When they come out against us as they did the first time, we will flee from them. They will come after us until we have drawn them away from the city, for they will say,
10 'They are fleeing from us as before.' While we are fleeing from them, you are to come out of your ambush and seize the city. The LORD your God will hand it over to you. After taking the city, set it on fire. Follow the LORD's command—see that you do as I have ordered you." So Joshua sent them out, and they went to the ambush site and waited between Bethel and Ai, to the west of Ai. But he spent that night with the troops.

Joshua started early the next morning and mobilized them. Then he and the elders of Israel led the people up to Ai. All the troops who were with him went up and approached the city, arriving opposite Ai, and camped to the north of it, with a valley between them and the city. Now Joshua had taken about five thousand men and set them in ambush between Bethel and Ai, to the west of the city. The troops were stationed in this way: the main camp to the north of the city and its rear
20 guard to the west of the city. And that night Joshua went into the valley.

When the king of Ai saw the Israelites, the men of the city hurried and went out early in the morning so that he and all his people could engage Israel in battle at a suitable place facing the Arabah. But he did not know there was an ambush waiting for him behind the city. Joshua and all Israel pretended to be beaten back by them and fled toward the wilderness. Then all the troops of

Ai were summoned to pursue them, and they pursued Joshua and were drawn away from the city. Not a man was left in Ai or Bethel who did not go out after Israel, leaving the city exposed while they pursued Israel.

Then the Lord said to Joshua, "Hold out the javelin in your hand toward Ai, for I will hand the city over to you." So Joshua held out his javelin toward it. When he held out his hand, the men in ambush rose quickly from their position. They ran, entered the city, captured it, and immediately set it on fire.

The men of Ai turned and looked back, and smoke from the city was rising to the sky! They could not escape in any direction, and the troops who had fled to the wilderness now became the pursuers. When Joshua and all Israel saw that the men in ambush had captured the city and that smoke was rising from it, they turned back and struck down the men of Ai. Then men in ambush came out of the city against them, and the men of Ai were trapped between the Israelite forces, some on one side and some on the other. They struck them down until no survivor or fugitive remained, but they captured the king of Ai alive and brought him to Joshua.

When Israel had finished killing everyone living in Ai who had pursued them into the open country, and when every last one of them had fallen by the sword, all Israel returned to Ai and struck it down with the sword. The total of those who fell that day, both men and women, was twelve thousand—all the people of Ai. Joshua did not draw back his hand that was holding the javelin until all the inhabitants of Ai were completely destroyed. Israel plundered only the cattle and spoil of that city for themselves, according to the Lord's command that he had given Joshua.

Joshua burned Ai and left it a permanent ruin, still desolate today. He hung the body of the king of Ai on a tree until evening, and at sunset Joshua commanded that they take his body down from the tree. They threw it down at the entrance of the city gate and put a large pile of rocks over it, which still remains today.

At that time Joshua built an altar on Mount Ebal to the Lord, the God of Israel, just as Moses the Lord's servant had commanded the Israelites. He built it according to what is written in the book of the law of Moses: an altar of uncut stones on which no iron tool has been used. Then they offered burnt offerings to the Lord and sacrificed fellowship offerings on it. There on the stones, Joshua copied the law of Moses, which he had written in the presence of the Israelites. All Israel—resident alien and citizen alike—with their elders, officers, and judges, stood on either side of the ark of the Lord's covenant facing the Levitical priests who carried it. Half of them were in front of Mount Gerizim and half in front of Mount Ebal, as Moses the Lord's servant had commanded earlier concerning blessing the people of Israel. Afterward, Joshua read aloud all the words of the law—the blessings as well as the curses—according to all that is written in the book of the law. There was not a word of all that Moses had commanded that Joshua did not read before the entire assembly of Israel, including the women, the dependents, and the resident aliens who lived among them.

9 When all the kings heard about Jericho and Ai, those who were west of the Jordan in the hill country, in the Judean foothills, and all along the coast of the Mediterranean Sea toward Lebanon—the Hethites, Amorites, Canaanites, Perizzites, Hivites, and Jebusites—they formed a unified alliance to fight against Joshua and Israel.

When the inhabitants of Gibeon heard what Joshua had done to Jericho and Ai, they acted deceptively. They gathered provisions and took worn-out sacks on their donkeys and old wineskins, cracked and mended. They wore old, patched sandals on their feet and threadbare clothing on their bodies. Their entire provision of bread was dry and crumbly. They went to Joshua in the camp at Gilgal and said to him and the men of Israel, "We have come from a distant
10 land. Please make a treaty with us."

The men of Israel replied to the Hivites, "Perhaps you live among us. How can we make a treaty with you?"

They said to Joshua, "We are your servants."

Then Joshua asked them, "Who are you and where do you come from?"

They replied to him, "Your servants have come from a faraway land because of the reputation of the LORD your God. For we have heard of his fame, and all that he did in Egypt, and all that he did to the two Amorite kings beyond the Jordan—King Sihon of Heshbon and King Og of Bashan, who was in Ashtaroth. So our elders and all the inhabitants of our land told us, 'Take provisions with you for the journey; go and meet them and say, "We are your servants. Please make a treaty with us."' This bread
20 of ours was warm when we took it from our houses as food on the day we left to come to you; but see, it is now dry and crumbly. These wineskins were new when we filled them; but see, they are cracked. And these clothes and sandals of ours are worn out from the extremely long journey." Then the men of Israel took some of their provisions, but did not seek the LORD's decision. So Joshua established peace with them and made a treaty to let them live, and the leaders of the community swore an oath to them.

Three days after making the treaty with them, they heard that the Gibeonites were their neighbors, living among them. So the Israelites set out and reached the Gibeonite cities on the third day. Now their cities were Gibeon, Chephirah, Beeroth, and Kiriath-jearim. But the Israelites did not attack them, because the leaders of the community had sworn an oath to them by the LORD, the God of Israel. Then the whole community grumbled against the leaders.
30 All the leaders answered them, "We have sworn an oath to them by the LORD, the God of Israel, and now we cannot touch them. This is how we will treat them: we will let them live, so that no wrath will fall on us because of the oath we swore to them." They also said, "Let them live." So the Gibeonites became woodcutters and water carriers for the whole community, as the leaders had promised them.

Joshua summoned the Gibeonites and said to them, "Why did you deceive us by telling us you live far away from us, when in fact you live among us? Therefore you are cursed and will always be slaves—woodcutters and water carriers for the house of my God."

The Gibeonites answered him, "It was clearly communicated to your servants that the LORD your God had commanded his servant Moses to give you all the land and to destroy all the
40   inhabitants of the land before you. We greatly feared for our lives because of you, and that is why we did this. Now we are in your hands. Do to us whatever you think is right." This is what Joshua did to them: he rescued them from the Israelites, and they did not kill them. On that day he made them woodcutters and water carriers—as they are today—for the community and for the LORD's altar at the place he would choose.

10   Now King Adoni-zedek of Jerusalem heard that Joshua had captured Ai and completely destroyed it, treating Ai and its king as he had Jericho and its king, and that the inhabitants of Gibeon had made peace with Israel and were living among them. So Adoni-zedek and his people were greatly alarmed because Gibeon was a large city like one of the royal cities; it was larger than Ai, and all its men were warriors. Therefore King Adoni-zedek of Jerusalem sent word to King Hoham of Hebron, King Piram of Jarmuth, King Japhia of Lachish, and King Debir of Eglon, saying, "Come up and help me. We will attack Gibeon, because they have made peace with Joshua and the Israelites." So the five Amorite kings—the kings of Jerusalem, Hebron, Jarmuth, Lachish, and Eglon—joined forces, advanced with all their armies, besieged Gibeon, and fought against it.
10   Then the men of Gibeon sent word to Joshua in the camp at Gilgal: "Don't give up on your servants. Come quickly and save us! Help us, for all the Amorite kings living in the hill country have joined forces against us." So Joshua and all his troops, including all his best soldiers, came from Gilgal.

The LORD said to Joshua, "Do not be afraid of them, for I have handed them over to you. Not one of them will be able to stand against you."

So Joshua caught them by surprise, after marching all night from Gilgal. The LORD threw them into confusion before Israel. He defeated them in a great slaughter at Gibeon, chased them through the ascent of Beth-horon, and struck them down as far as Azekah and Makkedah. As they fled before Israel, the LORD threw large hailstones on them from the sky along the descent
20   of Beth-horon all the way to Azekah, and they died. More of them died from the hail than the Israelites killed with the sword.

On the day the LORD gave the Amorites over to the Israelites, Joshua spoke to the LORD in the presence of Israel:

"Sun, stand still over Gibeon,
and moon, over the Valley of Aijalon."
And the sun stood still
and the moon stopped
until the nation took vengeance on its enemies.
Isn't this written in the Book of Jashar?
30   So the sun stopped

> in the middle of the sky
> and delayed its setting
> almost a full day.

There has been no day like it before or since, when the Lord listened to a man, because the Lord fought for Israel. Then Joshua and all Israel with him returned to the camp at Gilgal.

Now the five defeated kings had fled and hidden in the cave at Makkedah. It was reported to Joshua, "The five kings have been found; they are hiding in the cave at Makkedah."

Joshua said, "Roll large stones against the mouth of the cave, and station men by it to guard the kings. But as for the rest of you, don't stay there. Pursue your enemies and attack them from
40 behind. Don't let them enter their cities, for the Lord your God has handed them over to you." So Joshua and the Israelites finished inflicting a terrible slaughter on them until they were destroyed, although a few survivors ran away to the fortified cities. The people returned safely to Joshua in the camp at Makkedah. And no one dared to threaten the Israelites.

Then Joshua said, "Open the mouth of the cave, and bring those five kings to me out of there." That is what they did. They brought the five kings of Jerusalem, Hebron, Jarmuth, Lachish, and Eglon to Joshua out of the cave. When they had brought the kings to him, Joshua summoned all the men of Israel and said to the military commanders who had accompanied him, "Come here and put your feet on the necks of these kings." So the commanders came forward and put their feet on their necks. Joshua said to them, "Do not be
50 afraid or discouraged. Be strong and courageous, for the Lord will do this to all the enemies you fight."

After this, Joshua struck them down and executed them. He hung their bodies on five trees and they were there until evening. At sunset Joshua commanded that they be taken down from the trees and thrown into the cave where they had hidden. Then large stones were placed against the mouth of the cave, and the stones are still there today.

On that day Joshua captured Makkedah and struck it down with the sword, including its king. He completely destroyed it and everyone in it, leaving no survivors. So he treated the king of Makkedah as he had the king of Jericho.

Joshua and all Israel with him crossed from Makkedah to Libnah and fought against Libnah.
60 The Lord also handed it and its king over to Israel. He struck it down, putting everyone in it to the sword, and left no survivors in it. He treated Libnah's king as he had the king of Jericho.

From Libnah, Joshua and all Israel with him crossed to Lachish. They laid siege to it and attacked it. The Lord handed Lachish over to Israel, and Joshua captured it on the second day. He struck it down, putting everyone in it to the sword, just as he had done to Libnah. At that time King Horam of Gezer went to help Lachish, but Joshua struck him down along with his people, leaving no survivors.

Then Joshua crossed from Lachish to Eglon and all Israel with him. They laid siege to it and attacked it. On that day they captured it and struck it down, putting everyone in it to the sword. He completely destroyed it that day, just as he had done to Lachish.

70   Next, Joshua and all Israel with him went up from Eglon to Hebron and attacked it. They captured it and struck down its king, all its villages, and everyone in it with the sword. He left no survivors, just as he had done at Eglon. He completely destroyed Hebron and everyone in it.

Finally, Joshua turned toward Debir and attacked it. And all Israel was with him. He captured it—its king and all its villages. They struck them down with the sword and completely destroyed everyone in it, leaving no survivors. He treated Debir and its king as he had treated Hebron and as he had treated Libnah and its king.

So Joshua conquered the whole region—the hill country, the Negev, the Judean foothills, and the slopes—with all their kings, leaving no survivors. He completely destroyed every living being, as the Lord, the God of Israel, had commanded. Joshua conquered everyone from Kadesh-barnea
80   to Gaza, and all the land of Goshen as far as Gibeon. Joshua captured all these kings and their land in one campaign, because the Lord, the God of Israel, fought for Israel. Then Joshua returned with all Israel to the camp at Gilgal.

11 When King Jabin of Hazor heard this news, he sent a message to: King Jobab of Madon, the kings of Shimron and Achshaph, and the kings of the north in the hill country, the Arabah south of Chinnereth, the Judean foothills, and the Slopes of Dor to the west, the Canaanites in the east and west, the Amorites, Hethites, Perizzites, and Jebusites in the hill country, and the Hivites at the foot of Hermon in the land of Mizpah. They went out with all their armies—a multitude as numerous as the sand on the seashore—along with a vast number of horses and chariots. All these kings joined forces; they came and camped together at the Waters of Merom to attack Israel.

The Lord said to Joshua, "Do not be afraid of them, for at this time tomorrow I will cause all of them to be killed before Israel. You are to hamstring their horses and burn their chariots." So
10   Joshua and all his troops surprised them at the Waters of Merom and attacked them. The Lord handed them over to Israel, and they struck them down, pursuing them as far as greater Sidon and Misrephoth-maim, and to the east as far as the Valley of Mizpeh. They struck them down, leaving no survivors. Joshua treated them as the Lord had told him; he hamstrung their horses and burned their chariots.

At that time Joshua turned back, captured Hazor, and struck down its king with the sword, because Hazor had formerly been the leader of all these kingdoms. They struck down everyone in it with the sword, completely destroying them; he left no one alive. Then he burned Hazor.

Joshua captured all these kings and their cities and struck them down with the sword. He completely destroyed them, as Moses the Lord's servant had commanded. However, Israel did
20   not burn any of the cities that stood on their mounds except Hazor, which Joshua burned. The Israelites plundered all the spoils and cattle of these cities for themselves. But they struck down

every person with the sword until they had annihilated them, leaving no one alive. Just as the LORD had commanded his servant Moses, Moses commanded Joshua. That is what Joshua did, leaving nothing undone of all that the LORD had commanded Moses.

So Joshua took all this land—the hill country, all the Negev, all the land of Goshen, the foothills, the Arabah, and the hill country of Israel with its foothills—from Mount Halak, which ascends to Seir, as far as Baal-gad in the Valley of Lebanon at the foot of Mount Hermon. He captured all their kings and struck them down, putting them to death. Joshua waged war with all these kings for a long time. No city made peace with the Israelites except the Hivites who inhabited Gibeon;

30 all of them were taken in battle. For it was the LORD's intention to harden their hearts, so that they would engage Israel in battle, be completely destroyed without mercy, and be annihilated, just as the LORD had commanded Moses.

At that time Joshua proceeded to exterminate the Anakim from the hill country—Hebron, Debir, Anab—all the hill country of Judah and of Israel. Joshua completely destroyed them with their cities. No Anakim were left in the land of the Israelites, except for some remaining in Gaza, Gath, and Ashdod.

So Joshua took the entire land, in keeping with all that the LORD had told Moses. Joshua then gave it as an inheritance to Israel according to their tribal allotments. After this, the land had rest from war.

12 The Israelites struck down the following kings of the land and took possession of their land beyond the Jordan to the east and from the Arnon River to Mount Hermon, including all the Arabah eastward:

King Sihon of the Amorites lived in Heshbon. He ruled from Aroer on the rim of the Arnon River, along the middle of the valley, and half of Gilead up to the Jabbok River (the border of the Ammonites), the Arabah east of the Sea of Chinnereth to the Sea of Arabah (that is, the Dead Sea), eastward through Beth-jeshimoth and southward below the slopes of Pisgah.

King Og of Bashan, of the remnant of the Rephaim, lived in Ashtaroth and Edrei. He ruled over Mount Hermon, Salecah, all Bashan up to the Geshurite and Maacathite border, and half

10 of Gilead to the border of King Sihon of Heshbon. Moses the LORD's servant and the Israelites struck them down. And Moses the LORD's servant gave their land as an inheritance to the Reubenites, Gadites, and half the tribe of Manasseh.

Joshua and the Israelites struck down the following kings of the land beyond the Jordan to the west, from Baal-gad in the Valley of Lebanon to Mount Halak, which ascends toward Seir (Joshua gave their land as an inheritance to the tribes of Israel according to their allotments: the hill country, the Judean foothills, the Arabah, the slopes, the wilderness, and the Negev—the lands of the Hethites, Amorites, Canaanites, Perizzites, Hivites, and Jebusites):

the king of Jericho	one
the king of Ai, which is next to Bethel	one
the king of Jerusalem	one
the king of Hebron	one
the king of Jarmuth	one
the king of Lachish	one
the king of Eglon	one
the king of Gezer	one
the king of Debir	one
the king of Geder	one
the king of Hormah	one
the king of Arad	one
the king of Libnah	one
the king of Adullam	one
the king of Makkedah	one
the king of Bethel	one
the king of Tappuah	one
the king of Hepher	one
the king of Aphek	one
the king of Lasharon	one
the king of Madon	one
the king of Hazor	one
the king of Shimron-meron	one
the king of Achshaph	one
the king of Taanach	one
the king of Megiddo	one
the king of Kedesh	one
the king of Jokneam in Carmel	one
the king of Dor in Naphath-dor	one
the king of Goiim in Gilgal	one
the king of Tirzah	one
the total number of all kings:	thirty-one.

13 Joshua was now old, advanced in age, and the Lord said to him, "You have become old, advanced in age, but a great deal of the land remains to be possessed. This is the land that remains:

All the districts of the Philistines and the Geshurites: from the Shihor east of Egypt to the border of Ekron on the north (considered to be Canaanite territory)—the five Philistine rulers of Gaza, Ashdod, Ashkelon, Gath, and Ekron, as well as the Avvites in the south; all the land of the Canaanites, from Arah of the Sidonians to Aphek and as far as the border of the Amorites; the land of the Gebalites; and all Lebanon east from Baal-gad below Mount Hermon to the entrance of Hamath—all the inhabitants of the hill country from Lebanon to Misrephoth-maim, all the Sidonians.

10 I will drive them out before the Israelites, only distribute the land as an inheritance for Israel, as I have commanded you. Therefore, divide this land as an inheritance to the nine tribes and half the tribe of Manasseh."

With the other half of the tribe of Manasseh, the Reubenites and Gadites had received the inheritance Moses gave them beyond the Jordan to the east, just as Moses the LORD's servant had given them:

From Aroer on the rim of the Arnon Valley, along with the city in the middle of the valley, all the Medeba plateau as far as Dibon, and all the cities of King Sihon of the Amorites, who reigned in Heshbon, to the border of the Ammonites; also Gilead and the territory of the Geshurites and Maacathites, all Mount Hermon, and all Bashan to Salecah—the whole kingdom of Og in Bashan, who reigned in Ashtaroth and Edrei; he was one of the remaining Rephaim.

20 Moses struck them down and drove them out, but the Israelites did not drive out the Geshurites and Maacathites. So Geshur and Maacath still live in Israel today.

He did not, however, give any inheritance to the tribe of Levi. This was their inheritance, just as he had promised: the food offerings made to the LORD, the God of Israel.

To the tribe of Reuben's descendants by their clans, Moses gave this as their territory:

From Aroer on the rim of the Arnon Valley, along with the city in the middle of the valley, the whole plateau as far as Medeba, with Heshbon and all its cities on the plateau—Dibon, Bamoth-baal, Beth-baal-meon, Jahaz, Kedemoth, Mephaath, Kiriathaim, Sibmah, Zereth-shahar on the hill in the valley, Beth-peor, the slopes of Pisgah, and Beth-jeshimoth—all the cities of the plateau, and all the kingdom of King Sihon of the Amorites, who reigned in Heshbon. Moses had killed him and the chiefs of Midian—Evi, Rekem, Zur, Hur, and Reba— 30 the princes of Sihon who lived in the land. Along with those the Israelites put to death, they also killed the diviner, Balaam son of Beor, with the sword.

The border of the Reubenites was the Jordan and its plain. This was the inheritance of the Reubenites by their clans, with the cities and their settlements.

To the tribe of the Gadites by their clans, Moses gave this as their territory:

> Jazer and all the cities of Gilead, and half the land of the Ammonites to Aroer, near Rabbah; from Heshbon to Ramath-mizpeh and Betonim, and from Mahanaim to the border of Debir; in the valley: Beth-haram, Beth-nimrah, Succoth, and Zaphon—the rest of the kingdom of King Sihon of Heshbon. Their land also included the Jordan and its territory as far as the edge of the Sea of Chinnereth on the east side of the Jordan.

40 This was the inheritance of the Gadites by their clans, with the cities and their settlements.

And to half the tribe of Manasseh (that is, to half the tribe of Manasseh's descendants by their clans) Moses gave this as their territory:

> From Mahanaim through all Bashan—all the kingdom of King Og of Bashan, including all of Jair's Villages that are in Bashan—sixty cities. But half of Gilead, and Og's royal cities in Bashan—Ashtaroth and Edrei—are for the descendants of Machir son of Manasseh (that is, half the descendants of Machir by their clans).

These were the portions Moses gave them on the plains of Moab beyond the Jordan east of Jericho. But Moses did not give a portion to the tribe of Levi. The Lord, the God of Israel, was their inheritance, just as he had promised them.

14 The Israelites received these portions that the priest Eleazar, Joshua son of Nun, and the family heads of the Israelite tribes gave them in the land of Canaan. Their inheritance was by lot as the Lord commanded through Moses for the nine and a half tribes, because Moses had given the inheritance to the two and a half tribes beyond the Jordan. But he gave no inheritance among them to the Levites. The descendants of Joseph became two tribes, Manasseh and Ephraim. No portion of the land was given to the Levites except cities to live in, along with pasturelands for their cattle and livestock. So the Israelites did as the Lord commanded Moses, and they divided the land.

The descendants of Judah approached Joshua at Gilgal, and Caleb son of Jephunneh the Kenizzite said to him, "You know what the Lord promised Moses the man of God at Kadesh-barnea about you and me. I was forty years old when Moses the Lord's servant sent me from Kadesh-barnea to scout the land, and I brought back an honest report. My brothers who went with me caused the people to lose heart, but I followed the Lord my God completely. On that day Moses swore to me, 'The land where you have set foot will be an inheritance for you and your descendants forever, because you have followed the Lord my God completely.'

"As you see, the LORD has kept me alive these forty-five years as he promised, since the LORD spoke this word to Moses while Israel was journeying in the wilderness. Here I am today, eighty-five years old. I am still as strong today as I was the day Moses sent me out. My strength for battle and for daily tasks is now as it was then. Now give me this hill country the LORD promised me on that day, because you heard then that the Anakim are there, as well as large fortified cities.

20 Perhaps the LORD will be with me and I will drive them out as the LORD promised."

Then Joshua blessed Caleb son of Jephunneh and gave him Hebron as an inheritance. Therefore, Hebron still belongs to Caleb son of Jephunneh the Kenizzite as an inheritance today because he followed the LORD, the God of Israel, completely. Hebron's name used to be Kiriath-arba; Arba was the greatest man among the Anakim. After this, the land had rest from war.

15 Now the allotment for the tribe of the descendants of Judah by their clans was in the southernmost region, south to the Wilderness of Zin and over to the border of Edom.

Their southern border began at the tip of the Dead Sea on the south bay and went south of the Scorpions' Ascent, proceeded to Zin, ascended to the south of Kadesh-barnea, passed Hezron, ascended to Addar, and turned to Karka. It proceeded to Azmon and to the Brook of Egypt and so the border ended at the Mediterranean Sea. This is your southern border.

Now the eastern border was along the Dead Sea to the mouth of the Jordan.

The border on the north side was from the bay of the sea at the mouth of the Jordan. It ascended to Beth-hoglah, proceeded north of Beth-arabah, and ascended to the Stone of Bohan
10 son of Reuben. Then the border ascended to Debir from the Valley of Achor, turning north to the Gilgal that is opposite the Ascent of Adummim, which is south of the ravine. The border proceeded to the Waters of En-shemesh and ended at En-rogel. From there the border ascended Ben Hinnom Valley to the southern Jebusite slope (that is, Jerusalem) and ascended to the top of the hill that faces Hinnom Valley on the west, at the northern end of Rephaim Valley. From the top of the hill the border curved to the spring of the Waters of Nephtoah, went to the cities of Mount Ephron, and then curved to Baalah (that is, Kiriath-jearim). The border turned westward from Baalah to Mount Seir, went to the northern slope of Mount Jearim (that is, Chesalon), descended to Beth-shemesh, and proceeded to Timnah. Then the border reached to the slope north of Ekron, curved to Shikkeron, proceeded to Mount Baalah, went to Jabneel, and ended at
20 the Mediterranean Sea.

Now the western border was the coastline of the Mediterranean Sea.

This was the boundary of the descendants of Judah around their clans.

He gave Caleb son of Jephunneh the following portion among the descendants of Judah based on the Lord's instruction to Joshua: Kiriath-arba (that is, Hebron; Arba was the father of Anak). Caleb drove out from there the three sons of Anak: Sheshai, Ahiman, and Talmai, descendants of Anak. From there he marched against the inhabitants of Debir, which used to be called Kiriath-sepher, and Caleb said, "Whoever attacks and captures Kiriath-sepher, I will give my daughter Achsah to him as a wife." So Othniel son of Caleb's brother, Kenaz, captured it, and Caleb gave his daughter Achsah to him as a wife. When she arrived, she persuaded Othniel to ask her father for a field. As she got off her donkey, Caleb asked her, "What can I do for you?" She replied, "Give me a blessing. Since you have given me land in the Negev, give me the springs also." So he gave her the upper and lower springs.

This was the inheritance of the tribe of the descendants of Judah by their clans.

These were the outermost cities of the tribe of the descendants of Judah toward the border of Edom in the Negev: Kabzeel, Eder, Jagur, Kinah, Dimonah, Adadah, Kedesh, Hazor, Ithnan, Ziph, Telem, Bealoth, Hazor-hadattah, Kerioth-hezron (that is, Hazor), Amam, Shema, Moladah, Hazar-gaddah, Heshmon, Beth-pelet, Hazar-shual, Beer-sheba, Biziothiah, Baalah, Iim, Ezem, Eltolad, Chesil, Hormah, Ziklag, Madmannah, Sansannah, Lebaoth, Shilhim, Ain, and Rimmon—twenty-nine cities in all, with their settlements.

In the Judean foothills: Eshtaol, Zorah, Ashnah, Zanoah, En-gannim, Tappuah, Enam, Jarmuth, Adullam, Socoh, Azekah, Shaaraim, Adithaim, Gederah, and Gederothaim—fourteen cities, with their settlements; Zenan, Hadashah, Migdal-gad, Dilan, Mizpeh, Jokthe-el, Lachish, Bozkath, Eglon, Cabbon, Lahmam, Chitlish, Gederoth, Beth-dagon, Naamah, and Makkedah— sixteen cities, with their settlements; Libnah, Ether, Ashan, Iphtah, Ashnah, Nezib, Keilah, Achzib, and Mareshah—nine cities, with their settlements; Ekron, with its surrounding villages and settlements; from Ekron to the sea, all the cities near Ashdod, with their settlements; Ashdod, with its surrounding villages and settlements; Gaza, with its surrounding villages and settlements, to the Brook of Egypt and the coastline of the Mediterranean Sea.

In the hill country: Shamir, Jattir, Socoh, Dannah, Kiriath-sannah (that is, Debir), Anab, Eshtemoh, Anim, Goshen, Holon, and Giloh—eleven cities, with their settlements; Arab, Dumah, Eshan, Janim, Beth-tappuah, Aphekah, Humtah, Kiriath-arba (that is, Hebron), and Zior—nine cities, with their settlements; Maon, Carmel, Ziph, Juttah, Jezreel, Jokdeam, Zanoah, Kain, Gibeah, and Timnah—ten cities, with their settlements; Halhul, Beth-zur, Gedor, Maarath, Beth-anoth, and Eltekon—six cities, with their settlements; Kiriath-baal (that is, Kiriath-jearim), and Rabbah—two cities, with their settlements.

In the wilderness: Beth-arabah, Middin, Secacah, Nibshan, the City of Salt, and En-gedi—six cities, with their settlements.

But the descendants of Judah could not drive out the Jebusites who lived in Jerusalem. So the Jebusites still live in Jerusalem among the descendants of Judah today.

16 The allotment for the descendants of Joseph went from the Jordan at Jericho to the Waters of Jericho on the east, through the wilderness ascending from Jericho into the hill country of Bethel. From Bethel it went to Luz and proceeded to the border of the Archites by Ataroth. It then descended westward to the border of the Japhletites as far as the border of Lower Beth-horon, then to Gezer, and ended at the Mediterranean Sea. So Ephraim and Manasseh, the sons of Joseph, received their inheritance.

This was the territory of the descendants of Ephraim by their clans:

The border of their inheritance went from Ataroth-addar on the east to Upper Beth-horon. In the north the border went westward from Michmethath; it turned eastward from Taanath-shiloh and passed it east of Janoah. From Janoah it descended to Ataroth and Naarah, and then reached Jericho and went to the Jordan. From Tappuah the border went westward along the Brook of Kanah and ended at the Mediterranean Sea.

This was the inheritance of the tribe of the descendants of Ephraim by their clans, together with the cities set apart for the descendants of Ephraim within the inheritance of the descendants of Manasseh—all these cities with their settlements. However, they did not drive out the Canaanites who lived in Gezer. So the Canaanites still live in Ephraim today, but they are forced laborers.

17 This was the allotment for the tribe of Manasseh as Joseph's firstborn. Gilead and Bashan were given to Machir, the firstborn of Manasseh and the father of Gilead, because he was a man of war. So the allotment was for the rest of Manasseh's descendants by their clans, for the sons of Abiezer, Helek, Asriel, Shechem, Hepher, and Shemida. These are the male descendants of Manasseh son of Joseph, by their clans.

Now Zelophehad son of Hepher, son of Gilead, son of Machir, son of Manasseh, had no sons, only daughters. These are the names of his daughters: Mahlah, Noah, Hoglah, Milcah, and Tirzah. They came before the priest Eleazar, Joshua son of Nun, and the leaders, saying, "The LORD commanded Moses to give us an inheritance among our male relatives." So they gave them an inheritance among their father's brothers, in keeping with the LORD's instruction. As a result, ten tracts fell to Manasseh, besides the land of Gilead and Bashan, which are beyond the Jordan, because Manasseh's daughters received an inheritance among his sons. The land of Gilead belonged to the rest of Manasseh's sons.

The border of Manasseh went from Asher to Michmethath near Shechem. It then went southward toward the inhabitants of En-tappuah. The region of Tappuah belonged to Manasseh, but Tappuah itself on Manasseh's border belonged to the descendants of Ephraim. From there the border descended to the Brook of Kanah; south of the brook, cities belonged to Ephraim among Manasseh's cities. Manasseh's border was on the north side of the brook and ended at the Mediterranean Sea. Ephraim's territory was to the south and Manasseh's to the north, with the

20 Sea as its border. They reached Asher on the north and Issachar on the east. Within Issachar and Asher, Manasseh had Beth-shean, Ibleam, and the inhabitants of Dor with their surrounding villages; the inhabitants of En-dor, Taanach, and Megiddo—the three cities of Naphath—with their surrounding villages.

The descendants of Manasseh could not possess these cities, because the Canaanites were determined to stay in this land. However, when the Israelites grew stronger, they imposed forced labor on the Canaanites but did not drive them out completely.

Joseph's descendants said to Joshua, "Why did you give us only one tribal allotment as an inheritance? We have many people, because the LORD has been blessing us greatly."

"If you have so many people," Joshua replied to them, "go to the forest and clear an area for
30 yourselves there in the land of the Perizzites and the Rephaim, because Ephraim's hill country is too small for you."

But the descendants of Joseph said, "The hill country is not enough for us, and all the Canaanites who inhabit the valley area have iron chariots, both at Beth-shean with its surrounding villages and in the Jezreel Valley."

So Joshua replied to Joseph's family (that is, Ephraim and Manasseh), "You have many people and great strength. You will not have just one allotment, because the hill country will be yours also. It is a forest; clear it and its outlying areas will be yours. You can also drive out the Canaanites, even though they have iron chariots and are strong."

18 The entire Israelite community assembled at Shiloh and set up the tent of meeting there. The land had been subdued before them, but seven tribes among the Israelites were left who had not divided up their inheritance. So Joshua asked the Israelites, "How long will you delay going out to take possession of the land that the LORD, the God of your ancestors, gave you? Appoint for yourselves three men from each tribe, and I will send them out. They are to go and survey the land, write a description of it for the purpose of their inheritance, and return to me. Then they are to divide it into seven portions. Judah is to remain in its territory in the south and Joseph's family in their territory in the north. When you have written a description of the seven portions of land and brought it to me, I will cast lots for you here in the presence of the LORD our God. But the Levites among you do not get a portion, because
10 their inheritance is the priesthood of the LORD. Gad, Reuben, and half the tribe of Manasseh have taken their inheritance beyond the Jordan to the east, which Moses the LORD's servant gave them."

As the men prepared to go, Joshua commanded them to write down a description of the land, saying, "Go and survey the land, write a description of it, and return to me. I will then cast lots for you here in Shiloh in the presence of the Lord." So the men left, went through the land, and described it by towns in a document of seven sections. They returned to Joshua at the camp in Shiloh. Joshua cast lots for them at Shiloh in the presence of the Lord where he distributed the land to the Israelites according to their divisions.

The lot came up for the tribe of Benjamin's descendants by their clans, and their allotted territory lay between Judah's descendants and Joseph's descendants.

20   Their border on the north side began at the Jordan, ascended to the slope of Jericho on the north, through the hill country westward, and ended at the wilderness around Beth-aven. From there the border went toward Luz, to the southern slope of Luz (that is, Bethel); it then went down by Ataroth-addar, over the hill south of Lower Beth-horon.

On the west side, from the hill facing Beth-horon on the south, the border curved, turning southward, and ended at Kiriath-baal (that is, Kiriath-jearim), a city of the descendants of Judah. This was the west side of their border.

The south side began at the edge of Kiriath-jearim, and the border extended westward; it went to the spring at the Waters of Nephtoah. The border descended to the foot of the hill that faces Ben Hinnom Valley at the northern end of Rephaim Valley. It ran down Hinnom Valley toward 30   the south Jebusite slope and downward to En-rogel. It curved northward and went to En-shemesh and on to Geliloth, which is opposite the Ascent of Adummim, and continued down to the Stone of Bohan son of Reuben. Then it went north to the slope opposite the Arabah and proceeded into the plains. The border continued to the north slope of Beth-hoglah and ended at the northern bay of the Dead Sea, at the southern end of the Jordan. This was the southern border.

The Jordan formed the border on the east side.
This was the inheritance of Benjamin's descendants, by their clans, according to its surrounding borders.

These were the cities of the tribe of Benjamin's descendants by their clans:

Jericho, Beth-hoglah, Emek-keziz, Beth-arabah, Zemaraim, Bethel, Avvim, Parah, Ophrah, 40   Chephar-ammoni, Ophni, and Geba—twelve cities, with their settlements; Gibeon, Ramah, Beeroth, Mizpeh, Chephirah, Mozah, Rekem, Irpeel, Taralah, Zela, Haeleph, Jebus (that is, Jerusalem), Gibeah, and Kiriath—fourteen cities, with their settlements.

This was the inheritance for Benjamin's descendants by their clans.

19 The second lot came out for Simeon, for the tribe of his descendants by their clans, but their inheritance was within the inheritance given to Judah's descendants. Their inheritance included

Beer-sheba (or Sheba), Moladah, Hazar-shual, Balah, Ezem, Eltolad, Bethul, Hormah, Ziklag, Beth-marcaboth, Hazar-susah, Beth-lebaoth, and Sharuhen—thirteen cities, with their settlements; Ain, Rimmon, Ether, and Ashan—four cities, with their settlements; and all the settlements surrounding these cities as far as Baalath-beer (Ramah in the south).

This was the inheritance of the tribe of Simeon's descendants by their clans. The inheritance of Simeon's descendants was within the territory of Judah's descendants, because the share for Judah's descendants was too large. So Simeon's descendants received an inheritance within Judah's
10 portion.

The third lot came up for Zebulun's descendants by their clans.

The territory of their inheritance stretched as far as Sarid; their border went up westward to Maralah, reached Dabbesheth, and met the brook east of Jokneam. From Sarid, it turned due east along the border of Chisloth-tabor, went to Daberath, and went up to Japhia. From there, it went due east to Gath-hepher and to Eth-kazin; it extended to Rimmon, curving around to Neah. The border then circled around Neah on the north to Hannathon and ended at Iphtah-el Valley, along with Kattath, Nahalal, Shimron, Idalah, and Bethlehem—twelve cities, with their settlements. This was the inheritance of Zebulun's descendants by their clans, these cities, with their settlements.

The fourth lot came out for the tribe of Issachar's descendants by their clans.
20 Their territory went to Jezreel, and included Chesulloth, Shunem, Hapharaim, Shion, Anaharath, Rabbith, Kishion, Ebez, Remeth, En-gannim, En-haddah, and Beth-pazzez. The border reached Tabor, Shahazumah, and Beth-shemesh, and ended at the Jordan—sixteen cities, with their settlements.
This was the inheritance of the tribe of Issachar's descendants by their clans, the cities, with their settlements.

The fifth lot came out for the tribe of Asher's descendants by their clans.

Their boundary included Helkath, Hali, Beten, Achshaph, Allammelech, Amad, and Mishal and reached westward to Carmel and Shihor-libnath. It turned eastward to Beth-dagon, reached Zebulun and Iphtah-el Valley, north toward Beth-emek and Neiel, and went north to Cabul, Ebron,
30 Rehob, Hammon, and Kanah, as far as greater Sidon. The boundary then turned to Ramah as far as the fortified city of Tyre; it turned back to Hosah and ended at the Mediterranean Sea, including Mahalab, Achzib, Ummah, Aphek, and Rehob—twenty-two cities, with their settlements. This was the inheritance of the tribe of Asher's descendants by their clans, these cities with their settlements.

The sixth lot came out for Naphtali's descendants by their clans.

Their boundary went from Heleph and from the oak in Zaanannim, including Adami-nekeb and Jabneel, as far as Lakkum, and ended at the Jordan. To the west, the boundary turned to Aznoth-tabor and went from there to Hukkok, reaching Zebulun on the south, Asher on the west, and Judah at the Jordan on the east. The fortified cities were Ziddim, Zer, Hammath, Rakkath, Chinnereth, Adamah, Ramah, Hazor, Kedesh, Edrei, En-hazor, Iron, Migdal-el, Horem, Beth-anath, and Beth-shemesh—nineteen cities, with their settlements. This was the inheritance of the tribe of Naphtali's descendants by their clans, the cities with their settlements.

The seventh lot came out for the tribe of Dan's descendants by their clans.

The territory of their inheritance included Zorah, Eshtaol, Ir-shemesh, Shaalabbin, Aijalon, Ithlah, Elon, Timnah, Ekron, Eltekeh, Gibbethon, Baalath, Jehud, Bene-berak, Gath-rimmon, Me-jarkon, and Rakkon, with the territory facing Joppa. When the territory of the descendants of Dan slipped out of their control, they went up and fought against Leshem, captured it, and struck it down with the sword. So they took possession of it, lived there, and renamed Leshem after their ancestor Dan. This was the inheritance of the tribe of Dan's descendants by their clans, these cities with their settlements.

When they had finished distributing the land into its territories, the Israelites gave Joshua son of Nun an inheritance among them. By the LORD's command, they gave him the city Timnath-serah in the hill country of Ephraim, which he requested. He rebuilt the city and lived in it.

These were the portions that the priest Eleazar, Joshua son of Nun, and the family heads distributed to the Israelite tribes by lot at Shiloh in the LORD's presence at the entrance to the tent of meeting. So they finished dividing up the land.

20 Then the LORD spoke to Joshua, "Tell the Israelites: Select your cities of refuge, as I instructed you through Moses, so that a person who kills someone unintentionally or accidentally may flee there. These will be your refuge from the avenger of blood. When someone flees to one of these cities, stands at the entrance of the city gate, and states his case before the elders of that city, they are to bring him into the city and give him a place to live among them. And if the avenger of blood pursues him, they must not hand the one who committed manslaughter over to him, for he killed his neighbor accidentally and did not hate him beforehand. He is to stay in that city until he stands trial before the assembly and until the death of the high priest serving at that time. Then the one who committed manslaughter may return home to his own city from which he fled."

So they designated Kedesh in the hill country of Naphtali in Galilee, Shechem in the hill country of Ephraim, and Kiriath-arba (that is, Hebron) in the hill country of Judah. Across the

Jordan east of Jericho, they selected Bezer on the wilderness plateau from Reuben's tribe, Ramoth in Gilead from Gad's tribe, and Golan in Bashan from Manasseh's tribe.

These are the cities appointed for all the Israelites and the aliens residing among them, so that anyone who kills a person unintentionally may flee there and not die at the hand of the avenger of blood until he stands before the assembly.

21 The Levite family heads approached the priest Eleazar, Joshua son of Nun, and the family heads of the Israelite tribes. At Shiloh, in the land of Canaan, they told them, "The LORD commanded through Moses that we be given cities to live in, with their pasturelands for our livestock." So the Israelites, by the LORD's command, gave the Levites these cities with their pasturelands from their inheritance.

The lot came out for the Kohathite clans: The Levites who were the descendants of the priest Aaron received thirteen cities by lot from the tribes of Judah, Simeon, and Benjamin. The remaining descendants of Kohath received ten cities by lot from the clans of the tribes of Ephraim, Dan, and half the tribe of Manasseh.

10   Gershon's descendants received thirteen cities by lot from the clans of the tribes of Issachar, Asher, Naphtali, and half the tribe of Manasseh in Bashan.

Merari's descendants received twelve cities for their clans from the tribes of Reuben, Gad, and Zebulun.

The Israelites gave these cities with their pasturelands around them to the Levites by lot, as the LORD had commanded through Moses.

The Israelites gave these cities by name from the tribes of the descendants of Judah and Simeon to the descendants of Aaron from the Kohathite clans of the Levites, because they received the first lot. They gave them Kiriath-arba (that is, Hebron; Arba was the father of Anak) with its surrounding pasturelands in the hill country of Judah. But they gave the fields and settlements of 20 the city to Caleb son of Jephunneh as his possession.

They gave to the descendants of the priest Aaron:

Hebron, the city of refuge for the one who commits manslaughter, with its pasturelands, Libnah with its pasturelands, Jattir with its pasturelands, Eshtemoa with its pasturelands, Holon with its pasturelands, Debir with its pasturelands, Ain with its pasturelands, Juttah with its pasturelands, and Beth-shemesh with its pasturelands—nine cities from these two tribes.

From the tribe of Benjamin they gave:

Gibeon with its pasturelands, Geba with its pasturelands, Anathoth with its pasturelands, and Almon with its pasturelands—four cities. All thirteen cities with their pasturelands were for the priests, the descendants of Aaron.

The allotted cities to the remaining clans of Kohath's descendants, who were Levites, came from the tribe of Ephraim. The Israelites gave them:

Shechem, the city of refuge for the one who commits manslaughter, with its pasturelands in the hill country of Ephraim, Gezer with its pasturelands, Kibzaim with its pasturelands, and Beth-horon with its pasturelands—four cities.

From the tribe of Dan they gave:

Elteke with its pasturelands, Gibbethon with its pasturelands, Aijalon with its pasturelands, and Gath-rimmon with its pasturelands—four cities.

From half the tribe of Manasseh they gave:

Taanach with its pasturelands and Gath-rimmon with its pasturelands—two cities. All ten cities with their pasturelands were for the clans of Kohath's other descendants.

From half the tribe of Manasseh, they gave to the descendants of Gershon, who were one of the Levite clans:

Golan, the city of refuge for the one who commits manslaughter, with its pasturelands in Bashan, and Beeshterah with its pasturelands—two cities.

From the tribe of Issachar they gave:

Kishion with its pasturelands, Daberath with its pasturelands, Jarmuth with its pasturelands, and En-gannim with its pasturelands—four cities.

From the tribe of Asher they gave:

Mishal with its pasturelands, Abdon with its pasturelands, Helkath with its pasturelands, and Rehob with its pasturelands—four cities.

From the tribe of Naphtali they gave:

Kedesh in Galilee, the city of refuge for the one who commits manslaughter, with its pasturelands, Hammoth-dor with its pasturelands, and Kartan with its pasturelands—three cities. All thirteen cities with their pasturelands were for the Gershonites by their clans.

From the tribe of Zebulun, they gave to the clans of the descendants of Merari, who were the remaining Levites:

Jokneam with its pasturelands, Kartah with its pasturelands, Dimnah with its pasturelands, and Nahalal with its pasturelands—four cities.

60 From the tribe of Reuben they gave:
Bezer with its pasturelands, Jahzah with its pasturelands, Kedemoth with its pasturelands, and Mephaath with its pasturelands—four cities.

From the tribe of Gad they gave:
Ramoth in Gilead, the city of refuge for the one who commits manslaughter, with its pasturelands, Mahanaim with its pasturelands, Heshbon with its pasturelands, and Jazer with its pasturelands—four cities in all. All twelve cities were allotted to the clans of Merari's descendants, the remaining Levite clans.

Within the Israelite possession there were forty-eight cities in all with their pasturelands for the Levites. Each of these cities had its own surrounding pasturelands; this was true for all the 70 cities.

So the LORD gave Israel all the land he had sworn to give their ancestors, and they took possession of it and settled there. The LORD gave them rest on every side according to all he had sworn to their ancestors. None of their enemies were able to stand against them, for the LORD handed over all their enemies to them. None of the good promises the LORD had made to the house of Israel failed. Everything was fulfilled.

22 Joshua summoned the Reubenites, Gadites, and half the tribe of Manasseh and told them, "You have done everything Moses the LORD's servant commanded you and have obeyed me in everything I commanded you. You have not deserted your brothers even once this whole time but have carried out the requirement of the command of the LORD your God. Now that he has given your brothers rest, just as he promised them, return to your homes in your own land that Moses the LORD's servant gave you across the Jordan. Only carefully obey the command and instruction that Moses the LORD's servant gave you: to love the LORD your God, walk in all his ways, keep his commands, be loyal to him, and serve him with all your heart and all your soul."

Joshua blessed them and sent them on their way, and they went to their homes. Moses had 10 given territory to half the tribe of Manasseh in Bashan, but Joshua had given territory to the other half, with their brothers, on the west side of the Jordan. When Joshua sent them to their homes and blessed them, he said, "Return to your homes with great wealth: a huge number of cattle, and silver, gold, bronze, iron, and a large quantity of clothing. Share the spoil of your enemies with your brothers."

The Reubenites, Gadites, and half the tribe of Manasseh left the Israelites at Shiloh in the land of Canaan to return to their own land of Gilead, which they took possession of according to the LORD's command through Moses. When they came to the region of the Jordan in the land of Canaan, the Reubenites, Gadites, and half the tribe of Manasseh built a large, impressive altar there by the Jordan.

Then the Israelites heard it said, "Look, the Reubenites, Gadites, and half the tribe of
20 Manasseh have built an altar on the frontier of the land of Canaan at the region of the Jordan, on the Israelite side." When the Israelites heard this, the entire Israelite community assembled at Shiloh to go to war against them.

The Israelites sent Phinehas son of Eleazar the priest to the Reubenites, Gadites, and half the tribe of Manasseh, in the land of Gilead. They sent ten leaders with him—one family leader for each tribe of Israel. All of them were heads of their ancestral families among the clans of Israel. They went to the Reubenites, Gadites, and half the tribe of Manasseh, in the land of Gilead, and told them, "This is what the LORD's entire community says: 'What is this treachery you have committed today against the God of Israel by turning away from the LORD and building an altar for yourselves, so that you are in rebellion against the LORD today? Wasn't the iniquity of Peor,
30 which brought a plague on the LORD's community, enough for us? We have not cleansed ourselves from it even to this day, and now would you turn away from the LORD? If you rebel against the LORD today, tomorrow he will be angry with the entire community of Israel. But if the land you possess is defiled, cross over to the land the LORD possesses where the LORD's tabernacle stands, and take possession of it among us. But don't rebel against the LORD or against us by building for yourselves an altar other than the altar of the LORD our God. Wasn't Achan son of Zerah unfaithful regarding what was set apart for destruction, bringing wrath on the entire community of Israel? He was not the only one who perished because of his iniquity.'"

The Reubenites, Gadites, and half the tribe of Manasseh answered the heads of the Israelite clans, "The Mighty One, God, the LORD! The Mighty One, God, the LORD! He knows, and may
40 Israel also know. Do not spare us today, if it was in rebellion or treachery against the LORD that we have built for ourselves an altar to turn away from him. May the LORD himself hold us accountable if we intended to offer burnt offerings and grain offerings on it, or to sacrifice fellowship offerings on it. We actually did this from a specific concern that in the future your descendants might say to our descendants, 'What relationship do you have with the LORD, the God of Israel? For the LORD has made the Jordan a border between us and you descendants of Reuben and Gad. You have no share in the LORD!' So your descendants may cause our descendants to stop fearing the LORD.

"Therefore we said: Let's take action and build an altar for ourselves, but not for burnt offering or sacrifice. Instead, it is to be a witness between us and you, and between the generations after us, so that we may carry out the worship of the LORD in his presence with our burnt offerings,
50 sacrifices, and fellowship offerings. Then in the future, your descendants will not be able to say to our descendants, 'You have no share in the LORD!' We thought that if they said this to us or

to our generations in the future, we would reply: Look at the replica of the LORD's altar that our ancestors made, not for burnt offering or sacrifice, but as a witness between us and you. We would never ever rebel against the LORD or turn away from him today by building an altar for burnt offering, grain offering, or sacrifice, other than the altar of the LORD our God, which is in front of his tabernacle."

When the priest Phinehas and the community leaders, the heads of Israel's clans who were with him, heard what the descendants of Reuben, Gad, and Manasseh had to say, they were pleased. Phinehas son of Eleazar the priest said to the descendants of Reuben, Gad, and Manasseh, "Today

60 we know that the LORD is among us, because you have not committed this treachery against him. As a result, you have rescued the Israelites from the LORD's power."

Then the priest Phinehas son of Eleazar and the leaders returned from the Reubenites and Gadites in the land of Gilead to the Israelites in the land of Canaan and brought back a report to them. The Israelites were pleased with the report, and they blessed God. They spoke no more about going to war against them to ravage the land where the Reubenites and Gadites lived. So the Reubenites and Gadites named the altar: It is a witness between us that the LORD is God.

23 A long time after the LORD had given Israel rest from all the enemies around them, Joshua was old, advanced in age. So Joshua summoned all Israel, including its elders, leaders, judges, and officers, and said to them, "I am old, advanced in age, and you have seen for yourselves everything the LORD your God did to all these nations on your account, because it was the LORD your God who was fighting for you. See, I have allotted these remaining nations to you as an inheritance for your tribes, including all the nations I have destroyed, from the Jordan westward to the Mediterranean Sea. The LORD your God will force them back on your account and drive them out before you so that you can take possession of their land, as the LORD your God promised you.

"Be very strong and continue obeying all that is written in the book of the law of Moses, so

10 that you do not turn from it to the right or left and so that you do not associate with these nations remaining among you. Do not call on the names of their gods or make an oath to them; do not serve them or bow in worship to them. Instead, be loyal to the LORD your God, as you have been to this day.

"The LORD has driven out great and powerful nations before you, and no one is able to stand against you to this day. One of you routed a thousand because the LORD your God was fighting for you, as he promised. So diligently watch yourselves! Love the LORD your God! If you ever turn away and become loyal to the rest of these nations remaining among you, and if you intermarry or associate with them and they with you, know for certain that the LORD your God will not continue to drive these nations out before you. They will become a snare and a trap for you, a

20 sharp stick for your sides and thorns in your eyes, until you disappear from this good land the LORD your God has given you.

"I am now going the way of the whole earth, and you know with all your heart and all your soul that none of the good promises the LORD your God made to you has failed. Everything was fulfilled for you; not one promise has failed. Since every good thing the LORD your God promised you has come about, so he will bring on you every bad thing until he has annihilated you from this good land the LORD your God has given you. If you break the covenant of the LORD your God, which he commanded you, and go and serve other gods, and bow in worship to them, the LORD's anger will burn against you, and you will quickly disappear from this good land he has given you."

24 Joshua assembled all the tribes of Israel at Shechem and summoned Israel's elders, leaders, judges, and officers, and they presented themselves before God. Joshua said to all the people, "This is what the LORD, the God of Israel, says: 'Long ago your ancestors, including Terah, the father of Abraham and Nahor, lived beyond the Euphrates River and worshiped other gods. But I took your father Abraham from the region beyond the Euphrates River, led him throughout the land of Canaan, and multiplied his descendants. I gave him Isaac, and to Isaac I gave Jacob and Esau. I gave the hill country of Seir to Esau as a possession.

"'Jacob and his sons, however, went down to Egypt. I sent Moses and Aaron, and I defeated Egypt by what I did within it, and afterward I brought you out. When I brought your ancestors out of Egypt and you reached the Red Sea, the Egyptians pursued your ancestors with chariots and horsemen as far as the sea. Your ancestors cried out to the LORD, so he put darkness between you and the Egyptians, and brought the sea over them, engulfing them. Your own eyes saw what I did to Egypt. After that, you lived in the wilderness a long time.

"'Later, I brought you to the land of the Amorites who lived beyond the Jordan. They fought against you, but I handed them over to you. You possessed their land, and I annihilated them before you. Balak son of Zippor, king of Moab, set out to fight against Israel. He sent for Balaam son of Beor to curse you, but I would not listen to Balaam. Instead, he repeatedly blessed you, and I rescued you from him.

"'You then crossed the Jordan and came to Jericho. Jericho's citizens—as well as the Amorites, Perizzites, Canaanites, Hethites, Girgashites, Hivites, and Jebusites—fought against you, but I handed them over to you. I sent hornets ahead of you, and they drove out the two Amorite kings before you. It was not by your sword or bow. I gave you a land you did not labor for, and cities you did not build, though you live in them; you are eating from vineyards and olive groves you did not plant.'

"Therefore, fear the LORD and worship him in sincerity and truth. Get rid of the gods your ancestors worshiped beyond the Euphrates River and in Egypt, and worship the LORD. But if it doesn't please you to worship the LORD, choose for yourselves today: Which will you worship—the gods your ancestors worshiped beyond the Euphrates River or the gods of the Amorites in whose land you are living? As for me and my family, we will worship the LORD."

30 The people replied, "We will certainly not abandon the LORD to worship other gods! For the LORD our God brought us and our ancestors out of the land of Egypt, out of the place of slavery, and performed these great signs before our eyes. He also protected us all along the way we went and among all the peoples whose lands we traveled through. The LORD drove out before us all the peoples, including the Amorites who lived in the land. We too will worship the LORD, because he is our God."

But Joshua told the people, "You will not be able to worship the LORD, because he is a holy God. He is a jealous God; he will not forgive your transgressions and sins. If you abandon the LORD and worship foreign gods, he will turn against you, harm you, and completely destroy you, after he has been good to you."

40 "No!" the people answered Joshua. "We will worship the LORD."

Joshua then told the people, "You are witnesses against yourselves that you yourselves have chosen to worship the LORD."

"We are witnesses," they said.

"Then get rid of the foreign gods that are among you and turn your hearts to the LORD, the God of Israel."

So the people said to Joshua, "We will worship the LORD our God and obey him."

On that day Joshua made a covenant for the people at Shechem and established a statute and ordinance for them. Joshua recorded these things in the book of the law of God; he also took a large stone and set it up there under the oak at the sanctuary of the LORD. And Joshua said to all
50 the people, "You see this stone—it will be a witness against us, for it has heard all the words the LORD said to us, and it will be a witness against you, so that you will not deny your God." Then Joshua sent the people away, each to his own inheritance.

After these things, the LORD's servant, Joshua son of Nun, died at the age of 110. They buried him in his allotted territory at Timnath-serah, in the hill country of Ephraim north of Mount Gaash. Israel worshiped the LORD throughout Joshua's lifetime and during the lifetimes of the elders who outlived Joshua and who had experienced all the works the LORD had done for Israel.

Joseph's bones, which the Israelites had brought up from Egypt, were buried at Shechem in the parcel of land Jacob had purchased from the sons of Hamor, Shechem's father, for a hundred pieces of silver. It was an inheritance for Joseph's descendants.

60 And Eleazar son of Aaron died, and they buried him at Gibeah, which had been given to his son Phinehas in the hill country of Ephraim.

Introduction to Judges

Jillian L. Ross

Children's Sunday school literature often captures the imaginations of little ones by depicting the military triumphs of judges like Gideon and Samson as ancient superheroes. Adults reading Judges, however, see pages strewn with brutality and victimization. Often repulsed by such atrocities, they query, "Why all this violence?" Superheroes and oppressors make for interesting bedfellows, but the answer to the question lies in the theology of Judges and its development through the narrative.

Judges is a historical narrative, but it is not simply a report of the major events of the judges period (the period between Joshua's death and Saul's kingship). The book omits key figures like Ruth, Boaz, and the last judge Samuel, and instead focuses on accounts reflecting the progressive spiritual deterioration of Yahweh's people, including its leaders. Judges 2 characterizes the period as a cycle of idolatry, resulting in foreign oppression, leading to groans to Yahweh, and culminating with Yahweh's gracious deliverance, then Israel apostatizes again. This pattern repeats itself throughout the stories of the judges.

Judges begins with leaders and (infrequently) the people doing right in Yahweh's sight but as the book unfolds, Israel's righteousness diminishes and its brutality intensifies. The people start looking and acting like Canaanites. In the final story, "there is no one righteous" (see Rom 3:10); the episode is plagued with scheming half-truths, sexual exploitation, and successive bloody battles. Thus, Judges concludes darkly, "Everyone did whatever seemed right to him" (21.40). Judges dramatically details this theological truth: when Yahweh's people turn away from him, they act selfishly and barbarously, oppressing the weak and destroying society.

Israel's task had been to purify the land by ridding it of idolatry through demolishing pagan sites and expelling the pagan Canaanites (2.3–5). Israel tragically failed the task in its worship of Yahweh and its warfare for him. Judges develops this in three major sections: (1) a prologue, comprising two introductions; (2) the "cycles" (stories) of the judges; and (3) an epilogue, comprising two concluding stories. Israel begins by struggling with foreign idolatry and foreign wars, but by the middle Israel occasionally faces even greater infidelity: state-sponsored idolatry and civil wars. These become the norm by the end. This patterning can be visually depicted as follows.

Prologue	A	Warfare against Foreigners (1.1–2.7)
	B	Worship of Foreign Idols (2.8–3.9)
Center of Judges: Gideon	B	Worship of Foreign Idols (6.1–56)
	A	Warfare against Foreigners (6.57–7.51)
	A'	Warfare against Israelites (8.1–38)
	B'	Worship of Israelite Idols (8.39–55)
Epilogue	B'	Worship of Israelite Idols (17–18)
	A'	Warfare against Israelites (19–21)

Gideon is the pivotal character of Judges since he is the middle figure in the judges cycle. Those before him, like Othniel and Deborah, are faithful Israelites worth emulating. Those after him have serious failings. Gideon's life represents the arc of Israel's commitment to Yahweh in that period. Gideon, though flawed, begins by ridding his hometown of idolatry and leading Israel in battle for the Lord. Gideon triumphs despite being grossly outnumbered because Yahweh was with him. Yet afterwards, Gideon tortured Israelites in civil war and led Israel in worshiping the Lord in a pagan manner. Thus, Gideon began as a good judge but lacked stamina. His "superhero" strength was from Yahweh for his redemptive purposes, but Gideon is not a superhero to emulate. At the critical moment, he, as well as the later judges, exercised faith (see Heb 11:32–34), but their lives were not characterized by fidelity to Yahweh. Israel devalued Yahweh, thus superheroes and oppressors coexist in Judges.

Outline

1. Prologue: Israel's Incomplete Conquest and Idolatry (1.1–3.9)
    a. Warfare against Foreigners (1.1–2.7)
    b. Worship of Foreign Idols (2.8–3.9)

2. The Cycles of the Judges (3.10–16.67)
    a. Othniel (3.10–17)
    b. Ehud (3.18–48)
    c. Shamgar (3.49–50)
    d. Deborah with Barak (4.1–5.104)
    e. Gideon the Central Judge (6.1–8.59)
    f. Abimelech (9.1–110)
    g. Tola (10.1–3)
    h. Jair (10.4–6)

  i. Jephthah (10.7–12.15)
  j. Ibzan (12.16–18)
  k. Elon (12.19–20)
  l. Abdon (12.21–23)
  m. Samson (13.1–16.67)

3. Epilogue: Israel's Complete Spiritual and Moral Failure (17.1–21.40)
  a. The Micah Story (17.1–18.56)
  b. The Outrage at Gibeah (19.1–21.40)

Suggested Resources

Block, Daniel I. *Judges, Ruth.* New American Commentary. Nashville: Broadman & Holman, 1999.

Sasson, Jack M. *Judges 1–12.* Anchor Bible Commentary. New Haven: Yale University Press, 2014.

Schneider, Tammi J. *Judges.* Berit Olam. Collegeville, MN: Liturgical Press, 2000.

Webb, Barry G. *The Book of Judges.* New International Commentary on the Old Testament. Grand Rapids: Eerdmans, 2012.

Younger, K. Lawson, Jr. *Judges, Ruth.* NIV Application Commentary. Rev. ed. Grand Rapids: Zondervan, 2021.

Judges

1 After the death of Joshua, the Israelites inquired of the LORD, "Who will be the first to fight for us against the Canaanites?"

The LORD answered, "Judah is to go. I have handed the land over to him."

Judah said to his brother Simeon, "Come with me to my allotted territory, and let's fight against the Canaanites. I will also go with you to your allotted territory." So Simeon went with him.

When Judah attacked, the LORD handed the Canaanites and Perizzites over to them. They struck down ten thousand men in Bezek. They found Adoni-bezek in Bezek, fought against him, and struck down the Canaanites and Perizzites.

When Adoni-bezek fled, they pursued him, caught him, and cut off his thumbs and big toes. Adoni-bezek said, "Seventy kings with their thumbs and big toes cut off used to pick up scraps under my table. God has repaid me for what I have done." They brought him to Jerusalem, and he died there.

The men of Judah fought against Jerusalem, captured it, put it to the sword, and set the city on fire. Afterward, the men of Judah marched down to fight against the Canaanites who were living in the hill country, the Negev, and the Judean foothills. Judah also marched against the Canaanites who were living in Hebron (Hebron was formerly named Kiriath-arba). They struck down Sheshai, Ahiman, and Talmai. From there they marched against the residents of Debir (Debir was formerly named Kiriath-sepher).

Caleb said, "Whoever attacks and captures Kiriath-sepher, I will give my daughter Achsah to him as a wife." So Othniel son of Kenaz, Caleb's youngest brother, captured it, and Caleb gave his daughter Achsah to him as his wife.

When she arrived, she persuaded Othniel to ask her father for a field. As she got off her donkey, Caleb asked her, "What do you want?" She answered him, "Give me a blessing. Since you have given me land in the Negev, give me springs also." So Caleb gave her both the upper and lower springs.

The descendants of the Kenite, Moses's father-in-law, had gone up with the men of Judah from the City of Palms to the Wilderness of Judah, which was in the Negev of Arad. They went to live among the people.

Judah went with his brother Simeon, struck the Canaanites who were living in Zephath, and completely destroyed the town. So they named the town Hormah. Judah captured Gaza and its territory, Ashkelon and its territory, and Ekron and its territory. The LORD was with Judah and enabled them to take possession of the hill country, but they could not drive out the people who were living in the plain because those people had iron chariots.

Judah gave Hebron to Caleb, just as Moses had promised. Then Caleb drove out the three sons of Anak who lived there.

At the same time the Benjaminites did not drive out the Jebusites who were living in Jerusalem. The Jebusites have lived among the Benjaminites in Jerusalem to this day.

The house of Joseph also attacked Bethel, and the LORD was with them. They sent spies to Bethel
40 (the town was formerly named Luz). The spies saw a man coming out of the town and said to him, "Please show us how to get into town, and we will show you kindness." When he showed them the way into the town, they put the town to the sword but released the man and his entire family. Then the man went to the land of the Hittites, built a town, and named it Luz. That is its name still today.

At that time Manasseh failed to take possession of Beth-shean and Taanach and their surrounding villages, or the residents of Dor, Ibleam, and Megiddo and their surrounding villages; the Canaanites were determined to stay in this land. When Israel became stronger, they made the Canaanites serve as forced labor but never drove them out completely.

At that time Ephraim failed to drive out the Canaanites who were living in Gezer, so the Canaanites have lived among them in Gezer.
50 Zebulun failed to drive out the residents of Kitron or the residents of Nahalol, so the Canaanites lived among them and served as forced labor.

Asher failed to drive out the residents of Acco or of Sidon, or Ahlab, Achzib, Helbah, Aphik, or Rehob. The Asherites lived among the Canaanites who were living in the land, because they failed to drive them out.

Naphtali did not drive out the residents of Beth-shemesh or the residents of Beth-anath. They lived among the Canaanites who were living in the land, but the residents of Beth-shemesh and Beth-anath served as their forced labor.

The Amorites forced the Danites into the hill country and did not allow them to go down into the valley. The Amorites were determined to stay in Har-heres, Aijalon, and Shaalbim. When
60 the house of Joseph got the upper hand, the Amorites were made to serve as forced labor. The territory of the Amorites extended from the Scorpions' Ascent, that is from Sela upward.

2 The angel of the LORD went up from Gilgal to Bochim and said, "I brought you out of Egypt and led you into the land I had promised to your ancestors. I also said: I will never break my covenant with you. You are not to make a covenant with the inhabitants of this land. You are to tear down their altars. But you have not obeyed me. What have you done? Therefore, I now say: I will not drive out these people before you. They will be thorns in your sides, and their gods will be a trap for you." When the angel of the Lord had spoken these words to all the Israelites, the people wept loudly. So they named that place Bochim and offered sacrifices there to the Lord.

Previously, when Joshua had sent the people away, the Israelites had gone to take possession of the land, each to his own inheritance. The people worshiped the Lord throughout Joshua's lifetime and during the lifetimes of the elders who outlived Joshua. They had seen all the Lord's great works he had done for Israel.

Joshua son of Nun, the servant of the Lord, died at the age of 110. They buried him in the territory of his inheritance, in Timnath-heres, in the hill country of Ephraim, north of Mount Gaash. That whole generation was also gathered to their ancestors. After them another generation rose up who did not know the Lord or the works he had done for Israel.

The Israelites did what was evil in the Lord's sight. They worshiped the Baals and abandoned the Lord, the God of their ancestors, who had brought them out of Egypt. They followed other gods from the surrounding peoples and bowed down to them. They angered the Lord, for they abandoned him and worshiped Baal and the Ashtoreths.

The Lord's anger burned against Israel, and he handed them over to marauders who raided them. He sold them to the enemies around them, and they could no longer resist their enemies. Whenever the Israelites went out, the Lord was against them and brought disaster on them, just as he had promised and sworn to them. So they suffered greatly.

The Lord raised up judges, who saved them from the power of their marauders, but they did not listen to their judges. Instead, they prostituted themselves with other gods, bowing down to them. They quickly turned from the way of their ancestors, who had walked in obedience to the Lord's commands. They did not do as their ancestors did. Whenever the Lord raised up a judge for the Israelites, the Lord was with him and saved the people from the power of their enemies while the judge was still alive. The Lord was moved to pity whenever they groaned because of those who were oppressing and afflicting them. Whenever the judge died, the Israelites would act even more corruptly than their ancestors, following other gods to serve them and bow in worship to them. They did not turn from their evil practices or their obstinate ways.

The Lord's anger burned against Israel, and he declared, "Because this nation has violated my covenant that I made with their ancestors and disobeyed me, I will no longer drive out before them any of the nations Joshua left when he died. I did this to test Israel and to see whether or not they would keep the Lord's way by walking in it, as their ancestors had." The Lord left these nations and did not drive them out immediately. He did not hand them over to Joshua.

3 These are the nations the Lord left in order to test all those in Israel who had experienced none of the wars in Canaan. This was to teach the future generations of the Israelites how to fight in battle, especially those who had not fought before. These nations included the five rulers of the Philistines and all of the Canaanites, the Sidonians, and the Hivites who lived in the Lebanese mountains from Mount Baal-hermon as far as the entrance to Hamath. The LORD left them to test Israel, to determine if they would keep the LORD's commands he had given their ancestors through Moses. But they settled among the Canaanites, Hethites, Amorites, Perizzites, Hivites, and Jebusites. The Israelites took their daughters as wives for themselves, gave their own daughters to their sons, and worshiped their gods.

10 The Israelites did what was evil in the LORD's sight; they forgot the LORD their God and worshiped the Baals and the Asherahs. The LORD's anger burned against Israel, and he sold them to King Cushan-rishathaim of Aram-naharaim, and the Israelites served him eight years.

The Israelites cried out to the LORD. So the LORD raised up Othniel son of Kenaz, Caleb's youngest brother, as a deliverer to save the Israelites. The Spirit of the LORD came on him, and he judged Israel. Othniel went out to battle, and the LORD handed over King Cushan-rishathaim of Aram to him, so that Othniel overpowered him. Then the land had peace for forty years, and Othniel son of Kenaz died.

The Israelites again did what was evil in the LORD's sight. He gave King Eglon of Moab power over Israel, because they had done what was evil in the LORD's sight. After Eglon convinced the 20 Ammonites and the Amalekites to join forces with him, he attacked and defeated Israel and took possession of the City of Palms. The Israelites served King Eglon of Moab eighteen years.

Then the Israelites cried out to the LORD, and he raised up Ehud son of Gera, a left-handed Benjaminite, as a deliverer for them. The Israelites sent him with the tribute for King Eglon of Moab.

Ehud made himself a double-edged sword eighteen inches long. He strapped it to his right thigh under his clothes and brought the tribute to King Eglon of Moab, who was an extremely fat man. When Ehud had finished presenting the tribute, he dismissed the people who had carried it. At the carved images near Gilgal he returned and said, "King Eglon, I have a secret message for you." The king said, "Silence!" and all his attendants left him. Then Ehud approached him while 30 he was sitting alone in his upstairs room where it was cool. Ehud said, "I have a message from God for you," and the king stood up from his throne. Ehud reached with his left hand, took the sword from his right thigh, and plunged it into Eglon's belly. Even the handle went in after the blade, and Eglon's fat closed in over it, so that Ehud did not withdraw the sword from his belly. And the waste came out. Ehud escaped by way of the porch, closing and locking the doors of the upstairs room behind him.

Ehud was gone when Eglon's servants came in. They looked and found the doors of the upstairs room locked and thought he was relieving himself in the cool room. The servants waited until they became embarrassed and saw that he had still not opened the doors of the upstairs room. So they took the key and opened the doors—and there was their lord lying dead on the 40 floor!

Ehud escaped while the servants waited. He passed the Jordan near the carved images and reached Seirah. After he arrived, he sounded the rams' horn throughout the hill country of Ephraim. The Israelites came down with him from the hill country, and he became their leader. He told them, "Follow me, because the Lord has handed over your enemies, the Moabites, to you." So they followed him, captured the fords of the Jordan leading to Moab, and did not allow anyone to cross over. At that time they struck down about ten thousand Moabites, all stout and able-bodied men. Not one of them escaped. Moab became subject to Israel that day, and the land had peace for eighty years.

After Ehud, Shamgar son of Anath became judge. He also delivered Israel, striking down six hundred Philistines with a cattle prod.

4 The Israelites again did what was evil in the sight of the Lord after Ehud had died. So the Lord sold them to King Jabin of Canaan, who reigned in Hazor. The commander of his army was Sisera who lived in Harosheth of the Nations. Then the Israelites cried out to the Lord, because Jabin had nine hundred iron chariots, and he harshly oppressed them twenty years.

Deborah, a prophetess and the wife of Lappidoth, was judging Israel at that time. She would sit under the palm tree of Deborah between Ramah and Bethel in the hill country of Ephraim, and the Israelites went up to her to settle disputes.

She summoned Barak son of Abinoam from Kedesh in Naphtali and said to him, "Hasn't the Lord, the God of Israel, commanded you, 'Go, deploy the troops on Mount Tabor, and take with you ten thousand men from the Naphtalites and Zebulunites? Then I will lure Sisera commander of Jabin's army, his chariots, and his infantry at the Wadi Kishon to fight against you, and I will hand him over to you.'"

Barak said to her, "If you will go with me, I will go. But if you will not go with me, I will not go."

"I will gladly go with you," she said, "but you will receive no honor on the road you are about to take, because the Lord will sell Sisera to a woman." So Deborah got up and went with Barak to Kedesh. Barak summoned Zebulun and Naphtali to Kedesh; ten thousand men followed him, and Deborah also went with him.

Now Heber the Kenite had moved away from the Kenites, the sons of Hobab, Moses's father-in-law, and pitched his tent beside the oak tree of Zaanannim, which was near Kedesh.

It was reported to Sisera that Barak son of Abinoam had gone up Mount Tabor. Sisera summoned all his nine hundred iron chariots and all the troops who were with him from Harosheth of the Nations to the Wadi Kishon. Then Deborah said to Barak, "Go! This is the day the Lord has handed Sisera over to you. Hasn't the Lord gone before you?" So Barak came down from Mount Tabor with ten thousand men following him.

The Lord threw Sisera, all his charioteers, and all his army into a panic before Barak's assault. Sisera left his chariot and fled on foot. Barak pursued the chariots and the army as far as

Harosheth of the Nations, and the whole army of Sisera fell by the sword; not a single man was left.

Meanwhile, Sisera had fled on foot to the tent of Jael, the wife of Heber the Kenite, because
there was peace between King Jabin of Hazor and the family of Heber the Kenite. Jael went out
to greet Sisera and said to him, "Come in, my lord. Come in with me. Don't be afraid." So he went
into her tent, and she covered him with a blanket. He said to her, "Please give me a little water to
drink for I am thirsty." She opened a container of milk, gave him a drink, and covered him again.
Then he said to her, "Stand at the entrance to the tent. If a man comes and asks you, 'Is there a
man here?' say, 'No.'" While he was sleeping from exhaustion, Heber's wife, Jael, took a tent peg,
grabbed a hammer, and went silently to Sisera. She hammered the peg into his temple and drove it
into the ground, and he died.

When Barak arrived in pursuit of Sisera, Jael went out to greet him and said to him, "Come
and I will show you the man you are looking for." So he went in with her, and there was Sisera
lying dead with a tent peg through his temple!

That day God subdued King Jabin of Canaan before the Israelites. The power of the Israelites
continued to increase against King Jabin of Canaan until they destroyed him.

5 On that day Deborah and Barak son of Abinoam sang:

When the leaders lead in Israel,
when the people volunteer,
blessed be the LORD.
Listen, kings! Pay attention, princes!
I will sing to the LORD;
I will sing praise to the LORD God of Israel.
LORD, when you came from Seir,
when you marched from the fields of Edom,
the earth trembled,
the skies poured rain,
and the clouds poured water.
The mountains melted before the LORD,
even Sinai, before the LORD, the God of Israel.

In the days of Shamgar son of Anath,
in the days of Jael,
the main roads were deserted
because travelers kept to the side roads.
Villages were deserted,
they were deserted in Israel,

until I, Deborah, arose,
a mother in Israel.
Israel chose new gods,
then there was war in the city gates.
Not a shield or spear was seen
among forty thousand in Israel.
My heart is with the leaders of Israel,
with the volunteers of the people.
Blessed be the LORD!
30   You who ride on white donkeys,
who sit on saddle blankets,
and who travel on the road, give praise!
Let them tell the righteous acts of the LORD,
the righteous deeds of his villagers in Israel,
with the voices of the singers at the watering places.

Then the LORD's people went down to the city gates.
    "Awake! Awake, Deborah!
Awake! Awake, sing a song!
Arise, Barak,
40   and take your prisoners,
son of Abinoam!"
Then the survivors came down to the nobles;
the LORD's people came down to me against the warriors.
Those with their roots in Amalek came from Ephraim;
Benjamin came with your people after you.
The leaders came down from Machir,
and those who carry a marshal's staff came from Zebulun.
The princes of Issachar were with Deborah;
Issachar was with Barak;
50   they were under his leadership in the valley.
There was great searching of heart
among the clans of Reuben.
Why did you sit among the sheep pens
listening to the playing of pipes for the flocks?
There was great searching of heart
among the clans of Reuben.
Gilead remained beyond the Jordan.

Dan, why did you linger at the ships?
Asher remained at the seashore
and stayed in his harbors.
The people of Zebulun defied death,
Naphtali also, on the heights of the battlefield.

Kings came and fought.
Then the kings of Canaan fought
at Taanach by the Waters of Megiddo,
but they did not plunder the silver.
The stars fought from the heavens;
the stars fought with Sisera from their paths.
The river Kishon swept them away,
the ancient river, the river Kishon.
March on, my soul, in strength!
The horses' hooves then hammered—
the galloping, galloping of his stallions.
"Curse Meroz," says the angel of the LORD,
"Bitterly curse her inhabitants,
for they did not come to help the LORD,
to help the LORD with the warriors."

Most blessed of women is Jael,
the wife of Heber the Kenite;
she is most blessed among tent-dwelling women.
He asked for water; she gave him milk.
She brought him cream in a majestic bowl.
She reached for a tent peg,
her right hand, for a workman's hammer.
Then she hammered Sisera—
she crushed his head;
she shattered and pierced his temple.
He collapsed, he fell, he lay down between her feet;
he collapsed, he fell between her feet;
where he collapsed, there he fell—dead.

Sisera's mother looked through the window;
she peered through the lattice, crying out:

"Why is his chariot so long in coming?
Why don't I hear the hoofbeats of his horses?"
Her wisest princesses answer her;
she even answers herself:
"Are they not finding and dividing the spoil—
a girl or two for each warrior,
the spoil of colored garments for Sisera,
100   the spoil of an embroidered garment or two for my neck?"

Lord, may all your enemies perish as Sisera did.
But may those who love him
be like the rising of the sun in its strength.

And the land had peace for forty years.

6 The Israelites did what was evil in the sight of the Lord. So the Lord handed them over to Midian seven years, and they oppressed Israel. Because of Midian, the Israelites made hiding places for themselves in the mountains, caves, and strongholds. Whenever the Israelites planted crops, the Midianites, Amalekites, and the people of the east came and attacked them. They encamped against them and destroyed the produce of the land, even as far as Gaza. They left nothing for Israel to eat, as well as no sheep, ox, or donkey. For the Midianites came with their cattle and their tents like a great swarm of locusts. They and their camels were without number, and they entered the land to lay waste to it. So Israel became poverty-stricken because of Midian, and the Israelites cried out to the Lord.

When the Israelites cried out to him because of Midian, the Lord sent a prophet to them. He 10 said to them, "This is what the Lord God of Israel says: 'I brought you out of Egypt and out of the place of slavery. I rescued you from the power of Egypt and the power of all who oppressed you. I drove them out before you and gave you their land. I said to you: I am the Lord your God. Do not fear the gods of the Amorites whose land you live in. But you did not obey me.'"

The angel of the Lord came, and he sat under the oak that was in Ophrah, which belonged to Joash, the Abiezrite. His son Gideon was threshing wheat in the winepress in order to hide it from the Midianites. Then the angel of the Lord appeared to him and said, "The Lord is with you, valiant warrior."

Gideon said to him, "Please, my lord, if the Lord is with us, why has all this happened? And where are all his wonders that our ancestors told us about? They said, 'Hasn't the Lord brought 20 us out of Egypt?' But now the Lord has abandoned us and handed us over to Midian."

The Lord turned to him and said, "Go in the strength you have and deliver Israel from the grasp of Midian. I am sending you!"

He said to him, "Please, Lord, how can I deliver Israel? Look, my family is the weakest in Manasseh, and I am the youngest in my father's family."

"But I will be with you," the LORD said to him. "You will strike Midian down as if it were one man."

Then he said to him, "If I have found favor with you, give me a sign that you are speaking with me. Please do not leave this place until I return to you. Let me bring my gift and set it before you."

And he said, "I will stay until you return."

So Gideon went and prepared a young goat and unleavened bread from a half bushel of flour.
30 He placed the meat in a basket and the broth in a pot. He brought them out and offered them to him under the oak.

The angel of God said to him, "Take the meat with the unleavened bread, put it on this stone, and pour the broth on it." So he did that.

The angel of the LORD extended the tip of the staff that was in his hand and touched the meat and the unleavened bread. Fire came up from the rock and consumed the meat and the unleavened bread. Then the angel of the LORD vanished from his sight.

When Gideon realized that he was the angel of the LORD, he said, "Oh no, Lord GOD! I have seen the angel of the LORD face to face!"

But the LORD said to him, "Peace to you. Don't be afraid, for you will not die." So Gideon built an
40 altar to the LORD there and called it The LORD Is Peace. It is still in Ophrah of the Abiezrites today.

On that very night the LORD said to him, "Take your father's young bull and a second bull seven years old. Then tear down the altar of Baal that belongs to your father and cut down the Asherah pole beside it. Build a well-constructed altar to the LORD your God on the top of this mound. Take the second bull and offer it as a burnt offering with the wood of the Asherah pole you cut down." So Gideon took ten of his male servants and did as the LORD had told him. But because he was too afraid of his father's family and the men of the city to do it in the daytime, he did it at night.

When the men of the city got up in the morning, they found Baal's altar torn down, the Asherah pole beside it cut down, and the second bull offered up on the altar that had been built. They said to each other, "Who did this?" After they made a thorough investigation, they said,
50 "Gideon son of Joash did it."

Then the men of the city said to Joash, "Bring out your son. He must die, because he tore down Baal's altar and cut down the Asherah pole beside it."

But Joash said to all who stood against him, "Would you plead Baal's case for him? Would you save him? Whoever pleads his case will be put to death by morning! If he is a god, let him plead his own case because someone tore down his altar." That day Gideon was called Jerubbaal, since Joash said, "Let Baal contend with him," because he tore down his altar.

All the Midianites, Amalekites, and people of the east gathered together, crossed over the Jordan, and camped in the Jezreel Valley.

The Spirit of the LORD enveloped Gideon, and he blew the rams' horn and the Abiezrites
60 rallied behind him. He sent messengers throughout all of Manasseh, who rallied behind him. He
also sent messengers throughout Asher, Zebulun, and Naphtali, who also came to meet him.

Then Gideon said to God, "If you will deliver Israel by me, as you said, I will put a wool fleece
here on the threshing floor. If dew is only on the fleece, and all the ground is dry, I will know that
you will deliver Israel by me, as you said." And that is what happened. When he got up early in the
morning, he squeezed the fleece and wrung dew out of it, filling a bowl with water.

Gideon then said to God, "Don't be angry with me; let me speak one more time. Please
allow me to make one more test with the fleece. Let it remain dry, and the dew be all over the
ground." That night God did as Gideon requested: only the fleece was dry, and dew was all over
the ground.

7 Jerubbaal (that is, Gideon) and all the troops who were with him, got up early and camped beside
the spring of Harod. The camp of Midian was north of them, below the hill of Moreh, in the
valley. The LORD said to Gideon, "You have too many troops for me to hand the Midianites over
to them, or else Israel might elevate themselves over me and say, 'I saved myself.' Now announce to
the troops, 'Whoever is fearful and trembling may turn back and leave Mount Gilead.'" So twenty-
two thousand of the troops turned back, but ten thousand remained.

Then the LORD said to Gideon, "There are still too many troops. Take them down to the
water, and I will test them for you there. If I say to you, 'This one can go with you,' he can go.
But if I say about anyone, 'This one cannot go with you,' he cannot go." So he brought the troops
10 down to the water, and the LORD said to Gideon, "Separate everyone who laps water with his
tongue like a dog. Do the same with everyone who kneels to drink." The number of those who
lapped with their hands to their mouths was three hundred men, and all the rest of the troops
knelt to drink water. The LORD said to Gideon, "I will deliver you with the three hundred men
who lapped and hand the Midianites over to you. But everyone else is to go home." So Gideon
sent all the Israelites to their tents but kept the three hundred troops, who took the provisions and
their rams' horns. The camp of Midian was below him in the valley.

That night the LORD said to him, "Get up and attack the camp, for I have handed it over to you.
But if you are afraid to attack the camp, go down with Purah your servant. Listen to what they say,
and then you will be encouraged to attack the camp." So he went down with Purah his servant to
20 the outpost of the troops who were in the camp.

Now the Midianites, Amalekites, and all the people of the east had settled down in the valley
like a swarm of locusts, and their camels were as innumerable as the sand on the seashore. When
Gideon arrived, there was a man telling his friend about a dream. He said, "Listen, I had a dream:
a loaf of barley bread came tumbling into the Midianite camp, struck a tent, and it fell. The loaf
turned the tent upside down so that it collapsed."

His friend answered, "This is nothing less than the sword of Gideon son of Joash, the Israelite. God has handed the entire Midianite camp over to him."

When Gideon heard the account of the dream and its interpretation, he bowed in worship. He returned to Israel's camp and said, "Get up, for the LORD has handed the Midianite camp over to you." Then he divided the three hundred men into three companies and gave each of the men a ram's horn in one hand and an empty pitcher with a torch inside it in the other hand.

"Watch me," he said to them, "and do what I do. When I come to the outpost of the camp, do as I do. When I and everyone with me blow our rams' horns, you are also to blow your rams' horns all around the camp. Then you will say, 'For the LORD and for Gideon!'"

Gideon and the hundred men who were with him went to the outpost of the camp at the beginning of the middle watch after the sentries had been stationed. They blew their rams' horns and broke the pitchers that were in their hands. The three companies blew their rams' horns and shattered their pitchers. They held their torches in their left hands and their rams' horns to blow in their right hands, and they shouted, "A sword for the LORD and for Gideon!" Each Israelite took his position around the camp, and the entire Midianite army began to run, and they cried out as they fled. When Gideon's men blew their three hundred rams' horns, the LORD caused the men in the whole army to turn on each other with their swords. They fled to Acacia House in the direction of Zererah as far as the border of Abel-meholah near Tabbath. Then the men of Israel were called from Naphtali, Asher, and Manasseh, and they pursued the Midianites.

Gideon sent messengers throughout the hill country of Ephraim with this message: "Come down to intercept the Midianites and take control of the watercourses ahead of them as far as Beth-barah and the Jordan." So all the men of Ephraim were called out, and they took control of the watercourses as far as Beth-barah and the Jordan. They captured Oreb and Zeeb, the two princes of Midian; they killed Oreb at the rock of Oreb and Zeeb at the winepress of Zeeb, while they were pursuing the Midianites. They brought the heads of Oreb and Zeeb to Gideon across the Jordan.

8 The men of Ephraim said to him, "Why have you done this to us, not calling us when you went to fight against the Midianites?" And they argued with him violently.

So he said to them, "What have I done now compared to you? Is not the gleaning of Ephraim better than the grape harvest of Abiezer? God handed over to you Oreb and Zeeb, the two princes of Midian. What was I able to do compared to you?" When he said this, their anger against him subsided.

Gideon and the three hundred men came to the Jordan and crossed it. They were exhausted but still in pursuit. He said to the men of Succoth, "Please give some loaves of bread to the troops

9 under my command, because they are exhausted, for I am pursuing Zebah and Zalmunna, the kings of Midian."

But the princes of Succoth asked, "Are Zebah and Zalmunna now in your hands that we should give bread to your army?"

Gideon replied, "Very well, when the LORD has handed Zebah and Zalmunna over to me, I will tear your flesh with thorns and briers from the wilderness!" He went from there to Penuel and asked the same thing from them. The men of Penuel answered just as the men of Succoth had answered. He also told the men of Penuel, "When I return safely, I will tear down this tower!"

Now Zebah and Zalmunna were in Karkor, and with them was their army of about fifteen thousand men, who were all those left of the entire army of the people of the east. Those who had been killed were one hundred twenty thousand armed men. Gideon traveled on the caravan
20 route east of Nobah and Jogbehah and attacked their army while the army felt secure. Zebah and Zalmunna fled, and he pursued them. He captured these two kings of Midian and routed the entire army.

Gideon son of Joash returned from the battle by the Ascent of Heres. He captured a youth from the men of Succoth and interrogated him. The youth wrote down for him the names of the seventy-seven leaders and elders of Succoth. Then he went to the men of Succoth and said, "Here are Zebah and Zalmunna. You taunted me about them, saying, 'Are Zebah and Zalmunna now in your power that we should give bread to your exhausted men?'" So he took the elders of the city, and he took some thorns and briers from the wilderness, and he disciplined the men of Succoth with them. He also tore down the tower of Penuel and killed the men of the city.

30 He asked Zebah and Zalmunna, "What kind of men did you kill at Tabor?"

"They were like you," they said. "Each resembled the son of a king."

So he said, "They were my brothers, the sons of my mother! As the LORD lives, if you had let them live, I would not kill you." Then he said to Jether, his firstborn, "Get up and kill them." The youth did not draw his sword, for he was afraid because he was still a youth.

Zebah and Zalmunna said, "Get up and strike us down yourself, for a man is judged by his strength." So Gideon got up, killed Zebah and Zalmunna, and took the crescent ornaments that were on the necks of their camels.

Then the Israelites said to Gideon, "Rule over us, you as well as your sons and your grandsons, for you delivered us from the power of Midian."

40 But Gideon said to them, "I will not rule over you, and my son will not rule over you; the LORD will rule over you." Then he said to them, "Let me make a request of you: Everyone give me an earring from his plunder." Now the enemy had gold earrings because they were Ishmaelites.

They said, "We agree to give them." So they spread out a cloak, and everyone threw an earring from his plunder on it. The weight of the gold earrings he requested was forty-three pounds of gold, in addition to the crescent ornaments and ear pendants, the purple garments on the kings of

Midian, and the chains on the necks of their camels. Gideon made an ephod from all this and put it in Ophrah, his hometown. Then all Israel prostituted themselves by worshiping it there, and it became a snare to Gideon and his household.

So Midian was subdued before the Israelites, and they were no longer a threat. The land had
50 peace for forty years during the days of Gideon. Jerubbaal (that is, Gideon) son of Joash went back to live at his house.

Gideon had seventy sons, his own offspring, since he had many wives. His concubine who was in Shechem also bore him a son, and he named him Abimelech. Then Gideon son of Joash died at a good old age and was buried in the tomb of his father Joash in Ophrah of the Abiezrites.

When Gideon died, the Israelites turned and prostituted themselves by worshiping the Baals and made Baal-berith their god. The Israelites did not remember the LORD their God who had rescued them from the hand of the enemies around them. They did not show kindness to the house of Jerubbaal (that is, Gideon) for all the good he had done for Israel.

9 Abimelech son of Jerubbaal went to Shechem and spoke to his uncles and to his mother's whole clan, saying, "Please speak in the hearing of all the citizens of Shechem, 'Is it better for you that seventy men, all the sons of Jerubbaal, rule over you or that one man rule over you?' Remember that I am your own flesh and blood."

His mother's relatives spoke all these words about him in the hearing of all the citizens of Shechem, and they were favorable to Abimelech, for they said, "He is our brother." So they gave him seventy pieces of silver from the temple of Baal-berith. Abimelech used it to hire worthless and reckless men, and they followed him. He went to his father's house in Ophrah and killed his seventy brothers, the sons of Jerubbaal, on top of a large stone. But Jotham, the youngest son of
10 Jerubbaal, survived, because he hid. Then all the citizens of Shechem and of Beth-millo gathered together and proceeded to make Abimelech king at the oak of the pillar in Shechem.

When they told Jotham, he climbed to the top of Mount Gerizim, raised his voice, and called to them:
Listen to me, citizens of Shechem,
and may God listen to you:

The trees decided
to anoint a king over themselves.
They said to the olive tree, "Reign over us."
But the olive tree said to them,
"Should I stop giving my oil
20 that people use to honor both God and men,
and rule over the trees?"

Then the trees said to the fig tree,
"Come and reign over us."
But the fig tree said to them,
"Should I stop giving
my sweetness and my good fruit,
and rule over trees?"

Later, the trees said to the grapevine,
"Come and reign over us."
30   But the grapevine said to them,
"Should I stop giving my wine
that cheers both God and man,
and rule over trees?"

Finally, all the trees said to the bramble,
"Come and reign over us."
The bramble said to the trees,
"If you really are anointing me
as king over you,
come and find refuge in my shade.
40   But if not,
may fire come out from the bramble
and consume the cedars of Lebanon."

"Now if you have acted faithfully and honestly in making Abimelech king, if you have done well by Jerubbaal and his family, and if you have rewarded him appropriately for what he did—for my father fought for you, risked his life, and rescued you from Midian, and now you have attacked my father's family today, killed his seventy sons on top of a large stone, and made Abimelech, the son of his slave woman, king over the citizens of Shechem 'because he is your brother'—so if you have acted faithfully and honestly with Jerubbaal and his house this day, rejoice in Abimelech and may he also rejoice in you. But if not, may fire come from Abimelech and consume the citizens of 50   Shechem and Beth-millo, and may fire come from the citizens of Shechem and Beth-millo and consume Abimelech." Then Jotham fled, escaping to Beer, and lived there because of his brother Abimelech.

When Abimelech had ruled over Israel three years, God sent an evil spirit between Abimelech and the citizens of Shechem. They treated Abimelech deceitfully, so that the crime against the seventy sons of Jerubbaal might come to justice and their blood would be avenged on their brother Abimelech, who killed them, and on the citizens of Shechem, who had helped him kill his brothers. The citizens of Shechem rebelled against him by putting men in ambush on the tops of the mountains, and they robbed everyone who passed by them on the road. So this was reported to Abimelech.

Gaal son of Ebed came with his brothers and crossed into Shechem, and the citizens of Shechem trusted him. So they went out to the countryside and harvested grapes from their vineyards. They trampled the grapes and held a celebration. Then they went to the house of their god, and as they ate and drank, they cursed Abimelech. Gaal son of Ebed said, "Who is Abimelech and who is Shechem that we should serve him? Isn't he the son of Jerubbaal, and isn't Zebul his officer? You are to serve the men of Hamor, the father of Shechem. Why should we serve Abimelech? If only these people were in my power, I would remove Abimelech." So he said to Abimelech, "Gather your army and come out."

When Zebul, the ruler of the city, heard the words of Gaal son of Ebed, he was angry. So he secretly sent messengers to Abimelech, saying, "Beware! Gaal son of Ebed and his brothers have come to Shechem and are turning the city against you. Now tonight, you and the troops with you, come and wait in ambush in the countryside. Then get up early, and at sunrise attack the city. When he and the troops who are with him come out against you, do to him whatever you can." So Abimelech and all the troops with him got up at night and waited in ambush for Shechem in four units.

Gaal son of Ebed went out and stood at the entrance of the city gate. Then Abimelech and the troops who were with him got up from their ambush. When Gaal saw the troops, he said to Zebul, "Look, troops are coming down from the mountaintops!" But Zebul said to him, "The shadows of the mountains look like men to you."

Then Gaal spoke again, "Look, troops are coming down from the central part of the land, and one unit is coming from the direction of the Diviners' Oak." Zebul replied, "What do you have to say now? You said, 'Who is Abimelech that we should serve him?' Aren't these the troops you despised? Now go and fight them!"

So Gaal went out leading the citizens of Shechem and fought against Abimelech, but Abimelech pursued him, and Gaal fled before him. Numerous bodies were strewn as far as the entrance of the city gate. Abimelech stayed in Arumah, and Zebul drove Gaal and his brothers from Shechem.

The next day when the people of Shechem went into the countryside, this was reported to Abimelech. He took the troops, divided them into three companies, and waited in ambush in the countryside. He looked, and the people were coming out of the city, so he arose against them and struck them down. Then Abimelech and the units that were with him rushed forward and took their stand at the entrance of the city gate. The other two units rushed against all who were in the countryside and struck them down. So Abimelech fought against the city that entire day, captured it, and killed the people who were in it. Then he tore down the city and sowed it with salt.

When all the citizens of the Tower of Shechem heard, they entered the inner chamber of the temple of El-berith. Then it was reported to Abimelech that all the citizens of the Tower of

Shechem had gathered. So Abimelech and all the troops who were with him went up to Mount Zalmon. Abimelech took his ax in his hand and cut a branch from the trees. He picked up the branch, put it on his shoulder, and said to the troops who were with him, "Hurry and do what you have seen me do." Each of the troops also cut his own branch and followed Abimelech. They put the branches against the inner chamber and set it on fire; about a thousand men and women died, including all the men of the Tower of Shechem.

100   Abimelech went to Thebez, camped against it, and captured it. There was a strong tower inside the city, and all the men, women, and citizens of the city fled there. They locked themselves in and went up to the roof of the tower. When Abimelech came to attack the tower, he approached its entrance to set it on fire. But a woman threw the upper portion of a millstone on Abimelech's head and fractured his skull. He quickly called his armor-bearer and said to him, "Draw your sword and kill me, or they'll say about me, 'A woman killed him.'" So his armor-bearer ran him through, and he died. When the Israelites saw that Abimelech was dead, they all went home.

    In this way, God brought back Abimelech's evil—the evil that Abimelech had done to his father when he killed his seventy brothers. God also brought back to the men of Shechem all their evil. So the curse of Jotham son of Jerubbaal came upon them.

10   After Abimelech, Tola son of Puah, son of Dodo became judge and began to deliver Israel. He was from Issachar and lived in Shamir in the hill country of Ephraim. Tola judged Israel twenty-three years and when he died, was buried in Shamir.

    After him came Jair the Gileadite, who judged Israel twenty-two years. He had thirty sons who rode on thirty donkeys. They had thirty towns in Gilead, which are still called Jair's Villages today. When Jair died, he was buried in Kamon.

    Then the Israelites again did what was evil in the sight of the LORD. They worshiped the Baals and the Ashtoreths, the gods of Aram, Sidon, and Moab, and the gods of the Ammonites and the Philistines. They abandoned the LORD and did not worship him. So the LORD's anger
10 burned against Israel, and he sold them to the Philistines and the Ammonites. They shattered and crushed the Israelites that year, and for eighteen years they did the same to all the Israelites who were on the other side of the Jordan in the land of the Amorites in Gilead. The Ammonites also crossed the Jordan to fight against Judah, Benjamin, and the house of Ephraim. Israel was greatly oppressed, so they cried out to the LORD, saying, "We have sinned against you. We have abandoned our God and worshiped the Baals."

    The LORD said to the Israelites, "When the Egyptians, Amorites, Ammonites, Philistines, Sidonians, Amalekites, and Maonites oppressed you, and you cried out to me, did I not deliver you from them? But you have abandoned me and worshiped other gods. Therefore, I will not deliver you again. Go and cry out to the gods you have chosen. Let them deliver you whenever you
20 are oppressed."

But the Israelites said, "We have sinned. Deal with us as you see fit; only rescue us today!" So they got rid of the foreign gods among them and worshiped the LORD, and he became weary of Israel's misery.

The Ammonites were called together, and they camped in Gilead. So the Israelites assembled and camped at Mizpah. The rulers of Gilead said to one another, "Which man will begin the fight against the Ammonites? He will be the leader of all the inhabitants of Gilead."

11 Jephthah the Gileadite was a valiant warrior, but he was the son of a prostitute, and Gilead was his father. Gilead's wife bore him sons, and when they grew up, they drove Jephthah out and said to him, "You will have no inheritance in our father's family, because you are the son of another woman." So Jephthah fled from his brothers and lived in the land of Tob. Then some worthless men joined Jephthah and went on raids with him.

Some time later, the Ammonites fought against Israel. When the Ammonites made war with Israel, the elders of Gilead went to get Jephthah from the land of Tob. They said to him, "Come, be our commander, and let's fight the Ammonites."

Jephthah replied to the elders of Gilead, "Didn't you hate me and drive me out of my father's
10 family? Why then have you come to me now when you're in trouble?"

They answered Jephthah, "That's true. But now we turn to you. Come with us, fight the Ammonites, and you will become leader of all the inhabitants of Gilead."

So Jephthah said to them, "If you are bringing me back to fight the Ammonites and the LORD gives them to me, I will be your leader."

The elders of Gilead said to Jephthah, "The LORD is our witness if we don't do as you say." So Jephthah went with the elders of Gilead. The people made him their leader and commander, and Jephthah repeated all his terms in the presence of the LORD at Mizpah.

Jephthah sent messengers to the king of the Ammonites, asking, "What do you have against me that you have come to fight me in my land?"
20 The king of the Ammonites said to Jephthah's messengers, "When Israel came from Egypt, they seized my land from the Arnon to the Jabbok and the Jordan. Now restore it peaceably."

Jephthah again sent messengers to the king of the Ammonites to tell him, "This is what Jephthah says: Israel did not take away the land of Moab or the land of the Ammonites. But when they came from Egypt, Israel traveled through the wilderness to the Red Sea and came to Kadesh. Israel sent messengers to the king of Edom, saying, 'Please let us travel through your land,' but the king of Edom would not listen. They also sent messengers to the king of Moab, but he refused. So Israel stayed in Kadesh.

"Then they traveled through the wilderness and around the lands of Edom and Moab. They came to the east side of the land of Moab and camped on the other side of the Arnon but did not
30 enter into the territory of Moab, for the Arnon was the boundary of Moab.

"Then Israel sent messengers to Sihon king of the Amorites, king of Heshbon. Israel said to him, 'Please let us travel through your land to our country,' but Sihon would not trust Israel to pass through his territory. Instead, Sihon gathered all his troops, camped at Jahaz, and fought with Israel. Then the Lord God of Israel handed over Sihon and all his troops to Israel, and they defeated them. So Israel took possession of the entire land of the Amorites who lived in that country. They took possession of all the territory of the Amorites from the Arnon to the Jabbok and from the wilderness to the Jordan.

"The Lord God of Israel has now driven out the Amorites before his people Israel, and will you now force us out? Isn't it true that you can have whatever your god Chemosh conquers for you, and we can have whatever the Lord our God conquers for us? Now are you any better than Balak son of Zippor, king of Moab? Did he ever contend with Israel or fight against them? While Israel lived three hundred years in Heshbon and Aroer and their surrounding villages, and in all the cities that are on the banks of the Arnon, why didn't you take them back at that time? I have not sinned against you, but you are doing me wrong by fighting against me. Let the Lord who is the judge decide today between the Israelites and the Ammonites." But the king of the Ammonites would not listen to Jephthah's message that he sent him.

The Spirit of the Lord came on Jephthah, who traveled through Gilead and Manasseh, and then through Mizpah of Gilead. He crossed over to the Ammonites from Mizpah of Gilead. Jephthah made this vow to the Lord: "If you in fact hand over the Ammonites to me, whoever comes out the doors of my house to greet me when I return safely from the Ammonites will belong to the Lord, and I will offer that person as a burnt offering."

Jephthah crossed over to the Ammonites to fight against them, and the Lord handed them over to him. He defeated twenty of their cities with a great slaughter from Aroer all the way to the entrance of Minnith and to Abel-keramim. So the Ammonites were subdued before the Israelites.

When Jephthah went to his home in Mizpah, there was his daughter, coming out to meet him with tambourines and dancing! She was his only child; he had no other son or daughter besides her. When he saw her, he tore his clothes and said, "No! Not my daughter! You have devastated me! You have brought great misery on me. I have given my word to the Lord and cannot take it back."

Then she said to him, "My father, you have given your word to the Lord. Do to me as you have said, for the Lord brought vengeance on your enemies, the Ammonites." She also said to her father, "Let me do this one thing: Let me wander two months through the mountains with my friends and mourn my virginity."

"Go," he said. And he sent her away two months. So she left with her friends and mourned her virginity as she wandered through the mountains. At the end of two months, she returned to her father, and he kept the vow he had made about her. And she had never been intimate with a man. Now it became a custom in Israel that four days each year the young women of Israel would commemorate the daughter of Jephthah the Gileadite.

12 The men of Ephraim were called together and crossed the Jordan to Zaphon. They said to Jephthah, "Why have you crossed over to fight against the Ammonites but didn't call us to go with you? We will burn your house with you in it!"

Then Jephthah said to them, "My people and I had a bitter conflict with the Ammonites. So I called for you, but you didn't deliver me from their power. When I saw that you weren't going to deliver me, I took my life in my own hands and crossed over to the Ammonites, and the LORD handed them over to me. Why then have you come today to fight against me?"

Then Jephthah gathered all of the men of Gilead. They fought and defeated Ephraim, because Ephraim had said, "You Gileadites are Ephraimite fugitives in the territories of Ephraim and Manasseh." The Gileadites captured the fords of the Jordan leading to Ephraim. Whenever a fugitive from Ephraim said, "Let me cross over," the Gileadites asked him, "Are you an Ephraimite?" If he answered, "No," they told him, "Please say Shibboleth." If he said, "Sibboleth," because he could not pronounce it correctly, they seized him and executed him at the fords of the Jordan. At that time forty-two thousand from Ephraim died.

Jephthah judged Israel six years, and when he died, he was buried in one of the cities of Gilead.

Ibzan, who was from Bethlehem, judged Israel after Jephthah and had thirty sons. He gave his thirty daughters in marriage to men outside the tribe and brought back thirty wives for his sons from outside the tribe. Ibzan judged Israel seven years, and when he died, he was buried in Bethlehem.

Elon, who was from Zebulun, judged Israel after Ibzan. He judged Israel ten years, and when he died, he was buried in Aijalon in the land of Zebulun.

After Elon, Abdon son of Hillel, who was from Pirathon, judged Israel. He had forty sons and thirty grandsons, who rode on seventy donkeys. Abdon judged Israel eight years, and when he died, he was buried in Pirathon in the land of Ephraim, in the hill country of the Amalekites.

13 The Israelites again did what was evil in the LORD's sight, so the LORD handed them over to the Philistines forty years. There was a certain man from Zorah, from the family of Dan, whose name was Manoah; his wife was unable to conceive and had no children. The angel of the LORD appeared to the woman and said to her, "Although you are unable to conceive and have no children, you will conceive and give birth to a son. Now please be careful not to drink wine or beer, or to eat anything unclean; for indeed, you will conceive and give birth to a son. You must never cut his hair, because the boy will be a Nazirite to God from birth, and he will begin to save Israel from the power of the Philistines."

Then the woman went and told her husband, "A man of God came to me. He looked like the awe-inspiring angel of God. I didn't ask him where he came from, and he didn't tell me his name. He said to me, 'You will conceive and give birth to a son. Therefore, do not drink wine or beer, and do not eat anything unclean, because the boy will be a Nazirite to God from birth until the day of his death.'"

Manoah prayed to the LORD and said, "Please, Lord, let the man of God you sent come again to us and teach us what we should do for the boy who will be born."

God listened to Manoah, and the angel of God came again to the woman. She was sitting in the field, and her husband, Manoah, was not with her. The woman ran quickly to her husband and told him, "The man who came to me the other day has just come back!"

So Manoah got up and followed his wife. When he came to the man, he asked, "Are you the man who spoke to my wife?"

"I am," he said.

Then Manoah asked, "When your words come true, what will be the boy's responsibilities and work?"

The angel of the LORD answered Manoah, "Your wife needs to do everything I told her. She must not eat anything that comes from the grapevine or drink wine or beer. And she must not eat anything unclean. Your wife must do everything I have commanded her."

"Please stay here," Manoah told him, "and we will prepare a young goat for you."

The angel of the LORD said to him, "If I stay, I won't eat your food. But if you want to prepare a burnt offering, offer it to the LORD." (Manoah did not know he was the angel of the Lord.)

Then Manoah said to him, "What is your name, so that we may honor you when your words come true?"

"Why do you ask my name," the angel of the LORD asked him, "since it is beyond understanding?"

Manoah took a young goat and a grain offering and offered them on a rock to the LORD, who did something miraculous while Manoah and his wife were watching. When the flame went up from the altar to the sky, the angel of the LORD went up in its flame. When Manoah and his wife saw this, they fell facedown on the ground. The angel of the LORD did not appear again to Manoah and his wife. Then Manoah realized that it was the angel of the LORD.

"We're certainly going to die," he said to his wife, "because we have seen God!"

But his wife said to him, "If the LORD had intended to kill us, he wouldn't have accepted the burnt offering and the grain offering from us, and he would not have shown us all these things or spoken to us like this."

So the woman gave birth to a son and named him Samson. The boy grew, and the LORD blessed him. Then the Spirit of the LORD began to stir him in the Camp of Dan, between Zorah and Eshtaol.

14 Samson went down to Timnah and saw a young Philistine woman there. He went back and told his father and his mother, "I have seen a young Philistine woman in Timnah. Now get her for me as a wife."

But his father and mother said to him, "Can't you find a young woman among your relatives or among any of our people? Must you go to the uncircumcised Philistines for a wife?"

But Samson told his father, "Get her for me. She's the right one for me." Now his father and mother did not know this was from the LORD, who wanted the Philistines to provide an opportunity for a confrontation. At that time, the Philistines were ruling Israel.

Samson went down to Timnah with his father and mother and came to the vineyards of Timnah. Suddenly a young lion came roaring at him, the Spirit of the LORD came powerfully on him, and he tore the lion apart with his bare hands as he might have torn a young goat. But he did not tell his father or mother what he had done. Then he went and spoke to the woman, because she seemed right to Samson.

After some time, when he returned to marry her, he left the road to see the lion's carcass, and there was a swarm of bees with honey in the carcass. He scooped some honey into his hands and ate it as he went along. When he came to his father and mother, he gave some to them and they ate it. But he did not tell them that he had scooped the honey from the lion's carcass.

His father went to visit the woman, and Samson prepared a feast there, as young men were accustomed to do. When the Philistines saw him, they brought thirty men to accompany him.

"Let me tell you a riddle," Samson said to them. "If you can explain it to me during the seven days of the feast and figure it out, I will give you thirty linen garments and thirty changes of clothes. But if you can't explain it to me, you must give me thirty linen garments and thirty changes of clothes."

"Tell us your riddle," they replied. "Let's hear it."

So he said to them:

> Out of the eater came something to eat,
> and out of the strong came something sweet.

After three days, they were unable to explain the riddle. On the fourth day they said to Samson's wife, "Persuade your husband to explain the riddle to us, or we will burn you and your father's family to death. Did you invite us here to rob us?"

So Samson's wife came to him, weeping, and said, "You hate me and don't love me! You told my people the riddle, but haven't explained it to me."

"Look," he said, "I haven't even explained it to my father or mother, so why should I explain it to you?"

She wept the whole seven days of the feast, and at last, on the seventh day, he explained it to her, because she had nagged him so much. Then she explained it to her people. On the seventh day, before sunset, the men of the city said to him:

> What is sweeter than honey?
> What is stronger than a lion?

So he said to them:

> If you hadn't plowed with my young cow,
> you wouldn't know my riddle now!

The Spirit of the LORD came powerfully on him, and he went down to Ashkelon and killed thirty of their men. He stripped them and gave their clothes to those who had explained the riddle. In a rage, Samson returned to his father's house, and his wife was given to one of the men who had accompanied him.

15 Later on, during the wheat harvest, Samson took a young goat as a gift and visited his wife. "I want to go to my wife in her room," he said. But her father would not let him enter.

"I was sure you hated her," her father said, "so I gave her to one of the men who accompanied you. Isn't her younger sister more beautiful than she is? Why not take her instead?"

Samson said to them, "This time I will be blameless when I harm the Philistines." So he went out and caught three hundred foxes. He took torches, turned the foxes tail-to-tail, and put a torch between each pair of tails. Then he ignited the torches and released the foxes into the standing grain of the Philistines. He burned the piles of grain and the standing grain as well as the vineyards and olive groves.

10   Then the Philistines asked, "Who did this?"

They were told, "It was Samson, the Timnite's son-in-law, because he took Samson's wife and gave her to his companion." So the Philistines went to her and her father and burned them to death.

Then Samson told them, "Because you did this, I swear that I won't rest until I have taken vengeance on you." He tore them limb from limb and then went down and stayed in the cave at the rock of Etam.

The Philistines went up, camped in Judah, and raided Lehi. So the men of Judah said, "Why have you attacked us?"

They replied, "We have come to tie Samson up and pay him back for what he did to us."

20   Then three thousand men of Judah went to the cave at the rock of Etam, and they asked Samson, "Don't you realize that the Philistines rule us? What have you done to us?"

"I have done to them what they did to me," he answered.

They said to him, "We've come to tie you up and hand you over to the Philistines."

Then Samson told them, "Swear to me that you yourselves won't kill me."

"No," they said, "we won't kill you, but we will tie you up securely and hand you over to them." So they tied him up with two new ropes and led him away from the rock.

When he came to Lehi, the Philistines came to meet him shouting. The Spirit of the LORD came powerfully on him, and the ropes that were on his arms and wrists became like burnt flax and fell off. He found a fresh jawbone of a donkey, reached out his hand, took it, and killed a 30   thousand men with it. Then Samson said:

With the jawbone of a donkey
I have piled them in heaps.
With the jawbone of a donkey
I have killed a thousand men.

When he finished speaking, he threw away the jawbone and named that place Jawbone Hill. He became very thirsty and called out to the LORD, "You have accomplished this great victory through your servant. Must I now die of thirst and fall into the hands of the uncircumcised?" So God split a hollow place in the ground at Lehi, and water came out of it. After Samson drank, his strength returned, and he revived. That is why he named it Hakkore Spring, which is still in Lehi today.

40 And he judged Israel twenty years in the days of the Philistines.

16 Samson went to Gaza, where he saw a prostitute and went to bed with her. When the Gazites heard that Samson was there, they surrounded the place and waited in ambush for him all that night at the city gate. They kept quiet all night, saying, "Let's wait until dawn; then we will kill him." But Samson stayed in bed only until midnight. Then he got up, took hold of the doors of the city gate along with the two gateposts, and pulled them out, bar and all. He put them on his shoulders and took them to the top of the mountain overlooking Hebron.

Some time later, he fell in love with a woman named Delilah, who lived in the Sorek Valley. The Philistine leaders went to her and said, "Persuade him to tell you where his great strength comes from, so we can overpower him, tie him up, and make him helpless. Each of us will then

10 give you 1,100 pieces of silver."

So Delilah said to Samson, "Please tell me, where does your great strength come from? How could someone tie you up and make you helpless?"

Samson told her, "If they tie me up with seven fresh bowstrings that have not been dried, I will become weak and be like any other man."

The Philistine leaders brought her seven fresh bowstrings that had not been dried, and she tied him up with them. While the men in ambush were waiting in her room, she called out to him, "Samson, the Philistines are here!" But he snapped the bowstrings as a strand of yarn snaps when it touches fire. The secret of his strength remained unknown.

Then Delilah said to Samson, "You have mocked me and told me lies! Won't you please tell me

20 how you can be tied up?"

He told her, "If they tie me up with new ropes that have never been used, I will become weak and be like any other man."

Delilah took new ropes, tied him up with them, and shouted, "Samson, the Philistines are here!" But while the men in ambush were waiting in her room, he snapped the ropes off his arms like a thread.

Then Delilah said to Samson, "You have mocked me all along and told me lies! Tell me how you can be tied up."

He told her, "If you weave the seven braids on my head into the fabric on a loom—"

She fastened the braids with a pin and called to him, "Samson, the Philistines are here!" He awoke from his sleep and pulled out the pin, with the loom and the web.

30 "How can you say, 'I love you,'" she told him, "when your heart is not with me? This is the third time you have mocked me and not told me what makes your strength so great!"

Because she nagged him day after day and pleaded with him until she wore him out, he told her the whole truth and said to her, "My hair has never been cut, because I am a Nazirite to God from birth. If I am shaved, my strength will leave me, and I will become weak and be like any other man."

When Delilah realized that he had told her the whole truth, she sent this message to the Philistine leaders: "Come one more time, for he has told me the whole truth." The Philistine leaders came to her and brought the silver with them.

Then she let him fall asleep on her lap and called a man to shave off the seven braids on his
40 head. In this way, she made him helpless, and his strength left him. Then she cried, "Samson, the Philistines are here!" When he awoke from his sleep, he said, "I will escape as I did before and shake myself free." But he did not know that the Lord had left him.

The Philistines seized him and gouged out his eyes. They brought him down to Gaza and bound him with bronze shackles, and he was forced to grind grain in the prison. But his hair began to grow back after it had been shaved.

Now the Philistine leaders gathered together to offer a great sacrifice to their god Dagon. They rejoiced and said:

> Our god has handed over
> our enemy Samson to us.

50 When the people saw him, they praised their god and said:

> Our god has handed over to us
> our enemy who destroyed our land
> and who multiplied our dead.

When they were in good spirits, they said, "Bring Samson here to entertain us." So they brought Samson from prison, and he entertained them. They had him stand between the pillars.

Samson said to the young man who was leading him by the hand, "Lead me where I can feel the pillars supporting the temple, so I can lean against them." The temple was full of men and women; all the leaders of the Philistines were there, and about three thousand men and women were on the roof watching Samson entertain them. He called out to the Lord, "Lord
60 God, please remember me. Strengthen me, God, just once more. With one act of vengeance, let me pay back the Philistines for my two eyes." Samson took hold of the two middle pillars supporting the temple and leaned against them, one on his right hand and the other on his left. Samson said, "Let me die with the Philistines." He pushed with all his might, and the temple

fell on the leaders and all the people in it. And those he killed at his death were more than those he had killed in his life.

Then his brothers and his father's whole family came down, carried him back, and buried him between Zorah and Eshtaol in the tomb of his father Manoah. So he judged Israel twenty years.

17 There was a man from the hill country of Ephraim named Micah. He said to his mother, "The 1,100 pieces of silver taken from you, and that I heard you place a curse on—here's the silver. I took it."

Then his mother said, "My son, may you be blessed by the LORD!"

He returned the 1,100 pieces of silver to his mother, and his mother said, "I personally consecrate the silver to the LORD for my son's benefit to make a carved image and a silver idol. I will give it back to you." So he returned the silver to his mother, and she took five pounds of silver and gave it to a silversmith. He made it into a carved image and a silver idol, and it was in Micah's house.

This man Micah had a shrine, and he made an ephod and household idols, and installed one of his sons to be his priest. In those days there was no king in Israel; everyone did whatever seemed
10 right to him.

There was a young man, a Levite from Bethlehem in Judah, who was staying within the clan of Judah. The man left the town of Bethlehem in Judah to stay wherever he could find a place. On his way he came to Micah's home in the hill country of Ephraim.

"Where do you come from?" Micah asked him.

He answered him, "I am a Levite from Bethlehem in Judah, and I'm going to stay wherever I can find a place."

Micah replied, "Stay with me and be my father and priest, and I will give you four ounces of silver a year, along with your clothing and provisions." So the Levite went in and agreed to stay with the man, and the young man became like one of his sons. Micah consecrated the Levite, and
20 the young man became his priest and lived in Micah's house. Then Micah said, "Now I know that the LORD will be good to me, because a Levite has become my priest."

18 In those days, there was no king in Israel, and the Danite tribe was looking for territory to occupy. Up to that time no territory had been captured by them among the tribes of Israel. So the Danites sent out five brave men from all their clans, from Zorah and Eshtaol, to scout out the land and explore it. They told them, "Go and explore the land."

They came to the hill country of Ephraim as far as the home of Micah and spent the night there. While they were near Micah's home, they recognized the accent of the young Levite. So they went over to him and asked, "Who brought you here? What are you doing in this place? What is keeping you here?"

He told them, "This is what Micah has done for me: He has hired me, and I became his priest."
10 Then they said to him, "Please inquire of God for us to determine if we will have a successful journey."

The priest told them, "Go in peace. The Lord is watching over the journey you are going on."

The five men left and came to Laish. They saw that the people who were there were living securely, in the same way as the Sidonians, quiet and unsuspecting. There was nothing lacking in the land and no oppressive ruler. They were far from the Sidonians, having no alliance with anyone.

When the men went back to their relatives at Zorah and Eshtaol, their relatives asked them, "What did you find out?"

They answered, "Come on, let's attack them, for we have seen the land, and it is very good. Why wait? Don't hesitate to go and invade and take possession of the land! When you get there, you will come to an unsuspecting people and a spacious land, for God has handed it over to you. It is a place where nothing on earth is lacking." Six hundred Danites departed from Zorah and Eshtaol armed with weapons of war. They went up and camped at Kiriath-jearim in Judah. This is why the place is still called the Camp of Dan today; it is west of Kiriath-jearim. From there they traveled to the hill country of Ephraim and arrived at Micah's house.

The five men who had gone to scout out the land of Laish told their brothers, "Did you know that there are an ephod, household gods, and a carved image and a silver idol in these houses? Now think about what you should do." So they detoured there and went to the house of the young Levite at the home of Micah and greeted him. The six hundred Danite men were standing by the entrance of the city gate, armed with their weapons of war. Then the five men who had gone to scout out the land went in and took the carved image, the ephod, the household idols, and the silver idol, while the priest was standing by the entrance of the city gate with the six hundred men armed with weapons of war.

When they entered Micah's house and took the carved image, the ephod, the household idols, and the silver idol, the priest said to them, "What are you doing?"

They told him, "Be quiet. Keep your mouth shut. Come with us and be a father and a priest to us. Is it better for you to be a priest for the house of one person or for you to be a priest for a tribe and family in Israel?" So the priest was pleased and took the ephod, household idols, and carved image, and went with the people. They prepared to leave, putting their dependents, livestock, and possessions in front of them.

After they were some distance from Micah's house, the men who were in the houses near it were mustered and caught up with the Danites. They called to the Danites, who turned to face them, and said to Micah, "What's the matter with you that you mustered the men?"

He said, "You took the gods I had made and the priest, and went away. What do I have left? How can you say to me, 'What's the matter with you?'"

The Danites said to him, "Don't raise your voice against us, or angry men will attack you, and you and your family will lose your lives." The Danites went on their way, and Micah turned to go back home, because he saw that they were stronger than he was.

After they had taken the gods Micah had made and the priest that belonged to him, they went to Laish, to a quiet and unsuspecting people. They killed them with their swords and burned the

50 city. There was no one to rescue them because it was far from Sidon and they had no alliance with anyone. It was in a valley that belonged to Beth-rehob. They rebuilt the city and lived in it. They named the city Dan, after the name of their ancestor Dan, who was born to Israel. The city was formerly named Laish.

The Danites set up the carved image for themselves. Jonathan son of Gershom, son of Moses, and his sons were priests for the Danite tribe until the time of the exile from the land. So they set up for themselves Micah's carved image that he had made, and it was there as long as the house of God was in Shiloh.

19 In those days, when there was no king in Israel, a Levite staying in a remote part of the hill country of Ephraim acquired a woman from Bethlehem in Judah as his concubine. But she was unfaithful to him and left him for her father's house in Bethlehem in Judah. She was there for four months. Then her husband got up and followed her to speak kindly to her and bring her back. He had his servant with him and a pair of donkeys. So she brought him to her father's house, and when the girl's father saw him, he gladly welcomed him. His father-in-law, the girl's father, detained him, and he stayed with him for three days. They ate, drank, and spent the nights there.

On the fourth day, they got up early in the morning and prepared to go, but the girl's father said to his son-in-law, "Have something to eat to keep up your strength and then you can go." So 10 they sat down and the two of them ate and drank together. Then the girl's father said to the man, "Please agree to stay overnight and enjoy yourself." The man got up to go, but his father-in-law persuaded him, so he stayed and spent the night there again. He got up early in the morning of the fifth day to leave, but the girl's father said to him, "Please keep up your strength." So they waited until late afternoon and the two of them ate. The man got up to go with his concubine and his servant, when his father-in-law, the girl's father, said to him, "Look, night is coming. Please spend the night. See, the day is almost over. Spend the night here, enjoy yourself, then you can get up early tomorrow for your journey and go home."

But the man was unwilling to spend the night. He got up, departed, and arrived opposite Jebus (that is, Jerusalem). The man had his two saddled donkeys and his concubine with him. When 20 they were near Jebus and the day was almost gone, the servant said to his master, "Please, why not let us stop at this Jebusite city and spend the night here?"

But his master replied to him, "We will not stop at a foreign city where there are no Israelites. Let's move on to Gibeah." "Come on," he said, "let's try to reach one of these places and spend the night in Gibeah or Ramah." So they continued on their journey, and the sun set as they neared Gibeah in Benjamin. They stopped to go in and spend the night in Gibeah. The Levite went in and sat down in the city square, but no one took them into their home to spend the night.

In the evening, an old man came in from his work in the field. He was from the hill country of Ephraim, but he was residing in Gibeah where the people were Benjaminites. When he looked up

30 and saw the traveler in the city square, the old man asked, "Where are you going, and where do you come from?"

He answered him, "We're traveling from Bethlehem in Judah to the remote hill country of Ephraim, where I am from. I went to Bethlehem in Judah, and now I'm going to the house of the Lord. No one has taken me into his home, although there's straw and feed for the donkeys, and I have bread and wine for me, my concubine, and the servant with us. There is nothing we lack."

"Welcome!" said the old man. "I'll take care of everything you need. Only don't spend the night in the square." So he brought him to his house and fed the donkeys. Then they washed their feet and ate and drank. While they were enjoying themselves, all of a sudden, wicked men of the city surrounded the house and beat on the door. They said to the old man who was the owner of the 40 house, "Bring out the man who came to your house so we can have sex with him!"

The owner of the house went out and said to them, "Please don't do this evil, my brothers. After all, this man has come into my house. Don't commit this horrible outrage. Here, let me bring out my virgin daughter and the man's concubine now. Abuse them and do whatever you want to them. But don't commit this outrageous thing against this man."

But the men would not listen to him, so the man seized his concubine and took her outside to them. They raped her and abused her all night until morning. At daybreak they let her go. Early that morning, the woman made her way back, and as it was getting light, she collapsed at the doorway of the man's house where her master was.

When her master got up in the morning, opened the doors of the house, and went out to leave 50 on his journey, there was the woman, his concubine, collapsed near the doorway of the house with her hands on the threshold. "Get up," he told her. "Let's go." But there was no response. So the man put her on his donkey and set out for home.

When he entered his house, he picked up a knife, took hold of his concubine, cut her into twelve pieces, limb by limb, and then sent her throughout the territory of Israel. Everyone who saw it said, "Nothing like this has ever happened or has been seen since the day the Israelites came out of the land of Egypt until now. Think it over, discuss it, and speak up!"

20 All the Israelites from Dan to Beer-sheba and from the land of Gilead came out, and the community assembled as one body before the Lord at Mizpah. The leaders of all the people and of all the tribes of Israel presented themselves in the assembly of God's people: four hundred thousand armed foot soldiers. The Benjaminites heard that the Israelites had gone up to Mizpah.

The Israelites asked, "Tell us, how did this evil act happen?"

The Levite, the husband of the murdered woman, answered, "I went to Gibeah in Benjamin with my concubine to spend the night. Citizens of Gibeah came to attack me and surrounded the house at night. They intended to kill me, but they raped my concubine, and she died. Then I took my concubine and cut her in pieces, and sent her throughout Israel's territory, because they have committed a wicked 10 outrage in Israel. Look, all of you are Israelites. Give your judgment and verdict here and now."

Then all the people stood united and said, "None of us will go to his tent or return to his house. Now this is what we will do to Gibeah: we will attack it. By lot we will take ten men out of every hundred from all the tribes of Israel, and one hundred out of every thousand, and one thousand out of every ten thousand to get provisions for the troops when they go to Gibeah in Benjamin to punish them for all the outrage they committed in Israel."

So all the men of Israel gathered united against the city. Then the tribes of Israel sent men throughout the tribe of Benjamin, saying, "What is this evil act that has happened among you? Hand over the wicked men in Gibeah so we can put them to death and purge evil from Israel." But the Benjaminites would not listen to their fellow Israelites. Instead, the Benjaminites gathered 20 together from their cities to Gibeah to go out and fight against the Israelites. On that day the Benjaminites mobilized twenty-six thousand armed men from their cities, besides seven hundred fit young men rallied by the inhabitants of Gibeah. There were seven hundred fit young men who were left-handed among all these troops; all could sling a stone at a hair and not miss.

The Israelites, apart from Benjamin, mobilized four hundred thousand armed men, every one an experienced warrior. They set out, went to Bethel, and inquired of God. The Israelites asked, "Who is to go first to fight for us against the Benjaminites?"

And the LORD answered, "Judah will be first."

In the morning, the Israelites set out and camped near Gibeah. The men of Israel went out to fight against Benjamin and took their battle positions against Gibeah. The Benjaminites came 30 out of Gibeah and slaughtered twenty-two thousand men of Israel on the field that day. But the Israelite troops rallied and again took their battle positions in the same place where they positioned themselves on the first day. They went up, wept before the LORD until evening, and inquired of him, "Should we again attack our brothers the Benjaminites?"

And the LORD answered, "Fight against them."

On the second day the Israelites advanced against the Benjaminites. That same day the Benjaminites came out from Gibeah to meet them and slaughtered an additional eighteen thousand Israelites on the field; all were armed.

The whole Israelite army went to Bethel where they wept and sat before the LORD. They fasted that day until evening and offered burnt offerings and fellowship offerings to the LORD. Then 40 the Israelites inquired of the LORD. In those days, the ark of the covenant of God was there, and Phinehas son of Eleazar, son of Aaron, was serving before it. The Israelites asked, "Should we again fight against our brothers the Benjaminites or should we stop?"

The LORD answered, "Fight, because I will hand them over to you tomorrow." So Israel set up an ambush around Gibeah. On the third day the Israelites fought against the Benjaminites and took their battle positions against Gibeah as before. Then the Benjaminites came out against the troops and were drawn away from the city. They began to attack the troops as before, killing about thirty men of Israel on the highways, one of which goes up to Bethel and the other to Gibeah through the open country. The Benjaminites said, "We are defeating them as before."

But the Israelites said, "Let's flee and draw them away from the city to the highways." So all 50 the men of Israel got up from their places and took their battle positions at Baal-tamar, while the Israelites in ambush charged out of their places west of Geba. Then ten thousand fit young men from all Israel made a frontal assault against Gibeah, and the battle was fierce, but the Benjaminites did not know that disaster was about to strike them. The LORD defeated Benjamin in the presence of Israel, and on that day the Israelites slaughtered 25,100 men of Benjamin; all were armed. Then the Benjaminites realized they had been defeated.

The men of Israel had retreated before Benjamin, because they were confident in the ambush they had set against Gibeah. The men in ambush had rushed quickly against Gibeah; they advanced and put the whole city to the sword. The men of Israel had a prearranged signal with the men in ambush: when they sent up a great cloud of smoke from the city, the men of Israel would 60 return to the battle. When Benjamin had begun to strike them down, killing about thirty men of Israel, they said, "They're defeated before us, just as they were in the first battle." But when the column of smoke began to go up from the city, Benjamin looked behind them, and the whole city was going up in smoke. Then the men of Israel returned, and the men of Benjamin were terrified when they realized that disaster had struck them. They retreated before the men of Israel toward the wilderness, but the battle overtook them, and those who came out of the cities slaughtered those between them. They surrounded the Benjaminites, pursued them, and easily overtook them near Gibeah toward the east. There were eighteen thousand men who died from Benjamin; all were warriors. Then Benjamin turned and fled toward the wilderness to Rimmon Rock, and Israel killed five thousand men on the highways. They overtook them at Gidom and struck two 70 thousand more dead.

All the Benjaminites who died that day were twenty-five thousand armed men; all were warriors. But six hundred men escaped into the wilderness to Rimmon Rock and stayed there four months. The men of Israel turned back against the other Benjaminites and killed them with their swords—the entire city, the animals, and everything that remained. They also burned all the cities that remained.

21 The men of Israel had sworn an oath at Mizpah: "None of us will give his daughter to a Benjaminite in marriage." So the people went to Bethel and sat there before God until evening. They wept loudly and bitterly, and cried out, "Why, LORD God of Israel, has it occurred that one tribe is missing in Israel today?" The next day the people got up early, built an altar there, and offered burnt offerings and fellowship offerings. The Israelites asked, "Who of all the tribes of Israel didn't come to the LORD with the assembly?" For a great oath had been taken that anyone who had not come to the LORD at Mizpah would certainly be put to death.

But the Israelites had compassion on their brothers, the Benjaminites, and said, "Today a tribe has been cut off from Israel. What should we do about wives for the survivors? We've sworn to 10 the LORD not to give them any of our daughters as wives." They asked, "Which city among the tribes of Israel didn't come to the LORD at Mizpah?" It turned out that no one from Jabesh-gilead had come to the camp and the assembly. For when the roll was called, no men were there from the inhabitants of Jabesh-gilead.

The congregation sent twelve thousand brave warriors there and commanded them, "Go and kill the inhabitants of Jabesh-gilead with the sword, including women and dependents. This is what you should do: Completely destroy every male, as well as every woman who has gone to bed with a man." They found among the inhabitants of Jabesh-gilead four hundred young virgins, who had not been intimate with a man, and they brought them to the camp at Shiloh in the land of Canaan.

20 The whole congregation sent a message of peace to the Benjaminites who were at Rimmon Rock. Benjamin returned at that time, and Israel gave them the women they had kept alive from Jabesh-gilead. But there were not enough for them.

The people had compassion on Benjamin, because the LORD had made this gap in the tribes of Israel. The elders of the congregation said, "What should we do about wives for those who are left, since the women of Benjamin have been destroyed?" They said, "There must be heirs for the survivors of Benjamin, so that a tribe of Israel will not be wiped out. But we can't give them our daughters as wives." For the Israelites had sworn, "Anyone who gives a wife to a Benjaminite is cursed." They also said, "Look, there's an annual festival to the LORD in Shiloh, which is north of Bethel, east of the highway that goes up from Bethel to Shechem, and south of Lebonah."

30 Then they commanded the Benjaminites, "Go and hide in the vineyards. Watch, and when you see the young women of Shiloh come out to perform the dances, each of you leave the vineyards and catch a wife for yourself from the young women of Shiloh, and go to the land of Benjamin. When their fathers or brothers come to us and protest, we will tell them, 'Show favor to them, since we did not get enough wives for each of them in the battle. You didn't actually give the women to them, so you are not guilty of breaking your oath.'"

The Benjaminites did this and took the number of women they needed from the dancers they caught. They went back to their own inheritance, rebuilt their cities, and lived in them. At that time, each of the Israelites returned from there to his own tribe and family. Each returned from there to his own inheritance.

40 In those days there was no king in Israel; everyone did whatever seemed right to him.

Introduction to Samuel

Ben Johnson

The Samuel Corpus tells the story of the beginning of Israel's monarchy. Though a two-part book in our English Bibles, it was probably originally conceived as a single work and only divided into two separate books because of the restrictions of scroll length. In the HS, 1–2 Samuel is immediately preceded by the book of Judges. The final chapters of the book of Judges include a repeated refrain, "In those days there was no king in Israel; everyone did whatever seemed right to him" (Judg 17.9–10; 18.1–2; 19.1–2; 21.40). In the book of Samuel we get to see what happens when there is a king in Israel.

The Samuel Corpus begins with the birth and call of Samuel, a prophet and the last judge of Israel. Samuel becomes the kingmaker when, in response to the people's dubious request for a king like "all the other nations have" (1 Sam 8.4–6), he anoints Saul, son of Kish, king over Israel (1 Sam 10.1–2; 11.29–32). Though Saul starts off promising, he is quickly rejected for failing to fulfill what the Yahweh has given him to do (1 Sam 13; 15). In his place, Samuel anoints David (1 Sam 16) and from that moment on, the story is about David. The narrative shifts to David through his slaying of the Philistine giant, Goliath (1 Sam 17) and his early successes in the court of Saul (1 Sam 18). However, Saul's antagonism quickly puts David on the run (1 Sam 19–26), leading him to seek refuge as a vassal of the Philistines (1 Sam 27–30). After the death of Saul (1 Sam 31–2 Sam 1), David becomes king over Judah (2 Sam 2). After a civil war with Saul's son Ishbosheth, David becomes king over all Israel (2 Sam 5). As his reign is consolidated David decides to build a *house* or temple for Yahweh. However, Yahweh did not ask for a *house* from David but will instead build a *house* or dynasty for David (2 Sam 7). This is perhaps the most significant event in David's story and is subsequently one of the most important events in the entire HS. This covenant with David will become one of the most significant driving forces for the rest of the biblical narrative as Yahweh's commitment to David's house will be a theme throughout the Psalms and Prophets.

From the making of the covenant with David, the story takes a stark and negative turn. David's adultery with Bathsheba and murder of her husband Uriah (2 Sam 11) marks a turning point in the Samuel Corpus. The prophet Nathan tells David that from here on out "the sword will never leave your house" (2 Sam 12.17–18). David's eldest son Amnon rapes his half-sister Tamar (2 Sam 13.1–38). In retribution for this act, Tamar's brother Absalom murders Amnon (2 Sam 13.39–51). After this point Absalom's relationship with David never fully recovers and eventually Absalom rebels against his father, leading to civil war in Israel (2 Sam 14–19). David manages to defeat Absalom's rebellion, but it leaves him broken and mourning his son's death in his famous cry, "Oh, my son

Absalom! Oh, Absalom, my son! My son!" (2 Sam 19.3–4). Though David recovers the throne, he faces another rebellion, this time from a Benjamite named Sheba (2 Sam 20).

The Samuel Corpus ends with a concluding set of chapters that, at first glance, appear to contain a miscellaneous set of stories, poems, and lists. This section is actually carefully crafted (see the parallelism in the outline below). This section of text, though chronologically disjointed from the rest of the narrative, concludes the book with parallel stories that highlight David's capacity to intercede on behalf of Israel (2 Sam 21; 24), parallel sections that detail the military exploits of David's men (2 Sam 21.33–46; 23.25–89), and parallel poems that highlight David's dependence on Yahweh (2 Sam 22 and 23.1–24).

The Samuel Corpus is one of the most artistically powerful books in all of the HS. Its characters are memorable and very human. In Samuel we see a flawed prophet who hears the word of Yahweh and anoints the first kings of Israel. In Saul we see a flawed character, who may gain our sympathies in being put in a job he did not want, yet whose downward spiral is believable and tragic. In David we see a complex character who is capable of great evil in cases such as his dealings with Bathsheba and Uriah and yet who nevertheless repents and returns to Yahweh when he has erred (e.g. 1 Sam 24.8–10; 25.53–58; 2 Sam 12.22; 24.17–19). Their stories tend toward the tragic. As such, this powerful corpus explores what it means to be human and what it may mean to be a "man following after the Lord's own heart" (1 Sam 13.27–29). A key theme of the Samuel Corpus is the relationship between human leadership in the picture of the king and divine leadership. Yahweh sees the request for a human king as rejection of his own kingship in Israel (1 Sam 8.8–9). The two first examples of kingship, Saul and David, are both mixed characters who have high points and low points. Nevertheless, Yahweh commits to working through David and his line (2 Sam 7). What we see in the story of the Samuel Corpus is that human kingship can only work when it is submitted to Yahweh's will. The hope that is expressed in the book of Samuel, however, is Yahweh's commitment to David and his descendants (2 Sam 7). This commitment is the rock which anchors the prophetic hope of a coming Davidic king throughout the prophetic literature of the HS and is the promise which will reach its fulfillment in Jesus Christ, the son of David (see Matt 1:1).

Outline
1 Samuel
1. The Ministry of Samuel (1 Sam 1–7)
    a. Hannah and the Birth of Samuel (1 Sam 1–2)
    b. Samuel's Judgeship and the Loss of Ark (1 Sam 3–7)

2. The Rise and Rejection of Saul (1 Sam 8–15)
    a. The Institution of the Monarchy and Saul's Rise (1 Sam 8–12)
    b. Saul's Rejection (1 Sam 13–15)

3. The Rise of David (1 Sam 16–21)
    a. Introducing David (1 Sam 16–17)
    b. David and Saul's Court (1 Sam 18–21)

4. David on the Run (1 Sam 22–31)
    a. David on the Run (1 Sam 22–23)
    b. David Hiding and Confronting (1 Sam 24–26)
    c. David amongst the Philistines (1 Sam 27–31)

2 Samuel

1. David's Kingdom and Yahweh's Covenant (2 Sam 1–9)
    a. Consolidating David's Reign (2 Sam 1–4)
    b. David's Victories and God's Covenant (2 Sam 5–7)
    c. David's Justice and Kindness (2 Sam 8–9)

2. David's Transgression (2 Sam 10–12)

3. Rebellion in David's Kingdom (2 Sam 13–20)
    a. Amnon, Tamar, and Absalom (2 Sam 13–15)
    b. Absalom's Rebellion and Sheba's Rebellion (2 Sam 16–20)

4. David and His Reign in Chiastic Retrospect (2 Sam 21–24)
    a. Famine Account (2 Sam 21.1–14)
        b. Warrior Stories (2 Sam 21.15–22)
            c. David's Thanksgiving Psalm (2 Sam 22)
            c′ David's Last Words (2 Sam 23.1–7)
        b′ Warrior Stories (2 Sam 23.8–39)
    a′ Plague Account (2 Sam 24)

Suggested Resources

Brueggemann, Walter. *First and Second Samuel*. Interpretation. Louisville: John Knox, 1990.

Evans, Mary J. *1 & 2 Samuel*. Understanding the Bible Commentary Series. Grand Rapids: Baker Books, 2012.

Evans, Paul S. *1–2 Samuel*. The Story of God Bible Commentary. Grand Rapids: Zondervan, 2018.

Firth, David G. *1 & 2 Samuel*. Apollos Old Testament Commentary. Downers Grove, IL: InterVarsity Press, 2009.

Tsumura, David Toshio. *The First Book of Samuel.* New International Commentary on the Old Testament. Grand Rapids: Eerdmans, 2007.

———. *The Second Book of Samuel.* New International Commentary on the Old Testament, Grand Rapids: Eerdmans, 2019.

1 Samuel

I There was a man from Ramathaim-zophim in the hill country of Ephraim. His name was Elkanah son of Jeroham, son of Elihu, son of Tohu, son of Zuph, an Ephraimite. He had two wives, the first named Hannah and the second Peninnah. Peninnah had children, but Hannah was childless. This man would go up from his town every year to worship and to sacrifice to the Lord of Armies at Shiloh, where Eli's two sons, Hophni and Phinehas, were the Lord's priests.

Whenever Elkanah offered a sacrifice, he always gave portions of the meat to his wife Peninnah and to each of her sons and daughters. But he gave a double portion to Hannah, for he loved her even though the Lord had kept her from conceiving. Her rival would taunt her severely just to provoke her, because the Lord had kept Hannah from conceiving. Year after year, when she went
10 up to the Lord's house, her rival taunted her in this way. Hannah would weep and would not eat. "Hannah, why are you crying?" her husband, Elkanah, would ask. "Why won't you eat? Why are you troubled? Am I not better to you than ten sons?"

On one occasion, Hannah got up after they ate and drank at Shiloh. The priest Eli was sitting on a chair by the doorpost of the Lord's temple. Deeply hurt, Hannah prayed to the Lord and wept with many tears. Making a vow, she pleaded, "Lord of Armies, if you will take notice of your servant's affliction, remember and not forget me, and give your servant a son, I will give him to the Lord all the days of his life, and his hair will never be cut."

While she continued praying in the Lord's presence, Eli watched her mouth. Hannah was praying silently, and though her lips were moving, her voice could not be heard. Eli thought she
20 was drunk and said to her, "How long are you going to be drunk? Get rid of your wine!"

"No, my lord," Hannah replied. "I am a woman with a broken heart. I haven't had any wine or beer; I've been pouring out my heart before the Lord. Don't think of me as a wicked woman; I've been praying from the depth of my anguish and resentment."

Eli responded, "Go in peace, and may the God of Israel grant the request you've made of him."

"May your servant find favor with you," she replied. Then Hannah went on her way; she ate and no longer looked despondent.

The next morning Elkanah and Hannah got up early to worship before the Lord. Afterward, they returned home to Ramah. Then Elkanah was intimate with his wife Hannah, and the Lord
30 remembered her. After some time, Hannah conceived and gave birth to a son. She named him Samuel, because she said, "I requested him from the Lord."

When Elkanah and all his household went up to make the annual sacrifice and his vow offering to the Lord, Hannah did not go and explained to her husband, "After the child is weaned, I'll take him to appear in the Lord's presence and to stay there permanently."

Her husband, Elkanah, replied, "Do what you think is best, and stay here until you've weaned him. May the Lord confirm your word." So Hannah stayed there and nursed her son until she weaned him. When she had weaned him, she took him with her to Shiloh, as well as a three-year-old bull, half a bushel of flour, and a clay jar of wine. Though the boy was still young, she took him to the Lord's house at Shiloh. Then they slaughtered the bull and brought the boy to Eli.

40 "Please, my lord," she said, "as surely as you live, my lord, I am the woman who stood here beside you praying to the Lord. I prayed for this boy, and since the Lord gave me what I asked him for, I now give the boy to the Lord. For as long as he lives, he is given to the Lord." Then he worshiped the Lord there.

2 Hannah prayed:

> My heart rejoices in the Lord;
> my horn is lifted up by the Lord.
> My mouth boasts over my enemies,
> because I rejoice in your salvation.
> There is no one holy like the Lord.
> There is no one besides you!
> And there is no rock like our God.
> Do not boast so proudly,
10
> or let arrogant words come out of your mouth,
> for the Lord is a God of knowledge,
> and actions are weighed by him.
> The bows of the warriors are broken,
> but the feeble are clothed with strength.
> Those who are full hire themselves out for food,
> but those who are starving hunger no more.
> The woman who is childless gives birth to seven,
> but the woman with many sons pines away.
> The Lord brings death and gives life;
20
> he sends some down to Sheol, and he raises others up.
> The Lord brings poverty and gives wealth;
> he humbles and he exalts.
> He raises the poor from the dust
> and lifts the needy from the trash heap.
> He seats them with noblemen

and gives them a throne of honor.
For the foundations of the earth are the LORD's;
he has set the world on them.
He guards the steps of his faithful ones,
30   but the wicked perish in darkness,
for a person does not prevail by his own strength.
Those who oppose the LORD will be shattered;
he will thunder in the heavens against them.
The LORD will judge the ends of the earth.
He will give power to his king;
he will lift up the horn of his anointed.

Elkanah went home to Ramah, but the boy served the LORD in the presence of the priest Eli.

Eli's sons were wicked men; they did not respect the LORD or the priests' share of the sacrifices from the people. When anyone offered a sacrifice, the priest's servant would come with a three-
40 pronged meat fork while the meat was boiling and plunge it into the container, kettle, cauldron, or cooking pot. The priest would claim for himself whatever the meat fork brought up. This is the way they treated all the Israelites who came there to Shiloh. Even before the fat was burned, the priest's servant would come and say to the one who was sacrificing, "Give the priest some meat to roast, because he won't accept boiled meat from you—only raw." If that person said to him, "The fat must be burned first; then you can take whatever you want for yourself," the servant would reply, "No, I insist that you hand it over right now. If you don't, I'll take it by force!" So the servants' sin was very severe in the presence of the LORD, because the men treated the LORD's offering with contempt.

Samuel served in the LORD's presence—this mere boy was dressed in the linen ephod. Each
50 year his mother made him a little robe and took it to him when she went with her husband to offer the annual sacrifice. Eli would bless Elkanah and his wife: "May the LORD give you children by this woman in place of the one she has given to the LORD." Then they would go home.

The LORD paid attention to Hannah's need, and she conceived and gave birth to three sons and two daughters. Meanwhile, the boy Samuel grew up in the presence of the LORD.

Now Eli was very old. He heard about everything his sons were doing to all Israel and how they were sleeping with the women who served at the entrance to the tent of meeting. He said to them, "Why are you doing these things? I have heard about your evil actions from all these people. No, my sons, the news I hear the LORD's people spreading is not good. If one person sins against another, God can intercede for him, but if a person sins against the LORD, who can intercede for
60 him?" But they would not listen to their father, since the LORD intended to kill them. By contrast, the boy Samuel grew in stature and in favor with the LORD and with people.

A man of God came to Eli and said to him, "This is what the LORD says: 'Didn't I reveal myself to your forefather's family when they were in Egypt and belonged to Pharaoh's palace? Out of all the tribes of Israel, I chose your house to be my priests, to offer sacrifices on my altar, to burn incense, and to wear an ephod in my presence. I also gave your forefather's family all the Israelite food offerings. Why, then, do all of you despise my sacrifices and offerings that I require at the place of worship? You have honored your sons more than me, by making yourselves fat with the best part of all of the offerings of my people Israel.'

"Therefore, this is the declaration of the LORD, the God of Israel: 'I did say that your family and your forefather's family would walk before me forever. But now,' this is the LORD's declaration, 'no longer! For those who honor me I will honor, but those who despise me will be disgraced. Look, the days are coming when I will cut off your strength and the strength of your forefather's family, so that none in your family will reach old age. You will see distress in the place of worship, in spite of all that is good in Israel, and no one in your family will ever again reach old age. Any man from your family I do not cut off from my altar will bring grief and sadness to you. All your descendants will die violently. This will be the sign that will come to you concerning your two sons Hophni and Phinehas: both of them will die on the same day.

"'Then I will raise up a faithful priest for myself. He will do whatever is in my heart and mind. I will establish a lasting dynasty for him, and he will walk before my anointed one for all time. Anyone who is left in your family will come and bow down to him for a piece of silver or a loaf of bread. He will say: Please appoint me to some priestly office so I can have a piece of bread to eat.'"

3 The boy Samuel served the LORD in Eli's presence. In those days the word of the LORD was rare and prophetic visions were not widespread.

One day Eli, whose eyesight was failing, was lying in his usual place. Before the lamp of God had gone out, Samuel was lying down in the temple of the LORD, where the ark of God was located.

Then the LORD called Samuel, and he answered, "Here I am." He ran to Eli and said, "Here I am; you called me."

"I didn't call," Eli replied. "Go back and lie down." So he went and lay down.

Once again the LORD called, "Samuel!"

Samuel got up, went to Eli, and said, "Here I am; you called me."

"I didn't call, my son," he replied. "Go back and lie down."

Now Samuel did not yet know the LORD, because the word of the LORD had not yet been revealed to him. Once again, for the third time, the LORD called Samuel. He got up, went to Eli, and said, "Here I am; you called me."

Then Eli understood that the LORD was calling the boy. He told Samuel, "Go and lie down. If he calls you, say, 'Speak, LORD, for your servant is listening.'" So Samuel went and lay down in his place.

The Lord came, stood there, and called as before, "Samuel, Samuel!"

Samuel responded, "Speak, for your servant is listening."

20 The Lord said to Samuel, "I am about to do something in Israel that will cause everyone who hears about it to shudder. On that day I will carry out against Eli everything I said about his family, from beginning to end. I told him that I am going to judge his family forever because of the iniquity he knows about: his sons are cursing God, and he has not stopped them. Therefore, I have sworn to Eli's family: The iniquity of Eli's family will never be wiped out by either sacrifice or offering."

Samuel lay down until the morning; then he opened the doors of the Lord's house. He was afraid to tell Eli the vision, but Eli called him and said, "Samuel, my son."

"Here I am," answered Samuel.

"What was the message he gave you?" Eli asked. "Don't hide it from me. May God punish you 30 and do so severely if you hide anything from me that he told you." So Samuel told him everything and did not hide anything from him. Eli responded, "He is the Lord. Let him do what he thinks is good."

Samuel grew. The Lord was with him, and he fulfilled everything Samuel prophesied. All Israel from Dan to Beer-sheba knew that Samuel was a confirmed prophet of the Lord. The Lord continued to appear in Shiloh, because there he revealed himself to Samuel by his word.

4 And Samuel's words came to all Israel.

Israel went out to meet the Philistines in battle and camped at Ebenezer while the Philistines camped at Aphek. The Philistines lined up in battle formation against Israel, and as the battle intensified, Israel was defeated by the Philistines, who struck down about four thousand men on the battlefield.

When the troops returned to the camp, the elders of Israel asked, "Why did the Lord defeat us today before the Philistines? Let's bring the ark of the Lord's covenant from Shiloh. Then it will go with us and save us from our enemies." So the people sent men to Shiloh to bring back the ark of the covenant of the Lord of Armies, who is enthroned between the cherubim. Eli's two 10 sons, Hophni and Phinehas, were there with the ark of the covenant of God. When the ark of the covenant of the Lord entered the camp, all the Israelites raised such a loud shout that the ground shook.

The Philistines heard the sound of the war cry and asked, "What's this loud shout in the Hebrews' camp?" When the Philistines discovered that the ark of the Lord had entered the camp, they panicked. "A god has entered their camp!" they said. "Woe to us! Nothing like this has happened before. Woe to us! Who will rescue us from these magnificent gods? These are the gods that slaughtered the Egyptians with all kinds of plagues in the wilderness. Show some courage and be men, Philistines! Otherwise, you'll serve the Hebrews just as they served you. Now be men and fight!"

20 So the Philistines fought, and Israel was defeated, and each man fled to his tent. The slaughter was severe—thirty thousand of the Israelite foot soldiers fell. The ark of God was captured, and Eli's two sons, Hophni and Phinehas, died.

That same day, a Benjaminite man ran from the battle and came to Shiloh. His clothes were torn, and there was dirt on his head. When he arrived, there was Eli sitting on his chair beside the road waiting, because he was anxious about the ark of God. When the man entered the city to give a report, the entire city cried out.

Eli heard the outcry and asked, "Why this commotion?" The man quickly came and reported to Eli. At that time Eli was ninety-eight years old, and his eyes didn't move because he couldn't see.

The man said to Eli, "I'm the one who came from the battle. I fled from there today."

30 "What happened, my son?" Eli asked.

The messenger answered, "Israel has fled from the Philistines, and also there was a great slaughter among the people. Your two sons, Hophni and Phinehas, are both dead, and the ark of God has been captured." When he mentioned the ark of God, Eli fell backward off the chair by the city gate, and since he was old and heavy, his neck broke and he died. Eli had judged Israel forty years.

Eli's daughter-in-law, the wife of Phinehas, was pregnant and about to give birth. When she heard the news about the capture of God's ark and the deaths of her father-in-law and her husband, she collapsed and gave birth because her labor pains came on her. As she was dying, the women taking care of her said, "Don't be afraid. You've given birth to a son!" But she did not respond or pay 40 attention. She named the boy Ichabod, saying, "The glory has departed from Israel," referring to the capture of the ark of God and to the deaths of her father-in-law and her husband. "The glory has departed from Israel," she said, "because the ark of God has been captured."

5 After the Philistines had captured the ark of God, they took it from Ebenezer to Ashdod, brought it into the temple of Dagon and placed it next to his statue. When the people of Ashdod got up early the next morning, there was Dagon, fallen with his face to the ground before the ark of the Lord. So they took Dagon and returned him to his place. But when they got up early the next morning, there was Dagon, fallen with his face to the ground before the ark of the Lord. This time, Dagon's head and both of his hands were broken off and lying on the threshold. Only Dagon's torso remained. That is why, still today, the priests of Dagon and everyone who enters the temple of Dagon in Ashdod do not step on Dagon's threshold.

The Lord's hand was heavy on the people of Ashdod. He terrified the people of Ashdod 10 and its territory and afflicted them with tumors. When the people of Ashdod saw what was happening, they said, "The ark of Israel's God must not stay here with us, because his hand is strongly against us and our god Dagon." So they called all the Philistine rulers together and asked, "What should we do with the ark of Israel's God?"

"The ark of Israel's God should be moved to Gath," they replied. So they moved the ark of Israel's God. After they had moved it, the Lord's hand was against the city of Gath, causing a great panic. He afflicted the people of the city, from the youngest to the oldest, with an outbreak of tumors.

The people of Gath then sent the ark of God to Ekron, but when it got there, the Ekronites cried out, "They've moved the ark of Israel's God to us to kill us and our people!"

20 The Ekronites called all the Philistine rulers together. They said, "Send the ark of Israel's God away. Let it return to its place so it won't kill us and our people!" For the fear of death pervaded the city; God's hand was oppressing them. Those who did not die were afflicted with tumors, and the outcry of the city went up to heaven.

6 When the ark of the Lord had been in Philistine territory for seven months, the Philistines summoned the priests and the diviners and pleaded, "What should we do with the ark of the Lord? Tell us how we can send it back to its place."

They replied, "If you send the ark of Israel's God away, do not send it without an offering. Send back a guilt offering to him, and you will be healed. Then the reason his hand hasn't been removed from you will be revealed."

They asked, "What guilt offering should we send back to him?"

And they answered, "Five gold tumors and five gold mice corresponding to the number of Philistine rulers, since there was one plague for both you and your rulers. Make images of your
10 tumors and of your mice that are destroying the land. Give glory to Israel's God, and perhaps he will stop oppressing you, your gods, and your land. Why harden your hearts as the Egyptians and Pharaoh hardened theirs? When he afflicted them, didn't they send Israel away, and Israel left?

"Now then, prepare one new cart and two milk cows that have never been yoked. Hitch the cows to the cart, but take their calves away and pen them up. Take the ark of the Lord, place it on the cart, and put the gold objects that you're sending him as a guilt offering in a box beside the ark. Send it off and let it go its way. Then watch: If it goes up the road to its homeland toward Beth-shemesh, it is the Lord who has made this terrible trouble for us. However, if it doesn't, we will know that it was not his hand that punished us—it was just something that happened to us by chance."

20 The men did this: They took two milk cows, hitched them to the cart, and confined their calves in the pen. Then they put the ark of the Lord on the cart, along with the box containing the gold mice and the images of their tumors. The cows went straight up the road to Beth-shemesh. They stayed on that one highway, lowing as they went; they never strayed to the right or to the left. The Philistine rulers were walking behind them to the territory of Beth-shemesh.

The people of Beth-shemesh were harvesting wheat in the valley, and when they looked up and saw the ark, they were overjoyed to see it. The cart came to the field of Joshua of Beth-shemesh and stopped there near a large rock. The people of the city chopped up the cart and offered the cows as a burnt offering to the LORD. The Levites removed the ark of the LORD, along with the box containing the gold objects, and placed them on the large rock. That day the people of Beth-

30 shemesh offered burnt offerings and made sacrifices to the LORD. When the five Philistine rulers observed this, they returned to Ekron that same day.

As a guilt offering to the LORD, the Philistines had sent back one gold tumor for each city: Ashdod, Gaza, Ashkelon, Gath, and Ekron. The number of gold mice also corresponded to the number of Philistine cities of the five rulers, the fortified cities and the outlying villages. The large rock on which the ark of the LORD was placed is still in the field of Joshua of Beth-shemesh today.

God struck down the people of Beth-shemesh because they looked inside the ark of the LORD. He struck down seventy persons. The people mourned because the LORD struck them with a great slaughter. The people of Beth-shemesh asked, "Who is able to stand in the presence of the LORD

40 this holy God? To whom should the ark go from here?"

They sent messengers to the residents of Kiriath-jearim, saying, "The Philistines have returned the ark of the LORD. Come down and get it."

7 So the people of Kiriath-jearim came for the ark of the LORD and took it to Abinadab's house on the hill. They consecrated his son Eleazar to take care of it.

Time went by until twenty years had passed since the ark had been taken to Kiriath-jearim. Then the whole house of Israel longed for the LORD. Samuel told them, "If you are returning to the LORD with all your heart, get rid of the foreign gods and the Ashtoreths that are among you, set your hearts on the LORD, and worship only him. Then he will rescue you from the Philistines." So the Israelites removed the Baals and the Ashtoreths and only worshiped the LORD.

Samuel said, "Gather all Israel at Mizpah, and I will pray to the LORD on your behalf." When they gathered at Mizpah, they drew water and poured it out in the LORD's presence. They fasted

10 that day, and there they confessed, "We have sinned against the LORD." And Samuel judged the Israelites at Mizpah.

When the Philistines heard that the Israelites had gathered at Mizpah, their rulers marched up toward Israel. When the Israelites heard about it, they were afraid because of the Philistines. The Israelites said to Samuel, "Don't stop crying out to the LORD our God for us, so that he will save us from the Philistines."

Then Samuel took a young lamb and offered it as a whole burnt offering to the LORD. He cried out to the LORD on behalf of Israel, and the LORD answered him. Samuel was offering the burnt offering as the Philistines approached to fight against Israel. The LORD thundered loudly against the Philistines that day and threw them into such confusion that they were defeated by Israel.

20 Then the men of Israel charged out of Mizpah and pursued the Philistines striking them down all the way to a place below Beth-car.

Afterward, Samuel took a stone and set it upright between Mizpah and Shen. He named it Ebenezer, explaining, "The Lord has helped us to this point." So the Philistines were subdued and did not invade Israel's territory again. The Lord's hand was against the Philistines all of Samuel's life. The cities from Ekron to Gath, which they had taken from Israel, were restored; Israel even rescued their surrounding territories from Philistine control. There was also peace between Israel and the Amorites.

Samuel judged Israel throughout his life. Every year he would go on a circuit to Bethel, Gilgal, and Mizpah and would judge Israel at all these locations. Then he would return to Ramah because
30 his home was there, he judged Israel there, and he built an altar to the Lord there.

8 When Samuel grew old, he appointed his sons as judges over Israel. His firstborn son's name was Joel and his second was Abijah. They were judges in Beer-sheba. However, his sons did not walk in his ways—they turned toward dishonest profit, took bribes, and perverted justice.

So all the elders of Israel gathered together and went to Samuel at Ramah. They said to him, "Look, you are old, and your sons do not walk in your ways. Therefore, appoint a king to judge us the same as all the other nations have."

When they said, "Give us a king to judge us," Samuel considered their demand wrong, so he prayed to the Lord. But the Lord told him, "Listen to the people and everything they say to you. They have not rejected you; they have rejected me as their king. They are doing the same
10 thing to you that they have done to me, since the day I brought them out of Egypt until this day, abandoning me and worshiping other gods. Listen to them, but solemnly warn them and tell them about the customary rights of the king who will reign over them."

Samuel told all the Lord's words to the people who were asking him for a king. He said, "These are the rights of the king who will reign over you: He will take your sons and put them to his use in his chariots, on his horses, or running in front of his chariots. He can appoint them for his use as commanders of thousands or commanders of fifties, to plow his ground and reap his harvest, or to make his weapons of war and the equipment for his chariots. He can take your daughters to become perfumers, cooks, and bakers. He can take your best fields, vineyards, and olive orchards and give them to his servants. He can take a tenth of your grain and your vineyards
20 and give them to his officials and servants. He can take your male servants, your female servants, your best cattle, and your donkeys and use them for his work. He can take a tenth of your flocks, and you yourselves can become his servants. When that day comes, you will cry out because of the king you've chosen for yourselves, but the Lord won't answer you on that day."

The people refused to listen to Samuel. "No!" they said. "We must have a king over us. Then we'll be like all the other nations: our king will judge us, go out before us, and fight our battles."

Samuel listened to all the people's words and then repeated them to the Lord. "Listen to them," the Lord told Samuel. "Appoint a king for them."

Then Samuel told the men of Israel, "Each of you, go back to your city."

9 There was a prominent man of Benjamin named Kish son of Abiel, son of Zeror, son of Becorath, son of Aphiah, son of a Benjaminite. He had a son named Saul, an impressive young man. There was no one more impressive among the Israelites than he. He stood a head taller than anyone else.

One day the donkeys of Saul's father Kish wandered off. Kish said to his son Saul, "Take one of the servants with you and go look for the donkeys." Saul and his servant went through the hill country of Ephraim and then through the region of Shalishah, but they didn't find them. They went through the region of Shaalim—nothing. Then they went through the Benjaminite region but still didn't find them.

When they came to the land of Zuph, Saul said to the servant who was with him, "Come on, let's go back, or my father will stop worrying about the donkeys and start worrying about us."

"Look," the servant said, "there's a man of God in this city who is highly respected; everything he says is sure to come true. Let's go there now. Maybe he'll tell us which way we should go."

"Suppose we do go," Saul said to his servant, "what do we take the man? The food from our packs is gone, and there's no gift to take to the man of God. What do we have?"

The servant answered Saul, "Here, I have a little silver. I'll give it to the man of God, and he will tell us which way we should go."

Formerly in Israel, a man who was going to inquire of God would say, "Come, let's go to the seer," for the prophet of today was formerly called the seer.

"Good," Saul replied to his servant. "Come on, let's go." So they went to the city where the man of God was. As they were climbing the hill to the city, they found some young women coming out to draw water and asked, "Is the seer here?"

The women answered, "Yes, he is ahead of you. Hurry, he just now entered the city, because there's a sacrifice for the people at the high place today. As soon as you enter the city, you will find him before he goes to the high place to eat. The people won't eat until he comes because he must bless the sacrifice; after that, the guests can eat. Go up immediately—you can find him now." So they went up toward the city.

Saul and his servant were entering the city when they saw Samuel coming toward them on his way to the high place. Now the day before Saul's arrival, the Lord had informed Samuel, "At this time tomorrow I will send you a man from the land of Benjamin. Anoint him ruler over my people Israel. He will save them from the Philistines because I have seen the affliction of my people, for their cry has come to me." When Samuel saw Saul, the Lord told him, "Here is the man I told you about; he will govern my people."

Saul approached Samuel in the city gate and asked, "Would you please tell me where the seer's house is?"

"I am the seer," Samuel answered. "Go up ahead of me to the high place and eat with me today. When I send you off in the morning, I'll tell you everything that's in your heart. As for the donkeys that wandered away from you three days ago, don't worry about them because they've been found. And who does all Israel desire but you and all your father's family?"

Saul responded, "Am I not a Benjaminite from the smallest of Israel's tribes and isn't my clan
40 the least important of all the clans of the Benjaminite tribe? So why have you said something like
this to me?"

Samuel took Saul and his servant, brought them to the banquet hall, and gave them a place at
the head of the thirty or so men who had been invited. Then Samuel said to the cook, "Get the
portion of meat that I gave you and told you to set aside."

The cook picked up the thigh and what was attached to it and set it before Saul. Then Samuel
said, "Notice that the reserved piece is set before you. Eat it because it was saved for you for
this solemn event at the time I said, 'I've invited the people.'" So Saul ate with Samuel that day.
Afterward, they went down from the high place to the city, and Samuel spoke with Saul on the
roof.

50 They got up early, and just before dawn, Samuel called to Saul on the roof, "Get up, and I'll
send you on your way!" Saul got up, and both he and Samuel went outside. As they were going
down to the edge of the city, Samuel said to Saul, "Tell the servant to go on ahead of us, but you
stay for a while, and I'll reveal the word of God to you." So the servant went on.

10 Samuel took the flask of oil, poured it out on Saul's head, kissed him, and said, "Hasn't the LORD
anointed you ruler over his inheritance? Today when you leave me, you'll find two men at Rachel's
Grave at Zelzah in the territory of Benjamin. They will say to you, 'The donkeys you went looking
for have been found, and now your father has stopped being concerned about the donkeys and is
worried about you, asking: What should I do about my son?'

"You will proceed from there until you come to the oak of Tabor. Three men going up to God
at Bethel will meet you there, one bringing three goats, one bringing three loaves of bread, and one
bringing a clay jar of wine. They will ask how you are and give you two loaves of bread, which you
will accept from them.

10 "After that you will come to Gibeah of God where there are Philistine garrisons. When you
arrive at the city, you will meet a group of prophets coming down from the high place prophesying.
They will be preceded by harps, tambourines, flutes, and lyres. The Spirit of the LORD will come
powerfully on you, you will prophesy with them, and you will be transformed. When these
signs have happened to you, do whatever your circumstances require because God is with you.
Afterward, go ahead of me to Gilgal. I will come to you to offer burnt offerings and to sacrifice
fellowship offerings. Wait seven days until I come to you and show you what to do."

When Saul turned to leave Samuel, God changed his heart, and all the signs came about that
day. When Saul and his servant arrived at Gibeah, a group of prophets met him. Then the Spirit
of God came powerfully on him, and he prophesied along with them.

20 Everyone who knew him previously and saw him prophesy with the prophets asked each other,
"What has happened to the son of Kish? Is Saul also among the prophets?"

Then a man who was from there asked, "And who is their father?"

As a result, "Is Saul also among the prophets?" became a popular saying. Then Saul finished prophesying and went to the high place.

Saul's uncle asked him and his servant, "Where did you go?"

"To look for the donkeys," Saul answered. "When we saw they weren't there, we went to Samuel."

"Tell me," Saul's uncle asked, "what did Samuel say to you?"

Saul told him, "He assured us the donkeys had been found." However, Saul did not tell him
30 what Samuel had said about the matter of kingship.

Samuel summoned the people to the LORD at Mizpah and said to the Israelites, "This is what the LORD, the God of Israel, says: 'I brought Israel out of Egypt, and I rescued you from the power of the Egyptians and all the kingdoms that were oppressing you.' But today you have rejected your God, who saves you from all your troubles and afflictions. You said to him, 'You must set a king over us.' Now therefore present yourselves before the LORD by your tribes and clans."

Samuel had all the tribes of Israel come forward, and the tribe of Benjamin was selected. Then he had the tribe of Benjamin come forward by its clans, and the Matrite clan was selected. Finally, Saul son of Kish was selected. But when they searched for him, they could not find him. They again inquired of the LORD, "Has the man come here yet?"

40 The LORD replied, "There he is, hidden among the supplies."

They ran and got him from there. When he stood among the people, he stood a head taller than anyone else. Samuel said to all the people, "Do you see the one the LORD has chosen? There is no one like him among the entire population."

And all the people shouted, "Long live the king!"

Samuel proclaimed to the people the rights of kingship. He wrote them on a scroll, which he placed in the presence of the LORD. Then Samuel sent all the people home.

Saul also went to his home in Gibeah, and brave men whose hearts God had touched went with him. But some wicked men said, "How can this guy save us?" They despised him and did not bring him a gift, but Saul said nothing.

11 Nahash the Ammonite came up and laid siege to Jabesh-gilead. All the men of Jabesh said to him, "Make a treaty with us, and we will serve you."

Nahash the Ammonite replied, "I'll make one with you on this condition: that I gouge out everyone's right eye and humiliate all Israel."

"Don't do anything to us for seven days," the elders of Jabesh said to him, "and let us send messengers throughout the territory of Israel. If no one saves us, we will surrender to you."

When the messengers came to Gibeah, Saul's hometown, and told the terms to the people, all wept aloud. Just then Saul was coming in from the field behind his oxen. "What's the matter with the people? Why are they weeping?" Saul inquired, and they repeated to him the words of the men from Jabesh.

10 When Saul heard these words, the Spirit of God suddenly came powerfully on him, and his anger burned furiously. He took a team of oxen, cut them in pieces, and sent them throughout the territory of Israel by messengers who said, "This is what will be done to the ox of anyone who doesn't march behind Saul and Samuel." As a result, the terror of the LORD fell on the people, and they went out united.

Saul counted them at Bezek. There were three hundred thousand Israelites and thirty thousand men from Judah. He told the messengers who had come, "Tell this to the men of Jabesh-gilead: 'Deliverance will be yours tomorrow by the time the sun is hot.'" So the messengers told the men of Jabesh, and they rejoiced.

Then the men of Jabesh said to Nahash, "Tomorrow we will come out, and you can do 20 whatever you want to us."

The next day Saul organized the troops into three divisions. During the morning watch, they invaded the Ammonite camp and slaughtered them until the heat of the day. There were survivors, but they were so scattered that no two of them were left together.

Afterward, the people said to Samuel, "Who said that Saul should not reign over us? Give us those men so we can kill them!"

But Saul ordered, "No one will be executed this day, for today the LORD has provided deliverance in Israel."

Then Samuel said to the people, "Come, let's go to Gilgal, so we can renew the kingship there." 30 So all the people went to Gilgal, and there in the LORD's presence they made Saul king. There they sacrificed fellowship offerings in the LORD's presence, and Saul and all the men of Israel rejoiced greatly.

12 Then Samuel said to all Israel, "I have carefully listened to everything you said to me and placed a king over you. Now you can see that the king is leading you. As for me, I'm old and gray, and my sons are here with you. I have led you from my youth until now. Here I am. Bring charges against me before the LORD and his anointed: Whose ox or donkey have I taken? Who have I wronged or mistreated? Who gave me a bribe to overlook something? I will return it to you."

"You haven't wronged us, you haven't mistreated us, and you haven't taken anything from anyone," they responded.

He said to them, "The LORD is a witness against you, and his anointed is a witness today that you haven't found anything in my hand."

10 "He is a witness," they said.

Then Samuel said to the people, "The LORD, who appointed Moses and Aaron and who brought your ancestors up from the land of Egypt, is a witness. Now present yourselves, so I may confront you before the LORD about all the righteous acts he has done for you and your ancestors.

"When Jacob went to Egypt, your ancestors cried out to the LORD, and he sent them Moses and Aaron, who led your ancestors out of Egypt and settled them in this place. But they forgot the LORD their God, so he handed them over to Sisera commander of the army of Hazor, to the Philistines, and to the king of Moab. These enemies fought against them. Then they cried out to the LORD and said, 'We have sinned, for we abandoned the LORD and worshiped the Baals and the Ashtoreths. Now rescue us from the power of our enemies, and we will serve you.' So the LORD sent Jerubbaal, Barak, Jephthah, and Samuel. He rescued you from the power of the enemies around you, and you lived securely. But when you saw that Nahash king of the Ammonites was coming against you, you said to me, 'No, we must have a king reign over us'—even though the LORD your God is your king.

"Now here is the king you've chosen, the one you requested. Look, this is the king the LORD has placed over you. If you fear the LORD, worship and obey him, and if you don't rebel against the LORD's command, then both you and the king who reigns over you will follow the LORD your God. However, if you disobey the LORD and rebel against his command, the LORD's hand will be against you as it was against your ancestors.

"Now, therefore, present yourselves and see this great thing that the LORD will do before your eyes. Isn't the wheat harvest today? I will call on the LORD, and he will send thunder and rain so that you will recognize what an immense evil you committed in the LORD's sight by requesting a king for yourselves." Samuel called on the LORD, and on that day the LORD sent thunder and rain. As a result, all the people greatly feared the LORD and Samuel.

They pleaded with Samuel, "Pray to the LORD your God for your servants so we won't die! For we have added to all our sins the evil of requesting a king for ourselves."

Samuel replied, "Don't be afraid. Even though you have committed all this evil, don't turn away from following the LORD. Instead, worship the LORD with all your heart. Don't turn away to follow worthless things that can't profit or rescue you; they are worthless. The LORD will not abandon his people, because of his great name and because he has determined to make you his own people.

"As for me, I vow that I will not sin against the LORD by ceasing to pray for you. I will teach you the good and right way. Above all, fear the LORD and worship him faithfully with all your heart; consider the great things he has done for you. However, if you continue to do what is evil, both you and your king will be swept away."

13 Saul was thirty years old when he became king, and he reigned forty-two years over Israel. He chose three thousand men from Israel for himself: two thousand were with Saul at Michmash and in Bethel's hill country, and one thousand were with Jonathan in Gibeah of Benjamin. He sent the rest of the troops away, each to his own tent.

Jonathan attacked the Philistine garrison in Gibeah, and the Philistines heard about it. So Saul blew the ram's horn throughout the land saying, "Let the Hebrews hear!" And all Israel heard the news, "Saul has attacked the Philistine garrison, and Israel is now repulsive to the Philistines." Then the troops were summoned to join Saul at Gilgal.

The Philistines also gathered to fight against Israel: three thousand chariots, six thousand horsemen, and troops as numerous as the sand on the seashore. They went up and camped at Michmash, east of Beth-aven.

The men of Israel saw that they were in trouble because the troops were in a difficult situation. They hid in caves, in thickets, among rocks, and in holes and cisterns. Some Hebrews even crossed the Jordan to the land of Gad and Gilead.

Saul, however, was still at Gilgal, and all his troops were gripped with fear. He waited seven days for the appointed time that Samuel had set, but Samuel didn't come to Gilgal, and the troops were deserting him. So Saul said, "Bring me the burnt offering and the fellowship offerings." Then he offered the burnt offering.

Just as he finished offering the burnt offering, Samuel arrived. So Saul went out to greet him, and Samuel asked, "What have you done?"

Saul answered, "When I saw that the troops were deserting me and you didn't come within the appointed days and the Philistines were gathering at Michmash, I thought, 'The Philistines will now descend on me at Gilgal, and I haven't sought the LORD's favor.' So I forced myself to offer the burnt offering."

Samuel said to Saul, "You have been foolish. You have not kept the command the LORD your God gave you. It was at this time that the LORD would have permanently established your reign over Israel, but now your reign will not endure. The LORD has found a man after his own heart, and the LORD has appointed him as ruler over his people, because you have not done what the LORD commanded." Then Samuel went from Gilgal to Gibeah in Benjamin. Saul registered the troops who were with him, about six hundred men.

Saul, his son Jonathan, and the troops who were with them were staying in Geba of Benjamin, and the Philistines were camped at Michmash. Raiding parties went out from the Philistine camp in three divisions. One division headed toward the Ophrah road leading to the land of Shual. The next division headed toward the Beth-horon road, and the last division headed down the border road that looks out over the Zeboim Valley toward the wilderness.

No blacksmith could be found in all the land of Israel because the Philistines had said, "Otherwise, the Hebrews will make swords or spears." So all the Israelites went to the Philistines to sharpen their plows, mattocks, axes, and sickles. The price was two-thirds of a shekel for plows and mattocks, and one-third of a shekel for pitchforks and axes, and for putting a point on a cattle prod. So on the day of battle not a sword or spear could be found in the hand of any of the troops who were with Saul and Jonathan; only Saul and his son Jonathan had weapons.

14 Now a Philistine garrison took control of the pass at Michmash. That same day Saul's son Jonathan said to the attendant who carried his weapons, "Come on, let's cross over to the Philistine garrison on the other side." However, he did not tell his father.

Saul was staying under the pomegranate tree in Migron on the outskirts of Gibeah. The troops with him numbered about six hundred. Ahijah, who was wearing an ephod, was also there. He was the son of Ahitub, the brother of Ichabod son of Phinehas, son of Eli the LORD's priest at Shiloh. But the troops did not know that Jonathan had left.

There were sharp columns of rock on both sides of the pass that Jonathan intended to cross to reach the Philistine garrison. One was named Bozez and the other Seneh; one stood to the north
10 in front of Michmash and the other to the south in front of Geba. Jonathan said to the attendant who carried his weapons, "Come on, let's cross over to the garrison of these uncircumcised men. Perhaps the LORD will help us. Nothing can keep the LORD from saving, whether by many or by few."

His armor-bearer responded, "Do what is in your heart. Go ahead! I'm completely with you."

"All right," Jonathan replied, "we'll cross over to the men and then let them see us. If they say, 'Wait until we reach you,' then we will stay where we are and not go up to them. But if they say, 'Come on up,' then we'll go up, because the LORD has handed them over to us—that will be our sign."

They let themselves be seen by the Philistine garrison, and the Philistines said, "Look, the
20 Hebrews are coming out of the holes where they've been hiding!" The men of the garrison called to Jonathan and his armor-bearer. "Come on up, and we'll teach you a lesson!" they said.

"Follow me," Jonathan told his armor-bearer, "for the LORD has handed them over to Israel." Jonathan climbed up using his hands and feet, with his armor-bearer behind him. Jonathan cut them down, and his armor-bearer followed and finished them off. In that first assault Jonathan and his armor-bearer struck down about twenty men in a half-acre field.

Terror spread through the Philistine camp and the open fields to all the troops. Even the garrison and the raiding parties were terrified. The earth shook, and terror spread from God. When Saul's watchmen in Gibeah of Benjamin looked, they saw the panicking troops scattering in every direction. So Saul said to the troops with him, "Call the roll and determine who has left us." They
30 called the roll and saw that Jonathan and his armor-bearer were gone.

Saul told Ahijah, "Bring the ark of God," for it was with the Israelites at that time. While Saul spoke to the priest, the panic in the Philistine camp increased in intensity. So Saul said to the priest, "Stop what you're doing."

Saul and all the troops with him assembled and marched to the battle, and there the Philistines were, fighting against each other in great confusion! There were Hebrews from the area who had gone earlier into the camp to join the Philistines, but even they joined the Israelites who were with Saul and Jonathan. When all the Israelite men who had been hiding in the hill country of Ephraim heard that the Philistines were fleeing, they also joined Saul and Jonathan in the battle. So the Lord saved Israel that day.

40 The battle extended beyond Beth-aven, and the men of Israel were worn out that day, for Saul had placed the troops under an oath: "The man who eats food before evening, before I have taken vengeance on my enemies is cursed." So none of the troops tasted any food.

Everyone went into the forest, and there was honey on the ground. When the troops entered the forest, they saw the flow of honey, but none of them ate any of it because they feared the oath. However, Jonathan had not heard his father make the troops swear the oath. He reached out with the end of the staff he was carrying and dipped it into the honeycomb. When he ate the honey, he had renewed energy. Then one of the troops said, "Your father made the troops solemnly swear, 'The man who eats food today is cursed,' and the troops are exhausted."

Jonathan replied, "My father has brought trouble to the land. Just look at how I have renewed 50 energy because I tasted a little of this honey. How much better if the troops had eaten freely today from the plunder they took from their enemies! Then the slaughter of the Philistines would have been much greater."

The Israelites struck down the Philistines that day from Michmash all the way to Aijalon. Since the Israelites were completely exhausted, they rushed to the plunder, took sheep, goats, cattle, and calves, slaughtered them on the ground, and ate meat with the blood still in it. Some reported to Saul, "Look, the troops are sinning against the Lord by eating meat with the blood still in it."

Saul said, "You have been unfaithful. Roll a large stone over here at once." He then said, "Go among the troops and say to them, 'Let each man bring me his ox or his sheep. Do the slaughtering 60 here and then you can eat. Don't sin against the Lord by eating meat with the blood in it.'" So every one of the troops brought his ox that night and slaughtered it there. Then Saul built an altar to the Lord; it was the first time he had built an altar to the Lord.

Saul said, "Let's go down after the Philistines tonight and plunder them until morning. Don't let even one remain!"

"Do whatever you want," the troops replied.

But the priest said, "Let's approach God here."

So Saul inquired of God, "Should I go after the Philistines? Will you hand them over to Israel?" But God did not answer him that day.

Saul said, "All you leaders of the troops, come here. Let's investigate how this sin has occurred 70 today. As surely as the Lord lives who saves Israel, even if it is because of my son Jonathan, he must die!" Not one of the troops answered him.

So he said to all Israel, "You will be on one side, and I and my son Jonathan will be on the other side."

And the troops replied, "Do whatever you want."

So Saul said to the LORD, "God of Israel, why have you not answered your servant today? If the unrighteousness is in me or in my son Jonathan, LORD God of Israel, give Urim; but if the fault is in your people Israel, give Thummim." Jonathan and Saul were selected, and the troops were cleared of the charge.

Then Saul said, "Cast the lot between me and my son Jonathan," and Jonathan was selected. 80 Saul commanded him, "Tell me what you did."

Jonathan told him, "I tasted a little honey with the end of the staff I was carrying. I am ready to die!"

Saul declared to him, "May God punish me and do so severely if you do not die, Jonathan!"

But the people said to Saul, "Must Jonathan die? He accomplished such a great deliverance for Israel! No, as the LORD lives, not a hair of his head will fall to the ground, for he worked with God's help today." So the people redeemed Jonathan, and he did not die. Then Saul gave up the pursuit of the Philistines, and the Philistines returned to their own territory.

When Saul assumed the kingship over Israel, he fought against all his enemies in every direction: against Moab, the Ammonites, Edom, the kings of Zobah, and the Philistines. Wherever he 90 turned, he caused havoc. He fought bravely, defeated the Amalekites, and rescued Israel from those who plundered them.

Saul's sons were Jonathan, Ishvi, and Malchishua. The names of his two daughters were Merab, his firstborn, and Michal, the younger. The name of Saul's wife was Ahinoam daughter of Ahimaaz. The name of the commander of his army was Abner son of Saul's uncle Ner. Saul's father was Kish. Abner's father was Ner son of Abiel.

The conflict with the Philistines was fierce all of Saul's days, so whenever Saul noticed any strong or valiant man, he enlisted him.

15 Samuel told Saul, "The LORD sent me to anoint you as king over his people Israel. Now, listen to the words of the LORD. This is what the LORD of Armies says: 'I witnessed what the Amalekites did to the Israelites when they opposed them along the way as they were coming out of Egypt. Now go and attack the Amalekites and completely destroy everything they have. Do not spare them. Kill men and women, infants and nursing babies, oxen and sheep, camels and donkeys.'"

Then Saul summoned the troops and counted them at Telaim: two hundred thousand foot soldiers and ten thousand men from Judah. Saul came to the city of Amalek and set up an ambush in the wadi. He warned the Kenites, "Since you showed kindness to all the Israelites when they came out of Egypt, go on and leave! Get away from the Amalekites, or I'll sweep you away with 10 them." So the Kenites withdrew from the Amalekites.

Then Saul struck down the Amalekites from Havilah all the way to Shur, which is next to Egypt. He captured King Agag of Amalek alive, but he completely destroyed all the rest of the people with the sword. Saul and the troops spared Agag, and the best of the sheep, goats, cattle, and choice animals, as well as the young rams and the best of everything else. They were not willing to destroy them, but they did destroy all the worthless and unwanted things.

Then the word of the LORD came to Samuel, "I regret that I made Saul king, for he has turned away from following me and has not carried out my instructions." So Samuel became angry and cried out to the LORD all night.

Early in the morning Samuel got up to confront Saul, but it was reported to Samuel, "Saul
20 went to Carmel where he set up a monument for himself. Then he turned around and went down to Gilgal." When Samuel came to him, Saul said, "May the LORD bless you. I have carried out the LORD's instructions."

Samuel replied, "Then what is this sound of sheep, goats, and cattle I hear?"

Saul answered, "The troops brought them from the Amalekites and spared the best sheep, goats, and cattle in order to offer a sacrifice to the LORD your God, but the rest we destroyed."

"Stop!" exclaimed Samuel. "Let me tell you what the LORD said to me last night."

"Tell me," he replied.

Samuel continued, "Although you once considered yourself unimportant, haven't you become
30 the leader of the tribes of Israel? The LORD anointed you king over Israel and then sent you on a mission and said, 'Go and completely destroy the sinful Amalekites. Fight against them until you have annihilated them.' So why didn't you obey the LORD? Why did you rush on the plunder and do what was evil in the LORD's sight?"

"But I did obey the LORD!" Saul answered. "I went on the mission the LORD gave me: I brought back King Agag of Amalek, and I completely destroyed the Amalekites. The troops took sheep, goats, and cattle from the plunder—the best of what was set apart for destruction—to sacrifice to the LORD your God at Gilgal."

Then Samuel said:

Does the LORD take pleasure in burnt offerings and sacrifices
40   as much as in obeying the LORD?

Look: to obey is better than sacrifice,
    to pay attention is better than the fat of rams.
For rebellion is like the sin of divination,
    and defiance is like wickedness and idolatry.
Because you have rejected the word of the LORD,
    he has rejected you as king.

Saul answered Samuel, "I have sinned. I have transgressed the LORD's command and your words. Because I was afraid of the people, I obeyed them. Now therefore, please forgive my sin and return with me so I can worship the LORD."

50 Samuel replied to Saul, "I will not return with you. Because you rejected the word of the LORD, the LORD has rejected you from being king over Israel." When Samuel turned to go, Saul grabbed the corner of his robe, and it tore. Samuel said to him, "The LORD has torn the kingship of Israel away from you today and has given it to your neighbor who is better than you. Furthermore, the Eternal One of Israel does not lie or change his mind, for he is not man who changes his mind."

Saul said, "I have sinned. Please honor me now before the elders of my people and before Israel. Come back with me so I can bow in worship to the LORD your God." Then Samuel went back, following Saul, and Saul bowed down to the LORD.

Samuel said, "Bring me King Agag of Amalek."

Agag came to him trembling, for he thought, "Certainly the bitterness of death has come."

60 Samuel declared:

> As your sword has made women childless,
> so your mother will be childless among women.

Then he hacked Agag to pieces before the LORD at Gilgal.

Samuel went to Ramah, and Saul went up to his home in Gibeah of Saul. Even to the day of his death, Samuel never saw Saul again. Samuel mourned for Saul, and the LORD regretted he had made Saul king over Israel.

16 The LORD said to Samuel, "How long are you going to mourn for Saul, since I have rejected him as king over Israel? Fill your horn with oil and go. I am sending you to Jesse of Bethlehem because I have selected for myself a king from his sons."

Samuel asked, "How can I go? Saul will hear about it and kill me!"

The LORD answered, "Take a young cow with you and say, 'I have come to sacrifice to the LORD.' Then invite Jesse to the sacrifice, and I will let you know what you are to do. You are to anoint for me the one I indicate to you."

Samuel did what the LORD directed and went to Bethlehem. When the elders of the town met him, they trembled and asked, "Do you come in peace?"

10 "In peace," he replied. "I've come to sacrifice to the LORD. Consecrate yourselves and come with me to the sacrifice." Then he consecrated Jesse and his sons and invited them to the sacrifice. When they arrived, Samuel saw Eliab and said, "Certainly the LORD's anointed one is here before him."

But the LORD said to Samuel, "Do not look at his appearance or his stature because I have rejected him. Humans do not see what the LORD sees, for humans see what is visible, but the LORD sees the heart."

Jesse called Abinadab and presented him to Samuel. "The LORD hasn't chosen this one either," Samuel said. Then Jesse presented Shammah, but Samuel said, "The LORD hasn't chosen this one either." After Jesse presented seven of his sons to him, Samuel told Jesse, "The LORD hasn't chosen

20 any of these." Samuel asked him, "Are these all the sons you have?"

"There is still the youngest," he answered, "but right now he's tending the sheep." Samuel told Jesse, "Send for him. We won't sit down to eat until he gets here." So Jesse sent for him. He had beautiful eyes and a healthy, handsome appearance.

Then the LORD said, "Anoint him, for he is the one." So Samuel took the horn of oil and anointed him in the presence of his brothers, and the Spirit of the LORD came powerfully on David from that day forward. Then Samuel set out and went to Ramah.

Now the Spirit of the LORD had left Saul, and an evil spirit sent from the LORD began to torment him, so Saul's servants said to him, "You see that an evil spirit from God is tormenting you. Let our lord command your servants here in your presence to look for someone who knows how to 30 play the lyre. Whenever the evil spirit from God comes on you, that person can play the lyre, and you will feel better."

Then Saul commanded his servants, "Find me someone who plays well and bring him to me."

One of the young men answered, "I have seen a son of Jesse of Bethlehem who knows how to play the lyre. He is also a valiant man, a warrior, eloquent, handsome, and the LORD is with him."

Then Saul dispatched messengers to Jesse and said, "Send me your son David, who is with the sheep." So Jesse took a donkey loaded with bread, a wineskin, and one young goat and sent them by his son David to Saul. When David came to Saul and entered his service, Saul loved him very much, and David became his armor-bearer. Then Saul sent word to Jesse: "Let David remain in my service, for he has found favor with me." Whenever the spirit from God came on Saul, David 40 would pick up his lyre and play, and Saul would then be relieved, feel better, and the evil spirit would leave him.

17 The Philistines gathered their forces for war at Socoh in Judah and camped between Socoh and Azekah in Ephes-dammim. Saul and the men of Israel gathered and camped in the Valley of Elah; then they lined up in battle formation to face the Philistines.

The Philistines were standing on one hill, and the Israelites were standing on another hill with a ravine between them. Then a champion named Goliath, from Gath, came out from the Philistine camp. He was nine feet, nine inches tall and wore a bronze helmet and bronze scale armor that weighed one hundred twenty-five pounds. There was bronze armor on his shins, and a bronze javelin was slung between his shoulders. His spear shaft was like a weaver's beam, and the iron point of his spear weighed fifteen pounds. In addition, a shield-bearer was walking in front of 10 him.

He stood and shouted to the Israelite battle formations, "Why do you come out to line up in battle formation?" He asked them, "Am I not a Philistine and are you not servants of Saul? Choose one of your men and have him come down against me. If he wins in a fight against me and kills me, we will be your servants. But if I win against him and kill him, then you will be our servants and serve us." Then the Philistine said, "I defy the ranks of Israel today. Send me a man so we can fight each other!" When Saul and all Israel heard these words from the Philistine, they lost their courage and were terrified.

Now David was the son of the Ephrathite from Bethlehem of Judah named Jesse. Jesse had eight sons and during Saul's reign was already an old man. Jesse's three oldest sons had followed
20 Saul to the war, and their names were Eliab, the firstborn, Abinadab, the next, and Shammah, the third, and David was the youngest. The three oldest had followed Saul, but David kept going back and forth from Saul to tend his father's flock in Bethlehem.

Every morning and evening for forty days the Philistine came forward and took his stand. One day Jesse had told his son David, "Take this half-bushel of roasted grain along with these ten loaves of bread for your brothers and hurry to their camp. Also take these ten portions of cheese to the field commander. Check on the well-being of your brothers and bring a confirmation from them. They are with Saul and all the men of Israel in the Valley of Elah fighting with the Philistines."

So David got up early in the morning, left the flock with someone to keep it, loaded up, and set out as Jesse had charged him.

30 He arrived at the perimeter of the camp as the army was marching out to its battle formation shouting their battle cry. Israel and the Philistines lined up in battle formation facing each other. David left his supplies in the care of the quartermaster and ran to the battle line. When he arrived, he asked his brothers how they were. While he was speaking with them, suddenly the champion named Goliath, the Philistine from Gath, came forward from the Philistine battle line and shouted his usual words, which David heard. When all the Israelite men saw Goliath, they retreated from him terrified.

Previously, an Israelite man had declared, "Do you see this man who keeps coming out? He comes to defy Israel. The king will make the man who kills him very rich and will give him his daughter. The king will also make the family of that man's father exempt from paying taxes in Israel."

40 David spoke to the men who were standing with him: "What will be done for the man who kills that Philistine and removes this disgrace from Israel? Just who is this uncircumcised Philistine that he should defy the armies of the living God?"

The troops told him about the offer, concluding, "That is what will be done for the man who kills him."

David's oldest brother Eliab listened as he spoke to the men, and he became angry with him. "Why did you come down here?" he asked. "Who did you leave those few sheep with in the wilderness? I know your arrogance and your evil heart—you came down to see the battle!"

"What have I done now?" protested David. "It was just a question." Then he turned from those beside him to others in front of him and asked about the offer. The people gave him the same
50 answer as before.

What David said was overheard and reported to Saul, so he had David brought to him. David said to Saul, "Don't let anyone be discouraged by him; your servant will go and fight this Philistine!"

But Saul replied, "You can't go fight this Philistine. You're just a youth, and he's been a warrior since he was young."

David answered Saul, "Your servant has been tending his father's sheep. Whenever a lion or a bear came and carried off a lamb from the flock, I went after it, struck it down, and rescued the lamb from its mouth. If it reared up against me, I would grab it by its fur, strike it down, and kill it. Your servant has killed lions and bears; this uncircumcised Philistine will be like one of them, for he has defied the armies of the living God." Then David said, "The LORD who rescued me from the paw of the lion and the paw of the bear will rescue me from the hand of this Philistine."

Saul said to David, "Go, and may the LORD be with you."

Then Saul had his own military clothes put on David. He put a bronze helmet on David's head and had him put on armor. David strapped his sword on over the military clothes and tried to walk, but he was not used to them. "I can't walk in these," David said to Saul, "I'm not used to them." So David took them off. Instead, he took his staff in his hand and chose five smooth stones from the wadi and put them in the pouch, in his shepherd's bag. Then, with his sling in his hand, he approached the Philistine.

The Philistine came closer and closer to David, with the shield-bearer in front of him. When the Philistine looked and saw David, he despised him because he was just a youth, healthy and handsome. He said to David, "Am I a dog that you come against me with sticks?" Then he cursed David by his gods. "Come here," the Philistine called to David, "and I'll give your flesh to the birds of the sky and the wild beasts!"

David said to the Philistine, "You come against me with a sword, spear, and javelin, but I come against you in the name of the LORD of Armies, the God of the ranks of Israel—you have defied him. Today, the LORD will hand you over to me. Today, I'll strike you down, remove your head, and give the corpses of the Philistine camp to the birds of the sky and the wild creatures of the earth. Then all the world will know that Israel has a God, and this whole assembly will know that it is not by sword or by spear that the LORD saves, for the battle is the LORD's. He will hand you over to us."

When the Philistine started forward to attack him, David ran quickly to the battle line to meet the Philistine. David put his hand in the bag, took out a stone, slung it, and hit the Philistine on his forehead. The stone sank into his forehead, and he fell facedown to the ground. David defeated the Philistine with a sling and a stone. David overpowered the Philistine and killed him without having a sword. David ran and stood over him. He grabbed the Philistine's sword, pulled it from its sheath, and used it to kill him. Then he cut off his head. When the Philistines saw that their hero was dead, they fled. The men of Israel and Judah rallied, shouting their battle cry, and chased the Philistines to the entrance of the valley and to the gates of Ekron. Philistine bodies were strewn all along the Shaaraim road to Gath and Ekron.

When the Israelites returned from the pursuit of the Philistines, they plundered their camps. David took Goliath's head and brought it to Jerusalem, but he put Goliath's weapons in his own tent.

When Saul had seen David going out to confront the Philistine, he asked Abner the commander of the army, "Whose son is this youth, Abner?"

"Your Majesty, as surely as you live, I don't know," Abner replied.

The king said, "Find out whose son this young man is!"

When David returned from killing the Philistine, Abner took him and brought him before Saul with the Philistine's head still in his hand. Saul said to him, "Whose son are you, young man?"

"The son of your servant Jesse of Bethlehem," David answered.

18 When David had finished speaking with Saul, Jonathan was bound to David in close friendship, and loved him as much as he loved himself. Saul kept David with him from that day on and did not let him return to his father's house.

Jonathan made a covenant with David because he loved him as much as himself. Then Jonathan removed the robe he was wearing and gave it to David, along with his military tunic, his sword, his bow, and his belt.

David marched out with the army and was successful in everything Saul sent him to do. Saul put him in command of the fighting men, which pleased all the people and Saul's servants as well.

As the troops were coming back, when David was returning from killing the Philistine,
10 the women came out from all the cities of Israel to meet King Saul, singing and dancing with tambourines, with shouts of joy, and with three-stringed instruments. As they danced, the women sang:

> Saul has killed his thousands,
> but David his tens of thousands.

Saul was furious and resented this song. "They credited tens of thousands to David," he complained, "but they only credited me with thousands. What more can he have but the kingdom?" So Saul watched David jealously from that day forward.

The next day an evil spirit sent from God came powerfully on Saul, and he began to rave inside the palace. David was playing the lyre as usual, but Saul was holding a spear, and he threw it,
20 thinking, "I'll pin David to the wall." But David got away from him twice.

Saul was afraid of David, because the LORD was with David but had left Saul. Therefore, Saul sent David away from him and made him commander over a thousand men. David led the troops and continued to be successful in all his activities because the LORD was with him. When Saul observed that David was very successful, he dreaded him. But all Israel and Judah loved David because he was leading their troops. Saul told David, "Here is my oldest daughter Merab. I'll give her to you as a wife if you will be a warrior for me and fight the LORD's battles." But Saul was thinking, "I don't need to raise a hand against him; let the hand of the Philistines be against him."

Then David responded, "Who am I, and what is my family or my father's clan in Israel that I should become the king's son-in-law?" When it was time to give Saul's daughter Merab to David, she was given to Adriel the Meholathite as a wife.

Now Saul's daughter Michal loved David, and when it was reported to Saul, it pleased him. "I'll give her to him," Saul thought. "She'll be a trap for him, and the hand of the Philistines will be against him." So Saul said to David a second time, "You can now be my son-in-law."

Saul then ordered his servants, "Speak to David in private and tell him, 'Look, the king is pleased with you, and all his servants love you. Therefore, you should become the king's son-in-law.'"

Saul's servants reported these words directly to David, but he replied, "Is it trivial in your sight to become the king's son-in-law? I am a poor commoner."

The servants reported back to Saul, "These are the words David spoke."

Then Saul replied, "Say this to David: 'The king desires no other bride-price except a hundred Philistine foreskins, to take revenge on his enemies.'" Actually, Saul intended to cause David's death at the hands of the Philistines.

When the servants reported these terms to David, he was pleased to become the king's son-in-law. Before the wedding day arrived, David and his men went out and killed two hundred Philistines. He brought their foreskins and presented them as full payment to the king to become his son-in-law. Then Saul gave his daughter Michal to David as his wife. Saul realized that the LORD was with David and that his daughter Michal loved him, and he became even more afraid of David. As a result, Saul was David's enemy from then on.

Every time the Philistine commanders came out to fight, David was more successful than all of Saul's officers. So his name became well known.

19 Saul ordered his son Jonathan and all his servants to kill David. But Saul's son Jonathan liked David very much, so he told him, "My father, Saul, intends to kill you. Be on your guard in the morning and hide in a secret place and stay there. I'll go out and stand beside my father in the field where you are and talk to him about you. When I see what he says, I'll tell you."

Jonathan spoke well of David to his father, Saul. He said to him, "The king should not sin against his servant David. He hasn't sinned against you; in fact, his actions have been a great advantage to you. He took his life in his hands when he struck down the Philistine, and the LORD brought about a great victory for all Israel. You saw it and rejoiced, so why would you sin against innocent blood by killing David for no reason?"

Saul listened to Jonathan's advice and swore an oath: "As surely as the LORD lives, David will not be killed." So Jonathan summoned David and told him all these words. Then Jonathan brought David to Saul, and he served him as he did before.

When war broke out again, David went out and fought against the Philistines. He defeated them with such great force that they fled from him.

Now an evil spirit sent from the LORD came on Saul as he was sitting in his palace holding a spear. David was playing the lyre, and Saul tried to pin David to the wall with the spear. As the spear struck the wall, David eluded Saul, ran away, and escaped that night. Saul sent agents to David's house to watch for him and kill him in the morning. But his wife Michal warned David, "If you don't escape tonight, you will be dead tomorrow!" So she lowered David from the window, and he fled and escaped. Then Michal took the household idol and put it on the bed, placed some goat hair on its head, and covered it with a garment. When Saul sent agents to seize David, Michal said, "He's sick."

Saul sent the agents back to see David and said, "Bring him on his bed so I can kill him." When the agents arrived, to their surprise, the household idol was on the bed with some goat hair on its head.

Saul asked Michal, "Why did you deceive me like this? You sent my enemy away, and he has escaped!"

She answered him, "He said to me, 'Let me go! Why should I kill you?'"

So David fled and escaped and went to Samuel at Ramah and told him everything Saul had done to him. Then he and Samuel left and stayed at Naioth.

When it was reported to Saul that David was at Naioth in Ramah, he sent agents to seize David. However, when they saw the group of prophets prophesying with Samuel leading them, the Spirit of God came on Saul's agents, and they also started prophesying. When they reported to Saul, he sent other agents, and they also began prophesying. So Saul tried again and sent a third group of agents, and even they began prophesying. Then Saul himself went to Ramah. He came to the large cistern at Secu and asked, "Where are Samuel and David?"

"At Naioth in Ramah," someone said.

So he went to Naioth in Ramah. The Spirit of God also came on him, and as he walked along, he prophesied until he entered Naioth in Ramah. Saul then removed his clothes and also prophesied before Samuel; he collapsed and lay naked all that day and all that night. That is why they say, "Is Saul also among the prophets?"

20 David fled from Naioth in Ramah and came to Jonathan and asked, "What have I done? What did I do wrong? How have I sinned against your father so that he wants to take my life?"

Jonathan said to him, "No, you won't die. Listen, my father doesn't do anything, great or small, without telling me. So why would he hide this matter from me? This can't be true."

But David said, "Your father certainly knows that I have found favor with you. He has said, 'Jonathan must not know of this, or else he will be grieved.'" David also swore, "As surely as the LORD lives and as you yourself live, there is but a step between me and death."

Jonathan said to David, "Whatever you say, I will do for you."

So David told him, "Look, tomorrow is the New Moon, and I'm supposed to sit down and eat with the king. Instead, let me go, and I'll hide in the countryside for the next two nights. If your father misses me at all, say, 'David urgently requested my permission to go quickly to his hometown, Bethlehem, for an annual sacrifice there involving the whole clan.' If he says, 'Good,' then your servant is safe, but if he becomes angry, you will know he has evil intentions. Deal kindly with your servant, for you have brought me into a covenant with you before the LORD. If I have done anything wrong, then kill me yourself; why take me to your father?"

"No!" Jonathan responded. "If I ever find out my father has evil intentions against you, wouldn't I tell you about it?"

So David asked Jonathan, "Who will tell me if your father answers you harshly?"

He answered David, "Come on, let's go out to the countryside." So both of them went out to the countryside. "By the LORD, the God of Israel, I will sound out my father by this time tomorrow or the next day. If I find out that he is favorable toward you, will I not send for you and tell you? If my father intends to bring evil on you, may the LORD punish Jonathan and do so severely if I do not tell you and send you away so you may leave safely. May the LORD be with you, just as he was with my father. If I continue to live, show me kindness from the LORD, but if I die, don't ever withdraw your kindness from my household—not even when the LORD cuts off every one of David's enemies from the face of the earth." Then Jonathan made a covenant with the house of David, saying, "May the LORD hold David's enemies accountable." Jonathan once again swore to David in his love for him, because he loved him as he loved himself.

Then Jonathan said to him, "Tomorrow is the New Moon; you'll be missed because your seat will be empty. The following day hurry down and go to the place where you hid on the day this incident began and stay beside the rock Ezel. I will shoot three arrows beside it as if I'm aiming at a target. Then I will send a servant and say, 'Go and find the arrows!' Now, if I expressly say to the servant, 'Look, the arrows are on this side of you—get them,' then come, because as the LORD lives, it is safe for you and there is no problem. But if I say this to the youth, 'Look, the arrows are beyond you!' then go, for the LORD is sending you away. As for the matter you and I have spoken about, the LORD will be a witness between you and me forever." So David hid in the countryside.

At the New Moon, the king sat down to eat the meal. He sat at his usual place on the seat by the wall. Jonathan sat facing him and Abner took his place beside Saul, but David's place was empty. Saul did not say anything that day because he thought, "Something unexpected has happened; he must be ceremonially unclean—yes, that's it, he is unclean."

However, the day after the New Moon, the second day, David's place was still empty, and Saul asked his son Jonathan, "Why didn't Jesse's son come to the meal either yesterday or today?"

Jonathan answered, "David asked for my permission to go to Bethlehem. He said, 'Please let me go because our clan is holding a sacrifice in the town, and my brother has told me to be there. So now, if I have found favor with you, let me go so I can see my brothers.' That's why he didn't come to the king's table."

Then Saul became angry with Jonathan and shouted, "You son of a perverse and rebellious woman! Don't I know that you are siding with Jesse's son to your own shame and to the disgrace

of your mother? Every day Jesse's son lives on earth you and your kingship are not secure. Now
50 send for him and bring him to me—he must die!"

Jonathan answered his father back, "Why is he to be killed? What has he done?"

Then Saul threw his spear at Jonathan to kill him, so he knew that his father was determined to kill David. He got up from the table fiercely angry and did not eat any food that second day of the New Moon, for he was grieved because of his father's shameful behavior toward David.

In the morning Jonathan went out to the countryside for the appointed meeting with David. A young servant was with him. He said to the servant, "Run and find the arrows I'm shooting." As the servant ran, Jonathan shot an arrow beyond him. He came to the location of the arrow that Jonathan had shot, but Jonathan called to him and said, "The arrow is beyond you, isn't it?" Then Jonathan called to him, "Hurry up and don't stop!" Jonathan's servant picked up the
60 arrow and returned to his master. He did not know anything; only Jonathan and David knew the arrangement. Then Jonathan gave his equipment to the servant who was with him and said, "Go, take it back to the city."

When the servant had gone, David got up from the south side of the stone Ezel, fell facedown to the ground, and paid homage three times. Then he and Jonathan kissed each other and wept with each other, though David wept more.

Jonathan then said to David, "Go in the assurance the two of us pledged in the name of the Lord when we said, 'The Lord will be a witness between you and me and between my offspring and your offspring forever.'" Then David left, and Jonathan went into the city.

21 David went to the priest Ahimelech at Nob. Ahimelech was afraid to meet David, so he said to him, "Why are you alone and no one is with you?"

David answered the priest Ahimelech, "The king gave me a mission, but he told me, 'Don't let anyone know anything about the mission I'm sending you on or what I have ordered you to do.' I have stationed my young men at a certain place. Now what do you have on hand? Give me five loaves of bread or whatever can be found."

The priest told him, "There is no ordinary bread on hand. However, there is consecrated bread, but the young men may eat it only if they have kept themselves from women."

David answered him, "I swear that women are being kept from us, as always when I go out to
10 battle. The young men's bodies are consecrated even on an ordinary mission, so of course their bodies are consecrated today." So the priest gave him the consecrated bread, for there was no bread there except the Bread of the Presence that had been removed from the presence of the Lord. When the bread was removed, it had been replaced with warm bread.

One of Saul's servants, detained before the Lord, was there that day. His name was Doeg the Edomite, chief of Saul's shepherds.

David said to Ahimelech, "Do you have a spear or sword on hand? I didn't even bring my sword or my weapons since the king's mission was urgent."

The priest replied, "The sword of Goliath the Philistine, whom you killed in the Valley of Elah, is here, wrapped in a cloth behind the ephod. If you want to take it for yourself, then take it, for there isn't another one here."

"There's none like it!" David said. "Give it to me."

David fled that day from Saul's presence and went to King Achish of Gath. But Achish's servants said to him, "Isn't this David, the king of the land? Don't they sing about him during their dances:

> Saul has killed his thousands,
> but David his tens of thousands?"

David took this to heart and became very afraid of King Achish of Gath, so he pretended to be insane in their presence. He acted like a madman around them, scribbling on the doors of the city gate and letting saliva run down his beard.

"Look! You can see the man is crazy," Achish said to his servants. "Why did you bring him to me? Do I have such a shortage of crazy people that you brought this one to act crazy around me? Is this one going to come into my house?"

22 So David left Gath and took refuge in the cave of Adullam. When David's brothers and his father's whole family heard, they went down and joined him there. In addition, every man who was desperate, in debt, or discontented rallied around him, and he became their leader. About four hundred men were with him.

From there David went to Mizpeh of Moab where he said to the king of Moab, "Please let my father and mother stay with you until I know what God will do for me." So he left them in the care of the king of Moab, and they stayed with him the whole time David was in the stronghold.

Then the prophet Gad said to David, "Don't stay in the stronghold. Leave and return to the land of Judah." So David left and went to the forest of Hereth.

Saul heard that David and his men had been discovered. At that time Saul was in Gibeah, sitting under the tamarisk tree at the high place. His spear was in his hand, and all his servants were standing around him. Saul said to his servants, "Listen, men of Benjamin: Is Jesse's son going to give all of you fields and vineyards? Do you think he'll make all of you commanders of thousands and commanders of hundreds? That's why all of you have conspired against me! Nobody tells me when my own son makes a covenant with Jesse's son. None of you cares about me or tells me that my son has stirred up my own servant to wait in ambush for me, as is the case today."

Then Doeg the Edomite, who was in charge of Saul's servants, answered, "I saw Jesse's son come to Ahimelech son of Ahitub at Nob. Ahimelech inquired of the LORD for him and gave him provisions. He also gave him the sword of Goliath the Philistine."

The king sent messengers to summon the priest Ahimelech son of Ahitub, and his father's whole family, who were priests in Nob. All of them came to the king. Then Saul said, "Listen, son of Ahitub!"

"I'm at your service, my lord," he said.

Saul asked him, "Why did you and Jesse's son conspire against me? You gave him bread and a sword and inquired of God for him, so he could rise up against me and wait in ambush, as is the case today."

Ahimelech replied to the king, "Who among all your servants is as faithful as David? He is the king's son-in-law, captain of your bodyguard, and honored in your house. Was today the first time I inquired of God for him? Of course not! Please don't let the king make an accusation against your servant or any of my father's family, for your servant didn't have any idea about all this."

But the king said, "You will die, Ahimelech—you and your father's whole family!"

Then the king ordered the guards standing by him, "Turn and kill the priests of the LORD because they sided with David. For they knew he was fleeing, but they didn't tell me." But the king's servants would not lift a hand to execute the priests of the LORD.

So the king said to Doeg, "Go and execute the priests!" So Doeg the Edomite went and executed the priests himself. On that day, he killed eighty-five men who wore linen ephods. He also struck down Nob, the city of the priests, with the sword—both men and women, infants and nursing babies, oxen, donkeys, and sheep.

However, one of the sons of Ahimelech son of Ahitub escaped. His name was Abiathar, and he fled to David. Abiathar told David that Saul had killed the priests of the LORD. Then David said to Abiathar, "I knew that Doeg the Edomite was there that day and that he was sure to report to Saul. I myself am responsible for the lives of everyone in your father's family. Stay with me. Don't be afraid, for the one who wants to take my life wants to take your life. You will be safe with me."

23 It was reported to David, "Look, the Philistines are fighting against Keilah and raiding the threshing floors."

So David inquired of the LORD: "Should I launch an attack against these Philistines?"

The LORD answered David, "Launch an attack against the Philistines and rescue Keilah."

But David's men said to him, "Look, we're afraid here in Judah; how much more if we go to Keilah against the Philistine forces!"

Once again, David inquired of the LORD, and the LORD answered him, "Go at once to Keilah, for I will hand the Philistines over to you." Then David and his men went to Keilah, fought against the Philistines, drove their livestock away, and inflicted heavy losses on them. So David rescued the inhabitants of Keilah. Abiathar son of Ahimelech fled to David at Keilah, and he brought an ephod with him.

When it was reported to Saul that David had gone to Keilah, he said, "God has handed him over to me, for he has trapped himself by entering a town with barred gates." Then Saul summoned all the troops to go to war at Keilah and besiege David and his men.

When David learned that Saul was plotting evil against him, he said to the priest Abiathar, "Bring the ephod."

Then David said, "Lord God of Israel, your servant has reliable information that Saul intends to come to Keilah and destroy the town because of me. Will the citizens of Keilah hand me over to him? Will Saul come down as your servant has heard? Lord God of Israel, please tell your servant."

20 The Lord answered, "He will come down."

Then David asked, "Will the citizens of Keilah hand me and my men over to Saul?"

"They will," the Lord responded.

So David and his men, numbering about six hundred, left Keilah at once and moved from place to place. When it was reported to Saul that David had escaped from Keilah, he called off the expedition. David then stayed in the wilderness strongholds and in the hill country of the Wilderness of Ziph. Saul searched for him every day, but God did not hand David over to him.

David was in the Wilderness of Ziph in Horesh when he saw that Saul had come out to take his life. Then Saul's son Jonathan came to David in Horesh and encouraged him in his faith in God, saying, "Don't be afraid, for my father Saul will never lay a hand on you. You yourself will be king 30 over Israel, and I'll be your second-in-command. Even my father Saul knows it is true." Then the two of them made a covenant in the Lord's presence. Afterward, David remained in Horesh, while Jonathan went home.

Some Ziphites came up to Saul at Gibeah and said, "Isn't it true that David is hiding among us in the strongholds in Horesh on the hill of Hachilah south of Jeshimon? So now, whenever the king wants to come down, let him come down. As for us, we will be glad to hand him over to the king."

"May you be blessed by the Lord," replied Saul, "for you have shown concern for me. Go and check again. Investigate where he goes and who has seen him there; they tell me he is extremely cunning. Investigate all the places where he hides. Then come back to me with accurate information, and I'll go with you. If it turns out he really is in the region, I'll search for him among 40 all the clans of Judah." So they went to Ziph ahead of Saul.

Now David and his men were in the wilderness near Maon in the Arabah south of Jeshimon, and Saul and his men went to look for him. When David was told about it, he went down to the rock and stayed in the Wilderness of Maon. Saul heard of this and pursued David there.

Saul went along one side of the mountain and David and his men went along the other side. Even though David was hurrying to get away from Saul, Saul and his men were closing in on David and his men to capture them. Then a messenger came to Saul saying, "Come quickly, because the Philistines have raided the land!" So Saul broke off his pursuit of David and went to engage the Philistines. Therefore, that place was named the Rock of Separation. From there David went up and stayed in the strongholds of En-gedi.

24 When Saul returned from pursuing the Philistines, he was told, "David is in the wilderness near En-gedi." So Saul took three thousand of Israel's fit young men and went to look for David and his men in front of the Rocks of the Wild Goats. When Saul came to the sheep pens along the road, a cave was there, and he went in to relieve himself. David and his men were staying in the recesses of the cave, so they said to him, "Look, this is the day the LORD told you about: 'I will hand your enemy over to you so you can do to him whatever you desire.'" Then David got up and secretly cut off the corner of Saul's robe.

Afterward, David's conscience bothered him because he had cut off the corner of Saul's robe. He said to his men, "As the LORD is my witness, I would never do such a thing to my lord, the

10 LORD's anointed. I will never lift my hand against him, since he is the LORD's anointed." With these words David persuaded his men, and he did not let them rise up against Saul.

Then Saul left the cave and went on his way. After that, David got up, went out of the cave, and called to Saul, "My lord the king!" When Saul looked behind him, David knelt low with his face to the ground and paid homage. David said to Saul, "Why do you listen to the words of people who say, 'Look, David intends to harm you'? You can see with your own eyes that the LORD handed you over to me today in the cave. Someone advised me to kill you, but I took pity on you and said: I won't lift my hand against my lord, since he is the LORD's anointed. Look, my father! Look at the corner of your robe in my hand, for I cut it off, but I didn't kill you. Recognize that I've committed no crime or rebellion. I haven't sinned against you even though you are hunting me down to take

20 my life.

"May the LORD judge between me and you, and may the LORD take vengeance on you for me, but my hand will never be against you. As the old proverb says, 'Wickedness comes from wicked people.' My hand will never be against you. Who has the king of Israel come after? What are you chasing after? A dead dog? A single flea? May the LORD be judge and decide between you and me. May he take notice and plead my case and deliver me from you."

When David finished saying these things to him, Saul replied, "Is that your voice, David my son?" Then Saul wept aloud and said to David, "You are more righteous than I, for you have done what is good to me though I have done what is evil to you. You yourself have told me today what good you did for me: when the LORD handed me over to you, you didn't kill me. When a

30 man finds his enemy, does he let him go unharmed? May the LORD repay you with good for what you've done for me today.

"Now I know for certain you will be king, and the kingdom of Israel will be established in your hand. Therefore swear to me by the LORD that you will not cut off my descendants or wipe out my name from my father's family." So David swore to Saul. Then Saul went back home, and David and his men went up to the stronghold.

25 Samuel died, and all Israel assembled to mourn for him, and they buried him by his home in Ramah. David then went down to the Wilderness of Paran.

A man in Maon had a business in Carmel; he was a very rich man with three thousand sheep and one thousand goats and was shearing his sheep in Carmel. The man's name was Nabal, and his wife's name, Abigail. The woman was intelligent and beautiful, but the man, a Calebite, was harsh and evil in his dealings.

While David was in the wilderness, he heard that Nabal was shearing sheep, so David sent ten young men instructing them, "Go up to Carmel, and when you come to Nabal, greet him in my name. Then say this: 'Long life to you, and peace to you, peace to your family, and peace to all that is yours. I hear that you are shearing. When your shepherds were with us, we did not harass them, and nothing of theirs was missing the whole time they were in Carmel. Ask your young men, and they will tell you. So let my young men find favor with you, for we have come on a feast day. Please give whatever you have on hand to your servants and to your son David.'"

David's young men went and said all these things to Nabal on David's behalf, and they waited. Nabal asked them, "Who is David? Who is Jesse's son? Many slaves these days are running away from their masters. Am I supposed to take my bread, my water, and my meat that I butchered for my shearers and give them to these men? I don't know where they are from."

David's young men retraced their steps. When they returned to him, they reported all these words. He said to his men, "All of you, put on your swords!" So each man put on his sword, and David also put on his sword. About four hundred men followed David while two hundred stayed with the supplies.

One of Nabal's young men informed Abigail, Nabal's wife, "Look, David sent messengers from the wilderness to greet our master, but he screamed at them. The men treated us very well. When we were in the field, we weren't harassed and nothing of ours was missing the whole time we were living among them. They were a wall around us, both day and night, the entire time we were with them herding the sheep. Now consider carefully what you should do, because there is certain to be trouble for our master and his entire family. He is such a worthless fool nobody can talk to him!"

Abigail hurried, taking two hundred loaves of bread, two clay jars of wine, five butchered sheep, a bushel of roasted grain, one hundred clusters of raisins, and two hundred cakes of pressed figs, and loaded them on donkeys. Then she said to her male servants, "Go ahead of me. I will be right behind you." But she did not tell her husband, Nabal.

As she rode the donkey down a mountain pass hidden from view, she saw David and his men coming toward her and met them. David had just said, "I guarded everything that belonged to this man in the wilderness for nothing. He was not missing anything, yet he paid me back evil for good. May God punish me and do so severely if I let any of his males survive until morning."

When Abigail saw David, she quickly got off the donkey and knelt down with her face to the ground and paid homage to David. She knelt at his feet and said, "The guilt is mine, my lord, but please let your servant speak to you directly. Listen to the words of your servant. My lord should pay no attention to this worthless fool Nabal, for he lives up to his name: His name means 'stupid,' and stupidity is all he knows. I, your servant, didn't see my lord's young men whom you sent. Now my lord, as surely as the Lord lives and as you yourself live—it is the Lord who kept you from participating in bloodshed and avenging yourself by your own hand—may your enemies and those who intend to harm my lord be like Nabal. Let this gift your servant has brought to my lord be given to the young men who follow my lord. Please forgive your servant's offense, for the Lord is certain to make a lasting dynasty for my lord because he fights the Lord's battles. Throughout your life, may evil not be found in you.

"Someone is pursuing you and intends to take your life. My lord's life is tucked safely in the place where the Lord your God protects the living, but he is flinging away your enemies' lives like stones from a sling. When the Lord does for my lord all the good he promised you and appoints
50 you ruler over Israel, there will not be remorse or a troubled conscience for my lord because of needless bloodshed or my lord's revenge. And when the Lord does good things for my lord, may you remember me your servant."

Then David said to Abigail, "Blessed be the Lord God of Israel, who sent you to meet me today! May your discernment be blessed, and may you be blessed. Today you kept me from participating in bloodshed and avenging myself by my own hand. Otherwise, as surely as the Lord God of Israel lives, who prevented me from harming you, if you had not come quickly to meet me, Nabal wouldn't have had any males left by morning light." Then David accepted what she had brought him and said, "Go home in peace. See, I have heard what you said and have granted your request."

Then Abigail went to Nabal, and there he was in his house, holding a feast fit for a king. Nabal's
60 heart was cheerful, and he was very drunk, so she didn't say anything to him until morning light.

In the morning when Nabal sobered up, his wife told him about these events. His heart died and he became a stone. About ten days later, the Lord struck Nabal dead.

When David heard that Nabal was dead, he said, "Blessed be the Lord who championed my cause against Nabal's insults and restrained his servant from doing evil. The Lord brought Nabal's evil deeds back on his own head."

Then David sent messengers to speak to Abigail about marrying him. When David's servants came to Abigail at Carmel, they said to her, "David sent us to bring you to him as a wife."

She stood up, paid homage with her face to the ground, and said, "Here I am, your servant, a slave to wash the feet of my lord's servants." Then Abigail got up quickly, and with her five female
70 servants accompanying her, rode on the donkey following David's messengers. And so she became his wife.

David also married Ahinoam of Jezreel, and the two of them became his wives. But Saul gave his daughter Michal, David's wife, to Palti son of Laish, who was from Gallim.

26 Then the Ziphites came to Saul at Gibeah saying, "David is hiding on the hill of Hachilah opposite Jeshimon." So Saul, accompanied by three thousand of the fit young men of Israel, went immediately to the Wilderness of Ziph to search for David there. Saul camped beside the road at the hill of Hachilah opposite Jeshimon. David was living in the wilderness and discovered

Saul had come there after him. So David sent out spies and knew for certain that Saul had come. Immediately, David went to the place where Saul had camped. He saw the place where Saul and Abner son of Ner, the commander of his army, were lying down. Saul was lying inside the inner circle of the camp with the troops camped around him. Then David asked Ahimelech the Hethite and Joab's brother Abishai son of Zeruiah, "Who will go with me into the camp to Saul?"

10 "I'll go with you," answered Abishai.

That night, David and Abishai came to the troops, and Saul was lying there asleep in the inner circle of the camp with his spear stuck in the ground by his head. Abner and the troops were lying around him. Then Abishai said to David, "Today God has delivered your enemy to you. Let me thrust the spear through him into the ground just once. I won't have to strike him twice!"

But David said to Abishai, "Don't destroy him, for who can lift a hand against the LORD's anointed and be innocent?" David added, "As the LORD lives, the LORD will certainly strike him down: either his day will come and he will die, or he will go into battle and perish. However, as the LORD is my witness, I will never lift my hand against the LORD's anointed. Instead, take the spear and the water jug by his head, and let's go."

20 So David took the spear and the water jug by Saul's head, and they went their way. No one saw them, no one knew, and no one woke up; they all remained asleep because a deep sleep from the LORD came over them. David crossed to the other side and stood on top of the mountain at a distance; there was a considerable space between them. Then David shouted to the troops and to Abner son of Ner, "Aren't you going to answer, Abner?"

"Who are you who calls to the king?" Abner asked.

David called to Abner, "You're a man, aren't you? Who in Israel is your equal? So why didn't you protect your lord the king when one of the people came to destroy him? What you have done is not good. As the LORD lives, all of you deserve to die since you didn't protect your lord, the LORD's anointed. Now look around; where are the king's spear and water jug that were by his head?"

30 Saul recognized David's voice and asked, "Is that your voice, my son David?"

"It is my voice, my lord and king," David said. Then he continued, "Why is my lord pursuing his servant? What have I done? What crime have I committed? Now, may my lord the king please hear the words of his servant: If it is the LORD who has incited you against me, then may he accept an offering. But if it is people, may they be cursed in the presence of the LORD, for today they have banished me from sharing in the inheritance of the LORD, saying, 'Go and worship other gods.' So don't let my blood fall to the ground far from the LORD's presence, for the king of Israel has come out to search for a single flea, like one who pursues a partridge in the mountains."

Saul responded, "I have sinned. Come back, my son David, I will never harm you again because today you considered my life precious. I have been a fool! I've committed a grave error."

40 David answered, "Here is the king's spear; have one of the young men come over and get it. The LORD will repay every man for his righteousness and his loyalty. I wasn't willing to lift my hand against the LORD's anointed, even though the LORD handed you over to me today. Just as I

considered your life valuable today, so may the LORD consider my life valuable and rescue me from all trouble."

Saul said to him, "You are blessed, my son David. You will certainly do great things and will also prevail." Then David went on his way, and Saul returned home.

27 David said to himself, "One of these days I'll be swept away by Saul. There is nothing better for me than to escape immediately to the land of the Philistines. Then Saul will give up searching for me everywhere in Israel, and I'll escape from him." So David set out with his six hundred men and went over to Achish son of Maoch, the king of Gath. David and his men stayed with Achish in Gath. Each man had his family with him, and David had his two wives: Ahinoam of Jezreel and Abigail of Carmel, Nabal's widow. When it was reported to Saul that David had fled to Gath, he no longer searched for him.

Now David said to Achish, "If I have found favor with you, let me be given a place in one of the outlying towns, so I can live there. Why should your servant live in the royal city with you?" That day Achish gave Ziklag to him, and it still belongs to the kings of Judah today. The length of time
10 that David stayed in Philistine territory amounted to a year and four months.

David and his men went up and raided the Geshurites, the Girzites, and the Amalekites. From ancient times they had been the inhabitants of the region through Shur as far as the land of Egypt. Whenever David attacked the land, he did not leave a single person alive, either man or woman, but he took flocks, herds, donkeys, camels, and clothing. Then he came back to Achish, who inquired, "Where did you raid today?"

David replied, "The south country of Judah," "The south country of the Jerahmeelites," or "The south country of the Kenites."

David did not let a man or woman live to be brought to Gath, for he said, "Or they will inform on us and say, 'This is what David did.'" This was David's custom during the whole time he stayed
20 in the Philistine territory. So Achish trusted David, thinking, "Since he has made himself repulsive to his people Israel, he will be my servant forever."

28 At that time, the Philistines gathered their military units into one army to fight against Israel. So Achish said to David, "You know, of course, that you and your men must march out in the army with me."

David replied to Achish, "Good, you will find out what your servant can do."

So Achish said to David, "Very well, I will appoint you as my permanent bodyguard."

By this time Samuel had died, all Israel had mourned for him and buried him in Ramah, his city, and Saul had removed the mediums and spiritists from the land. The Philistines gathered and camped at Shunem. So Saul gathered all Israel, and they camped at Gilboa. When Saul saw the Philistine camp, he was afraid and his heart pounded. He inquired of the LORD, but the LORD did
10 not answer him in dreams or by the Urim or by the prophets. Saul then said to his servants, "Find me a woman who is a medium, so I can go and consult her."

His servants replied, "There is a woman at En-dor who is a medium."

Saul disguised himself by putting on different clothes and set out with two of his men. They came to the woman at night, and Saul said, "Consult a spirit for me. Bring up for me the one I tell you."

But the woman said to him, "You surely know what Saul has done, how he has cut off the mediums and spiritists from the land. Why are you setting a trap for me to get me killed?"

Then Saul swore to her by the LORD: "As surely as the LORD lives, no punishment will come to you from this."

"Who is it that you want me to bring up for you?" the woman asked.

"Bring up Samuel for me," he answered.

When the woman saw Samuel, she screamed, and then she asked Saul, "Why did you deceive me? You are Saul!"

But the king said to her, "Don't be afraid. What do you see?"

"I see a spirit form coming up out of the earth," the woman answered.

Then Saul asked her, "What does he look like?"

"An old man is coming up," she replied. "He's wearing a robe." Then Saul knew that it was Samuel, and he knelt low with his face to the ground and paid homage.

"Why have you disturbed me by bringing me up?" Samuel asked Saul.

"I'm in serious trouble," replied Saul. "The Philistines are fighting against me and God has turned away from me. He doesn't answer me anymore, either through the prophets or in dreams. So I've called on you to tell me what I should do."

Samuel answered, "Since the LORD has turned away from you and has become your enemy, why are you asking me? The LORD has done exactly what he said through me: The LORD has torn the kingship out of your hand and given it to your neighbor David. You did not obey the LORD and did not carry out his burning anger against Amalek; therefore the LORD has done this to you today. The LORD will also hand Israel over to the Philistines along with you. Tomorrow you and your sons will be with me, and the LORD will hand Israel's army over to the Philistines."

Immediately, Saul fell flat on the ground. He was terrified by Samuel's words and was also weak because he had not eaten anything all day and all night. The woman came over to Saul, and she saw that he was terrified and said to him, "Look, your servant has obeyed you. I took my life in my hands and did what you told me to do. Now please listen to your servant. Let me set some food in front of you. Eat and it will give you strength so you can go on your way."

He refused, saying, "I won't eat," but when his servants and the woman urged him, he listened to them. He got up off the ground and sat on the bed.

The woman had a fattened calf at her house, and she quickly slaughtered it. She also took flour, kneaded it, and baked unleavened bread. She served it to Saul and his servants, and they ate. Afterward, they got up and left that night.

29 The Philistines brought all their military units together at Aphek while Israel was camped by the spring in Jezreel. As the Philistine leaders were passing in review with their units of hundreds and thousands, David and his men were passing in review behind them with Achish. Then the Philistine commanders asked, "What are these Hebrews doing here?"

Achish answered the Philistine commanders, "That is David, servant of King Saul of Israel. He has been with me a considerable period of time. From the day he defected until today, I've found no fault with him."

The Philistine commanders, however, were enraged with Achish and told him, "Send that man back and let him return to the place you assigned him. He must not go down with us into
10 battle only to become our adversary during the battle. What better way could he ingratiate himself with his master than with the heads of our men? Isn't this the David they sing about during their dances:

> Saul has killed his thousands,
> but David his tens of thousands?"

So Achish summoned David and told him, "As the LORD lives, you are an honorable man. I think it is good to have you fighting in this unit with me, because I have found no fault in you from the day you came to me until today. But the leaders don't think you are reliable. Now go back quietly and you won't be doing anything the Philistine leaders think is wrong."

"But what have I done?" David replied to Achish. "From the first day I entered your service
20 until today, what have you found against your servant to keep me from going to fight against the enemies of my lord the king?"

Achish answered David, "I'm convinced that you are as reliable as an angel of God. But the Philistine commanders have said, 'He must not go into battle with us.' So get up early in the morning, you and your masters' servants who came with you. When you've all gotten up early, go as soon as it's light." So David and his men got up early in the morning to return to the land of the Philistines. And the Philistines went up to Jezreel.

30 David and his men arrived in Ziklag on the third day. The Amalekites had raided the Negev and attacked and burned Ziklag. They also had kidnapped the women and everyone in it from youngest to oldest. They had killed no one but had carried them off as they went on their way.

When David and his men arrived at the town, they found it burned. Their wives, sons, and daughters had been kidnapped. David and the troops with him wept loudly until they had no strength left to weep. David's two wives, Ahinoam the Jezreelite and Abigail the widow of Nabal the Carmelite, had also been kidnapped. David was in an extremely difficult position because the troops talked about stoning him, for they were all very bitter over the loss of their sons and daughters. But David found strength in the LORD his God.

10 David said to the priest Abiathar son of Ahimelech, "Bring me the ephod." So Abiathar brought it to him, and David asked the LORD, "Should I pursue these raiders? Will I overtake them?"

The LORD replied to him, "Pursue them, for you will certainly overtake them and rescue the people."

So David and the six hundred men with him went. They came to the Wadi Besor, where some stayed behind. David and four hundred of the men continued the pursuit, while two hundred stopped because they were too exhausted to cross the Wadi Besor.

David's men found an Egyptian in the open country and brought him to David. They gave him some bread to eat and water to drink. Then they gave him some pressed figs and two clusters of 20 raisins. After he ate he revived, for he hadn't eaten food or drunk water for three days and three nights.

Then David said to him, "Who do you belong to? Where are you from?"

"I'm an Egyptian, the slave of an Amalekite man," he said. "My master abandoned me when I got sick three days ago. We raided the south country of the Cherethites, the territory of Judah, and the south country of Caleb, and we burned Ziklag."

David then asked him, "Will you lead me to these raiders?"

He said, "Swear to me by God that you won't kill me or turn me over to my master, and I will lead you to them."

So he led him, and there were the Amalekites, spread out over the entire area, eating, drinking, 30 and celebrating because of the great amount of plunder they had taken from the land of the Philistines and the land of Judah. David slaughtered them from twilight until the evening of the next day. None of them escaped, except four hundred young men who got on camels and fled.

David recovered everything the Amalekites had taken; he also rescued his two wives. Nothing of theirs was missing from the youngest to the oldest, including the sons and daughters, and all the plunder the Amalekites had taken. David got everything back. He took all the flocks and herds, which were driven ahead of the other livestock, and the people shouted, "This is David's plunder!"

When David came to the two hundred men who had been too exhausted to go with him and had been left at the Wadi Besor, they came out to meet him and to meet the troops with him. When David approached the men, he greeted them, but all the corrupt and worthless men among 40 those who had gone with David argued, "Because they didn't go with us, we will not give any of the plunder we recovered to them except for each man's wife and children. They may take them and go."

But David said, "My brothers, you must not do this with what the LORD has given us. He protected us and handed over to us the raiders who came against us. Who can agree to your proposal? The share of the one who goes into battle is to be the same as the share of the one who remains with the supplies. They will share equally." And it has been so from that day forward. David established this policy as a law and an ordinance for Israel and it still continues today.

When David came to Ziklag, he sent some of the plunder to his friends, the elders of Judah, saying, "Here is a gift for you from the plunder of the LORD's enemies." He sent gifts to those in 50 Bethel, in Ramoth of the Negev, and in Jattir; to those in Aroer, in Siphmoth, and in Eshtemoa; to those in Racal, in the towns of the Jerahmeelites, and in the towns of the Kenites; to those in Hormah, in Bor-ashan, and in Athach; to those in Hebron, and to those in all the places where David and his men had roamed.

31 The Philistines fought against Israel, and Israel's men fled from them and were killed on Mount Gilboa. The Philistines pursued Saul and his sons and killed his sons, Jonathan, Abinadab, and Malchishua. When the battle intensified against Saul, the archers found him and severely wounded him. Then Saul said to his armor-bearer, "Draw your sword and run me through with it, or these uncircumcised men will come and run me through and torture me!" But his armor-bearer would not do it because he was terrified. Then Saul took his sword and fell on it. When his armor-bearer saw that Saul was dead, he also fell on his own sword and died with him. So on that day, Saul died together with his three sons, his armor-bearer, and all his men.

When the men of Israel on the other side of the valley and on the other side of the Jordan saw 10 that Israel's men had fled and that Saul and his sons were dead, they abandoned the cities and fled. So the Philistines came and settled in them.

The next day when the Philistines came to strip the slain, they found Saul and his three sons dead on Mount Gilboa. They cut off Saul's head, stripped off his armor, and sent messengers throughout the land of the Philistines to spread the good news in the temples of their idols and among the people. Then they put his armor in the temple of the Ashtoreths and hung his body on the wall of Beth-shan.

When the residents of Jabesh-gilead heard what the Philistines had done to Saul, all their brave men set out, journeyed all night, and retrieved the body of Saul and the bodies of his sons from the wall of Beth-shan. When they arrived at Jabesh, they burned the bodies there. Afterward, they 20 took their bones and buried them under the tamarisk tree in Jabesh and fasted seven days.

2 Samuel

1 After the death of Saul, David returned from defeating the Amalekites and stayed at Ziklag two days. On the third day a man with torn clothes and dust on his head came from Saul's camp. When he came to David, he fell to the ground and paid homage. David asked him, "Where have you come from?"

He replied to him, "I've escaped from the Israelite camp."

"What was the outcome? Tell me," David asked him.

"The troops fled from the battle," he answered. "Many of the troops have fallen and are dead. Also, Saul and his son Jonathan are dead."

David asked the young man who had brought him the report, "How do you know Saul and his son Jonathan are dead?"

"I happened to be on Mount Gilboa," he replied, "and there was Saul, leaning on his spear. At that very moment the chariots and the cavalry were closing in on him. When he turned around and saw me, he called out to me, so I answered: I'm at your service. He asked me, 'Who are you?' I told him: I'm an Amalekite. Then he begged me, 'Stand over me and kill me, for I'm mortally wounded, but my life still lingers.' So I stood over him and killed him because I knew that after he had fallen he couldn't survive. I took the crown that was on his head and the armband that was on his arm, and I've brought them here to my lord."

Then David took hold of his clothes and tore them, and all the men with him did the same. They mourned, wept, and fasted until the evening for those who died by the sword—for Saul, his son Jonathan, the Lord's people, and the house of Israel.

David inquired of the young man who had brought him the report, "Where are you from?"

"I'm the son of a resident alien," he said. "I'm an Amalekite."

David questioned him, "How is it that you were not afraid to lift your hand to destroy the Lord's anointed?" Then David summoned one of his servants and said, "Come here and kill him!" The servant struck him, and he died. For David had said to the Amalekite, "Your blood is on your own head because your own mouth testified against you by saying, 'I killed the Lord's anointed.'"

David sang the following lament for Saul and his son Jonathan, and he ordered that the Judahites be taught The Song of the Bow. It is written in the Book of Jashar:

> The splendor of Israel lies slain on your heights.
> How the mighty have fallen!
> Do not tell it in Gath,
>   don't announce it in the marketplaces of Ashkelon,
>   or the daughters of the Philistines will rejoice,

and the daughters of the uncircumcised will celebrate.
Mountains of Gilboa,
let no dew or rain be on you,
or fields of offerings,
for there the shield of the mighty was defiled—
the shield of Saul, no longer anointed with oil.
Jonathan's bow never retreated,
40 Saul's sword never returned unstained,
from the blood of the slain,
from the flesh of the mighty.
Saul and Jonathan,
loved and delightful,
they were not parted in life or in death.
They were swifter than eagles, stronger than lions.
Daughters of Israel, weep for Saul,
who clothed you in scarlet, with luxurious things,
who decked your garments with gold ornaments.
50 How the mighty have fallen in the thick of battle!
Jonathan lies slain on your heights.
I grieve for you, Jonathan, my brother.
You were such a friend to me.
Your love for me was more wondrous
than the love of women.
How the mighty have fallen
and the weapons of war have perished!

2 Some time later, David inquired of the LORD: "Should I go to one of the towns of Judah?"

The LORD answered him, "Go."

Then David asked, "Where should I go?"

"To Hebron," the LORD replied.

So David went there with his two wives, Ahinoam the Jezreelite and Abigail, the widow of Nabal the Carmelite. In addition, David brought the men who were with him, each one with his family, and they settled in the towns near Hebron. Then the men of Judah came, and there they anointed David king over the house of Judah. They told David, "It was the men of Jabesh-gilead who buried Saul."

10 David sent messengers to the men of Jabesh-gilead and said to them, "The LORD bless you because you have shown this kindness to Saul your lord when you buried him. Now, may the LORD show kindness and faithfulness to you, and I will also show the same goodness to you

because you have done this deed. Therefore, be strong and valiant, for though Saul your lord is dead, the house of Judah has anointed me king over them."

Abner son of Ner, commander of Saul's army, took Saul's son Ish-bosheth and moved him to Mahanaim. He made him king over Gilead, Asher, Jezreel, Ephraim, Benjamin—over all Israel. Saul's son Ish-bosheth was forty years old when he became king over Israel; he reigned for two years. The house of Judah, however, followed David. The length of time that David was king in Hebron over the house of Judah was seven years and six months.

20 Abner son of Ner and soldiers of Ish-bosheth son of Saul marched out from Mahanaim to Gibeon. So Joab son of Zeruiah and David's soldiers marched out and met them by the pool of Gibeon. The two groups took up positions on opposite sides of the pool.

Then Abner said to Joab, "Let's have the young men get up and compete in front of us."

"Let them get up," Joab replied.

So they got up and were counted off—twelve for Benjamin and Ish-bosheth son of Saul, and twelve from David's soldiers. Then each man grabbed his opponent by the head and thrust his sword into his opponent's side so that they all died together. So this place, which is in Gibeon, is named Field of Blades.

The battle that day was extremely fierce, and Abner and the men of Israel were defeated by 30 David's soldiers. The three sons of Zeruiah were there: Joab, Abishai, and Asahel. Asahel was a fast runner, like one of the wild gazelles. He chased Abner and did not turn to the right or the left in his pursuit of him. Abner glanced back and said, "Is that you, Asahel?"

"Yes it is," Asahel replied.

Abner said to him, "Turn to your right or left, seize one of the young soldiers, and take whatever you can get from him." But Asahel would not stop chasing him. Once again, Abner warned Asahel, "Stop chasing me. Why should I strike you to the ground? How could I ever look your brother Joab in the face?"

But Asahel refused to turn away, so Abner hit him in the stomach with the butt of his spear. The spear went through his body, and he fell and died right there. As they all came to the place 40 where Asahel had fallen and died, they stopped, but Joab and Abishai pursued Abner. By sunset, they had gone as far as the hill of Ammah, which is opposite Giah on the way to the wilderness of Gibeon.

The Benjaminites rallied to Abner; they formed a unit and took their stand on top of a hill. Then Abner called out to Joab, "Must the sword devour forever? Don't you realize this will only end in bitterness? How long before you tell the troops to stop pursuing their brothers?"

"As God lives," Joab replied, "if you had not spoken up, the troops wouldn't have stopped pursuing their brothers until morning." Then Joab blew the ram's horn, and all the troops stopped; they no longer pursued Israel or continued to fight. So Abner and his men marched through the Arabah all that night. They crossed the Jordan, marched all morning, and arrived at 50 Mahanaim.

When Joab had turned back from pursuing Abner, he gathered all the troops. In addition to Asahel, nineteen of David's soldiers were missing, but they had killed 360 of the Benjaminites and Abner's men. Afterward, they carried Asahel to his father's tomb in Bethlehem and buried him. Then Joab and his men marched all night and reached Hebron at dawn.

3 During the long war between the house of Saul and the house of David, David was growing stronger and the house of Saul was becoming weaker.

Sons were born to David in Hebron:

His firstborn was Amnon,

by Ahinoam the Jezreelite;

his second was Chileab,

by Abigail, the widow of Nabal the Carmelite;

the third was Absalom,

son of Maacah the daughter of King Talmai of Geshur;

10 the fourth was Adonijah,

son of Haggith;

the fifth was Shephatiah,

son of Abital;

the sixth was Ithream,

by David's wife Eglah.

These were born to David in Hebron.

During the war between the house of Saul and the house of David, Abner kept acquiring more power in the house of Saul. Now Saul had a concubine whose name was Rizpah daughter of Aiah, and Ish-bosheth questioned Abner, "Why did you sleep with my father's concubine?"

20 Abner was very angry about Ish-bosheth's accusation. "Am I a dog's head who belongs to Judah?" he asked. "All this time I've been loyal to the family of your father Saul, to his brothers, and to his friends and haven't betrayed you to David, but now you accuse me of wrongdoing with this woman! May God punish Abner and do so severely if I don't do for David what the LORD swore to him: to transfer the kingdom from the house of Saul and establish the throne of David over Israel and Judah from Dan to Beer-sheba." Ish-bosheth did not dare respond to Abner because he was afraid of him.

Abner sent messengers as his representatives to say to David, "Whose land is it? Make your covenant with me, and you can be certain I am on your side to turn all Israel over to you."

David replied, "Good, I will make a covenant with you. However, there's one thing I require of 30 you: You will not see my face unless you first bring Saul's daughter Michal when you come to see me."

Then David sent messengers to say to Ish-bosheth son of Saul, "Give me back my wife Michal. I was engaged to her for the price of a hundred Philistine foreskins."

So Ish-bosheth sent someone to take her away from her husband, Paltiel son of Laish. Her husband followed her, weeping all the way to Bahurim. Abner said to him, "Go back." So he went back.

Abner conferred with the elders of Israel: "In the past you wanted David to be king over you. Now take action, because the LORD has spoken concerning David: 'Through my servant David I will save my people Israel from the power of the Philistines and the power of all Israel's enemies.'"

40 Abner also informed the Benjaminites and went to Hebron to inform David about all that was agreed on by Israel and the whole house of Benjamin. When Abner and twenty men came to David at Hebron, David held a banquet for him and his men.

Abner said to David, "Let me now go and I will gather all Israel to my lord the king. They will make a covenant with you, and you will reign over all you desire." So David dismissed Abner, and he went in peace.

Just then David's soldiers and Joab returned from a raid and brought a large amount of plundered goods with them. Abner was not with David in Hebron because David had dismissed him, and he had gone in peace. When Joab and his whole army arrived, Joab was informed, "Abner son of Ner came to see the king, the king dismissed him, and he went in peace."

50 Joab went to the king and said, "What have you done? Look here, Abner came to you. Why did you dismiss him? Now he's getting away. You know that Abner son of Ner came to deceive you and to find out about your military activities and everything you're doing." Then Joab left David and sent messengers after Abner. They brought him back from the well of Sirah, but David was unaware of it. When Abner returned to Hebron, Joab pulled him aside to the middle of the city gate, as if to speak to him privately, and there Joab stabbed him in the stomach. So Abner died in revenge for the death of Asahel, Joab's brother.

David heard about it later and said, "I and my kingdom are forever innocent before the LORD concerning the blood of Abner son of Ner. May it hang over Joab's head and his father's whole family, and may the house of Joab never be without someone who has a discharge or a skin disease,
60 or a man who can only work a spindle, or someone who falls by the sword or starves." Joab and his brother Abishai killed Abner because he had put their brother Asahel to death in the battle at Gibeon.

David then ordered Joab and all the people who were with him, "Tear your clothes, put on sackcloth, and mourn over Abner." And King David walked behind the coffin.

When they buried Abner in Hebron, the king wept aloud at Abner's tomb. All the people wept, and the king sang a lament for Abner:

> Should Abner die as a fool dies?
> Your hands were not bound,
> your feet not placed in bronze shackles.
70 > You fell like one who falls victim to criminals.

And all the people wept over him even more.

Then they came to urge David to eat food while it was still day, but David took an oath: "May God punish me and do so severely if I taste bread or anything else before sunset!" All the people took note of this, and it pleased them. In fact, everything the king did pleased them. On that day all the troops and all Israel were convinced that the king had no part in the killing of Abner son of Ner.

Then the king said to his soldiers, "You must know that a great leader has fallen in Israel today. As for me, even though I am the anointed king, I have little power today. These men, the sons of Zeruiah, are too fierce for me. May the Lord repay the evildoer according to his evil!"

4 When Saul's son Ish-bosheth heard that Abner had died in Hebron, he gave up, and all Israel was dismayed. Saul's son had two men who were leaders of raiding parties: one named Baanah and the other Rechab, sons of Rimmon the Beerothite of the Benjaminites. Beeroth is also considered part of Benjamin, and the Beerothites fled to Gittaim and still reside there as aliens today.

Saul's son Jonathan had a son whose feet were crippled. He was five years old when the report about Saul and Jonathan came from Jezreel. His nanny picked him up and fled, but as she was hurrying to flee, he fell and became lame. His name was Mephibosheth.

Rechab and Baanah, the sons of Rimmon the Beerothite, set out and arrived at Ish-bosheth's house during the heat of the day while the king was taking his midday nap. They entered the

10 interior of the house as if to get wheat and stabbed him in the stomach. Then Rechab and his brother Baanah escaped. They had entered the house while Ish-bosheth was lying on his bed in his bedroom and stabbed and killed him. They removed his head, took it, and traveled by way of the Arabah all night. They brought Ish-bosheth's head to David at Hebron and said to the king, "Here's the head of Ish-bosheth son of Saul, your enemy who intended to take your life. Today the Lord has granted vengeance to my lord the king against Saul and his offspring."

But David answered Rechab and his brother Baanah, sons of Rimmon the Beerothite, "As the Lord lives, the one who has redeemed my life from every distress, when the person told me, 'Look, Saul is dead,' he thought he was a bearer of good news, but I seized him and put him to death at Ziklag. That was my reward to him for his news! How much more when wicked men kill

20 a righteous man in his own house on his own bed! So now, should I not require his blood from you and purge you from the earth?"

So David gave orders to the young men, and they killed Rechab and Baanah. They cut off their hands and feet and hung their bodies by the pool in Hebron, but they took Ish-bosheth's head and buried it in Abner's tomb in Hebron.

5 All the tribes of Israel came to David at Hebron and said, "Here we are, your own flesh and blood. Even while Saul was king over us, you were the one who led us out to battle and brought us back. The Lord also said to you, 'You will shepherd my people Israel, and you will be ruler over Israel.'"

So all the elders of Israel came to the king at Hebron. King David made a covenant with them at Hebron in the Lord's presence, and they anointed David king over Israel.

David was thirty years old when he began his reign; he reigned forty years. In Hebron he reigned over Judah seven years and six months, and in Jerusalem he reigned thirty-three years over all Israel and Judah.

The king and his men marched to Jerusalem against the Jebusites who inhabited the land. The Jebusites had said to David, "You will never get in here. Even the blind and lame can repel you" thinking, "David can't get in here."

Yet David did capture the stronghold of Zion, that is, the city of David. He said that day, "Whoever attacks the Jebusites must go through the water shaft to reach the lame and the blind who are despised by David." For this reason it is said, "The blind and the lame will never enter the house."

David took up residence in the stronghold, which he named the city of David. He built it up all the way around from the supporting terraces inward. David became more and more powerful, and the Lord God of Armies was with him. King Hiram of Tyre sent envoys to David; he also sent cedar logs, carpenters, and stonemasons, and they built a palace for David. Then David knew that the Lord had established him as king over Israel and had exalted his kingdom for the sake of his people Israel.

After he arrived from Hebron, David took more concubines and wives from Jerusalem, and more sons and daughters were born to him. These are the names of those born to him in Jerusalem: Shammua, Shobab, Nathan, Solomon, Ibhar, Elishua, Nepheg, Japhia, Elishama, Eliada, and Eliphelet.

When the Philistines heard that David had been anointed king over Israel, they all went in search of David, but he heard about it and went down to the stronghold. So the Philistines came and spread out in Rephaim Valley.

Then David inquired of the Lord: "Should I attack the Philistines? Will you hand them over to me?"

The Lord replied to David, "Attack, for I will certainly hand the Philistines over to you."

So David went to Baal-perazim and defeated them there and said, "Like a bursting flood, the Lord has burst out against my enemies before me." Therefore, he named that place The Lord Bursts Out. The Philistines abandoned their idols there, and David and his men carried them off.

The Philistines came up again and spread out in Rephaim Valley. So David inquired of the Lord, and he answered, "Do not attack directly, but circle around behind them and come at them opposite the balsam trees. When you hear the sound of marching in the tops of the balsam trees, act decisively, for then the Lord will have gone out ahead of you to strike down the army of the Philistines." So David did exactly as the Lord commanded him, and he struck down the Philistines all the way from Geba to Gezer.

6 David again assembled all the fit young men in Israel: thirty thousand. He and all his troops set out to bring the ark of God from Baale-judah. The ark bears the Name, the name of the Lord of Armies who is enthroned between the cherubim. They set the ark of God on a new cart and transported it from Abinadab's house, which was on the hill. Uzzah and Ahio, sons of Abinadab, were guiding the cart and brought it with the ark of God from Abinadab's house on the hill. Ahio walked in front of the ark. David and the whole house of Israel were dancing before the Lord with all kinds of fir wood instruments, lyres, harps, tambourines, sistrums, and cymbals.

When they came to Nacon's threshing floor, Uzzah reached out to the ark of God and took hold of it because the oxen had stumbled. Then the Lord's anger burned against Uzzah, and God struck him dead on the spot for his irreverence, and he died there next to the ark of God. David was angry because of the Lord's outburst against Uzzah, so he named that place Outburst Against Uzzah, as it is today. David feared the Lord that day and said, "How can the ark of the Lord ever come to me?" So he was not willing to bring the ark of the Lord to the city of David; instead, he diverted it to the house of Obed-edom of Gath. The ark of the Lord remained in his house three months, and the Lord blessed Obed-edom and his whole family.

It was reported to King David, "The Lord has blessed Obed-edom's family and all that belongs to him because of the ark of God." So David went and had the ark of God brought up from Obed-edom's house to the city of David with rejoicing. When those carrying the ark of the Lord advanced six steps, he sacrificed an ox and a fattened calf. David was dancing with all his might before the Lord wearing a linen ephod. He and the whole house of Israel were bringing up the ark of the Lord with shouts and the sound of the ram's horn. As the ark of the Lord was entering the city of David, Saul's daughter Michal looked down from the window and saw King David leaping and dancing before the Lord, and she despised him in her heart.

They brought the ark of the Lord and set it in its place inside the tent David had pitched for it. Then David offered burnt offerings and fellowship offerings in the Lord's presence. When David had finished offering the burnt offering and the fellowship offerings, he blessed the people in the name of the Lord of Armies. Then he distributed a loaf of bread, a date cake, and a raisin cake to each one in the entire Israelite community, both men and women. Then all the people went home.

When David returned home to bless his household, Saul's daughter Michal came out to meet him. "How the king of Israel honored himself today!" she said. "He exposed himself today in the sight of the slave girls of his subjects like a vulgar person would expose himself."

David replied to Michal, "It was before the Lord who chose me over your father and his whole family to appoint me ruler over the Lord's people Israel. I will dance before the Lord, and I will dishonor myself and humble myself even more. However, by the slave girls you spoke about, I will be honored." And Saul's daughter Michal had no child to the day of her death.

7 When the king had settled into his palace and the LORD had given him rest on every side from all his enemies, the king said to the prophet Nathan, "Look, I am living in a cedar house while the ark of God sits inside tent curtains."

So Nathan told the king, "Go and do all that is on your mind, for the LORD is with you."

But that night the word of the LORD came to Nathan: "Go to my servant David and say, 'This is what the LORD says: Are you to build me a house to dwell in? From the time I brought the Israelites out of Egypt until today I have not dwelt in a house; instead, I have been moving around with a tent as my dwelling. In all my journeys with all the Israelites, have I ever spoken a word to one of the tribal leaders of Israel, whom I commanded to shepherd my people Israel, asking: Why 10 haven't you built me a house of cedar?'

"So now this is what you are to say to my servant David: 'This is what the LORD of Armies says: I took you from the pasture, from tending the flock, to be ruler over my people Israel. I have been with you wherever you have gone, and I have destroyed all your enemies before you. I will make a great name for you like that of the greatest on the earth. I will designate a place for my people Israel and plant them, so that they may live there and not be disturbed again. Evildoers will not continue to oppress them as they have done ever since the day I ordered judges to be over my people Israel. I will give you rest from all your enemies.

"'The LORD declares to you: The LORD himself will make a house for you. When your time comes and you rest with your ancestors, I will raise up after you your descendant, who will come 20 from your body, and I will establish his kingdom. He is the one who will build a house for my name, and I will establish the throne of his kingdom forever. I will be his father, and he will be my son. When he does wrong, I will discipline him with a rod of men and blows from mortals. But my faithful love will never leave him as it did when I removed it from Saul, whom I removed from before you. Your house and kingdom will endure before me forever, and your throne will be established forever.'"

Nathan reported all these words and this entire vision to David.

Then King David went in, sat in the LORD's presence, and said,

Who am I, Lord GOD, and what is my house that you have brought me this far? What you have done so far was a little thing to you, Lord GOD, for you have also spoken about your 30 servant's house in the distant future. And this is a revelation for mankind, Lord GOD. What more can David say to you? You know your servant, Lord GOD. Because of your word and according to your will, you have revealed all these great things to your servant.

This is why you are great, Lord GOD. There is no one like you, and there is no God besides you, as all we have heard confirms. And who is like your people Israel? God came to one nation on earth in order to redeem a people for himself, to make a name for himself, and to perform for them great and awesome acts, driving out nations and their gods before your people you redeemed for yourself from Egypt. You established your people Israel to be your own people forever, and you, LORD, have become their God.

Now, LORD God, fulfill the promise forever that you have made to your servant and his house. Do as you have promised, so that your name will be exalted forever, when it is said, "The LORD of Armies is God over Israel." The house of your servant David will be established before you since you, LORD of Armies, God of Israel, have revealed this to your servant when you said, "I will build a house for you." Therefore, your servant has found the courage to pray this prayer to you. Lord GOD, you are God; your words are true, and you have promised this good thing to your servant. Now, please bless your servant's house so that it will continue before you forever. For you, Lord GOD, have spoken, and with your blessing your servant's house will be blessed forever.

8 After this, David defeated the Philistines, subdued them, and took Metheg-ammah from Philistine control. He also defeated the Moabites, and after making them lie down on the ground, he measured them off with a cord. He measured every two cord lengths of those to be put to death and one full length of those to be kept alive. So the Moabites became David's subjects and brought tribute.

David also defeated Hadadezer son of Rehob, king of Zobah, when he went to restore his control at the Euphrates River. David captured seventeen hundred horsemen and twenty thousand foot soldiers from him, and he hamstrung all the horses and kept a hundred chariots.

When the Arameans of Damascus came to assist King Hadadezer of Zobah, David struck down twenty-two thousand Aramean men. Then he placed garrisons in Aram of Damascus, and the Arameans became David's subjects and brought tribute. The LORD made David victorious wherever he went.

David took the gold shields of Hadadezer's officers and brought them to Jerusalem. King David also took huge quantities of bronze from Betah and Berothai, Hadadezer's cities.

When King Toi of Hamath heard that David had defeated the entire army of Hadadezer, he sent his son Joram to King David to greet him and to congratulate him because David had fought against Hadadezer and defeated him, for Toi and Hadadezer had fought many wars. Joram had items of silver, gold, and bronze with him. King David also dedicated these to the LORD, along with the silver and gold he had dedicated from all the nations he had subdued—from Edom, Moab, the Ammonites, the Philistines, the Amalekites, and the spoil of Hadadezer son of Rehob, king of Zobah.

David made a reputation for himself when he returned from striking down eighteen thousand Edomites in Salt Valley. He placed garrisons throughout Edom, and all the Edomites were subject to David. The LORD made David victorious wherever he went.

So David reigned over all Israel, administering justice and righteousness for all his people.

> Joab son of Zeruiah was over the army;
>
> Jehoshaphat son of Ahilud was court historian;
>
> Zadok son of Ahitub and Ahimelech son of Abiathar were priests;
>
> Seraiah was court secretary;
>
> Benaiah son of Jehoiada was over the Cherethites and the Pelethites;
>
> and David's sons were chief officials.

9 David asked, "Is there anyone remaining from the family of Saul I can show kindness to for Jonathan's sake?" There was a servant of Saul's family named Ziba. They summoned him to David, and the king said to him, "Are you Ziba?"

"I am your servant," he replied.

So the king asked, "Is there anyone left of Saul's family that I can show the kindness of God to?"

Ziba said to the king, "There is still Jonathan's son who was injured in both feet."

The king asked him, "Where is he?"

Ziba answered the king, "You'll find him in Lo-debar at the house of Machir son of Ammiel."

So King David had him brought from the house of Machir son of Ammiel in Lo-debar.

¹⁰ Mephibosheth son of Jonathan son of Saul came to David, fell facedown, and paid homage. David said, "Mephibosheth!"

"I am your servant," he replied.

"Don't be afraid," David said to him, "since I intend to show you kindness for the sake of your father Jonathan. I will restore to you all your grandfather Saul's fields, and you will always eat meals at my table."

Mephibosheth paid homage and said, "What is your servant that you take an interest in a dead dog like me?"

Then the king summoned Saul's attendant Ziba and said to him, "I have given to your master's grandson all that belonged to Saul and his family. You, your sons, and your servants are to work the ground for him, and you are to bring in the crops so your master's grandson will have food to eat. But Mephibosheth, your master's grandson, is always to eat at my table." Now Ziba had fifteen sons and twenty servants.

Ziba said to the king, "Your servant will do all my lord the king commands."

So Mephibosheth ate at David's table just like one of the king's sons. Mephibosheth had a young son whose name was Mica. All those living in Ziba's house were Mephibosheth's servants. However, Mephibosheth lived in Jerusalem because he always ate at the king's table. His feet had been injured.

10 Some time later, the king of the Ammonites died, and his son Hanun became king in his place. Then David said, "I'll show kindness to Hanun son of Nahash, just as his father showed kindness to me."

So David sent his emissaries to console Hanun concerning his father. However, when they arrived in the land of the Ammonites, the Ammonite leaders said to Hanun their lord, "Just because David has sent men with condolences for you, do you really believe he's showing respect for your father? Instead, hasn't David sent his emissaries in order to scout out the city, spy on it, and demolish it?" So Hanun took David's emissaries, shaved off half their beards, cut their clothes in half at the hips, and sent them away.

When this was reported to David, he sent someone to meet them, since they were deeply humiliated. The king said, "Stay in Jericho until your beards grow back; then return."

When the Ammonites realized they had become repulsive to David, they hired twenty thousand foot soldiers from the Arameans of Beth-rehob and Zobah, one thousand men from the king of Maacah, and twelve thousand men from Tob.

David heard about it and sent Joab and all the elite troops. The Ammonites marched out and lined up in battle formation at the entrance to the city gate while the Arameans of Zobah and Rehob and the men of Tob and Maacah were in the field by themselves. When Joab saw that there was a battle line in front of him and another behind him, he chose some of Israel's finest young men and lined up in formation to engage the Arameans. He placed the rest of the forces under the command of his brother Abishai. They lined up in formation to engage the Ammonites.

"If the Arameans are too strong for me," Joab said, "then you will be my help. However, if the Ammonites are too strong for you, I'll come to help you. Be strong! Let's prove ourselves strong for our people and for the cities of our God. May the LORD's will be done."

Joab and his troops advanced to fight against the Arameans, and they fled before him. When the Ammonites saw that the Arameans had fled, they too fled before Abishai and entered the city. So Joab withdrew from the attack against the Ammonites and went to Jerusalem.

When the Arameans saw that they had been defeated by Israel, they regrouped. Hadadezer sent messengers to bring the Arameans who were beyond the Euphrates River, and they came to Helam with Shobach, commander of Hadadezer's army, leading them.

When this was reported to David, he gathered all Israel, crossed the Jordan, and went to Helam. Then the Arameans lined up to engage David in battle and fought against him. But the Arameans fled before Israel, and David killed seven hundred of their charioteers and forty thousand foot soldiers. He also struck down Shobach commander of their army, who died there. When all the kings who were Hadadezer's subjects saw that they had been defeated by Israel, they made peace with Israel and became their subjects. After this, the Arameans were afraid to ever help the Ammonites again.

11 In the spring when kings march out to war, David sent Joab with his officers and all Israel. They destroyed the Ammonites and besieged Rabbah, but David remained in Jerusalem.

One evening David got up from his bed and strolled around on the roof of the palace. From the roof he saw a woman bathing—a very beautiful woman. So David sent someone to inquire about her, and he said, "Isn't this Bathsheba, daughter of Eliam and wife of Uriah the Hethite?"

David sent messengers to get her, and when she came to him, he slept with her. Now she had just been purifying herself from her uncleanness. Afterward, she returned home. The woman conceived and sent word to inform David, "I am pregnant."

10 David sent orders to Joab: "Send me Uriah the Hethite." So Joab sent Uriah to David. When Uriah came to him, David asked how Joab and the troops were doing and how the war was going. Then he said to Uriah, "Go down to your house and wash your feet." So Uriah left the palace, and a gift from the king followed him. But Uriah slept at the door of the palace with all his master's servants; he did not go down to his house.

When it was reported to David, "Uriah didn't go home," David questioned Uriah, "Haven't you just come from a journey? Why didn't you go home?"

Uriah answered David, "The ark, Israel, and Judah are dwelling in tents, and my master Joab and his soldiers are camping in the open field. How can I enter my house to eat and drink and sleep with my wife? As surely as you live and by your life, I will not do this!"

20 "Stay here today also," David said to Uriah, "and tomorrow I will send you back." So Uriah stayed in Jerusalem that day and the next. Then David invited Uriah to eat and drink with him, and David got him drunk. He went out in the evening to lie down on his cot with his master's servants, but he did not go home.

The next morning David wrote a letter to Joab and sent it with Uriah. In the letter he wrote:

Put Uriah at the front of the fiercest fighting, then withdraw from him so that he is struck down and dies.

When Joab was besieging the city, he put Uriah in the place where he knew the best enemy soldiers were. Then the men of the city came out and attacked Joab, and some of the men from David's soldiers fell in battle; Uriah the Hethite also died.

30 Joab sent someone to report to David all the details of the battle. He commanded the messenger, "When you've finished telling the king all the details of the battle—if the king's anger gets stirred up and he asks you, 'Why did you get so close to the city to fight? Didn't you realize they would shoot from the top of the wall? At Thebez, who struck Abimelech son of Jerubbesheth? Didn't a woman drop an upper millstone on him from the top of the wall so that he died? Why did you get so close to the wall?'—then say, 'Your servant Uriah the Hethite is dead also.'" Then the messenger left.

When he arrived, he reported to David all that Joab had sent him to tell. The messenger reported to David, "The men gained the advantage over us and came out against us in the field, but we counterattacked right up to the entrance of the city gate. However, the archers shot down

40 on your servants from the top of the wall, and some of the king's servants died. Your servant Uriah the Hethite is also dead."

David told the messenger, "Say this to Joab: 'Don't let this matter upset you because the sword devours all alike. Intensify your fight against the city and demolish it.' Encourage him."

When Uriah's wife heard that her husband, Uriah, had died, she mourned for him. When the time of mourning ended, David had her brought to his house. She became his wife and bore him a son. However, the LORD considered what David had done to be evil.

12 So the LORD sent Nathan to David. When he arrived, he said to him:

There were two men in a certain city, one rich and the other poor. The rich man had very large flocks and herds, but the poor man had nothing except one small ewe lamb that he had bought. He raised her, and she grew up with him and with his children. From his meager food she would eat, from his cup she would drink, and in his arms she would sleep. She was like a daughter to him. Now a traveler came to the rich man, but the rich man could not bring himself to take one of his own sheep or cattle to prepare for the traveler who had come to him. Instead, he took the poor man's lamb and prepared it for his guest.

David was infuriated with the man and said to Nathan, "As the LORD lives, the man who did
10 this deserves to die! Because he has done this thing and shown no pity, he must pay four lambs for that lamb."

Nathan replied to David, "You are the man! This is what the LORD God of Israel says: 'I anointed you king over Israel, and I rescued you from Saul. I gave your master's house to you and your master's wives into your arms, and I gave you the house of Israel and Judah, and if that was not enough, I would have given you even more. Why then have you despised the LORD's command by doing what I consider evil? You struck down Uriah the Hethite with the sword and took his wife as your own wife—you murdered him with the Ammonite's sword. Now therefore, the sword will never leave your house because you despised me and took the wife of Uriah the Hethite to be your own wife.'

"This is what the LORD says, 'I am going to bring disaster on you from your own family: I will
20 take your wives and give them to another before your very eyes, and he will sleep with them in broad daylight. You acted in secret, but I will do this before all Israel and in broad daylight.'"

David responded to Nathan, "I have sinned against the LORD."

Then Nathan replied to David, "And the LORD has taken away your sin; you will not die. However, because you treated the LORD with such contempt in this matter, the son born to you will die." Then Nathan went home.

The LORD struck the baby that Uriah's wife had borne to David, and he became deathly ill. David pleaded with God for the boy. He fasted, went home, and spent the night lying on the ground. The elders of his house stood beside him to get him up from the ground, but he was unwilling and would not eat anything with them.

30 On the seventh day the baby died. But David's servants were afraid to tell him the baby was dead. They said, "Look, while the baby was alive, we spoke to him, and he wouldn't listen to us. So how can we tell him the baby is dead? He may do something desperate."

When David saw that his servants were whispering to each other, he guessed that the baby was dead. So he asked his servants, "Is the baby dead?"

"He is dead," they replied.

Then David got up from the ground. He washed, anointed himself, changed his clothes, went to the LORD's house, and worshiped. Then he went home and requested something to eat. So they served him food, and he ate.

His servants asked him, "Why have you done this? While the baby was alive, you fasted and
40 wept, but when he died, you got up and ate food."

He answered, "While the baby was alive, I fasted and wept because I thought, 'Who knows? The LORD may be gracious to me and let him live.' But now that he is dead, why should I fast? Can I bring him back again? I'll go to him, but he will never return to me."

Then David comforted his wife Bathsheba; he went to her and slept with her. She gave birth to a son and named him Solomon. The LORD loved him, and he sent a message through the prophet Nathan, who named him Jedidiah, because of the LORD.

Joab fought against Rabbah of the Ammonites and captured the royal fortress. Then Joab sent
50 messengers to David to say, "I have fought against Rabbah and have also captured its water supply. Now therefore, assemble the rest of the troops, lay siege to the city, and capture it. Otherwise I will be the one to capture the city, and it will be named after me." So David assembled all the troops and went to Rabbah; he fought against it and captured it. He took the crown from the head of their king, and it was placed on David's head. The crown weighed seventy-five pounds of gold, and it had a precious stone in it. In addition, David took away a large quantity of plunder from the city. He removed the people who were in the city and put them to work with saws, iron picks, and iron axes, and to labor at brickmaking. He did the same to all the Ammonite cities. Then he and all his troops returned to Jerusalem.

13 Some time passed. David's son Absalom had a beautiful sister named Tamar, and David's son Amnon was infatuated with her. Amnon was frustrated to the point of making himself sick over his sister Tamar because she was a virgin, but it seemed impossible to do anything to her. Amnon had a friend named Jonadab, a son of David's brother Shimeah. Jonadab was a very shrewd man, and he asked Amnon, "Why are you, the king's son, so miserable every morning? Won't you tell me?"

Amnon replied, "I'm in love with Tamar, my brother Absalom's sister."

Jonadab said to him, "Lie down on your bed and pretend you're sick. When your father comes to see you, say to him, 'Please let my sister Tamar come and give me something to eat. Let her prepare a meal in my presence so I can watch and eat from her hand.'"

10   So Amnon lay down and pretended to be sick. When the king came to see him, Amnon said to him, "Please let my sister Tamar come and make a couple of cakes in my presence so I can eat from her hand."

     David sent word to Tamar at the palace: "Please go to your brother Amnon's house and prepare a meal for him."

     Then Tamar went to his house while Amnon was lying down. She took dough, kneaded it, made cakes in his presence, and baked them. She brought the pan and set it down in front of him, but he refused to eat. Amnon said, "Everyone leave me!" And everyone left him. "Bring the meal to the bedroom," Amnon told Tamar, "so I can eat from your hand." Tamar took the cakes she had made and went to her brother Amnon's bedroom. When she brought them to him to eat, he

20 grabbed her and said, "Come sleep with me, my sister!"

     "Don't, my brother!" she cried. "Don't disgrace me, for such a thing should never be done in Israel. Don't commit this outrage! Where could I ever go with my humiliation? And you—you would be like one of the outrageous fools in Israel! Please, speak to the king, for he won't keep me from you." But he refused to listen to her, and because he was stronger than she was, he disgraced her by raping her.

     So Amnon hated Tamar with such intensity that the hatred he hated her with was greater than the love he had loved her with. "Get out of here!" he said.

     "No," she cried, "sending me away is much worse than the great wrong you've already done to me!"

     But he refused to listen to her. Instead, he called to the servant who waited on him, "Get this

30 away from me, throw her out, and bolt the door behind her!" Amnon's servant threw her out and bolted the door behind her. Now Tamar was wearing a long-sleeved robe, because this is what the king's virgin daughters wore. Tamar put ashes on her head and tore the long-sleeved robe she was wearing. She put her hand on her head and went away crying out.

     Her brother Absalom said to her, "Has your brother Amnon been with you? Be quiet for now, my sister. He is your brother. Don't take this thing to heart." So Tamar lived as a desolate woman in the house of her brother Absalom.

When King David heard about all these things, he was furious. Absalom didn't say anything to Amnon, either good or bad, because he hated Amnon since he disgraced his sister Tamar.

     Two years later, Absalom's sheepshearers were at Baal-hazor near Ephraim, and Absalom

40 invited all the king's sons. Then he went to the king and said, "Your servant has just hired sheepshearers. Will the king and his servants please come with your servant?"

     The king replied to Absalom, "No, my son, we should not all go, or we would be a burden to you." Although Absalom urged him, he wasn't willing to go, though he did bless him.

     "If not," Absalom said, "please let my brother Amnon go with us."

     The king asked him, "Why should he go with you?" But Absalom urged him, so he sent Amnon and all the king's sons.

Now Absalom commanded his young men, "Watch Amnon until he is in a good mood from the wine. When I order you to strike Amnon, then kill him. Don't be afraid. Am I not the one who has commanded you? Be strong and valiant!" So Absalom's young men did to Amnon just as Absalom had commanded. Then all the rest of the king's sons got up, and each fled on his mule.

While they were on the way, a report reached David: "Absalom struck down all the king's sons; not even one of them survived!" In response the king stood up, tore his clothes, and lay down on the ground, and all his servants stood by with their clothes torn.

But Jonadab, son of David's brother Shimeah, spoke up: "My lord must not think they have killed all the young men, the king's sons, because only Amnon is dead. In fact, Absalom has planned this ever since the day Amnon disgraced his sister Tamar. So now, my lord the king, don't take seriously the report that says all the king's sons are dead. Only Amnon is dead."

Meanwhile, Absalom had fled. When the young man who was standing watch looked up, there were many people coming from the road west of him from the side of the mountain. Jonadab said to the king, "Look, the king's sons have come! It's exactly like your servant said." Just as he finished speaking, the king's sons entered and wept loudly. Then the king and all his servants also wept very bitterly. But Absalom fled and went to Talmai son of Ammihud, king of Geshur. And David mourned for his son every day.

After Absalom had fled to Geshur and had been there three years, King David longed to go to Absalom, for David had finished grieving over Amnon's death.

14 Joab son of Zeruiah realized that the king's mind was on Absalom. So Joab sent someone to Tekoa to bring a wise woman from there. He told her, "Pretend to be in mourning: dress in mourning clothes and don't put on any oil. Act like a woman who has been mourning for the dead for a long time. Go to the king and speak these words to him." Then Joab told her exactly what to say.

When the woman from Tekoa came to the king, she fell facedown to the ground, paid homage, and said, "Help me, Your Majesty!"

"What's the matter?" the king asked her.

"Sadly, I am a widow; my husband died," she said. "Your servant had two sons. They were fighting in the field with no one to separate them, and one struck the other and killed him. Now the whole clan has risen up against your servant and said, 'Hand over the one who killed his brother so we may put him to death for the life of the brother he murdered. We will eliminate the heir!' They would extinguish my one remaining ember by not preserving my husband's name or posterity on earth."

The king told the woman, "Go home. I will issue a command on your behalf."

Then the woman of Tekoa said to the king, "My lord the king, may any blame be on me and my father's family, and may the king and his throne be innocent."

"Whoever speaks to you," the king said, "bring him to me. He will not trouble you again!"

She replied, "Please, may the king invoke the LORD your God, so that the avenger of blood will not increase the loss, and they will not eliminate my son!"

20 "As the LORD lives," he vowed, "not a hair of your son will fall to the ground."

Then the woman said, "Please, may your servant speak a word to my lord the king?"

"Speak," he replied.

The woman asked, "Why have you devised something similar against the people of God? When the king spoke as he did about this matter, he has pronounced his own guilt. The king has not brought back his own banished one. We will certainly die and be like water poured out on the ground, which can't be recovered. But God would not take away a life; he would devise plans so that the one banished from him does not remain banished.

"Now therefore, I've come to present this matter to my lord the king because the people have made me afraid. Your servant thought: I must speak to the king. Perhaps the king will grant his 30 servant's request. The king will surely listen in order to keep his servant from the grasp of this man who would eliminate both me and my son from God's inheritance. Your servant thought: May the word of my lord the king bring relief, for my lord the king is able to discern the good and the bad like the angel of God. May the LORD your God be with you."

Then the king answered the woman, "I'm going to ask you something; don't conceal it from me!"

"Let my lord the king speak," the woman replied.

The king asked, "Did Joab put you up to all this?"

The woman answered. "As you live, my lord the king, no one can turn to the right or left from all my lord the king says. Yes, your servant Joab is the one who gave orders to me; he told your 40 servant exactly what to say. Joab your servant has done this to address the issue indirectly, but my lord has wisdom like the wisdom of the angel of God, knowing everything on earth."

Then the king said to Joab, "I hereby grant this request. Go, bring back the young man Absalom."

Joab fell with his face to the ground in homage and blessed the king. "Today," Joab said, "your servant knows I have found favor with you, my lord the king, because the king has granted the request of your servant."

So Joab got up, went to Geshur, and brought Absalom to Jerusalem. However, the king added, "He may return to his house, but he may not see my face." So Absalom returned to his house, but he did not see the king.

50 No man in all Israel was as handsome and highly praised as Absalom. From the sole of his foot to the top of his head, he did not have a single flaw. When he shaved his head—he shaved it at the end of every year because his hair got so heavy for him that he had to shave it off—he would weigh the hair from his head and it would be five pounds according to the royal standard.

Three sons were born to Absalom, and a daughter named Tamar, who was a beautiful woman. Absalom resided in Jerusalem two years but never saw the king. Then Absalom sent for Joab in order to send him to the king, but Joab was unwilling to come to him. So he sent again, a second time, but he still would not come. Then Absalom said to his servants, "See, Joab has a field right next to mine, and he has barley there. Go and set fire to it!" So Absalom's servants set the field on fire.

60 Then Joab came to Absalom's house and demanded, "Why did your servants set my field on fire?"

"Look," Absalom explained to Joab, "I sent for you and said, 'Come here. I want to send you to the king to ask: Why have I come back from Geshur? I'd be better off if I were still there.' So now, let me see the king. If I am guilty, let him kill me."

Joab went to the king and told him. So David summoned Absalom, who came to the king and paid homage with his face to the ground before him. Then the king kissed Absalom.

15 After this, Absalom got himself a chariot, horses, and fifty men to run before him. He would get up early and stand beside the road leading to the city gate. Whenever anyone had a grievance to bring before the king for settlement, Absalom called out to him and asked, "What city are you from?" If he replied, "Your servant is from one of the tribes of Israel," Absalom said to him, "Look, your claims are good and right, but the king does not have anyone to listen to you." He added, "If only someone would appoint me judge in the land. Then anyone who had a grievance or dispute could come to me, and I would make sure he received justice." When a person approached to pay homage to him, Absalom reached out his hand, took hold of him, and kissed him. Absalom did this to all the Israelites who came to the king for a settlement. So Absalom stole the hearts of the men of Israel.

10 When four years had passed, Absalom said to the king, "Please let me go to Hebron to fulfill a vow I made to the LORD. For your servant made a vow when I lived in Geshur of Aram, saying, 'If the LORD really brings me back to Jerusalem, I will worship the LORD in Hebron.'"

"Go in peace," the king said to him. So he went to Hebron.

Then Absalom sent agents throughout the tribes of Israel with this message: "When you hear the sound of the ram's horn, you are to say, 'Absalom has become king in Hebron!'"

Two hundred men from Jerusalem went with Absalom. They had been invited and were going innocently, for they did not know the whole situation. While he was offering the sacrifices, Absalom sent for David's adviser Ahithophel the Gilonite, from his city of Giloh. So the conspiracy grew strong, and the people supporting Absalom continued to increase.

20 Then an informer came to David and reported, "The hearts of the men of Israel are with Absalom."

David said to all the servants with him in Jerusalem, "Get up. We have to flee, or we will not escape from Absalom! Leave quickly, or he will overtake us quickly, heap disaster on us, and strike the city with the edge of the sword."

The king's servants said to the king, "Whatever my lord the king decides, we are your servants." Then the king set out, and his entire household followed him. But he left behind ten concubines to take care of the palace. So the king set out, and all the people followed him. They stopped at the last house while all his servants marched past him. Then all the Cherethites, the Pelethites, and the people of Gath—six hundred men who came with him from there—marched past the king.

30 The king said to Ittai of Gath, "Why are you also going with us? Go back and stay with the new king since you're both a foreigner and an exile from your homeland. Besides, you only arrived yesterday; should I make you wander around with us today while I go wherever I can? Go back and take your brothers with you. May the LORD show you kindness and faithfulness."

But in response, Ittai vowed to the king, "As the LORD lives and as my lord the king lives, wherever my lord the king is, whether it means life or death, your servant will be there!"

"March on," David replied to Ittai. So Ittai of Gath marched past with all his men and the dependents who were with him. Everyone in the countryside was weeping loudly while all the people were marching out of the city. As the king was crossing the Kidron Valley, all the people were marching past on the road that leads to the wilderness.

40 Zadok was also there, and all the Levites with him were carrying the ark of the covenant of God. They set the ark of God down, and Abiathar offered sacrifices until the people had finished marching past. Then the king instructed Zadok, "Return the ark of God to the city. If I find favor with the LORD, he will bring me back and allow me to see both it and its dwelling place. However, if he should say, 'I do not delight in you,' then here I am—he can do with me whatever pleases him."

The king also said to the priest Zadok, "Look, return to the city in peace and your two sons with you: your son Ahimaaz and Abiathar's son Jonathan. Remember, I'll wait at the fords of the wilderness until word comes from you to inform me." So Zadok and Abiathar returned the ark of God to Jerusalem and stayed there.

50 David was climbing the slope of the Mount of Olives, weeping as he ascended. His head was covered, and he was walking barefoot. All of the people with him covered their heads and went up, weeping as they ascended.

Then someone reported to David, "Ahithophel is among the conspirators with Absalom."

"LORD," David pleaded, "please turn the counsel of Ahithophel into foolishness!"

When David came to the summit where he used to worship God, Hushai the Archite was there to meet him with his robe torn and dust on his head. David said to him, "If you go away with me, you'll be a burden to me, but if you return to the city and tell Absalom, 'I will be your servant, Your Majesty! Previously, I was your father's servant, but now I will be your servant,' then you can counteract Ahithophel's counsel for me. Won't the priests Zadok and Abiathar be there with you?

60 Report everything you hear from the palace to the priests Zadok and Abiathar. Take note: their two sons are there with them—Zadok's son Ahimaaz and Abiathar's son Jonathan. Send them to tell me everything you hear." So Hushai, David's personal adviser, entered Jerusalem just as Absalom was entering the city.

16 When David had gone a little beyond the summit, Ziba, Mephibosheth's servant, was right there to meet him. He had a pair of saddled donkeys loaded with two hundred loaves of bread, one hundred clusters of raisins, one hundred bunches of summer fruit, and a clay jar of wine. The king said to Ziba, "Why do you have these?"

Ziba answered, "The donkeys are for the king's household to ride, the bread and summer fruit are for the young men to eat, and the wine is for those to drink who become exhausted in the wilderness."

"Where is your master's grandson?" the king asked.

"Why, he's staying in Jerusalem," Ziba replied to the king, "for he said, 'Today, the house of Israel will restore my grandfather's kingdom to me.'"

The king said to Ziba, "All that belongs to Mephibosheth is now yours!"

"I bow before you," Ziba said. "May I find favor with you, my lord the king!"

When King David got to Bahurim, a man belonging to the family of the house of Saul was just coming out. His name was Shimei son of Gera, and he was yelling curses as he approached. He threw stones at David and at all the royal servants, the people and the warriors on David's right and left. Shimei said as he cursed, "Get out, get out, you man of bloodshed, you wicked man! The LORD has paid you back for all the blood of the house of Saul in whose place you became king, and the LORD has handed the kingdom over to your son Absalom. Look, you are in trouble because you're a man of bloodshed!"

Then Abishai son of Zeruiah said to the king, "Why should this dead dog curse my lord the king? Let me go over and remove his head!"

The king replied, "Sons of Zeruiah, do we agree on anything? He curses me this way because the LORD told him, 'Curse David!' Therefore, who can say, 'Why did you do that?'" Then David said to Abishai and all his servants, "Look, my own son, my own flesh and blood, intends to take my life—how much more now this Benjaminite! Leave him alone and let him curse me; the LORD has told him to. Perhaps the LORD will see my affliction and restore goodness to me instead of Shimei's curses today." So David and his men proceeded along the road as Shimei was going along the ridge of the hill opposite him. As Shimei went, he cursed David, threw stones at him, and kicked up dust. Finally, the king and all the people with him arrived exhausted, so they rested there.

Now Absalom and all the Israelites came to Jerusalem. Ahithophel was also with him. When David's friend Hushai the Archite came to Absalom, Hushai said to Absalom, "Long live the king! Long live the king!"

"Is this your loyalty to your friend?" Absalom asked Hushai. "Why didn't you go with your friend?"

"Not at all," Hushai answered Absalom. "I am on the side of the one that the LORD, this people, and all the men of Israel have chosen. I will stay with him. Furthermore, whom will I serve if not his son? As I served in your father's presence, I will also serve in yours."

Then Absalom said to Ahithophel, "Give me your advice. What should we do?"

Ahithophel replied to Absalom, "Sleep with your father's concubines whom he left to take care of the palace. When all Israel hears that you have become repulsive to your father, everyone with you will be encouraged." So they pitched a tent for Absalom on the roof, and he slept with his
40 father's concubines in the sight of all Israel.

Now the advice Ahithophel gave in those days was like someone asking about a word from God—such was the regard that both David and Absalom had for Ahithophel's advice. Ahithophel
17 said to Absalom, "Let me choose twelve thousand men, and I will set out in pursuit of David tonight. I will attack him while he is weary and discouraged, throw him into a panic, and all the people with him will scatter. I will strike down only the king and bring all the people back to you. When everyone returns except the man you're looking for, all the people will be at peace." This proposal seemed right to Absalom and all the elders of Israel.

Then Absalom said, "Summon Hushai the Archite also. Let's hear what he has to say as well."

So Hushai came to Absalom, and Absalom told him, "Ahithophel offered this proposal. Should we carry out his proposal? If not, what do you say?"

Hushai replied to Absalom, "The advice Ahithophel has given this time is not good." Hushai
10 continued, "You know your father and his men. They are warriors and are desperate like a wild bear robbed of her cubs. Your father is an experienced soldier who won't spend the night with the people. He's probably already hiding in one of the caves or some other place. If some of our troops fall first, someone is sure to hear and say, 'There's been a slaughter among the people who follow Absalom.' Then, even a brave man with the heart of a lion will lose heart because all Israel knows that your father and the valiant men with him are warriors. Instead, I advise that all Israel from Dan to Beer-sheba—as numerous as the sand by the sea—be gathered to you and that you personally go into battle. Then we will attack David wherever we find him, and we will descend on him like dew on the ground. Not even one will be left—neither he nor any of the men with him. If he retreats to some city, all Israel will bring ropes to that city, and we
20 will drag its stones into the valley until not even a pebble can be found there." Since the LORD had decreed that Ahithophel's good advice be undermined in order to bring about Absalom's ruin, Absalom and all the men of Israel said, "The advice of Hushai the Archite is better than Ahithophel's advice."

Hushai then told the priests Zadok and Abiathar, "This is what Ahithophel advised Absalom and the elders of Israel, and this is what I advised. Now send someone quickly and tell David, 'Don't spend the night at the wilderness ford, but be sure to cross over the Jordan, or the king and all the people with him will be devoured.'"

Jonathan and Ahimaaz were staying at En-rogel, where a servant girl would come and pass along information to them. They in turn would go and inform King David, because they dared
30 not be seen entering the city. However, a young man did see them and informed Absalom. So the two left quickly and came to the house of a man in Bahurim. He had a well in his courtyard, and

they climbed down into it. Then his wife took the cover, placed it over the mouth of the well, and scattered grain on it so nobody would know anything.

Absalom's servants came to the woman at the house and asked, "Where are Ahimaaz and Jonathan?"

"They passed by toward the water," the woman replied to them. The men searched but did not find them, so they returned to Jerusalem.

After they had gone, Ahimaaz and Jonathan climbed out of the well and went and informed King David. They told him, "Get up and immediately ford the river, for Ahithophel has given this advice against you." So David and all the people with him got up and crossed the Jordan. By daybreak, there was no one who had not crossed the Jordan.

When Ahithophel realized that his advice had not been followed, he saddled his donkey and set out for his house in his hometown. He set his house in order and hanged himself. So he died and was buried in his father's tomb.

David had arrived at Mahanaim by the time Absalom crossed the Jordan with all the men of Israel. Now Absalom had appointed Amasa over the army in Joab's place. Amasa was the son of a man named Ithra the Israelite; Ithra had married Abigail daughter of Nahash. Abigail was a sister to Zeruiah, Joab's mother. And Israel and Absalom camped in the land of Gilead. When David came to Mahanaim, Shobi son of Nahash from Rabbah of the Ammonites, Machir son of Ammiel from Lo-debar, and Barzillai the Gileadite from Rogelim brought beds, basins, and pottery items. They also brought wheat, barley, flour, roasted grain, beans, lentils, honey, curds, sheep, goats, and cheese from the herd for David and the people with him to eat. They had reasoned, "The people must be hungry, exhausted, and thirsty in the wilderness."

18 David reviewed his troops and appointed commanders of thousands and of hundreds over them. He then sent out the troops, a third under Joab, a third under Joab's brother Abishai son of Zeruiah, and a third under Ittai of Gath. The king said to the troops, "I must also march out with you."

"You must not go!" the people pleaded. "If we have to flee, they will not pay any attention to us. Even if half of us die, they will not pay any attention to us because you are worth ten thousand of us. Therefore, it is better if you support us from the city."

"I will do whatever you think is best," the king replied to them. So he stood beside the city gate while all the troops marched out by hundreds and thousands. The king commanded Joab, Abishai, and Ittai, "Treat the young man Absalom gently for my sake." All the people heard the king's orders to all the commanders about Absalom.

Then David's forces marched into the field to engage Israel in battle, which took place in the forest of Ephraim. Israel's army was defeated by David's soldiers, and the slaughter there was vast that day—twenty thousand dead. The battle spread over the entire area, and that day the forest claimed more people than the sword.

Absalom was riding on his mule when he happened to meet David's soldiers. When the mule went under the tangled branches of a large oak tree, Absalom's head was caught fast in the tree. The mule under him kept going, so he was suspended in midair. One of the men saw him and informed Joab. He said, "I just saw Absalom hanging in an oak tree!"

"You just saw him!" Joab exclaimed. "Why didn't you strike him to the ground right there? I would have given you ten silver pieces and a belt!"

The man replied to Joab, "Even if I had the weight of a thousand pieces of silver in my hand, I would not raise my hand against the king's son. For we heard the king command you, Abishai, and Ittai, 'Protect the young man Absalom for me.' If I had jeopardized my own life—and nothing is hidden from the king—you would have abandoned me."

Joab said, "I'm not going to waste time with you!" He then took three spears in his hand and thrust them into Absalom's chest. While Absalom was still alive in the oak tree, ten young men who were Joab's armor-bearers surrounded Absalom, struck him, and killed him. Joab blew the ram's horn, and the troops broke off their pursuit of Israel because Joab restrained them. They took Absalom, threw him into a large pit in the forest, and raised up a huge mound of stones over him. And all Israel fled, each to his tent.

When he was alive, Absalom had taken a pillar and raised it up for himself in the King's Valley, since he thought, "I have no son to preserve the memory of my name." So he named the pillar after himself. It is still called Absalom's Monument today.

Ahimaaz son of Zadok said, "Please let me run and tell the king the good news that the LORD has vindicated him by freeing him from his enemies."

Joab replied to him, "You are not the man to take good news today. You may do it another day, but today you aren't taking good news, because the king's son is dead." Joab then said to a Cushite, "Go tell the king what you have seen." The Cushite bowed to Joab and took off running.

However, Ahimaaz son of Zadok persisted and said to Joab, "No matter what, please let me also run behind the Cushite!"

Joab replied, "My son, why do you want to run since you won't get a reward?"

"No matter what, I want to run!"

"Then run!" Joab said to him. So Ahimaaz ran by way of the plain and outran the Cushite.

David was sitting between the city gates when the watchman went up to the roof of the city gate and over to the wall. The watchman looked out and saw a man running alone. He called out and told the king.

The king said, "If he's alone, he bears good news."

As the first runner came closer, the watchman saw another man running. He called out to the gatekeeper, "Look! Another man is running alone!"

"This one is also bringing good news," said the king.

The watchman said, "The way the first man runs looks to me like the way Ahimaaz son of Zadok runs."

"This is a good man; he comes with good news," the king commented.

Ahimaaz called out to the king, "All is well," and paid homage to the king with his face to the ground. He continued, "Blessed be the LORD your God! He delivered up the men who rebelled against my lord the king."

The king asked, "Is the young man Absalom all right?"

Ahimaaz replied, "When Joab sent the king's servant and your servant, I saw a big disturbance, but I don't know what it was."

60 The king said, "Move aside and stand here." So he stood to one side.

Just then the Cushite came and said, "May my lord the king hear the good news: The LORD has vindicated you today by freeing you from all who rise against you!"

The king asked the Cushite, "Is the young man Absalom all right?"

The Cushite replied, "I wish that the enemies of my lord the king, along with all who rise up against you with evil intent, would become like that young man."

The king was deeply moved and went up to the chamber above the city gate and wept. As he walked, he cried, "My son Absalom! My son, my son Absalom! If only I had died instead of you, Absalom, my son, my son!"

19 It was reported to Joab, "The king is weeping. He's mourning over Absalom." That day's victory was turned into mourning for all the troops because on that day the troops heard, "The king is grieving over his son." So they returned to the city quietly that day like troops come in when they are humiliated after fleeing in battle. But the king covered his face and cried loudly, "My son Absalom! Absalom, my son, my son!"

Then Joab went into the house to the king and said, "Today you have shamed all your soldiers—those who saved your life as well as your sons, your wives, and your concubines—by loving your enemies and hating those who love you! Today you have made it clear that the commanders and soldiers mean nothing to you. In fact, today I know that if Absalom were alive 10 and all of us were dead, it would be fine with you!

"Now get up! Go out and encourage your soldiers, for I swear by the LORD that if you don't go out, not a man will remain with you tonight. This will be worse for you than all the trouble that has come to you from your youth until now!"

So the king got up and sat in the city gate, and all the people were told, "Look, the king is sitting in the city gate." Then they all came into the king's presence.

Meanwhile, each Israelite had fled to his tent. People throughout all the tribes of Israel were arguing among themselves, saying, "The king rescued us from the grasp of our enemies, and he saved us from the grasp of the Philistines, but now he has fled from the land because of Absalom. But Absalom, the man we anointed over us, has died in battle. So why do you say nothing about restoring the king?"

20 King David sent word to the priests Zadok and Abiathar: "Say to the elders of Judah, 'Why should you be the last to restore the king to his palace? The talk of all Israel has reached the king

at his house. You are my brothers, my flesh and blood. So why should you be the last to restore the king?' And tell Amasa, 'Aren't you my flesh and blood? May God punish me and do so severely if you don't become commander of my army from now on instead of Joab!'"

So he won over all the men of Judah, and they unanimously sent word to the king: "Come back, you and all your servants." Then the king returned. When he arrived at the Jordan, Judah came to Gilgal to meet the king and escort him across the Jordan.

Shimei son of Gera, the Benjaminite from Bahurim, hurried down with the men of Judah to meet King David. There were a thousand men from Benjamin with him. Ziba, an attendant from the
30 house of Saul, with his fifteen sons and twenty servants also rushed down to the Jordan ahead of the king. They forded the Jordan to bring the king's household across and do whatever the king desired.

When Shimei son of Gera crossed the Jordan, he fell facedown before the king and said to him, "My lord, don't hold me guilty, and don't remember your servant's wrongdoing on the day my lord the king left Jerusalem. May the king not take it to heart. For your servant knows that I have sinned. But look! Today I am the first one of the entire house of Joseph to come down to meet my lord the king."

Abishai son of Zeruiah asked, "Shouldn't Shimei be put to death for this, because he cursed the LORD's anointed?"

David answered, "Sons of Zeruiah, do we agree on anything? Have you become my adversary today? Should any man be killed in Israel today? Am I not aware that today I'm king over Israel?"
40 So the king said to Shimei, "You will not die." Then the king gave him his oath.

Mephibosheth, Saul's grandson, also went down to meet the king. He had not taken care of his feet, trimmed his mustache, or washed his clothes from the day the king left until the day he returned safely. When he came from Jerusalem to meet the king, the king asked him, "Mephibosheth, why didn't you come with me?"

"My lord the king," he replied, "my servant Ziba betrayed me. Actually your servant said, 'I'll saddle the donkey for myself so that I may ride it and go with the king'—for your servant is lame. Ziba slandered your servant to my lord the king. But my lord the king is like the angel of God, so do whatever you think best. For my grandfather's entire family deserves death from my lord the king, but you set your servant among those who eat at your table. So what further right do I have
50 to keep on making appeals to the king?"

The king said to him, "Why keep on speaking about these matters of yours? I hereby declare: you and Ziba are to divide the land."

Mephibosheth said to the king, "Instead, since my lord the king has come to his palace safely, let Ziba take it all!"

Barzillai the Gileadite had come down from Rogelim and accompanied the king to the Jordan River to see him off at the Jordan. Barzillai was a very old man—eighty years old—and since he was a very wealthy man, he had provided for the needs of the king while he stayed in Mahanaim.

The king said to Barzillai, "Cross over with me, and I'll provide for you at my side in Jerusalem."

60 Barzillai replied to the king, "How many years of my life are left that I should go up to Jerusalem with the king? I'm now eighty years old. Can I discern what is pleasant and what is not? Can your servant taste what he eats or drinks? Can I still hear the voice of male and female singers? Why should your servant be an added burden to my lord the king? Since your servant is only going with the king a little way across the Jordan, why should the king repay me with such a reward? Please let your servant return so that I may die in my own city near the tomb of my father and mother. But here is your servant Chimham; let him cross over with my lord the king. Do for him what seems good to you."

The king replied, "Chimham will cross over with me, and I will do for him what seems good to you, and whatever you desire from me I will do for you." So all the people crossed the Jordan, 70 and then the king crossed. The king kissed Barzillai and blessed him, and Barzillai returned to his home.

The king went on to Gilgal, and Chimham went with him. All the troops of Judah and half of Israel's escorted the king. Suddenly, all the men of Israel came to the king. They asked him, "Why did our brothers, the men of Judah, take you away secretly and transport the king and his household across the Jordan, along with all of David's men?"

All the men of Judah responded to the men of Israel, "Because the king is our relative. Why does this make you angry? Have we ever eaten anything of the king's or been honored at all?"

The men of Israel answered the men of Judah, "We have ten shares in the king, so we have a greater claim to David than you. Why then do you despise us? Weren't we the first to speak of 80 restoring our king?" But the words of the men of Judah were harsher than those of the men of Israel.

20 Now a wicked man, a Benjaminite named Sheba son of Bichri, happened to be there. He blew the ram's horn and shouted:

> We have no portion in David,
> no inheritance in Jesse's son.
> Each man to his tent, Israel!

So all the men of Israel deserted David and followed Sheba son of Bichri, but the men of Judah from the Jordan all the way to Jerusalem remained loyal to their king.

When David came to his palace in Jerusalem, he took the ten concubines he had left to take care of the palace and placed them under guard. He provided for them, but he was not intimate 10 with them. They were confined until the day of their death, living as widows.

The king said to Amasa, "Summon the men of Judah to me within three days and be here yourself." Amasa went to summon Judah, but he took longer than the time allotted him. So David said to Abishai, "Sheba son of Bichri will do more harm to us than Absalom. Take your lord's soldiers and pursue him, or he will find fortified cities and elude us."

So Joab's men, the Cherethites, the Pelethites, and all the warriors marched out under Abishai's command; they left Jerusalem to pursue Sheba son of Bichri. They were at the great stone in Gibeon when Amasa joined them. Joab was wearing his uniform and over it was a belt around his waist with a sword in its sheath. As he approached, the sword fell out. Joab asked Amasa, "Are you well, my brother?" Then with his right hand Joab grabbed Amasa by the beard to kiss him. Amasa was not on guard against the sword in Joab's hand, and Joab stabbed him in the stomach with it and spilled his intestines out on the ground. Joab did not stab him again, and Amasa died.

Joab and his brother Abishai pursued Sheba son of Bichri. One of Joab's young men had stood over Amasa saying, "Whoever favors Joab and whoever is for David, follow Joab!" Now Amasa had been writhing in his blood in the middle of the highway, and the man had seen that all the troops stopped. So he moved Amasa from the highway to the field and threw a garment over him because he realized that all those who encountered Amasa were stopping. When he was removed from the highway, all the men passed by and followed Joab to pursue Sheba son of Bichri.

Sheba passed through all the tribes of Israel to Abel of Beth-maacah. All the Berites came together and followed him. Joab's troops came and besieged Sheba in Abel of Beth-maacah. They built a siege ramp against the outer wall of the city. While all the troops with Joab were battering the wall to make it collapse, a wise woman called out from the city, "Listen! Listen! Please tell Joab to come here and let me speak with him."

When he had come near her, the woman asked, "Are you Joab?"

"I am," he replied.

"Listen to the words of your servant," she said to him.

He answered, "I'm listening."

She said, "In the past they used to say, 'Seek counsel in Abel,' and that's how they settled disputes. I am one of the peaceful and faithful in Israel, but you're trying to destroy a city that is like a mother in Israel. Why would you devour the LORD's inheritance?"

Joab protested: "Never! I would never devour or demolish! That is not the case. There is a man named Sheba son of Bichri, from the hill country of Ephraim, who has rebelled against King David. Deliver this one man, and I will withdraw from the city."

The woman replied to Joab, "Watch! His head will be thrown over the wall to you." The woman went to all the people with her wise counsel, and they cut off the head of Sheba son of Bichri and threw it to Joab. So he blew the ram's horn, and they dispersed from the city, each to his own tent. Joab returned to the king in Jerusalem.

> Joab commanded the whole army of Israel;
> Benaiah son of Jehoiada was over the Cherethites and Pelethites;
> Adoram was over forced labor;
> Jehoshaphat son of Ahilud was court historian;
> Sheva was court secretary;
> Zadok and Abiathar were priests;
> and in addition, Ira the Jairite was David's priest.

21 During David's reign there was a famine for three successive years, so David inquired of the LORD. The LORD answered, "It is due to Saul and to his bloody family, because he killed the Gibeonites."

The Gibeonites were not Israelites but rather a remnant of the Amorites. The Israelites had taken an oath concerning them, but Saul had tried to kill them in his zeal for the Israelites and Judah. So David summoned the Gibeonites and spoke to them. He asked the Gibeonites, "What should I do for you? How can I make atonement so that you will bring a blessing on the LORD's inheritance?"

The Gibeonites said to him, "We are not asking for silver and gold from Saul or his family, and we cannot put anyone to death in Israel."

10 "Whatever you say, I will do for you," he said.

They replied to the king, "As for the man who annihilated us and plotted to destroy us so we would not exist within the whole territory of Israel, let seven of his male descendants be handed over to us so we may hang them in the presence of the LORD at Gibeah of Saul, the LORD's chosen."

The king answered, "I will hand them over."

David spared Mephibosheth, the son of Saul's son Jonathan, because of the oath of the LORD that was between David and Jonathan, Saul's son. But the king took Armoni and Mephibosheth, who were the two sons whom Rizpah daughter of Aiah had borne to Saul, and the five sons whom Merab daughter of Saul had borne to Adriel son of Barzillai the Meholathite and handed them 20 over to the Gibeonites. They hanged them on the hill in the presence of the LORD; the seven of them died together. They were executed in the first days of the harvest at the beginning of the barley harvest.

Rizpah, Aiah's daughter, took sackcloth and spread it out for herself on the rock from the beginning of the harvest until the rain poured down from heaven on the bodies. She kept the birds of the sky from them by day and the wild animals by night.

When it was reported to David what Saul's concubine Rizpah daughter of Aiah had done, he went and got the bones of Saul and his son Jonathan from the citizens of Jabesh-gilead. They had stolen them from the public square of Beth-shan where the Philistines had hung the bodies the day the Philistines killed Saul at Gilboa. David had the bones brought from there. They gathered 30 up the bones of Saul's family who had been hanged and buried the bones of Saul and his son Jonathan at Zela in the land of Benjamin in the tomb of Saul's father Kish. They did everything the king commanded. After this, God was receptive to prayer for the land.

The Philistines again waged war against Israel. David went down with his soldiers, and they fought the Philistines, but David became exhausted. Then Ishbi-benob, one of the descendants of the giant, whose bronze spear weighed about eight pounds and who wore new armor, intended to kill David. But Abishai son of Zeruiah came to his aid, struck the Philistine, and killed him.

Then David's men swore to him, "You must never again go out with us to battle. You must not extinguish the lamp of Israel."

After this, there was another battle with the Philistines at Gob. At that time Sibbecai the

40 Hushathite killed Saph, who was one of the descendants of the giant.

Once again there was a battle with the Philistines at Gob, and Elhanan son of Jaare-oregim the Bethlehemite killed Goliath of Gath. The shaft of his spear was like a weaver's beam.

At Gath there was still another battle. A huge man was there with six fingers on each hand and six toes on each foot—twenty-four in all. He, too, was descended from the giant. When he taunted Israel, Jonathan, son of David's brother Shimei, killed him.

These four were descended from the giant in Gath and were killed by David and his soldiers.

22 David spoke the words of this song to the LORD on the day the LORD rescued him from the grasp of all his enemies and from the grasp of Saul. He said:

> The LORD is my rock, my fortress, and my deliverer,
> my God, my rock where I seek refuge.
> My shield, the horn of my salvation, my stronghold, my refuge,
> and my Savior, you save me from violence.
> I called to the LORD, who is worthy of praise,
> and I was saved from my enemies.
> For the waves of death engulfed me;
10   the torrents of destruction terrified me.
> The ropes of Sheol entangled me;
> the snares of death confronted me.
>
> I called to the LORD in my distress;
> I called to my God.
> From his temple he heard my voice,
> and my cry for help reached his ears.
> Then the earth shook and quaked;
> the foundations of the heavens trembled;
> they shook because he burned with anger.
20 Smoke rose from his nostrils,
> and consuming fire came from his mouth;
> coals were set ablaze by it.
> He bent the heavens and came down,
> total darkness beneath his feet.
> He rode on a cherub and flew,
> soaring on the wings of the wind.

He made darkness a canopy around him,
a gathering of water and thick clouds.
From the radiance of his presence,
30 blazing coals were ignited.
The LORD thundered from heaven;
the Most High made his voice heard.
He shot arrows and scattered them;
he hurled lightning bolts and routed them.
The depths of the sea became visible,
the foundations of the world were exposed
at the rebuke of the LORD,
at the blast of the breath of his nostrils.

He reached down from on high
40 and took hold of me;
he pulled me out of deep water.
He rescued me from my powerful enemy
and from those who hated me,
for they were too strong for me.
They confronted me in the day of my calamity,
but the LORD was my support.
He brought me out to a spacious place;
he rescued me because he delighted in me.

The LORD rewarded me
50 according to my righteousness;
he repaid me
according to the cleanness of my hands.
For I have kept the ways of the LORD
and have not turned from my God to wickedness.
Indeed, I let all his ordinances guide me
and have not disregarded his statutes.
I was blameless before him
and kept myself from my iniquity.
So the LORD repaid me
60 according to my righteousness,
according to my cleanness in his sight.

With the faithful
you prove yourself faithful,
with the blameless
you prove yourself blameless,
with the pure
you prove yourself pure,
but with the crooked
you prove yourself shrewd.

70　You rescue an oppressed people,
but your eyes are set against the proud—
you humble them.
LORD, you are my lamp;
the LORD illuminates my darkness.
With you I can attack a barricade,
and with my God I can leap over a wall.
God—his way is perfect;
the word of the LORD is pure.
He is a shield to all who take refuge in him.

80　For who is God besides the LORD?
And who is a rock? Only our God.
God is my strong refuge;
he makes my way perfect.
He makes my feet like the feet of a deer
and sets me securely on the heights.
He trains my hands for war;
my arms can bend a bow of bronze.
You have given me the shield of your salvation;
your help exalts me.

90　You make a spacious place beneath me for my steps,
and my ankles do not give way.
I pursue my enemies and destroy them;
I do not turn back until they are wiped out.
I wipe them out and crush them,
and they do not rise;
they fall beneath my feet.
You have clothed me with strength for battle;
you subdue my adversaries beneath me.

You have made my enemies retreat before me;
100   I annihilate those who hate me.
They look, but there is no one to save them—
they look to the Lord, but he does not answer them.
I pulverize them like dust of the earth;
I crush them and trample them like mud in the streets.

You have freed me from the feuds among my people;
you have preserved me as head of nations;
a people I had not known serve me.
Foreigners submit to me cringing;
as soon as they hear, they obey me.
110   Foreigners lose heart
and come trembling from their fortifications.

The Lord lives—blessed be my rock!
God, the rock of my salvation, is exalted.
God—he grants me vengeance
and casts down peoples under me.
He frees me from my enemies.
You exalt me above my adversaries;
you rescue me from violent men.

Therefore I will give thanks to you among the nations, Lord;
120   I will sing praises about your name.
He is a tower of salvation for his king;
he shows loyalty to his anointed,
to David and his descendants forever.

23 These are the last words of David:
The declaration of David son of Jesse,
the declaration of the man raised on high,
the one anointed by the God of Jacob.
This is the most delightful of Israel's songs.
The Spirit of the Lord spoke through me,
his word was on my tongue.
The God of Israel spoke;
the Rock of Israel said to me,

10 "The one who rules the people with justice,
who rules in the fear of God,
is like the morning light when the sun rises
on a cloudless morning,
the glisten of rain on sprouting grass."

Is it not true my house is with God?
For he has established a permanent covenant with me,
ordered and secured in every detail.
Will he not bring about
my whole salvation and my every desire?
20 But all the wicked are like thorns raked aside;
they can never be picked up by hand.
The man who touches them
must be armed with iron and the shaft of a spear.
They will be completely burned up on the spot.

These are the names of David's warriors:

Josheb-basshebeth the Tahchemonite was chief of the officers. He wielded his spear against eight hundred men that he killed at one time.

After him, Eleazar son of Dodo son of an Ahohite was among the three warriors with David when they defied the Philistines. The men of Israel retreated in the place they had gathered for 30 battle, but Eleazar stood his ground and attacked the Philistines until his hand was tired and stuck to his sword. The LORD brought about a great victory that day. Then the troops came back to him, but only to plunder the dead.

After him was Shammah son of Agee the Hararite. The Philistines had assembled in formation where there was a field full of lentils. The troops fled from the Philistines, but Shammah took his stand in the middle of the field, defended it, and struck down the Philistines. So the LORD brought about a great victory.

Three of the thirty leading warriors went down at harvest time and came to David at the cave of Adullam, while a company of Philistines was camping in Rephaim Valley. At that time David was in the stronghold, and a Philistine garrison was at Bethlehem. David was extremely 40 thirsty and said, "If only someone would bring me water to drink from the well at the city gate of Bethlehem!" So three of the warriors broke through the Philistine camp and drew water from the well at the gate of Bethlehem. They brought it back to David, but he refused to drink it. Instead, he poured it out to the LORD. David said, "LORD, I would never do such a thing! Is this not the blood of men who risked their lives?" So he refused to drink it. Such were the exploits of the three warriors.

Abishai, Joab's brother and son of Zeruiah, was leader of the Three. He wielded his spear against three hundred men and killed them, gaining a reputation among the Three. Was he not more honored than the Three? He became their commander even though he did not become one of the Three.

50 Benaiah son of Jehoiada was the son of a brave man from Kabzeel, a man of many exploits. Benaiah killed two sons of Ariel of Moab, and he went down into a pit on a snowy day and killed a lion. He also killed an Egyptian, an impressive man. Even though the Egyptian had a spear in his hand, Benaiah went down to him with a staff, snatched the spear out of the Egyptian's hand, and then killed him with his own spear. These were the exploits of Benaiah son of Jehoiada, who had a reputation among the three warriors. He was the most honored of the Thirty, but he did not become one of the Three. David put him in charge of his bodyguard.

Among the Thirty were
Joab's brother Asahel,
Elhanan son of Dodo of Bethlehem,
60 Shammah the Harodite,
Elika the Harodite,
Helez the Paltite,
Ira son of Ikkesh the Tekoite,
Abiezer the Anathothite,
Mebunnai the Hushathite,
Zalmon the Ahohite,
Maharai the Netophathite,
Heleb son of Baanah the Netophathite,
Ittai son of Ribai from Gibeah of the Benjaminites,
70 Benaiah the Pirathonite,
Hiddai from the wadis of Gaash,
Abi-albon the Arbathite,
Azmaveth the Barhumite,
Eliahba the Shaalbonite,
the sons of Jashen,
Jonathan son of Shammah the Hararite,
Ahiam son of Sharar the Hararite,
Eliphelet son of Ahasbai son of the Maacathite,
Eliam son of Ahithophel the Gilonite,
80 Hezro the Carmelite,
Paarai the Arbite,
Igal son of Nathan from Zobah,
Bani the Gadite,

Zelek the Ammonite,
Naharai the Beerothite, the armor-bearer for Joab son of Zeruiah,
Ira the Ithrite,
Gareb the Ithrite,
and Uriah the Hethite.
There were thirty-seven in all.

24 The Lord's anger burned against Israel again, and he stirred up David against them to say, "Go, count the people of Israel and Judah."

So the king said to Joab, the commander of his army, "Go through all the tribes of Israel from Dan to Beer-sheba and register the troops so I can know their number."

Joab replied to the king, "May the Lord your God multiply the troops a hundred times more than they are—while my lord the king looks on! But why does my lord the king want to do this?"

Yet the king's order prevailed over Joab and the commanders of the army. So Joab and the commanders of the army left the king's presence to register the troops of Israel.

They crossed the Jordan and camped in Aroer, south of the town in the middle of the valley, and then proceeded toward Gad and Jazer. They went to Gilead and to the land of the Hittites and continued on to Dan-jaan and around to Sidon. They went to the fortress of Tyre and all the cities of the Hivites and Canaanites. Afterward, they went to the Negev of Judah at Beer-sheba.

When they had gone through the whole land, they returned to Jerusalem at the end of nine months and twenty days. Joab gave the king the total of the registration of the troops. There were eight hundred thousand valiant armed men from Israel and five hundred thousand men from Judah.

David's conscience troubled him after he had taken a census of the troops. He said to the Lord, "I have sinned greatly in what I've done. Now, Lord, because I've been very foolish, please take away your servant's guilt."

When David got up in the morning, the word of the Lord had come to the prophet Gad, David's seer: "Go and say to David, 'This is what the Lord says: I am offering you three choices. Choose one of them, and I will do it to you.'"

So Gad went to David, told him the choices, and asked him, "Do you want three years of famine to come on your land, to flee from your foes three months while they pursue you, or to have a plague in your land three days? Now, consider carefully what answer I should take back to the one who sent me."

David answered Gad, "I have great anxiety. Please, let us fall into the Lord's hands because his mercies are great, but don't let me fall into human hands."

So the Lord sent a plague on Israel from that morning until the appointed time, and from Dan to Beer-sheba seventy thousand men died. Then the angel extended his hand toward Jerusalem to destroy it, but the LORD relented concerning the destruction and said to the angel who was destroying the people, "Enough, withdraw your hand now!" The angel of the LORD was then at the threshing floor of Araunah the Jebusite.

When David saw the angel striking the people, he said to the LORD, "Look, I am the one who has sinned; I am the one who has done wrong. But these sheep, what have they done? Please, let your hand be against me and my father's family."

Gad came to David that day and said to him, "Go up and set up an altar to the LORD on the threshing floor of Araunah the Jebusite." David went up in obedience to Gad's command, just as the LORD had commanded. Araunah looked down and saw the king and his servants coming 40 toward him, so he went out and paid homage to the king with his face to the ground.

Araunah said, "Why has my lord the king come to his servant?"

David replied, "To buy the threshing floor from you in order to build an altar to the LORD, so the plague on the people may be halted."

Araunah said to David, "My lord the king may take whatever he wants and offer it. Here are the oxen for a burnt offering and the threshing sledges and ox yokes for the wood. Your Majesty, Araunah gives everything here to the king." Then he said to the king, "May the LORD your God accept you."

The king answered Araunah, "No, I insist on buying it from you for a price, for I will not offer to the LORD my God burnt offerings that cost me nothing." David bought the threshing floor 50 and the oxen for twenty ounces of silver. He built an altar to the LORD there and offered burnt offerings and fellowship offerings. Then the LORD was receptive to prayer for the land, and the plague on Israel ended.

Introduction to Kings

Ralph K. Hawkins

The Kings Corpus recounts the history of Israel under a monarchy. The books survey more than four centuries of history, tracking the united and divided monarchies from Solomon in the 10th century BC to Zedekiah in the 6th century BC. Israel's national story is a tragic one that ends in destruction due to failure to maintain covenant with Yahweh.

The Kings Corpus contains no information about its author and is essentially anonymous. The books could not have been completed until after 561 BC, since that is the date of its last recorded historical event (see 2 Kgs 25.48–53). The author does not mention the edict of Cyrus, which ended the exile in 539 BC (2 Chr 36.40–45). The Kings Corpus, therefore, must have been completed between 561–539 BC, during the final decades of the exile.

The primary literary genre of the Kings Corpus is historical narrative. The books are more than history, however, but view Israel's past through a Deuteronomistic lens. This means that they understand and interpret Israel's history in light of Deuteronomy, ancient Israel's constitutional document. The author assumes a theology of retribution, in which obedience to the covenant results in blessings and disobedience in curses (see Deut 28). From the perspective of exile, the author looks back over Israel's national history and links its demise to covenant unfaithfulness. Following the division of the united monarchy into the Northern and Southern Kingdoms (Israel and Judah, respectively), their kings are evaluated on the basis of a regnal formula consisting of: (1) introductory sentences (e.g., 1 Kgs 15.1–2); (2) an evaluation sentence (1 Kgs 15.3–4); (3) a reference to the royal annals (1 Kgs 15.9–11); and (4) a death, burial, and successor account (1 Kgs 15.11–12). The author's survey of Israel and Judah's kings proves his thesis, since the vast majority of them were unfaithful to Yahweh.

The narrative of the Kings Corpus has three main parts. The first part narrates the reign of Solomon (1 Kgs 1–11). He experienced two theophanies (1 Kgs 3.7–23; 9.1–25), was a great builder, and a pioneer in international commerce (1 Kgs 9.26–47). His reign was viewed as a magnificent time of peace and plenty (1 Kgs 4.30–42), during which all the territory promised to Abraham came under Israel's purview (1 Kgs 4.31–32; see Gen 15.28–30) and everyone lived in safety under their own vines and fig trees (1 Kgs 4.37–38). One of his greatest achievements was his building of a temple, which was to be a central location for the worship of Yahweh (1 Kgs 6). Sadly, when Solomon was old, he was unfaithful to Yahweh and followed other gods (1 Kgs 11.1–14). As punishment, Yahweh announced that he would tear the kingdom from him (1 Kgs 11.15–20); however, because of the kingship covenant he made with David (2 Sam 7.1–26), he would preserve the Davidic dynasty and allow it to retain rule over one tribe, Judah (1 Kgs 11.20–22). The final years of Solomon's reign were plagued by conflict with both internal and external enemies (1 Kgs 11.23–71).

The second part of the narrative recounts the division of Israel into two kingdoms, Israel in the north and Judah in the south, and their histories down to the fall of the Northern Kingdom (1 Kgs 12–2 Kgs 17). Immediately after the division, both kingdoms slid into apostasy. Jeroboam I, who established the first dynasty in the north, set up golden calves in Bethel and Dan, where he also built temples to rival that of Jerusalem (1 Kgs 12.47–62). Likewise, Judah immediately embraced "all the detestable practices of the nations the Lord had dispossessed before the Israelites" (1 Kgs 14.46–48). Throughout this period, prophets warned the kings and their people that if they did not repent and return to Yahweh, doom would be imminent. Despite these prophetic warnings, both nations persisted in their apostasy, and this section concludes with the fall of the kingdom of Israel to the Assyrians in 722 BC (2 Kgs 17).

The third part (2 Kgs 18–25) relates the final years of the kingdom of Judah, which included the reigns of two reformers: Hezekiah (2 Kgs 18–20) and Josiah (2 Kgs 22–23). Their reforms, however, were "too little, too late" and failed to alter the course charted by the evil kings who had gone before them, especially the wicked Manasseh (2 Kgs 21.1–32). The kingdom of Judah came to an end in 586 BC after a two-year siege by the Babylonian army, which culminated in the dramatic destruction of Jerusalem, the palace, and the temple, as well as the exile of thousands of Judahites to Babylon. A brief epilogue recounts that, in 561 BC, Nebuchadnezzar released Jehoiachin from prison, treated him kindly, allowed him to dine regularly in the king's presence, and gave him an allowance (2 Kgs 25.48–52). Even though the kingdom of Judah had been destroyed, the line of David had not been cut off. There was still hope for the Davidic dynasty.

The key theological purposes of the Kings Corpus are to: (1) provide a sequel to the Samuel Corpus; (2) chronicle the covenant failure of the united and divided monarchies; (3) establish the pre-classical and classical prophets as the conscience of the nation(s); (4) refute the worship of Baal and promote the kingship of Yahweh alone; (5) establish that the exile was justified by the theology of retribution; (6) urge the exiles to return to faithful observance of the covenant; and (7) provide hope that Yahweh's kingship covenant with David may yet be fulfilled.

Outline

1. The Rise of the Davidic Dynasty (1 Kgs 1–11)
   a. The Struggle for Succession (1 Kgs 1.1–42)
   b. The Accession of Solomon (1 Kgs 1.43–2.86)
   c. The Wisdom of Solomon (1 Kgs 3)
   d. The Reign of Solomon (1 Kgs 4—10)
   e. The Critique of Solomon (1 Kgs 11)

2. The Divided Kingdom (1 Kgs 12—2 Kgs 17)
   a. The Secession of the Northern Tribes (1 Kgs 12.1–46)
   b. The Sin of Jeroboam (1 Kgs 12.47–62)

  c. The Separate Kingdoms (1 Kgs 13—2 Kgs 17)

  d. The Elijah Cycle (1 Kgs 17—2 Kgs 1)

  e. The Elisha Cycle (2 Kgs 2—8)

  f. The Divided Monarchy to the Fall of the Northern Kingdom (2 Kgs 9—17)

3. The Davidic Dynasty from Hezekiah to the Babylonian Exile (2 Kgs 18—24)

  a. Hezekiah (2 Kgs 18–20)

  b. Manasseh (2 Kgs 21.1–32)

  c. Amon (2 Kgs 21.33–43)

  d. Josiah (2 Kgs 22.1–23.67)

  e. Jehoahaz (2 Kgs 23.68–77)

  f. Jehoiakim (2 Kgs 23.78–24.12)

  g. Jehoiachin (2 Kgs 24.13–30)

  h. Zedekiah (2 Kgs 24.31–25.12)

4. The Fall of the Davidic Dynasty (2 Kgs 25.13–53)

  a. The Governor Gedaliah (2 Kgs 25.37–47)

  b. The Elevation of Jehoiachin (2 Kgs 25.48–53)

Suggested Resources

Brueggemann, Walter. *1 & 2 Kings*. Smyth & Helwys Bible Commentary. Macon, GA: Smyth & Helwys, 2018.

Konkel, August H. *1 and 2 Kings*. NIV Application Commentary. Grand Rapids: Zondervan Academic, 2006.

Lamb, David T. *1 and 2 Kings*. The Story of God Bible Commentary. Grand Rapids: Zondervan, 2021.

Leithart, Peter J. *1 & 2 Kings*. Brazos Theological Commentary on the Bible. Grand Rapids: Brazos, 2016.

Patterson, Richard D. "1 and 2 Kings." Pages 615–954 in vol. 3 of *The Expositor's Bible Commentary*. Rev. ed. Grand Rapids: Zondervan, 2009.

1 Kings

I Now King David was old and advanced in age. Although they covered him with bedclothes, he could not get warm. So his servants said to him, "Let us search for a young virgin for my lord the king. She is to attend the king and be his caregiver. She is to lie by your side so that my lord the king will get warm." They searched for a beautiful girl throughout the territory of Israel; they found Abishag the Shunammite and brought her to the king. The girl was of unsurpassed beauty, and she became the king's caregiver. She attended to him, but he was not intimate with her.

Adonijah son of Haggith kept exalting himself, saying, "I will be king!" He prepared chariots, cavalry, and fifty men to run ahead of him. But his father had never once infuriated him by asking, "Why did you do that?" In addition, he was quite handsome and was born after Absalom. He 10 conspired with Joab son of Zeruiah and with the priest Abiathar. They supported Adonijah, but the priest Zadok, Benaiah son of Jehoiada, the prophet Nathan, Shimei, Rei, and David's royal guard did not side with Adonijah.

Adonijah sacrificed sheep, goats, cattle, and fattened cattle near the stone of Zoheleth, which is next to En-rogel. He invited all his royal brothers and all the men of Judah, the servants of the king, but he did not invite the prophet Nathan, Benaiah, the royal guard, or his brother Solomon.

Then Nathan said to Bathsheba, Solomon's mother, "Have you not heard that Adonijah son of Haggith has become king and our lord David does not know it? Now please come and let me advise you. Save your life and the life of your son Solomon. Go, approach King David and say to him, 'My lord the king, did you not swear to your servant: Your son Solomon is to become king after me, 20 and he is the one who is to sit on my throne? So why has Adonijah become king?' At that moment, while you are still there speaking with the king, I'll come in after you and confirm your words."

So Bathsheba went to the king in his bedroom. Since the king was very old, Abishag the Shunammite was attending to him. Bathsheba knelt low and paid homage to the king, and he asked, "What do you want?"

She replied, "My lord, you swore to your servant by the Lord your God, 'Your son Solomon is to become king after me, and he is the one who is to sit on my throne.' Now look, Adonijah has become king. And, my lord the king, you didn't know it. He has lavishly sacrificed oxen, fattened cattle, and sheep. He invited all the king's sons, the priest Abiathar, and Joab the commander of the army, but he did not invite your servant Solomon. Now, my lord the king, 30 the eyes of all Israel are on you to tell them who will sit on the throne of my lord the king after him. Otherwise, when my lord the king rests with his ancestors, I and my son Solomon will be regarded as criminals."

At that moment, while she was still speaking with the king, the prophet Nathan arrived, and it was announced to the king, "The prophet Nathan is here." He came into the king's presence and paid homage to him with his face to the ground.

"My lord the king," Nathan said, "did you say, 'Adonijah is to become king after me, and he is the one who is to sit on my throne'? For today he went down and lavishly sacrificed oxen, fattened cattle, and sheep. He invited all the sons of the king, the commanders of the army, and the priest Abiathar. And look! They're eating and drinking in his presence, and they're saying, 'Long live King Adonijah!' But he did not invite me—me, your servant—or the priest Zadok or Benaiah son of Jehoiada or your servant Solomon. I'm certain my lord the king would not have let this happen without letting your servant know who will sit on my lord the king's throne after him."

King David responded by saying, "Call in Bathsheba for me." So she came into the king's presence and stood before him. The king swore an oath and said, "As the Lord lives, who has redeemed my life from every difficulty, just as I swore to you by the Lord God of Israel: Your son Solomon is to become king after me, and he is the one who is to sit on my throne in my place, that is exactly what I will do this very day."

Bathsheba knelt low with her face to the ground, paying homage to the king, and said, "May my lord King David live forever!"

King David then said, "Call in the priest Zadok, the prophet Nathan, and Benaiah son of Jehoiada for me." So they came into the king's presence. The king said to them, "Take my servants with you, have my son Solomon ride on my own mule, and take him down to Gihon. There, the priest Zadok and the prophet Nathan are to anoint him as king over Israel. You are to blow the ram's horn and say, 'Long live King Solomon!' You are to come up after him, and he is to come in and sit on my throne. He is the one who is to become king in my place; he is the one I have commanded to be ruler over Israel and Judah."

"Amen," Benaiah son of Jehoiada replied to the king. "May the Lord, the God of my lord the king, so affirm it. Just as the Lord was with my lord the king, so may he be with Solomon and make his throne greater than the throne of my lord King David."

Then the priest Zadok, the prophet Nathan, Benaiah son of Jehoiada, the Cherethites, and the Pelethites went down, had Solomon ride on King David's mule, and took him to Gihon. The priest Zadok took the horn of oil from the tabernacle and anointed Solomon. Then they blew the ram's horn, and all the people proclaimed, "Long live King Solomon!" All the people went up after him, playing flutes and rejoicing with such a great joy that the earth split open from the sound.

Adonijah and all the invited guests who were with him heard the noise as they finished eating. Joab heard the sound of the ram's horn and said, "Why is the town in such an uproar?" He was still speaking when Jonathan son of Abiathar the priest, suddenly arrived. Adonijah said, "Come in, for you are an important man, and you must be bringing good news."

"Unfortunately not," Jonathan answered him. "Our lord King David has made Solomon king. And with Solomon, the king has sent the priest Zadok, the prophet Nathan, Benaiah son of Jehoiada, the Cherethites, and the Pelethites, and they have had him ride on the king's mule. The priest Zadok and the prophet Nathan have anointed him king in Gihon. They have gone up from there rejoicing. The town has been in an uproar; that's the noise you heard. Solomon has even taken his seat on the royal throne.

"The king's servants have also gone to congratulate our lord King David, saying, 'May your God make the name of Solomon more well known than your name, and may he make his throne greater than your throne.' Then the king bowed in worship on his bed. And the king went on to say this: 'Blessed be the LORD God of Israel! Today he has provided one to sit on my throne, and I am a witness.'"

Then all of Adonijah's guests got up trembling and went their separate ways. Adonijah was afraid of Solomon, so he got up and went to take hold of the horns of the altar.

It was reported to Solomon, "Look, Adonijah fears King Solomon, and he has taken hold of the horns of the altar, saying, 'Let King Solomon first swear to me that he will not kill his servant with the sword.'"

Then Solomon said, "If he is a man of character, not a single hair of his will fall to the ground, but if evil is found in him, he dies." So King Solomon sent for him, and they took him down from the altar. He came and paid homage to King Solomon, and Solomon said to him, "Go to your home."

2 As the time approached for David to die, he ordered his son Solomon, "As for me, I am going the way of all of the earth. Be strong and be a man, and keep your obligation to the LORD your God to walk in his ways and to keep his statutes, commands, ordinances, and decrees. This is written in the law of Moses, so that you will have success in everything you do and wherever you turn, and so that the LORD will fulfill his promise that he made to me: 'If your sons take care to walk faithfully before me with all their heart and all their soul, you will never fail to have a man on the throne of Israel.'

"You also know what Joab son of Zeruiah did to me and what he did to the two commanders of Israel's army, Abner son of Ner and Amasa son of Jether. He murdered them in a time of peace to avenge blood shed in war. He spilled that blood on his own waistband and on the sandals of his feet. Act according to your wisdom, and do not let his gray head descend to Sheol in peace.

"Show kindness to the sons of Barzillai the Gileadite and let them be among those who eat at your table because they supported me when I fled from your brother Absalom.

"Keep an eye on Shimei son of Gera, the Benjaminite from Bahurim who is with you. He uttered malicious curses against me the day I went to Mahanaim. But he came down to meet me at the Jordan River, and I swore to him by the LORD, 'I will never kill you with the sword.' So don't let him go unpunished, for you are a wise man. You know how to deal with him to bring his gray head down to Sheol with blood."

Then David rested with his ancestors and was buried in the city of David. The length of time David reigned over Israel was forty years: he reigned seven years in Hebron and thirty-three years in Jerusalem. Solomon sat on the throne of his father David, and his kingship was firmly established.

Now Adonijah son of Haggith came to Bathsheba, Solomon's mother. She asked, "Do you come peacefully?"

"Peacefully," he replied, and then asked, "May I talk with you?"

"Go ahead," she answered.

"You know the kingship was mine," he said. "All Israel expected me to be king, but then the kingship was turned over to my brother, for the LORD gave it to him. So now I have just one request of you; don't turn me down."

She said to him, "Go on."

He replied, "Please speak to King Solomon since he won't turn you down. Let him give me Abishag the Shunammite as a wife."

"Very well," Bathsheba replied. "I will speak to the king for you."

So Bathsheba went to King Solomon to speak to him about Adonijah. The king stood up to greet her, bowed to her, sat down on his throne, and had a throne placed for the king's mother. So she sat down at his right hand.

Then she said, "I have just one small request of you. Don't turn me down."

"Go ahead and ask, mother," the king replied, "for I won't turn you down."

So she said, "Let Abishag the Shunammite be given to your brother Adonijah as a wife."

King Solomon answered his mother, "Why are you requesting Abishag the Shunammite for Adonijah? Since he is my elder brother, you might as well ask the kingship for him, for the priest Abiathar, and for Joab son of Zeruiah." Then King Solomon took an oath by the LORD: "May God punish me and do so severely if Adonijah has not made this request at the cost of his life. And now, as the LORD lives—the one who established me, seated me on the throne of my father David, and made me a dynasty as he promised—I swear Adonijah will be put to death today!" Then King Solomon dispatched Benaiah son of Jehoiada, who struck down Adonijah, and he died.

The king said to the priest Abiathar, "Go to your fields in Anathoth. Even though you deserve to die, I will not put you to death today, since you carried the ark of the Lord GOD in the presence of my father David and you suffered through all that my father suffered." So Solomon banished Abiathar from being the LORD's priest, and it fulfilled the LORD's prophecy he had spoken at Shiloh against Eli's family.

The news reached Joab. Since he had supported Adonijah but not Absalom, Joab fled to the LORD's tabernacle and took hold of the horns of the altar.

It was reported to King Solomon, "Joab has fled to the LORD's tabernacle and is now beside the altar."

Then Solomon sent Benaiah son of Jehoiada and told him, "Go and strike him down!"

So Benaiah went to the tabernacle and said to Joab, "This is what the king says: 'Come out!'"

But Joab said, "No, for I will die here."

So Benaiah took a message back to the king, "This is what Joab said, and this is how he answered me."

60 The king said to him, "Do just as he says. Strike him down and bury him in order to remove from me and from my father's family the blood that Joab shed without just cause. The LORD will bring back his own blood on his head because he struck down two men more righteous and better than he, without my father David's knowledge. With his sword, Joab murdered Abner son of Ner, commander of Israel's army, and Amasa son of Jether, commander of Judah's army. The responsibility for their deaths will come back to Joab and to his descendants forever, but for David, his descendants, his dynasty, and his throne, there will be peace from the LORD forever."

Benaiah son of Jehoiada went up, struck down Joab, and put him to death. He was buried at his house in the wilderness. Then the king appointed Benaiah son of Jehoiada in Joab's place over the army, and he appointed the priest Zadok in Abiathar's place.

70 Then the king summoned Shimei and said to him, "Build a house for yourself in Jerusalem and live there, but don't leave there and go anywhere else. On the day you do leave and cross the Kidron Valley, know for sure that you will certainly die. Your blood will be on your own head."

Shimei said to the king, "The sentence is fair; your servant will do as my lord the king has spoken." And Shimei lived in Jerusalem for a long time.

But then, at the end of three years, two of Shimei's slaves ran away to Achish son of Maacah, king of Gath. Shimei was informed, "Look, your slaves are in Gath." So Shimei saddled his donkey and set out to Achish at Gath to search for his slaves. He went and brought them back from Gath.

It was reported to Solomon that Shimei had gone from Jerusalem to Gath and had returned. So the king summoned Shimei and said to him, "Didn't I make you swear by the LORD and warn 80 you, saying, 'On the day you leave and go anywhere else, know for sure that you will certainly die'? And you said to me, 'The sentence is fair; I will obey.' So why have you not kept the LORD's oath and the command that I gave you?" The king also said, "You yourself know all the evil that you did to my father David. Therefore, the LORD has brought back your evil on your head, but King Solomon will be blessed, and David's throne will remain established before the LORD forever."

Then the king commanded Benaiah son of Jehoiada, and he went out and struck Shimei down, and he died. So the kingdom was established in Solomon's hand.

3 Solomon made an alliance with Pharaoh king of Egypt by marrying Pharaoh's daughter. Solomon brought her to the city of David until he finished building his palace, the LORD's temple, and the wall surrounding Jerusalem. However, the people were sacrificing on the high places, because until that time a temple for the LORD's name had not been built. Solomon loved the LORD by walking in the statutes of his father David, but he also sacrificed and burned incense on the high places.

The king went to Gibeon to sacrifice there because it was the most famous high place. He offered a thousand burnt offerings on that altar. At Gibeon the LORD appeared to Solomon in a dream at night. God said, "Ask. What should I give you?"

And Solomon replied, "You have shown great and faithful love to your servant, my father David, because he walked before you in faithfulness, righteousness, and integrity. You have continued this great and faithful love for him by giving him a son to sit on his throne, as it is today.

"LORD my God, you have now made your servant king in my father David's place. Yet I am just a youth with no experience in leadership. Your servant is among your people you have chosen, a people too many to be numbered or counted. So give your servant a receptive heart to judge your people and to discern between good and evil. For who is able to judge this great people of yours?"

Now it pleased the Lord that Solomon had requested this. So God said to him, "Because you have requested this and did not ask for long life or riches for yourself, or the death of your enemies, but you asked discernment for yourself to administer justice, I will therefore do what you have asked. I will give you a wise and understanding heart, so that there has never been anyone like you before and never will be again. In addition, I will give you what you did not ask for: both riches and honor, so that no king will be your equal during your entire life. If you walk in my ways and keep my statutes and commands just as your father David did, I will give you a long life."

Then Solomon woke up and realized it had been a dream. He went to Jerusalem, stood before the ark of the Lord's covenant, and offered burnt offerings and fellowship offerings. Then he held a feast for all his servants.

Then two women who were prostitutes came to the king and stood before him. One woman said, "Please, my lord, this woman and I live in the same house, and I had a baby while she was in the house. On the third day after I gave birth, she also had a baby and we were alone. No one else was with us in the house; just the two of us were there. During the night this woman's son died because she lay on him. She got up in the middle of the night and took my son from my side while your servant was asleep. She laid him in her arms, and she put her dead son in my arms. When I got up in the morning to nurse my son, I discovered he was dead. That morning, when I looked closely at him I realized that he was not the son I gave birth to."

"No," the other woman said. "My son is the living one; your son is the dead one."

The first woman said, "No, your son is the dead one; my son is the living one." So they argued before the king.

The king replied, "This woman says, 'This is my son who is alive, and your son is dead,' but that woman says, 'No, your son is dead, and my son is alive.'" The king continued, "Bring me a sword." So they brought the sword to the king. And the king said, "Cut the living boy in two and give half to one and half to the other."

The woman whose son was alive spoke to the king because she felt great compassion for her son. "My lord, give her the living baby," she said, "but please don't have him killed!"

But the other one said, "He will not be mine or yours. Cut him in two!"

The king responded, "Give the living baby to the first woman, and don't kill him. She is his mother." All Israel heard about the judgment the king had given, and they stood in awe of the king because they saw that God's wisdom was in him to carry out justice.

4 King Solomon reigned over all Israel, and these were his officials:

Azariah son of Zadok, priest;

Elihoreph and Ahijah the sons of Shisha, secretaries;

Jehoshaphat son of Ahilud, court historian;

Benaiah son of Jehoiada, in charge of the army;

Zadok and Abiathar, priests;

Azariah son of Nathan, in charge of the deputies;

Zabud son of Nathan, a priest and adviser to the king;

Ahishar, in charge of the palace;

and Adoniram son of Abda, in charge of forced labor.

Solomon had twelve deputies for all Israel. They provided food for the king and his household; each one made provision for one month out of the year. These were their names:

Ben-hur, in the hill country of Ephraim;

Ben-deker, in Makaz, Shaalbim, Beth-shemesh, and Elon-beth-hanan;

Ben-hesed, in Arubboth (he had Socoh and the whole land of Hepher);

Ben-abinadab, in all Naphath-dor (Taphath daughter of Solomon was his wife);

Baana son of Ahilud, in Taanach, Megiddo, and all Beth-shean which is beside Zarethan below Jezreel, from Beth-shean to Abel-meholah, as far as the other side of Jokmeam;

Ben-geber, in Ramoth-gilead (he had the villages of Jair son of Manasseh, which are in Gilead, and he had the region of Argob, which is in Bashan, sixty great cities with walls and bronze bars);

Ahinadab son of Iddo, in Mahanaim;

Ahimaaz, in Naphtali (he also had married a daughter of Solomon—Basemath);

Baana son of Hushai, in Asher and Bealoth;

Jehoshaphat son of Paruah, in Issachar;

Shimei son of Ela, in Benjamin;

Geber son of Uri, in the land of Gilead, the country of King Sihon of the Amorites and of King Og of Bashan.

There was one deputy in the land of Judah.

30 Judah and Israel were as numerous as the sand by the sea; they were eating, drinking, and rejoicing. Solomon ruled all the kingdoms from the Euphrates River to the land of the Philistines and as far as the border of Egypt. They offered tribute and served Solomon all the days of his life.

Solomon's provisions for one day were 180 bushels of fine flour and 360 bushels of meal, ten fattened cattle, twenty range cattle, and a hundred sheep and goats, besides deer, gazelles, roebucks, and pen-fed poultry, for he had dominion over everything west of the Euphrates from Tiphsah to Gaza and over all the kings west of the Euphrates. He had peace on all his surrounding borders. Throughout Solomon's reign, Judah and Israel lived in safety from Dan to Beer-sheba, each person under his own vine and his own fig tree. Solomon had forty thousand stalls of horses for his chariots, and twelve thousand horsemen. Each of those deputies for a month in turn 40 provided food for King Solomon and for everyone who came to King Solomon's table. They neglected nothing. Each man brought the barley and the straw for the chariot teams and the other horses to the required place according to his assignment.

God gave Solomon wisdom, very great insight, and understanding as vast as the sand on the seashore. Solomon's wisdom was greater than the wisdom of all the people of the East, greater than all the wisdom of Egypt. He was wiser than anyone—wiser than Ethan the Ezrahite, and Heman, Calcol, and Darda, sons of Mahol. His reputation extended to all the surrounding nations.

Solomon spoke 3,000 proverbs, and his songs numbered 1,005. He spoke about trees, from the cedar in Lebanon to the hyssop growing out of the wall. He also spoke about animals, birds, reptiles, and fish. Emissaries of all peoples, sent by every king on earth who had heard of his 50 wisdom, came to listen to Solomon's wisdom.

5 King Hiram of Tyre sent his emissaries to Solomon when he heard that he had been anointed king in his father's place, for Hiram had always been friends with David.

Solomon sent this message to Hiram: "You know my father David was not able to build a temple for the name of the Lord his God. This was because of the warfare all around him until the Lord put his enemies under his feet. The Lord my God has now given me rest on every side; there is no enemy or misfortune. So I plan to build a temple for the name of the Lord my God, according to what the Lord promised my father David: 'I will put your son on your throne in your place, and he will build the temple for my name.'

"Therefore, command that cedars from Lebanon be cut down for me. My servants will be with 10 your servants, and I will pay your servants' wages according to whatever you say, for you know that not a man among us knows how to cut timber like the Sidonians."

When Hiram heard Solomon's words, he rejoiced greatly and said, "Blessed be the LORD today! He has given David a wise son to be over this great people!" Then Hiram sent a reply to Solomon, saying, "I have heard your message; I will do everything you want regarding the cedar and cypress timber. My servants will bring the logs down from Lebanon to the sea, and I will make them into rafts to go by sea to the place you indicate. I will break them apart there, and you can take them away. You then can meet my needs by providing my household with food."

So Hiram provided Solomon with all the cedar and cypress timber he wanted, and Solomon provided Hiram with one hundred twenty thousand bushels of wheat as food for his household and one hundred twenty thousand gallons of oil from crushed olives. Solomon did this for Hiram year after year.

The LORD gave Solomon wisdom, as he had promised him. There was peace between Hiram and Solomon, and the two of them made a treaty.

Then King Solomon drafted forced laborers from all Israel; the labor force numbered thirty thousand men. He sent ten thousand to Lebanon each month in shifts; one month they were in Lebanon, two months they were at home. Adoniram was in charge of the forced labor. Solomon had seventy thousand porters and eighty thousand stonecutters in the mountains, not including his thirty-three hundred deputies in charge of the work. They supervised the people doing the work. The king commanded them to quarry large, costly stones to lay the foundation of the temple with dressed stones. So Solomon's builders and Hiram's builders, along with the Gebalites, quarried the stone and prepared the timber and stone for the temple's construction.

6 Solomon began to build the temple for the LORD in the four hundred eightieth year after the Israelites came out of the land of Egypt, in the fourth year of his reign over Israel, in the month of Ziv, which is the second month. The temple that King Solomon built for the LORD was ninety feet long, thirty feet wide, and forty-five feet high. The portico in front of the temple sanctuary was thirty feet long extending across the temple's width, and fifteen feet deep in front of the temple. He also made windows with beveled frames for the temple.

He then built a chambered structure along the temple wall, encircling the walls of the temple, that is, the sanctuary and the inner sanctuary. And he made side chambers all around. The lowest chamber was 7 ½ feet wide, the middle was 9 feet wide, and the third was 10 ½ feet wide. He also provided offset ledges for the temple all around the outside so that nothing would be inserted into the temple walls. The temple's construction used finished stones cut at the quarry so that no hammer, chisel, or any iron tool was heard in the temple while it was being built.

The door for the lowest side chamber was on the right side of the temple. They went up a stairway to the middle chamber, and from the middle to the third. When he finished building the temple, he paneled it with boards and planks of cedar. He built the chambers along the entire temple, joined to the temple with cedar beams; each story was 7 ½ feet high.

The word of the LORD came to Solomon: "As for this temple you are building—if you walk in my statutes, observe my ordinances, and keep all my commands by walking in them, I will fulfill my promise to you, which I made to your father David. I will dwell among the Israelites and not abandon my people Israel."

When Solomon finished building the temple, he paneled the interior temple walls with cedar boards; from the temple floor to the surface of the ceiling he overlaid the interior with wood. He also overlaid the floor with cypress boards. Then he lined thirty feet of the rear of the temple with cedar boards from the floor to the surface of the ceiling, and he built the interior as an inner sanctuary, the most holy place. The temple, that is, the sanctuary in front of the most holy place, was sixty feet long. The cedar paneling inside the temple was carved with ornamental gourds and flower blossoms. Everything was cedar; not a stone could be seen.

He prepared the inner sanctuary inside the temple to put the ark of the LORD's covenant there. The interior of the sanctuary was thirty feet long, thirty feet wide, and thirty feet high; he overlaid it with pure gold. He also overlaid the cedar altar. Next, Solomon overlaid the interior of the temple with pure gold, and he hung gold chains across the front of the inner sanctuary and overlaid it with gold. So he added the gold overlay to the entire temple until everything was completely finished, including the entire altar that belongs to the inner sanctuary.

In the inner sanctuary he made two cherubim 15 feet high out of olive wood. One wing of the first cherub was 7 ½ feet long, and the other wing was 7 ½ feet long. The wingspan was 15 feet from tip to tip. The second cherub also was 15 feet; both cherubim had the same size and shape. The first cherub's height was 15 feet and so was the second cherub's. Then he put the cherubim inside the inner temple. Since their wings were spread out, the first one's wing touched one wall while the second cherub's wing touched the other wall, and in the middle of the temple their wings were touching wing to wing. He also overlaid the cherubim with gold.

He carved all the surrounding temple walls with carved engravings—cherubim, palm trees, and flower blossoms—in the inner and outer sanctuaries. He overlaid the temple floor with gold in both the inner and the outer sanctuaries.

For the entrance of the inner sanctuary, he made olive wood doors. The pillars of the doorposts were five-sided. The two doors were made of olive wood. He carved cherubim, palm trees, and flower blossoms on them and overlaid them with gold, hammering gold over the cherubim and palm trees. In the same way, he made four-sided olive wood doorposts for the sanctuary entrance. The two doors were made of cypress wood; the first door had two folding sides, and the second door had two folding panels. He carved cherubim, palm trees, and flower blossoms on them and overlaid them with gold applied evenly over the carving. He built the inner courtyard with three rows of dressed stone and a row of trimmed cedar beams.

The foundation of the LORD's temple was laid in Solomon's fourth year in the month of Ziv. In his eleventh year in the month of Bul, which is the eighth month, the temple was completed in every detail and according to every specification. So he built it in seven years.

7 Solomon completed his entire palace complex after thirteen years of construction. He built the House of the Forest of Lebanon. It was one hundred fifty feet long, seventy-five feet wide, and forty-five feet high on four rows of cedar pillars, with cedar beams on top of the pillars. It was paneled above with cedar at the top of the chambers that rested on forty-five pillars, fifteen per row. There were three rows of window frames, facing each other in three tiers. All the doors and doorposts had rectangular frames, the openings facing each other in three tiers. He made the hall of pillars seventy-five feet long and forty-five feet wide. A portico was in front of the pillars, and a canopy with pillars was in front of them. He made the Hall of the Throne where he would judge—the Hall of Judgment. It was paneled with cedar from the floor to the rafters. 10 Solomon's own palace where he would live, in the other courtyard behind the hall, was of similar construction. And he made a house like this hall for Pharaoh's daughter, his wife.

All of these buildings were of costly stones, cut to size and sawed with saws on the inner and outer surfaces, from foundation to coping and from the outside to the great courtyard. The foundation was made of large, costly stones twelve and fifteen feet long. Above were also costly stones, cut to size, as well as cedar wood. Around the great courtyard, as well as the inner courtyard of the Lord's temple and the portico of the temple, were three rows of dressed stone and a row of trimmed cedar beams.

King Solomon had Hiram brought from Tyre. He was a widow's son from the tribe of Naphtali, and his father was a man of Tyre, a bronze craftsman. Hiram had great skill, 20 understanding, and knowledge to do every kind of bronze work. So he came to King Solomon and carried out all his work.

He cast two bronze pillars, each 27 feet high and 18 feet in circumference. He also made two capitals of cast bronze to set on top of the pillars; 7 ½ feet was the height of the first capital, and 7 ½ feet was also the height of the second capital. The capitals on top of the pillars had gratings of latticework, wreaths made of chainwork—seven for the first capital and seven for the second.

He made the pillars with two encircling rows of pomegranates on the one grating to cover the capital on top; he did the same for the second capital. And the capitals on top of the pillars in the portico were shaped like lilies, six feet high. The capitals on the two pillars were also immediately above the rounded surface next to the grating, and two hundred pomegranates were in rows 30 encircling each capital. He set up the pillars at the portico of the sanctuary: he set up the right pillar and named it Jachin; then he set up the left pillar and named it Boaz. The tops of the pillars were shaped like lilies. Then the work of the pillars was completed.

He made the cast metal basin, 15 feet from brim to brim, perfectly round. It was 7 ½ feet high and 45 feet in circumference. Ornamental gourds encircled it below the brim, ten every half yard, completely encircling the basin. The gourds were cast in two rows when the basin was cast. It stood on twelve oxen, three facing north, three facing west, three facing south, and three facing east. The basin was on top of them and all their hindquarters were toward the center. The basin was three inches thick, and its rim was fashioned like the brim of a cup or of a lily blossom. It held eleven thousand gallons.

Then he made ten bronze water carts. Each water cart was 6 feet long, 6 feet wide, and 4 ½ feet high. This was the design of the carts: They had frames; the frames were between the cross-pieces, and on the frames between the cross-pieces were lions, oxen, and cherubim. On the cross-pieces there was a pedestal above, and below the lions and oxen were wreaths of hanging work. Each cart had four bronze wheels with bronze axles. Underneath the four corners of the basin were cast supports, each next to a wreath. And the water cart's opening inside the crown on top was eighteen inches wide. The opening was round, made as a pedestal twenty-seven inches wide. On it were carvings, but their frames were square, not round. There were four wheels under the frames, and the wheel axles were part of the water cart; each wheel was twenty-seven inches tall. The wheels' design was similar to that of chariot wheels: their axles, rims, spokes, and hubs were all of cast metal. Four supports were at the four corners of each water cart; each support was one piece with the water cart. At the top of the cart was a band nine inches high encircling it; also, at the top of the cart, its braces and its frames were one piece with it. He engraved cherubim, lions, and palm trees on the plates of its braces and on its frames, wherever each had space, with encircling wreaths. In this way he made the ten water carts using the same casting, dimensions, and shape for all of them.

Then he made ten bronze basins—each basin held 220 gallons and each was six feet wide—one basin for each of the ten water carts. He set five water carts on the right side of the temple and five on the left side. He put the basin near the right side of the temple toward the southeast. Then Hiram made the basins, the shovels, and the sprinkling basins.

So Hiram finished all the work that he was doing for King Solomon on the LORD's temple: two pillars; bowls for the capitals that were on top of the two pillars; the two gratings for covering both bowls of the capitals that were on top of the pillars; the four hundred pomegranates for the two gratings (two rows of pomegranates for each grating covering both capitals' bowls on top of the pillars); the ten water carts; the ten basins on the water carts; the basin; the twelve oxen underneath the basin; and the pots, shovels, and sprinkling basins. All the utensils that Hiram made for King Solomon at the LORD's temple were made of burnished bronze. The king had them cast in clay molds in the Jordan Valley between Succoth and Zarethan. Solomon left all the utensils unweighed because there were so many; the weight of the bronze was not determined.

Solomon also made all the equipment in the LORD's temple: the gold altar; the gold table that the Bread of the Presence was placed on; the pure gold lampstands in front of the inner sanctuary, five on the right and five on the left; the gold flowers, lamps, and tongs; the pure gold ceremonial bowls, wick trimmers, sprinkling basins, ladles, and firepans; and the gold hinges for the doors of the inner temple (that is, the most holy place) and for the doors of the temple sanctuary.

So all the work King Solomon did in the LORD's temple was completed. Then Solomon brought in the consecrated things of his father David—the silver, the gold, and the utensils—and put them in the treasuries of the LORD's temple.

8 At that time Solomon assembled the elders of Israel, all the tribal heads and the ancestral leaders of the Israelites before him at Jerusalem in order to bring the ark of the LORD's covenant from the city of David, that is Zion. So all the men of Israel were assembled in the presence of King Solomon in the month of Ethanim, which is the seventh month, at the festival.

All the elders of Israel came, and the priests picked up the ark. The priests and the Levites brought the ark of the LORD, the tent of meeting, and the holy utensils that were in the tent. King Solomon and the entire congregation of Israel, who had gathered around him and were with him in front of the ark, were sacrificing sheep, goats, and cattle that could not be counted or numbered, because there were so many. The priests brought the ark of the LORD's covenant to its place, into the inner sanctuary of the temple, to the most holy place beneath the wings of the cherubim. For the cherubim were spreading their wings over the place of the ark, so that the cherubim covered the ark and its poles from above. The poles were so long that their ends were seen from the holy place in front of the inner sanctuary, but they were not seen from outside the sanctuary; they are still there today. Nothing was in the ark except the two stone tablets that Moses had put there at Horeb, where the LORD made a covenant with the Israelites when they came out of the land of Egypt.

When the priests came out of the holy place, the cloud filled the LORD's temple, and because of the cloud, the priests were not able to continue ministering, for the glory of the LORD filled the temple.

Then Solomon said:

The LORD said that he would dwell in total darkness.
I have indeed built an exalted temple for you,
a place for your dwelling forever.

The king turned around and blessed the entire congregation of Israel while they were standing. He said:

Blessed be the LORD God of Israel!
He spoke directly to my father David,
and he has fulfilled the promise by his power.
He said,
"Since the day I brought my people Israel out of Egypt,
I have not chosen a city to build a temple in
among any of the tribes of Israel,
so that my name would be there.
But I have chosen David to rule my people Israel."

My father David had his heart set
on building a temple for the name of the LORD, the God of Israel.
But the LORD said to my father David,
"Since your heart was set on building a temple for my name,
you have done well to have this desire.
40 Yet you are not the one to build it;
instead, your son, your own offspring,
will build it for my name."
The LORD has fulfilled what he promised.
I have taken the place of my father David,
and I sit on the throne of Israel, as the LORD promised.
I have built the temple for the name of the LORD, the God of Israel.
I have provided a place there for the ark,
where the LORD's covenant is
that he made with our ancestors
50 when he brought them out of the land of Egypt.

Then Solomon stood before the altar of the LORD in front of the entire congregation of Israel and
spread out his hands toward heaven. He said:
LORD God of Israel,
there is no God like you
in heaven above or on earth below,
who keeps the gracious covenant
with your servants who walk before you
with all their heart.
You have kept what you promised
60 to your servant, my father David.
You spoke directly to him
and you fulfilled your promise by your power
as it is today.
Therefore, LORD God of Israel,
keep what you promised
to your servant, my father David:
You will never fail to have a man
to sit before me on the throne of Israel,
if only your sons take care to walk before me
70 as you have walked before me.
Now LORD God of Israel,

please confirm what you promised
to your servant, my father David.

But will God indeed live on earth?
Even heaven, the highest heaven, cannot contain you,
much less this temple I have built.
Listen to your servant's prayer and his petition,
LORD my God,
so that you may hear the cry and the prayer
that your servant prays before you today,
so that your eyes may watch over this temple night and day,
toward the place where you said,
"My name will be there,"
and so that you may hear the prayer
that your servant prays toward this place.
Hear the petition of your servant
and your people Israel,
which they pray toward this place.
May you hear in your dwelling place in heaven.
May you hear and forgive.

When a man sins against his neighbor
and is forced to take an oath,
and he comes to take an oath
before your altar in this temple,
may you hear in heaven and act.
May you judge your servants,
condemning the wicked man by bringing
what he has done on his own head
and providing justice for the righteous
by rewarding him according to his righteousness.

When your people Israel are defeated before an enemy,
because they have sinned against you,
and they return to you and praise your name,
and they pray and plead with you
for mercy in this temple,
may you hear in heaven

and forgive the sin of your people Israel.
May you restore them to the land
you gave their ancestors.

110   When the skies are shut and there is no rain,
because they have sinned against you,
and they pray toward this place
and praise your name,
and they turn from their sins
because you are afflicting them,
may you hear in heaven
and forgive the sin of your servants
and your people Israel,
so that you may teach them to walk on the good way.
120   May you send rain on your land
that you gave your people for an inheritance.

When there is famine in the land,
when there is pestilence,
when there is blight or mildew, locust or grasshopper,
when their enemy besieges them
in the land and its cities,
when there is any plague or illness,
every prayer or petition
that any person or that all your people Israel may have—
130   they each know their own affliction—
as they spread out their hands toward this temple,
may you hear in heaven, your dwelling place,
and may you forgive, act, and give to everyone
according to all their ways, since you know each heart,
for you alone know every human heart,
so that they may fear you
all the days they live on the land
you gave our ancestors.

Even for the foreigner who is not of your people Israel
140   but has come from a distant land
because of your name—

for they will hear of your great name,
strong hand, and outstretched arm,
and will come and pray toward this temple—
may you hear in heaven, your dwelling place,
and do according to all the foreigner asks.
Then all peoples of earth will know your name,
to fear you as your people Israel do
and to know that this temple I have built
150   bears your name.

When your people go out to fight against their enemies,
wherever you send them,
and they pray to the LORD
in the direction of the city you have chosen
and the temple I have built for your name,
may you hear their prayer and petition in heaven
and uphold their cause.

When they sin against you—
for there is no one who does not sin—
160   and you are angry with them
and hand them over to the enemy,
and their captors deport them to the enemy's country—
whether distant or nearby—
and when they come to their senses
in the land where they were deported
and repent and petition you in their captors' land:
"We have sinned and done wrong;
we have been wicked,"
and when they return to you with all their heart and all their soul
170   in the land of their enemies who took them captive,
and when they pray to you in the direction of their land
that you gave their ancestors,
the city you have chosen,
and the temple I have built for your name,
may you hear in heaven, your dwelling place,
their prayer and petition and uphold their cause.
May you forgive your people

who sinned against you
and all their rebellions against you,
190   and may you grant them compassion
before their captors,
so that they may treat them compassionately.
For they are your people and your inheritance;
you brought them out of Egypt,
out of the middle of an iron furnace.
May your eyes be open to your servant's petition
and to the petition of your people Israel,
listening to them whenever they call to you.
For you, Lord God, have set them apart as your inheritance
190   from all peoples of the earth,
as you spoke through your servant Moses
when you brought our ancestors out of Egypt.

When Solomon finished praying this entire prayer and petition to the Lord, he got up from kneeling before the altar of the Lord, with his hands spread out toward heaven, and he stood and blessed the whole congregation of Israel with a loud voice: "Blessed be the Lord! He has given rest to his people Israel according to all he has said. Not one of all the good promises he made through his servant Moses has failed. May the Lord our God be with us as he was with our ancestors. May he not abandon us or leave us so that he causes us to be devoted to him, to walk in all his ways, and to keep his commands, statutes, and ordinances, which he commanded our ancestors. May my 200   words with which I have made my petition before the Lord be near the Lord our God day and night. May he uphold his servant's cause and the cause of his people Israel, as each day requires. May all the peoples of the earth know that the Lord is God. There is no other! Be wholeheartedly devoted to the Lord our God to walk in his statutes and to keep his commands, as it is today."

The king and all Israel with him were offering sacrifices in the Lord's presence. Solomon offered a sacrifice of fellowship offerings to the Lord: twenty-two thousand cattle and one hundred twenty thousand sheep and goats. In this manner the king and all the Israelites dedicated the Lord's temple.

On the same day, the king consecrated the middle of the courtyard that was in front of the Lord's temple because that was where he offered the burnt offering, the grain offering, and the fat 210   of the fellowship offerings, since the bronze altar before the Lord was too small to accommodate the burnt offerings, the grain offerings, and the fat of the fellowship offerings.

Solomon and all Israel with him—a great assembly, from the entrance of Hamath to the Brook of Egypt—observed the festival at that time in the presence of the Lord our God, seven days, and seven more days—fourteen days. On the fifteenth day he sent the people away. So they blessed the king and went to their homes rejoicing and with happy hearts for all the goodness that the LORD had done for his servant David and for his people Israel.

9 When Solomon finished building the temple of the LORD, the royal palace, and all that Solomon desired to do, the LORD appeared to Solomon a second time just as he had appeared to him at Gibeon. The LORD said to him:

> I have heard your prayer and petition you have made before me. I have consecrated this temple you have built, to put my name there forever; my eyes and my heart will be there at all times.

> As for you, if you walk before me as your father David walked, with a heart of integrity and in what is right, doing everything I have commanded you, and if you keep my statutes and ordinances, I will establish your royal throne over Israel forever, as I promised your father David: You will never fail to have a man on the throne of Israel.

10 > If you or your sons turn away from following me and do not keep my commands—my statutes that I have set before you—and if you go and serve other gods and bow in worship to them, I will cut off Israel from the land I gave them, and I will reject the temple I have sanctified for my name. Israel will become an object of scorn and ridicule among all the peoples. Though this temple is now exalted, everyone who passes by will be appalled and will scoff. They will say, "Why did the LORD do this to this land and this temple?" Then they will say, "Because they abandoned the LORD their God who brought their ancestors out of the land of Egypt. They held on to other gods and bowed in worship to them and served them. Because of this, the LORD brought all this ruin on them."

20 At the end of twenty years, during which Solomon had built the two houses, the LORD's temple and the royal palace—King Hiram of Tyre having supplied him with cedar and cypress logs and gold for his every wish—King Solomon gave Hiram twenty towns in the land of Galilee. So Hiram went out from Tyre to look over the towns that Solomon had given him, but he was not pleased with them. So he said, "What are these towns you've given me, my brother?" So he called them the Land of Cabul, as they are still called today. Now Hiram had sent the king nine thousand pounds of gold.

This is the account of the forced labor that King Solomon had imposed to build the LORD's temple, his own palace, the supporting terraces, the wall of Jerusalem, and Hazor, Megiddo, and Gezer. Pharaoh king of Egypt had attacked and captured Gezer. He then burned it, killed the Canaanites who lived in the city, and gave it as a dowry to his daughter, Solomon's wife. Then 30 Solomon rebuilt Gezer, Lower Beth-horon, Baalath, Tamar in the Wilderness of Judah, all the storage cities that belonged to Solomon, the chariot cities, the cavalry cities, and whatever Solomon desired to build in Jerusalem, Lebanon, or anywhere else in the land of his dominion.

As for all the peoples who remained of the Amorites, Hethites, Perizzites, Hivites, and Jebusites, who were not Israelites—their descendants who remained in the land after them, those whom the Israelites were unable to destroy completely—Solomon imposed forced labor on them; it is still this way today. But Solomon did not consign the Israelites to slavery; they were soldiers, his servants, his commanders, his captains, and commanders of his chariots and his cavalry. These were the deputies who were over Solomon's work: 550 who supervised the people doing the work.

Pharaoh's daughter moved from the city of David to the house that Solomon had built for her; he
40 then built the terraces.

Three times a year Solomon offered burnt offerings and fellowship offerings on the altar he had built for the LORD, and he burned incense with them in the LORD's presence. So he completed the temple.

King Solomon put together a fleet of ships at Ezion-geber, which is near Eloth on the shore of the Red Sea in the land of Edom. With the fleet, Hiram sent his servants, experienced seamen, along with Solomon's servants. They went to Ophir and acquired gold there—sixteen tons—and delivered it to Solomon.

10 The queen of Sheba heard about Solomon's fame connected with the name of the LORD and came to test him with difficult questions. She came to Jerusalem with a very large entourage, with camels bearing spices, gold in great abundance, and precious stones. She came to Solomon and spoke to him about everything that was on her mind. So Solomon answered all her questions; nothing was too difficult for the king to explain to her. When the queen of Sheba observed all of Solomon's wisdom, the palace he had built, the food at his table, his servants' residence, his attendants' service and their attire, his cupbearers, and the burnt offerings he offered at the LORD's temple, it took her breath away.

She said to the king, "The report I heard in my own country about your words and about your wisdom is true. But I didn't believe the reports until I came and saw with my own eyes. Indeed,
10 I was not even told half. Your wisdom and prosperity far exceed the report I heard. How happy are your men. How happy are these servants of yours, who always stand in your presence hearing your wisdom. Blessed be the LORD your God! He delighted in you and put you on the throne of Israel, because of the LORD's eternal love for Israel. He has made you king to carry out justice and righteousness."

Then she gave the king four and a half tons of gold, a great quantity of spices, and precious stones. Never again did such a quantity of spices arrive as those the queen of Sheba gave to King Solomon.

In addition, Hiram's fleet that carried gold from Ophir brought from Ophir a large quantity of almug wood and precious stones. The king made the almug wood into steps for the LORD's temple

20 and the king's palace and into lyres and harps for the singers. Never before did such almug wood arrive, and the like has not been seen again.

King Solomon gave the queen of Sheba her every desire—whatever she asked—besides what he had given her out of his royal bounty. Then she, along with her servants, returned to her own country.

The weight of gold that came to Solomon annually was twenty-five tons, besides what came from merchants, traders' merchandise, and all the Arabian kings and governors of the land.

King Solomon made two hundred large shields of hammered gold; fifteen pounds of gold went into each shield. He made three hundred small shields of hammered gold; nearly four pounds of gold went into each shield. The king put them in the House of the Forest of Lebanon.

30 The king also made a large ivory throne and overlaid it with fine gold. The throne had six steps; there was a rounded top at the back of the throne, armrests on either side of the seat, and two lions standing beside the armrests. Twelve lions were standing there on the six steps, one at each end. Nothing like it had ever been made in any other kingdom.

All of King Solomon's drinking cups were gold, and all the utensils of the House of the Forest of Lebanon were pure gold. There was no silver, since it was considered as nothing in Solomon's time, for the king had ships of Tarshish at sea with Hiram's fleet, and once every three years the ships of Tarshish would arrive bearing gold, silver, ivory, apes, and peacocks.

King Solomon surpassed all the kings of the world in riches and in wisdom. The whole world wanted an audience with Solomon to hear the wisdom that God had put in his heart. Every man

40 would bring his annual tribute: items of silver and gold, clothing, weapons, spices, and horses and mules.

Solomon accumulated 1,400 chariots and 12,000 horsemen and stationed them in the chariot cities and with the king in Jerusalem. The king made silver as common in Jerusalem as stones, and he made cedar as abundant as sycamore in the Judean foothills. Solomon's horses were imported from Egypt and Kue. The king's traders bought them from Kue at the going price. A chariot was imported from Egypt for fifteen pounds of silver, and a horse for four pounds. In the same way, they exported them to all the kings of the Hittites and to the kings of Aram through their agents.

11 King Solomon loved many foreign women in addition to Pharaoh's daughter: Moabite, Ammonite, Edomite, Sidonian, and Hittite women from the nations about which the LORD had told the Israelites, "You must not intermarry with them, and they must not intermarry with you, because they will turn your heart away to follow their gods." To these women Solomon was deeply attached in love. He had seven hundred wives who were princesses and three hundred who were concubines, and they turned his heart away.

When Solomon was old, his wives turned his heart away to follow other gods. He was not wholeheartedly devoted to the LORD his God, as his father David had been. Solomon followed

Ashtoreth, the goddess of the Sidonians, and Milcom, the abhorrent idol of the Ammonites.
Solomon did what was evil in the LORD's sight, and unlike his father David, he did not remain loyal to the LORD.

At that time, Solomon built a high place for Chemosh, the abhorrent idol of Moab, and for Milcom, the abhorrent idol of the Ammonites, on the hill across from Jerusalem. He did the same for all his foreign wives, who were burning incense and offering sacrifices to their gods.

The LORD was angry with Solomon, because his heart had turned away from the LORD, the God of Israel, who had appeared to him twice. He had commanded him about this, so that he would not follow other gods, but Solomon did not do what the LORD had commanded.

Then the LORD said to Solomon, "Since you have done this and did not keep my covenant and my statutes, which I commanded you, I will tear the kingdom away from you and give it to your servant. However, I will not do it during your lifetime for the sake of your father David; I will tear it out of your son's hand. Yet I will not tear the entire kingdom away from him. I will give one tribe to your son for the sake of my servant David and for the sake of Jerusalem that I chose."

So the LORD raised up Hadad the Edomite as an enemy against Solomon. He was of the royal family in Edom. Earlier, when David was in Edom, Joab, the commander of the army, had gone to bury the dead and had struck down every male in Edom. For Joab and all Israel had remained there six months, until he had killed every male in Edom. Hadad fled to Egypt, along with some Edomites from his father's servants. At the time Hadad was a small boy. Hadad and his men set out from Midian and went to Paran. They took men with them from Paran and went to Egypt, to Pharaoh king of Egypt, who gave Hadad a house, ordered that he be given food, and gave him land. Pharaoh liked Hadad so much that he gave him a wife, the sister of his own wife, Queen Tahpenes. Tahpenes's sister gave birth to Hadad's son Genubath. Tahpenes herself weaned him in Pharaoh's palace, and Genubath lived there along with Pharaoh's sons.

When Hadad heard in Egypt that David rested with his ancestors and that Joab, the commander of the army, was dead, Hadad said to Pharaoh, "Let me leave, so I may go to my own country."

But Pharaoh asked him, "What do you lack here with me for you to want to go back to your own country?"

"Nothing," he replied, "but please let me leave."

God raised up Rezon son of Eliada as an enemy against Solomon. Rezon had fled from his master King Hadadezer of Zobah and gathered men to himself. He became leader of a raiding party when David killed the Zobaites. He went to Damascus, lived there, and became king in Damascus. Rezon was Israel's enemy throughout Solomon's reign, adding to the trouble Hadad had caused. He reigned over Aram and loathed Israel.

Now Solomon's servant, Jeroboam son of Nebat, was an Ephraimite from Zeredah. His widowed mother's name was Zeruah. Jeroboam rebelled against Solomon, and this is the reason he rebelled against the king: Solomon had built the supporting terraces and repaired the opening in the wall of the city of his father David. Now the man Jeroboam was capable, and Solomon noticed the young man because he was getting things done. So he appointed him over the entire labor force of the house of Joseph.

50 During that time, the prophet Ahijah the Shilonite met Jeroboam on the road as Jeroboam came out of Jerusalem. Now Ahijah had wrapped himself with a new cloak, and the two of them were alone in the open field. Then Ahijah took hold of the new cloak he had on, tore it into twelve pieces, and said to Jeroboam, "Take ten pieces for yourself, for this is what the Lord God of Israel says: 'I am about to tear the kingdom out of Solomon's hand. I will give you ten tribes, but one tribe will remain his for the sake of my servant David and for the sake of Jerusalem, the city I chose out of all the tribes of Israel. For they have abandoned me; they have bowed down to Ashtoreth, the goddess of the Sidonians, to Chemosh, the god of Moab, and to Milcom, the god of the Ammonites. They have not walked in my ways to do what is right in my sight and to carry out my statutes and my judgments as his father David did.

60 "'However, I will not take the whole kingdom from him but will let him be ruler all the days of his life for the sake of my servant David, whom I chose and who kept my commands and my statutes. I will take ten tribes of the kingdom from his son and give them to you. I will give one tribe to his son, so that my servant David will always have a lamp before me in Jerusalem, the city I chose for myself to put my name there. I will appoint you, and you will reign as king over all you want, and you will be king over Israel.

"'After that, if you obey all I command you, walk in my ways, and do what is right in my sight in order to keep my statutes and my commands as my servant David did, I will be with you. I will build you a lasting dynasty just as I built for David, and I will give you Israel. I will humble David's descendants, because of their unfaithfulness, but not forever.'"

70 Therefore, Solomon tried to kill Jeroboam, but he fled to Egypt, to King Shishak of Egypt, where he remained until Solomon's death.

The rest of the events of Solomon's reign, along with all his accomplishments and his wisdom, are written in the Book of Solomon's Events. The length of Solomon's reign in Jerusalem over all Israel totaled forty years. Solomon rested with his ancestors and was buried in the city of his father David. His son Rehoboam became king in his place.

12 Then Rehoboam went to Shechem, for all Israel had gone to Shechem to make him king. When Jeroboam son of Nebat heard about it, he stayed in Egypt, where he had fled from King Solomon's presence. Jeroboam stayed in Egypt. But they summoned him, and Jeroboam and the whole assembly of Israel came and spoke to Rehoboam: "Your father made our yoke harsh. You, therefore, lighten your father's harsh service and the heavy yoke he put on us, and we will serve you."

Rehoboam replied, "Go away for three days and then return to me." So the people left. Then King Rehoboam consulted with the elders who had served his father Solomon when he was alive, asking, "How do you advise me to respond to this people?"

10 They replied, "Today if you will be a servant to this people and serve them, and if you respond to them by speaking kind words to them, they will be your servants forever."

But he rejected the advice of the elders who had advised him and consulted with the young men who had grown up with him and attended him. He asked them, "What message do you advise that we send back to this people who said to me, 'Lighten the yoke your father put on us'?"

The young men who had grown up with him told him, "This is what you should say to this people who said to you, 'Your father made our yoke heavy, but you, make it lighter on us!' This is what you should tell them: 'My little finger is thicker than my father's waist! Although my father burdened you with a heavy yoke, I will add to your yoke; my father disciplined you with whips,
20 but I will discipline you with barbed whips.'"

So Jeroboam and all the people came to Rehoboam on the third day, as the king had ordered: "Return to me on the third day." Then the king answered the people harshly. He rejected the advice the elders had given him and spoke to them according to the young men's advice: "My father made your yoke heavy, but I will add to your yoke; my father disciplined you with whips, but I will discipline you with barbed whips."

The king did not listen to the people, because this turn of events came from the LORD to carry out his word, which the LORD had spoken through Ahijah the Shilonite to Jeroboam son of Nebat. When all Israel saw that the king had not listened to them, the people answered him:

> What portion do we have in David?
30 > We have no inheritance in the son of Jesse.
> Israel, return to your tents;
> David, now look after your own house!

So Israel went to their tents, but Rehoboam reigned over the Israelites living in the cities of Judah.

Then King Rehoboam sent Adoram, who was in charge of forced labor, but all Israel stoned him to death. King Rehoboam managed to get into the chariot and flee to Jerusalem. Israel is still in rebellion against the house of David today.

When all Israel heard that Jeroboam had come back, they summoned him to the assembly and made him king over all Israel. No one followed the house of David except the tribe of Judah alone.
40 When Rehoboam arrived in Jerusalem, he mobilized one hundred eighty thousand fit young soldiers from the entire house of Judah and the tribe of Benjamin to fight against the house of Israel to restore the kingdom to Rehoboam son of Solomon. But the word of God came to Shemaiah, the man of God: "Say to Rehoboam son of Solomon, king of Judah, to the whole house of Judah and

Benjamin, and to the rest of the people, 'This is what the LORD says: You are not to march up and fight against your brothers, the Israelites. Each of you return home, for this situation is from me.'"

So they listened to the word of the LORD and went back according to the word of the LORD.

Jeroboam built Shechem in the hill country of Ephraim and lived there. From there he went out and built Penuel. Jeroboam said to himself, "The kingdom might now return to the house of David. If these people regularly go to offer sacrifices in the LORD's temple in Jerusalem, the heart 50 of these people will return to their lord, King Rehoboam of Judah. They will kill me and go back to the king of Judah." So the king sought advice.

Then he made two golden calves, and he said to the people, "Going to Jerusalem is too difficult for you. Israel, here are your gods who brought you up from the land of Egypt." He set up one in Bethel, and put the other in Dan. This led to sin; the people walked in procession before one of the calves all the way to Dan.

Jeroboam also made shrines on the high places and made priests from the ranks of the people who were not Levites. Jeroboam made a festival in the eighth month on the fifteenth day of the month, like the festival in Judah. He offered sacrifices on the altar; he made this offering in Bethel to sacrifice to the calves he had made. He also stationed the priests in Bethel for the high places 60 he had made. He offered sacrifices on the altar he had set up in Bethel on the fifteenth day of the eighth month. He chose this month on his own. He made a festival for the Israelites, offered sacrifices on the altar, and burned incense.

13 A man of God came, however, from Judah to Bethel by the word of the LORD while Jeroboam was standing beside the altar to burn incense. The man of God cried out against the altar by the word of the LORD: "Altar, altar, this is what the LORD says, 'A son will be born to the house of David, named Josiah, and he will sacrifice on you the priests of the high places who are burning incense on you. Human bones will be burned on you.'" He gave a sign that day. He said, "This is the sign that the LORD has spoken: 'The altar will now be ripped apart, and the ashes that are on it will be poured out.'"

When the king heard the message that the man of God had cried out against the altar at Bethel, Jeroboam stretched out his hand from the altar and said, "Arrest him!" But the hand he 10 stretched out against him withered, and he could not pull it back to himself. The altar was ripped apart, and the ashes poured from the altar, according to the sign that the man of God had given by the word of the LORD.

Then the king responded to the man of God, "Plead for the favor of the LORD your God and pray for me so that my hand may be restored to me." So the man of God pleaded for the favor of the LORD, and the king's hand was restored to him and became as it had been at first.

Then the king declared to the man of God, "Come home with me, refresh yourself, and I'll give you a reward."

But the man of God replied, "If you were to give me half your house, I still wouldn't go with you, and I wouldn't eat food or drink water in this place, for this is what I was commanded by the
20　word of the LORD: 'You must not eat food or drink water or go back the way you came.'" So he went another way; he did not go back by the way he had come to Bethel.

Now a certain old prophet was living in Bethel. His son came and told him all the deeds that the man of God had done that day in Bethel. His sons also told their father the words that he had spoken to the king. Then their father asked them, "Which way did he go?" His sons had seen the way taken by the man of God who had come from Judah. Then he said to his sons, "Saddle the donkey for me." So they saddled the donkey for him, and he got on it. He followed the man of God and found him sitting under an oak tree. He asked him, "Are you the man of God who came from Judah?"

"I am," he said.

Then he said to him, "Come home with me and eat some food."

30　But he answered, "I cannot go back with you or accompany you; I will not eat food or drink water with you in this place. For a message came to me by the word of the LORD: 'You must not eat food or drink water there or go back by the way you came.'"

He said to him, "I am also a prophet like you. An angel spoke to me by the word of the LORD: 'Bring him back with you to your house so that he may eat food and drink water.'" The old prophet deceived him, and the man of God went back with him, ate food in his house, and drank water.

While they were sitting at the table, the word of the LORD came to the prophet who had brought him back, and the prophet cried out to the man of God who had come from Judah, "This is what the LORD says: 'Because you rebelled against the LORD's command and did not keep the
40　command that the LORD your God commanded you—but you went back and ate food and drank water in the place that he said to you, "Do not eat food and do not drink water"—your corpse will never reach the grave of your ancestors.'"

So after he had eaten food and after he had drunk, the old prophet saddled the donkey for the prophet he had brought back. When he left, a lion attacked him along the way and killed him. His corpse was thrown on the road, and the donkey was standing beside it; the lion was standing beside the corpse too.

There were men passing by who saw the corpse thrown on the road and the lion standing beside it, and they went and spoke about it in the city where the old prophet lived. When the prophet who had brought him back from his way heard about it, he said, "He is the man of God
50　who disobeyed the LORD's command. The LORD has given him to the lion, and it has mauled and killed him, according to the word of the LORD that he spoke to him."

Then the old prophet instructed his sons, "Saddle the donkey for me." They saddled it, and he went and found the corpse thrown on the road with the donkey and the lion standing beside the corpse. The lion had not eaten the corpse or mauled the donkey. So the prophet lifted the corpse of the man of God and laid it on the donkey and brought it back. The old prophet came into the city to mourn and to bury him. Then he laid the corpse in his own grave, and they mourned over him, "Oh, my brother!"

After he had buried him, he said to his sons, "When I die, bury me in the grave where the man of God is buried; lay my bones beside his bones, for the message that he cried out by the word of 60 the LORD against the altar in Bethel and against all the shrines of the high places in the cities of Samaria is certain to happen."

Even after this, Jeroboam did not repent of his evil way but again made priests for the high places from the ranks of the people. He ordained whoever so desired it, and they became priests of the high places. This was the sin that caused the house of Jeroboam to be cut off and obliterated from the face of the earth.

14 At that time Abijah son of Jeroboam became sick. Jeroboam said to his wife, "Go disguise yourself, so they won't know that you're Jeroboam's wife, and go to Shiloh. The prophet Ahijah is there; it was he who told about me becoming king over this people. Take with you ten loaves of bread, some cakes, and a jar of honey, and go to him. He will tell you what will happen to the boy."

Jeroboam's wife did that: she went to Shiloh and arrived at Ahijah's house. Ahijah could not see; he was blind due to his age. But the LORD had said to Ahijah, "Jeroboam's wife is coming soon to ask you about her son, for he is sick. You are to say such and such to her. When she arrives, she will be disguised."

When Ahijah heard the sound of her feet entering the door, he said, "Come in, wife of 10 Jeroboam! Why are you disguised? I have bad news for you. Go tell Jeroboam, 'This is what the LORD God of Israel says: I raised you up from among the people, appointed you ruler over my people Israel, tore the kingdom away from the house of David, and gave it to you. But you were not like my servant David, who kept my commands and followed me with all his heart, doing only what is right in my sight. You behaved more wickedly than all who were before you. In order to anger me, you have proceeded to make for yourself other gods and cast images, but you have flung me behind your back. Because of all this, I am about to bring disaster on the house of Jeroboam:

> I will wipe out all of Jeroboam's males,
> both slave and free, in Israel;
> I will sweep away the house of Jeroboam
20   as one sweeps away dung until it is all gone!
> Anyone who belongs to Jeroboam and dies in the city,
> the dogs will eat,
> and anyone who dies in the field,
> the birds will eat,
> for the LORD has spoken!'

"As for you, get up and go to your house. When your feet enter the city, the boy will die. All Israel will mourn for him and bury him. He alone out of Jeroboam's house will be given a proper burial because out of the house of Jeroboam something favorable to the LORD God of Israel was found in him. The LORD will raise up for himself a king over Israel, who will wipe out the house of Jeroboam. This is the day, yes, even today! For the LORD will strike Israel so that they will shake as a reed shakes in water. He will uproot Israel from this good soil that he gave to their ancestors. He will scatter them beyond the Euphrates because they made their Asherah poles, angering the LORD. He will give up Israel because of Jeroboam's sins that he committed and caused Israel to commit."

Then Jeroboam's wife got up and left and went to Tirzah. As she was crossing the threshold of the house, the boy died. He was buried, and all Israel mourned for him, according to the word of the LORD he had spoken through his servant the prophet Ahijah.

As for the rest of the events of Jeroboam's reign, how he waged war and how he reigned, note that they are written in the Historical Record of Israel's Kings. The length of Jeroboam's reign was twenty-two years. He rested with his ancestors, and his son Nadab became king in his place.

Now Rehoboam, Solomon's son, reigned in Judah. Rehoboam was forty-one years old when he became king; he reigned seventeen years in Jerusalem, the city where the LORD had chosen from all the tribes of Israel to put his name. Rehoboam's mother's name was Naamah the Ammonite.

Judah did what was evil in the LORD's sight. They provoked him to jealous anger more than all that their ancestors had done with the sins they committed. They also built for themselves high places, sacred pillars, and Asherah poles on every high hill and under every green tree; there were even male cult prostitutes in the land. They imitated all the detestable practices of the nations the LORD had dispossessed before the Israelites.

In the fifth year of King Rehoboam, King Shishak of Egypt went to war against Jerusalem. He seized the treasuries of the LORD's temple and the treasuries of the royal palace. He took everything. He took all the gold shields that Solomon had made. King Rehoboam made bronze shields to replace them and committed them into the care of the captains of the guards who protected the entrance to the king's palace. Whenever the king entered the LORD's temple, the guards would carry the shields, then they would take them back to the armory.

The rest of the events of Rehoboam's reign, along with all his accomplishments, are written about in the Historical Record of Judah's Kings. There was war between Rehoboam and Jeroboam throughout their reigns. Rehoboam rested with his ancestors and was buried with his ancestors in the city of David. His mother's name was Naamah the Ammonite. His son Abijam became king in his place.

15 In the eighteenth year of Israel's King Jeroboam son of Nebat, Abijam became king over Judah, and he reigned three years in Jerusalem. His mother's name was Maacah daughter of Abishalom.

Abijam walked in all the sins his father before him had committed, and he was not wholeheartedly devoted to the LORD his God as his ancestor David had been. But for the sake of David, the LORD his God gave him a lamp in Jerusalem by raising up his son after him and by preserving Jerusalem. For David did what was right in the LORD's sight, and he did not turn aside from anything he had commanded him all the days of his life, except in the matter of Uriah the Hethite.

There had been war between Rehoboam and Jeroboam all the days of Rehoboam's life. The rest of the events of Abijam's reign, along with all his accomplishments, are written in the Historical Record of Judah's Kings. There was also war between Abijam and Jeroboam. Abijam rested with his ancestors and was buried in the city of David. His son Asa became king in his place.

In the twentieth year of Israel's King Jeroboam, Asa became king of Judah, and he reigned forty-one years in Jerusalem. His grandmother's name was Maacah daughter of Abishalom.

Asa did what was right in the LORD's sight, as his ancestor David had done. He banished the male cult prostitutes from the land and removed all of the idols that his ancestors had made. He also removed his grandmother Maacah from being queen mother because she had made an obscene image of Asherah. Asa chopped down her obscene image and burned it in the Kidron Valley. The high places were not taken away, but Asa was wholeheartedly devoted to the LORD his entire life. He brought his father's consecrated gifts and his own consecrated gifts into the LORD's temple: silver, gold, and utensils.

There was war between Asa and King Baasha of Israel throughout their reigns. Israel's King Baasha went to war against Judah. He built Ramah in order to keep anyone from leaving or coming to King Asa of Judah. So Asa withdrew all the silver and gold that remained in the treasuries of the LORD's temple and the treasuries of the royal palace and gave it to his servants. Then King Asa sent them to Ben-hadad son of Tabrimmon son of Hezion king of Aram who lived in Damascus, saying, "There is a treaty between me and you, between my father and your father. Look, I have sent you a gift of silver and gold. Go and break your treaty with King Baasha of Israel so that he will withdraw from me."

Ben-hadad listened to King Asa and sent the commanders of his armies against the cities of Israel. He attacked Ijon, Dan, Abel-beth-maacah, all Chinnereth, and the whole land of Naphtali. When Baasha heard about it, he quit building Ramah and stayed in Tirzah. Then King Asa gave a command to everyone without exception in Judah, and they carried away the stones of Ramah and the timbers Baasha had built it with. Then King Asa built Geba of Benjamin and Mizpah with them.

The rest of all the events of Asa's reign, along with all his might, all his accomplishments, and the cities he built, are written in the Historical Record of Judah's Kings. But in his old age he developed a disease in his feet. Then Asa rested with his ancestors and was buried in the city of his ancestor David. His son Jehoshaphat became king in his place.

Nadab son of Jeroboam became king over Israel in the second year of Judah's King Asa; he reigned
40 over Israel two years. Nadab did what was evil in the LORD's sight and walked in the ways of his
father and the sin he had caused Israel to commit.

Then Baasha son of Ahijah of the house of Issachar conspired against Nadab, and Baasha
struck him down at Gibbethon of the Philistines while Nadab and all Israel were besieging
Gibbethon. In the third year of Judah's King Asa, Baasha killed Nadab and reigned in his place.

When Baasha became king, he struck down the entire house of Jeroboam. He did not leave
Jeroboam any survivors but destroyed his family according to the word of the LORD he had spoken
through his servant Ahijah the Shilonite. This was because Jeroboam had angered the LORD God
of Israel by the sins he had committed and had caused Israel to commit.

The rest of the events of Nadab's reign, along with all his accomplishments, are written in
50 the Historical Record of Israel's Kings. There was war between Asa and King Baasha of Israel
throughout their reigns.

In the third year of Judah's King Asa, Baasha son of Ahijah became king over all Israel, and he
reigned in Tirzah twenty-four years. He did what was evil in the LORD's sight and walked in the
ways of Jeroboam and the sin he had caused Israel to commit.

16 Now the word of the LORD came to Jehu son of Hanani against Baasha: "Because I raised you
up from the dust and made you ruler over my people Israel, but you have walked in the ways of
Jeroboam and have caused my people Israel to sin, angering me with their sins, take note: I will
eradicate Baasha and his house, and I will make your house like the house of Jeroboam son of Nebat:

> Anyone who belongs to Baasha and dies in the city,
> the dogs will eat,
> and anyone who is his and dies in the field,
> the birds will eat."

The rest of the events of Baasha's reign, along with all his accomplishments and might, are
10 written in the Historical Record of Israel's Kings. Baasha rested with his ancestors and was buried
in Tirzah. His son Elah became king in his place. But through the prophet Jehu son of Hanani the
word of the LORD also had come against Baasha and against his house because of all the evil he had
done in the LORD's sight. His actions angered the LORD, and Baasha's house became like the house
of Jeroboam, because he had struck it down.

In the twenty-sixth year of Judah's King Asa, Elah son of Baasha became king over Israel, and he
reigned in Tirzah two years.

His servant Zimri, commander of half his chariots, conspired against him while Elah was in
Tirzah getting drunk in the house of Arza, who was in charge of the household at Tirzah. In the

twenty-seventh year of Judah's King Asa, Zimri went in and struck Elah down, killing him. Then Zimri became king in his place.

When he became king, as soon as he was seated on his throne, Zimri struck down the entire house of Baasha. He did not leave a single male, including his kinsmen and his friends. So Zimri destroyed the entire house of Baasha, according to the word of the LORD he had spoken against Baasha through the prophet Jehu. This happened because of all the sins of Baasha and those of his son Elah, which they committed and caused Israel to commit, angering the LORD God of Israel with their worthless idols.

The rest of the events of Elah's reign, along with all his accomplishments, are written in the Historical Record of Israel's Kings.

In the twenty-seventh year of Judah's King Asa, Zimri became king for seven days in Tirzah. Now the troops were encamped against Gibbethon of the Philistines. When these troops heard that Zimri had not only conspired but had also struck down the king, then all Israel made Omri, the army commander, king over Israel that very day in the camp. Omri along with all Israel marched up from Gibbethon and besieged Tirzah. When Zimri saw that the city was captured, he entered the citadel of the royal palace and burned it down over himself. He died because of the sin he committed by doing what was evil in the LORD's sight and by walking in the ways of Jeroboam and the sin he caused Israel to commit.

The rest of the events of Zimri's reign, along with the conspiracy that he instigated, are written in the Historical Record of Israel's Kings. At that time the people of Israel were divided: half the people followed Tibni son of Ginath, to make him king, and half followed Omri. However, the people who followed Omri proved stronger than those who followed Tibni son of Ginath. So Tibni died and Omri became king.

In the thirty-first year of Judah's King Asa, Omri became king over Israel, and he reigned twelve years. He reigned six years in Tirzah, then he bought the hill of Samaria from Shemer for 150 pounds of silver, and he built up the hill. He named the city he built Samaria based on the name Shemer, the owner of the hill.

Omri did what was evil in the LORD's sight; he did more evil than all who were before him. He walked in all the ways of Jeroboam son of Nebat in every respect and continued in his sins that he caused Israel to commit, angering the LORD God of Israel with their worthless idols. The rest of the events of Omri's reign, along with his accomplishments and the might he exercised, are written in the Historical Record of Israel's Kings. Omri rested with his ancestors and was buried in Samaria. His son Ahab became king in his place.

Ahab son of Omri became king over Israel in the thirty-eighth year of Judah's King Asa; Ahab son of Omri reigned over Israel in Samaria twenty-two years. But Ahab son of Omri did what was evil in the LORD's sight more than all who were before him. Then, as if following the sin of Jeroboam son of Nebat were not enough, he married Jezebel, the daughter of Ethbaal king of the Sidonians, and then proceeded to serve Baal and bow in worship to him. He set up an altar for Baal in the temple of Baal that he had built in Samaria. Ahab also made an Asherah pole. Ahab did more to anger the Lord God of Israel than all the kings of Israel who were before him.

During his reign, Hiel the Bethelite built Jericho. At the cost of Abiram his firstborn, he laid its foundation, and at the cost of Segub his youngest, he finished its gates, according to the word of the Lord he had spoken through Joshua son of Nun.

17 Now Elijah the Tishbite, from the Gilead settlers, said to Ahab, "As the Lord God of Israel lives, in whose presence I stand, there will be no dew or rain during these years except by my command!"

Then the word of the Lord came to him: "Leave here, turn eastward, and hide at the Wadi Cherith where it enters the Jordan. You are to drink from the wadi. I have commanded the ravens to provide for you there."

So he proceeded to do what the Lord commanded. Elijah left and lived at the Wadi Cherith where it enters the Jordan. The ravens kept bringing him bread and meat in the morning and in the evening, and he would drink from the wadi. After a while, the wadi dried up because there had been no rain in the land.

10 Then the word of the Lord came to him: "Get up, go to Zarephath that belongs to Sidon and stay there. Look, I have commanded a woman who is a widow to provide for you there." So Elijah got up and went to Zarephath. When he arrived at the city gate, there was a widow gathering wood. Elijah called to her and said, "Please bring me a little water in a cup and let me drink." As she went to get it, he called to her and said, "Please bring me a piece of bread in your hand."

But she said, "As the Lord your God lives, I don't have anything baked—only a handful of flour in the jar and a bit of oil in the jug. Just now, I am gathering a couple of sticks in order to go prepare it for myself and my son so we can eat it and die."

Then Elijah said to her, "Don't be afraid; go and do as you have said. But first make me a small loaf from it and bring it out to me. Afterward, you may make some for yourself and your son, for 20 this is what the Lord God of Israel says, 'The flour jar will not become empty and the oil jug will not run dry until the day the Lord sends rain on the surface of the land.'"

So she proceeded to do according to the word of Elijah. Then the woman, Elijah, and her household ate for many days. The flour jar did not become empty, and the oil jug did not run dry, according to the word of the Lord he had spoken through Elijah.

After this, the son of the woman who owned the house became ill. His illness got worse until he stopped breathing. She said to Elijah, "Man of God, what do you have against me? Have you come to call attention to my iniquity so that my son is put to death?"

But Elijah said to her, "Give me your son." So he took him from her arms, brought him up to the upstairs room where he was staying, and laid him on his own bed. Then he cried out to the

30 LORD and said, "LORD my God, have you also brought tragedy on the widow I am staying with by killing her son?" Then he stretched himself out over the boy three times. He cried out to the LORD and said, "LORD my God, please let this boy's life come into him again!"

So the LORD listened to Elijah, and the boy's life came into him again, and he lived. Then Elijah took the boy, brought him down from the upstairs room into the house, and gave him to his mother. Elijah said, "Look, your son is alive."

Then the woman said to Elijah, "Now I know you are a man of God and the LORD's word from your mouth is true."

18 After a long time, the word of the LORD came to Elijah in the third year: "Go and present yourself to Ahab. I will send rain on the surface of the land." So Elijah went to present himself to Ahab.

The famine was severe in Samaria. Ahab called for Obadiah, who was in charge of the palace. Obadiah was a man who greatly feared the LORD and took a hundred prophets and hid them, fifty men to a cave, and provided them with food and water when Jezebel slaughtered the LORD's prophets. Ahab said to Obadiah, "Go throughout the land to every spring and to every wadi. Perhaps we'll find grass so we can keep the horses and mules alive and not have to destroy any cattle." They divided the land between them in order to cover it. Ahab went one way by himself, and Obadiah went the other way by himself.

10 While Obadiah was walking along the road, Elijah suddenly met him. When Obadiah recognized him, he fell facedown and said, "Is it you, my lord Elijah?"

"It is I," he replied. "Go tell your lord, 'Elijah is here!'"

But Obadiah said, "What sin have I committed, that you are handing your servant over to Ahab to put me to death? As the LORD your God lives, there is no nation or kingdom where my lord has not sent someone to search for you. When they said, 'He is not here,' he made that kingdom or nation swear they had not found you.

"Now you say, 'Go tell your lord, "Elijah is here!"' But when I leave you, the Spirit of the LORD may carry you off to some place I don't know. Then when I go report to Ahab and he doesn't find you, he will kill me. But I, your servant, have feared the LORD from my youth. Wasn't it reported

20 to my lord what I did when Jezebel slaughtered the LORD's prophets? I hid a hundred of the prophets of the LORD, fifty men to a cave, and I provided them with food and water. Now you say, 'Go tell your lord, "Elijah is here!"' He will kill me!"

Then Elijah said, "As the LORD of Armies lives, in whose presence I stand, today I will present myself to Ahab."

Obadiah went to meet Ahab and told him. Then Ahab went to meet Elijah. When Ahab saw Elijah, Ahab said to him, "Is that you, the one ruining Israel?"

He replied, "I have not ruined Israel, but you and your father's family have, because you have abandoned the LORD's commands and followed the Baals. Now summon all Israel to meet me at Mount Carmel, along with the 450 prophets of Baal and the 400 prophets of Asherah who eat at Jezebel's table."

30 So Ahab summoned all the Israelites and gathered the prophets at Mount Carmel. Then Elijah approached all the people and said, "How long will you waver between two opinions? If the LORD is God, follow him. But if Baal, follow him." But the people didn't answer him a word.

Then Elijah said to the people, "I am the only remaining prophet of the LORD, but Baal's prophets are 450 men. Let two bulls be given to us. They are to choose one bull for themselves, cut it in pieces, and place it on the wood but not light the fire. I will prepare the other bull and place it on the wood but not light the fire. Then you call on the name of your god, and I will call on the name of the LORD. The God who answers with fire, he is God."

All the people answered, "That's fine."

Then Elijah said to the prophets of Baal, "Since you are so numerous, choose for yourselves one
40 bull and prepare it first. Then call on the name of your god but don't light the fire."

So they took the bull that he gave them, prepared it, and called on the name of Baal from morning until noon, saying, "Baal, answer us!" But there was no sound; no one answered. Then they danced around the altar they had made.

At noon Elijah mocked them. He said, "Shout loudly, for he's a god! Maybe he's thinking it over; maybe he has wandered away; or maybe he's on the road. Perhaps he's sleeping and will wake up!" They shouted loudly, and cut themselves with knives and spears, according to their custom, until blood gushed over them. All afternoon they kept on raving until the offering of the evening sacrifice, but there was no sound; no one answered, no one paid attention.

Then Elijah said to all the people, "Come near me." So all the people approached him.
50 Then he repaired the LORD's altar that had been torn down: Elijah took twelve stones— according to the number of the tribes of the sons of Jacob, to whom the word of the LORD had come, saying, "Israel will be your name"—and he built an altar with the stones in the name of the LORD. Then he made a trench around the altar large enough to hold about four gallons. Next, he arranged the wood, cut up the bull, and placed it on the wood. He said, "Fill four water pots with water and pour it on the offering to be burned and on the wood." Then he said, "A second time!" and they did it a second time. And then he said, "A third time!" and they did it a third time. So the water ran all around the altar; he even filled the trench with water.

At the time for offering the evening sacrifice, the prophet Elijah approached the altar and said,
60 "LORD, the God of Abraham, Isaac, and Israel, today let it be known that you are God in Israel and I am your servant, and that at your word I have done all these things. Answer me, LORD! Answer me so that this people will know that you, the LORD, are God and that you have turned their hearts back."

Then the LORD's fire fell and consumed the burnt offering, the wood, the stones, and the dust, and it licked up the water that was in the trench. When all the people saw it, they fell facedown and said, "The LORD, he is God! The LORD, he is God!"

Then Elijah ordered them, "Seize the prophets of Baal! Do not let even one of them escape." So they seized them, and Elijah brought them down to the Wadi Kishon and slaughtered them there. Elijah said to Ahab, "Go up, eat and drink, for there is the sound of a rainstorm."

70 So Ahab went to eat and drink, but Elijah went up to the summit of Carmel. He bent down on the ground and put his face between his knees. Then he said to his servant, "Go up and look toward the sea."

So he went up, looked, and said, "There's nothing."

Seven times Elijah said, "Go back."

On the seventh time, he reported, "There's a cloud as small as a man's hand coming up from the sea."

Then Elijah said, "Go and tell Ahab, 'Get your chariot ready and go down so the rain doesn't stop you.'"

In a little while, the sky grew dark with clouds and wind, and there was a downpour. So Ahab 80 got in his chariot and went to Jezreel. The power of the LORD was on Elijah, and he tucked his mantle under his belt and ran ahead of Ahab to the entrance of Jezreel.

19 Ahab told Jezebel everything that Elijah had done and how he had killed all the prophets with the sword. So Jezebel sent a messenger to Elijah, saying, "May the gods punish me and do so severely if I don't make your life like the life of one of them by this time tomorrow!"

Then Elijah became afraid and immediately ran for his life. When he came to Beer-sheba that belonged to Judah, he left his servant there, but he went on a day's journey into the wilderness. He sat down under a broom tree and prayed that he might die. He said, "I have had enough! LORD, take my life, for I'm no better than my ancestors." Then he lay down and slept under the broom tree.

Suddenly, an angel touched him. The angel told him, "Get up and eat." Then he looked, and 10 there at his head was a loaf of bread baked over hot stones, and a jug of water. So he ate and drank and lay down again. Then the angel of the LORD returned for a second time and touched him. He said, "Get up and eat, or the journey will be too much for you." So he got up, ate, and drank. Then on the strength from that food, he walked forty days and forty nights to Horeb, the mountain of God. He entered a cave there and spent the night.

Suddenly, the word of the LORD came to him, and he said to him, "What are you doing here, Elijah?"

He replied, "I have been very zealous for the LORD God of Armies, but the Israelites have abandoned your covenant, torn down your altars, and killed your prophets with the sword. I alone am left, and they are looking for me to take my life."

20 Then he said, "Go out and stand on the mountain in the LORD's presence."

At that moment, the LORD passed by. A great and mighty wind was tearing at the mountains and was shattering cliffs before the LORD, but the LORD was not in the wind. After the wind there was an earthquake, but the LORD was not in the earthquake. After the earthquake there was a fire, but the LORD was not in the fire. And after the fire there was a voice, a soft whisper. When Elijah heard it, he wrapped his face in his mantle and went out and stood at the entrance of the cave.

Suddenly, a voice came to him and said, "What are you doing here, Elijah?"

"I have been very zealous for the LORD God of Armies," he replied, "but the Israelites have abandoned your covenant, torn down your altars, and killed your prophets with the sword. I alone am left, and they're looking for me to take my life."

Then the LORD said to him, "Go and return by the way you came to the Wilderness of Damascus. When you arrive, you are to anoint Hazael as king over Aram. You are to anoint Jehu son of Nimshi as king over Israel and Elisha son of Shaphat from Abel-meholah as prophet in your place. Then Jehu will put to death whoever escapes the sword of Hazael, and Elisha will put to death whoever escapes the sword of Jehu. But I will leave seven thousand in Israel—every knee that has not bowed to Baal and every mouth that has not kissed him."

Elijah left there and found Elisha son of Shaphat as he was plowing. Twelve teams of oxen were in front of him, and he was with the twelfth team. Elijah walked by him and threw his mantle over him. Elisha left the oxen, ran to follow Elijah, and said, "Please let me kiss my father and mother, and then I will follow you."

"Go on back," he replied, "for what have I done to you?"

So he turned back from following him, took the team of oxen, and slaughtered them. With the oxen's wooden yoke and plow, he cooked the meat and gave it to the people, and they ate. Then he left, followed Elijah, and served him.

20 Now King Ben-hadad of Aram assembled his entire army. Thirty-two kings, along with horses and chariots, were with him. He marched up, besieged Samaria, and fought against it. He sent messengers into the city to King Ahab of Israel and said to him, "This is what Ben-hadad says: 'Your silver and your gold are mine! And your best wives and children are mine as well!'"

Then the king of Israel answered, "Just as you say, my lord the king: I am yours, along with all that I have."

The messengers then returned and said, "This is what Ben-hadad says: 'I have sent messengers to you, saying, "You are to give me your silver, your gold, your wives, and your children." But at this time tomorrow I will send my servants to you, and they will search your palace and your servants' houses. They will lay their hands on and take away whatever is precious to you.'"

Then the king of Israel called for all the elders of the land and said, "Recognize that this one is only looking for trouble, for he demanded my wives, my children, my silver, and my gold, and I didn't turn him down."

All the elders and all the people said to him, "Don't listen or agree."

So he said to Ben-hadad's messengers, "Say to my lord the king, 'Everything you demanded of your servant the first time, I will do, but this thing I cannot do.'" So the messengers left and took word back to him.

Then Ben-hadad sent messengers to him and said, "May the gods punish me and do so severely if Samaria's dust amounts to a handful for each of the people who follow me."

20 The king of Israel answered, "Say this: 'Don't let the one who puts on his armor boast like the one who takes it off.'"

When Ben-hadad heard this response, while he and the kings were drinking in their quarters, he said to his servants, "Take your positions." So they took their positions against the city.

A prophet approached King Ahab of Israel and said, "This is what the LORD says: 'Do you see this whole huge army? Watch, I am handing it over to you today so that you may know that I am the LORD.'"

Ahab asked, "By whom?"

And the prophet said, "This is what the LORD says: 'By the young men of the provincial leaders.'"

Then he asked, "Who is to start the battle?"

30 He said, "You."

So Ahab mobilized the young men of the provincial leaders, and there were 232. After them he mobilized all the Israelite troops: 7,000. They marched out at noon while Ben-hadad and the thirty-two kings who were helping him were getting drunk in their quarters. The young men of the provincial leaders marched out first. Then Ben-hadad sent out scouts, and they reported to him, saying, "Men are marching out of Samaria."

So he said, "If they have marched out in peace, take them alive, and if they have marched out for battle, take them alive."

The young men of the provincial leaders and the army behind them marched out from the city, and each one struck down his opponent. So the Arameans fled and Israel pursued them, but King

40 Ben-hadad of Aram escaped on a horse with the cavalry. Then the king of Israel marched out and attacked the cavalry and the chariots. He inflicted a severe slaughter on Aram.

The prophet approached the king of Israel and said to him, "Go and strengthen yourself, then consider carefully what you should do, for in the spring the king of Aram will attack you."

Now the king of Aram's servants said to him, "Their gods are gods of the hill country. That's why they were stronger than we were. Instead, we should fight with them on the plain; then we will certainly be stronger than they are. Also do this: remove each king from his position and appoint captains in their place. Raise another army for yourself like the army you lost—horse for horse, chariot for chariot—and let's fight with them on the plain; and we will certainly be stronger than they are." The king listened to them and did it.

50 In the spring, Ben-hadad mobilized the Arameans and went up to Aphek to battle Israel. The Israelites mobilized, gathered supplies, and went to fight them. The Israelites camped in front of them like two little flocks of goats, while the Arameans filled the landscape.

Then the man of God approached and said to the king of Israel, "This is what the Lord says: 'Because the Arameans have said, "The Lord is a god of the mountains and not a god of the valleys," I will hand over all this whole huge army to you. Then you will know that I am the Lord.'"

They camped opposite each other for seven days. On the seventh day, the battle took place, and the Israelites struck down the Arameans—one hundred thousand foot soldiers in one day. The ones who remained fled into the city of Aphek, and the wall fell on those twenty-seven thousand 60 remaining men.

Ben-hadad also fled and went into an inner room in the city. His servants said to him, "Consider this: we have heard that the kings of the house of Israel are merciful kings. So let's put sackcloth around our waists and ropes around our heads, and let's go out to the king of Israel. Perhaps he will spare your life."

So they dressed with sackcloth around their waists and ropes around their heads, went to the king of Israel, and said, "Your servant Ben-hadad says, 'Please spare my life.'"

So he said, "Is he still alive? He is my brother."

Now the men were looking for a sign of hope, so they quickly picked up on this and responded, "Yes, it is your brother Ben-hadad."

70 Then he said, "Go and bring him."

So Ben-hadad came out to him, and Ahab had him come up into the chariot. Then Ben-hadad said to him, "I restore to you the cities that my father took from your father, and you may set up marketplaces for yourself in Damascus, like my father set up in Samaria."

Ahab responded, "On the basis of this treaty, I release you." So he made a treaty with him and released him.

One of the sons of the prophets said to his fellow prophet by the word of the Lord, "Strike me!" But the man refused to strike him.

He told him, "Because you did not listen to the Lord, mark my words: When you leave me, a lion will kill you." When he left him, a lion attacked and killed him.

80 The prophet found another man and said to him, "Strike me!" So the man struck him, inflicting a wound. Then the prophet went and waited for the king on the road. He disguised himself with a bandage over his eyes. As the king was passing by, he cried out to the king and said, "Your servant marched out into the middle of the battle. Suddenly, a man turned aside and brought someone to me and said, 'Guard this man! If he is ever missing, it will be your life in place of his life, or you will weigh out seventy-five pounds of silver.' But while your servant was busy here and there, he disappeared."

The king of Israel said to him, "That will be your sentence; you yourself have decided it."

He quickly removed the bandage from his eyes. The king of Israel recognized that he was one of the prophets. The prophet said to him, "This is what the Lord says: 'Because you released from

90 your hand the man I had set apart for destruction, it will be your life in place of his life and your people in place of his people.'" The king of Israel left for home resentful and angry, and he entered Samaria.

21 Some time passed after these events. Naboth the Jezreelite had a vineyard; it was in Jezreel next to the palace of King Ahab of Samaria. So Ahab spoke to Naboth, saying, "Give me your vineyard so I can have it for a vegetable garden, since it is right next to my palace. I will give you a better vineyard in its place, or if you prefer, I will give you its value in silver."

But Naboth said to Ahab, "As the Lord is my witness, I will never give my ancestors' inheritance to you."

So Ahab went to his palace resentful and angry because of what Naboth the Jezreelite had told him. He had said, "I will not give you my ancestors' inheritance." He lay down on his bed, turned his face away, and didn't eat any food.

10 Then his wife Jezebel came to him and said to him, "Why are you so upset that you refuse to eat?"

"Because I spoke to Naboth the Jezreelite," he replied. "I told him, 'Give me your vineyard for silver, or if you wish, I will give you a vineyard in its place.' But he said, 'I won't give you my vineyard!'"

Then his wife Jezebel said to him, "Now, exercise your royal power over Israel. Get up, eat some food, and be happy. For I will give you the vineyard of Naboth the Jezreelite." So she wrote letters in Ahab's name and sealed them with his seal. She sent the letters to the elders and nobles who lived with Naboth in his city. In the letters, she wrote:

Proclaim a fast and seat Naboth at the head of the people. Then seat two wicked men opposite him and have them testify against him, saying, "You have cursed God and the king!" Then take
20 him out and stone him to death.

The men of his city, the elders and nobles who lived in his city, did as Jezebel had sent word to them, just as it was written in the letters she had sent them. They proclaimed a fast and seated Naboth at the head of the people. The two wicked men came in and sat opposite him. Then the wicked men testified against Naboth in the presence of the people, saying, "Naboth has cursed God and the king!" So they took him outside the city and stoned him to death with stones. Then they sent word to Jezebel: "Naboth has been stoned to death."

When Jezebel heard that Naboth had been stoned to death, she said to Ahab, "Get up and take possession of the vineyard of Naboth the Jezreelite who refused to give it to you for silver, since Naboth isn't alive, but dead." When Ahab heard that Naboth was dead, he got up to go down to
30 the vineyard of Naboth the Jezreelite to take possession of it.

Then the word of the Lord came to Elijah the Tishbite: "Get up and go to meet King Ahab of Israel, who is in Samaria. He's in Naboth's vineyard, where he has gone to take possession of it.

Tell him, 'This is what the LORD says: Have you murdered and also taken possession?' Then tell him, 'This is what the LORD says: In the place where the dogs licked up Naboth's blood, the dogs will also lick up your blood!'"

Ahab said to Elijah, "So, my enemy, you've found me, have you?"

He replied, "I have found you because you devoted yourself to do what is evil in the LORD's sight. This is what the LORD says: 'I am about to bring disaster on you and will eradicate your descendants:

40   I will wipe out all of Ahab's males,
                   both slave and free, in Israel;

I will make your house like the house of Jeroboam son of Nebat and like the house of Baasha son of Ahijah, because you have angered me and caused Israel to sin.' The LORD also speaks of Jezebel: 'The dogs will eat Jezebel in the plot of land at Jezreel:

       Anyone who belongs to Ahab and dies in the city, the dogs will eat,
       and anyone who dies in the field, the birds will eat.'"

Still, there was no one like Ahab, who devoted himself to do what was evil in the LORD's sight, because his wife Jezebel incited him. He committed the most detestable acts by following idols as the Amorites had, whom the LORD had dispossessed before the Israelites.

50   When Ahab heard these words, he tore his clothes, put sackcloth over his body, and fasted. He lay down in sackcloth and walked around subdued. Then the word of the LORD came to Elijah the Tishbite: "Have you seen how Ahab has humbled himself before me? I will not bring the disaster during his lifetime, because he has humbled himself before me. I will bring the disaster on his house during his son's lifetime."

22 There was a lull of three years without war between Aram and Israel. However, in the third year, King Jehoshaphat of Judah went to visit the king of Israel. The king of Israel had said to his servants, "Don't you know that Ramoth-gilead is ours, but we're doing nothing to take it from the king of Aram?" So he asked Jehoshaphat, "Will you go with me to fight Ramoth-gilead?"

Jehoshaphat replied to the king of Israel, "I am as you are, my people as your people, my horses as your horses." But Jehoshaphat said to the king of Israel, "First, please ask what the LORD's will is."

So the king of Israel gathered the prophets, about four hundred men, and asked them, "Should I go against Ramoth-gilead for war or should I refrain?"

10   They replied, "March up, and the Lord will hand it over to the king."

But Jehoshaphat asked, "Isn't there a prophet of the LORD here anymore? Let's ask him."

The king of Israel said to Jehoshaphat, "There is still one man who can inquire of the LORD, but I hate him because he never prophesies good about me, but only disaster. He is Micaiah son of Imlah."

"The king shouldn't say that!" Jehoshaphat replied.

So the king of Israel called an officer and said, "Hurry and get Micaiah son of Imlah!"

Now the king of Israel and King Jehoshaphat of Judah, clothed in royal attire, were each sitting on his own throne. They were on the threshing floor at the entrance to the gate of Samaria, and all the prophets were prophesying in front of them. Then Zedekiah son of Chenaanah made iron horns and said, "This is what the Lord says: 'You will gore the Arameans with these until they are finished off.'" And all the prophets were prophesying the same: "March up to Ramoth-gilead and succeed, for the Lord will hand it over to the king."

The messenger who went to call Micaiah instructed him, "Look, the words of the prophets are unanimously favorable for the king. So let your words be like theirs, and speak favorably."

But Micaiah said, "As the Lord lives, I will say whatever the Lord says to me."

So he went to the king, and the king asked him, "Micaiah, should we go to Ramoth-gilead for war, or should we refrain?"

Micaiah told him, "March up and succeed. The Lord will hand it over to the king."

But the king said to him, "How many times must I make you swear not to tell me anything but the truth in the name of the Lord?"

So Micaiah said:

> I saw all Israel scattered on the hills
> like sheep without a shepherd.
> And the Lord said,
> "They have no master;
> let everyone return home in peace."

So the king of Israel said to Jehoshaphat, "Didn't I tell you he never prophesies good about me, but only disaster?"

Then Micaiah said, "Therefore, hear the word of the Lord: I saw the Lord sitting on his throne, and the whole heavenly army was standing by him at his right hand and at his left hand. And the Lord said, 'Who will entice Ahab to march up and fall at Ramoth-gilead?' So one was saying this and another was saying that.

"Then a spirit came forward, stood in the Lord's presence, and said, 'I will entice him.'

"The Lord asked him, 'How?'

"He said, 'I will go and become a lying spirit in the mouth of all his prophets.'

"Then he said, 'You will certainly entice him and prevail. Go and do that.'

"You see, the Lord has put a lying spirit into the mouth of all these prophets of yours, and the Lord has pronounced disaster against you."

Then Zedekiah son of Chenaanah came up, hit Micaiah on the cheek, and demanded, "Did the Spirit of the Lord leave me to speak to you?"

Micaiah replied, "You will soon see when you go to hide in an inner chamber on that day."

Then the king of Israel ordered, "Take Micaiah and return him to Amon, the governor of the city, and to Joash, the king's son, and say, 'This is what the king says: Put this guy in prison and feed him only a little bread and water until I come back safely.'"

But Micaiah said, "If you ever return safely, the LORD has not spoken through me." Then he said, "Listen, all you people!"

Then the king of Israel and Judah's King Jehoshaphat went up to Ramoth-gilead. But the king of Israel said to Jehoshaphat, "I will disguise myself and go into battle, but you wear your royal attire." So the king of Israel disguised himself and went into battle.

60 Now the king of Aram had ordered his thirty-two chariot commanders, "Do not fight with anyone at all except the king of Israel."

When the chariot commanders saw Jehoshaphat, they shouted, "He must be the king of Israel!" So they turned to fight against him, but Jehoshaphat cried out. When the chariot commanders saw that he was not the king of Israel, they turned back from pursuing him.

But a man drew his bow without taking special aim and struck the king of Israel through the joints of his armor. So he said to his charioteer, "Turn around and take me out of the battle, for I am badly wounded!" The battle raged throughout that day, and the king was propped up in his chariot facing the Arameans. He died that evening, and blood from his wound flowed into the bottom of the chariot. Then the cry rang out in the army as the sun set, declaring:

70   Each man to his own city,
        and each man to his own land!

So the king died and was brought to Samaria. They buried the king in Samaria. Then someone washed the chariot at the pool of Samaria. The dogs licked up his blood, and the prostitutes bathed in it, according to the word of the LORD that he had spoken.

The rest of the events of Ahab's reign, along with all his accomplishments, including the ivory palace he built, and all the cities he built, are written in the Historical Record of Israel's Kings. Ahab rested with his ancestors, and his son Ahaziah became king in his place.

Jehoshaphat son of Asa became king over Judah in the fourth year of Israel's King Ahab. Jehoshaphat was thirty-five years old when he became king; he reigned twenty-five years in 80 Jerusalem. His mother's name was Azubah daughter of Shilhi. He walked in all the ways of his father Asa; he did not turn away from them but did what was right in the LORD's sight. However, the high places were not taken away; the people still sacrificed and burned incense on the high places. Jehoshaphat also made peace with the king of Israel.

The rest of the events of Jehoshaphat's reign, along with the might he exercised and how he waged war, are written in the Historical Record of Judah's Kings. He eradicated from the land the rest of the male cult prostitutes who were left from the days of his father Asa. There was no king in Edom; a deputy served as king. Jehoshaphat made ships of Tarshish to go to Ophir for gold, but they did not go because the ships were wrecked at Ezion-geber. At that time, Ahaziah son of Ahab said to Jehoshaphat, "Let my servants go with your servants in the ships," but Jehoshaphat was not willing. Jehoshaphat rested with his ancestors and was buried with them in the city of his ancestor David. His son Jehoram became king in his place.

Ahaziah son of Ahab became king over Israel in Samaria in the seventeenth year of Judah's King Jehoshaphat, and he reigned over Israel two years. He did what was evil in the LORD's sight. He walked in the ways of his father, in the ways of his mother, and in the ways of Jeroboam son of Nebat, who had caused Israel to sin. He served Baal and bowed in worship to him. He angered the LORD God of Israel just as his father had done.

2 Kings

1 After Ahab's death, Moab rebelled against Israel. Ahaziah had fallen through the latticed window of his upstairs room in Samaria and was injured. So he sent messengers, instructing them, "Go inquire of Baal-zebub, the god of Ekron, whether I will recover from this injury."

But the angel of the LORD said to Elijah the Tishbite, "Go and meet the messengers of the king of Samaria and say to them, 'Is it because there is no God in Israel that you are going to inquire of Baal-zebub, the god of Ekron? Therefore, this is what the LORD says: You will not get up from your sickbed; you will certainly die.'" Then Elijah left.

The messengers returned to the king, who asked them, "Why have you come back?"

They replied, "A man came to meet us and said, 'Go back to the king who sent you and declare
10 to him, "This is what the LORD says: Is it because there is no God in Israel that you're sending these men to inquire of Baal-zebub, the god of Ekron? Therefore, you will not get up from your sickbed; you will certainly die."'"

The king asked them, "What sort of man came up to meet you and spoke those words to you?"

They replied, "A hairy man with a leather belt around his waist."

He said, "It's Elijah the Tishbite."

So King Ahaziah sent a captain with his fifty men to Elijah. When the captain went up to him, he was sitting on top of the hill. He announced, "Man of God, the king declares, 'Come down!'"

Elijah responded to the captain, "If I am a man of God, may fire come down from heaven and
20 consume you and your fifty men." Then fire came down from heaven and consumed him and his fifty men.

So the king sent another captain with his fifty men to Elijah. He took in the situation and announced, "Man of God, this is what the king says: 'Come down immediately!'"

Elijah responded, "If I am a man of God, may fire come down from heaven and consume you and your fifty men." So a divine fire came down from heaven and consumed him and his fifty men.

Then the king sent a third captain with his fifty men. The third captain went up and fell on his knees in front of Elijah and begged him, "Man of God, please let my life and the lives of these fifty servants of yours be precious to you. Already fire has come down from heaven and consumed the
30 first two captains with their companies, but this time let my life be precious to you."

The angel of the LORD said to Elijah, "Go down with him. Don't be afraid of him." So he got up and went down with him to the king.

Then Elijah said to King Ahaziah, "This is what the LORD says: 'Because you have sent messengers to inquire of Baal-zebub, the god of Ekron—is it because there is no God in Israel for you to inquire of his will?—you will not get up from your sickbed; you will certainly die.'"

Ahaziah died according to the word of the LORD that Elijah had spoken. Since he had no son, Joram became king in his place. This happened in the second year of Judah's King Jehoram son of Jehoshaphat. The rest of the events of Ahaziah's reign, along with his accomplishments, are written in the Historical Record of Israel's Kings.

2 The time had come for the LORD to take Elijah up to heaven in a whirlwind. Elijah and Elisha were traveling from Gilgal, and Elijah said to Elisha, "Stay here; the LORD is sending me on to Bethel."

But Elisha replied, "As the LORD lives and as you yourself live, I will not leave you." So they went down to Bethel.

Then the sons of the prophets who were at Bethel came out to Elisha and said, "Do you know that the LORD will take your master away from you today?"

He said, "Yes, I know. Be quiet."

Elijah said to him, "Elisha, stay here; the LORD is sending me to Jericho."

But Elisha said, "As the LORD lives and as you yourself live, I will not leave you." So they went
10 to Jericho.

Then the sons of the prophets who were in Jericho came up to Elisha and said, "Do you know that the LORD will take your master away from you today?"

He said, "Yes, I know. Be quiet."

Elijah said to him, "Stay here; the LORD is sending me to the Jordan."

But Elisha said, "As the LORD lives and as you yourself live, I will not leave you." So the two of them went on.

Fifty men from the sons of the prophets came and stood observing them at a distance while the two of them stood by the Jordan. Elijah took his mantle, rolled it up, and struck the water, which parted to the right and left. Then the two of them crossed over on dry ground. When they had
20 crossed over, Elijah said to Elisha, "Tell me what I can do for you before I am taken from you."

So Elisha answered, "Please, let me inherit two shares of your spirit."

Elijah replied, "You have asked for something difficult. If you see me being taken from you, you will have it. If not, you won't."

As they continued walking and talking, a chariot of fire with horses of fire suddenly appeared and separated the two of them. Then Elijah went up into heaven in the whirlwind. As Elisha watched, he kept crying out, "My father, my father, the chariots and horsemen of Israel!"

When he could see him no longer, he took hold of his own clothes, tore them in two, picked up the mantle that had fallen off Elijah, and went back and stood on the bank of the Jordan. He took the mantle Elijah had dropped, and he struck the water. "Where is the LORD God of

30 Elijah?" he asked. He struck the water himself, and it parted to the right and the left, and Elisha crossed over.

When the sons of the prophets from Jericho who were observing saw him, they said, "The spirit of Elijah rests on Elisha." They came to meet him and bowed down to the ground in front of him.

Then the sons of the prophets said to Elisha, "Since there are fifty strong men here with your servants, please let them go and search for your master. Maybe the Spirit of the LORD has carried him away and put him on one of the mountains or into one of the valleys."

He answered, "Don't send them."

However, they urged him to the point of embarrassment, so he said, "Send them." They sent 40 fifty men, who looked for three days but did not find him. When they returned to him in Jericho where he was staying, he said to them, "Didn't I tell you not to go?"

The men of the city said to Elisha, "My lord can see that even though the city's location is good, the water is bad and the land unfruitful."

He replied, "Bring me a new bowl and put salt in it."

After they had brought him one, Elisha went out to the spring, threw salt in it, and said, "This is what the LORD says: 'I have healed this water. No longer will death or unfruitfulness result from it.'" Therefore, the water still remains healthy today according to the word that Elisha spoke.

From there Elisha went up to Bethel. As he was walking up the path, some small boys came out of the city and jeered at him, chanting, "Go up, baldy! Go up, baldy!" He turned around, looked 50 at them, and cursed them in the name of the LORD. Then two female bears came out of the woods and mauled forty-two of the children. From there Elisha went to Mount Carmel, and then he returned to Samaria.

3 Joram son of Ahab became king over Israel in Samaria during the eighteenth year of Judah's King Jehoshaphat, and he reigned twelve years. He did what was evil in the LORD's sight, but not like his father and mother, for he removed the sacred pillar of Baal his father had made. Nevertheless, Joram clung to the sins that Jeroboam son of Nebat had caused Israel to commit. He did not turn away from them.

King Mesha of Moab was a sheep breeder. He used to pay the king of Israel one hundred thousand lambs and the wool of one hundred thousand rams, but when Ahab died, the king of Moab rebelled against the king of Israel. So King Joram marched out from Samaria at that time and mobilized all Israel. Then he sent a message to King Jehoshaphat of Judah: "The king of 10 Moab has rebelled against me. Will you go with me to fight against Moab?"

Jehoshaphat said, "I will go. I am as you are, my people as your people, my horses as your horses."

He asked, "Which route should we take?"

He replied, "The route of the Wilderness of Edom."

So the king of Israel, the king of Judah, and the king of Edom set out. After they had traveled their indirect route for seven days, they had no water for the army or the animals with them.

Then the king of Israel said, "Oh no, the LORD has summoned these three kings, only to hand them over to Moab."

But Jehoshaphat said, "Isn't there a prophet of the LORD here? Let's inquire of the LORD
20 through him."

One of the servants of the king of Israel answered, "Elisha son of Shaphat, who used to pour water on Elijah's hands, is here."

Jehoshaphat affirmed, "The word of the LORD is with him." So the king of Israel and Jehoshaphat and the king of Edom went to him.

However, Elisha said to King Joram of Israel, "What do we have in common? Go to the prophets of your father and your mother!"

But the king of Israel replied, "No, because it is the LORD who has summoned these three kings to hand them over to Moab."

Elisha responded, "By the life of the LORD of Armies, before whom I stand: If I did not have
30 respect for King Jehoshaphat of Judah, I wouldn't look at you; I would not take notice of you. Now, bring me a musician."

While the musician played, the LORD's hand came on Elisha. Then he said, "This is what the LORD says: 'Dig ditch after ditch in this wadi.' For the LORD says, 'You will not see wind or rain, but the wadi will be filled with water, and you will drink—you and your cattle and your animals.' This is easy in the LORD's sight. He will also hand Moab over to you. Then you will attack every fortified city and every choice city. You will cut down every good tree and stop up every spring. You will ruin every good piece of land with stones."

About the time for the grain offering the next morning, water suddenly came from the direction of Edom and filled the land.

40 All Moab had heard that the kings had come up to fight against them. So all who could bear arms, from the youngest to the oldest, were summoned and took their stand at the border. When they got up early in the morning, the sun was shining on the water, and the Moabites saw that the water across from them was red like blood. "This is blood!" they exclaimed. "The kings have crossed swords and their men have killed one another. So, to the spoil, Moab!"

However, when the Moabites came to Israel's camp, the Israelites attacked them, and they fled from them. So Israel went into the land attacking the Moabites. They would destroy the cities, and each of them would throw a stone to cover every good piece of land. They would stop up every spring and cut down every good tree. This went on until only the buildings of Kir-hareseth were left. Then men with slings surrounded the city and attacked it.

50 When the king of Moab saw that the battle was too fierce for him, he took seven hundred swordsmen with him to try to break through to the king of Edom, but they could not do it. So he

took his firstborn son, who was to become king in his place, and offered him as a burnt offering on the city wall. Great wrath was on the Israelites, and they withdrew from him and returned to their land.

4 One of the wives of the sons of the prophets cried out to Elisha, "Your servant, my husband, has died. You know that your servant feared the LORD. Now the creditor is coming to take my two children as his slaves."

Elisha asked her, "What can I do for you? Tell me, what do you have in the house?"

She said, "Your servant has nothing in the house except a jar of oil."

Then he said, "Go out and borrow empty containers from all your neighbors. Do not get just a few. Then go in and shut the door behind you and your sons, and pour oil into all these containers. Set the full ones to one side." So she left.

After she had shut the door behind her and her sons, they kept bringing her containers, and 10 she kept pouring. When they were full, she said to her son, "Bring me another container."

But he replied, "There aren't any more." Then the oil stopped.

She went and told the man of God, and he said, "Go sell the oil and pay your debt; you and your sons can live on the rest."

One day Elisha went to Shunem. A prominent woman who lived there persuaded him to eat some food. So whenever he passed by, he stopped there to eat. Then she said to her husband, "I know that the one who often passes by here is a holy man of God, so let's make a small, walled-in upper room and put a bed, a table, a chair, and a lamp there for him. Whenever he comes, he can stay there."

One day he came there and stopped at the upstairs room to lie down. He ordered his attendant Gehazi, "Call this Shunammite woman." So he called her and she stood before him.

20 Then he said to Gehazi, "Say to her, 'Look, you've gone to all this trouble for us. What can we do for you? Can we speak on your behalf to the king or to the commander of the army?'"

She answered, "I am living among my own people."

So he asked, "Then what should be done for her?"

Gehazi answered, "Well, she has no son, and her husband is old."

"Call her," Elisha said. So Gehazi called her, and she stood in the doorway. Elisha said, "At this time next year you will have a son in your arms."

Then she said, "No, my lord. Man of God, do not lie to your servant."

The woman conceived and gave birth to a son at the same time the following year, as Elisha had promised her.

30 The child grew and one day went out to his father and the harvesters. Suddenly he complained to his father, "My head! My head!"

His father told his servant, "Carry him to his mother." So he picked him up and took him to his mother. The child sat on her lap until noon and then died. She went up and laid him on the bed of the man of God, shut him in, and left.

She summoned her husband and said, "Please send me one of the servants and one of the donkeys, so I can hurry to the man of God and come back again."

But he said, "Why go to him today? It's not a New Moon or a Sabbath."

She replied, "It's all right."

Then she saddled the donkey and said to her servant, "Go fast; don't slow the pace for me unless I tell you." So she came to the man of God at Mount Carmel.

When the man of God saw her at a distance, he said to his attendant Gehazi, "Look, there's the Shunammite woman. Run out to meet her and ask, 'Are you all right? Is your husband all right? Is your son all right?'"

And she answered, "It's all right."

When she came up to the man of God at the mountain, she clung to his feet. Gehazi came to push her away, but the man of God said, "Leave her alone—she is in severe anguish, and the Lord has hidden it from me. He hasn't told me."

Then she said, "Did I ask my lord for a son? Didn't I say, 'Do not lie to me?'"

So Elisha said to Gehazi, "Tuck your mantle under your belt, take my staff with you, and go. If you meet anyone, don't stop to greet him, and if a man greets you, don't answer him. Then place my staff on the boy's face."

The boy's mother said to Elisha, "As the Lord lives and as you yourself live, I will not leave you." So he got up and followed her.

Gehazi went ahead of them and placed the staff on the boy's face, but there was no sound or sign of life, so he went back to meet Elisha and told him, "The boy didn't wake up."

When Elisha got to the house, he discovered the boy lying dead on his bed. So he went in, closed the door behind the two of them, and prayed to the Lord. Then he went up and lay on the boy: he put mouth to mouth, eye to eye, hand to hand. While he bent down over him, the boy's flesh became warm. Elisha got up, went into the house, and paced back and forth. Then he went up and bent down over him again. The boy sneezed seven times and opened his eyes.

Elisha called Gehazi and said, "Call the Shunammite woman." He called her and she came. Then Elisha said, "Pick up your son." She came, fell at his feet, and bowed to the ground; she picked up her son and left.

When Elisha returned to Gilgal, there was a famine in the land. The sons of the prophets were sitting before him. He said to his attendant, "Put on the large pot and make stew for the sons of the prophets."

One went out to the field to gather herbs and found a wild vine from which he gathered as many wild gourds as his garment would hold. Then he came back and cut them up into the pot of stew, but they were unaware of what they were.

They served some for the men to eat, but when they ate the stew they cried out, "There's death in the pot, man of God!" And they were unable to eat it.

Then Elisha said, "Get some flour." He threw it into the pot and said, "Serve it for the people to eat." And there was nothing bad in the pot.

A man from Baal-shalishah came to the man of God with his sack full of twenty loaves of barley bread from the first bread of the harvest. Elisha said, "Give it to the people to eat."

But Elisha's attendant asked, "What? Am I to set this before a hundred men?"

"Give it to the people to eat," Elisha said, "for this is what the LORD says: 'They will eat, and they will have some left over.'" So he set it before them, and as the LORD had promised, they ate and had some left over.

5 Naaman, commander of the army for the king of Aram, was a man important to his master and highly regarded because through him, the LORD had given victory to Aram. The man was a valiant warrior, but he had a skin disease.

Aram had gone on raids and brought back from the land of Israel a young girl who served Naaman's wife. She said to her mistress, "If only my master were with the prophet who is in Samaria, he would cure him of his skin disease."

So Naaman went and told his master what the girl from the land of Israel had said. Therefore, the king of Aram said, "Go, and I will send a letter with you to the king of Israel."

So he went and took with him 750 pounds of silver, 150 pounds of gold, and ten sets of clothing. He brought the letter to the king of Israel, and it read:

When this letter comes to you, note that I have sent you my servant Naaman for you to cure him of his skin disease.

When the king of Israel read the letter, he tore his clothes and asked, "Am I God, killing and giving life, that this man expects me to cure a man of his skin disease? Recognize that he is only picking a fight with me."

When Elisha the man of God heard that the king of Israel had torn his clothes, he sent a message to the king: "Why have you torn your clothes? Have him come to me, and he will know there is a prophet in Israel." So Naaman came with his horses and chariots and stood at the door of Elisha's house.

Then Elisha sent him a messenger, who said, "Go wash seven times in the Jordan and your skin will be restored and you will be clean."

But Naaman got angry and left, saying, "I was telling myself: He will surely come out, stand and call on the name of the LORD his God, and wave his hand over the place and cure the skin disease. Aren't Abana and Pharpar, the rivers of Damascus, better than all the waters of Israel? Couldn't I wash in them and be clean?" So he turned and left in a rage.

But his servants approached and said to him, "My father, if the prophet had told you to do some great thing, would you not have done it? How much more should you do it when he only tells you, 'Wash and be clean'?" So Naaman went down and dipped himself in the Jordan seven times, according to the command of the man of God. Then his skin was restored and became like the skin of a small boy, and he was clean.

Then Naaman and his whole company went back to the man of God, stood before him, and declared, "I know there's no God in the whole world except in Israel. Therefore, please accept a gift from your servant."

But Elisha said, "As the LORD lives, in whose presence I stand, I will not accept it." Naaman urged him to accept it, but he refused.

Naaman responded, "If not, please let your servant be given as much soil as a pair of mules can carry, for your servant will no longer offer a burnt offering or a sacrifice to any other god but the LORD. However, in a particular matter may the LORD pardon your servant: When my master, the king of Aram, goes into the temple of Rimmon to bow in worship while he is leaning on my arm, and I have to bow in the temple of Rimmon—when I bow in the temple of Rimmon, may the LORD pardon your servant in this matter."

So he said to him, "Go in peace."

After Naaman had traveled a short distance from Elisha, Gehazi, the attendant of Elisha the man of God, thought, "My master has let this Aramean Naaman off lightly by not accepting from him what he brought. As the LORD lives, I will run after him and get something from him."

So Gehazi pursued Naaman. When Naaman saw someone running after him, he got down from the chariot to meet him and asked, "Is everything all right?"

Gehazi said, "It's all right. My master has sent me to say, 'I have just now discovered that two young men from the sons of the prophets have come to me from the hill country of Ephraim. Please give them seventy-five pounds of silver and two sets of clothing.'"

But Naaman insisted, "Please, accept one hundred fifty pounds." He urged Gehazi and then packed one hundred fifty pounds of silver in two bags with two sets of clothing. Naaman gave them to two of his attendants who carried them ahead of Gehazi. When Gehazi came to the hill, he took the gifts from them and deposited them in the house. Then he dismissed the men, and they left.

Gehazi came and stood by his master. "Where did you go, Gehazi?" Elisha asked him.

He replied, "Your servant didn't go anywhere."

"And my heart didn't go when the man got down from his chariot to meet you," Elisha said. "Is this a time to accept silver and clothing, olive orchards and vineyards, flocks and herds, and male and female slaves? Therefore, Naaman's skin disease will cling to you and your descendants forever." So Gehazi went out from his presence diseased, resembling snow.

6 The sons of the prophets said to Elisha, "Please notice that the place where we live under your supervision is too small for us. Please let us go to the Jordan where we can each get a log and can build ourselves a place to live there."

"Go," he said.

Then one said, "Please come with your servants."

"I'll come," he answered.

So he went with them, and when they came to the Jordan, they cut down trees. As one of them was cutting down a tree, the iron ax head fell into the water, and he cried out, "Oh, my master, it was borrowed!"

10 Then the man of God asked, "Where did it fall?"

When he showed him the place, the man of God cut a piece of wood, threw it there, and made the iron float. Then he said, "Pick it up." So he reached out and took it.

When the king of Aram was waging war against Israel, he conferred with his servants, "My camp will be at such and such a place."

But the man of God sent word to the king of Israel: "Be careful passing by this place, for the Arameans are going down there." Consequently, the king of Israel sent word to the place the man of God had told him about. The man of God repeatedly warned the king, so the king would be on his guard.

The king of Aram was enraged because of this matter, and he called his servants and demanded 20 of them, "Tell me, which one of us is for the king of Israel?"

One of his servants said, "No one, my lord the king. Elisha, the prophet in Israel, tells the king of Israel even the words you speak in your bedroom."

So the king said, "Go and see where he is, so I can send men to capture him."

When he was told, "Elisha is in Dothan," he sent horses, chariots, and a massive army there. They went by night and surrounded the city.

When the servant of the man of God got up early and went out, he discovered an army with horses and chariots surrounding the city. So he asked Elisha, "Oh, my master, what are we to do?"

Elisha said, "Don't be afraid, for those who are with us outnumber those who are with them."

Then Elisha prayed, "Lord, please open his eyes and let him see." So the Lord opened the 30 servant's eyes, and he saw that the mountain was covered with horses and chariots of fire all around Elisha.

When the Arameans came against him, Elisha prayed to the Lord, "Please strike this nation with blindness." So he struck them with blindness, according to Elisha's word. Then Elisha said to them, "This is not the way, and this is not the city. Follow me, and I will take you to the man you're looking for." And he led them to Samaria. When they entered Samaria, Elisha said, "Lord, open these men's eyes and let them see." So the Lord opened their eyes, and they saw that they were in the middle of Samaria.

When the king of Israel saw them, he said to Elisha, "Should I kill them, should I kill them, my father?"

40 Elisha replied, "Don't kill them. Do you kill those you have captured with your sword or your bow? Set food and water in front of them so they can eat and drink and go to their master."

So he prepared a big feast for them. When they had eaten and drunk, he sent them away, and they went to their master. The Aramean raiders did not come into Israel's land again.

Some time later, King Ben-hadad of Aram brought all his military units together and marched up and laid siege to Samaria. So there was a severe famine in Samaria, and they continued the siege against it until a donkey's head sold for thirty-four ounces of silver, and a cup of dove's dung sold for two ounces of silver.

As the king of Israel was passing by on the wall, a woman cried out to him, "My lord the king, help!"

He answered, "If the LORD doesn't help you, where can I get help for you? From the threshing 50 floor or the winepress?" Then the king asked her, "What's the matter?"

She said, "This woman said to me, 'Give up your son, and we will eat him today. Then we will eat my son tomorrow.' So we boiled my son and ate him, and I said to her the next day, 'Give up your son, and we will eat him,' but she has hidden her son."

When the king heard the woman's words, he tore his clothes. Then, as he was passing by on the wall, the people saw that there was sackcloth under his clothes next to his skin. He announced, "May God punish me and do so severely if the head of Elisha son of Shaphat remains on his shoulders today."

Elisha was sitting in his house, and the elders were sitting with him. The king sent a man ahead of him, but before the messenger got to him, Elisha said to the elders, "Do you see how this 60 murderer has sent someone to remove my head? Look, when the messenger comes, shut the door to keep him out. Isn't the sound of his master's feet behind him?"

While Elisha was still speaking with them, the messenger came down to him. Then he said, "This disaster is from the LORD. Why should I wait for the LORD any longer?"

7 Elisha replied, "Hear the word of the LORD! This is what the LORD says: 'About this time tomorrow at Samaria's gate, six quarts of fine flour will sell for a half ounce of silver and twelve quarts of barley will sell for a half ounce of silver.'"

Then the captain, the king's right-hand man, responded to the man of God, "Look, even if the LORD were to make windows in heaven, could this really happen?"

Elisha announced, "You will in fact see it with your own eyes, but you won't eat any of it."

Now four men with a skin disease were at the entrance to the city gate. They said to each other, "Why just sit here until we die? If we say, 'Let's go into the city,' we will die there because the famine is in the city, but if we sit here, we will also die. So now, come on. Let's surrender to the 10 Arameans' camp. If they let us live, we will live; if they kill us, we will die."

So the diseased men got up at twilight to go to the Arameans' camp. When they came to the camp's edge, they discovered that no one was there, for the Lord had caused the Aramean camp to hear the sound of chariots, horses, and a large army. The Arameans had said to each other, "The king of Israel must have hired the kings of the Hittites and the kings of Egypt to attack us." So they had gotten up and fled at twilight, abandoning their tents, horses, and donkeys. The camp was intact, and they had fled for their lives.

When these diseased men came to the edge of the camp, they went into a tent to eat and drink. Then they picked up the silver, gold, and clothing and went off and hid them. They came back and entered another tent, picked things up, and hid them. Then they said to each other, "We're not 20 doing what is right. Today is a day of good news. If we are silent and wait until morning light, our punishment will catch up with us. So let's go tell the king's household."

The diseased men came and called to the city's gatekeepers and told them, "We went to the Aramean camp and no one was there—no human sounds. There was nothing but tethered horses and donkeys, and the tents were intact." The gatekeepers called out, and the news was reported to the king's household.

So the king got up in the night and said to his servants, "Let me tell you what the Arameans have done to us. They know we are starving, so they have left the camp to hide in the open country, thinking, 'When they come out of the city, we will take them alive and go into the city.'"

But one of his servants responded, "Please, let messengers take five of the horses that are left in 30 the city. Their fate is like the entire Israelite community who will die, so let's send them and see."

The messengers took two chariots with horses, and the king sent them after the Aramean army, saying, "Go and see." So they followed them as far as the Jordan. They saw that the whole way was littered with clothes and equipment the Arameans had thrown off in their haste. The messengers returned and told the king.

Then the people went out and plundered the Aramean camp. It was then that six quarts of fine flour sold for a half ounce of silver and twelve quarts of barley sold for a half ounce of silver, according to the word of the LORD. The king had appointed the captain, his right-hand man, to be in charge of the city gate, but the people trampled him in the gate. He died, just as the man of God had predicted when the king had come to him. When the man of God had said to the king, 40 "About this time tomorrow twelve quarts of barley will sell for a half ounce of silver and six quarts of fine flour will sell for a half ounce of silver at Samaria's gate," this captain had answered the man of God, "Look, even if the LORD were to make windows in heaven, could this really happen?" Elisha had said, "You will in fact see it with your own eyes, but you won't eat any of it." This is what happened to him: the people trampled him in the city gate, and he died.

8 Elisha said to the woman whose son he had restored to life, "Get ready, you and your household, and go live as a resident alien wherever you can. For the LORD has announced a seven-year famine, and it has already come to the land."

So the woman got ready and did what the man of God said. She and her household lived as resident aliens in the land of the Philistines for seven years. When the woman returned from the land of the Philistines at the end of seven years, she went to appeal to the king for her house and field.

The king had been speaking to Gehazi, the attendant of the man of God, saying, "Tell me all the great things Elisha has done."

While he was telling the king how Elisha restored the dead son to life, the woman whose son he had restored to life came to appeal to the king for her house and field. So Gehazi said, "My lord the king, this is the woman and this is the son Elisha restored to life."

When the king asked the woman, she told him the story. So the king appointed a court official for her, saying, "Restore all that was hers, along with all the income from the field from the day she left the country until now."

Elisha came to Damascus while King Ben-hadad of Aram was sick, and the king was told, "The man of God has come here." So the king said to Hazael, "Take a gift with you and go meet the man of God. Inquire of the LORD through him, 'Will I recover from this sickness?'"

Hazael went to meet Elisha, taking with him a gift: forty camel-loads of all the finest products of Damascus. When he came and stood before him, he said, "Your son, King Ben-hadad of Aram, has sent me to ask you, 'Will I recover from this sickness?'"

Elisha told him, "Go say to him, 'You are sure to recover.' But the LORD has shown me that he is sure to die." Then he stared steadily at him until he was ashamed.

The man of God wept, and Hazael asked, "Why is my lord weeping?"

He replied, "Because I know the evil you will do to the people of Israel. You will set their fortresses on fire. You will kill their young men with the sword. You will dash their children to pieces. You will rip open their pregnant women."

Hazael said, "How could your servant, a mere dog, do such a mighty deed?"

Elisha answered, "The LORD has shown me that you will be king over Aram."

Hazael left Elisha and went to his master, who asked him, "What did Elisha say to you?"

He responded, "He told me you are sure to recover." The next day Hazael took a heavy cloth, dipped it in water, and spread it over the king's face. Ben-hadad died, and Hazael reigned in his place.

In the fifth year of Israel's King Joram son of Ahab, Jehoram son of Jehoshaphat became king of Judah, replacing his father. He was thirty-two years old when he became king, and he reigned eight years in Jerusalem. He walked in the ways of the kings of Israel, as the house of Ahab had done, for Ahab's daughter was his wife. He did what was evil in the LORD's sight. For the sake of his servant David, the LORD was unwilling to destroy Judah, since he had promised to give a lamp to David and his sons forever.

40 During Jehoram's reign, Edom rebelled against Judah's control and appointed their own king. So Jehoram crossed over to Zair with all his chariots. Then at night he set out to attack the Edomites who had surrounded him and the chariot commanders, but his troops fled to their tents. So Edom is still in rebellion against Judah's control today. Libnah also rebelled at that time.

The rest of the events of Jehoram's reign, along with all his accomplishments, are written in the Historical Record of Judah's Kings. Jehoram rested with his ancestors and was buried with his ancestors in the city of David, and his son Ahaziah became king in his place.

In the twelfth year of Israel's King Joram son of Ahab, Ahaziah son of Jehoram became king of Judah. Ahaziah was twenty-two years old when he became king, and he reigned one year in Jerusalem. His mother's name was Athaliah, granddaughter of Israel's King Omri. He walked in 50 the ways of the house of Ahab and did what was evil in the LORD's sight like the house of Ahab, for his father had married into the house of Ahab.

Ahaziah went with Joram son of Ahab to fight against King Hazael of Aram in Ramoth-gilead, and the Arameans wounded Joram. So King Joram returned to Jezreel to recover from the wounds that the Arameans had inflicted on him in Ramoth-gilead when he fought against Aram's King Hazael. Then Judah's King Ahaziah son of Jehoram went down to Jezreel to visit Joram son of Ahab since Joram was ill.

9 The prophet Elisha called one of the sons of the prophets and said, "Tuck your mantle under your belt, take this flask of oil with you, and go to Ramoth-gilead. When you get there, look for Jehu son of Jehoshaphat, son of Nimshi. Go in, get him away from his colleagues, and take him to an inner room. Then take the flask of oil, pour it on his head, and say, 'This is what the LORD says: "I anoint you king over Israel."' Open the door and escape. Don't wait." So the young prophet went to Ramoth-gilead.

When he arrived, the army commanders were sitting there, so he said, "I have a message for you, commander."

Jehu asked, "For which one of us?"

He answered, "For you, commander."

10 So Jehu got up and went into the house. The young prophet poured the oil on his head and said, "This is what the LORD God of Israel says: 'I anoint you king over the LORD's people, Israel. You are to strike down the house of your master Ahab so that I may avenge the blood shed by the hand of Jezebel—the blood of my servants the prophets and of all the servants of the LORD. The whole house of Ahab will perish, and I will wipe out all of Ahab's males, both slave and free, in Israel. I will make the house of Ahab like the house of Jeroboam son of Nebat and like the house of Baasha son of Ahijah. The dogs will eat Jezebel in the plot of land at Jezreel—no one will bury her.'" Then the young prophet opened the door and escaped.

When Jehu came out to his master's servants, they asked, "Is everything all right? Why did this crazy person come to you?"

20 Then he said to them, "You know the sort and their ranting."

But they replied, "That's a lie! Tell us!"

So Jehu said, "He talked to me about this and that and said, 'This is what the LORD says: I anoint you king over Israel.'"

Each man quickly took his garment and put it under Jehu on the bare steps. They blew the ram's horn and proclaimed, "Jehu is king!"

Then Jehu son of Jehoshaphat, son of Nimshi, conspired against Joram. Joram and all Israel had been at Ramoth-gilead on guard against King Hazael of Aram. But King Joram had returned to Jezreel to recover from the wounds that the Arameans had inflicted on him when he fought against Aram's King Hazael. Jehu said, "If you commanders wish to make me king, then don't let 30 anyone escape from the city to go tell about it in Jezreel."

Jehu got into his chariot and went to Jezreel since Joram was laid up there and King Ahaziah of Judah had gone down to visit Joram. Now the watchman was standing on the tower in Jezreel. He saw Jehu's mob approaching and shouted, "I see a mob!"

Joram responded, "Choose a rider and send him to meet them and have him ask, 'Do you come in peace?'"

So a horseman went to meet Jehu and said, "This is what the king asks: 'Do you come in peace?'"

Jehu replied, "What do you have to do with peace? Fall in behind me."

The watchman reported, "The messenger reached them but hasn't started back."

40 So he sent out a second horseman, who went to them and said, "This is what the king asks: 'Do you come in peace?'"

Jehu answered, "What do you have to do with peace? Fall in behind me."

Again the watchman reported, "He reached them but hasn't started back. Also, the driving is like that of Jehu son of Nimshi—he drives like a madman."

"Get the chariot ready!" Joram shouted, and they got it ready. Then King Joram of Israel and King Ahaziah of Judah set out, each in his own chariot, and met Jehu at the plot of land of Naboth the Jezreelite. When Joram saw Jehu he asked, "Do you come in peace, Jehu?"

He answered, "What peace can there be as long as there is so much prostitution and sorcery from your mother Jezebel?"

50 Joram turned around and fled, shouting to Ahaziah, "It's treachery, Ahaziah!"

Then Jehu drew his bow and shot Joram between the shoulders. The arrow went through his heart, and he slumped down in his chariot. Jehu said to Bidkar his aide, "Pick him up and throw him on the plot of ground belonging to Naboth the Jezreelite. For remember when you and I were riding side by side behind his father Ahab, and the LORD uttered this pronouncement against him: 'As surely as I saw the blood of Naboth and the blood of his sons yesterday'— this is the LORD's declaration—'so will I repay you on this plot of land'—this is the LORD's declaration. So now, according to the word of the LORD, pick him up and throw him on the plot of land."

When King Ahaziah of Judah saw what was happening, he fled up the road toward Beth-
60 haggan. Jehu pursued him, shouting, "Shoot him too!" So they shot him in his chariot at Gur Pass near Ibleam, but he fled to Megiddo and died there. Then his servants carried him to Jerusalem in a chariot and buried him in his ancestors' tomb in the city of David. It was in the eleventh year of Joram son of Ahab that Ahaziah had become king over Judah.

When Jehu came to Jezreel, Jezebel heard about it, so she painted her eyes, fixed her hair, and looked down from the window. As Jehu entered the city gate, she said, "Do you come in peace, Zimri, killer of your master?"

He looked up toward the window and said, "Who is on my side? Who?" Two or three eunuchs looked down at him, and he said, "Throw her down!" So they threw her down, and some of her blood splattered on the wall and on the horses, and Jehu rode over her.

70 Then he went in, ate and drank, and said, "Take care of this cursed woman and bury her, since she's a king's daughter." But when they went out to bury her, they did not find anything but the skull, the feet, and the hands. So they went back and told him, and he said, "This fulfills the LORD's word that he spoke through his servant Elijah the Tishbite: 'In the plot of land at Jezreel, the dogs will eat Jezebel's flesh. Jezebel's corpse will be like manure on the surface of the ground in the plot of land at Jezreel so that no one will be able to say: This is Jezebel.'"

10 Since Ahab had seventy sons in Samaria, Jehu wrote letters and sent them to Samaria to the rulers of Jezreel, to the elders, and to the guardians of Ahab's sons, saying:

Your master's sons are with you, and you have chariots, horses, a fortified city, and weaponry, so when this letter arrives select the most qualified of your master's sons, set him on his father's throne, and fight for your master's house.

However, they were terrified and reasoned, "Look, two kings couldn't stand against him; how can we?"

So the overseer of the palace, the overseer of the city, the elders, and the guardians sent a message to Jehu: "We are your servants, and we will do whatever you tell us. We will not make
10 anyone king. Do whatever you think is right."

Then Jehu wrote them a second letter, saying:

If you are on my side, and if you will obey me, bring me the heads of your master's sons at this time tomorrow at Jezreel.

All seventy of the king's sons were being cared for by the city's prominent men. When the letter came to them, they took the king's sons and slaughtered all seventy, put their heads in baskets, and sent them to Jehu at Jezreel. When the messenger came and told him, "They have brought the heads of the king's sons," the king said, "Pile them in two heaps at the entrance of the city gate until morning."

20 The next morning when he went out and stood at the gate, he said to all the people, "You are innocent. It was I who conspired against my master and killed him. But who struck down all these? Know, then, that not a word the LORD spoke against the house of Ahab will fail, for the LORD has done what he promised through his servant Elijah." So Jehu killed all who remained of the house of Ahab in Jezreel—all his great men, close friends, and priests—leaving him no survivors.

Then he set out and went to Samaria. On the way, while he was at Beth-eked of the Shepherds, Jehu met the relatives of King Ahaziah of Judah and asked, "Who are you?"

They answered, "We're Ahaziah's relatives. We've come down to greet the king's sons and the queen mother's sons."

30 Then Jehu ordered, "Take them alive." So they took them alive and then slaughtered them at the pit of Beth-eked—forty-two men. He didn't spare any of them.

When he left there, he found Jehonadab son of Rechab coming to meet him. He greeted him and then asked, "Is your heart one with mine?"

"It is," Jehonadab replied.

Jehu said, "If it is, give me your hand."

So he gave him his hand, and Jehu pulled him up into the chariot with him. Then he said, "Come with me and see my zeal for the LORD!" So he let him ride with him in his chariot. When Jehu came to Samaria, he struck down all who remained from the house of Ahab in Samaria until he had annihilated his house, according to the word of the LORD spoken to Elijah.

40 Then Jehu brought all the people together and said to them, "Ahab served Baal a little, but Jehu will serve him a lot. Now, therefore, summon to me all the prophets of Baal, all his servants, and all his priests. None must be missing, for I have a great sacrifice for Baal. Whoever is missing will not live." However, Jehu was acting deceptively in order to destroy the servants of Baal. Jehu commanded, "Consecrate a solemn assembly for Baal." So they called one.

Then Jehu sent messengers throughout all Israel, and all the servants of Baal came; no one failed to come. They entered the temple of Baal, and it was filled from one end to the other. Then he said to the custodian of the wardrobe, "Bring out the garments for all the servants of Baal." So he brought out their garments.

Then Jehu and Jehonadab son of Rechab entered the temple of Baal, and Jehu said to the servants of Baal, "Look carefully to see that there are no servants of the LORD here among you—

50 only servants of Baal." Then they went in to offer sacrifices and burnt offerings.

Now Jehu had stationed eighty men outside, and he warned them, "Whoever allows any of the men I am placing in your hands to escape will forfeit his life for theirs." When he finished offering the burnt offering, Jehu said to the guards and officers, "Go in and kill them. Don't let anyone out." So they struck them down with the sword. Then the guards and officers threw the bodies out and went into the inner room of the temple of Baal. They brought out the pillar of the temple of Baal and burned it, and they tore down the pillar of Baal. Then they tore down the temple of Baal and made it a latrine—which it still is today.

Jehu eliminated Baal worship from Israel, but he did not turn away from the sins that Jeroboam son of Nebat had caused Israel to commit—worshiping the gold calves that were in Bethel and

60 Dan. Nevertheless, the LORD said to Jehu, "Because you have done well in carrying out what is right in my sight and have done to the house of Ahab all that was in my heart, four generations of your sons will sit on the throne of Israel."

Yet Jehu was not careful to follow the instruction of the LORD God of Israel with all his heart. He did not turn from the sins that Jeroboam had caused Israel to commit.

In those days the LORD began to reduce the size of Israel. Hazael defeated the Israelites throughout their territory from the Jordan eastward: the whole land of Gilead—the Gadites, the Reubenites, and the Manassites—from Aroer which is by the Arnon Valley through Gilead to Bashan.

The rest of the events of Jehu's reign, along with all his accomplishments and all his might, are written in the Historical Record of Israel's Kings. Jehu rested with his ancestors and was buried

70 in Samaria. His son Jehoahaz became king in his place. The length of Jehu's reign over Israel in Samaria was twenty-eight years.

11 When Athaliah, Ahaziah's mother, saw that her son was dead, she proceeded to annihilate all the royal heirs. Jehosheba, who was King Jehoram's daughter and Ahaziah's sister, secretly rescued Joash son of Ahaziah from among the king's sons who were being killed and put him and the one who nursed him in a bedroom. So he was hidden from Athaliah and was not killed. Joash was in hiding with her in the LORD's temple six years while Athaliah reigned over the land.

In the seventh year, Jehoiada sent for the commanders of hundreds, the Carites, and the guards. He had them come to him in the LORD's temple, where he made a covenant with them and put them under oath. He showed them the king's son and commanded them, "This is what you are to do: A third of you who come on duty on the Sabbath are to provide protection for the king's

10 palace. A third are to be at the Foundation Gate and a third at the gate behind the guards. You are to take turns providing protection for the palace.

"Your two divisions that go off duty on the Sabbath are to provide the king protection at the LORD's temple. Completely surround the king with weapons in hand. Anyone who approaches the ranks is to be put to death. Be with the king in all his daily tasks."

So the commanders of hundreds did everything the priest Jehoiada commanded. They each brought their men—those coming on duty on the Sabbath and those going off duty—and came to the priest Jehoiada. The priest gave to the commanders of hundreds King David's spears and shields that were in the Lord's temple. Then the guards stood with their weapons in hand surrounding the king—from the right side of the temple to the left side, by the altar and by the temple.

Jehoiada brought out the king's son, put the crown on him, gave him the testimony, and made him king. They anointed him and clapped their hands and cried, "Long live the king!"

When Athaliah heard the noise from the guard and the crowd, she went out to the people at the Lord's temple. She looked, and there was the king standing by the pillar according to the custom. The commanders and the trumpeters were by the king, and all the people of the land were rejoicing and blowing trumpets. Athaliah tore her clothes and screamed "Treason! Treason!"

Then the priest Jehoiada ordered the commanders of hundreds in charge of the army, "Take her out between the ranks, and put to death by the sword anyone who follows her," for the priest had said, "She is not to be put to death in the Lord's temple." So they arrested her, and she went through the horse entrance to the king's palace, where she was put to death.

Then Jehoiada made a covenant between the Lord, the king, and the people that they would be the Lord's people and another covenant between the king and the people. So all the people of the land went to the temple of Baal and tore it down. They smashed its altars and images to pieces, and they killed Mattan, the priest of Baal, at the altars.

Then Jehoiada the priest appointed guards for the Lord's temple. He took the commanders of hundreds, the Carites, the guards, and all the people of the land, and they brought the king from the Lord's temple. They entered the king's palace by way of the guards' gate. Then Joash sat on the throne of the kings. All the people of the land rejoiced, and the city was quiet, for they had put Athaliah to death by the sword in the king's palace.

12 Joash was seven years old when he became king. In the seventh year of Jehu, Joash became king, and he reigned forty years in Jerusalem. His mother's name was Zibiah; she was from Beer-sheba. Throughout the time the priest Jehoiada instructed him, Joash did what was right in the Lord's sight. Yet the high places were not taken away; the people continued sacrificing and burning incense on the high places.

Then Joash said to the priests, "All the dedicated silver brought to the Lord's temple, census silver, silver from vows, and all silver voluntarily given for the Lord's temple—each priest is to take it from his assessor and repair whatever damage is found in the temple."

But by the twenty-third year of the reign of King Joash, the priests had not repaired the damage to the temple. So King Joash called the priest Jehoiada and the other priests and asked,

"Why haven't you repaired the temple's damage? Since you haven't, don't take any silver from your assessors; instead, hand it over for the repair of the temple." So the priests agreed that they would receive no silver from the people and would not be the ones to repair the temple's damage.

Then the priest Jehoiada took a chest, bored a hole in its lid, and set it beside the altar on the right side as one enters the LORD's temple; the priests who guarded the threshold put into the chest all the silver that was brought to the LORD's temple. Whenever they saw there was a large amount of silver in the chest, the king's secretary and the high priest would go bag up and tally the silver found in the LORD's temple. Then they would give the weighed silver to those doing the work—those who oversaw the LORD's temple. They in turn would pay it out to those working on the LORD's temple—the carpenters, the builders, the masons, and the stonecutters—and would use it to buy timber and quarried stone to repair the damage to the LORD's temple and for all expenses for temple repairs.

However, no silver bowls, wick trimmers, sprinkling basins, trumpets, or any articles of gold or silver were made for the LORD's temple from the contributions brought to the LORD's temple. Instead, it was given to those doing the work, and they repaired the LORD's temple with it. No accounting was required from the men who received the silver to pay those doing the work, since they worked with integrity. The silver from the guilt offering and the sin offering was not brought to the LORD's temple since it belonged to the priests.

At that time King Hazael of Aram marched up and fought against Gath and captured it. Then he planned to attack Jerusalem. So King Joash of Judah took all the items consecrated by himself and by his ancestors—Judah's kings Jehoshaphat, Jehoram, and Ahaziah—as well as all the gold found in the treasuries of the LORD's temple and in the king's palace, and he sent them to King Hazael of Aram. Then Hazael withdrew from Jerusalem.

The rest of the events of Joash's reign, along with all his accomplishments, are written in the Historical Record of Judah's Kings. Joash's servants conspired against him and attacked him at Beth-millo on the road that goes down to Silla. It was his servants Jozabad son of Shimeath and Jehozabad son of Shomer who attacked him. He died and they buried him with his ancestors in the city of David, and his son Amaziah became king in his place.

13 In the twenty-third year of Judah's King Joash son of Ahaziah, Jehoahaz son of Jehu became king over Israel in Samaria, and he reigned seventeen years. He did what was evil in the LORD's sight and followed the sins that Jeroboam son of Nebat had caused Israel to commit; he did not turn away from them. So the LORD's anger burned against Israel, and he handed them over to King Hazael of Aram and to his son Ben-hadad during their reigns.

Then Jehoahaz sought the LORD's favor, and the LORD heard him, for he saw the oppression the king of Aram inflicted on Israel. Therefore, the LORD gave Israel a deliverer, and they escaped from the power of the Arameans. Then the people of Israel returned to their former way of life, but they didn't turn away from the sins that the house of Jeroboam had caused Israel to commit. Jehoahaz continued them, and the Asherah pole also remained standing in Samaria. Jehoahaz did not have an army left, except for fifty horsemen, ten chariots, and ten thousand foot soldiers, because the king of Aram had destroyed them, making them like dust at threshing.

The rest of the events of Jehoahaz's reign, along with all his accomplishments and his might, are written in the Historical Record of Israel's Kings. Jehoahaz rested with his ancestors, and he was buried in Samaria. His son Jehoash became king in his place.

In the thirty-seventh year of Judah's King Joash, Jehoash son of Jehoahaz became king over Israel in Samaria, and he reigned sixteen years. He did what was evil in the LORD's sight. He did not turn away from all the sins that Jeroboam son of Nebat had caused Israel to commit, but he continued them.

The rest of the events of Jehoash's reign, along with all his accomplishments and the power he had to wage war against Judah's King Amaziah, are written in the Historical Record of Israel's Kings. Jehoash rested with his ancestors, and Jeroboam sat on his throne. Jehoash was buried in Samaria with the kings of Israel.

When Elisha became sick with the illness from which he died, King Jehoash of Israel went down and wept over him and said, "My father, my father, the chariots and horsemen of Israel!"

Elisha responded, "Get a bow and arrows." So he got a bow and arrows. Then Elisha said to the king of Israel, "Grasp the bow." So the king grasped it, and Elisha put his hands on the king's hands. Elisha said, "Open the east window." So he opened it. Elisha said, "Shoot!" So he shot. Then Elisha said, "The LORD's arrow of victory, yes, the arrow of victory over Aram. You are to strike down the Arameans in Aphek until you have put an end to them."

Then Elisha said, "Take the arrows!" So he took them. Then Elisha said to the king of Israel, "Strike the ground!" So he struck the ground three times and stopped. The man of God was angry with him and said, "You should have struck the ground five or six times. Then you would have struck down Aram until you had put an end to them, but now you will strike down Aram only three times." Then Elisha died and was buried.

Now Moabite raiders used to come into the land in the spring of the year. Once, as the Israelites were burying a man, suddenly they saw a raiding party, so they threw the man into Elisha's tomb. When he touched Elisha's bones, the man revived and stood up!

King Hazael of Aram oppressed Israel throughout the reign of Jehoahaz, but the LORD was gracious to them, had compassion on them, and turned toward them because of his covenant with Abraham, Isaac, and Jacob. He was not willing to destroy them. Even now he has not banished them from his presence.

King Hazael of Aram died, and his son Ben-hadad became king in his place. Then Jehoash son of Jehoahaz took back from Ben-hadad son of Hazael the cities that Hazael had taken in war from Jehoash's father Jehoahaz. Jehoash defeated Ben-hadad three times and recovered the cities of Israel.

14 In the second year of Israel's King Jehoash son of Jehoahaz, Amaziah son of Joash became king of Judah. He was twenty-five years old when he became king, and he reigned twenty-nine years in Jerusalem. His mother's name was Jehoaddan; she was from Jerusalem. He did what was right in the LORD's sight, but not like his ancestor David. He did everything his father Joash had done. Yet the high places were not taken away, and the people continued sacrificing and burning incense on the high places.

As soon as the kingdom was firmly in his grasp, Amaziah killed his servants who had killed his father the king. However, he did not put the children of the killers to death, as it is written in the book of the law of Moses where the LORD commanded, "Fathers are not to be put to death
10 because of children, and children are not to be put to death because of fathers; instead, each one will be put to death for his own sin."

Amaziah killed ten thousand Edomites in Salt Valley. He took Sela in battle and called it Joktheel, which is still its name today. Amaziah then sent messengers to Jehoash son of Jehoahaz, son of Jehu, king of Israel, and challenged him: "Come, let's meet face to face."

King Jehoash of Israel sent word to King Amaziah of Judah, saying, "The thistle in Lebanon once sent a message to the cedar in Lebanon, saying, 'Give your daughter to my son as a wife.' Then a wild animal in Lebanon passed by and trampled the thistle. You have indeed defeated Edom, and you have become overconfident. Enjoy your glory and stay at home. Why should you stir up such trouble that you fall—you and Judah with you?"

20 But Amaziah would not listen, so King Jehoash of Israel advanced. He and King Amaziah of Judah met face to face at Beth-shemesh that belonged to Judah. Judah was routed before Israel, and each man fled to his own tent. King Jehoash of Israel captured Judah's King Amaziah son of Joash, son of Ahaziah, at Beth-shemesh. Then Jehoash went to Jerusalem and broke down two hundred yards of Jerusalem's wall from the Ephraim Gate to the Corner Gate. He took all the gold and silver, all the articles found in the LORD's temple and in the treasuries of the king's palace, and some hostages. Then he returned to Samaria.

The rest of the events of Jehoash's reign, along with his accomplishments, his might, and how he waged war against King Amaziah of Judah, are written in the Historical Record of Israel's Kings. Jehoash rested with his ancestors, and he was buried in Samaria with the kings of Israel. His son Jeroboam became king in his place.

30 Judah's King Amaziah son of Joash lived fifteen years after the death of Israel's King Jehoash son of Jehoahaz. The rest of the events of Amaziah's reign are written in the Historical Record

of Judah's Kings. A conspiracy was formed against him in Jerusalem, and he fled to Lachish. However, men were sent after him to Lachish, and they put him to death there. They carried him back on horses, and he was buried in Jerusalem with his ancestors in the city of David.

Then all the people of Judah took Azariah, who was sixteen years old, and made him king in place of his father Amaziah. After Amaziah the king rested with his ancestors, Azariah rebuilt Elath and restored it to Judah.

In the fifteenth year of Judah's King Amaziah son of Joash, Jeroboam son of Jehoash became king of Israel in Samaria, and he reigned forty-one years. He did what was evil in the LORD's sight. He did not turn away from all the sins Jeroboam son of Nebat had caused Israel to commit.

He restored Israel's border from Lebo-hamath as far as the Sea of the Arabah, according to the word the LORD, the God of Israel, had spoken through his servant, the prophet Jonah son of Amittai from Gath-hepher. For the LORD saw that the affliction of Israel was very bitter for both slaves and free people. There was no one to help Israel. The LORD had not said he would blot out the name of Israel under heaven, so he delivered them by the hand of Jeroboam son of Jehoash.

The rest of the events of Jeroboam's reign—along with all his accomplishments, the power he had to wage war, and how he recovered for Israel Damascus and Hamath, which had belonged to Judah—are written in the Historical Record of Israel's Kings. Jeroboam rested with his ancestors, the kings of Israel. His son Zechariah became king in his place.

15 In the twenty-seventh year of Israel's King Jeroboam, Azariah son of Amaziah became king of Judah. He was sixteen years old when he became king, and he reigned fifty-two years in Jerusalem. His mother's name was Jecoliah; she was from Jerusalem. Azariah did what was right in the LORD's sight just as his father Amaziah had done. Yet the high places were not taken away; the people continued sacrificing and burning incense on the high places.

The LORD afflicted the king, and he had a serious skin disease until the day of his death. He lived in quarantine, while Jotham, the king's son, was over the household governing the people of the land.

The rest of the events of Azariah's reign, along with all his accomplishments, are written in the Historical Record of Judah's Kings. Azariah rested with his ancestors and was buried with his ancestors in the city of David. His son Jotham became king in his place.

In the thirty-eighth year of Judah's King Azariah, Zechariah son of Jeroboam reigned over Israel in Samaria for six months. He did what was evil in the LORD's sight as his predecessors had done. He did not turn away from the sins Jeroboam son of Nebat had caused Israel to commit.

Shallum son of Jabesh conspired against Zechariah. He struck him down publicly, killed him, and became king in his place. As for the rest of the events of Zechariah's reign, they are written in the Historical Record of Israel's Kings. The word of the LORD that he spoke to Jehu was, "Four generations of your sons will sit on the throne of Israel," and it was so.

In the thirty-ninth year of Judah's King Uzziah, Shallum son of Jabesh became king; he reigned in Samaria a full month. Then Menahem son of Gadi came up from Tirzah to Samaria and struck down Shallum son of Jabesh there. He killed him and became king in his place. As for the rest of the events of Shallum's reign, along with the conspiracy that he formed, they are written in the Historical Record of Israel's Kings.

At that time, starting from Tirzah, Menahem attacked Tiphsah, all who were in it, and its territory because they wouldn't surrender. He ripped open all the pregnant women.

In the thirty-ninth year of Judah's King Azariah, Menahem son of Gadi became king over Israel, and he reigned ten years in Samaria. He did what was evil in the Lord's sight. Throughout his reign, he did not turn away from the sins Jeroboam son of Nebat had caused Israel to commit.

King Pul of Assyria invaded the land, so Menahem gave Pul seventy-five thousand pounds of silver so that Pul would support him to strengthen his grasp on the kingdom. Then Menahem exacted twenty ounces of silver from each of the prominent men of Israel to give to the king of Assyria. So the king of Assyria withdrew and did not stay there in the land.

The rest of the events of Menahem's reign, along with all his accomplishments, are written in the Historical Record of Israel's Kings. Menahem rested with his ancestors, and his son Pekahiah became king in his place.

In the fiftieth year of Judah's King Azariah, Pekahiah son of Menahem became king over Israel in Samaria, and he reigned two years. He did what was evil in the Lord's sight and did not turn away from the sins Jeroboam son of Nebat had caused Israel to commit.

Then his officer, Pekah son of Remaliah, conspired against him and struck him down in Samaria at the citadel of the king's palace—with Argob and Arieh. There were fifty Gileadite men with Pekah. He killed Pekahiah and became king in his place.

As for the rest of the events of Pekahiah's reign, along with all his accomplishments, they are written in the Historical Record of Israel's Kings.

In the fifty-second year of Judah's King Azariah, Pekah son of Remaliah became king over Israel in Samaria, and he reigned twenty years. He did what was evil in the Lord's sight. He did not turn away from the sins Jeroboam son of Nebat had caused Israel to commit.

In the days of King Pekah of Israel, King Tiglath-pileser of Assyria came and captured Ijon, Abel-beth-maacah, Janoah, Kedesh, Hazor, Gilead, and Galilee—all the land of Naphtali—and deported the people to Assyria.

Then Hoshea son of Elah organized a conspiracy against Pekah son of Remaliah. He attacked him, killed him, and became king in his place in the twentieth year of Jotham son of Uzziah.

As for the rest of the events of Pekah's reign, along with all his accomplishments, they are written in the Historical Record of Israel's Kings.

In the second year of Israel's King Pekah son of Remaliah, Jotham son of Uzziah became king of Judah. He was twenty-five years old when he became king, and he reigned sixteen years in Jerusalem. His mother's name was Jerusha daughter of Zadok. He did what was right in the LORD's sight just as his father Uzziah had done. Yet the high places were not taken away; the people continued sacrificing and burning incense on the high places.

Jotham built the Upper Gate of the LORD's temple. The rest of the events of Jotham's reign, along with all his accomplishments, are written in the Historical Record of Judah's Kings. In those days the LORD began sending Aram's King Rezin and Pekah son of Remaliah against Judah. 60 Jotham rested with his ancestors and was buried with his ancestors in the city of his ancestor David. His son Ahaz became king in his place.

16 In the seventeenth year of Pekah son of Remaliah, Ahaz son of Jotham became king of Judah. Ahaz was twenty years old when he became king, and he reigned sixteen years in Jerusalem. He did not do what was right in the sight of the LORD his God like his ancestor David but walked in the ways of the kings of Israel. He even sacrificed his son in the fire, imitating the detestable practices of the nations the LORD had dispossessed before the Israelites. He sacrificed and burned incense on the high places, on the hills, and under every green tree.

Then Aram's King Rezin and Israel's King Pekah son of Remaliah came to wage war against Jerusalem. They besieged Ahaz but were not able to conquer him. At that time Aram's King Rezin recovered Elath for Aram and expelled the Judahites from Elath. Then the Arameans came 10 to Elath, and they still live there today.

So Ahaz sent messengers to King Tiglath-pileser of Assyria, saying, "I am your servant and your son. March up and save me from the grasp of the king of Aram and of the king of Israel, who are rising up against me." Ahaz also took the silver and gold found in the LORD's temple and in the treasuries of the king's palace and sent them to the king of Assyria as a bribe. So the king of Assyria listened to him and marched up to Damascus and captured it. He deported its people to Kir but put Rezin to death.

King Ahaz went to Damascus to meet King Tiglath-pileser of Assyria. When he saw the altar that was in Damascus, King Ahaz sent a model of the altar and complete plans for its construction to the priest Uriah. Uriah built the altar according to all the instructions King Ahaz sent from 20 Damascus. Therefore, by the time King Ahaz came back from Damascus, the priest Uriah had completed it. When the king came back from Damascus, he saw the altar. Then he approached the altar and ascended it. He offered his burnt offering and his grain offering, poured out his drink offering, and splattered the blood of his fellowship offerings on the altar. He took the bronze altar that was before the LORD in front of the temple between his altar and the LORD's temple, and put it on the north side of his altar.

Then King Ahaz commanded the priest Uriah, "Offer on the great altar the morning burnt offering, the evening grain offering, and the king's burnt offering and his grain offering. Also offer the burnt offering of all the people of the land, their grain offering, and their drink offerings. Splatter on the altar all the blood of the burnt offering and all the blood of sacrifice. The bronze altar will be for me to seek guidance." The priest Uriah did everything King Ahaz commanded.

Then King Ahaz cut off the frames of the water carts and removed the bronze basin from each of them. He took the basin from the bronze oxen that were under it and put it on a stone pavement. To satisfy the king of Assyria, he removed from the Lord's temple the Sabbath canopy they had built in the palace, and he closed the outer entrance for the king.

The rest of the events of Ahaz's reign, along with his accomplishments, are written in the Historical Record of Judah's Kings. Ahaz rested with his ancestors and was buried with his ancestors in the city of David, and his son Hezekiah became king in his place.

17 In the twelfth year of Judah's King Ahaz, Hoshea son of Elah became king over Israel in Samaria, and he reigned nine years. He did what was evil in the Lord's sight, but not like the kings of Israel who preceded him.

King Shalmaneser of Assyria attacked him, and Hoshea became his vassal and paid him tribute. But the king of Assyria caught Hoshea in a conspiracy: He had sent envoys to So king of Egypt and had not paid tribute to the king of Assyria as in previous years. Therefore the king of Assyria arrested him and put him in prison. The king of Assyria invaded the whole land, marched up to Samaria, and besieged it for three years.

In the ninth year of Hoshea, the king of Assyria captured Samaria. He deported the Israelites to Assyria and settled them in Halah, along the Habor (Gozan's river), and in the cities of the Medes.

This disaster happened because the people of Israel sinned against the Lord their God who had brought them out of the land of Egypt from the power of Pharaoh king of Egypt and because they worshiped other gods. They lived according to the customs of the nations that the Lord had dispossessed before the Israelites and according to what the kings of Israel did. The Israelites secretly did things against the Lord their God that were not right. They built high places in all their towns from watchtower to fortified city. They set up for themselves sacred pillars and Asherah poles on every high hill and under every green tree. They burned incense there on all the high places just like the nations that the Lord had driven out before them had done. They did evil things, angering the Lord. They served idols, although the Lord had told them, "You must not do this." Still, the Lord warned Israel and Judah through every prophet and every seer, saying, "Turn from your evil ways and keep my commands and statutes according to the whole law I commanded your ancestors and sent to you through my servants the prophets."

But they would not listen. Instead they became obstinate like their ancestors who did not believe the LORD their God. They rejected his statutes and his covenant he had made with their ancestors and the warnings he had given them. They followed worthless idols and became worthless themselves, following the surrounding nations the LORD had commanded them not to imitate.

They abandoned all the commands of the LORD their God. They made cast images for themselves, two calves, and an Asherah pole. They bowed in worship to all the stars in the sky ³⁰ and served Baal. They sacrificed their sons and daughters in the fire and practiced divination and interpreted omens. They devoted themselves to do what was evil in the LORD's sight and angered him.

Therefore, the LORD was very angry with Israel, and he removed them from his presence. Only the tribe of Judah remained. Even Judah did not keep the commands of the LORD their God but lived according to the customs Israel had practiced. So the LORD rejected all the descendants of Israel, punished them, and handed them over to plunderers until he had banished them from his presence.

When the LORD tore Israel from the house of David, Israel made Jeroboam son of Nebat king. Then Jeroboam led Israel away from following the LORD and caused them to commit grave sin. ⁴⁰ The Israelites persisted in all the sins that Jeroboam committed and did not turn away from them. Finally, the LORD removed Israel from his presence just as he had declared through all his servants the prophets. So Israel has been exiled to Assyria from their homeland to this very day.

Then the king of Assyria brought people from Babylon, Cuthah, Avva, Hamath, and Sepharvaim and settled them in place of the Israelites in the cities of Samaria. The settlers took possession of Samaria and lived in its cities. When they first lived there, they did not fear the LORD. So the LORD sent lions among them, which killed some of them. The settlers said to the king of Assyria, "The nations that you have deported and placed in the cities of Samaria do not know the requirements of the god of the land. Therefore he has sent lions among them that are killing them because the people don't know the requirements of the god of the land."

⁵⁰ Then the king of Assyria issued a command: "Send back one of the priests you deported. Have him go and live there so he can teach them the requirements of the god of the land." So one of the priests they had deported came and lived in Bethel, and he began to teach them how they should fear the LORD.

But the people of each nation were still making their own gods in the cities where they lived and putting them in the shrines of the high places that the people of Samaria had made. The men of Babylon made Succoth-benoth, the men of Cuth made Nergal, the men of Hamath made Ashima, the Avvites made Nibhaz and Tartak, and the Sepharvites burned their children in the fire to Adrammelech and Anammelech, the gods of Sepharvaim. They feared the LORD, but they

60 also made from their ranks priests for the high places, who were working for them at the shrines of the high places. They feared the LORD, but they also worshiped their own gods according to the practice of the nations from which they had been deported.

They are still observing the former practices to this day. None of them fear the LORD or observe the statutes and ordinances, the law and commandments that the LORD had commanded the descendants of Jacob, whom he had given the name Israel. The LORD made a covenant with Jacob's descendants and commanded them, "Do not fear other gods; do not bow in worship to them; do not serve them; do not sacrifice to them. Instead fear the LORD, who brought you up from the land of Egypt with great power and an outstretched arm. You are to bow down to him, and you are to sacrifice to him. You are to be careful always to observe the statutes, the ordinances, the law, and the commandments he wrote for you; do not fear other gods. Do not forget the covenant that I have made with you. Do not fear other gods, but fear the LORD your God, and he will rescue you from all your enemies."

However, these nations would not listen but continued observing their former practices. They feared the LORD but also served their idols. Still today, their children and grandchildren continue doing as their ancestors did.

18 In the third year of Israel's King Hoshea son of Elah, Hezekiah son of Ahaz became king of Judah. He was twenty-five years old when he became king, and he reigned twenty-nine years in Jerusalem. His mother's name was Abi daughter of Zechariah. He did what was right in the LORD's sight just as his ancestor David had done. He removed the high places, shattered the sacred pillars, and cut down the Asherah poles. He broke into pieces the bronze snake that Moses made, for until then the Israelites were burning incense to it. It was called Nehushtan.

Hezekiah relied on the LORD God of Israel; not one of the kings of Judah was like him, either before him or after him. He remained faithful to the LORD and did not turn from following him but kept the commands the LORD had commanded Moses.

10 The LORD was with him, and wherever he went he prospered. He rebelled against the king of Assyria and did not serve him. He defeated the Philistines as far as Gaza and its borders, from watchtower to fortified city.

In the fourth year of King Hezekiah, which was the seventh year of Israel's King Hoshea son of Elah, Assyria's King Shalmaneser marched against Samaria and besieged it. The Assyrians captured it at the end of three years. In the sixth year of Hezekiah, which was the ninth year of Israel's King Hoshea, Samaria was captured. The king of Assyria deported the Israelites to Assyria and put them in Halah, along the Habor (Gozan's river), and in the cities of the Medes, because they did not listen to the LORD their God but violated his covenant—all he had commanded Moses the servant of the LORD. They did not listen, and they did not obey.

20 In the fourteenth year of King Hezekiah, Assyria's King Sennacherib attacked all the fortified cities of Judah and captured them. So King Hezekiah of Judah sent word to the king of Assyria at Lachish: "I have done wrong; withdraw from me. Whatever you demand from me, I will pay." The king of Assyria demanded eleven tons of silver and one ton of gold from King Hezekiah of Judah. So Hezekiah gave him all the silver found in the LORD's temple and in the treasuries of the king's palace.

At that time Hezekiah stripped the gold from the doors of the LORD's sanctuary and from the doorposts he had overlaid and gave it to the king of Assyria.

Then the king of Assyria sent the field marshal, the chief of staff, and his royal spokesman, along with a massive army, from Lachish to King Hezekiah at Jerusalem. They advanced and came to Jerusalem, and they took their position by the aqueduct of the upper pool, by the road to the
30 Launderer's Field. They called for the king, but Eliakim son of Hilkiah, who was in charge of the palace, Shebnah the court secretary, and Joah son of Asaph, the court historian, came out to them.

Then the royal spokesman said to them, "Tell Hezekiah this is what the great king, the king of Assyria, says: 'What are you relying on? You think mere words are strategy and strength for war. Who are you now relying on so that you have rebelled against me? Now look, you are relying on Egypt, that splintered reed of a staff that will pierce the hand of anyone who grabs it and leans on it. This is what Pharaoh king of Egypt is to all who rely on him. Suppose you say to me, "We rely on the LORD our God." Isn't he the one whose high places and altars Hezekiah has removed, saying to Judah and to Jerusalem, "You must worship at this altar in Jerusalem"?'

"So now, make a bargain with my master the king of Assyria. I'll give you two thousand horses
40 if you're able to supply riders for them! How then can you drive back a single officer among the least of my master's servants? How can you rely on Egypt for chariots and for horsemen? Now, have I attacked this place to destroy it without the LORD's approval? The LORD said to me, 'Attack this land and destroy it.'"

Then Eliakim son of Hilkiah, Shebnah, and Joah said to the royal spokesman, "Please speak to your servants in Aramaic, since we understand it. Don't speak with us in Hebrew within earshot of the people on the wall."

But the royal spokesman said to them, "Has my master sent me to speak these words only to your master and to you? Hasn't he also sent me to the men who sit on the wall, destined with you to eat their own excrement and drink their own urine?"

50 The royal spokesman stood and called out loudly in Hebrew: "Hear the word of the great king, the king of Assyria. This is what the king says: 'Don't let Hezekiah deceive you; he can't rescue you from my power. Don't let Hezekiah persuade you to rely on the LORD by saying, "Certainly the LORD will rescue us! This city will not be handed over to the king of Assyria."'

"Don't listen to Hezekiah, for this is what the king of Assyria says: 'Make peace with me and surrender to me. Then each of you may eat from his own vine and his own fig tree, and each may drink water from his own cistern until I come and take you away to a land like your own land—a land of grain and new wine, a land of bread and vineyards, a land of olive trees and honey—so that you may live and not die. But don't listen to Hezekiah when he misleads you, saying, "The LORD will rescue us." Has any of the gods of the nations ever rescued his land from the power of the king of Assyria? Where are the gods of Hamath and Arpad? Where are the gods of Sepharvaim, Hena, and Ivvah? Have they rescued Samaria from my power? Who among all the gods of the lands has rescued his land from my power? So will the LORD rescue Jerusalem from my power?'"

But the people kept silent; they did not answer him at all, for the king's command was, "Don't answer him." Then Eliakim son of Hilkiah, who was in charge of the palace, Shebna the court secretary, and Joah son of Asaph, the court historian, came to Hezekiah with their clothes torn and reported to him the words of the royal spokesman.

19 When King Hezekiah heard their report, he tore his clothes, covered himself with sackcloth, and went into the LORD's temple. He sent Eliakim, who was in charge of the palace, Shebna the court secretary, and the leading priests, who were covered with sackcloth, to the prophet Isaiah son of Amoz. They said to him, "This is what Hezekiah says: 'Today is a day of distress, rebuke, and disgrace, for children have come to the point of birth, but there is no strength to deliver them. Perhaps the LORD your God will hear all the words of the royal spokesman, whom his master the king of Assyria sent to mock the living God, and will rebuke him for the words that the LORD your God has heard. Therefore, offer a prayer for the surviving remnant.'"

So the servants of King Hezekiah went to Isaiah, who said to them, "Tell your master, 'The LORD says this: Don't be afraid because of the words you have heard, with which the king of Assyria's attendants have blasphemed me. I am about to put a spirit in him, and he will hear a rumor and return to his own land, where I will cause him to fall by the sword.'"

When the royal spokesman heard that the king of Assyria had pulled out of Lachish, he left and found him fighting against Libnah. The king had heard concerning King Tirhakah of Cush, "Look, he has set out to fight against you." So he again sent messengers to Hezekiah, saying, "Say this to King Hezekiah of Judah: 'Don't let your God, on whom you rely, deceive you by promising that Jerusalem will not be handed over to the king of Assyria. Look, you have heard what the kings of Assyria have done to all the countries: They completely destroyed them. Will you be rescued? Did the gods of the nations that my predecessors destroyed rescue them—nations such as Gozan, Haran, Rezeph, and the Edenites in Telassar? Where is the king of Hamath, the king of Arpad, the king of the city of Sepharvaim, Hena, or Ivvah?'"

Hezekiah took the letter from the messengers' hands, read it, then went up to the LORD's temple, and spread it out before the LORD. Then Hezekiah prayed before the LORD:

LORD God of Israel, enthroned between the cherubim, you are God—you alone—of all the kingdoms of the earth. You made the heavens and the earth. Listen closely, LORD, and hear;

open your eyes, LORD, and see. Hear the words that Sennacherib has sent to mock the living
God. LORD, it is true that the kings of Assyria have devastated the nations and their lands.
They have thrown their gods into the fire, for they were not gods but made by human hands—
wood and stone. So they have destroyed them. Now, LORD our God, please save us from his
power so that all the kingdoms of the earth may know that you, LORD, are God—you alone.

30 Then Isaiah son of Amoz sent a message to Hezekiah: "The LORD, the God of Israel says, 'I have
heard your prayer to me about King Sennacherib of Assyria.' This is the word the LORD has
spoken against him:

> Virgin Daughter Zion
> despises you and scorns you;
> Daughter Jerusalem
> shakes her head behind your back.
> Who is it you mocked and blasphemed?
> Against whom have you raised your voice
> and lifted your eyes in pride?
40 Against the Holy One of Israel!
> You have mocked the Lord through your messengers.
> You have said, 'With my many chariots
> I have gone up to the heights of the mountains,
> to the far recesses of Lebanon.
> I cut down its tallest cedars,
> its choice cypress trees.
> I came to its farthest outpost,
> its densest forest.
> I dug wells
50 and drank water in foreign lands.
> I dried up all the streams of Egypt
> with the soles of my feet.'
>
> Have you not heard?
> I designed it long ago;
> I planned it in days gone by.
> I have now brought it to pass,
> and you have crushed fortified cities
> into piles of rubble.
> Their inhabitants have become powerless,
60 dismayed, and ashamed.

They are plants of the field,
tender grass,
grass on the rooftops,
blasted by the east wind.

But I know your sitting down,
your going out and your coming in,
and your raging against me.
Because your raging against me
and your arrogance have reached my ears,
70 I will put my hook in your nose
and my bit in your mouth;
I will make you go back
the way you came.

"This will be the sign for you: This year you will eat what grows on its own, and in the second year what grows from that. But in the third year sow and reap, plant vineyards and eat their fruit. The surviving remnant of the house of Judah will again take root downward and bear fruit upward. For a remnant will go out from Jerusalem, and survivors, from Mount Zion. The zeal of the LORD of Armies will accomplish this.

Therefore, this is what the LORD says about the king of Assyria:
80 He will not enter this city,
shoot an arrow here,
come before it with a shield,
or build up a siege ramp against it.
He will go back
the way he came,
and he will not enter this city.

This is the LORD's declaration.

I will defend this city and rescue it
for my sake and for the sake of my servant David."

90 That night the angel of the LORD went out and struck down one hundred eighty-five thousand in the camp of the Assyrians. When the people got up the next morning—there were all the dead bodies! So King Sennacherib of Assyria broke camp and left. He returned home and lived in Nineveh.

One day, while he was worshiping in the temple of his god Nisroch, his sons Adrammelech and Sharezer struck him down with the sword and escaped to the land of Ararat. Then his son Esarhaddon became king in his place.

20 In those days Hezekiah became terminally ill. The prophet Isaiah son of Amoz came and said to him, "This is what the LORD says: 'Set your house in order, for you are about to die; you will not recover.'"

Then Hezekiah turned his face to the wall and prayed to the LORD, "Please, LORD, remember how I have walked before you faithfully and wholeheartedly and have done what pleases you." And Hezekiah wept bitterly.

Isaiah had not yet gone out of the inner courtyard when the word of the LORD came to him: "Go back and tell Hezekiah, the leader of my people, 'This is what the LORD God of your ancestor David says: I have heard your prayer; I have seen your tears. Look, I will heal you. On the third day from now you will go up to the LORD's temple. I will add fifteen years to your life. I will rescue
10 you and this city from the grasp of the king of Assyria. I will defend this city for my sake and for the sake of my servant David.'"

Then Isaiah said, "Bring a lump of pressed figs." So they brought it and applied it to his infected skin, and he recovered.

Hezekiah had asked Isaiah, "What is the sign that the LORD will heal me and that I will go up to the LORD's temple on the third day?"

Isaiah said, "This is the sign to you from the LORD that he will do what he has promised: Should the shadow go ahead ten steps or go back ten steps?"

Then Hezekiah answered, "It's easy for the shadow to lengthen ten steps. No, let the shadow go back ten steps." So the prophet Isaiah called out to the LORD, and he brought the shadow back
20 the ten steps it had descended on the stairway of Ahaz.

At that time Merodach-baladan son of Baladan, king of Babylon, sent letters and a gift to Hezekiah since he heard that he had been sick. Hezekiah listened to the letters and showed the envoys his whole treasure house—the silver, the gold, the spices, and the precious oil—and his armory, and everything that was found in his treasuries. There was nothing in his palace and in all his realm that Hezekiah did not show them.

Then the prophet Isaiah came to King Hezekiah and asked him, "Where did these men come from and what did they say to you?"

Hezekiah replied, "They came from a distant country, from Babylon."

Isaiah asked, "What have they seen in your palace?"

30 Hezekiah answered, "They have seen everything in my palace. There isn't anything in my treasuries that I didn't show them."

Then Isaiah said to Hezekiah, "Hear the word of the LORD: 'Look, the days are coming when everything in your palace and all that your predecessors have stored up until today will be carried off to Babylon; nothing will be left,' says the LORD. 'Some of your descendants—who come from you, whom you father—will be taken away, and they will become eunuchs in the palace of the king of Babylon.'"

Then Hezekiah said to Isaiah, "The word of the LORD that you have spoken is good," for he thought, "Why not, if there will be peace and security during my lifetime?"

The rest of the events of Hezekiah's reign, along with all his might and how he made the pool and
40 the tunnel and brought water into the city, are written in the Historical Record of Judah's Kings. Hezekiah rested with his ancestors, and his son Manasseh became king in his place.

21 Manasseh was twelve years old when he became king, and he reigned fifty-five years in Jerusalem. His mother's name was Hephzibah. He did what was evil in the LORD's sight, imitating the detestable practices of the nations that the LORD had dispossessed before the Israelites. He rebuilt the high places that his father Hezekiah had destroyed and reestablished the altars for Baal. He made an Asherah, as King Ahab of Israel had done; he also bowed in worship to all the stars in the sky and served them. He built altars in the LORD's temple, where the LORD had said, "Jerusalem is where I will put my name." He built altars to all the stars in the sky in both courtyards of the LORD's temple. He sacrificed his son in the fire, practiced witchcraft and divination, and consulted mediums and spiritists. He did a huge amount of evil in the LORD's sight, angering him.

10 Manasseh set up the carved image of Asherah, which he made, in the temple that the LORD had spoken about to David and his son Solomon: "I will establish my name forever in this temple and in Jerusalem, which I have chosen out of all the tribes of Israel. I will never again cause the feet of the Israelites to wander from the land I gave to their ancestors if only they will be careful to do all I have commanded them—the whole law that my servant Moses commanded them." But they did not listen; Manasseh caused them to stray so that they did worse evil than the nations the LORD had destroyed before the Israelites.

The LORD said through his servants the prophets, "Since King Manasseh of Judah has committed all these detestable acts—worse evil than the Amorites who preceded him had done—and by means of his idols has also caused Judah to sin, this is what the LORD God of Israel says:
20 'I am about to bring such a disaster on Jerusalem and Judah that everyone who hears about it will shudder. I will stretch over Jerusalem the measuring line used on Samaria and the mason's level used on the house of Ahab, and I will wipe Jerusalem clean as one wipes a bowl—wiping it and turning it upside down. I will abandon the remnant of my inheritance and hand them over to their enemies. They will become plunder and spoil to all their enemies, because they have done what is evil in my sight and have angered me from the day their ancestors came out of Egypt until today.'"

Manasseh also shed so much innocent blood that he filled Jerusalem with it from one end to another. This was in addition to his sin that he caused Judah to commit, so that they did what was evil in the LORD's sight.

The rest of the events of Manasseh's reign, along with all his accomplishments and the sin that
he committed, are written in the Historical Record of Judah's Kings. Manasseh rested with his
ancestors and was buried in the garden of his own house, the garden of Uzza. His son Amon
became king in his place.

Amon was twenty-two years old when he became king, and he reigned two years in Jerusalem.
His mother's name was Meshullemeth daughter of Haruz; she was from Jotbah. He did what
was evil in the LORD's sight, just as his father Manasseh had done. He walked in all the ways his
father had walked; he served the idols his father had served, and he bowed in worship to them. He
abandoned the LORD God of his ancestors and did not walk in the ways of the LORD.

Amon's servants conspired against him and put the king to death in his own house. The
common people killed all who had conspired against King Amon, and they made his son Josiah
king in his place.

The rest of the events of Amon's reign, along with his accomplishments, are written in the
Historical Record of Judah's Kings. He was buried in his tomb in the garden of Uzza, and his son
Josiah became king in his place.

22 Josiah was eight years old when he became king, and he reigned thirty-one years in Jerusalem. His
mother's name was Jedidah the daughter of Adaiah; she was from Bozkath. He did what was right
in the LORD's sight and walked in all the ways of his ancestor David; he did not turn to the right or
the left.

In the eighteenth year of King Josiah, the king sent the court secretary Shaphan son of Azaliah,
son of Meshullam, to the LORD's temple, saying, "Go up to the high priest Hilkiah so that he may
total up the silver brought into the LORD's temple—the silver the doorkeepers have collected from
the people. It is to be given to those doing the work—those who oversee the LORD's temple. They
in turn are to give it to the workmen in the LORD's temple to repair the damage. They are to give
it to the carpenters, builders, and masons to buy timber and quarried stone to repair the temple.
But no accounting is to be required from them for the silver given to them since they work with
integrity."

The high priest Hilkiah told the court secretary Shaphan, "I have found the book of the law in the
LORD's temple," and he gave the book to Shaphan, who read it.

Then the court secretary Shaphan went to the king and reported, "Your servants have emptied
out the silver that was found in the temple and have given it to those doing the work—those who
oversee the LORD's temple." Then the court secretary Shaphan told the king, "The priest Hilkiah
has given me a book," and Shaphan read it in the presence of the king.

When the king heard the words of the book of the law, he tore his clothes. Then he
20 commanded the priest Hilkiah, Ahikam son of Shaphan, Achbor son of Micaiah, the court
secretary Shaphan, and the king's servant Asaiah, "Go and inquire of the LORD for me, for the
people, and for all Judah about the words in this book that has been found. For great is the LORD's
wrath that is kindled against us because our ancestors have not obeyed the words of this book in
order to do everything written about us."

So the priest Hilkiah, Ahikam, Achbor, Shaphan, and Asaiah went to the prophetess Huldah,
wife of Shallum son of Tikvah, son of Harhas, keeper of the wardrobe. She lived in Jerusalem in
the Second District. They spoke with her.

She said to them, "This is what the LORD God of Israel says: Say to the man who sent you to
me, 'This is what the LORD says: I am about to bring disaster on this place and on its inhabitants,
30 fulfilling all the words of the book that the king of Judah has read, because they have abandoned
me and burned incense to other gods in order to anger me with all the work of their hands. My
wrath will be kindled against this place, and it will not be quenched.' Say this to the king of Judah
who sent you to inquire of the LORD: 'This is what the LORD God of Israel says: As for the words
that you heard, because your heart was tender and you humbled yourself before the LORD when
you heard what I spoke against this place and against its inhabitants, that they would become a
desolation and a curse, and because you have torn your clothes and wept before me, I myself have
heard'—this is the LORD's declaration. 'Therefore, I will indeed gather you to your ancestors,
and you will be gathered to your grave in peace. Your eyes will not see all the disaster that I am
bringing on this place.'"
40 Then they reported to the king.

23 So the king sent messengers, and they gathered all the elders of Judah and Jerusalem to him. Then
the king went to the LORD's temple with all the men of Judah and all the inhabitants of Jerusalem, as
well as the priests and the prophets—all the people from the youngest to the oldest. He read in their
hearing all the words of the book of the covenant that had been found in the LORD's temple. Next, the
king stood by the pillar and made a covenant in the LORD's presence to follow the LORD and to keep
his commands, his decrees, and his statutes with all his heart and with all his soul in order to carry out
the words of this covenant that were written in this book; all the people agreed to the covenant.

Then the king commanded the high priest Hilkiah and the priests of the second rank and the
doorkeepers to bring out of the LORD's sanctuary all the articles made for Baal, Asherah, and all
10 the stars in the sky. He burned them outside Jerusalem in the fields of the Kidron and carried
their ashes to Bethel. Then he did away with the idolatrous priests the kings of Judah had
appointed to burn incense at the high places in the cities of Judah and in the areas surrounding
Jerusalem. They had burned incense to Baal, and to the sun, moon, constellations, and all the stars

in the sky. He brought out the Asherah pole from the LORD's temple to the Kidron Valley outside Jerusalem. He burned it at the Kidron Valley, beat it to dust, and threw its dust on the graves of the common people. He also tore down the houses of the male cult prostitutes that were in the LORD's temple, in which the women were weaving tapestries for Asherah.

Then Josiah brought all the priests from the cities of Judah, and he defiled the high places from Geba to Beer-sheba, where the priests had burned incense. He tore down the high places of the city gates at the entrance of the gate of Joshua the governor of the city (on the left at the city gate). The priests of the high places, however, did not come up to the altar of the LORD in Jerusalem; instead, they ate unleavened bread with their fellow priests.

He defiled Topheth, which is in Ben Hinnom Valley, so that no one could sacrifice his son or daughter in the fire to Molech. He did away with the horses that the kings of Judah had dedicated to the sun. They had been at the entrance of the LORD's temple in the precincts by the chamber of Nathan-melech, the eunuch. He also burned the chariots of the sun.

The king tore down the altars that the kings of Judah had made on the roof of Ahaz's upper chamber. He also tore down the altars that Manasseh had made in the two courtyards of the LORD's temple. Then he smashed them there and threw their dust into the Kidron Valley. The king also defiled the high places that were across from Jerusalem, to the south of the Mount of Destruction, which King Solomon of Israel had built for Ashtoreth, the abhorrent idol of the Sidonians; for Chemosh, the abhorrent idol of Moab; and for Milcom, the detestable idol of the Ammonites. He broke the sacred pillars into pieces, cut down the Asherah poles, then filled their places with human bones.

He even tore down the altar at Bethel and the high place that had been made by Jeroboam son of Nebat, who caused Israel to sin. He burned the high place, crushed it to dust, and burned the Asherah. As Josiah turned, he saw the tombs there on the mountain. He sent someone to take the bones out of the tombs, and he burned them on the altar. He defiled it according to the word of the LORD proclaimed by the man of God who proclaimed these things. Then he said, "What is this monument I see?"

The men of the city told him, "It is the tomb of the man of God who came from Judah and proclaimed these things that you have done to the altar at Bethel."

So he said, "Let him rest. Don't let anyone disturb his bones." So they left his bones undisturbed with the bones of the prophet who came from Samaria.

Josiah also removed all the shrines of the high places that were in the cities of Samaria, which the kings of Israel had made to anger the LORD. Josiah did the same things to them that he had done at Bethel. He slaughtered on the altars all the priests of those high places, and he burned human bones on the altars. Then he returned to Jerusalem.

The king commanded all the people, "Observe the Passover of the LORD your God as written in the book of the covenant." No such Passover had ever been observed from the time of the judges who judged Israel through the entire time of the kings of Israel and Judah. But in the eighteenth year of King Josiah, the Lord's Passover was observed in Jerusalem.

In addition, Josiah eradicated the mediums, the spiritists, household idols, images, and all the abhorrent things that were seen in the land of Judah and in Jerusalem. He did this in order to carry out the words of the law that were written in the book that the priest Hilkiah found in the Lord's temple. Before him there was no king like him who turned to the Lord with all his heart and with all his soul and with all his strength according to all the law of Moses, and no one like him arose after him.

In spite of all that, the Lord did not turn from the fury of his intense burning anger, which burned against Judah because of all the affronts with which Manasseh had angered him. For the 60 Lord had said, "I will also remove Judah from my presence just as I have removed Israel. I will reject this city Jerusalem, that I have chosen, and the temple about which I said, 'My name will be there.'"

The rest of the events of Josiah's reign, along with all his accomplishments, are written in the Historical Record of Judah's Kings. During his reign, Pharaoh Neco king of Egypt marched up to help the king of Assyria at the Euphrates River. King Josiah went to confront him, and at Megiddo when Neco saw him he killed him. From Megiddo his servants carried his dead body in a chariot, brought him into Jerusalem, and buried him in his own tomb. Then the common people took Jehoahaz son of Josiah, anointed him, and made him king in place of his father.

Jehoahaz was twenty-three years old when he became king, and he reigned three months in Jerusalem. His mother's name was Hamutal daughter of Jeremiah; she was from Libnah. He did 70 what was evil in the Lord's sight just as his ancestors had done. Pharaoh Neco imprisoned him at Riblah in the land of Hamath to keep him from reigning in Jerusalem, and he imposed on the land a fine of seventy-five hundred pounds of silver and seventy-five pounds of gold.

Then Pharaoh Neco made Eliakim son of Josiah king in place of his father Josiah and changed Eliakim's name to Jehoiakim. But Neco took Jehoahaz and went to Egypt, and he died there. So Jehoiakim gave the silver and the gold to Pharaoh, but at Pharaoh's command he taxed the land to give it. He exacted the silver and the gold from the common people, each according to his assessment, to give it to Pharaoh Neco.

Jehoiakim was twenty-five years old when he became king, and he reigned eleven years in Jerusalem. His mother's name was Zebidah daughter of Pedaiah; she was from Rumah. He did 80 what was evil in the Lord's sight just as his ancestors had done.

24 During Jehoiakim's reign, King Nebuchadnezzar of Babylon attacked. Jehoiakim became his vassal for three years, and then he turned and rebelled against him. The Lord sent Chaldean, Aramean, Moabite, and Ammonite raiders against Jehoiakim. He sent them against Judah to destroy it, according to the word of the LORD he had spoken through his servants the prophets. Indeed, this happened to Judah at the LORD's command to remove them from his presence. It was because of the sins of Manasseh, according to all he had done, and also because of all the innocent blood he had shed. He had filled Jerusalem with innocent blood, and the LORD was not willing to forgive.

The rest of the events of Jehoiakim's reign, along with all his accomplishments, are written in the Historical Record of Judah's Kings. Jehoiakim rested with his ancestors, and his son Jehoiachin became king in his place.

Now the king of Egypt did not march out of his land again, for the king of Babylon took everything that had belonged to the king of Egypt, from the Brook of Egypt to the Euphrates River.

Jehoiachin was eighteen years old when he became king, and he reigned three months in Jerusalem. His mother's name was Nehushta daughter of Elnathan; she was from Jerusalem. He did what was evil in the LORD's sight just as his father had done.

At that time the servants of King Nebuchadnezzar of Babylon marched up to Jerusalem, and the city came under siege. King Nebuchadnezzar of Babylon came to the city while his servants were besieging it. King Jehoiachin of Judah, along with his mother, his servants, his commanders, and his officials, surrendered to the king of Babylon.

So the king of Babylon took him captive in the eighth year of his reign. He also carried off from there all the treasures of the LORD's temple and the treasures of the king's palace, and he cut into pieces all the gold articles that King Solomon of Israel had made for the LORD's sanctuary, just as the LORD had predicted. He deported all Jerusalem and all the commanders and all the best soldiers—ten thousand captives including all the craftsmen and metalsmiths. Except for the poorest people of the land, no one remained.

Nebuchadnezzar deported Jehoiachin to Babylon. He took the king's mother, the king's wives, his officials, and the leading men of the land into exile from Jerusalem to Babylon. The king of Babylon brought captive into Babylon all seven thousand of the best soldiers and one thousand craftsmen and metalsmiths—all strong and fit for war. And the king of Babylon made Mattaniah, Jehoiachin's uncle, king in his place and changed his name to Zedekiah.

Zedekiah was twenty-one years old when he became king, and he reigned eleven years in Jerusalem. His mother's name was Hamutal daughter of Jeremiah; she was from Libnah. Zedekiah did what was evil in the LORD's sight just as Jehoiakim had done. Because of the LORD's anger, it came to the point in Jerusalem and Judah that he finally banished them from his presence. Then Zedekiah rebelled against the king of Babylon.

25 In the ninth year of Zedekiah's reign, on the tenth day of the tenth month, King Nebuchadnezzar of Babylon advanced against Jerusalem with his entire army. They laid siege to the city and built a siege wall against it all around. The city was under siege until King Zedekiah's eleventh year.

By the ninth day of the fourth month the famine was so severe in the city that the common people had no food. Then the city was broken into, and all the warriors fled at night by way of the city gate between the two walls near the king's garden, even though the Chaldeans surrounded the city. As the king made his way along the route to the Arabah, the Chaldean army pursued him and overtook him in the plains of Jericho. Zedekiah's entire army left him and scattered. The

10 Chaldeans seized the king and brought him up to the king of Babylon at Riblah, and they passed sentence on him. They slaughtered Zedekiah's sons before his eyes. Finally, the king of Babylon blinded Zedekiah, bound him in bronze chains, and took him to Babylon.

On the seventh day of the fifth month—which was the nineteenth year of King Nebuchadnezzar of Babylon—Nebuzaradan, the captain of the guards, a servant of the king of Babylon, entered Jerusalem. He burned the LORD's temple, the king's palace, and all the houses of Jerusalem; he burned down all the great houses. The whole Chaldean army with the captain of the guards tore down the walls surrounding Jerusalem. Nebuzaradan, the captain of the guards, deported the rest of the people who remained in the city, the deserters who had defected to the king of Babylon, and the rest of the population. But the captain of the guards left some of the poorest of the land to be

20 vinedressers and farmers.

Now the Chaldeans broke into pieces the bronze pillars of the LORD's temple, the water carts, and the bronze basin, which were in the LORD's temple, and carried the bronze to Babylon. They also took the pots, shovels, wick trimmers, dishes, and all the bronze articles used in the priests' service. The captain of the guards took away the firepans and sprinkling basins—whatever was gold or silver.

As for the two pillars, the one basin, and the water carts that Solomon had made for the LORD's temple, the weight of the bronze of all these articles was beyond measure. One pillar was twenty-seven feet tall and had a bronze capital on top of it. The capital, encircled by a grating and pomegranates of bronze, stood five feet high. The second pillar was the same, with its own grating.

30 The captain of the guards also took away Seraiah the chief priest, Zephaniah the priest of the second rank, and the three doorkeepers. From the city he took a court official who had been appointed over the warriors; five trusted royal aides found in the city; the secretary of the commander of the army, who enlisted the people of the land for military duty; and sixty men from the common people who were found within the city. Nebuzaradan, the captain of the guards, took them and brought them to the king of Babylon at Riblah. The king of Babylon put them to death at Riblah in the land of Hamath. So Judah went into exile from its land.

King Nebuchadnezzar of Babylon appointed Gedaliah son of Ahikam, son of Shaphan, over the rest of the people he left in the land of Judah. When all the commanders of the armies—they and

their men—heard that the king of Babylon had appointed Gedaliah, they came to Gedaliah at
40 Mizpah. The commanders included Ishmael son of Nethaniah, Johanan son of Kareah, Seraiah
son of Tanhumeth the Netophathite, and Jaazaniah son of the Maacathite—they and their men.
Gedaliah swore an oath to them and their men, assuring them, "Don't be afraid of the servants of
the Chaldeans. Live in the land and serve the king of Babylon, and it will go well for you."

In the seventh month, however, Ishmael son of Nethaniah, son of Elishama, of the royal family,
came with ten men and struck down Gedaliah, and he died. Also, they killed the Judeans and the
Chaldeans who were with him at Mizpah. Then all the people, from the youngest to the oldest,
and the commanders of the army, left and went to Egypt, for they were afraid of the Chaldeans.

On the twenty-seventh day of the twelfth month of the thirty-seventh year of the exile of Judah's
King Jehoiachin, in the year Evil-merodach became king of Babylon, he pardoned King Jehoiachin
50 of Judah and released him from prison. He spoke kindly to him and set his throne over the
thrones of the kings who were with him in Babylon. So Jehoiachin changed his prison clothes,
and he dined regularly in the presence of the king of Babylon for the rest of his life. As for his
allowance, a regular allowance was given to him by the king, a portion for each day, for the rest of
his life.

Introduction to Isaiah

Cory Barnes

Unlike the Former Prophets (Joshua—2 Kings), which are narrative in genre, Isaiah and the "writing prophets" are prophetic in genre as well as content. Like the rest of the prophetic books, the message of Isaiah comes to us as the words of Yahweh spoken through his prophet.

Despite the simplicity of the book's introduction, which identifies the author as Isaiah son of Amoz, and locates him in the mid to late 8th century (ca. 770–700 BC), the historical background of Isaiah is complex. The dramatic shift in historical perspective between Isaiah 1–39 and 40–66 leads many scholars to propose that multiple authors across several centuries composed the prophecies in Isaiah. The debate over the nature of authorship and composition of the book has dominated the study of Isaiah over the past century, though the discussion provides limited insight into the message of the book.

What Isaiah presents with absolute clarity is a prophetic call to Yahweh's people to understand his role in upholding justice. Yahweh's message is clear from the beginning of Isaiah that he will not tolerate sinfulness among Judah and Israel; if they fail to repent, he will judge them and will use the global powers that surround them as his instruments of discipline (Isa 5.101–127; 8.51–55). Isaiah 1–39 contains two historical narratives, one of which focuses on a geopolitical crisis in the time of Ahaz (Isa 7–8), while the other recounts an even more tumultuous national crisis during the reign of Hezekiah (Isa 36–39). Hezekiah heeds Isaiah's prophecy and experiences Yahweh's deliverance only to take actions that will lead Judah into conflict with a new enemy—Babylon (Isa 39).

The prophecies of Isa 40–66 speak in a different tone than the earlier chapters. The historical perspective of these prophecies shifts from a focus on Assyria to Babylon. Chapters 40–66 speak comfort to those exiled in Babylon by revealing Yahweh's plan to restore his people after their time in exile is complete. Just as Yahweh has raised nations to judge his people, so he will raise pagan kings to restore his people to the land he has promised. In a powerful reminder of the sovereignty of Yahweh over global events, Cyrus of Persia is referenced by name and is called both Yahweh's shepherd and his anointed (Isa 44.114–45.6).

Four passages in Isa 42–53, often called the "Servant Songs," introduce the servant of the Lord (42.1–12; 49.1–26; 50.18–32; 52.54–53.51). The second song identifies the servant as Israel when Yahweh says: "He said to me, 'You are my servant, Israel, in whom I will be glorified'" (Isa 49.9–10). Other passages in the songs, however, seem to speak of an individual servant. In the final servant song, Isaiah speaks of a servant who suffers on behalf of Yahweh's people: "He was taken away because of oppression and judgment, and who considered his fate? For he was cut off from the land of the living; he was struck because of my people's rebellion" (Isa 53.29–32). Ultimately, the suffering of the servant will result in his vindication and in the redemption of many (Isa 53.37–51).

The difficult nature of identifying the servant has led some, especially in Christian interpretation, to view the servant songs as predictive prophecies disconnected from the broader context of Isaiah. When the servant songs are read in context with the rest of Isaiah, however, they demonstrate continuity with Isaiah's broader theme of judgment and restoration. Yahweh will use the servant to bring about his redemptive purposes. This complements passages from Isa 1–39 that speak of a Davidic king playing a part in Yahweh's restorative work (e.g., Isa 11.1–23). In Isaiah, therefore, we are told that Yahweh is bringing about justice through global events, the covenant kingship of David, and the servant who will somehow bring about redemption through suffering (Isa 53.8–51). Christians see in Isaiah powerful images that point them toward the redemptive work of Jesus. Jesus himself identifies his ministry with Isaiah's proclamation of the one who is anointed with the Spirit of the Lord to bring good news to the ones in Zion (Isa 61.1–16; Luke 4:18–19).

Outline

1. The indictment of injustice among Yahweh's people and his promise to use the nations to chastise his people (1.1–5.127)

2. Isaiah commissioned to his prophetic task (6.1–45)

3. The sign of Immanuel (7.1–12.21)

4. Judgment and Restoration Cycle 1 (13.1–27.49)
    a. Oracles against the nations (13.1–24.83)
    b. Restoration of the world: Death is swallowed up, Judah sings, Leviathan dies (25.1–27.49)

5. Judgment and Restoration Cycle 2 (28.1–35.38)
    a. Woe to Yahweh's people (28.1–30.71)
    b. The restoration of Yahweh's people and judgment of their enemies (30.72–35.38)

6. Hezekiah's Story, Assyria humbled, Babylon emerges (36.1–39.18)

7. Restoration from Babylonian exile promised (40.1–55.52)

8. Yahweh promises to righteously rule over his restored people (56.1–66.96)

Suggested Resources

Childs, Brevard S. *Isaiah*. Old Testament Library. Louisville: Westminster John Knox, 2000.

Goldingay, John. *Isaiah for Everyone*. Old Testament for Everyone. Louisville: Westminster John Knox, 2015.

———. *The Theology of Isaiah*. Downers Grove, IL: InterVarsity Press, 2014.

Oswalt, John N. *Isaiah*. NIV Application Commentary. Grand Rapids: Zondervan, 2003.

Witherington, Ben, III. *Isaiah Old and New: Exegesis, Intertextuality, and Hermeneutics*. Minneapolis: Fortress, 2017.

Isaiah

I The vision concerning Judah and Jerusalem that Isaiah son of Amoz saw during the reigns of Kings Uzziah, Jotham, Ahaz, and Hezekiah of Judah.

> Listen, heavens, and pay attention, earth,
> for the LORD has spoken:
> "I have raised children and brought them up,
> but they have rebelled against me.
> The ox knows its owner,
> and the donkey its master's feeding trough,
> but Israel does not know;
> my people do not understand."

> Oh sinful nation,
> people weighed down with iniquity,
> brood of evildoers,
> depraved children!
> They have abandoned the LORD;
> they have despised the Holy One of Israel;
> they have turned their backs on him.

> Why do you want more beatings?
> Why do you keep on rebelling?
> The whole head is hurt,
> and the whole heart is sick.
> From the sole of the foot even to the head,
> no spot is uninjured—
> wounds, welts, and festering sores
> not cleansed, bandaged,
> or soothed with oil.

> Your land is desolate,
> your cities burned down;

foreigners devour your fields
right in front of you—
a desolation, like a place demolished by foreigners.
Daughter Zion is abandoned
like a shelter in a vineyard,
like a shack in a cucumber field,
like a besieged city.
If the LORD of Armies
had not left us a few survivors,
we would be like Sodom,
we would resemble Gomorrah.

Hear the word of the LORD,
you rulers of Sodom!
Listen to the instruction of our God,
you people of Gomorrah!
"What are all your sacrifices to me?"
asks the LORD.
"I have had enough of burnt offerings and rams
and the fat of well-fed cattle;
I have no desire for the blood of bulls,
lambs, or male goats.
When you come to appear before me,
who requires this from you—
this trampling of my courts?
Stop bringing useless offerings.
Your incense is detestable to me.
New Moons and Sabbaths,
and the calling of solemn assemblies—
I cannot stand iniquity with a festival.
I hate your New Moons and prescribed festivals.
They have become a burden to me;
I am tired of putting up with them.
When you spread out your hands in prayer,
I will refuse to look at you;
even if you offer countless prayers,
I will not listen.
Your hands are covered with blood.

"Wash yourselves. Cleanse yourselves.
Remove your evil deeds from my sight.
Stop doing evil.
Learn to do what is good.
70   Pursue justice.
Correct the oppressor.
Defend the rights of the fatherless.
Plead the widow's cause.

"Come, let's settle this,"
says the LORD.
"Though your sins are scarlet,
they will be as white as snow;
though they are crimson red,
they will be like wool.
80   If you are willing and obedient,
you will eat the good things of the land.
But if you refuse and rebel,
you will be devoured by the sword."
For the mouth of the LORD has spoken.

The faithful town—
what an adulteress she has become!
She was once full of justice.
Righteousness once dwelt in her,
but now, murderers!
90   Your silver has become dross to be discarded,
your beer is diluted with water.
Your rulers are rebels,
friends of thieves.
They all love graft
and chase after bribes.
They do not defend the rights of the fatherless,
and the widow's case never comes before them.

Therefore the Lord GOD of Armies,
the Mighty One of Israel, declares:

100   "Ah, I will get even with my foes;
         I will take revenge against my enemies.
         I will turn my hand against you
         and will burn away your dross completely;
         I will remove all your impurities.
         I will restore your judges to what they were at first,
         and your advisers to what they were at the start.
         Afterward you will be called the Righteous City,
         a Faithful Town."

         Zion will be redeemed by justice,
110   those who repent, by righteousness.
         At the same time both rebels and sinners will be broken,
         and those who abandon the LORD will perish.
         Indeed, they will be ashamed of the sacred trees
         you desired,
         and you will be embarrassed because of the garden shrines
         you have chosen.
         For you will become like an oak
         whose leaves are withered,
         and like a garden without water.
120   The strong one will become tinder,
         and his work a spark;
         both will burn together,
         with no one to extinguish the flames.

2   The vision that Isaiah son of Amoz saw concerning Judah and Jerusalem:
         In the last days
         the mountain of the LORD's house will be established
         at the top of the mountains
         and will be raised above the hills.
         All nations will stream to it,
         and many peoples will come and say,
         "Come, let's go up to the mountain of the LORD,
         to the house of the God of Jacob.
10   He will teach us about his ways
         so that we may walk in his paths."
         For instruction will go out of Zion

and the word of the Lord from Jerusalem.
He will settle disputes among the nations
and provide arbitration for many peoples.
They will beat their swords into plows
and their spears into pruning knives.
Nation will not take up the sword against nation,
and they will never again train for war.

20 House of Jacob,
come and let's walk in the Lord's light.
For you have abandoned your people,
the house of Jacob,
because they are full of divination from the East
and of fortune-tellers like the Philistines.
They are in league with foreigners.
Their land is full of silver and gold,
and there is no limit to their treasures;
their land is full of horses,
30 and there is no limit to their chariots.
Their land is full of worthless idols;
they worship the work of their hands,
what their fingers have made.
So humanity is brought low,
and each person is humbled.
Do not forgive them!
Go into the rocks
and hide in the dust
from the terror of the Lord
40 and from his majestic splendor.
The pride of mankind will be humbled,
and human loftiness will be brought low;
the Lord alone will be exalted on that day.

For a day belonging to the Lord of Armies is coming
against all that is proud and lofty,
against all that is lifted up—it will be humbled—
against all the cedars of Lebanon,
lofty and lifted up,

against all the oaks of Bashan,
50   against all the high mountains,
against all the lofty hills,
against every high tower,
against every fortified wall,
against every ship of Tarshish,
and against every splendid sea vessel.
The pride of mankind will be brought low,
and human loftiness will be humbled;
the LORD alone will be exalted on that day.
The worthless idols will vanish completely.

60   People will go into caves in the rocks
and holes in the ground,
away from the terror of the LORD
and from his majestic splendor,
when he rises to terrify the earth.
On that day people will throw
their worthless idols of silver and gold,
which they made to worship,
to the moles and the bats.
They will go into the caves of the rocks
70   and the crevices in the cliffs,
away from the terror of the LORD
and from his majestic splendor,
when he rises to terrify the earth.
Put no more trust in a mere human,
who has only the breath in his nostrils.
What is he really worth?

3   Note this: The Lord GOD of Armies
is about to remove from Jerusalem and from Judah
every kind of security:
the entire supply of bread and water,
heroes and warriors,
judges and prophets,
fortune-tellers and elders,
commanders of fifty and dignitaries,

counselors, cunning magicians, and necromancers.
10 "I will make youths their leaders,
and unstable rulers will govern them."
The people will oppress one another,
man against man, neighbor against neighbor;
the young will act arrogantly toward the old,
and the worthless toward the honorable.
A man will even seize his brother
in his father's house, saying,
"You have a cloak—you be our leader!
This heap of rubble will be under your control."
20 On that day he will cry out, saying,
"I'm not a healer.
I don't even have food or clothing in my house.
Don't make me the leader of the people!"
For Jerusalem has stumbled
and Judah has fallen
because they have spoken and acted against the Lord,
defying his glorious presence.
The look on their faces testifies against them,
and like Sodom, they flaunt their sin;
30 they do not conceal it.
Woe to them,
for they have brought disaster on themselves.
Tell the righteous that it will go well for them,
for they will eat the fruit of their labor.
Woe to the wicked—it will go badly for them,
for what they have done will be done to them.
Youths oppress my people,
and women rule over them.
My people, your leaders mislead you;
40 they confuse the direction of your paths.

The Lord rises to argue the case
and stands to judge the people.
The Lord brings this charge
against the elders and leaders of his people:
"You have devastated the vineyard.

The plunder from the poor is in your houses.
Why do you crush my people
and grind the faces of the poor?"
This is the declaration
50   of the Lord God of Armies.

The Lord also says:
Because the daughters of Zion are haughty,
walking with heads held high
and seductive eyes,
prancing along,
jingling their ankle bracelets,
the Lord will put scabs on the heads
of the daughters of Zion,
and the Lord will shave their foreheads bare.

60   On that day the Lord will strip their finery: ankle bracelets, headbands, crescents, pendants, bracelets, veils, headdresses, ankle jewelry, sashes, perfume bottles, amulets, signet rings, nose rings, festive robes, capes, cloaks, purses, garments, linen clothes, turbans, and shawls.

Instead of perfume there will be a stench;
instead of a belt, a rope;
instead of beautifully styled hair, baldness;
instead of fine clothes, sackcloth;
instead of beauty, branding.
Your men will fall by the sword,
your warriors in battle.
70   Then her gates will lament and mourn;
deserted, she will sit on the ground.

4   On that day seven women
will seize one man, saying,
"We will eat our own bread
and provide our own clothing.
Just let us bear your name.
Take away our disgrace."

On that day the Branch of the Lord will be beautiful and glorious, and the fruit of the land will be the pride and glory of Israel's survivors. Whoever remains in Zion and whoever is left in Jerusalem

will be called holy—all in Jerusalem written in the book of life—when the Lord has washed away
10   the filth of the daughters of Zion and cleansed the bloodguilt from the heart of Jerusalem by a
spirit of judgment and a spirit of burning. Then the LORD will create a cloud of smoke by day and
a glowing flame of fire by night over the entire site of Mount Zion and over its assemblies. For
there will be a canopy over all the glory, and there will be a shelter for shade from heat by day and
a refuge and shelter from storm and rain.

5

     I will sing about the one I love,
     a song about my loved one's vineyard:
     The one I love had a vineyard
     on a very fertile hill.
     He broke up the soil, cleared it of stones,
     and planted it with the finest vines.
     He built a tower in the middle of it
     and even dug out a winepress there.
     He expected it to yield good grapes,
10   but it yielded worthless grapes.

     So now, residents of Jerusalem
     and men of Judah,
     please judge between me
     and my vineyard.
     What more could I have done for my vineyard
     than I did?
     Why, when I expected a yield of good grapes,
     did it yield worthless grapes?
     Now I will tell you
20   what I am about to do to my vineyard:
     I will remove its hedge,
     and it will be consumed;
     I will tear down its wall,
     and it will be trampled.
     I will make it a wasteland.
     It will not be pruned or weeded;
     thorns and briers will grow up.
     I will also give orders to the clouds
     that rain should not fall on it.
30   For the vineyard of the LORD of Armies

is the house of Israel,
and the men of Judah,
the plant he delighted in.
He expected justice
but saw injustice;
he expected righteousness
but heard cries of despair.

Woe to those who add house to house
and join field to field
40 until there is no more room
and you alone are left in the land.

I heard the LORD of Armies say:
Indeed, many houses will become desolate,
grand and lovely ones without inhabitants.
For a ten-acre vineyard will yield
only six gallons of wine,
and ten bushels of seed will yield
only one bushel of grain.

Woe to those who rise early in the morning
50 in pursuit of beer,
who linger into the evening,
inflamed by wine.
At their feasts they have lyre, harp,
tambourine, flute, and wine.
They do not perceive the LORD's actions,
and they do not see the work of his hands.

Therefore my people will go into exile
because they lack knowledge;
her dignitaries are starving,
60 and her masses are parched with thirst.
Therefore Sheol enlarges its throat
and opens wide its enormous jaws,
and down go Zion's dignitaries, her masses,
her crowds, and those who celebrate in her!

Humanity is brought low, each person is humbled,
and haughty eyes are humbled.
But the LORD of Armies is exalted by his justice,
and the holy God demonstrates his holiness through his righteousness.
Lambs will graze
70   as if in their own pastures,
and resident aliens will eat
among the ruins of the rich.

Woe to those who drag iniquity
with cords of deceit
and pull sin along with cart ropes,
to those who say,
"Let him hurry up and do his work quickly
so that we can see it!
Let the plan of the Holy One of Israel take place
80   so that we can know it!"
Woe to those who call evil good
and good evil,
who substitute darkness for light
and light for darkness,
who substitute bitter for sweet
and sweet for bitter.
Woe to those who consider themselves wise
and judge themselves clever.
Woe to those who are heroes at drinking wine,
90   who are champions at pouring beer,
who acquit the guilty for a bribe
and deprive the innocent of justice.

Therefore, as a tongue of fire consumes straw
and as dry grass shrivels in the flame,
so their roots will become like something rotten
and their blossoms will blow away like dust,
for they have rejected
the instruction of the LORD of Armies,
and they have despised
100   the word of the Holy One of Israel.

Therefore the LORD's anger burned against his people.
He raised his hand against them and struck them;
the mountains quaked,
and their corpses were like garbage in the streets.
In all this, his anger has not turned away,
and his hand is still raised to strike.

He raises a signal flag for the distant nations
and whistles for them from the ends of the earth.
Look—how quickly and swiftly they come!
110   None of them grows weary or stumbles;
no one slumbers or sleeps.
No belt is loose
and no sandal strap broken.
Their arrows are sharpened,
and all their bows strung.
Their horses' hooves are like flint;
their chariot wheels are like a whirlwind.
Their roaring is like a lion's;
they roar like young lions;
120   they growl and seize their prey
and carry it off,
and no one can rescue it.
On that day they will roar over it,
like the roaring of the sea.
When one looks at the land,
there will be darkness and distress;
light will be obscured by clouds.

6 In the year that King Uzziah died, I saw the Lord seated on a high and lofty throne, and the hem of his robe filled the temple. Seraphim were standing above him; they each had six wings: with two they covered their faces, with two they covered their feet, and with two they flew. And one called to another:

Holy, holy, holy is the LORD of Armies;
his glory fills the whole earth.

The foundations of the doorways shook at the sound of their voices, and the temple was filled with smoke.

Then I said:

10 Woe is me for I am ruined
    because I am a man of unclean lips
    and live among a people of unclean lips,
    and because my eyes have seen the King,
    the LORD of Armies.

Then one of the seraphim flew to me, and in his hand was a glowing coal that he had taken
from the altar with tongs. He touched my mouth with it and said:
    Now that this has touched your lips,
    your iniquity is removed
    and your sin is atoned for.

20 Then I heard the voice of the Lord asking:
    Who will I send?
    Who will go for us?

I said:
    Here I am. Send me.

And he replied:
    Go! Say to these people:
    Keep listening, but do not understand;
    keep looking, but do not perceive.
    Make the minds of these people dull;
30 deafen their ears and blind their eyes;
    otherwise they might see with their eyes
    and hear with their ears,
    understand with their minds,
    turn back, and be healed.

Then I said, "Until when, Lord?" And he replied:
    Until cities lie in ruins without inhabitants,
    houses are without people,
    the land is ruined and desolate,
    and the LORD drives the people far away,
40 leaving great emptiness in the land.
    Though a tenth will remain in the land,
    it will be burned again.

> Like the terebinth or the oak
> that leaves a stump when felled,
> the holy seed is the stump.

7 This took place during the reign of Ahaz, son of Jotham, son of Uzziah king of Judah: Aram's King Rezin and Israel's King Pekah son of Remaliah went to fight against Jerusalem, but they were not able to conquer it.

When it became known to the house of David that Aram had occupied Ephraim, the heart of Ahaz and the hearts of his people trembled like trees of a forest shaking in the wind.

The LORD said to Isaiah, "Go out with your son Shear-jashub to meet Ahaz at the end of the conduit of the upper pool, by the road to the Launderer's Field. Say to him: Calm down and be quiet. Don't be afraid or cowardly because of these two smoldering sticks, the fierce anger of Rezin and Aram, and the son of Remaliah. For Aram, along with Ephraim and the son of Remaliah,
10 has plotted harm against you. They say, 'Let's go up against Judah, terrorize it, and conquer it for ourselves. Then we can install Tabeel's son as king in it.'"

This is what the Lord GOD says:

> It will not happen; it will not occur.
> The chief city of Aram is Damascus,
> the chief of Damascus is Rezin
> (within sixty-five years
> Ephraim will be too shattered to be a people),
> the chief city of Ephraim is Samaria,
> and the chief of Samaria is the son of Remaliah.
20 > If you do not stand firm in your faith,
> then you will not stand at all.

Then the LORD spoke again to Ahaz: "Ask for a sign from the LORD your God—it can be as deep as Sheol or as high as heaven."

But Ahaz replied, "I will not ask. I will not test the LORD."

Isaiah said, "Listen, house of David! Is it not enough for you to try the patience of men? Will you also try the patience of my God? Therefore, the Lord himself will give you a sign: See, the virgin will conceive, have a son, and name him Immanuel. By the time he learns to reject what is bad and choose what is good, he will be eating curds and honey. For before the boy knows to reject what is bad and choose what is good, the land of the two kings you dread will be abandoned. The
30 LORD will bring on you, your people, and your father's house such a time as has never been since Ephraim separated from Judah: He will bring the king of Assyria."

> On that day
> the LORD will whistle to flies

at the farthest streams of the Nile
and to bees in the land of Assyria.
All of them will come and settle
in the steep ravines, in the clefts of the rocks,
in all the thornbushes, and in all the water holes.

On that day the Lord will use a razor hired from beyond the Euphrates River—the king of
40 Assyria—to shave the hair on your heads, the hair on your legs, and even your beards.
On that day
a man will raise a young cow and two sheep,
and from the abundant milk they give
he will eat curds,
for every survivor in the land will eat curds and honey.

And on that day
every place where there were a thousand vines,
worth a thousand pieces of silver,
will become thorns and briers.
50 A man will go there with bow and arrows
because the whole land will be thorns and briers.
You will not go to all the hills
that were once tilled with a hoe,
for fear of the thorns and briers.
Those hills will be places for oxen to graze
and for sheep to trample.

8 Then the LORD said to me, "Take a large piece of parchment and write on it with an ordinary pen:
Maher-shalal-hash-baz. I have appointed trustworthy witnesses—the priest Uriah and Zechariah
son of Jeberechiah."

I was then intimate with the prophetess, and she conceived and gave birth to a son. The LORD
said to me, "Name him Maher-shalal-hash-baz, for before the boy knows how to call 'Father,'
or 'Mother,' the wealth of Damascus and the spoils of Samaria will be carried off to the king of
Assyria."

The LORD spoke to me again:
Because these people rejected
10 the slowly flowing water of Shiloah
and rejoiced with Rezin
and the son of Remaliah,

the Lord will certainly bring against them
the mighty rushing water of the Euphrates River—
the king of Assyria and all his glory.
It will overflow its channels
and spill over all its banks.
It will pour into Judah,
flood over it, and sweep through,
reaching up to the neck;
and its flooded banks
will fill your entire land, Immanuel!

Band together, peoples, and be broken;
pay attention, all you distant lands;
prepare for war, and be broken;
prepare for war, and be broken.
Devise a plan; it will fail.
Make a prediction; it will not happen.
For God is with us.

For this is what the LORD said to me with great power, to keep me from going the way of this people:
Do not call everything a conspiracy
that these people say is a conspiracy.
Do not fear what they fear;
do not be terrified.
You are to regard only the LORD of Armies as holy.
Only he should be feared;
only he should be held in awe.
He will be a sanctuary;
but for the two houses of Israel,
he will be a stone to stumble over
and a rock to trip over,
and a trap and a snare to the inhabitants of Jerusalem.
Many will stumble over these;
they will fall and be broken;
they will be snared and captured.

Bind up the testimony.
Seal up the instruction among my disciples.

> I will wait for the LORD,
> who is hiding his face from the house of Jacob.
> 50 I will wait for him.

Here I am with the children the LORD has given me to be signs and wonders in Israel from the LORD of Armies who dwells on Mount Zion. When they say to you, "Inquire of the mediums and the spiritists who chirp and mutter," shouldn't a people inquire of their God? Should they inquire of the dead on behalf of the living? Go to God's instruction and testimony! If they do not speak according to this word, there will be no dawn for them.

They will wander through the land, dejected and hungry. When they are famished, they will become enraged, and, looking upward, will curse their king and their God. They will look toward the earth and see only distress, darkness, and the gloom of affliction, and they will be driven into thick darkness.

9 Nevertheless, the gloom of the distressed land will not be like that of the former times when he humbled the land of Zebulun and the land of Naphtali. But in the future he will bring honor to the way of the sea, to the land east of the Jordan, and to Galilee of the nations.

> The people walking in darkness
> have seen a great light;
> a light has dawned
> on those living in the land of darkness.
> You have enlarged the nation
> and increased its joy.
> 10 The people have rejoiced before you
> as they rejoice at harvest time
> and as they rejoice when dividing spoils.
> For you have shattered their oppressive yoke
> and the rod on their shoulders,
> the staff of their oppressor,
> just as you did on the day of Midian.
> For every trampling boot of battle
> and the bloodied garments of war
> will be burned as fuel for the fire.
> 20 For a child will be born for us,
> a son will be given to us,
> and the government will be on his shoulders.
> He will be named
> Wonderful Counselor, Mighty God,

Eternal Father, Prince of Peace.
The dominion will be vast,
and its prosperity will never end.
He will reign on the throne of David
and over his kingdom,
30   to establish and sustain it
with justice and righteousness from now on and forever.
The zeal of the LORD of Armies will accomplish this.

The Lord sent a message against Jacob;
it came against Israel.
All the people—
Ephraim and the inhabitants of Samaria—will know it.
They will say with pride and arrogance,
"The bricks have fallen,
but we will rebuild with cut stones;
40   the sycamores have been cut down,
but we will replace them with cedars."
The LORD has raised up Rezin's adversaries against him
and stirred up his enemies.
Aram from the east and Philistia from the west
have consumed Israel with open mouths.
In all this, his anger has not turned away,
and his hand is still raised to strike.

The people did not turn to him who struck them;
they did not seek the LORD of Armies.
50   So the LORD cut off Israel's head and tail,
palm branch and reed in a single day.
The head is the elder, the honored one;
the tail is the prophet, the one teaching lies.
The leaders of the people mislead them,
and those they mislead are swallowed up.
Therefore the Lord does not rejoice
over Israel's young men
and has no compassion
on its fatherless and widows,
60   for everyone is a godless evildoer,

and every mouth speaks folly.
In all this, his anger has not turned away,
and his hand is still raised to strike.

For wickedness burns like a fire
that consumes thorns and briers
and kindles the forest thickets
so that they go up in a column of smoke.
The land is scorched
by the wrath of the LORD of Armies,
70 and the people are like fuel for the fire.
No one has compassion on his brother.
They carve meat on the right,
but they are still hungry;
they have eaten on the left,
but they are still not satisfied.
Each one eats the flesh of his arm.
Manasseh eats Ephraim,
and Ephraim, Manasseh;
together, both are against Judah.
80 In all this, his anger has not turned away,
and his hand is still raised to strike.

10 Woe to those enacting crooked statutes
and writing oppressive laws
to keep the poor from getting a fair trial
and to deprive the needy among my people of justice,
so that widows can be their spoil
and they can plunder the fatherless.
What will you do on the day of punishment
when devastation comes from far away?
Who will you run to for help?
10 Where will you leave your wealth?
There will be nothing to do
except crouch among the prisoners
or fall among the slain.
In all this, his anger has not turned away,
and his hand is still raised to strike.

Woe to Assyria, the rod of my anger—
the staff in their hands is my wrath.
I will send him against a godless nation;
I will command him to go
against a people destined for my rage,
to take spoils, to plunder,
and to trample them down like clay in the streets.
But this is not what he intends;
this is not what he plans.
It is his intent to destroy
and to cut off many nations.
For he says,
"Aren't all my commanders kings?
Isn't Calno like Carchemish?
Isn't Hamath like Arpad?
Isn't Samaria like Damascus?
As my hand seized the kingdoms of worthless images,
kingdoms whose idols exceeded those of Jerusalem and Samaria,
and as I did to Samaria and its worthless images
will I not also do to Jerusalem and its idols?"

But when the Lord finishes all his work against Mount Zion and Jerusalem, he will say, "I will punish the king of Assyria for his arrogant acts and the proud look in his eyes." For he said:
I have done this by my own strength
and wisdom, for I am clever.
I abolished the borders of nations
and plundered their treasures;
like a mighty warrior, I subjugated the inhabitants.
My hand has reached out, as if into a nest,
to seize the wealth of the nations.
Like one gathering abandoned eggs,
I gathered the whole earth.
No wing fluttered;
no beak opened or chirped.

Does an ax exalt itself
above the one who chops with it?

Does a saw magnify itself
above the one who saws with it?
It would be like a rod waving the ones who lift it!
It would be like a staff lifting the one who isn't wood!
Therefore the Lord God of Armies
will inflict an emaciating disease
on the well-fed of Assyria,
and he will kindle a burning fire
under its glory.
60   Israel's Light will become a fire,
and its Holy One, a flame.
In one day it will burn and consume Assyria's thorns and thistles.
He will completely destroy
the glory of its forests and orchards
as a sickness consumes a person.
The remaining trees of its forest
will be so few in number
that a child could count them.

On that day the remnant of Israel and the survivors of the house of Jacob will no longer depend on
70 the one who struck them, but they will faithfully depend on the Lord, the Holy One of Israel.
   The remnant will return, the remnant of Jacob,
to the Mighty God.
Israel, even if your people were as numerous
as the sand of the sea,
only a remnant of them will return.
Destruction has been decreed;
justice overflows.
For throughout the land
the Lord God of Armies
80   is carrying out a destruction that was decreed.

Therefore, the Lord God of Armies says this: "My people who dwell in Zion, do not fear Assyria, though they strike you with a rod and raise their staff over you as the Egyptians did. In just a little while my wrath will be spent and my anger will turn to their destruction." And the Lord of Armies will brandish a whip against him as he did when he struck Midian at the rock of Oreb; and he will raise his staff over the sea as he did in Egypt.

On that day
his burden will fall from your shoulders,
and his yoke from your neck.
The yoke will be broken because your neck will be too large.
90 Assyria has come to Aiath
and has gone through Migron,
storing their equipment at Michmash.
They crossed over at the ford, saying,
"We will spend the night at Geba."
The people of Ramah are trembling;
those at Gibeah of Saul have fled.
Cry aloud, daughter of Gallim!
Listen, Laishah!
Anathoth is miserable.
100 Madmenah has fled.
The inhabitants of Gebim have sought refuge.
Today the Assyrians will stand at Nob,
shaking their fists at the mountain of Daughter Zion,
the hill of Jerusalem.
Look, the Lord God of Armies
will chop off the branches with terrifying power,
and the tall trees will be cut down,
the high trees felled.
He is clearing the thickets of the forest with an ax,
110 and Lebanon with its majesty will fall.

11 Then a shoot will grow from the stump of Jesse,
and a branch from his roots will bear fruit.
The Spirit of the Lord will rest on him—
a Spirit of wisdom and understanding,
a Spirit of counsel and strength,
a Spirit of knowledge and of the fear of the Lord.
His delight will be in the fear of the Lord.
He will not judge
by what he sees with his eyes,
10 he will not execute justice
by what he hears with his ears,
but he will judge the poor righteously

and execute justice for the oppressed of the land.
He will strike the land
with a scepter from his mouth,
and he will kill the wicked
with a command from his lips.
Righteousness will be a belt around his hips;
faithfulness will be a belt around his waist.
20 The wolf will dwell with the lamb,
and the leopard will lie down with the goat.
The calf, the young lion, and the fattened calf will be together,
and a child will lead them.
The cow and the bear will graze,
their young ones will lie down together,
and the lion will eat straw like cattle.
An infant will play beside the cobra's pit,
and a toddler will put his hand into a snake's den.
They will not harm or destroy each other
30 on my entire holy mountain,
for the land will be as full
of the knowledge of the LORD
as the sea is filled with water.

On that day the root of Jesse
will stand as a banner for the peoples.
The nations will look to him for guidance,
and his resting place will be glorious.

On that day the Lord will extend his hand a second time to recover the remnant of his people
who survive—from Assyria, Egypt, Pathros, Cush, Elam, Shinar, Hamath, and the coasts and
40 islands of the west.
He will lift up a banner for the nations
and gather the dispersed of Israel;
he will collect the scattered of Judah
from the four corners of the earth.
Ephraim's envy will cease;
Judah's harassing will end.
Ephraim will no longer be envious of Judah,
and Judah will not harass Ephraim.

But they will swoop down
50   on the Philistine flank to the west.
Together they will plunder the people of the east.
They will extend their power over Edom and Moab,
and the Ammonites will be their subjects.
The LORD will divide the Gulf of Suez.
He will wave his hand over the Euphrates
with his mighty wind
and will split it into seven streams,
letting people walk through on foot.
There will be a highway for the remnant of his people
60   who will survive from Assyria,
as there was for Israel
when they came up from the land of Egypt.

12   On that day you will say:
"I will give thanks to you, LORD,
although you were angry with me.
Your anger has turned away,
and you have comforted me.
Indeed, God is my salvation;
I will trust him and not be afraid,
for the LORD, the LORD himself,
is my strength and my song.
10   He has become my salvation."
You will joyfully draw water
from the springs of salvation,
and on that day you will say,
"Give thanks to the LORD; proclaim his name!
Make his works known among the peoples.
Declare that his name is exalted.
Sing to the LORD, for he has done glorious things.
Let this be known throughout the earth.
Cry out and sing, citizen of Zion,
20   for the Holy One of Israel is among you
in his greatness."

13 A pronouncement concerning Babylon that Isaiah son of Amoz saw:

> Lift up a banner on a barren mountain.
> Call out to them.
> Signal with your hand, and they will go
> through the gates of the nobles.
> I have commanded my consecrated ones;
> yes, I have called my warriors,
> who celebrate my triumph,
> to execute my wrath.
> Listen, a commotion on the mountains,
> like that of a mighty people!
> Listen, an uproar among the kingdoms,
> like nations being gathered together!
> The Lord of Armies is mobilizing an army for war.
> They are coming from a distant land,
> from the farthest horizon—
> the Lord and the weapons of his wrath—
> to destroy the whole country.

> Wail! For the day of the Lord is near.
> It will come as destruction from the Almighty.
> Therefore everyone's hands will become weak,
> and every man will lose heart.
> They will be horrified;
> pain and agony will seize them;
> they will be in anguish like a woman in labor.
> They will look at each other,
> their faces flushed with fear.
> Look, the day of the Lord is coming—
> cruel, with fury and burning anger—
> to make the earth a desolation
> and to destroy its sinners.
> Indeed, the stars of the sky and its constellations
> will not give their light.
> The sun will be dark when it rises,
> and the moon will not shine.
> I will punish the world for its evil,
> and wicked people for their iniquities.

I will put an end to the pride of the arrogant
and humiliate the insolence of tyrants.
40 I will make a human more scarce than fine gold,
and mankind more rare than the gold of Ophir.
Therefore I will make the heavens tremble,
and the earth will shake from its foundations
at the wrath of the LORD of Armies,
on the day of his burning anger.
Like wandering gazelles
and like sheep without a shepherd,
each one will turn to his own people,
each one will flee to his own land.
50 Whoever is found will be stabbed,
and whoever is caught will die by the sword.
Their children will be dashed to pieces before their eyes;
their houses will be looted,
and their wives raped.
Look! I am stirring up the Medes against them,
who cannot be bought off with silver
and who have no desire for gold.
Their bows will cut young men to pieces.
They will have no compassion on offspring;
60 they will not look with pity on children.

And Babylon, the jewel of the kingdoms,
the glory of the pride of the Chaldeans,
will be like Sodom and Gomorrah
when God overthrew them.
It will never be inhabited
or lived in from generation to generation;
a nomad will not pitch his tent there,
and shepherds will not let their flocks rest there.
But desert creatures will lie down there,
70 and owls will fill the houses.
Ostriches will dwell there,
and wild goats will leap about.
Hyenas will howl in the fortresses,
and jackals, in the luxurious palaces.

Babylon's time is almost up;
her days are almost over.

14 For the LORD will have compassion on Jacob and will choose Israel again. He will settle them on their own land. The resident alien will join them and be united with the house of Jacob. The nations will escort Israel and bring it to its homeland. Then the house of Israel will possess them as male and female slaves in the LORD's land. They will make captives of their captors and will rule over their oppressors.

When the LORD gives you rest from your pain, torment, and the hard labor you were forced to do, you will sing this song of contempt about the king of Babylon and say:

How the oppressor has quieted down,
and how the raging has become quiet!
The LORD has broken the staff of the wicked,
the scepter of the rulers.
It struck the peoples in anger
with unceasing blows.
It subdued the nations in rage
with relentless persecution.
The whole earth is calm and at rest;
people shout with a ringing cry.
Even the cypresses and the cedars of Lebanon
rejoice over you:
"Since you have been laid low,
no lumberjack has come against us."

Sheol below is eager to greet your coming,
stirring up the spirits of the departed for you—
all the rulers of the earth—
making all the kings of the nations
rise from their thrones.
They all respond to you, saying,
"You too have become as weak as we are;
you have become like us!
Your splendor has been brought down to Sheol,
along with the music of your harps.
Maggots are spread out under you,
and worms cover you."

Shining morning star,
how you have fallen from the heavens!
You destroyer of nations,
you have been cut down to the ground.
You said to yourself,
"I will ascend to the heavens;
I will set up my throne
40   above the stars of God.
I will sit on the mount of the gods' assembly,
in the remotest parts of the North.
I will ascend above the highest clouds;
I will make myself like the Most High."
But you will be brought down to Sheol
into the deepest regions of the Pit.

Those who see you will stare at you;
they will look closely at you:
"Is this the man who caused the earth to tremble,
50   who shook the kingdoms,
who turned the world into a wilderness,
who destroyed its cities
and would not release the prisoners to return home?"
All the kings of the nations
lie in splendor, each in his own tomb.
But you are thrown out without a grave,
like a worthless branch,
covered by those slain with the sword
and dumped into a rocky pit like a trampled corpse.
60   You will not join them in burial,
because you destroyed your land
and slaughtered your own people.
The offspring of evildoers
will never be mentioned again.
Prepare a place of slaughter for his sons,
because of the iniquity of their ancestors.
They will never rise up to possess a land
or fill the surface of the earth with cities.

"I will rise up against them"—this is the declaration of the Lord of Armies—"and I will cut off from
70 Babylon her reputation, remnant, offspring, and posterity"—this is the Lord's declaration. "I will make
her a swampland and a region for herons, and I will sweep her away with the broom of destruction."
This is the declaration of the Lord of Armies.

The Lord of Armies has sworn:
    As I have purposed, so it will be;
    as I have planned it, so it will happen.
    I will break Assyria in my land;
    I will tread him down on my mountain.
    Then his yoke will be taken from them,
    and his burden will be removed from their shoulders.
80   This is the plan prepared
    for the whole earth,
    and this is the hand stretched out
    against all the nations.
    The Lord of Armies himself has planned it;
    therefore, who can stand in its way?
    It is his hand that is outstretched,
    so who can turn it back?

In the year that King Ahaz died, this pronouncement came:
    Don't rejoice, all of you in Philistia,
90   because the rod of the one who struck you is broken.
    For a viper will come from the root of a snake,
    and from its egg comes a flying serpent.
    Then the firstborn of the poor will be well fed,
    and the impoverished will lie down in safety,
    but I will kill your root with hunger,
    and your remnant will be slain.
    Wail, you gates! Cry out, city!
    Tremble with fear, all Philistia!
    For a cloud of dust is coming from the north,
100   and there is no one missing from the invader's ranks.
    What answer will be given to the messengers from that nation?
    The Lord has founded Zion,
    and his oppressed people find refuge in her.

15   A pronouncement concerning Moab:

> Ar in Moab is devastated,
> destroyed in a night.
> Kir in Moab is devastated,
> destroyed in a night.
> Dibon went up to its temple
> to weep at its high places.
> Moab wails on Nebo and at Medeba.
> Every head is shaved;
> every beard is chopped short.
> In its streets they wear sackcloth;
> on its rooftops and in its public squares everyone wails,
> falling down and weeping.
> Heshbon and Elealeh cry out;
> their voices are heard as far away as Jahaz.
> Therefore the soldiers of Moab cry out,
> and they tremble.
> My heart cries out over Moab,
> whose fugitives flee as far as Zoar,
> to Eglath-shelishiyah;
> they go up the Ascent of Luhith weeping;
> they raise a cry of destruction
> on the road to Horonaim.
> The Waters of Nimrim are desolate;
> the grass is withered, the foliage is gone,
> and the vegetation has vanished.
> So they carry their wealth and belongings
> over the Wadi of the Willows.
> For their cry echoes
> throughout the territory of Moab.
> Their wailing reaches Eglaim;
> their wailing reaches Beer-elim.
> The Waters of Dibon are full of blood,
> but I will bring on Dibon even more than this—
> a lion for those who escape from Moab,
> and for the survivors in the land.

16 Send lambs to the ruler of the land,
from Sela in the desert
to the mountain of Daughter Zion.
Like a bird fleeing,
forced from the nest,
the daughters of Moab
will be at the fords of the Arnon.

Give us counsel and make a decision.
Shelter us at noonday
10 with shade that is as dark as night.
Hide the refugees;
do not betray the one who flees.
Let my refugees stay with you;
be a refuge for Moab from the aggressor.

When the oppressor has gone,
destruction has ended,
and marauders have vanished from the land,
a throne will be established in love,
and one will sit on it faithfully
20 in the tent of David,
judging and pursuing what is right,
quick to execute justice.

We have heard of Moab's pride—
how very proud he is—
his haughtiness, his pride, his arrogance,
and his empty boasting.
Therefore let Moab wail;
let every one of them wail for Moab.
You who are completely devastated, mourn
30 for the raisin cakes of Kir-hareseth.
For Heshbon's terraced vineyards
and the grapevines of Sibmah have withered.
The rulers of the nations
have trampled its choice vines
that reached as far as Jazer

and spread to the desert.
Their shoots spread out
and reached the sea.
So I join with Jazer
40 to weep for the vines of Sibmah;
I drench Heshbon and Elealeh with my tears.
Triumphant shouts have fallen silent
over your summer fruit and your harvest.
Joy and rejoicing have been removed from the orchard;
no one is singing or shouting for joy in the vineyards.
No one tramples grapes in the winepresses.
I have put an end to the shouting.
Therefore I moan like the sound of a lyre for Moab,
as does my innermost being for Kir-heres.
50 When Moab appears
and tires himself out on the high place
and comes to his sanctuary to pray,
it will do him no good.

This is the message that the Lord previously announced about Moab. And now the Lord says, "In three years, as a hired worker counts years, Moab's splendor will become an object of contempt, in spite of a very large population. And those who are left will be few and weak."

17 A pronouncement concerning Damascus:
Look, Damascus is no longer a city.
It has become a ruined heap.
The cities of Aroer are abandoned;
they will be places for flocks.
They will lie down without fear.
The fortress disappears from Ephraim,
and a kingdom from Damascus.
The remnant of Aram will be
10 like the splendor of the Israelites.
This is the declaration of the Lord of Armies.

On that day
the splendor of Jacob will fade,
and his healthy body will become emaciated.

It will be as if a reaper had gathered standing grain—
his arm harvesting the heads of grain—
and as if one had gleaned heads of grain
in Rephaim Valley.
Only gleanings will be left in Israel,
20   as if an olive tree had been beaten—
two or three olives at the very top of the tree,
four or five on its fruitful branches.
This is the declaration of the Lord,
the God of Israel.

On that day people will look to their Maker and will turn their eyes to the Holy One of Israel. They will not look to the altars they made with their hands or to the Asherahs and shrines they made with their fingers.

On that day their strong cities will be
like the abandoned woods and mountaintops
30   that were abandoned because of the Israelites;
there will be desolation.
For you have forgotten the God of your salvation,
and you have failed to remember
the rock of your strength;
therefore you will plant beautiful plants
and set out cuttings from exotic vines.
On the day that you plant,
you will help them to grow,
and in the morning
40   you will help your seed to sprout,
but the harvest will vanish
on the day of disease and incurable pain.

Ah! The roar of many peoples—
they roar like the roaring of the seas.
The raging of the nations—
they rage like the rumble of rushing water.
The nations rage like the rumble of a huge torrent.
He rebukes them, and they flee far away,
driven before the wind like chaff on the hills
50   and like tumbleweeds before a gale.

In the evening—sudden terror!
Before morning—it is gone!
This is the fate of those who plunder us
and the lot of those who ravage us.

18   Woe to the land of buzzing insect wings
beyond the rivers of Cush,
which sends envoys by sea,
in reed vessels over the water.

Go, swift messengers,
to a nation tall and smooth-skinned,
to a people feared far and near,
a powerful nation with a strange language,
whose land is divided by rivers.
10   All you inhabitants of the world
and you who live on the earth,
when a banner is raised on the mountains, look!
When a ram's horn sounds, listen!

For the LORD said to me:
I will quietly look out from my place,
like shimmering heat in sunshine,
like a rain cloud in harvest heat.
For before the harvest, when the blossoming is over
and the blossom becomes a ripening grape,
20   he will cut off the shoots with a pruning knife,
and tear away and remove the branches.
They will all be left for the birds of prey on the hills
and for the wild animals of the land.
The birds of prey will spend the summer feeding on them,
and all the wild animals the winter.

At that time a gift will be brought to the LORD of Armies from a people tall and smooth-skinned, a people feared far and near, a powerful nation with a strange language, whose land is divided by rivers—to Mount Zion, the place of the name of the LORD of Armies.

19 A pronouncement concerning Egypt:

Look, the LORD rides on a swift cloud
and is coming to Egypt.
Egypt's worthless idols will tremble before him,
and Egypt will lose heart.
I will provoke Egyptians against Egyptians;
each will fight against his brother
and each against his friend,
city against city, kingdom against kingdom.
Egypt's spirit will be disturbed within it,
and I will frustrate its plans.
Then they will inquire of worthless idols, ghosts,
mediums, and spiritists.
I will hand over Egypt to harsh masters,
and a strong king will rule it.
This is the declaration of the Lord GOD of Armies.

The water of the sea will dry up,
and the river will be parched and dry.
The channels will stink;
they will dwindle, and Egypt's canals will be parched.
Reed and rush will wilt.
The reeds by the Nile, by the mouth of the river,
and all the cultivated areas of the Nile
will wither, blow away, and vanish.
Then the fishermen will mourn.
All those who cast hooks into the Nile will lament,
and those who spread nets on the water will give up.
Those who work with flax will be dismayed;
those combing it and weaving linen will turn pale.
Egypt's weavers will be dejected;
all her wage earners will be demoralized.

The princes of Zoan are complete fools;
Pharaoh's wisest advisers give stupid advice!
How can you say to Pharaoh,
"I am one of the wise,
a student of eastern kings"?

Where then are your wise men?
Let them tell you and reveal
what the Lord of Armies has planned against Egypt.

40 The princes of Zoan have been fools;
the princes of Memphis are deceived.
Her tribal chieftains have led Egypt astray.
The Lord has mixed within her a spirit of confusion.
The leaders have made Egypt stagger in all she does,
as a drunkard staggers in his vomit.
No head or tail, palm or reed,
will be able to do anything for Egypt.

On that day Egypt will be like women and will tremble with fear because of the threatening hand of the Lord of Armies when he raises it against them. The land of Judah will terrify Egypt; whenever 50 Judah is mentioned, Egypt will tremble because of what the Lord of Armies has planned against it.

On that day five cities in the land of Egypt will speak the language of Canaan and swear loyalty to the Lord of Armies. One of the cities will be called the City of the Sun.

On that day there will be an altar to the Lord in the center of the land of Egypt and a pillar to the Lord near her border. It will be a sign and witness to the Lord of Armies in the land of Egypt. When they cry out to the Lord because of their oppressors, he will send them a savior and leader, and he will rescue them. The Lord will make himself known to Egypt, and Egypt will know the Lord on that day. They will offer sacrifices and offerings; they will make vows to the Lord and fulfill them. The Lord will strike Egypt, striking and healing. Then they will turn to the Lord, and he will be receptive to their prayers and heal them.

60 On that day there will be a highway from Egypt to Assyria. Assyria will go to Egypt, Egypt to Assyria, and Egypt will worship with Assyria.

On that day Israel will form a triple alliance with Egypt and Assyria—a blessing within the land. The Lord of Armies will bless them, saying, "Egypt my people, Assyria my handiwork, and Israel my inheritance are blessed."

20 In the year that the chief commander, sent by King Sargon of Assyria, came to Ashdod and attacked and captured it—during that time the Lord had spoken through Isaiah son of Amoz, saying, "Go, take off your sackcloth from your waist and remove the sandals from your feet," and he did that, going stripped and barefoot—the Lord said, "As my servant Isaiah has gone stripped and barefoot three years as a sign and omen against Egypt and Cush, so the king of Assyria will lead the captives of Egypt and the exiles of Cush, young and old alike, stripped and barefoot, with bared buttocks—to Egypt's shame. Those who made Cush their hope and Egypt their boast will be dismayed and ashamed. And the inhabitants of this coastland will say on that day, 'Look, this is

what has happened to those we relied on and fled to for help to rescue us from the king of Assyria!
10 Now, how will we escape?'"

21 A pronouncement concerning the desert by the sea:
Like storms that pass over the Negev,
it comes from the desert, from the land of terror.
A troubling vision is declared to me:
"The treacherous one acts treacherously,
and the destroyer destroys.
Advance, Elam! Lay siege, you Medes!
I will put an end to all the groaning."

Therefore I am filled with anguish.
10 Pain grips me, like the pain of a woman in labor.
I am too perplexed to hear,
too dismayed to see.
My heart staggers;
horror terrifies me.
He has turned my last glimmer of hope
into sheer terror.
Prepare a table, and spread out a carpet!
Eat and drink!
Rise up, you princes, and oil the shields!

20 For the Lord has said to me,
"Go, post a lookout;
let him report what he sees.
When he sees riders—
pairs of horsemen,
riders on donkeys,
riders on camels—
he must pay close attention."
Then the lookout reported,
"Lord, I stand on the watchtower all day,
30 and I stay at my post all night.
Look, riders come—
horsemen in pairs."
And he answered, saying,

"Babylon has fallen, has fallen.
All the images of her gods
have been shattered on the ground."

My people who have been crushed
on the threshing floor,
I have declared to you
what I have heard from the LORD of Armies,
the God of Israel.

A pronouncement concerning Dumah:
One calls to me from Seir,
"Watchman, what is left of the night?
Watchman, what is left of the night?"
The watchman said,
"Morning has come, and also night.
If you want to ask, ask!
Come back again."

A pronouncement concerning Arabia:
In the desert brush
you will camp for the night,
you caravans of Dedanites.
Bring water for the thirsty.
The inhabitants of the land of Tema
meet the refugees with food.
For they have fled from swords,
from the drawn sword,
from the bow that is strung,
and from the stress of battle.

For the Lord said this to me: "Within one year, as a hired worker counts years, all the glory of
Kedar will be gone. The remaining Kedarite archers will be few in number." For the LORD, the
God of Israel, has spoken.

22 A pronouncement concerning the Valley of Vision:
What's the matter with you?
Why have all of you gone up to the rooftops?

The noisy city, the jubilant town,
is filled with celebration.
Your dead did not die by the sword;
they were not killed in battle.
All your rulers have fled together,
captured without a bow.
10   All your fugitives were captured together;
they had fled far away.
Therefore I said,
"Look away from me! Let me weep bitterly!
Do not try to comfort me
about the destruction of my dear people."
For the Lord GOD of Armies
had a day of tumult, trampling, and confusion
in the Valley of Vision—
people shouting and crying to the mountains;
20   Elam took up a quiver
with chariots and horsemen,
and Kir uncovered the shield.
Your best valleys were full of chariots,
and horsemen were positioned at the city gates.
He removed the defenses of Judah.

On that day you looked to the weapons in the House of the Forest. You saw that there were many breaches in the walls of the city of David. You collected water from the lower pool. You counted the houses of Jerusalem so that you could tear them down to fortify the wall. You made a reservoir between the walls for the water of the ancient pool, but you did not look to the one who
30   made it, or consider the one who created it long ago.

On that day the Lord GOD of Armies
called for weeping, for wailing, for shaven heads,
and for the wearing of sackcloth.
But look: joy and gladness,
butchering of cattle, slaughtering of sheep and goats,
eating of meat, and drinking of wine—
"Let's eat and drink, for tomorrow we die!"
The LORD of Armies has directly revealed to me:
"This iniquity will not be wiped out for you people as long as you live."
40   The Lord GOD of Armies has spoken.

The Lord God of Armies said, "Go to Shebna, that steward who is in charge of the palace, and say to him: What are you doing here? Who authorized you to carve out a tomb for yourself here, carving your tomb on the height and cutting a resting place for yourself out of rock? Look, you strong man! The Lord is about to shake you violently. He will take hold of you, wind you up into a ball, and sling you into a wide land. There you will die, and there your glorious chariots will be—a disgrace to the house of your lord. I will remove you from your office; you will be ousted from your position.

"On that day I will call for my servant, Eliakim son of Hilkiah. I will clothe him with your robe and tie your sash around him. I will hand your authority over to him, and he will be like a father to the inhabitants of Jerusalem and to the house of Judah. I will place the key of the house of David on his shoulder; what he opens, no one can close; what he closes, no one can open. I will drive him, like a peg, into a firm place. He will be a throne of honor for his father's family. They will hang on him all the glory of his father's family: the descendants and the offshoots—all the small vessels, from bowls to every kind of jar. On that day"—the declaration of the Lord of Armies—"the peg that was driven into a firm place will give way, be cut off, and fall, and the load on it will be destroyed." Indeed, the Lord has spoken.

23 A pronouncement concerning Tyre:

Wail, ships of Tarshish,
for your haven has been destroyed.
Word has reached them from the land of Cyprus.
Mourn, inhabitants of the coastland,
you merchants of Sidon;
your agents have crossed the sea
over deep water.
Tyre's revenue was the grain from Shihor—
the harvest of the Nile.
She was the merchant among the nations.
Be ashamed, Sidon, the stronghold of the sea,
for the sea has spoken:
"I have not been in labor or given birth.
I have not raised young men
or brought up young women."
When the news reaches Egypt,
they will be in anguish over the news about Tyre.
Cross over to Tarshish;
wail, inhabitants of the coastland!
Is this your jubilant city,

whose origin was in ancient times,
whose feet have taken her
to reside far away?
Who planned this against Tyre,
the bestower of crowns,
whose traders are princes,
whose merchants are the honored ones of the earth?
The Lord of Armies planned it,
30   to desecrate all its glorious beauty,
to disgrace all the honored ones of the earth.
Overflow your land like the Nile, daughter of Tarshish;
there is no longer anything to restrain you.
He stretched out his hand over the sea;
he made kingdoms tremble.
The Lord has commanded
that the Canaanite fortresses be destroyed.
He said,
"You will not celebrate anymore,
40   ravished young woman, daughter of Sidon.
Get up and cross over to Cyprus—
even there you will have no rest!"
Look at the land of the Chaldeans—
a people who no longer exist.
Assyria destined it for desert creatures.
They set up their siege towers
and stripped its palaces.
They made it a ruin.
Wail, ships of Tarshish,
50   because your fortress is destroyed!

On that day Tyre will be forgotten for seventy years—the life span of one king. At the end of seventy years, what the song says about the prostitute will happen to Tyre:
Pick up your lyre,
stroll through the city,
you forgotten prostitute.
Play skillfully,
sing many a song
so that you will be remembered.

And at the end of the seventy years, the LORD will restore Tyre and she will go back into
60 business, prostituting herself with all the kingdoms of the world throughout the earth. But her
profits and wages will be dedicated to the LORD. They will not be stored or saved, for her profit will
go to those who live in the LORD's presence, to provide them with ample food and sacred clothing.

24   Look, the LORD is stripping the earth bare
      and making it desolate.
      He will twist its surface and scatter its inhabitants:
      people and priest alike,
      servant and master,
      female servant and mistress,
      buyer and seller,
      lender and borrower,
      creditor and debtor.
10   The earth will be stripped completely bare
      and will be totally plundered,
      for the LORD has spoken this message.

      The earth mourns and withers;
      the world wastes away and withers;
      the exalted people of the earth waste away.
      The earth is polluted by its inhabitants,
      for they have transgressed teachings,
      overstepped decrees,
      and broken the permanent covenant.
20   Therefore a curse has consumed the earth,
      and its inhabitants have become guilty;
      the earth's inhabitants have been burned,
      and only a few survive.
      The new wine mourns;
      the vine withers.
      All the carousers now groan.
      The joyful tambourines have ceased.
      The noise of the jubilant has stopped.
      The joyful lyre has ceased.
30   They no longer sing and drink wine;
      beer is bitter to those who drink it.

The city of chaos is shattered;
every house is closed to entry.
In the streets they cry for wine.
All joy grows dark;
earth's rejoicing goes into exile.
Only desolation remains in the city;
its gate has collapsed in ruins.
For this is how it will be on earth
40   among the nations:
like a harvested olive tree,
like a gleaning after a grape harvest.

They raise their voices, they sing out;
they proclaim in the west
the majesty of the Lord.
Therefore, in the east honor the Lord!
In the coasts and islands of the west
honor the name of the Lord,
the God of Israel.
50   From the ends of the earth we hear songs:
The Splendor of the Righteous One.

But I said, "I waste away! I waste away!
Woe is me."
The treacherous act treacherously;
the treacherous deal very treacherously.

Panic, pit, and trap await you
who dwell on the earth.
Whoever flees at the sound of panic
will fall into a pit,
60   and whoever escapes from the pit
will be caught in a trap.
For the floodgates on high are opened,
and the foundations of the earth are shaken.
The earth is completely devastated;
the earth is split open;
the earth is violently shaken.

The earth staggers like a drunkard
and sways like a hut.
Earth's rebellion weighs it down,
70   and it falls, never to rise again.

On that day the LORD will punish
the army of the heights in the heights
and the kings of the ground on the ground.
They will be gathered together
like prisoners in a pit.
They will be confined to a dungeon;
after many days they will be punished.
The moon will be put to shame
and the sun disgraced,
80   because the LORD of Armies will reign as king
on Mount Zion in Jerusalem,
and he will display his glory
in the presence of his elders.

25   LORD, you are my God;
I will exalt you. I will praise your name,
for you have accomplished wonders,
plans formed long ago, with perfect faithfulness.
For you have turned the city into a pile of rocks,
a fortified city, into ruins;
the fortress of barbarians is no longer a city;
it will never be rebuilt.
Therefore, a strong people will honor you.
10   The cities of violent nations will fear you.
For you have been a stronghold for the poor person,
a stronghold for the needy in his distress,
a refuge from storms and a shade from heat.
When the breath of the violent
is like a storm against a wall,
like heat in a dry land,
you will subdue the uproar of barbarians.
As the shade of a cloud cools the heat of the day,
so he will silence the song of the violent.

20 On this mountain,
    the Lord of Armies will prepare for all the peoples a feast of choice meat,
    a feast with aged wine, prime cuts of choice meat, fine vintage wine.
    On this mountain
    he will swallow up the burial shroud,
    the shroud over all the peoples,
    the sheet covering all the nations.
    When he has swallowed up death once and for all,
    the Lord God will wipe away the tears
    from every face
30 and remove his people's disgrace
    from the whole earth,
    for the Lord has spoken.

    On that day it will be said,
    "Look, this is our God;
    we have waited for him, and he has saved us.
    This is the Lord; we have waited for him.
    Let's rejoice and be glad in his salvation."
    For the Lord's power will rest on this mountain.

    But Moab will be trampled in his place
40 as straw is trampled in a dung pile.
    He will spread out his arms in the middle of it,
    as a swimmer spreads out his arms to swim.
    His pride will be brought low,
    along with the trickery of his hands.
    The high-walled fortress will be brought down,
    thrown to the ground, to the dust.

26 On that day this song will be sung in the land of Judah:
    We have a strong city.
    Salvation is established as walls and ramparts.
    Open the gates
    so a righteous nation can come in—
    one that remains faithful.
    You will keep the mind that is dependent on you

in perfect peace,
for it is trusting in you.
10   Trust in the LORD forever,
because in the LORD, the LORD himself, is an everlasting rock!
For he has humbled those who live in lofty places—
an inaccessible city.
He brings it down; he brings it down to the ground;
he throws it to the dust.
Feet trample it,
the feet of the humble,
the steps of the poor.

The path of the righteous is level;
20   you clear a straight path for the righteous.
Yes, LORD, we wait for you
in the path of your judgments.
Our desire is for your name and renown.
I long for you in the night;
yes, my spirit within me diligently seeks you,
for when your judgments are in the land,
the inhabitants of the world will learn righteousness.
But if the wicked man is shown favor,
he does not learn righteousness.
30   In a righteous land he acts unjustly
and does not see the majesty of the LORD.

LORD, your hand is lifted up to take action,
but they do not see it.
Let them see your zeal for your people
and be put to shame.
Let fire consume your adversaries.
LORD, you will establish peace for us,
for you have also done all our work for us.
LORD our God, lords other than you have owned us,
40   but we remember your name alone.

The dead do not live;
departed spirits do not rise up.

Indeed, you have punished and destroyed them;
you have wiped out all memory of them.
You have added to the nation, LORD.
You have added to the nation; you are honored.
You have expanded all the borders of the land.
LORD, they went to you in their distress;
they poured out whispered prayers
50   because your discipline fell on them.
As a pregnant woman about to give birth
writhes and cries out in her pains,
so we were before you, LORD.
We became pregnant, we writhed in pain;
we gave birth to wind.
We have won no victories on earth,
and the earth's inhabitants have not fallen.

Your dead will live; their bodies will rise.
Awake and sing, you who dwell in the dust!
60   For you will be covered with the morning dew,
and the earth will bring out the departed spirits.

Go, my people, enter your rooms
and close your doors behind you.
Hide for a little while until the wrath has passed.
For look, the LORD is coming from his place
to punish the inhabitants of the earth for their iniquity.
The earth will reveal the blood shed on it
and will no longer conceal her slain.

27 On that day the LORD with his relentless, large, strong sword will bring judgment on Leviathan, the fleeing serpent—Leviathan, the twisting serpent. He will slay the monster that is in the sea.

On that day
sing about a desirable vineyard:
I am the LORD, who watches over it
to water it regularly.
So that no one disturbs it,
I watch over it night and day.

I am not angry.

10   If only there were thorns and briers for me to battle,

I would trample them

and burn them to the ground.

Or let it take hold of my strength;

let it make peace with me—

make peace with me.

In days to come, Jacob will take root.

Israel will blossom and bloom

and fill the whole world with fruit.

Did the LORD strike Israel

20   as he struck the one who struck Israel?

Was Israel killed like those killed by the LORD?

You disputed with Israel

by banishing and driving her away.

He removed her with his severe storm

on the day of the east wind.

Therefore Jacob's iniquity will be atoned for in this way,

and the result of the removal of his sin will be this:

when he makes all the altar stones

like crushed bits of chalk,

30   no Asherah poles or incense altars will remain standing.

For the fortified city will be desolate,

pastures deserted and abandoned like a wilderness.

Calves will graze there,

and there they will spread out and strip its branches.

When its branches dry out, they will be broken off.

Women will come and make fires with them,

for they are not a people with understanding.

Therefore their Maker will not have compassion on them,

and their Creator will not be gracious to them.

40   On that day

the LORD will thresh grain from the Euphrates River

as far as the Wadi of Egypt,

and you Israelites will be gathered one by one.

On that day

a great ram's horn will be blown,
and those lost in the land of Assyria will come,
as well as those dispersed in the land of Egypt;
and they will worship the LORD
at Jerusalem on the holy mountain.

28   Woe to the majestic crown of Ephraim's drunkards,
and to the fading flower of its beautiful splendor,
which is on the summit above the rich valley.
Woe to those overcome with wine.
Look, the Lord has a strong and mighty one—
like a devastating hail storm,
like a storm with strong flooding water.
He will bring it across the land with his hand.
The majestic crown of Ephraim's drunkards
10   will be trampled underfoot.
The fading flower of his beautiful splendor,
which is on the summit above the rich valley,
will be like a ripe fig before the summer harvest.
Whoever sees it will swallow it
while it is still in his hand.
On that day
the LORD of Armies will become a crown of beauty
and a diadem of splendor
to the remnant of his people,
20   a spirit of justice
to the one who sits in judgment,
and strength
to those who repel attacks at the city gate.

Even these stagger because of wine
and stumble under the influence of beer:
Priest and prophet stagger because of beer.
They are confused by wine.
They stumble because of beer.
They are muddled in their visions.
30   They stumble in their judgments.
Indeed, all their tables are covered with vomit;

there is no place without a stench.
Who is he trying to teach?
Who is he trying to instruct?
Infants just weaned from milk?
Babies removed from the breast?
"Law after law, law after law,
line after line, line after line,
a little here, a little there."
40   For he will speak to this people
with stammering speech
and in a foreign language.
He had said to them,
"This is the place of rest;
let the weary rest;
this is the place of repose."
But they would not listen.

The word of the LORD will come to them:
"Law after law, law after law,
50   line after line, line after line,
a little here, a little there,"
so they go stumbling backward,
to be broken, trapped, and captured.

Therefore hear the word of the LORD, you scoffers
who rule this people in Jerusalem.
For you said, "We have made a covenant with Death,
and we have an agreement with Sheol;
when the overwhelming catastrophe passes through,
it will not touch us,
60   because we have made falsehood our refuge
and have hidden behind treachery."
Therefore the Lord GOD said:
"Look, I have laid a stone in Zion,
a tested stone,
a precious cornerstone, a sure foundation;
the one who believes will be unshakable.
And I will make justice the measuring line

and righteousness the mason's level."
Hail will sweep away the false refuge,
70   and water will flood your hiding place.
Your covenant with Death will be dissolved,
and your agreement with Sheol will not last.
When the overwhelming catastrophe passes through,
you will be trampled.
Every time it passes through,
it will carry you away;
it will pass through every morning—
every day and every night.
Only terror will cause you
80   to understand the message.
Indeed, the bed is too short to stretch out on,
and its cover too small to wrap up in.
For the LORD will rise up as he did at Mount Perazim.
He will rise in wrath, as at the Valley of Gibeon,
to do his work, his unexpected work,
and to perform his task, his unfamiliar task.
So now, do not scoff,
or your shackles will become stronger.
Indeed, I have heard from the Lord GOD of Armies
90   a decree of destruction for the whole land.

Listen and hear my voice.
Pay attention and hear what I say.
Does the plowman plow every day to plant seed?
Does he continuously break up and cultivate the soil?
When he has leveled its surface,
does he not then scatter black cumin and sow cumin?
He plants wheat in rows and barley in plots,
with spelt as their border.
His God teaches him order;
100   he instructs him.
Certainly black cumin is not threshed
with a threshing board,
and a cart wheel is not rolled over the cumin.
But black cumin is beaten out with a stick,

and cumin with a rod.
Bread grain is crushed,
but is not threshed endlessly.
Though the wheel of the farmer's cart rumbles,
his horses do not crush it.
110 This also comes from the LORD of Armies.
He gives wondrous advice;
he gives great wisdom.

29 Woe to Ariel, Ariel,
the city where David camped!
Continue year after year;
let the festivals recur.
I will oppress Ariel,
and there will be mourning and crying,
and she will be to me like an Ariel.
I will camp in a circle around you;
I will besiege you with earth ramps,
10 and I will set up my siege towers against you.
You will be brought down;
you will speak from the ground,
and your words will come from low in the dust.
Your voice will be like that of a spirit from the ground;
your speech will whisper from the dust.

Your many foes will be like fine dust,
and many of the ruthless, like blowing chaff.
Then suddenly, in an instant,
you will be punished by the LORD of Armies
20 with thunder, earthquake, and loud noise,
storm, tempest, and a flame of consuming fire.
All the many nations
going out to battle against Ariel—
all the attackers, the siege works against her,
and those who oppress her—
will then be like a dream, a vision in the night.
It will be like a hungry one who dreams he is eating,
then wakes and is still hungry;

and like a thirsty one who dreams he is drinking,
30　　then wakes and is still thirsty, longing for water.
So it will be for all the many nations
who go to battle against Mount Zion.

Stop and be astonished;
blind yourselves and be blind!
They are drunk, but not with wine;
they stagger, but not with beer.
For the LORD has poured out on you
an overwhelming urge to sleep;
he has shut your eyes (the prophets)
40　　and covered your heads (the seers).

For you the entire vision will be like the words of a sealed document. If it is given to one who can read and he is asked to read it, he will say, "I can't read it, because it is sealed." And if the document is given to one who cannot read and he is asked to read it, he will say, "I can't read."

The Lord said:

These people approach me with their speeches
to honor me with lip-service,
yet their hearts are far from me,
and human rules direct their worship of me.
Therefore, I will again confound these people
50　　with wonder after wonder.
The wisdom of their wise will vanish,
and the perception of their perceptive will be hidden.

Woe to those who go to great lengths
to hide their plans from the LORD.
They do their works in the dark,
and say, "Who sees us? Who knows us?"
You have turned things around,
as if the potter were the same as the clay.
How can what is made say about its maker,
60　　"He didn't make me"?
How can what is formed
say about the one who formed it,
"He doesn't understand what he's doing"?

Isn't it true that in just a little while
Lebanon will become an orchard,
and the orchard will seem like a forest?
On that day the deaf will hear
the words of a document,
and out of a deep darkness
70   the eyes of the blind will see.
The humble will have joy
after joy in the Lord,
and the poor people will rejoice
in the Holy One of Israel.
For the ruthless one will vanish,
the scorner will disappear,
and all those who lie in wait with evil intent
will be killed—
those who, with their speech,
80   accuse a person of wrongdoing,
who set a trap for the one mediating at the city gate
and without cause deprive the righteous of justice.

Therefore, the Lord who redeemed Abraham says this about the house of Jacob:
Jacob will no longer be ashamed,
and his face will no longer be pale.
For when he sees his children,
the work of my hands within his nation,
they will honor my name,
they will honor the Holy One of Jacob
90   and stand in awe of the God of Israel.
Those who are confused will gain understanding,
and those who grumble will accept instruction.

30   Woe to the rebellious children!
This is the Lord's declaration.
They carry out a plan, but not mine;
they make an alliance,
but against my will,
piling sin on top of sin.
Without asking my advice

they set out to go down to Egypt
in order to seek shelter under Pharaoh's protection
and take refuge in Egypt's shadow.
10 But Pharaoh's protection will become your shame,
and refuge in Egypt's shadow your humiliation.
For though his princes are at Zoan
and his messengers reach as far as Hanes,
everyone will be ashamed
because of a people who can't help.
They are of no benefit, they are no help;
they are good for nothing but shame and disgrace.

A pronouncement concerning the animals of the Negev:
20   Through a land of trouble and distress,
of lioness and lion,
of viper and flying serpent,
they carry their wealth on the backs of donkeys
and their treasures on the humps of camels,
to a people who will not help them.
Egypt's help is completely worthless;
therefore, I call her:
Rahab Who Just Sits.

Go now, write it on a tablet in their presence
30   and inscribe it on a scroll;
it will be for the future,
forever and ever.
They are a rebellious people,
deceptive children,
children who do not want to listen to the LORD's instruction.
They say to the seers, "Do not see,"
and to the prophets,
"Do not prophesy the truth to us.
Tell us flattering things.
40   Prophesy illusions.
Get out of the way!
Leave the pathway.
Rid us of the Holy One of Israel."

Therefore the Holy One of Israel says:
"Because you have rejected this message
and have trusted in oppression and deceit,
and have depended on them,
this iniquity of yours will be
like a crumbling gap,
50   a bulge in a high wall
whose collapse will come in an instant—suddenly!
Its collapse will be like the shattering
of a potter's jar, crushed to pieces,
so that not even a fragment of pottery
will be found among its shattered remains—
no fragment large enough to take fire from a hearth
or scoop water from a cistern."
For the Lord God, the Holy One of Israel, has said:
"You will be delivered by returning and resting;
60   your strength will lie in quiet confidence.
But you are not willing."
You say, "No!
We will escape on horses"—
therefore you will escape!—
and, "We will ride on fast horses"—
but those who pursue you will be faster.
One thousand will flee at the threat of one,
at the threat of five you will flee,
until you remain
70   like a solitary pole on a mountaintop
or a banner on a hill.

Therefore the Lord is waiting to show you mercy,
and is rising up to show you compassion,
for the Lord is a just God.
All who wait patiently for him are happy.

For people will live on Zion in Jerusalem. You will never weep again; he will show favor to
you at the sound of your outcry; as soon as he hears, he will answer you. The Lord will give you
meager bread and water during oppression, but your Teacher will not hide any longer. Your
eyes will see your Teacher, and whenever you turn to the right or to the left, your ears will hear

80 this command behind you: "This is the way. Walk in it." Then you will defile your silver-plated idols and your gold-plated images. You will throw them away like menstrual cloths, and call them filth.

Then he will send rain for your seed that you have sown in the ground, and the food, the produce of the ground, will be rich and plentiful. On that day your cattle will graze in open pastures. The oxen and donkeys that work the ground will eat salted fodder scattered with winnowing shovel and fork. Streams flowing with water will be on every high mountain and every raised hill on the day of great slaughter when the towers fall. The moonlight will be as bright as the sunlight, and the sunlight will be seven times brighter—like the light of seven days—on the day that the LORD bandages his people's injuries and heals the wounds he inflicted.

90
    Look! The name of the Lord is coming from far away,
    his anger burning and heavy with smoke.
    His lips are full of fury,
    and his tongue is like a consuming fire.
    His breath is like an overflowing torrent
    that rises to the neck.
    He comes to sift the nations in a sieve of destruction
    and to put a bridle on the jaws of the peoples
    to lead them astray.
    Your singing will be like that
100
    on the night of a holy festival,
    and your heart will rejoice
    like one who walks to the music of a flute,
    going up to the mountain of the LORD,
    to the Rock of Israel.
    And the LORD will make the splendor of his voice heard
    and reveal his arm striking in angry wrath
    and a flame of consuming fire,
    in driving rain, a torrent, and hailstones.
    Assyria will be shattered by the voice of the LORD.
110
    He will strike with a rod.
    And every stroke of the appointed staff
    that the LORD brings down on him
    will be to the sound of tambourines and lyres;
    he will fight against him with brandished weapons.
    Indeed! Topheth has been ready
    for the king for a long time.

Its funeral pyre is deep and wide,
with plenty of fire and wood.
The breath of the Lord, like a torrent of burning sulfur,
kindles it.

31 Woe to those who go down to Egypt for help
and who depend on horses!
They trust in the abundance of chariots
and in the large number of horsemen.
They do not look to the Holy One of Israel,
and they do not seek the Lord.
But he also is wise and brings disaster.
He does not go back on what he says;
he will rise up against the house of the wicked
and against the allies of evildoers.
Egyptians are men, not God;
their horses are flesh, not spirit.
When the Lord raises his hand to strike,
the helper will stumble
and the one who is helped will fall;
both will perish together.

For this is what the Lord said to me:
As a lion or young lion growls over its prey
when a band of shepherds is called out against it,
and it is not terrified by their shouting
or subdued by their noise,
so the Lord of Armies will come down
to fight on Mount Zion
and on its hill.

Like hovering birds,
so the Lord of Armies will protect Jerusalem;
by protecting it, he will rescue it;
by passing over it, he will deliver it.

Return to the one the Israelites have greatly rebelled against. For on that day, every one of you
will reject the worthless idols of silver and gold that your own hands have sinfully made.

Then Assyria will fall,
but not by human sword;
a sword will devour him,
but not one made by man.
He will flee from the sword;
his young men will be put to forced labor.
His rock will pass away because of fear,
and his officers will be afraid because of the signal flag.
This is the LORD's declaration—whose fire is in Zion and whose furnace is in Jerusalem.

32 Indeed, a king will reign righteously,
and rulers will rule justly.
Each will be like a shelter from the wind,
a refuge from the rain,
like flowing streams in a dry land
and the shade of a massive rock in an arid land.
Then the eyes of those who see will not be closed,
and the ears of those who hear will listen.
The reckless mind will gain knowledge,
10 and the stammering tongue will speak clearly and fluently.
A fool will no longer be called a noble,
nor a scoundrel said to be important.
For a fool speaks foolishness
and his mind plots iniquity.
He lives in a godless way
and speaks falsely about the LORD.
He leaves the hungry empty
and deprives the thirsty of drink.
The scoundrel's weapons are destructive;
20 he hatches plots to destroy the needy with lies,
even when the poor person says what is right.
But a noble person plans noble things;
he stands up for noble causes.

Stand up, you complacent women;
listen to me.
Pay attention to what I say,
you overconfident daughters.

In a little more than a year
you overconfident ones will shudder,
for the grapes will fail
and the harvest will not come.
Shudder, you complacent ones;
tremble, you overconfident ones!
Strip yourselves bare
and put sackcloth around your waists.
Beat your breasts in mourning
for the delightful fields and the fruitful vines,
for the ground of my people
growing thorns and briers,
40 indeed, for every joyous house in the jubilant city.
For the palace will be deserted,
the busy city abandoned.
The hill and the watchtower will become
barren places forever,
the joy of wild donkeys,
and a pasture for flocks,
until the Spirit from on high is poured out on us.
Then the desert will become an orchard,
and the orchard will seem like a forest.
50 Then justice will inhabit the wilderness,
and righteousness will dwell in the orchard.
The result of righteousness will be peace;
the effect of righteousness
will be quiet confidence forever.
Then my people will dwell in a peaceful place,
in safe and secure dwellings.
But hail will level the forest,
and the city will sink into the depths.
You will be happy as you sow seed
60 beside abundant water,
and as you let oxen and donkeys range freely.

33 Woe, you destroyer never destroyed,
you traitor never betrayed!
When you have finished destroying,

you will be destroyed.
When you have finished betraying,
they will betray you.

Lord, be gracious to us! We wait for you.
Be our strength every morning
and our salvation in time of trouble.
The peoples flee at the thunderous noise;
the nations scatter when you rise in your majesty.
Your spoil will be gathered as locusts are gathered;
people will swarm over it like an infestation of locusts.
The Lord is exalted, for he dwells on high;
he has filled Zion with justice and righteousness.
There will be times of security for you—
a storehouse of salvation, wisdom, and knowledge.
The fear of the Lord is Zion's treasure.

Listen! Their warriors cry loudly in the streets;
the messengers of peace weep bitterly.
The highways are deserted;
travel has ceased.
An agreement has been broken,
cities despised,
and human life disregarded.
The land mourns and withers;
Lebanon is ashamed and wilted.
Sharon is like a desert;
Bashan and Carmel shake off their leaves.
"Now I will rise up," says the Lord.
"Now I will lift myself up.
Now I will be exalted.
You will conceive chaff;
you will give birth to stubble.
Your breath is fire that will consume you.
The peoples will be burned to ashes,
like thorns cut down and burned in a fire.
You who are far off, hear what I have done;
you who are near, know my strength."

40 The sinners in Zion are afraid;
trembling seizes the ungodly:
"Who among us can dwell with a consuming fire?
Who among us can dwell with ever-burning flames?"
The one who lives righteously
and speaks rightly,
who refuses profit from extortion,
whose hand never takes a bribe,
who stops his ears from listening to murderous plots
and shuts his eyes against evil schemes—
50 he will dwell on the heights;
his refuge will be the rocky fortresses,
his food provided, his water assured.

Your eyes will see the King in his beauty;
you will see a vast land.
Your mind will meditate on the past terror:
"Where is the accountant?
Where is the tribute collector?
Where is the one who spied out our defenses?"
You will no longer see the barbarians,
60 a people whose speech is difficult to comprehend—
who stammer in a language that is not understood.
Look at Zion, the city of our festival times.
Your eyes will see Jerusalem,
a peaceful pasture, a tent that does not wander;
its tent pegs will not be pulled up
nor will any of its cords be loosened.
For the majestic one, our LORD, will be there,
a place of rivers and broad streams
where ships that are rowed will not go,
70 and majestic vessels will not pass.
For the LORD is our Judge,
the LORD is our Lawgiver,
the LORD is our King.
He will save us.
Your ropes are slack;

they cannot hold the base of the mast
or spread out the flag.
Then abundant spoil will be divided,
the lame will plunder it,
80 and none there will say, "I am sick."
The people who dwell there
will be forgiven their iniquity.

34 You nations, come here and listen;
you peoples, pay attention!
Let the earth and all that fills it hear,
the world and all that comes from it.
The LORD is angry with all the nations,
furious with all their armies.
He will set them apart for destruction,
giving them over to slaughter.
Their slain will be thrown out,
10 and the stench of their corpses will rise;
the mountains will flow with their blood.
All the stars in the sky will dissolve.
The sky will roll up like a scroll,
and its stars will all wither
as leaves wither on the vine,
and foliage on the fig tree.

When my sword has drunk its fill in the heavens,
it will then come down on Edom
and on the people I have set apart for destruction.
20 The LORD's sword is covered with blood.
It drips with fat,
with the blood of lambs and goats,
with the fat of the kidneys of rams.
For the LORD has a sacrifice in Bozrah,
a great slaughter in the land of Edom.
The wild oxen will be struck down with them,
and young bulls with the mighty bulls.
Their land will be soaked with blood,
and their soil will be saturated with fat.

30 For the LORD has a day of vengeance,
a time of paying back Edom
for its hostility against Zion.
Edom's streams will be turned into pitch,
her soil into sulfur;
her land will become burning pitch.
It will never go out—day or night.
Its smoke will go up forever.
It will be desolate, from generation to generation;
no one will pass through it forever and ever.
40 Eagle owls and herons will possess it,
and long-eared owls and ravens will dwell there.
The LORD will stretch out a measuring line
and a plumb line over her
for her destruction and chaos.
No nobles will be left to proclaim a king,
and all her princes will come to nothing.
Her palaces will be overgrown with thorns;
her fortified cities, with thistles and briers.
She will become a dwelling for jackals,
50 an abode for ostriches.
The desert creatures will meet hyenas,
and one wild goat will call to another.
Indeed, the night birds will stay there
and will find a resting place.
Sand partridges will make their nests there;
they will lay and hatch their eggs
and will gather their broods under their shadows.
Indeed, the birds of prey will gather there,
each with its mate.
60 Search and read the scroll of the LORD:
Not one of them will be missing,
none will be lacking its mate,
because he has ordered it by my mouth,
and he will gather them by his Spirit.
He has cast the lot for them;
his hand allotted their portion with a measuring line.

They will possess it forever;
they will dwell in it from generation to generation.

35 The wilderness and the dry land will be glad;
the desert will rejoice and blossom like a wildflower.
It will blossom abundantly
and will also rejoice with joy and singing.
The glory of Lebanon will be given to it,
the splendor of Carmel and Sharon.
They will see the glory of the Lord,
the splendor of our God.
Strengthen the weak hands,
10 steady the shaking knees!
Say to the cowardly:
"Be strong; do not fear!
Here is your God; vengeance is coming.
God's retribution is coming; he will save you."
Then the eyes of the blind will be opened,
and the ears of the deaf unstopped.
Then the lame will leap like a deer,
and the tongue of the mute will sing for joy,
for water will gush in the wilderness,
20 and streams in the desert;
the parched ground will become a pool,
and the thirsty land, springs.
In the haunt of jackals, in their lairs,
there will be grass, reeds, and papyrus.
A road will be there and a way;
it will be called the Holy Way.
The unclean will not travel on it,
but it will be for the one who walks the path.
Fools will not wander on it.
30 There will be no lion there,
and no vicious beast will go up on it;
they will not be found there.
But the redeemed will walk on it,
and the ransomed of the Lord will return
and come to Zion with singing,

> crowned with unending joy.
> Joy and gladness will overtake them,
> and sorrow and sighing will flee.

36 In the fourteenth year of King Hezekiah, King Sennacherib of Assyria attacked all the fortified cities of Judah and captured them. Then the king of Assyria sent his royal spokesman, along with a massive army, from Lachish to King Hezekiah at Jerusalem. The Assyrian stood near the conduit of the upper pool, by the road to Launderer's Field. Eliakim son of Hilkiah, who was in charge of the palace, Shebna the court secretary, and Joah son of Asaph, the court historian, came out to him.

The royal spokesman said to them, "Tell Hezekiah:

The great king, the king of Assyria, says this: What are you relying on? You think mere words are strategy and strength for war. Who are you now relying on that you have rebelled against me? Look, you are relying on Egypt, that splintered reed of a staff that will pierce the hand of anyone who grabs it and leans on it. This is how Pharaoh king of Egypt is to all who rely on him. Suppose you say to me, 'We rely on the LORD our God.' Isn't he the one whose high places and altars Hezekiah has removed, saying to Judah and Jerusalem, 'You are to worship at this altar'?

"Now make a deal with my master, the king of Assyria. I'll give you two thousand horses if you're able to supply riders for them! How then can you drive back a single officer among the least of my master's servants? How can you rely on Egypt for chariots and horsemen? Have I attacked this land to destroy it without the LORD's approval? The LORD said to me, 'Attack this land and destroy it.'"

Then Eliakim, Shebna, and Joah said to the royal spokesman, "Please speak to your servants in Aramaic, since we understand it. Don't speak to us in Hebrew within earshot of the people who are on the wall."

But the royal spokesman replied, "Has my master sent me to speak these words to your master and to you, and not to the men who are sitting on the wall, who are destined with you to eat their own excrement and drink their own urine?"

Then the royal spokesman stood and called out loudly in Hebrew:

Listen to the words of the great king, the king of Assyria! This is what the king says: "Don't let Hezekiah deceive you, for he cannot rescue you. Don't let Hezekiah persuade you to rely on the LORD, saying, 'The LORD will certainly rescue us! This city will not be handed over to the king of Assyria.'"

Don't listen to Hezekiah, for this is what the king of Assyria says: "Make peace with me and surrender to me. Then every one of you may eat from his own vine and his own fig tree and drink water from his own cistern until I come and take you away to a land like your own land—a land of grain and new wine, a land of bread and vineyards. Beware that Hezekiah does not mislead you by saying, 'The LORD will rescue us.' Has any one of the gods of the nations rescued his land from the power of the king of Assyria? Where are the gods of Hamath and Arpad? Where are the gods of Sepharvaim? Have they rescued Samaria from my power? Who among all the gods of these lands ever rescued his land from my power? So will the LORD rescue Jerusalem from my power?"

But they kept silent; they didn't say anything, for the king's command was, "Don't answer him." Then Eliakim son of Hilkiah, who was in charge of the palace, Shebna the court secretary, and Joah son of Asaph, the court historian, came to Hezekiah with their clothes torn and reported to 40 him the words of the royal spokesman.

37 When King Hezekiah heard their report, he tore his clothes, covered himself with sackcloth, and went to the LORD's temple. He sent Eliakim, who was in charge of the palace, Shebna the court secretary, and the leading priests, who were covered with sackcloth, to the prophet Isaiah son of Amoz. They said to him, "This is what Hezekiah says: 'Today is a day of distress, rebuke, and disgrace. It is as if children have come to the point of birth, and there is no strength to deliver them. Perhaps the LORD your God will hear all the words of the royal spokesman, whom his master the king of Assyria sent to mock the living God, and will rebuke him for the words that the LORD your God has heard. Therefore offer a prayer for the surviving remnant.'"

So the servants of King Hezekiah went to Isaiah, who said to them, "Tell your master, 'The 10 LORD says this: Don't be afraid because of the words you have heard, with which the king of Assyria's attendants have blasphemed me. I am about to put a spirit in him and he will hear a rumor and return to his own land, where I will cause him to fall by the sword.'"

When the royal spokesman heard that the king of Assyria had pulled out of Lachish, he left and found him fighting against Libnah. The king had heard concerning King Tirhakah of Cush, "He has set out to fight against you." So when he heard this, he sent messengers to Hezekiah, saying, "Say this to King Hezekiah of Judah: 'Don't let your God, on whom you rely, deceive you by promising that Jerusalem won't be handed over to the king of Assyria. Look, you have heard what the kings of Assyria have done to all the countries: they completely destroyed them. Will you be rescued? Did the gods of the nations that my predecessors destroyed rescue them—Gozan, 20 Haran, Rezeph, and the Edenites in Telassar? Where is the king of Hamath, the king of Arpad, the king of the city of Sepharvaim, Hena, or Ivvah?'"

Hezekiah took the letter from the messengers' hands, read it, then went up to the LORD's temple and spread it out before the LORD. Then Hezekiah prayed to the LORD:

LORD of Armies, God of Israel, enthroned between the cherubim, you are God—you alone—of all the kingdoms of the earth. You made the heavens and the earth. Listen closely, LORD, and hear; open your eyes, LORD, and see. Hear all the words that Sennacherib has sent to mock the living God. LORD, it is true that the kings of Assyria have devastated all these countries and their lands. They have thrown their gods into the fire, for they were not gods but made from wood and stone by human hands. So they have destroyed them. Now, LORD our God, save us from his

30 power so that all the kingdoms of the earth may know that you, LORD, are God—you alone.

Then Isaiah son of Amoz sent a message to Hezekiah: "The LORD, the God of Israel, says, 'Because you prayed to me about King Sennacherib of Assyria, this is the word the LORD has spoken against him:

Virgin Daughter Zion
despises you and scorns you;
Daughter Jerusalem shakes her head
behind your back.
Who is it you have mocked and blasphemed?
Against whom have you raised your voice
and lifted your eyes in pride?
40 Against the Holy One of Israel!
You have mocked the LORD through your servants.
You have said, "With my many chariots
I have gone up to the heights of the mountains,
to the far recesses of Lebanon.
I cut down its tallest cedars,
its choice cypress trees.
I came to its distant heights,
its densest forest.
I dug wells and drank water in foreign lands.
50 I dried up all the streams of Egypt
with the soles of my feet."

Have you not heard?
I designed it long ago;
I planned it in days gone by.
I have now brought it to pass,
and you have crushed fortified cities
into piles of rubble.
Their inhabitants have become powerless,
dismayed, and ashamed.
60 They are plants of the field,
tender grass,

grass on the rooftops,
blasted by the east wind.

But I know your sitting down,
your going out and your coming in,
and your raging against me.
Because your raging against me
and your arrogance have reached my ears,
I will put my hook in your nose
70   and my bit in your mouth;
I will make you go back
the way you came.

"'This will be the sign for you: This year you will eat what grows on its own, and in the second year what grows from that. But in the third year sow and reap, plant vineyards and eat their fruit. The surviving remnant of the house of Judah will again take root downward and bear fruit upward. For a remnant will go out from Jerusalem, and survivors from Mount Zion. The zeal of the LORD of Armies will accomplish this.'

"Therefore, this is what the LORD says about the king of Assyria:
He will not enter this city,
80   shoot an arrow here,
come before it with a shield,
or build up a siege ramp against it.
He will go back
the way he came,
and he will not enter this city.
This is the LORD's declaration.
I will defend this city and rescue it
for my sake
and for the sake of my servant David."

90 Then the angel of the LORD went out and struck down one hundred eighty-five thousand in the camp of the Assyrians. When the people got up the next morning, there were all the dead bodies! So King Sennacherib of Assyria broke camp and left. He returned home and lived in Nineveh.

One day, while he was worshiping in the temple of his god Nisroch, his sons Adrammelech and Sharezer struck him down with the sword and escaped to the land of Ararat. Then his son Esar-haddon became king in his place.

38 In those days Hezekiah became terminally ill. The prophet Isaiah son of Amoz came and said to him, "This is what the LORD says: 'Set your house in order, for you are about to die; you will not recover.'"

Then Hezekiah turned his face to the wall and prayed to the LORD. He said, "Please, LORD, remember how I have walked before you faithfully and wholeheartedly, and have done what pleases you." And Hezekiah wept bitterly.

Then the word of the LORD came to Isaiah: "Go and tell Hezekiah, 'This is what the LORD God of your ancestor David says: I have heard your prayer; I have seen your tears. Look, I am going to add fifteen years to your life. And I will rescue you and this city from the grasp of the king of Assyria; I will defend this city. This is the sign to you from the LORD that he will do what he
10 has promised: I am going to make the sun's shadow that goes down on the stairway of Ahaz go back by ten steps.'" So the sun's shadow went back the ten steps it had descended.

A poem by King Hezekiah of Judah after he had been sick and had recovered from his illness:

> I said: In the prime of my life
> I must go to the gates of Sheol;
> I am deprived of the rest of my years.
> I said: I will never see the LORD,
> the LORD in the land of the living;
> I will not look on humanity any longer
> with the inhabitants of what is passing away.
20 My dwelling is plucked up and removed from me
> like a shepherd's tent.
> I have rolled up my life like a weaver;
> he cuts me off from the loom.
> By nightfall you make an end of me.
> I thought until the morning:
> He will break all my bones like a lion.
> By nightfall you make an end of me.
> I chirp like a swallow or a crane;
> I moan like a dove.
30 My eyes grow weak looking upward.
> Lord, I am oppressed; support me.
>
> What can I say?
> He has spoken to me,
> and he himself has done it.
> I walk along slowly all my years
> because of the bitterness of my soul.
> Lord, by such things people live,

and in every one of them my spirit finds life;
40   you have restored me to health
and let me live.
Indeed, it was for my own well-being
that I had such intense bitterness;
but your love has delivered me
from the Pit of destruction,
for you have thrown all my sins behind your back.
For Sheol cannot thank you;
Death cannot praise you.
Those who go down to the Pit
50   cannot hope for your faithfulness.
The living, only the living can thank you,
as I do today;
a father will make your faithfulness known to children.
The LORD is ready to save me;
we will play stringed instruments
all the days of our lives
at the house of the LORD.

Now Isaiah had said, "Let them take a lump of pressed figs and apply it to his infected skin, so that he may recover." And Hezekiah had asked, "What is the sign that I will go up to the LORD's
60 temple?"

39 At that time Merodach-baladan son of Baladan, king of Babylon, sent letters and a gift to Hezekiah since he heard that he had been sick and had recovered. Hezekiah was pleased with the letters, and he showed the envoys his treasure house—the silver, the gold, the spices, and the precious oil—and all his armory, and everything that was found in his treasuries. There was nothing in his palace and in all his realm that Hezekiah did not show them.

Then the prophet Isaiah came to King Hezekiah and asked him, "What did these men say, and where did they come to you from?"

Hezekiah replied, "They came to me from a distant country, from Babylon."

Isaiah asked, "What have they seen in your palace?"

10 Hezekiah answered, "They have seen everything in my palace. There isn't anything in my treasuries that I didn't show them."

Then Isaiah said to Hezekiah, "Hear the word of the LORD of Armies: 'Look, the days are coming when everything in your palace and all that your predecessors have stored up until today will be carried off to Babylon; nothing will be left,' says the LORD. 'Some of your descendants—who come from you, whom you father—will be taken away, and they will become eunuchs in the palace of the king of Babylon.'"

Then Hezekiah said to Isaiah, "The word of the LORD that you have spoken is good," for he thought: There will be peace and security during my lifetime.

40
    "Comfort, comfort my people,"
says your God.
"Speak tenderly to Jerusalem,
and announce to her
that her time of hard service is over,
her iniquity has been pardoned,
and she has received from the LORD's hand
double for all her sins."

A voice of one crying out:
10   Prepare the way of the LORD in the wilderness;
make a straight highway for our God in the desert.
Every valley will be lifted up,
and every mountain and hill will be leveled;
the uneven ground will become smooth
and the rough places, a plain.
And the glory of the LORD will appear,
and all humanity together will see it,
for the mouth of the LORD has spoken.

A voice was saying, "Cry out!"
20   Another said, "What should I cry out?"
"All humanity is grass,
and all its goodness is like the flower of the field.
The grass withers, the flowers fade
when the breath of the LORD blows on them;
indeed, the people are grass.
The grass withers, the flowers fade,
but the word of our God remains forever."

Zion, herald of good news,
go up on a high mountain.
30   Jerusalem, herald of good news,

raise your voice loudly.
Raise it, do not be afraid!
Say to the cities of Judah,
"Here is your God!"
See, the Lord GOD comes with strength,
and his power establishes his rule.
His wages are with him,
and his reward accompanies him.
He protects his flock like a shepherd;
he gathers the lambs in his arms
and carries them in the fold of his garment.
He gently leads those that are nursing.

Who has measured the waters in the hollow of his hand
or marked off the heavens with the span of his hand?
Who has gathered the dust of the earth in a measure
or weighed the mountains on a balance
and the hills on the scales?
Who has directed the Spirit of the LORD,
or who gave him counsel?
Who did he consult?
Who gave him understanding
and taught him the paths of justice?
Who taught him knowledge
and showed him the way of understanding?
Look, the nations are like a drop in a bucket;
they are considered as a speck of dust on the scales;
he lifts up the islands like fine dust.
Lebanon's cedars are not enough for fuel,
or its animals enough for a burnt offering.
All the nations are as nothing before him;
they are considered by him
as empty nothingness.

With whom will you compare God?
What likeness will you set up for comparison with him?
An idol?—something that a smelter casts
and a metalworker plates with gold

and makes silver chains for?
A poor person contributes wood for a pedestal
that will not rot.
He looks for a skilled craftsman
to set up an idol that will not fall over.

Do you not know?
Have you not heard?
Has it not been declared to you
from the beginning?
Have you not considered
the foundations of the earth?
God is enthroned above the circle of the earth;
its inhabitants are like grasshoppers.
He stretches out the heavens like thin cloth
and spreads them out like a tent to live in.
He reduces princes to nothing
and makes judges of the earth like a wasteland.
They are barely planted, barely sown,
their stem hardly takes root in the ground
when he blows on them and they wither,
and a whirlwind carries them away like stubble.

"To whom will you compare me,
or who is my equal?" asks the Holy One.
Look up and see!
Who created these?
He brings out the stars by number;
he calls all of them by name.
Because of his great power and strength,
not one of them is missing.

Jacob, why do you say,
and Israel, why do you assert,
"My way is hidden from the LORD,
and my claim is ignored by my God"?
Do you not know?
Have you not heard?

The Lord is the everlasting God,
the Creator of the whole earth.
He never becomes faint or weary;
there is no limit to his understanding.
He gives strength to the faint
and strengthens the powerless.
Youths may become faint and weary,
and young men stumble and fall,
but those who trust in the Lord
will renew their strength;
they will soar on wings like eagles;
they will run and not become weary,
they will walk and not faint.

41 "Be silent before me, coasts and islands!
And let peoples renew their strength.
Let them approach; let them testify;
let's come together for the trial.
Who has stirred up someone from the east?
In righteousness he calls him to serve.
The Lord hands nations over to him,
and he subdues kings.
He makes them like dust with his sword,
like wind-driven stubble with his bow.
He pursues them, going on safely,
hardly touching the path with his feet.
Who has performed and done this,
calling the generations from the beginning?
I am the Lord, the first
and with the last—I am he."

The coasts and islands see and are afraid,
the whole earth trembles.
They approach and arrive.
Each one helps the other,
and says to another, "Take courage!"
The craftsman encourages the metalworker;
the one who flattens with the hammer

encourages the one who strikes the anvil,
saying of the soldering, "It is good."
He fastens it with nails so that it will not fall over.

But you, Israel, my servant,
Jacob, whom I have chosen,
descendant of Abraham, my friend—
30 I brought you from the ends of the earth
and called you from its farthest corners.
I said to you: You are my servant;
I have chosen you; I haven't rejected you.
Do not fear, for I am with you;
do not be afraid, for I am your God.
I will strengthen you; I will help you;
I will hold on to you with my righteous right hand.

Be sure that all who are enraged against you
will be ashamed and disgraced;
40 those who contend with you
will become as nothing and will perish.
You will look for those who contend with you,
but you will not find them.
Those who war against you
will become absolutely nothing.
For I am the LORD your God,
who holds your right hand,
who says to you, "Do not fear,
I will help you.
50 Do not fear, you worm Jacob,
you men of Israel.
I will help you"—
this is the LORD's declaration.
Your Redeemer is the Holy One of Israel.
See, I will make you into a sharp threshing board,
new, with many teeth.
You will thresh mountains and pulverize them
and make hills into chaff.
You will winnow them

60 and a wind will carry them away,
 a whirlwind will scatter them.
 But you will rejoice in the LORD;
 you will boast in the Holy One of Israel.

 The poor and the needy seek water, but there is none;
 their tongues are parched with thirst.
 I will answer them.
 I am the LORD, the God of Israel. I will not abandon them.
 I will open rivers on the barren heights,
 and springs in the middle of the plains.
70 I will turn the desert into a pool
 and dry land into springs.
 I will plant cedar, acacia, myrtle, and olive trees
 in the wilderness.
 I will put juniper, elm, and cypress trees together
 in the desert,
 so that all may see and know,
 consider and understand,
 that the hand of the LORD has done this,
 the Holy One of Israel has created it.

80 "Submit your case," says the LORD.
 "Present your arguments," says Jacob's King.
 "Let them come and tell us
 what will happen.
 Tell us the past events,
 so that we may reflect on them
 and know the outcome,
 or tell us the future.
 Tell us the coming events,
 then we will know that you are gods.
90 Indeed, do something good or bad,
 then we will be in awe when we see it.
 Look, you are nothing
 and your work is worthless.
 Anyone who chooses you is detestable.

"I have stirred up one from the north, and he has come,
one from the east who invokes my name.
He will march over rulers as if they were mud,
like a potter who treads the clay.
Who told about this from the beginning,
so that we might know,
and from times past,
so that we might say, 'He is right'?
No one announced it,
no one told it,
no one heard your words.
I was the first to say to Zion,
'Look! Here they are!'
And I gave Jerusalem a herald with good news.
When I look, there is no one;
there is no counselor among them;
when I ask them, they have nothing to say.
Look, all of them are a delusion;
their works are nonexistent;
their images are wind and emptiness.

42   "This is my servant; I strengthen him,
this is my chosen one; I delight in him.
I have put my Spirit on him;
he will bring justice to the nations.
He will not cry out or shout
or make his voice heard in the streets.
He will not break a bruised reed,
and he will not put out a smoldering wick;
he will faithfully bring justice.
He will not grow weak or be discouraged
until he has established justice on earth.
The coasts and islands will wait for his instruction."

This is what God, the LORD, says—
who created the heavens and stretched them out,
who spread out the earth and what comes from it,
who gives breath to the people on it

and spirit to those who walk on it—
"I am the LORD. I have called you
for a righteous purpose,
20   and I will hold you by your hand.
I will watch over you, and I will appoint you
to be a covenant for the people
and a light to the nations,
in order to open blind eyes,
to bring out prisoners from the dungeon,
and those sitting in darkness from the prison house.
I am the LORD. That is my name,
and I will not give my glory to another
or my praise to idols.
30   The past events have indeed happened.
Now I declare new events;
I announce them to you before they occur."

Sing a new song to the LORD;
sing his praise from the ends of the earth,
you who go down to the sea with all that fills it,
you coasts and islands with your inhabitants.
Let the desert and its cities shout,
the settlements where Kedar dwells cry aloud.
Let the inhabitants of Sela sing for joy;
40   let them cry out from the mountaintops.
Let them give glory to the LORD
and declare his praise in the coasts and islands.
The LORD advances like a warrior;
he stirs up his zeal like a soldier.
He shouts, he roars aloud,
he prevails over his enemies.

"I have kept silent from ages past;
I have been quiet and restrained myself.
But now, I will groan like a woman in labor,
50   gasping breathlessly.
I will lay waste mountains and hills
and dry up all their vegetation.

I will turn rivers into islands
and dry up marshes.
I will lead the blind by a way they did not know;
I will guide them on paths they have not known.
I will turn darkness to light in front of them
and rough places into level ground.
This is what I will do for them,
60 and I will not abandon them.
They will be turned back and utterly ashamed—
those who trust in an idol
and say to a cast image,
'You are our gods!'

"Listen, you deaf!
Look, you blind, so that you may see.
Who is blind but my servant,
or deaf like my messenger I am sending?
Who is blind like my dedicated one,
70 or blind like the servant of the LORD?
Though seeing many things, you pay no attention.
Though his ears are open, he does not listen."

Because of his righteousness, the LORD was pleased
to magnify his instruction and make it glorious.
But this is a people plundered and looted,
all of them trapped in holes
or imprisoned in dungeons.
They have become plunder
with no one to rescue them
80 and loot, with no one saying, "Give it back!"
Who among you will hear this?
Let him listen and obey in the future.
Who gave Jacob to the robber,
and Israel to the plunderers?
Was it not the LORD?
Have we not sinned against him?
They were not willing to walk in his ways,
and they would not listen to his instruction.

So he poured out his furious anger
90 and the power of war on Jacob.
It surrounded him with fire, but he did not know it;
it burned him, but he didn't take it to heart.

43 Now this is what the LORD says—
the one who created you, Jacob,
and the one who formed you, Israel—
"Do not fear, for I have redeemed you;
I have called you by your name; you are mine.
When you pass through the waters,
I will be with you,
and the rivers will not overwhelm you.
When you walk through the fire,
10 you will not be scorched,
and the flame will not burn you.
For I am the LORD your God,
the Holy One of Israel, and your Savior.
I have given Egypt as a ransom for you,
Cush and Seba in your place.
Because you are precious in my sight
and honored, and I love you,
I will give people in exchange for you
and nations instead of your life.
20 Do not fear, for I am with you;
I will bring your descendants from the east,
and gather you from the west.
I will say to the north, 'Give them up!'
and to the south, 'Do not hold them back!'
Bring my sons from far away,
and my daughters from the ends of the earth—
everyone who bears my name
and is created for my glory.
I have formed them; indeed, I have made them."

30 Bring out a people who are blind, yet have eyes,
and are deaf, yet have ears.
All the nations are gathered together,

and the peoples are assembled.
Who among them can declare this,
and tell us the former things?
Let them present their witnesses
to vindicate themselves,
so that people may hear and say, "It is true."
"You are my witnesses"—
40   this is the LORD's declaration—
"and my servant whom I have chosen,
so that you may know and believe me
and understand that I am he.
No god was formed before me,
and there will be none after me.
I—I am the LORD.
Besides me, there is no Savior.
I alone declared, saved, and proclaimed—
and not some foreign god among you.
50   So you are my witnesses"—
this is the LORD's declaration—
"and I am God.
Also, from today on I am he alone,
and none can rescue from my power.
I act, and who can reverse it?"

This is what the LORD, your Redeemer, the Holy One of Israel says:
    Because of you, I will send an army to Babylon
    and bring all of them as fugitives,
    even the Chaldeans in the ships in which they rejoice.
60   I am the LORD, your Holy One,
    the Creator of Israel, your King.

This is what the LORD says—
who makes a way in the sea,
and a path through raging water,
who brings out the chariot and horse,
the army and the mighty one together
(they lie down, they do not rise again;
they are extinguished, put out like a wick)—

"Do not remember the past events;
pay no attention to things of old.
Look, I am about to do something new;
even now it is coming. Do you not see it?
Indeed, I will make a way in the wilderness,
rivers in the desert.
Wild animals—
jackals and ostriches—will honor me,
because I provide water in the wilderness,
and rivers in the desert,
to give drink to my chosen people.
The people I formed for myself
will declare my praise.

"But, Jacob, you have not called on me,
because, Israel, you have become weary of me.
You have not brought me your sheep for burnt offerings
or honored me with your sacrifices.
I have not burdened you with offerings
or wearied you with incense.
You have not bought me aromatic cane with silver,
or satisfied me with the fat of your sacrifices.
But you have burdened me with your sins;
you have wearied me with your iniquities.

"I am the one, I sweep away your transgressions
for my own sake
and remember your sins no more.
Remind me. Let's argue the case together.
Recount the facts, so that you may be vindicated.
Your first father sinned,
and your mediators have rebelled against me.
So I defiled the officers of the sanctuary,
and set Jacob apart for destruction
and Israel for scorn.

44   "And now listen, Jacob my servant,
Israel whom I have chosen.

This is the word of the LORD
your Maker, the one who formed you from the womb:
He will help you.
Do not fear, Jacob my servant,
Jeshurun whom I have chosen.
For I will pour water on the thirsty land
and streams on the dry ground;
10   I will pour out my Spirit on your descendants
and my blessing on your offspring.
They will sprout among the grass
like poplars by flowing streams.
This one will say, 'I am the LORD's';
another will use the name of Jacob;
still another will write on his hand, 'The LORD's,'
and take on the name of Israel."

This is what the LORD, the King of Israel and its Redeemer, the LORD of Armies, says:
I am the first and I am the last.
20   There is no God but me.
Who, like me, can announce the future?
Let him say so and make a case before me,
since I have established an ancient people.
Let these gods declare the coming things,
and what will take place.
Do not be startled or afraid.
Have I not told you and declared it long ago?
You are my witnesses!
Is there any God but me?
30   There is no other Rock; I do not know any.

All who make idols are nothing,
and what they treasure benefits no one.
Their witnesses do not see or know anything,
so they will be put to shame.
Who makes a god or casts a metal image
that benefits no one?
Look, all its worshipers will be put to shame,
and the craftsmen are humans.

They all will assemble and stand;
40   they all will be startled and put to shame.

The ironworker labors over the coals,
shapes the idol with hammers,
and works it with his strong arm.
Also he grows hungry and his strength fails;
he doesn't drink water and is faint.
The woodworker stretches out a measuring line,
he outlines it with a stylus;
he shapes it with chisels
and outlines it with a compass.
50   He makes it according to a human form,
like a beautiful person,
to dwell in a temple.
He cuts down cedars for his use,
or he takes a cypress or an oak.
He lets it grow strong among the trees of the forest.
He plants a laurel, and the rain makes it grow.
A person can use it for fuel.
He takes some of it and warms himself;
also he kindles a fire and bakes bread;
60   he even makes it into a god and worships it;
he makes an idol from it and bows down to it.
He burns half of it in a fire,
and he roasts meat on that half.
He eats the roast and is satisfied.
He warms himself and says, "Ah!
I am warm, I see the blaze."
He makes a god or his idol with the rest of it.
He bows down to it and worships;
he prays to it, "Save me, for you are my god."
70   Such people do not comprehend
and cannot understand,
for he has shut their eyes so they cannot see,
and their minds so they cannot understand.
No one comes to his senses;
no one has the perception or insight to say,

"I burned half of it in the fire,
I also baked bread on its coals,
I roasted meat and ate.
Should I make something detestable with the rest of it?
80   Should I bow down to a block of wood?"
He feeds on ashes.
His deceived mind has led him astray,
and he cannot rescue himself,
or say, "Isn't there a lie in my right hand?"

Remember these things, Jacob,
and Israel, for you are my servant;
I formed you, you are my servant;
Israel, you will never be forgotten by me.
I have swept away your transgressions like a cloud,
90   and your sins like a mist.
Return to me,
for I have redeemed you.
Rejoice, heavens, for the Lord has acted;
shout, depths of the earth.
Break out into singing, mountains,
forest, and every tree in it.
For the Lord has redeemed Jacob,
and glorifies himself through Israel.

This is what the Lord, your Redeemer who formed you from the womb, says:
100   I am the Lord, who made everything;
who stretched out the heavens by myself;
who alone spread out the earth;
who destroys the omens of the false prophets
and makes fools of diviners;
who confounds the wise
and makes their knowledge foolishness;
who confirms the message of his servant
and fulfills the counsel of his messengers;
who says to Jerusalem, "She will be inhabited,"
110   and to the cities of Judah, "They will be rebuilt,"
and I will restore her ruins;

who says to the depths of the sea, "Be dry,"
and I will dry up your rivers;
who says to Cyrus, "My shepherd,
he will fulfill all my pleasure"
and says to Jerusalem, "She will be rebuilt,"
and of the temple, "Its foundation will be laid."

45   The LORD says this to Cyrus, his anointed,
whose right hand I have grasped
to subdue nations before him
and disarm kings,
to open doors before him,
and even city gates will not be shut:
"I will go before you
and level the uneven places;
I will shatter the bronze doors
10   and cut the iron bars in two.
I will give you the treasures of darkness
and riches from secret places,
so that you may know that I am the LORD.
I am the God of Israel, who calls you by your name.
I call you by your name,
for the sake of my servant Jacob
and Israel my chosen one.
I give a name to you,
though you do not know me.
20   I am the LORD, and there is no other;
there is no God but me.
I will strengthen you,
though you do not know me,
so that all may know from the rising of the sun to its setting
that there is no one but me.
I am the LORD, and there is no other.
I form light and create darkness,
I make success and create disaster;
I am the LORD, who does all these things.

30 "Heavens, sprinkle from above,
    and let the skies shower righteousness.
    Let the earth open up
    so that salvation will sprout
    and righteousness will spring up with it.
    I, the Lord, have created it.

    "Woe to the one who argues with his Maker—
    one clay pot among many.
    Does clay say to the one forming it,
    'What are you making?'
40 Or does your work say,
    'He has no hands'?
    Woe to the one who says to his father,
    'What are you fathering?'
    or to his mother,
    'What are you giving birth to?'"
    This is what the Lord,
    the Holy One of Israel and its Maker, says:
    "Ask me what is to happen to my sons,
    and instruct me about the work of my hands.
50 I made the earth,
    and created humans on it.
    It was my hands that stretched out the heavens,
    and I commanded everything in them.
    I have stirred him up in righteousness,
    and will level all roads for him.
    He will rebuild my city,
    and set my exiles free,
    not for a price or a bribe,"
    says the Lord of Armies.

60 This is what the Lord says:
        "The products of Egypt and the merchandise of Cush
        and the Sabeans, men of stature,
        will come over to you
        and will be yours;
        they will follow you,

622

they will come over in chains
and bow down to you.
They will confess to you,
'God is indeed with you, and there is no other;
70   there is no other God.'"

Yes, you are a God who hides,
God of Israel, Savior.
All of them are put to shame, even humiliated;
the makers of idols go in humiliation together.
Israel will be saved by the LORD
with an everlasting salvation;
you will not be put to shame or humiliated
for all eternity.

For this is what the LORD says—
80   the Creator of the heavens,
the God who formed the earth and made it,
the one who established it
(he did not create it to be a wasteland,
but formed it to be inhabited)—
he says, "I am the LORD,
and there is no other.
I have not spoken in secret,
somewhere in a land of darkness.
I did not say to the descendants of Jacob:
90   Seek me in a wasteland.
I am the LORD, who speaks righteously,
who declares what is right.

"Come, gather together,
and approach, you fugitives of the nations.
Those who carry their wooden idols
and pray to a god who cannot save
have no knowledge.
Speak up and present your case—
yes, let them consult each other.
100   Who predicted this long ago?

Who announced it from ancient times?
Was it not I, the LORD?
There is no other God but me,
a righteous God and Savior;
there is no one except me.
Turn to me and be saved,
all the ends of the earth.
For I am God,
and there is no other.
110   By myself I have sworn;
truth has gone from my mouth,
a word that will not be revoked:
Every knee will bow to me,
every tongue will swear allegiance.
It will be said about me, 'Righteousness and strength
are found only in the LORD.'"
All who are enraged against him
will come to him and be put to shame.
All the descendants of Israel
120   will be justified and boast in the Lord.

46   Bel crouches; Nebo cowers.
Idols depicting them are consigned to beasts and cattle.
The images you carry are loaded,
as a burden for the weary animal.
The gods cower; they crouch together;
they are not able to rescue the burden,
but they themselves go into captivity.

"Listen to me, house of Jacob,
all the remnant of the house of Israel,
10   who have been sustained from the womb,
carried along since birth.
I will be the same until your old age,
and I will bear you up when you turn gray.
I have made you, and I will carry you;
I will bear and rescue you.

"To whom will you compare me or make me equal?
Who will you measure me with,
so that we should be like each other?
Those who pour out their bags of gold
20 and weigh out silver on scales—
they hire a goldsmith and he makes it into a god.
Then they kneel and bow down to it.
They lift it to their shoulder and bear it along;
they set it in its place, and there it stands;
it does not budge from its place.
They cry out to it but it doesn't answer;
it saves no one from his trouble.

"Remember this and be brave;
take it to heart, you transgressors!
30 Remember what happened long ago,
for I am God, and there is no other;
I am God, and no one is like me.
I declare the end from the beginning,
and from long ago what is not yet done,
saying: my plan will take place,
and I will do all my will.
I call a bird of prey from the east,
a man for my purpose from a far country.
Yes, I have spoken; so I will also bring it about.
40 I have planned it; I will also do it.
Listen to me, you hardhearted,
far removed from justice:
I am bringing my justice near;
it is not far away,
and my salvation will not delay.
I will put salvation in Zion,
my splendor in Israel.

47 "Go down and sit in the dust,
Virgin Daughter Babylon.
Sit on the ground without a throne,
Daughter Chaldea!

For you will no longer be called pampered and spoiled.
Take millstones and grind flour;
remove your veil,
strip off your skirt, bare your thigh,
wade through the streams.
Your nakedness will be uncovered,
and your disgrace will be exposed.
I will take vengeance;
I will spare no one."
The Holy One of Israel is our Redeemer;
The Lord of Armies is his name.

"Daughter Chaldea,
sit in silence and go into darkness.
For you will no longer be called mistress of kingdoms.
I was angry with my people;
I profaned my possession,
and I handed them over to you.
You showed them no mercy;
you made your yoke very heavy on the elderly.
You said, 'I will be the queen forever.'
You did not take these things to heart
or think about their outcome.

"So now hear this, lover of luxury,
who sits securely,
who says to herself,
'I am, and there is no one else.
I will never be a widow
or know the loss of children.'
These two things will happen to you
suddenly, in one day:
loss of children and widowhood.
They will happen to you in their entirety,
in spite of your many sorceries
and the potency of your spells.
You were secure in your wickedness;
you said, 'No one sees me.'

Your wisdom and knowledge
led you astray.
You said to yourself,
'I am, and there is no one else.'
But disaster will happen to you;
you will not know how to avert it.
And it will fall on you,
but you will be unable to ward it off.
Devastation will happen to you suddenly
50   and unexpectedly.
So take your stand with your spells
and your many sorceries,
which you have wearied yourself with from your youth.
Perhaps you will be able to succeed;
perhaps you will inspire terror!
You are worn out with your many consultations.
So let the astrologers stand and save you—
those who observe the stars,
those who predict monthly
60   what will happen to you.
Look, they are like stubble;
fire burns them.
They cannot rescue themselves
from the power of the flame.
This is not a coal for warming themselves,
or a fire to sit beside!
This is what they are to you—
those who have wearied you
and have traded with you from your youth—
70   each wanders on his own way;
no one can save you.

48   "Listen to this, house of Jacob—
those who are called by the name Israel
and have descended from Judah,
who swear by the name of the LORD
and declare the God of Israel,
but not in truth or righteousness.

For they are named after the holy city,
and lean on the God of Israel;
his name is the LORD of Armies.
10 I declared the past events long ago;
they came out of my mouth; I proclaimed them.
Suddenly I acted, and they occurred.
Because I know that you are stubborn,
and your neck is iron
and your forehead bronze,
therefore I declared to you long ago.
I announced it to you before it occurred,
so you could not claim, 'My idol caused them;
my carved image and cast idol control them.'
20 You have heard it. Observe it all.
Will you not acknowledge it?
From now on I will announce new things to you,
hidden things that you have not known.
They have been created now, and not long ago;
you have not heard of them before today,
so you could not claim, 'I already knew them!'
You have never heard; you have never known;
for a long time your ears have not been open.
For I knew that you were very treacherous,
30 and were known as a rebel from birth.
I will delay my anger for the sake of my name,
and I will restrain myself for your benefit and for my praise,
so that you will not be destroyed.
Look, I have refined you, but not as silver;
I have tested you in the furnace of affliction.
I will act for my own sake, indeed, my own,
for how can I be defiled?
I will not give my glory to another.

"Listen to me, Jacob,
40 and Israel, the one called by me:
I am he; I am the first,
I am also the last.
My own hand founded the earth,

and my right hand spread out the heavens;
when I summoned them,
they stood up together.
All of you, assemble and listen!
Who among the idols has declared these things?
The Lord loves him;
50 he will accomplish his will against Babylon,
and his arm will be against the Chaldeans.
I—I have spoken;
yes, I have called him;
I have brought him,
and he will succeed in his mission.
Approach me and listen to this.
From the beginning I have not spoken in secret;
from the time anything existed, I was there."
And now the Lord God
60 has sent me and his Spirit.

This is what the Lord, your Redeemer, the Holy One of Israel says:
I am the Lord your God,
who teaches you for your benefit,
who leads you in the way you should go.
If only you had paid attention to my commands.
Then your peace would have been like a river,
and your righteousness like the waves of the sea.
Your descendants would have been as countless as the sand,
and the offspring of your body like its grains;
70 their name would not be cut off
or eliminated from my presence.

Leave Babylon,
flee from the Chaldeans!
Declare with a shout of joy,
proclaim this,
let it go out to the end of the earth;
announce,
"The Lord has redeemed his servant Jacob!"
They did not thirst

80   when he led them through the deserts;
he made water flow from the rock for them;
he split the rock, and water gushed out.
"There is no peace for the wicked," says the Lord.

49   Coasts and islands, listen to me;
distant peoples, pay attention.
The Lord called me before I was born.
He named me while I was in my mother's womb.
He made my words like a sharp sword;
he hid me in the shadow of his hand.
He made me like a sharpened arrow;
he hid me in his quiver.
He said to me, "You are my servant,
10   Israel, in whom I will be glorified."
But I myself said: I have labored in vain,
I have spent my strength for nothing and futility;
yet my vindication is with the Lord,
and my reward is with my God.
And now, says the Lord,
who formed me from the womb to be his servant,
to bring Jacob back to him
so that Israel might be gathered to him;
for I am honored in the sight of the Lord,
20   and my God is my strength—
he says,
"It is not enough for you to be my servant
raising up the tribes of Jacob
and restoring the protected ones of Israel.
I will also make you a light for the nations,
to be my salvation to the ends of the earth."
This is what the Lord,
the Redeemer of Israel, his Holy One, says
to one who is despised,
30   to one abhorred by people,
to a servant of rulers:
"Kings will see, princes will stand up,
and they will all bow down

because of the LORD, who is faithful,
the Holy One of Israel—and he has chosen you."

This is what the LORD says:
I will answer you in a time of favor,
and I will help you in the day of salvation.
I will keep you, and I will appoint you
40 to be a covenant for the people,
to restore the land,
to make them possess the desolate inheritances,
saying to the prisoners, "Come out,"
and to those who are in darkness, "Show yourselves."
They will feed along the pathways,
and their pastures will be on all the barren heights.
They will not hunger or thirst,
the scorching heat or sun will not strike them;
for their compassionate one will guide them,
50 and lead them to springs.
I will make all my mountains into a road,
and my highways will be raised up.
See, these will come from far away,
from the north and from the west,
and from the land of Sinim.

Shout for joy, you heavens!
Earth, rejoice!
Mountains break into joyful shouts!
For the LORD has comforted his people,
60 and will have compassion on his afflicted ones.

Zion says, "The LORD has abandoned me;
the Lord has forgotten me!"
"Can a woman forget her nursing child,
or lack compassion for the child of her womb?
Even if these forget,
yet I will not forget you.
Look, I have inscribed you on the palms of my hands;
your walls are continually before me.

Your builders hurry;
70 those who destroy and devastate you will leave you.
Look up, and look around.
They all gather together; they come to you.
As I live"—
this is the LORD's declaration—
"you will wear all your children as jewelry,
and put them on as a bride does.
For your waste and desolate places
and your land marked by ruins
will now be indeed too small for the inhabitants,
80 and those who swallowed you up will be far away.
Yet as you listen, the children
that you have been deprived of will say,
'This place is too small for me;
make room for me so that I may settle.'
Then you will say within yourself,
'Who fathered these for me?
I was deprived of my children and unable to conceive,
exiled and wandering—
but who brought them up?
90 See, I was left by myself—
but these, where did they come from?'"

This is what the Lord GOD says:
Look, I will lift up my hand to the nations,
and raise my banner to the peoples.
They will bring your sons in their arms,
and your daughters will be carried on their shoulders.
Kings will be your guardians
and their queens your nursing mothers.
They will bow down to you
100 with their faces to the ground
and lick the dust at your feet.
Then you will know that I am the LORD;
those who put their hope in me
will not be put to shame.

Can the prey be taken from a mighty man,
or the captives of a tyrant be delivered?
For this is what the LORD says:
"Even the captives of a mighty man will be taken,
and the prey of a tyrant will be delivered;
110   I will contend with the one who contends with you,
and I will save your children.
I will make your oppressors eat their own flesh,
and they will be drunk with their own blood
as with sweet wine.
Then all humanity will know
that I, the LORD, am your Savior,
and your Redeemer, the Mighty One of Jacob."

50   This is what the LORD says:
Where is your mother's divorce certificate
that I used to send her away?
Or to which of my creditors did I sell you?
Look, you were sold for your iniquities,
and your mother was sent away
because of your transgressions.
Why was no one there when I came?
Why was there no one to answer when I called?
10   Is my arm too weak to redeem?
Or do I have no power to rescue?
Look, I dry up the sea by my rebuke;
I turn the rivers into a wilderness;
their fish rot because of lack of water
and die of thirst.
I dress the heavens in black
and make sackcloth their covering.

The Lord GOD has given me
the tongue of those who are instructed
20   to know how to sustain the weary with a word.
He awakens me each morning;
he awakens my ear to listen like those being instructed.
The Lord GOD has opened my ear,

and I was not rebellious;
I did not turn back.
I gave my back to those who beat me,
and my cheeks to those who tore out my beard.
I did not hide my face from scorn and spitting.
The Lord GOD will help me;
30   therefore I have not been humiliated;
therefore I have set my face like flint,
and I know I will not be put to shame.
The one who vindicates me is near;
who will contend with me?
Let us confront each other.
Who has a case against me?
Let him come near me!
In truth, the Lord GOD will help me;
who will condemn me?
40   Indeed, all of them will wear out like a garment;
a moth will devour them.
Who among you fears the LORD
and listens to his servant?
Who among you walks in darkness,
and has no light?
Let him trust in the name of the LORD;
let him lean on his God.
Look, all you who kindle a fire,
who encircle yourselves with torches;
50   walk in the light of your fire
and of the torches you have lit!
This is what you'll get from my hand:
you will lie down in a place of torment.

51   Listen to me, you who pursue righteousness,
you who seek the LORD:
Look to the rock from which you were cut,
and to the quarry from which you were dug.
Look to Abraham your father,
and to Sarah who gave birth to you.
When I called him, he was only one;

I blessed him and made him many.
For the Lord will comfort Zion;
he will comfort all her waste places,
and he will make her wilderness like Eden,
and her desert like the garden of the Lord.
Joy and gladness will be found in her,
thanksgiving and melodious song.

Pay attention to me, my people,
and listen to me, my nation;
for instruction will come from me,
and my justice for a light to the nations.
I will bring it about quickly.
My righteousness is near,
my salvation appears,
and my arms will bring justice to the nations.
The coasts and islands will put their hope in me,
and they will look to my strength.
Look up to the heavens,
and look at the earth beneath;
for the heavens will vanish like smoke,
the earth will wear out like a garment,
and its inhabitants will die like gnats.
But my salvation will last forever,
and my righteousness will never be shattered.

Listen to me, you who know righteousness,
the people in whose heart is my instruction:
do not fear disgrace by men,
and do not be shattered by their taunts.
For moths will devour them like a garment,
and worms will eat them like wool.
But my righteousness will last forever,
and my salvation for all generations.

Wake up, wake up!
Arm of the Lord, clothe yourself with strength.
Wake up as in days past,

as in generations long ago.
Wasn't it you who hacked Rahab to pieces,
who pierced the sea monster?
Wasn't it you who dried up the sea,
the waters of the great deep,
who made the sea-bed into a road
for the redeemed to pass over?
50 And the ransomed of the LORD will return
and come to Zion with singing,
crowned with unending joy.
Joy and gladness will overtake them,
and sorrow and sighing will flee.

I—I am the one who comforts you.
Who are you that you should fear humans who die,
or a son of man who is given up like grass?
But you have forgotten the LORD, your Maker,
who stretched out the heavens
60 and laid the foundations of the earth.
You are in constant dread all day long
because of the fury of the oppressor,
who has set himself to destroy.
But where is the fury of the oppressor?
The prisoner is soon to be set free;
he will not die and go to the Pit,
and his food will not be lacking.
For I am the LORD your God
who stirs up the sea so that its waves roar—
70 his name is the LORD of Armies.
I have put my words in your mouth,
and covered you in the shadow of my hand,
in order to plant the heavens,
to found the earth,
and to say to Zion, "You are my people."

Wake yourself, wake yourself up!
Stand up, Jerusalem,
you who have drunk the cup of his fury

from the LORD's hand;
you who have drunk the goblet to the dregs—
the cup that causes people to stagger.
There is no one to guide her
among all the children she has raised;
there is no one to take hold of her hand
among all the offspring she has brought up.
These two things have happened to you:
devastation and destruction,
famine and sword.
Who will grieve for you?
How can I comfort you?
Your children have fainted;
they lie at the head of every street
like an antelope in a net.
They are full of the LORD's fury,
the rebuke of your God.

So listen to this, suffering
and drunken one—but not with wine.
This is what your Lord says—
the LORD, even your God,
who defends his people—
"Look, I have removed from your hand
the cup that causes staggering;
that goblet, the cup of my fury.
You will never drink it again.
I will put it into the hands of your tormentors,
who said to you,
'Lie down, so we can walk over you.'
You made your back like the ground,
and like a street for those who walk on it.

52 "Wake up, wake up;
put on your strength, Zion!
Put on your beautiful garments,
Jerusalem, the holy city!
For the uncircumcised and the unclean

will no longer enter you.
Stand up, shake the dust off yourself!
Take your seat, Jerusalem.
Remove the bonds from your neck,
10   captive Daughter Zion."
For this is what the LORD says:
"You were sold for nothing,
and you will be redeemed without silver."
For this is what the Lord GOD says:
"At first my people went down to Egypt to reside there,
then Assyria oppressed them without cause.
So now what have I here"—
this is the LORD's declaration—
"that my people are taken away for nothing?
20   Its rulers wail"—
this is the LORD's declaration—
"and my name is continually blasphemed all day long.
Therefore my people will know my name;
therefore they will know on that day
that I am he who says,
'Here I am.'"

How beautiful on the mountains
are the feet of the herald,
who proclaims peace,
30   who brings news of good things,
who proclaims salvation,
who says to Zion, "Your God reigns!"
The voices of your watchmen—
they lift up their voices,
shouting for joy together;
for every eye will see
when the LORD returns to Zion.
Be joyful, rejoice together,
you ruins of Jerusalem!
40   For the LORD has comforted his people;
he has redeemed Jerusalem.
The LORD has displayed his holy arm

in the sight of all the nations;
all the ends of the earth will see
the salvation of our God.

Leave, leave, go out from there!
Do not touch anything unclean;
go out from her, purify yourselves,
you who carry the vessels of the LORD.
50   For you will not leave in a hurry,
and you will not have to take flight;
because the LORD is going before you,
and the God of Israel is your rear guard.

See, my servant will be successful;
he will be raised and lifted up and greatly exalted.
Just as many were appalled at you—
his appearance was so disfigured
that he did not look like a man,
and his form did not resemble a human being—
60   so he will sprinkle many nations.
Kings will shut their mouths because of him,
for they will see what had not been told them,
and they will understand what they had not heard.

53   Who has believed what we have heard?
And to whom has the arm of the LORD been revealed?
He grew up before him like a young plant
and like a root out of dry ground.
He didn't have an impressive form
or majesty that we should look at him,
no appearance that we should desire him.
He was despised and rejected by men,
a man of suffering who knew what sickness was.
10   He was like someone people turned away from;
he was despised, and we didn't value him.

Yet he himself bore our sicknesses,
and he carried our pains;

but we in turn regarded him stricken,
struck down by God, and afflicted.
But he was pierced because of our rebellion,
crushed because of our iniquities;
punishment for our peace was on him,
and we are healed by his wounds.
20   We all went astray like sheep;
we all have turned to our own way;
and the LORD has punished him
for the iniquity of us all.

He was oppressed and afflicted,
yet he did not open his mouth.
Like a lamb led to the slaughter
and like a sheep silent before her shearers,
he did not open his mouth.
He was taken away because of oppression and judgment,
30   and who considered his fate?
For he was cut off from the land of the living;
he was struck because of my people's rebellion.
He was assigned a grave with the wicked,
but he was with a rich man at his death,
because he had done no violence
and had not spoken deceitfully.

Yet the LORD was pleased to crush him severely.
When you make him a guilt offering,
he will see his seed, he will prolong his days,
40   and by his hand, the LORD's pleasure will be accomplished.
After his anguish,
he will see light and be satisfied.
By his knowledge,
my righteous servant will justify many,
and he will carry their iniquities.
Therefore I will give him the many as a portion,
and he will receive the mighty as spoil,
because he willingly submitted to death,
and was counted among the rebels;

50 yet he bore the sin of many
and interceded for the rebels.

54 "Rejoice, childless one, who did not give birth;
burst into song and shout,
you who have not been in labor!
For the children of the desolate one will be more
than the children of the married woman,"
says the Lord.
"Enlarge the site of your tent,
and let your tent curtains be stretched out;
do not hold back;
10 lengthen your ropes,
and drive your pegs deep.
For you will spread out to the right and to the left,
and your descendants will dispossess nations
and inhabit the desolate cities.

"Do not be afraid, for you will not be put to shame;
don't be humiliated, for you will not be disgraced.
For you will forget the shame of your youth,
and you will no longer remember
the disgrace of your widowhood.
20 Indeed, your husband is your Maker—
his name is the Lord of Armies—
and the Holy One of Israel is your Redeemer;
he is called the God of the whole earth.
For the Lord has called you,
like a wife deserted and wounded in spirit,
a wife of one's youth when she is rejected,"
says your God.
"I deserted you for a brief moment,
but I will take you back with abundant compassion.
30 In a surge of anger
I hid my face from you for a moment,
but I will have compassion on you
with everlasting love,"
says the Lord your Redeemer.

"For this is like the days of Noah to me:
when I swore that the water of Noah
would never flood the earth again,
so I have sworn that I will not be angry with you
or rebuke you.
40   Though the mountains move
and the hills shake,
my love will not be removed from you
and my covenant of peace will not be shaken,"
says your compassionate Lord.

"Poor Jerusalem, storm-tossed, and not comforted,
I will set your stones in black mortar,
and lay your foundations in lapis lazuli.
I will make your fortifications out of rubies,
your gates out of sparkling stones,
50   and all your walls out of precious stones.
Then all your children will be taught by the Lord,
their prosperity will be great,
and you will be established
on a foundation of righteousness.
You will be far from oppression,
you will certainly not be afraid;
you will be far from terror,
it will certainly not come near you.
If anyone attacks you,
60   it is not from me;
whoever attacks you
will fall before you.
Look, I have created the craftsman
who blows on the charcoal fire
and produces a weapon suitable for its task;
and I have created the destroyer to cause havoc.
No weapon formed against you will succeed,
and you will refute any accusation
raised against you in court.
70   This is the heritage of the Lord's servants,
and their vindication is from me."

This is the LORD's declaration.

55   "Come, everyone who is thirsty,
come to the water;
and you without silver,
come, buy, and eat!
Come, buy wine and milk
without silver and without cost!
Why do you spend silver on what is not food,
and your wages on what does not satisfy?
Listen carefully to me, and eat what is good,
and you will enjoy the choicest of foods.
Pay attention and come to me;
listen, so that you will live.
I will make a permanent covenant with you
on the basis of the faithful kindnesses of David.
Since I have made him a witness to the peoples,
a leader and commander for the peoples,
so you will summon a nation you do not know,
and nations who do not know you will run to you.
For the LORD your God,
even the Holy One of Israel,
has glorified you."

Seek the LORD while he may be found;
call to him while he is near.
Let the wicked one abandon his way
and the sinful one his thoughts;
let him return to the LORD,
so he may have compassion on him,
and to our God, for he will freely forgive.

"For my thoughts are not your thoughts,
and your ways are not my ways."
This is the LORD's declaration.
"For as heaven is higher than earth,
so my ways are higher than your ways,

and my thoughts than your thoughts.
For just as rain and snow fall from heaven
and do not return there
without saturating the earth
and making it germinate and sprout,
and providing seed to sow
40   and food to eat,
so my word that comes from my mouth
will not return to me empty,
but it will accomplish what I please
and will prosper in what I send it to do."

You will indeed go out with joy
and be peacefully guided;
the mountains and the hills will break into singing before you,
and all the trees of the field will clap their hands.
Instead of the thornbush, a cypress will come up,
50   and instead of the brier, a myrtle will come up;
this will stand as a monument for the LORD,
an everlasting signs that will not be destroyed.

56 This is what the LORD says:
Preserve justice and do what is right,
for my salvation is coming soon,
and my righteousness will be revealed.
Happy is the person who does this,
the son of man who holds it fast,
who keeps the Sabbath without desecrating it,
and keeps his hand from doing any evil.

No foreigner who has joined himself to the LORD
10   should say,
"The LORD will exclude me from his people,"
and the eunuch should not say,
"Look, I am a dried-up tree."
For the LORD says this:
"For the eunuchs who keep my Sabbaths,
and choose what pleases me,

and hold firmly to my covenant,
I will give them, in my house and within my walls,
a memorial and a name

20 better than sons and daughters.
I will give each of them an everlasting name
that will never be cut off.
As for the foreigners who join themselves to the LORD
to minister to him, to love the name of the LORD,
and to become his servants—
all who keep the Sabbath without desecrating it
and who hold firmly to my covenant—
I will bring them to my holy mountain
and let them rejoice in my house of prayer.

30 Their burnt offerings and sacrifices
will be acceptable on my altar,
for my house will be called a house of prayer
for all nations."
This is the declaration of the Lord GOD,
who gathers the dispersed of Israel:
"I will gather to them still others
besides those already gathered."

All you animals of the field and forest,
come and eat!

40 Israel's watchmen are blind, all of them,
they know nothing;
all of them are mute dogs,
they cannot bark;
they dream, lie down,
and love to sleep.
These dogs have fierce appetites;
they never have enough.
And they are shepherds
who have no discernment;

50 all of them turn to their own way,
every last one for his own profit.
"Come, let me get some wine,
let's guzzle some beer;

and tomorrow will be like today,
only far better!"

57 The righteous person perishes,
and no one takes it to heart;
the faithful are taken away,
with no one realizing
that the righteous person is taken away
because of evil.
He will enter into peace—
they will rest on their beds—
everyone who lives uprightly.

10 But come here,
you witch's sons,
offspring of an adulterer and a prostitute!
Who are you mocking?
Who are you opening your mouth
and sticking out your tongue at?
Isn't it you, you rebellious children,
you offspring of liars,
who burn with lust among the oaks,
under every green tree,
20 who slaughter children in the wadis
below the clefts of the rocks?
Your portion is among the smooth stones of the wadi;
indeed, they are your lot.
You have even poured out a drink offering to them;
you have offered a grain offering;
should I be satisfied with these?
You have placed your bed
on a high and lofty mountain;
you also went up there to offer sacrifice.
30 You have set up your memorial
behind the door and doorpost.
For away from me, you stripped,
went up, and made your bed wide,
and you have made a bargain for yourself with them.

You have loved their bed;
you have gazed on their genitals.
You went to the king with oil
and multiplied your perfumes;
you sent your envoys far away
40   and sent them down even to Sheol.
You became weary on your many journeys,
but you did not say, "It's hopeless!"
You found a renewal of your strength;
therefore you did not grow weak.
Who was it you dreaded and feared,
so that you lied and didn't remember me
or take it to heart?
I have kept silent for a long time, haven't I?
So you do not fear me.
50   I will announce your righteousness,
and your works—they will not profit you.
When you cry out,
let your collection of idols rescue you!
The wind will carry all of them off,
a breath will take them away.
But whoever takes refuge in me
will inherit the land
and possess my holy mountain.

He said,
60   "Build it up, build it up, prepare the way,
remove every obstacle from my people's way."
For the High and Exalted One,
who lives forever, whose name is holy, says this:
"I live in a high and holy place,
and with the oppressed and lowly of spirit,
to revive the spirit of the lowly
and revive the heart of the oppressed.
For I will not accuse you forever,
and I will not always be angry;
70   for then the spirit would grow weak before me,
even the breath, which I have made.

Because of his sinful greed I was angry,
so I struck him; I was angry and hid;
but he went on turning back to the desires of his heart.
I have seen his ways, but I will heal him;
I will lead him and restore comfort
to him and his mourners,
creating words of praise."
The LORD says,
80 "Peace, peace to the one who is far or near,
and I will heal him.
But the wicked are like the storm-tossed sea,
for it cannot be still,
and its water churns up mire and muck.
There is no peace for the wicked,"
says my God.

58 "Cry out loudly, don't hold back!
Raise your voice like a ram's horn.
Tell my people their transgression
and the house of Jacob their sins.
They seek me day after day
and delight to know my ways,
like a nation that does what is right
and does not abandon the justice of their God.
They ask me for righteous judgments;
10 they delight in the nearness of God."
"Why have we fasted, but you have not seen?
We have denied ourselves, but you haven't noticed!"
"Look, you do as you please on the day of your fast,
and oppress all your workers.
You fast with contention and strife
to strike viciously with your fist.
You cannot fast as you do today,
hoping to make your voice heard on high.
Will the fast I choose be like this:
20 A day for a person to deny himself,
to bow his head like a reed,
and to spread out sackcloth and ashes?

Will you call this a fast
and a day acceptable to the LORD?
Isn't this the fast I choose:
To break the chains of wickedness,
to untie the ropes of the yoke,
to set the oppressed free,
and to tear off every yoke?
Is it not to share your bread with the hungry,
to bring the poor and homeless into your house,
to clothe the naked when you see him,
and not to ignore your own flesh and blood?
Then your light will appear like the dawn,
and your recovery will come quickly.
Your righteousness will go before you,
and the LORD's glory will be your rear guard.
At that time, when you call, the LORD will answer;
when you cry out, he will say, 'Here I am.'
If you get rid of the yoke among you,
the finger-pointing and malicious speaking,
and if you offer yourself to the hungry,
and satisfy the afflicted one,
then your light will shine in the darkness,
and your night will be like noonday.
The LORD will always lead you,
satisfy you in a parched land,
and strengthen your bones.
You will be like a watered garden
and like a spring whose water never runs dry.
Some of you will rebuild the ancient ruins;
you will restore the foundations laid long ago;
you will be called the repairer of broken walls,
the restorer of streets where people live.

"If you keep from desecrating the Sabbath,
from doing whatever you want on my holy day;
if you call the Sabbath a delight,
and the holy day of the LORD honorable;
if you honor it, not going your own ways,

60   seeking your own pleasure, or talking business;
    then you will delight in the LORD,
    and I will make you ride over the heights of the land,
    and let you enjoy the heritage of your father Jacob."
    For the mouth of the LORD has spoken.

59   Indeed, the LORD's arm is not too weak to save,
    and his ear is not too deaf to hear.
    But your iniquities are separating you
    from your God,
    and your sins have hidden his face from you
    so that he does not listen.
    For your hands are defiled with blood
    and your fingers, with iniquity;
    your lips have spoken lies,
10   and your tongues mutter injustice.
    No one makes claims justly;
    no one pleads honestly.
    They trust in empty and worthless words;
    they conceive trouble and give birth to iniquity.
    They hatch viper's eggs
    and weave spider's webs.
    Whoever eats their eggs will die;
    crack one open, and a viper is hatched.
    Their webs cannot become clothing,
20   and they cannot cover themselves with their works.
    Their works are sinful works,
    and violent acts are in their hands.
    Their feet run after evil,
    and they rush to shed innocent blood.
    Their thoughts are sinful thoughts;
    ruin and wretchedness are in their paths.
    They have not known the path of peace,
    and there is no justice in their ways.
    They have made their roads crooked;
30   no one who walks on them will know peace.

    Therefore justice is far from us,

and righteousness does not reach us.
We hope for light, but there is darkness;
for brightness, but we live in the night.
We grope along a wall like the blind;
we grope like those without eyes.
We stumble at noon as though it were twilight;
we are like the dead among those who are healthy.
We all growl like bears
40 and moan like doves.
We hope for justice, but there is none;
for salvation, but it is far from us.
For our transgressions have multiplied before you,
and our sins testify against us.
For our transgressions are with us,
and we know our iniquities:
transgression and deception against the Lord,
turning away from following our God,
speaking oppression and revolt,
50 conceiving and uttering lying words from the heart.
Justice is turned back,
and righteousness stands far off.
For truth has stumbled in the public square,
and honesty cannot enter.
Truth is missing,
and whoever turns from evil is plundered.

The Lord saw that there was no justice,
and he was offended.
He saw that there was no man—
60 he was amazed that there was no one interceding;
so his own arm brought salvation,
and his own righteousness supported him.
He put on righteousness as body armor,
and a helmet of salvation on his head;
he put on garments of vengeance for clothing,
and he wrapped himself in zeal as in a cloak.
So he will repay according to their deeds:
fury to his enemies,

retribution to his foes,
70   and he will repay the coasts and islands.
They will fear the name of the LORD in the west
and his glory in the east;
for he will come like a rushing stream
driven by the wind of the LORD.
"The Redeemer will come to Zion,
and to those in Jacob who turn from transgression."
This is the LORD's declaration.

"As for me, this is my covenant with them," says the LORD: "My Spirit who is on you, and my words that I have put in your mouth, will not depart from your mouth, or from the mouths of your
80 children, or from the mouths of your children's children, from now on and forever," says the LORD.

60

Arise, shine, for your light has come,
and the glory of the LORD shines over you.
For look, darkness will cover the earth,
and total darkness the peoples;
but the LORD will shine over you,
and his glory will appear over you.
Nations will come to your light,
and kings to your shining brightness.
Raise your eyes and look around:
10   they all gather and come to you;
your sons will come from far away,
and your daughters on the hips of nursing mothers.
Then you will see and be radiant,
and your heart will tremble and rejoice,
because the riches of the sea will become yours
and the wealth of the nations will come to you.
Caravans of camels will cover your land—
young camels of Midian and Ephah—
all of them will come from Sheba.
20   They will carry gold and frankincense
and proclaim the praises of the LORD.
All the flocks of Kedar will be gathered to you;
the rams of Nebaioth will serve you
and go up on my altar as an acceptable sacrifice.
I will glorify my beautiful house.

Who are these who fly like a cloud,
like doves to their shelters?
Yes, the coasts and islands will wait for me
with the ships of Tarshish in the lead,
30   to bring your children from far away,
their silver and gold with them,
for the honor of the LORD your God,
the Holy One of Israel,
who has glorified you.
Foreigners will rebuild your walls,
and their kings will serve you.
Although I struck you in my wrath,
yet I will show mercy to you with my favor.
Your city gates will always be open;
40   they will never be shut day or night
so that the wealth of the nations
may be brought into you,
with their kings being led in procession.
For the nation and the kingdom
that will not serve you will perish;
those nations will be annihilated.
The glory of Lebanon will come to you—
its pine, elm, and cypress together—
to beautify the place of my sanctuary,
50   and I will glorify my dwelling place.
The sons of your oppressors
will come and bow down to you;
all who reviled you
will fall facedown at your feet.
They will call you the City of the LORD,
Zion of the Holy One of Israel.
Instead of your being deserted and hated,
with no one passing through,
I will make you an object of eternal pride,
60   a joy from age to age.
You will nurse on the milk of nations,
and nurse at the breast of kings;

you will know that I, the LORD, am your Savior
and Redeemer, the Mighty One of Jacob.

I will bring gold instead of bronze;
I will bring silver instead of iron,
bronze instead of wood,
and iron instead of stones.
I will appoint peace as your government
70   and righteousness as your overseers.
Violence will never again be heard of in your land;
devastation and destruction
will be gone from your borders.
You will call your walls Salvation
and your city gates Praise.
The sun will no longer be your light by day,
and the brightness of the moon will not shine on you.
The LORD will be your everlasting light,
and your God will be your splendor.
80   Your sun will no longer set,
and your moon will not fade;
for the LORD will be your everlasting light,
and the days of your sorrow will be over.
All your people will be righteous;
they will possess the land forever;
they are the branch I planted,
the work of my hands,
so that I may be glorified.
The least will become a thousand,
90   the smallest a mighty nation.
I am the LORD;
I will accomplish it quickly in its time.

61   The Spirit of the Lord GOD is on me,
because the LORD has anointed me
to bring good news to the poor.
He has sent me to heal the brokenhearted,
to proclaim liberty to the captives
and freedom to the prisoners;

to proclaim the year of the LORD's favor,
and the day of our God's vengeance;
to comfort all who mourn,
to provide for those who mourn in Zion;
to give them a crown of beauty instead of ashes,
festive oil instead of mourning,
and splendid clothes instead of despair.
And they will be called righteous trees,
planted by the LORD
to glorify him.

They will rebuild the ancient ruins;
they will restore the former devastations;
they will renew the ruined cities,
the devastations of many generations.
Strangers will stand and feed your flocks,
and foreigners will be your plowmen and vinedressers.
But you will be called the LORD's priests;
they will speak of you as ministers of our God;
you will eat the wealth of the nations,
and you will boast in their riches.
In place of your shame, you will have a double portion;
in place of disgrace, they will rejoice over their share.
So they will possess double in their land,
and eternal joy will be theirs.

For I the LORD love justice;
I hate robbery and injustice;
I will faithfully reward my people
and make a permanent covenant with them.
Their descendants will be known among the nations,
and their posterity among the peoples.
All who see them will recognize
that they are a people the LORD has blessed.

I rejoice greatly in the LORD,
I exult in my God;
for he has clothed me with the garments of salvation

and wrapped me in a robe of righteousness,
as a groom wears a turban
and as a bride adorns herself with her jewels.
For as the earth produces its growth,
and as a garden enables what is sown to spring up,
so the Lord God will cause righteousness and praise
to spring up before all the nations.

62
I will not keep silent because of Zion,
and I will not keep still because of Jerusalem,
until her righteousness shines like a bright light
and her salvation, like a flaming torch.
Nations will see your righteousness
and all kings, your glory.
You will be given a new name
that the Lord's mouth will announce.
You will be a glorious crown in the Lord's hand,
10 and a royal diadem in the palm of your God's hand.
You will no longer be called Deserted,
and your land will not be called Desolate;
instead, you will be called My Delight Is in Her,
and your land Married;
for the Lord delights in you,
and your land will be married.
For as a young man marries a young woman,
so your sons will marry you;
and as a groom rejoices over his bride,
20 so your God will rejoice over you.

Jerusalem,
I have appointed watchmen on your walls;
they will never be silent, day or night.
There is no rest for you,
who remind the Lord.
Do not give him rest
until he establishes and makes Jerusalem
the praise of the earth.

The LORD has sworn with his right hand
and his strong arm:
I will no longer give your grain
to your enemies for food,
and foreigners will not drink the new wine
for which you have labored.
For those who gather grain will eat it
and praise the LORD,
and those who harvest the grapes will drink the wine
in my holy courts.

Go out, go out through the city gates;
prepare a way for the people!
Build it up, build up the highway;
clear away the stones!
Raise a banner for the peoples.
Look, the LORD has proclaimed
to the ends of the earth,
"Say to Daughter Zion:
Look, your salvation is coming,
his wages are with him,
and his reward accompanies him."
And they will be called the Holy People,
the LORD's Redeemed;
and you will be called Cared For,
A City Not Deserted.

63 Who is this coming from Edom
in crimson-stained garments from Bozrah—
this one who is splendid in his apparel,
striding in his formidable might?

It is I, proclaiming vindication,
powerful to save.

Why are your clothes red,
and your garments like one who treads a winepress?

I trampled the winepress alone,
10   and no one from the nations was with me.
I trampled them in my anger
and ground them underfoot in my fury;
their blood spattered my garments,
and all my clothes were stained.
For I planned the day of vengeance,
and the year of my redemption came.
I looked, but there was no one to help,
and I was amazed that no one assisted;
so my arm accomplished victory for me,
20   and my wrath assisted me.
I crushed nations in my anger;
I made them drunk with my wrath
and poured out their blood on the ground.

I will make known the LORD's faithful love
and the LORD's praiseworthy acts,
because of all the LORD has done for us—
even the many good things
he has done for the house of Israel,
which he did for them based on his compassion
30   and the abundance of his faithful love.
He said, "They are indeed my people,
children who will not be disloyal,"
and he became their Savior.
In all their suffering, he suffered,
and the angel of his presence saved them.
He redeemed them
because of his love and compassion;
he lifted them up and carried them
all the days of the past.
40   But they rebelled
and grieved his Holy Spirit.
So he became their enemy
and fought against them.
Then he remembered the days of the past,
the days of Moses and his people.

Where is he who brought them out of the sea
with the shepherds of his flock?
Where is he who put his Holy Spirit among the flock?
He made his glorious strength
50   available at the right hand of Moses,
divided the water before them
to make an eternal name for himself,
and led them through the depths
like a horse in the wilderness,
so that they did not stumble.
Like cattle that go down into the valley,
the Spirit of the LORD gave them rest.
You led your people this way
to make a glorious name for yourself.

60   Look down from heaven and see
from your lofty home—holy and beautiful.
Where is your zeal and your might?
Your yearning and your compassion
are withheld from me.
Yet you are our Father,
even though Abraham does not know us
and Israel doesn't recognize us.
You, LORD, are our Father;
your name is Our Redeemer
70   from Ancient Times.
Why, LORD, do you make us stray from your ways?
You harden our hearts so we do not fear you.
Return, because of your servants,
the tribes of your heritage.
Your holy people had a possession
for a little while,
but our enemies have trampled down
your sanctuary.
We have become like those you never ruled,
80   like those who did not bear your name.

64
If only you would tear the heavens open
and come down,
so that mountains would quake at your presence—
just as fire kindles brushwood,
and fire boils water—
to make your name known to your enemies,
so that nations would tremble at your presence!
When you did awesome works
that we did not expect,
10 you came down,
and the mountains quaked at your presence.
From ancient times no one has heard,
no one has listened to,
no eye has seen any God except you
who acts on behalf of the one who waits for him.
You welcome the one who joyfully does what is right;
they remember you in your ways.
But we have sinned, and you were angry.
How can we be saved if we remain in our sins?
20 All of us have become like something unclean,
and all our righteous acts are like a polluted garment;
all of us wither like a leaf,
and our iniquities carry us away like the wind.
No one calls on your name,
striving to take hold of you.
For you have hidden your face from us
and made us melt because of our iniquity.

Yet LORD, you are our Father;
we are the clay, and you are our potter;
30 we all are the work of your hands.
LORD, do not be terribly angry
or remember our iniquity forever.
Please look—all of us are your people!
Your holy cities have become a wilderness;
Zion has become a wilderness,
Jerusalem a desolation.
Our holy and beautiful temple,

where our ancestors praised you,
has been burned down,
40   and all that was dear to us lies in ruins.
Lord, after all this, will you restrain yourself?
Will you keep silent and afflict us severely?

65   "I was sought by those who did not ask;
I was found by those who did not seek me.
I said, 'Here I am, here I am,'
to a nation that did not call on my name.
I spread out my hands all day long
to a rebellious people
who walk in the path that is not good,
following their own thoughts.
These people continually anger me
10   to my face,
sacrificing in gardens,
burning incense on bricks,
sitting among the graves,
spending nights in secret places,
eating the meat of pigs,
and putting polluted broth in their bowls.
They say, 'Keep to yourself,
don't come near me, for I am too holy for you!'
These practices are smoke in my nostrils,
20   a fire that burns all day long.
Look, it is written in front of me:
I will not keep silent, but I will repay;
I will repay them fully
for your iniquities and the iniquities
of your ancestors together,"
says the Lord.
"Because they burned incense on the mountains
and reproached me on the hills,
I will reward them fully
30   for their former deeds."

The Lord says this:
"As the new wine is found in a bunch of grapes,
and one says, 'Don't destroy it,
for there's some good in it,'
so I will act because of my servants
and not destroy them all.
I will produce descendants from Jacob,
and heirs to my mountains from Judah;
my chosen ones will possess it,
and my servants will dwell there.

40   Sharon will be a pasture for flocks,
and the Valley of Achor a place for herds to lie down,
for my people who have sought me.
But you who abandon the Lord,
who forget my holy mountain,
who prepare a table for Fortune
and fill bowls of mixed wine for Destiny,
I will destine you for the sword,
and all of you will kneel down to be slaughtered,

50   because I called and you did not answer,
I spoke and you did not hear;
you did what was evil in my sight
and chose what I did not delight in."

Therefore, this is what the Lord God says:
"Look! My servants will eat,
but you will be hungry.
Look! My servants will drink,
but you will be thirsty.
Look! My servants will rejoice,

60   but you will be put to shame.
Look! My servants will shout for joy from a glad heart,
but you will cry out from an anguished heart,
and you will lament out of a broken spirit.
You will leave your name behind
as a curse for my chosen ones,
and the Lord God will kill you;
but he will give his servants another name.

Whoever asks for a blessing in the land
will ask for a blessing by the God of truth,
and whoever swears in the land
will swear by the God of truth.
For the former troubles will be forgotten
and hidden from my sight.

"For I will create new heavens and a new earth;
the past events will not be remembered or come to mind.
Then be glad and rejoice forever
in what I am creating;
for I will create Jerusalem to be a joy
and its people to be a delight.
I will rejoice in Jerusalem
and be glad in my people.
The sound of weeping and crying
will no longer be heard in her.
In her, a nursing infant will no longer live
only a few days,
or an old man not live out his days.
Indeed, the one who dies at a hundred years old
will be mourned as a young man,
and the one who misses a hundred years
will be considered cursed.
People will build houses and live in them;
they will plant vineyards and eat their fruit.
They will not build and others live in them;
they will not plant and others eat.
For my people's lives will be
like the lifetime of a tree.
My chosen ones will fully enjoy
the work of their hands.
They will not labor without success
or bear children destined for disaster,
for they will be a people blessed by the LORD
along with their descendants.
Even before they call, I will answer;
while they are still speaking, I will hear.

The wolf and the lamb will feed together,
and the lion will eat straw like cattle,
but the serpent's food will be dust!
They will not do what is evil or destroy
on my entire holy mountain,"
110   says the LORD.

66 This is what the LORD says:

Heaven is my throne,
and earth is my footstool.
Where could you possibly build a house for me?
And where would my resting place be?
My hand made all these things,
and so they all came into being.
This is the LORD's declaration.
I will look favorably on this kind of person:
10   one who is humble, submissive in spirit,
and trembles at my word.
One person slaughters an ox, another kills a person;
one person sacrifices a lamb, another breaks a dog's neck;
one person offers a grain offering, another offers pig's blood;
one person offers incense, another praises an idol—
all these have chosen their ways
and delight in their abhorrent practices.
So I will choose their punishment,
and I will bring on them what they dread
20   because I called and no one answered;
I spoke and they did not listen;
they did what was evil in my sight
and chose what I did not delight in.

You who tremble at his word,
hear the word of the LORD:
"Your brothers who hate and exclude you
for my name's sake have said,
'Let the LORD be glorified
so that we can see your joy!'
30   But they will be put to shame."

A sound of uproar from the city!
A voice from the temple—
the voice of the LORD,
paying back his enemies what they deserve!

Before Zion was in labor, she gave birth;
before she was in pain, she delivered a boy.
Who has heard of such a thing?
Who has seen such things?
Can a land be born in one day
40   or a nation be delivered in an instant?
Yet as soon as Zion was in labor,
she gave birth to her sons.
"Will I bring a baby to the point of birth
and not deliver it?"
says the LORD;
"or will I who deliver, close the womb?"
says your God.
Be glad for Jerusalem and rejoice over her,
all who love her.
50   Rejoice greatly with her,
all who mourn over her—
so that you may nurse and be satisfied
from her comforting breast
and drink deeply and delight yourselves
from her glorious breasts.

For this is what the LORD says:
I will make peace flow to her like a river,
and the wealth of nations like a flood;
you will nurse and be carried on her hip
60   and bounced on her lap.
As a mother comforts her son,
so I will comfort you,
and you will be comforted in Jerusalem.

You will see, you will rejoice,
and you will flourish like grass;
then the LORD's power will be revealed to his servants,
but he will show his wrath against his enemies.
Look, the LORD will come with fire—
his chariots are like the whirlwind—
70   to execute his anger with fury
and his rebuke with flames of fire.
For the LORD will execute judgment
on all humanity with his fiery sword,
and many will be slain by the LORD.

"Those who dedicate and purify themselves to enter the groves following their leader, eating meat from pigs, vermin, and rats, will perish together."

This is the LORD's declaration.

"Knowing their works and their thoughts, I have come to gather all nations and languages; they will come and see my glory. I will establish a sign among them, and I will send survivors from them 80   to the nations—to Tarshish, Put, Lud (who are archers), Tubal, Javan, and the coasts and islands far away—who have not heard about me or seen my glory. And they will proclaim my glory among the nations. They will bring all your brothers from all the nations as a gift to the LORD on horses and chariots, in litters, and on mules and camels, to my holy mountain Jerusalem," says the LORD, "just as the Israelites bring an offering in a clean vessel to the house of the LORD. I will also take some of them as priests and Levites," says the LORD.

"For just as the new heavens and the new earth,
which I will make,
will remain before me"—
this is the LORD's declaration—
90   "so your offspring and your name will remain.
All humanity will come to worship me
from one New Moon to another
and from one Sabbath to another,"
says the LORD.

"As they leave, they will see the dead bodies of those who have rebelled against me; for their worm will never die, their fire will never go out, and they will be a horror to all mankind."

Introduction to Jeremiah

Jill Firth

Jeremiah lived in a time of crisis in the kingdom of Judah. The Northern Kingdom fell to the Assyrians in the eighth century BC, and a century later, the Babylonians threatened the existence of the Southern Kingdom. Jeremiah's ministry spans the reigns of the last kings of Judah: Josiah, his sons Jehoahaz, Jehoiakim, and Zedekiah, and his grandson, Jehoiachin. Jeremiah is distinctive among the prophetic books because of the unusual amount of detail on the life of the prophet, who embodies the suffering of Israel and of Yahweh, sharing their tears (8.74–9.4).

This book begins with the call of Jeremiah and ends with the tragedy of the fall of Jerusalem in 587 BC. Prophecies against Judah (2.1–11.39) and against the nations (chs. 46–51) form an inner frame, though these sections also include some promises of hope (e.g., 3.50–57; 49.30–31). Jeremiah pours out his fears and anxiety to Yahweh in his prayers and laments often called his "confessions" (11.40–20.62). A central section (chs. 21–39) compares the reigns of Jehoiakim, an arrogant and godless king, and his younger brother Zedekiah, a weak and ineffectual leader. The aftermath of the fall of Jerusalem includes the appointment of a wise and godly governor who is soon assassinated, and two military coups (chs. 40–44).

Almost everyone in Judah is complicit in rebelling against Yahweh, including men, women, and children, poor and rich, (5.16–26; 7.24–26). In the reign of Jehoiakim, Jeremiah calls for repentance but is not heeded (25.1–12). In the reign of Zedekiah, those who remain in Jerusalem are invited to surrender to Nebuchadnezzar and retain their lives "like the spoils of war" (21.15–19; 38.2–5), but few accept Yahweh's gracious offer and most persist in rebellion. After the fall of Jerusalem, the people are invited to remain in the land (40.21–30; 42.13–30), but they go down to Egypt, rejecting all Yahweh's efforts to save them from destruction (43.1–14).

Jeremiah challenges Judah's complacency, emphasising the ugliness of her sins using feminine caricature (2.92–107, 136–157) and negative masculine imagery (2.35–59, 111). He then seeks to elicit pity, with a dystopia featuring destruction of the land (4.89–108) and danger for "Daughter Zion" (4.122–127; 6.7–8, 96–101). In later chapters, words of comfort accompany warnings of judgment. People who have been deported to Babylon are exhorted to flourish there (29.1–24), and Jeremiah reassures the reader of Yahweh's love for women and men and his good plans for their future welfare (31.7–106). The book looks forward to a "new covenant" (31.116–139) and ends with future hope for the line of Davidic kings (52.53–59).

The prophet dictated his prophecies to Baruch the scribe (36.6–7; 29–33), and Baruch or later writers may have edited the final document. Our English versions are based on the Hebrew Masoretic Text (MT). The ancient Greek (LXX) version is shorter than MT, but most differences are due to details such as longer forms of some descriptive titles. More noticeably, in the LXX, the oracles about the nations (chs. 46–51) are found in the middle of the book (25.23–24).

The book of Jeremiah as a whole illustrates Yahweh's invitation to trust in him, "the fountain of living water" (2.48–52), and demonstrates how he continues to reach out in persistent "faithful love, justice, and righteousness on the earth" (9.81–90), despite the rebellion of his people. A division into warnings of judgment (chs. 1–25) and promises of restoration (chs. 26–52) can be a helpful starting point in reading the book.

Outline

1. Jeremiah's call: a prophet to the nations (1.1–44)

2. Prophecies and sermons about judgment and hope (2.1–11.39)
    a. Broken relationships and invitations to "return" (2.1–4.19)
    b. Warnings of warfare and suffering (4.20–11.39)

3. Jeremiah's "confessions," sign acts, and sermons (11.40–20.62)
    a. Jeremiah fears for his life (11.40–12.66)
    b. Judgment on Judah (13.1–15.38)
    c. Jeremiah fears that Yahweh will fail him (15.39–95)
    d. Jeremiah trusts despite danger and disgrace (16.1–20.61)

4. Condemnation of rebellious kings and prophets (21.1–23.107)

5. Prophecies and narratives of judgment and hope (24.1–39.31)
    a. Hope in Babylon (24.1–19)
    b. Judgment in Judah for Jehoiakim and Zedekiah (25.1–28.31)
    c. Hope in Babylon (29.1–59)
    d. Promise of future restoration and a new covenant (30.1–33.60)
    e. Treachery by Zedekiah and Jehoiakim (34.1–36.58)
    f. Last days of Judah (37.1–39.31)

6. Aftermath of the fall of Jerusalem (40.1–44.64)
    a. Hope under governor Gedaliah (40.1–38)
    b. Rebellions of Ishmael (41.1–34) and Johanan (42.1–44.64)

7. Promise to Baruch (45.1–10)

8. Oracles about the nations (46.1–51.253)

9. Epilogue: the fall of Jerusalem reprised (52.1–52)

10. Hope for Jehoiachin (52.53–59)

Suggested Resources

Craigie, Peter C., Page H. Kelley, and Joel F. Drinkard, Jr. *Jeremiah 1–25*. Word Biblical Commentary. Nashville: Thomas Nelson, 1991.

Keown, Gerald L., Pamela J. Scalise, and Thomas G. Smothers. *Jeremiah 26–52*. Word Biblical Commentary. Nashville: Thomas Nelson, 1995.

Lalleman, Hetty. *Jeremiah and Lamentations*. Tyndale Old Testament Commentaries. Downers Grove, IL: InterVarsity Press, 2013.

Thompson, J. A. *The Book of Jeremiah*. New International Commentary on the Old Testament. Grand Rapids: Eerdmans, 1980.

Wright, Christopher J. H. *The Message of Jeremiah*. The Bible Speaks Today. Downers Grove, IL: InterVarsity Press, 2014.

Jeremiah

1 The words of Jeremiah, the son of Hilkiah, one of the priests living in Anathoth in the territory of Benjamin. The word of the Lord came to him in the thirteenth year of the reign of Josiah son of Amon, king of Judah. It also came throughout the days of Jehoiakim son of Josiah, king of Judah, until the fifth month of the eleventh year of Zedekiah son of Josiah, king of Judah, when the people of Jerusalem went into exile.

The word of the Lord came to me:
> I chose you before I formed you in the womb;
> I set you apart before you were born.
> I appointed you a prophet to the nations.

But I protested, "Oh no, Lord God! Look, I don't know how to speak since I am only a youth."
Then the Lord said to me:
> Do not say, "I am only a youth,"
> for you will go to everyone I send you to
> and speak whatever I tell you.
> Do not be afraid of anyone,
> for I will be with you to rescue you.
> This is the Lord's declaration.

Then the Lord reached out his hand, touched my mouth, and told me:
> I have now filled your mouth with my words.
> See, I have appointed you today
> over nations and kingdoms
> to uproot and tear down,
> to destroy and demolish,
> to build and plant.

Then the word of the Lord came to me, asking, "What do you see, Jeremiah?"
I replied, "I see a branch of an almond tree."
The Lord said to me, "You have seen correctly, for I watch over my word to accomplish it."
Again the word of the Lord came to me asking, "What do you see?"

And I replied, "I see a boiling pot, its lip tilted from the north to the south."

30 Then the LORD said to me, "Disaster will be poured out from the north on all who live in the land. Indeed, I am about to summon all the clans and kingdoms of the north."

This is the LORD's declaration.

> They will come, and each king will set up his throne
> at the entrance to Jerusalem's gates.
> They will attack all her surrounding walls
> and all the other cities of Judah.

"I will pronounce my judgments against them for all the evil they did when they abandoned me to burn incense to other gods and to worship the works of their own hands.

"Now, get ready. Stand up and tell them everything that I command you. Do not be
40 intimidated by them or I will cause you to cower before them. Today, I am the one who has made you a fortified city, an iron pillar, and bronze walls against the whole land—against the kings of Judah, its officials, its priests, and the population. They will fight against you but never prevail over you, since I am with you to rescue you."

This is the LORD's declaration.

2 The word of the LORD came to me: "Go and announce directly to Jerusalem that this is what the LORD says:

> I remember the loyalty of your youth,
> your love as a bride—
> how you followed me in the wilderness,
> in a land not sown.
> Israel was holy to the LORD,
> the firstfruits of his harvest.
> All who ate of it found themselves guilty;
10 > disaster came on them."

This is the LORD's declaration.

> Hear the word of the LORD, house of Jacob
> and all families of the house of Israel.
> This is what the LORD says:

> What fault did your ancestors find in me
> that they went so far from me,
> followed worthless idols,
> and became worthless themselves?

They stopped asking, "Where is the LORD
who brought us from the land of Egypt,
who led us through the wilderness,
through a land of deserts and ravines,
through a land of drought and darkness,
a land no one traveled through
and where no one lived?"
I brought you to a fertile land
to eat its fruit and bounty,
but after you entered, you defiled my land;
you made my inheritance detestable.
The priests quit asking, "Where is the LORD?"
The experts in the law no longer knew me,
and the rulers rebelled against me.
The prophets prophesied by Baal
and followed useless idols.

Therefore, I will bring a case against you again.
This is the LORD's declaration.
I will bring a case against your children's children.
Cross over to the coasts of Cyprus and take a look.
Send someone to Kedar and consider carefully;
see if there has ever been anything like this:
Has a nation ever exchanged its gods?
(But they were not gods!)
Yet my people have exchanged their Glory
for useless idols.
Be appalled at this, heavens;
be shocked and utterly desolated!
This is the LORD's declaration.

For my people have committed a double evil:
They have abandoned me,
the fountain of living water,
and dug cisterns for themselves—
cracked cisterns that cannot hold water.

Is Israel a slave?
Was he born into slavery?
Why else has he become a prey?
The young lions have roared at him;
they have roared loudly.
They have laid waste his land.
His cities are in ruins, without inhabitants.
60 The men of Memphis and Tahpanhes
have also broken your skull.
Have you not brought this on yourself
by abandoning the LORD your God
while he was leading you along the way?
Now what will you gain
by traveling along the way to Egypt
to drink the water of the Nile?
What will you gain
by traveling along the way to Assyria
70 to drink the water of the Euphrates?
Your own evil will discipline you;
your own apostasies will reprimand you.
Recognize how evil and bitter it is
for you to abandon the LORD your God
and to have no fear of me.
This is the declaration
of the Lord GOD of Armies.

For long ago I broke your yoke;
I tore off your chains.
80 You insisted, "I will not serve!"
On every high hill
and under every green tree
you lay down like a prostitute.

I planted you, a choice vine
from the very best seed.
How then could you turn into
a degenerate, foreign vine?

Even if you wash with lye
and use a great amount of bleach,
the stain of your iniquity is still in front of me.
This is the Lord God's declaration.
How can you protest, "I am not defiled;
I have not followed the Baals"?
Look at your behavior in the valley;
acknowledge what you have done.
You are a swift young camel
twisting and turning on her way,
a wild donkey at home in the wilderness.
She sniffs the wind in the heat of her desire.
Who can control her passion?
All who look for her will not become weary;
they will find her in her mating season.
Keep your feet from going bare
and your throat from thirst.
But you say, "It's hopeless;
I love strangers,
and I will continue to follow them."

Like the shame of a thief when he is caught,
so the house of Israel has been put to shame.
They, their kings, their officials,
their priests, and their prophets
say to a tree, "You are my father,"
and to a stone, "You gave birth to me."
For they have turned their back to me
and not their face,
yet in their time of disaster they beg,
"Rise up and save us!"
But where are your gods you made for yourself?
Let them rise up and save you
in your time of disaster if they can,
for your gods are as numerous as your cities, Judah.

Why do you bring a case against me?
All of you have rebelled against me.

This is the Lord's declaration.
I have struck down your children in vain;
they would not accept discipline.
Your own sword has devoured your prophets
like a ravaging lion.
Evil generation,
130 pay attention to the word of the Lord!
Have I been a wilderness to Israel
or a land of dense darkness?
Why do my people claim,
"We will go where we want;
we will no longer come to you"?
Can a young woman forget her jewelry
or a bride her wedding sash?
Yet my people have forgotten me
for countless days.
140 How skillfully you pursue love;
you also teach evil women your ways.
Moreover, your skirts are stained
with the blood of the innocent poor.
You did not catch them breaking and entering.
But in spite of all these things
you claim, "I am innocent.
His anger is sure to turn away from me."
But I will certainly judge you
because you have said, "I have not sinned."
150 How unstable you are,
constantly changing your ways!
You will be put to shame by Egypt
just as you were put to shame by Assyria.
Moreover, you will be led out from here
with your hands on your head
since the Lord has rejected those you trust;
you will not succeed even with their help.

3 If a man divorces his wife
and she leaves him to marry another,
can he ever return to her?

Wouldn't such a land become totally defiled?
But you!
You have prostituted yourself with many partners—
can you return to me?
This is the LORD's declaration.
Look to the barren heights and see.
10   Where have you not been immoral?
You sat waiting for them beside the highways
like a nomad in the desert.
You have defiled the land
with your prostitution and wickedness.
This is why the showers haven't come—
why there has been no spring rain.
You have the brazen look of a prostitute
and refuse to be ashamed.
Haven't you recently called to me, "My Father!
20   You were my friend in my youth.
Will he bear a grudge forever?
Will he be endlessly infuriated?"
This is what you have said,
but you have done the evil things
you are capable of.

In the days of King Josiah the LORD asked me, "Have you seen what unfaithful Israel has done?
She has ascended every high hill and gone under every green tree to prostitute herself there. I
thought, 'After she has done all these things, she will return to me.' But she didn't return, and her
treacherous sister Judah saw it. I observed that it was because unfaithful Israel had committed
30 adultery that I had sent her away and had given her a certificate of divorce. Nevertheless, her
treacherous sister Judah was not afraid but also went and prostituted herself. Indifferent to her
prostitution, she defiled the land and committed adultery with stones and trees. Yet in spite of all
this, her treacherous sister Judah didn't return to me with all her heart—only in pretense."
    This is the LORD's declaration.
    The LORD announced to me, "Unfaithful Israel has shown herself more righteous than
treacherous Judah. Go, proclaim these words to the north, and say,
        'Return, unfaithful Israel.
    This is the LORD's declaration.
I will not look on you with anger,
40   for I am unfailing in my love.

This is the Lord's declaration.
I will not be angry forever.
Only acknowledge your guilt—
you have rebelled against the Lord your God.
You have scattered your favors to strangers
under every green tree
and have not obeyed me.
This is the Lord's declaration.

50 "'Return, you faithless children—this is the Lord's declaration—for I am your master, and I will take you, one from a city and two from a family, and I will bring you to Zion. I will give you shepherds who are loyal to me, and they will shepherd you with knowledge and skill. When you multiply and increase in the land, in those days—this is the Lord's declaration—no one will say again, "The ark of the Lord's covenant." It will never come to mind, and no one will remember or miss it. Another one will not be made. At that time Jerusalem will be called The Lord's Throne, and all the nations will be gathered to it, to the name of the Lord in Jerusalem. They will cease to follow the stubbornness of their evil hearts. In those days the house of Judah will join with the house of Israel, and they will come together from the land of the north to the land I have given your ancestors to inherit.'"

I thought, "How I long to make you my sons
and give you a desirable land,
60 the most beautiful inheritance of all the nations."
I thought, "You will call me 'My Father'
and never turn away from me."
However, as a woman may betray her lover,
so you have betrayed me, house of Israel.
This is the Lord's declaration.

A sound is heard on the barren heights:
the children of Israel weeping and begging for mercy,
for they have perverted their way;
they have forgotten the Lord their God.
70 Return, you faithless children.
I will heal your unfaithfulness.
"Here we are, coming to you,
for you are the Lord our God.
Surely, falsehood comes from the hills,
commotion from the mountains,

but the salvation of Israel
is only in the LORD our God.
From the time of our youth
the shameful one has consumed
80   what our ancestors have worked for—
their flocks and their herds,
their sons and their daughters.
Let us lie down in our shame;
let our disgrace cover us.
We have sinned against the LORD our God,
both we and our ancestors,
from the time of our youth even to this day.
We have not obeyed the LORD our God."

4   If you return, Israel—
this is the LORD's declaration—
you will return to me,
if you remove your abhorrent idols
from my presence
and do not waver,
then you can swear, "As the LORD lives,"
in truth, justice, and righteousness,
and then the nations will be blessed by him
10   and will boast in him.

For this is what the LORD says to the men of Judah and Jerusalem:
Break up the unplowed ground;
do not sow among the thorns.
Circumcise yourselves to the LORD;
remove the foreskin of your hearts,
men of Judah and residents of Jerusalem.
Otherwise, my wrath will break out like fire
and burn with no one to extinguish it
because of your evil deeds.

20   Declare in Judah, proclaim in Jerusalem, and say,
Blow the ram's horn throughout the land.
Cry out loudly and say,

"Assemble yourselves,
and let's flee to the fortified cities."
Lift up a signal flag toward Zion.
Run for cover! Don't stand still!
For I am bringing disaster from the north—
a crushing blow.
A lion has gone up from his thicket;
30   a destroyer of nations has set out.
He has left his lair
to make your land a waste.
Your cities will be reduced to uninhabited ruins.
Because of this, put on sackcloth;
mourn and wail,
for the LORD's burning anger
has not turned away from us.

"On that day"—this is the LORD's declaration—"the king and the officials will lose their courage. The priests will tremble in fear, and the prophets will be scared speechless."

I said, "Oh no, Lord GOD, you have certainly deceived this people and Jerusalem, by announcing, 'You will have peace,' while a sword is at our throats."

"At that time it will be said to this people and to Jerusalem, 'A searing wind blows from the barren heights in the wilderness on the way to my dear people. It comes not to winnow or to sift; a wind too strong for this comes at my call. Now I will also pronounce judgments against them.'"

Look, he advances like clouds;
his chariots are like a storm.
His horses are swifter than eagles.
Woe to us, for we are ruined!
50   Wash the evil from your heart, Jerusalem,
so that you will be delivered.
How long will you harbor
malicious thoughts?
For a voice announces from Dan,
proclaiming malice from Mount Ephraim.
Warn the nations: Look!
Proclaim to Jerusalem:
Those who besiege are coming
from a distant land;

60   they raise their voices
against the cities of Judah.
They have her surrounded
like those who guard a field,
because she has rebelled against me.
This is the Lord's declaration.
Your way and your actions
have brought this on you.
This is your punishment. It is very bitter,
because it has reached your heart!

70   My anguish, my anguish! I writhe in agony!
Oh, the pain in my heart!
My heart pounds;
I cannot be silent.
For you, my soul,
have heard the sound of the ram's horn—
the shout of battle.
Disaster after disaster is reported
because the whole land is destroyed.
Suddenly my tents are destroyed,
80   my tent curtains, in a moment.
How long must I see the signal flag
and hear the sound of the ram's horn?

"For my people are fools;
they do not know me.
They are foolish children,
without understanding.
They are skilled in doing what is evil,
but they do not know how to do what is good."

I looked at the earth,
90   and it was formless and empty.
I looked to the heavens,
and their light was gone.
I looked at the mountains,
and they were quaking;

all the hills shook.
I looked, and there was no human being,
and all the birds of the sky had fled.
I looked, and the fertile field was a wilderness.
All its cities were torn down
100 because of the LORD
and his burning anger.

For this is what the LORD says:
"The whole land will be a desolation,
but I will not finish it off.
Because of this, the earth will mourn;
the skies above will grow dark.
I have spoken; I have planned,
and I will not relent or turn back from it."

Every city flees
110 at the sound of the horseman and the archer.
They enter the thickets
and climb among the rocks.
Every city is abandoned;
no inhabitant is left.
And you, devastated one, what are you doing
that you dress yourself in scarlet,
that you adorn yourself with gold jewelry,
that you enhance your eyes with makeup?
You beautify yourself for nothing.
120 Your lovers reject you;
they intend to take your life.
I hear a cry like a woman in labor,
a cry of anguish like one bearing her first child.
The cry of Daughter Zion gasping for breath,
stretching out her hands:
"Woe is me, for my life is weary
because of the murderers!"

5   Roam through the streets of Jerusalem.
     Investigate;

search in her squares.
If you find one person,
any who acts justly,
who pursues faithfulness,
then I will forgive her.
When they say, "As the LORD lives,"
they are swearing falsely.
LORD, don't your eyes look for faithfulness?
You have struck them, but they felt no pain.
You finished them off,
but they refused to accept discipline.
They made their faces harder than rock,
and they refused to return.

Then I thought:
They are just the poor;
they have been foolish.
For they don't understand the way of the LORD,
the justice of their God.
I will go to the powerful
and speak to them.
Surely they know the way of the LORD,
the justice of their God.
However, these also had broken the yoke
and torn off the chains.
Therefore, a lion from the forest will strike them down.
A wolf from arid plains will ravage them.
A leopard stalks their cities.
Anyone who leaves them will be torn to pieces
because their rebellious acts are many,
their unfaithful deeds numerous.

Why should I forgive you?
Your children have abandoned me
and sworn by those who are not gods.
I satisfied their needs, yet they committed adultery;
they gashed themselves at the prostitute's house.
They are well-fed, eager stallions,

each neighing after someone else's wife.

40 Should I not punish them for these things?
This is the LORD's declaration.
Should I not avenge myself
on such a nation as this?

Go up among her vineyard terraces and destroy them,
but do not finish them off.
Prune away her shoots,
for they do not belong to the LORD.
They, the house of Israel and the house of Judah,
have dealt very treacherously with me.
50 This is the LORD's declaration.
They have contradicted the LORD
and insisted, "It won't happen.
Harm won't come to us;
we won't see sword or famine."
The prophets become only wind,
for the LORD's word is not in them.
This will in fact happen to them.

Therefore, this is what the Lord GOD of Armies says:
Because you have spoken this word,
60 I am going to make my words
become fire in your mouth.
These people are the wood,
and the fire will consume them.
I am about to bring a nation
from far away against you,
house of Israel.
This is the LORD's declaration.
It is an established nation,
an ancient nation,
70 a nation whose language you do not know
and whose speech you do not understand.
Their quiver is like an open grave;
they are all warriors.
They will consume your harvest and your food.

They will consume your sons and your daughters.
They will consume your flocks and your herds.
They will consume your vines and your fig trees.
With the sword they will destroy
your fortified cities in which you trust.

80 "But even in those days"—this is the LORD's declaration—"I will not finish you off. When people ask, 'For what offense has the LORD our God done all these things to us?' You will respond to them, 'Just as you abandoned me and served foreign gods in your land, so will you serve strangers in a land that is not yours.'

"Declare this in the house of Jacob; proclaim it in Judah, saying:

Hear this,
you foolish and senseless people.
They have eyes, but they don't see.
They have ears, but they don't hear.
Do you not fear me?
90 This is the LORD's declaration.
Do you not tremble before me,
the one who set the sand as the boundary of the sea,
an enduring barrier that it cannot cross?
The waves surge, but they cannot prevail.
They roar but cannot pass over it.
But these people have stubborn and rebellious hearts.
They have turned aside and have gone away.
They have not said to themselves,
'Let's fear the LORD our God,
100 who gives the seasonal rains, both autumn and spring,
who guarantees to us the fixed weeks of the harvest.'
Your guilty acts have diverted these things from you.
Your sins have withheld my bounty from you,
for wicked men live among my people.
They watch like hunters lying in wait.
They set a trap;
they catch men.
Like a cage full of birds,
so their houses are full of deceit.
110 Therefore they have grown powerful and rich.
They have become fat and sleek.

They have also excelled in evil matters.
They have not taken up cases,
such as the case of the fatherless, so they might prosper,
and they have not defended the rights of the needy.
Should I not punish them for these things?
This is the Lord's declaration.
Should I not avenge myself
on such a nation as this?

120 "An appalling, horrible thing
has taken place in the land.
The prophets prophesy falsely,
and the priests rule by their own authority.
My people love it like this.
But what will you do at the end of it?

6 "Run for cover
out of Jerusalem, Benjaminites.
Sound the ram's horn in Tekoa;
raise a smoke signal over Beth-haccherem,
for disaster threatens from the north,
even a crushing blow.
Though she is beautiful and delicate,
I will destroy Daughter Zion.
Shepherds and their flocks will come against her;
10 they will pitch their tents all around her.
Each will pasture his own portion.
Set them apart for war against her;
rise up, let's attack at noon.
Woe to us, for the day is passing;
the evening shadows grow long.
Rise up, let's attack by night.
Let's destroy her fortresses."

For this is what the Lord of Armies says:
Cut down the trees;
20 raise a siege ramp against Jerusalem.
This city must be punished.

There is nothing but oppression within her.
As a well gushes out its water,
so she pours out her evil.
Violence and destruction resound in her.
Sickness and wounds keep coming to my attention.
Be warned, Jerusalem,
or I will turn away from you;
I will make you a desolation,
30   a land without inhabitants.

This is what the Lord of Armies says:
Glean the remnant of Israel
as thoroughly as a vine.
Pass your hand once more like a grape gatherer
over the branches.

Who can I speak to and give such a warning
that they will listen?
Look, their ear is uncircumcised,
so they cannot pay attention.
40   See, the word of the Lord has become contemptible to them—
they find no pleasure in it.
But I am full of the Lord's wrath;
I am tired of holding it back.
Pour it out on the children in the street,
on the gathering of young men as well.
For both husband and wife will be captured,
the old with the very old.
Their houses will be turned over to others,
their fields and wives as well,
50   for I will stretch out my hand
against the inhabitants of the land.
This is the Lord's declaration.

For from the least to the greatest of them,
everyone is making profit dishonestly.
From prophet to priest,
everyone deals falsely.

They have treated my people's brokenness superficially,
claiming, "Peace, peace,"
when there is no peace.
60   Were they ashamed when they acted so detestably?
They weren't at all ashamed.
They can no longer feel humiliation.
Therefore, they will fall among the fallen.
When I punish them, they will collapse,
says the LORD.

This is what the LORD says:
Stand by the roadways and look.
Ask about the ancient paths,
"Which is the way to what is good?"
70   Then take it
and find rest for yourselves.
But they protested, "We won't!"
I appointed watchmen over you
and said, "Listen for the sound of the ram's horn."
But they protested, "We won't listen!"

Therefore listen, you nations
and you witnesses,
learn what the charge is against them.
Listen, earth!
80   I am about to bring disaster on these people,
the fruit of their own plotting,
for they have paid no attention to my words.
They have rejected my instruction.
What use to me is frankincense from Sheba
or sweet cane from a distant land?
Your burnt offerings are not acceptable;
your sacrifices do not please me.
Therefore, this is what the LORD says:
I am going to place stumbling blocks before these people;
90   fathers and sons together will stumble over them;
friends and neighbors will also perish.

This is what the LORD says:
    Look, an army is coming from a northern land;
    a great nation will be stirred up
    from the remote regions of the earth.
    They grasp bow and javelin.
    They are cruel and show no mercy.
    Their voice roars like the sea,
    and they ride on horses,
100   lined up like men in battle formation
    against you, Daughter Zion.

    We have heard about it,
    and our hands have become weak.
    Distress has seized us—
    pain, like a woman in labor.
    Don't go out to the fields;
    don't walk on the road.
    For the enemy has a sword;
    terror is on every side.

110   My dear people, dress yourselves in sackcloth
    and roll in the dust.
    Mourn as you would for an only son,
    a bitter lament,
    for suddenly the destroyer will come on us.

    I have appointed you to be an assayer among my people—
    a refiner—
    so you may know and assay their way of life.
    All are stubborn rebels
    spreading slander.
120   They are bronze and iron;
    all of them are corrupt.
    The bellows blow,
    blasting the lead with fire.
    The refining is completely in vain;
    the evil ones are not separated out.

> They are called rejected silver,
> for the LORD has rejected them.

7 This is the word that came to Jeremiah from the LORD: "Stand in the gate of the house of the LORD and there call out this word: 'Hear the word of the LORD, all you people of Judah who enter through these gates to worship the LORD.

"'This is what the LORD of Armies, the God of Israel, says: Correct your ways and your actions, and I will allow you to live in this place. Do not trust deceitful words, chanting, "This is the temple of the LORD, the temple of the LORD, the temple of the LORD." Instead, if you really correct your ways and your actions, if you act justly toward one another, if you no longer oppress the resident alien, the fatherless, and the widow and no longer shed innocent blood in this place or follow other gods, bringing harm on yourselves, I will allow you to live in this place, the land I gave to your ancestors long ago and forever. But look, you keep trusting in deceitful words that cannot help.

"'Do you steal, murder, commit adultery, swear falsely, burn incense to Baal, and follow other gods that you have not known? Then do you come and stand before me in this house that bears my name and say, "We are rescued, so we can continue doing all these detestable acts"? Has this house, which bears my name, become a den of robbers in your view? Yes, I too have seen it.

This is the LORD's declaration.

"'But return to my place that was at Shiloh, where I made my name dwell at first. See what I did to it because of the evil of my people Israel. Now, because you have done all these things—this is the LORD's declaration—and because I have spoken to you time and time again but you wouldn't listen, and I have called to you, but you wouldn't answer, what I did to Shiloh I will do to the house that bears my name, the house in which you trust, the place that I gave you and your ancestors. I will banish you from my presence, just as I banished all of your brothers, all the descendants of Ephraim.'

"As for you, do not pray for these people. Do not offer a cry or a prayer on their behalf, and do not beg me, for I will not listen to you. Don't you see how they behave in the cities of Judah and in the streets of Jerusalem? The sons gather wood, the fathers light the fire, and the women knead dough to make cakes for the queen of heaven, and they pour out drink offerings to other gods so that they provoke me to anger. But are they really provoking me?" This is the LORD's declaration. "Isn't it they themselves being provoked to disgrace?"

Therefore, this is what the Lord GOD says: "Look, my anger—my burning wrath—is about to be poured out on this place, on people and animals, on the tree of the field, and on the produce of the land. My wrath will burn and not be quenched."

This is what the LORD of Armies, the God of Israel, says: "Add your burnt offerings to your other sacrifices, and eat the meat yourselves, for when I brought your ancestors out of the land of Egypt,

I did not speak with them or command them concerning burnt offering and sacrifice. However, I did give them this command: 'Obey me, and then I will be your God, and you will be my people. Follow every way I command you so that it may go well with you.' Yet they didn't listen or pay attention but followed their own advice and their own stubborn, evil heart. They went backward and not forward. Since the day your ancestors came out of the land of Egypt until today, I have sent all my servants the prophets to you time and time again. However, my people wouldn't listen to me or pay attention but became obstinate; they did more evil than their ancestors.

40 "When you speak all these things to them, they will not listen to you. When you call to them, they will not answer you. Therefore, declare to them, 'This is the nation that would not listen to the Lord their God and would not accept discipline. Truth has perished—it has disappeared from their mouths. Cut off the hair of your sacred vow and throw it away. Raise up a dirge on the barren heights, for the Lord has rejected and abandoned the generation under his wrath.'

"For the Judeans have done what is evil in my sight." This is the Lord's declaration. "They have set up their abhorrent things in the house that bears my name in order to defile it. They have built the high places of Topheth in Ben Hinnom Valley in order to burn their sons and daughters in the fire, a thing I did not command; I never entertained the thought.

"Therefore, look, the days are coming"—the Lord's declaration—"when this place will no
50 longer be called Topheth and Ben Hinnom Valley, but Slaughter Valley. Topheth will become a cemetery, because there will be no other burial place. The corpses of these people will become food for the birds of the sky and for the wild animals of the land, with no one to scare them away. I will remove from the cities of Judah and the streets of Jerusalem the sound of joy and gladness and the voices of the groom and the bride, for the land will become a desolate waste.

8 "At that time"—this is the Lord's declaration—"the bones of the kings of Judah, the bones of her officials, the bones of the priests, the bones of the prophets, and the bones of the residents of Jerusalem will be brought out of their graves. They will be exposed to the sun, the moon, and all the stars in the sky, which they have loved, served, followed, consulted, and worshiped. Their bones will not be collected and buried but will become like manure on the soil's surface. Death will be chosen over life by all the survivors of this evil family, those who remain wherever I have banished them." This is the declaration of the Lord of Armies.

"You are to say to them: This is what the Lord says:

Do people fall and not get up again?
10 If they turn away, do they not return?
Why have these people turned away?
Why is Jerusalem always turning away?
They take hold of deceit;
they refuse to return.

I have paid careful attention.
They do not speak what is right.
No one regrets his evil,
asking, 'What have I done?'
Everyone has stayed his course
20 like a horse rushing into battle.
Even storks in the sky
know their seasons.
Turtledoves, swallows, and cranes
are aware of their migration,
but my people do not know
the requirements of the LORD.

"How can you claim, 'We are wise;
the law of the LORD is with us'?
In fact, the lying pen of scribes
30 has produced falsehood.
The wise will be put to shame;
they will be dismayed and snared.
They have rejected the word of the LORD,
so what wisdom do they really have?
Therefore, I will give their wives to other men,
their fields to new occupants,
for from the least to the greatest,
everyone is making profit dishonestly.
From prophet to priest,
40 everyone deals falsely.
They have treated the brokenness
of my dear people superficially,
claiming, 'Peace, peace,'
when there is no peace.
Were they ashamed when they acted so detestably?
They weren't at all ashamed.
They can no longer feel humiliation.
Therefore, they will fall among the fallen.
When I punish them, they will collapse,"
50 says the LORD.

"I will gather them and bring them to an end."
This is the LORD's declaration.
"There will be no grapes on the vine,
no figs on the fig tree,
and even the leaf will wither.
Whatever I have given them will be lost to them."

Why are we just sitting here?
Gather together; let's enter the fortified cities
and perish there,
for the LORD our God has destroyed us.
He has given us poisoned water to drink,
because we have sinned against the LORD.
We hoped for peace, but there was nothing good;
for a time of healing, but there was only terror.

From Dan, the snorting of horses is heard.
At the sound of the neighing of mighty steeds,
the whole land quakes.
They come to devour the land and everything in it,
the city and all its residents.
Indeed, I am about to send snakes among you,
poisonous vipers that cannot be charmed.
They will bite you.
This is the LORD's declaration.

My joy has flown away;
grief has settled on me.
My heart is sick.
Listen—the cry of my dear people
from a faraway land,
"Is the LORD no longer in Zion,
her King not within her?"
Why have they angered me
with their carved images,
with their worthless foreign idols?
Harvest has passed, summer has ended,
but we have not been saved.

I am broken by the brokenness
of my dear people.
I mourn; horror has taken hold of me.
Is there no balm in Gilead?
90 Is there no physician there?
So why has the healing of my dear people
not come about?

9 If my head were a flowing spring,
my eyes a fountain of tears,
I would weep day and night
over the slain of my dear people.
If only I had a traveler's lodging place
in the wilderness,
I would abandon my people
and depart from them,
for they are all adulterers,
10 a solemn assembly of treacherous people.

They bent their tongues like their bows;
lies and not faithfulness prevail in the land,
for they proceed from one evil to another,
and they do not take me into account.
This is the LORD's declaration.

Everyone has to be on guard against his friend.
Don't trust any brother,
for every brother will certainly deceive,
and every friend spread slander.
20 Each one betrays his friend;
no one tells the truth.
They have taught their tongues to speak lies;
they wear themselves out doing wrong.
You live in a world of deception.
In their deception they refuse to know me.
This is the LORD's declaration.

Therefore, this is what the LORD of Armies says:
> I am about to refine them and test them,
> for what else can I do
30 > because of my dear people?
> Their tongues are deadly arrows—
> they speak deception.
> With his mouth
> one speaks peaceably with his friend,
> but inwardly he sets up an ambush.
> Should I not punish them for these things?
> This is the LORD's declaration.
> Should I not avenge myself
> on such a nation as this?

40 > I will raise weeping and a lament
> over the mountains,
> a dirge over the wilderness grazing land,
> for they have been so scorched
> that no one passes through.
> The sound of cattle is no longer heard.
> From the birds of the sky to the animals,
> everything has fled—they have gone away.
> I will make Jerusalem a heap of rubble,
> a jackals' den.
50 > I will make the cities of Judah a desolation,
> an uninhabited place.

Who is the person wise enough to understand this? Who has the LORD spoken to, that he may explain it? Why is the land destroyed and scorched like a wilderness, so no one can pass through?

The LORD said, "It is because they abandoned my instruction, which I set before them, and did not obey my voice or walk according to it. Instead, they followed the stubbornness of their hearts and followed the Baals as their ancestors taught them." Therefore, this is what the LORD of Armies, the God of Israel, says: "I am about to feed this people wormwood and give them poisonous water to drink. I will scatter them among the nations that they and their ancestors have not known. I will send a sword after them until I have finished them off."

60 This is what the LORD of Armies says:
> Consider, and summon the women who mourn;

send for the skillful women.
Let them come quickly to raise a lament over us
so that our eyes may overflow with tears,
our eyelids be soaked with weeping.
For a sound of lamentation is heard from Zion:
How devastated we are.
We are greatly ashamed,
for we have abandoned the land;
70   our dwellings have been torn down.

Now hear the word of the Lord, you women.
Pay attention to the words from his mouth.
Teach your daughters a lament
and one another a dirge,
for Death has climbed through our windows;
it has entered our fortresses,
cutting off children from the streets,
young men from the squares.

"Speak as follows: 'This is what the Lord declares: Human corpses will fall like manure on the
80 surface of the field, like newly cut grain after the reaper with no one to gather it.

"'This is what the Lord says:
The wise person should not boast in his wisdom;
the strong should not boast in his strength;
the wealthy should not boast in his wealth.
But the one who boasts should boast in this:
that he understands and knows me—
that I am the Lord, showing faithful love,
justice, and righteousness on the earth,
for I delight in these things.
90   This is the Lord's declaration.

"'Look, the days are coming—this is the Lord's declaration—when I will punish all the
circumcised yet uncircumcised: Egypt, Judah, Edom, the Ammonites, Moab, and all the
inhabitants of the desert who clip the hair on their temples. All these nations are uncircumcised,
and the whole house of Israel is uncircumcised in heart.'"

10 Hear the word that the LORD has spoken to you, house of Israel. This is what the LORD says:

Do not learn the way of the nations
or be terrified by signs in the heavens,
although the nations are terrified by them,
for the customs of the peoples are worthless.
Someone cuts down a tree from the forest;
it is worked by the hands of a craftsman with a chisel.
He decorates it with silver and gold.
It is fastened with hammer and nails,
so it won't totter.
Like scarecrows in a cucumber patch,
their idols cannot speak.
They must be carried because they cannot walk.
Do not fear them for they can do no harm—
and they cannot do any good.

LORD, there is no one like you.
You are great;
your name is great in power.
Who should not fear you,
King of the nations?
It is what you deserve.
For among all the wise people of the nations
and among all their kingdoms,
there is no one like you.
They are both stupid and foolish,
instructed by worthless idols
made of wood!
Beaten silver is brought from Tarshish
and gold from Uphaz.
The work of a craftsman
and of a goldsmith's hands
is clothed in blue and purple,
all the work of skilled artisans.
But the LORD is the true God;
he is the living God and eternal King.
The earth quakes at his wrath,
and the nations cannot endure his fury.

You are to say this to them: "The gods that did not make the heavens and the earth will perish from the earth and from under these heavens."

40   He made the earth by his power,
        established the world by his wisdom,
        and spread out the heavens by his understanding.
        When he thunders,
        the waters in the heavens are in turmoil,
        and he causes the clouds to rise
        from the ends of the earth.
        He makes lightning for the rain
        and brings the wind from his storehouses.

        Everyone is stupid and ignorant.
50   Every goldsmith is put to shame
        by his carved image,
        for his cast images are a lie;
        there is no breath in them.
        They are worthless, a work to be mocked.
        At the time of their punishment
        they will be destroyed.
        Jacob's Portion is not like these
        because he is the one who formed all things.
        Israel is the tribe of his inheritance;
60   the Lord of Armies is his name.

        Gather up your belongings from the ground,
        you who live under siege.

For this is what the Lord says:
        Look, I am flinging away
        the land's residents at this time
        and bringing them such distress
        that they will feel it.

        Woe to me because of my brokenness—
        I am severely wounded!
70   I exclaimed, "This is my intense suffering,

but I must bear it."
My tent is destroyed;
all my tent cords are snapped.
My sons have departed from me and are no more.
I have no one to pitch my tent again
or to hang up my curtains.
For the shepherds are stupid:
They don't seek the Lord.
Therefore they have not prospered,
80 and their whole flock is scattered.
Listen! A noise—it is coming—
a great commotion from the land to the north.
The cities of Judah will be made desolate,
a jackals' den.

I know, Lord,
that a person's way of life is not his own;
no one who walks determines his own steps.
Discipline me, Lord, but with justice—
not in your anger,
90 or you will reduce me to nothing.
Pour out your wrath on the nations
that don't recognize you
and on the families
that don't call on your name,
for they have consumed Jacob;
they have consumed him and finished him off
and made his homeland desolate.

11 This is the word that came to Jeremiah from the Lord: "Listen to the words of this covenant and tell them to the men of Judah and the residents of Jerusalem. Tell them, 'This is what the Lord, the God of Israel, says: "Let a curse be on the man who does not obey the words of this covenant, which I commanded your ancestors when I brought them out of the land of Egypt, out of the iron furnace." I declared, "Obey me, and do everything that I command you, and you will be my people, and I will be your God," in order to establish the oath I swore to your ancestors, to give them a land flowing with milk and honey, as it is today.'"

I answered, "Amen, Lord."

The Lord said to me, "Proclaim all these words in the cities of Judah and in the streets of Jerusalem: 'Obey the words of this covenant and carry them out.' For I strongly warned your

10 ancestors when I brought them out of the land of Egypt until today, warning them time and time again, 'Obey me.' Yet they would not obey or pay attention; each one followed the stubbornness of his evil heart. So I brought on them all the curses of this covenant, because they had not done what I commanded them to do."

The LORD said to me, "A conspiracy has been discovered among the men of Judah and the residents of Jerusalem. They have returned to the iniquities of their ancestors who refused to obey my words and have followed other gods to worship them. The house of Israel and the house of Judah broke my covenant I made with their ancestors.

"Therefore, this is what the LORD says: I am about to bring on them disaster that they cannot escape. They will cry out to me, but I will not hear them. Then the cities of Judah and
20 the residents of Jerusalem will go and cry out to the gods they have been burning incense to, but they certainly will not save them in their time of disaster. Your gods are indeed as numerous as your cities, Judah, and the altars you have set up to Shame—altars to burn incense to Baal—as numerous as the streets of Jerusalem.

"As for you, do not pray for these people. Do not raise up a cry or a prayer on their behalf, for I will not be listening when they call out to me at the time of their disaster.

> What right does my beloved have
> to be in my house,
> having carried out so many evil schemes?
> Can holy meat prevent your disaster
30 > so you can celebrate?
> The LORD named you
> a flourishing olive tree,
> beautiful with well-formed fruit.
> He has set fire to it,
> and its branches are consumed
> with the sound of a mighty tumult.

"The LORD of Armies who planted you has decreed disaster against you, because of the disaster the house of Israel and the house of Judah brought on themselves when they angered me by burning incense to Baal."
40 > The LORD informed me, so I knew.
> Then you helped me to see their deeds,
> for I was like a docile lamb led to slaughter.
> I didn't know that they had devised plots against me:
> "Let's destroy the tree with its fruit;
> let's cut him off from the land of the living
> so that his name will no longer be remembered."

But, Lord of Armies, who judges righteously,
who tests heart and mind,
let me see your vengeance on them,
50   for I have presented my case to you.

Therefore, here is what the Lord says concerning the people of Anathoth who intend to take your life. They warn, "Do not prophesy in the name of the Lord, or you will certainly die at our hand." Therefore, this is what the Lord of Armies says: "I am about to punish them. The young men will die by the sword; their sons and daughters will die by famine. They will have no remnant, for I will bring disaster on the people of Anathoth in the year of their punishment."

12   You will be righteous, Lord,
even if I bring a case against you.
Yet, I wish to contend with you:
Why does the way of the wicked prosper?
Why do all the treacherous live at ease?
You planted them, and they have taken root.
They have grown and produced fruit.
You are ever on their lips,
but far from their conscience.
10   As for you, Lord, you know me; you see me.
You test whether my heart is with you.
Drag the wicked away like sheep to slaughter
and set them apart for the day of killing.
How long will the land mourn
and the grass of every field wither?
Because of the evil of its residents,
animals and birds have been swept away,
for the people have said,
"He cannot see what our end will be."

20   If you have raced with runners
and they have worn you out,
how can you compete with horses?
If you stumble in a peaceful land,
what will you do in the thickets of the Jordan?
Even your brothers—your own father's family—
even they were treacherous to you;

even they have cried out loudly after you.
Do not have confidence in them,
though they speak well of you.

30   I have abandoned my house;
I have deserted my inheritance.
I have handed the love of my life
over to her enemies.
My inheritance has behaved toward me
like a lion in the forest.
She has roared against me.
Therefore, I hate her.
Is my inheritance like a hyena to me?
Are birds of prey circling her?

40   Go, gather all the wild animals;
bring them to devour her.
Many shepherds have destroyed my vineyard;
they have trampled my plot of land.
They have turned my desirable plot
into a desolate wasteland.
They have made it a desolation.
It mourns, desolate, before me.
All the land is desolate,
but no one takes it to heart.

50   Over all the barren heights in the wilderness
the destroyers have come,
for the LORD has a sword that devours
from one end of the earth to the other.
No one has peace.
They have sown wheat but harvested thorns.
They have exhausted themselves but have no profit.
Be put to shame by your harvests
because of the LORD's burning anger.

This is what the LORD says: "Concerning all my evil neighbors who attack the inheritance that
60 I bequeathed to my people, Israel, I am about to uproot them from their land, and I will uproot
the house of Judah from them. After I have uprooted them, I will once again have compassion on
them and return each one to his inheritance and to his land. If they will diligently learn the ways of

my people—to swear by my name, 'As the LORD lives,' just as they taught my people to swear by Baal—they will be built up among my people. However, if they will not obey, then I will uproot and destroy that nation."

This is the LORD's declaration.

13 This is what the LORD said to me: "Go and buy yourself a linen undergarment and put it on. But do not put it in water." So I bought underwear as the LORD instructed me and put it on.

Then the word of the LORD came to me a second time: "Take the underwear that you bought and are wearing, and go at once to the Euphrates and hide it in a rocky crevice." So I went and hid it by the Euphrates, as the LORD commanded me.

A long time later the LORD said to me, "Go at once to the Euphrates and get the underwear that I commanded you to hide there." So I went to the Euphrates and dug up the underwear and got it from the place where I had hidden it, but it was ruined—of no use at all.

Then the word of the LORD came to me: "This is what the LORD says: Just like this I will
10 ruin the great pride of both Judah and Jerusalem. These evil people, who refuse to listen to me, who follow the stubbornness of their own hearts, and who have followed other gods to serve and bow in worship—they will be like this underwear, of no use at all. Just as underwear clings to one's waist, so I fastened the whole house of Israel and of Judah to me"—this is the LORD's declaration—"so that they might be my people for my fame, praise, and glory, but they would not obey.

"Say this to them: 'This is what the LORD, the God of Israel, says: Every jar should be filled with wine.' Then they will respond to you, 'Don't we know that every jar should be filled with wine?' And you will say to them, 'This is what the LORD says: I am about to fill all who live in this land— the kings who reign for David on his throne, the priests, the prophets, and all the residents of
20 Jerusalem—with drunkenness. I will smash them against each other, fathers and sons alike—this is the LORD's declaration. I will allow no mercy, pity, or compassion to keep me from destroying them.'"

> Listen and pay attention. Do not be proud,
> for the LORD has spoken.
> Give glory to the LORD your God
> before he brings darkness,
> before your feet stumble
> on the mountains at dusk.
> You wait for light,
> but he brings darkest gloom
> and makes total darkness.
30 But if you will not listen,

my innermost being will weep in secret
because of your pride.
My eyes will overflow with tears,
for the LORD's flock has been taken captive.

Say to the king and the queen mother:
Take a humble seat,
for your glorious crowns
have fallen from your heads.
40 The cities of the Negev are under siege;
no one can help them.
All of Judah has been taken into exile,
taken completely into exile.
Look up and see
those coming from the north.
Where is the flock entrusted to you,
the sheep that were your pride?

What will you say when he appoints
close friends as leaders over you,
50 ones you yourself trained?
Won't labor pains seize you,
as they do a woman in labor?
And when you ask yourself,
"Why have these things happened to me?"
it is because of your great guilt
that your skirts have been stripped off,
your body exposed.
Can the Cushite change his skin,
or a leopard his spots?
60 If so, you might be able to do what is good,
you who are instructed in evil.
I will scatter you like drifting chaff
before the desert wind.
This is your lot,
what I have decreed for you—
this is the LORD's declaration—
because you have forgotten me

and trusted in lies.
I will pull your skirts up over your face
70   so that your shame might be seen.
Your adulteries and your lustful neighing,
your depraved prostitution
on the hills, in the fields—
I have seen your abhorrent acts.
Woe to you, Jerusalem!
You are unclean—
for how long yet?

14 This is the word of the LORD that came to Jeremiah concerning the drought:
Judah mourns;
her city gates languish.
Her people are on the ground in mourning;
Jerusalem's cry rises up.
Their nobles send their servants for water.
They go to the cisterns;
they find no water;
their containers return empty.
10   They are ashamed and humiliated;
they cover their heads.
The ground is cracked
since no rain has fallen on the land.
The farmers are ashamed;
they cover their heads.
Even the doe in the field
gives birth and abandons her fawn
since there is no grass.
Wild donkeys stand on the barren heights
20   panting for air like jackals.
Their eyes fail
because there are no green plants.

Though our iniquities testify against us,
LORD, act for your name's sake.
Indeed, our rebellions are many;
we have sinned against you.

Hope of Israel,
its Savior in time of distress,
why are you like a resident alien in the land,
30   like a traveler stopping only for the night?
Why are you like a helpless man,
like a warrior unable to save?
Yet you are among us, Lord,
and we bear your name.
Don't leave us!

This is what the Lord says concerning these people:
Truly they love to wander;
they never rest their feet.
So the Lord does not accept them.
40   Now he will remember their iniquity
and punish their sins.

Then the Lord said to me, "Do not pray for the well-being of these people. If they fast, I will not hear their cry of despair. If they offer burnt offering and grain offering, I will not accept them. Rather, I will finish them off by sword, famine, and plague."

And I replied, "Oh no, Lord God! The prophets are telling them, 'You won't see sword or suffer famine. I will certainly give you lasting peace in this place.'"

But the Lord said to me, "These prophets are prophesying a lie in my name. I did not send them, nor did I command them or speak to them. They are prophesying to you a false vision, worthless divination, the deceit of their own minds.

50   "Therefore, this is what the Lord says concerning the prophets who prophesy in my name, though I did not send them, and who say, 'There will never be sword or famine in this land.' By sword and famine these prophets will meet their end. The people they are prophesying to will be thrown into the streets of Jerusalem because of the famine and the sword. There will be no one to bury them—they, their wives, their sons, and their daughters. I will pour out their own evil on them."

You are to speak this word to them:
Let my eyes overflow with tears;
day and night may they not stop,
for my dearest people
60   have been destroyed by a crushing blow,
an extremely severe wound.

If I go out to the field,
look—those slain by the sword!
If I enter the city,
look—those ill from famine!
For both prophet and priest
travel to a land they do not know.

Have you completely rejected Judah?
Do you detest Zion?
Why do you strike us
with no hope of healing for us?
We hoped for peace,
but there was nothing good;
for a time of healing,
but there was only terror.
We acknowledge our wickedness, Lord,
the iniquity of our ancestors;
indeed, we have sinned against you.
For your name's sake, don't despise us.
Don't disdain your glorious throne.
Remember your covenant with us;
do not break it.
Can any of the worthless idols of the nations bring rain?
Or can the skies alone give showers?
Are you not the Lord our God?
We therefore put our hope in you,
for you have done all these things.

15 Then the Lord said to me, "Even if Moses and Samuel should stand before me, my compassions would not reach out to these people. Send them from my presence, and let them go. If they ask you, 'Where will we go?' tell them: This is what the Lord says:

Those destined for death, to death;
those destined for the sword, to the sword.
Those destined for famine, to famine;
those destined for captivity, to captivity.

"I will ordain four kinds of judgment for them"—this is the Lord's declaration—"the sword to kill, the dogs to drag away, and the birds of the sky and the wild animals of the land to devour and

10   destroy. I will make them a horror to all the kingdoms of the earth because of Manasseh son of
Hezekiah, the king of Judah, for what he did in Jerusalem.

> Who will have pity on you, Jerusalem?
> Who will show sympathy toward you?
> Who will turn aside
> to ask about your well-being?
> You have left me."
> This is the Lord's declaration.
> "You have turned your back,
> so I have stretched out my hand against you
> and destroyed you.
> I am tired of showing compassion.
> I scattered them with a winnowing fork
> at the city gates of the land.
> I made them childless; I destroyed my people.
> They would not turn from their ways.
> I made their widows more numerous
> than the sand of the seas.
> I brought a destroyer at noon
> against the mother of young men.
> I suddenly released on her
> agitation and terrors.
> The mother of seven grew faint;
> she breathed her last breath.
> Her sun set while it was still day;
> she was ashamed and humiliated.
> The rest of them I will give over to the sword
> in the presence of their enemies."
> This is the Lord's declaration.

> Woe is me, my mother,
> that you gave birth to me,
> a man who incites dispute and conflict
> in all the land.
> I did not lend or borrow,
> yet everyone curses me.

The Lord said:

Haven't I set you loose for your good?
Haven't I punished you
in a time of trouble,
in a time of distress with the enemy?
Can anyone smash iron,
50   iron from the north, or bronze?
I will give up your wealth
and your treasures as plunder,
without cost, for all your sins
in all your borders.
Then I will make you serve your enemies
in a land you do not know,
for my anger will kindle a fire
that will burn against you.

You know, Lord;
60   remember me and take note of me.
Avenge me against my persecutors.
In your patience, don't take me away.
Know that I suffer disgrace for your honor.
Your words were found, and I ate them.
Your words became a delight to me
and the joy of my heart,
for I bear your name,
Lord God of Armies.
I never sat with the band of revelers,
70   and I did not celebrate with them.
Because your hand was on me, I sat alone,
for you filled me with indignation.
Why has my pain become unending,
my wound incurable,
refusing to be healed?
You truly have become like a mirage to me—
water that is not reliable.

Therefore, this is what the Lord says:
If you return, I will take you back;
80   you will stand in my presence.

And if you speak noble words,
rather than worthless ones,
you will be my spokesman.
It is they who must return to you;
you must not return to them.
Then I will make you a fortified wall of bronze
to this people.
They will fight against you
but will not overcome you,
90   for I am with you
to save you and rescue you.
This is the Lord's declaration.
I will rescue you from the power of evil people
and redeem you from the grasp of the ruthless.

16 The word of the Lord came to me: "Do not marry or have sons or daughters in this place. For this is what the Lord says concerning sons and daughters born in this place as well as concerning the mothers who bear them and the fathers who father them in this land: They will die from deadly diseases. They will not be mourned or buried but will be like manure on the soil's surface. They will be finished off by sword and famine. Their corpses will become food for the birds of the sky and for the wild animals of the land.

"For this is what the Lord says: Don't enter a house where a mourning feast is taking place. Don't go to lament or sympathize with them, for I have removed my peace from these people as well as my faithful love and compassion." This is the Lord's declaration. "Both great and small will die in this land without burial. No lament will be made for them, nor will anyone cut himself or
10   shave his head for them. Food won't be provided for the mourner to comfort him because of the dead. A consoling drink won't be given him for the loss of his father or mother. Do not enter the house where feasting is taking place to sit with them to eat and drink. For this is what the Lord of Armies, the God of Israel, says: I am about to eliminate from this place, before your very eyes and in your time, the sound of joy and gladness, the voice of the groom and the bride.

"When you tell these people all these things, they will say to you, 'Why has the Lord declared all this terrible disaster against us? What is our iniquity? What is our sin that we have committed against the Lord our God?' Then you will answer them, 'Because your ancestors abandoned me— this is the Lord's declaration—and followed other gods, served them, and bowed in worship to them. Indeed, they abandoned me and did not keep my instruction. You did more evil than your
20   ancestors. Look, each one of you was following the stubbornness of his evil heart, not obeying me.

So I will hurl you from this land into a land that you and your ancestors have not known. There you will worship other gods both day and night, for I will not grant you grace.'

"However, look, the days are coming"—the LORD's declaration—"when it will no longer be said, 'As the LORD lives who brought the Israelites from the land of Egypt,' but rather, 'As the LORD lives who brought the Israelites from the land of the north and from all the other lands where he had banished them.' For I will return them to their land that I gave to their ancestors.

"I am about to send for many fishermen"—this is the LORD's declaration—"and they will fish for them. Then I will send for many hunters, and they will hunt them down on every mountain and hill and out of the clefts of the rocks, for my gaze takes in all their ways. They are not concealed from me, and their iniquity is not hidden from my sight. I will first repay them double for their iniquity and sin because they have polluted my land. They have filled my inheritance with the carcasses of their abhorrent and detestable idols."

LORD, my strength and my stronghold,
my refuge in a time of distress,
the nations will come to you
from the ends of the earth, and they will say,
"Our ancestors inherited only lies,
worthless idols of no benefit at all."
Can one make gods for himself?
But they are not gods.
"Therefore, I am about to inform them,
and this time I will make them know
my power and my might;
then they will know that my name is the LORD."

17 The sin of Judah is inscribed
with an iron stylus.
With a diamond point
it is engraved on the tablet of their hearts
and on the horns of their altars,
while their children remember their altars
and their Asherah poles, by the green trees
on the high hills—
my mountains in the countryside.
I will give up your wealth
and all your treasures as plunder
because of the sin of your high places

in all your borders.
    You will, on your own, relinquish your inheritance
    that I gave you.
    I will make you serve your enemies
    in a land you do not know,
    for you have set my anger on fire;
    it will burn forever.

20 This is what the LORD says:
    Cursed is the person who trusts in mankind.
    He makes human flesh his strength,
    and his heart turns from the LORD.
    He will be like a juniper in the Arabah;
    he cannot see when good comes
    but dwells in the parched places in the wilderness,
    in a salt land where no one lives.
    The person who trusts in the LORD,
    whose confidence indeed is the LORD, is blessed.
30   He will be like a tree planted by water:
    it sends its roots out toward a stream,
    it doesn't fear when heat comes,
    and its foliage remains green.
    It will not worry in a year of drought
    or cease producing fruit.

    The heart is more deceitful than anything else,
    and incurable—who can understand it?
    I, the LORD, examine the mind,
    I test the heart
40   to give to each according to his way,
    according to what his actions deserve.
    He who makes a fortune unjustly
    is like a partridge that hatches eggs it didn't lay.
    In the middle of his life
    his riches will abandon him,
    so in the end he will be a fool.

A glorious throne
on high from the beginning
is the place of our sanctuary.
50   Lord, the hope of Israel,
all who abandon you
will be put to shame.
All who turn away from me
will be written in the dirt,
for they have abandoned
the Lord, the fountain of living water.

Heal me, Lord, and I will be healed;
save me, and I will be saved,
for you are my praise.
60   Hear how they keep challenging me,
"Where is the word of the Lord?
Let it come!"
But I have not run away from being your shepherd,
and I have not longed for the fatal day.
You know my words were spoken in your presence.
Don't become a terror to me.
You are my refuge in the day of disaster.
Let my persecutors be put to shame,
but don't let me be put to shame.
70   Let them be terrified, but don't let me be terrified.
Bring on them the day of disaster;
shatter them with total destruction.

This is what the Lord said to me, "Go and stand at the People's Gate, through which the kings of Judah enter and leave, as well as at all the gates of Jerusalem. Announce to them, 'Hear the word of the Lord, kings of Judah, all Judah, and all the residents of Jerusalem who enter through these gates. This is what the Lord says: Watch yourselves; do not pick up a load and bring it in through Jerusalem's gates on the Sabbath day. Do not carry a load out of your houses on the Sabbath day or do any work, but keep the Sabbath day holy, just as I commanded your ancestors. They wouldn't listen or pay attention but became obstinate, not listening or accepting discipline.

80   "However, if you listen to me—this is the Lord's declaration—and do not bring loads through the gates of this city on the Sabbath day, but keep the Sabbath day holy and do no work on it, kings and princes will enter through the gates of this city. They will sit on the throne of David;

they will ride in chariots and on horses with their officials, the men of Judah, and the residents of Jerusalem. This city will be inhabited forever. Then people will come from the cities of Judah and from the area around Jerusalem, from the land of Benjamin and from the Judean foothills, from the hill country and from the Negev bringing burnt offerings and sacrifices, grain offerings and frankincense, and thanksgiving sacrifices to the house of the LORD. But if you do not listen to me to keep the Sabbath day holy by not carrying a load while entering the gates of Jerusalem on the Sabbath day, I will set fire to its gates, and it will consume the citadels of Jerusalem and not be 90 extinguished.'"

18 This is the word that came to Jeremiah from the LORD: "Go down at once to the potter's house; there I will reveal my words to you." So I went down to the potter's house, and there he was, working away at the wheel. But the jar that he was making from the clay became flawed in the potter's hand, so he made it into another jar, as it seemed right for him to do.

The word of the LORD came to me: "House of Israel, can I not treat you as this potter treats his clay?"—this is the LORD's declaration. "Just like clay in the potter's hand, so are you in my hand, house of Israel. At one moment I might announce concerning a nation or a kingdom that I will uproot, tear down, and destroy it. However, if that nation about which I have made the announcement turns from its evil, I will relent concerning the disaster I had planned to do to it. 10 At another time I might announce concerning a nation or a kingdom that I will build and plant it. However, if it does what is evil in my sight by not listening to me, I will relent concerning the good I had said I would do to it. So now, say to the men of Judah and to the residents of Jerusalem, 'This is what the LORD says: Look, I am about to bring harm to you and make plans against you. Turn now, each from your evil way, and correct your ways and your deeds.' But they will say, 'It's hopeless. We will continue to follow our plans, and each of us will continue to act according to the stubbornness of his evil heart.'"

Therefore, this is what the LORD says:
> Ask among the nations,
> who has heard things like these?
20 Virgin Israel has done a most horrible thing.
> Does the snow of Lebanon ever leave the highland crags?
> Or does cold water flowing from a distance ever fail?
> Yet my people have forgotten me.
> They burn incense to worthless idols
> that make them stumble in their ways
> on the ancient roads,
> and make them walk on new paths, not the highway.
> They have made their land a horror,

a perpetual object of scorn;
30 all who pass by it will be appalled
and shake their heads.
I will scatter them before the enemy like the east wind.
I will show them my back and not my face
on the day of their calamity.

Then certain ones said, "Come, let's make plans against Jeremiah, for instruction will never be lost from the priest, or counsel from the wise, or a word from the prophet. Come, let's denounce him and pay no attention to all his words."

Pay attention to me, LORD.
Hear what my opponents are saying!
40 Should good be repaid with evil?
Yet they have dug a pit for me.
Remember how I stood before you
to speak good on their behalf,
to turn your anger from them.
Therefore, hand their children over to famine,
and give them over to the power of the sword.
Let their wives become childless and widowed,
their husbands slain by deadly disease,
their young men struck down by the sword in battle.
50 Let a cry be heard from their houses
when you suddenly bring raiders against them,
for they have dug a pit to capture me
and have hidden snares for my feet.
But you, LORD, know
all their deadly plots against me.
Do not wipe out their iniquity;
do not blot out their sin before you.
Let them be forced to stumble before you;
deal with them in the time of your anger.

19 This is what the LORD says: "Go, buy a potter's clay jar. Take some of the elders of the people and some of the leading priests and go out to Ben Hinnom Valley near the entrance of the Potsherd Gate. Proclaim there the words I speak to you. Say, 'Hear the word of the LORD, kings of Judah and residents of Jerusalem. This is what the LORD of Armies, the God of Israel, says: I am going to bring such a disaster on this place that everyone who hears about it will shudder because they have abandoned me and made this a foreign place. They have burned incense in it to other gods that they, their ancestors, and the kings of Judah have never known. They have filled this place with the blood of the innocent. They have built high places to Baal on which to burn their children in the fire as burnt offerings to Baal, something I have never commanded or mentioned; I never entertained the thought.

10 "'Therefore, look, the days are coming—this is the Lord's declaration—when this place will no longer be called Topheth and Ben Hinnom Valley, but Slaughter Valley. I will spoil the plans of Judah and Jerusalem in this place. I will make them fall by the sword before their enemies, by the hand of those who intend to take their life. I will provide their corpses as food for the birds of the sky and for the wild animals of the land. I will make this city desolate, an object of scorn. Everyone who passes by it will be appalled and scoff because of all its wounds. I will make them eat the flesh of their sons and their daughters, and they will eat each other's flesh in the distressing siege inflicted on them by their enemies who intend to take their life.'

"Then you are to shatter the jar in the presence of the people going with you, and you are to proclaim to them, 'This is what the Lord of Armies says: I will shatter these people and this city, like 20 one shatters a potter's jar that can never again be mended. They will bury the dead in Topheth because there is no other place for burials. That is what I will do to this place—this is the declaration of the Lord—and to its residents, making this city like Topheth. The houses of Jerusalem and the houses of the kings of Judah will become impure like that place Topheth—all the houses on whose rooftops they have burned incense to all the stars in the sky and poured out drink offerings to other gods.'"

Jeremiah returned from Topheth, where the Lord had sent him to prophesy, stood in the courtyard of the Lord's temple, and proclaimed to all the people, "This is what the Lord of Armies, the God of Israel, says: 'I am about to bring on this city—and on all its cities—every disaster that I spoke against it, for they have become obstinate, not obeying my words.'"

20 Pashhur the priest, the son of Immer and chief official in the temple of the Lord, heard Jeremiah prophesying these things. So Pashhur had the prophet Jeremiah beaten and put him in the stocks at the Upper Benjamin Gate in the Lord's temple. The next day, when Pashhur released Jeremiah from the stocks, Jeremiah said to him, "The Lord does not call you Pashhur, but Terror Is on Every Side, for this is what the Lord says, 'I am about to make you a terror to both yourself and those you love. They will fall by the sword of their enemies before your very eyes. I will hand Judah over to the king of Babylon, and he will deport them to Babylon and put them to the sword. I will give away all the wealth of this city, all its products and valuables. Indeed, I will hand all the treasures of the kings of Judah over to their enemies. They will plunder them, seize them, and carry them off to Babylon. As for you, 10 Pashhur, and all who live in your house, you will go into captivity. You will go to Babylon. There you will die, and there you will be buried, you and all your friends to whom you prophesied lies.'"

> You deceived me, Lord, and I was deceived.
> You seized me and prevailed.

I am a laughingstock all the time;
everyone ridicules me.
For whenever I speak, I cry out,
I proclaim, "Violence and destruction!"
so the word of the Lord has become my
constant disgrace and derision.

20 I say, "I won't mention him
or speak any longer in his name."
But his message becomes a fire burning in my heart,
shut up in my bones.
I become tired of holding it in,
and I cannot prevail.
For I have heard the gossip of many people,
"Terror is on every side!
Report him; let's report him!"
Everyone I trusted watches for my fall.

30 "Perhaps he will be deceived
so that we might prevail against him
and take our vengeance on him."
But the Lord is with me like a violent warrior.
Therefore, my persecutors will stumble and not prevail.
Since they have not succeeded, they will be utterly shamed,
an everlasting humiliation that will never be forgotten.
Lord of Armies, testing the righteous
and seeing the heart and mind,
let me see your vengeance on them,

40 for I have presented my case to you.
Sing to the Lord!
Praise the Lord,
for he rescues the life of the needy
from evil people.

May the day I was born
be cursed.
May the day my mother bore me
never be blessed.
May the man be cursed

50 who brought the news to my father, saying,

"A male child is born to you,"
bringing him great joy.
Let that man be like the cities
the LORD demolished without compassion.
Let him hear an outcry in the morning
and a war cry at noontime
because he didn't kill me in the womb
so that my mother might have been my grave,
her womb eternally pregnant.
Why did I come out of the womb
to see only struggle and sorrow,
to end my life in shame?

21 This is the word that came to Jeremiah from the LORD when King Zedekiah sent Pashhur son of Malchijah and the priest Zephaniah son of Maaseiah to Jeremiah, asking, "Inquire of the LORD on our behalf, since King Nebuchadnezzar of Babylon is making war against us. Perhaps the LORD will perform for us something like all his past wondrous works so that Nebuchadnezzar will withdraw from us."

But Jeremiah answered, "This is what you are to say to Zedekiah: 'This is what the LORD, the God of Israel, says: I am about to repel the weapons of war in your hands, those you are using to fight the king of Babylon and the Chaldeans who are besieging you outside the wall, and I will bring them into the center of this city. I myself will fight against you with an outstretched hand and a strong arm, with anger, fury, and intense wrath. I will strike the residents of this city, both

10 people and animals. They will die in a severe plague. Afterward—this is the LORD's declaration— King Zedekiah of Judah, his officers, and the people—those in this city who survive the plague, the sword, and the famine—I will hand over to King Nebuchadnezzar of Babylon, to their enemies, yes, to those who intend to take their lives. He will put them to the sword; he won't spare them or show pity or compassion.'

"But tell this people, 'This is what the LORD says: Look, I am setting before you the way of life and the way of death. Whoever stays in this city will die by the sword, famine, and plague, but whoever goes out and surrenders to the Chaldeans who are besieging you will live and will retain his life like the spoils of war. For I have set my face against this city to bring disaster and not good—this is the LORD's declaration. It will be handed over to the king of Babylon, who will burn it.'

20 "And to the house of the king of Judah say this: 'Hear the word of the LORD! House of David, this is what the LORD says:

Administer justice every morning,
and rescue the victim of robbery
from his oppressor,

or my anger will flare up like fire
and burn unquenchably
because of your evil deeds.
Beware! I am against you,
you who sit above the valley,
you atop the rocky plateau—
this is the LORD's declaration—
you who say, "Who can come down against us?
Who can enter our hiding places?"
I will punish you according to what you have done—
this is the LORD's declaration.
I will kindle a fire in your forest
that will consume everything around it.'"

22 This is what the LORD says: "Go down to the palace of the king of Judah and announce this word there. You are to say, 'Hear the word of the LORD, king of Judah, you who sit on the throne of David—you, your officers, and your people who enter these gates. This is what the LORD says: Administer justice and righteousness. Rescue the victim of robbery from his oppressor. Don't exploit or brutalize the resident alien, the fatherless, or the widow. Don't shed innocent blood in this place. For if you conscientiously carry out this word, then kings sitting on David's throne will enter through the gates of this palace riding on chariots and horses—they, their officers, and their people. But if you do not obey these words, then I swear by myself—this is the LORD's declaration—that this house will become a ruin.'"

For this is what the LORD says concerning the house of the king of Judah:

"You are like Gilead to me,
or the summit of Lebanon,
but I will certainly turn you into a wilderness,
uninhabited cities.
I will set apart destroyers against you,
each with his weapons.
They will cut down the choicest of your cedars
and throw them into the fire.

"Many nations will pass by this city and ask one another, 'Why did the LORD do such a thing to this great city?' They will answer, 'Because they abandoned the covenant of the LORD their God and bowed in worship to other gods and served them.'"

Do not weep for the dead;
do not mourn for him.

Weep bitterly for the one who has gone away,
for he will never return again
and see his native land.

For this is what the LORD says concerning Shallum son of Josiah, king of Judah, who became king in place of his father Josiah, and who has left this place: "He will never return here again, but he will die in the place where they deported him, never seeing this land again."

Woe for the one who builds his palace
30 through unrighteousness,
his upstairs rooms through injustice,
who makes his neighbor serve without pay
and will not give him his wages,
who says, "I will build myself a massive palace,
with spacious upstairs rooms."
He will cut windows in it,
and it will be paneled with cedar
and painted bright red.
Are you a king because you excel in cedar?
40 Didn't your father eat and drink
and administer justice and righteousness?
Then it went well with him.
He took up the case of the poor and needy;
then it went well.
Is this not what it means to know me?
This is the LORD's declaration.
But you have eyes and a heart for nothing
except your own dishonest profit,
shedding innocent blood
50 and committing extortion and oppression.

Therefore, this is what the LORD says concerning Jehoiakim son of Josiah, king of Judah:
They will not mourn for him, saying,
"Woe, my brother!" or "Woe, my sister!"
They will not mourn for him, saying,
"Woe, lord! Woe, his majesty!"
He will be buried like a donkey,
dragged off and thrown

outside Jerusalem's gates.
Go up to Lebanon and cry out;
60   raise your voice in Bashan;
cry out from Abarim,
for all your lovers have been crushed.
I spoke to you when you were secure.
You said, "I will not listen."
This has been your way since youth;
indeed, you have never listened to me.
The wind will take charge of all your shepherds,
and your lovers will go into captivity.
Then you will be ashamed and humiliated
70   because of all your evil.
You residents of Lebanon,
nestled among the cedars,
how you will groan when pains come on you,
agony like a woman in labor.

"As I live"—this is the LORD's declaration—"though you, Coniah son of Jehoiakim, the king of Judah, were a signet ring on my right hand, I would tear you from it. In fact, I will hand you over to those you dread, who intend to take your life, to Nebuchadnezzar king of Babylon and the Chaldeans. I will hurl you and the mother who gave birth to you into another land, where neither of you were born, and there you will both die. They will never return to the land they long to
80   return to."
Is this man Coniah a despised, shattered pot,
a jar no one wants?
Why are he and his descendants hurled out
and cast into a land they have not known?
Earth, earth, earth,
hear the word of the LORD!

This is what the LORD says:
Record this man as childless,
a man who will not be successful in his lifetime.
90   None of his descendants will succeed
in sitting on the throne of David
or ruling again in Judah.

23 "Woe to the shepherds who destroy and scatter the sheep of my pasture!" This is the LORD's declaration. "Therefore, this is what the LORD, the God of Israel, says about the shepherds who tend my people: You have scattered my flock, banished them, and have not attended to them. I am about to attend to you because of your evil acts"—this is the LORD's declaration. "I will gather the remnant of my flock from all the lands where I have banished them, and I will return them to their grazing land. They will become fruitful and numerous. I will raise up shepherds over them who will tend them. They will no longer be afraid or discouraged, nor will any be missing." This is the LORD's declaration.

> "Look, the days are coming"—this is the LORD's declaration—
> "when I will raise up a Righteous Branch for David.
> He will reign wisely as king
> and administer justice and righteousness in the land.
> In his days Judah will be saved,
> and Israel will dwell securely.
> This is the name he will be called:
> The LORD Is Our Righteousness.

"Look, the days are coming"—the LORD's declaration—"when it will no longer be said, 'As the LORD lives who brought the Israelites from the land of Egypt,' but, 'As the LORD lives, who brought and led the descendants of the house of Israel from the land of the north and from all the other countries where I had banished them.' They will dwell once more in their own land."

Concerning the prophets:
> My heart is broken within me,
> and all my bones tremble.
> I have become like a drunkard,
> like a man overcome by wine,
> because of the LORD,
> because of his holy words.
> For the land is full of adulterers;
> the land mourns because of the curse,
> and the grazing lands in the wilderness have dried up.
> Their way of life has become evil,
> and their power is not rightly used
> because both prophet and priest are ungodly,
> even in my house I have found their evil.
> This is the LORD's declaration.

Therefore, their way will seem
like slippery paths in the gloom.
They will be driven away and fall down there,
for I will bring disaster on them,
40 the year of their punishment.
This is the Lord's declaration.

Among the prophets of Samaria
I saw something disgusting:
They prophesied by Baal
and led my people Israel astray.
Among the prophets of Jerusalem also
I saw a horrible thing:
They commit adultery and walk in lies.
They strengthen the hands of evildoers,
50 and none turns his back on evil.
They are all like Sodom to me;
Jerusalem's residents are like Gomorrah.

Therefore, this is what the Lord of Armies says concerning the prophets:
I am about to feed them wormwood
and give them poisoned water to drink,
for from the prophets of Jerusalem
ungodliness has spread throughout the land.

This is what the Lord of Armies says: "Do not listen to the words of the prophets who
prophesy to you. They are deluding you. They speak visions from their own minds, not from the
60 Lord's mouth. They keep on saying to those who despise me, 'The Lord has spoken: You will
have peace.' They have said to everyone who follows the stubbornness of his heart, 'No harm will
come to you.'"
For who has stood in the council of the Lord
to see and hear his word?
Who has paid attention to his word and obeyed?
Look, a storm from the Lord!
Wrath has gone out,
a whirling storm.
It will whirl about the heads of the wicked.
70 The Lord's anger will not turn away

723

until he has completely fulfilled the purposes of his heart.
In time to come you will understand it clearly.

I did not send out these prophets,
yet they ran.
I did not speak to them,
yet they prophesied.
If they had really stood in my council,
they would have enabled my people to hear my words
and would have turned them from their evil ways
80 and their evil deeds.

"Am I a God who is only near"—this is the Lord's declaration—"and not a God who is far away? Can a person hide in secret places where I cannot see him?"—the Lord's declaration. "Do I not fill the heavens and the earth?"—the Lord's declaration.

"I have heard what the prophets who prophesy a lie in my name have said: 'I had a dream! I had a dream!' How long will this continue in the minds of the prophets prophesying lies, prophets of the deceit of their own minds? Through their dreams that they tell one another, they plan to cause my people to forget my name as their ancestors forgot my name through Baal worship. The prophet who has only a dream should recount the dream, but the one who has my word should speak my word truthfully, for what is straw compared to grain?"—this is the Lord's declaration.
90 "Is not my word like fire"—this is the Lord's declaration—"and like a hammer that pulverizes rock? Therefore, take note! I am against the prophets"—the Lord's declaration—"who steal my words from each other. I am against the prophets"—the Lord's declaration—"who use their own tongues to make a declaration. I am against those who prophesy false dreams"—the Lord's declaration—"telling them and leading my people astray with their reckless lies. It was not I who sent or commanded them, and they are of no benefit at all to these people"—this is the Lord's declaration.

"Now when these people or a prophet or a priest asks you, 'What is the burden of the Lord?' you will respond to them, 'What is the burden? I will throw you away! This is the Lord's declaration.' As for the prophet, priest, or people who say, 'The burden of the Lord,' I will punish that man and
100 his household. This is what each man is to say to his friend and to his brother: 'What has the Lord answered?' or 'What has the Lord spoken?' But no longer refer to the burden of the Lord, for each man's word becomes his burden and you pervert the words of the living God, the Lord of Armies, our God. Say to the prophet, 'What has the Lord answered you?' or 'What has the Lord spoken?' But if you say, 'The burden of the Lord,' then this is what the Lord says: Because you have said, 'The burden of the Lord,' and I specifically told you not to say, 'The burden of the Lord,' I will

surely forget you. I will throw you away from my presence—both you and the city that I gave you and your ancestors. I will bring on you everlasting disgrace and humiliation that will never be forgotten."

24 After King Nebuchadnezzar of Babylon had deported Jeconiah son of Jehoiakim king of Judah, the officials of Judah, and the craftsmen and metalsmiths from Jerusalem and had brought them to Babylon, the LORD showed me two baskets of figs placed in front of the temple of the LORD. One basket contained very good figs, like early figs, but the other basket contained very bad figs, so bad they were inedible. The LORD said to me, "What do you see, Jeremiah?"

I said, "Figs! The good figs are very good, but the bad figs are extremely bad, so bad they are inedible."

The word of the LORD came to me: "This is what the LORD, the God of Israel, says: Like these good figs, so I regard as good the exiles from Judah I sent away from this place to the land of the
10 Chaldeans. I will keep my eyes on them for their good and will return them to this land. I will build them up and not demolish them; I will plant them and not uproot them. I will give them a heart to know me, that I am the LORD. They will be my people, and I will be their God because they will return to me with all their heart.

"But as for the bad figs, so bad they are inedible, this is what the LORD says: In this way I will deal with King Zedekiah of Judah, his officials, and the remnant of Jerusalem those remaining in this land or living in the land of Egypt. I will make them an object of horror and a disaster to all the kingdoms of the earth, an example for disgrace, scorn, ridicule, and cursing, wherever I have banished them. I will send the sword, famine, and plague against them until they have perished from the land I gave to them and their ancestors."

25 This is the word that came to Jeremiah concerning all the people of Judah in the fourth year of Jehoiakim son of Josiah, king of Judah (which was the first year of King Nebuchadnezzar of Babylon). The prophet Jeremiah spoke concerning all the people of Judah and all the residents of Jerusalem as follows: "From the thirteenth year of Josiah son of Amon, king of Judah, until this very day—twenty-three years—the word of the LORD has come to me, and I have spoken to you time and time again, but you have not obeyed. The LORD sent all his servants the prophets to you time and time again, but you have not obeyed or even paid attention. He announced, 'Turn, each of you, from your evil way of life and from your evil deeds. Live in the land the LORD gave to you and your ancestors long ago and forever. Do not follow other gods to serve them and to bow in
10 worship to them, and do not anger me by the work of your hands. Then I will do you no harm.

"'But you have not obeyed me'—this is the LORD's declaration—'with the result that you have angered me by the work of your hands and brought disaster on yourselves.'

"Therefore, this is what the LORD of Armies says: 'Because you have not obeyed my words, I am going to send for all the families of the north'—this is the LORD's declaration—'and send for my servant Nebuchadnezzar king of Babylon, and I will bring them against this land, against its residents, and against all these surrounding nations, and I will completely destroy them and make them an example of horror and scorn, and ruins forever. I will eliminate the sound of joy and gladness from them—the voice of the groom and the bride, the sound of the millstones and the light of the lamp. This whole land will become a desolate ruin, and these nations will serve the king of Babylon for seventy years. When the seventy years are completed, I will punish the king of Babylon and that nation'—this is the LORD's declaration—'the land of the Chaldeans, for their iniquity, and I will make it a ruin forever. I will bring on that land all my words I have spoken against it, all that is written in this book that Jeremiah prophesied against all the nations. For many nations and great kings will enslave them, and I will repay them according to their deeds and the work of their hands.'"

This is what the LORD, the God of Israel, said to me: "Take this cup of the wine of wrath from my hand and make all the nations to whom I am sending you drink from it. They will drink, stagger, and go out of their minds because of the sword I am sending among them."

So I took the cup from the LORD's hand and made all the nations to whom the LORD sent me drink from it.

Jerusalem and the other cities of Judah, its kings and its officials, to make them a desolate ruin, an example for scorn and cursing—as it is today;

Pharaoh king of Egypt, his officers, his leaders, all his people,

and all the mixed peoples;

all the kings of the land of Uz;

all the kings of the land of the Philistines—Ashkelon, Gaza, Ekron, and the remnant of Ashdod;

Edom, Moab, and the Ammonites;

all the kings of Tyre,

all the kings of Sidon,

and the kings of the coasts and islands;

Dedan, Tema, Buz, and all those who clip the hair on their temples;

all the kings of Arabia,

and all the kings of the mixed peoples who have settled in the desert;

all the kings of Zimri,

all the kings of Elam,

and all the kings of Media;

all the kings of the north, both near and far from one another;

that is, all the kingdoms of the world throughout the earth.

Finally, the king of Sheshak will drink after them.

"Then you are to say to them, 'This is what the LORD of Armies, the God of Israel, says: Drink, get drunk, and vomit. Fall down and never get up again, as a result of the sword I am sending among you.' If they refuse to accept the cup from your hand and drink, you are to say to them, 'This is what the LORD of Armies says: You must drink! For I am already bringing disaster on the city that bears my name, so how could you possibly go unpunished? You will not go unpunished, for I am summoning a sword against all the inhabitants of the earth. This is the declaration of the LORD of Armies.'

"As for you, you are to prophesy all these things to them, and say to them:
> The LORD roars from on high;
> he makes his voice heard from his holy dwelling.
60   He roars loudly over his grazing land;
> he calls out with a shout, like those who tread grapes,
> against all the inhabitants of the earth.
> The tumult reaches to the ends of the earth
> because the LORD brings a case against the nations.
> He enters into judgment with all humanity.
> As for the wicked, he hands them over to the sword—
> this is the LORD's declaration.

> "This is what the LORD of Armies says:
> Pay attention! Disaster spreads
70   from nation to nation.
> A huge storm is stirred up
> from the ends of the earth."

Those slain by the LORD on that day will be scattered from one end of the earth to the other. They will not be mourned, gathered, or buried. They will be like manure on the soil's surface.
> Wail, you shepherds, and cry out.
> Roll in the dust, you leaders of the flock.
> Because the days of your slaughter have come,
> you will fall and become shattered like a precious vase.
> Flight will be impossible for the shepherds,
80   and escape, for the leaders of the flock.
> Hear the sound of the shepherds' cry,
> the wail of the leaders of the flock,
> for the LORD is destroying their pasture.
> Peaceful grazing land will become lifeless
> because of the LORD's burning anger.
> He has left his den like a lion,

for their land has become a desolation
because of the sword of the oppressor,
because of his burning anger.

26 At the beginning of the reign of Jehoiakim son of Josiah, king of Judah, this word came from the LORD: "This is what the LORD says: Stand in the courtyard of the LORD's temple and speak all the words I have commanded you to speak to all Judah's cities that are coming to worship there. Do not hold back a word. Perhaps they will listen and turn—each from his evil way of life—so that I might relent concerning the disaster that I plan to do to them because of the evil of their deeds. You are to say to them, 'This is what the LORD says: If you do not listen to me by living according to my instruction that I set before you and by listening to the words of my servants the prophets—whom I have been sending to you time and time again, though you did not listen—I will make this temple like Shiloh. I will make this city an example for cursing for all the nations of
10 the earth.'"

The priests, the prophets, and all the people heard Jeremiah speaking these words in the temple of the LORD. When he finished the address the LORD had commanded him to deliver to all the people, immediately the priests, the prophets, and all the people took hold of him, yelling, "You must surely die! How dare you prophesy in the name of the LORD, 'This temple will become like Shiloh and this city will become an uninhabited ruin'!" Then all the people crowded around Jeremiah at the LORD's temple.

When the officials of Judah heard about these things, they went from the king's palace to the LORD's temple and sat at the entrance of the New Gate of the LORD's temple. Then the priests and prophets said to the officials and all the people, "This man deserves the death sentence
20 because he has prophesied against this city, as you have heard with your own ears."

Then Jeremiah said to all the officials and all the people, "The LORD sent me to prophesy all the words that you have heard against this temple and city. So now, correct your ways and deeds, and obey the LORD your God so that he might relent concerning the disaster he had pronounced against you. As for me, here I am in your hands; do to me what you think is good and right. But know for certain that if you put me to death, you will bring innocent blood on yourselves, on this city, and on its residents, for it is certain the LORD has sent me to speak all these things directly to you."

Then the officials and all the people told the priests and prophets, "This man doesn't deserve the death sentence, for he has spoken to us in the name of the LORD our God!"

Some of the elders of the land stood up and said to all the assembled people, "Micah the
30 Moreshite prophesied in the days of King Hezekiah of Judah and said to all the people of Judah, 'This is what the LORD of Armies says:

> Zion will be plowed like a field,
> Jerusalem will become ruins,
> and the temple's mountain will be a high thicket.'

Did King Hezekiah of Judah and all the people of Judah put him to death? Did not the king fear the LORD and plead for the LORD's favor, and did not the LORD relent concerning the disaster he had pronounced against them? We are about to bring a terrible disaster on ourselves!"

Another man was also prophesying in the name of the LORD—Uriah son of Shemaiah from Kiriath-jearim. He prophesied against this city and against this land in words like all those of
40 Jeremiah. King Jehoiakim, all his warriors, and all the officials heard his words, and the king tried to put him to death. When Uriah heard, he fled in fear and went to Egypt. But King Jehoiakim sent men to Egypt: Elnathan son of Achbor and certain other men with him went to Egypt. They brought Uriah out of Egypt and took him to King Jehoiakim, who executed him with the sword and threw his corpse into the burial place of the common people.

But Ahikam son of Shaphan supported Jeremiah, so he was not handed over to the people to be put to death.

27 At the beginning of the reign of Zedekiah son of Josiah, king of Judah, this word came to Jeremiah from the LORD: This is what the LORD said to me: "Make chains and yoke bars for yourself and put them on your neck. Send word to the king of Edom, the king of Moab, the king of the Ammonites, the king of Tyre, and the king of Sidon through messengers who are coming to King Zedekiah of Judah in Jerusalem. Command them to go to their masters, saying, 'This is what the LORD of Armies, the God of Israel, says: Tell this to your masters: "By my great strength and outstretched arm, I made the earth, and the people, and animals on the face of the earth. I give it to anyone I please. So now I have placed all these lands under the authority of my servant Nebuchadnezzar, king of Babylon. I have even given him the wild animals to serve him. All
10 nations will serve him, his son, and his grandson until the time for his own land comes, and then many nations and great kings will enslave him.

""As for the nation or kingdom that does not serve King Nebuchadnezzar of Babylon and does not place its neck under the yoke of the king of Babylon, that nation I will punish by sword, famine, and plague—this is the LORD's declaration—until through him I have destroyed it. So you should not listen to your prophets, diviners, dreamers, fortune-tellers, or sorcerers who say to you, 'Don't serve the king of Babylon!' They are prophesying a lie to you so that you will be removed from your land. I will banish you, and you will perish. But as for the nation that will put its neck under the yoke of the king of Babylon and serve him, I will leave it in its own land, and that nation will cultivate it and reside in it. This is the LORD's declaration.'"

20 I spoke to King Zedekiah of Judah in the same way: "Put your necks under the yoke of the king of Babylon, serve him and his people, and live! Why should you and your people die by the sword, famine, and plague as the LORD has threatened against any nation that does not serve the king of Babylon? Do not listen to the words of the prophets who are telling you, 'Don't serve the king of Babylon,' for they are prophesying a lie to you. 'I have not sent them'—this is the LORD's declaration—'and they are prophesying falsely in my name; therefore, I will banish you, and you will perish—you and the prophets who are prophesying to you.'"

Then I spoke to the priests and all these people, saying, "This is what the LORD says: 'Do not listen to the words of your prophets. They are prophesying to you, claiming, "Look, very soon now the articles of the LORD's temple will be brought back from Babylon." They are prophesying a lie to 30 you. Do not listen to them. Serve the king of Babylon and live! Why should this city become a ruin? If they are indeed prophets and if the word of the LORD is with them, let them intercede with the LORD of Armies not to let the articles that remain in the LORD's temple, in the palace of the king of Judah, and in Jerusalem go to Babylon.' For this is what the LORD of Armies says about the pillars, the basin, the water carts, and the rest of the articles that still remain in this city, those King Nebuchadnezzar of Babylon did not take when he deported Jeconiah son of Jehoiakim, king of Judah, from Jerusalem to Babylon along with all the nobles of Judah and Jerusalem. Yes, this is what the LORD of Armies, the God of Israel, says about the articles that remain in the temple of the LORD, in the palace of the king of Judah, and in Jerusalem: 'They will be taken to Babylon and will remain there until I attend to them again.' This is the LORD's declaration. 'Then I will bring them up and restore them to this place.'"

28 In that same year, at the beginning of the reign of King Zedekiah of Judah, in the fifth month of the fourth year, the prophet Hananiah son of Azzur from Gibeon said to me in the temple of the LORD in the presence of the priests and all the people, "This is what the LORD of Armies, the God of Israel, says: 'I have broken the yoke of the king of Babylon. Within two years I will restore to this place all the articles of the LORD's temple that King Nebuchadnezzar of Babylon took from here and transported to Babylon. And I will restore to this place Jeconiah son of Jehoiakim, king of Judah, and all the exiles from Judah who went to Babylon'—this is the LORD's declaration—'for I will break the yoke of the king of Babylon.'"

10 The prophet Jeremiah replied to the prophet Hananiah in the presence of the priests and all the people who were standing in the temple of the LORD. The prophet Jeremiah said, "Amen! May the LORD do that. May the LORD make the words you have prophesied come true and may he restore the articles of the LORD's temple and all the exiles from Babylon to this place! Only listen to this message I am speaking in your hearing and in the hearing of all the people. The prophets who preceded you and me from ancient times prophesied war, disaster, and plague against many lands and great kingdoms. As for the prophet who prophesies peace—only when the word of the prophet comes true will the prophet be recognized as one the LORD has truly sent."

The prophet Hananiah then took the yoke bar from the neck of the prophet Jeremiah and broke it. In the presence of all the people Hananiah proclaimed, "This is what the LORD says: 'In this way, within two years I will break the yoke of King Nebuchadnezzar of Babylon from the neck of all the nations.'" The prophet Jeremiah then went on his way.

After the prophet Hananiah had broken the yoke bar from the neck of the prophet Jeremiah, the word of the LORD came to Jeremiah: "Go say to Hananiah, 'This is what the LORD says: You broke a wooden yoke bar, but in its place you will make an iron yoke bar. For this is what the LORD of Armies, the God of Israel, says: I have put an iron yoke on the neck of all these nations that they might serve King Nebuchadnezzar of Babylon, and they will serve him. I have even put the wild animals under him.'"

The prophet Jeremiah said to the prophet Hananiah, "Listen, Hananiah! The LORD did not send you, but you have led these people to trust in a lie. Therefore, this is what the LORD says: 'I am about to send you off the face of the earth. You will die this year because you have preached rebellion against the LORD.'" And the prophet Hananiah died that year in the seventh month.

29 This is the text of the letter that the prophet Jeremiah sent from Jerusalem to the remaining exiled elders, the priests, the prophets, and all the people Nebuchadnezzar had deported from Jerusalem to Babylon. This was after King Jeconiah, the queen mother, the court officials, the officials of Judah and Jerusalem, the craftsmen, and the metalsmiths had left Jerusalem. He sent the letter with Elasah son of Shaphan and Gemariah son of Hilkiah, whom Zedekiah king of Judah sent to Babylon to King Nebuchadnezzar of Babylon. The letter stated:

This is what the LORD of Armies, the God of Israel, says to all the exiles I deported from Jerusalem to Babylon: "Build houses and live in them. Plant gardens and eat their produce. Find wives for yourselves, and have sons and daughters. Find wives for your sons and give your daughters to men in marriage so that they may bear sons and daughters. Multiply there; do not decrease. Pursue the well-being of the city I have deported you to. Pray to the LORD on its behalf, for when it thrives, you will thrive."

For this is what the LORD of Armies, the God of Israel, says: "Don't let your prophets who are among you and your diviners deceive you, and don't listen to the dreams you elicit from them, for they are prophesying falsely to you in my name. I have not sent them." This is the LORD's declaration.

For this is what the LORD says: "When seventy years for Babylon are complete, I will attend to you and will confirm my promise concerning you to restore you to this place. For I know the plans I have for you"—this is the LORD's declaration—"plans for your well-being, not for disaster,

20 to give you a future and a hope. You will call to me and come and pray to me, and I will listen to you. You will seek me and find me when you search for me with all your heart. I will be found by you"—this is the Lord's declaration—"and I will restore your fortunes and gather you from all the nations and places where I banished you"—this is the Lord's declaration. "I will restore you to the place from which I deported you."

You have said, "The Lord has raised up prophets for us in Babylon!" But this is what the Lord says concerning the king sitting on David's throne and concerning all the people living in this city—that is, concerning your brothers who did not go with you into exile. This is what the Lord of Armies says: "I am about to send sword, famine, and plague against them, and I will make them like rotten figs that are inedible because they are so bad. I will pursue them with sword, famine,
30 and plague. I will make them a horror to all the kingdoms of the earth—a curse and a desolation, an object of scorn and a disgrace among all the nations where I have banished them. I will do this because they have not listened to my words"—this is the Lord's declaration—"the words that I sent to them with my servants the prophets time and time again. And you too have not listened." This is the Lord's declaration.

Hear the word of the Lord, all you exiles I have sent from Jerusalem to Babylon. This is what the Lord of Armies, the God of Israel, says about Ahab son of Kolaiah and concerning Zedekiah son of Maaseiah, the ones prophesying a lie to you in my name: "I am about to hand them over to King Nebuchadnezzar of Babylon, and he will kill them before your very eyes. Based on what happens to them, all the exiles of Judah who are in Babylon will create a curse that says, 'May the
40 Lord make you like Zedekiah and Ahab, whom the king of Babylon roasted in the fire!' because they have committed an outrage in Israel by committing adultery with their neighbors' wives and have spoken in my name a lie, which I did not command them. I am he who knows, and I am a witness." This is the Lord's declaration.

To Shemaiah the Nehelamite you are to say, "This is what the Lord of Armies, the God of Israel, says: You in your own name have sent out letters to all the people of Jerusalem, to the priest Zephaniah son of Maaseiah, and to all the priests, saying, 'The Lord has appointed you priest in place of the priest Jehoiada to be the chief officer in the temple of the Lord, responsible for every madman who acts like a prophet. You must confine him in the stocks and an iron collar. So now, why have you not rebuked Jeremiah of Anathoth who has been acting like a prophet among you?
50 For he has sent word to us in Babylon, claiming, "The exile will be long. Build houses and settle down. Plant gardens and eat their produce."'"

The priest Zephaniah read this letter in the hearing of the prophet Jeremiah.

Then the word of the LORD came to Jeremiah: "Send a message to all the exiles, saying, 'This is what the LORD says concerning Shemaiah the Nehelamite. Because Shemaiah prophesied to you, though I did not send him, and made you trust a lie, this is what the LORD says: I am about to punish Shemaiah the Nehelamite and his descendants. There will not be even one of his descendants living among these people, nor will any ever see the good that I will bring to my people—this is the LORD's declaration—for he has preached rebellion against the LORD.'"

30 This is the word that came to Jeremiah from the LORD. "This is what the LORD, the God of Israel, says: Write on a scroll all the words that I have spoken to you, for look, the days are coming"—this is the LORD's declaration—"when I will restore the fortunes of my people Israel and Judah," says the LORD. "I will restore them to the land I gave to their ancestors and they will possess it."

These are the words the LORD spoke to Israel and Judah. This is what the LORD says:

> We have heard a cry of terror,
> of dread—there is no peace.
> Ask and see
> whether a male can give birth.
> Why then do I see every man
> with his hands on his stomach like a woman in labor
> and every face turned pale?
> How awful that day will be!
> There will be no other like it!
> It will be a time of trouble for Jacob,
> but he will be saved out of it.
>
> On that day—
> this is the declaration of the LORD of Armies—
> I will break his yoke from your neck
> and tear off your chains,
> and strangers will never again enslave him.
> They will serve the LORD their God
> and David their king,
> whom I will raise up for them.
>
> As for you, my servant Jacob,
> do not be afraid—
> this is the LORD's declaration—
> and do not be discouraged, Israel,

for without fail I will save you out of a distant place,
30   your descendants, from the land of their captivity!
Jacob will return and have calm and quiet
with no one to frighten him.
For I will be with you—
this is the LORD's declaration—
to save you!
I will bring destruction on all the nations
where I have scattered you;
however, I will not bring destruction on you.
I will discipline you justly,
40   and I will by no means leave you unpunished.

For this is what the LORD says:
Your injury is incurable;
your wound most severe.
You have no defender for your case.
There is no remedy for your sores,
and no healing for you.
All your lovers have forgotten you;
they no longer look for you,
for I have struck you as an enemy would,
50   with the discipline of someone cruel,
because of your enormous guilt
and your innumerable sins.
Why do you cry out about your injury?
Your pain has no cure!
I have done these things to you
because of your enormous guilt
and your innumerable sins.
Nevertheless, all who devoured you will be devoured,
and all your adversaries—all of them—
60   will go off into exile.
Those who plunder you will be plundered,
and all who raid you will be raided.
But I will bring you health
and will heal you of your wounds—
this is the LORD's declaration—

for they call you Outcast,
Zion whom no one cares about.

This is what the LORD says:

I will certainly restore the fortunes of Jacob's tents
70 and show compassion on his dwellings.
Every city will be rebuilt on its mound;
every citadel will stand on its proper site.
Thanksgiving will come out of them,
a sound of rejoicing.
I will multiply them, and they will not decrease;
I will honor them, and they will not be insignificant.
His children will be as in past days;
his congregation will be established in my presence.
I will punish all his oppressors.
80 Jacob's leader will be one of them;
his ruler will issue from him.
I will invite him to me, and he will approach me,
for who would otherwise risk his life to approach me?
This is the LORD's declaration.
You will be my people,
and I will be your God.

Look, a storm from the LORD!
Wrath has gone out,
a churning storm.
90 It will whirl about the heads of the wicked.
The LORD's burning anger will not turn back
until he has completely fulfilled the purposes of his heart.
In time to come you will understand it.

31 "At that time"—this is the LORD's declaration—"I will be the God of all the families of Israel, and they will be my people."

This is what the LORD says:

The people who survived the sword
found favor in the wilderness.
When Israel went to find rest,
the LORD appeared to him from far away.

I have loved you with an everlasting love;
therefore, I have continued to extend faithful love to you.
10 Again I will build you so that you will be rebuilt,
Virgin Israel.
You will take up your tambourines again
and go out in joyful dancing.
You will plant vineyards again
on the mountains of Samaria;
the planters will plant and will enjoy the fruit.
For there will be a day when watchmen will call out
in the hill country of Ephraim,
"Come, let's go up to Zion,
20 to the LORD our God!"

For this is what the LORD says:
Sing with joy for Jacob;
shout for the foremost of the nations!
Proclaim, praise, and say,
"LORD, save your people,
the remnant of Israel!"
Watch! I am going to bring them from the northern land.
I will gather them from remote regions of the earth—
the blind and the lame will be with them,
30 along with those who are pregnant and those about to give birth.
They will return here as a great assembly!
They will come weeping,
but I will bring them back with consolation.
I will lead them to wadis filled with water,
by a smooth way where they will not stumble,
for I am Israel's Father,
and Ephraim is my firstborn.
Nations, hear the word of the LORD,
and tell it among the far off coasts and islands!
40 Say, "The one who scattered Israel will gather him.
He will watch over him as a shepherd guards his flock,
for the LORD has ransomed Jacob
and redeemed him from the power of one stronger than he."
They will come and shout for joy on the heights of Zion;

they will be radiant with joy
because of the Lord's goodness,
because of the grain, the new wine, the fresh oil,
and because of the young of the flocks and herds.
Their life will be like an irrigated garden,
50   and they will no longer grow weak from hunger.
Then the young women will rejoice with dancing,
while young and old men rejoice together.
I will turn their mourning into joy,
give them consolation,
and bring happiness out of grief.
I will refresh the priests with an abundance,
and my people will be satisfied with my goodness.
This is the Lord's declaration.

This is what the Lord says:
60   A voice was heard in Ramah,
a lament with bitter weeping—
Rachel weeping for her children,
refusing to be comforted for her children
because they are no more.

This is what the Lord says:
Keep your voice from weeping
and your eyes from tears,
for the reward for your work will come—
this is the Lord's declaration—
70   and your children will return from the enemy's land.
There is hope for your future—
this is the Lord's declaration—
and your children will return to their own territory.
I have surely heard Ephraim moaning,
"You disciplined me, and I have been disciplined
like an untrained calf.
Take me back, so that I can return,
for you, Lord, are my God.
After my return, I felt regret;
80   After I was instructed, I struck my thigh in grief.

I was ashamed and humiliated
because I bore the disgrace of my youth."
Isn't Ephraim a precious son to me,
a delightful child?
Whenever I speak against him,
I certainly still think about him.
Therefore, my inner being yearns for him;
I will truly have compassion on him.
This is the LORD's declaration.

90   Set up road markers for yourself;
establish signposts!
Keep the highway in mind,
the way you have traveled.
Return, Virgin Israel!
Return to these cities of yours.
How long will you turn here and there,
faithless daughter?
For the LORD creates something new in the land—
a female will shelter a man.

This is what the LORD of Armies, the God of Israel, says: "When I restore their fortunes, they
100 will once again speak this word in the land of Judah and in its cities: 'May the LORD bless you,
righteous settlement, holy mountain.' Judah and all its cities will live in it together—also farmers
and those who move with the flocks—for I satisfy the thirsty person and feed all those who are
weak."

At this I awoke and looked around. My sleep had been most pleasant to me.

"Look, the days are coming"—this is the LORD's declaration—"when I will sow the house of
Israel and the house of Judah with the seed of people and the seed of animals. Just as I watched
over them to uproot and to tear them down, to demolish and to destroy, and to cause disaster, so
will I watch over them to build and to plant them"—this is the LORD's declaration. "In those days,
it will never again be said,

110   'The fathers have eaten sour grapes,
and the children's teeth are set on edge.'

Rather, each will die for his own iniquity. Anyone who eats sour grapes—his own teeth will be
set on edge.

"Look, the days are coming"—this is the LORD's declaration—"when I will make a new covenant with the house of Israel and with the house of Judah. This one will not be like the covenant I made with their ancestors on the day I took them by the hand to lead them out of the land of Egypt— my covenant that they broke even though I am their master"—the LORD's declaration. "Instead, this is the covenant I will make with the house of Israel after those days"—the LORD's declaration. "I will put my teaching within them and write it on their hearts. I will be their God, and they will be my people. No longer will one teach his neighbor or his brother, saying, 'Know the LORD,' for they will all know me, from the least to the greatest of them"—this is the LORD's declaration. "For I will forgive their iniquity and never again remember their sin.

"This is what the LORD says:

The one who gives the sun for light by day,
the fixed order of moon and stars for light by night,
who stirs up the sea and makes its waves roar—
the LORD of Armies is his name:
If this fixed order departs from before me—
this is the LORD's declaration—
only then will Israel's descendants cease
to be a nation before me forever.

"This is what the LORD says:

Only if the heavens above can be measured
and the foundations of the earth below explored,
will I reject all of Israel's descendants
because of all they have done—
this is the LORD's declaration.

"Look, the days are coming"—the LORD's declaration—"when the city from the Tower of Hananel to the Corner Gate will be rebuilt for the LORD. A measuring line will once again stretch out straight to the hill of Gareb and then turn toward Goah. The whole valley—the corpses, the ashes, and all the fields as far as the Kidron Valley to the corner of the Horse Gate to the east— will be holy to the LORD. It will never be uprooted or demolished again."

32 This is the word that came to Jeremiah from the LORD in the tenth year of King Zedekiah of Judah, which was the eighteenth year of Nebuchadnezzar. At that time, the army of the king of Babylon was besieging Jerusalem, and the prophet Jeremiah was imprisoned in the guard's courtyard in the palace of the king of Judah. King Zedekiah of Judah had imprisoned him, saying, "Why are you prophesying as you do? You say, 'This is what the LORD says: Look, I am about to hand this city over to Babylon's king, and he will capture it. King Zedekiah of Judah will not escape from the Chaldeans; indeed, he will certainly be handed over to Babylon's king. They will speak face to face and meet eye to eye. He will take Zedekiah to Babylon, where he will stay until I attend to him—this is the LORD's declaration. For you will fight the Chaldeans, but you will not succeed.'"

10 Jeremiah replied, "The word of the LORD came to me: Watch! Hanamel, the son of your uncle Shallum, is coming to you to say, 'Buy my field in Anathoth for yourself, for you own the right of redemption to buy it.'

"Then, as the LORD had said, my cousin Hanamel came to the guard's courtyard and urged me, 'Please buy my field in Anathoth in the land of Benjamin, for you own the right of inheritance and redemption. Buy it for yourself.' Then I knew that this was the word of the LORD. So I bought the field in Anathoth from my cousin Hanamel, and I weighed out the silver to him—seventeen shekels of silver. I recorded it on a scroll, sealed it, called in witnesses, and weighed out the silver on the scales. I took the purchase agreement—the sealed copy with its terms and conditions and the open copy—and gave the purchase agreement to Baruch son of Neriah, son of Mahseiah. I did 20 this in the sight of my cousin Hanamel, the witnesses who had signed the purchase agreement, and all the Judeans sitting in the guard's courtyard.

"I charged Baruch in their sight, 'This is what the LORD of Armies, the God of Israel, says: Take these scrolls—this purchase agreement with the sealed copy and this open copy—and put them in an earthen storage jar so they will last a long time. For this is what the LORD of Armies, the God of Israel, says: Houses, fields, and vineyards will again be bought in this land.'

"After I had given the purchase agreement to Baruch, son of Neriah, I prayed to the LORD: Oh, Lord GOD! You yourself made the heavens and earth by your great power and with your outstretched arm. Nothing is too difficult for you! You show faithful love to thousands but lay the fathers' iniquity on their sons' laps after them, great and mighty God whose name is the LORD of 30 Armies, the one great in counsel and powerful in action. Your eyes are on all the ways of the children of men in order to reward each person according to his ways and as the result of his actions. You performed signs and wonders in the land of Egypt and still do today, both in Israel and among all mankind. You made a name for yourself, as is the case today. You brought your people Israel out of Egypt with signs and wonders, with a strong hand and an outstretched arm, and with great terror. You gave them this land you swore to give to their ancestors, a land flowing with milk and honey. They entered and possessed it, but they did not obey you or live according to your instructions. They failed to perform all you commanded them to do, and so you have brought all this disaster on them. Look! Siege ramps have come against the city to capture it, and the city, as a result of the sword, famine, and plague, has been handed over to the Chaldeans who are fighting against it. What 40 you have spoken has happened. Look, you can see it! Yet you, Lord GOD, have said to me, 'Purchase the field and call in witnesses'—even though the city has been handed over to the Chaldeans!"

The word of the LORD came to Jeremiah: "Look, I am the LORD, the God over every creature. Is anything too difficult for me? Therefore, this is what the LORD says: I am about to hand this city over to the Chaldeans, to Babylon's king Nebuchadnezzar, and he will capture it. The

Chaldeans who are fighting against this city will come and set this city on fire. They will burn it, including the houses where incense has been burned to Baal on their rooftops and where drink offerings have been poured out to other gods to anger me. From their youth, the Israelites and Judeans have done nothing but what is evil in my sight! They have done nothing but anger me by the work of their hands"—this is the LORD's declaration—"for this city has caused my wrath and fury from the day it was built until now. I will therefore remove it from my presence because of all the evil the Israelites and Judeans have done to anger me—they, their kings, their officials, their priests, and their prophets, the men of Judah, and the residents of Jerusalem. They have turned their backs to me and not their faces. Though I taught them time and time again, they do not listen and receive discipline. They have placed their abhorrent things in the house that bears my name and have defiled it. They have built the high places of Baal in Ben Hinnom Valley to sacrifice their sons and daughters in the fire to Molech—something I had not commanded them. I had never entertained the thought that they do this detestable act causing Judah to sin!

"Now therefore, this is what the LORD, the God of Israel, says to this city about which you said, 'It has been handed over to Babylon's king through sword, famine, and plague': I will certainly gather them from all the lands where I have banished them in my anger, fury, and intense wrath, and I will return them to this place and make them live in safety. They will be my people, and I will be their God. I will give them integrity of heart and action so that they will fear me always, for their good and for the good of their descendants after them.

"I will make a permanent covenant with them: I will never turn away from doing good to them, and I will put fear of me in their hearts so they will never again turn away from me. I will take delight in them to do what is good for them, and with all my heart and mind I will faithfully plant them in this land.

"For this is what the LORD says: Just as I have brought all this terrible disaster on these people, so am I about to bring on them all the good I am promising them. Fields will be bought in this land about which you are saying, 'It's a desolation without people or animals; it has been handed over to the Chaldeans!' Fields will be purchased, the transaction written on a scroll and sealed, and witnesses will be called on in the land of Benjamin, in the areas surrounding Jerusalem, and in Judah's cities—the cities of the hill country, the cities of the Judean foothills, and the cities of the Negev—because I will restore their fortunes."

This is the LORD's declaration.

33 While he was still confined in the guard's courtyard, the word of the LORD came to Jeremiah a second time: "The LORD who made the earth, the LORD who forms it to establish it, the LORD is his name, says this: Call to me and I will answer you and tell you great and incomprehensible things you do not know. For this is what the LORD, the God of Israel, says concerning the houses of this city and the palaces of Judah's kings, the ones torn down for defense against the assault ramps and the sword: The people coming to fight the Chaldeans will fill the houses with the corpses of their own men that I strike down in my wrath and fury. I have hidden my face from this city because of all their evil. Yet I will certainly bring health and healing to it and will indeed heal them. I will let them experience the abundance of true peace. I will restore the fortunes of Judah and of Israel and will rebuild them as in former times. I will purify them from all the iniquity they have committed against me, and I will forgive all the iniquities they have committed against me, rebelling against me. This city will bear on my behalf a name of joy, praise, and glory before all the nations of the earth, who will hear of all the prosperity I will give them. They will tremble with awe because of all the good and all the peace I will bring about for them.

"This is what the Lord says: In this place, which you say is a ruin, without people or animals—that is, in Judah's cities and Jerusalem's streets that are a desolation without people, without inhabitants, and without animals—there will be heard again a sound of joy and gladness, the voice of the groom and the bride, and the voice of those saying,

> Give thanks to the Lord of Armies,
> for the Lord is good;
> his faithful love endures forever

as they bring thanksgiving sacrifices to the temple of the Lord. For I will restore the fortunes of the land as in former times, says the Lord.

"This is what the Lord of Armies says: In this desolate place—without people or animals—and in all its cities there will once more be a grazing land where shepherds may rest flocks. The flocks will again pass under the hands of the one who counts them in the cities of the hill country, the cities of the Judean foothills, the cities of the Negev, the land of Benjamin—the areas around Jerusalem and in Judah's cities, says the Lord.

> "Look, the days are coming"—
> this is the Lord's declaration—
> "when I will fulfill the good promise
> that I have spoken
> concerning the house of Israel
> and the house of Judah.
> In those days and at that time
> I will cause a Righteous Branch
> to sprout up for David,
> and he will administer justice
> and righteousness in the land.
> In those days Judah will be saved,
> and Jerusalem will dwell securely,
> and this is what she will be named:
> The Lord Is Our Righteousness.

"For this is what the LORD says: David will never fail to have a man sitting on the throne of the house of Israel. The Levitical priests will never fail to have a man always before me to offer burnt offerings, to burn grain offerings, and to make sacrifices."

The word of the LORD came to Jeremiah: "This is what the LORD says: If you can break my covenant with the day and my covenant with the night so that day and night cease to come at their regular time, then also my covenant with my servant David may be broken. If that could happen, then he would not have a son reigning on his throne and the Levitical priests would not be my ministers. Even as the stars of heaven cannot be counted, and the sand of the sea cannot be measured, so too I will make innumerable the descendants of my servant David and the Levites who minister to me."

The word of the LORD came to Jeremiah: "Have you not noticed what these people have said? They say, 'The LORD has rejected the two families he had chosen.' My people are treated with contempt and no longer regarded as a nation among them. This is what the LORD says: If I do not keep my covenant with the day and with the night, and if I fail to establish the fixed order of heaven and earth, then I might also reject the descendants of Jacob and of my servant David. That is, I would not take rulers from his descendants to rule over the descendants of Abraham, Isaac, and Jacob. But in fact, I will restore their fortunes and have compassion on them."

34 This is the word that came to Jeremiah from the LORD when King Nebuchadnezzar of Babylon, his whole army, all the kingdoms of the lands under his control, and all other peoples were fighting against Jerusalem and all its surrounding cities: "This is what the LORD, the God of Israel, says: Go, speak to King Zedekiah of Judah, and tell him, 'This is what the LORD says: I am about to hand this city over to the king of Babylon, and he will burn it. As for you, you will not escape from him but are certain to be captured and handed over to him. You will meet the king of Babylon eye to eye and speak face to face; you will go to Babylon.

"'Yet hear the LORD's word, King Zedekiah of Judah. This is what the LORD says concerning you: You will not die by the sword; you will die peacefully. There will be a burning ceremony for you just like the burning ceremonies for your ancestors, the kings of old who came before you. "Oh, master!" will be the lament for you, for I have spoken this word. This is the LORD's declaration.'"

So the prophet Jeremiah related all these words to King Zedekiah of Judah in Jerusalem while the king of Babylon's army was attacking Jerusalem and all of Judah's remaining cities—that is, Lachish and Azekah, for they were the only ones left of Judah's fortified cities.

This is the word that came to Jeremiah from the LORD after King Zedekiah made a covenant with all the people who were in Jerusalem to proclaim freedom to them. As a result, each was to let his male and female Hebrew slaves go free, and no one was to enslave his fellow Judean. All the officials and

people who entered into covenant to let their male and female slaves go free—in order not to enslave
20   them any longer—obeyed and let them go free. Afterward, however, they changed their minds and
took back their male and female slaves they had let go free and forced them to become slaves again.

Then the word of the LORD came to Jeremiah from the LORD: "This is what the LORD, the
God of Israel, says: I made a covenant with your ancestors when I brought them out of the land of
Egypt, out of the place of slavery, saying, 'At the end of seven years, each of you must let his fellow
Hebrew who sold himself to you go. He may serve you six years, but then you must let him go free
from your service.' But your ancestors did not obey me or pay any attention. Today you repented
and did what pleased me, each of you proclaiming freedom for his neighbor. You made a covenant
before me at the house that bears my name. But you have changed your minds and profaned my
name. Each has taken back his male and females slaves who had been set free to go wherever they
30   wanted, and you have again forced them to be your slaves.

"Therefore, this is what the LORD says: You have not obeyed me by proclaiming freedom,
each for his fellow Hebrew and for his neighbor. I hereby proclaim freedom for you—this is the
LORD's declaration—to the sword, to plague, and to famine! I will make you a horror to all the
earth's kingdoms. As for those who disobeyed my covenant, not keeping the terms of the covenant
they made before me, I will treat them like the calf they cut in two in order to pass between its
pieces. The officials of Judah and Jerusalem, the court officials, the priests, and all the people of
the land who passed between the pieces of the calf—all these I will hand over to their enemies,
to those who intend to take their life. Their corpses will become food for the birds of the sky and
for the wild animals of the land. I will hand King Zedekiah of Judah and his officials over to their
40   enemies, to those who intend to take their lives, to the king of Babylon's army that is withdrawing.
I am about to give the command—this is the LORD's declaration—and I will bring them back to
this city. They will fight against it, capture it, and burn it. I will make Judah's cities a desolation,
without inhabitant."

35   This is the word that came to Jeremiah from the LORD in the days of Jehoiakim son of Josiah,
king of Judah: "Go to the house of the Rechabites, speak to them, and bring them to one of the
chambers of the temple of the LORD to offer them a drink of wine."

So I took Jaazaniah son of Jeremiah, son of Habazziniah, and his brothers and all his sons—
the entire house of the Rechabites—and I brought them into the temple of the LORD to a chamber
occupied by the sons of Hanan son of Igdaliah, a man of God, who had a chamber near the
officials' chamber, which was above the chamber of Maaseiah son of Shallum the doorkeeper. I
set jars filled with wine and some cups before the sons of the house of the Rechabites and said to
them, "Drink wine!"

10   But they replied, "We do not drink wine, for Jonadab, son of our ancestor Rechab,
commanded, 'You and your descendants must never drink wine. You must not build a house or
sow seed or plant a vineyard. Those things are not for you. Rather, you must live in tents your

whole life, so you may live a long time on the soil where you stay as a resident alien.' We have obeyed Jonadab, son of our ancestor Rechab, in all he commanded us. So we haven't drunk wine our whole life—we, our wives, our sons, and our daughters. We also have not built houses to live in and do not have vineyard, field, or seed. But we have lived in tents and have obeyed and done everything our ancestor Jonadab commanded us. However, when King Nebuchadnezzar of Babylon marched into the land, we said, 'Come, let's go into Jerusalem to get away from the Chaldean and Aramean armies.' So we have been living in Jerusalem."

20   Then the word of the LORD came to Jeremiah: "This is what the LORD of Armies, the God of Israel, says: Go, say to the men of Judah and the residents of Jerusalem, 'Will you not accept discipline by listening to my words?—this is the LORD's declaration. The words of Jonadab, son of Rechab, have been carried out. He commanded his descendants not to drink wine, and they have not drunk to this day because they have obeyed their ancestor's command. But I have spoken to you time and time again, and you have not obeyed me! Time and time again I have sent you all my servants the prophets, proclaiming, "Turn, each one from his evil way, and correct your actions. Stop following other gods to serve them. Live in the land that I gave you and your ancestors." But you did not pay attention or obey me. Yes, the sons of Jonadab son of Rechab carried out their ancestor's command he gave them, but these people have not obeyed me. Therefore, this is what
30   the LORD, the God of Armies, the God of Israel, says: I will certainly bring on Judah and on all the residents of Jerusalem all the disaster I have pronounced against them because I have spoken to them, but they have not obeyed, and I have called to them, but they did not answer.'"

But to the house of the Rechabites Jeremiah said, "This is what the LORD of Armies, the God of Israel, says: 'Because you have obeyed the command of your ancestor Jonadab and have kept all his commands and have done everything he commanded you, this is what the LORD of Armies, the God of Israel, says: Jonadab son of Rechab will never fail to have a man to stand before me always.'"

36   In the fourth year of Jehoiakim son of Josiah, king of Judah, this word came to Jeremiah from the LORD: "Take a scroll, and write on it all the words I have spoken to you concerning Israel, Judah, and all the nations from the time I first spoke to you during Josiah's reign until today. Perhaps when the house of Judah hears about all the disaster I am planning to bring on them, each one of them will turn from his evil way. Then I will forgive their iniquity and their sin."

So Jeremiah summoned Baruch son of Neriah. At Jeremiah's dictation, Baruch wrote on a scroll all the words the LORD had spoken to Jeremiah. Then Jeremiah commanded Baruch, "I am restricted; I cannot enter the temple of the LORD, so you must go and read from the scroll—which you wrote at my dictation—the words of the LORD in the hearing of the people at the temple of
10   the LORD on a day of fasting. Read his words in the hearing of all the Judeans who are coming from their cities. Perhaps their petition will come before the LORD, and each one will turn from his evil way, for the anger and fury that the LORD has pronounced against this people are intense."

So Baruch son of Neriah did everything the prophet Jeremiah had commanded him. At the Lord's temple he read the Lord's words from the scroll.

In the fifth year of Jehoiakim son of Josiah, king of Judah, in the ninth month, all the people of Jerusalem and all those coming in from Judah's cities into Jerusalem proclaimed a fast before the Lord. Then at the Lord's temple, in the chamber of Gemariah son of Shaphan the scribe, in the upper courtyard at the opening of the New Gate of the Lord's temple, in the hearing of all the people, Baruch read Jeremiah's words from the scroll.

20 When Micaiah son of Gemariah, son of Shaphan, heard all the words of the Lord from the scroll, he went down to the scribe's chamber in the king's palace. All the officials were sitting there—Elishama the scribe, Delaiah son of Shemaiah, Elnathan son of Achbor, Gemariah son of Shaphan, Zedekiah son of Hananiah, and all the other officials. Micaiah reported to them all the words he had heard when Baruch read from the scroll in the hearing of the people. Then all the officials sent word to Baruch through Jehudi son of Nethaniah, son of Shelemiah, son of Cushi, saying, "Bring the scroll that you read in the hearing of the people, and come." So Baruch son of Neriah took the scroll and went to them. They said to him, "Sit down and read it in our hearing." So Baruch read it in their hearing.

When they had heard all the words, they turned to each other in fear and said to Baruch, "We 30 must surely tell the king all these things." Then they asked Baruch, "Tell us, how did you write all these words? At his dictation?"

Baruch said to them, "At his dictation. He recited all these words to me while I was writing on the scroll in ink."

The officials said to Baruch, "You and Jeremiah must hide and tell no one where you are." Then, after depositing the scroll in the chamber of Elishama the scribe, the officials came to the king at the courtyard and reported everything in the hearing of the king. The king sent Jehudi to get the scroll, and he took it from the chamber of Elishama the scribe. Jehudi then read it in the hearing of the king and all the officials who were standing by the king. Since it was the ninth month, the king was sitting in his winter quarters with a fire burning in front of him. As soon as Jehudi would read three 40 or four columns, Jehoiakim would cut the scroll with a scribe's knife and throw the columns into the fire in the hearth until the entire scroll was consumed by the fire in the hearth. As they heard all these words, the king and all his servants did not become terrified or tear their clothes. Even though Elnathan, Delaiah, and Gemariah had urged the king not to burn the scroll, he did not listen to them. Then the king commanded Jerahmeel the king's son, Seraiah son of Azriel, and Shelemiah son of Abdeel to seize the scribe Baruch and the prophet Jeremiah, but the Lord hid them.

After the king had burned the scroll and the words Baruch had written at Jeremiah's dictation, the word of the Lord came to Jeremiah: "Take another scroll, and once again write on it the original

words that were on the original scroll that King Jehoiakim of Judah burned. You are to proclaim concerning King Jehoiakim of Judah, 'This is what the LORD says: You have burned the scroll,
₅₀ asking, "Why have you written on it that the king of Babylon will certainly come and destroy this land and cause it to be without people or animals?" Therefore, this is what the LORD says concerning King Jehoiakim of Judah: He will have no one to sit on David's throne, and his corpse will be thrown out to be exposed to the heat of day and the frost of night. I will punish him, his descendants, and his officers for their iniquity. I will bring on them, on the residents of Jerusalem, and on the people of Judah all the disaster, which I warned them about but they did not listen.'"

Then Jeremiah took another scroll and gave it to Baruch son of Neriah, the scribe, and he wrote on it at Jeremiah's dictation all the words of the scroll that Jehoiakim, Judah's king, had burned in the fire. And many other words like them were added.

37 Zedekiah son of Josiah reigned as king in the land of Judah in place of Coniah son of Jehoiakim, for King Nebuchadnezzar of Babylon made him king. He and his officers and the people of the land did not obey the words of the LORD that he spoke through the prophet Jeremiah.

Nevertheless, King Zedekiah sent Jehucal son of Shelemiah and Zephaniah son of Maaseiah, the priest, to the prophet Jeremiah, requesting, "Please pray to the LORD our God on our behalf!" Jeremiah was going about his daily tasks among the people, for he had not yet been put into the prison. Pharaoh's army had left Egypt, and when the Chaldeans, who were besieging Jerusalem, heard the report, they withdrew from Jerusalem.

The word of the LORD came to the prophet Jeremiah: "This is what the LORD, the God of
₁₀ Israel, says: This is what you will say to Judah's king, who is sending you to inquire of me: 'Watch: Pharaoh's army, which has come out to help you, is going to return to its own land of Egypt. The Chaldeans will then return and fight against this city. They will capture it and burn it. This is what the LORD says: Don't deceive yourselves by saying, "The Chaldeans will leave us for good," for they will not leave. Indeed, if you were to strike down the entire Chaldean army that is fighting with you, and there remained among them only the badly wounded men, each in his tent, they would get up and burn this city.'"

When the Chaldean army withdrew from Jerusalem because of Pharaoh's army, Jeremiah started to leave Jerusalem to go to the land of Benjamin to claim his portion there among the people. But when he was at the Benjamin Gate, an officer of the guard was there, whose name was
₂₀ Irijah son of Shelemiah, son of Hananiah, and he apprehended the prophet Jeremiah, saying, "You are defecting to the Chaldeans."

"That's a lie," Jeremiah replied. "I am not defecting to the Chaldeans!" Irijah would not listen to him but apprehended Jeremiah and took him to the officials. The officials were angry at Jeremiah and beat him and placed him in jail in the house of Jonathan the scribe, for it had been made into a prison. So Jeremiah went into a cell in the dungeon and stayed there many days.

King Zedekiah later sent for him and received him, and in his house privately asked him, "Is there a word from the LORD?"

"There is," Jeremiah responded. He continued, "You will be handed over to the king of Babylon." Then Jeremiah said to King Zedekiah, "How have I sinned against you or your servants or these people that you have put me in prison? Where are your prophets who prophesied to you, claiming, 'The king of Babylon will not come against you and this land'? So now please listen, my lord the king. May my petition come before you. Don't send me back to the house of Jonathan the scribe, or I will die there."

So King Zedekiah gave orders, and Jeremiah was placed in the guard's courtyard. He was given a loaf of bread each day from the bakers' street until all the bread was gone from the city. So Jeremiah remained in the guard's courtyard.

38 Now Shephatiah son of Mattan, Gedaliah son of Pashhur, Jucal son of Shelemiah, and Pashhur son of Malchijah heard the words Jeremiah was speaking to all the people: "This is what the LORD says: 'Whoever stays in this city will die by the sword, famine, and plague, but whoever surrenders to the Chaldeans will live. He will retain his life like the spoils of war and will live.' This is what the LORD says: 'This city will most certainly be handed over to the king of Babylon's army, and he will capture it.'"

The officials then said to the king, "This man ought to die, because he is weakening the morale of the warriors who remain in this city and of all the people by speaking to them in this way. This man is not pursuing the welfare of this people, but their harm."

King Zedekiah said, "Here he is; he's in your hands since the king can't do anything against you." So they took Jeremiah and dropped him into the cistern of Malchiah the king's son, which was in the guard's courtyard, lowering Jeremiah with ropes. There was no water in the cistern, only mud, and Jeremiah sank in the mud.

But Ebed-melech, a Cushite court official in the king's palace, heard Jeremiah had been put into the cistern. While the king was sitting at the Benjamin Gate, Ebed-melech went from the king's palace and spoke to the king: "My lord the king, these men have been evil in all they have done to the prophet Jeremiah. They have dropped him into the cistern where he will die from hunger, because there is no more bread in the city."

So the king commanded Ebed-melech, the Cushite, "Take from here thirty men under your authority and pull the prophet Jeremiah up from the cistern before he dies."

So Ebed-melech took the men under his authority and went to the king's palace to a place below the storehouse. From there he took old rags and worn-out clothes and lowered them by ropes to Jeremiah in the cistern. Ebed-melech the Cushite called down to Jeremiah, "Place these old rags and clothes between your armpits and the ropes." Jeremiah did this. They pulled him up with the ropes and lifted him out of the cistern, but he remained in the guard's courtyard.

King Zedekiah sent for the prophet Jeremiah and received him at the third entrance of the Lord's temple. The king said to Jeremiah, "I am going to ask you something; don't hide anything from me."

Jeremiah replied to Zedekiah, "If I tell you, you will kill me, won't you? Besides, if I give you advice, you won't listen to me anyway."

King Zedekiah swore to Jeremiah in private, "As the Lord lives, who has given us this life, I will not kill you or hand you over to these men who intend to take your life."

Jeremiah therefore said to Zedekiah, "This is what the Lord, the God of Armies, the God of Israel, says: 'If indeed you surrender to the officials of the king of Babylon, then you will live, this city will not be burned, and you and your household will survive. But if you do not surrender to the officials of the king of Babylon, then this city will be handed over to the Chaldeans. They will burn it, and you yourself will not escape from them.'"

But King Zedekiah said to Jeremiah, "I am worried about the Judeans who have defected to the Chaldeans. They may hand me over to the Judeans to abuse me."

"They will not hand you over," Jeremiah replied. "Obey the Lord in what I am telling you, so it may go well for you and you can live. But if you refuse to surrender, this is the verdict that the Lord has shown me: 'All the women who remain in the palace of Judah's king will be brought out to the officials of the king of Babylon and will say to you,

> "Your trusted friends misled you
> and overcame you.
> Your feet sank into the mire,
> and they deserted you."

All your wives and children will be brought out to the Chaldeans. You yourself will not escape from them, for you will be seized by the king of Babylon and this city will burn.'"

Then Zedekiah warned Jeremiah, "Don't let anyone know about this conversation or you will die. The officials may hear that I have spoken with you and come and demand of you, 'Tell us what you said to the king; don't hide anything from us and we won't kill you. Also, what did the king say to you?' If they do, tell them, 'I was bringing before the king my petition that he not return me to the house of Jonathan to die there.'" All the officials did come to Jeremiah, and they questioned him. He reported the exact words to them the king had commanded, and they quit speaking with him because the conversation had not been overheard. Jeremiah remained in the guard's courtyard until the day Jerusalem was captured, and he was there when it happened.

39 In the ninth year of King Zedekiah of Judah, in the tenth month, King Nebuchadnezzar of Babylon advanced against Jerusalem with his entire army and laid siege to it. In the fourth month of Zedekiah's eleventh year, on the ninth day of the month, the city was broken into. All the officials of the king of Babylon entered and sat at the Middle Gate: Nergal-sharezer, Samgar, Nebusarsechim the chief of staff, Nergal-sharezer the chief soothsayer, and all the rest of the officials of Babylon's king.

When King Zedekiah of Judah and all the fighting men saw them, they fled. They left the city at night by way of the king's garden through the city gate between the two walls. They left along the route to the Arabah. However, the Chaldean army pursued them and overtook Zedekiah in the plains of Jericho. They arrested him and brought him up to Nebuchadnezzar, Babylon's king,

10 at Riblah in the land of Hamath. The king passed sentence on him there.

At Riblah the king of Babylon slaughtered Zedekiah's sons before his eyes, and he also slaughtered all Judah's nobles. Then he blinded Zedekiah and put him in bronze chains to take him to Babylon. The Chaldeans next burned down the king's palace and the people's houses and tore down the walls of Jerusalem. Nebuzaradan, the captain of the guards, deported the rest of the people to Babylon—those who had remained in the city and those deserters who had defected to him along with the rest of the people who remained. However, Nebuzaradan, the captain of the guards, left in the land of Judah some of the poor people who owned nothing, and he gave them vineyards and fields at that time.

Speaking through Nebuzaradan, captain of the guards, King Nebuchadnezzar of Babylon gave

20 orders concerning Jeremiah: "Take him and look after him. Don't do him any harm, but do for him whatever he says." Nebuzaradan, captain of the guards, Nebushazban the chief of staff, Nergal-sharezer the chief soothsayer, and all the captains of Babylon's king had Jeremiah brought from the guard's courtyard and turned him over to Gedaliah son of Ahikam, son of Shaphan, to take him home. So he settled among his own people.

Now the word of the Lord had come to Jeremiah when he was confined in the guard's courtyard: "Go tell Ebed-melech the Cushite, 'This is what the Lord of Armies, the God of Israel, says: I am about to fulfill my words for disaster and not for good against this city. They will take place before your eyes on that day. But I will rescue you on that day—this is the Lord's declaration—and you will not be handed over to the men you dread. Indeed, I will certainly

30 deliver you so that you do not fall by the sword. Because you have trusted in me, you will retain your life like the spoils of war. This is the Lord's declaration.'"

40 This is the word that came to Jeremiah from the Lord after Nebuzaradan, captain of the guards, released him at Ramah. When he found him, he was bound in chains with all the exiles of Jerusalem and Judah who were being exiled to Babylon. The captain of the guards took Jeremiah and said to him, "The Lord your God decreed this disaster on this place, and the Lord has fulfilled it. He has done just what he decreed. Because you people have sinned against the Lord and have not obeyed him, this thing has happened. Now pay attention: Today I am setting you free from the chains that were on your hands. If it pleases you to come with me to Babylon, come, and I will take care of you. But if it seems wrong to you to come with me to Babylon, go no farther. Look—the whole land is in front of you. Wherever it seems good and right for you to go, go

10 there." When Jeremiah had not yet turned to go, Nebuzaradan said to him, "Return to Gedaliah

son of Ahikam, son of Shaphan, whom the king of Babylon has appointed over the cities of Judah, and stay with him among the people or go wherever it seems right for you to go." So the captain of the guards gave him a ration and a gift and released him. Jeremiah therefore went to Gedaliah son of Ahikam at Mizpah, and he stayed with him among the people who remained in the land.

All the commanders of the armies that were in the countryside—they and their men—heard that the king of Babylon had appointed Gedaliah son of Ahikam over the land. He had been put in charge of the men, women, and children from among the poorest of the land, who had not been deported to Babylon. So they came to Gedaliah at Mizpah. The commanders included Ishmael son of Nethaniah, Johanan and Jonathan the sons of Kareah, Seraiah son of Tanhumeth, the sons
20 of Ephai the Netophathite, and Jezaniah son of the Maacathite—they and their men.

Gedaliah son of Ahikam, son of Shaphan, swore an oath to them and their men, assuring them, "Don't be afraid to serve the Chaldeans. Live in the land and serve the king of Babylon, and it will go well for you. As for me, I am going to live in Mizpah to represent you before the Chaldeans who come to us. As for you, gather wine, summer fruit, and oil, place them in your storage jars, and live in the cities you have captured."

When all the Judeans in Moab and among the Ammonites and in Edom and in all the other lands also heard that the king of Babylon had left a remnant in Judah and had appointed Gedaliah son of Ahikam, son of Shaphan, over them, they all returned from all the places where they had been banished and came to the land of Judah, to Gedaliah at Mizpah, and harvested a great
30 amount of wine and summer fruit.

Meanwhile, Johanan son of Kareah and all the commanders of the armies in the countryside came to Gedaliah at Mizpah and warned him, "Don't you realize that Baalis, king of the Ammonites, has sent Ishmael son of Nethaniah to kill you?" But Gedaliah son of Ahikam would not believe them. Then Johanan son of Kareah suggested to Gedaliah in private at Mizpah, "Let me go kill Ishmael son of Nethaniah. No one will know it. Why should he kill you and allow all of Judah that has gathered around you to scatter and the remnant of Judah to perish?"

But Gedaliah son of Ahikam responded to Johanan son of Kareah, "Don't do that! What you're saying about Ishmael is a lie."

41 In the seventh month, Ishmael son of Nethaniah, son of Elishama, of the royal family and one of the king's chief officers, came with ten men to Gedaliah son of Ahikam at Mizpah. They ate a meal together there in Mizpah, but then Ishmael son of Nethaniah and the ten men who were with him got up and struck down Gedaliah son of Ahikam, son of Shaphan, with the sword; he killed the one the king of Babylon had appointed in the land. Ishmael also struck down all the Judeans who were with Gedaliah at Mizpah, as well as the Chaldean soldiers who were there.

On the day after he had killed Gedaliah, when no one knew yet, eighty men came from Shechem, Shiloh, and Samaria who had shaved their beards, torn their clothes, and gashed themselves, and who were carrying grain and incense offerings to bring to the temple of the LORD.

10 Ishmael son of Nethaniah came out of Mizpah to meet them, weeping as he came. When he encountered them, he said, "Come to Gedaliah son of Ahikam!" But when they came into the city, Ishmael son of Nethaniah and the men with him slaughtered them and threw them into a cistern.

However, there were ten men among them who said to Ishmael, "Don't kill us, for we have hidden treasure in the field—wheat, barley, oil, and honey!" So he stopped and did not kill them along with their companions. Now the cistern where Ishmael had thrown all the corpses of the men he had struck down was a large one that King Asa had made in the encounter with King Baasha of Israel. Ishmael son of Nethaniah filled it with the slain.

Then Ishmael took captive all the rest of the people of Mizpah including the daughters of the king—all those who remained in Mizpah over whom Nebuzaradan, captain of the guards, had
20 appointed Gedaliah son of Ahikam. Ishmael son of Nethaniah took them captive and set off to cross over to the Ammonites.

When Johanan son of Kareah and all the commanders of the armies with him heard of all the evil that Ishmael son of Nethaniah had done, they took all their men and went to fight with Ishmael son of Nethaniah. They found him by the great pool in Gibeon. When all the people held by Ishmael saw Johanan son of Kareah and all the commanders of the army with him, they rejoiced. All the people whom Ishmael had taken captive from Mizpah turned around and rejoined Johanan son of Kareah. But Ishmael son of Nethaniah escaped from Johanan with eight men and went to the Ammonites. Johanan son of Kareah and all the commanders of the armies with him then took from Mizpah all the remnant of the people whom he had recovered from Ishmael son of
30 Nethaniah after Ishmael had killed Gedaliah son of Ahikam—men, soldiers, women, children, and court officials whom he brought back from Gibeon. They left, stopping in Geruth Chimham, which is near Bethlehem, in order to make their way into Egypt, away from the Chaldeans. For they feared them because Ishmael son of Nethaniah had struck down Gedaliah son of Ahikam, whom the king of Babylon had appointed over the land.

42 Then all the commanders of the armies, along with Johanan son of Kareah, Jezaniah son of Hoshaiah, and all the people from the least to the greatest, approached the prophet Jeremiah and said, "May our petition come before you; pray to the LORD your God on our behalf, on behalf of this entire remnant (for few of us remain out of the many, as you can see with your own eyes), that the LORD your God may tell us the way we should go and the thing we should do."

So the prophet Jeremiah said to them, "I have heard. I will now pray to the LORD your God according to your words, and I will tell you every word that the LORD answers you; I won't withhold a word from you."

And they said to Jeremiah, "May the LORD be a true and faithful witness against us if we don't
10 act according to every word the LORD your God sends you to tell us. Whether it is pleasant or

unpleasant, we will obey the LORD our God to whom we are sending you so that it may go well with us. We will certainly obey the LORD our God!"

At the end of ten days, the word of the LORD came to Jeremiah, and he summoned Johanan son of Kareah, all the commanders of the armies who were with him, and all the people from the least to the greatest.

He said to them, "This is what the LORD says, the God of Israel to whom you sent me to bring your petition before him: 'If you will indeed stay in this land, then I will rebuild and not demolish you, and I will plant and not uproot you, because I relent concerning the disaster that I have brought on you. Don't be afraid of the king of Babylon whom you now fear; don't be afraid
20 of him'—this is the LORD's declaration—'because I am with you to save you and rescue you from him. I will grant you compassion, and he will have compassion on you and allow you to return to your own soil.'

"But if you say, 'We will not stay in this land,' in order to disobey the LORD your God, and if you say, 'No, instead we'll go to the land of Egypt where we will not see war or hear the sound of the ram's horn or hunger for food, and we'll live there,' then hear the word of the LORD, remnant of Judah! This is what the LORD of Armies, the God of Israel, says: 'If you are firmly resolved to go to Egypt and stay there for a while, then the sword you fear will overtake you there in the land of Egypt, and the famine you are worried about will follow on your heels there to Egypt, and you will die there. All who resolve to go to Egypt to stay there for a while will die by the sword, famine,
30 and plague. They will have no survivor or fugitive from the disaster I will bring on them.'

"For this is what the LORD of Armies, the God of Israel, says: 'Just as my anger and fury were poured out on Jerusalem's residents, so will my fury pour out on you if you go to Egypt. You will become an example for cursing, scorn, execration, and disgrace, and you will never see this place again.' The LORD has spoken concerning you, remnant of Judah: 'Don't go to Egypt.' Know for certain that I have warned you today! You have gone astray at the cost of your lives because you are the ones who sent me to the LORD your God, saying, 'Pray to the LORD our God on our behalf, and as for all that the LORD our God says, tell it to us, and we'll act accordingly.' For I have told you today, but you have not obeyed the LORD your God in everything he has sent me to tell you. Now therefore, know for certain that by the sword, famine, and plague you will die in the place
40 where you desired to go to stay for a while."

43 When Jeremiah had finished speaking to all the people all the words of the LORD their God—all these words the LORD their God had sent him to give them—then Azariah son of Hoshaiah, Johanan son of Kareah, and all the other arrogant men responded to Jeremiah, "You are speaking a lie! The LORD our God has not sent you to say, 'You must not go to Egypt to stay there for a while!' Rather, Baruch son of Neriah is inciting you against us to hand us over to the Chaldeans to put us to death or to deport us to Babylon!"

So Johanan son of Kareah, all the commanders of the armies, and all the people failed to obey the LORD's command to stay in the land of Judah. Instead, Johanan son of Kareah and all the commanders of the armies led away the whole remnant of Judah, those who had returned to stay in the land of Judah from all the nations where they had been banished. They led away the men, women, children, king's daughters, and everyone whom Nebuzaradan, captain of the guards, had allowed to remain with Gedaliah son of Ahikam son of Shaphan. They also led the prophet Jeremiah and Baruch son of Neriah away. They went to the land of Egypt because they did not obey the LORD. They went as far as Tahpanhes.

Then the word of the LORD came to Jeremiah at Tahpanhes: "Pick up some large stones and set them in the mortar of the brick pavement that is at the opening of Pharaoh's palace at Tahpanhes. Do this in the sight of the Judean men and tell them, 'This is what the LORD of Armies, the God of Israel, says: I will send for my servant Nebuchadnezzar king of Babylon, and I will place his throne on these stones that I have embedded, and he will pitch his pavilion over them. He will come and strike down the land of Egypt—those destined for death, to death; those destined for captivity, to captivity; and those destined for the sword, to the sword. I will kindle a fire in the temples of Egypt's gods, and he will burn them and take them captive. He will clean the land of Egypt as a shepherd picks lice off his clothes, and he will leave there unscathed. He will smash the sacred pillars of the sun temple in the land of Egypt and burn the temples of the Egyptian gods.'"

44 This is the word that came to Jeremiah for all the Jews living in the land of Egypt—at Migdol, Tahpanhes, Memphis, and in the land of Pathros: "This is what the LORD of Armies, the God of Israel, says: You have seen all the disaster I brought against Jerusalem and all Judah's cities. Look, they are a ruin today without an inhabitant in them because of the evil they committed to anger me, by going and burning incense to serve other gods that they, you, and your ancestors did not know. So I sent you all my servants the prophets time and time again, saying, 'Don't commit this detestable action that I hate.' But they did not listen or pay attention; they did not turn from their evil or stop burning incense to other gods. So my fierce wrath poured out and burned in Judah's cities and Jerusalem's streets so that they became the desolate ruin they are today.

"So now, this is what the LORD, the God of Armies, the God of Israel, says: Why are you doing such terrible harm to yourselves? You are cutting off man and woman, infant and nursing baby from Judah, leaving yourselves without a remnant. You are angering me by the work of your hands. You are burning incense to other gods in the land of Egypt where you have gone to stay for a while. As a result, you will be cut off and become an example for cursing and insult among all the nations of earth. Have you forgotten the evils of your ancestors, the evils of Judah's kings, the evils of their wives, your own evils, and the evils of your wives that were committed in the land of Judah and in the streets of Jerusalem? They have not become humble to this day, and they have not feared or followed my instruction or my statutes that I set before you and your ancestors.

"Therefore, this is what the LORD of Armies, the God of Israel, says: I am about to set my face
20 against you to bring disaster, to cut off all Judah. And I will take away the remnant of Judah, those
who have set their face to go to the land of Egypt to stay there. All of them will meet their end in
the land of Egypt. They will fall by the sword; they will meet their end by famine. From the least
to the greatest, they will die by the sword and by famine. Then they will become an example for
cursing, scorn, execration, and disgrace. I will punish those living in the land of Egypt just as I
punished Jerusalem by sword, famine, and plague. Then the remnant of Judah—those going to
live for a while there in the land of Egypt—will have no fugitive or survivor to return to the land of
Judah where they are longing to return to stay, for they will not return except for a few fugitives."

However, all the men who knew that their wives were burning incense to other gods, all the women
standing by—a great assembly—and all the people who were living in the land of Egypt at Pathros
30 answered Jeremiah, "As for the word you spoke to us in the name of the LORD, we are not going
to listen to you! Instead, we will do everything we promised: we will burn incense to the queen of
heaven and offer drink offerings to her just as we, our ancestors, our kings, and our officials did in
Judah's cities and in Jerusalem's streets. Then we had enough food, we were well off, and we saw no
disaster, but from the time we ceased to burn incense to the queen of heaven and to offer her drink
offerings, we have lacked everything, and through sword and famine we have met our end."

And the women said, "When we burned incense to the queen of heaven and poured out drink
offerings to her, was it apart from our husbands' knowledge that we made sacrificial cakes in her
image and poured out drink offerings to her?"

But Jeremiah responded to all the people—the men, women, and all the people who were
40 answering him: "As for the incense you burned in Judah's cities and in Jerusalem's streets—you,
your ancestors, your kings, your officials, and the people of the land—did the LORD not remember
them? He brought this to mind. The LORD can no longer bear your evil deeds and the detestable
acts you have committed, so your land has become a waste, a desolation, and an example for
cursing, without inhabitant, as you see today. Because you burned incense and sinned against the
LORD and didn't obey the LORD and didn't follow his instruction, his statutes, and his testimonies,
this disaster has come to you, as you see today."

Then Jeremiah said to all the people, including all the women, "Hear the word of the LORD, all
you people of Judah who are in the land of Egypt. This is what the LORD of Armies, the God of
Israel, says: 'As for you and your wives, you women have spoken with your mouths, and you men
50 fulfilled it by your deeds, saying, "We will keep our vows that we have made to burn incense to the
queen of heaven and to pour out drink offerings for her." Go ahead, confirm your vows! Keep your
vows!'

"Therefore, hear the word of the LORD, all you Judeans who live in the land of Egypt: 'I have
sworn by my great name, says the LORD, that my name will never again be invoked by anyone
of Judah in all the land of Egypt, saying, "As the Lord GOD lives." I am watching over them for

disaster and not for good, and everyone from Judah who is in the land of Egypt will meet his end by sword or famine until they are finished off. Those who escape the sword will return from the land of Egypt to the land of Judah only few in number, and the whole remnant of Judah, the ones going to the land of Egypt to stay there for a while, will know whose word stands, mine or theirs! 60 This will be a sign to you'—this is the Lord's declaration—'that I will punish you in this place, so you may know that my words of disaster concerning you will certainly come to pass. This is what the Lord says: I am about to hand over Pharaoh Hophra, Egypt's king, to his enemies, to those who intend to take his life, just as I handed over Judah's King Zedekiah to Babylon's King Nebuchadnezzar, who was his enemy, the one who intended to take his life.'"

45 This is the word that the prophet Jeremiah spoke to Baruch son of Neriah when he wrote these words on a scroll at Jeremiah's dictation in the fourth year of Jehoiakim son of Josiah, king of Judah: "This is what the Lord, the God of Israel, says to you, Baruch: 'You have said, "Woe is me, because the Lord has added misery to my pain! I am worn out with groaning and have found no rest.'"

"This is what you are to say to him: 'This is what the Lord says: "What I have built I am about to demolish, and what I have planted I am about to uproot—the whole land! But as for you, do you pursue great things for yourself? Stop pursuing! For I am about to bring disaster on all humanity"—this is the Lord's declaration—"but I will grant you your life like the spoils of war 10 wherever you go."'"

Prophecies against the Nations

46 This is the word of the Lord that came to the prophet Jeremiah about the nations:

About Egypt and the army of Pharaoh Neco, Egypt's king, which was defeated at Carchemish on the Euphrates River by King Nebuchadnezzar of Babylon in the fourth year of Judah's King Jehoiakim son of Josiah:

> Deploy small shields and large;
> approach for battle!
> Harness the horses;
> mount the steeds;
> take your positions with helmets on!
> 10 Polish the lances;
> put on armor!
> Why have I seen this?
> They are terrified,
> they are retreating,
> their warriors are crushed,
> they flee headlong,

they never look back,
terror is on every side!
This is the LORD's declaration.
20 The swift cannot flee,
and the warrior cannot escape!
In the north by the bank of the Euphrates River,
they stumble and fall.

Who is this, rising like the Nile,
with waters that churn like rivers?
Egypt rises like the Nile,
and its waters churn like rivers.
He boasts, "I will go up, I will cover the earth;
I will destroy cities with their residents."
30 Rise up, you cavalry!
Race furiously, you chariots!
Let the warriors march out—
Cush and Put,
who are able to handle shields,
and the men of Lud,
who are able to handle and string the bow.
That day belongs to the Lord, the GOD of Armies,
a day of vengeance to avenge himself
against his adversaries.
40 The sword will devour and be satisfied;
it will drink its fill of their blood,
because it will be a sacrifice to the Lord, the GOD of Armies,
in the northern land by the Euphrates River.

Go up to Gilead and get balm,
Virgin Daughter Egypt!
You have multiplied remedies in vain;
there is no healing for you.
The nations have heard of your dishonor,
and your cries fill the earth,
50 because warrior stumbles against warrior
and together both of them have fallen.

This is the word the LORD spoke to the prophet Jeremiah about the coming of King Nebuchadnezzar of Babylon to defeat the land of Egypt:

> Announce it in Egypt, and proclaim it in Migdol!
> Proclaim it in Memphis and in Tahpanhes!
> Say, "Take positions! Prepare yourself,
> for the sword devours all around you."
> Why have your strong ones been swept away?
> Each has not stood,
> for the LORD has thrust him down.
> He continues to stumble.
> Indeed, each falls over the other.
> They say, "Get up! Let's return to our people
> and to our native land,
> away from the oppressor's sword."
> There they will cry out,
> "Pharaoh king of Egypt was all noise;
> he let the opportune moment pass."

> As I live—
> this is the King's declaration;
> the LORD of Armies is his name—
> the king of Babylon will come like Tabor among the mountains
> and like Carmel by the sea.
> Get your bags ready for exile,
> inhabitant of Daughter Egypt!
> For Memphis will become a desolation,
> uninhabited ruins.

> Egypt is a beautiful young cow,
> but a horsefly from the north is coming against her.
> Even her mercenaries among her
> are like stall-fed calves.
> They too will turn back;
> together they will flee;
> they will not take their stand,
> for the day of their calamity is coming on them,
> the time of their punishment.
> Egypt will hiss like a slithering snake,

for the enemy will come with an army;
with axes they will come against her
like those who cut trees.
90 They will cut down her forest—
this is the Lord's declaration—
though it is dense,
for they are more numerous than locusts;
they cannot be counted.
Daughter Egypt will be put to shame,
handed over to a northern people.

The Lord of Armies, the God of Israel, says, "I am about to punish Amon, god of Thebes, along with Pharaoh, Egypt, her gods, and her kings—Pharaoh and those trusting in him. I will 100 hand them over to those who intend to take their lives—to King Nebuchadnezzar of Babylon and his officers. But after this, Egypt will be inhabited again as in ancient times."

This is the Lord's declaration.

But you, my servant Jacob, do not be afraid,
and do not be discouraged, Israel,
for without fail I will save you from far away,
and your descendants from the land of their captivity!
Jacob will return and have calm and quiet
with no one to frighten him.
And you, my servant Jacob, do not be afraid—
110 this is the Lord's declaration—
for I will be with you.
I will bring destruction on all the nations
where I have banished you,
but I will not bring destruction on you.
I will discipline you with justice,
and I will by no means leave you unpunished.

47 This is the word of the Lord that came to the prophet Jeremiah about the Philistines before Pharaoh defeated Gaza. This is what the Lord says:
Look, water is rising from the north
and becoming an overflowing wadi.
It will overflow the land and everything in it,
the cities and their inhabitants.

The people will cry out,
and every inhabitant of the land will wail.
At the sound of the stomping hooves of his stallions,
10   the rumbling of his chariots,
and the clatter of their wheels,
fathers will not turn back for their sons.
They will be utterly helpless
on account of the day that is coming
to destroy all the Philistines,
to cut off from Tyre and Sidon
every remaining ally.
Indeed, the Lord is about to destroy the Philistines,
the remnant of the coastland of Caphtor.
20   Baldness is coming to Gaza;
Ashkelon will become silent.
Remnant of their valley,
how long will you gash yourself?

Oh, sword of the Lord!
How long will you be restless?
Go back to your sheath;
be still; be silent!
How can it rest
when the Lord has given it a command?
30   He has assigned it
against Ashkelon and the shore of the sea.

48 About Moab, this is what the Lord of Armies, the God of Israel, says:
Woe to Nebo, because it is about to be destroyed;
Kiriathaim will be put to shame; it will be taken captive.
The fortress will be put to shame and dismayed!
There is no longer praise for Moab;
they plan harm against her in Heshbon:
Come, let's cut her off from nationhood.
Also, Madmen, you will be silenced;
the sword will follow you.
10   A voice cries out from Horonaim,
"devastation and a crushing blow!"

Moab will be shattered;
her little ones will cry out.
For on the Ascent to Luhith
they will be weeping continually,
and on the descent to Horonaim
will be heard cries of distress over the destruction:
Flee! Save your lives!
Be like a juniper bush in the wilderness.
20 Because you trust in your works and treasures,
you will be captured also.
Chemosh will go into exile
with his priests and officials.
The destroyer will move against every town;
not one town will escape.
The valley will perish,
and the plain will be annihilated,
as the Lord has said.
Make Moab a salt marsh,
30 for she will run away;
her towns will become a desolation,
without inhabitant.

The one who does
the Lord's business deceitfully is cursed,
and the one who withholds
his sword from bloodshed is cursed.

Moab has been left quiet since his youth,
settled like wine on its dregs.
He hasn't been poured from one container to another
40 or gone into exile.
So his taste has remained the same,
and his aroma hasn't changed.
Therefore look, the days are coming—
this is the Lord's declaration—
when I will send pourers to him, who will pour him out.
They will empty his containers
and smash his jars.

Moab will be put to shame because of Chemosh,
just as the house of Israel was put to shame
50   because of Bethel that they trusted in.

How can you say, "We are warriors—
valiant men for battle"?
The destroyer of Moab and its towns
has come up,
and the best of its young men
have gone down to slaughter.
This is the King's declaration;
the LORD of Armies is his name.
Moab's calamity is near at hand;
60   his disaster is rushing swiftly.
Mourn for him, all you surrounding nations,
everyone who knows his name.
Say, "How the mighty scepter is shattered,
the glorious staff!"

Come down from glory; sit on parched ground,
resident of the daughter of Dibon,
for the destroyer of Moab has come against you;
he has destroyed your fortresses.
Stand by the highway and watch,
70   resident of Aroer!
Ask him who is fleeing or her who is escaping,
"What happened?"
Moab is put to shame, indeed dismayed.
Wail and cry out!
Declare by the Arnon
that Moab is destroyed.

"Judgment has come to the land of the plateau—to Holon, Jahzah, Mephaath, Dibon, Nebo, Beth-diblathaim, Kiriathaim, Beth-gamul, Beth-meon, Kerioth, Bozrah, and all the towns of the land of Moab, those far and near. Moab's horn is chopped off; his arm is shattered."
80   This is the LORD's declaration.
"Make him drunk, because he has exalted himself against the LORD. Moab will wallow in his own vomit, and he will also become a laughingstock. Wasn't Israel a laughingstock

to you? Was he ever found among thieves? For whenever you speak of him you shake your head."

Abandon the towns! Live in the cliffs,
residents of Moab!
Be like a dove
that nests inside the mouth of a cave.

90 We have heard of Moab's pride,
great pride, indeed—
his insolence, arrogance, pride,
and haughty heart.
I know his outburst.
This is the LORD's declaration.
It is empty.
His boast is empty.
Therefore, I will wail over Moab.
I will cry out for Moab, all of it;
he will moan for the men of Kir-heres.
100 I will weep for you, vine of Sibmah,
with more than the weeping for Jazer.
Your tendrils have extended to the sea;
they have reached to the sea and to Jazer.
The destroyer has fallen on your summer fruit and grape harvest.
Gladness and celebration are taken from the fertile field
and from the land of Moab.
I have stopped the flow of wine from the winepresses;
no one will tread with shouts of joy.
The shouting is not a shout of joy.

110 "There is a cry from Heshbon to Elealeh; they make their voices heard as far as Jahaz— from Zoar to Horonaim and Eglath-shelishiyah—because even the Waters of Nimrim have become desolate. In Moab, I will stop"—this is the LORD's declaration—"the one who offers sacrifices on the high place and burns incense to his gods. Therefore, my heart moans like flutes for Moab, and my heart moans like flutes for the people of Kir-heres. And therefore, the wealth he has gained has perished. Indeed, every head is bald and every beard is chopped short. On every hand is a gash and sackcloth around the waist. On all the rooftops of Moab and in her public squares, everyone is mourning because I have shattered Moab like a jar no one wants." This is the LORD's declaration. "How broken it is! They wail! How Moab has turned

his back! He is ashamed. Moab will become a laughingstock and a shock to all those around
120   him."

For this is what the LORD says:

Look! He will swoop down like an eagle
and spread his wings against Moab.
The towns have been captured,
and the strongholds seized.
In that day the heart of Moab's warriors
will be like the heart of a woman with contractions.
Moab will be destroyed as a people
because he has exalted himself against the LORD.
130   Panic, pit, and trap
await you, resident of Moab.
This is the LORD's declaration.
He who flees from the panic will fall in the pit,
and he who climbs from the pit
will be captured in the trap,
for I will bring against Moab
the year of their punishment.
This is the LORD's declaration.

Those who flee will stand exhausted in Heshbon's shadow
140   because fire has come out from Heshbon
and a flame from within Sihon.
It will devour Moab's forehead
and the skull of the noisemakers.
Woe to you, Moab!
The people of Chemosh have perished
because your sons have been taken captive
and your daughters have gone into captivity.
Yet, I will restore the fortunes of Moab in the last days.
This is the LORD's declaration.
150   The judgment on Moab ends here.

49 About the Ammonites, this is what the LORD says:

Does Israel have no sons?
Is he without an heir?
Why then has Milcom dispossessed Gad

and his people settled in their cities?
Therefore look, the days are coming—
this is the Lord's declaration—
when I will make the shout of battle heard
against Rabbah of the Ammonites.
It will become a desolate mound,
and its surrounding villages will be set on fire.
Israel will dispossess their dispossessors,
says the Lord.
Wail, Heshbon, for Ai is devastated;
cry out, daughters of Rabbah!
Clothe yourselves with sackcloth, and lament;
run back and forth within your walls,
because Milcom will go into exile
together with his priests and officials.
Why do you boast about your valleys,
your flowing valley,
you faithless daughter—
you who trust in your treasures
and say, "Who can attack me?"
Look, I am about to bring terror on you—
this is the declaration of the Lord God of Armies—
from all those around you.
You will be banished, each person headlong,
with no one to gather up the fugitives.
But after that, I will restore the fortunes of the Ammonites.
This is the Lord's declaration.

About Edom, this is what the Lord of Armies says:
Is there no longer wisdom in Teman?
Has counsel perished from the prudent?
Has their wisdom rotted away?
Run! Turn back! Lie low,
residents of Dedan,
for I will bring Esau's calamity on him
at the time I punish him.
If grape harvesters came to you,
wouldn't they leave a few grapes?

Were thieves to come in the night,
they would destroy only what they wanted.
But I will strip Esau bare;
I will uncover his secret places.
He will try to hide, but he will be unable.
His descendants will be destroyed
along with his relatives and neighbors.
He will exist no longer.
50   Abandon your fatherless; I will preserve them;
let your widows trust in me.

For this is what the LORD says: "If those who do not deserve to drink the cup must drink it,
can you possibly remain unpunished? You will not remain unpunished, for you must drink it too.
For by myself I have sworn"—this is the LORD's declaration—"Bozrah will become a desolation, a
disgrace, a ruin, and an example for cursing, and all its surrounding cities will become ruins forever."
I have heard an envoy from the LORD;
a messenger has been sent among the nations:
Assemble yourselves to come against her.
Rise up for war!

60   I will certainly make you insignificant among the nations,
despised among humanity.
As to the terror you cause,
your arrogant heart has deceived you.
You who live in the clefts of the rock,
you who occupy the mountain summit,
though you elevate your nest like the eagles,
even from there I will bring you down.
This is the LORD's declaration.

"Edom will become a desolation. Everyone who passes by her will be appalled and scoff
70   because of all her wounds. As when Sodom and Gomorrah were overthrown along with
their neighbors," says the LORD, "no one will live there; no human being will stay in it even
temporarily.
"Look, it will be like a lion coming from the thickets of the Jordan to the watered grazing
land. I will chase Edom away from her land in a flash. I will appoint whoever is chosen for her.
For who is like me? Who will issue me a summons? Who is the shepherd who can stand against
me?"

Therefore, hear the plans that the LORD has drawn up against Edom and the strategies he has devised against the people of Teman: The flock's little lambs will certainly be dragged away, and their grazing land will be made desolate because of them. At the sound of their fall the earth will quake; the sound of her cry will be heard at the Red Sea. Look! It will be like an eagle soaring upward, then swooping down and spreading its wings over Bozrah. In that day the hearts of Edom's warriors will be like the heart of a woman with contractions.

About Damascus:

> Hamath and Arpad are put to shame,
> for they have heard a bad report and are agitated,
> like the anxious sea that cannot be calmed.
> Damascus has become weak;
> she has turned to run;
> panic has gripped her.
> Distress and labor pains have seized her
> like a woman in labor.
> How can the city of praise not be abandoned,
> the town that brings me joy?
> Therefore, her young men will fall in her public squares;
> all the warriors will perish in that day.
> This is the declaration of the LORD of Armies.
> I will set fire to the wall of Damascus;
> it will consume Ben-hadad's citadels.

About Kedar and the kingdoms of Hazor, which King Nebuchadnezzar of Babylon defeated, this is what the LORD says:

> Rise up, attack Kedar,
> and destroy the people of the east!
> They will take their tents and their flocks
> along with their tent curtains and all their equipment.
> They will take their camels for themselves.
> They will call out to them,
> "Terror is on every side!"
> Run! Escape quickly! Lie low,
> residents of Hazor—
> this is the LORD's declaration—
> for King Nebuchadnezzar of Babylon

has drawn up a plan against you;
he has devised a strategy against you.

Rise up, attack a nation at ease,
one living in security.
This is the Lord's declaration.
They have no doors, not even a gate bar;
they live alone.
120 Their camels will become plunder,
and their massive herds of cattle will become spoil.
I will scatter them to the wind in every direction,
those who clip the hair on their temples;
I will bring calamity on them across all their borders.
This is the Lord's declaration.
Hazor will become a jackals' den,
a desolation forever.
No one will live there;
no human being will stay in it even temporarily.

130 This is the word of the Lord that came to the prophet Jeremiah about Elam at the beginning of
the reign of King Zedekiah of Judah. This is what the Lord of Armies says:
I am about to shatter Elam's bow,
the source of their might.
I will bring the four winds against Elam
from the four corners of the heavens,
and I will scatter them to all these winds.
There will not be a nation
to which Elam's banished ones will not go.
I will devastate Elam before their enemies,
140 before those who intend to take their lives.
I will bring disaster on them,
my burning anger.
This is the Lord's declaration.
I will send the sword after them
until I finish them off.
I will set my throne in Elam,
and I will destroy the king and officials from there.
This is the Lord's declaration.

Yet, in the last days,
150   I will restore the fortunes of Elam.
This is the Lord's declaration.

50 This is the word the Lord spoke about Babylon, the land of the Chaldeans, through the prophet
Jeremiah:

Announce to the nations;
proclaim and raise up a signal flag;
proclaim, and hide nothing.
Say, "Babylon is captured;
Bel is put to shame;
Marduk is terrified."
Her idols are put to shame;
10   her false gods, devastated.
For a nation from the north will attack her;
it will make her land desolate.
No one will be living in it—
both people and animals will escape.
In those days and at that time—
this is the Lord's declaration—
the Israelites and Judeans will come together,
weeping as they come,
and will seek the Lord their God.
20   They will ask about Zion,
turning their faces to this road.
They will come and join themselves to the Lord
in a permanent covenant that will never be forgotten.

My people were lost sheep;
their shepherds led them astray,
guiding them the wrong way in the mountains.
They wandered from mountain to hill;
they forgot their resting place.
Whoever found them devoured them.
30   Their adversaries said, "We're not guilty;
instead, they have sinned against the Lord,
their righteous grazing land,
the hope of their ancestors, the Lord."

Escape from Babylon;
depart from the Chaldeans' land.
Be like the rams that lead the flock.
For I will soon stir up and bring against Babylon
an assembly of great nations from the north country.
They will line up in battle formation against her;
40   from there she will be captured.
Their arrows will be like a skilled warrior
who does not return empty-handed.
The Chaldeans will become plunder;
all Babylon's plunderers will be fully satisfied.
This is the Lord's declaration.
Because you rejoice,
because you celebrate—
you who plundered my inheritance—
because you frolic like a young cow treading grain
50   and neigh like stallions,
your mother will be utterly humiliated;
she who bore you will be put to shame.
Look! She will lag behind all the nations—
an arid wilderness, a desert.
Because of the Lord's wrath,
she will not be inhabited;
she will become a desolation, every bit of her.
Everyone who passes through Babylon
will be appalled
60   and scoff because of all her wounds.
Line up in battle formation around Babylon,
all you archers!
Shoot at her! Do not spare an arrow,
for she has sinned against the Lord.
Raise a war cry against her on every side!
She has thrown up her hands in surrender;
her defense towers have fallen;
her walls are demolished.
Since this is the Lord's vengeance,
70   take your vengeance on her;

as she has done, do the same to her.
Cut off the sower from Babylon
as well as him who wields the sickle at harvest time.
Because of the oppressor's sword,
each will turn to his own people,
each will flee to his own land.

Israel is a stray lamb, chased by lions.
The first who devoured him was the king of Assyria;
the last who crushed his bones
was King Nebuchadnezzar of Babylon.

Therefore, this is what the LORD of Armies, the God of Israel, says: I am about to punish the king of Babylon and his land just as I punished the king of Assyria.
I will return Israel to his grazing land,
and he will feed on Carmel and Bashan;
he will be satisfied
in the hill country of Ephraim and of Gilead.
In those days and at that time—
this is the LORD's declaration—
one will search for Israel's iniquity,
but there will be none,
and for Judah's sins,
but they will not be found,
for I will forgive those I leave as a remnant.

Attack the land of Merathaim,
and those living in Pekod.
Put them to the sword;
completely destroy them—
this is the LORD's declaration—
do everything I have commanded you.
The sound of war is in the land—
a crushing blow!
How the hammer of the whole earth
is cut down and smashed!
What a horror Babylon has become
among the nations!

Babylon, I laid a trap for you, and you were caught,
but you did not even know it.
You were found and captured
because you pitted yourself against the LORD.
110 The LORD opened his armory
and brought out his weapons of wrath,
because it is a task of the Lord GOD of Armies
in the land of the Chaldeans.
Come against her from the most distant places.
Open her granaries;
pile her up like mounds of grain
and completely destroy her.
Leave her no survivors.
Put all her young bulls to the sword;
120 let them go down to the slaughter.
Woe to them because their day has come,
the time of their punishment.

There is a voice of fugitives and refugees
from the land of Babylon.
The voice announces in Zion the vengeance of the LORD our God,
the vengeance for his temple.
Summon the archers to Babylon,
all who string the bow;
camp all around her; let none escape.
130 Repay her according to her deeds;
just as she has done, do the same to her,
for she has acted arrogantly against the LORD,
against the Holy One of Israel.
Therefore, her young men will fall
in her public squares;
all the warriors will perish in that day.
This is the LORD's declaration.
Look, I am against you, you arrogant one—
this is the declaration of
140 the Lord GOD of Armies—
for your day has come,
the time when I will punish you.

The arrogant will stumble and fall
with no one to pick him up.
I will set fire to his cities,
and it will consume everything around him.

This is what the LORD of Armies says:
    Israelites and Judeans alike have been oppressed.
    All their captors hold them fast;
150   they refuse to release them.
    Their Redeemer is strong;
    the LORD of Armies is his name.
    He will fervently champion their cause
    so that he might bring rest to the earth
    but turmoil to those who live in Babylon.
    A sword is over the Chaldeans—
    this is the LORD's declaration—
    against those who live in Babylon,
    against her officials, and against her sages.
160   A sword is against the diviners,
    and they will act foolishly.
    A sword is against her heroic warriors,
    and they will be terrified.
    A sword is against his horses and chariots
    and against all the foreigners among them,
    and they will be like women.
    A sword is against her treasuries,
    and they will be plundered.
    A drought will come on her waters,
170   and they will be dried up.
    For it is a land of carved images,
    and they go mad because of terrifying things.

Therefore, desert creatures will live with hyenas,
and ostriches will also live in her.
It will never again be inhabited
or lived in through all generations.
Just as God demolished Sodom and Gomorrah
and their neighboring towns—

this is the LORD's declaration—
180   so no one will live there;
no human being will stay in it even temporarily
as a temporary resident.

Look! A people comes from the north.
A great nation and many kings will be stirred up
from the remote regions of the earth.
They grasp bow and javelin.
They are cruel and show no mercy.
Their voice roars like the sea,
and they ride on horses,
190   lined up like men in battle formation
against you, Daughter Babylon.
The king of Babylon has heard about them;
his hands have become weak.
Distress has seized him—
pain, like a woman in labor.

"Look, it will be like a lion coming from the thickets of the Jordan to the watered grazing land. I will chase Babylon away from her land in a flash. I will appoint whoever is chosen for her. For who is like me? Who will issue me a summons? Who is the shepherd who can stand against me?"

200   Therefore, hear the plans that the LORD has drawn up against Babylon and the strategies he has devised against the land of the Chaldeans: Certainly the flock's little lambs will be dragged away; certainly the grazing land will be made desolate because of them. At the sound of Babylon's conquest the earth will quake; a cry will be heard among the nations.

51   This is what the LORD says:
I am about to rouse the spirit of a destroyer against Babylon
and against the population of Leb-qamai.
I will send strangers to Babylon
who will scatter her and strip her land bare,
for they will come against her
from every side in the day of disaster.
Don't let the archer string his bow;
don't let him put on his armor.
10   Don't spare her young men;

completely destroy her entire army!
Those who were slain will fall in the land of the Chaldeans,
those who were pierced through, in her streets.
For Israel and Judah are not left widowed
by their God, the LORD of Armies,
though their land is full of guilt
against the Holy One of Israel.

Leave Babylon;
save your lives, each of you!
20   Don't perish because of her guilt.
For this is the time of the LORD's vengeance—
he will pay her what she deserves.
Babylon was a gold cup in the LORD's hand,
making the whole earth drunk.
The nations drank her wine;
therefore, the nations go mad.
Suddenly Babylon fell and was shattered.
Wail for her;
get balm for her wound—
30   perhaps she can be healed.

We tried to heal Babylon,
but she could not be healed.
Abandon her!
Let each of us go to his own land,
for her judgment extends to the sky
and reaches as far as the clouds.

The LORD has brought about our vindication;
come, let's tell in Zion
what the LORD our God has accomplished.

40   Sharpen the arrows!
Fill the quivers!
The LORD has roused the spirit
of the kings of the Medes
because his plan is aimed at Babylon

to destroy her,
for it is the LORD's vengeance,
vengeance for his temple.
Raise up a signal flag
against the walls of Babylon;
50   fortify the watch post;
set the watchmen in place;
prepare the ambush.
For the LORD has both planned and accomplished
what he has threatened
against those who live in Babylon.
You who reside by abundant water,
rich in treasures,
your end has come,
your life thread is cut.

60   The LORD of Armies has sworn by himself:
I will fill you up with men as with locusts,
and they will sing the victory song over you.

He made the earth by his power,
established the world by his wisdom,
and spread out the heavens by his understanding.
When he thunders,
the waters in the heavens are tumultuous,
and he causes the clouds
to rise from the ends of the earth.
70   He makes lightning for the rain
and brings the wind from his storehouses.

Everyone is stupid and ignorant.
Every goldsmith is put to shame by his carved image,
for his cast images are a lie;
there is no breath in them.
They are worthless, a work to be mocked.
At the time of their punishment they will be destroyed.
Jacob's Portion is not like these
because he is the one who formed all things.

80 Israel is the tribe of his inheritance;
the Lord of Armies is his name.

You are my war club,
my weapons of war.
With you I will smash nations;
with you I will bring kingdoms to ruin.
With you I will smash the horse and its rider;
with you I will smash the chariot and its rider.
With you I will smash man and woman;
with you I will smash the old man and the youth;
90 with you I will smash the young man and the young woman.
With you I will smash the shepherd and his flock;
with you I will smash the farmer and his ox-team.
With you I will smash governors and officials.

"Before your very eyes, I will repay Babylon and all the residents of Chaldea for all their evil they have done in Zion."
This is the Lord's declaration.

Look, I am against you, devastating mountain.
This is the Lord's declaration.
You devastate the whole earth.
100 I will stretch out my hand against you,
roll you down from the cliffs,
and turn you into a charred mountain.
No one will be able to retrieve a cornerstone
or a foundation stone from you,
because you will become desolate forever.
This is the Lord's declaration.

Raise a signal flag in the land;
blow a ram's horn among the nations;
set apart the nations against her.
110 Summon kingdoms against her—
Ararat, Minni, and Ashkenaz.
Appoint a marshal against her;
bring up horses like a swarm of locusts.

Set apart the nations for battle against her—
the kings of Media,
her governors and all her officials,
and all the lands they rule.
The earth quakes and trembles
because the LORD's intentions against Babylon stand:
120   to make the land of Babylon a desolation, without inhabitant.
Babylon's warriors have stopped fighting;
they sit in their strongholds.
Their might is exhausted;
they have become like women.
Babylon's homes have been set ablaze,
her gate bars are shattered.
Messenger races to meet messenger,
and herald to meet herald,
to announce to the king of Babylon
130   that his city has been captured
from end to end.
The fords have been seized,
the marshes set on fire,
and the fighting men are terrified.

For this is what the LORD of Armies, the God of Israel, says:
Daughter Babylon is like a threshing floor
at the time it is trampled.
In just a little while her harvest time will come.

"King Nebuchadnezzar of Babylon has devoured me;
140   he has crushed me.
He has set me aside like an empty dish;
he has swallowed me like a sea monster;
he filled his belly with my delicacies;
he has vomited me out.
Let the violence done to me and my family be done to Babylon,"
says the inhabitant of Zion.
"Let my blood be on the inhabitants of Chaldea,"
says Jerusalem.

Therefore, this is what the LORD says:
> I am about to champion your cause
> and take vengeance on your behalf;
> I will dry up her sea
> and make her fountain run dry.
> Babylon will become a heap of rubble,
> a jackals' den,
> a desolation and an object of scorn,
> without inhabitant.
> They will roar together like young lions;
> they will growl like lion cubs.
> While they are flushed with heat, I will serve them a feast,
> and I will make them drunk so that they celebrate.
> Then they will fall asleep forever
> and never wake up.
> This is the LORD's declaration.
> I will bring them down like lambs to the slaughter,
> like rams together with male goats.

> How Sheshak has been captured,
> the praise of the whole earth seized.
> What a horror Babylon has become
> among the nations!
> The sea has risen over Babylon;
> she is covered with its tumultuous waves.
> Her cities have become a desolation,
> an arid desert,
> a land where no one lives,
> where no human being even passes through.
> I will punish Bel in Babylon.
> I will make him vomit what he swallowed.
> The nations will no longer stream to him;
> even Babylon's wall will fall.

> Come out from among her, my people!
> Save your lives, each of you,
> from the LORD's burning anger.
> May you not become cowardly and fearful

when the report is proclaimed in the land,
for the report will come one year,
and then another the next year.
There will be violence in the land
with ruler against ruler.
190 Therefore, look, the days are coming
when I will punish Babylon's carved images.
Her entire land will suffer shame,
and all her slain will lie fallen within her.
Heaven and earth and everything in them
will shout for joy over Babylon
because the destroyers from the north
will come against her.
This is the Lord's declaration.

Babylon must fall because of the slain of Israel,
200 even as the slain of the whole earth fell
because of Babylon.
You who have escaped the sword,
go and do not stand still!
Remember the Lord from far away,
and let Jerusalem come to your mind.

We are ashamed
because we have heard insults.
Humiliation covers our faces
because foreigners have entered
210 the holy places of the Lord's temple.

Therefore, look, the days are coming—
this is the Lord's declaration—
when I will punish her carved images,
and the wounded will groan
throughout her land.
Even if Babylon should ascend to the heavens
and fortify her tall fortresses,
destroyers will come against her from me.
This is the Lord's declaration.

220 The sound of a cry from Babylon!
The sound of terrible destruction
from the land of the Chaldeans!
For the Lord is going to devastate Babylon;
he will silence her mighty voice.
Their waves roar like a huge torrent;
the tumult of their voice resounds,
for a destroyer is coming against her,
against Babylon.
Her warriors will be captured,
230 their bows shattered,
for the Lord is a God of retribution;
he will certainly repay.
I will make her princes and sages drunk,
along with her governors, officials, and warriors.
Then they will fall asleep forever
and never wake up.
This is the King's declaration;
the Lord of Armies is his name.

This is what the Lord of Armies says:
240 Babylon's thick walls will be totally demolished,
and her high gates set ablaze.
The peoples will have labored for nothing;
the nations will weary themselves only to feed the fire.

This is what the prophet Jeremiah commanded Seraiah son of Neriah son of Mahseiah, the quartermaster, when he went to Babylon with King Zedekiah of Judah in the fourth year of Zedekiah's reign. Jeremiah wrote on one scroll about all the disaster that would come to Babylon; all these words were written against Babylon.

Jeremiah told Seraiah, "When you get to Babylon, see that you read all these words aloud. Say, 'Lord, you have threatened to cut off this place so that no one will live in it—people or animals.
250 Indeed, it will remain desolate forever.' When you have finished reading this scroll, tie a stone to it and throw it into the middle of the Euphrates River. Then say, 'In the same way, Babylon will sink and never rise again because of the disaster I am bringing on her. They will grow weary.'"

The words of Jeremiah end here.

52 Zedekiah was twenty-one years old when he became king, and he reigned eleven years in Jerusalem. His mother's name was Hamutal daughter of Jeremiah; she was from Libnah. Zedekiah did what was evil in the LORD's sight just as Jehoiakim had done. Because of the LORD's anger, it came to the point in Jerusalem and Judah that he finally banished them from his presence. Then Zedekiah rebelled against the king of Babylon.

In the ninth year of Zedekiah's reign, on the tenth day of the tenth month, King Nebuchadnezzar of Babylon advanced against Jerusalem with his entire army. They laid siege to the city and built a siege wall against it all around. The city was under siege until King Zedekiah's eleventh year.

10 By the ninth day of the fourth month the famine was so severe in the city that the common people had no food. Then the city was broken into, and all the warriors fled. They left the city at night by way of the city gate between the two walls near the king's garden, though the Chaldeans surrounded the city. They made their way along the route to the Arabah. The Chaldean army pursued the king and overtook Zedekiah in the plains of Jericho. Zedekiah's entire army left him and scattered. The Chaldeans seized the king and brought him to the king of Babylon at Riblah in the land of Hamath, and he passed sentence on him.

At Riblah the king of Babylon slaughtered Zedekiah's sons before his eyes, and he also slaughtered the Judean commanders. Then he blinded Zedekiah and bound him with bronze chains. The king of Babylon brought Zedekiah to Babylon, where he kept him in custody until his 20 dying day.

On the tenth day of the fifth month — which was the nineteenth year of King Nebuchadnezzar, king of Babylon — Nebuzaradan, the captain of the guards, entered Jerusalem as the representative of the king of Babylon. He burned the LORD's temple, the king's palace, all the houses of Jerusalem; he burned down all the great houses. The whole Chaldean army with the captain of the guards tore down all the walls surrounding Jerusalem. Nebuzaradan, the captain of the guards, deported some of the poorest of the people, as well as the rest of the people who remained in the city, the deserters who had defected to the king of Babylon, and the rest of the craftsmen. But Nebuzaradan, the captain of the guards, left some of the poorest of the land to be vinedressers and farmers.

30 Now the Chaldeans broke into pieces the bronze pillars for the LORD's temple and the water carts and the bronze basin that were in the LORD's temple, and they carried all the bronze to Babylon. They also took the pots, shovels, wick trimmers, sprinkling basins, dishes, and all the bronze articles used in the temple service. The captain of the guards took away the bowls, firepans, sprinkling basins, pots, lampstands, pans, and drink offering bowls — whatever was gold or silver.

As for the two pillars, the one basin, with the twelve bronze oxen under it, and the water carts that King Solomon had made for the LORD's temple, the weight of the bronze of all these articles was beyond measure. One pillar was 27 feet tall, had a circumference of 18 feet, was hollow — four fingers thick— and had a bronze capital on top of it. One capital, encircled by bronze grating

and pomegranates, stood 7 ½ feet high. The second pillar was the same, with pomegranates.
40 Each capital had ninety-six pomegranates all around it. All the pomegranates around the grating numbered one hundred.

The captain of the guards also took away Seraiah the chief priest, Zephaniah the priest of the second rank, and the three doorkeepers. From the city he took a court official who had been appointed over the warriors; seven trusted royal aides found in the city; the secretary of the commander of the army, who enlisted the people of the land for military duty; and sixty men from the common people who were found within the city. Nebuzaradan, the captain of the guards, took them and brought them to the king of Babylon at Riblah. The king of Babylon put them to death at Riblah in the land of Hamath. So Judah went into exile from its land.

These are the people Nebuchadnezzar deported: in the seventh year, 3,023 Jews; in
50 his eighteenth year, 832 people from Jerusalem; in Nebuchadnezzar's twenty-third year, Nebuzaradan, the captain of the guards, deported 745 Jews. Altogether, 4,600 people were deported.

On the twenty-fifth day of the twelfth month of the thirty-seventh year of the exile of Judah's King Jehoiachin, King Evil-merodach of Babylon, in the first year of his reign, pardoned King Jehoiachin of Judah and released him from prison. He spoke kindly to him and set his throne above the thrones of the kings who were with him in Babylon. So Jehoiachin changed his prison clothes, and he dined regularly in the presence of the king of Babylon for the rest of his life. As for his allowance, a regular allowance was given to him by the king of Babylon, a portion for each day until the day of his death, for the rest of his life.

Introduction to Ezekiel

William R. Osborne

The book of Ezekiel has challenged interpreters for thousands of years. Both Jewish rabbis and Christians have long struggled with various elements of the book (e.g., the prophet's temple vision and the enigmatic prophecies about Gog and Magog). Despite its notorious difficulties, it would be inaccurate to describe the book as inaccessible or beyond our grasp. While Ezekiel does at times place high demands upon its readers, the effort is well rewarded with rich reflections on the nature and work of Yahweh, the seriousness of human sin, and the glorious future for Yahweh's people.

Ezekiel provides fourteen specific dates that mark moments of time throughout the prophet's life and ministry from approximately 627 BC (birth?)–573 BC. The book opens with the call of the Judean priest-prophet living among the exiles in Babylon in 593 BC. The glory of Yahweh appears to Ezekiel in an otherworldly vision on the banks of the Chebar River and calls him to be his mouthpiece to the rebellious house of Judah (Ezek 1–3). Ezekiel is appointed as a "watchman" for the house of Israel (3.23–25; 33.10–11). Yahweh calls him to deliver to his people the warning of judgment, whether they respond to it or not (3.27–29). Despite the stubbornness of the people and the difficulty of the task, the book presents Ezekiel's faithfulness in proclaiming—in word and act—Yahweh's words of judgment against the people of Judah and the nations.

The theological direction of the book moves from judgment to salvation and centers around the presence of Yahweh among his people. The opening vision of the storm-theophany is a striking portrayal of Yahweh's presence outside of the temple, capable of carrying out judgment in Babylon. The sovereign Yahweh of the universe arrives in Babylon upon his angel-borne chariot throne, diminishing the gods of Babylon to mere puppets. Aside from a few brief diversions, chs. 4–32 communicate Yahweh's disgust over the sins of his people and the nations and his subsequent commitment to judge them for their wicked deeds.

In chs. 8–11 Ezekiel receives yet another vision, similar to the one he had at the Chebar River. Only in this vision, he is taken to Jerusalem, shown the secret idolatry of the people (8.15–19), beholds Yahweh's execution of judgment upon the city (9.9–17), and witnesses the glory of Yahweh depart from the temple in Jerusalem (10.23–31). Yahweh's presence among his people is compromised because of the wickedness of their ways, and the vision of the judgment against Jerusalem becomes reality at the hands of the Babylonians in ch. 33. After Ezekiel's watchman role is reiterated (33.1–36), the prophet receives word from a fugitive of Jerusalem that the city had been destroyed (33.37–38). Divine judgment did indeed fall upon the house of Judah, raising the question, now what?

In many ways the book of Ezekiel depicts a community wrestling with the reality of exile and judgment. In light of the Babylonian destruction and captivity, is Yahweh still powerful? Does he still hear the prayers of his people? Is there a future for the house of David? Is there a hope for the people of Yahweh? Such questions loom large in the background and give shape to the latter part of the book. In these final chapters, the message shifts from the inevitability of judgment to the promise and hope of restoration. Unlike the wicked leaders of Israel, Yahweh himself will shepherd his people, gathering them from the nations where they were scattered (34.17–26). The Yahweh who withdrew from the temple in Jerusalem will pursue his scattered sheep and cleanse them from their iniquity, giving them a new heart and placing his Spirit within them (36.38–48). Yahweh will restore his people, transforming them from death to life (37.1–21), and ultimately dwelling among them as their Lord. The book concludes with Ezekiel's magnificent vision of a heavenly temple where Yahweh's glory returns (43.1–5) and he establishes a new city for the people of Yahweh, whose name will forever be *Yahweh Shamah*—Yahweh is There.

Outline

1. The Call of Ezekiel (1.1–3.42)
   a. The Glory of Yahweh in Exile (1.1–43)
   b. Speak to this House of Rebels (1.44–3.22)
   c. Ezekiel, the Watchman (3.23–42)

2. The Judgement of Jerusalem (4.1–7.110)
   a. Acting the Part: Ezekiel's Sign-Act Siege (4.1–27)
   b. A Razor and Fire Comes against Jerusalem (5.1–33)
   c. Judgement against the Mountains of Judah (6.1–23)
   d. Disaster is Coming (7.1–110)

3. Vision of Jerusalem's Sin and Divine Visitation (8.1–11.39)
   a. The Corruption of the Temple Exposed (8.1–33)
   b. The Judgement and the Glory (9.1–10.35)
   c. The Death of Pelatiah (11.1–19)
   d. One Heart and a New Spirit (11.20–39)

4. Parable and Allegories about Jerusalem's Coming Judgment (12.1–24.74)
   a. Headed for Exile (12.1–31)
   b. Empty Wisdom (12.32–44)
   c. Wicked Prophets (13.1–42)
   d. "I Will Set My Face against Them" (14.1–15.11)
   e. Jerusalem's Shocking Story (16.1–103)
   f. From Jehoiachin to Zedekiah to Messiah (17.1–54)
   g. The Soul Who Sins Will Die (18.1–54)

Suggested Resources

Block, Daniel I. *The Book of Ezekiel.* New International Commentary on the Old Testament. 2 vols. Grand Rapids: Eerdmans, 1997–1998.

Cook, Stephen L. *Ezekiel 38–48.* Anchor Bible Commentary. New Haven: Yale University Press, 2018.

Duguid, Iain M. *Ezekiel.* NIV Application Commentary. Grand Rapids: Zondervan, 1999.

Greenberg, Moshe. *Ezekiel.* Anchor Bible Commentary. 2 vols. New York: Doubleday, 1983–1995.

Joyce, Paul M. *Ezekiel: A Commentary.* Library of Hebrew Bible/Old Testament Studies. New York: T&T Clark, 2007.

Wright, Christopher J. H. *The Message of Ezekiel: A New Heart and a New Spirit.* The Bible Speaks Today. Downers Grove, IL: InterVarsity Press, 2001.

Ezekiel

I In the thirtieth year, in the fourth month, on the fifth day of the month, while I was among the exiles by the Chebar Canal, the heavens were opened and I saw visions of God. On the fifth day of the month — it was the fifth year of King Jehoiachin's exile— the word of the LORD came directly to the priest Ezekiel son of Buzi, in the land of the Chaldeans by the Chebar Canal. The LORD's hand was on him there.

I looked, and there was a whirlwind coming from the north, a huge cloud with fire flashing back and forth and brilliant light all around it. In the center of the fire, there was a gleam like amber. The likeness of four living creatures came from it, and this was their appearance: They looked something like a human, but each of them had four faces and four wings. Their legs were straight, and the soles of their feet were like the hooves of a calf, sparkling like the gleam of polished bronze. They had human hands under their wings on their four sides. All four of them had faces and wings. Their wings were touching. The creatures did not turn as they moved; each one went straight ahead. Their faces looked something like the face of a human, and each of the four had the face of a lion on the right, the face of an ox on the left, and the face of an eagle. That is what their faces were like. Their wings were spread upward; each had two wings touching that of another and two wings covering its body. Each creature went straight ahead. Wherever the Spirit wanted to go, they went without turning as they moved.

The likeness of the living creatures was like the appearance of blazing coals of fire or like torches. Fire was moving back and forth between the living creatures; it was bright, with lightning coming out of it. The creatures were darting back and forth like flashes of lightning.

When I looked at the living creatures, there was one wheel on the ground beside each of the four-faced creatures. The appearance of the wheels and their craftsmanship was like the gleam of beryl, and all four had the same likeness. Their appearance and craftsmanship was like a wheel within a wheel. When they moved, they went in any of the four directions, without turning as they moved. Their four rims were tall and awe-inspiring, completely covered with eyes. When the living creatures moved, the wheels moved beside them, and when the creatures rose from the earth, the wheels also rose. Wherever the Spirit wanted to go, the creatures went in the direction the Spirit was moving. The wheels rose alongside them, for the spirit of the living creatures was in the wheels. When the creatures moved, the wheels moved; when the creatures stopped, the wheels stopped; and when the creatures rose from the earth, the wheels rose alongside them, for the spirit of the living creatures was in the wheels.

Over the heads of the living creatures the likeness of an expanse was spread out. It gleamed like awe-inspiring crystal, and under the expanse their wings extended one toward another. They each also had two wings covering their bodies. When they moved, I heard the sound of their wings like the roar of a huge torrent, like the voice of the Almighty, and a sound of tumult like the noise of an army. When they stopped, they lowered their wings.

A voice came from above the expanse over their heads; when they stopped, they lowered their wings. Something like a throne with the appearance of lapis lazuli was above the expanse over their heads. On the throne, high above, was someone who looked like a human. From what seemed to be his waist up, I saw a gleam like amber, with what looked like fire enclosing it all around. From what seemed to be his waist down, I also saw what looked like fire. There was a brilliant light all around him. The appearance of the brilliant light all around was like that of a rainbow in a cloud on a rainy day. This was the appearance of the likeness of the Lord's glory. When I saw it, I fell facedown and heard a voice speaking.

2 He said to me, "Son of man, stand up on your feet and I will speak with you." As he spoke to me, the Spirit entered me and set me on my feet, and I listened to the one who was speaking to me. He said to me, "Son of man, I am sending you to the Israelites, to the rebellious pagans who have rebelled against me. The Israelites and their ancestors have transgressed against me to this day. The descendants are obstinate and hardhearted. I am sending you to them, and you must say to them, 'This is what the Lord God says.' Whether they listen or refuse to listen — for they are a rebellious house — they will know that a prophet has been among them.

"But you, son of man, do not be afraid of them and do not be afraid of their words, even though briers and thorns are beside you and you live among scorpions. Don't be afraid of their words or discouraged by the look on their faces, for they are a rebellious house. Speak my words to them whether they listen or refuse to listen, for they are rebellious.

"And you, son of man, listen to what I tell you: Do not be rebellious like that rebellious house. Open your mouth and eat what I am giving you." So I looked and saw a hand reaching out to me, and there was a written scroll in it. When he unrolled it before me, it was written on the front and back; words of lamentation, mourning, and woe were written on it.

3 He said to me, "Son of man, eat what you find here. Eat this scroll, then go and speak to the house of Israel." So I opened my mouth, and he fed me the scroll. "Son of man," he said to me, "feed your stomach and fill your belly with this scroll I am giving you." So I ate it, and it was as sweet as honey in my mouth.

Then he said to me, "Son of man, go to the house of Israel and speak my words to them. For you are not being sent to a people of unintelligible speech or a difficult language but to the house of Israel—not to the many peoples of unintelligible speech or a difficult language, whose words you cannot understand. No doubt, if I sent you to them, they would listen to you. But the house

of Israel will not want to listen to you because they do not want to listen to me. For the whole
house of Israel is hardheaded and hardhearted. Look, I have made your face as hard as their faces
and your forehead as hard as their foreheads. I have made your forehead like a diamond, harder
than flint. Don't be afraid of them or discouraged by the look on their faces, though they are a
rebellious house."

Next he said to me, "Son of man, listen carefully to all my words that I speak to you and take
them to heart. Go to your people, the exiles, and speak to them. Tell them, 'This is what the Lord
God says,' whether they listen or refuse to listen."

The Spirit then lifted me up, and I heard a loud rumbling sound behind me — bless the glory
of the Lord in his place!— with the sound of the living creatures' wings brushing against each
other and the sound of the wheels beside them, a loud rumbling sound. The Spirit lifted me up
and took me away. I left in bitterness and in an angry spirit, and the Lord's hand was on me
powerfully. I came to the exiles at Tel-abib, who were living by the Chebar Canal, and I sat there
among them stunned for seven days.

Now at the end of seven days the word of the Lord came to me: "Son of man, I have made you a
watchman over the house of Israel. When you hear a word from my mouth, give them a warning
from me. If I say to the wicked person, 'You will surely die,' but you do not warn him — you don't
speak out to warn him about his wicked way in order to save his life — that wicked person will die
for his iniquity. Yet I will hold you responsible for his blood. But if you warn a wicked person and
he does not turn from his wickedness or his wicked way, he will die for his iniquity, but you will
have rescued yourself. Now if a righteous person turns from his righteousness and acts unjustly,
and I put a stumbling block in front of him, he will die. If you did not warn him, he will die because
of his sin, and the righteous acts he did will not be remembered. Yet I will hold you responsible for
his blood. But if you warn the righteous person that he should not sin, and he does not sin, he will
indeed live because he listened to your warning, and you will have rescued yourself."

The hand of the Lord was on me there, and he said to me, "Get up, go out to the plain, and I
will speak with you there." So I got up and went out to the plain. The Lord's glory was present
there, like the glory I had seen by the Chebar Canal, and I fell facedown. The Spirit entered me
and set me on my feet. He spoke with me and said, "Go, shut yourself inside your house. As for
you, son of man, they will put ropes on you and bind you with them so you cannot go out among
them. I will make your tongue stick to the roof of your mouth, and you will be mute and unable
to be a mediator for them, for they are a rebellious house. But when I speak with you, I will open
your mouth, and you will say to them, 'This is what the Lord God says.' Let the one who listens,
listen, and let the one who refuses, refuse — for they are a rebellious house.

4 "Now you, son of man, take a brick, set it in front of you, and draw the city of Jerusalem on it. Then
lay siege against it: Construct a siege wall, build a ramp, pitch military camps, and place battering

rams against it on all sides. Take an iron plate and set it up as an iron wall between yourself and the city. Face it so that it is under siege, and besiege it. This will be a sign for the house of Israel.

"Then lie down on your left side and place the iniquity of the house of Israel on it. You will bear their iniquity for the number of days you lie on your side. For I have assigned you the years of their iniquity according to the number of days you lie down, 390 days; so you will bear the iniquity of the house of Israel. When you have completed these days, lie down again, but on your right side, and bear the iniquity of the house of Judah. I have assigned you forty days, a day for each

10 year. Face the siege of Jerusalem with your arm bared, and prophesy against it. Be aware that I will put cords on you so you cannot turn from side to side until you have finished the days of your siege.

"Also take wheat, barley, beans, lentils, millet, and spelt. Put them in a single container and make them into bread for yourself. You are to eat it during the number of days you lie on your side, 390 days. The food you eat each day will weigh eight ounces; you will eat it at set times. You will also drink a ration of water, a sixth of a gallon, which you will drink at set times. You will eat it as you would a barley cake and bake it over dried human excrement in their sight." The Lord said, "This is how the Israelites will eat their bread — ceremonially unclean — among the nations where I will banish them."

20 But I said, "Oh, Lord God, I have never been defiled. From my youth until now I have not eaten anything that died naturally or was mauled by wild beasts. And impure meat has never entered my mouth."

He replied to me, "Look, I will let you use cow dung instead of human excrement, and you can make your bread over that." He said to me, "Son of man, I am going to cut off the supply of bread in Jerusalem. They will anxiously eat food they have weighed out and in dread drink rationed water for lack of bread and water. Everyone will be devastated and waste away because of their iniquity.

5 "Now you, son of man, take a sharp sword, use it as you would a barber's razor, and shave your head and beard. Then take a set of scales and divide the hair. You are to burn a third of it in the city when the days of the siege have ended; you are to take a third and slash it with the sword all around the city; and you are to scatter a third to the wind, for I will draw a sword to chase after them. But you are to take a few strands from the hair and secure them in the folds of your robe. Take some more of them, throw them into the fire, and burn them in it. A fire will spread from it to the whole house of Israel.

"This is what the Lord God says: I have set this Jerusalem in the center of the nations, with countries all around her. She has rebelled against my ordinances with more wickedness than the nations, and against my statutes more than the countries that surround her. For her people have

10 rejected my ordinances and have not walked in my statutes.

"Therefore, this is what the Lord God says: Because you have been more insubordinate than the nations around you — you have not walked in my statutes or kept my ordinances; you have not even kept the ordinances of the nations around you— therefore, this is what the Lord God says: See, I myself am against you, Jerusalem, and I will execute judgments within you in the sight of the nations. Because of all your detestable practices, I will do to you what I have never done before and what I will never do again. As a result, fathers will eat their sons within Jerusalem, and sons will eat their fathers. I will execute judgments against you and scatter all your survivors to every direction of the wind.

20 "Therefore, as I live" — this is the declaration of the Lord God — "I will withdraw and show you no pity, because you have defiled my sanctuary with all your abhorrent acts and detestable practices. Yes, I will not spare you. A third of your people will die by plague and be consumed by famine within you; a third will fall by the sword all around you; and I will scatter a third to every direction of the wind, and I will draw a sword to chase after them. When my anger is spent and I have vented my wrath on them, I will be appeased. Then after I have spent my wrath on them, they will know that I, the Lord, have spoken in my jealousy.

"I will make you a ruin and a disgrace among the nations around you, in the sight of everyone who passes by. So you will be a disgrace and a taunt, a warning and a horror, to the nations around you when I execute judgments against you in anger, wrath, and furious rebukes. I, the Lord, have spoken. When I shoot deadly arrows of famine at them, arrows for destruction that I will 30 send to destroy you, inhabitants of Jerusalem, I will intensify the famine against you and cut off your supply of bread. I will send famine and dangerous animals against you. They will leave you childless. Plague and bloodshed will sweep through you, and I will bring a sword against you. I, the Lord, have spoken."

6 The word of the Lord came to me: "Son of man, face the mountains of Israel and prophesy against them. You are to say: Mountains of Israel, hear the word of the Lord God! This is what the Lord God says to the mountains and the hills, to the ravines and the valleys: I am about to bring a sword against you, and I will destroy your high places. Your altars will be desolated and your shrines smashed. I will throw down your slain in front of your idols. I will lay the corpses of the Israelites in front of their idols and scatter your bones around your altars. Wherever you live the cities will be in ruins and the high places will be desolate, so that your altars will lie in ruins and be desecrated, your idols smashed and obliterated, your shrines cut down, and what you have made wiped out. The slain will fall among you, and you will know that I am the Lord.

10 "Yet I will leave a remnant when you are scattered among the nations, for throughout the countries there will be some of you who will escape the sword. Then your survivors will remember me among the nations where they are taken captive, how I was crushed by their promiscuous hearts that turned away from me and by their eyes that lusted after their idols. They will loathe themselves because of the evil things they did, their detestable actions of every kind. And they will know that I am the Lord; I did not threaten to bring this disaster on them without a reason.

"This is what the Lord GOD says: Clap your hands, stamp your feet, and cry out over all the evil and detestable practices of the house of Israel, who will fall by the sword, famine, and plague. The one who is far off will die by plague; the one who is near will fall by the sword; and the one who remains and is spared will die of famine. In this way I will exhaust my wrath on them. You will all know that

20 I am the LORD when their slain lie among their idols around their altars, on every high hill, on all the mountaintops, and under every green tree and every leafy oak — the places where they offered pleasing aromas to all their idols. I will stretch out my hand against them, and wherever they live I will make the land a desolate waste, from the wilderness to Riblah. Then they will know that I am the LORD."

7 The word of the LORD came to me: "Son of man, this is what the Lord GOD says to the land of Israel:

> An end! The end has come
> on the four corners of the earth.
> The end is now upon you;
> I will send my anger against you
> and judge you according to your ways.
> I will punish you for all your detestable practices.
> I will not look on you with pity or spare you,
> but I will punish you for your ways

10
> and for your detestable practices within you.
> Then you will know that I am the LORD."

This is what the Lord GOD says:

> Look, one disaster after another is coming!
> An end has come; the end has come!
> It has awakened against you.
> Look, it is coming!
> Doom has come on you,
> inhabitants of the land.
> The time has come; the day is near.

20
> There will be panic on the mountains
> and not celebration.

> I will pour out my wrath on you very soon;
> I will exhaust my anger against you
> and judge you according to your ways.
> I will punish you for all your detestable practices.
> I will not look on you with pity or spare you.
> I will punish you for your ways

and for your detestable practices within you.
Then you will know
30   that it is I, the Lord, who strikes.

Here is the day! Here it comes!
Doom is on its way.
The rod has blossomed;
arrogance has bloomed.
Violence has grown into a rod of wickedness.
None of them will remain:
none of that crowd,
none of their wealth,
and none of the eminent among them.

40   The time has come; the day has arrived.
Let the buyer not rejoice
and the seller not mourn,
for wrath is on her whole crowd.
The seller will certainly not return
to what was sold
as long as he and the buyer remain alive.
For the vision concerning her whole crowd
will not be revoked,
and because of the iniquity of each one,
50   none will preserve his life.

They have blown the trumpet
and prepared everything,
but no one goes to war,
for my wrath is on her whole crowd.
The sword is on the outside;
plague and famine are on the inside.
Whoever is in the field will die by the sword,
and famine and plague will devour
whoever is in the city.

60   The survivors among them will escape
and live on the mountains.

Like doves of the valley,
all of them will moan,
each over his own iniquity.
All their hands will become weak,
and all their knees will run with urine.
They will put on sackcloth,
and horror will overwhelm them.
Shame will cover all their faces,
70   and all their heads will be bald.

They will throw their silver into the streets,
and their gold will seem like something filthy.
Their silver and gold will be unable to save them
in the day of the LORD's wrath.
They will not satisfy their appetites
or fill their stomachs,
for these were the stumbling blocks
that brought about their iniquity.

He appointed his beautiful ornaments for majesty,
80   but they made their detestable images from them,
their abhorrent things.
Therefore, I have made these
into something filthy to them.
I will hand these things over
to foreigners as plunder
and to the wicked of the earth as spoil,
and they will profane them.
I will turn my face from them
as they profane my treasured place.
90   Violent men will enter it and profane it.

Forge the chain,
for the land is filled with crimes of bloodshed,
and the city is filled with violence.
So I will bring the most evil of nations
to take possession of their houses.
I will put an end to the pride of the strong,

and their sacred places will be profaned.
Anguish is coming!
They will look for peace, but there will be none.
100 Disaster after disaster will come,
and there will be rumor after rumor.
Then they will look for a vision from a prophet,
but instruction will perish from the priests
and counsel from the elders.
The king will mourn;
the prince will be clothed in grief;
and the hands of the people of the land will tremble.
I will deal with them according to their own conduct,
and I will judge them by their own standards.
110 Then they will know that I am the Lord.

8 In the sixth year, in the sixth month, on the fifth day of the month, I was sitting in my house and the elders of Judah were sitting in front of me, and there the hand of the Lord God came down on me. I looked, and there was someone who looked like a man. From what seemed to be his waist down was fire, and from his waist up was something that looked bright, like the gleam of amber. He stretched out what appeared to be a hand and took me by the hair of my head. Then the Spirit lifted me up between earth and heaven and carried me in visions of God to Jerusalem, to the entrance of the inner gate that faces north, where the offensive statue that provokes jealousy was located. I saw the glory of the God of Israel there, like the vision I had seen in the plain.

The Lord said to me, "Son of man, look toward the north." I looked to the north, and there was
10 this offensive statue north of the Altar Gate, at the entrance. He said to me, "Son of man, do you see what they are doing here — more detestable acts that the house of Israel is committing — so that I must depart from my sanctuary? You will see even more detestable acts."

Then he brought me to the entrance of the court, and when I looked there was a hole in the wall. He said to me, "Son of man, dig through the wall." So I dug through the wall and discovered a doorway. He said to me, "Go in and see the detestable, wicked acts they are committing here."

I went in and looked, and there engraved all around the wall was every kind of abhorrent thing — crawling creatures and beasts — as well as all the idols of the house of Israel. Seventy elders from the house of Israel were standing before them, with Jaazaniah son of Shaphan standing among them. Each had a firepan in his hand, and a fragrant cloud of incense was rising up. He said to me,
20 "Son of man, do you see what the elders of the house of Israel are doing in the darkness, each at the shrine of his idol? For they are saying, 'The Lord does not see us. The Lord has abandoned the land.'" Again he said to me, "You will see even more detestable acts that they are committing."

Then he brought me to the entrance of the north gate of the LORD's house, and I saw women sitting there weeping for Tammuz. And he said to me, "Do you see this, son of man? You will see even more detestable acts than these."

So he brought me to the inner court of the LORD's house, and there were about twenty-five men at the entrance of the LORD's temple, between the portico and the altar, with their backs to the LORD's temple and their faces turned to the east. They were bowing to the east in worship of the sun. And he said to me, "Do you see this, son of man? Is it not enough for the house of Judah 30 to commit the detestable acts they are doing here, that they must also fill the land with violence and repeatedly anger me, even putting the branch to their nose? Therefore I will respond with wrath. I will not show pity or spare them. Though they call loudly in my hearing, I will not listen to them."

9 Then he called loudly in my hearing, "Come near, executioners of the city, each of you with a destructive weapon in his hand." And I saw six men coming from the direction of the Upper Gate, which faces north, each with a war club in his hand. There was another man among them, clothed in linen, carrying writing equipment. They came and stood beside the bronze altar.

Then the glory of the God of Israel rose from above the cherub where it had been, to the threshold of the temple. He called to the man clothed in linen and carrying writing equipment. "Pass throughout the city of Jerusalem," the LORD said to him, "and put a mark on the foreheads of the men who sigh and groan over all the detestable practices committed in it."

He spoke to the others in my hearing: "Pass through the city after him and start killing; 10 do not show pity or spare them! Slaughter the old men, the young men and women, as well as the children and older women, but do not come near anyone who has the mark. Begin at my sanctuary." So they began with the elders who were in front of the temple. Then he said to them, "Defile the temple and fill the courts with the slain. Go!" So they went out killing people in the city.

While they were killing, I was left alone. And I fell facedown and cried out, "Oh, Lord GOD! Are you going to destroy the entire remnant of Israel when you pour out your wrath on Jerusalem?"

He answered me, "The iniquity of the house of Israel and Judah is extremely great; the land is full of bloodshed, and the city full of perversity. For they say, 'The LORD has abandoned the land; 20 he does not see.' But as for me, I will not show pity or spare them. I will bring their conduct down on their own heads."

Then the man clothed in linen and carrying writing equipment reported back, "I have done all that you commanded me."

10 Then I looked, and there above the expanse over the heads of the cherubim was something like a throne with the appearance of lapis lazuli. The LORD spoke to the man clothed in linen and said,

"Go inside the wheelwork beneath the cherubim. Fill your hands with blazing coals from among the cherubim and scatter them over the city." So he went in as I watched.

Now the cherubim were standing to the south of the temple when the man went in, and the cloud filled the inner court. Then the glory of the LORD rose from above the cherub to the threshold of the temple. The temple was filled with the cloud, and the court was filled with the brightness of the LORD's glory. The sound of the cherubim's wings could be heard as far as the outer court; it was like the voice of God Almighty when he speaks.

10 After the LORD commanded the man clothed in linen, saying, "Take fire from inside the wheelwork, from among the cherubim," the man went in and stood beside a wheel. Then the cherub reached out his hand to the fire that was among them. He took some and put it into the hands of the man clothed in linen, who took it and went out. The cherubim appeared to have the form of human hands under their wings.

I looked, and there were four wheels beside the cherubim, one wheel beside each cherub. The luster of the wheels was like the gleam of beryl. In appearance, all four looked alike, like a wheel within a wheel. When they moved, they would go in any of the four directions, without pivoting as they moved. But wherever the head faced, they would go in that direction, without pivoting as they went. Their entire bodies, including their backs, hands, wings, and the wheels that the four of

20 them had, were full of eyes all around. As I listened the wheels were called "the wheelwork." Each one had four faces: one was the face of a cherub, the second the face of a human, the third the face of a lion, and the fourth the face of an eagle.

The cherubim ascended; these were the living creatures I had seen by the Chebar Canal. When the cherubim moved, the wheels moved beside them, and when they lifted their wings to rise from the earth, even then the wheels did not veer away from them. When the cherubim stopped, the wheels stood still, and when they ascended, the wheels ascended with them, for the spirit of the living creatures was in them.

Then the glory of the LORD moved away from the threshold of the temple and stopped above the cherubim. The cherubim lifted their wings and ascended from the earth right before my eyes;

30 the wheels were beside them as they went. The glory of the God of Israel was above them, and it stopped at the entrance to the eastern gate of the LORD's house.

These were the living creatures I had seen beneath the God of Israel by the Chebar Canal, and I recognized that they were cherubim. Each had four faces and each had four wings, with what looked something like human hands under their wings. Their faces looked like the same faces I had seen by the Chebar Canal. Each creature went straight ahead.

11 The Spirit then lifted me up and brought me to the eastern gate of the LORD's house, which faces east, and at the gate's entrance were twenty-five men. Among them I saw Jaazaniah son of Azzur, and Pelatiah son of Benaiah, leaders of the people. The LORD said to me, "Son of man, these are the men who plot evil and give wicked advice in this city. They are saying, 'Isn't the time near

to build houses? The city is the pot, and we are the meat.' Therefore, prophesy against them. Prophesy, son of man!"

Then the Spirit of the LORD came on me, and he told me, "You are to say, 'This is what the LORD says: That is what you are thinking, house of Israel; and I know the thoughts that arise in your mind. You have multiplied your slain in this city, filling its streets with them.

10 "'Therefore, this is what the Lord GOD says: The slain you have put within it are the meat, and the city is the pot, but I will take you out of it. You fear the sword, so I will bring the sword against you. This is the declaration of the Lord GOD. I will take you out of the city and hand you over to foreigners; I will execute judgments against you. You will fall by the sword, and I will judge you at the border of Israel. Then you will know that I am the LORD. The city will not be a pot for you, and you will not be the meat within it. I will judge you at the border of Israel, so you will know that I am the LORD, whose statutes you have not followed and whose ordinances you have not practiced. Instead, you have acted according to the ordinances of the nations around you.'"

Now while I was prophesying, Pelatiah son of Benaiah died. Then I fell facedown and cried out loudly, "Oh, Lord GOD! You are bringing the remnant of Israel to an end!"

20 The word of the LORD came to me again: "Son of man, your own relatives, those who have the right to redeem your property, along with the entire house of Israel — all of them — are those to whom the residents of Jerusalem have said, 'You are far from the LORD; this land has been given to us as a possession.'

"Therefore say, 'This is what the Lord GOD says: Though I sent them far away among the nations and scattered them among the countries, yet for a little while I have been a sanctuary for them in the countries where they have gone.'

"Therefore say, 'This is what the Lord GOD says: I will gather you from the peoples and assemble you from the countries where you have been scattered, and I will give you the land of Israel.'

"When they arrive there, they will remove all its abhorrent acts and detestable practices from 30 it. I will give them integrity of heart and put a new spirit within them; I will remove their heart of stone from their bodies and give them a heart of flesh, so that they will follow my statutes, keep my ordinances, and practice them. They will be my people, and I will be their God. But as for those whose hearts pursue their desire for abhorrent acts and detestable practices, I will bring their conduct down on their own heads." This is the declaration of the Lord GOD.

Then the cherubim, with the wheels beside them, lifted their wings, and the glory of the God of Israel was above them. The glory of the LORD rose up from within the city and stopped on the mountain east of the city. The Spirit lifted me up and brought me to Chaldea and to the exiles in a vision from the Spirit of God. After the vision I had seen left me, I spoke to the exiles about all the things the LORD had shown me.

12 The word of the LORD came to me: "Son of man, you are living among a rebellious house. They have eyes to see but do not see, and ears to hear but do not hear, for they are a rebellious house.

"Now you, son of man, get your bags ready for exile and go into exile in their sight during the day. You will go into exile from your place to another place while they watch; perhaps they will understand, though they are a rebellious house. During the day, bring out your bags like an exile's bags while they look on. Then in the evening go out in their sight like those going into exile. As they watch, dig through the wall and take the bags out through it. And while they look on, lift the bags to your shoulder and take them out in the dark; cover your face so that you cannot see the land. For I have made you a sign to the house of Israel."

¹⁰ So I did just as I was commanded. In the daytime I brought out my bags like an exile's bags. In the evening I dug through the wall by hand; I took them out in the dark, carrying them on my shoulder in their sight.

In the morning the word of the LORD came to me: "Son of man, hasn't the house of Israel, that rebellious house, asked you, 'What are you doing?' Say to them, 'This is what the Lord GOD says: This pronouncement concerns the prince in Jerusalem and the whole house of Israel living there.' You are to say, 'I am a sign for you. Just as I have done, it will be done to them; they will go into exile, into captivity.' The prince who is among them will lift his bags to his shoulder in the dark and go out. They will dig through the wall to bring him out through it. He will cover his face so he cannot see the land with his eyes. But I will spread my net over him, and he will be caught in my ²⁰ snare. I will bring him to Babylon, the land of the Chaldeans, yet he will not see it, and he will die there. I will also scatter all the attendants who surround him and all his troops to every direction of the wind, and I will draw a sword to chase after them. They will know that I am the LORD when I disperse them among the nations and scatter them among the countries. But I will spare a few of them from the sword, famine, and plague, so that among the nations where they go they can tell about all their detestable practices. Then they will know that I am the LORD."

The word of the LORD came to me: "Son of man, eat your bread with trembling and drink your water with anxious shaking. Then say to the people of the land, 'This is what the Lord GOD says about the residents of Jerusalem in the land of Israel: They will eat their bread with anxiety and drink their water in dread, for their land will be stripped of everything in it because of the violence ³⁰ of all who live there. The inhabited cities will be destroyed, and the land will become dreadful. Then you will know that I am the LORD.'"

Again the word of the LORD came to me: "Son of man, what is this proverb you people have about the land of Israel, which goes, 'The days keep passing by, and every vision fails'? Therefore say to them, 'This is what the Lord GOD says: I will put a stop to this proverb, and they will not use it again in Israel.' But say to them, 'The days have arrived, as well as the fulfillment of every vision. For there will no longer be any false vision or flattering divination within the house of Israel. But

I, the LORD, will speak whatever message I will speak, and it will be done. It will no longer be delayed. For in your days, rebellious house, I will speak a message and bring it to pass. This is the declaration of the Lord GOD.'"

40

The word of the LORD came to me: "Son of man, notice that the house of Israel is saying, 'The vision that he sees concerns many years from now; he prophesies about distant times.' Therefore say to them, 'This is what the Lord GOD says: None of my words will be delayed any longer. The message I speak will be fulfilled. This is the declaration of the Lord GOD.'"

13 The word of the LORD came to me: "Son of man, prophesy against the prophets of Israel who are prophesying. Say to those who prophesy out of their own imagination, 'Hear the word of the LORD! This is what the Lord GOD says: Woe to the foolish prophets who follow their own spirit and have seen nothing. Your prophets, Israel, are like jackals among ruins. You did not go up to the gaps or restore the wall around the house of Israel so that it might stand in battle on the day of the LORD. They saw false visions and their divinations were a lie. They claimed, "This is the LORD's declaration," when the LORD did not send them, yet they wait for the fulfillment of their message. Didn't you see a false vision and speak a lying divination when you proclaimed, "This is the LORD's declaration," even though I had not spoken?

10

"'Therefore, this is what the Lord GOD says: You have spoken falsely and had lying visions; that's why you discover that I am against you. This is the declaration of the Lord GOD. My hand will be against the prophets who see false visions and speak lying divinations. They will not be present in the council of my people or be recorded in the register of the house of Israel, and they will not enter the land of Israel. Then you will know that I am the Lord GOD.

"'Since they have led my people astray by saying, "Peace," when there is no peace, and since when a flimsy wall is being built, they plaster it with whitewash, therefore, tell those plastering it with whitewash that it will fall. Torrential rain will come, and I will send hailstones plunging down, and a whirlwind will be released. When the wall has fallen, will you not be asked, "Where's the whitewash you plastered on it?"

20

"'So this is what the Lord GOD says: I will release a whirlwind in my wrath. Torrential rain will come in my anger, and hailstones will fall in destructive fury. I will demolish the wall you plastered with whitewash and knock it to the ground so that its foundation is exposed. The city will fall, and you will be destroyed within it. Then you will know that I am the LORD. After I exhaust my wrath against the wall and against those who plaster it with whitewash, I will say to you, "The wall is no more and neither are those who plastered it— those prophets of Israel who prophesied to Jerusalem and saw a vision of peace for her when there was no peace." This is the declaration of the Lord GOD.'

"Now you, son of man, face the women among your people who prophesy out of their own imagination, and prophesy against them. Say, 'This is what the Lord GOD says: Woe to the

30

women who sew magic bands on the wrist of every hand and who make veils for the heads of people of every size in order to ensnare lives. Will you ensnare the lives of my people but preserve your own? You profane me among my people for handfuls of barley and scraps of bread; you put those to death who should not die and spare those who should not live, when you lie to my people, who listen to lies.

"'Therefore, this is what the Lord God says: I am against your magic bands with which you ensnare people like birds, and I will tear them from your arms. I will free the people you have ensnared like birds. I will also tear off your veils and rescue my people from your hands, so that they will no longer be prey in your hands. Then you will know that I am the Lord. Because you have disheartened the righteous person with lies (when I intended no distress), and because you have supported the wicked person so that he does not turn from his evil way to save his life, therefore you will no longer see false visions or practice divination. I will rescue my people from your hands. Then you will know that I am the Lord.'"

14 Some of the elders of Israel came to me and sat down in front of me. Then the word of the Lord came to me: "Son of man, these men have set up idols in their hearts and have put their sinful stumbling blocks in front of themselves. Should I actually let them inquire of me?

"Therefore, speak to them and tell them, 'This is what the Lord God says: When anyone from the house of Israel sets up idols in his heart and puts his sinful stumbling block in front of himself, and then comes to the prophet, I, the Lord, will answer him appropriately. I will answer him according to his many idols, so that I may take hold of the house of Israel by their hearts. They are all estranged from me because of their idols.'

"Therefore, say to the house of Israel, 'This is what the Lord God says: Repent and turn away from your idols; turn your faces away from all your detestable things. For when anyone from the house of Israel or from the aliens who reside in Israel separates himself from me, setting up idols in his heart and putting his sinful stumbling block in front of himself, and then comes to the prophet to inquire of me, I, the Lord, will answer him myself. I will turn against that one and make him a sign and a proverb; I will cut him off from among my people. Then you will know that I am the Lord.

"'But if the prophet is deceived and speaks a message, it was I, the Lord, who deceived that prophet. I will stretch out my hand against him and destroy him from among my people Israel. They will bear their punishment — the punishment of the one who inquires will be the same as that of the prophet— in order that the house of Israel may no longer stray from following me and no longer defile themselves with all their transgressions. Then they will be my people and I will be their God. This is the declaration of the Lord God.'"

The word of the Lord came to me: "Son of man, suppose a land sins against me by acting faithlessly, and I stretch out my hand against it to cut off its supply of bread, to send famine through it, and to wipe out both people and animals from it. Even if these three men — Noah,

Daniel, and Job — were in it, they would rescue only themselves by their righteousness." This is the declaration of the Lord God.

"Suppose I allow dangerous animals to pass through the land and depopulate it so that it becomes desolate, with no one passing through it for fear of the animals. Even if these three men were in it, as I live" — the declaration of the Lord God — "they could not rescue their sons or 30 daughters. They alone would be rescued, but the land would be desolate.

"Or suppose I bring a sword against that land and say, 'Let a sword pass through it,' so that I wipe out both people and animals from it. Even if these three men were in it, as I live" — the declaration of the Lord God — "they could not rescue their sons or daughters, but they alone would be rescued.

"Or suppose I send a plague into that land and pour out my wrath on it with bloodshed to wipe out both people and animals from it. Even if Noah, Daniel, and Job were in it, as I live" — the declaration of the Lord God — "they could not rescue their son or daughter. They would rescue only themselves by their righteousness.

"For this is what the Lord God says: How much worse will it be when I send my four 40 devastating judgments against Jerusalem — sword, famine, dangerous animals, and plague — in order to wipe out both people and animals from it! Even so, there will be survivors left in it, sons and daughters who will be brought out. Indeed, they will come out to you, and you will observe their conduct and actions. Then you will be consoled about the devastation I have brought on Jerusalem, about all I have brought on it. They will bring you consolation when you see their conduct and actions, and you will know that it was not without cause that I have done what I did to it." This is the declaration of the Lord God.

15 Then the word of the Lord came to me: "Son of man, how does the wood of the vine, that branch among the trees of the forest, compare to any other wood? Can wood be taken from it to make something useful? Or can anyone make a peg from it to hang things on? In fact, it is put into the fire as fuel. The fire devours both of its ends, and the middle is charred. Can it be useful for anything? Even when it was whole it could not be made into a useful object. How much less can it ever be made into anything useful when the fire has devoured it and it is charred!"

Therefore, this is what the Lord God says, "Like the wood of the vine among the trees of the forest, which I have given to the fire as fuel, so I will give up the residents of Jerusalem. I will turn against them. They may have escaped from the fire, but it will still consume them. And you will 10 know that I am the Lord when I turn against them. I will make the land desolate because they have acted unfaithfully." This is the declaration of the Lord God.

16 The word of the Lord came to me again: "Son of man, confront Jerusalem with her detestable practices. You are to say, 'This is what the Lord God says to Jerusalem: Your origin and your birth were in the land of the Canaanites. Your father was an Amorite and your mother a Hethite.

As for your birth, your umbilical cord wasn't cut on the day you were born, and you weren't washed clean with water. You were not rubbed with salt or wrapped in cloths. No one cared enough about you to do even one of these things out of compassion for you. But you were thrown out into the open field because you were despised on the day you were born.

"'I passed by you and saw you thrashing around in your blood, and I said to you as you lay in your blood, "Live!" Yes, I said to you as you lay in your blood, "Live!" I made you thrive like plants of the field. You grew up and matured and became very beautiful. Your breasts were formed and your hair grew, but you were stark naked.

"'Then I passed by you and saw you, and you were indeed at the age for love. So I spread the edge of my garment over you and covered your nakedness. I pledged myself to you, entered into a covenant with you — this is the declaration of the Lord God — and you became mine. I washed you with water, rinsed off your blood, and anointed you with oil. I clothed you in embroidered cloth and provided you with fine leather sandals. I also wrapped you in fine linen and covered you with silk. I adorned you with jewelry, putting bracelets on your wrists and a necklace around your neck. I put a ring in your nose, earrings on your ears, and a beautiful crown on your head. So you were adorned with gold and silver, and your clothing was made of fine linen, silk, and embroidered cloth. You ate fine flour, honey, and oil. You became extremely beautiful and attained royalty. Your fame spread among the nations because of your beauty, for it was perfect through my splendor, which I had bestowed on you. This is the declaration of the Lord God.

"'But you trusted in your beauty and acted like a prostitute because of your fame. You lavished your sexual favors on everyone who passed by. Your beauty became his. You took some of your clothing and made colorful high places for yourself, and you engaged in prostitution on them. These places should not have been built, and this should never have happened! You also took your beautiful jewelry made from the gold and silver I had given you, and you made male images so that you could engage in prostitution with them. Then you took your embroidered clothing to cover them and set my oil and incense before them. The food that I gave you — the fine flour, oil, and honey that I fed you — you set it before them as a pleasing aroma. That is what happened. This is the declaration of the Lord God.

"'You even took your sons and daughters you bore to me and sacrificed them to these images as food. Wasn't your prostitution enough? You slaughtered my children and gave them up when you passed them through the fire to the images. In all your detestable practices and acts of prostitution, you did not remember the days of your youth when you were stark naked and thrashing around in your blood.

"'Then after all your evil — Woe, woe to you! — the declaration of the Lord God— you built yourself a mound and made yourself an elevated place in every square. You built your elevated place at the head of every street and turned your beauty into a detestable thing. You spread your legs to everyone who passed by and increased your prostitution. You engaged in promiscuous acts with Egyptian men, your well-endowed neighbors, and increased your prostitution to anger me.

"'Therefore, I stretched out my hand against you and reduced your provisions. I gave you over to the desire of those who hate you, the Philistine women, who were embarrassed by your indecent conduct. Then you engaged in prostitution with the Assyrian men because you were not satisfied. Even though you did this with them, you were still not satisfied. So you extended your prostitution to Chaldea, the land of merchants, but you were not even satisfied with this!

"'How your heart was inflamed with lust — the declaration of the Lord God — when you did all these things, the acts of a brazen prostitute, building your mound at the head of every street and making your elevated place in every square. But you were unlike a prostitute because you scorned payment. You adulterous wife, who receives strangers instead of her husband! Men give gifts to all prostitutes, but you gave gifts to all your lovers. You bribed them to come to you from all around for your sexual favors. So you were the opposite of other women in your acts of prostitution; no one solicited you. When you paid a fee instead of one being paid to you, you were the opposite.

"'Therefore, you prostitute, hear the word of the Lord! This is what the Lord God says: Because your lust was poured out and your nakedness exposed by your acts of prostitution with your lovers, and because of all your detestable idols and the blood of your children that you gave to them, I am therefore going to gather all the lovers you pleased — all those you loved as well as all those you hated. I will gather them against you from all around and expose your nakedness to them so they see you completely naked. I will judge you the way adulteresses and those who shed blood are judged. Then I will bring about the shedding of your blood in jealous wrath. I will hand you over to them, and they will demolish your mounds and tear down your elevated places. They will strip off your clothes, take your beautiful jewelry, and leave you stark naked. They will bring a mob against you to stone you and to cut you to pieces with their swords. They will burn your houses and execute judgments against you in the sight of many women. I will stop you from being a prostitute, and you will never again pay fees for lovers. So I will satisfy my wrath against you, and my jealousy will turn away from you. Then I will be calm and no longer angry. Because you did not remember the days of your youth but enraged me with all these things, I will also bring your conduct down on your own head. This is the declaration of the Lord God. Haven't you committed depravity in addition to all your detestable practices?

"'Look, everyone who uses proverbs will quote this proverb about you: "Like mother, like daughter." You are the daughter of your mother, who despised her husband and children. You are the sister of your sisters, who despised their husbands and children. Your mother was a Hethite and your father an Amorite. Your older sister was Samaria, who lived with her daughters to the north of you, and your younger sister was Sodom, who lived with her daughters to the south of you. Didn't you walk in their ways and do their detestable practices? It was only a short time before all your ways were more corrupt than theirs.

"'As I live — the declaration of the Lord God — your sister Sodom and her daughters have not behaved as you and your daughters have. Now this was the iniquity of your sister Sodom: She and

80 her daughters had pride, plenty of food, and comfortable security, but didn't support the poor and needy. They were haughty and did detestable acts before me, so I removed them when I saw this. But Samaria did not commit even half your sins. You have multiplied your detestable practices beyond theirs and made your sisters appear righteous by all the detestable acts you have committed. You must also bear your disgrace, since you have helped your sisters out. For they appear more righteous than you because of your sins, which you committed more detestably than they did. So you also, be ashamed and bear your disgrace, since you have made your sisters appear righteous.

"'I will restore their fortunes, the fortunes of Sodom and her daughters and those of Samaria and her daughters. I will also restore your fortunes among them, so you will bear your disgrace and be ashamed of all you did when you comforted them. As for your sisters, Sodom and

90 her daughters and Samaria and her daughters will return to their former state. You and your daughters will also return to your former state. Didn't you treat your sister Sodom as an object of scorn when you were proud, before your wickedness was exposed? It was like the time you were scorned by the daughters of Aram and all those around her, and by the daughters of the Philistines — those who treated you with contempt from every side. You yourself must bear the consequences of your depravity and detestable practices — this is the LORD's declaration.

"'For this is what the Lord GOD says: I will deal with you according to what you have done, since you have despised the oath by breaking the covenant. But I will remember the covenant I made with you in the days of your youth, and I will establish a permanent covenant with you. Then you will remember your ways and be ashamed when you receive your older and younger

100 sisters. I will give them to you as daughters, but not because of your covenant. I will establish my covenant with you, and you will know that I am the LORD, so that when I make atonement for all you have done, you will remember and be ashamed, and never open your mouth again because of your disgrace. This is the declaration of the Lord GOD.'"

17 The word of the LORD came to me: "Son of man, pose a riddle and speak a parable to the house of Israel. You are to say, 'This is what the Lord GOD says: A huge eagle with powerful wings, long feathers, and full plumage of many colors came to Lebanon and took the top of the cedar. He plucked off its topmost shoot, brought it to the land of merchants, and set it in a city of traders. Then he took some of the land's seed and put it in a fertile field; he set it like a willow, a plant by abundant water. It sprouted and became a spreading vine, low in height with its branches turned toward him, yet its roots stayed under it. So it became a vine, produced branches, and sent out shoots.

"'But there was another huge eagle with powerful wings and thick plumage. And this vine bent its roots toward him! It stretched out its branches to him from the plot where it was planted, so

10 that he might water it. It had been planted in a good field by abundant water in order to produce branches, bear fruit, and become a splendid vine.'

"You are to say, 'This is what the Lord GOD says: Will it flourish? Will he not tear out its roots and strip off its fruit so that it shrivels? All its fresh leaves will wither! Great strength and many people will not be needed to pull it from its roots. Even though it is planted, will it flourish? Won't it wither completely when the east wind strikes it? It will wither on the plot where it sprouted.'"

The word of the LORD came to me: "Now say to that rebellious house, 'Don't you know what these things mean?' Tell them, 'The king of Babylon came to Jerusalem, took its king and officials, and brought them back with him to Babylon. He took one of the royal family and made a covenant with him, putting him under oath. Then he took away the leading men of the land, so that the kingdom would be humble and not exalt itself but would keep his covenant in order to endure. However, this king revolted against him by sending his ambassadors to Egypt so they might give him horses and a large army. Will he flourish? Will the one who does such things escape? Can he break a covenant and still escape?

"'As I live — this is the declaration of the Lord GOD — he will die in Babylon, in the land of the king who put him on the throne, whose oath he despised and whose covenant he broke. Pharaoh with his mighty army and vast company will not help him in battle, when ramps are built and siege walls constructed to destroy many lives. He despised the oath by breaking the covenant. He did all these things even though he gave his hand in pledge. He will not escape!

"'Therefore, this is what the Lord GOD says: As I live, I will bring down on his head my oath that he despised and my covenant that he broke. I will spread my net over him, and he will be caught in my snare. I will bring him to Babylon and execute judgment on him there for the treachery he committed against me. All the fugitives among his troops will fall by the sword, and those who survive will be scattered to every direction of the wind. Then you will know that I, the LORD, have spoken.

"'This is what the Lord GOD says:

> I will take a sprig
> from the lofty top of the cedar and plant it.
> I will pluck a tender sprig
> from its topmost shoots,
> and I will plant it
> on a high towering mountain.
> I will plant it on Israel's high mountain
> so that it may bear branches, produce fruit,
> and become a majestic cedar.
> Birds of every kind will nest under it,
> taking shelter in the shade of its branches.
> Then all the trees of the field will know
> that I am the LORD.
> I bring down the tall tree,
> and make the low tree tall.
> I cause the green tree to wither

and make the withered tree thrive.
I, the LORD, have spoken
and I will do it.'"

18 The word of the LORD came to me: "What do you mean by using this proverb concerning the land of Israel:

'The fathers eat sour grapes,
and the children's teeth are set on edge'?

As I live" — this is the declaration of the Lord GOD — "you will no longer use this proverb in Israel. Look, every life belongs to me. The life of the father is like the life of the son — both belong to me. The person who sins is the one who will die.

"Suppose a man is righteous and does what is just and right: He does not eat at the mountain shrines or look to the idols of the house of Israel. He does not defile his neighbor's wife or approach
10 a woman during her menstrual impurity. He doesn't oppress anyone but returns his collateral to the debtor. He does not commit robbery, but gives his bread to the hungry and covers the naked with clothing. He doesn't lend at interest or for profit but keeps his hand from injustice and carries out true justice between men. He follows my statutes and keeps my ordinances, acting faithfully. Such a person is righteous; he will certainly live." This is the declaration of the Lord GOD.

"But suppose the man has a violent son, who sheds blood and does any of these things, though the father has done none of them. Indeed, when the son eats at the mountain shrines and defiles his neighbor's wife, and when he oppresses the poor and needy, commits robbery, and does not return collateral, and when he looks to the idols, commits detestable acts, and lends at interest or for profit, will he live? He will not live! Since he has committed all these detestable acts, he will
20 certainly die. His death will be his own fault.

"Now suppose he has a son who sees all the sins his father has committed, and though he sees them, he does not do likewise. He does not eat at the mountain shrines or look to the idols of the house of Israel. He does not defile his neighbor's wife. He doesn't oppress anyone, hold collateral, or commit robbery. He gives his bread to the hungry and covers the naked with clothing. He keeps his hand from harming the poor, not taking interest or profit on a loan. He practices my ordinances and follows my statutes. Such a person will not die for his father's iniquity. He will certainly live.

"As for his father, he will die for his own iniquity because he practiced fraud, robbed his brother, and did among his people what was not good. But you may ask, 'Why doesn't the son
30 suffer punishment for the father's iniquity?' Since the son has done what is just and right, carefully observing all my statutes, he will certainly live. The person who sins is the one who will die. A son won't suffer punishment for the father's iniquity, and a father won't suffer punishment for the son's iniquity. The righteousness of the righteous person will be on him, and the wickedness of the wicked person will be on him.

"But if the wicked person turns from all the sins he has committed, keeps all my statutes, and does what is just and right, he will certainly live; he will not die. None of the transgressions he has committed will be held against him. He will live because of the righteousness he has practiced. Do I take any pleasure in the death of the wicked?" This is the declaration of the Lord God. "Instead, don't I take pleasure when he turns from his ways and lives? But when a righteous person turns
40 from his righteousness and acts unjustly, committing the same detestable acts that the wicked do, will he live? None of the righteous acts he did will be remembered. He will die because of the treachery he has engaged in and the sin he has committed.

"But you say, 'The Lord's way isn't fair.' Now listen, house of Israel: Is it my way that is unfair? Instead, isn't it your ways that are unfair? When a righteous person turns from his righteousness and acts unjustly, he will die for this. He will die because of the injustice he has committed. But if a wicked person turns from the wickedness he has committed and does what is just and right, he will preserve his life. He will certainly live because he thought it over and turned from all the transgressions he had committed; he will not die. But the house of Israel says, 'The Lord's way isn't fair.' Is it my ways that are unfair, house of Israel? Instead, isn't it your ways that are unfair?

50 "Therefore, house of Israel, I will judge each one of you according to his ways." This is the declaration of the Lord God. "Repent and turn from all your rebellious acts, so they will not become a sinful stumbling block to you. Throw off all the transgressions you have committed, and get yourselves a new heart and a new spirit. Why should you die, house of Israel? For I take no pleasure in anyone's death." This is the declaration of the Lord God. "So repent and live!

19 "As for you, take up a lament for the princes of Israel, and say:
> What was your mother? A lioness!
> She lay down among the lions;
> she reared her cubs among the young lions.
> She brought up one of her cubs,
> and he became a young lion.
> After he learned to tear prey,
> he devoured people.
> When the nations heard about him,
10 > he was caught in their pit.
> Then they led him away with hooks
> to the land of Egypt.
>
> When she saw that she waited in vain,
> that her hope was lost,
> she took another of her cubs
> and made him a young lion.

He prowled among the lions,
and he became a young lion.
After he learned to tear prey,
20   he devoured people.
He devastated their strongholds
and destroyed their cities.
The land and everything in it shuddered
at the sound of his roaring.
Then the nations from the surrounding provinces
set out against him.
They spread their net over him;
he was caught in their pit.
They put a wooden yoke on him with hooks
30   and led him away to the king of Babylon.
They brought him into the fortresses
so his roar could no longer be heard
on the mountains of Israel.

Your mother was like a vine in your vineyard,
planted by the water;
it was fruitful and full of branches
because of abundant water.
It had strong branches, fit for the scepters of rulers;
its height towered among the clouds.
40   So it was conspicuous for its height
as well as its many branches.
But it was uprooted in fury,
thrown to the ground,
and the east wind dried up its fruit.
Its strong branches were torn off and dried up;
fire consumed them.
Now it is planted in the wilderness,
in a dry and thirsty land.
Fire has gone out from its main branch
50   and has devoured its fruit,
so that it no longer has a strong branch,
a scepter for ruling.
This is a lament and should be used as a lament."

20 In the seventh year, in the fifth month, on the tenth day of the month, some of Israel's elders came to inquire of the Lord, and they sat down in front of me. Then the word of the Lord came to me: "Son of man, speak with the elders of Israel and tell them, 'This is what the Lord God says: Are you coming to inquire of me? As I live, I will not let you inquire of me. This is the declaration of the Lord God.'

"Will you pass judgment against them, will you pass judgment, son of man? Explain the detestable practices of their ancestors to them. Say to them, 'This is what the Lord God says: On the day I chose Israel, I swore an oath to the descendants of Jacob's house and made myself known to them in the land of Egypt. I swore to them, saying, "I am the Lord your God." On that day I swore to them that I would bring them out of the land of Egypt into a land I had searched out

10 for them, a land flowing with milk and honey, the most beautiful of all lands. I also said to them, "Throw away, each of you, the abhorrent things that you prize, and do not defile yourselves with the idols of Egypt. I am the Lord your God."

"'But they rebelled against me and were unwilling to listen to me. None of them threw away the abhorrent things that they prized, and they did not abandon the idols of Egypt. So I considered pouring out my wrath on them, exhausting my anger against them within the land of Egypt. But I acted for the sake of my name, so that it would not be profaned in the eyes of the nations they were living among, in whose sight I had made myself known to Israel by bringing them out of Egypt.

"'So I brought them out of the land of Egypt and led them into the wilderness. Then I gave

20 them my statutes and explained my ordinances to them — the person who does them will live by them. I also gave them my Sabbaths to serve as a sign between me and them, so that they would know that I am the Lord who consecrates them.

"'But the house of Israel rebelled against me in the wilderness. They did not follow my statutes and they rejected my ordinances — the person who does them will live by them. They also completely profaned my Sabbaths. So I considered pouring out my wrath on them in the wilderness to put an end to them. But I acted for the sake of my name, so that it would not be profaned in the eyes of the nations in whose sight I had brought them out. However, I swore to them in the wilderness that I would not bring them into the land I had given them — the most beautiful of all lands, flowing with milk and honey— because they rejected my ordinances,

30 profaned my Sabbaths, and did not follow my statutes. For their hearts went after their idols. Yet I spared them from destruction and did not bring them to an end in the wilderness.

"'Then I said to their children in the wilderness, "Don't follow the statutes of your fathers, defile yourselves with their idols, or keep their ordinances. I am the Lord your God. Follow my statutes, keep my ordinances, and practice them. Keep my Sabbaths holy, and they will be a sign between me and you, so you may know that I am the Lord your God."

"'But the children rebelled against me. They did not follow my statutes or carefully keep my ordinances — the person who does them will live by them. They also profaned my Sabbaths. So I considered pouring out my wrath on them and exhausting my anger against them in the

wilderness. But I withheld my hand and acted for the sake of my name, so that it would not
be profaned in the eyes of the nations in whose sight I brought them out. However, I swore to
them in the wilderness that I would disperse them among the nations and scatter them among
the countries. For they did not practice my ordinances but rejected my statutes and profaned
my Sabbaths, and their eyes were fixed on their fathers' idols. I also gave them statutes that were
not good and ordinances they could not live by. When they sacrificed every firstborn in the fire,
I defiled them through their gifts in order to devastate them so they would know that I am the
Lord.'

"Therefore, son of man, speak to the house of Israel, and tell them, 'This is what the Lord God
says: In this way also your ancestors blasphemed me by committing treachery against me: When
I brought them into the land that I swore to give them and they saw any high hill or leafy tree,
they offered their sacrifices and presented their offensive offerings there. They also sent up their
pleasing aromas and poured out their drink offerings there. So I asked them, "What is this high
place you are going to?" And it is still called Bamah today.'

"Therefore say to the house of Israel, 'This is what the Lord God says: Are you defiling
yourselves the way your ancestors did, and prostituting yourselves with their abhorrent things?
When you offer your gifts, sacrificing your children in the fire, you still continue to defile
yourselves with all your idols today. So should I let you inquire of me, house of Israel? As I live —
this is the declaration of the Lord God — I will not let you inquire of me!

"'When you say, "Let's be like the nations, like the clans of other countries, serving wood and
stone," what you have in mind will never happen. As I live — the declaration of the Lord God —
I will reign over you with a strong hand, an outstretched arm, and outpoured wrath. I will bring
you from the peoples and gather you from the countries where you were scattered, with a strong
hand, an outstretched arm, and outpoured wrath. I will lead you into the wilderness of the peoples
and enter into judgment with you there face to face. Just as I entered into judgment with your
ancestors in the wilderness of the land of Egypt, so I will enter into judgment with you. This is the
declaration of the Lord God. I will make you pass under the rod and will bring you into the bond
of the covenant. I will purge you of those who rebel and transgress against me. I will bring them
out of the land where they live as foreign residents, but they will not enter the land of Israel. Then
you will know that I am the Lord.

"'As for you, house of Israel, this is what the Lord God says: Go and serve your idols, each of
you. But afterward you will surely listen to me, and you will no longer defile my holy name with
your gifts and idols. For on my holy mountain, Israel's high mountain — the declaration of the
Lord God — there the entire house of Israel, all of them, will serve me in the land. There I will
accept them and will require your contributions and choicest gifts, all your holy offerings. When
I bring you from the peoples and gather you from the countries where you have been scattered, I
will accept you as a pleasing aroma. And I will demonstrate my holiness through you in the sight

of the nations. When I lead you into the land of Israel, the land I swore to give your ancestors, you will know that I am the LORD. There you will remember your ways and all your deeds by which you have defiled yourself, and you will loathe yourselves for all the evil things you have done. You will know that I am the LORD, house of Israel, when I have dealt with you for the sake of my name 80 rather than according to your evil ways and corrupt acts. This is the declaration of the Lord GOD.'"

The word of the LORD came to me: "Son of man, face the south and preach against it. Prophesy against the forest land in the Negev, and say to the forest there, 'Hear the word of the LORD! This is what the Lord GOD says: I am about to ignite a fire in you, and it will devour every green tree and every dry tree in you. The blazing flame will not be extinguished, and every face from the south to the north will be scorched by it. Then all humanity will see that I, the LORD, have kindled it. It will not be extinguished.'"

Then I said, "Oh, Lord GOD, they are saying of me, 'Isn't he just composing parables?'"

21 The word of the LORD came to me again: "Son of man, face Jerusalem and preach against the sanctuaries. Prophesy against the land of Israel, and say to it, 'This is what the LORD says: I am against you. I will draw my sword from its sheath and cut off from you both the righteous and the wicked. Since I will cut off both the righteous and the wicked, my sword will therefore come out of its sheath against all humanity from the south to the north. So all humanity will know that I, the LORD, have taken my sword from its sheath — it will not be sheathed again.'

"But you, son of man, groan! Groan bitterly with a broken heart right before their eyes. And when they ask you, 'Why are you groaning?' then say, 'Because of the news that is coming. Every heart will melt, and every hand will become weak. Every spirit will be discouraged, and all knees 10 will run with urine. Yes, it is coming and it will happen. This is the declaration of the Lord GOD.'"

The word of the LORD came to me: "Son of man, prophesy, 'This is what the Lord says!' You are to proclaim,

'A sword! A sword is sharpened
and also polished.
It is sharpened for slaughter,
polished to flash like lightning!
Should we rejoice?
The scepter of my son,
the sword despises every tree.
20 The sword is given to be polished,
to be grasped in the hand.
It is sharpened, and it is polished,
to be put in the hand of the slayer.'

"Cry out and wail, son of man, for it is against my people. It is against all the princes of Israel! They are given over to the sword with my people. Therefore strike your thigh in grief. Surely it will be a trial! And what if the sword despises even the scepter? The scepter will not continue." This is the declaration of the Lord GOD.

"So you, son of man, prophesy and clap your hands together:

> Let the sword strike two times, even three.
> It is a sword for massacre,
> a sword for great massacre—
> it surrounds them!
> I have appointed a sword for slaughter
> at all their gates,
> so that their hearts may melt
> and many may stumble.
> Yes! It is ready to flash like lightning;
> it is drawn for slaughter.
> Slash to the right;
> turn to the left—
> wherever your blade is directed.

I also will clap my hands together, and I will satisfy my wrath. I, the LORD, have spoken."

The word of the LORD came to me: "Now you, son of man, mark out two roads that the sword of Babylon's king can take. Both of them should originate from the same land. And make a signpost at the fork in the road to each city. Mark out a road that the sword can take to Rabbah of the Ammonites and to Judah into fortified Jerusalem. For the king of Babylon stands at the split in the road, at the fork of the two roads, to practice divination: he shakes the arrows, consults the idols, and observes the liver. The answer marked Jerusalem appears in his right hand, indicating that he should set up battering rams, give the order to slaughter, raise a battle cry, set battering rams against the gates, build a ramp, and construct a siege wall. It will seem like false divination to those who have sworn an oath to the Babylonians, but it will draw attention to their guilt so that they will be captured.

"Therefore, this is what the Lord GOD says: Because you have drawn attention to your guilt, exposing your transgressions, so that your sins are revealed in all your actions — since you have done this, you will be captured by them. And you, profane and wicked prince of Israel, the day has come for your punishment.

"This is what the Lord GOD says:

> Remove the turban, and take off the crown.
> Things will not remain as they are;
> exalt the lowly and bring down the exalted.

A ruin, a ruin,
I will make it a ruin!
Yet this will not happen
until he comes;
I have given the judgment to him.

"Now you, son of man, prophesy, and say, 'This is what the Lord God says concerning the Ammonites and their contempt.' You are to proclaim,

'A sword! A sword
is drawn for slaughter,
70   polished to consume, to flash like lightning.
While they offer false visions
and lying divinations about you,
the time has come to put you
to the necks of the profane wicked ones;
the day has come
for final punishment.

"'Return it to its sheath!
"'I will judge you
in the place where you were created,
80   in the land of your origin.
I will pour out my indignation on you;
I will blow the fire of my fury on you.
I will hand you over to brutal men,
skilled at destruction.
You will be fuel for the fire.
Your blood will be spilled within the land.
You will not be remembered,
for I, the Lord, have spoken.'"

22 The word of the Lord came to me: "As for you, son of man, will you pass judgment? Will you pass judgment against the city of blood? Then explain all her detestable practices to her. You are to say, 'This is what the Lord God says: A city that sheds blood within her walls so that her time of judgment has come and who makes idols for herself so that she is defiled! You are guilty of the blood you have shed, and you are defiled from the idols you have made. You have brought your judgment days near and have come to your years of punishment. Therefore, I have made you a disgrace to the nations and a mockery to all the lands. Those who are near and those far away from you will mock you, you infamous one full of turmoil.

"'Look, every prince of Israel within you has used his strength to shed blood. Father and mother are treated with contempt, and the resident alien is exploited within you. The fatherless and widow are oppressed in you. You despise my holy things and profane my Sabbaths. There are men within you who slander in order to shed blood. People who live in you eat at the mountain shrines; they commit depraved acts within you. Men within you have sexual intercourse with their father's wife and violate women during their menstrual impurity. One man within you commits a detestable act with his neighbor's wife; another defiles his daughter-in-law with depravity; and yet another violates his sister, his father's daughter. People who live in you accept bribes in order to shed blood. You take interest and profit on a loan and brutally extort your neighbors. You have forgotten me. This is the declaration of the Lord God.

"'Now look, I clap my hands together against the dishonest profit you have made and against the blood shed among you. Will your courage endure or your hands be strong in the days when I deal with you? I, the Lord, have spoken, and I will act. I will disperse you among the nations and scatter you among the countries; I will purge your uncleanness. You will be profaned in the sight of the nations. Then you will know that I am the Lord.'"

The word of the Lord came to me: "Son of man, the house of Israel has become merely dross to me. All of them are copper, tin, iron, and lead inside the furnace; they are just dross from silver. Therefore, this is what the Lord God says: Because all of you have become dross, I am about to gather you into Jerusalem. Just as one gathers silver, copper, iron, lead, and tin into the furnace to blow fire on them and melt them, so I will gather you in my anger and wrath, put you inside, and melt you. Yes, I will gather you together and blow on you with the fire of my fury, and you will be melted within the city. As silver is melted inside a furnace, so you will be melted inside the city. Then you will know that I, the Lord, have poured out my wrath on you."

The word of the Lord came to me: "Son of man, say to her, 'You are a land that has not been cleansed, that has not received rain in the day of indignation.' The conspiracy of her prophets within her is like a roaring lion tearing its prey: they devour people, seize wealth and valuables, and multiply the widows within her. Her priests do violence to my instruction and profane my holy things. They make no distinction between the holy and the common, and they do not explain the difference between the clean and the unclean. They close their eyes to my Sabbaths, and I am profaned among them.

"Her officials within her are like wolves tearing their prey, shedding blood, and destroying lives in order to make profit dishonestly. Her prophets plaster for them with whitewash by seeing false visions and lying divinations, saying, 'This is what the Lord God says,' when the Lord has not spoken. The people of the land have practiced extortion and committed robbery. They have oppressed the poor and needy and unlawfully exploited the resident alien. I searched for a man among them who would repair the wall and stand in the gap before me on behalf of the land so that I might not destroy it, but I found no one. So I have poured out my indignation on them and consumed them with the fire of my fury. I have brought their conduct down on their own heads." This is the declaration of the Lord God.

23 The word of the Lord came to me again: "Son of man, there were two women, daughters of the same mother, who acted like prostitutes in Egypt, behaving promiscuously in their youth. Their breasts were fondled there, and their virgin nipples caressed. The older one was named Oholah, and her sister was Oholibah. They became mine and gave birth to sons and daughters. As for their names, Oholah represents Samaria and Oholibah represents Jerusalem.

"Oholah acted like a prostitute even though she was mine. She lusted after her lovers, the Assyrians: warriors dressed in blue, governors and prefects, all of them desirable young men, horsemen riding on steeds. She offered her sexual favors to them; all of them were the elite of Assyria. She defiled herself with all those she lusted after and with all their idols. She didn't give

10 up her promiscuity that began in Egypt, when men slept with her in her youth, caressed her virgin nipples, and poured out their lust on her. Therefore, I handed her over to her lovers, the Assyrians she lusted for. They exposed her nakedness, seized her sons and daughters, and killed her with the sword. Since they executed judgment against her, she became notorious among women.

"Now her sister Oholibah saw this, but she was even more depraved in her lust than Oholah, and made her promiscuous acts worse than those of her sister. She lusted after the Assyrians: governors and prefects, warriors splendidly dressed, horsemen riding on steeds, all of them desirable young men. And I saw that she had defiled herself; both of them had taken the same path. But she increased her promiscuity when she saw male figures carved on the wall, images of the Chaldeans, engraved in bright red, wearing belts on their waists and flowing turbans

20 on their heads; all of them looked like officers, a depiction of the Babylonians in Chaldea, their native land. At the sight of them she lusted after them and sent messengers to them in Chaldea. Then the Babylonians came to her, to the bed of love, and defiled her with their lust. But after she was defiled by them, she turned away from them in disgust. When she flaunted her promiscuity and exposed her nakedness, I turned away from her in disgust just as I turned away from her sister. Yet she multiplied her acts of promiscuity, remembering the days of her youth when she acted like a prostitute in the land of Egypt and lusted after their lovers, whose sexual members were like those of donkeys and whose emission was like that of stallions. So you revisited the depravity of your youth, when the Egyptians caressed your nipples to enjoy your youthful breasts.

30 "Therefore, Oholibah, this is what the Lord God says: I am going to incite your lovers against you, those you turned away from in disgust. I will bring them against you from every side: the Babylonians and all the Chaldeans; Pekod, Shoa, and Koa; and all the Assyrians with them — desirable young men, all of them governors and prefects, officers and administrators, all of them riding on steeds. They will come against you with an assembly of peoples and with weapons,

chariots, and wagons. They will set themselves against you on every side with large and small shields and helmets. I will delegate judgment to them, and they will judge you by their own standards. When I vent my jealous fury on you, they will deal with you in wrath. They will cut off your nose and ears, and the rest of you will fall by the sword. They will seize your sons and daughters, and the rest of you will be consumed by fire. They will strip off your clothes and take

40   your beautiful jewelry. So I will put an end to your depravity and sexual immorality, which began in the land of Egypt, and you will not look longingly at them or remember Egypt anymore.

"For this is what the Lord God says: I am going to hand you over to those you hate, to those you turned away from in disgust. They will treat you with hatred, take all you have worked for, and leave you stark naked, so that the shame of your debauchery will be exposed, both your depravity and promiscuity. These things will be done to you because you acted like a prostitute with the nations, defiling yourself with their idols. You have followed the path of your sister, so I will put her cup in your hand."

This is what the Lord God says:

> "You will drink your sister's cup,
50   which is deep and wide.
> You will be an object of ridicule and scorn,
> for it holds so much.
> You will be filled with drunkenness and grief,
> with a cup of devastation and desolation,
> the cup of your sister Samaria.
> You will drink it and drain it;
> then you will gnaw its broken pieces,
> and tear your breasts.
> For I have spoken."
60   This is the declaration of the Lord God.

Therefore, this is what the Lord God says: "Because you have forgotten me and cast me behind your back, you must bear the consequences of your indecency and promiscuity."

Then the Lord said to me, "Son of man, will you pass judgment against Oholah and Oholibah? Then declare their detestable practices to them. For they have committed adultery, and blood is on their hands; they have committed adultery with their idols. And the children they bore to me they have sacrificed in the fire as food for the idols. They also did this to me: they defiled my sanctuary on that same day and profaned my Sabbaths. On the same day they slaughtered their children for their idols, they entered my sanctuary to profane it. Yes, that is what they did inside my house.

70   "In addition, they sent for men who came from far away when a messenger was dispatched to them. And look how they came! You bathed, painted your eyes, and adorned yourself with jewelry

for them. You sat on a luxurious couch with a table spread before it, on which you had set my incense and oil. The sound of a carefree crowd was there. Drunkards from the desert were brought in, along with common men. They put bracelets on the women's hands and beautiful tiaras on their heads. Then I said concerning this woman worn out by adultery: Will they now have illicit sex with her, even her? Yet they had sex with her as one does with a prostitute. This is how they had sex with Oholah and Oholibah, those depraved women. But righteous men will judge them the way adulteresses and those who shed blood are judged, for they are adulteresses and blood is on their hands.

80   "This is what the Lord God says: Summon an assembly against them and consign them to terror and plunder. The assembly will stone them and cut them down with their swords. They will kill their sons and daughters and burn their houses. So I will put an end to depravity in the land, and all the women will be admonished not to imitate your depraved behavior. They will punish you for your depravity, and you will bear the consequences for your sins of idolatry. Then you will know that I am the Lord God."

24   The word of the Lord came to me in the ninth year, in the tenth month, on the tenth day of the month: "Son of man, write down today's date, this very day. The king of Babylon has laid siege to Jerusalem this very day. Now speak a parable to the rebellious house. Tell them, 'This is what the Lord God says:

> Put the pot on the fire—
> put it on,
> and then pour water into it!
> Place the pieces of meat in it,
> every good piece—
10   thigh and shoulder.
> Fill it with choice bones.
> Take the choicest of the flock
> and also pile up the fuel under it.
> Bring it to a boil
> and cook the bones in it.

"'Therefore, this is what the Lord God says:

> Woe to the city of bloodshed,
> the pot that has corrosion inside it,
> and its corrosion has not come out of it!
20   Empty it piece by piece;
> lots should not be cast for its contents.
> For the blood she shed is still within her.

She put it out on the bare rock;
she didn't pour it on the ground
to cover it with dust.
In order to stir up wrath and take vengeance,
I have put her blood on the bare rock,
so that it would not be covered.

""Therefore, this is what the Lord God says:
30   Woe to the city of bloodshed!
I myself will make the pile of kindling large.
Pile on the logs and kindle the fire!
Cook the meat well
and mix in the spices!
Let the bones be burned!
Set the empty pot on its coals
so that it becomes hot and its copper glows.
Then its impurity will melt inside it;
its corrosion will be consumed.
40   It has frustrated every effort;
its thick corrosion will not come off.
Into the fire with its corrosion!
Because of the depravity of your uncleanness—
since I tried to purify you,
but you would not be purified from your uncleanness—
you will not be pure again
until I have satisfied my wrath on you.
I, the Lord, have spoken.
It is coming, and I will do it!
50   I will not refrain, I will not show pity,
and I will not relent.
I will judge you
according to your ways and deeds.
This is the declaration of the Lord God.'"

Then the word of the Lord came to me: "Son of man, I am about to take the delight of your eyes away from you with a fatal blow. But you must not lament or weep or let your tears flow. Groan quietly; do not observe mourning rites for the dead. Put on your turban and strap your sandals on your feet; do not cover your mustache or eat the bread of mourners."

I spoke to the people in the morning, and my wife died in the evening. The next morning I did
just as I was commanded. Then the people asked me, "Won't you tell us what these things you are
doing mean for us?"

So I answered them, "The word of the LORD came to me: Say to the house of Israel, 'This
is what the Lord GOD says: I am about to desecrate my sanctuary, the pride of your power, the
delight of your eyes, and the desire of your heart. Also, the sons and daughters you left behind
will fall by the sword. Then you will do just as I have done: You will not cover your mustache or
eat the bread of mourners. Your turbans will remain on your heads and your sandals on your feet.
You will not lament or weep but will waste away because of your iniquities and will groan to one
another. Now Ezekiel will be a sign for you. You will do everything that he has done. When this
happens, you will know that I am the Lord GOD.'

"As for you, son of man, know that on that day I will take from them their stronghold — their
pride and joy, the delight of their eyes, and the longing of their hearts — as well as their sons and
daughters. On that day a fugitive will come to you and report the news. On that day your mouth
will be opened to talk with him; you will speak and no longer be mute. So you will be a sign for
them, and they will know that I am the LORD."

25 Then the word of the LORD came to me: "Son of man, face the Ammonites and prophesy against
them. Say to the Ammonites, 'Hear the word of the Lord GOD: This is what the Lord GOD says:
Because you said, "Aha!" about my sanctuary when it was desecrated, about the land of Israel
when it was laid waste, and about the house of Judah when they went into exile, therefore I am
about to give you to the people of the east as a possession. They will set up their encampments and
pitch their tents among you. They will eat your fruit and drink your milk. I will make Rabbah a
pasture for camels and Ammon a resting place for sheep. Then you will know that I am the LORD.

"'For this is what the Lord GOD says: Because you clapped your hands, stamped your feet, and
rejoiced over the land of Israel with wholehearted contempt, therefore I am about to stretch out
my hand against you and give you as plunder to the nations. I will cut you off from the peoples and
eliminate you from the countries. I will destroy you, and you will know that I am the LORD.

"'This is what the Lord GOD says: Because Moab and Seir said, "Look, the house of Judah is like
all the other nations." Therefore I am about to expose Moab's flank beginning with its frontier
cities, the splendor of the land: Beth-jeshimoth, Baal-meon, and Kiriathaim. I will give it along with
Ammon to the people of the east as a possession, so that Ammon will not be remembered among
the nations. So I will execute judgments against Moab, and they will know that I am the LORD.

"'This is what the Lord GOD says: Because Edom acted vengefully against the house of Judah and
incurred grievous guilt by taking revenge on them, therefore this is what the Lord GOD says: I will

stretch out my hand against Edom and cut off both people and animals from it. I will make it a

20 wasteland; they will fall by the sword from Teman to Dedan. I will take my vengeance on Edom through my people Israel, and they will deal with Edom according to my anger and wrath. So they will know my vengeance. This is the declaration of the Lord God.

"'This is what the Lord God says: Because the Philistines acted in vengeance and took revenge with deep contempt, destroying because of their perpetual hatred, therefore this is what the Lord God says: I am about to stretch out my hand against the Philistines, cutting off the Cherethites and wiping out what remains of the coastal peoples. I will execute severe vengeance against them with furious rebukes. They will know that I am the Lord when I take my vengeance on them.'"

26 In the eleventh year, on the first day of the month, the word of the Lord came to me: "Son of man, because Tyre said about Jerusalem, 'Aha! The gateway to the peoples is shattered. She has been turned over to me. I will be filled now that she lies in ruins,' therefore this is what the Lord God says: See, I am against you, Tyre! I will raise up many nations against you, just as the sea raises its waves. They will destroy the walls of Tyre and demolish her towers. I will scrape the soil from her and turn her into a bare rock. She will become a place in the sea to spread nets, for I have spoken." This is the declaration of the Lord God. "She will become plunder for the nations, and her villages on the mainland will be slaughtered by the sword. Then they will know that I am the Lord."

For this is what the Lord God says: "See, I am about to bring King Nebuchadnezzar of

10 Babylon, king of kings, against Tyre from the north with horses, chariots, cavalry, and a huge assembly of troops. He will slaughter your villages on the mainland with the sword. He will set up siege works, build a ramp, and raise a wall of shields against you. He will direct the blows of his battering rams against your walls and tear down your towers with his iron tools. His horses will be so numerous that their dust will cover you. When he enters your gates as an army entering a breached city, your walls will shake from the noise of cavalry, wagons, and chariots. He will trample all your streets with the hooves of his horses. He will slaughter your people with the sword, and your mighty pillars will fall to the ground. They will take your wealth as spoil and plunder your merchandise. They will also demolish your walls and tear down your beautiful homes. Then they will throw your stones, timber, and soil into the water. I will put an end to

20 the noise of your songs, and the sound of your lyres will no longer be heard. I will turn you into a bare rock, and you will be a place to spread nets. You will never be rebuilt, for I, the Lord, have spoken." This is the declaration of the Lord God.

This is what the Lord God says to Tyre: "Won't the coasts and islands quake at the sound of your downfall, when the wounded groan and slaughter occurs within you? All the princes of the sea will descend from their thrones, remove their robes, and strip off their embroidered garments. They will clothe themselves with trembling; they will sit on the ground, tremble continually, and be appalled at you. Then they will lament for you and say of you,

'How you have perished, city of renown,
you who were populated from the seas!
30 She who was powerful on the sea,
she and all of her inhabitants
inflicted their terror.
Now the coastlands tremble
on the day of your downfall;
the islands in the sea
are alarmed by your demise.'"

For this is what the Lord God says: "When I make you a ruined city like other deserted cities, when I raise up the deep against you so that the mighty waters cover you, then I will bring you down to be with those who descend to the Pit, to the people of antiquity. I will make you dwell 40 in the underworld like the ancient ruins, with those who descend to the Pit, so that you will no longer be inhabited or display your splendor in the land of the living. I will make you an object of horror, and you will no longer exist. You will be sought but will never be found again." This is the declaration of the Lord God.

27 The word of the Lord came to me: "Now, son of man, lament for Tyre. Say to Tyre, who is situated at the entrance of the sea, merchant of the peoples to many coasts and islands, 'This is what the Lord God says:

Tyre, you declared,
"I am perfect in beauty."
Your realm was in the heart of the sea;
your builders perfected your beauty.
They constructed all your planking
with pine trees from Senir.
10 They took a cedar from Lebanon
to make a mast for you.
They made your oars of oaks from Bashan.
They made your deck of cypress wood
from the coasts of Cyprus,
inlaid with ivory.
Your sail was made of
fine embroidered linen from Egypt,
and served as your banner.
Your awning was of blue and purple fabric
20 from the coasts of Elishah.

The inhabitants of Sidon and Arvad
were your rowers.
Your wise men were within you, Tyre;
they were your captains.
The elders of Gebal and its wise men
were within you, repairing your leaks.

"'All the ships of the sea and their sailors
came to you to barter for your goods.
Men of Persia, Lud, and Put
were in your army, serving as your warriors.
They hung shields and helmets in you;
they gave you splendor.
Men of Arvad and Helech
were stationed on your walls all around,
and Gammadites were in your towers.
They hung their shields all around your walls;
they perfected your beauty.

"'Tarshish was your trading partner because of your abundant wealth of every kind. They exchanged silver, iron, tin, and lead for your merchandise. Javan, Tubal, and Meshech were your merchants. They exchanged slaves and bronze utensils for your goods. Those from Beth-togarmah exchanged horses, war horses, and mules for your merchandise. Men of Dedan were also your merchants; many coasts and islands were your regular markets. They brought back ivory tusks and ebony as your payment. Aram was your trading partner because of your numerous products. They exchanged turquoise, purple and embroidered cloth, fine linen, coral, and rubies for your merchandise. Judah and the land of Israel were your merchants. They exchanged wheat from Minnith, meal, honey, oil, and balm, for your goods. Damascus was also your trading partner because of your numerous products and your abundant wealth of every kind, trading in wine from Helbon and white wool. Vedan and Javan from Uzal dealt in your merchandise; wrought iron, cassia, and aromatic cane were exchanged for your goods. Dedan was your merchant in saddlecloths for riding. Arabia and all the princes of Kedar were your business partners, trading with you in lambs, rams, and goats. The merchants of Sheba and Raamah traded with you. For your merchandise they exchanged the best of all spices and all kinds of precious stones as well as gold. Haran, Canneh, Eden, the merchants of Sheba, Asshur, and Chilmad traded with you. They were your merchants in choice garments, cloaks of blue and embroidered materials, and multicolored carpets, which were bound and secured with cords in your marketplace. Ships of Tarshish were the carriers for your goods.

"'So you became full and heavily loaded
in the heart of the sea.
Your rowers have brought you
60   onto the high seas,
but the east wind has wrecked you
in the heart of the sea.
Your wealth, merchandise, and goods,
your sailors and captains,
those who repair your leaks,
those who barter for your goods,
and all the warriors on board,
with all the other people within you,
sink into the heart of the sea
70   on the day of your downfall.

"'The countryside shakes
at the sound of your sailors' cries.
All the oarsmen
disembark from their ships.
The sailors and all the captains of the sea
stand on the shore.
Because of you, they raise their voices
and cry out bitterly.
They throw dust on their heads;
80   they roll in ashes.
They shave their heads because of you
and wrap themselves in sackcloth.
They weep over you
with deep anguish and bitter mourning.

"'In their wailing they lament for you,
mourning over you:
"Who was like Tyre,
silenced in the middle of the sea?
When your merchandise was unloaded from the seas,
90   you satisfied many peoples.
You enriched the kings of the earth
with your abundant wealth and goods.

Now you are wrecked by the sea
in the depths of the waters;
your goods and the people within you
have gone down.
All the inhabitants of the coasts and islands
are appalled at you.
Their kings shudder with fear;
their faces are contorted.
Those who trade among the peoples
scoff at you;
you have become an object of horror
and will never exist again."'"

28 The word of the LORD came to me: "Son of man, say to the ruler of Tyre, 'This is what the Lord GOD says: Your heart is proud, and you have said, "I am a god; I sit in the seat of gods in the heart of the sea." Yet you are a man and not a god, though you have regarded your heart as that of a god. Yes, you are wiser than Daniel; no secret is hidden from you! By your wisdom and understanding you have acquired wealth for yourself. You have acquired gold and silver for your treasuries. By your great skill in trading you have increased your wealth, but your heart has become proud because of your wealth.

"'Therefore, this is what the Lord GOD says:

Because you regard your heart as that of a god,
I am about to bring strangers against you,
ruthless men from the nations.
They will draw their swords
against your magnificent wisdom
and will pierce your splendor.
They will bring you down to the Pit,
and you will die a violent death
in the heart of the sea.
Will you still say, "I am a god,"
in the presence of those who slay you?
Yet you will be only a man, not a god,
in the hands of those who kill you.
You will die the death of the uncircumcised
at the hands of strangers.
For I have spoken.
This is the declaration of the Lord GOD.'"

The word of the LORD came to me: "Son of man, lament for the king of Tyre and say to him, 'This
is what the Lord GOD says:

> You were the seal of perfection,
> full of wisdom and perfect in beauty.
> You were in Eden, the garden of God.

30
> Every kind of precious stone covered you:
> carnelian, topaz, and diamond,
> beryl, onyx, and jasper,
> lapis lazuli, turquoise and emerald.
> Your mountings and settings were crafted in gold;
> they were prepared on the day you were created.
> You were an anointed guardian cherub,
> for I had appointed you.
> You were on the holy mountain of God;
> you walked among the fiery stones.

40
> From the day you were created
> you were blameless in your ways
> until wickedness was found in you.
> Through the abundance of your trade,
> you were filled with violence, and you sinned.
> So I expelled you in disgrace
> from the mountain of God,
> and banished you, guardian cherub,
> from among the fiery stones.
> Your heart became proud because of your beauty;

50
> For the sake of your splendor
> you corrupted your wisdom.
> So I threw you down to the ground;
> I made you a spectacle before kings.
> You profaned your sanctuaries
> by the magnitude of your iniquities
> in your dishonest trade.
> So I made fire come from within you,
> and it consumed you.
> I reduced you to ashes on the ground

60
> in the sight of everyone watching you.
> All those who know you among the peoples
> are appalled at you.

You have become an object of horror
and will never exist again.'"

The word of the LORD came to me: "Son of man, face Sidon and prophesy against it. You are to say, 'This is what the Lord GOD says:

Look! I am against you, Sidon,
and I will display my glory within you.
They will know that I am the LORD
70   when I execute judgments against her
and demonstrate my holiness through her.
I will send a plague against her
and bloodshed in her streets;
the slain will fall within her,
while the sword is against her on every side.
Then they will know that I am the LORD.

"'The house of Israel will no longer be hurt by prickly briers or painful thorns from all their neighbors who treat them with contempt. Then they will know that I am the Lord GOD.

"'This is what the Lord GOD says: When I gather the house of Israel from the peoples where 80 they are scattered, I will demonstrate my holiness through them in the sight of the nations, and they will live in their own land, which I gave to my servant Jacob. They will live there securely, build houses, and plant vineyards. They will live securely when I execute judgments against all their neighbors who treat them with contempt. Then they will know that I am the LORD their God.'"

29 In the tenth year, in the tenth month on the twelfth day of the month, the word of the LORD came to me: "Son of man, face Pharaoh king of Egypt and prophesy against him and against all of Egypt. Speak to him and say, 'This is what the Lord GOD says:

Look, I am against you, Pharaoh king of Egypt,
the great monster lying in the middle of his Nile,
who says, "My Nile is my own;
I made it for myself."
I will put hooks in your jaws
and make the fish of your streams
10   cling to your scales.
I will haul you up
from the middle of your Nile,
and all the fish of your streams

will cling to your scales.
I will leave you in the desert,
you and all the fish of your streams.
You will fall on the open ground
and will not be taken away
or gathered for burial.
20 I have given you
to the wild creatures of the earth
and the birds of the sky as food.

"'Then all the inhabitants of Egypt
will know that I am the Lord,
for they have been a staff made of reed
to the house of Israel.
When Israel grasped you by the hand,
you splintered, tearing all their shoulders;
when they leaned on you,
30 you shattered and made all their hips unsteady.

"'Therefore, this is what the Lord God says: I am going to bring a sword against you and cut off both people and animals from you. The land of Egypt will be a desolate ruin. Then they will know that I am the Lord. Because you said, "The Nile is my own; I made it," therefore, I am against you and your Nile. I will turn the land of Egypt into ruins, a desolate waste from Migdol to Syene, as far as the border of Cush. No human foot will pass through it, and no animal foot will pass through it. It will be uninhabited for forty years. I will make the land of Egypt a desolation among desolate lands, and its cities will be a desolation among ruined cities for forty years. I will disperse the Egyptians among the nations and scatter them throughout the lands.

"'For this is what the Lord God says: At the end of forty years I will gather the Egyptians from
40 the peoples where they were dispersed. I will restore the fortunes of Egypt and bring them back to the land of Pathros, the land of their origin. There they will be a lowly kingdom. Egypt will be the lowliest of kingdoms and will never again exalt itself over the nations. I will make them so small they cannot rule over the nations. It will never again be an object of trust for the house of Israel, drawing attention to their iniquity of turning to the Egyptians. Then they will know that I am the Lord God.'"

In the twenty-seventh year, in the first month, on the first day of the month, the word of the Lord came to me: "Son of man, King Nebuchadnezzar of Babylon made his army labor strenuously against Tyre. Every head was made bald and every shoulder chafed, but he and his army received no compensation from Tyre for the labor he expended against it. Therefore, this

is what the Lord God says: I am going to give the land of Egypt to King Nebuchadnezzar of
50 Babylon, and he will carry off its wealth, seizing its spoil and taking its plunder. This will be his
army's compensation. I have given him the land of Egypt as the pay he labored for, since they
worked for me." This is the declaration of the Lord God. "In that day I will cause a horn to sprout
for the house of Israel, and I will enable you to speak out among them. Then they will know that I
am the Lord."

30 The word of the Lord came to me: "Son of man, prophesy and say, 'This is what the Lord God says:
Wail, "Woe because of that day!"
For a day is near;
a day belonging to the Lord is near.
It will be a day of clouds,
a time of doom for the nations.
A sword will come against Egypt,
and there will be anguish in Cush
when the slain fall in Egypt,
10 and its wealth is taken away,
and its foundations are demolished.
Cush, Put, and Lud,
and all the various foreign troops,
plus Libya and the men of the covenant land
will fall by the sword along with them.
This is what the Lord says:
Those who support Egypt will fall,
and its proud strength will collapse.
From Migdol to Syene
20 they will fall within it by the sword.
This is the declaration of the Lord God.
They will be desolate
among desolate lands,
and their cities will lie
among ruined cities.
They will know that I am the Lord
when I set fire to Egypt
and all its allies are shattered.

On that day, messengers will go out from me in ships to terrify confident Cush. Anguish will
30 come over them on the day of Egypt's doom. For indeed it is coming.

"'This is what the Lord God says:
    I will put an end to the hordes of Egypt
    by the hand of King Nebuchadnezzar of Babylon.
    He along with his people,
    ruthless men from the nations,
    will be brought in to destroy the land.
    They will draw their swords against Egypt
    and fill the land with the slain.
    I will make the streams dry
40   and sell the land to evil men.
    I will bring desolation
    on the land and everything in it
    by the hands of foreigners.
    I, the Lord, have spoken.

"'This is what the Lord God says:
    I will destroy the worthless idols
    and put an end to the false gods in Memphis.
    There will no longer be
    a prince from the land of Egypt.
50   And I will instill fear in that land.
    I will make Pathros desolate,
    set fire to Zoan,
    and execute judgments on Thebes.
    I will pour out my wrath on Pelusium,
    the stronghold of Egypt,
    and will wipe out the hordes of Thebes.
    I will set fire to Egypt;
    Pelusium will writhe in anguish,
    Thebes will be breached,
60   and Memphis will face foes in broad daylight.
    The young men of On and Pi-beseth
    will fall by the sword,
    and those cities will go into captivity.
    The day will be dark in Tehaphnehes,
    when I break the yoke of Egypt there
    and its proud strength
    comes to an end in the city.

A cloud will cover Tehaphnehes,
and its surrounding villages will go into captivity.
70 So I will execute judgments against Egypt,
and they will know that I am the LORD.'"

In the eleventh year, in the first month, on the seventh day of the month, the word of the LORD came to me: "Son of man, I have broken the arm of Pharaoh king of Egypt. Look, it has not been bandaged — no medicine has been applied and no splint put on to bandage it so that it can grow strong enough to handle a sword. Therefore, this is what the Lord GOD says: Look! I am against Pharaoh king of Egypt. I will break his arms, both the strong one and the one already broken, and will make the sword fall from his hand. I will disperse the Egyptians among the nations and scatter them among the countries. I will strengthen the arms of Babylon's king and place my sword in his hand. But I will break the arms of Pharaoh, and he will groan before him as a mortally wounded
80 man. I will strengthen the arms of Babylon's king, but Pharaoh's arms will fall. They will know that I am the LORD when I place my sword in the hand of Babylon's king and he wields it against the land of Egypt. When I disperse the Egyptians among the nations and scatter them among the countries, they will know that I am the LORD."

31 In the eleventh year, in the third month, on the first day of the month, the word of the LORD came to me: "Son of man, say to Pharaoh king of Egypt and to his hordes,
'Who are you like in your greatness?
Think of Assyria, a cedar in Lebanon,
with beautiful branches and shady foliage
and of lofty height.
Its top was among the clouds.
The waters caused it to grow;
the underground springs made it tall,
10 directing their rivers all around
the place where the tree was planted
and sending their channels
to all the trees of the field.
Therefore the cedar became greater in height
than all the trees of the field.
Its branches multiplied,
and its boughs grew long
as it spread them out
because of the abundant water.
20 All the birds of the sky

nested in its branches,
and all the animals of the field
gave birth beneath its boughs;
all the great nations lived in its shade.
It was beautiful in its size,
in the length of its limbs,
for its roots extended to abundant water.
The cedars in God's garden could not eclipse it;
the pine trees couldn't compare with its branches,
30   nor could the plane trees match its boughs.
No tree in the garden of God
could compare with it in beauty.
I made it beautiful with its many limbs,
and all the trees of Eden,
which were in God's garden, envied it.

"'Therefore, this is what the Lord God says: Since it towered high in stature and set its top among the clouds, and it grew proud on account of its height, I determined to hand it over to a ruler of nations; he would surely deal with it. I banished it because of its wickedness. Foreigners, ruthless men from the nations, cut it down and left it lying. Its limbs fell on the mountains and 40 in every valley; its boughs lay broken in all the earth's ravines. All the peoples of the earth left its shade and abandoned it. All the birds of the sky nested on its fallen trunk, and all the animals of the field were among its boughs. This happened so that no trees planted beside water would become great in height and set their tops among the clouds, and so that no other well-watered trees would reach them in height. For they have all been consigned to death, to the underworld, among the people who descend to the Pit.

"'This is what the Lord God says: I caused grieving on the day the cedar went down to Sheol. I closed off the underground deep because of it: I held back the rivers of the deep, and its abundant water was restrained. I made Lebanon mourn on account of it, and all the trees of the field fainted because of it. I made the nations quake at the sound of its downfall, when I threw it down to 50 Sheol to be with those who descend to the Pit. Then all the trees of Eden, the choice and best of Lebanon, all the well-watered trees, were comforted in the underworld. They too descended with it to Sheol, to those slain by the sword. As its allies they had lived in its shade among the nations.

"'Who then are you like in glory and greatness among Eden's trees? You also will be brought down to the underworld to be with the trees of Eden. You will lie among the uncircumcised with those slain by the sword. This is Pharaoh and all his hordes. This is the declaration of the Lord God.'"

32 In the twelfth year, in the twelfth month, on the first day of the month, the word of the Lord
came to me: "Son of man, lament for Pharaoh king of Egypt and say to him,

'You compare yourself to a lion of the nations,
but you are like a monster in the seas.
You thrash about in your rivers,
churn up the waters with your feet,
and muddy the rivers.

'"This is what the Lord God says:
I will spread my net over you
with an assembly of many peoples,
and they will haul you up in my net.
I will abandon you on the land
and throw you onto the open field.
I will cause all the birds of the sky
to settle on you
and let the wild creatures of the entire earth
eat their fill of you.
I will put your flesh on the mountains
and fill the valleys with your carcass.
I will drench the land
with the flow of your blood,
even to the mountains;
the ravines will be filled with your gore.

'"When I snuff you out,
I will cover the heavens
and darken their stars.
I will cover the sun with a cloud,
and the moon will not give its light.
I will darken all the shining lights
in the heavens over you,
and will bring darkness on your land.
This is the declaration of the Lord God.

'"I will trouble the hearts of many peoples,
when I bring about your destruction
among the nations,

in countries you have not known.
I will cause many peoples to be appalled at you,
and their kings will shudder with fear because of you
when I brandish my sword in front of them.
40   On the day of your downfall
each of them will tremble
every moment for his life.

"'For this is what the Lord God says:
The sword of Babylon's king
will come against you!
I will make your hordes fall
by the swords of warriors,
all of them ruthless men from the nations.
They will ravage Egypt's pride,
50   and all its hordes will be destroyed.
I will slaughter all its cattle
that are beside many waters.
No human foot will churn them again,
and no cattle hooves will disturb them.
Then I will let their waters settle
and will make their rivers flow like oil.
This is the declaration of the Lord God.
When I make the land of Egypt a desolation,
so that it is emptied of everything in it,
60   when I strike down all who live there,
then they will know that I am the Lord.

"'The daughters of the nations will chant that lament. They will chant it over Egypt and all its hordes. This is the declaration of the Lord God.'"

In the twelfth year, on the fifteenth day of the month, the word of the Lord came to me: "Son of man, wail over the hordes of Egypt and bring Egypt and the daughters of mighty nations down to the underworld, to be with those who descend to the Pit:
Who do you surpass in loveliness?
Go down and be laid to rest with the uncircumcised!
They will fall among those slain by the sword.
70   A sword is appointed!

They drag her and all her hordes away.
Warrior leaders will speak
from the middle of Sheol
about him and his allies:
'They have come down;
the uncircumcised lie
slain by the sword.'

"Assyria is there with her whole assembly;
her graves are all around her.
80 All of them are slain, fallen by the sword.
Her graves are set in the deepest regions of the Pit,
and her assembly is all around her burial place.
All of them are slain, fallen by the sword—
those who once spread terror
in the land of the living.

"Elam is there
with all her hordes around her grave.
All of them are slain, fallen by the sword—
those who went down to the underworld uncircumcised,
90 who once spread their terror
in the land of the living.
They bear their disgrace
with those who descend to the Pit.
Among the slain
they prepare a bed for Elam
with all her hordes.
Her graves are all around her.
All of them are uncircumcised,
slain by the sword,
100 although their terror was once spread
in the land of the living.
They bear their disgrace
with those who descend to the Pit.
They are placed among the slain.

"Meshech and Tubal are there,
with all their hordes.
Their graves are all around them.
All of them are uncircumcised, slain by the sword,
although their terror was once spread
110   in the land of the living.
They do not lie down
with the fallen warriors of the uncircumcised,
who went down to Sheol
with their weapons of war,
whose swords were placed under their heads
and their shields
rested on their bones,
although the terror of these warriors
was once in the land of the living.
120   But you will be shattered
and will lie down among the uncircumcised,
with those slain by the sword.

"Edom is there, her kings and all her princes,
who, despite their strength, have been placed
among those slain by the sword.
They lie down with the uncircumcised,
with those who descend to the Pit.
All the leaders of the north
and all the Sidonians are there.
130   They went down in shame with the slain,
despite the terror their strength inspired.
They lie down uncircumcised
with those slain by the sword.
They bear their disgrace
with those who descend to the Pit.

"Pharaoh will see them
and be comforted over all his hordes—
Pharaoh and his whole army,
slain by the sword."
140   This is the declaration of the Lord God.

"For I will spread my terror
in the land of the living,
so Pharaoh and all his hordes
will be laid to rest among the uncircumcised,
with those slain by the sword."
This is the declaration of the Lord God.

33 The word of the Lord came to me: "Son of man, speak to your people and tell them, 'Suppose I bring the sword against a land, and the people of that land select a man from among them, appointing him as their watchman. And suppose he sees the sword coming against the land and blows his ram's horn to warn the people. Then, if anyone hears the sound of the ram's horn but ignores the warning, and the sword comes and takes him away, his death will be his own fault. Since he heard the sound of the ram's horn but ignored the warning, his death is his own fault. If he had taken warning, he would have saved his life. However, suppose the watchman sees the sword coming but doesn't blow the ram's horn, so that the people aren't warned, and the sword comes and takes away their lives. Then they have been taken away because of their iniquity, but I will hold the watchman accountable for their blood.'

"As for you, son of man, I have made you a watchman for the house of Israel. When you hear a word from my mouth, give them a warning from me. If I say to the wicked, 'Wicked one, you will surely die,' but you do not speak out to warn him about his way, that wicked person will die for his iniquity, yet I will hold you responsible for his blood. But if you warn a wicked person to turn from his way and he doesn't turn from it, he will die for his iniquity, but you will have rescued yourself.

"Now as for you, son of man, say to the house of Israel, 'You have said this: "Our transgressions and our sins are heavy on us, and we are wasting away because of them! How then can we survive?"' Tell them, 'As I live — this is the declaration of the Lord God — I take no pleasure in the death of the wicked, but rather that the wicked person should turn from his way and live. Repent, repent of your evil ways! Why will you die, house of Israel?'

"Now, son of man, say to your people, 'The righteousness of the righteous person will not save him on the day of his transgression; neither will the wickedness of the wicked person cause him to stumble on the day he turns from his wickedness. The righteous person won't be able to survive by his righteousness on the day he sins. When I tell the righteous person that he will surely live, but he trusts in his righteousness and acts unjustly, then none of his righteousness will be remembered, and he will die because of the injustice he has committed.

"'So when I tell the wicked person, "You will surely die," but he repents of his sin and does what is just and right— he returns collateral, makes restitution for what he has stolen, and walks in the statutes of life without committing injustice — he will certainly live; he will not die. None of the sins he committed will be held against him. He has done what is just and right; he will certainly live.

"'But your people say, "The Lord's way isn't fair," even though it is their own way that isn't fair. When a righteous person turns from his righteousness and commits injustice, he will die for it. But if a wicked person turns from his wickedness and does what is just and right, he will live because of it. Yet you say, "The Lord's way isn't fair." I will judge each of you according to his ways, house of Israel.'"

In the twelfth year of our exile, in the tenth month, on the fifth day of the month, a fugitive from Jerusalem came to me and reported, "The city has been taken!" Now the hand of the LORD had been on me the evening before the fugitive arrived, and he opened my mouth before the man came 40 to me in the morning. So my mouth was opened and I was no longer mute.

Then the word of the LORD came to me: "Son of man, those who live in the ruins in the land of Israel are saying, 'Abraham was only one person, yet he received possession of the land. But we are many; surely the land has been given to us as a possession.' Therefore say to them, 'This is what the Lord GOD says: You eat meat with blood in it, you look to your idols, and you shed blood. Should you then receive possession of the land? You have relied on your swords, you have committed detestable acts, and each of you has defiled his neighbor's wife. Should you then receive possession of the land?'

"Tell them this: 'This is what the Lord GOD says: As surely as I live, those who are in the ruins will fall by the sword, those in the open field I have given to wild animals to be devoured, and those in the strongholds and caves will die by plague. I will make the land a desolate waste, and 50 its proud strength will come to an end. The mountains of Israel will become desolate, with no one passing through. They will know that I am the LORD when I make the land a desolate waste because of all the detestable acts they have committed.'

"As for you, son of man, your people are talking about you near the city walls and in the doorways of their houses. One person speaks to another, each saying to his brother, 'Come and hear what the message is that comes from the LORD!' So my people come to you in crowds, sit in front of you, and hear your words, but they don't obey them. Their mouths go on passionately, but their hearts pursue dishonest profit. Yes, to them you are like a singer of passionate songs who has a beautiful voice and plays skillfully on an instrument. They hear your words, but they don't obey them. Yet when all this comes true — and it definitely will — then they will know that a 60 prophet has been among them."

34 The word of the LORD came to me: "Son of man, prophesy against the shepherds of Israel. Prophesy, and say to them, 'This is what the Lord GOD says to the shepherds: Woe to the shepherds of Israel, who have been feeding themselves! Shouldn't the shepherds feed their flock? You eat the fat, wear the wool, and butcher the fattened animals, but you do not tend the flock. You have not strengthened the weak, healed the sick, bandaged the injured, brought back the strays, or sought the lost. Instead, you have ruled them with violence and cruelty. They were scattered for lack of a shepherd; they became food for all the wild animals when they were scattered. My flock went astray on all the mountains and every high hill. My flock was scattered over the whole face of the earth, and there was no one searching or seeking for them.

10 "'Therefore, you shepherds, hear the word of the LORD. As I live — this is the declaration of the Lord GOD — because my flock, lacking a shepherd, has become prey and food for every wild animal, and because my shepherds do not search for my flock, and because the shepherds feed themselves rather than my flock, therefore, you shepherds, hear the word of the LORD!

"'This is what the Lord GOD says: Look, I am against the shepherds. I will demand my flock from them and prevent them from shepherding the flock. The shepherds will no longer feed themselves, for I will rescue my flock from their mouths so that they will not be food for them.

"'For this is what the Lord GOD says: See, I myself will search for my flock and look for them. As a shepherd looks for his sheep on the day he is among his scattered flock, so I will look for my flock. I will rescue them from all the places where they have been scattered on a day of clouds 20 and total darkness. I will bring them out from the peoples, gather them from the countries, and bring them to their own soil. I will shepherd them on the mountains of Israel, in the ravines, and in all the inhabited places of the land. I will tend them in good pasture, and their grazing place will be on Israel's lofty mountains. There they will lie down in a good grazing place; they will feed in rich pasture on the mountains of Israel. I will tend my flock and let them lie down. This is the declaration of the Lord GOD. I will seek the lost, bring back the strays, bandage the injured, and strengthen the weak, but I will destroy the fat and the strong. I will shepherd them with justice.

"'As for you, my flock, the Lord GOD says this: Look, I am going to judge between one sheep and another, between the rams and goats. Isn't it enough for you to feed on the good pasture? Must you also trample the rest of the pasture with your feet? Or isn't it enough that you drink the 30 clear water? Must you also muddy the rest with your feet? Yet my flock has to feed on what your feet have trampled, and drink what your feet have muddied.

"'Therefore, this is what the Lord GOD says to them: See, I myself will judge between the fat sheep and the lean sheep. Since you have pushed with flank and shoulder and butted all the weak ones with your horns until you scattered them all over, I will save my flock. They will no longer be prey, and I will judge between one sheep and another. I will establish over them one shepherd, my servant David, and he will shepherd them. He will tend them himself and will be their shepherd. I, the LORD, will be their God, and my servant David will be a prince among them. I, the LORD, have spoken.

"'I will make a covenant of peace with them and eliminate dangerous creatures from the land, 40 so that they may live securely in the wilderness and sleep in the forest. I will make them and the area around my hill a blessing: I will send down showers in their season; they will be showers of blessing. The trees of the field will yield their fruit, and the land will yield its produce; my flock will be secure in their land. They will know that I am the LORD when I break the bars of their yoke and rescue them from the power of those who enslave them. They will no longer be prey for the nations, and the wild creatures of the earth will not consume them. They will live securely, and no one will frighten them. I will establish for them a place renowned for its agriculture, and they will no longer be victims of famine in the land. They will no longer endure the insults of the nations. Then they will know that I, the Lord their God, am with them, and that they, the house of Israel, are my people. This is the declaration of the Lord God. You are my flock, the human flock of my 50 pasture, and I am your God. This is the declaration of the Lord God.'"

35 The word of the Lord came to me: "Son of man, face Mount Seir and prophesy against it. Say to it, 'This is what the Lord God says:

> Look! I am against you, Mount Seir.
> I will stretch out my hand against you
> and make you a desolate waste.
> I will turn your cities into ruins,
> and you will become a desolation.
> Then you will know that I am the Lord.

"'Because you maintained a perpetual hatred and gave the Israelites over to the power of the 10 sword in the time of their disaster, the time of final punishment, therefore, as I live — this is the declaration of the Lord God — I will destine you for bloodshed, and it will pursue you. Since you did not hate bloodshed, it will pursue you. I will make Mount Seir a desolate waste and will cut off from it those who come and go. I will fill its mountains with the slain; those slain by the sword will fall on your hills, in your valleys, and in all your ravines. I will make you a perpetual desolation; your cities will not be inhabited. Then you will know that I am the Lord.

"'Because you said, "These two nations and two lands will be mine, and we will possess them" — though the Lord was there — therefore, as I live — this is the declaration of the Lord God — I will treat you according to the anger and jealousy you showed in your hatred of them. I will make myself known among them when I judge you. Then you will know that I, the Lord, have heard all 20 the blasphemies you uttered against the mountains of Israel, saying, "They are desolate. They have been given to us to devour!" You boasted against me with your mouth, and spoke many words against me. I heard it myself!

"'This is what the Lord God says: While the whole world rejoices, I will make you a desolation. Just as you rejoiced over the inheritance of the house of Israel because it became a desolation, I will deal the same way with you: you will become a desolation, Mount Seir, and so will all Edom in its entirety. Then they will know that I am the Lord.'

36 "Son of man, prophesy to the mountains of Israel and say, 'Mountains of Israel, hear the word of the Lord. This is what the Lord God says: Because the enemy has said about you, "Aha! The ancient heights have become our possession,"' therefore, prophesy and say, 'This is what the Lord

GOD says: Because they have made you desolate and have trampled you from every side, so that you became a possession for the rest of the nations and an object of people's gossip and slander, therefore, mountains of Israel, hear the word of the Lord GOD. This is what the Lord GOD says to the mountains and hills, to the ravines and valleys, to the desolate ruins and abandoned cities, which have become plunder and a mockery to the rest of the nations all around.

"'This is what the Lord GOD says: Certainly in my burning zeal I speak against the rest of the nations and all of Edom, who took my land as their own possession with wholehearted rejoicing and utter contempt so that its pastureland became plunder. Therefore, prophesy concerning Israel's land, and say to the mountains and hills, to the ravines and valleys: This is what the Lord GOD says: Look, I speak in my burning zeal because you have endured the insults of the nations. Therefore, this is what the Lord GOD says: I swear that the nations all around you will endure their own insults.

"'You, mountains of Israel, will produce your branches and bear your fruit for my people Israel, since their arrival is near. Look! I am on your side; I will turn toward you, and you will be tilled and sown. I will fill you with people, with the whole house of Israel in its entirety. The cities will be inhabited and the ruins rebuilt. I will fill you with people and animals, and they will increase and be fruitful. I will make you inhabited as you once were and make you better off than you were before. Then you will know that I am the LORD. I will cause people, my people Israel, to walk on you; they will possess you, and you will be their inheritance. You will no longer deprive them of their children.

"'This is what the Lord GOD says: Because some are saying to you, "You devour people and deprive your nation of children," therefore, you will no longer devour people and deprive your nation of children. This is the declaration of the Lord GOD. I will no longer allow the insults of the nations to be heard against you, and you will not have to endure the reproach of the peoples anymore; you will no longer cause your nation to stumble. This is the declaration of the Lord GOD.'"

The word of the LORD came to me: "Son of man, while the house of Israel lived in their land, they defiled it with their conduct and actions. Their behavior before me was like menstrual impurity. So I poured out my wrath on them because of the blood they had shed on the land, and because they had defiled it with their idols. I dispersed them among the nations, and they were scattered among the countries. I judged them according to their conduct and actions. When they came to the nations where they went, they profaned my holy name, because it was said about them, 'These are the people of the LORD, yet they had to leave his land in exile.' Then I had concern for my holy name, which the house of Israel profaned among the nations where they went.

"Therefore, say to the house of Israel, 'This is what the Lord GOD says: It is not for your sake that I will act, house of Israel, but for my holy name, which you profaned among the nations where you went. I will honor the holiness of my great name, which has been profaned among the nations

— the name you have profaned among them. The nations will know that I am the LORD — this is the declaration of the Lord GOD — when I demonstrate my holiness through you in their sight.

"'For I will take you from the nations and gather you from all the countries, and will bring you into your own land. I will also sprinkle clean water on you, and you will be clean. I will cleanse you from all your impurities and all your idols. I will give you a new heart and put a new spirit within you; I will remove your heart of stone and give you a heart of flesh. I will place my Spirit within you and cause you to follow my statutes and carefully observe my ordinances. You will live in the land that I gave your ancestors; you will be my people, and I will be your God. I will save you from all your uncleanness. I will summon the grain and make it plentiful, and I will not bring famine on
50 you. I will also make the fruit of the trees and the produce of the field plentiful, so that you will no longer experience reproach among the nations on account of famine.

"'You will remember your evil ways and your deeds that were not good, and you will loathe yourselves for your iniquities and detestable practices. It is not for your sake that I will act — this is the declaration of the Lord GOD — let this be known to you. Be ashamed and humiliated because of your ways, house of Israel!

"'This is what the Lord GOD says: On the day I cleanse you from all your iniquities, I will cause the cities to be inhabited, and the ruins will be rebuilt. The desolate land will be cultivated instead of lying desolate in the sight of everyone who passes by. They will say, "This land that was desolate has become like the garden of Eden. The cities that were once ruined, desolate, and demolished are now fortified
60 and inhabited." Then the nations that remain around you will know that I, the LORD, have rebuilt what was demolished and have replanted what was desolate. I, the LORD, have spoken and I will do it.

"'This is what the Lord GOD says: I will respond to the house of Israel and do this for them: I will multiply them in number like a flock. So the ruined cities will be filled with a flock of people, just as Jerusalem is filled with a flock of sheep for sacrifice during its appointed festivals. Then they will know that I am the LORD.'"

37 The hand of the LORD was on me, and he brought me out by his Spirit and set me down in the middle of the valley; it was full of bones. He led me all around them. There were a great many of them on the surface of the valley, and they were very dry. Then he said to me, "Son of man, can these bones live?"

I replied, "Lord GOD, only you know."

He said to me, "Prophesy concerning these bones and say to them: Dry bones, hear the word of the LORD! This is what the Lord GOD says to these bones: I will cause breath to enter you, and you will live. I will put tendons on you, make flesh grow on you, and cover you with skin. I will put breath in you so that you come to life. Then you will know that I am the LORD."

10 So I prophesied as I had been commanded. While I was prophesying, there was a noise, a rattling sound, and the bones came together, bone to bone. As I looked, tendons appeared on them, flesh grew, and skin covered them, but there was no breath in them. He said to me, "Prophesy to

the breath, prophesy, son of man. Say to it: This is what the Lord God says: Breath, come from the four winds and breathe into these slain so that they may live!" So I prophesied as he commanded me; the breath entered them, and they came to life and stood on their feet, a vast army.

Then he said to me, "Son of man, these bones are the whole house of Israel. Look how they say, 'Our bones are dried up, and our hope has perished; we are cut off.' Therefore, prophesy and say to them, 'This is what the Lord God says: I am going to open your graves and bring you up from them, my people, and lead you into the land of Israel. You will know that I am the Lord, my
20 people, when I open your graves and bring you up from them. I will put my Spirit in you, and you will live, and I will settle you in your own land. Then you will know that I am the Lord. I have spoken, and I will do it. This is the declaration of the Lord.'"

The word of the Lord came to me: "Son of man, take a single stick and write on it: Belonging to Judah and the Israelites associated with him. Then take another stick and write on it: Belonging to Joseph — the stick of Ephraim — and all the house of Israel associated with him. Then join them together into a single stick so that they become one in your hand. When your people ask you, 'Won't you explain to us what you mean by these things?'— tell them, 'This is what the Lord God says: I am going to take the stick of Joseph, which is in the hand of Ephraim, and the tribes of Israel associated with him, and put them together with the stick of Judah. I will make them into
30 a single stick so that they become one in my hand.'

"When the sticks you have written on are in your hand and in full view of the people, tell them, 'This is what the Lord God says: I am going to take the Israelites out of the nations where they have gone. I will gather them from all around and bring them into their own land. I will make them one nation in the land, on the mountains of Israel, and one king will rule over all of them. They will no longer be two nations and will no longer be divided into two kingdoms. They will not defile themselves anymore with their idols, their abhorrent things, and all their transgressions. I will save them from all their apostasies by which they sinned, and I will cleanse them. Then they will be my people, and I will be their God. My servant David will be king over them, and there will be one shepherd for all of them. They will follow my ordinances, and keep my statutes and obey
40 them.

"'They will live in the land that I gave to my servant Jacob, where your ancestors lived. They will live in it forever with their children and grandchildren, and my servant David will be their prince forever. I will make a covenant of peace with them; it will be a permanent covenant with them. I will establish and multiply them and will set my sanctuary among them forever. My dwelling place will be with them; I will be their God, and they will be my people. When my sanctuary is among them forever, the nations will know that I, the Lord, sanctify Israel.'"

38 The word of the Lord came to me: "Son of man, face Gog, of the land of Magog, the chief prince of Meshech and Tubal. Prophesy against him and say, 'This is what the Lord God says: Look, I am against you, Gog, chief prince of Meshech and Tubal. I will turn you around, put hooks in your jaws, and bring you out with all your army, including horses and riders, who are all splendidly dressed, a huge assembly armed with large and small shields, all of them brandishing swords. Persia, Cush, and Put are with them, all of them with shields and helmets; Gomer with all its troops; and Beth-togarmah from the remotest parts of the north along with all its troops — many peoples are with you.

"'Be prepared and get yourself ready, you and your whole assembly that has been mobilized around you; you will be their guard. After a long time you will be summoned. In the last years
10 you will enter a land that has been restored from war and regathered from many peoples to the mountains of Israel, which had long been a ruin. They were brought out from the peoples, and all of them now live securely. You, all of your troops, and many peoples with you will advance, coming like a thunderstorm; you will be like a cloud covering the land.

"'This is what the Lord God says: On that day, thoughts will arise in your mind, and you will devise an evil plan. You will say, "I will advance against a land of open villages; I will come against a tranquil people who are living securely, all of them living without walls and without bars or gates" — in order to seize spoil and carry off plunder, to turn your hand against ruins now inhabited and against a people gathered from the nations, who have been acquiring cattle and possessions and who live at the center of the world. Sheba and Dedan and the merchants of Tarshish with all its
20 rulers will ask you, "Have you come to seize spoil? Have you mobilized your assembly to carry off plunder, to make off with silver and gold, to take cattle and possessions, to seize plenty of spoil?"'

"Therefore prophesy, son of man, and say to Gog, 'This is what the Lord God says: On that day when my people Israel are dwelling securely, will you not know this and come from your place in the remotest parts of the north — you and many peoples with you, who are all riding horses — a huge assembly, a powerful army? You will advance against my people Israel like a cloud covering the land. It will happen in the last days, Gog, that I will bring you against my land so that the nations may know me, when I demonstrate my holiness through you in their sight.

"'This is what the Lord God says: Are you the one I spoke about in former times through my servants, the prophets of Israel, who for years prophesied in those times that I would bring you against
30 them? Now on that day, the day when Gog comes against the land of Israel — this is the declaration of the Lord God — my wrath will flare up. I swear in my zeal and fiery wrath: On that day there will be a great earthquake in the land of Israel. The fish of the sea, the birds of the sky, the animals of the field, every creature that crawls on the ground, and every human being on the face of the earth will tremble before me. The mountains will be demolished, the cliffs will collapse, and every wall will fall to the ground. I will call for a sword against him on all my mountains — this is the declaration of the Lord God — and every man's sword will be against his brother. I will execute judgment on him with plague and bloodshed. I will pour out torrential rain, hailstones, fire, and burning sulfur on him, as well as his troops and the many peoples who are with him. I will display my greatness and holiness, and I will reveal myself in the sight of many nations. Then they will know that I am the Lord.'

39 "As for you, son of man, prophesy against Gog and say, 'This is what the Lord GOD says: Look, I am against you, Gog, chief prince of Meshech and Tubal. I will turn you around, drive you on, and lead you up from the remotest parts of the north. I will bring you against the mountains of Israel. Then I will knock your bow from your left hand and make your arrows drop from your right hand. You, all your troops, and the peoples who are with you will fall on the mountains of Israel. I will give you as food to every kind of predatory bird and to the wild animals. You will fall on the open field, for I have spoken. This is the declaration of the Lord GOD.

"'I will send fire against Magog and those who live securely on the coasts and islands. Then they will know that I am the LORD. So I will make my holy name known among my people Israel and will no longer allow it to be profaned. Then the nations will know that I am the LORD, the Holy One in Israel. Yes, it is coming, and it will happen. This is the declaration of the Lord GOD. This is the day I have spoken about.

"'Then the inhabitants of Israel's cities will go out, kindle fires, and burn the weapons — the small and large shields, the bows and arrows, the clubs and spears. For seven years they will use them to make fires. They will not gather wood from the countryside or cut it down from the forests, for they will use the weapons to make fires. They will take the loot from those who looted them and plunder those who plundered them. This is the declaration of the Lord GOD.

"'Now on that day I will give Gog a burial place there in Israel — the Travelers' Valley east of the Sea. It will block those who travel through, for Gog and all his hordes will be buried there. So it will be called Hordes of Gog Valley. The house of Israel will spend seven months burying them in order to cleanse the land. All the people of the land will bury them and their fame will spread on the day I display my glory. This is the declaration of the Lord GOD.

"'They will appoint men on a full-time basis to pass through the land and bury the invaders who remain on the surface of the ground, in order to cleanse it. They will make their search at the end of the seven months. When they pass through the land and one of them sees a human bone, he will set up a marker next to it until the buriers have buried it in Hordes of Gog Valley. There will even be a city named Hamonah there. So they will cleanse the land.'

"Son of man, this is what the Lord GOD says: Tell every kind of bird and all the wild animals, 'Assemble and come! Gather from all around to my sacrificial feast that I am slaughtering for you, a great feast on the mountains of Israel; you will eat flesh and drink blood. You will eat the flesh of mighty men and drink the blood of the earth's princes: rams, lambs, male goats, and all the fattened bulls of Bashan. You will eat fat until you are satisfied and drink blood until you are drunk, at my sacrificial feast that I have prepared for you. At my table you will eat your fill of horses and riders, of mighty men and all the warriors. This is the declaration of the Lord GOD.'

"I will display my glory among the nations, and all the nations will see the judgment I have executed and the hand I have laid on them. From that day forward the house of Israel will know that I am the LORD their God. And the nations will know that the house of Israel went into exile

on account of their iniquity, because they dealt unfaithfully with me. Therefore, I hid my face from them and handed them over to their enemies, so that they all fell by the sword. I dealt with
40 them according to their uncleanness and transgressions, and I hid my face from them.

"So this is what the Lord God says: Now I will restore the fortunes of Jacob and have compassion on the whole house of Israel, and I will be jealous for my holy name. They will feel remorse for their disgrace and all the unfaithfulness they committed against me, when they live securely in their land with no one to frighten them. When I bring them back from the peoples and gather them from the countries of their enemies, I will demonstrate my holiness through them in the sight of many nations. They will know that I am the Lord their God when I regather them to their own land after having exiled them among the nations. I will leave none of them behind. I will no longer hide my face from them, for I will pour out my Spirit on the house of Israel." This is the declaration of the Lord God.

40 In the twenty-fifth year of our exile, at the beginning of the year, on the tenth day of the month in the fourteenth year after Jerusalem had been captured, on that very day the Lord's hand was on me, and he brought me there. In visions of God he took me to the land of Israel and set me down on a very high mountain. On its southern slope was a structure resembling a city. He brought me there, and I saw a man whose appearance was like bronze, with a linen cord and a measuring rod in his hand. He was standing by the city gate. He spoke to me: "Son of man, look with your eyes, listen with your ears, and pay attention to everything I am going to show you, for you have been brought here so that I might show it to you. Report everything you see to the house of Israel."

Now there was a wall surrounding the outside of the temple. The measuring rod in the man's
10 hand was six units of twenty-one inches; each unit was the standard length plus three inches. He measured the thickness of the wall structure; it was 10 ½ feet, and its height was the same. Then he came to the gate that faced east and climbed its steps. He measured the threshold of the gate; it was 10 ½ feet deep — one threshold was 10 ½ feet deep. Each recess was 10 ½ feet long and 10 ½ feet deep, and there was a space of 8 ¾ feet between the recesses. The inner threshold of the gate on the temple side next to the gate's portico was 10 ½ feet. Next he measured the gate's portico; it was 14 feet, and its jambs were 3 ½ feet. The gate's portico was on the temple side.

There were three recesses on each side of the east gate, each with the same measurements, and the jambs on either side also had the same measurements. Then he measured the width of the gate's entrance; it was 17 ½ feet, while the width of the gate was 22 ¾ feet. There was a barrier
20 of 21 inches in front of the recesses on both sides, and the recesses on each side were 10 ½ feet square. Then he measured the gate from the roof of one recess to the roof of the opposite one; the distance was 43 ¾ feet. The openings of the recesses faced each other. Next, he measured the porch — 105 feet. The distance from the front of the gate at the entrance to the front of the gate's portico on the inside was 87 ½ feet. The recesses and their jambs had beveled windows all around

the inside of the gate. The porticoes also had windows all around on the inside. Each jamb was decorated with palm trees.

Then he brought me into the outer court, and there were chambers and a paved surface laid out all around the court. Thirty chambers faced the pavement, which flanked the courtyard's gates and corresponded to the length of the gates; this was the lower pavement. Then he measured the distance from the front of the lower gate to the exterior front of the inner court; it was 175 feet. This was the east; next the north is described.

He measured the gate of the outer court facing north, both its length and width. Its three recesses on each side, its jambs, and its portico had the same measurements as the first gate: 87 ½ feet long and 43 ¾ feet wide. Its windows, portico, and palm trees had the same measurements as those of the gate that faced east. Seven steps led up to the gate, and its portico was ahead of them. The inner court had a gate facing the north gate, like the one on the east. He measured the distance from gate to gate; it was 175 feet.

He brought me to the south side, and there was also a gate on the south. He measured its jambs and portico; they had the same measurements as the others. Both the gate and its portico had windows all around, like the other windows. It was 87 ½ feet long and 43 ¾ feet wide. Its stairway had seven steps, and its portico was ahead of them. It had palm trees on its jambs, one on each side. The inner court had a gate on the south. He measured from gate to gate on the south; it was 175 feet.

Then he brought me to the inner court through the south gate. When he measured the south gate, it had the same measurements as the others. Its recesses, jambs, and portico had the same measurements as the others. Both it and its portico had windows all around. It was 87 ½ feet long and 43 ¾ feet wide. (There were porticoes all around, 43 ¾ feet long and 8 ¾ feet wide.) Its portico faced the outer court, and its jambs were decorated with palm trees. Its stairway had eight steps.

Then he brought me to the inner court on the east side. When he measured the gate, it had the same measurements as the others. Its recesses, jambs, and portico had the same measurements as the others. Both it and its portico had windows all around. It was 87 ½ feet long and 43 ¾ feet wide. Its portico faced the outer court, and its jambs were decorated with palm trees on each side. Its stairway had eight steps.

Then he brought me to the north gate. When he measured it, it had the same measurements as the others, as did its recesses, jambs, and portico. It also had windows all around. It was 87 ½ feet long and 43 ¾ feet wide. Its portico faced the outer court, and its jambs were decorated with palm trees on each side. Its stairway had eight steps.

There was a chamber whose door opened into the gate's portico. The burnt offering was to be washed there. Inside the gate's portico there were two tables on each side, on which to slaughter the burnt offering, sin offering, and guilt offering. Outside, as one approaches the entrance of the north gate, there were two tables on one side and two more tables on the other side of the gate's portico. So there were four tables inside the gate and four outside, eight tables in all on which the slaughtering was to be done. There were also four tables of cut stone for the burnt offering, each 31 ½ inches long, 31 ½ inches wide, and 21 inches high. The utensils used to slaughter the burnt offerings and other sacrifices were placed on them. There were three-inch hooks fastened all around the inside of the room, and the flesh of the offering was to be laid on the tables.

Outside the inner gate, within the inner court, there were chambers for the singers: one beside the north gate, facing south, and another beside the south gate, facing north. Then the man said to me, "This chamber that faces south is for the priests who keep charge of the temple. The chamber
70 that faces north is for the priests who keep charge of the altar. These are the sons of Zadok, the ones from the sons of Levi who may approach the LORD to serve him." Next he measured the court. It was square, 175 feet long and 175 feet wide. The altar was in front of the temple.

Then he brought me to the portico of the temple and measured the jambs of the portico; they were 8 ¾ feet thick on each side. The width of the gate was 24 ½ feet, and the side walls of the gate were 5 ¼ feet wide on each side. The portico was 35 feet across and 21 feet deep, and 10 steps led up to it. There were pillars by the jambs, one on each side.

41 Next he brought me into the great hall and measured the jambs; on each side the width of the jamb was 10 ½ feet. The width of the entrance was 17 ½ feet, and the side walls of the entrance were 8 ¾ feet wide on each side. He also measured the length of the great hall, 70 feet, and the width, 35 feet. He went inside the next room and measured the jambs at the entrance; they were 3 ½ feet wide. The entrance was 10 ½ feet wide, and the width of the entrance's side walls on each side was 12 ¼ feet. He then measured the length of the room adjacent to the great hall, 35 feet, and the width, 35 feet. And he said to me, "This is the most holy place."

Then he measured the wall of the temple; it was 10 ½ feet thick. The width of the side rooms all around the temple was 7 feet. The side rooms were arranged one above another in three stories
10 of thirty rooms each. There were ledges on the wall of the temple all around to serve as supports for the side rooms, so that the supports would not be in the temple wall itself. The side rooms surrounding the temple widened at each successive story, for the structure surrounding the temple went up by stages. This was the reason for the temple's broadness as it rose. And so, one would go up from the lowest story to the highest by means of the middle one.

I saw that the temple had a raised platform surrounding it; this foundation for the side rooms was 10 ½ feet high. The thickness of the outer wall of the side rooms was 8 ¾ feet. The free space between the side rooms of the temple and the outer chambers was 35 feet wide all around the temple. The side rooms opened into the free space, one entrance toward the north and another to the south. The area of free space was 8 ¾ feet wide all around.

20 Now the building that faced the temple yard toward the west was 122 ½ feet wide. The wall of the building was 8 ¾ feet thick on all sides, and the building's length was 157 ½ feet.

Then the man measured the temple; it was 175 feet long. In addition, the temple yard and the building, including its walls, were 175 feet long. The width of the front of the temple along with the temple yard to the east was 175 feet. Next he measured the length of the building facing the temple yard to the west, with its galleries on each side; it was 175 feet.

The interior of the great hall and the porticoes of the court— the thresholds, the beveled windows, and the balconies all around with their three levels opposite the threshold — were overlaid with wood on all sides. They were paneled from the ground to the windows (but the windows were covered), reaching to the top of the entrance, and as far as the inner temple and
30 on the outside. On every wall all around, on the inside and outside, was a pattern carved with cherubim and palm trees. There was a palm tree between each pair of cherubim. Each cherub had two faces: a human face turned toward the palm tree on one side, and a lion's face turned toward it on the other. They were carved throughout the temple on all sides. Cherubim and palm trees were carved from the ground to the top of the entrance and on the wall of the great hall.

The doorposts of the great hall were square, and the front of the sanctuary had the same appearance. The altar was made of wood, 5 ¼ feet high and 3 ½ feet long. It had corners, and its length and sides were of wood. The man told me, "This is the table that stands before the Lord."

The great hall and the sanctuary each had a double door, and each of the doors had two swinging panels. There were two panels for one door and two for the other. Cherubim and palm
40 trees were carved on the doors of the great hall like those carved on the walls. There was a wooden canopy outside, in front of the portico. There were beveled windows and palm trees on both sides, on the side walls of the portico, the side rooms of the temple, and the canopies.

42 Then the man led me out by way of the north gate into the outer court. He brought me to the group of chambers opposite the temple yard and opposite the building to the north. Along the length of the chambers, which was 175 feet, there was an entrance on the north; the width was 87 ½ feet. Opposite the 35 foot space belonging to the inner court and opposite the paved surface belonging to the outer court, the structure rose gallery by gallery in three tiers. In front of the chambers was a walkway toward the inside, 17 ½ feet wide and 175 feet long, and their entrances were on the north. The upper chambers were narrower because the galleries took away more space from them than from the lower and middle stories of the building. For they were arranged in three stories and had no pillars like the pillars of the courts; therefore the upper chambers were set back
10 from the ground more than the lower and middle stories. A wall on the outside ran in front of the chambers, parallel to them, toward the outer court; it was 87 ½ feet long. For the chambers on the outer court were 87 ½ feet long, while those facing the great hall were 175 feet long. At the base of these chambers there was an entryway on the east side as one enters them from the outer court.

In the thickness of the wall of the court toward the south, there were chambers facing the temple yard and the western building, with a passageway in front of them, just like the chambers that faced north. Their length and width, as well as all their exits, measurements, and entrances, were identical. The entrance at the beginning of the passageway, the way in front of the corresponding wall as one enters on the east side, was similar to the entrances of the chambers that were on the south side.

20 Then the man said to me, "The northern and southern chambers that face the courtyard are the holy chambers where the priests who approach the LORD will eat the most holy offerings. There they will deposit the most holy offerings — the grain offerings, sin offerings, and guilt offerings — for the place is holy. Once the priests have entered, they are not to go out from the holy area to the outer court until they have removed the clothes they minister in, for these are holy. They are to put on other clothes before they approach the public area."

When he finished measuring inside the temple complex, he led me out by way of the gate that faced east and measured all around the complex.

He measured the east side with a measuring rod;
it was 875 feet by the measuring rod.
30 He measured the north side;
it was 875 feet by the measuring rod.
He measured the south side;
it was 875 feet by the measuring rod.
Then he turned to the west side
and measured 875 feet by the measuring rod.

He measured the temple complex on all four sides. It had a wall all around it, 875 feet long and 875 feet wide, to separate the holy from the common.

43 He led me to the gate, the one that faces east, and I saw the glory of the God of Israel coming from the east. His voice sounded like the roar of a huge torrent, and the earth shone with his glory. The vision I saw was like the one I had seen when he came to destroy the city, and like the ones I had seen by the Chebar Canal. I fell facedown. The glory of the LORD entered the temple by way of the gate that faced east. Then the Spirit lifted me up and brought me to the inner court, and the glory of the LORD filled the temple.

While the man was standing beside me, I heard someone speaking to me from the temple. He said to me, "Son of man, this is the place of my throne and the place for the soles of my feet, where I will dwell among the Israelites forever. The house of Israel and their kings will no longer 10 defile my holy name by their religious prostitution and by the corpses of their kings at their high places. Whenever they placed their threshold next to my threshold and their doorposts beside my doorposts, with only a wall between me and them, they were defiling my holy name by the detestable acts they committed. So I destroyed them in my anger. Now let them remove their prostitution and the corpses of their kings far from me, and I will dwell among them forever.

"As for you, son of man, describe the temple to the house of Israel, so that they may be ashamed of their iniquities. Let them measure its pattern, and they will be ashamed of all that they have done. Reveal the design of the temple to them — its layout with its exits and entrances — its complete design along with all its statutes, design specifications, and laws. Write it down in their sight so that they may observe its complete design and all its statutes and may carry them
20 out. This is the law of the temple: All its surrounding territory on top of the mountain will be especially holy. Yes, this is the law of the temple.

"These are the measurements of the altar in units of length (each unit being the standard length plus three inches): The gutter is 21 inches deep and 21 inches wide, with a rim of nine inches around its edge. This is the base of the altar. The distance from the gutter on the ground to the lower ledge is 3 ½ feet, and the width of the ledge is 21 inches. There are 7 feet from the small ledge to the large ledge, whose width is also 21 inches. The altar hearth is 7 feet high, and four horns project upward from the hearth. The hearth is square, 21 feet long by 21 feet wide. The ledge is 24 ½ feet long by 24 ½ feet wide, with four equal sides. The rim all around it is 10 ½ inches, and its gutter is 21 inches all around it. The altar's steps face east."

30   Then he said to me, "Son of man, this is what the Lord God says: These are the statutes for the altar on the day it is constructed, so that burnt offerings may be sacrificed on it and blood may be splattered on it: You are to give a bull from the herd as a sin offering to the Levitical priests who are from the offspring of Zadok, who approach me in order to serve me." This is the declaration of the Lord God. "You are to take some of its blood and apply it to the four horns of the altar, the four corners of the ledge, and all around the rim. In this way you will purify the altar and make atonement for it. Then you are to take away the bull for the sin offering, and it must be burned outside the sanctuary in the place appointed for the temple.

"On the second day you are to present an unblemished male goat as a sin offering. They will purify the altar just as they did with the bull. When you have finished the purification, you are
40   to present a young, unblemished bull and an unblemished ram from the flock. You are to present them before the Lord; the priests will throw salt on them and sacrifice them as a burnt offering to the Lord. You will offer a goat for a sin offering each day for seven days. A young bull and a ram from the flock, both unblemished, are also to be offered. For seven days the priests are to make atonement for the altar and cleanse it. In this way they will consecrate it and complete the days of purification. Then on the eighth day and afterward, the priests will offer your burnt offerings and fellowship offerings on the altar, and I will accept you." This is the declaration of the Lord God.

44 The man then brought me back toward the sanctuary's outer gate that faced east, and it was closed. The Lord said to me, "This gate will remain closed. It will not be opened, and no one will enter through it, because the Lord, the God of Israel, has entered through it. Therefore it will remain closed. The prince himself will sit in the gate to eat a meal before the Lord. He is to enter by way of the portico of the gate and go out the same way."

Then the man brought me by way of the north gate to the front of the temple. I looked, and the glory of the Lord filled his temple. And I fell facedown. The Lord said to me, "Son of man, pay attention; look with your eyes and listen with your ears to everything I tell you about all the statutes and laws of the Lord's temple. Take careful note of the entrance of the temple along with all the exits of the sanctuary.

"Say to the rebellious people, the house of Israel, 'This is what the Lord God says: I have had enough of all your detestable practices, house of Israel. When you brought in foreigners, uncircumcised in both heart and flesh, to occupy my sanctuary, you defiled my temple while you offered my food — the fat and the blood. You broke my covenant by all your detestable practices. You have not kept charge of my holy things but have appointed others to keep charge of my sanctuary for you.'

"This is what the Lord God says: No foreigner, uncircumcised in heart and flesh, may enter my sanctuary, not even a foreigner who is among the Israelites. Surely the Levites who wandered away from me when Israel went astray, and who strayed from me after their idols, will bear the consequences of their iniquity. Yet they will occupy my sanctuary, serving as guards at the temple gates and ministering at the temple. They will slaughter the burnt offerings and other sacrifices for the people and will stand before them to serve them. Because they ministered to the house of Israel before their idols and became a sinful stumbling block to them, therefore I swore an oath against them" — this is the declaration of the Lord God — "that they would bear the consequences of their iniquity. They must not approach me to serve me as priests or come near any of my holy things or the most holy things. They will bear their disgrace and the consequences of the detestable acts they committed. Yet I will make them responsible for the duties of the temple — for all its work and everything done in it.

"But the Levitical priests descended from Zadok, who kept charge of my sanctuary when the Israelites went astray from me, will approach me to serve me. They will stand before me to offer me fat and blood." This is the declaration of the Lord God. "They are the ones who may enter my sanctuary and approach my table to serve me. They will keep my mandate. When they enter the gates of the inner court they are to wear linen garments; they must not have on them anything made of wool when they minister at the gates of the inner court and within it. They are to wear linen turbans on their heads and linen undergarments around their waists. They are not to put on anything that makes them sweat. Before they go out to the outer court, to the people, they must take off the clothes they have been ministering in, leave them in the holy chambers, and dress in other clothes so that they do not transmit holiness to the people through their clothes.

"They may not shave their heads or let their hair grow long, but are to carefully trim their hair. No priest may drink wine before he enters the inner court. He is not to marry a widow or a divorced woman, but may marry only a virgin from the offspring of the house of Israel, or a widow
40 who is the widow of a priest. They are to teach my people the difference between the holy and the common, and explain to them the difference between the clean and the unclean.

"In a dispute, they will officiate as judges and decide the case according to my ordinances. They are to observe my laws and statutes regarding all my appointed festivals, and keep my Sabbaths holy. A priest may not come near a dead person so that he becomes defiled. However, he may defile himself for a father, a mother, a son, a daughter, a brother, or an unmarried sister. After he is cleansed, he is to count off seven days for himself. On the day he goes into the sanctuary, into the inner court to minister in the sanctuary, he is to present his sin offering." This is the declaration of the Lord God.

"This will be their inheritance: I am their inheritance. You are to give them no possession
50 in Israel; I am their possession. They will eat the grain offering, the sin offering, and the guilt offering. Everything in Israel that is permanently dedicated to the Lord will belong to them. The best of all the firstfruits of every kind and contribution of every kind from all your gifts will belong to the priests. You are to give your first batch of dough to the priest so that a blessing may rest on your homes. The priests may not eat any bird or animal that died naturally or was mauled by wild beasts.

45 "When you divide the land by lot as an inheritance, set aside a donation to the Lord, a holy portion of the land, 8 ⅓ miles long and 6 ⅔ miles wide. This entire region will be holy. In this area there will be a square section for the sanctuary, 875 by 875 feet, with 87 ½ feet of open space all around it. From this holy portion, you will measure off an area 8 ⅓ miles long and 3 ⅓ miles wide, in which the sanctuary, the most holy place, will stand. It will be a holy area of the land to be used by the priests who minister in the sanctuary, who approach to serve the Lord. It will be a place for their houses, as well as a holy area for the sanctuary. There will be another area 8 ⅓ miles long and 3 ⅓ miles wide for the Levites who minister in the temple; it will be their possession for towns to live in.

"As the property of the city, set aside an area 1 ⅔ miles wide and 8 ⅓ miles long, adjacent to
10 the holy donation of land. It will be for the whole house of Israel. And the prince will have the area on each side of the holy donation of land and the city's property, adjacent to the holy donation and the city's property, stretching to the west on the west side and to the east on the east side. Its length will correspond to one of the tribal portions from the western boundary to the eastern boundary. This will be his land as a possession in Israel. My princes will no longer oppress my people but give the rest of the land to the house of Israel according to their tribes.

"This is what the Lord God says: You have gone too far, princes of Israel! Put away violence and oppression and do what is just and right. Put an end to your evictions of my people." This is the declaration of the Lord God. "You are to have honest scales, an honest dry measure, and an

honest liquid measure. The dry measure and the liquid measure will be uniform, with the liquid
measure containing 5 ½ gallons and the dry measure holding half a bushel. Their measurement
will be a tenth of the standard larger capacity measure. The shekel will weigh twenty gerahs. Your
mina will equal sixty shekels.

"This is the contribution you are to offer: Three quarts from six bushels of wheat and three
quarts from six bushels of barley. The quota of oil in liquid measures will be one percent of
every cor. The cor equals ten liquid measures or one standard larger capacity measure, since ten
liquid measures equal one standard larger capacity measure. And the quota from the flock is one
animal out of every two hundred from the well-watered pastures of Israel. These are for the grain
offerings, burnt offerings, and fellowship offerings, to make atonement for the people." This is
the declaration of the Lord GOD. "All the people of the land must take part in this contribution
for the prince in Israel. Then the burnt offerings, grain offerings, and drink offerings for the
festivals, New Moons, and Sabbaths — for all the appointed times of the house of Israel — will be
the prince's responsibility. He will provide the sin offerings, grain offerings, burnt offerings, and
fellowship offerings to make atonement on behalf of the house of Israel.

"This is what the Lord GOD says: In the first month, on the first day of the month, you are to
take a young, unblemished bull and purify the sanctuary. The priest is to take some of the blood
from the sin offering and apply it to the temple doorposts, the four corners of the altar's ledge, and
the doorposts of the gate of the inner court. You are to do the same thing on the seventh day of
the month for everyone who sins unintentionally or through ignorance. In this way you will make
atonement for the temple.

"In the first month, on the fourteenth day of the month, you are to celebrate the Passover, a
festival of seven days during which unleavened bread will be eaten. On that day the prince will provide
a bull as a sin offering on behalf of himself and all the people of the land. During the seven days of the
festival, he will provide seven bulls and seven rams without blemish as a burnt offering to the LORD
on each of the seven days, along with a male goat each day for a sin offering. He will also provide a
grain offering of half a bushel per bull and half a bushel per ram, along with a gallon of oil for every
half bushel. At the festival that begins on the fifteenth day of the seventh month, he will provide the
same things for seven days — the same sin offerings, burnt offerings, grain offerings, and oil.

46 "This is what the Lord GOD says: The gate of the inner court that faces east is to be closed during
the six days of work, but it will be opened on the Sabbath day and opened on the day of the New
Moon. The prince should enter from the outside by way of the gate's portico and stand at the
gate's doorpost while the priests sacrifice his burnt offerings and fellowship offerings. He will bow
in worship at the gate's threshold and then depart, but the gate is not to be closed until evening.
The people of the land will also bow in worship before the LORD at the entrance of that gate on
the Sabbaths and New Moons.

"The burnt offering that the prince presents to the Lord on the Sabbath day is to be six unblemished lambs and an unblemished ram. The grain offering will be half a bushel with the ram, and the grain offering with the lambs will be whatever he wants to give, as well as a gallon of oil for every half bushel. On the day of the New Moon, the burnt offering is to be a young, unblemished bull, as well as six lambs and a ram without blemish. He will provide a grain offering of half a bushel with the bull, half a bushel with the ram, and whatever he can afford with the lambs, together with a gallon of oil for every half bushel. When the prince enters, he is to go in by way of the gate's portico and go out the same way.

"When the people of the land come before the Lord at the appointed times, whoever enters by way of the north gate to worship is to go out by way of the south gate, and whoever enters by way of the south gate is to go out by way of the north gate. No one may return through the gate by which he entered, but is to go out by the opposite gate. When the people enter, the prince will enter with them, and when they leave, he will leave. At the festivals and appointed times, the grain offering will be half a bushel with the bull, half a bushel with the ram, and whatever he wants to give with the lambs, along with a gallon of oil for every half bushel.

"When the prince makes a freewill offering, whether a burnt offering or a fellowship offering as a freewill offering to the Lord, the gate that faces east is to be opened for him. He is to offer his burnt offering or fellowship offering just as he does on the Sabbath day. Then he will go out, and the gate is to be closed after he leaves.

"You are to offer an unblemished year-old male lamb as a daily burnt offering to the Lord; you will offer it every morning. You are also to prepare a grain offering every morning along with it: three quarts, with one-third of a gallon of oil to moisten the fine flour — a grain offering to the Lord. This is a permanent statute to be observed regularly. They will offer the lamb, the grain offering, and the oil every morning as a regular burnt offering.

"This is what the Lord God says: If the prince gives a gift to each of his sons as their inheritance, it will belong to his sons. It will become their property by inheritance. But if he gives a gift from his inheritance to one of his servants, it will belong to that servant until the year of freedom, when it will revert to the prince. His inheritance belongs only to his sons; it is theirs. The prince must not take any of the people's inheritance, evicting them from their property. He is to provide an inheritance for his sons from his own property, so that none of my people will be displaced from his own property."

Then he brought me through the entrance that was at the side of the gate, into the priests' holy chambers, which faced north. I saw a place there at the far western end. He said to me, "This is the place where the priests will boil the guilt offering and the sin offering, and where they will bake the grain offering, so that they do not bring them into the outer court and transmit holiness to the people." Next he brought me into the outer court and led me past its four corners. There was a separate court in each of its corners. In the four corners of the outer court there were enclosed

857

courts, 70 feet long by 52 ½ feet wide. All four corner areas had the same dimensions. There was a stone wall around the inside of them, around the four of them, with ovens built at the base of the walls on all sides. He said to me, "These are the kitchens where those who minister at the temple will cook the people's sacrifices."

47 Then he brought me back to the entrance of the temple and there was water flowing from under the threshold of the temple toward the east, for the temple faced east. The water was coming down from under the south side of the threshold of the temple, south of the altar. Next he brought me out by way of the north gate and led me around the outside to the outer gate that faced east; there the water was trickling from the south side. As the man went out east with a measuring line in his hand, he measured off a third of a mile and led me through the water. It came up to my ankles. Then he measured off a third of a mile and led me through the water. It came up to my knees. He measured off another third of a mile and led me through the water. It came up to my waist. Again he measured off a third of a mile, and it was a river that I could not cross on foot.
10 For the water had risen; it was deep enough to swim in, a river that could not be crossed on foot.

He asked me, "Do you see this, son of man?" Then he led me back to the bank of the river. When I had returned, I saw a very large number of trees along both sides of the riverbank. He said to me, "This water flows out to the eastern region and goes down to the Arabah. When it enters the sea, the sea of foul water, the water of the sea becomes fresh. Every kind of living creature that swarms will live wherever the river flows, and there will be a huge number of fish because this water goes there. Since the water will become fresh, there will be life everywhere the river goes. Fishermen will stand beside it from En-gedi to En-eglaim. These will become places where nets are spread out to dry. Their fish will consist of many different kinds, like the fish of the Mediterranean Sea. Yet its swamps and marshes will not be healed; they will be left for salt. All
20 kinds of trees providing food will grow along both banks of the river. Their leaves will not wither, and their fruit will not fail. Each month they will bear fresh fruit because the water comes from the sanctuary. Their fruit will be used for eating and their leaves for healing."

This is what the Lord God says: "This is the border you will use to divide the land as an inheritance for the twelve tribes of Israel. Joseph will receive two shares. You will inherit it in equal portions, since I swore to give it to your ancestors. So this land will fall to you as an inheritance.

This is to be the border of the land:

On the north side it will extend from the Mediterranean Sea by way of Hethlon and Lebo-hamath to Zedad, Berothah, and Sibraim (which is between the border of Damascus and the border of Hamath), as far as Hazer-hatticon, which is on the border of Hauran. So the border
30 will run from the sea to Hazar-enon at the border of Damascus, with the territory of Hamath to the north. This will be the northern side.

On the east side it will run between Hauran and Damascus, along the Jordan between Gilead and the land of Israel; you will measure from the northern border to the eastern sea. This will be the eastern side.

On the south side it will run from Tamar to the Waters of Meribath-kadesh, and on to the Brook of Egypt as far as the Mediterranean Sea. This will be the southern side.

On the west side the Mediterranean Sea will be the border, from the southern border up to a point opposite Lebo-hamath. This will be the western side.

"You are to divide this land among yourselves according to the tribes of Israel. You will allot it as an inheritance for yourselves and for the aliens residing among you, who have fathered children among you. You will treat them like native-born Israelites; along with you, they will be allotted an inheritance among the tribes of Israel. In whatever tribe the alien resides, you will assign his inheritance there." This is the declaration of the Lord God.

48 "Now these are the names of the tribes:
From the northern end, along the road of Hethlon, to Lebo-hamath as far as Hazar-enon, at the northern border of Damascus, alongside Hamath and extending from the eastern side to the sea, will be Dan — one portion.
Next to the territory of Dan, from the east side to the west, will be Asher — one portion.
Next to the territory of Asher, from the east side to the west, will be Naphtali — one portion.
Next to the territory of Naphtali, from the east side to the west, will be Manasseh — one portion.
Next to the territory of Manasseh, from the east side to the west, will be Ephraim — one portion.
Next to the territory of Ephraim, from the east side to the west, will be Reuben — one portion.
Next to the territory of Reuben, from the east side to the west, will be Judah — one portion.

"Next to the territory of Judah, from the east side to the west, will be the portion you donate to the Lord, 8 ⅓ miles wide, and as long as one of the tribal portions from the east side to the west. The sanctuary will be in the middle of it.
"The special portion you donate to the Lord will be 8 ⅓ miles long and 3 ⅓ miles wide. This holy donation will be set apart for the priests alone. It will be 8 ⅓ miles long on the northern side, 3 ⅓ miles wide on the western side, 3 ⅓ miles wide on the eastern side, and 8 ⅓ miles long on the southern side. The Lord's sanctuary will be in the middle of it. It is for the consecrated priests, the sons of Zadok, who kept my charge and did not go astray as the Levites did when the Israelites went astray. It will be a special donation for them out of the holy donation of the land, a most holy place adjacent to the territory of the Levites.

"Next to the territory of the priests, the Levites will have an area 8 ⅓ miles long and 3 ⅓ miles wide. The total length will be 8 ⅓ miles and the width 3 ⅓ miles. They must not sell or exchange any of it, and they must not transfer this choice part of the land, for it is holy to the LORD.

"The remaining area, 1 ⅔ miles wide and 8 ⅓ miles long, will be for common use by the city, for both residential and open space. The city will be in the middle of it. These are the city's measurements:

1 ½ miles on the north side;

1 ½ miles on the south side;

1 ½ miles on the east side;

and 1 ½ miles on the west side.

The city's open space will extend:

425 feet to the north,

425 feet to the south,

425 feet to the east,

and 425 feet to the west.

"The remainder of the length alongside the holy donation will be 3 ⅓ miles to the east and 3 ⅓ miles to the west. It will run alongside the holy donation. Its produce will be food for the workers of the city. The city's workers from all the tribes of Israel will cultivate it. The entire donation will be 8 ⅓ miles by 8 ⅓ miles; you are to set apart the holy donation along with the city property as a square area.

"The remaining area on both sides of the holy donation and the city property will belong to the prince. He will own the land adjacent to the tribal portions, next to the 8 ⅓ miles of the donation as far as the eastern border and next to the 8 ⅓ miles of the donation as far as the western border. The holy donation and the sanctuary of the temple will be in the middle of it. Except for the Levitical property and the city property in the middle of the area belonging to the prince, the area between the territory of Judah and that of Benjamin will belong to the prince.

"As for the rest of the tribes:

From the east side to the west, will be Benjamin — one portion.

Next to the territory of Benjamin, from the east side to the west, will be Simeon — one portion.

Next to the territory of Simeon, from the east side to the west, will be Issachar — one portion.

Next to the territory of Issachar, from the east side to the west, will be Zebulun — one portion.

Next to the territory of Zebulun, from the east side to the west, will be Gad — one portion.

Next to the territory of Gad toward the south side, the border will run from Tamar to the Waters of Meribath-kadesh, to the Brook of Egypt, and out to the Mediterranean Sea. This is the land you are to allot as an inheritance to Israel's tribes, and these will be their portions." This is the declaration of the Lord God.

60 "These are the exits of the city:

On the north side, which measures 1 ½ miles, there will be three gates facing north, the gates of the city being named for the tribes of Israel: one, the gate of Reuben; one, the gate of Judah; and one, the gate of Levi.

On the east side, which is 1 ½ miles, there will be three gates: one, the gate of Joseph; one, the gate of Benjamin; and one, the gate of Dan.

On the south side, which measures 1 ½ miles, there will be three gates: one, the gate of Simeon; one, the gate of Issachar; and one, the gate of Zebulun.

On the west side, which is 1 ½ miles, there will be three gates: one, the gate of Gad; one, the gate of Asher; and one, the gate of Naphtali.

70 The perimeter of the city will be six miles, and the name of the city from that day on will be The Lord Is There."

Introduction to Hosea

A. Lauren Brown

First in the Book of the Twelve, Hosea is a retelling of Israel's covenant failure portrayed most memorably through the prophet's marriage. This marriage serves as a parable, a vision, and ultimately an act of sympathy toward the divine. The purpose of Hosea's marriage is to educate the prophet himself in empathy with the divine sensibility. Hosea guides the reader on the path to this understanding.

The Book of the Twelve is organized thematically rather than chronologically. Hosea sets the stage for dominant themes and movement in the Book of the Twelve with a narrative that alternates between judgment and hope for Israel's repentance. Comparatively, Amos, a chronological contemporary to Hosea, assumes judgment and has no hope of imminent repentance. While Amos may pack a more powerful punch to the conscience, Hosea forces the reader to consider the depths of Yahweh's emotional response to Israel's rebellion. No other book describes Yahweh's innermost feelings like Hosea. Through extensive relational metaphors, the evocative betrayals and surprising restorations of an adulterous spouse and rebellious child communicate to the reader such heights and depths of tenderness and mercy not seen elsewhere in the Hebrew canon.

In the HS, Hosea follows Ezekiel. Reading Hosea directly after Ezekiel amplifies the futility, yet the necessity, of hope. Hosea repeats Ezekiel's continuous call to repentance in order to avoid disaster, while the reader knows that disaster has already befallen Israel. Hosea reminds Israel that they had multiple chances to repent and did not, but still offers his audience hope in a way that echoes Ezekiel's renewal (Ezek 34–37) and is vital for the overarching narrative of the Book of the Twelve. Hosea builds on Ezekiel's portrayal of idolatry leading to social injustice through even grander sign acts and parables. Ezekiel ends in new Edenic creation and Hosea turns to how Israel might arrive in that new Eden, reflecting the wider narrative arc of wilderness to paradise, when he calls his beloved out into the wilderness to speak tenderly to her.

Joel follows Hosea, with Joel's first two chapters dovetailing with Hosea's call to repentance in ch. 14. While Hosea elaborately portrays Yahweh's justice and compassion, Joel makes the reader ask: how do we respond to Yahweh's justice and compassion? If Hosea is a retelling of Israel's covenant failure, Joel expounds on that failure through the practice of prophet as scriptural interpreter, where the prophet elaborates on coming judgment by looking at those present failures through the lens of covenant details in the Scriptures.

Hosea knows that worship and justice are inextricably linked; improper worship leads to social injustice. The principal sin of Israel, according to Hosea, is idolatry, and the sexual immortality of the faithless spouse is a metaphor for socio-economic immorality. Hosea connects worship of foreign gods with economic oppression, agrarian instability, and political infidelity. Hosea takes Israel to task over hiring foreign allies, actions which Hosea understands as blasphemy. Israel breaks the third commandment when they have no faith in Yahweh who brought them out of Egypt.

Hosea contains many shocking moments that trouble different readers for different reasons. Modern Western sensibilities may be appalled by Hosea's harsh treatment of his adulterous wife. The best practice to avoid misunderstanding and misappropriating the text of Hosea is to remember to whom Hosea is speaking. Is Hosea speaking to the wives of Israel? No. The metaphor of an adulterous wife is mapped onto the book's male audience. The metaphor bends gender norms as it assaults and accuses the Israelite male elite in charge of the nation's political, economic, and religious spheres.

Hosea speaks the language of his time to pack the biggest punch. Hosea's ancient Near East cultural context would not have been shocked at such violence against the cheating spouse. They would, however, have been floored to find at the conclusion of Hosea's story that his wife was not executed, but is restored! This is the real shock of Hosea: the hope of restoration to Yahweh after covenant infidelity. Hosea's 8th century message concludes with a timeless word about the truth of human nature and the divine sensibility of Yahweh's character: "Let whoever is wise understand these things, and whoever is insightful recognize them. For the ways of the Lord are right, and the righteous walk in them, but the rebellious stumble in them."

Outline

1. Marriage Metaphors and Symbolic Actions (1.1–3.8)
   a. Narrates a prophetic sign act where the prophet identifies with Yahweh (1.1–41)
   b. Poetically describes Yahweh's relationship with Israel (2.1–93)
   c. A second metaphor with the prophet as a spouse, clarifying the judgment and promise implied in ch. 1 (3.1–8)

2. Accusations, Judgment, Calls to Return (4.1–6.33)
   a. Accuses Israel's leadership of adultery and confronts/rebukes their covenantal failures (4.1–5.57)
   b. Calls for Israel to return to the Yahweh who has passed judgment on them but still longs for their loyalty and fidelity (6.1–33)

3. Politics, Idolatry, Punishment, and a Paternal Metaphor (7.1–10.69)
   a. Calls out Israel's errant political policies and punishes Israel's errant worship practices (7.1–8.53)
   b. Details Israel's punishment and retribution for their covenant failings (9.1–10.69)

4. Father and son relational metaphor for Israel's rebellion and shows Israel what it means for Assyria to be their king instead of Yahweh (11.1–46)

5. Judgment and a Call to Return (12.1–14.36)
   a. History lesson and reminder that Jacob is no longer a deceiver (12.1–13.63)
   b. Final call to repentance and the final word of hope. One day Israel will be healed of their wayward ways and Yahweh will no longer need to punish them for breaking covenant (14.1–36)

Suggested Resources

Fretheim, Terence. *Reading Hosea–Micah: A Literary and Theological Commentary*. Macon, GA: Smyth & Helwys, 2013.

Heschel, Abraham J. *The Prophets*. New York: HarperCollins, 2001.

Lim, Bo H., and Daniel Castelo. *Hosea*. Two Horizons Old Testament Commentary. Grand Rapids: Eerdmans, 2015.

Limburg, James. *Hosea–Micah*. Interpretation. Atlanta: John Knox Press, 1988.

O'Brien, Julia M., ed. *The Oxford Handbook of the Minor Prophets*. Oxford: Oxford University Press, 2021.

Stuart, Douglas. *Hosea–Jonah*. Word Biblical Commentary. Dallas: Thomas Nelson, 1987.

Zvi, Ehud Ben. *Hosea*. Forms of the Old Testament Literature. Grand Rapids: Eerdmans, 2005.

Hosea

1   The word of the Lord that came to Hosea son of Beeri during the reigns of Uzziah, Jotham, Ahaz, and Hezekiah, kings of Judah, and of Jeroboam son of Jehoash, king of Israel.

When the Lord first spoke to Hosea, he said this to him:
>Go and marry a woman of promiscuity,
>and have children of promiscuity,
>for the land is committing blatant acts of promiscuity
>by abandoning the Lord.

So he went and married Gomer daughter of Diblaim, and she conceived and bore him a son.
10 Then the Lord said to him:
>Name him Jezreel, for in a little while
>I will bring the bloodshed of Jezreel
>on the house of Jehu
>and put an end to the kingdom of the house of Israel.
>On that day I will break the bow of Israel
>in Jezreel Valley.

She conceived again and gave birth to a daughter, and the Lord said to him:
>Name her Lo-ruhamah,
>for I will no longer have compassion
20 on the house of Israel.
>I will certainly take them away.
>But I will have compassion on the house of Judah,
>and I will deliver them by the Lord their God.
>I will not deliver them by bow, sword, or war,
>or by horses and cavalry.

After Gomer had weaned Lo-ruhamah, she conceived and gave birth to a son. Then the Lord said:
>Name him Lo-ammi,
>for you are not my people,

867

30　　　and I will not be your God.
　　　　Yet the number of the Israelites
　　　　will be like the sand of the sea,
　　　　which cannot be measured or counted.
　　　　And in the place where they were told:
　　　　You are not my people,
　　　　they will be called: Sons of the living God.
　　　　And the Judeans and the Israelites
　　　　will be gathered together.
　　　　They will appoint for themselves a single ruler
40　　　and go up from the land.
　　　　For the day of Jezreel will be great.

2　　Call your brothers: My People
　　　　and your sisters: Compassion.

　　　　Rebuke your mother; rebuke her.
　　　　For she is not my wife and I am not her husband.
　　　　Let her remove the promiscuous look from her face
　　　　and her adultery from between her breasts.
　　　　Otherwise, I will strip her naked
　　　　and expose her as she was on the day of her birth.
　　　　I will make her like a desert
10　　　and like a parched land,
　　　　and I will let her die of thirst.
　　　　I will have no compassion on her children
　　　　because they are the children of promiscuity.
　　　　Yes, their mother is promiscuous;
　　　　she conceived them and acted shamefully.
　　　　For she thought, "I will follow my lovers,
　　　　the men who give me my food and water,
　　　　my wool and flax, my oil and drink."
　　　　Therefore, this is what I will do:
20　　　I will block her way with thorns;
　　　　I will enclose her with a wall,
　　　　so that she cannot find her paths.
　　　　She will pursue her lovers but not catch them;
　　　　she will look for them but not find them.

Then she will think,
"I will go back to my former husband,
for then it was better for me than now."
She does not recognize
that it is I who gave her the grain,
30 the new wine, and the fresh oil.
I lavished silver and gold on her,
which they used for Baal.
Therefore, I will take back my grain in its time
and my new wine in its season;
I will take away my wool and linen,
which were to cover her nakedness.
Now I will expose her shame
in the sight of her lovers,
and no one will rescue her from my power.
40 I will put an end to all her celebrations:
her feasts, New Moons, and Sabbaths—
all her festivals.
I will devastate her vines and fig trees.
She thinks that these are her wages
that her lovers have given her.
I will turn them into a thicket,
and the wild animals will eat them.
And I will punish her for the days of the Baals,
to which she burned incense.
50 She put on her rings and her jewelry
and followed her lovers,
but she forgot me.
This is the Lord's declaration.

Therefore, I am going to persuade her,
lead her to the wilderness,
and speak tenderly to her.
There I will give her vineyards back to her
and make the Valley of Achor
into a gateway of hope.
60 There she will respond as she did
in the days of her youth,

as in the day she came out of the land of Egypt.
In that day—
this is the LORD's declaration—
you will call me "my husband"
and no longer call me "my Baal."
For I will remove the names of the Baals
from her mouth;
they will no longer be remembered by their names.

70   On that day I will make a covenant for them
with the wild animals, the birds of the sky,
and the creatures that crawl on the ground.
I will shatter bow, sword,
and weapons of war in the land
and will enable the people to rest securely.
I will take you to be my wife forever.
I will take you to be my wife in righteousness,
justice, love, and compassion.
I will take you to be my wife in faithfulness,

80   and you will know the LORD.
On that day I will respond—
this is the LORD's declaration.
I will respond to the sky,
and it will respond to the earth.
The earth will respond to the grain,
the new wine, and the fresh oil,
and they will respond to Jezreel.
I will sow her in the land for myself,
and I will have compassion

90   on Lo-ruhamah;
I will say to Lo-ammi:
You are my people,
and he will say, "You are my God."

3 Then the LORD said to me, "Go again; show love to a woman who is loved by another man and is an adulteress, just as the LORD loves the Israelites though they turn to other gods and love raisin cakes."

So I bought her for fifteen shekels of silver and nine bushels of barley. I said to her, "You are to live with me many days. You must not be promiscuous or belong to any man, and I will act the same way toward you."

For the Israelites must live many days without king or prince, without sacrifice or sacred pillar, and without ephod or household idols. Afterward, the people of Israel will return and seek the LORD their God and David their king. They will come with awe to the LORD and to his goodness in the last days.

4 Hear the word of the LORD, people of Israel,
   for the LORD has a case
   against the inhabitants of the land:
   There is no truth, no faithful love,
   and no knowledge of God in the land!
   Cursing, lying, murder, stealing,
   and adultery are rampant;
   one act of bloodshed follows another.
   For this reason the land mourns,
10 and everyone who lives in it languishes,
   along with the wild animals and the birds of the sky;
   even the fish of the sea disappear.
   But let no one dispute; let no one argue,
   for my case is against you priests.
   You will stumble by day;
   the prophet will also stumble with you by night.
   And I will destroy your mother.
   My people are destroyed for lack of knowledge.
   Because you have rejected knowledge,
20 I will reject you from serving as my priest.
   Since you have forgotten the law of your God,
   I will also forget your sons.

   The more they multiplied,
   the more they sinned against me.
   I will change their honor into disgrace.
   They feed on the sin of my people;
   they have an appetite for their iniquity.
   The same judgment will happen
   to both people and priests.
30 I will punish them for their ways
   and repay them for their deeds.
   They will eat but not be satisfied;
   they will be promiscuous but not multiply.

For they have abandoned their devotion to the LORD.
Promiscuity, wine, and new wine
take away one's understanding.

My people consult their wooden idols,
and their divining rods inform them.
For a spirit of promiscuity leads them astray;
they act promiscuously
in disobedience to their God.
They sacrifice on the mountaintops,
and they burn offerings on the hills,
and under oaks, poplars, and terebinths,
because their shade is pleasant.
And so your daughters act promiscuously
and your daughters-in-law commit adultery.
I will not punish your daughters
when they act promiscuously
or your daughters-in-law
when they commit adultery,
for the men themselves go off with prostitutes
and make sacrifices with cult prostitutes.
People without discernment are doomed.

Israel, if you act promiscuously,
don't let Judah become guilty!
Do not go to Gilgal
or make a pilgrimage to Beth-aven,
and do not swear an oath: As the LORD lives!
For Israel is as obstinate as a stubborn cow.
Can the LORD now shepherd them
like a lamb in an open meadow?
Ephraim is attached to idols;
leave him alone!
When their drinking is over,
they turn to promiscuity.
Israel's leaders fervently love disgrace.
A wind with its wings will carry them off,
and they will be ashamed of their sacrifices.

5 Hear this, priests!
Pay attention, house of Israel!
Listen, royal house!
For the judgment applies to you
because you have been a snare at Mizpah
and a net spread out on Tabor.
Rebels are deeply involved in slaughter;
I will be a punishment for all of them.
I know Ephraim,
10 and Israel is not hidden from me.
For now, Ephraim,
you have acted promiscuously;
Israel is defiled.
Their actions do not allow them
to return to their God,
for a spirit of promiscuity is among them,
and they do not know the LORD.
Israel's arrogance testifies against them.
Both Israel and Ephraim stumble
20 because of their iniquity;
even Judah will stumble with them.
They go with their flocks and herds
to seek the LORD
but do not find him;
he has withdrawn from them.
They betrayed the LORD;
indeed, they gave birth to illegitimate children.
Now the New Moon will devour them
along with their fields.

30 Blow the ram's horn in Gibeah,
the trumpet in Ramah;
raise the war cry in Beth-aven:
Look behind you, Benjamin!
Ephraim will become a desolation
on the day of punishment;
I announce what is certain
among the tribes of Israel.

The princes of Judah are like those
who move boundary markers;
40 I will pour out my fury on them like water.
Ephraim is oppressed, crushed in judgment,
for he is determined to follow what is worthless.
So I am like rot to Ephraim
and like decay to the house of Judah.
When Ephraim saw his sickness
and Judah his wound,
Ephraim went to Assyria
and sent a delegation to the great king.
But he cannot cure you or heal your wound.
50 For I am like a lion to Ephraim
and like a young lion to the house of Judah.
Yes, I will tear them to pieces and depart.
I will carry them off,
and no one can rescue them.
I will depart and return to my place
until they recognize their guilt and seek my face;
they will search for me in their distress.

6 Come, let's return to the LORD.
For he has torn us,
and he will heal us;
he has wounded us,
and he will bind up our wounds.
He will revive us after two days,
and on the third day he will raise us up
so we can live in his presence.
Let's strive to know the LORD.
10 His appearance is as sure as the dawn.
He will come to us like the rain,
like the spring showers that water the land.

What am I going to do with you, Ephraim?
What am I going to do with you, Judah?
Your love is like the morning mist
and like the early dew that vanishes.

This is why I have used the prophets
to cut them down;
I have killed them with the words from my mouth.
My judgment strikes like lightning.
For I desire faithful love and not sacrifice,
the knowledge of God rather than burnt offerings.

But they, like Adam, have violated the covenant;
there they have betrayed me.
Gilead is a city of evildoers,
tracked with bloody footprints.
Like raiders who wait in ambush for someone,
a band of priests murders on the road to Shechem.
They commit atrocities.
I have seen something horrible in the house of Israel:
Ephraim's promiscuity is there; Israel is defiled.
A harvest is also appointed for you, Judah.

When I restore the fortunes of my people,

when I heal Israel,
the iniquity of Ephraim and the crimes of Samaria
will be exposed.
For they practice fraud;
a thief breaks in;
a raiding party pillages outside.
But they never consider that I remember all their evil.
Now their actions are all around them;
they are right in front of my face.

They please the king with their evil,
the princes with their lies.
All of them commit adultery;
they are like an oven heated by a baker
who stops stirring the fire
from the kneading of the dough until it is leavened.
On the day of our king,
the princes are sick with the heat of wine—

there is a conspiracy with traitors.
For they — their hearts like an oven—
draw him into their oven.
Their anger smolders all night;
in the morning it blazes like a flaming fire.
All of them are as hot as an oven,
and they consume their rulers.
All their kings fall;
not one of them calls on me.

Ephraim has allowed himself to get mixed up with the nations.
Ephraim is unturned bread baked on a griddle.
Foreigners consume his strength,
but he does not notice.
Even his hair is streaked with gray,
but he does not notice.
Israel's arrogance testifies against them,
yet they do not return to the LORD their God,
and for all this, they do not seek him.

So Ephraim has become like a silly, senseless dove;
they call to Egypt, and they go to Assyria.
As they are going, I will spread my net over them;
I will bring them down like birds of the sky.
I will discipline them in accordance
with the news that reaches their assembly.

Woe to them, for they fled from me;
destruction to them, for they rebelled against me!
Though I want to redeem them,
they speak lies against me.
They do not cry to me from their hearts;
rather, they wail on their beds.
They slash themselves for grain and new wine;
they turn away from me.
I trained and strengthened their arms,
but they plot evil against me.
They turn, but not to what is above;

they are like a faulty bow.
Their leaders will fall by the sword
because of their insolent tongue.
They will be ridiculed for this in the land of Egypt.

8   Put the ram's horn to your mouth!
One like an eagle comes
against the house of the LORD,
because they transgress my covenant
and rebel against my law.
Israel cries out to me,
"My God, we know you!"
Israel has rejected what is good;
an enemy will pursue him.

10   They have installed kings,
but not through me.
They have appointed leaders,
but without my approval.
They make their silver and gold
into idols for themselves
for their own destruction.
Your calf-idol is rejected, Samaria.
My anger burns against them.
How long will they be incapable of innocence?
20   For this thing is from Israel—
a craftsman made it, and it is not God.
The calf of Samaria will be smashed to bits!

Indeed, they sow the wind
and reap the whirlwind.
There is no standing grain;
what sprouts fails to yield flour.
Even if they did,
foreigners would swallow it up.
Israel is swallowed up!
30   Now they are among the nations
like discarded pottery.

For they have gone up to Assyria
like a wild donkey going off on its own.
Ephraim has paid for love.
Even though they hire lovers among the nations,
I will now round them up,
and they will begin to decrease in number
under the burden of the king and leaders.

When Ephraim multiplied his altars for sin,
40   they became his altars for sinning.
Though I were to write out for him
ten thousand points of my instruction,
they would be regarded as something strange.
Though they offer sacrificial gifts
and eat the flesh,
the Lord does not accept them.
Now he will remember their guilt
and punish their sins;
they will return to Egypt.
50   Israel has forgotten his Maker and built palaces;
Judah has also multiplied fortified cities.
I will send fire on their cities,
and it will consume their citadels.

9   Israel, do not rejoice jubilantly as the nations do,
for you have acted promiscuously, leaving your God.
You love the wages of a prostitute
on every grain-threshing floor.
Threshing floor and wine vat will not sustain them,
and the new wine will fail them.
They will not stay in the land of the Lord.
Instead, Ephraim will return to Egypt,
and they will eat unclean food in Assyria.

10   They will not pour out
their wine offerings to the Lord,
and their sacrifices will not please him.
Their food will be like the bread of mourners;

all who eat it become defiled.
For their bread will be for their appetites alone;
it will not enter the house of the LORD.
What will you do on a festival day,
on the day of the LORD's feast?
For even if they flee from devastation,
Egypt will gather them, and Memphis will bury them.
Thistles will take possession of their precious silver;
thorns will invade their tents.

The days of punishment have come;
the days of retribution have come.
Let Israel recognize it!
The prophet is a fool,
and the inspired man is insane,
because of the magnitude
of your iniquity and hostility.
Ephraim's watchman is with my God.
Yet the prophet encounters a bird trap
on all his pathways.
Hostility is in the house of his God!
They have deeply corrupted themselves
as in the days of Gibeah.
He will remember their iniquity;
he will punish their sins.

I discovered Israel
like grapes in the wilderness.
I saw your ancestors
like the first fruit of the fig tree in its first season.
But they went to Baal-peor,
consecrated themselves to Shame,
and became abhorrent,
like the thing they loved.
Ephraim's glory will fly away like a bird:
no birth, no pregnancy, no conception.
Even if they raise children,
I will bereave them of each one.

50   Yes, woe to them when I depart from them!
    I have seen Ephraim like Tyre,
    planted in a meadow,
    so Ephraim will bring out his children
    to the executioner.
    Give them, Lord—
    What should you give?
    Give them a womb that miscarries
    and breasts that are dry!

    All their evil appears at Gilgal,
60   for there I began to hate them.
    I will drive them from my house
    because of their evil, wicked actions.
    I will no longer love them;
    all their leaders are rebellious.
    Ephraim is struck down;
    their roots are withered;
    they cannot bear fruit.
    Even if they bear children,
    I will kill the precious offspring of their wombs.
70   My God will reject them
    because they have not listened to him;
    they will become wanderers among the nations.

10   Israel is a lush vine;
    it yields fruit for itself.
    The more his fruit increased,
    the more he increased the altars.
    The better his land produced,
    the better they made the sacred pillars.
    Their hearts are devious;
    now they must bear their guilt.
    The Lord will break down their altars
10   and demolish their sacred pillars.
    In fact, they are now saying,
    "We have no king!
    For we do not fear the Lord.

What can a king do for us?"
They speak mere words,
taking false oaths while making covenants.
So lawsuits break out
like poisonous weeds in the furrows of a field.

The residents of Samaria will have anxiety
over the calf of Beth-aven.
Indeed, its idolatrous priests rejoiced over it;
the people will mourn over it,
over its glory.
It will certainly go into exile.
The calf itself will be taken to Assyria
as an offering to the great king.
Ephraim will experience shame;
Israel will be ashamed of its counsel.
Samaria's king will disappear
like foam on the surface of the water.
The high places of Aven, the sin of Israel,
will be destroyed;
thorns and thistles will grow over their altars.
They will say to the mountains, "Cover us!"
and to the hills, "Fall on us!"

Israel, you have sinned
since the days of Gibeah;
they have taken their stand there.
Will not war against the unjust
overtake them in Gibeah?
I will discipline them at my discretion;
nations will be gathered against them
to put them in bondage
for their double iniquity.

Ephraim is a well-trained calf
that loves to thresh,
but I will place a yoke on her fine neck.
I will harness Ephraim;

50

Judah will plow;
Jacob will do the final plowing.
Sow righteousness for yourselves
and reap faithful love;
break up your unplowed ground.
It is time to seek the LORD
until he comes and sends righteousness
on you like the rain.

You have plowed wickedness and reaped injustice;
you have eaten the fruit of lies.
Because you have trusted in your own way

60

and in your large number of soldiers,
the roar of battle will rise against your people,
and all your fortifications will be demolished
in a day of war,
like Shalman's destruction of Beth-arbel.
Mothers will be dashed to pieces
along with their children.
So it will be done to you, Bethel,
because of your extreme evil.
At dawn the king of Israel will be totally destroyed.

11

When Israel was a child, I loved him,
and out of Egypt I called my son.
Israel called to the Egyptians
even as Israel was leaving them.
They kept sacrificing to the Baals
and burning offerings to idols.
It was I who taught Ephraim to walk,
taking them by the hand,
but they never knew that I healed them.

10

I led them with human cords,
with ropes of love.
To them I was like one
who eases the yoke from their jaws;
I bent down to give them food.
Israel will not return to the land of Egypt

and Assyria will be his king,
because they refused to repent.
A sword will whirl through his cities;
it will destroy and devour the bars of his gates,
because of their schemes.
My people are bent on turning from me.
Though they call to him on high,
he will not exalt them at all.

How can I give you up, Ephraim?
How can I surrender you, Israel?
How can I make you like Admah?
How can I treat you like Zeboiim?
I have had a change of heart;
my compassion is stirred!
I will not vent the full fury of my anger;
I will not turn back to destroy Ephraim.
For I am God and not man,
the Holy One among you;
I will not come in rage.
They will follow the LORD;
he will roar like a lion.
When he roars,
his children will come trembling from the west.
They will be roused like birds from Egypt
and like doves from the land of Assyria.
Then I will settle them in their homes.
This is the LORD's declaration.
Ephraim surrounds me with lies,
the house of Israel, with deceit.
Judah still wanders with God
and is faithful to the holy ones.

12 Ephraim chases the wind
and pursues the east wind.
He continually multiplies lies and violence.
He makes a covenant with Assyria,
and olive oil is carried to Egypt.

The LORD also has a dispute with Judah.
He is about to punish Jacob according to his conduct;
he will repay him based on his actions.
In the womb he grasped his brother's heel,
and as an adult he wrestled with God.
Jacob struggled with the angel and prevailed;
he wept and sought his favor.
He found him at Bethel,
and there he spoke with him.
The LORD is the God of Armies;
the LORD is his name.
But you must return to your God.
Maintain love and justice,
and always put your hope in God.

A merchant loves to extort
with dishonest scales in his hands.
But Ephraim thinks,
"How rich I have become;
I made it all myself.
In all my earnings,
no one can find any iniquity in me
that I can be punished for!"

I have been the LORD your God
ever since the land of Egypt.
I will make you live in tents again,
as in the festival days.
I will speak through the prophets
and grant many visions;
I will give parables through the prophets.
Since Gilead is full of evil,
they will certainly come to nothing.
They sacrifice bulls in Gilgal;
even their altars will be like piles of rocks
on the furrows of a field.

40 Jacob fled to the territory of Aram.
Israel worked to earn a wife;
he tended flocks for a wife.
The Lord brought Israel from Egypt by a prophet,
and Israel was tended by a prophet.

Ephraim has provoked bitter anger,
so his Lord will leave his bloodguilt on him
and repay him for his contempt.

13 When Ephraim spoke, there was trembling;
he was exalted in Israel.
But he incurred guilt through Baal and died.

Now they continue to sin
and make themselves a cast image,
idols skillfully made from their silver,
all of them the work of craftsmen.
People say about them,
"Let the men who sacrifice kiss the calves."
10 Therefore, they will be like the morning mist,
like the early dew that vanishes,
like chaff blown from a threshing floor,
or like smoke from a window.

I have been the Lord your God
ever since the land of Egypt;
you know no God but me,
and no Savior exists besides me.
I knew you in the wilderness,
in the land of drought.
20 When they had pasture,
they became satisfied;
they were satisfied,
and their hearts became proud.
Therefore they forgot me.
So I will be like a lion to them;
I will lurk like a leopard on the path.

I will attack them
like a bear robbed of her cubs
and tear open the rib cage over their hearts.
30   I will devour them there like a lioness,
like a wild beast that would rip them open.
I will destroy you, Israel;
you have no help but me.

Where now is your king,
that he may save you in all your cities,
and the rulers you demanded, saying,
"Give me a king and leaders"?
I give you a king in my anger
and take away a king in my wrath.
40   Ephraim's guilt is preserved;
his sin is stored up.
Labor pains come on him.
He is not a wise son;
when the time comes,
he will not be born.

I will ransom them from the power of Sheol.
I will redeem them from death.
Death, where are your barbs?
Sheol, where is your sting?
50   Compassion is hidden from my eyes.

Although he flourishes among his brothers,
an east wind will come,
a wind from the LORD rising up from the desert.
His water source will fail,
and his spring will run dry.
The wind will plunder the treasury
of every precious item.

Samaria will bear her guilt
because she has rebelled against her God.
60   They will fall by the sword;

their children will be dashed to pieces,
and their pregnant women ripped open.

14 Israel, return to the LORD your God,
for you have stumbled in your iniquity.
Take words of repentance with you
and return to the LORD.
Say to him, "Forgive all our iniquity
and accept what is good,
so that we may repay you
with praise from our lips.
Assyria will not save us,
10 we will not ride on horses,
and we will no longer proclaim, 'Our gods!'
to the work of our hands.
For the fatherless receives compassion in you."

I will heal their apostasy;
I will freely love them,
for my anger will have turned from him.
I will be like the dew to Israel;
he will blossom like the lily
and take root like the cedars of Lebanon.
20 His new branches will spread,
and his splendor will be like the olive tree,
his fragrance, like the forest of Lebanon.
The people will return and live beneath his shade.
They will grow grain
and blossom like the vine.
His renown will be like the wine of Lebanon.

Ephraim, why should I have anything more
to do with idols?
It is I who answer and watch over him.
30 I am like a flourishing pine tree;
your fruit comes from me.

Let whoever is wise understand these things,
and whoever is insightful recognize them.
For the ways of the LORD are right,
and the righteous walk in them,
but the rebellious stumble in them.

Introduction to Joel

Joel Barker

The book of Joel captivates its readers with images of ravenous locusts, invading armies, and upheaval in the heavenly realm. They also provide the backdrop for Joel to reflect on the nature of Yahweh and his relationship with his people. The book of Joel brings together terrifying portraits of divine judgment and reassuring promises of divine compassion and presence as it explores the essence of Yahweh's character.

The specific temporal setting of Joel is unknowable given its lack of identifying historical markers. Some view it as preexilic, with the locust imagery foretelling Babylonian soldiers; others consider it postexilic, with the locusts reflecting an actual locust plague. Against either backdrop, we see its core message come through: in times of crisis, Yahweh's people are invited to cry out to him for deliverance.

Thematically, Joel introduces a series of calamities in the first half of the book that are resolved in the latter half. These include the desolation of the landscape brought about by the locusts, an extensive drought, and the threat of the destruction of Zion by an invading horde. These disasters give way to hope in the latter part of the book when Yahweh promises to restore the land and its bounty, pour out his spirit among his people, and remove the threat of foreign nations by residing in Zion. Joel calls his audience to despair before promising deliverance rooted in Yahweh's presence. The Day of the Lord is essential to this progression. The prophet uses the Day of the Lord initially as a threat of judgment (1.58–60; 2.1–5, 43–48), before turning it into a promise of restoration (2.123–127; 3.40–43).

Joel transitions between these two perspectives on the Day of the Lord by reflecting upon Yahweh's essential qualities of mercy and compassion. In doing so, he borrows from Yahweh's own declaration of his character to Moses on Mount Sinai (Exod 34.9–13). With that reminder, Joel calls his audience to put their trust in Yahweh and to cry out to him. The latter half of the book suggests that Yahweh will respond in keeping with his character. The Day of the Lord thus no longer portends destruction, but rather deliverance and hope.

Joel is also valuable commentary on the HS on account of its many allusions. Most notable is the reversal in Joel 3.24–26 of the "swords into plowshares" motif from Isa 2.14–19 and Mic 4.14–20. Whereas Isaiah and Micah envision the nations peacefully gathering in Zion under Yahweh's sovereignty, Joel articulates that Yahweh can also break the power of the nations who stand against him. Further, both Joel and Jonah reflect on human inability to fully comprehend Yahweh, sharing the question: "Who knows?" In both cases, seekers learn that appeals to Yahweh do not go unheard and that compassion and mercy are close at hand. Joel and Amos both use the image of Yahweh roaring from Zion but assign it different implications in accordance with their intended messages.

Ultimately, Joel reminds the reader of Yahweh's sovereignty over his creation and his people. He uses the natural forces of the world to bring judgment and to enact restoration. He stands above all nations, including those who threaten his people. The people of Yahweh are called to appeal to him in the face of calamity, trusting that he will respond to their cries with mercy and compassion.

Outline

1. Despair (1.1–2.48)
    a. A call to cry out in response to a locust invasion (1.1–57)
    b. The initial announcement of the Day of the Lord and a warning of drought (1.58–81)
    c. The Day of the Lord envisioned as an attack against Zion (2.1–48)

2. Turning Point: The prophet's call for the people to respond by appealing to Yahweh's gracious and compassionate nature (2.49–80)

3. Deliverance (2.81–3.70)
    a. Promised restoration for the calamities caused by the locusts (2.81–122)
    b. Promised restoration through the presence of Yahweh's spirit (2.123–141)
    c. Promised deliverance from foreign enemies through Yahweh's presence in Zion (3.1–70)

Suggested Resources

Baker, David W. *Joel, Obadiah, Malachi*. NIV Application Commentary. Grand Rapids: Zondervan, 2006.

Barker, Joel. *Joel*. Zondervan Exegetical Commentary of the Old Testament. Grand Rapids: Zondervan, 2020.

Coggins, Richard J. *Joel and Amos*. New Century Bible Commentary. Sheffield: Sheffield Academic, 2000.

Crenshaw, James L. *Joel*. Anchor Bible Commentary. New York: Doubleday, 1995.

Garrett, Duane A. *Hosea, Joel*. New American Commentary. Nashville: Broadman & Holman, 1995.

Joel

1 The word of the Lord that came to Joel son of Pethuel:

> Hear this, you elders;
> listen, all you inhabitants of the land.
> Has anything like this ever happened in your days
> or in the days of your ancestors?
> Tell your children about it,
> and let your children tell their children,
> and their children the next generation.
> What the devouring locust has left,
> the swarming locust has eaten;
> what the swarming locust has left,
> the young locust has eaten;
> and what the young locust has left,
> the destroying locust has eaten.
>
> Wake up, you drunkards, and weep;
> wail, all you wine drinkers,
> because of the sweet wine,
> for it has been taken from your mouth.
> For a nation has invaded my land,
> powerful and without number;
> its teeth are the teeth of a lion,
> and it has the fangs of a lioness.
> It has devastated my grapevine
> and splintered my fig tree.
> It has stripped off its bark and thrown it away;
> its branches have turned white.
> Grieve like a young woman dressed in sackcloth,
> mourning for the husband of her youth.
> Grain and drink offerings have been cut off
> from the house of the Lord;

the priests, who are ministers of the LORD, mourn.
The fields are destroyed;
the land grieves;
indeed, the grain is destroyed;
the new wine is dried up;
and the fresh oil fails.
Be ashamed, you farmers,
wail, you vinedressers,
over the wheat and the barley,
40   because the harvest of the field has perished.
The grapevine is dried up,
and the fig tree is withered;
the pomegranate, the date palm, and the apple—
all the trees of the orchard — have withered.
Indeed, human joy has dried up.

Dress in sackcloth and lament, you priests;
wail, you ministers of the altar.
Come and spend the night in sackcloth,
you ministers of my God,
50   because grain and drink offerings
are withheld from the house of your God.
Announce a sacred fast;
proclaim a solemn assembly!
Gather the elders
and all the residents of the land
at the house of the LORD your God,
and cry out to the LORD.

Woe because of that day!
For the day of the LORD is near
60   and will come as devastation from the Almighty.
Hasn't the food been cut off
before our eyes,
joy and gladness
from the house of our God?
The seeds lie shriveled in their casings.
The storehouses are in ruin,

and the granaries are broken down,
because the grain has withered away.
How the animals groan!
70　The herds of cattle wander in confusion
since they have no pasture.
Even the flocks of sheep and goats suffer punishment.
I call to you, Lord,
for fire has consumed
the pastures of the wilderness,
and flames have devoured
all the trees of the orchard.
Even the wild animals cry out to you,
for the river beds are dried up,
80　and fire has consumed
the pastures of the wilderness.

2　　Blow the ram's horn in Zion;
sound the alarm on my holy mountain!
Let all the residents of the land tremble,
for the day of the Lord is coming;
in fact, it is near—
a day of darkness and gloom,
a day of clouds and total darkness,
like the dawn spreading over the mountains;
a great and strong people appears,
10　such as never existed in ages past
and never will again
in all the generations to come.

A fire devours in front of them,
and behind them a flame blazes.
The land in front of them
is like the garden of Eden,
but behind them,
it is like a desert wasteland;
there is no escape from them.
20　Their appearance is like that of horses,
and they gallop like war horses.

They bound on the tops of the mountains.
Their sound is like the sound of chariots,
like the sound of fiery flames consuming stubble,
like a mighty army deployed for war.

Nations writhe in horror before them;
all faces turn pale.
They attack as warriors attack;
they scale walls as men of war do.
30   Each goes on his own path,
and they do not change their course.
They do not push each other;
each proceeds on his own path.
They dodge the arrows, never stopping.
They storm the city;
they run on the wall;
they climb into the houses;
they enter through the windows like thieves.

The earth quakes before them;
40   the sky shakes.
The sun and moon grow dark,
and the stars cease their shining.
The LORD makes his voice heard
in the presence of his army.
His camp is very large;
those who carry out his command are powerful.
Indeed, the day of the LORD is terrible and dreadful—
who can endure it?

Even now—
50   this is the LORD's declaration—
turn to me with all your heart,
with fasting, weeping, and mourning.
Tear your hearts,
not just your clothes,
and return to the LORD your God.
For he is gracious and compassionate,

slow to anger, abounding in faithful love,
and he relents from sending disaster.
Who knows? He may turn and relent
60 and leave a blessing behind him,
so you can offer a grain offering and a drink offering
to the LORD your God.

Blow the ram's horn in Zion!
Announce a sacred fast;
proclaim a solemn assembly.
Gather the people;
sanctify the congregation;
assemble the aged;
gather the infants,
70 even babies nursing at the breast.
Let the groom leave his bedroom,
and the bride her honeymoon chamber.
Let the priests, the LORD's ministers,
weep between the portico and the altar.
Let them say,
"Have pity on your people, LORD,
and do not make your inheritance a disgrace,
an object of scorn among the nations.
Why should it be said among the peoples,
80 'Where is their God?'"

Then the LORD became jealous for his land and spared his people. The LORD answered his people:
Look, I am about to send you
grain, new wine, and fresh oil.
You will be satiated with them,
and I will no longer make you
a disgrace among the nations.

I will drive the northerner far from you
and banish him to a dry and desolate land,
his front ranks into the Dead Sea,
90 and his rear guard into the Mediterranean Sea.
His stench will rise;

yes, his rotten smell will rise,
for he has done astonishing things.

Don't be afraid, land;
rejoice and be glad,
for the LORD has done astonishing things.
Don't be afraid, wild animals,
for the wilderness pastures have turned green,
the trees bear their fruit,
100 and the fig tree and grapevine yield their riches.
Children of Zion, rejoice and be glad
in the LORD your God,
because he gives you the autumn rain
for your vindication.
He sends showers for you,
both autumn and spring rain as before.
The threshing floors will be full of grain,
and the vats will overflow
with new wine and fresh oil.

110 I will repay you for the years
that the swarming locust ate,
the young locust, the destroying locust,
and the devouring locust—
my great army that I sent against you.
You will have plenty to eat and be satisfied.
You will praise the name of the LORD your God,
who has dealt wondrously with you.
My people will never again be put to shame.
You will know that I am present in Israel
120 and that I am the LORD your God,
and there is no other.
My people will never again be put to shame.

After this
I will pour out my Spirit on all humanity;
then your sons and your daughters will prophesy,
your old men will have dreams,

and your young men will see visions.
I will even pour out my Spirit
on the male and female slaves in those days.
130 I will display wonders
in the heavens and on the earth:
blood, fire, and columns of smoke.
The sun will be turned to darkness
and the moon to blood
before the great and terrible day of the Lord comes.
Then everyone who calls
on the name of the Lord will be saved,
for there will be an escape
for those on Mount Zion and in Jerusalem,
140 as the Lord promised,
among the survivors the Lord calls.

3 Yes, in those days and at that time,
when I restore the fortunes of Judah and Jerusalem,
I will gather all the nations
and take them to the Valley of Jehoshaphat.
I will enter into judgment with them there
because of my people, my inheritance Israel.
The nations have scattered the Israelites
in foreign countries
and divided up my land.
10 They cast lots for my people;
they bartered a boy for a prostitute
and sold a girl for wine to drink.

And also: Tyre, Sidon, and all the territories of Philistia — what are you to me? Are you paying me back or trying to get even with me? I will quickly bring retribution on your heads. For you took my silver and gold and carried my finest treasures to your temples. You sold the people of Judah and Jerusalem to the Greeks to remove them far from their own territory. Look, I am about to rouse them up from the place where you sold them; I will bring retribution on your heads. I will sell your sons and daughters to the people of Judah, and they will sell them to the Sabeans, to a distant nation, for the Lord has spoken.

20 Proclaim this among the nations:
Prepare for holy war;

rouse the warriors;
let all the men of war advance and attack!
Beat your plows into swords
and your pruning knives into spears.
Let even the weakling say, "I am a warrior."
Come quickly, all you surrounding nations;
gather yourselves.
Bring down your warriors there, LORD.

30   Let the nations be roused
and come to the Valley of Jehoshaphat,
for there I will sit down
to judge all the surrounding nations.
Swing the sickle
because the harvest is ripe.
Come and trample the grapes
because the winepress is full;
the wine vats overflow
because the wickedness of the nations is extreme.

40   Multitudes, multitudes
in the valley of decision!
For the day of the LORD is near
in the valley of decision.
The sun and moon will grow dark,
and the stars will cease their shining.
The LORD will roar from Zion
and make his voice heard from Jerusalem;
heaven and earth will shake.
But the LORD will be a refuge for his people,
50   a stronghold for the Israelites.

Then you will know
that I am the LORD your God,
who dwells in Zion, my holy mountain.
Jerusalem will be holy,
and foreigners will never overrun it again.
In that day

the mountains will drip with sweet wine,
and the hills will flow with milk.
All the streams of Judah will flow with water,
60 and a spring will issue from the LORD's house,
watering the Valley of Acacias.
Egypt will become desolate,
and Edom a desert wasteland,
because of the violence done to the people of Judah
in whose land they shed innocent blood.
But Judah will be inhabited forever,
and Jerusalem from generation to generation.
I will pardon their bloodguilt,
which I have not pardoned,
70 for the LORD dwells in Zion.

Introduction to Amos

Archie W. England

The book of Amos has three primary units: oracles against the nations (1.8–2.62), the prophet's words and woes (3.1–6.51), and the prophet's visions (7.1–9.58). In many ways, Amos structures his message around the call to repentance through lament.

Like many other prophetic books, the message of Amos is carefully crafted with numerous literary devices, which highlight three predominant literary tropes woven through his message. In the oracles against the nations, Amos singles out six neighbors plus Judah and Israel by employing a formulaic expression (chs. 1–2). The prophet repeats, "For three sins of . . . and for four, I will not turn back," eight times and, in doing so, establishes the reasons and provides the justification for Yahweh's judgment.

Amos marks his message in chs. 3–6 with a series of commands ("Hear this word") to draw the readers' attention to the identified sin and, then, to evoke a response. Chapter 5 culminates this command-driven structure with a chiasm that leads the reader to "seek" Yahweh (5.12, 50–54), as well as to "seek good." In other words, to seek Yahweh and/or his goodness brings life; if not, death. Amos 5.67–92 unpacks that overwhelming Day of the Lord, segueing from their present decadence to a future of despair in ch. 6.

In the visions of the prophet (7.1–9.58), Amos intertwines the four poetic visions of Judah with a judgment narrative. Each vision begins with the formulaic, "Thus the Lord God showed me," and concludes with "it shall not be" in the first three. The fourth vision begins the same way, but invokes the imperative idea of Amos 3–6 to issue Yahweh's coming judgment.

Amos strings together imperatives, meditations, poetic vision, "that day" imagery, and a theme shared by several prophets—the Day of the Lord—to create a hard-hitting message. Amos's vision of Yahweh in ch. 9 completes his prophecy from 4.12: when Yahweh comes, there will be nowhere to hide (9.1–4). The sinfulness of all Israel (9.7–8) demands judgment. Nonetheless, God's promises mercy (9.9–10) to his remnant. His faithfulness will bring restoration and hope (9.11–15).

Amos attests to Israel's abuse of the sacrificial system and Yahweh's character to punish sin. Similar to his contemporaries Isaiah and Micah, Amos understood that relationship, not religious ritual, was the intent of the sacrificial system, decrying the rote ritual and it's nearing end.

Amos is indeed the prophet of justice (how Yahweh's people behave toward others) and righteousness (one's covenant relationship with Yahweh). From this, Amos powerfully depicts how wealth, power, prestige, and possessions are never reliable indicators that Yahweh is pleased with someone's life and behavior. Only the righteousness that results in justice (for all others) is what pleases Yahweh!

This prophetic message is masterfully organized to convey that Yahweh indeed sees all sin (chs. 1–2), confronts such sin (chs. 3–6), and judges that sin (chs. 7–9). After Yahweh's judgment, there is hope (9.59–83)! The hope that Yahweh will restore his people (imagery of the restored "fallen booth of David") is worked out in the NT (Acts 15:16–18). The God of Amos brings judgment but offers redemption: on "that day" when Yahweh acts, repentance will result in life to a people shaken and sifted, who will yet be spared and blessed by restoration and abundance, one day—on that day!

Outline

1. Introduction (1.1–7)

2. Eight Judgments: Against Israel and Her Neighbors
   a. Against the Neighboring Nations (1.8–2.12)
   b. Against Yahweh's People (2.13–62)

3. Five Exhortations to the Wayward Northern Tribes
   a. First Word: Judgment (3.1–59)
   b. Second Word: Judgment (4.1–66)
   c. Third Word: Lament (5.1–66)
   d. First Woe: The Day of the Lord (5.67–92)
   e. Second Woe: Exile and Despair (6.1–51)

4. Six Visions of the Future
   a. Vision of the Swarm of Locusts (7.1–4)
   b. Vision of the Fiery Judgment (7.5–9)
   c. Vision of the Plumb Line (7.10–17)
   d. Vision of Amaziah's Plight (7.18–37)
   e. Vision of the Basket of Summer Fruit (8.1–50)
   f. Vision of the Lord Standing by the Altar and Its Impact (9.1–58)

5. Conclusion (9.59–83)

Suggested Resources

Anderson, Francis. *Amos*. Anchor Bible Commentary. New York: Yale University Press, 1989.

Carroll, Daniel. *Amos*. New International Commentary on the Old Testament. Grand Rapids: Eerdmans, 2020.

Goldingay, John. *Hosea–Micah*. Baker Commentary on the Old Testament Prophetic Books. Grand Rapids: Baker Academic, 2021.

Shepherd, Michael. *Commentary on the Book of the Twelve*. Grand Rapids: Kregel, 2018.

Smith, Gary V. *Hosea, Amos, and Micah*. NIV Application Commentary. Grand Rapids: Zondervan, 2001.

Stuart, Douglas. *Hosea–Jonah*. Word Biblical Commentary. Dallas: Thomas Nelson, 1987.

Amos

I The words of Amos, who was one of the sheep breeders from Tekoa — what he saw regarding Israel in the
days of King Uzziah of Judah and Jeroboam son of Jehoash, king of Israel, two years before the earthquake.

He said:

> The LORD roars from Zion
> and makes his voice heard from Jerusalem;
> the pastures of the shepherds mourn,
> and the summit of Carmel withers.

The LORD says:

> I will not relent from punishing Damascus
> for three crimes, even four,
> because they threshed Gilead with iron sledges.
> Therefore, I will send fire against Hazael's palace,
> and it will consume Ben-hadad's citadels.
> I will break down the gates of Damascus.
> I will cut off the ruler from the Valley of Aven,
> and the one who wields the scepter from Beth-eden.
> The people of Aram will be exiled to Kir.
> The LORD has spoken.

The LORD says:

> I will not relent from punishing Gaza
> for three crimes, even four,
> because they exiled a whole community,
> handing them over to Edom.
> Therefore, I will send fire against the walls of Gaza,
> and it will consume its citadels.
> I will cut off the ruler from Ashdod,
> and the one who wields the scepter from Ashkelon.
> I will also turn my hand against Ekron,
> and the remainder of the Philistines will perish.
> The Lord GOD has spoken.

The Lord says:

    I will not relent from punishing Tyre
    for three crimes, even four,
    because they handed over
    a whole community of exiles to Edom
    and broke a treaty of brotherhood.
    Therefore, I will send fire against the walls of Tyre,
    and it will consume its citadels.

The Lord says:

    I will not relent from punishing Edom
    for three crimes, even four,
    because he pursued his brother with the sword.
    He stifled his compassion,
    his anger tore at him continually,
    and he harbored his rage incessantly.
    Therefore, I will send fire against Teman,
    and it will consume the citadels of Bozrah.

The Lord says:

    I will not relent from punishing the Ammonites
    for three crimes, even four,
    because they ripped open
    the pregnant women of Gilead
    in order to enlarge their territory.
    Therefore, I will set fire to the walls of Rabbah,
    and it will consume its citadels.
    There will be shouting on the day of battle
    and a violent wind on the day of the storm.
    Their king and his princes
    will go into exile together.
    The Lord has spoken.

2 The Lord says:

    I will not relent from punishing Moab
    for three crimes, even four,
    because he burned the bones

of the king of Edom to lime.
Therefore, I will send fire against Moab,
and it will consume the citadels of Kerioth.
Moab will die with a tumult,
with shouting and the sound of the ram's horn.
I will cut off the judge from the land
and kill all its officials with him.
The Lord has spoken.

The Lord says:
I will not relent from punishing Judah
for three crimes, even four,
because they have rejected the instruction of the Lord
and have not kept his statutes.
The lies that their ancestors followed
have led them astray.
Therefore, I will send fire against Judah,
and it will consume the citadels of Jerusalem.

The Lord says:
I will not relent from punishing Israel
for three crimes, even four,
because they sell a righteous person for silver
and a needy person for a pair of sandals.
They trample the heads of the poor
on the dust of the ground
and obstruct the path of the needy.
A man and his father have sexual relations
with the same girl,
profaning my holy name.
They stretch out beside every altar
on garments taken as collateral,
and in the house of their God
they drink wine obtained through fines.

Yet I destroyed the Amorite as Israel advanced;
his height was like the cedars,
and he was as sturdy as the oaks;

40   I destroyed his fruit above and his roots beneath.
    And I brought you from the land of Egypt
    and led you forty years in the wilderness
    in order to possess the land of the Amorite.
    I raised up some of your sons as prophets
    and some of your young men as Nazirites.
    Is this not the case, Israelites?

This is the Lord's declaration.
    But you made the Nazirites drink wine
    and commanded the prophets,
50   "Do not prophesy."
    Look, I am about to crush you in your place
    as a wagon crushes when full of grain.
    Escape will fail the swift,
    the strong one will not maintain his strength,
    and the warrior will not save his life.
    The archer will not stand his ground,
    the one who is swift of foot
    will not save himself,
    and the one riding a horse will not save his life.
60   Even the most courageous of the warriors
    will flee naked on that day—

this is the Lord's declaration.

3 Listen to this message that the Lord has spoken against you, Israelites, against the entire clan that
 I brought from the land of Egypt:
    I have known only you
    out of all the clans of the earth;
    therefore, I will punish you for all your iniquities.
    Can two walk together
    without agreeing to meet?
    Does a lion roar in the forest
    when it has no prey?
10   Does a young lion growl from its lair
    unless it has captured something?
    Does a bird land in a trap on the ground

if there is no bait for it?
Does a trap spring from the ground
when it has caught nothing?
If a ram's horn is blown in a city,
aren't people afraid?
If a disaster occurs in a city,
hasn't the LORD done it?

20   Indeed, the Lord GOD does nothing
without revealing his counsel
to his servants the prophets.
A lion has roared;
who will not fear?
The Lord GOD has spoken;
who will not prophesy?

Proclaim on the citadels in Ashdod
and on the citadels in the land of Egypt:
Assemble on the mountains of Samaria,

30   and see the great turmoil in the city
and the acts of oppression within it.
The people are incapable of doing right—
this is the LORD's declaration—
those who store up violence and destruction
in their citadels.

Therefore, the Lord GOD says:
An enemy will surround the land;
he will destroy your strongholds
and plunder your citadels.

40   The LORD says:
As the shepherd snatches two legs
or a piece of an ear
from the lion's mouth,
so the Israelites who live in Samaria
will be rescued
with only the corner of a bed
or the cushion of a couch.

Listen and testify against the house of Jacob—
this is the declaration of the Lord God,
50   the God of Armies.
I will punish the altars of Bethel
on the day I punish Israel for its crimes;
the horns of the altar will be cut off
and fall to the ground.
I will demolish the winter house
and the summer house;
the houses inlaid with ivory will be destroyed,
and the great houses will come to an end.

This is the Lord's declaration.

4   Listen to this message, you cows of Bashan
who are on the hill of Samaria,
women who oppress the poor
and crush the needy,
who say to their husbands,
"Bring us something to drink."

The Lord God has sworn by his holiness:
Look, the days are coming
when you will be taken away with hooks,
10   every last one of you with fishhooks.
You will go through breaches in the wall,
each woman straight ahead,
and you will be driven along toward Harmon.
This is the Lord's declaration.

Come to Bethel and rebel;
rebel even more at Gilgal!
Bring your sacrifices every morning,
your tenths every three days.
Offer leavened bread as a thanksgiving sacrifice,
20   and loudly proclaim your freewill offerings,

for that is what you Israelites love to do!
This is the declaration of the Lord God.

I gave you absolutely nothing to eat in all your cities,
a shortage of food in all your communities,
yet you did not return to me.
This is the Lord's declaration.

I also withheld the rain from you
while there were still three months until harvest.
I sent rain on one city
30 but no rain on another.
One field received rain
while a field with no rain withered.
Two or three cities staggered
to another city to drink water
but were not satisfied,
yet you did not return to me.
This is the Lord's declaration.

I struck you with blight and mildew;
the locust devoured
40 your many gardens and vineyards,
your fig trees and olive trees,
yet you did not return to me.
This is the Lord's declaration.

I sent plagues like those of Egypt;
I killed your young men with the sword,
along with your captured horses.
I caused the stench of your camp
to fill your nostrils,
yet you did not return to me.
50 This is the Lord's declaration.

I overthrew some of you
as I overthrew Sodom and Gomorrah,
and you were like a burning stick

snatched from a fire,
yet you did not return to me—
This is the LORD's declaration.

Therefore, Israel, that is what I will do to you,
and since I will do that to you,
Israel, prepare to meet your God!
60　He is here:
the one who forms the mountains,
creates the wind,
and reveals his thoughts to man,
the one who makes the dawn out of darkness
and strides on the heights of the earth.
The LORD, the God of Armies, is his name.

5 Listen to this message that I am singing for you, a lament, house of Israel:
She has fallen;
Virgin Israel will never rise again.
She lies abandoned on her land
with no one to raise her up.

For the Lord GOD says:
The city that marches out a thousand strong
will have only a hundred left,
and the one that marches out a hundred strong
10　will have only ten left in the house of Israel.

For the LORD says to the house of Israel:
Seek me and live!
Do not seek Bethel
or go to Gilgal
or journey to Beer-sheba,
for Gilgal will certainly go into exile,
and Bethel will come to nothing.
Seek the LORD and live,
or he will spread like fire
20　throughout the house of Joseph;
it will consume everything

with no one at Bethel to extinguish it.
Those who turn justice into wormwood
also throw righteousness to the ground.

The one who made the Pleiades and Orion,
who turns darkness into dawn
and darkens day into night,
who summons the water of the sea
and pours it out over the surface of the earth—
30 the LORD is his name.
He brings destruction on the strong,
and it falls on the fortress.

They hate the one who convicts the guilty
at the city gate,
and they despise the one who speaks with integrity.
Therefore, because you trample on the poor
and exact a grain tax from him,
you will never live in the houses of cut stone
you have built;
40 you will never drink the wine
from the lush vineyards
you have planted.
For I know your crimes are many
and your sins innumerable.
They oppress the righteous, take a bribe,
and deprive the poor of justice at the city gates.
Therefore, those who have insight will keep silent
at such a time,
for the days are evil.

50 Pursue good and not evil
so that you may live,
and the LORD, the God of Armies,
will be with you
as you have claimed.
Hate evil and love good;
establish justice at the city gate.

Perhaps the Lord, the God of Armies, will be gracious
to the remnant of Joseph.

Therefore the Lord, the God of Armies, the Lord, says:
60   There will be wailing in all the public squares;
they will cry out in anguish in all the streets.
The farmer will be called on to mourn,
and professional mourners to wail.
There will be wailing in all the vineyards,
for I will pass among you.
The Lord has spoken.

Woe to you who long for the day of the Lord!
What will the day of the Lord be for you?
It will be darkness and not light.
70   It will be like a man who flees from a lion
only to have a bear confront him.
He goes home and rests his hand against the wall
only to have a snake bite him.
Won't the day of the Lord
be darkness rather than light,
even gloom without any brightness in it?
I hate, I despise, your feasts!
I can't stand the stench
of your solemn assemblies.
80   Even if you offer me
your burnt offerings and grain offerings,
I will not accept them;
I will have no regard
for your fellowship offerings of fattened cattle.
Take away from me the noise of your songs!
I will not listen to the music of your harps.
But let justice flow like water,
and righteousness, like an unfailing stream.

"House of Israel, was it sacrifices and grain offerings that you presented to me during the forty
90   years in the wilderness? But you have taken up Sakkuth your king and Kaiwan your star god,

images you have made for yourselves. So I will send you into exile beyond Damascus." The LORD, the God of Armies, is his name. He has spoken.

6	Woe to those who are at ease in Zion
	and to those who feel secure on the hill of Samaria—
	the notable people in this first of the nations,
	those the house of Israel comes to.
	Cross over to Calneh and see;
	go from there to great Hamath;
	then go down to Gath of the Philistines.
	Are you better than these kingdoms?
	Is their territory larger than yours?
10	You dismiss any thought of the evil day
	and bring in a reign of violence.

	They lie on beds inlaid with ivory,
	sprawled out on their couches,
	and dine on lambs from the flock
	and calves from the stall.
	They improvise songs to the sound of the harp
	and invent their own musical instruments like David.
	They drink wine by the bowlful
20	and anoint themselves with the finest oils
	but do not grieve over the ruin of Joseph.
	Therefore, they will now go into exile
	as the first of the captives,
	and the feasting of those who sprawl out
	will come to an end.

The Lord GOD has sworn by himself — this is the declaration of the LORD, the God of Armies:
	I loathe Jacob's pride
	and hate his citadels,
	so I will hand over the city and everything in it.

30	And if there are ten men left in one house, they will die. A close relative and burner will remove his corpse from the house. He will call to someone in the inner recesses of the house, "Any more with you?"
	That person will reply, "None."

Then he will say, "Silence, because the LORD's name must not be invoked."
For the LORD commands:
> The large house will be smashed to pieces,
> and the small house to rubble.

> Do horses gallop on the cliffs?
> Does anyone plow there with oxen?
> Yet you have turned justice into poison
> and the fruit of righteousness into wormwood—
> you who rejoice over Lo-debar
> and say, "Didn't we capture Karnaim
> for ourselves by our own strength?"
> But look, I am raising up a nation
> against you, house of Israel—
> this is the declaration of the Lord,
> the GOD of Armies—
> and they will oppress you
> from the entrance of Hamath
> to the Brook of the Arabah.

7 The Lord GOD showed me this: He was forming a swarm of locusts at the time the spring crop first began to sprout — after the cutting of the king's hay. When the locusts finished eating the vegetation of the land, I said, "Lord GOD, please forgive! How will Jacob survive since he is so small?"

The LORD relented concerning this. "It will not happen," he said.

The Lord GOD showed me this: The Lord GOD was calling for a judgment by fire. It consumed the great deep and devoured the land. Then I said, "Lord GOD, please stop! How will Jacob survive since he is so small?"

The LORD relented concerning this. "This will not happen either," said the Lord GOD.

10 He showed me this: The Lord was standing there by a vertical wall with a plumb line in his hand. The LORD asked me, "What do you see, Amos?"

I replied, "A plumb line."

Then the Lord said, "I am setting a plumb line among my people Israel; I will no longer spare them:
> Isaac's high places will be deserted,
> and Israel's sanctuaries will be in ruins;
> I will rise up against the house of Jeroboam
> with a sword."

Amaziah the priest of Bethel sent word to King Jeroboam of Israel, saying, "Amos has conspired against you right here in the house of Israel. The land cannot endure all his words, for Amos has
20 said this: 'Jeroboam will die by the sword, and Israel will certainly go into exile from its homeland.'"

Then Amaziah said to Amos, "Go away, you seer! Flee to the land of Judah. Earn your living and give your prophecies there, but don't ever prophesy at Bethel again, for it is the king's sanctuary and a royal temple."

So Amos answered Amaziah, "I was not a prophet or the son of a prophet; rather, I was a herdsman, and I took care of sycamore figs. But the Lord took me from following the flock and said to me, 'Go, prophesy to my people Israel.'"

Now hear the word of the Lord. You say:

> Do not prophesy against Israel;
>
> do not preach against the house of Isaac.

30 Therefore, this is what the Lord says:

> Your wife will be a prostitute in the city,
>
> your sons and daughters will fall by the sword,
>
> and your land will be divided up
>
> with a measuring line.
>
> You yourself will die on pagan soil,
>
> and Israel will certainly go into exile
>
> from its homeland.

8 The Lord God showed me this: a basket of summer fruit. He asked me, "What do you see, Amos?"

I replied, "A basket of summer fruit."

The Lord said to me, "The end has come for my people Israel; I will no longer spare them. In that day the temple songs will become wailing" — this is the Lord God's declaration. "Many dead bodies, thrown everywhere! Silence!"

> Hear this, you who trample on the needy
>
> and do away with the poor of the land,
>
> asking, "When will the New Moon be over
>
> so we may sell grain,
>
10 > and the Sabbath,
>
> so we may market wheat?
>
> We can reduce the measure
>
> while increasing the price
>
> and cheat with dishonest scales.
>
> We can buy the poor with silver

and the needy for a pair of sandals
and even sell the chaff!"

The Lord has sworn by the Pride of Jacob:
    I will never forget all their deeds.
20   Because of this, won't the land quake
    and all who dwell in it mourn?
    All of it will rise like the Nile;
    it will surge and then subside
    like the Nile in Egypt.

    And in that day—
    this is the declaration of the Lord God—
    I will make the sun go down at noon;
    I will darken the land in the daytime.
    I will turn your feasts into mourning
30   and all your songs into lamentation;
    I will cause everyone to wear sackcloth
    and every head to be shaved.
    I will make that grief
    like mourning for an only son
    and its outcome like a bitter day.

    Look, the days are coming—
    this is the declaration of the Lord God—
    when I will send a famine through the land:
    not a famine of bread or a thirst for water,
40   but of hearing the words of the Lord.
    People will stagger from sea to sea
    and roam from north to east
    seeking the word of the Lord,
    but they will not find it.
    In that day the beautiful young women,
    the young men also, will faint from thirst.
    Those who swear by the guilt of Samaria
    and say, "As your god lives, Dan,"
    or, "As the way of Beer-sheba lives"—
50   they will fall, never to rise again.

9 I saw the Lord standing beside the altar, and he said:

Strike the capitals of the pillars
so that the thresholds shake;
knock them down on the heads of all the people.
Then I will kill the rest of them with the sword.
None of those who flee will get away;
none of the fugitives will escape.
If they dig down to Sheol,
from there my hand will take them;
if they climb up to heaven,
from there I will bring them down.
If they hide
on the top of Carmel,
from there I will track them down
and seize them;
if they conceal themselves
from my sight on the sea floor,
from there I will command
the sea serpent to bite them.
And if they are driven
by their enemies into captivity,
from there I will command
the sword to kill them.
I will keep my eye on them
for harm and not for good.

The Lord, the God of Armies—
he touches the earth;
it melts, and all who dwell in it mourn;
all of it rises like the Nile
and subsides like the Nile of Egypt.
He builds his upper chambers
in the heavens
and lays the foundation of his vault
on the earth.
He summons the water of the sea
and pours it out over the surface of the earth.
The Lord is his name.

Israelites, are you not like the Cushites to me?
This is the LORD's declaration.
40 Didn't I bring Israel from the land of Egypt,
the Philistines from Caphtor,
and the Arameans from Kir?
Look, the eyes of the Lord GOD
are on the sinful kingdom,
and I will obliterate it
from the face of the earth.
However, I will not totally destroy
the house of Jacob—
this is the LORD's declaration—
50 for I am about to give the command,
and I will shake the house of Israel
among all the nations,
as one shakes a sieve,
but not a pebble will fall to the ground.
All the sinners among my people
who say, "Disaster will never overtake
or confront us,"
will die by the sword.

In that day
60 I will restore the fallen shelter of David:
I will repair its gaps,
restore its ruins,
and rebuild it as in the days of old,
so that they may possess
the remnant of Edom
and all the nations
that bear my name—
this is the declaration of the LORD; he will do this.

Look, the days are coming—
70 this is the LORD's declaration—
when the plowman will overtake the reaper
and the one who treads grapes,

the sower of seed.
The mountains will drip with sweet wine,
and all the hills will flow with it.
I will restore the fortunes of my people Israel.
They will rebuild and occupy ruined cities,
plant vineyards and drink their wine,
make gardens and eat their produce.
80   I will plant them on their land,
and they will never again be uprooted
from the land I have given them.
The LORD your God has spoken.

Introduction to Obadiah

A. Lauren Brown

As the shortest book in the HS, Obadiah is often forgotten or relegated to trivia knowledge. Short as it may be, Obadiah plays an important role in the narrative of the HS. After Amos' diatribe against Israel, Obadiah narrows the prophetic focus from the surrounding nations to Edom alone in an oracle against the nations *par excellence* brimming with themes of judgment, justice, and the coming Day of the Lord.

Obadiah is an exposition of comeuppance for brotherly betrayal. The prophet proclaims judgment upon Edom for passively standing by Israel's destruction at the hands of the Babylonians. Obadiah then scorns Edom's arrogant confidence in their own city's safety and security. The prophet's attention is especially on Edom's exploitation of Israel's vulnerable state. After Babylon left Israel beaten and crippled, Edom rushed to plunder their neighbor Israel and revel in their brother Israel's downfall. They profited from Israel's defeat and even turned over Israel's refugees to Babylon. Obadiah answers the question that plagues any oppressed and abused people after such an event: Will Edom get away with it forever?

A vision composed of poetry and concluding in several lines of Hebrew prose, Obadiah's short message has teeth. Obadiah's literary themes of vengeance for brotherly betrayal in the first half of the book precede eschatological expectations in the second half. These themes dovetail with theological themes of judgment, justice, and the Day of the Lord. The Day of the Lord will usher in Yahweh's justice on behalf of the righteous and Yahweh's punishment for the wicked. Edom is judged for the arrogance of their national pride and self-reliance in their defenses, as well as for Edom's actions against Israel in their moment of need.

In the Book of the Twelve, Amos' bleak word of judgment to Israel precedes Obadiah's vision for Edom. The worst has happened for Israel, deservedly so according to Amos, and now Obadiah must address the brother who profited from Israel's desolation. The two nations' previous roles are now reversed: instead of Israel as the target of Yahweh's judgment, Edom is now on trial. Instead of the vulnerable nation, Israel will be Yahweh's tool of justice. Whereas Israel's fortunes will be restored according to Amos, Obadiah has no such promise for Edom. The force of Obadiah's message to Edom, a typology of Yahweh's wrath against all of Israel's neighbors, is tempered by the next prophet in the Book of the Twelve. Jonah shifts the reader's focus from Yahweh's wrath to Yahweh's mercy with Nineveh's penitent response.

Obadiah's brevity is also the book's clarity: Edom's destruction is imminent. Unlike Nineveh, there is no call for repentance. This shortest HS book is clear that arrogance and exploitation are not a part of Yahweh's kingdom. Obadiah's concluding line that "the kingdom will be the Lord's," reflects

Obadiah's message where, in the kingdom of God, all evil will be answered and a holy remnant will be restored to their inheritance. One day, the Edoms of the world will be no more and the kingdom will be Yahweh's.

Outline

1. Obadiah's oracle addresses Edom directly. The prophet proclaims Yahweh's judgment upon Edom and gives specific examples of actions Edom took against Judah. (1–64)

2. As you have done, so it will be done to you. (65–68)

3. Obadiah's oracle shifts from Edom to address Judah. The coming judgment of the Day of the Lord expands the oracle against Edom to encompass the judgment of all the nations around Israel. Israel will not only be spared but will be Yahweh's instrument of wrath against their neighbors. (69–97)

Suggested Resources

Barton, John. *Joel and Obadiah*. Old Testament Library. Louisville: Westminster John Knox, 2001.

Goldingay, John. *Hosea–Micah*. Baker Commentary on the Old Testament Prophetic Books. Grand Rapids: Baker Academic, 2021.

Jenson, Philip Peter. *Obadiah, Jonah, Micah: A Theological Commentary*. New York: T&T Clark, 2008.

O'Brien, Julia M., ed. *The Oxford Handbook of the Minor Prophets*. Oxford: Oxford University Press, 2021.

Raabe, Paul R. *Obadiah*. Anchor Bible Commentary. New York: Doubleday, 1996.

Obadiah

I   The vision of Obadiah.

This is what the Lord GOD has said about Edom:
>   We have heard a message from the LORD;
>   an envoy has been sent among the nations:
>   "Rise up, and let's go to war against her."
>   Look, I will make you insignificant
>   among the nations;
>   you will be deeply despised.
>   Your arrogant heart has deceived you,
>   you who live in clefts of the rock
>   in your home on the heights,
>   who say to yourself,
>   "Who can bring me down to the ground?"
>   Though you seem to soar like an eagle
>   and make your nest among the stars,
>   even from there I will bring you down.
>   This is the LORD's declaration.
>
>   If thieves came to you,
>   if marauders by night—
>   how ravaged you would be!—
>   wouldn't they steal only what they wanted?
>   If grape harvesters came to you,
>   wouldn't they leave a few grapes?
>   How Esau will be pillaged,
>   his hidden treasures searched out!
>   Everyone who has a treaty with you
>   will drive you to the border;
>   everyone at peace with you
>   will deceive and conquer you.
>   Those who eat your bread

will set a trap for you.
He will be unaware of it.
In that day—
this is the Lord's declaration—
will I not eliminate the wise ones of Edom
and those who understand
from the hill country of Esau?
Teman, your warriors will be terrified
so that everyone from the hill country of Esau
40   will be destroyed by slaughter.

You will be covered with shame
and destroyed forever
because of violence done to your brother Jacob.
On the day you stood aloof,
on the day strangers captured his wealth,
while foreigners entered his city gate
and cast lots for Jerusalem,
you were just like one of them.
Do not gloat over your brother
50   in the day of his calamity;
do not rejoice over the people of Judah
in the day of their destruction;
do not boastfully mock
in the day of distress.
Do not enter my people's city gate
in the day of their disaster.
Yes, you — do not gloat over their misery
in the day of their disaster,
and do not appropriate their possessions
60   in the day of their disaster.
Do not stand at the crossroads
to cut off their fugitives,
and do not hand over their survivors
in the day of distress.

For the day of the Lord is near,
against all the nations.

As you have done, it will be done to you;
what you deserve will return on your own head.
As you have drunk on my holy mountain,
70   so all the nations will drink continually.
They will drink and gulp down
and be as though they had never been.
But there will be a deliverance on Mount Zion,
and it will be holy;
the house of Jacob will dispossess
those who dispossessed them.
Then the house of Jacob will be a blazing fire,
and the house of Joseph, a burning flame,
but the house of Esau will be stubble;
80   Jacob will set them on fire and consume Edom.
Therefore no survivor will remain
of the house of Esau,
for the LORD has spoken.

People from the Negev will possess
the hill country of Esau;
those from the Judean foothills will possess
the land of the Philistines.
They will possess
the territories of Ephraim and Samaria,
90   while Benjamin will possess Gilead.
The exiles of the Israelites who are in Halah
and who are among the Canaanites as far as Zarephath
as well as the exiles of Jerusalem who are in Sepharad
will possess the cities of the Negev.
Saviors will ascend Mount Zion
to rule over the hill country of Esau,
but the kingdom will be the LORD's.

Introduction to Jonah

Bob Cole

The book of Jonah, fifth among the Book of the Twelve, is unusual among these prophets because it is not composed of the teaching and preaching of the prophet, neither does it include a "word from Yahweh." Instead, it is a story about Yahweh's interaction with Jonah and the city of Nineveh. Jonah's story is told in parallel units. Yahweh's first and second calls to the prophet open the units. Yahweh's mercy on Jonah and Jonah's prayer of thanks and praise complete the first unit. Yahweh's mercy on Nineveh and Jonah's complaint about that mercy complete the second. The comparison between Jonah's response to his own redemption and that of the Ninevites provides the main message of the book of Jonah.

The prophets reveal Yahweh's work through Israel to bless all the nations of the earth. The prophets share the message that all nations will be judged but will also enjoy a future restoration as they turn to Yahweh in worship. Within the Book of the Twelve, Hosea does not deal with the nations. Joel proclaims judgment upon the nations but does not mention their future restoration. Amos points to a future restoration of David's dynasty and a return of Israel to the land and prosperity. Obadiah proclaims the end of Edom, a hostile foreign nation that aided in Judah's oppression. These are followed by the book of Jonah, which qualifies the message of the first four prophets of the Book of the Twelve with the message that a loving, compassionate, and merciful Yahweh could offer repentance even to the nations. If the Ninevites could become followers of Yahweh, so any of the nations could likewise participate in the future restoration and worship of him.

The narrative presents theological truths concerning Yahweh that are common to the other prophets. First, Yahweh's grace, compassion, and faithful love extend beyond the boundaries of Israel/Judah to encompass the nations (4.1–4). The reader should understand that Yahweh's love for the nations is the same as his love for Israel.

Second, Yahweh is portrayed as sovereign over pagans, nature, and the residents of Nineveh. The pagan sailors come to fear Jonah's God greatly, offer a sacrifice, and make vows to Yahweh after he calms the sea (1.25–26). The sailors clearly recognized the work of Yahweh, a work that Jonah wanted to reject. Yahweh also demonstrated his sovereignty by throwing a great wind upon the sea (1.5–6) before he calms it (1.25–26) and by appointing the following: (1) a great fish to swallow Jonah (1.27–28), (2) a plant to shade Jonah (4.8–10), (3) a worm to eat the plant (4.10–11), and (4) a scorching east wind and beating sun to cause Jonah to become faint (4.12–14). Yahweh spared Nineveh as a result of the actions of the residents (3.15–16). When sinners repent, Yahweh relents.

Finally, Yahweh is portrayed as a redeemer. The author portrayed Jonah's disobedience as a series of steps down. Jonah went down to Joppa (1.4–5), went down into the ship (1.4–5), went down to the lowest part of the vessel (1.6–8), fell into a deep sleep (1.6–8), and sunk to the foundations of the mountains (2.17–19). Jonah's steps downward are the author's way of depicting the course of a life that refuses Yahweh's will. The steps downward led Jonah to a place of repentance. Failure to repent would have been fatal. Following Jonah's repentance, Yahweh redeemed Jonah from the pit (2.17–19). In a similar way, Nineveh's repentance led to Yahweh (lit. *Elohim*) relenting concerning the disaster he threatened through the prophet (3.15–16).

Jonah's failure to see his own sin and that of the Ninevites through the same lens puts Jonah at odds with his redeemer. Yahweh's challenge to Jonah provides the story's conclusion. He asks Jonah to consider whether Jonah's concerns aligned with Yahweh's concerns for the nations, a challenge that is as relevant for today's reader as it was for Jonah.

Outline

1. Yahweh's first call to Jonah (1.1–28)
   a. Yahweh's call and Jonah's flight (1.1–4)
   b. Yahweh's intervention (1.5–18)
   c. Yahweh calms the sea (1.18–26)
   d. Yahweh's judgment on Jonah (1.27–28)

2. Jonah's response to Yahweh's mercy (2.1–30)
   a. Jonah's prayer of thanksgiving (2.1–29)
   b. Jonah's deliverance (2.30)

3. Yahweh's second call to Jonah (3.1–16)
   a. Yahweh's second call and Jonah's mission (3.1–5)
   b. Nineveh's response to Jonah's message (3.5–14)
   c. Yahweh's response to Nineveh's repentance (3.15–16)

4. Jonah's response to Yahweh's mercy (4.1–8)
   a. Jonah's prayer and Yahweh's response (4.1–6)
   b. Jonah's vigil (4.7–8)

5. Yahweh's challenge to Jonah (4.8–20)

Suggested Resources

Allen, Leslie C. *The Books of Joel, Obadiah, Micah, and Jonah.* New International Commentary on the Old Testament. Grand Rapids: Eerdmans, 1976.

Bruckner, James. *Jonah, Nahum, Habakkuk, Zephaniah.* NIV Application Commentary. Grand Rapids: Zondervan, 2004.

Hays, J. Daniel. *The Message of the Prophets*. Grand Rapids: Zondervan, 2010.

Stuart, Douglas. *Hosea–Jonah*. Word Biblical Commentary. Dallas: Thomas Nelson, 1987.

Timmer, Daniel C. *A Gracious and Compassionate God: Mission, Salvation, and Spirituality in the Book of Jonah*. Downers Grove, IL: InterVarsity Press, 2011.

Jonah

1 The word of the LORD came to Jonah son of Amittai: "Get up! Go to the great city of Nineveh and preach against it because their evil has come up before me." Jonah got up to flee to Tarshish from the LORD's presence. He went down to Joppa and found a ship going to Tarshish. He paid the fare and went down into it to go with them to Tarshish from the LORD's presence.

But the LORD threw a great wind onto the sea, and such a great storm arose on the sea that the ship threatened to break apart. The sailors were afraid, and each cried out to his god. They threw the ship's cargo into the sea to lighten the load. Meanwhile, Jonah had gone down to the lowest part of the vessel and had stretched out and fallen into a deep sleep.

The captain approached him and said, "What are you doing sound asleep? Get up! Call to your god. Maybe this god will consider us, and we won't perish."

"Come on!" the sailors said to each other. "Let's cast lots. Then we'll know who is to blame for this trouble we're in." So they cast lots, and the lot singled out Jonah. Then they said to him, "Tell us who is to blame for this trouble we're in. What is your business, and where are you from? What is your country, and what people are you from?"

He answered them, "I'm a Hebrew. I worship the LORD, the God of the heavens, who made the sea and the dry land."

Then the men were seized by a great fear and said to him, "What have you done?" The men knew he was fleeing from the LORD's presence because he had told them. So they said to him, "What should we do to you so that the sea will calm down for us?" For the sea was getting worse and worse.

He answered them, "Pick me up and throw me into the sea so that it will calm down for you, for I know that I'm to blame for this great storm that is against you." Nevertheless, the men rowed hard to get back to dry land, but they couldn't because the sea was raging against them more and more.

So they called out to the LORD, "Please, LORD, don't let us perish because of this man's life, and don't charge us with innocent blood! For you, LORD, have done just as you pleased." Then they picked up Jonah and threw him into the sea, and the sea stopped its raging. The men were seized by great fear of the LORD, and they offered a sacrifice to the LORD and made vows.

The LORD appointed a great fish to swallow Jonah, and Jonah was in the belly of the fish three days and three nights.

2 Jonah prayed to the LORD his God from the belly of the fish:

> I called to the LORD in my distress,
> and he answered me.

I cried out for help from deep inside Sheol;
you heard my voice.
When you threw me into the depths,
into the heart of the seas,
the current overcame me.
All your breakers and your billows swept over me.

10 And I said, "I have been banished
from your sight,
yet I will look once more
toward your holy temple."
The water engulfed me up to the neck;
the watery depths overcame me;
seaweed was wrapped around my head.
I sank to the foundations of the mountains,
the earth's gates shut behind me forever!
Then you raised my life from the Pit, Lord my God!

20 As my life was fading away,
I remembered the Lord,
and my prayer came to you,
to your holy temple.
Those who cherish worthless idols
abandon their faithful love,
but as for me, I will sacrifice to you
with a voice of thanksgiving.
I will fulfill what I have vowed.
Salvation belongs to the Lord.

30 Then the Lord commanded the fish, and it vomited Jonah onto dry land.

3 The word of the Lord came to Jonah a second time: "Get up! Go to the great city of Nineveh and preach the message that I tell you." Jonah got up and went to Nineveh according to the Lord's command.

Now Nineveh was an extremely great city, a three-day walk. Jonah set out on the first day of his walk in the city and proclaimed, "In forty days Nineveh will be demolished!" Then the people of Nineveh believed God. They proclaimed a fast and dressed in sackcloth — from the greatest of them to the least.

When word reached the king of Nineveh, he got up from his throne, took off his royal robe, covered himself with sackcloth, and sat in ashes. Then he issued a decree in Nineveh:

10   By order of the king and his nobles: No person or animal, herd or flock, is to taste anything at all. They must not eat or drink water. Furthermore, both people and animals must be covered with sackcloth, and everyone must call out earnestly to God. Each must turn from his evil ways and from his wrongdoing. Who knows? God may turn and relent; he may turn from his burning anger so that we will not perish.

God saw their actions — that they had turned from their evil ways — so God relented from the disaster he had threatened them with. And he did not do it.

4 Jonah was greatly displeased and became furious. He prayed to the LORD, "Please, LORD, isn't this what I said while I was still in my own country? That's why I fled toward Tarshish in the first place. I knew that you are a gracious and compassionate God, slow to anger, abounding in faithful love, and one who relents from sending disaster. And now, LORD, take my life from me, for it is better for me to die than to live."

The LORD asked, "Is it right for you to be angry?"

Jonah left the city and found a place east of it. He made himself a shelter there and sat in its shade to see what would happen to the city. Then the LORD God appointed a plant, and it grew over Jonah to provide shade for his head to rescue him from his trouble. Jonah was greatly pleased

10 with the plant. When dawn came the next day, God appointed a worm that attacked the plant, and it withered.

As the sun was rising, God appointed a scorching east wind. The sun beat down on Jonah's head so much that he almost fainted, and he wanted to die. He said, "It's better for me to die than to live."

Then God asked Jonah, "Is it right for you to be angry about the plant?"

"Yes, it's right!" he replied. "I'm angry enough to die!"

So the LORD said, "You cared about the plant, which you did not labor over and did not grow. It appeared in a night and perished in a night. But may I not care about the great city of Nineveh, which has more than a hundred and twenty thousand people who cannot distinguish between

20 their right and their left, as well as many animals?"

Introduction to Micah

Andrew M. King

The book of Micah is a revelation "seen" by the prophet in the 8th century BC (1.1–2). The scope of the vision concerns both the Northern and Southern Kingdoms ("Samaria and Jerusalem"), as well as the nations. Like his near contemporaries Amos, Hosea, and Isaiah, Micah's prophecy targets both the spiritual and social dynamics in Israel and Judah. Although Yahweh had declared his expectation of justice, mercy, and covenant fidelity (6.28–32), corruption, oppression, and idolatry characterized the life of the people. Micah proclaims a coming judgment that will destroy the wicked and purify a faithful remnant. Thus, like other canonical prophets, Micah envisions hope beyond judgment. In particular, the messianic reign of a coming Davidic king will advance Yahweh's covenant promises (5.6–11). At this time, many nations will be joined with the people of Yahweh, their sin will be removed, and they will reside in the exalted Zion. All of this is possible because Yahweh is the "Lord of the whole earth" (4.62–68).

The opening verses of Micah provide the context for the prophetic oracle, namely the rebellion of Jacob and the sins of the house of Israel (1.14–19). The specific manifestation of these sins includes both idolatry and social injustice. The actions of the people have positioned them as Yahweh's enemy (2.32–36). Indeed, the prophet laments the seeming absence of the godly from the earth (7.1–10). Rebellion is entrenched at every level of society, but especially with respect to the leadership. Rather than shepherding the people with justice, the leaders devour the flesh of Yahweh's people (3.1–12). Furthermore, empty worship is perpetuated by religious functionaries who sell their services for a price (3.18–24, 46–51). In essence, "justice" and "truth" go to the highest bidder. The book underscores the severity of sin both in relation to Yahweh and to other people.

The power of corrupt and oppressive leaders is nullified, however, as Yahweh, the true king, comes forth from his throne (1.7–9). As he treads on the high places, creation convulses under his feet (1.10–13). Similarly, the impotence of idols is shown as they are easily crushed and burned (1.25–29) while Yahweh sets creation aflame with his very coming (1.10–13). In this way, Micah carries forward the motifs of Yahweh's universal sovereignty and justice witnessed in the first five prophets of the Book of the Twelve.

Moreover, Micah continues the motif of true and false representations of divine revelation. In contrast to the false prophets, Micah stands as a spirit-filled spokesman for Yahweh (3.35–39). Micah employs courtroom language to express the divine complaint (6.1–7). The authoritative declaration, in line with the covenant curses in the Torah (see Lev 26; Deut 28), is divine punishment and dispersion. Babylon is named explicitly in 4.47–54 as the destination for exile. But from exile, Yahweh's purpose is to redeem and restore his people in the sight of the nations. The remnant motif surfaces as the vehicle through which future hope is framed (2.49–53; 4.35–38; 5.32–43; 7.76–80). Yahweh will lead the restored remnant through a new exodus and to a renewed land (7.58–66). The inclusion of the nations in Yahweh's saving purposes echoes the Abrahamic promise (Mic 4.1–13; see Gen 12.10–13). The book concludes by celebrating Yahweh's compassion and forgiveness. Though he treads the earth underfoot in judgment in the opening chapter, he ends by treading the sins of people underfoot in forgiveness (7.76–84). In this way the spiritual and social failings would be reversed when Yahweh rules as king.

Outline

1. Title (1.1–2)

2. Yahweh comes to judge idolatry and oppression, and to regather a faithful remnant (1.3–2.54)

3. Yahweh condemns the political and spiritual leadership for their sin and exposes their false security. While wicked are brought down, Yahweh exalts Zion in the Latter Days, regathering the faithful remnant and nations under the coming messianic rule (3.1–5.61)

4. Yahweh presents his case against the faithless nation and the prophet laments the condition of the people. Nevertheless, Yahweh's covenant faithfulness, compassion, and forgiveness are the hope of his people (6.1–7.88)

Suggested Resources

Andersen, Francis I., and David Noel Freedman. *Micah*. Anchor Bible Commentary. New York: Doubleday, 2000.

Dempster, Stephen G. *Micah*. Two Horizons Old Testament Commentary. Grand Rapids: Eerdmans, 2017.

Gignilliat, Mark S. *Micah*. International Theological Commentary. London: T&T Clark, 2019.

Waltke, Bruce K. *A Commentary on Micah*. Grand Rapids: Eerdmans, 2007.

Wolff, Hans Walter. *Micah: A Commentary*. Continental Commentary. Minneapolis: Fortress, 1990.

Micah

1 The word of the LORD that came to Micah the Moreshite — what he saw regarding Samaria and Jerusalem in the days of Jotham, Ahaz, and Hezekiah, kings of Judah.

Listen, all you peoples;
pay attention, earth and everyone in it!
The Lord GOD will be a witness against you,
the Lord, from his holy temple.
Look, the LORD is leaving his place
and coming down to trample
the heights of the earth.
10 The mountains will melt beneath him,
and the valleys will split apart,
like wax near a fire,
like water cascading down a mountainside.
All this will happen because of Jacob's rebellion
and the sins of the house of Israel.
What is the rebellion of Jacob?
Isn't it Samaria?
And what is the high place of Judah?
Isn't it Jerusalem?
20 Therefore, I will make Samaria
a heap of ruins in the countryside,
a planting area for a vineyard.
I will roll her stones into the valley
and expose her foundations.
All her carved images will be smashed to pieces;
all her wages will be burned in the fire,
and I will destroy all her idols.
Since she collected the wages of a prostitute,
they will be used again for a prostitute.

30 Because of this I will lament and wail;
I will walk barefoot and naked.
I will howl like the jackals
and mourn like ostriches.
For her wound is incurable
and has reached even Judah;
it has approached my people's city gate,
as far as Jerusalem.

Don't announce it in Gath,
don't weep at all.
40 Roll in the dust in Beth-leaphrah.
Depart in shameful nakedness,
you residents of Shaphir;
the residents of Zaanan will not come out.
Beth-ezel is lamenting;
its support is taken from you.
Though the residents of Maroth
anxiously wait for something good,
disaster has come from the LORD
to the gate of Jerusalem.
50 Harness the horses to the chariot,
you residents of Lachish.
This was the beginning of sin for Daughter Zion
because Israel's acts of rebellion can be traced to you.
Therefore, send farewell gifts to Moresheth-gath;
the houses of Achzib are a deception
to the kings of Israel.
I will again bring a conqueror
against you who live in Mareshah.
The nobility of Israel will come to Adullam.
60 Shave yourselves bald and cut off your hair
in sorrow for your precious children;
make yourselves as bald as an eagle,
for they have been taken from you into exile.

2 Woe to those who dream up wickedness
and prepare evil plans on their beds!

At morning light they accomplish it
because the power is in their hands.
They covet fields and seize them;
they also take houses.
They deprive a man of his home,
a person of his inheritance.

Therefore, the LORD says:
I am now planning a disaster
against this nation;
you cannot free your necks from it.
Then you will not walk so proudly
because it will be an evil time.
In that day one will take up a taunt against you
and lament mournfully, saying,
"We are totally ruined!
He measures out the allotted land of my people.
How he removes it from me!
He allots our fields to traitors."
Therefore, there will be no one
in the assembly of the LORD
to divide the land by casting lots.

"Quit your preaching," they preach.
"They should not preach these things;
shame will not overtake us."
House of Jacob, should it be asked,
"Is the Spirit of the LORD impatient?
Are these the things he does?"
Don't my words bring good
to the one who walks uprightly?
But recently my people have risen up
like an enemy:
You strip off the splendid robe
from those who are passing through confidently,
like those returning from war.
You force the women of my people
out of their comfortable homes,

and you take my blessing
40   from their children forever.
Get up and leave,
for this is not your place of rest
because defilement brings destruction—
a grievous destruction!
If a man comes
and utters empty lies—
"I will preach to you about wine and beer"—
he would be just the preacher for this people!

I will indeed gather all of you, Jacob;
50   I will collect the remnant of Israel.
I will bring them together like sheep in a pen,
like a flock in the middle of its pasture.
It will be noisy with people.
One who breaks open the way
will advance before them;
they will break out, pass through the city gate,
and leave by it.
Their King will pass through before them,
the LORD as their leader.

3   Then I said, "Now listen, leaders of Jacob,
you rulers of the house of Israel.
Aren't you supposed to know what is just?
You hate good and love evil.
You tear off people's skin
and strip their flesh from their bones.
You eat the flesh of my people
after you strip their skin from them
and break their bones.
10   You chop them up
like flesh for the cooking pot,
like meat in a cauldron."
Then they will cry out to the LORD,
but he will not answer them.

He will hide his face from them at that time
because of the crimes they have committed.

This is what the Lord says
concerning the prophets
who lead my people astray,
who proclaim peace
when they have food to sink their teeth into
but declare war against the one
who puts nothing in their mouths.
Therefore, it will be night for you—
without visions;
it will grow dark for you—
without divination.
The sun will set on these prophets,
and the daylight will turn black over them.
Then the seers will be ashamed
and the diviners disappointed.
They will all cover their mouths
because there will be no answer from God.

As for me, however, I am filled with power
by the Spirit of the Lord,
with justice and courage,
to proclaim to Jacob his rebellion
and to Israel his sin.

Listen to this, leaders of the house of Jacob,
you rulers of the house of Israel,
who abhor justice
and pervert everything that is right,
who build Zion with bloodshed
and Jerusalem with injustice.
Her leaders issue rulings for a bribe,
her priests teach for payment,
and her prophets practice divination for silver.
Yet they lean on the Lord, saying,
"Isn't the Lord among us?

No disaster will overtake us."
Therefore, because of you,
Zion will be plowed like a field,
Jerusalem will become ruins,
and the temple's mountain
will be a high thicket.

4   In the last days
the mountain of the LORD's house
will be established
at the top of the mountains
and will be raised above the hills.
Peoples will stream to it,
and many nations will come and say,
"Come, let's go up to the mountain of the LORD,
to the house of the God of Jacob.
10   He will teach us about his ways
so we may walk in his paths."
For instruction will go out of Zion
and the word of the LORD from Jerusalem.
He will settle disputes among many peoples
and provide arbitration for strong nations
that are far away.
They will beat their swords into plows
and their spears into pruning knives.
Nation will not take up the sword against nation,
20   and they will never again train for war.
But each person will sit under his grapevine
and under his fig tree
with no one to frighten him.
For the mouth of the LORD of Armies
has spoken.
Though all the peoples walk
in the name of their own gods,
we will walk in the name of the LORD our God
forever and ever.

On that day—
this is the LORD's declaration—
I will assemble the lame
and gather the scattered,
those I have injured.
I will make the lame into a remnant,
those far removed into a strong nation.
Then the LORD will reign over them in Mount Zion
from this time on and forever.
And you, watchtower for the flock,
fortified hill of Daughter Zion,
the former rule will come to you;
sovereignty will come to Daughter Jerusalem.

Now, why are you shouting loudly?
Is there no king with you?
Has your counselor perished
so that anguish grips you like a woman in labor?
Writhe and cry out, Daughter Zion,
like a woman in labor,
for now you will leave the city
and camp in the open fields.
You will go to Babylon;
there you will be rescued;
there the LORD will redeem you
from the grasp of your enemies!
Many nations have now assembled against you;
they say, "Let her be defiled,
and let us feast our eyes on Zion."
But they do not know the LORD's intentions
or understand his plan,
that he has gathered them
like sheaves to the threshing floor.
Rise and thresh, Daughter Zion,
for I will make your horns iron
and your hooves bronze
so you can crush many peoples.
Then you will set apart their plunder

for the LORD,
their wealth for the Lord of the whole earth.

5 Now, daughter who is under attack,
you slash yourself in grief;
a siege is set against us!
They are striking the judge of Israel
on the cheek with a rod.
Bethlehem Ephrathah,
you are small among the clans of Judah;
one will come from you
to be ruler over Israel for me.

His origin is from antiquity,
from ancient times.
Therefore, Israel will be abandoned until the time
when she who is in labor has given birth;
then the rest of the ruler's brothers will return
to the people of Israel.
He will stand and shepherd them
in the strength of the LORD,
in the majestic name of the LORD his God.
They will live securely,
for then his greatness will extend
to the ends of the earth.
He will be their peace.
When Assyria invades our land,
when it marches against our fortresses,
we will raise against it seven shepherds,
even eight leaders of men.
They will shepherd the land of Assyria with the sword,
the land of Nimrod with a drawn blade.
So he will rescue us from Assyria
when it invades our land,
when it marches against our territory.

Then the remnant of Jacob
will be among many peoples
like dew from the LORD,

like showers on the grass,
which do not wait for anyone
or linger for mankind.
Then the remnant of Jacob
will be among the nations, among many peoples,
40   like a lion among animals of the forest,
like a young lion among flocks of sheep,
which tramples and tears as it passes through,
and there is no one to rescue them.
Your hand will be lifted up against your adversaries,
and all your enemies will be destroyed.

In that day—
this is the LORD's declaration—
I will remove your horses from you
and wreck your chariots.
50   I will remove the cities of your land
and tear down all your fortresses.
I will remove sorceries from your hands,
and you will not have any more fortune-tellers.
I will remove your carved images
and sacred pillars from you
so that you will no longer worship
the work of your hands.
I will pull up the Asherah poles from among you
and demolish your cities.
60   I will take vengeance in anger and wrath
against the nations that have not obeyed me.

6 Now listen to what the LORD is saying:
Rise, plead your case before the mountains,
and let the hills hear your complaint.
Listen to the LORD's lawsuit,
you mountains and enduring foundations of the earth,
because the LORD has a case against his people,
and he will argue it against Israel.
My people, what have I done to you,
or how have I wearied you?

10   Testify against me!
     Indeed, I brought you up from the land of Egypt
     and redeemed you from that place of slavery.
     I sent Moses, Aaron, and Miriam ahead of you.
     My people,
     remember what King Balak of Moab proposed,
     what Balaam son of Beor answered him,
     and what happened from the Acacia Grove to Gilgal
     so that you may acknowledge
     the Lord's righteous acts.

20   What should I bring before the Lord
     when I come to bow before God on high?
     Should I come before him with burnt offerings,
     with year-old calves?
     Would the Lord be pleased with thousands of rams
     or with ten thousand streams of oil?
     Should I give my firstborn for my transgression,
     the offspring of my body for my own sin?

     Mankind, he has told each of you what is good
     and what it is the Lord requires of you:
30   to act justly,
     to love faithfulness,
     and to walk humbly with your God.

     The voice of the Lord calls out to the city
     (and it is wise to fear your name):
     "Pay attention to the rod
     and the one who ordained it.
     Are there still the treasures of wickedness
     and the accursed short measure
     in the house of the wicked?
40   Can I excuse wicked scales
     or bags of deceptive weights?
     For the wealthy of the city are full of violence,
     and its residents speak lies;
     the tongues in their mouths are deceitful.

"As a result, I have begun to strike you severely,
bringing desolation because of your sins.
You will eat but not be satisfied,
for there will be hunger within you.
What you acquire, you cannot save,
50   and what you do save,
I will give to the sword.
You will sow but not reap;
you will press olives
but not anoint yourself with oil;
and you will tread grapes
but not drink the wine.
The statutes of Omri
and all the practices of Ahab's house
have been observed;
60   you have followed their policies.
Therefore, I will make you a desolate place
and the city's residents an object of contempt;
you will bear the scorn of my people."

7   How sad for me!
For I am like one who—
when the summer fruit has been gathered
after the gleaning of the grape harvest—
finds no grape cluster to eat,
no early fig, which I crave.
Faithful people have vanished from the land;
there is no one upright among the people.
All of them wait in ambush to shed blood;
10   they hunt each other with a net.
Both hands are good at accomplishing evil:
the official and the judge demand a bribe;
when the powerful man communicates his evil desire,
they plot it together.
The best of them is like a brier;
the most upright is worse than a hedge of thorns.
The day of your watchmen,

the day of your punishment, is coming;
at this time their panic is here.
20 Do not rely on a friend;
don't trust in a close companion.
Seal your mouth
from the woman who lies in your arms.
Surely a son considers his father a fool,
a daughter opposes her mother,
and a daughter-in-law is against her mother-in-law;
a man's enemies are the men of his own household.
But I will look to the LORD;
I will wait for the God of my salvation.
30 My God will hear me.

Do not rejoice over me, my enemy!
Though I have fallen, I will stand up;
though I sit in darkness,
the LORD will be my light.
Because I have sinned against him,
I must endure the LORD's fury
until he champions my cause
and establishes justice for me.
He will bring me into the light;
40 I will see his salvation.
Then my enemy will see,
and she will be covered with shame,
the one who said to me,
"Where is the LORD your God?"
My eyes will look at her in triumph;
at that time she will be trampled
like mud in the streets.

A day will come for rebuilding your walls;
on that day your boundary will be extended.
50 On that day people will come to you
from Assyria and the cities of Egypt,
even from Egypt to the Euphrates River
and from sea to sea

and mountain to mountain.
Then the earth will become a wasteland
because of its inhabitants
and as a result of their actions.

Shepherd your people with your staff,
the flock that is your possession.
60 They live alone in a woodland
surrounded by pastures.
Let them graze in Bashan and Gilead
as in ancient times.

I will perform miracles for them
as in the days of your exodus
from the land of Egypt.
Nations will see and be ashamed
of all their power.
They will put their hands over their mouths,
70 and their ears will become deaf.
They will lick the dust like a snake;
they will come trembling out of their hiding places
like reptiles slithering on the ground.
They will tremble in the presence of the LORD our God;
they will stand in awe of you.

Who is a God like you,
forgiving iniquity and passing over rebellion
for the remnant of his inheritance?
He does not hold on to his anger forever
80 because he delights in faithful love.
He will again have compassion on us;
he will vanquish our iniquities.
You will cast all our sins
into the depths of the sea.
You will show loyalty to Jacob
and faithful love to Abraham,
as you swore to our ancestors
from days long ago.

Introduction to Nahum

Andrew M. King

Well over a century after the reluctant prophet Jonah visited the Assyrian city of Nineveh, the prophet Nahum announced its downfall. The book is situated historically between the fall of Thebes (663 BC), mentioned in 3.32–36, and the fall of Nineveh (612 BC), which was a future event from the perspective of the book. While Jonah records Nineveh's previous repentance (Jon 3.11–13), by the time of Nahum, evil and violence once again characterized the city in the sight of the nations. Yet unlike the book of Jonah, which emphasizes hope for Nineveh, the "book of the vision of Nahum" announces its ultimate doom. Nahum declares in no uncertain terms that Yahweh's vengeance will be unleashed upon Assyria for their violence and cruelty, including towards Yahweh's people. Nineveh will be humiliated and destroyed without anyone to mourn her passing. Assyria's destruction, however, will result in blessing and security for all who take refuge in Yahweh (1.23–25).

As the seventh prophet in the Book of the Twelve, Nahum, with great poetic skill, continues many themes from previous prophets. For instance, Yahweh's universal sovereignty (see Amos 4.60–66; Mic 1.3–6, 57–59) is displayed in several ways. The opening hymn (1.2–28) describes a theophany in which creation responds to Yahweh's presence. He alone makes the mountains tremble and the earth heave. Before Nineveh comes into view, Yahweh's power is shown to be global in scope. Furthermore, Nahum reiterates Yahweh's authority over both Israelite and non-Israelite nations. Isaiah described Assyria as the rod of Yahweh's anger sent against his rebellious people (Isa 10.16–110). Now that they had served their purpose, Yahweh's justice required his opposition to Assyria's predatory and licentious behavior (3.1–4, 16–19). Though the Assyrians were strong and numerous (1.39–44), the horrors of war would be seen in their gates when Yahweh stands against them (2.52–58). Several taunts in Nah 3 magnify the certainty of the coming judgment. For example, Nahum poses a rhetorical question of whether Nineveh is better than the Egyptian city of Thebes, who, though once secure, was violently exiled (3.32–44). The point is clear: if Thebes can fall, so can Nineveh. This taunt shows the futility of Assyria's hope in its infrastructure and military might.

The interweaving of judgment and hope in the book invites reflection. At the very beginning of the oracle, Yahweh is described in canonically familiar terms: jealous, avenging, slow to anger, and not leaving the guilty unpunished (1.2–10). This echo of the divine revelation in Exodus (see Exod 20.6–9; 34.9–13) furthers the characterization seen in both Jonah and Micah (see Jonah 4.1–4; Mic 7.76–88). Nahum's emphasis on Yahweh's commitment to divine justice engenders hope for those oppressed by enemies. The delayed mention of Nineveh may indicate that Yahweh's vengeance is more broadly applicable to all peoples characterized by violence, not simply Assyria. Conversely, the brief delay in naming Judah (see 1.54–61) perhaps expands the boundaries of those who can take refuge in Yahweh (1.23–25). Alongside the vast scope of judgment, Nahum may advance the theme in the Book of the Twelve of Yahweh's global salvation beyond the borders of Judah. The early presentation of this global perspective counters a nationalistic and xenophobic interpretation of the following indictment of Nineveh. For Yahweh is not just concerned with Israel, but is God of all the earth. Moreover, Nineveh is not indicted on ethnic grounds in the book, but in terms of their gross violence and oppression of others. Their treatment of Yahweh's people betrays their view of Yahweh. And though Yahweh "is furious with his enemies" (1.2–6), as seen in Jonah, even enemies are able to find refuge in him (1.25–25).

Outline

1. Title (1.1)

2. Nahum's theophanic hymn emphasizes both Yahweh's character and power to judge and to save (1.2–28)

3. Nahum focuses on Assyria's destruction and Judah's deliverance (1.29–61)

4. Nahum graphicly portrays the invasion of Nineveh. The city's defenses are shown to be powerless against its assailants. Ironically, the lion who feasted on others is itself devoured (2)

5. Nahum proclaims a woe oracle. Nineveh is compared to a prostitute who will be subjected to open shame in the sight of the nations (3.1–31)

6. Nineveh is likened to the fallen Egyptian city of Thebes. Though it appears strong, its security is fleeting. Its officials and people will dissipate like locust when the wind blows (3.32–83)

Suggested Resources

Christensen, Duane L. *Nahum*. Anchor Bible Commentary. New York: Doubleday, 2009.

Robertson, O. Palmer. *The Books of Nahum, Habakkuk, and Zephaniah*. New International Commentary on the Old Testament. Grand Rapids: Eerdmans, 1990.

Spronk, Klaas. *Nahum*. Historical Commentary on the Old Testament. Kampen: Kok Pharos, 1997.

Timmer, Daniel C. *Nahum*. Zondervan Exegetical Commentary on the Old Testament. Grand Rapids: Zondervan Academic, 2020.

Nahum

I The pronouncement concerning Nineveh. The book of the vision of Nahum the Elkoshite.

> The LORD is a jealous and avenging God;
> the LORD takes vengeance
> and is fierce in wrath.
> The LORD takes vengeance against his foes;
> he is furious with his enemies.
> The LORD is slow to anger but great in power;
> the LORD will never leave the guilty unpunished.
> His path is in the whirlwind and storm,
> and clouds are the dust beneath his feet.
> He rebukes the sea and dries it up,
> and he makes all the rivers run dry.
> Bashan and Carmel wither;
> even the flower of Lebanon withers.
> The mountains quake before him,
> and the hills melt;
> the earth trembles at his presence—
> the world and all who live in it.
> Who can withstand his indignation?
> Who can endure his burning anger?
> His wrath is poured out like fire;
> even rocks are shattered before him.

> The LORD is good,
> a stronghold in a day of distress;
> he cares for those who take refuge in him.
> But he will completely destroy Nineveh
> with an overwhelming flood,
> and he will chase his enemies into darkness.

Whatever you plot against the LORD,
he will bring it to complete destruction;
oppression will not rise up a second time.
For they will be consumed
like entangled thorns,
like the drink of a drunkard
and like straw that is fully dry.
One has gone out from you,
who plots evil against the LORD,
and is a wicked counselor.

This is what the LORD says:
Though they are strong and numerous,
they will still be mowed down,
and he will pass away.
Though I have punished you,
I will punish you no longer.
For I will now break off his yoke from you
and tear off your shackles.

The LORD has issued an order concerning you:
There will be no offspring
to carry on your name.
I will eliminate the carved idol and cast image
from the house of your gods;
I will prepare your grave,
for you are contemptible.

Look to the mountains—
the feet of the herald,
who proclaims peace.
Celebrate your festivals, Judah;
fulfill your vows.
For the wicked one will never again
march through you;
he will be entirely wiped out.

2 One who scatters is coming up against you.
Man the fortifications!
Watch the road!
Brace yourself!
Summon all your strength!

For the Lord will restore the majesty of Jacob,
yes, the majesty of Israel,
though ravagers have ravaged them
and ruined their vine branches.

10 The shields of his warriors are dyed red;
the valiant men are dressed in scarlet.
The fittings of the chariot flash like fire
on the day of its battle preparations,
and the spears are brandished.
The chariots dash madly through the streets;
they rush around in the plazas.
They look like torches;
they dart back and forth like lightning.
He gives orders to his officers;
20 they stumble as they advance.
They race to its wall;
the protective shield is set in place.
The river gates are opened,
and the palace erodes away.

Beauty is stripped;
she is carried away;
her ladies-in-waiting moan
like the sound of doves
and beat their breasts.
30 Nineveh has been like a pool of water
from her first days,
but they are fleeing.
"Stop! Stop!" they cry,
but no one turns back.
"Plunder the silver! Plunder the gold!"

There is no end to the treasure,
an abundance of every precious thing.
Desolation, decimation, devastation!
Hearts melt,
40   knees tremble,
insides churn,
every face grows pale!

Where is the lions' lair,
or the feeding ground of the young lions,
where the lion and lioness prowled,
and the lion's cub,
with nothing to frighten them away?
The lion mauled whatever its cubs needed
and strangled prey for its lionesses.
50   It filled up its dens with the kill,
and its lairs with mauled prey.
Beware, I am against you.
This is the declaration of the LORD of Armies.
I will make your chariots go up in smoke,
and the sword will devour your young lions.
I will cut off your prey from the earth,
and the sound of your messengers
will never be heard again.

3   Woe to the city of blood,
totally deceitful,
full of plunder,
never without prey.
The crack of the whip
and rumble of the wheel,
galloping horse
and jolting chariot!
Charging horseman,
10   flashing sword,
shining spear;
heaps of slain,
mounds of corpses,

dead bodies without end—
they stumble over their dead.
Because of the continual prostitution of the prostitute,
the attractive mistress of sorcery,
who treats nations and clans like merchandise
by her prostitution and sorcery,
I am against you.
This is the declaration of the Lord of Armies.
I will lift your skirts over your face
and display your nakedness to nations,
your shame to kingdoms.
I will throw filth on you
and treat you with contempt;
I will make a spectacle of you.
Then all who see you will recoil from you, saying,
"Nineveh is devastated;
who will show sympathy to her?"
Where can I find anyone to comfort you?

Are you better than Thebes
that sat along the Nile
with water surrounding her,
whose rampart was the sea,
the river her wall?
Cush and Egypt were her endless source of strength;
Put and Libya were among her allies.
Yet she became an exile;
she went into captivity.
Her children were also dashed to pieces
at the head of every street.
They cast lots for her dignitaries,
and all her nobles were bound in chains.
You also will become drunk;
you will hide.
You also will seek refuge from the enemy.

All your fortresses are fig trees
with figs that ripened first;

50   when shaken, they fall—
right into the mouth of the eater!

Look, your troops are like women among you;
your land's city gates
are wide open to your enemies.
Fire will devour the bars of your gates.

Draw water for the siege;
strengthen your fortresses.
Step into the clay and tread the mortar;
take hold of the brick-mold!
60   The fire will devour you there;
the sword will cut you down.
It will devour you like the young locust.
Multiply yourselves like the young locust;
multiply like the swarming locust!
You have made your merchants
more numerous than the stars of the sky.
The young locust strips the land
and flies away.
Your court officials are like the swarming locust,
70   and your scribes like clouds of locusts,
which settle on the walls on a cold day;
when the sun rises, they take off,
and no one knows where they are.

King of Assyria, your shepherds slumber;
your officers sleep.
Your people are scattered across the mountains
with no one to gather them together.
There is no remedy for your injury;
your wound is severe.
80   All who hear the news about you
will clap their hands because of you,
for who has not experienced
your constant cruelty?

Introduction to Habakkuk

Myrto Theocharous

The book of Habakkuk is about a prophets wrestling with two apparently contradictory realities: a world where evil prevails and an all-powerful Yahweh who loves justice. The book opens with a prayer of lament by the prophet who is struggling to make sense of Yahweh's silence and inaction in the face of his suffering. Yahweh reveals to him a well-known way of dealing with the wicked throughout the HS: raising up a nation as an agent of justice against the sinful people. In Habakkuk's case, the prophet's *own* people, Judah, are the wrongdoers and Babylon (*the Chaldeans*) is Yahweh's rod of judgment.

Regardless of how deserving this retributive punishment is for Judah, the prophet is not satisfied by Yahweh's solution. He realizes that the agents of judgment chosen by Yahweh are themselves evil and comparatively worse than their object of attack. Habakkuk cannot accept that the world's mighty empires that devour weaker nations are Yahweh's ultimate response to the problem of evil. The big fish devouring the smaller fish is by no means the definitive justice the prophet longs for. The futility in the image of the defenseless masses falling prey to the hands of the mightiest military powers cannot be the vision Habakkuk's God had in mind for his world.

Yahweh's response to Habakkuk comes with a message for the end times, offering the prophet a vision of ultimate justice, the kind he has been seeking all along. This vision, which is essentially Yahweh himself coming to save his faithful ones in person, will require strong perseverance from them in the face of its apparent delay. Their patience will be tested as they are called to depend on the faithfulness of Yahweh who assures them of his promise. This divine faithfulness is what the righteous must "live by" (2.14–16) while the unjust continue in their violent ways and store up wrath for themselves.

The book begins with a vision or an oracle that the prophet saw (1.1) and leaves us in silence (2.80–82). Habakkuk prays in 3.1 to break this silence and invites us into the prophet's response to the terrifying vision, the only appropriate response in the light of Yahweh's salvific coming: a prayer. This prayer speaks of the same God of the exodus galloping across the heavens, marching across the earth, and this vision of his coming fills the prophet and, hopefully, his readers with great awe, as well as with joyful determination to wait for him against all odds (3.62–67).

While the book of Nahum gives us a clear picture of Yahweh's fury against the evil empire of Assyria, a book that would have been readily welcomed by any Israelite acquainted with this historic enemy, Habakkuk refuses to allow for any sense of superiority to arise in his fellow Judahites. They are guilty as well, and Zephaniah, following Habakkuk, will demonstrate this leveling of Judah with the nations in the final day of judgment very dramatically.

In the midst of these glum images of Nahum and Zephaniah, however, Habakkuk invites us to rejoice in Yahweh and wait patiently for him because his coming will mean salvation for those who hunger and thirst for justice (Matt 5:6). This is, in fact, the same encouragement that the author of Hebrews gives to the believers in Heb 10:38 when he quotes Hab 2.14–16, encouraging them to persevere against all odds until the second coming of Christ.

Outline

1. The Burden of the Prophet (1.1)

2. The Dialogue Between the Prophet and Yahweh (1.2–63)
   a. The Prophet's First Complaint (1.2–13)
   b. Yahweh's First Response (1.14–40)
   c. The Prophet's Dissatisfaction with Yahweh's Response (1.41–63)

3. The Vision for the End and the Oracle for Judgment (2.1–82)
   a. The Prophet's Anticipation for the Divine Answer (2.1–4)
   b. Yahweh's Vision for the End (2.5–22)
   c. Woe Oracle for the Wicked of the Earth (2.23–82)

4. The Prophet's Expectant Prayer (3.1–67)
   a. The Prayer of the Prophet (3.1)
   b. The Prophet Fearfully Requests Yahweh's Act (3.2–6)
   c. The Prophet Exults Yahweh's Majesty (3.7–49)
   d. The Prophet Fearfully Anticipates Yahweh's Act (3.50–55)
   e. The Prophet Persists in Trust and Joy (3.56–67)

Suggested Resources

Bruckner, James K. *Jonah, Nahum, Habakkuk, Zephaniah*. NIV Application Commentary. Grand Rapids: Zondervan, 2004.

Coggins, Richard, and Jin H. Han. *Nahum, Habakkuk, Zephaniah, Haggai, Zechariah, and Malachi*. Blackwell Bible Commentaries. Hoboken, NJ: Wiley-Blackwell, 2011.

Kassis, Riad A. *Frustrated with God: A Syrian Theologian's Reflections on Habakkuk*. Scotts Valley, CA: CreateSpace, 2016.

Thomas, Heath A. *Habakkuk*. Two Horizons Old Testament Commentary. Grand Rapids: Eerdmans, 2018.

Habakkuk

I The pronouncement that the prophet Habakkuk saw.

How long, LORD, must I call for help
and you do not listen
or cry out to you about violence
and you do not save?
Why do you force me to look at injustice?
Why do you tolerate wrongdoing?
Oppression and violence are right in front of me.
Strife is ongoing, and conflict escalates.
10 This is why the law is ineffective
and justice never emerges.
For the wicked restrict the righteous;
therefore, justice comes out perverted.

Look at the nations and observe—
be utterly astounded!
For I am doing something in your days
that you will not believe
when you hear about it.
Look! I am raising up the Chaldeans,
20 that bitter, impetuous nation
that marches across the earth's open spaces
to seize territories not its own.
They are fierce and terrifying;
their views of justice and sovereignty
stem from themselves.
Their horses are swifter than leopards
and more fierce than wolves of the night.
Their horsemen charge ahead;
their horsemen come from distant lands.
30 They fly like eagles, swooping to devour.

All of them come to do violence;
their faces are set in determination.
They gather prisoners like sand.
They mock kings,
and rulers are a joke to them.
They laugh at every fortress
and build siege ramps to capture it.
Then they sweep by like the wind
and pass through.
40 They are guilty; their strength is their god.

Are you not from eternity, Lord my God?
My Holy One, you will not die.
Lord, you appointed them to execute judgment;
my Rock, you destined them to punish us.
Your eyes are too pure to look on evil,
and you cannot tolerate wrongdoing.
So why do you tolerate those who are treacherous?
Why are you silent
while one who is wicked swallows up
50 one who is more righteous than himself?
You have made mankind
like the fish of the sea,
like marine creatures that have no ruler.
The Chaldeans pull them all up with a hook,
catch them in their dragnet,
and gather them in their fishing net;
that is why they are glad and rejoice.
That is why they sacrifice to their dragnet
and burn incense to their fishing net,
60 for by these things their portion is rich
and their food plentiful.
Will they therefore empty their net
and continually slaughter nations without mercy?

2   I will stand at my guard post
and station myself on the lookout tower.

I will watch to see what he will say to me
and what I should reply about my complaint.

The Lord answered me:
    Write down this vision;
    clearly inscribe it on tablets
    so one may easily read it.
    For the vision is yet for the appointed time;
    it testifies about the end and will not lie.
    Though it delays, wait for it,
    since it will certainly come and not be late.
    Look, his ego is inflated;
    he is without integrity.
    But the righteous one will live by his faith.
    Moreover, wine betrays;
    an arrogant man is never at rest.
    He enlarges his appetite like Sheol,
    and like Death he is never satisfied.
    He gathers all the nations to himself;
    he collects all the peoples for himself.

    Won't all of these take up a taunt against him,
    with mockery and riddles about him?
    They will say,

    "Woe to him who amasses what is not his—
    how much longer?—
    and loads himself with goods taken in pledge."
    Won't your creditors suddenly arise,
    and those who disturb you wake up?
    Then you will become spoil for them.
    Since you have plundered many nations,
    all the peoples who remain will plunder you—
    because of human bloodshed
    and violence against lands, cities,
    and all who live in them.

Woe to him who dishonestly makes
wealth for his house
to place his nest on high,
40   to escape the grasp of disaster!
You have planned shame for your house
by wiping out many peoples
and sinning against your own self.
For the stones will cry out from the wall,
and the rafters will answer them
from the woodwork.

Woe to him who builds a city with bloodshed
and founds a town with injustice!
Is it not from the Lord of Armies
50   that the peoples labor only to fuel the fire
and countries exhaust themselves for nothing?
For the earth will be filled
with the knowledge of the Lord's glory,
as the water covers the sea.

Woe to him who gives his neighbors drink,
pouring out your wrath
and even making them drunk,
in order to look at their nakedness!
You will be filled with disgrace instead of glory.
60   You also — drink,
and expose your uncircumcision!
The cup in the Lord's right hand
will come around to you,
and utter disgrace will cover your glory.
For your violence against Lebanon
will overwhelm you;
the destruction of animals will terrify you
because of your human bloodshed and violence
against lands, cities, and all who live in them.

70   What use is a carved idol
after its craftsman carves it?

It is only a cast image, a teacher of lies.
For the one who crafts its shape trusts in it
and makes worthless idols that cannot speak.
Woe to him who says to wood: Wake up!
or to mute stone: Come alive!
Can it teach?
Look! It may be plated with gold and silver,
yet there is no breath in it at all.

80   But the Lord is in his holy temple;
let the whole earth
be silent in his presence.

3 A prayer of the prophet Habakkuk. According to *Shigionoth.*
       Lord, I have heard the report about you;
       Lord, I stand in awe of your deeds.
       Revive your work in these years;
       make it known in these years.
       In your wrath remember mercy!

       God comes from Teman,
       the Holy One from Mount Paran. *Selah*
       His splendor covers the heavens,
10   and the earth is full of his praise.
       His brilliance is like light;
       rays are flashing from his hand.
       This is where his power is hidden.
       Plague goes before him,
       and pestilence follows in his steps.
       He stands and shakes the earth;
       he looks and startles the nations.
       The age-old mountains break apart;
       the ancient hills sink down.
20   His pathways are ancient.
       I see the tents of Cushan in distress;
       the tent curtains of the land of Midian tremble.
       Are you angry at the rivers, Lord?
       Is your wrath against the rivers?

Or is your fury against the sea
when you ride on your horses,
your victorious chariot?
You took the sheath from your bow;
the arrows are ready to be used with an oath. *Selah*
30   You split the earth with rivers.
The mountains see you and shudder;
a downpour of water sweeps by.
The deep roars with its voice
and lifts its waves high.
Sun and moon stand still in their lofty residence,
at the flash of your flying arrows,
at the brightness of your shining spear.
You march across the earth with indignation;
you trample down the nations in wrath.
40   You come out to save your people,
to save your anointed.
You crush the leader of the house of the wicked
and strip him from foot to neck. *Selah*
You pierce his head
with his own spears;
his warriors storm out to scatter us,
gloating as if ready to secretly devour the weak.
You tread the sea with your horses,
stirring up the vast water.

50   I heard, and I trembled within;
my lips quivered at the sound.
Rottenness entered my bones;
I trembled where I stood.
Now I must quietly wait for the day of distress
to come against the people invading us.
Though the fig tree does not bud
and there is no fruit on the vines,
though the olive crop fails
and the fields produce no food,
60   though the flocks disappear from the pen
and there are no herds in the stalls,

yet I will celebrate in the LORD;
I will rejoice in the God of my salvation!
The LORD my Lord is my strength;
he makes my feet like those of a deer
and enables me to walk on mountain heights!

For the choir director: on stringed instruments.

Introduction to Zephaniah

Jason S. DeRouchie

Zephaniah ("Yahweh has hidden") grew up during the dark days of King Manasseh (2 Kgs 20.41–21.31), son of reformer King Hezekiah (2 Kgs 18–20; Isa 36–38), who was Zephaniah's great-great grandfather (1.1–2). As a member of the royal family, Zephaniah's life highlighted the hope of the Davidic Messiah.

The prophet was also likely a black Judean, for he was "son of Cushi" (1.1–2), a proper name related to the ethnic title "Cushite" and the place designation "Cush," ancient black Africa (tagged "Ethiopia" in the New Testament period and centered in modern Sudan). Probably Cushi's mother, Gedaliah's wife, was a Cushite, and the parents named their son "my black one" likely to celebrate his racial heritage. Zephaniah's father's name, therefore, introduces the book's motifs of sin's seriousness (2.51) and of international reconciliation with Yahweh (see 2.34–42; 3.41–48).

Zephaniah prophesied during the reign of King Josiah (641/40–609 BC), and the prophet's preaching would have advanced the king's reforms (2 Kgs 22.5–23.57; 2 Chr 34.14–35.38). The immediate oracle likely arose in 622 BC after Josiah found the Book of the Law but before reform had fully taken effect. Zephaniah exhorted all covenant violators in Judah to repent and patiently pursue the Lord (2.1–11; 3.32–40). He also addressed other nations (2.16–20, 51) and spoke of global punishment (1.3–12, 52–76; 2.16–71) and restoration (e.g., 3.32–48), which suggests his charges targeted those beyond Judah as well.

Within the Book of the Twelve, Zephaniah portrays Yahweh as the only savior of the world who invites his readers to seek him together (2.1–11) and to wait upon him for a satisfying salvation. The superscription in Zeph 1.1–2 identifies Zephaniah's message as Yahweh's word. Then 1.3–76 provides the setting by calling the audience to revere Yahweh in light of his encroaching day of wrath. The primary prophetic exhortation that shapes the savior's invitation then comes in 2.1–3.96. The prophet first charges his audience to seek Yahweh together in order to avoid punishment (2.1–3.25). He then infers the need to wait for Yahweh in order to enjoy deliverance and lasting life (3.32–96). Zephaniah uses predictions of future punishment and promises of global restoration to motivate readers to accept his exhortations. A subscription concludes the book in 3.96, recalling 1.1–2 and reinforcing that all that precedes is Yahweh's word.

Zephaniah highlights Yahweh's wrath against sin yet identifies the possibility of deliverance and delight for a remnant. On the coming Day of the Lord (1.26, 52), Yahweh will execute just vengeance against sinners and he will establish peace and joy in his presence for a multi-ethnic remnant patiently seeking him (2.1–11; 3.32–48). Babylon's imminent destruction of Judah for her wickedness (e.g., 1.13–51) provides a foretaste of when Yahweh will eradicate all evil-doers (e.g.,

1.52–76; see Deut 30.10–11; Isa 24.16–23). Nevertheless, Yahweh will also reverse the effects of the Tower of Babel (Gen 11.1–12) and restore a global remnant of "peoples," transforming their speech so that they "call on the name of the LORD and serve him with a single purpose" (3.41–48). Only those who seek and wait for Yahweh will enjoy his divine protection and provision. Sustained satisfaction in Yahweh's presence is only for those in Judah and beyond who flee idolatry and look to Yahweh in prayer and devotion, who seek righteousness and humility, who embrace his instruction and respond in humble trust, and who fear him. As a bi-racial Jew, Zephaniah celebrates that Yahweh will gather to himself a multi-ethnic remnant who will find refuge and delight in his presence at the mountain of his holiness, even as he celebrates over these who will never again have reason to fear (3.41–95).

Zephaniah portrays the Day of the Lord as both sacrifice (e.g., 1.25–28) and war (1.52–63), and both images foreshadow the sacrificial death of Jesus by which he bears for all in him the just penalty of Yahweh's wrath (2 Cor 5:21; Gal 3:13; Col 2:13–15). With allusions to Zeph 3.65–72, John identifies Jesus as the end-times king through whom Yahweh secures salvation for the world (John 12:13–15; see Zech 9.34–39). Also, with links to Zeph 3.32–48, Luke treats Jesus's death and resurrection and Pentecost as initiating the Tower of Babel's reversal and the fulfillment of Zephaniah's Day of the Lord judgment and restoration (Acts 2:5–6, 19–21). The salvation of the Ethiopian eunuch in Acts 8:26–39 also marks the initial fulfillment of God's drawing in peoples "from beyond the rivers of Cush" (Zeph 3.46). In the following outline, the language of "savior" speaks first of Yahweh but also anticipates the work of Christ.

Outline

1. The Superscription of the Savior's Invitation to Satisfaction (1.1–2)

2. The Setting of the Savior's Invitation to Satisfaction: A Call to Revere Yahweh in Light of the Coming Day of the Lord (1.3–76)
   a. The Context for the Call to Revere Yahweh: Coming Punishment (1.3–28)
   b. The Makeup of the Call to Revere Yahweh (1.29–76)

3. The Substance of the Savior's Invitation to Satisfaction (2.1–3.95)
   a. Stage 1: Seek Yahweh Together to Avoid Punishment (2.1–3.31)
   b. Stage 2: Wait for Yahweh to Enjoy Satisfying Salvation (3.32–95)

4. The Subscription of the Savior's Invitation to Satisfaction (3.96)

Suggested Resources

Berlin, Adele. *Zephaniah*. Anchor Bible Commentary. New Haven: Yale University Press, 1994.

DeRouchie, Jason S. "Zephaniah." Pages 561–604 in vol. 7 of *ESV Expository Commentary*. Wheaton, IL: Crossway, 2018.

Floyd, Michael H. *Minor Prophets, Part 2*. Forms of Old Testament Literature. Grand Rapids: Eerdmans, 2000.

Motyer, J. Alec. "Zephaniah." Pages 897–962 in *The Minor Prophets: An Exegetical and Expository Commentary*. Grand Rapids: Baker Academic, 1998.

Patterson, Richard D. *Nahum, Habakkuk, Zephaniah: An Exegetical Commentary*. Minor Prophets Exegetical Commentary. Dallas: Biblical Studies Press, 2003.

Sweeney, Marvin A. *Zephaniah: A Commentary*. Hermeneia. Minneapolis: Fortress, 2003.

Zephaniah

1 The word of the Lord that came to Zephaniah son of Cushi, son of Gedaliah, son of Amariah, son of Hezekiah, in the days of Josiah son of Amon, king of Judah.

> I will completely sweep away everything
> from the face of the earth—
> this is the Lord's declaration.
> I will sweep away people and animals;
> I will sweep away the birds of the sky
> and the fish of the sea,
> and the ruins along with the wicked.
> I will cut off mankind
> from the face of the earth.
> This is the Lord's declaration.
>
> I will stretch out my hand against Judah
> and against all the residents of Jerusalem.
> I will cut off every vestige of Baal
> from this place,
> the names of the pagan priests
> along with the priests;
> those who bow in worship on the rooftops
> to the stars in the sky;
> those who bow and pledge loyalty to the Lord
> but also pledge loyalty to Milcom;
> and those who turn back from following the Lord,
> who do not seek the Lord or inquire of him.
> Be silent in the presence of the Lord God,
> for the day of the Lord is near.
> Indeed, the Lord has prepared a sacrifice;
> he has consecrated his guests.

On the day of the LORD's sacrifice

30   I will punish the officials, the king's sons,
and all who are dressed in foreign clothing.
On that day I will punish
all who skip over the threshold,
who fill their master's house
with violence and deceit.

On that day—
this is the LORD's declaration—
there will be an outcry from the Fish Gate,
a wailing from the Second District,

40   and a loud crashing from the hills.
Wail, you residents of the Hollow,
for all the merchants will be silenced;
all those loaded with silver will be cut off.

And at that time I will search Jerusalem with lamps
and punish those who settle down comfortably,
who say to themselves:
The LORD will do nothing—good or bad.
Their wealth will become plunder
and their houses a ruin.

50   They will build houses but never live in them,
plant vineyards but never drink their wine.

The great day of the LORD is near,
near and rapidly approaching.
Listen, the day of the LORD—
then the warrior's cry is bitter.
That day is a day of wrath,
a day of trouble and distress,
a day of destruction and desolation,
a day of darkness and gloom,

60   a day of clouds and total darkness,
a day of ram's horn and battle cry
against the fortified cities,
and against the high corner towers.

I will bring distress on mankind,
and they will walk like the blind
because they have sinned against the LORD.
Their blood will be poured out like dust
and their flesh like dung.
Their silver and their gold
70   will be unable to rescue them
on the day of the LORD's wrath.
The whole earth will be consumed
by the fire of his jealousy,
for he will make a complete,
yes, a horrifying end
of all the inhabitants of the earth.

2   Gather yourselves together;
gather together, undesirable nation,
before the decree takes effect
and the day passes like chaff,
before the burning of the LORD's anger overtakes you,
before the day of the LORD's anger overtakes you.
Seek the LORD, all you humble of the earth,
who carry out what he commands.
Seek righteousness, seek humility;
10   perhaps you will be concealed
on the day of the LORD's anger.

For Gaza will be abandoned,
and Ashkelon will become a ruin.
Ashdod will be driven out at noon,
and Ekron will be uprooted.
Woe, inhabitants of the seacoast,
nation of the Cherethites!
The word of the LORD is against you,
Canaan, land of the Philistines:
20   I will destroy you until there is no one left.
The seacoast will become pasturelands
with caves for shepherds and pens for sheep.
The coastland will belong

to the remnant of the house of Judah;
they will find pasture there.
They will lie down in the evening
among the houses of Ashkelon,
for the LORD their God will return to them
and restore their fortunes.

30   I have heard the taunting of Moab
and the insults of the Ammonites,
who have taunted my people
and threatened their territory.
Therefore, as I live—
this is the declaration of the LORD of Armies,
the God of Israel—
Moab will be like Sodom
and the Ammonites like Gomorrah:
a place overgrown with weeds,
40   a salt pit, and a perpetual wasteland.
The remnant of my people will plunder them;
the remainder of my nation will dispossess them.
This is what they get for their pride,
because they have taunted and acted arrogantly
against the people of the LORD of Armies.
The LORD will be terrifying to them
when he starves all the gods of the earth.
Then all the distant coasts and islands of the nations
will bow in worship to him,
50   each in its own place.

You Cushites will also be slain by my sword.

He will also stretch out his hand against the north
and destroy Assyria;
he will make Nineveh a desolate ruin,
dry as the desert.
Herds will lie down in the middle of it,
every kind of wild animal.
Both eagle owls and herons

60 will roost in the capitals of its pillars.
Their calls will sound from the window,
but devastation will be on the threshold,
for he will expose the cedar work.
This is the jubilant city
that lives in security,
that says to herself:
I exist, and there is no one else.
What a desolation she has become,
a place for wild animals to lie down!
70 Everyone who passes by her
scoffs and shakes his fist.

3 Woe to the city that is rebellious and defiled,
the oppressive city!
She has not obeyed;
she has not accepted discipline.
She has not trusted in the Lord;
she has not drawn near to her God.
The princes within her are roaring lions;
her judges are wolves of the night,
which leave nothing for the morning.
10 Her prophets are reckless—
treacherous men.
Her priests profane the sanctuary;
they do violence to instruction.
The righteous Lord is in her;
he does no wrong.
He applies his justice morning by morning;
he does not fail at dawn,
yet the one who does wrong knows no shame.

I have cut off nations;
20 their corner towers are destroyed.
I have laid waste their streets,
with no one to pass through.
Their cities lie devastated,
without a person, without an inhabitant.

I said: You will certainly fear me
and accept correction.
Then her dwelling place
would not be cut off
based on all that I had allocated to her.
30 However, they became more corrupt
in all their actions.
Therefore, wait for me—
this is the LORD's declaration—
until the day I rise up for plunder.
For my decision is to gather nations,
to assemble kingdoms,
in order to pour out my indignation on them,
all my burning anger;
for the whole earth will be consumed
40 by the fire of my jealousy.

For I will then restore
pure speech to the peoples
so that all of them may call
on the name of the LORD
and serve him with a single purpose.
From beyond the rivers of Cush
my supplicants, my dispersed people,
will bring an offering to me.
On that day you will not be put to shame
50 because of everything you have done
in rebelling against me.
For then I will remove
from among you your jubilant, arrogant people,
and you will never again be haughty
on my holy mountain.
I will leave
a meek and humble people among you,
and they will take refuge in the name of the LORD.
The remnant of Israel will no longer
60 do wrong or tell lies;
a deceitful tongue will not be found

in their mouths.
They will pasture and lie down,
with nothing to make them afraid.

Sing for joy, Daughter Zion;
shout loudly, Israel!
Be glad and celebrate with all your heart,
Daughter Jerusalem!
The Lord has removed your punishment;
70   he has turned back your enemy.
The King of Israel, the Lord, is among you;
you need no longer fear harm.
On that day it will be said to Jerusalem:
"Do not fear;
Zion, do not let your hands grow weak.
The Lord your God is among you,
a warrior who saves.
He will rejoice over you with gladness.
He will be quiet in his love.
80   He will delight in you with singing."

I will gather those who have been driven
from the appointed festivals;
they will be a tribute from you
and a reproach on her.
Yes, at that time
I will deal with all who oppress you.
I will save the lame and gather the outcasts;
I will make those who were disgraced
throughout the earth
90   receive praise and fame.
At that time I will bring you back,
yes, at the time I will gather you.
I will give you fame and praise
among all the peoples of the earth,
when I restore your fortunes before your eyes.
The Lord has spoken.

Introduction to Haggai

David G. Firth

The message of Haggai is dominated by one central concern—Judah needs to be faithful to Yahweh and rebuild the temple. Haggai's date can be worked out with some precision. The book consists of four sermons preached by Haggai plus a response to the first sermon, all given between August 29 and December 18, 520 BC. This is consistent with the information about his preaching (along with Zechariah) in Ezra 5.1–5 in encouraging those who have returned from the exile to build the temple. Almost certainly, the book was compiled very soon after this.

Haggai provides an important bridge within the Book of the Twelve. The preceding books (Nahum, Habakkuk, Zephaniah) are concerned with the end of the Assyrian empire and rise of the Babylonians. With Haggai, we move to the generation after the exile, the period also covered by Zechariah and Malachi. Yahweh has shown himself greater than Assyria and Babylon, but now the Persians are the dominant world power. How should those who have returned from exile respond to this? Haggai's answer is that the people must commit themselves to Yahweh first because when they do, they will see his purposes being fulfilled among them. Yahweh is greater than all world powers.

We know virtually nothing about Haggai himself. It is possible that 2.3–4 hints at Haggai having seen the first temple. If so, he would have been an old man by the time of his preaching. Though uncertain, it would explain why his ministry was so brief.

Though we know little about Haggai himself, his message is clear, with a consistent focus on building the second temple since its construction would demonstrate their commitment to Yahweh. In his first sermon, he challenges the people to change their priorities and rebuild the temple, pointing to a famine as a sign that the failure to do so was discipline from Yahweh. The reported response to this sermon shows that work started on the temple only twenty-three days later.

The three sermons in ch. 2 are addressed to a community who has responded to the initial challenge, providing encouragement to continue. The community (and especially its governor and priest, Zerubbabel and Joshua) needed to understand that though the new temple was not as outwardly impressive as its predecessor, Yahweh would still be present within. Due to the people's response to Haggai's message, Yahweh promises that he will bless them for their action. The final sermon, preached the same day as the third, assures Zerubbabel that, as a descendant of David, he would have a part in Yahweh's future purposes. This emphasizes a continuing messianic hope, showing that the rebuilding of the temple was not the end but rather looking forward to the greater work Yahweh would still do. In sum, the book is a powerful call to faith that expresses itself in commitment to the work that Yahweh set before his people, while also showing that Yahweh continued to be present with his people in their challenges.

Outline

1. Sermon One — On the Ruins of the Temple (1.1–32)

2. Response to Sermon 1 (1.33–41)

3. Sermon Two — Glory for the New House (1.42–2.14)

4. Sermon Three — Blessings in Future (2.15–32)

5. Sermon Four — A Future for Zerubbabel (2.33–39)

Suggested Resources

Boda, Mark J. *Haggai, Zechariah*. NIV Application Commentary. Grand Rapids: Zondervan, 2004.

Boda, Mark J., and Michael H. Floyd, eds. *Haggai and Zechariah 1–8 in the Trajectory of Hebrew Theology*. Library of the Hebrew Bible/Old Testament Studies. London: T&T Clark, 2008.

Hill, Andrew E. *Haggai, Zechariah, and Malachi*. Tyndale Old Testament Commentaries. Downers Grove, IL: InterVarsity, 2012.

Jacobs, Mignon R. *The Books of Haggai and Malachi*. New International Commentary on the Old Testament. Grand Rapids: Eerdmans, 2018.

Petersen, David L. *Haggai, Zechariah 1–8*. Old Testament Library. London: SCM Press, 1984.

Petterson, Anthony R. *Haggai, Zechariah & Malachi*. Apollos Old Testament Commentary. Downers Grove, IL: InterVarsity Press, 2015.

Haggai

I In the second year of King Darius, on the first day of the sixth month, the word of the Lord came through the prophet Haggai to Zerubbabel son of Shealtiel, the governor of Judah, and to Joshua son of Jehozadak, the high priest:

"The Lord of Armies says this: These people say: The time has not come for the house of the Lord to be rebuilt."

The word of the Lord came through the prophet Haggai: "Is it a time for you yourselves to live in your paneled houses, while this house lies in ruins?" Now, the Lord of Armies says this: "Think carefully about your ways:

> You have planted much
> but harvested little.
> You eat
> but never have enough to be satisfied.
> You drink
> but never have enough to be happy.
> You put on clothes
> but never have enough to get warm.
> The wage earner puts his wages
> into a bag with a hole in it."

The Lord of Armies says this: "Think carefully about your ways. Go up into the hills, bring down lumber, and build the house; and I will be pleased with it and be glorified," says the Lord. "You expected much, but then it amounted to little. When you brought the harvest to your house, I ruined it. Why?" This is the declaration of the Lord of Armies. "Because my house still lies in ruins, while each of you is busy with his own house.

> So on your account,
> the skies have withheld the dew
> and the land its crops.
> I have summoned a drought
> on the fields and the hills,
> on the grain, new wine, fresh oil,
> and whatever the ground yields,

> on people and animals,
> and on all that your hands produce."

Then Zerubbabel son of Shealtiel, the high priest Joshua son of Jehozadak, and the entire remnant of the people obeyed the LORD their God and the words of the prophet Haggai, because the LORD their God had sent him. So the people feared the LORD.

Then Haggai, the LORD's messenger, delivered the LORD's message to the people: "I am with you — this is the LORD's declaration."

The LORD roused the spirit of Zerubbabel son of Shealtiel, governor of Judah, the spirit of the high priest Joshua son of Jehozadak, and the spirit of all the remnant of the people. They 40 began work on the house of the LORD of Armies, their God, on the twenty-fourth day of the sixth month, in the second year of King Darius.

2 On the twenty-first day of the seventh month, the word of the LORD came through the prophet Haggai: "Speak to Zerubbabel son of Shealtiel, governor of Judah, to the high priest Joshua son of Jehozadak, and to the remnant of the people: 'Who is left among you who saw this house in its former glory? How does it look to you now? Doesn't it seem to you like nothing by comparison? Even so, be strong, Zerubbabel — this is the LORD's declaration. Be strong, Joshua son of Jehozadak, high priest. Be strong, all you people of the land — this is the LORD's declaration. Work! For I am with you — the declaration of the LORD of Armies. This is the promise I made to you when you came out of Egypt, and my Spirit is present among you; don't be afraid.'"

For the LORD of Armies says this: "Once more, in a little while, I am going to shake the heavens 10 and the earth, the sea and the dry land. I will shake all the nations so that the treasures of all the nations will come, and I will fill this house with glory," says the LORD of Armies. "The silver and gold belong to me" — this is the declaration of the LORD of Armies. "The final glory of this house will be greater than the first," says the LORD of Armies. "I will provide peace in this place" — this is the declaration of the LORD of Armies.

On the twenty-fourth day of the ninth month, in the second year of Darius, the word of the LORD came to the prophet Haggai: "This is what the LORD of Armies says: Ask the priests for a ruling. If a man is carrying consecrated meat in the fold of his garment, and it touches bread, stew, wine, oil, or any other food, does it become holy?"

The priests answered, "No."

20 Then Haggai asked, "If someone defiled by contact with a corpse touches any of these, does it become defiled?"

The priests answered, "It becomes defiled."

Then Haggai replied, "So is this people, and so is this nation before me — this is the LORD's declaration. And so is every work of their hands; even what they offer there is defiled.

"Now from this day on, think carefully: Before one stone was placed on another in the LORD's temple, what state were you in? When someone came to a grain heap of twenty measures, it only amounted to ten; when one came to the winepress to dip fifty measures from the vat, it only amounted to twenty. I struck you — all the work of your hands — with blight, mildew, and hail, but you didn't turn to me — this is the LORD's declaration. From this day on, think carefully; from the twenty-fourth day of the ninth month, from the day the foundation of the LORD's temple was laid; think carefully. Is there still seed left in the granary? The vine, the fig, the pomegranate, and the olive tree have not yet produced. But from this day on I will bless you."

30

The word of the LORD came to Haggai a second time on the twenty-fourth day of the month: "Speak to Zerubbabel, governor of Judah: I am going to shake the heavens and the earth. I will overturn royal thrones and destroy the power of the Gentile kingdoms. I will overturn chariots and their riders. Horses and their riders will fall, each by his brother's sword. On that day" — this is the declaration of the LORD of Armies — "I will take you, Zerubbabel son of Shealtiel, my servant" — this is the LORD's declaration — "and make you like my signet ring, for I have chosen you." This is the declaration of the LORD of Armies.

Introduction to Zechariah

Casey B. Hough

Zechariah's referential history may span roughly eighty years from 520–440 BC. During this period, the Jews who survived Babylonian captivity returned to their land under the oversight of the Persian Empire. The book of Zechariah overlaps with the time period of the book of Haggai. Zechariah, the son of Berechiah, the son of Iddo, called the people of Israel to repent in the hope of restoration in the land after exile (1.1–11). The prominent message of Zechariah is how Israel's God will restore his people through his presence by judging their enemies and renewing the worship of the community.

The book of Zechariah is best divided into two sections: chs. 1–8 and chs. 9–14. In chapters 1–8, explicit references are made to dates that accord with a specific historical setting during the reign of Darius (1.1–2, 12–13; 7.1–2). Chapters 9–14 have no such dates referencing a specific time in the history of the people of Israel. Given the change in style and content between the two major sections of Zechariah, it is reasonable to interpret the sections separately. This, however, does not mean that the material does not belong together or that a literary unity cannot be established between the two sections. Instead, it is better to assume that chs. 1–8 bore a contemporary significance for the immediate audience of a people returning from exiles while chs. 9–14 looked forward to a time of greater restoration among the remnant of Israelites. The sense of greater, future restoration would seem to be confirmed by the way that New Testament authors felt significantly more comfortable using Zech 9–14 as opposed to Zech 1–8.

The language of repentance and restoration fill the book of Zechariah and harks back to earlier prophets like Isaiah, Jeremiah, and Ezekiel. According to the night visions (Zech 1–6), the subsequent instructions (Zech 7–8), and the concluding prophecies (Zech 9–14), Yahweh would restore the people but not apart from repentance and obedience. The first eight chapters of Zechariah reveal that the hope for restoration would entail a cleansing and forgiving of the sins of the people through active work of Yahweh's priest under the reign of Yahweh's Davidic king. This hope of restoration and cleansing is revealed to the people in the form of eight different night visions. In the first vision (1.12–33), the people are confronted with the dilemma of their enemies being at peace. In the second vision (1.34–41), the hope of judgment on the nation that oppressed them is revealed. In the third vision (2.1–18), the abundance of Yahweh's restoration is disclosed. In the fourth vision (3.1–17), the purification of the priesthood, which was essential to the people's flourishing in the land, is foretold. In the fifth vision (4.1–23), Yahweh reveals how he will provide everything that the people need for the fulfillment of their mission in the land. With the sixth (5.1–8) and seventh visions (5.9–19), the certainty of Yahweh's judgment against evil in the land is declared. Finally, with the eighth vision (6.1–10), there is hope of peace as the Spirit rests, bringing a conclusion to the visions which began in Zech 1.12–23. A prophetic sign-act follows the final vision, then Zechariah is approached by messengers from Bethel with questions about cultic observations in the community. Zechariah responds with ten oracles that summarize the concerns of the first seven chapters. Five whole chapters of Zechariah address Yahweh's coming judgment and deliverance of His people.

Outline

1. Introduction to the Prophetic Ministry of Zechariah (1.1–11)

2. Eight Night Visions regarding the Restoration of the People of Yahweh (1.12–6.10)
   a. The Man among the Myrtle Trees (1.12–33)
   b. Horns and Craftsmen (1.34–41)
   c. The Measuring Line (2.1–18)
   d. The Purification of the Priesthood (3.1–17)
   e. The Golden Lampstand among the Olive Trees (4.1–23)
   f. The Flying Scroll (5.1–8)
   g. Wickedness in a Basket (5.9–19)
   h. Roving Chariots (6.1–10)

3. Zechariah's Prophetic Sign–Act: Fashioning a Crown for the Priest (6.11–20)

4. Messengers from Bethel Asking Questions about Fasting (7.1–21)

5. Ten Oracles Regarding Yahweh's Intention to Bless His People Again (8.1–34)

6. An Oracle Regarding the Judgment of the Enemies of Yahweh's People and the Fulfillment of Yahweh's Promise to Care for His People (9.1–11.37)

7. An Oracle Revealing the Triumph of Yahweh over His Enemies and His Arrival to Reign among His People (12.1–14.37)

Suggested Resources

Baldwin, Joyce G. *Haggai, Zechariah, Malachi*. Tyndale Old Testament Commentaries. Downers Grove, IL: InterVarsity Press, 1988.

Boda, Mark J. *The Book of Zechariah*. New International Commentary on the Old Testament. Grand Rapids: Eerdmans, 2016.

McComiskey, Thomas Edward. "Zechariah." Pages 1003–244 in *The Minor Prophets: An Exegetical and Expository Commentary*. Grand Rapids: Baker Academic, 1992.

Petterson, Anthony R. *Haggai, Zechariah & Malachi*. Apollos Old Testament Commentary. Downers Grove, IL: InterVarsity Press, 2015.

Shepherd, Michael B. *A Commentary on the Book of the Twelve*. Grand Rapids: Kregel, 2018.

Wolters, Albert M. *Zechariah*. Historical Commentary on the Old Testament. Leuven: Peeters, 2014.

Zechariah

I In the eighth month, in the second year of Darius, the word of the Lord came to the prophet Zechariah son of Berechiah, son of Iddo: "The Lord was extremely angry with your ancestors. So tell the people, 'This is what the Lord of Armies says: Return to me — this is the declaration of the Lord of Armies — and I will return to you, says the Lord of Armies. Do not be like your ancestors; the earlier prophets proclaimed to them: This is what the Lord of Armies says: Turn from your evil ways and your evil deeds. But they did not listen or pay attention to me — this is the Lord's declaration. Where are your ancestors now? And do the prophets live forever? But didn't my words and my statutes that I commanded my servants the prophets overtake your ancestors?'"

10   So the people repented and said, "As the Lord of Armies decided to deal with us for our ways and our deeds, so he has dealt with us."

On the twenty-fourth day of the eleventh month, which is the month of Shebat, in the second year of Darius, the word of the Lord came to the prophet Zechariah son of Berechiah, son of Iddo:

I looked out in the night and saw a man riding on a chestnut horse. He was standing among the myrtle trees in the valley. Behind him were chestnut, brown, and white horses. I asked, "What are these, my lord?"

The angel who was talking to me replied, "I will show you what they are."

Then the man standing among the myrtle trees explained, "They are the ones the Lord has
20   sent to patrol the earth."

They reported to the angel of the Lord standing among the myrtle trees, "We have patrolled the earth, and right now the whole earth is calm and quiet."

Then the angel of the Lord responded, "How long, Lord of Armies, will you withhold mercy from Jerusalem and the cities of Judah that you have been angry with these seventy years?" The Lord replied with kind and comforting words to the angel who was speaking with me.

So the angel who was speaking with me said, "Proclaim: The Lord of Armies says: I am extremely jealous for Jerusalem and Zion. I am fiercely angry with the nations that are at ease, for I was a little angry, but they made the destruction worse. Therefore, this is what the Lord says: In mercy, I have returned to Jerusalem; my house will be rebuilt within it — this
30   is the declaration of the Lord of Armies — and a measuring line will be stretched out over Jerusalem.

"Proclaim further: This is what the LORD of Armies says: My cities will again overflow with prosperity; the LORD will once more comfort Zion and again choose Jerusalem."

Then I looked up and saw four horns. So I asked the angel who was speaking with me, "What are these?"

And he said to me, "These are the horns that scattered Judah, Israel, and Jerusalem."

Then the LORD showed me four craftsmen. I asked, "What are they coming to do?"

He replied, "These are the horns that scattered Judah so no one could raise his head. These craftsmen have come to terrify them, to cut off the horns of the nations that raised a horn against the land of Judah to scatter it."

2 I looked up and saw a man with a measuring line in his hand. I asked, "Where are you going?"

He answered me, "To measure Jerusalem to determine its width and length."

Then the angel who was speaking with me went out, and another angel went out to meet him. He said to him, "Run and tell this young man: Jerusalem will be inhabited without walls because of the number of people and animals in it." The declaration of the LORD: "I myself will be a wall of fire around it, and I will be the glory within it."

"Listen! Listen! Flee from the land of the north" — this is the LORD's declaration — "for I have scattered you like the four winds of heaven" — this is the LORD's declaration. "Listen, Zion! Escape, you who are living with Daughter Babylon." For the LORD of Armies says this: "In pursuit of his glory, he sent me against the nations plundering you, for whoever touches you touches the pupil of my eye. For look, I am raising my hand against them, and they will become plunder for their own servants. Then you will know that the LORD of Armies has sent me.

"Daughter Zion, shout for joy and be glad, for I am coming to dwell among you" — this is the LORD's declaration. "Many nations will join themselves to the LORD on that day and become my people. I will dwell among you, and you will know that the LORD of Armies has sent me to you. The LORD will take possession of Judah as his portion in the Holy Land, and he will once again choose Jerusalem. Let all humanity be silent before the LORD, for from his holy dwelling he has roused himself."

3 Then he showed me the high priest Joshua standing before the angel of the LORD, with Satan standing at his right side to accuse him. The LORD said to Satan, "The LORD rebuke you, Satan! May the LORD who has chosen Jerusalem rebuke you! Isn't this man a burning stick snatched from the fire?"

Now Joshua was dressed with filthy clothes as he stood before the angel. So the angel of the LORD spoke to those standing before him, "Take off his filthy clothes!" Then he said to him, "See, I have removed your iniquity from you, and I will clothe you with festive robes."

Then I said, "Let them put a clean turban on his head." So a clean turban was placed on his head, and they clothed him in garments while the angel of the LORD was standing nearby.

10   Then the angel of the Lord charged Joshua, "This is what the Lord of Armies says: If you walk in my ways and keep my mandates, you will both rule my house and take care of my courts; I will also grant you access among these who are standing here.

"Listen, High Priest Joshua, you and your colleagues sitting before you; indeed, these men are a sign that I am about to bring my servant, the Branch. Notice the stone I have set before Joshua; on that one stone are seven eyes. I will engrave an inscription on it" — this is the declaration of the Lord of Armies — "and I will take away the iniquity of this land in a single day. On that day, each of you will invite his neighbor to sit under his vine and fig tree." This is the declaration of the Lord of Armies.

4   The angel who was speaking with me then returned and roused me as one awakened out of sleep. He asked me, "What do you see?"

I replied, "I see a solid gold lampstand with a bowl at the top. The lampstand also has seven lamps at the top with seven spouts for each of the lamps. There are also two olive trees beside it, one on the right of the bowl and the other on its left."

Then I asked the angel who was speaking with me, "What are these, my lord?"

"Don't you know what they are?" replied the angel who was speaking with me.

I said, "No, my lord."

So he answered me, "This is the word of the Lord to Zerubbabel: 'Not by strength or by
10 might, but by my Spirit,' says the Lord of Armies. 'What are you, great mountain? Before Zerubbabel you will become a plain. And he will bring out the capstone accompanied by shouts of: Grace, grace to it!'"

Then the word of the Lord came to me: "Zerubbabel's hands have laid the foundation of this house, and his hands will complete it. Then you will know that the Lord of Armies has sent me to you. For who despises the day of small things? These seven eyes of the Lord, which scan throughout the whole earth, will rejoice when they see the ceremonial stone in Zerubbabel's hand."

I asked him, "What are the two olive trees on the right and left of the lampstand?" And I
questioned him further, "What are the two streams of the olive trees, from which the golden oil is
20 pouring through the two golden conduits?"

Then he inquired of me, "Don't you know what these are?"

"No, my lord," I replied.

"These are the two anointed ones," he said, "who stand by the Lord of the whole earth."

5 I looked up again and saw a flying scroll. "What do you see?" he asked me.

"I see a flying scroll," I replied, "thirty feet long and fifteen feet wide."

Then he said to me, "This is the curse that is going out over the whole land, for everyone who is a thief, contrary to what is written on one side, has gone unpunished, and everyone who swears

falsely, contrary to what is written on the other side, has gone unpunished. I will send it out," —
this is the declaration of the LORD of Armies — "and it will enter the house of the thief and the
house of the one who swears falsely by my name. It will stay inside his house and destroy it along
with its timbers and stones."

Then the angel who was speaking with me came forward and told me, "Look up and see what this
10   is that is approaching."

    So I asked, "What is it?"

    He responded, "It's a measuring basket that is approaching." And he continued, "This is their
iniquity in all the land." Then a lead cover was lifted, and there was a woman sitting inside the
basket. "This is Wickedness," he said. He shoved her down into the basket and pushed the lead
weight over its opening. Then I looked up and saw two women approaching with the wind in their
wings. Their wings were like those of a stork, and they lifted up the basket between earth and sky.

    So I asked the angel who was speaking with me, "Where are they taking the basket?"

    "To build a shrine for it in the land of Shinar," he told me. "When that is ready, the basket will
be placed there on its pedestal."

6   Then I looked up again and saw four chariots coming from between two mountains. The
mountains were made of bronze. The first chariot had chestnut horses, the second chariot black
horses, the third chariot white horses, and the fourth chariot dappled horses — all strong horses.
So I inquired of the angel who was speaking with me, "What are these, my lord?"

    The angel told me, "These are the four spirits of heaven going out after presenting themselves
to the Lord of the whole earth. The one with the black horses is going to the land of the north, the
white horses are going after them, but the dappled horses are going to the land of the south." As
the strong horses went out, they wanted to go patrol the earth, and the LORD said, "Go, patrol the
earth." So they patrolled the earth. Then he summoned me saying, "See, those going to the land of
10   the north have pacified my Spirit in the northern land."

The word of the LORD came to me: "Take an offering from the exiles, from Heldai, Tobijah,
and Jedaiah, who have arrived from Babylon, and go that same day to the house of Josiah son of
Zephaniah. Take silver and gold, make a crown, and place it on the head of Joshua son of Jehozadak,
the high priest. You are to tell him: This is what the LORD of Armies says: Here is a man whose
name is Branch; he will branch out from his place and build the LORD's temple. Yes, he will build the
LORD's temple; he will bear royal splendor and will sit on his throne and rule. There will be a priest
on his throne, and there will be peaceful counsel between the two of them. The crown will reside in
the LORD's temple as a memorial to Heldai, Tobijah, Jedaiah, and Hen son of Zephaniah. People
who are far off will come and build the LORD's temple, and you will know that the LORD of Armies
20   has sent me to you. This will happen when you fully obey the LORD your God."

7 In the fourth year of King Darius, the word of the LORD came to Zechariah on the fourth day of the ninth month, which is Chislev. Now the people of Bethel had sent Sharezer, Regem-melech, and their men to plead for the LORD's favor by asking the priests who were at the house of the LORD of Armies as well as the prophets, "Should we mourn and fast in the fifth month as we have done these many years?"

Then the word of the LORD of Armies came to me: "Ask all the people of the land and the priests: When you fasted and lamented in the fifth and in the seventh months for these seventy years, did you really fast for me? When you eat and drink, don't you eat and drink simply for yourselves? Aren't these the words that the LORD proclaimed through the earlier prophets when
10 Jerusalem was inhabited and secure, along with its surrounding cities, and when the southern region and the Judean foothills were inhabited?"

The word of the LORD came to Zechariah: "The LORD of Armies says this: 'Make fair decisions. Show faithful love and compassion to one another. Do not oppress the widow or the fatherless, the resident alien or the poor, and do not plot evil in your hearts against one another.' But they refused to pay attention and turned a stubborn shoulder; they closed their ears so they could not hear. They made their hearts like a rock so as not to obey the law or the words that the LORD of Armies had sent by his Spirit through the earlier prophets. Therefore intense anger came from the LORD of Armies. Just as he had called, and they would not listen, so when they called, I would not listen, says the LORD of Armies. I scattered them with a windstorm over all the nations
20 that had not known them, and the land was left desolate behind them, with no one coming or going. They turned a pleasant land into a desolation."

8 The word of the LORD of Armies came: The LORD of Armies says this: "I am extremely jealous for Zion; I am jealous for her with great wrath." The LORD says this: "I will return to Zion and live in Jerusalem. Then Jerusalem will be called the Faithful City; the mountain of the LORD of Armies will be called the Holy Mountain." The LORD of Armies says this: "Old men and women will again sit along the streets of Jerusalem, each with a staff in hand because of advanced age. The streets of the city will be filled with boys and girls playing in them." The LORD of Armies says this: "Though it may seem impossible to the remnant of this people in those days, should it also seem impossible to me?" — this is the declaration of the LORD of Armies. The LORD of Armies says this: "I will save my people from the land of the east and the land of the west. I will bring them
10 back to live in Jerusalem. They will be my people, and I will be their faithful and righteous God."

The LORD of Armies says this: "Let your hands be strong, you who now hear these words that the prophets spoke when the foundations were laid for the rebuilding of the temple, the house of the LORD of Armies. For prior to those days neither people nor animals had wages. There was no safety from the enemy for anyone who came or went, for I turned everyone against his neighbor. But now, I will not treat the remnant of this people as in the former days" — this is the declaration of the LORD of Armies. "For they will sow in peace: the vine will yield its fruit, the land will yield its produce, and the skies will yield their dew. I will give the remnant of this people all these things as an inheritance. As you have been a curse among the nations, house of Judah and house of Israel, so I will save you, and you will be a blessing. Don't be afraid; let your hands be strong." For the

20 LORD of Armies says this: "As I resolved to treat you badly when your ancestors provoked me to anger, and I did not relent," says the LORD of Armies, "so I have resolved again in these days to do what is good to Jerusalem and the house of Judah. Don't be afraid. These are the things you must do: Speak truth to one another; make true and sound decisions within your city gates. Do not plot evil in your hearts against your neighbor, and do not love perjury, for I hate all this" — this is the LORD's declaration.

Then the word of the LORD of Armies came to me: The LORD of Armies says this: "The fast of the fourth month, the fast of the fifth, the fast of the seventh, and the fast of the tenth will become times of joy, gladness, and cheerful festivals for the house of Judah. Therefore, love truth and peace." The LORD of Armies says this: "Peoples will yet come, the residents of many cities; the

30 residents of one city will go to another, saying: Let's go at once to plead for the LORD's favor and to seek the LORD of Armies. I am also going. Many peoples and strong nations will come to seek the LORD of Armies in Jerusalem and to plead for the LORD's favor." The LORD of Armies says this: "In those days, ten men from nations of every language will grab the robe of a Jewish man tightly, urging: Let us go with you, for we have heard that God is with you."

9 A pronouncement:

> The word of the LORD
> is against the land of Hadrach,
> and Damascus is its resting place—
> for the eyes of humanity
> and all the tribes of Israel
> are on the LORD—
> and also against Hamath, which borders it,
> as well as Tyre and Sidon,
10 > though they are very shrewd.
> Tyre has built herself a fortress;
> she has heaped up silver like dust
> and gold like the dirt of the streets.
> Listen! The Lord will impoverish her
> and cast her wealth into the sea;
> she herself will be consumed by fire.
> Ashkelon will see it and be afraid;
> Gaza too, and will writhe in great pain,
> as will Ekron, for her hope will fail.

20 There will cease to be a king in Gaza,
and Ashkelon will become uninhabited.
A mongrel people will live in Ashdod,
and I will destroy the pride of the Philistines.
I will remove the blood from their mouths
and the abhorrent things
from between their teeth.
Then they too will become a remnant for our God;
they will become like a clan in Judah
and Ekron like the Jebusites.
30 I will encamp at my house as a guard,
against those who march back and forth,
and no oppressor will march against them again,
for now I have seen with my own eyes.

Rejoice greatly, Daughter Zion!
Shout in triumph, Daughter Jerusalem!
Look, your King is coming to you;
he is righteous and victorious,
humble and riding on a donkey,
on a colt, the foal of a donkey.
40 I will cut off the chariot from Ephraim
and the horse from Jerusalem.
The bow of war will be removed,
and he will proclaim peace to the nations.
His dominion will extend from sea to sea,
from the Euphrates River
to the ends of the earth.
As for you,
because of the blood of your covenant,
I will release your prisoners
50 from the waterless cistern.
Return to a stronghold,
you prisoners who have hope;
today I declare that I will restore double to you.
For I will bend Judah as my bow;
I will fill that bow with Ephraim.
I will rouse your sons, Zion,

against your sons, Greece.
I will make you like a warrior's sword.
Then the LORD will appear over them,
60 and his arrow will fly like lightning.
The Lord GOD will sound the ram's horn
and advance with the southern storms.
The LORD of Armies will defend them.
They will consume and conquer with slingstones;
they will drink and be rowdy as if with wine.
They will be as full as the sprinkling basin,
like those at the corners of the altar.
The LORD their God will save them on that day
as the flock of his people;
70 for they are like jewels in a crown,
sparkling over his land.
How lovely and beautiful!
Grain will make the young men flourish,
and new wine, the young women.

10 Ask the LORD for rain
in the season of spring rain.
The LORD makes the rain clouds,
and he will give them showers of rain
and crops in the field for everyone.
For the idols speak falsehood,
and the diviners see illusions;
they relate empty dreams
and offer empty comfort.
10 Therefore the people wander like sheep;
they suffer affliction because there is no shepherd.
My anger burns against the shepherds,
so I will punish the leaders.
For the LORD of Armies has tended his flock,
the house of Judah;
he will make them like his majestic steed in battle.
The cornerstone, the tent peg,
the battle bow, and every ruler—
all will go out from him together.

They will be like warriors in battle
trampling down the mud of the streets.
They will fight because the LORD is with them,
and they will put horsemen to shame.
I will strengthen the house of Judah
and deliver the house of Joseph.
I will restore them
because I have compassion on them,
and they will be
as though I had never rejected them.
For I am the LORD their God,
and I will answer them.
Ephraim will be like a warrior,
and their hearts will be glad as if with wine.
Their children will see it and be glad;
their hearts will rejoice in the LORD.

I will whistle and gather them
because I have redeemed them;
they will be as numerous as they once were.
Though I sow them among the nations,
they will remember me in the distant lands;
they and their children will live and return.
I will bring them back from the land of Egypt
and gather them from Assyria.
I will bring them to the land of Gilead
and to Lebanon,
but it will not be enough for them.
The LORD will pass through the sea of distress
and strike the waves of the sea;
all the depths of the Nile will dry up.
The pride of Assyria will be brought down,
and the scepter of Egypt will come to an end.
I will strengthen them in the LORD,
and they will march in his name—

this is the LORD's declaration.

11   Open your gates, Lebanon,
     and fire will consume your cedars.
     Wail, cypress, for the cedar has fallen;
     the glorious trees are destroyed!
     Wail, oaks of Bashan,
     for the stately forest has fallen!
     Listen to the wail of the shepherds,
     for their glory is destroyed.
     Listen to the roar of young lions,
10   for the thickets of the Jordan are destroyed.

The Lord my God says this: "Shepherd the flock intended for slaughter. Those who buy them slaughter them but are not punished. Those who sell them say, 'Blessed be the Lord because I have become rich!' Even their own shepherds have no compassion for them. Indeed, I will no longer have compassion on the inhabitants of the land" — this is the Lord's declaration. "Instead, I will turn everyone over to his neighbor and his king. They will devastate the land, and I will not rescue it from their hand."

So I shepherded the flock intended for slaughter, the oppressed of the flock. I took two staffs, calling one Favor and the other Union, and I shepherded the flock. In one month I got rid of three shepherds. I became impatient with them, and they also detested me. Then I said, "I will no longer shepherd you. Let what is dying die, and let what is perishing perish; let the rest devour each other's flesh." Next I took my staff called Favor and cut it in two, annulling the covenant I had made with all the peoples. It was annulled on that day, and so the oppressed of the flock who were watching me knew that it was the word of the Lord. Then I said to them, "If it seems right to you, give me my wages; but if not, keep them." So they weighed my wages, thirty pieces of silver.

"Throw it to the potter," the Lord said to me — this magnificent price I was valued by them. So I took the thirty pieces of silver and threw it into the house of the Lord, to the potter. Then I cut in two my second staff, Union, annulling the brotherhood between Judah and Israel.

The Lord also said to me, "Take the equipment of a foolish shepherd. I am about to raise up a shepherd in the land who will not care for those who are perishing, and he will not seek the lost or heal the broken. He will not sustain the healthy, but he will devour the flesh of the fat sheep and tear off their hooves.

     Woe to the worthless shepherd
     who deserts the flock!
     May a sword strike his arm
     and his right eye!
     May his arm wither away
     and his right eye go completely blind!"

12 A pronouncement:

> The word of the LORD concerning Israel.
> A declaration of the LORD,
> who stretched out the heavens,
> laid the foundation of the earth,
> and formed the spirit of man within him.

"Look, I will make Jerusalem a cup that causes staggering for the peoples who surround the city. The siege against Jerusalem will also involve Judah. On that day I will make Jerusalem a heavy stone for all the peoples; all who try to lift it will injure themselves severely when all the nations of the earth gather against her. On that day" — this is the LORD's declaration — "I will strike every horse with panic and its rider with madness. I will keep a watchful eye on the house of Judah but strike all the horses of the nations with blindness. Then each of the leaders of Judah will think to himself: The residents of Jerusalem are my strength through the LORD of Armies, their God. On that day I will make the leaders of Judah like a firepot in a woodpile, like a flaming torch among sheaves; they will consume all the peoples around them on the right and the left, while Jerusalem continues to be inhabited on its site, in Jerusalem. The LORD will save the tents of Judah first, so that the glory of David's house and the glory of Jerusalem's residents may not be greater than that of Judah. On that day the LORD will defend the inhabitants of Jerusalem, so that on that day the one who is weakest among them will be like David on that day, and the house of David will be like God, like the angel of the LORD, before them. On that day I will set out to destroy all the nations that come against Jerusalem.

"Then I will pour out a spirit of grace and prayer on the house of David and the residents of Jerusalem, and they will look at me whom they pierced. They will mourn for him as one mourns for an only child and weep bitterly for him as one weeps for a firstborn. On that day the mourning in Jerusalem will be as great as the mourning of Hadad-rimmon in the plain of Megiddo. The land will mourn, every family by itself: the family of David's house by itself and their women by themselves; the family of Nathan's house by itself and their women by themselves; the family of Levi's house by itself and their women by themselves; the family of Shimei by itself and their women by themselves; all the remaining families, every family by itself, and their women by themselves.

13 "On that day a fountain will be opened for the house of David and for the residents of Jerusalem, to wash away sin and impurity. On that day" — this is the declaration of the LORD of Armies — "I will remove the names of the idols from the land, and they will no longer be remembered. I will banish the prophets and the unclean spirit from the land. If a man still prophesies, his father and his mother who bore him will say to him, 'You cannot remain alive because you have spoken a lie in the name of the LORD.' When he prophesies, his father and his mother who bore him will

pierce him through. On that day every prophet will be ashamed of his vision when he prophesies; they will not put on a hairy cloak in order to deceive. He will say, 'I am not a prophet; I work the land, for a man purchased me as a servant since my youth.' If someone asks him, 'What are these
10 wounds on your chest?' — then he will answer, 'I received the wounds in the house of my friends.'

> Sword, awake against my shepherd,
> against the man who is my associate—
> this is the declaration of the LORD of Armies.
> Strike the shepherd, and the sheep will be scattered;
> I will turn my hand against the little ones.
> In the whole land—
> this is the LORD's declaration—
> two-thirds will be cut off and die,
> but a third will be left in it.
20 I will put this third through the fire;
> I will refine them as silver is refined
> and test them as gold is tested.
> They will call on my name,
> and I will answer them.
> I will say, 'They are my people,'
> and they will say, 'The LORD is our God.'"

14 Look, a day belonging to the LORD is coming when the plunder taken from you will be divided in your presence. I will gather all the nations against Jerusalem for battle. The city will be captured, the houses looted, and the women raped. Half the city will go into exile, but the rest of the people will not be removed from the city.

Then the LORD will go out to fight against those nations as he fights on a day of battle. On that day his feet will stand on the Mount of Olives, which faces Jerusalem on the east. The Mount of Olives will be split in half from east to west, forming a huge valley, so that half the mountain will move to the north and half to the south. You will flee by my mountain valley, for the valley of the mountains will extend to Azal. You will flee as you fled from the earthquake in the days of King
10 Uzziah of Judah. Then the LORD my God will come and all the holy ones with him.

On that day there will be no light; the sunlight and moonlight will diminish. It will be a unique day known only to the LORD, without day or night, but there will be light at evening.

On that day living water will flow out from Jerusalem, half of it toward the eastern sea and the other half toward the western sea, in summer and winter alike. On that day the LORD will become King over the whole earth — the LORD alone, and his name alone. All the land from Geba to Rimmon south of Jerusalem will be changed into a plain. But Jerusalem will be raised up and will remain on its site from the Benjamin Gate to the place of the First Gate, to the Corner Gate, and from the Tower of Hananel to the royal winepresses. People will live there, and never again will there be a curse of complete destruction. So Jerusalem will dwell in security.

20 This will be the plague with which the LORD strikes all the people who have warred against Jerusalem: their flesh will rot while they stand on their feet, their eyes will rot in their sockets, and their tongues will rot in their mouths. On that day a great panic from the LORD will be among them, so that each will seize the hand of another, and the hand of one will rise against the other. Judah will also fight at Jerusalem, and the wealth of all the surrounding nations will be collected: gold, silver, and clothing in great abundance. The same plague as the previous one will strike the horses, mules, camels, donkeys, and all the animals that are in those camps.

Then all the survivors from the nations that came against Jerusalem will go up year after year to worship the King, the LORD of Armies, and to celebrate the Festival of Shelters. Should any of the families of the earth not go up to Jerusalem to worship the King, the LORD of Armies, rain will not 30 fall on them. And if the people of Egypt will not go up and enter, then rain will not fall on them; this will be the plague the LORD inflicts on the nations who do not go up to celebrate the Festival of Shelters. This will be the punishment of Egypt and all the nations that do not go up to celebrate the Festival of Shelters.

On that day, the words HOLY TO THE LORD will be on the bells of the horses. The pots in the house of the LORD will be like the sprinkling basins before the altar. Every pot in Jerusalem and in Judah will be holy to the LORD of Armies. All who sacrifice will come and use the pots to cook in. And on that day there will no longer be a Canaanite in the house of the LORD of Armies.

Introduction to Malachi

Tremper Longman III

Malachi is the twelfth and final book in the Book of the Twelve and, since the twelve are in roughly chronological order, reflects the final editor of the Book of the Twelve's view that Malachi was the last prophet in terms of date. Various internal indications, including the fact that the temple has been rebuilt (1.21–24; completed 515 BC) and has been around long enough for dissatisfaction to settle in among the people of Yahweh, again indicates that the prophet wrote late in the HS time period.

The book derives its name from the author who is identified as Malachi. Some believe that Malachi, which means "my messenger," is not a personal name but rather a generic description of the author. In any case, Malachi is not known elsewhere in scripture, so whether a personal name or a generic, we know nothing much about him except that Yahweh commissioned him to bring a message to his contemporaries.

Malachi's message is primarily in the form of six disputations between Yahweh and his people, each showing Yahweh's displeasure with his people and the people's dissatisfaction with him. In the first disputation, the people question Yahweh's love for them based on the fact that their enemy, Edom, thrives while they languish. Yahweh informs them that Edom will not get away with their bad treatment of his people (1.3–11). The longest dispute, the second, is against the priests. Yahweh accuses them of contempt in the shoddy way that they observe the rituals that were supposed to glorify Yahweh (1.12–2.15). The third disputation concerns the people's violation of the covenant, which is likened to a divorce (2.16–30). In response to the fourth disputation that he is unjust, Yahweh responds by saying a day is coming when he will set all things straight (2.31–3.12). Yahweh calls the people who steal Yahweh's tithes to repentance in the fifth disputation (3.13–24). In the sixth and final disputation, Yahweh accuses his people of speaking arrogantly against him when they say they get nothing from serving him (3.25–4.6). Again they think that wicked people prosper and not them. Yahweh again informs them that he will punish the wicked and reward those who follow him.

The use of the disputation form shows Yahweh's extreme displeasure with his people's attitudes and behavior. The people's request for clarification of the command shows just how spiritually dull they are in their relationship with Yahweh and how much they need to repent and obey. In clarifying his initial statement, Yahweh also details the charge in a way that further implicates the people.

The book ends with two short statements, the first is a call to obey the law of Moses (4.7–8) since the previous disputations indicate that they have been disobedient. The second announces that he will send the prophet Elijah before the "Day of the Lord," which is a day of judgment (4.8–10), thus warning them that if they do not obey the law of Moses Yahweh will punish them. On the positive side, here at the end of the book, Yahweh not only calls on his people to repent but also gives hope to "those who fear my name" (4.3). For them, "the sun of righteousness will rise with healing it its wings, and you will go out and playfully jump like calves from the stall." (4.3–4).

Significantly, the gospel of Mark cites Mal 3.1–3 along with Isa 40.9–11 to announce the arrival of a messenger, John the Baptist, who will precede Jesus, the Messiah. Jesus also associates the messenger John the Baptist with Elijah (Matt 11:4; 17:2, see Mal 4.8–10). In his coming, Jesus initiates the day of the Lord that will be fully realized in his second coming when the wicked are punished and the righteous rewarded. The eschatological hopes of the book of Malachi find realization in the Gospels.

Outline

1. Superscription (1.1–2)

2. Yahweh Disputes the People's Charge that He Does Not Love Them (1.3–11)

3. Yahweh Disputes the Contempt of Priests (1.12–2.15)

4. Yahweh Disputes Israel for Breaking the Covenant (2.16–30)

5. Yahweh Disputes the Charge of Injustice (2.31–3.12)

6. Yahweh Disputes His People over Repentance (3.13–24)

7. Yahweh Disputes Israel over Their Harsh Words (3.25–4.6)

8. Command to Obey the Law (4.7–8)

9. Announcement of Coming Day of the Lord (4.8–10)

Suggested Resources

Baker, David W. *Joel, Obadiah, Malachi*. NIV Application Commentary. Grand Rapids: Zondervan, 2006.

Hill, Andrew E. *Malachi*. Anchor Bible Commentary. New Haven: Yale University Press, 1998.

Merrill, Eugene H. "Malachi." Pages 835–63 in vol. 8 of *The Expositor's Bible Commentary*. Rev. ed. Grand Rapids: Zondervan, 2008.

Stuart, Duane. "Malachi." Pages 1245–396 of *The Minor Prophets: An Exegetical and Expository Commentary*. Grand Rapids: Baker Academic, 1998.

Malachi

1 A pronouncement:

The word of the LORD to Israel through Malachi.

"I have loved you," says the LORD.

Yet you ask, "How have you loved us?"

"Wasn't Esau Jacob's brother?" This is the LORD's declaration. "Even so, I loved Jacob, but I hated Esau. I turned his mountains into a wasteland, and gave his inheritance to the desert jackals."

Though Edom says, "We have been devastated, but we will rebuild the ruins," the LORD of Armies says this: "They may build, but I will demolish. They will be called a wicked country and the people the LORD has cursed forever. Your own eyes will see this, and you yourselves will say, 'The LORD is great, even beyond the borders of Israel.'

"A son honors his father, and a servant his master. But if I am a father, where is my honor? And if I am a master, where is your fear of me? says the LORD of Armies to you priests, who despise my name."

Yet you ask, "How have we despised your name?"

"By presenting defiled food on my altar."

"How have we defiled you?" you ask.

When you say, "The LORD's table is contemptible."

"When you present a blind animal for sacrifice, is it not wrong? And when you present a lame or sick animal, is it not wrong? Bring it to your governor! Would he be pleased with you or show you favor?" asks the LORD of Armies. "And now plead for God's favor. Will he be gracious to us? Since this has come from your hands, will he show any of you favor?" asks the LORD of Armies. "I wish one of you would shut the temple doors, so that you would no longer kindle a useless fire on my altar! I am not pleased with you," says the LORD of Armies, "and I will accept no offering from your hands.

"My name will be great among the nations, from the rising of the sun to its setting. Incense and pure offerings will be presented in my name in every place because my name will be great among the nations," says the LORD of Armies.

"But you are profaning it when you say, 'The Lord's table is defiled, and its product, its food, is contemptible.' You also say, 'Look, what a nuisance!' And you scorn it," says the LORD of Armies. "You bring stolen, lame, or sick animals. You bring this as an offering! Am I to accept that from your hands?" asks the LORD.

"The deceiver is cursed who has an acceptable male in his flock and makes a vow but sacrifices a defective animal to the Lord. For I am a great King," says the LORD of Armies, "and my name will be feared among the nations.

2 "Therefore, this decree is for you priests: If you don't listen, and if you don't take it to heart to honor my name," says the LORD of Armies, "I will send a curse among you, and I will curse your blessings. In fact, I have already begun to curse them because you are not taking it to heart.

"Look, I am going to rebuke your descendants, and I will spread animal waste over your faces, the waste from your festival sacrifices, and you will be taken away with it. Then you will know that I sent you this decree, so that my covenant with Levi may continue," says the LORD of Armies. "My covenant with him was one of life and peace, and I gave these to him; it called for reverence, and he revered me and stood in awe of my name. True instruction was in his mouth, and nothing wrong was found on his lips. He walked with me in peace and integrity and turned many from iniquity. For the lips of a priest should guard knowledge, and people should desire instruction from his mouth, because he is the messenger of the LORD of Armies.

"You, on the other hand, have turned from the way. You have caused many to stumble by your instruction. You have violated the covenant of Levi," says the LORD of Armies. "So I in turn have made you despised and humiliated before all the people because you are not keeping my ways but are showing partiality in your instruction."

Don't all of us have one Father? Didn't one God create us? Why then do we act treacherously against one another, profaning the covenant of our ancestors? Judah has acted treacherously, and a detestable act has been done in Israel and in Jerusalem. For Judah has profaned the LORD's sanctuary, which he loves, and has married the daughter of a foreign god. May the LORD cut off from the tents of Jacob the man who does this, whoever he may be, even if he presents an offering to the LORD of Armies.

This is another thing you do. You are covering the LORD's altar with tears, with weeping and groaning, because he no longer respects your offerings or receives them gladly from your hands.

And you ask, "Why?" Because even though the LORD has been a witness between you and the wife of your youth, you have acted treacherously against her. She was your marriage partner and your wife by covenant. Didn't God make them one and give them a portion of spirit? What is the one seeking? Godly offspring. So watch yourselves carefully, so that no one acts treacherously against the wife of his youth.

"If he hates and divorces his wife," says the LORD God of Israel, "he covers his garment with injustice," says the LORD of Armies. Therefore, watch yourselves carefully, and do not act treacherously.

You have wearied the LORD with your words.

Yet you ask, "How have we wearied him?"

When you say, "Everyone who does what is evil is good in the Lord's sight, and he is delighted with them, or else where is the God of justice?"

3 "See, I am going to send my messenger, and he will clear the way before me. Then the Lord you seek will suddenly come to his temple, the Messenger of the covenant you delight in — see, he is coming," says the Lord of Armies. But who can endure the day of his coming? And who will be able to stand when he appears? For he will be like a refiner's fire and like launderer's bleach. He will be like a refiner and purifier of silver; he will purify the sons of Levi and refine them like gold and silver. Then they will present offerings to the Lord in righteousness. And the offerings of Judah and Jerusalem will please the Lord as in days of old and years gone by.

"I will come to you in judgment, and I will be ready to witness against sorcerers and adulterers; against those who swear falsely; against those who oppress the hired worker, the widow, and the fatherless; and against those who deny justice to the resident alien. They do not fear me," says the Lord of Armies. "Because I, the Lord, have not changed, you descendants of Jacob have not been destroyed.

"Since the days of your ancestors, you have turned from my statutes; you have not kept them. Return to me, and I will return to you," says the Lord of Armies.

Yet you ask, "How can we return?"

"Will a man rob God? Yet you are robbing me!"

"How do we rob you?" you ask.

"By not making the payments of the tenth and the contributions. You are suffering under a curse, yet you — the whole nation — are still robbing me. Bring the full tenth into the storehouse so that there may be food in my house. Test me in this way," says the Lord of Armies. "See if I will not open the floodgates of heaven and pour out a blessing for you without measure. I will rebuke the devourer for you, so that it will not ruin the produce of your land and your vine in your field will not fail to produce fruit," says the Lord of Armies. "Then all the nations will consider you fortunate, for you will be a delightful land," says the Lord of Armies.

"Your words against me are harsh," says the Lord.

Yet you ask, "What have we spoken against you?"

You have said, "It is useless to serve God. What have we gained by keeping his requirements and walking mournfully before the Lord of Armies? So now we consider the arrogant to be fortunate. Not only do those who commit wickedness prosper, they even test God and escape."

At that time those who feared the Lord spoke to one another. The Lord took notice and listened. So a book of remembrance was written before him for those who feared the Lord and had high regard for his name. "They will be mine," says the Lord of Armies, "my own possession on the day I am preparing. I will have compassion on them as a man has compassion on his son who serves him. So you will again see the difference between the righteous and the wicked, between one who serves God and one who does not serve him.

4 "For look, the day is coming, burning like a furnace, when all the arrogant and everyone who commits wickedness will become stubble. The coming day will consume them," says the LORD of Armies, "not leaving them root or branches. But for you who fear my name, the sun of righteousness will rise with healing in its wings, and you will go out and playfully jump like calves from the stall. You will trample the wicked, for they will be ashes under the soles of your feet on the day I am preparing," says the LORD of Armies.

"Remember the instruction of Moses my servant, the statutes and ordinances I commanded him at Horeb for all Israel. Look, I am going to send you the prophet Elijah before the great and terrible day of the LORD comes. And he will turn the hearts of fathers to their children and the hearts of 10 children to their fathers. Otherwise, I will come and strike the land with a curse."

The Ketuvim
(Writings)

Introduction to the Writings

Joshua E. Stewart

The Writings (*Ketuvim*) section of the HS is often regarded as a place in which later literary works found their home. The order witnessed in English translations is vastly different from the HS. Essentially all the books of the Writings appear in a different location from those witnessed in English Bibles. Even though it is true that most of these works, or at least their final form, did come about in the later period of Israel's history (after the destruction of the temple in 586 BC), their placement in this section is much more than an orphan needing a home. The books therein contain many different genres: poetry, narrative, apocalyptic, and wisdom. The genres included in the Writings are unique in the sense that they do not fit neatly in the Torah or the Prophets.

In the HS, as witnessed in the standard critical Hebrew Bible (*Biblia Hebraica Stuttgartensia* or BHS) the books appear as such: Psalms, Job, Proverbs, Ruth, Song of Songs, Ecclesiastes, Lamentations, Esther, Daniel, Ezra-Nehemiah, and the Chronicles Corpus. However, within this section of the HS there is a variety in the ordering of the books. In *Baba Bathra* 14b, the Writings are arranged as follows: Ruth, Psalms, Job, Proverbs, Ecclesiastes, Song of Songs, Lamentations, Daniel, Esther, Ezra-Nehemiah, and the Chronicles Corpus.[1] A few later codices (i.e., Aleppo Codex) present another option of ordering the same books; this order is currently used in the *Biblia Hebraica Quinta*. Although the arrangement of the books differs, the books within the Writings remain consistent. The order found in the BHS is the topic of this introduction.

Although these books are placed in English translations according to supposed chronology and at times based upon the literary character of a book, in the HS these books are placed in the Writings because of the later date of their final form. Similarities exist between books in the Writings and books in the Torah and Prophets. For example, the Chronicles Corpus is historical literature much like Samuel and Kings. The books in the Writings are loosely arranged according to genre and liturgical function. Psalms, Job, and Proverbs are poetic in nature. These books are followed by the Megilloth (the five scrolls)—Ruth, Song of Songs, Ecclesiastes, Lamentations, and Esther—which is used in Jewish worship to remember important times in their history. Esther is followed by the uniquely apocalyptic book of Daniel. The section is rounded out by two literary historiographies (Ezra-Nehemiah and the Chronicles Corpus).

The multiple available orders of this section point to the needs and views of different communities. Each of these orderings, and this applies to the traditional ordering of the English versions as well, are liturgical in nature. Within this project as a whole, and the Writings in particular, one thing remains

---

1. See the note on *Baba Bathra 14b* in the Introduction to the Hebrew Scriptures.

the same: the books in the Writings are forward-looking for the Israelite community and assume the existence of the Torah and the Prophets. In essence, the Writings look forward to how Israel might best make sense of life and the lessons learned from exile. We shall see in our exploration of the HS order of the writing that we risk missing out on this forward-looking aspect witnessed in the literary nature of this collection when read in the traditional English order.

We will briefly turn to each book in the Writings with the aim of understanding how each book functions in the context of the post-exilic period. The first book is the Psalms. The Psalter shows the significance of prayer and expressing one's emotions to Yahweh. Vital to our discussion here is how the Psalms open with a reflection on the necessity of the Torah (Ps 1) followed by Yahweh's chosen king (Ps 2), which reflects a theme of the Prophets. From the onset of the Writings, the reader is made aware of the dual necessity of Torah and king. The shape of the Psalter as a whole focuses on the absolute rule and reign of Yahweh, with a renewal of the Davidic reign, no matter the circumstances facing Yahweh's people.

The book of Job follows the Psalter. Job is the first of the wisdom books found in the Writings (see Proverbs and Ecclesiastes). Much of the book is about the problem of evil, especially why the righteous suffer tragedy. In HS terms, this book is a challenge to retribution theology. However, the book is more about how one responds to suffering and the goal of that response is wisdom. In a sense, explaining the how and why of suffering is not the primary concern of the book. In the end, Job realizes that Yahweh is in control, and who better to have in control than the creator of the universe (see Job 42.5–6). This is a most fitting ideology for the Jewish people in the period after the exile and for us to remember when difficult times come upon us.

Proverbs is an anthology of short sayings broadly associated with wisdom. These sayings are short and easily remembered with the aim of providing a general truth about life. At least about an idyllic life or the way things should be. The goal is to teach the reader from the wisdom of those who have gone before, wisdom from those who have faced and learned from the difficulties of life. As Proverbs stands in the HS, the book aims for the reader to learn from the past with the hope of living a wise future and trusting Yahweh.

The next five books after Proverbs are known as the Megilloth.[2] Each of these books are traditionally used to garner theological reflection related to an annual festival commemorating major events in the life of Israel, especially in light of the postexilic period.[3] They are used for remembrance, reenactment, and theological reflection—pointing to the hope of renewal of the ideals of Torah.

---

2. Sailhamer notes that these five books are the only books in the HS with a feminine singular subject throughout. He suggests this is an effort to group these books following the theme of wisdom as a young woman found in Proverbs. See Sailhamer, *Old Testament Theology*, 214.

3. For the ritual festivals of the Feast of Weeks, Passover, and Feast of Tabernacles see Lev 23. Here in Leviticus these festivals become part of the law code as appointed festivals. One of the major points of these festivals is remembrance of Yahweh's good works for his people. By reading these books in that context readers are brought to a place in which they should remember how Yahweh worked in the past with the hope that he will continue to act as long as faithfulness remains.

Traditionally, Ruth is connected to the Feast of Weeks/Pentecost and the giving of the Torah to Moses. This connection is through the story's setting during the wheat and barley harvest, which also according to tradition, aligns with the giving of the Torah. The story of Ruth provides a positive view on the inclusion of foreigners into the community of faith. As well as an interest in the Davidic ideal for the time to come, a royal messianic line.

Song of Songs connects the people to the exodus and the Passover. Passover is tied to the grain harvest in the spring and commemorates the exodus from Egypt. For centuries, Songs was understood by both Jews and Christians to be an allegory, but the book is no longer read this way in most circles. The intimacy conveyed in the poetry of the book can be thematically related to the passion and love that prompted Yahweh to deliver his people from Egypt. Songs functions in this placement as an aid for people to remember and uphold the principles of true love as given by Yahweh for all kinds of times.

Ecclesiastes functions as a means of reflecting upon the forty years in the wilderness as witnessed in the Feast of Tabernacles. During this festival the people built temporary shelters as a means of remembering their time of living in shelters when they came out of Egypt. Living in these temporary shelters is a twofold act of reflection. The first recalls the unfaithfulness that required the wilderness wandering. Secondly, living in these shelters was only temporary since Yahweh did bring them to the promised land eventually. Ecclesiastes reflects upon the world when it does not seem to make sense, especially when life is harder than it should be. By remembering the wilderness journey through Ecclesiastes, faith in Yahweh aids the reader to be assured that they have not been abandoned and prompts a forward-looking ethos for readers of all ages.

Lamentations recalls the destruction of the temple in 586 BC on the ninth of Av.[4] The book is a protest or complaint to Yahweh for what he allowed to happen to the temple and his people. The book is graphic in the details befallen the people by the Babylonians. In ways similar to Ecclesiastes, the people, and even modern readers, try to make sense of the tragic and unknown realities of the world. How do these things happen when Yahweh is in control? Has Yahweh rejected his people? The future seems dim in this book, but in an odd way this book looks forward to a better time, because from its perspective things cannot be any worse.

The final book of the Megilloth, Esther, is connected to the deliverance of the Jews by the Persians, celebrated by the Feast of Purim. Since Lamentations is dim and protesting with Yahweh, Esther provides the answer in its retelling of the deliverance of Yahweh's people. The book does this even in the midst of recalling how the Jews were the outsiders and treated poorly. The book calls readers to affirm their position as Yahweh's people even when they are in an environment hostile to the very idea. Esther conveys the necessity of hope and faithfulness.

---

4. According to some Jewish traditions the ninth of Av (a Jewish month) was the day the spies brought back their report to Moses (Num 13–14), the destruction of the first temple in 586 BC, and the destruction of the second temple in 70 AD. In essence this date and the festival are related to despair and even failures.

Daniel is apocalyptic in genre. Although the book is full of interpretive difficulties, the theological impetus of the book is clear: Yahweh is the Lord of history. He has his hands on the present (chs. 1–6) and he is active in the events to come (chs. 7–12). The wise man Daniel (Ezek 28.3) trusted Yahweh despite his circumstances, which gave him and his readers confidence in the visions of things to come.

The Writings conclude with a telling of Israel's return to the land (Ezra-Nehemiah) and a retelling of their history from the beginning (Chronicles Corpus). These books together, often identified as the Chronicler's History, reflect upon how Israel would seek to regain its former glory. Chronologically speaking, the ending of Chronicles precedes the stories of Ezra-Nehemiah. The focus of these works should remind the reader of Pss 1–2 (Torah and king). Ezra-Nehemiah reflects upon the Torah and Moses as the giver of Torah. Chronicles highlights the design and building of the temple by kings David and Solomon. Both Torah and temple garner hope that Yahweh will restore his kingdom on earth (see Ezra 1.2; 2 Chron 36.23).

Overall, the books in the Writings are full of people trying to make sense of Israel's past all the while looking forward to Yahweh's continued work for both Israel and all the kingdoms of the world (2 Chron 32.23). The Writings, often present challenges to traditional Israelite theology. These books contain the narratives and responses of followers of Yahweh as they attempt to live faithfully in a chaotic world.

The Writings as a literary unit look back on the troubles brought about by the exile, and in doing so, the result is an eye toward the future. The process of looking back is not without difficulties and questions (e.g., psalms of lament, Job, Ecclesiastes, etc.). The bookends of the Writings (Psalms, Chronicles Corpus) remind the reader of the importance of the Torah (instructions) and the Prophets (Yahweh's king's relationship to the temple and proper worship). No matter what comes Yahweh always prevails, whether by enforcing egregious covenant failures or upholding covenant faithfulness.

When reading the final third of the HS as an intentional unit, the path to the NT is paved differently. Not to say that the English order of these books is wrong; rather, it presents a different perspective. The English canon ends with Malachi, while the HS ends with Chronicles. Both of these endings encourage hope that Yahweh is still at work. The English order ends with a call to Torah obedience and the coming of Elijah (i.e., prophet with a message of repentance), which is a call to faith. The HS ends with a hope in a Davidic messianic kingdom. These hopes are important for Jesus and his followers, a hope that is instilled as a means of adapting to any circumstance this world may bring.

Suggested Resources:

Bandstra, Barry L. *Reading the Old Testament*. 3rd ed. Belmont, CA: Wadsworth, 2004.

Rendtorff, Rolf. *The Canonical Hebrew Bible: A Theology of the Old Testament*. Tools for Biblical Study. Dorset, UK: Deo, 2011.

Sailhamer, John H. *Introduction to Old Testament Theology: A Canonical Approach*. Grand Rapids: Zondervan, 1999.

Seitz, Christopher R. *The Elder Testament: Canon, Theology, Trinity*. Waco, TX: Baylor University Press, 2018.

Steinberg, Julius, and Timothy J. Stone, eds. *The Shape of the Writings*. Siphrut: Literature and Theology of the Hebrew Scriptures. Winona Lake, IN: Eisenbrauns, 2015.

Sweeney, Marvin A. *TANAK: A Theological and Critical Introduction to the Jewish Bible*. Minneapolis: Fortress, 2011.

Introduction to Psalms

Nancy L. deClaissé-Walford

The Hebrew name of the book we call "Psalms" is *Tehillim*, which means "Praises." The book names in the English translation of the OT are taken from the names of the books as they occur in Greek manuscripts. The name "Psalms" and "The Psalter" come from the Greek words *psalmoi* and *psalterion*. Both Greek words mean "song," a translation of the Hebrew term *mizmor*, which occurs in the superscriptions of fifty-seven psalms.

The Psalter, *Tehillim*, is a rich collection of poetry, expressing the joys, sorrows, fears, oppressions, hurts, amazements, and yearnings of the people of Yahweh. The psalms address interpersonal relationships, enemies, illnesses, national crises, the wonders of creation, the goodness of Yahweh, Israel's history, and personal sins; but rarely do we find any specific reference to an easily-identified historical or personal event. Rather, the psalms have to do with humanity's relationship with God and with one another in all times and all places.

Scholars have identified various types of psalms in the Psalter. Most numerous are psalms of lament, either Individual Laments, in which an individual voice cries out to Yahweh (see Pss 13 and 71), or Community Laments, in which the gathered people of Yahweh cry out (see Pss 80 and 106). Community Hymns contain expressions of praise for who Yahweh is and what Yahweh does on behalf of the people (see Pss 29 and 135). Individual Hymns of Thanksgiving are words of thanks offered by a psalmist to Yahweh for goodness to or on behalf of the individual, usually deliverance from some trying situation (see Pss 30 and 103). Other psalm types are Creation Psalms, musings over the creative work of Yahweh in the world (see Pss 8 and 104); Enthronement Psalms that celebrate Yahweh as sovereign over all peoples (see Pss 93-99); Royal Psalms that address human kingship/rule (see Pss 2 and 110); and Wisdom Psalms, reflecting the wisdom tradition of ancient Israel and the ancient Near East (see Pss 1 and 73).

The Psalter's ascription as the hymnbook of ancient Israel is an apt one. As with the hymn books in churches today that offer a multitude of ways to sing to Yahweh, so does the Psalter. The psalms in the Psalter, however, are not grouped together by type, but rather move fluidly back and forth between expressions of lament, of praise, of wonder, of thanksgiving, and so forth. That leads us to ask, why these 150 psalms and why in this particular order? Are they simply a random collection of the songs of our ancestors in the faith?

During the past thirty years, those who study the psalms have pondered these questions, and suggest a way to understand the ordering of the psalms in the book. The Psalter is divided into five books, modeled, it seems, on the five books of Moses—Genesis, Exodus, Leviticus, Numbers, and Deuteronomy: five books of Moses, the great lawgiver, and five books of David, the great musician. It opens with Psalm 1, a wisdom psalm stating that the path to wisdom is meditation on the Torah (the law, the instruction); Psalm 2 follows, a royal psalm maintaining that Yahweh will provide a king, a sovereign, for the people, but only one of God's choosing. These two psalms provide a "dual lens" for reading the Psalter—adherence to Torah and God's role in sovereignty over the people.

Book One of the Psalter (Pss 1–41) narrates the kingship of David, the legendary ideal king of the people; in Book Two (Pss 42–72) David is still present, but other voices mingle with David's as David recedes to the background and turns the reins of the kingdom over to Solomon (Pss 71 and 72); Book Three (Pss 73–89) recounts the days of the divided monarchy, the fall of the northern kingdom to the Assyrians, and the final destruction of Jerusalem at the hands of the Babylonians (Ps 89). The setting of Book Four (Pss 90–106) is the exile in Babylon and a search by the people for a means to remain the distinct people of Yahweh in their altered circumstances. The Enthronement Psalms (Pss 93–100) provide the answer—Yahweh is sovereign, not an earthly king. Book Five (Pss 107–150) reflects the return from exile and resettlement in the land of promise. The temple is rebuilt, worship resumes, and perhaps instills a glimmer of hope for the restoration of a Davidic kingship. In conclusion, how then shall we read the Psalter? It is the timeless words of the people of Yahweh addressed to their God in all times and all life situations.

Outline

1. Book 1: The reign of King David (Pss 1–41)
2. Book 2: The end of the reign of David and Solomon becomes king (Pss 42–72)
3. Book 3: The divided kingdoms; the fall of the Northern Kingdom; the fall of the Southern Kingdom (Pss 73–89)
4. Book 4: The exile in Babylon (Pss 90–106)
5. Book 5: The return from Exile and re-establishing temple worship (Pss 107–150)

Suggested Resources

Bellinger, William H., Jr. and Walter Brueggemann. *Psalms.* New Cambridge Bible Commentary. Cambridge: Cambridge University Press, 2014.

Brueggemann, Walter. *From Whom No Secrets Are Hidden: Introducing the Psalms.* Louisville: Westminster John Knox, 2014.

deClaissé-Walford, Nancy L. *Introduction to the Psalms: A Song from Ancient Israel.* St. Louis: Chalice Press, 2004.

deClaissé-Walford, Nancy L., Rolf A. Jacobson, and Beth LaNeel Tanner. *The Book of Psalms.* New International Commentary on the Old Testament. Grand Rapids: Eerdmans, 2014.

Jacobson, Rolf A., and Karl N. Jacobson. *Invitation to the Psalms: A Reader's Guide for Discovery and Engagement.* Grand Rapids: Baker Academic, 2013.

Mays, James L. *Psalms.* Interpretation. Louisville: John Knox, 1994.

Psalms

Book I

(Psalms 1–41)

1 How happy is the one who does not
walk in the advice of the wicked
or stand in the pathway with sinners
or sit in the company of mockers!
Instead, his delight is in the Lord's instruction,
and he meditates on it day and night.
He is like a tree planted beside flowing streams
that bears its fruit in its season,
and its leaf does not wither.
10 Whatever he does prospers.

The wicked are not like this;
instead, they are like chaff that the wind blows away.
Therefore the wicked will not stand up in the judgment,
nor sinners in the assembly of the righteous.

For the Lord watches over the way of the righteous,
but the way of the wicked leads to ruin.

2 Why do the nations rage
and the peoples plot in vain?
The kings of the earth take their stand,
and the rulers conspire together
against the Lord and his Anointed One:
"Let's tear off their chains
and throw their ropes off of us."

The one enthroned in heaven laughs;
the Lord ridicules them.
10 Then he speaks to them in his anger
and terrifies them in his wrath:

"I have installed my king
on Zion, my holy mountain."

I will declare the LORD's decree.
He said to me, "You are my Son;
today I have become your Father.
Ask of me,
and I will make the nations your inheritance
and the ends of the earth your possession.
You will break them with an iron scepter;
you will shatter them like pottery."

So now, kings, be wise;
receive instruction, you judges of the earth.
Serve the LORD with reverential awe
and rejoice with trembling.
Pay homage to the Son or he will be angry
and you will perish in your rebellion,
for his anger may ignite at any moment.
All who take refuge in him are happy.

3   A psalm of David when he fled from his son Absalom.

LORD, how my foes increase!
There are many who attack me.
Many say about me,
    "There is no help for him in God." *Selah*

But you, LORD, are a shield around me,
my glory, and the one who lifts up my head.
I cry aloud to the LORD,
    and he answers me from his holy mountain. *Selah*

I lie down and sleep;
I wake again because the LORD sustains me.
I will not be afraid of thousands of people
who have taken their stand against me on every side.

Rise up, Lord!
Save me, my God!
You strike all my enemies on the cheek;
you break the teeth of the wicked.
Salvation belongs to the Lord;
    may your blessing be on your people.*Selah*

4 For the choir director: with stringed instruments. A psalm of David.

Answer me when I call,
God, who vindicates me.
You freed me from affliction;
be gracious to me and hear my prayer.

How long, exalted ones, will my honor be insulted?
How long will you love what is worthless
    and pursue a lie?*Selah*
Know that the Lord has set apart
10   the faithful for himself;
the Lord will hear when I call to him.
Be angry and do not sin;
reflect in your heart while on your bed and be silent.*Selah*
Offer sacrifices in righteousness
and trust in the Lord.

Many are asking, "Who can show us anything good?"
Let the light of your face shine on us, Lord.

You have put more joy in my heart
than they have when their grain and new wine abound.
20 I will both lie down and sleep in peace,
for you alone, Lord, make me live in safety.

5 For the choir director: with the flutes. A psalm of David.

Listen to my words, Lord;
consider my sighing.
Pay attention to the sound of my cry,

my King and my God,
for I pray to you.

In the morning, LORD, you hear my voice;
in the morning I plead my case to you and watch expectantly.

For you are not a God who delights in wickedness;
10   evil cannot dwell with you.
The boastful cannot stand in your sight;
you hate all evildoers.
You destroy those who tell lies;
the LORD abhors violent and treacherous people.

But I enter your house
by the abundance of your faithful love;
I bow down toward your holy temple
in reverential awe of you.
LORD, lead me in your righteousness
20   because of my adversaries;
make your way straight before me.

For there is nothing reliable in what they say;
destruction is within them;
their throat is an open grave;
they flatter with their tongues.
Punish them, God;
let them fall by their own schemes.
Drive them out because of their many crimes,
for they rebel against you.

30   But let all who take refuge in you rejoice;
let them shout for joy forever.
May you shelter them,
and may those who love your name boast about you.
For you, LORD, bless the righteous one;
you surround him with favor like a shield.

6   For the choir director: with stringed instruments, according to *Sheminith*. A psalm of David.

> Lᴏʀᴅ, do not rebuke me in your anger;
> do not discipline me in your wrath.
> Be gracious to me, Lᴏʀᴅ, for I am weak;
> heal me, Lᴏʀᴅ, for my bones are shaking;
> my whole being is shaken with terror.
> And you, Lᴏʀᴅ — how long?
>
> Turn, Lᴏʀᴅ! Rescue me;
> save me because of your faithful love.
10 For there is no remembrance of you in death;
> who can thank you in Sheol?
>
> I am weary from my groaning;
> with my tears I dampen my bed
> and drench my couch every night.
> My eyes are swollen from grief;
> they grow old because of all my enemies.
>
> Depart from me, all evildoers,
> for the Lᴏʀᴅ has heard the sound of my weeping.
> The Lᴏʀᴅ has heard my plea for help;
20 the Lᴏʀᴅ accepts my prayer.
> All my enemies will be ashamed and shake with terror;
> they will turn back and suddenly be disgraced.

7   A *Shiggaion* of David, which he sang to the Lᴏʀᴅ concerning the words of Cush, a Benjaminite.

> Lᴏʀᴅ my God, I seek refuge in you;
> save me from all my pursuers and rescue me,
> or they will tear me like a lion,
> ripping me apart with no one to rescue me.
>
> Lᴏʀᴅ my God, if I have done this,
> if there is injustice on my hands,
> if I have done harm to one at peace with me
> or have plundered my adversary without cause,

10 may an enemy pursue and overtake me;
may he trample me to the ground
and leave my honor in the dust.*Selah*

Rise up, Lord, in your anger;
lift yourself up against the fury of my adversaries;
awake for me;
you have ordained a judgment.
Let the assembly of peoples gather around you;
take your seat on high over it.
The Lord judges the peoples;
20 vindicate me, Lord,
according to my righteousness and my integrity.

Let the evil of the wicked come to an end,
but establish the righteous.
The one who examines the thoughts and emotions
is a righteous God.
My shield is with God,
who saves the upright in heart.
God is a righteous judge
and a God who shows his wrath every day.

30 If anyone does not repent,
he will sharpen his sword;
he has strung his bow and made it ready.
He has prepared his deadly weapons;
he tips his arrows with fire.

See, the wicked one is pregnant with evil,
conceives trouble, and gives birth to deceit.
He dug a pit and hollowed it out
but fell into the hole he had made.
His trouble comes back on his own head;
40 his own violence comes down on top of his head.

I will thank the Lord for his righteousness;
I will sing about the name of the Lord Most High.

8 For the choir director: on the *Gittith*. A psalm of David.

> LORD, our Lord,
> how magnificent is your name throughout the earth!
>
> You have covered the heavens with your majesty.
> From the mouths of infants and nursing babies,
> you have established a stronghold
> on account of your adversaries
> in order to silence the enemy and the avenger.
>
> When I observe your heavens,
> the work of your fingers,
> the moon and the stars,
> which you set in place,
> what is a human being that you remember him,
> a son of man that you look after him?
> You made him little less than God
> and crowned him with glory and honor.
> You made him ruler over the works of your hands;
> you put everything under his feet:
> all the sheep and oxen,
> as well as the animals in the wild,
> the birds of the sky,
> and the fish of the sea
> that pass through the currents of the seas.
>
> LORD, our Lord,
> how magnificent is your name throughout the earth!

9 For the choir director: according to *Muth-labben*. A psalm of David.

> I will thank the LORD with all my heart;
> I will declare all your wondrous works.
> I will rejoice and boast about you;
> I will sing about your name, Most High.

When my enemies retreat,
they stumble and perish before you.
For you have upheld my just cause;
you are seated on your throne as a righteous judge.
You have rebuked the nations:
You have destroyed the wicked;
you have erased their name forever and ever.
The enemy has come to eternal ruin;
you have uprooted the cities,
and the very memory of them has perished.

But the Lord sits enthroned forever;
he has established his throne for judgment.
And he judges the world with righteousness;
he executes judgment on the nations with fairness.
The Lord is a refuge for the persecuted,
a refuge in times of trouble.
Those who know your name trust in you
because you have not abandoned
those who seek you, Lord.

Sing to the Lord, who dwells in Zion;
proclaim his deeds among the nations.
For the one who seeks an accounting
for bloodshed remembers them;
he does not forget the cry of the oppressed.

Be gracious to me, Lord;
consider my affliction at the hands of those who hate me.
Lift me up from the gates of death,
so that I may declare all your praises.
I will rejoice in your salvation
within the gates of Daughter Zion.

The nations have fallen into the pit they made;
their foot is caught in the net they have concealed.
The Lord has made himself known;
he has executed justice,

40   snaring the wicked
            by the work of their hands.*Higgaion. Selah*

The wicked will return to Sheol—
all the nations that forget God.
For the needy will not always be forgotten;
the hope of the oppressed will not perish forever.

Rise up, LORD! Do not let mere humans prevail;
let the nations be judged in your presence.
Put terror in them, LORD;
            let the nations know they are only humans.*Selah*

10   LORD, why do you stand so far away?
Why do you hide in times of trouble?
In arrogance the wicked relentlessly pursue their victims;
let them be caught in the schemes they have devised.

For the wicked one boasts about his own cravings;
the one who is greedy curses and despises the LORD.
In all his scheming,
the wicked person arrogantly thinks,
"There's no accountability,
10   since there's no God."
His ways are always secure;
your lofty judgments have no effect on him;
he scoffs at all his adversaries.
He says to himself, "I will never be moved—
from generation to generation I will be without calamity."
Cursing, deceit, and violence fill his mouth;
trouble and malice are under his tongue.
He waits in ambush near settlements;
he kills the innocent in secret places.
20   His eyes are on the lookout for the helpless;
he lurks in secret like a lion in a thicket.
He lurks in order to seize a victim;
he seizes a victim and drags him in his net.
So he is oppressed and beaten down;

helpless people fall because of the wicked one's strength.
He says to himself, "God has forgotten;
he hides his face and will never see."

Rise up, Lord God! Lift up your hand.
Do not forget the oppressed.
30   Why has the wicked person despised God?
He says to himself, "You will not demand an account."
But you yourself have seen trouble and grief,
observing it in order to take the matter into your hands.
The helpless one entrusts himself to you;
you are a helper of the fatherless.
Break the arm of the wicked, evil person,
until you look for his wickedness,
but it can't be found.

The Lord is King forever and ever;
40   the nations will perish from his land.
Lord, you have heard the desire of the humble;
you will strengthen their hearts.
You will listen carefully,
doing justice for the fatherless and the oppressed
so that mere humans from the earth may terrify them no more.

11   For the choir director. Of David.

I have taken refuge in the Lord.
How can you say to me,
"Escape to the mountains like a bird!
For look, the wicked string bows;
they put their arrows on bowstrings
to shoot from the shadows at the upright in heart.
When the foundations are destroyed,
what can the righteous do?"

10   The Lord is in his holy temple;
the Lord—his throne is in heaven.
His eyes watch;

his gaze examines everyone.
The LORD examines the righteous,
but he hates the wicked
and those who love violence.
Let him rain burning coals and sulfur on the wicked;
let a scorching wind be the portion in their cup.
For the LORD is righteous; he loves righteous deeds.
20 The upright will see his face.

12 For the choir director: according to *Sheminith*. A psalm of David.

Help, LORD, for no faithful one remains;
the loyal have disappeared from the human race.
They lie to one another;
they speak with flattering lips and deceptive hearts.
May the LORD cut off all flattering lips
and the tongue that speaks boastfully.
They say, "Through our tongues we have power;
our lips are our own — who can be our master?"

10 "Because of the devastation of the needy
and the groaning of the poor,
I will now rise up," says the LORD.
"I will provide safety for the one who longs for it."

The words of the LORD are pure words,
like silver refined in an earthen furnace,
purified seven times.

You, LORD, will guard us;
you will protect us from this generation forever.
The wicked prowl all around,
20 and what is worthless is exalted by the human race.

13 For the choir director. A psalm of David.

How long, LORD? Will you forget me forever?
How long will you hide your face from me?

How long will I store up anxious concerns within me,
agony in my mind every day?
How long will my enemy dominate me?

Consider me and answer, LORD my God.
Restore brightness to my eyes;
otherwise, I will sleep in death.
10 My enemy will say, "I have triumphed over him,"
and my foes will rejoice because I am shaken.

But I have trusted in your faithful love;
my heart will rejoice in your deliverance.
I will sing to the LORD
because he has treated me generously.

14 For the choir director. Of David.

The fool says in his heart, "There's no God."
They are corrupt; they do vile deeds.
There is no one who does good.
The LORD looks down from heaven on the human race
to see if there is one who is wise,
one who seeks God.
All have turned away;
all alike have become corrupt.
10 There is no one who does good,
not even one.

Will evildoers never understand?
They consume my people as they consume bread;
they do not call on the LORD.

Then they will be filled with dread,
for God is with those who are righteous.
You sinners frustrate the plans of the oppressed,
but the LORD is his refuge.

Oh, that Israel's deliverance would come from Zion!
20 When the LORD restores the fortunes of his people,
let Jacob rejoice, let Israel be glad.

15 A psalm of David.

LORD, who can dwell in your tent?
Who can live on your holy mountain?

The one who lives blamelessly, practices righteousness,
and acknowledges the truth in his heart—
who does not slander with his tongue,
who does not harm his friend
or discredit his neighbor,
who despises the one rejected by the LORD
10 but honors those who fear the LORD,
who keeps his word whatever the cost,
who does not lend his silver at interest
or take a bribe against the innocent—
the one who does these things will never be shaken.

16 A *Miktam* of David.

Protect me, God, for I take refuge in you.
I said to the LORD, "You are my Lord;
I have nothing good besides you."
As for the holy people who are in the land,
they are the noble ones.
All my delight is in them.
The sorrows of those who take another god
for themselves will multiply;
10 I will not pour out their drink offerings of blood,
and I will not speak their names with my lips.

LORD, you are my portion
and my cup of blessing;
you hold my future.
The boundary lines have fallen for me

in pleasant places;
indeed, I have a beautiful inheritance.

I will bless the LORD who counsels me—
even at night when my thoughts trouble me.
20   I always let the LORD guide me.
Because he is at my right hand,
I will not be shaken.

Therefore my heart is glad
and my whole being rejoices;
my body also rests securely.
For you will not abandon me to Sheol;
you will not allow your faithful one to see decay.
You reveal the path of life to me;
in your presence is abundant joy;
30   at your right hand are eternal pleasures.

17   A prayer of David.

LORD, hear a just cause;
pay attention to my cry;
listen to my prayer—
from lips free of deceit.
Let my vindication come from you,
for you see what is right.
You have tested my heart;
you have examined me at night.
10   You have tried me and found nothing evil;
I have determined that my mouth will not sin.
Concerning what people do:
by the words from your lips
I have avoided the ways of the violent.
My steps are on your paths;
my feet have not slipped.

I call on you, God,
because you will answer me;

listen closely to me; hear what I say.
20 Display the wonders of your faithful love,
Savior of all who seek refuge
from those who rebel against your right hand.
Protect me as the pupil of your eye;
hide me in the shadow of your wings
from the wicked who treat me violently,
my deadly enemies who surround me.

They are uncaring;
their mouths speak arrogantly.
They advance against me; now they surround me.
30 They are determined
to throw me to the ground.
They are like a lion eager to tear,
like a young lion lurking in ambush.

Rise up, LORD!
Confront him; bring him down.
With your sword, save me from the wicked.
With your hand, LORD, save me from men,
from men of the world
whose portion is in this life:
40 You fill their bellies with what you have in store;
their sons are satisfied,
and they leave their surplus to their children.

But I will see your face in righteousness;
when I awake, I will be satisfied with your presence.

18 For the choir director. Of the servant of the LORD, David, who spoke the words of this song to the LORD on the day the LORD rescued him from the grasp of all his enemies and from the power of Saul. He said:

I love you, LORD, my strength.
The LORD is my rock,
my fortress, and my deliverer,
my God, my rock where I seek refuge,

my shield and the horn of my salvation,
my stronghold.
10 I called to the LORD, who is worthy of praise,
and I was saved from my enemies.

The ropes of death were wrapped around me;
the torrents of destruction terrified me.
The ropes of Sheol entangled me;
the snares of death confronted me.
I called to the LORD in my distress,
and I cried to my God for help.
From his temple he heard my voice,
and my cry to him reached his ears.

20 Then the earth shook and quaked;
the foundations of the mountains trembled;
they shook because he burned with anger.
Smoke rose from his nostrils,
and consuming fire came from his mouth;
coals were set ablaze by it.
He bent the heavens and came down,
total darkness beneath his feet.
He rode on a cherub and flew,
soaring on the wings of the wind.
30 He made darkness his hiding place,
dark storm clouds his canopy around him.
From the radiance of his presence,
his clouds swept onward with hail and blazing coals.
The LORD thundered from heaven;
the Most High made his voice heard.
He shot his arrows and scattered them;
he hurled lightning bolts and routed them.
The depths of the sea became visible,
the foundations of the world were exposed,
40 at your rebuke, LORD,
at the blast of the breath of your nostrils.

He reached down from on high
and took hold of me;
he pulled me out of deep water.
He rescued me from my powerful enemy
and from those who hated me,
for they were too strong for me.
They confronted me in the day of my calamity,
but the LORD was my support.
50   He brought me out to a spacious place;
he rescued me because he delighted in me.

The LORD rewarded me
according to my righteousness;
he repaid me
according to the cleanness of my hands.
For I have kept the ways of the LORD
and have not turned from my God to wickedness.
Indeed, I let all his ordinances guide me
and have not disregarded his statutes.
60   I was blameless toward him
and kept myself from my iniquity.
So the LORD repaid me
according to my righteousness,
according to the cleanness of my hands in his sight.

With the faithful
you prove yourself faithful,
with the blameless
you prove yourself blameless,
with the pure
70   you prove yourself pure,
but with the crooked
you prove yourself shrewd.
For you rescue an oppressed people,
but you humble those with haughty eyes.
LORD, you light my lamp;
my God illuminates my darkness.

With you I can attack a barricade,
and with my God I can leap over a wall.

God — his way is perfect;
80 the word of the LORD is pure.
He is a shield to all who take refuge in him.
For who is God besides the LORD?
And who is a rock? Only our God.
God — he clothes me with strength
and makes my way perfect.
He makes my feet like the feet of a deer
and sets me securely on the heights.
He trains my hands for war;
my arms can bend a bow of bronze.
90 You have given me the shield of your salvation;
your right hand upholds me,
and your humility exalts me.
You make a spacious place beneath me for my steps,
and my ankles do not give way.

I pursue my enemies and overtake them;
I do not turn back until they are wiped out.
I crush them, and they cannot get up;
they fall beneath my feet.
You have clothed me with strength for battle;
100 you subdue my adversaries beneath me.
You have made my enemies retreat before me;
I annihilate those who hate me.
They cry for help, but there is no one to save them—
they cry to the LORD, but he does not answer them.
I pulverize them like dust before the wind;
I trample them like mud in the streets.

You have freed me from the feuds among the people;
you have appointed me the head of nations;
a people I had not known serve me.
110 Foreigners submit to me cringing;
as soon as they hear they obey me.

Foreigners lose heart
and come trembling from their fortifications.

The LORD lives — blessed be my rock!
The God of my salvation is exalted.
God — he grants me vengeance
and subdues peoples under me.
He frees me from my enemies.
You exalt me above my adversaries;
120   you rescue me from violent men.
Therefore I will give thanks to you among the nations, LORD;
I will sing praises about your name.
He gives great victories to his king;
he shows loyalty to his anointed,
to David and his descendants forever.

19   For the choir director. A psalm of David.

The heavens declare the glory of God,
and the expanse proclaims the work of his hands.
Day after day they pour out speech;
night after night they communicate knowledge.
There is no speech; there are no words;
their voice is not heard.
Their message has gone out to the whole earth,
and their words to the ends of the world.

10   In the heavens he has pitched a tent for the sun.
It is like a bridegroom coming from his home;
it rejoices like an athlete running a course.
It rises from one end of the heavens
and circles to their other end;
nothing is hidden from its heat.

The instruction of the LORD is perfect,
renewing one's life;
the testimony of the LORD is trustworthy,
making the inexperienced wise.

20 The precepts of the LORD are right,
making the heart glad;
the command of the LORD is radiant,
making the eyes light up.
The fear of the LORD is pure,
enduring forever;
the ordinances of the LORD are reliable
and altogether righteous.
They are more desirable than gold—
than an abundance of pure gold;
30 and sweeter than honey
dripping from a honeycomb.
In addition, your servant is warned by them,
and in keeping them there is an abundant reward.

Who perceives his unintentional sins?
Cleanse me from my hidden faults.
Moreover, keep your servant from willful sins;
do not let them rule me.
Then I will be blameless
and cleansed from blatant rebellion.
40 May the words of my mouth
and the meditation of my heart
be acceptable to you,
LORD, my rock and my Redeemer.

20 For the choir director. A psalm of David.

May the LORD answer you in a day of trouble;
may the name of Jacob's God protect you.
May he send you help from the sanctuary
and sustain you from Zion.
May he remember all your offerings
and accept your burnt offering.*Selah*

May he give you what your heart desires
and fulfill your whole purpose.
10 Let us shout for joy at your victory

and lift the banner in the name of our God.
May the LORD fulfill all your requests.

Now I know that the LORD gives victory to his anointed;
he will answer him from his holy heaven
with mighty victories from his right hand.
Some take pride in chariots, and others in horses,
but we take pride in the name of the LORD our God.
They collapse and fall,
but we rise and stand firm.

20 LORD, give victory to the king!
May he answer us on the day that we call.

21 For the choir director. A psalm of David.

LORD, the king finds joy in your strength.
How greatly he rejoices in your victory!
You have given him his heart's desire
and have not denied the request of his lips.*Selah*
For you meet him with rich blessings;
you place a crown of pure gold on his head.
He asked you for life, and you gave it to him—
length of days forever and ever.

10 His glory is great through your victory;
you confer majesty and splendor on him.
You give him blessings forever;
you cheer him with joy in your presence.
For the king relies on the LORD;
through the faithful love of the Most High
he is not shaken.

Your hand will capture all your enemies;
your right hand will seize those who hate you.
You will make them burn

20 like a fiery furnace when you appear;
the LORD will engulf them in his wrath,
and fire will devour them.
You will wipe their progeny from the earth

and their offspring from the human race.
Though they intend to harm you
and devise a wicked plan, they will not prevail.
Instead, you will put them to flight
when you ready your bowstrings to shoot at them.

Be exalted, Lord, in your strength;
30   we will sing and praise your might.

22   For the choir director: according to "The Deer of the Dawn." A psalm of David.

My God, my God, why have you abandoned me?
Why are you so far from my deliverance
and from my words of groaning?
My God, I cry by day, but you do not answer,
by night, yet I have no rest.
But you are holy,
enthroned on the praises of Israel.
Our ancestors trusted in you;
10   they trusted, and you rescued them.
They cried to you and were set free;
they trusted in you and were not disgraced.

But I am a worm and not a man,
scorned by mankind and despised by people.
Everyone who sees me mocks me;
they sneer and shake their heads:
"He relies on the Lord;
let him save him;
let the Lord rescue him,
20   since he takes pleasure in him."

It was you who brought me out of the womb,
making me secure at my mother's breast.
I was given over to you at birth;
you have been my God from my mother's womb.

Don't be far from me, because distress is near
and there's no one to help.

Many bulls surround me;
strong ones of Bashan encircle me.
They open their mouths against me—
30   lions, mauling and roaring.
I am poured out like water,
and all my bones are disjointed;
my heart is like wax,
melting within me.
My strength is dried up like baked clay;
my tongue sticks to the roof of my mouth.
You put me into the dust of death.
For dogs have surrounded me;
a gang of evildoers has closed in on me;
40   they pierced my hands and my feet.
I can count all my bones;
people look and stare at me.
They divided my garments among themselves,
and they cast lots for my clothing.

But you, Lord, don't be far away.
My strength, come quickly to help me.
Rescue my life from the sword,
my only life from the power of these dogs.
Save me from the lion's mouth,
50   from the horns of wild oxen.

You answered me!
    I will proclaim your name to my brothers and sisters;
    I will praise you in the assembly.
    You who fear the Lord, praise him!
    All you descendants of Jacob, honor him!
    All you descendants of Israel, revere him!
    For he has not despised or abhorred
    the torment of the oppressed.

He did not hide his face from him
but listened when he cried to him for help.

I will give praise in the great assembly
because of you;
I will fulfill my vows
before those who fear you.
The humble will eat and be satisfied;
those who seek the LORD will praise him.
May your hearts live forever!

All the ends of the earth will remember
and turn to the LORD.
All the families of the nations
will bow down before you,
for kingship belongs to the LORD;
he rules the nations.
All who prosper on earth will eat and bow down;
all those who go down to the dust
will kneel before him—
even the one who cannot preserve his life.
Their descendants will serve him;
the next generation will be told about the Lord.
They will come and declare his righteousness;
to a people yet to be born
they will declare what he has done.

23   A psalm of David.

The LORD is my shepherd;
I have what I need.
He lets me lie down in green pastures;
he leads me beside quiet waters.
He renews my life;
he leads me along the right paths
for his name's sake.
Even when I go through the darkest valley,
I fear no danger,

for you are with me;
your rod and your staff — they comfort me.

You prepare a table before me
in the presence of my enemies;
you anoint my head with oil;
my cup overflows.
Only goodness and faithful love will pursue me
all the days of my life,
and I will dwell in the house of the Lord
20   as long as I live.

24   A psalm of David.

The earth and everything in it,
the world and its inhabitants,
belong to the Lord;
for he laid its foundation on the seas
and established it on the rivers.

Who may ascend the mountain of the Lord?
Who may stand in his holy place?
The one who has clean hands and a pure heart,
10   who has not appealed to what is false,
and who has not sworn deceitfully.
He will receive blessing from the Lord,
and righteousness from the God of his salvation.
Such is the generation of those who inquire of him,
      who seek the face of the God of Jacob.*Selah*

Lift up your heads, you gates!
Rise up, ancient doors!
Then the King of glory will come in.
Who is this King of glory?
20   The Lord, strong and mighty,
the Lord, mighty in battle.
Lift up your heads, you gates!
Rise up, ancient doors!

Then the King of glory will come in.
Who is he, this King of glory?
The Lord of Armies,
    he is the King of glory. *Selah*

25   Of David.

Lord, I appeal to you.
My God, I trust in you.
Do not let me be disgraced;
do not let my enemies gloat over me.
No one who waits for you
will be disgraced;
those who act treacherously without cause
will be disgraced.

10   Make your ways known to me, Lord;
teach me your paths.
Guide me in your truth and teach me,
for you are the God of my salvation;
I wait for you all day long.
Remember, Lord, your compassion
and your faithful love,
for they have existed from antiquity.
Do not remember the sins of my youth
or my acts of rebellion;
20   in keeping with your faithful love, remember me
because of your goodness, Lord.

The Lord is good and upright;
therefore he shows sinners the way.
He leads the humble in what is right
and teaches them his way.
All the Lord's ways show faithful love and truth
to those who keep his covenant and decrees.
Lord, for the sake of your name,
forgive my iniquity, for it is immense.

30 Who is this person who fears the LORD?
He will show him the way he should choose.
He will live a good life,
and his descendants will inherit the land.
The secret counsel of the LORD
is for those who fear him,
and he reveals his covenant to them.
My eyes are always on the LORD,
for he will pull my feet out of the net.

Turn to me and be gracious to me,
40 for I am alone and afflicted.
The distresses of my heart increase;
bring me out of my sufferings.
Consider my affliction and trouble,
and forgive all my sins.
Consider my enemies; they are numerous,
and they hate me violently.
Guard me and rescue me;
do not let me be disgraced,
for I take refuge in you.
50 May integrity and what is right
watch over me,
for I wait for you.

God, redeem Israel, from all its distresses.

26 Of David.

Vindicate me, LORD,
because I have lived with integrity
and have trusted in the LORD without wavering.
Test me, LORD, and try me;
examine my heart and mind.
For your faithful love guides me,
and I live by your truth.

I do not sit with the worthless
or associate with hypocrites.
I hate a crowd of evildoers,
and I do not sit with the wicked.
I wash my hands in innocence
and go around your altar, LORD,
raising my voice in thanksgiving
and telling about your wondrous works.

LORD, I love the house where you dwell,
the place where your glory resides.
Do not destroy me along with sinners,
or my life along with men of bloodshed
in whose hands are evil schemes
and whose right hands are filled with bribes.

But I live with integrity;
redeem me and be gracious to me.
My foot stands on level ground;
I will bless the LORD in the assemblies.

27 Of David.

The LORD is my light and my salvation—
whom should I fear?
The LORD is the stronghold of my life—
whom should I dread?
When evildoers came against me to devour my flesh,
my foes and my enemies stumbled and fell.
Though an army deploys against me,
my heart will not be afraid;
though a war breaks out against me,
I will still be confident.

I have asked one thing from the LORD;
it is what I desire:
to dwell in the house of the LORD
all the days of my life,

gazing on the beauty of the LORD
and seeking him in his temple.
For he will conceal me in his shelter
in the day of adversity;
20 he will hide me under the cover of his tent;
he will set me high on a rock.
Then my head will be high
above my enemies around me;
I will offer sacrifices in his tent with shouts of joy.
I will sing and make music to the LORD.

LORD, hear my voice when I call;
be gracious to me and answer me.
My heart says this about you:
"Seek his face."
30 LORD, I will seek your face.
Do not hide your face from me;
do not turn your servant away in anger.
You have been my helper;
do not leave me or abandon me,
God of my salvation.
Even if my father and mother abandon me,
the LORD cares for me.

Because of my adversaries,
show me your way, LORD,
40 and lead me on a level path.
Do not give me over to the will of my foes,
for false witnesses rise up against me,
breathing violence.

I am certain that I will see the LORD's goodness
in the land of the living.
Wait for the LORD;
be strong, and let your heart be courageous.
Wait for the LORD.

28   Of David.

LORD, I call to you;
my rock, do not be deaf to me.
If you remain silent to me,
I will be like those going down to the Pit.
Listen to the sound of my pleading
when I cry to you for help,
when I lift up my hands
toward your holy sanctuary.

10   Do not drag me away with the wicked,
with the evildoers,
who speak in friendly ways with their neighbors
while malice is in their hearts.
Repay them according to what they have done—
according to the evil of their deeds.
Repay them according to the work of their hands;
give them back what they deserve.
Because they do not consider
what the LORD has done
20   or the work of his hands,
he will tear them down and not rebuild them.

Blessed be the LORD,
for he has heard the sound of my pleading.
The LORD is my strength and my shield;
my heart trusts in him, and I am helped.
Therefore my heart celebrates,
and I give thanks to him with my song.

The LORD is the strength of his people;
he is a stronghold of salvation for his anointed.
30   Save your people, bless your possession,
shepherd them, and carry them forever.

29   A psalm of David.

> Ascribe to the LORD, you heavenly beings,
> ascribe to the LORD glory and strength.
> Ascribe to the LORD the glory due his name;
> worship the LORD
> in the splendor of his holiness.
>
> The voice of the LORD is above the waters.
> The God of glory thunders—
> the LORD, above the vast water,
> the voice of the LORD in power,
> the voice of the LORD in splendor.
> The voice of the LORD breaks the cedars;
> the LORD shatters the cedars of Lebanon.
> He makes Lebanon skip like a calf,
> and Sirion, like a young wild ox.
> The voice of the LORD flashes flames of fire.
> The voice of the LORD shakes the wilderness;
> the LORD shakes the wilderness of Kadesh.
> The voice of the LORD makes the deer give birth
> and strips the woodlands bare.

In his temple all cry, "Glory!"

> The LORD sits enthroned over the flood;
> the LORD sits enthroned, King forever.
> The LORD gives his people strength;
> the LORD blesses his people with peace.

30   A psalm; a dedication song for the house. Of David.

> I will exalt you, LORD,
> because you have lifted me up
> and have not allowed my enemies
> to triumph over me.
> LORD my God,
> I cried to you for help, and you healed me.

Lord, you brought me up from Sheol;
you spared me from among those
going down to the Pit.

Sing to the Lord, you his faithful ones,
and praise his holy name.
For his anger lasts only a moment,
but his favor, a lifetime.
Weeping may stay overnight,
but there is joy in the morning.

When I was secure, I said,
"I will never be shaken."
Lord, when you showed your favor,
you made me stand like a strong mountain;
when you hid your face, I was terrified.
Lord, I called to you;
I sought favor from my Lord:
"What gain is there in my death,
if I go down to the Pit?
Will the dust praise you?
Will it proclaim your truth?
Lord, listen and be gracious to me;
Lord, be my helper."

You turned my lament into dancing;
you removed my sackcloth
and clothed me with gladness,
so that I can sing to you and not be silent.
Lord my God, I will praise you forever.

31   For the choir director. A psalm of David.

Lord, I seek refuge in you;
let me never be disgraced.
Save me by your righteousness.
Listen closely to me; rescue me quickly.
Be a rock of refuge for me,

a mountain fortress to save me.
For you are my rock and my fortress;
you lead and guide me
10   for your name's sake.
You will free me from the net
that is secretly set for me,
for you are my refuge.
Into your hand I entrust my spirit;
you have redeemed me, LORD, God of truth.

I hate those who are devoted to worthless idols,
but I trust in the LORD.
I will rejoice and be glad in your faithful love
because you have seen my affliction.
20   You know the troubles of my soul
and have not handed me over to the enemy.
You have set my feet in a spacious place.

Be gracious to me, LORD,
because I am in distress;
my eyes are worn out from frustration—
my whole being as well.
Indeed, my life is consumed with grief
and my years with groaning;
my strength has failed
30   because of my iniquity,
and my bones waste away.
I am ridiculed by all my adversaries
and even by my neighbors.
I am dreaded by my acquaintances;
those who see me in the street run from me.
I am forgotten: gone from memory
like a dead person — like broken pottery.
I have heard the gossip of many;
terror is on every side.
40   When they conspired against me,
they plotted to take my life.

But I trust in you, Lord;
I say, "You are my God."
The course of my life is in your power;
rescue me from the power of my enemies
and from my persecutors.
Make your face shine on your servant;
save me by your faithful love.
Lord, do not let me be disgraced when I call on you.
50 Let the wicked be disgraced;
let them be quiet in Sheol.
Let lying lips
that arrogantly speak against the righteous
in proud contempt be silenced.

How great is your goodness,
which you have stored up for those who fear you.
In the presence of everyone you have acted
for those who take refuge in you.
You hide them in the protection of your presence;
60 you conceal them in a shelter
from human schemes,
from quarrelsome tongues.
Blessed be the Lord,
for he has wondrously shown his faithful love to me
in a city under siege.
In my alarm I said,
"I am cut off from your sight."
But you heard the sound of my pleading
when I cried to you for help.

70 Love the Lord, all his faithful ones.
The Lord protects the loyal,
but fully repays the arrogant.
Be strong, and let your heart be courageous,
all you who put your hope in the Lord.

32   Of David. A *Maskil*.

How joyful is the one
whose transgression is forgiven,
whose sin is covered!
How joyful is a person whom
the LORD does not charge with iniquity
and in whose spirit is no deceit!

When I kept silent, my bones became brittle
from my groaning all day long.
10   For day and night your hand was heavy on me;
my strength was drained
     as in the summer's heat.*Selah*
Then I acknowledged my sin to you
and did not conceal my iniquity.
I said, "I will confess my transgressions to the LORD,"
     and you forgave the guilt of my sin.*Selah*

Therefore let everyone who is faithful pray to you immediately.
When great floodwaters come,
they will not reach him.
20   You are my hiding place;
you protect me from trouble.
You surround me with joyful shouts of deliverance.*Selah*

I will instruct you and show you the way to go;
with my eye on you, I will give counsel.
Do not be like a horse or mule,
without understanding,
that must be controlled with bit and bridle
or else it will not come near you.

Many pains come to the wicked,
30   but the one who trusts in the LORD
will have faithful love surrounding him.
Be glad in the LORD and rejoice,
you righteous ones;

shout for joy,
all you upright in heart.

33 Rejoice in the LORD, you righteous ones;
praise from the upright is beautiful.
Praise the LORD with the lyre;
make music to him with a ten-stringed harp.
Sing a new song to him;
play skillfully on the strings, with a joyful shout.

For the word of the LORD is right,
and all his work is trustworthy.
He loves righteousness and justice;
10   the earth is full of the LORD's unfailing love.

The heavens were made by the word of the LORD,
and all the stars, by the breath of his mouth.
He gathers the water of the sea into a heap;
he puts the depths into storehouses.
Let the whole earth fear the LORD;
let all the inhabitants of the world stand in awe of him.
For he spoke, and it came into being;
he commanded, and it came into existence.

The LORD frustrates the counsel of the nations;
20   he thwarts the plans of the peoples.
The counsel of the LORD stands forever,
the plans of his heart from generation to generation.
Happy is the nation whose God is the LORD—
the people he has chosen to be his own possession!

The LORD looks down from heaven;
he observes everyone.
He gazes on all the inhabitants of the earth
from his dwelling place.
He forms the hearts of them all;
30   he considers all their works.
A king is not saved by a large army;

a warrior will not be rescued by great strength.
The horse is a false hope for safety;
it provides no escape by its great power.

But look, the LORD keeps his eye on those who fear him—
those who depend on his faithful love
to rescue them from death
and to keep them alive in famine.

We wait for the LORD;
40   he is our help and shield.
For our hearts rejoice in him
because we trust in his holy name.
May your faithful love rest on us, LORD,
for we put our hope in you.

34   **Concerning David, when he pretended to be insane in the presence of Abimelech, who drove him out, and he departed.**

I will bless the LORD at all times;
his praise will always be on my lips.
I will boast in the LORD;
the humble will hear and be glad.
Proclaim the LORD's greatness with me;
let us exalt his name together.

I sought the LORD, and he answered me
10   and rescued me from all my fears.
Those who look to him are radiant with joy;
their faces will never be ashamed.
This poor man cried, and the LORD heard him
and saved him from all his troubles.
The angel of the LORD encamps
around those who fear him, and rescues them.

Taste and see that the LORD is good.
How happy is the person who takes refuge in him!
You who are his holy ones, fear the LORD,

20   for those who fear him lack nothing.
Young lions lack food and go hungry,
but those who seek the LORD
will not lack any good thing.

Come, children, listen to me;
I will teach you the fear of the LORD.
Who is someone who desires life,
loving a long life to enjoy what is good?
Keep your tongue from evil
and your lips from deceitful speech.

30   Turn away from evil and do what is good;
seek peace and pursue it.

The eyes of the LORD are on the righteous,
and his ears are open to their cry for help.
The face of the LORD is set
against those who do what is evil,
to remove all memory of them from the earth.
The righteous cry out, and the LORD hears,
and rescues them from all their troubles.
The LORD is near the brokenhearted;

40   he saves those crushed in spirit.

One who is righteous has many adversities,
but the LORD rescues him from them all.
He protects all his bones;
not one of them is broken.
Evil brings death to the wicked,
and those who hate the righteous will be punished.
The LORD redeems the life of his servants,
and all who take refuge in him will not be punished.

35   Of David.

Oppose my opponents, LORD;
fight those who fight me.
Take your shields — large and small—

and come to my aid.
Draw the spear and javelin against my pursuers,
and assure me, "I am your deliverance."

Let those who intend to take my life
be disgraced and humiliated;
let those who plan to harm me
be turned back and ashamed.
Let them be like chaff in the wind,
with the angel of the Lᴏʀᴅ driving them away.
Let their way be dark and slippery,
with the angel of the Lᴏʀᴅ pursuing them.
They hid their net for me without cause;
they dug a pit for me without cause.
Let ruin come on him unexpectedly,
and let the net that he hid ensnare him;
let him fall into it — to his ruin.

Then I will rejoice in the Lᴏʀᴅ;
I will delight in his deliverance.
All my bones will say,
"Lᴏʀᴅ, who is like you,
rescuing the poor from one too strong for him,
the poor or the needy from one who robs him?"

Malicious witnesses come forward;
they question me about things I do not know.
They repay me evil for good,
making me desolate.
Yet when they were sick,
my clothing was sackcloth;
I humbled myself with fasting,
and my prayer was genuine.
I went about mourning as if for my friend or brother;
I was bowed down with grief,
like one mourning for a mother.
But when I stumbled, they gathered in glee;
they gathered against me.

40   Assailants I did not know
tore at me and did not stop.
With godless mockery
they gnashed their teeth at me.

Lord, how long will you look on?
Rescue me from their ravages;
rescue my precious life from the young lions.
I will praise you in the great assembly;
I will exalt you among many people.
Do not let my deceitful enemies rejoice over me;
50   do not let those who hate me without cause
wink at me maliciously.
For they do not speak in friendly ways,
but contrive fraudulent schemes
against those who live peacefully in the land.
They open their mouths wide against me and say,
"Aha, aha! We saw it!"

You saw it, Lord; do not be silent.
Lord, do not be far from me.
Wake up and rise to my defense,
60   to my cause, my God and my Lord!
Vindicate me, Lord my God,
in keeping with your righteousness,
and do not let them rejoice over me.
Do not let them say in their hearts,
"Aha! Just what we wanted."
Do not let them say,
"We have swallowed him up!"
Let those who rejoice at my misfortune
be disgraced and humiliated;
70   let those who exalt themselves over me
be clothed with shame and reproach.

Let those who want my vindication
shout for joy and be glad;
let them continually say,

"The LORD be exalted.
He takes pleasure in his servant's well-being."
And my tongue will proclaim your righteousness,
your praise all day long.

36 For the choir director. Of David, the LORD's servant.

An oracle within my heart
concerning the transgression of the wicked person:
Dread of God has no effect on him.
For with his flattering opinion of himself,
he does not discover and hate his iniquity.
The words from his mouth are malicious and deceptive;
he has stopped acting wisely and doing good.
Even on his bed he makes malicious plans.
10 He sets himself on a path that is not good,
and he does not reject evil.

LORD, your faithful love reaches to heaven,
your faithfulness to the clouds.
Your righteousness is like the highest mountains,
your judgments like the deepest sea.
LORD, you preserve people and animals.
How priceless your faithful love is, God!
People take refuge in the shadow of your wings.
They are filled from the abundance of your house.
20 You let them drink from your refreshing stream.
For the wellspring of life is with you.
By means of your light we see light.

Spread your faithful love over those who know you,
and your righteousness over the upright in heart.
Do not let the foot of the arrogant come near me
or the hand of the wicked drive me away.
There! The evildoers have fallen.
They have been thrown down and cannot rise.

37   Of David.

Do not be agitated by evildoers;
do not envy those who do wrong.
For they wither quickly like grass
and wilt like tender green plants.

Trust in the LORD and do what is good;
dwell in the land and live securely.
Take delight in the LORD,
and he will give you your heart's desires.

Commit your way to the LORD;
trust in him, and he will act,
making your righteousness shine like the dawn,
your justice like the noonday.

Be silent before the LORD and wait expectantly for him;
do not be agitated by one who prospers in his way,
by the person who carries out evil plans.

Refrain from anger and give up your rage;
do not be agitated — it can only bring harm.
For evildoers will be destroyed,
but those who put their hope in the LORD
will inherit the land.

A little while, and the wicked person will be no more;
though you look for him, he will not be there.
But the humble will inherit the land
and will enjoy abundant prosperity.

The wicked person schemes against the righteous
and gnashes his teeth at him.
The Lord laughs at him
because he sees that his day is coming.

30 The wicked have drawn the sword and strung the bow
to bring down the poor and needy
and to slaughter those whose way is upright.
Their swords will enter their own hearts,
and their bows will be broken.

The little that the righteous person has is better
than the abundance of many wicked people.
For the arms of the wicked will be broken,
but the Lord supports the righteous.

The Lord watches over the blameless all their days,
40 and their inheritance will last forever.
They will not be disgraced in times of adversity;
they will be satisfied in days of hunger.

But the wicked will perish;
the Lord's enemies, like the glory of the pastures,
will fade away—
they will fade away like smoke.

The wicked person borrows and does not repay,
but the righteous one is gracious and giving.
Those who are blessed by the Lord will inherit the land,
50 but those cursed by him will be destroyed.

A person's steps are established by the Lord,
and he takes pleasure in his way.
Though he falls, he will not be overwhelmed,
because the Lord supports him with his hand.

I have been young and now I am old,
yet I have not seen the righteous abandoned
or his children begging for bread.
He is always generous, always lending,
and his children are a blessing.

60   Turn away from evil, do what is good,
      and settle permanently.
      For the Lord loves justice
      and will not abandon his faithful ones.
      They are kept safe forever,
      but the children of the wicked will be destroyed.
      The righteous will inherit the land
      and dwell in it permanently.

      The mouth of the righteous utters wisdom;
      his tongue speaks what is just.
70   The instruction of his God is in his heart;
      his steps do not falter.

      The wicked one lies in wait for the righteous
      and intends to kill him;
      the Lord will not leave him
      in the power of the wicked one
      or allow him to be condemned when he is judged.

      Wait for the Lord and keep his way,
      and he will exalt you to inherit the land.
      You will watch when the wicked are destroyed.

80   I have seen a wicked, violent person
      well-rooted, like a flourishing native tree.
      Then I passed by and noticed he was gone;
      I searched for him, but he could not be found.

      Watch the blameless and observe the upright,
      for the person of peace will have a future.
      But transgressors will all be eliminated;
      the future of the wicked will be destroyed.

      The salvation of the righteous is from the Lord,
      their refuge in a time of distress.
90   The Lord helps and delivers them;

he will deliver them from the wicked and will save them
because they take refuge in him.

38   A psalm of David to bring remembrance.

Lord, do not punish me in your anger
or discipline me in your wrath.
For your arrows have sunk into me,
and your hand has pressed down on me.

There is no soundness in my body
because of your indignation;
there is no health in my bones
because of my sin.
10   For my iniquities have flooded over my head;
they are a burden too heavy for me to bear.
My wounds are foul and festering
because of my foolishness.
I am bent over and brought very low;
all day long I go around in mourning.
For my insides are full of burning pain,
and there is no soundness in my body.
I am faint and severely crushed;
I groan because of the anguish of my heart.

20   Lord, my every desire is in front of you;
my sighing is not hidden from you.
My heart races, my strength leaves me,
and even the light of my eyes has faded.
My loved ones and friends stand back from my affliction,
and my relatives stand at a distance.
Those who intend to kill me set traps,
and those who want to harm me threaten to destroy me;
they plot treachery all day long.

I am like a deaf person; I do not hear.
30   I am like a speechless person
who does not open his mouth.

I am like a man who does not hear
and has no arguments in his mouth.
For I put my hope in you, LORD;
you will answer me, my Lord, my God.
For I said, "Don't let them rejoice over me—
those who are arrogant toward me when I stumble."
For I am about to fall,
and my pain is constantly with me.
So I confess my iniquity;
I am anxious because of my sin.
But my enemies are vigorous and powerful;
many hate me for no reason.
Those who repay evil for good
attack me for pursuing good.

LORD, do not abandon me;
my God, do not be far from me.
Hurry to help me,
my Lord, my salvation.

39 For the choir director, for Jeduthun. A psalm of David.

I said, "I will guard my ways
so that I may not sin with my tongue;
I will guard my mouth with a muzzle
as long as the wicked are in my presence."
I was speechless and quiet;
I kept silent, even from speaking good,
and my pain intensified.
My heart grew hot within me;
as I mused, a fire burned.
I spoke with my tongue:
"LORD, make me aware of my end
and the number of my days
so that I will know how short-lived I am.
In fact, you have made my days just inches long,
and my life span is as nothing to you.
    Yes, every human being stands as only a vapor. *Selah*

Yes, a person goes about like a mere shadow.
Indeed, they rush around in vain,
20 gathering possessions
without knowing who will get them.

"Now, Lord, what do I wait for?
My hope is in you.
Rescue me from all my transgressions;
do not make me the taunt of fools.
I am speechless; I do not open my mouth
because of what you have done.
Remove your torment from me.
Because of the force of your hand I am finished.
30 You discipline a person with punishment for iniquity,
consuming like a moth what is precious to him;
        yes, every human being is only a vapor. *Selah*

"Hear my prayer, LORD,
and listen to my cry for help;
do not be silent at my tears.
For I am here with you as an alien,
a temporary resident like all my ancestors.
Turn your angry gaze from me
so that I may be cheered up
40 before I die and am gone."

40 For the choir director. A psalm of David.

I waited patiently for the LORD,
and he turned to me and heard my cry for help.
He brought me up from a desolate pit,
out of the muddy clay,
and set my feet on a rock,
making my steps secure.
He put a new song in my mouth,
a hymn of praise to our God.
10 Many will see and fear,
and they will trust in the LORD.

How happy is anyone
who has put his trust in the Lord
and has not turned to the proud
or to those who run after lies!
Lord my God, you have done many things—
your wondrous works and your plans for us;
none can compare with you.
If I were to report and speak of them,
20   they are more than can be told.

You do not delight in sacrifice and offering;
you open my ears to listen.
You do not ask for a whole burnt offering or a sin offering.
Then I said, "See, I have come;
in the scroll it is written about me.
I delight to do your will, my God,
and your instruction is deep within me."

I proclaim righteousness in the great assembly;
see, I do not keep my mouth closed—
30   as you know, Lord.
I did not hide your righteousness in my heart;
I spoke about your faithfulness and salvation;
I did not conceal your constant love and truth
from the great assembly.

Lord, you do not withhold your compassion from me.
Your constant love and truth will always guard me.
For troubles without number have surrounded me;
my iniquities have overtaken me; I am unable to see.
They are more than the hairs of my head,
40   and my courage leaves me.
Lord, be pleased to rescue me;
hurry to help me, Lord.

Let those who intend to take my life
be disgraced and confounded.

Let those who wish me harm
be turned back and humiliated.
Let those who say to me, "Aha, aha!"
be appalled because of their shame.

Let all who seek you rejoice and be glad in you;
50   let those who love your salvation continually say,
"The LORD is great!"
I am oppressed and needy;
may the Lord think of me.
You are my helper and my deliverer;
my God, do not delay.

41   For the choir director. A psalm of David.

Happy is one who is considerate of the poor;
the LORD will save him in a day of adversity.
The LORD will keep him and preserve him;
he will be blessed in the land.
You will not give him over to the desire of his enemies.
The LORD will sustain him on his sickbed;
you will heal him on the bed where he lies.

I said, "LORD, be gracious to me;
10   heal me, for I have sinned against you."
My enemies speak maliciously about me:
"When will he die and be forgotten?"
When one of them comes to visit, he speaks deceitfully;
he stores up evil in his heart;
he goes out and talks.
All who hate me whisper together about me;
they plan to harm me.
"Something awful has overwhelmed him,
and he won't rise again from where he lies!"
20   Even my friend in whom I trusted,
one who ate my bread,
has raised his heel against me.

But you, Lord, be gracious to me and raise me up;
then I will repay them.
By this I know that you delight in me:
my enemy does not shout in triumph over me.
You supported me because of my integrity
and set me in your presence forever.

Blessed be the Lord God of Israel,
30   from everlasting to everlasting.
Amen and amen.

Book II
(Psalms 42–72)

42   For the choir director. A *Maskil* of the sons of Korah.

As a deer longs for flowing streams,
so I long for you, God.
I thirst for God, the living God.
When can I come and appear before God?
My tears have been my food day and night,
while all day long people say to me,
"Where is your God?"
I remember this as I pour out my heart:
how I walked with many,
leading the festive procession to the house of God,
with joyful and thankful shouts.

Why, my soul, are you so dejected?
Why are you in such turmoil?
Put your hope in God, for I will still praise him,
my Savior and my God.
I am deeply depressed;
therefore I remember you from the land of Jordan
and the peaks of Hermon, from Mount Mizar.
Deep calls to deep in the roar of your waterfalls;
all your breakers and your billows have swept over me.
The LORD will send his faithful love by day;
his song will be with me in the night—
a prayer to the God of my life.

I will say to God, my rock,
"Why have you forgotten me?
Why must I go about in sorrow
because of the enemy's oppression?"
My adversaries taunt me,

30   as if crushing my bones,
while all day long they say to me,
"Where is your God?"
Why, my soul, are you so dejected?
Why are you in such turmoil?
Put your hope in God, for I will still praise him,
my Savior and my God.

43   Vindicate me, God, and champion my cause
against an unfaithful nation;
rescue me from the deceitful and unjust person.
For you are the God of my refuge.
Why have you rejected me?
Why must I go about in sorrow
because of the enemy's oppression?

Send your light and your truth; let them lead me.
Let them bring me to your holy mountain,
10   to your dwelling place.
Then I will come to the altar of God,
to God, my greatest joy.
I will praise you with the lyre,
God, my God.

Why, my soul, are you so dejected?
Why are you in such turmoil?
Put your hope in God, for I will still praise him,
my Savior and my God.

44   For the choir director. A *Maskil* of the sons of Korah.

God, we have heard with our ears—
our ancestors have told us—
the work you accomplished in their days,
in days long ago:
In order to plant them,
you displaced the nations by your hand;
in order to settle them,

you brought disaster on the peoples.
10 For they did not take the land by their sword—
their arm did not bring them victory—
but by your right hand, your arm,
and the light of your face,
because you were favorable toward them.

You are my King, my God,
who ordains victories for Jacob.
Through you we drive back our foes;
through your name we trample our enemies.
For I do not trust in my bow,
20 and my sword does not bring me victory.
But you give us victory over our foes
and let those who hate us be disgraced.
We boast in God all day long;
    we will praise your name forever. *Selah*

But you have rejected and humiliated us;
you do not march out with our armies.
You make us retreat from the foe,
and those who hate us
have taken plunder for themselves.
30 You hand us over to be eaten like sheep
and scatter us among the nations.
You sell your people for nothing;
you make no profit from selling them.
You make us an object of reproach to our neighbors,
a source of mockery and ridicule to those around us.
You make us a joke among the nations,
a laughingstock among the peoples.
My disgrace is before me all day long,
and shame has covered my face,
40 because of the taunts of the scorner and reviler,
because of the enemy and avenger.

All this has happened to us,
but we have not forgotten you

or betrayed your covenant.
Our hearts have not turned back;
our steps have not strayed from your path.
But you have crushed us in a haunt of jackals
and have covered us with deepest darkness.
If we had forgotten the name of our God
50 and spread out our hands to a foreign god,
wouldn't God have found this out,
since he knows the secrets of the heart?
Because of you we are being put to death all day long;
we are counted as sheep to be slaughtered.

Wake up, LORD! Why are you sleeping?
Get up! Don't reject us forever!
Why do you hide
and forget our affliction and oppression?
For we have sunk down to the dust;
60 our bodies cling to the ground.
Rise up! Help us!
Redeem us because of your faithful love.

45 For the choir director: according to "The Lilies." A *Maskil* of the sons of Korah. A love song.

My heart is moved by a noble theme
as I recite my verses to the king;
my tongue is the pen of a skillful writer.
You are the most handsome of men;
grace flows from your lips.
Therefore God has blessed you forever.

Mighty warrior, strap your sword at your side.
In your majesty and splendor—
10 in your splendor ride triumphantly
in the cause of truth, humility, and justice.
May your right hand show your awe-inspiring acts.
Your sharpened arrows pierce the hearts of the king's enemies;
the peoples fall under you.

Your throne, God, is forever and ever;
the scepter of your kingdom is a scepter of justice.
You love righteousness and hate wickedness;
therefore God, your God, has anointed you with the oil of joy
more than your companions.
20 Myrrh, aloes, and cassia perfume all your garments;
from ivory palaces harps bring you joy.
Kings' daughters are among your honored women;
the queen, adorned with gold from Ophir,
stands at your right hand.

Listen, daughter, pay attention and consider:
Forget your people and your father's house,
and the king will desire your beauty.
Bow down to him, for he is your lord.
The daughter of Tyre, the wealthy people,
30 will seek your favor with gifts.

In her chamber, the royal daughter is all glorious,
her clothing embroidered with gold.
In colorful garments she is led to the king;
after her, the virgins, her companions, are brought to you.
They are led in with gladness and rejoicing;
they enter the king's palace.

Your sons will succeed your ancestors;
you will make them princes throughout the land.
I will cause your name to be remembered for all generations;
40 therefore the peoples will praise you forever and ever.

46 For the choir director. A song of the sons of Korah. According to *Alamoth*.

God is our refuge and strength,
a helper who is always found
in times of trouble.
Therefore we will not be afraid,
though the earth trembles
and the mountains topple

into the depths of the seas,
though its water roars and foams
10   and the mountains quake with its turmoil.*Selah*

There is a river—
its streams delight the city of God,
the holy dwelling place of the Most High.
God is within her; she will not be toppled.
God will help her when the morning dawns.
Nations rage, kingdoms topple;
the earth melts when he lifts his voice.
The Lord of Armies is with us;
   the God of Jacob is our stronghold.*Selah*

20 Come, see the works of the Lord,
who brings devastation on the earth.
He makes wars cease throughout the earth.
He shatters bows and cuts spears to pieces;
he sets wagons ablaze.
"Stop fighting, and know that I am God,
exalted among the nations, exalted on the earth."
The Lord of Armies is with us;
   the God of Jacob is our stronghold.*Selah*

47 For the choir director. A psalm of the sons of Korah.

Clap your hands, all you peoples;
shout to God with a jubilant cry.
For the Lord, the Most High, is awe-inspiring,
a great King over the whole earth.
He subdues peoples under us
and nations under our feet.
He chooses for us our inheritance—
   the pride of Jacob, whom he loves.*Selah*

10 God ascends among shouts of joy,
the Lord, with the sound of a ram's horn.
Sing praise to God, sing praise;

sing praise to our King, sing praise!
Sing a song of wisdom,
for God is King of the whole earth.

God reigns over the nations;
God is seated on his holy throne.
The nobles of the peoples have assembled
with the people of the God of Abraham.
20   For the leaders of the earth belong to God;
he is greatly exalted.

48   A song. A psalm of the sons of Korah.

The LORD is great and highly praised
in the city of our God.
His holy mountain, rising splendidly,
is the joy of the whole earth.
Mount Zion — the summit of Zaphon —
is the city of the great King.
God is known as a stronghold
in its citadels.

10   Look! The kings assembled;
they advanced together.
They looked and froze with fear;
they fled in terror.
Trembling seized them there,
agony like that of a woman in labor,
as you wrecked the ships of Tarshish
with the east wind.

Just as we heard, so we have seen
in the city of the LORD of Armies,
20   in the city of our God;
        God will establish it forever. *Selah*

God, within your temple,
we contemplate your faithful love.

Like your name, God, so your praise
reaches to the ends of the earth;
your right hand is filled with justice.
Mount Zion is glad.
Judah's villages rejoice
because of your judgments.

30 Go around Zion, encircle it;
count its towers,
note its ramparts; tour its citadels
so that you can tell a future generation:
"This God, our God forever and ever—
he will always lead us."

49 For the choir director. A psalm of the sons of Korah.

Hear this, all you peoples;
listen, all who inhabit the world,
both low and high,
rich and poor together.
My mouth speaks wisdom;
my heart's meditation brings understanding.
I turn my ear to a proverb;
I explain my riddle with a lyre.

10 Why should I fear in times of trouble?
The iniquity of my foes surrounds me.
They trust in their wealth
and boast of their abundant riches.
Yet these cannot redeem a person
or pay his ransom to God—
since the price of redeeming him is too costly,
one should forever stop trying—
so that he may live forever
and not see the Pit.

20 For one can see that the wise die;
the foolish and stupid also pass away.

Then they leave their wealth to others.
Their graves are their permanent homes,
their dwellings from generation to generation,
though they have named estates after themselves.
But despite his assets, mankind will not last;
he is like the animals that perish.

This is the way of those who are arrogant,
and of their followers,
     who approve of their words. *Selah*
Like sheep they are headed for Sheol;
Death will shepherd them.
The upright will rule over them in the morning,
and their form will waste away in Sheol,
far from their lofty abode.
But God will redeem me
from the power of Sheol,
     for he will take me. *Selah*

Do not be afraid when a person gets rich,
when the wealth of his house increases.
For when he dies, he will take nothing at all;
his wealth will not follow him down.
Though he blesses himself during his lifetime—
and you are acclaimed when you do well for yourself—
he will go to the generation of his ancestors;
they will never see the light.
Mankind, with his assets
but without understanding,
is like the animals that perish.

50   A psalm of Asaph.

The Mighty One, God, the Lord, speaks;
he summons the earth
from the rising of the sun to its setting.
From Zion, the perfection of beauty,
God appears in radiance.

Our God is coming; he will not be silent!
Devouring fire precedes him,
and a storm rages around him.
On high, he summons heaven and earth
in order to judge his people:
"Gather my faithful ones to me,
those who made a covenant with me by sacrifice."
The heavens proclaim his righteousness,
     for God is the Judge.*Selah*

"Listen, my people, and I will speak;
I will testify against you, Israel.
I am God, your God.
I do not rebuke you for your sacrifices
or for your burnt offerings,
which are continually before me.
I will not take a bull from your household
or male goats from your pens,
for every animal of the forest is mine,
the cattle on a thousand hills.
I know every bird of the mountains,
and the creatures of the field are mine.
If I were hungry, I would not tell you,
for the world and everything in it is mine.
Do I eat the flesh of bulls
or drink the blood of goats?
Offer a thanksgiving sacrifice to God,
and pay your vows to the Most High.
Call on me in a day of trouble;
I will rescue you, and you will honor me."

But God says to the wicked:
"What right do you have to recite my statutes
and to take my covenant on your lips?
You hate instruction
and fling my words behind you.
When you see a thief,
you make friends with him,

and you associate with adulterers.
You unleash your mouth for evil
and harness your tongue for deceit.
You sit, maligning your brother,
slandering your mother's son.
You have done these things, and I kept silent;
you thought I was just like you.

50 But I will rebuke you
and lay out the case before you.

"Understand this, you who forget God,
or I will tear you apart,
and there will be no one to rescue you.
Whoever offers a thanksgiving sacrifice honors me,
and whoever orders his conduct,
I will show him the salvation of God."

51 For the choir director. A psalm of David, when the prophet Nathan came to him after he had gone to Bathsheba.

Be gracious to me, God,
according to your faithful love;
according to your abundant compassion,
blot out my rebellion.
Completely wash away my guilt
and cleanse me from my sin.
For I am conscious of my rebellion,

10 and my sin is always before me.
Against you — you alone — I have sinned
and done this evil in your sight.
So you are right when you pass sentence;
you are blameless when you judge.
Indeed, I was guilty when I was born;
I was sinful when my mother conceived me.

Surely you desire integrity in the inner self,
and you teach me wisdom deep within.
Purify me with hyssop, and I will be clean;

20   wash me, and I will be whiter than snow.
Let me hear joy and gladness;
let the bones you have crushed rejoice.
Turn your face away from my sins
and blot out all my guilt.

God, create a clean heart for me
and renew a steadfast spirit within me.
Do not banish me from your presence
or take your Holy Spirit from me.
Restore the joy of your salvation to me,
30   and sustain me by giving me a willing spirit.
Then I will teach the rebellious your ways,
and sinners will return to you.

Save me from the guilt of bloodshed, God—
God of my salvation—
and my tongue will sing of your righteousness.
Lord, open my lips,
and my mouth will declare your praise.
You do not want a sacrifice, or I would give it;
you are not pleased with a burnt offering.
40   The sacrifice pleasing to God is a broken spirit.
You will not despise a broken and humbled heart, God.

In your good pleasure, cause Zion to prosper;
build the walls of Jerusalem.
Then you will delight in righteous sacrifices,
whole burnt offerings;
then bulls will be offered on your altar.

52   For the choir director. A *Maskil* of David. When Doeg the Edomite went and reported to Saul, telling him, "David went to Ahimelech's house."

Why boast about evil, you hero!
God's faithful love is constant.
Like a sharpened razor,
your tongue devises destruction,

working treachery.
You love evil instead of good,
    lying instead of speaking truthfully.*Selah*
10   You love any words that destroy,
you treacherous tongue!

This is why God will bring you down forever.
He will take you, ripping you out of your tent;
    he will uproot you from the land of the living.*Selah*
The righteous will see and fear,
and they will derisively say about that hero,
"Here is the man
who would not make God his refuge,
but trusted in the abundance of his riches,
20   taking refuge in his destructive behavior."

But I am like a flourishing olive tree
in the house of God;
I trust in God's faithful love forever and ever.
I will praise you forever for what you have done.
In the presence of your faithful people,
I will put my hope in your name, for it is good.

53   For the choir director: on *Mahalath*. A *Maskil* of David.

The fool says in his heart, "There's no God."
They are corrupt, and they do vile deeds.
There is no one who does good.
God looks down from heaven on the human race
to see if there is one who is wise,
one who seeks God.
All have turned away;
all alike have become corrupt.
10   There is no one who does good,
not even one.

Will evildoers never understand?
They consume my people as they consume bread;

they do not call on God.
Then they will be filled with dread—
dread like no other—
because God will scatter
the bones of those who besiege you.
You will put them to shame,
20   for God has rejected them.

Oh, that Israel's deliverance would come from Zion!
When God restores the fortunes of his people,
let Jacob rejoice, let Israel be glad.

54   For the choir director: with stringed instruments. A *Maskil* of David. When the Ziphites went and said to Saul, "Is David not hiding among us?"

God, save me by your name,
and vindicate me by your might!
God, hear my prayer;
listen to the words from my mouth.
For strangers rise up against me,
and violent men intend to kill me.
       They do not let God guide them. *Selah*

10   God is my helper;
the Lord is the sustainer of my life.
He will repay my adversaries for their evil.
Because of your faithfulness, annihilate them.

I will sacrifice a freewill offering to you.
I will praise your name, Lord,
because it is good.
For he has rescued me from every trouble,
and my eye has looked down on my enemies.

55   For the choir director: with stringed instruments. A *Maskil* of David.

God, listen to my prayer
and do not hide from my plea for help.

Pay attention to me and answer me.
I am restless and in turmoil with my complaint,
because of the enemy's words,
because of the pressure of the wicked.
For they bring down disaster on me
and harass me in anger.

10   My heart shudders within me;
terrors of death sweep over me.
Fear and trembling grip me;
horror has overwhelmed me.
I said, "If only I had wings like a dove!
I would fly away and find rest.
How far away I would flee;
        I would stay in the wilderness.Selah
I would hurry to my shelter
from the raging wind and the storm."

20   Lord, confuse and confound their speech,
for I see violence and strife in the city;
day and night they make the rounds on its walls.
Crime and trouble are within it;
destruction is inside it;
oppression and deceit never leave its marketplace.

Now it is not an enemy who insults me—
otherwise I could bear it;
it is not a foe who rises up against me—
otherwise I could hide from him.
30   But it is you, a man who is my peer,
my companion and good friend!
We used to have close fellowship;
we walked with the crowd into the house of God.

Let death take them by surprise;
let them go down to Sheol alive,
because evil is in their homes and within them.
But I call to God,

and the LORD will save me.
I complain and groan morning, noon, and night,
and he hears my voice.
40 Though many are against me,
he will redeem me from my battle unharmed.
God, the one enthroned from long ago,
will hear and will humiliate them*Selah*
because they do not change
and do not fear God.

My friend acts violently
against those at peace with him;
he violates his covenant.
50 His buttery words are smooth,
but war is in his heart.
His words are softer than oil,
but they are drawn swords.

Cast your burden on the LORD,
and he will sustain you;
he will never allow the righteous to be shaken.

God, you will bring them down
to the Pit of destruction;
men of bloodshed and treachery
60 will not live out half their days.
But I will trust in you.

56 For the choir director: according to "A Silent Dove Far Away." A *Miktam* of David. When the Philistines seized him in Gath.

Be gracious to me, God, for a man is trampling me;
he fights and oppresses me all day long.
My adversaries trample me all day,
for many arrogantly fight against me.

When I am afraid,
I will trust in you.

In God, whose word I praise,
10 in God I trust; I will not be afraid.
What can mere mortals do to me?

They twist my words all day long;
all their thoughts against me are evil.
They stir up strife, they lurk,
they watch my steps
while they wait to take my life.
Will they escape in spite of such sin?
God, bring down the nations in wrath.

You yourself have recorded my wanderings.
20 Put my tears in your bottle.
Are they not in your book?
Then my enemies will retreat on the day when I call.
This I know: God is for me.

In God, whose word I praise,
in the LORD, whose word I praise,
in God I trust; I will not be afraid.
What can mere humans do to me?

I am obligated by vows to you, God;
I will make my thanksgiving sacrifices to you.
30 For you rescued me from death,
even my feet from stumbling,
to walk before God in the light of life.

57 For the choir director: "Do Not Destroy." A *Miktam* of David. When he fled before Saul into the cave.

Be gracious to me, God, be gracious to me,
for I take refuge in you.
I will seek refuge in the shadow of your wings
until danger passes.
I call to God Most High,
to God who fulfills his purpose for me.

He reaches down from heaven and saves me,
      challenging the one who tramples me.*Selah*
God sends his faithful love and truth.
I am surrounded by lions;
I lie down among devouring lions—
people whose teeth are spears and arrows,
whose tongues are sharp swords.
God, be exalted above the heavens;
let your glory be over the whole earth.
They prepared a net for my steps;
I was despondent.
They dug a pit ahead of me,
      but they fell into it!*Selah*

My heart is confident, God, my heart is confident.
I will sing; I will sing praises.
Wake up, my soul!
Wake up, harp and lyre!
I will wake up the dawn.
I will praise you, Lord, among the peoples;
I will sing praises to you among the nations.
For your faithful love is as high as the heavens;
your faithfulness reaches the clouds.
God, be exalted above the heavens;
let your glory be over the whole earth.

58   For the choir director: "Do Not Destroy." A *Miktam* of David.

Do you really speak righteously, you mighty ones?
Do you judge people fairly?
No, you practice injustice in your hearts;
with your hands you weigh out violence in the land.

The wicked go astray from the womb;
liars wander about from birth.
They have venom like the venom of a snake,
like the deaf cobra that stops up its ears,

10   that does not listen to the sound of the charmers
who skillfully weave spells.

God, knock the teeth out of their mouths;
LORD, tear out the young lions' fangs.
May they vanish like water that flows by;
may they aim their blunted arrows.
Like a slug that moves along in slime,
like a woman's miscarried child,
may they not see the sun.

Before your pots can feel the heat of the thorns—
20   whether green or burning—
he will sweep them away.
The righteous one will rejoice
when he sees the retribution;
he will wash his feet in the blood of the wicked.
Then people will say,
"Yes, there is a reward for the righteous!
There is a God who judges on earth!"

59   For the choir director: "Do Not Destroy." A *Miktam* of David. When Saul sent agents to watch the house and kill him.

Rescue me from my enemies, my God;
protect me from those who rise up against me.
Rescue me from evildoers,
and save me from men of bloodshed.
Because look, LORD, they set an ambush for me.
Powerful men attack me,
but not because of any sin or rebellion of mine.
10   For no fault of mine,
they run and take up a position.
Awake to help me, and take notice.
LORD God of Armies, you are the God of Israel.
Rise up to punish all the nations;
    do not show favor to any wicked traitors.*Selah*

They return at evening, snarling like dogs
and prowling around the city.
Look, they spew from their mouths—
sharp words from their lips.
"For who," they say, "will hear?"
But you laugh at them, LORD;
you ridicule all the nations.
I will keep watch for you, my strength,
because God is my stronghold.
My faithful God will come to meet me;
God will let me look down on my adversaries.

Do not kill them; otherwise, my people will forget.
By your power, make them homeless wanderers
and bring them down,
Lord, our shield.
For the sin of their mouths and the words of their lips,
let them be caught in their pride.
They utter curses and lies.
Consume them in fury;
consume them until they are gone.
Then people will know throughout the earth
        that God rules over Jacob.*Selah*

And they return at evening, snarling like dogs
and prowling around the city.
They scavenge for food;
they growl if they are not satisfied.

But I will sing of your strength
and will joyfully proclaim
your faithful love in the morning.
For you have been a stronghold for me,
a refuge in my day of trouble.
To you, my strength, I sing praises,
because God is my stronghold—
my faithful God.

60   For the choir director: according to "The Lily of Testimony." A *Miktam* of David for teaching.
When he fought with Aram-naharaim and Aram-zobah, and Joab returned and struck Edom in
Salt Valley, killing twelve thousand.

> God, you have rejected us;
> you have broken us down;
> you have been angry. Restore us!
> You have shaken the land and split it open.
> Heal its fissures, for it shudders.
> You have made your people suffer hardship;
> you have given us wine to drink
> that made us stagger.
> You have given a signal flag to those who fear you,
>   so that they can flee before the archers.*Selah*
> Save with your right hand, and answer me,
> so that those you love may be rescued.
>
> God has spoken in his sanctuary:
> "I will celebrate!
> I will divide up Shechem.
> I will apportion the Valley of Succoth.
> Gilead is mine, Manasseh is mine,
> and Ephraim is my helmet;
> Judah is my scepter.
> Moab is my washbasin.
> I throw my sandal on Edom;
> I shout in triumph over Philistia."
>
> Who will bring me to the fortified city?
> Who will lead me to Edom?
> God, haven't you rejected us?
> God, you do not march out with our armies.
> Give us aid against the foe,
> for human help is worthless.
> With God we will perform valiantly;
> he will trample our foes.

61   For the choir director: on stringed instruments. Of David.

God, hear my cry;
pay attention to my prayer.
I call to you from the ends of the earth
when my heart is without strength.
Lead me to a rock that is high above me,
for you have been a refuge for me,
a strong tower in the face of the enemy.
I will dwell in your tent forever
      and take refuge under the shelter of your wings. *Selah*

God, you have heard my vows;
you have given a heritage
to those who fear your name.
Add days to the king's life;
may his years span many generations.
May he sit enthroned before God forever.
Appoint faithful love and truth to guard him.
Then I will continually sing of your name,
fulfilling my vows day by day.

62   For the choir director: according to Jeduthun. A psalm of David.

I am at rest in God alone;
my salvation comes from him.
He alone is my rock and my salvation,
my stronghold; I will never be shaken.

How long will you threaten a man?
Will all of you attack
as if he were a leaning wall
or a tottering fence?
They only plan to bring him down
from his high position.
They take pleasure in lying;
they bless with their mouths,
      but they curse inwardly. *Selah*

Rest in God alone, my soul,
for my hope comes from him.
He alone is my rock and my salvation,
my stronghold; I will not be shaken.
My salvation and glory depend on God, my strong rock.
20   My refuge is in God.
Trust in him at all times, you people;
pour out your hearts before him.
   God is our refuge.*Selah*

Common people are only a vapor;
important people, an illusion.
Together on a scale,
they weigh less than a vapor.
Place no trust in oppression
or false hope in robbery.
30   If wealth increases,
don't set your heart on it.

God has spoken once;
I have heard this twice:
strength belongs to God,
and faithful love belongs to you, LORD.
For you repay each according to his works.

63 A psalm of David. When he was in the Wilderness of Judah.

  God, you are my God; I eagerly seek you.
  I thirst for you;
  my body faints for you
  in a land that is dry, desolate, and without water.
  So I gaze on you in the sanctuary
  to see your strength and your glory.

  My lips will glorify you
  because your faithful love is better than life.
10 So I will bless you as long as I live;

at your name, I will lift up my hands.
You satisfy me as with rich food;
my mouth will praise you with joyful lips.

When I think of you as I lie on my bed,
I meditate on you during the night watches
because you are my helper;
I will rejoice in the shadow of your wings.
I follow close to you;
your right hand holds on to me.

20   But those who intend to destroy my life
will go into the depths of the earth.
They will be given over to the power of the sword;
they will become a meal for jackals.
But the king will rejoice in God;
all who swear by him will boast,
for the mouths of liars will be shut.

64   For the choir director. A psalm of David.

God, hear my voice when I am in anguish.
Protect my life from the terror of the enemy.
Hide me from the scheming of wicked people,
from the mob of evildoers,
who sharpen their tongues like swords
and aim bitter words like arrows,
shooting from concealed places at the blameless.
They shoot at him suddenly and are not afraid.
10   They adopt an evil plan;
they talk about hiding traps and say,
"Who will see them?"
They devise crimes and say,
"We have perfected a secret plan."
The inner man and the heart are mysterious.

But God will shoot them with arrows;
suddenly, they will be wounded.

They will be made to stumble;
their own tongues work against them.
20   All who see them will shake their heads.
Then everyone will fear
and will tell about God's work,
for they will understand what he has done.

The righteous one rejoices in the LORD
and takes refuge in him;
all those who are upright in heart
will offer praise.

65   For the choir director. A psalm of David. A song.

Praise is rightfully yours,
God, in Zion;
vows to you will be fulfilled.
All humanity will come to you,
the one who hears prayer.
Iniquities overwhelm me;
only you can atone for our rebellions.
How happy is the one you choose
10   and bring near to live in your courts!
We will be satisfied with the goodness of your house,
the holiness of your temple.

You answer us in righteousness,
with awe-inspiring works,
God of our salvation,
the hope of all the ends of the earth
and of the distant seas.
You establish the mountains by your power;
you are robed with strength.
20   You silence the roar of the seas,
the roar of their waves,
and the tumult of the nations.
Those who live far away are awed by your signs;
you make east and west shout for joy.

You visit the earth and water it abundantly,
enriching it greatly.
God's stream is filled with water,
for you prepare the earth in this way,
providing people with grain.
30 You soften it with showers and bless its growth,
soaking its furrows and leveling its ridges.
You crown the year with your goodness;
your carts overflow with plenty.
The wilderness pastures overflow,
and the hills are robed with joy.
The pastures are clothed with flocks
and the valleys covered with grain.
They shout in triumph; indeed, they sing.

66 For the choir director. A song. A psalm.

Let the whole earth shout joyfully to God!
Sing about the glory of his name;
make his praise glorious.
Say to God, "How awe-inspiring are your works!
Your enemies will cringe before you
because of your great strength.
The whole earth will worship you
and sing praise to you.
10 They will sing praise to your name." *Selah*

Come and see the wonders of God;
his acts for humanity are awe-inspiring.
He turned the sea into dry land,
and they crossed the river on foot.
There we rejoiced in him.
He rules forever by his might;
he keeps his eye on the nations.
The rebellious should not exalt themselves. *Selah*
Bless our God, you peoples;
20 let the sound of his praise be heard.

He keeps us alive
and does not allow our feet to slip.

For you, God, tested us;
you refined us as silver is refined.
You lured us into a trap;
you placed burdens on our backs.
You let men ride over our heads;
we went through fire and water,
but you brought us out to abundance.

30   I will enter your house with burnt offerings;
I will pay you my vows
that my lips promised
and my mouth spoke during my distress.
I will offer you fattened sheep as burnt offerings,
with the fragrant smoke of rams;
        I will sacrifice bulls with goats. *Selah*

Come and listen, all who fear God,
and I will tell what he has done for me.
I cried out to him with my mouth,
40   and praise was on my tongue.
If I had been aware of malice in my heart,
the Lord would not have listened.
However, God has listened;
he has paid attention to the sound of my prayer.
Blessed be God!
He has not turned away my prayer
or turned his faithful love from me.

67   For the choir director: with stringed instruments. A psalm. A song.

May God be gracious to us and bless us;
        may he make his face shine upon us *Selah*
so that your way may be known on earth,
your salvation among all nations.

Let the peoples praise you, God;
let all the peoples praise you.
Let the nations rejoice and shout for joy,
for you judge the peoples with fairness
10   and lead the nations on earth.*Selah*
Let the peoples praise you, God,
let all the peoples praise you.

The earth has produced its harvest;
God, our God, blesses us.
God will bless us,
and all the ends of the earth will fear him.

68   For the choir director. A psalm of David. A song.

God arises. His enemies scatter,
and those who hate him flee from his presence.
As smoke is blown away,
so you blow them away.
As wax melts before the fire,
so the wicked are destroyed before God.
But the righteous are glad;
they rejoice before God and celebrate with joy.

10   Sing to God! Sing praises to his name.
Exalt him who rides on the clouds —
his name is the Lord — and celebrate before him.
God in his holy dwelling is
a father of the fatherless
and a champion of widows.
God provides homes for those who are deserted.
He leads out the prisoners to prosperity,
but the rebellious live in a scorched land.

God, when you went out before your people,
20   when you marched through the desert,*Selah*
the earth trembled and the skies poured rain
before God, the God of Sinai,

before God, the God of Israel.
You, God, showered abundant rain;
you revived your inheritance when it languished.
Your people settled in it;
God, you provided for the poor by your goodness.

The Lord gave the command;
a great company of women brought the good news:
30 "The kings of the armies flee — they flee!"
She who stays at home divides the spoil.
While you lie among the sheep pens,
the wings of a dove are covered with silver,
and its feathers with glistening gold.
When the Almighty scattered kings in the land,
it snowed on Zalmon.

Mount Bashan is God's towering mountain;
Mount Bashan is a mountain of many peaks.
Why gaze with envy, you mountain peaks,
40 at the mountain God desired for his abode?
The Lord will dwell there forever!
God's chariots are tens of thousands,
thousands and thousands;
the Lord is among them in the sanctuary
as he was at Sinai.
You ascended to the heights, taking away captives;
you received gifts from people,
even from the rebellious,
so that the Lord God might dwell there.

50 Blessed be the Lord!
Day after day he bears our burdens;
    God is our salvation. *Selah*
Our God is a God of salvation,
and escape from death belongs to the Lord my Lord.
Surely God crushes the heads of his enemies,
the hairy brow of one who goes on in his guilty acts.
The Lord said, "I will bring them back from Bashan;

I will bring them back from the depths of the sea
so that your foot may wade in blood
60   and your dogs' tongues may have their share
from the enemies."
People have seen your procession, God,
the procession of my God,
my King, in the sanctuary.
Singers lead the way,
with musicians following;
among them are young women
playing tambourines.
Bless God in the assemblies;
70   bless the Lord from the fountain of Israel.
There is Benjamin, the youngest, leading them,
the rulers of Judah in their assembly,
the rulers of Zebulun, the rulers of Naphtali.

Your God has decreed your strength.
Show your strength, God,
you who have acted on our behalf.
Because of your temple at Jerusalem,
kings will bring tribute to you.
Rebuke the beast in the reeds,
80   the herd of bulls with the calves of the peoples.
Trample underfoot those with bars of silver.
Scatter the peoples who take pleasure in war.
Ambassadors will come from Egypt;
Cush will stretch out its hands to God.

Sing to God, you kingdoms of the earth;
    sing praise to the Lord, *Selah*
to him who rides in the ancient, highest heavens.
Look, he thunders with his powerful voice!
Ascribe power to God.
90   His majesty is over Israel;
his power is among the clouds.
God, you are awe-inspiring in your sanctuaries.

The God of Israel gives power and strength to his people.
Blessed be God!

69 For the choir director: according to "The Lilies." Of David.

Save me, God,
for the water has risen to my neck.
I have sunk in deep mud, and there is no footing;
I have come into deep water,
and a flood sweeps over me.
I am weary from my crying;
my throat is parched.
My eyes fail, looking for my God.

10   Those who hate me without cause
are more numerous than the hairs of my head;
my deceitful enemies, who would destroy me,
are powerful.
Though I did not steal, I must repay.

God, you know my foolishness,
and my guilty acts are not hidden from you.
Do not let those who put their hope in you
be disgraced because of me,
Lord GOD of Armies;

20   do not let those who seek you
be humiliated because of me,
God of Israel.
For I have endured insults because of you,
and shame has covered my face.
I have become a stranger to my brothers
and a foreigner to my mother's sons
because zeal for your house has consumed me,
and the insults of those who insult you
have fallen on me.

30   I mourned and fasted,
but it brought me insults.
I wore sackcloth as my clothing,
and I was a joke to them.

Those who sit at the city gate talk about me,
and drunkards make up songs about me.

But as for me, Lord,
my prayer to you is for a time of favor.
In your abundant, faithful love, God,
answer me with your sure salvation.
40　Rescue me from the miry mud; don't let me sink.
Let me be rescued from those who hate me
and from the deep water.
Don't let the floodwaters sweep over me
or the deep swallow me up;
don't let the Pit close its mouth over me.
Answer me, Lord,
for your faithful love is good.
In keeping with your abundant compassion,
turn to me.
50　Don't hide your face from your servant,
for I am in distress.
Answer me quickly!
Come near to me and redeem me;
ransom me because of my enemies.

You know the insults I endure—
my shame and disgrace.
You are aware of all my adversaries.
Insults have broken my heart,
and I am in despair.
60　I waited for sympathy,
but there was none;
for comforters, but found no one.
Instead, they gave me gall for my food,
and for my thirst
they gave me vinegar to drink.

Let their table set before them be a snare,
and let it be a trap for their allies.
Let their eyes grow too dim to see,

and let their hips continually quake.

70 Pour out your rage on them,
and let your burning anger overtake them.
Make their fortification desolate;
may no one live in their tents.
For they persecute the one you struck
and talk about the pain of those you wounded.
Charge them with crime on top of crime;
do not let them share in your righteousness.
Let them be erased from the book of life
and not be recorded with the righteous.

80 But as for me — poor and in pain—
let your salvation protect me, God.
I will praise God's name with song
and exalt him with thanksgiving.
That will please the LORD more than an ox,
more than a bull with horns and hooves.
The humble will see it and rejoice.
You who seek God, take heart!
For the LORD listens to the needy
and does not despise
90 his own who are prisoners.

Let heaven and earth praise him,
the seas and everything that moves in them,
for God will save Zion
and build up the cities of Judah.
They will live there and possess it.
The descendants of his servants will inherit it,
and those who love his name will live in it.

70 For the choir director. Of David. To bring remembrance.

God, hurry to rescue me.
LORD, hurry to help me!

Let those who seek to kill me
be disgraced and confounded;
let those who wish me harm
be turned back and humiliated.
Let those who say, "Aha, aha!"
retreat because of their shame.

10   Let all who seek you rejoice and be glad in you;
let those who love your salvation
continually say, "God is great!"
I am oppressed and needy;
hurry to me, God.
You are my help and my deliverer;
Lord, do not delay.

71   Lord, I seek refuge in you;
let me never be disgraced.
In your justice, rescue and deliver me;
listen closely to me and save me.
Be a rock of refuge for me,
where I can always go.
Give the command to save me,
for you are my rock and fortress.
Deliver me, my God, from the power of the wicked,
10   from the grasp of the unjust and oppressive.
For you are my hope, Lord God,
my confidence from my youth.
I have leaned on you from birth;
you took me from my mother's womb.
My praise is always about you.
I am like a miraculous sign to many,
and you are my strong refuge.
My mouth is full of praise
and honor to you all day long.

20   Don't discard me in my old age.
As my strength fails, do not abandon me.
For my enemies talk about me,

and those who spy on me plot together,
saying, "God has abandoned him;
chase him and catch him,
for there is no one to rescue him."
God, do not be far from me;
my God, hurry to help me.
May my adversaries be disgraced and destroyed;
30   may those who intend to harm me
be covered with disgrace and humiliation.
But I will hope continually
and will praise you more and more.
My mouth will tell about your righteousness
and your salvation all day long,
though I cannot sum them up.
I come because of the mighty acts of the Lord GOD;
I will proclaim your righteousness, yours alone.

God, you have taught me from my youth,
40   and I still proclaim your wondrous works.
Even while I am old and gray,
God, do not abandon me,
while I proclaim your power
to another generation,
your strength to all who are to come.
Your righteousness reaches the heights, God,
you who have done great things;
God, who is like you?
You caused me to experience
50   many troubles and misfortunes,
but you will revive me again.
You will bring me up again,
even from the depths of the earth.
You will increase my honor
and comfort me once again.
Therefore, I will praise you with a harp
for your faithfulness, my God;
I will sing to you with a lyre,
Holy One of Israel.

60   My lips will shout for joy
when I sing praise to you
because you have redeemed me.
Therefore, my tongue will proclaim
your righteousness all day long,
for those who intend to harm me
will be disgraced and confounded.

72   Of Solomon.

God, give your justice to the king
and your righteousness to the king's son.
He will judge your people with righteousness
and your afflicted ones with justice.
May the mountains bring well-being to the people
and the hills, righteousness.
May he vindicate the afflicted among the people,
help the poor,
10   and crush the oppressor.

May they fear you while the sun endures
and as long as the moon, throughout all generations.
May the king be like rain that falls on the cut grass,
like spring showers that water the earth.
May the righteous flourish in his days
and well-being abound
until the moon is no more.

May he rule from sea to sea
and from the Euphrates
20   to the ends of the earth.
May desert tribes kneel before him
and his enemies lick the dust.
May the kings of Tarshish
and the coasts and islands bring tribute,
the kings of Sheba and Seba offer gifts.
Let all kings bow in homage to him,
all nations serve him.

For he will rescue the poor who cry out
and the afflicted who have no helper.
He will have pity on the poor and helpless
and save the lives of the poor.
He will redeem them from oppression and violence,
for their lives are precious in his sight.

May he live long!
May gold from Sheba be given to him.
May prayer be offered for him continually,
and may he be blessed all day long.
May there be plenty of grain in the land;
may it wave on the tops of the mountains.
May its crops be like Lebanon.
May people flourish in the cities
like the grass of the field.
May his name endure forever;
as long as the sun shines,
may his fame increase.
May all nations be blessed by him
and call him blessed.

Blessed be the Lord God, the God of Israel,
who alone does wonders.
Blessed be his glorious name forever;
the whole earth is filled with his glory.
Amen and amen.
The prayers of David son of Jesse are concluded.

Book III
(Psalms 73–89)

73   A psalm of Asaph.

God is indeed good to Israel,
to the pure in heart.
But as for me, my feet almost slipped;
my steps nearly went astray.
For I envied the arrogant;
I saw the prosperity of the wicked.

They have an easy time until they die,
and their bodies are well fed.
They are not in trouble like others;
they are not afflicted like most people.
Therefore, pride is their necklace,
and violence covers them like a garment.
Their eyes bulge out from fatness;
the imaginations of their hearts run wild.
They mock, and they speak maliciously;
they arrogantly threaten oppression.
They set their mouths against heaven,
and their tongues strut across the earth.
Therefore his people turn to them
and drink in their overflowing words.
The wicked say, "How can God know?
Does the Most High know everything?"
Look at them — the wicked!
They are always at ease,
and they increase their wealth.

Did I purify my heart
and wash my hands in innocence for nothing?
For I am afflicted all day long

30 and punished every morning.
  If I had decided to say these things aloud,
  I would have betrayed your people.
  When I tried to understand all this,
  it seemed hopeless
  until I entered God's sanctuary.
  Then I understood their destiny.
  Indeed, you put them in slippery places;
  you make them fall into ruin.
  How suddenly they become a desolation!
40 They come to an end, swept away by terrors.
  Like one waking from a dream,
  Lord, when arising, you will despise their image.

  When I became embittered
  and my innermost being was wounded,
  I was stupid and didn't understand;
  I was an unthinking animal toward you.
  Yet I am always with you;
  you hold my right hand.
  You guide me with your counsel,
50 and afterward you will take me up in glory.
  Who do I have in heaven but you?
  And I desire nothing on earth but you.
  My flesh and my heart may fail,
  but God is the strength of my heart,
  my portion forever.
  Those far from you will certainly perish;
  you destroy all who are unfaithful to you.
  But as for me, God's presence is my good.
  I have made the Lord GOD my refuge,
60 so I can tell about all you do.

74 A *Maskil* of Asaph.

  Why have you rejected us forever, God?
  Why does your anger burn
  against the sheep of your pasture?

Remember your congregation,
which you purchased long ago
and redeemed as the tribe for your own possession.
Remember Mount Zion where you dwell.
Make your way to the perpetual ruins,
10   to all that the enemy has destroyed in the sanctuary.
Your adversaries roared in the meeting place
where you met with us.
They set up their emblems as signs.
It was like men in a thicket of trees,
wielding axes,
then smashing all the carvings
with hatchets and picks.
They set your sanctuary on fire;
they utterly desecrated
20   the dwelling place of your name.
They said in their hearts,
"Let's oppress them relentlessly."
They burned every place throughout the land
where God met with us.
There are no signs for us to see.
There is no longer a prophet.
And none of us knows how long this will last.
God, how long will the enemy mock?
Will the foe insult your name forever?
30   Why do you hold back your hand?
Stretch out your right hand and destroy them!

God my King is from ancient times,
performing saving acts on the earth.
You divided the sea with your strength;
you smashed the heads of the sea monsters in the water;
you crushed the heads of Leviathan;
you fed him to the creatures of the desert.
You opened up springs and streams;
you dried up ever-flowing rivers.
40   The day is yours, also the night;
you established the moon and the sun.

You set all the boundaries of the earth;
you made summer and winter.

Remember this: the enemy has mocked the LORD,
and a foolish people has insulted your name.
Do not give to beasts the life of your dove;
do not forget the lives of your poor people forever.
Consider the covenant,
for the dark places of the land are full of violence.
Do not let the oppressed turn away in shame;
let the poor and needy praise your name.
Rise up, God, champion your cause!
Remember the insults
that fools bring against you all day long.
Do not forget the clamor of your adversaries,
the tumult of your opponents that goes up constantly.

75 For the choir director: "Do Not Destroy." A psalm of Asaph. A song.

We give thanks to you, God;
we give thanks to you, for your name is near.
People tell about your wondrous works.

"When I choose a time,
I will judge fairly.
When the earth and all its inhabitants shake,
    I am the one who steadies its pillars. *Selah*
I say to the boastful, 'Do not boast,'
and to the wicked, 'Do not lift up your horn.
Do not lift up your horn against heaven
or speak arrogantly.'"

Exaltation does not come
from the east, the west, or the desert,
for God is the Judge:
He brings down one and exalts another.
For there is a cup in the LORD's hand,
full of wine blended with spices, and he pours from it.

All the wicked of the earth will drink,
20   draining it to the dregs.

As for me, I will tell about him forever;
I will sing praise to the God of Jacob.

"I will cut off all the horns of the wicked,
but the horns of the righteous will be lifted up."

76   For the choir director: with stringed instruments. A psalm of Asaph. A song.

God is known in Judah;
his name is great in Israel.
His tent is in Salem,
his dwelling place in Zion.
There he shatters the bow's flaming arrows,
    the shield, the sword, and the weapons of war.*Selah*

You are resplendent and majestic
coming down from the mountains of prey.
10   The brave-hearted have been plundered;
they have slipped into their final sleep.
None of the warriors was able to lift a hand.
At your rebuke, God of Jacob,
both chariot and horse lay still.

And you — you are to be feared.
When you are angry,
who can stand before you?
From heaven you pronounced judgment.
The earth feared and grew quiet
20   when God rose up to judge
    and to save all the lowly of the earth.*Selah*
Even human wrath will praise you;
you will clothe yourself
with the wrath that remains.

Make and keep your vows
to the LORD your God;
let all who are around him bring tribute
to the awe-inspiring one.
He humbles the spirit of leaders;
30   he is feared by the kings of the earth.

77   For the choir director: according to Jeduthun. Of Asaph. A psalm.

I cry aloud to God,
aloud to God, and he will hear me.
I sought the Lord in my day of trouble.
My hands were continually lifted up
all night long;
I refused to be comforted.
I think of God; I groan;
    I meditate; my spirit becomes weak. *Selah*

10   You have kept me from closing my eyes;
I am troubled and cannot speak.
I consider days of old,
years long past.
At night I remember my music;
I meditate in my heart, and my spirit ponders.

"Will the Lord reject forever
and never again show favor?
Has his faithful love ceased forever?
Is his promise at an end for all generations?
20   Has God forgotten to be gracious?
    Has he in anger withheld his compassion?" *Selah*

So I say, "I am grieved
that the right hand of the Most High has changed."
I will remember the LORD's works;
yes, I will remember your ancient wonders.
I will reflect on all you have done
and meditate on your actions.

God, your way is holy.
What god is great like God?
30   You are the God who works wonders;
you revealed your strength among the peoples.
With power you redeemed your people,
    the descendants of Jacob and Joseph.*Selah*

The water saw you, God.
The water saw you; it trembled.
Even the depths shook.
The clouds poured down water.
The storm clouds thundered;
your arrows flashed back and forth.
40   The sound of your thunder was in the whirlwind;
lightning lit up the world.
The earth shook and quaked.
Your way went through the sea
and your path through the vast water,
but your footprints were unseen.
You led your people like a flock
by the hand of Moses and Aaron.

78   A *Maskil* of Asaph.

My people, hear my instruction;
listen to the words from my mouth.
I will declare wise sayings;
I will speak mysteries from the past—
things we have heard and known
and that our ancestors have passed down to us.
We will not hide them from their children,
but will tell a future generation
10   the praiseworthy acts of the LORD,
his might, and the wondrous works
he has performed.
He established a testimony in Jacob
and set up a law in Israel,

which he commanded our ancestors
to teach to their children
so that a future generation—
children yet to be born — might know.
They were to rise and tell their children
20   so that they might put their confidence in God
and not forget God's works,
but keep his commands.
Then they would not be like their ancestors,
a stubborn and rebellious generation,
a generation whose heart was not loyal
and whose spirit was not faithful to God.

The Ephraimite archers turned back
on the day of battle.
They did not keep God's covenant
30   and refused to live by his law.
They forgot what he had done,
the wondrous works he had shown them.
He worked wonders in the sight of their ancestors
in the land of Egypt, the territory of Zoan.
He split the sea and brought them across;
the water stood firm like a wall.
He led them with a cloud by day
and with a fiery light throughout the night.
He split rocks in the wilderness
40   and gave them drink as abundant as the depths.
He brought streams out of the stone
and made water flow down like rivers.

But they continued to sin against him,
rebelling in the desert against the Most High.
They deliberately tested God,
demanding the food they craved.
They spoke against God, saying,
"Is God able to provide food in the wilderness?
Look! He struck the rock and water gushed out;
50   torrents overflowed.

But can he also provide bread
or furnish meat for his people?"
Therefore, the LORD heard and became furious;
then fire broke out against Jacob,
and anger flared up against Israel
because they did not believe God
or rely on his salvation.
He gave a command to the clouds above
and opened the doors of heaven.
60 He rained manna for them to eat;
he gave them grain from heaven.
People ate the bread of angels.
He sent them an abundant supply of food.
He made the east wind blow in the skies
and drove the south wind by his might.
He rained meat on them like dust,
and winged birds like the sand of the seas.
He made them fall in the camp,
all around the tents.
70 The people ate and were completely satisfied,
for he gave them what they craved.
Before they had turned from what they craved,
while the food was still in their mouths,
God's anger flared up against them,
and he killed some of their best men.
He struck down Israel's fit young men.

Despite all this, they kept sinning
and did not believe his wondrous works.
He made their days end in futility,
80 their years in sudden disaster.
When he killed some of them,
the rest began to seek him;
they repented and searched for God.
They remembered that God was their rock,
the Most High God, their Redeemer.
But they deceived him with their mouths,
they lied to him with their tongues,

their hearts were insincere toward him,
and they were unfaithful to his covenant.
90   Yet he was compassionate;
he atoned for their iniquity
and did not destroy them.
He often turned his anger aside
and did not unleash all his wrath.
He remembered that they were only flesh,
a wind that passes and does not return.

How often they rebelled against him
in the wilderness
and grieved him in the desert.
100   They constantly tested God
and provoked the Holy One of Israel.
They did not remember his power shown
on the day he redeemed them from the foe,
when he performed his miraculous signs in Egypt
and his wonders in the territory of Zoan.
He turned their rivers into blood,
and they could not drink from their streams.
He sent among them swarms of flies,
which fed on them,
110   and frogs, which devastated them.
He gave their crops to the caterpillar
and the fruit of their labor to the locust.
He killed their vines with hail
and their sycamore fig trees with a flood.
He handed over their livestock to hail
and their cattle to lightning bolts.
He sent his burning anger against them:
fury, indignation, and calamity—
a band of deadly messengers.
120   He cleared a path for his anger.
He did not spare them from death
but delivered their lives to the plague.
He struck all the firstborn in Egypt,
the first progeny of the tents of Ham.

He led his people out like sheep
and guided them like a flock in the wilderness.
He led them safely, and they were not afraid;
but the sea covered their enemies.
He brought them to his holy territory,
130   to the mountain his right hand acquired.
He drove out nations before them.
He apportioned their inheritance by lot
and settled the tribes of Israel in their tents.

But they rebelliously tested the Most High God,
for they did not keep his decrees.
They treacherously turned away like their ancestors;
they became warped like a faulty bow.
They enraged him with their high places
and provoked his jealousy with their carved images.
140   God heard and became furious;
he completely rejected Israel.
He abandoned the tabernacle at Shiloh,
the tent where he resided among mankind.
He gave up his strength to captivity
and his splendor to the hand of a foe.
He surrendered his people to the sword
because he was enraged with his heritage.
Fire consumed his chosen young men,
and his young women had no wedding songs.
150   His priests fell by the sword,
and the widows could not lament.

The Lord awoke as if from sleep,
like a warrior from the effects of wine.
He beat back his foes;
he gave them lasting disgrace.
He rejected the tent of Joseph
and did not choose the tribe of Ephraim.
He chose instead the tribe of Judah,
Mount Zion, which he loved.
160   He built his sanctuary like the heights,

like the earth that he established forever.
He chose David his servant
and took him from the sheep pens;
he brought him from tending ewes
to be shepherd over his people Jacob—
over Israel, his inheritance.
He shepherded them with a pure heart
and guided them with his skillful hands.

79   A psalm of Asaph.

God, the nations have invaded your inheritance,
desecrated your holy temple,
and turned Jerusalem into ruins.
They gave the corpses of your servants
to the birds of the sky for food,
the flesh of your faithful ones
to the beasts of the earth.
They poured out their blood
10   like water all around Jerusalem,
and there was no one to bury them.
We have become an object of reproach
to our neighbors,
a source of mockery and ridicule
to those around us.

How long, Lord? Will you be angry forever?
Will your jealousy keep burning like fire?
Pour out your wrath on the nations
that don't acknowledge you,
20   on the kingdoms that don't call on your name,
for they have devoured Jacob
and devastated his homeland.
Do not hold past iniquities against us;
let your compassion come to us quickly,
for we have become very weak.

God of our salvation, help us,
for the glory of your name.
Rescue us and atone for our sins,
for your name's sake.
30 Why should the nations ask,
"Where is their God?"
Before our eyes,
let vengeance for the shed blood of your servants
be known among the nations.
Let the groans of the prisoners reach you;
according to your great power,
preserve those condemned to die.

Pay back sevenfold to our neighbors
the reproach they have hurled at you, Lord.
40 Then we, your people, the sheep of your pasture,
will thank you forever;
we will declare your praise
to generation after generation.

80 For the choir director: according to "The Lilies." A testimony of Asaph. A psalm.

Listen, Shepherd of Israel,
who leads Joseph like a flock;
you who sit enthroned between the cherubim,
shine on Ephraim,
Benjamin, and Manasseh.
Rally your power and come to save us.
Restore us, God;
make your face shine on us,
10 so that we may be saved.

LORD God of Armies,
how long will you be angry
with your people's prayers?
You fed them the bread of tears
and gave them a full measure
of tears to drink.

You put us at odds with our neighbors;
our enemies mock us.
Restore us, God of Armies;
make your face shine on us, so that we may be saved.

You dug up a vine from Egypt;
you drove out the nations and planted it.
You cleared a place for it;
it took root and filled the land.
The mountains were covered by its shade,
and the mighty cedars with its branches.
It sent out sprouts toward the Sea
and shoots toward the River.

Why have you broken down its walls
so that all who pass by pick its fruit?
Boars from the forest tear at it
and creatures of the field feed on it.
Return, God of Armies.
Look down from heaven and see;
take care of this vine,
the root your right hand planted,
the son that you made strong for yourself.
It was cut down and burned;
they perish at the rebuke of your countenance.
Let your hand be with the man at your right hand,
with the son of man
you have made strong for yourself.
Then we will not turn away from you;
revive us, and we will call on your name.
Restore us, Lord, God of Armies;
make your face shine on us, so that we may be saved.

81 For the choir director: on the *Gittith*. Of Asaph.

Sing for joy to God our strength;
shout in triumph to the God of Jacob.
Lift up a song — play the tambourine,

the melodious lyre, and the harp.
Blow the ram's horn on the day of our feasts
during the new moon
and during the full moon.
For this is a statute for Israel,
10   an ordinance of the God of Jacob.
He set it up as a decree for Joseph
when he went throughout the land of Egypt.

I heard an unfamiliar language:
    "I relieved his shoulder from the burden;
his hands were freed from carrying the basket.
You called out in distress, and I rescued you;
I answered you from the thundercloud.
       I tested you at the Waters of Meribah. *Selah*
Listen, my people, and I will admonish you.
20   Israel, if you would only listen to me!
There must not be a strange god among you;
you must not bow down to a foreign god.
I am the LORD your God,
who brought you up from the land of Egypt.
Open your mouth wide, and I will fill it.

"But my people did not listen to my voice;
Israel did not obey me.
So I gave them over to their stubborn hearts
to follow their own plans.
30   If only my people would listen to me
and Israel would follow my ways,
I would quickly subdue their enemies
and turn my hand against their foes."
Those who hate the LORD
would cower to him;
their doom would last forever.
But he would feed Israel with the best wheat.
"I would satisfy you with honey from the rock."

82 A psalm of Asaph.

> God stands in the divine assembly;
> he pronounces judgment among the gods:
> "How long will you judge unjustly
>   and show partiality to the wicked?*Selah*
> Provide justice for the needy and the fatherless;
> uphold the rights of the oppressed and the destitute.
> Rescue the poor and needy;
> save them from the power of the wicked."
>
> They do not know or understand;
> they wander in darkness.
> All the foundations of the earth are shaken.
>
> I said, "You are gods;
> you are all sons of the Most High.
> However, you will die like humans
> and fall like any other ruler."
>
> Rise up, God, judge the earth,
> for all the nations belong to you.

83 A song. A psalm of Asaph.

> God, do not keep silent.
> Do not be deaf, God; do not be quiet.
> See how your enemies make an uproar;
> those who hate you have acted arrogantly.
> They devise clever schemes against your people;
> they conspire against your treasured ones.
> They say, "Come, let's wipe them out as a nation
> so that Israel's name will no longer be remembered."
> For they have conspired with one mind;
> they form an alliance against you—
> the tents of Edom and the Ishmaelites,
> Moab and the Hagrites,
> Gebal, Ammon, and Amalek,

Philistia with the inhabitants of Tyre.
Even Assyria has joined them;
　　they lend support to the sons of Lot.*Selah*

Deal with them as you did with Midian,
as you did with Sisera
20　and Jabin at the Kishon River.
They were destroyed at En-dor;
they became manure for the ground.
Make their nobles like Oreb and Zeeb,
and all their tribal leaders like Zebah and Zalmunna,
who said, "Let's seize God's pastures for ourselves."

Make them like tumbleweed, my God,
like straw before the wind.
As fire burns a forest,
as a flame blazes through mountains,
30　so pursue them with your tempest
and terrify them with your storm.
Cover their faces with shame
so that they will seek your name, LORD.
Let them be put to shame and terrified forever;
let them perish in disgrace.
May they know that you alone—
whose name is the LORD—
are the Most High over the whole earth.

84　For the choir director: on the *Gittith*. A psalm of the sons of Korah.

How lovely is your dwelling place,
LORD of Armies.
I long and yearn
for the courts of the LORD;
my heart and flesh cry out for the living God.

Even a sparrow finds a home,
and a swallow, a nest for herself
where she places her young—

10 near your altars, Lord of Armies,
my King and my God.
How happy are those who reside in your house,
     who praise you continually.*Selah*

Happy are the people whose strength is in you,
whose hearts are set on pilgrimage.
As they pass through the Valley of Baca,
they make it a source of spring water;
even the autumn rain will cover it with blessings.
They go from strength to strength;
20 each appears before God in Zion.

Lord God of Armies, hear my prayer;
     listen, God of Jacob.*Selah*
Consider our shield, God;
look on the face of your anointed one.

Better a day in your courts
than a thousand anywhere else.
I would rather stand at the threshold of the house of my God
than live in the tents of wicked people.
For the Lord God is a sun and shield.
30 The Lord grants favor and honor;
he does not withhold the good
from those who live with integrity.
Happy is the person who trusts in you,
Lord of Armies!

85 For the choir director. A psalm of the sons of Korah.

Lord, you showed favor to your land;
you restored the fortunes of Jacob.
You forgave your people's guilt;
     you covered all their sin.*Selah*
You withdrew all your fury;
you turned from your burning anger.

Return to us, God of our salvation,
and abandon your displeasure with us.
10   Will you be angry with us forever?
Will you prolong your anger for all generations?
Will you not revive us again
so that your people may rejoice in you?
Show us your faithful love, LORD,
and give us your salvation.

I will listen to what God will say;
surely the LORD will declare peace
to his people, his faithful ones,
and not let them go back to foolish ways.
20   His salvation is very near those who fear him,
so that glory may dwell in our land.

Faithful love and truth will join together;
righteousness and peace will embrace.
Truth will spring up from the earth,
and righteousness will look down from heaven.
Also, the LORD will provide what is good,
and our land will yield its crops.
Righteousness will go before him
to prepare the way for his steps.

86   A prayer of David.

Listen, LORD, and answer me,
for I am poor and needy.
Protect my life, for I am faithful.
You are my God; save your servant who trusts in you.
Be gracious to me, Lord,
for I call to you all day long.
Bring joy to your servant's life,
because I appeal to you, Lord.

10   For you, Lord, are kind and ready to forgive,
abounding in faithful love to all who call on you.

LORD, hear my prayer;
listen to my cries for mercy.
I call on you in the day of my distress,
for you will answer me.

Lord, there is no one like you among the gods,
and there are no works like yours.
All the nations you have made
will come and bow down before you, Lord,
20   and will honor your name.
For you are great and perform wonders;
you alone are God.

Teach me your way, LORD,
and I will live by your truth.
Give me an undivided mind to fear your name.
I will praise you with all my heart, Lord my God,
and will honor your name forever.
For your faithful love for me is great,
and you rescue my life from the depths of Sheol.

30   God, arrogant people have attacked me;
a gang of ruthless men intends to kill me.
They do not let you guide them.
But you, Lord, are a compassionate and gracious God,
slow to anger and abounding in faithful love and truth.
Turn to me and be gracious to me.
Give your strength to your servant;
save the son of your female servant.
Show me a sign of your goodness;
my enemies will see and be put to shame
40   because you, LORD, have helped and comforted me.

87   A psalm of the sons of Korah. A song.

The city he founded is on the holy mountains.
The LORD loves Zion's city gates
more than all the dwellings of Jacob.

Glorious things are said about you,
    city of God.*Selah*

"I will make a record of those who know me:
Rahab, Babylon, Philistia, Tyre, and Cush—
each one was born there."

10 And it will be said of Zion,
"This one and that one were born in her."
The Most High himself will establish her.
When he registers the peoples,
the LORD will record,
    "This one was born there."*Selah*
Singers and dancers alike will say,
"My whole source of joy is in you."

88   A song. A psalm of the sons of Korah. For the choir director: according to *Mahalath Leannoth*.
A *Maskil* of Heman the Ezrahite.

LORD, God of my salvation,
I cry out before you day and night.
May my prayer reach your presence;
listen to my cry.

For I have had enough troubles,
and my life is near Sheol.
I am counted among those going down to the Pit.
10 I am like a man without strength,
abandoned among the dead.
I am like the slain lying in the grave,
whom you no longer remember,
and who are cut off from your care.

You have put me in the lowest part of the Pit,
in the darkest places, in the depths.
Your wrath weighs heavily on me;
    you have overwhelmed me with all your waves.*Selah*
You have distanced my friends from me;
20 you have made me repulsive to them.

I am shut in and cannot go out.
My eyes are worn out from crying.
LORD, I cry out to you all day long;
I spread out my hands to you.

Do you work wonders for the dead?
    Do departed spirits rise up to praise you?*Selah*
Will your faithful love be declared in the grave,
your faithfulness in Abaddon?
Will your wonders be known in the darkness
30   or your righteousness in the land of oblivion?

But I call to you for help, LORD;
in the morning my prayer meets you.
LORD, why do you reject me?
Why do you hide your face from me?
From my youth,
I have been suffering and near death.
I suffer your horrors; I am desperate.
Your wrath sweeps over me;
your terrors destroy me.
40   They surround me like water all day long;
they close in on me from every side.
You have distanced loved one and neighbor from me;
darkness is my only friend.

89   A *Maskil* of Ethan the Ezrahite.

I will sing about the LORD's faithful love forever;
I will proclaim your faithfulness to all generations
with my mouth.
For I will declare,
"Faithful love is built up forever;
you establish your faithfulness in the heavens."

The LORD said,
"I have made a covenant with my chosen one;
10   I have sworn an oath to David my servant:

'I will establish your offspring forever
  and build up your throne for all generations.'"*Selah*

Lord, the heavens praise your wonders—
your faithfulness also—
in the assembly of the holy ones.
For who in the skies can compare with the Lord?
Who among the heavenly beings is like the Lord?
God is greatly feared in the council of the holy ones,
more awe-inspiring than all who surround him.
20 Lord God of Armies,
who is strong like you, Lord?
Your faithfulness surrounds you.
You rule the raging sea;
when its waves surge, you still them.
You crushed Rahab like one who is slain;
you scattered your enemies with your powerful arm.
The heavens are yours; the earth also is yours.
The world and everything in it — you founded them.
North and south — you created them.
30 Tabor and Hermon shout for joy at your name.
You have a mighty arm;
your hand is powerful;
your right hand is lifted high.
Righteousness and justice are the foundation
of your throne;
faithful love and truth go before you.
Happy are the people who know the joyful shout;
Lord, they walk in the light from your face.
They rejoice in your name all day long,
40 and they are exalted by your righteousness.
For you are their magnificent strength;
by your favor our horn is exalted.
Surely our shield belongs to the Lord,
our king to the Holy One of Israel.

You once spoke in a vision to your faithful ones
and said, "I have granted help to a warrior;

I have exalted one chosen from the people.
I have found David my servant;
I have anointed him with my sacred oil.

50 My hand will always be with him,
and my arm will strengthen him.
The enemy will not oppress him;
the wicked will not afflict him.
I will crush his foes before him
and strike those who hate him.
My faithfulness and love will be with him,
and through my name
his horn will be exalted.
I will extend his power to the sea

60 and his right hand to the rivers.
He will call to me, 'You are my Father,
my God, the rock of my salvation.'
I will also make him my firstborn,
greatest of the kings of the earth.
I will always preserve my faithful love for him,
and my covenant with him will endure.
I will establish his line forever,
his throne as long as heaven lasts.
If his sons abandon my instruction

70 and do not live by my ordinances,
if they dishonor my statutes
and do not keep my commands,
then I will call their rebellion
to account with the rod,
their iniquity with blows.
But I will not withdraw
my faithful love from him
or betray my faithfulness.
I will not violate my covenant

80 or change what my lips have said.
Once and for all
I have sworn an oath by my holiness;
I will not lie to David.
His offspring will continue forever,

his throne like the sun before me,
like the moon, established forever,
    a faithful witness in the sky."*Selah*

But you have spurned and rejected him;
you have become enraged with your anointed.
90   You have repudiated the covenant with your servant;
you have completely dishonored his crown.
You have broken down all his walls;
you have reduced his fortified cities to ruins.
All who pass by plunder him;
he has become an object of ridicule
to his neighbors.
You have lifted high the right hand of his foes;
you have made all his enemies rejoice.
You have also turned back his sharp sword
100 and have not let him stand in battle.
You have made his splendor cease
and have overturned his throne.
You have shortened the days of his youth;
    you have covered him with shame.*Selah*

How long, Lord? Will you hide forever?
Will your anger keep burning like fire?
Remember how short my life is.
Have you created everyone for nothing?
What courageous person can live and never see death?
110   Who can save himself from the power of Sheol?*Selah*
Lord, where are the former acts of your faithful love
that you swore to David in your faithfulness?
Remember, Lord, the ridicule against your servants—
in my heart I carry abuse from all the peoples—
how your enemies have ridiculed, Lord,
how they have ridiculed every step of your anointed.

Blessed be the Lord forever.
Amen and amen.

Book IV
(Psalms 90–106)

90   A prayer of Moses, the man of God.

Lord, you have been our refuge
in every generation.
Before the mountains were born,
before you gave birth to the earth and the world,
from eternity to eternity, you are God.

You return mankind to the dust,
saying, "Return, descendants of Adam."
For in your sight a thousand years
10   are like yesterday that passes by,
like a few hours of the night.
You end their lives; they sleep.
They are like grass that grows in the morning—
in the morning it sprouts and grows;
by evening it withers and dries up.

For we are consumed by your anger;
we are terrified by your wrath.
You have set our iniquities before you,
our secret sins in the light of your presence.
20   For all our days ebb away under your wrath;
we end our years like a sigh.
Our lives last seventy years
or, if we are strong, eighty years.
Even the best of them are struggle and sorrow;
indeed, they pass quickly and we fly away.
Who understands the power of your anger?
Your wrath matches the fear that is due you.
Teach us to number our days carefully
so that we may develop wisdom in our hearts.

30 Lord — how long?
Turn and have compassion on your servants.
Satisfy us in the morning with your faithful love
so that we may shout with joy and be glad all our days.
Make us rejoice for as many days as you have humbled us,
for as many years as we have seen adversity.
Let your work be seen by your servants,
and your splendor by their children.
Let the favor of the Lord our God be on us;
establish for us the work of our hands—
40 establish the work of our hands!

91 The one who lives under the protection of the Most High
dwells in the shadow of the Almighty.

I will say concerning the Lord, who is my refuge and my fortress,
my God in whom I trust:
He himself will rescue you from the bird trap,
from the destructive plague.
He will cover you with his feathers;
you will take refuge under his wings.
His faithfulness will be a protective shield.
10 You will not fear the terror of the night,
the arrow that flies by day,
the plague that stalks in darkness,
or the pestilence that ravages at noon.
Though a thousand fall at your side
and ten thousand at your right hand,
the pestilence will not reach you.
You will only see it with your eyes
and witness the punishment of the wicked.

Because you have made the Lord — my refuge,
20 the Most High — your dwelling place,
no harm will come to you;
no plague will come near your tent.
For he will give his angels orders concerning you,

to protect you in all your ways.
They will support you with their hands
so that you will not strike your foot against a stone.
You will tread on the lion and the cobra;
you will trample the young lion and the serpent.

Because he has his heart set on me,
I will deliver him;   30
I will protect him because he knows my name.
When he calls out to me, I will answer him;
I will be with him in trouble.
I will rescue him and give him honor.
I will satisfy him with a long life
and show him my salvation.

92   A psalm. A song for the Sabbath day.

It is good to give thanks to the LORD,
to sing praise to your name, Most High,
to declare your faithful love in the morning
and your faithfulness at night,
with a ten-stringed harp
and the music of a lyre.

For you have made me rejoice, LORD,
by what you have done;
I will shout for joy   10
because of the works of your hands.
How magnificent are your works, LORD,
how profound your thoughts!
A stupid person does not know,
a fool does not understand this:
though the wicked sprout like grass
and all evildoers flourish,
they will be eternally destroyed.
But you, LORD, are exalted forever.
For indeed, LORD, your enemies—   20
indeed, your enemies will perish;

all evildoers will be scattered.
You have lifted up my horn
like that of a wild ox;
I have been anointed with the finest oil.
My eyes look at my enemies;
when evildoers rise against me,
my ears hear them.

The righteous thrive like a palm tree
and grow like a cedar tree in Lebanon.
Planted in the house of the Lord,
they thrive in the courts of our God.
They will still bear fruit in old age,
healthy and green,
to declare, "The Lord is just;
he is my rock,
and there is no unrighteousness in him."

93   The Lord reigns! He is robed in majesty;
the Lord is robed, enveloped in strength.
The world is firmly established;
it cannot be shaken.
Your throne has been established
from the beginning;
you are from eternity.
The floods have lifted up, Lord,
the floods have lifted up their voice;
the floods lift up their pounding waves.
Greater than the roar of a huge torrent—
the mighty breakers of the sea—
the Lord on high is majestic.

Lord, your testimonies are completely reliable;
holiness adorns your house
for all the days to come.

94   Lord, God of vengeance—
God of vengeance, shine!

Rise up, Judge of the earth;
repay the proud what they deserve.
Lord, how long will the wicked—
how long will the wicked celebrate?

They pour out arrogant words;
all the evildoers boast.
Lord, they crush your people;
10   they oppress your heritage.
They kill the widow and the resident alien
and murder the fatherless.
They say, "The Lord doesn't see it.
The God of Jacob doesn't pay attention."

Pay attention, you stupid people!
Fools, when will you be wise?
Can the one who shaped the ear not hear,
the one who formed the eye not see?
The one who instructs nations,
20   the one who teaches mankind knowledge—
does he not discipline?
The Lord knows the thoughts of mankind;
they are futile.

Lord, how happy is anyone you discipline
and teach from your law
to give him relief from troubled times
until a pit is dug for the wicked.
The Lord will not leave his people
or abandon his heritage,
30   for the administration of justice will again be righteous,
and all the upright in heart will follow it.

Who stands up for me against the wicked?
Who takes a stand for me against evildoers?
If the Lord had not been my helper,
I would soon rest in the silence of death.
If I say, "My foot is slipping,"

your faithful love will support me, LORD.
When I am filled with cares,
your comfort brings me joy.

40   Can a corrupt throne be your ally,
a throne that makes evil laws?
They band together against the life of the righteous
and condemn the innocent to death.
But the LORD is my refuge;
my God is the rock of my protection.
He will pay them back for their sins
and destroy them for their evil.
The LORD our God will destroy them.

95   Come, let's shout joyfully to the LORD,
shout triumphantly to the rock of our salvation!
Let's enter his presence with thanksgiving;
let's shout triumphantly to him in song.

For the LORD is a great God,
a great King above all gods.
The depths of the earth are in his hand,
and the mountain peaks are his.
The sea is his; he made it.
10   His hands formed the dry land.

Come, let's worship and bow down;
let's kneel before the LORD our Maker.
For he is our God,
and we are the people of his pasture,
the sheep under his care.

Today, if you hear his voice:
Do not harden your hearts as at Meribah,
as on that day at Massah in the wilderness
where your ancestors tested me;
20   they tried me, though they had seen what I did.
For forty years I was disgusted with that generation;

I said, "They are a people whose hearts go astray;
they do not know my ways."
So I swore in my anger,
"They will not enter my rest."

96

Sing a new song to the Lord;
let the whole earth sing to the Lord.
Sing to the Lord, bless his name;
proclaim his salvation from day to day.
Declare his glory among the nations,
his wondrous works among all peoples.

For the Lord is great and is highly praised;
he is feared above all gods.
For all the gods of the peoples are worthless idols,
but the Lord made the heavens.
Splendor and majesty are before him;
strength and beauty are in his sanctuary.

Ascribe to the Lord, you families of the peoples,
ascribe to the Lord glory and strength.
Ascribe to the Lord the glory of his name;
bring an offering and enter his courts.
Worship the Lord in the splendor of his holiness;
let the whole earth tremble before him.

Say among the nations, "The Lord reigns.
The world is firmly established; it cannot be shaken.
He judges the peoples fairly."
Let the heavens be glad and the earth rejoice;
let the sea and all that fills it resound.
Let the fields and everything in them celebrate.
Then all the trees of the forest will shout for joy
before the Lord, for he is coming—
for he is coming to judge the earth.
He will judge the world with righteousness
and the peoples with his faithfulness.

97
The LORD reigns! Let the earth rejoice;
let the many coasts and islands be glad.

Clouds and total darkness surround him;
righteousness and justice are the foundation of his throne.
Fire goes before him
and burns up his foes on every side.
His lightning lights up the world;
the earth sees and trembles.
The mountains melt like wax
at the presence of the LORD—
at the presence of the Lord of the whole earth.

The heavens proclaim his righteousness;
all the peoples see his glory.

All who serve carved images,
those who boast in worthless idols, will be put to shame.
All the gods must worship him.

Zion hears and is glad,
Judah's villages rejoice
because of your judgments, LORD.
For you, LORD,
are the Most High over the whole earth;
you are exalted above all the gods.

You who love the LORD, hate evil!
He protects the lives of his faithful ones;
he rescues them from the power of the wicked.
Light dawns for the righteous,
gladness for the upright in heart.
Be glad in the LORD, you righteous ones,
and give thanks to his holy name.

98   A psalm.

> Sing a new song to the Lord,
> for he has performed wonders;
> his right hand and holy arm
> have won him victory.
> The Lord has made his victory known;
> he has revealed his righteousness
> in the sight of the nations.
> He has remembered his love
> and faithfulness to the house of Israel;
> all the ends of the earth
> have seen our God's victory.
>
> Let the whole earth shout to the Lord;
> be jubilant, shout for joy, and sing.
> Sing to the Lord with the lyre,
> with the lyre and melodious song.
> With trumpets and the blast of the ram's horn
> shout triumphantly
> in the presence of the Lord, our King.
>
> Let the sea and all that fills it,
> the world and those who live in it, resound.
> Let the rivers clap their hands;
> let the mountains shout together for joy
> before the Lord,
> for he is coming to judge the earth.
> He will judge the world righteously
> and the peoples fairly.

99   The Lord reigns! Let the peoples tremble.

> He is enthroned between the cherubim.
> Let the earth quake.
> The Lord is great in Zion;
> he is exalted above all the peoples.
> Let them praise your great

and awe-inspiring name.
He is holy.

The mighty King loves justice.
10 You have established fairness;
you have administered justice
and righteousness in Jacob.
Exalt the LORD our God;
bow in worship at his footstool.
He is holy.

Moses and Aaron were among his priests;
Samuel also was among those calling on his name.
They called to the LORD and he answered them.
He spoke to them in a pillar of cloud;
20 they kept his decrees and the statutes he gave them.
LORD our God, you answered them.
You were a forgiving God to them,
but an avenger of their sinful actions.

Exalt the LORD our God;
bow in worship at his holy mountain,
for the LORD our God is holy.

100 A psalm of thanksgiving.

Let the whole earth shout triumphantly to the LORD!
Serve the LORD with gladness;
come before him with joyful songs.
Acknowledge that the LORD is God.
He made us, and we are his—
his people, the sheep of his pasture.
Enter his gates with thanksgiving
and his courts with praise.
10 Give thanks to him and bless his name.
For the LORD is good, and his faithful love endures forever;
his faithfulness, through all generations.

101 A psalm of David.

> I will sing of faithful love and justice;
> I will sing praise to you, Lord.
> I will pay attention to the way of integrity.
> When will you come to me?
> I will live with a heart of integrity in my house.
> I will not let anything worthless guide me.
> I hate the practice of transgression;
> it will not cling to me.

10
> A devious heart will be far from me;
> I will not be involved with evil.
>
> I will destroy anyone
> who secretly slanders his neighbor;
> I cannot tolerate anyone
> with haughty eyes or an arrogant heart.
> My eyes favor the faithful of the land
> so that they may sit down with me.
> The one who follows the way of integrity
> may serve me.

20
> No one who acts deceitfully
> will live in my palace;
> the one who tells lies
> will not be retained here to guide me.
> Every morning I will destroy
> all the wicked of the land,
> wiping out all evildoers from the Lord's city.

102 A prayer of a suffering person who is weak and pours out his lament before the Lord.

> Lord, hear my prayer;
> let my cry for help come before you.
> Do not hide your face from me in my day of trouble.
> Listen closely to me;
> answer me quickly when I call.

For my days vanish like smoke,
and my bones burn like a furnace.
My heart is suffering, withered like grass;
I even forget to eat my food.
Because of the sound of my groaning,
my flesh sticks to my bones.
I am like an eagle owl,
like a little owl among the ruins.
I stay awake;
I am like a solitary bird on a roof.
My enemies taunt me all day long;
they ridicule and use my name as a curse.
I eat ashes like bread
and mingle my drinks with tears
because of your indignation and wrath;
for you have picked me up and thrown me aside.
My days are like a lengthening shadow,
and I wither away like grass.

But you, Lord, are enthroned forever;
your fame endures to all generations.
You will rise up and have compassion on Zion,
for it is time to show favor to her—
the appointed time has come.
For your servants take delight in its stones
and favor its dust.

Then the nations will fear the name of the Lord,
and all the kings of the earth your glory,
for the Lord will rebuild Zion;
he will appear in his glory.
He will pay attention to the prayer of the destitute
and will not despise their prayer.

This will be written for a later generation,
and a people who have not yet been created will praise the Lord:
He looked down from his holy heights—
the Lord gazed out from heaven to earth—

to hear a prisoner's groaning,
to set free those condemned to die,
so that they might declare
the name of the Lord in Zion
and his praise in Jerusalem
when peoples and kingdoms are assembled
to serve the Lord.

He has broken my strength in midcourse;
50   he has shortened my days.
I say, "My God, do not take me
in the middle of my life!
Your years continue through all generations.
Long ago you established the earth,
and the heavens are the work of your hands.
They will perish, but you will endure;
all of them will wear out like clothing.
You will change them like a garment,
and they will pass away.
60   But you are the same,
and your years will never end.
Your servants' children will dwell securely,
and their offspring will be established before you."

103   Of David.

My soul, bless the Lord,
and all that is within me, bless his holy name.
My soul, bless the Lord,
and do not forget all his benefits.

He forgives all your iniquity;
he heals all your diseases.
He redeems your life from the Pit;
he crowns you with faithful love and compassion.
10   He satisfies you with good things;
your youth is renewed like the eagle.

The LORD executes acts of righteousness
and justice for all the oppressed.
He revealed his ways to Moses,
his deeds to the people of Israel.
The LORD is compassionate and gracious,
slow to anger and abounding in faithful love.
He will not always accuse us
or be angry forever.
20 He has not dealt with us as our sins deserve
or repaid us according to our iniquities.

For as high as the heavens are above the earth,
so great is his faithful love
toward those who fear him.
As far as the east is from the west,
so far has he removed
our transgressions from us.
As a father has compassion on his children,
so the LORD has compassion on those who fear him.
30 For he knows what we are made of,
remembering that we are dust.

As for man, his days are like grass—
he blooms like a flower of the field;
when the wind passes over it, it vanishes,
and its place is no longer known.
But from eternity to eternity
the LORD's faithful love is toward those who fear him,
and his righteousness toward the grandchildren
of those who keep his covenant,
40 who remember to observe his precepts.
The LORD has established his throne in heaven,
and his kingdom rules over all.

Bless the LORD,
all his angels of great strength,
who do his word,
obedient to his command.

Bless the LORD, all his armies,
his servants who do his will.
Bless the LORD, all his works

50 in all the places where he rules.
My soul, bless the LORD!

104 My soul, bless the LORD!
LORD my God, you are very great;
you are clothed with majesty and splendor.
He wraps himself in light as if it were a robe,
spreading out the sky like a canopy,
laying the beams of his palace
on the waters above,
making the clouds his chariot,
walking on the wings of the wind,

10 and making the winds his messengers,
flames of fire his servants.

He established the earth on its foundations;
it will never be shaken.
You covered it with the deep
as if it were a garment;
the water stood above the mountains.
At your rebuke the water fled;
at the sound of your thunder they hurried away—
mountains rose and valleys sank—

20 to the place you established for them.
You set a boundary they cannot cross;
they will never cover the earth again.

He causes the springs to gush into the valleys;
they flow between the mountains.
They supply water for every wild beast;
the wild donkeys quench their thirst.
The birds of the sky live beside the springs;
they make their voices heard among the foliage.
He waters the mountains from his palace;

30 the earth is satisfied by the fruit of your labor.

He causes grass to grow for the livestock
and provides crops for man to cultivate,
producing food from the earth,
wine that makes human hearts glad—
making his face shine with oil—
and bread that sustains human hearts.

The trees of the LORD flourish,
the cedars of Lebanon that he planted.
There the birds make their nests;
40   storks make their homes in the pine trees.
The high mountains are for the wild goats;
the cliffs are a refuge for hyraxes.

He made the moon to mark the festivals;
the sun knows when to set.
You bring darkness, and it becomes night,
when all the forest animals stir.
The young lions roar for their prey
and seek their food from God.
The sun rises; they go back
50   and lie down in their dens.
Man goes out to his work
and to his labor until evening.

How countless are your works, LORD!
In wisdom you have made them all;
the earth is full of your creatures.
Here is the sea, vast and wide,
teeming with creatures beyond number—
living things both large and small.
There the ships move about,
60   and Leviathan, which you formed to play there.

All of them wait for you
to give them their food at the right time.
When you give it to them,

they gather it;
when you open your hand,
they are satisfied with good things.
When you hide your face,
they are terrified;
when you take away their breath,
70   they die and return to the dust.
When you send your breath,
they are created,
and you renew the surface of the ground.

May the glory of the LORD endure forever;
may the LORD rejoice in his works.
He looks at the earth, and it trembles;
he touches the mountains,
and they pour out smoke.
I will sing to the LORD all my life;
80   I will sing praise to my God while I live.
May my meditation be pleasing to him;
I will rejoice in the LORD.
May sinners vanish from the earth
and wicked people be no more.
My soul, bless the LORD!
Hallelujah!

105   Give thanks to the LORD, call on his name;
proclaim his deeds among the peoples.
Sing to him, sing praise to him;
tell about all his wondrous works!
Boast in his holy name;
let the hearts of those who seek the LORD rejoice.
Seek the LORD and his strength;
seek his face always.
Remember the wondrous works he has done,
10   his wonders, and the judgments he has pronounced,
you offspring of Abraham his servant,
Jacob's descendants — his chosen ones.

He is the LORD our God;
his judgments govern the whole earth.
He remembers his covenant forever,
the promise he ordained
for a thousand generations—
the covenant he made with Abraham,
swore to Isaac,
20 and confirmed to Jacob as a decree
and to Israel as a permanent covenant:
"I will give the land of Canaan to you
as your inherited portion."

When they were few in number,
very few indeed,
and resident aliens in Canaan,
wandering from nation to nation
and from one kingdom to another,
he allowed no one to oppress them;
30 he rebuked kings on their behalf:
"Do not touch my anointed ones,
or harm my prophets."

He called down famine against the land
and destroyed the entire food supply.
He had sent a man ahead of them—
Joseph, who was sold as a slave.
They hurt his feet with shackles;
his neck was put in an iron collar.
Until the time his prediction came true,
40 the word of the LORD tested him.
The king sent for him and released him;
the ruler of peoples set him free.
He made him master of his household,
ruler over all his possessions—
binding his officials at will
and instructing his elders.

Then Israel went to Egypt;
Jacob lived as an alien in the land of Ham.
The LORD made his people very fruitful;
50 he made them more numerous than their foes,
whose hearts he turned to hate his people
and to deal deceptively with his servants.
He sent Moses his servant,
and Aaron, whom he had chosen.
They performed his miraculous signs among them
and wonders in the land of Ham.
He sent darkness, and it became dark—
for did they not defy his commands?
He turned their water into blood
60 and caused their fish to die.
Their land was overrun with frogs,
even in their royal chambers.
He spoke, and insects came—
gnats throughout their country.
He gave them hail for rain,
and lightning throughout their land.
He struck their vines and fig trees
and shattered the trees of their territory.
He spoke, and locusts came—
70 young locusts without number.
They devoured all the vegetation in their land
and consumed the produce of their land.
He struck all the firstborn in their land,
all their first progeny.

Then he brought Israel out with silver and gold,
and no one among his tribes stumbled.
Egypt was glad when they left,
for the dread of Israel had fallen on them.
He spread a cloud as a covering
80 and gave a fire to light up the night.
They asked, and he brought quail
and satisfied them with bread from heaven.
He opened a rock, and water gushed out;

it flowed like a stream in the desert.
For he remembered his holy promise
to Abraham his servant.
He brought his people out with rejoicing,
his chosen ones with shouts of joy.
He gave them the lands of the nations,
90 and they inherited
what other peoples had worked for.

All this happened
so that they might keep his statutes
and obey his instructions.
Hallelujah!

106 Hallelujah!
Give thanks to the LORD, for he is good;
his faithful love endures forever.
Who can declare the LORD's mighty acts
or proclaim all the praise due him?
How happy are those who uphold justice,
who practice righteousness at all times.

Remember me, LORD,
when you show favor to your people.
10 Come to me with your salvation
so that I may enjoy the prosperity
of your chosen ones,
rejoice in the joy of your nation,
and boast about your heritage.

Both we and our ancestors have sinned;
we have done wrong and have acted wickedly.
Our ancestors in Egypt did not grasp
the significance of your wondrous works
or remember your many acts of faithful love;
20 instead, they rebelled by the sea — the Red Sea.
Yet he saved them for his name's sake,
to make his power known.

He rebuked the Red Sea, and it dried up;
he led them through the depths as through a desert.
He saved them from the power of the adversary;
he redeemed them from the power of the enemy.
Water covered their foes;
not one of them remained.
Then they believed his promises
30   and sang his praise.

They soon forgot his works
and would not wait for his counsel.
They were seized with craving in the wilderness
and tested God in the desert.
He gave them what they asked for,
but sent a wasting disease among them.

In the camp they were envious of Moses
and of Aaron, the LORD's holy one.
The earth opened up and swallowed Dathan;
40   it covered the assembly of Abiram.
Fire blazed throughout their assembly;
flames consumed the wicked.

At Horeb they made a calf
and worshiped the cast metal image.
They exchanged their glory
for the image of a grass-eating ox.
They forgot God their Savior,
who did great things in Egypt,
wondrous works in the land of Ham,
50   awe-inspiring acts at the Red Sea.
So he said he would have destroyed them—
if Moses his chosen one
had not stood before him in the breach
to turn his wrath away from destroying them.

They despised the pleasant land
and did not believe his promise.

They grumbled in their tents
and did not listen to the LORD.
So he raised his hand against them with an oath

60   that he would make them fall in the desert
and would disperse their descendants
among the nations,
scattering them throughout the lands.

They aligned themselves with Baal of Peor
and ate sacrifices offered to lifeless gods.
They angered the LORD with their deeds,
and a plague broke out against them.
But Phinehas stood up and intervened,
and the plague was stopped.

70   It was credited to him as righteousness
throughout all generations to come.

They angered the LORD at the Waters of Meribah,
and Moses suffered because of them,
for they embittered his spirit,
and he spoke rashly with his lips.

They did not destroy the peoples
as the LORD had commanded them
but mingled with the nations
and adopted their ways.

80   They served their idols,
which became a snare to them.
They sacrificed their sons and daughters to demons.
They shed innocent blood—
the blood of their sons and daughters
whom they sacrificed to the idols of Canaan;
so the land became polluted with blood.
They defiled themselves by their actions
and prostituted themselves by their deeds.

Therefore the LORD's anger burned against his people,

90   and he abhorred his own inheritance.

He handed them over to the nations;
those who hated them ruled over them.
Their enemies oppressed them,
and they were subdued under their power.
He rescued them many times,
but they continued to rebel deliberately
and were beaten down by their iniquity.

When he heard their cry,
he took note of their distress,
remembered his covenant with them,
and relented according to the abundance
of his faithful love.
He caused them to be pitied
before all their captors.

Save us, LORD our God,
and gather us from the nations,
so that we may give thanks to your holy name
and rejoice in your praise.

Blessed be the LORD God of Israel,
from everlasting to everlasting.
Let all the people say, "Amen!"
Hallelujah!

Book V

(Psalms 107–150)

107 Give thanks to the LORD, for he is good;
his faithful love endures forever.
Let the redeemed of the LORD proclaim
that he has redeemed them from the power of the foe
and has gathered them from the lands—
from the east and the west,
from the north and the south.

Some wandered in the desolate wilderness,
finding no way to a city where they could live.
10 They were hungry and thirsty;
their spirits failed within them.
Then they cried out to the LORD in their trouble;
he rescued them from their distress.
He led them by the right path
to go to a city where they could live.
Let them give thanks to the LORD
for his faithful love
and his wondrous works for all humanity.
For he has satisfied the thirsty
20 and filled the hungry with good things.

Others sat in darkness and gloom—
prisoners in cruel chains—
because they rebelled against God's commands
and despised the counsel of the Most High.
He broke their spirits with hard labor;
they stumbled, and there was no one to help.
Then they cried out to the LORD in their trouble;
he saved them from their distress.
He brought them out of darkness and gloom
30 and broke their chains apart.

Let them give thanks to the Lord
for his faithful love
and his wondrous works for all humanity.
For he has broken down the bronze gates
and cut through the iron bars.

Fools suffered affliction
because of their rebellious ways and their iniquities.
They loathed all food
and came near the gates of death.
40   Then they cried out to the Lord in their trouble;
he saved them from their distress.
He sent his word and healed them;
he rescued them from their traps.
Let them give thanks to the Lord
for his faithful love
and his wondrous works for all humanity.
Let them offer thanksgiving sacrifices
and announce his works with shouts of joy.

Others went to sea in ships,
50   conducting trade on the vast water.
They saw the Lord's works,
his wondrous works in the deep.
He spoke and raised a stormy wind
that stirred up the waves of the sea.
Rising up to the sky, sinking down to the depths,
their courage melting away in anguish,
they reeled and staggered like a drunkard,
and all their skill was useless.
Then they cried out to the Lord in their trouble,
60   and he brought them out of their distress.
He stilled the storm to a whisper,
and the waves of the sea were hushed.
They rejoiced when the waves grew quiet.
Then he guided them to the harbor they longed for.
Let them give thanks to the Lord
for his faithful love

and his wondrous works for all humanity.
Let them exalt him in the assembly of the people
and praise him in the council of the elders.

70   He turns rivers into desert,
springs into thirsty ground,
and fruitful land into salty wasteland,
because of the wickedness of its inhabitants.
He turns a desert into a pool,
dry land into springs.
He causes the hungry to settle there,
and they establish a city where they can live.
They sow fields and plant vineyards
that yield a fruitful harvest.
80   He blesses them, and they multiply greatly;
he does not let their livestock decrease.

When they are diminished and are humbled
by cruel oppression and sorrow,
he pours contempt on nobles
and makes them wander in a trackless wasteland.
But he lifts the needy out of their suffering
and makes their families multiply like flocks.
The upright see it and rejoice,
and all injustice shuts its mouth.

90   Let whoever is wise pay attention to these things
and consider the Lord's acts of faithful love.

108   A song. A psalm of David.

My heart is confident, God;
I will sing; I will sing praises
with the whole of my being.
Wake up, harp and lyre!
I will wake up the dawn.
I will praise you, Lord, among the peoples;
I will sing praises to you among the nations.

For your faithful love is higher than the heavens,
10   and your faithfulness reaches to the clouds.
God, be exalted above the heavens,
and let your glory be over the whole earth.
Save with your right hand and answer me
so that those you love may be rescued.

God has spoken in his sanctuary:
"I will celebrate!
I will divide up Shechem.
I will apportion the Valley of Succoth.
Gilead is mine, Manasseh is mine,
20   and Ephraim is my helmet;
Judah is my scepter.
Moab is my washbasin;
I throw my sandal on Edom.
I shout in triumph over Philistia."

Who will bring me to the fortified city?
Who will lead me to Edom?
God, haven't you rejected us?
God, you do not march out with our armies.
Give us aid against the foe,
30   for human help is worthless.
With God we will perform valiantly;
he will trample our foes.

109   For the choir director. A psalm of David.

God of my praise, do not be silent.

For wicked and deceitful mouths open against me;
they speak against me with lying tongues.
They surround me with hateful words
and attack me without cause.
In return for my love they accuse me,
but I continue to pray.

They repay me evil for good,
and hatred for my love.

Set a wicked person over him;
let an accuser stand at his right hand.
When he is judged, let him be found guilty,
and let his prayer be counted as sin.
Let his days be few;
let another take over his position.
Let his children be fatherless
and his wife a widow.
Let his children wander as beggars,
searching for food far from their demolished homes.
Let a creditor seize all he has;
let strangers plunder what he has worked for.
Let no one show him kindness,
and let no one be gracious to his fatherless children.
Let the line of his descendants be cut off;
let their name be blotted out in the next generation.
Let the iniquity of his fathers
be remembered before the LORD,
and do not let his mother's sin be blotted out.
Let their sins always remain before the LORD,
and let him remove all memory of them from the earth.

For he did not think to show kindness,
but pursued the suffering, needy, and brokenhearted
in order to put them to death.
He loved cursing — let it fall on him;
he took no delight in blessing — let it be far from him.
He wore cursing like his coat—
let it enter his body like water
and go into his bones like oil.
Let it be like a robe he wraps around himself,
like a belt he always wears.
Let this be the LORD's payment to my accusers,
to those who speak evil against me.

But you, LORD, my Lord,
deal kindly with me for your name's sake;
because your faithful love is good, rescue me.
For I am suffering and needy;
my heart is wounded within me.
I fade away like a lengthening shadow;
50   I am shaken off like a locust.
My knees are weak from fasting,
and my body is emaciated.
I have become an object of ridicule to my accusers;
when they see me, they shake their heads in scorn.

Help me, LORD my God;
save me according to your faithful love
so they may know that this is your hand
and that you, LORD, have done it.
Though they curse, you will bless.
60   When they rise up, they will be put to shame,
but your servant will rejoice.
My accusers will be clothed with disgrace;
they will wear their shame like a cloak.
I will fervently thank the LORD with my mouth;
I will praise him in the presence of many.
For he stands at the right hand of the needy
to save him from those who would condemn him.

110   A psalm of David.

This is the declaration of the LORD
to my Lord:
"Sit at my right hand
until I make your enemies your footstool."
The LORD will extend your mighty scepter from Zion.
Rule over your surrounding enemies.
Your people will volunteer
on your day of battle.
10   In holy splendor, from the womb of the dawn,
the dew of your youth belongs to you.

The LORD has sworn an oath and will not take it back:
"You are a priest forever
according to the pattern of Melchizedek."

The Lord is at your right hand;
he will crush kings on the day of his anger.
He will judge the nations, heaping up corpses;
he will crush leaders over the entire world.
He will drink from the brook by the road;
20   therefore, he will lift up his head.

III   Hallelujah!
I will praise the LORD with all my heart
in the assembly of the upright and in the congregation.

The LORD's works are great,
studied by all who delight in them.
All that he does is splendid and majestic;
his righteousness endures forever.
He has caused his wondrous works to be remembered.
The LORD is gracious and compassionate.
10   He has provided food for those who fear him;
he remembers his covenant forever.
He has shown his people the power of his works
by giving them the inheritance of the nations.
The works of his hands are truth and justice;
all his instructions are trustworthy.
They are established forever and ever,
enacted in truth and in uprightness.
He has sent redemption to his people.
He has ordained his covenant forever.
20   His name is holy and awe-inspiring.

The fear of the LORD is the beginning of wisdom;
all who follow his instructions have good insight.
His praise endures forever.

112   Hallelujah!
Happy is the person who fears the Lord,
taking great delight in his commands.

His descendants will be powerful in the land;
the generation of the upright will be blessed.
Wealth and riches are in his house,
and his righteousness endures forever.
Light shines in the darkness for the upright.
He is gracious, compassionate, and righteous.
10   Good will come to the one who lends generously
and conducts his business fairly.
He will never be shaken.
The righteous one will be remembered forever.
He will not fear bad news;
his heart is confident, trusting in the Lord.
His heart is assured; he will not fear.
In the end he will look in triumph on his foes.
He distributes freely to the poor;
his righteousness endures forever.
20   His horn will be exalted in honor.

The wicked one will see it and be angry;
he will gnash his teeth in despair.
The desire of the wicked leads to ruin.

113   Hallelujah!
Give praise, servants of the Lord;
praise the name of the Lord.
Let the name of the Lord be blessed
both now and forever.
From the rising of the sun to its setting,
let the name of the Lord be praised.

The Lord is exalted above all the nations,
his glory above the heavens.
10   Who is like the Lord our God—
the one enthroned on high,

who stoops down to look
on the heavens and the earth?
He raises the poor from the dust
and lifts the needy from the trash heap
in order to seat them with nobles—
with the nobles of his people.
He gives the childless woman a household,
making her the joyful mother of children.
Hallelujah!

114   When Israel came out of Egypt—
the house of Jacob from a people
who spoke a foreign language—
Judah became his sanctuary,
Israel, his dominion.

The sea looked and fled;
the Jordan turned back.
The mountains skipped like rams,
the hills, like lambs.
Why was it, sea, that you fled?
Jordan, that you turned back?
Mountains, that you skipped like rams?
Hills, like lambs?

Tremble, earth, at the presence of the Lord,
at the presence of the God of Jacob,
who turned the rock into a pool,
the flint into a spring.

115   Not to us, Lord, not to us,
but to your name give glory
because of your faithful love, because of your truth.
Why should the nations say,
"Where is their God?"
Our God is in heaven
and does whatever he pleases.

Their idols are silver and gold,
made by human hands.
10   They have mouths but cannot speak,
eyes, but cannot see.
They have ears but cannot hear,
noses, but cannot smell.
They have hands but cannot feel,
feet, but cannot walk.
They cannot make a sound with their throats.
Those who make them are just like them,
as are all who trust in them.

Israel, trust in the LORD!
20   He is their help and shield.
House of Aaron, trust in the LORD!
He is their help and shield.
You who fear the LORD, trust in the LORD!
He is their help and shield.
The LORD remembers us and will bless us.
He will bless the house of Israel;
he will bless the house of Aaron;
he will bless those who fear the LORD—
small and great alike.

30   May the LORD add to your numbers,
both yours and your children's.
May you be blessed by the LORD,
the Maker of heaven and earth.
The heavens are the LORD's,
but the earth he has given to the human race.
It is not the dead who praise the LORD,
nor any of those descending into the silence of death.
But we will bless the LORD,
both now and forever.
40   Hallelujah!

116   I love the LORD because he has heard
my appeal for mercy.

Because he has turned his ear to me,
I will call out to him as long as I live.

The ropes of death were wrapped around me,
and the torments of Sheol overcame me;
I encountered trouble and sorrow.
Then I called on the name of the LORD:
"LORD, save me!"

10 The LORD is gracious and righteous;
our God is compassionate.
The LORD guards the inexperienced;
I was helpless, and he saved me.
Return to your rest, my soul,
for the LORD has been good to you.
For you, LORD, rescued me from death,
my eyes from tears,
my feet from stumbling.
I will walk before the LORD
20 in the land of the living.
I believed, even when I said,
"I am severely oppressed."
In my alarm I said,
"Everyone is a liar."

How can I repay the LORD
for all the good he has done for me?
I will take the cup of salvation
and call on the name of the LORD.
I will fulfill my vows to the LORD
30 in the presence of all his people.

The death of his faithful ones
is valuable in the LORD's sight.
LORD, I am indeed your servant;
I am your servant, the son of your female servant.
You have loosened my bonds.

I will offer you a thanksgiving sacrifice
and call on the name of the LORD.
I will fulfill my vows to the LORD
in the presence of all his people,
40   in the courts of the LORD's house—
within you, Jerusalem.
Hallelujah!

117   Praise the LORD, all nations!
Glorify him, all peoples!
For his faithful love to us is great;
the LORD's faithfulness endures forever.
Hallelujah!

118   Give thanks to the LORD, for he is good;
his faithful love endures forever.
Let Israel say,
"His faithful love endures forever."
Let the house of Aaron say,
"His faithful love endures forever."
Let those who fear the LORD say,
"His faithful love endures forever."

I called to the LORD in distress;
10   the LORD answered me
and put me in a spacious place.
The LORD is for me; I will not be afraid.
What can a mere mortal do to me?
The LORD is my helper;
therefore, I will look in triumph on those who hate me.

It is better to take refuge in the LORD
than to trust in humanity.
It is better to take refuge in the LORD
than to trust in nobles.

20   All the nations surrounded me;
in the name of the LORD I destroyed them.

They surrounded me, yes, they surrounded me;
in the name of the LORD I destroyed them.
They surrounded me like bees;
they were extinguished like a fire among thorns;
in the name of the LORD I destroyed them.
They pushed me hard to make me fall,
but the LORD helped me.
The LORD is my strength and my song;
30   he has become my salvation.

There are shouts of joy and victory
in the tents of the righteous:
"The LORD's right hand performs valiantly!
The LORD's right hand is raised.
The LORD's right hand performs valiantly!"
I will not die, but I will live
and proclaim what the LORD has done.
The LORD disciplined me severely
but did not give me over to death.

40   Open the gates of righteousness for me;
I will enter through them
and give thanks to the LORD.
This is the LORD's gate;
the righteous will enter through it.
I will give thanks to you
because you have answered me
and have become my salvation.
The stone that the builders rejected
has become the cornerstone.
50   This came from the LORD;
it is wondrous in our sight.
This is the day the LORD has made;
let's rejoice and be glad in it.

LORD, save us!
LORD, please grant us success!
He who comes in the name

of the LORD is blessed.
From the house of the LORD we bless you.
The LORD is God and has given us light.

60   Bind the festival sacrifice with cords
to the horns of the altar.
You are my God, and I will give you thanks.
You are my God; I will exalt you.
Give thanks to the LORD, for he is good;
his faithful love endures forever.

119   א *Aleph*

How happy are those whose way is blameless,
who walk according to the LORD's instruction!
Happy are those who keep his decrees
and seek him with all their heart.
They do nothing wrong,
they walk in his ways.
You have commanded that your precepts
be diligently kept.

10   If only my ways were committed
to keeping your statutes!
Then I would not be ashamed
when I think about all your commands.
I will praise you with an upright heart
when I learn your righteous judgments.
I will keep your statutes;
never abandon me.

ב *Beth*

How can a young man keep his way pure?
20   By keeping your word.
I have sought you with all my heart;
don't let me wander from your commands.
I have treasured your word in my heart
so that I may not sin against you.
LORD, may you be blessed;

teach me your statutes.
With my lips I proclaim
all the judgments from your mouth.
I rejoice in the way revealed by your decrees
30   as much as in all riches.
I will meditate on your precepts
and think about your ways.
I will delight in your statutes;
I will not forget your word.

ג Gimel

Deal generously with your servant
so that I might live;
then I will keep your word.
Open my eyes so that I may contemplate
40   wondrous things from your instruction.
I am a resident alien on earth;
do not hide your commands from me.
I am continually overcome
with longing for your judgments.
You rebuke the arrogant,
the ones under a curse,
who wander from your commands.
Take insult and contempt away from me,
for I have kept your decrees.
50   Though princes sit together speaking against me,
your servant will think about your statutes;
your decrees are my delight
and my counselors.

ד Daleth

My life is down in the dust;
give me life through your word.
I told you about my life,
and you answered me;
teach me your statutes.

60 Help me understand
the meaning of your precepts
so that I can meditate on your wonders.
I am weary from grief;
strengthen me through your word.
Keep me from the way of deceit
and graciously give me your instruction.
I have chosen the way of truth;
I have set your ordinances before me.
I cling to your decrees;
70 LORD, do not put me to shame.
I pursue the way of your commands,
for you broaden my understanding.

ה *He*

Teach me, LORD, the meaning of your statutes,
and I will always keep them.
Help me understand your instruction,
and I will obey it
and follow it with all my heart.
Help me stay on the path of your commands,
80 for I take pleasure in it.
Turn my heart to your decrees
and not to dishonest profit.
Turn my eyes
from looking at what is worthless;
give me life in your ways.
Confirm what you said to your servant,
for it produces reverence for you.
Turn away the disgrace I dread;
indeed, your judgments are good.
90 How I long for your precepts!
Give me life through your righteousness.

ו *Waw*

> Let your faithful love come to me, LORD,
> your salvation, as you promised.
> Then I can answer the one who taunts me,
> for I trust in your word.
> Never take the word of truth from my mouth,
> for I hope in your judgments.
> I will always obey your instruction,
> forever and ever.
> I will walk freely in an open place
> because I study your precepts.
> I will speak of your decrees before kings
> and not be ashamed.
> I delight in your commands,
> which I love.
> I will lift up my hands to your commands,
> which I love,
> and will meditate on your statutes.

100

ז *Zayin*

110

> Remember your word to your servant;
> you have given me hope through it.
> This is my comfort in my affliction:
> Your promise has given me life.
> The arrogant constantly ridicule me,
> but I do not turn away from your instruction.
> LORD, I remember your judgments from long ago
> and find comfort.
> Fury seizes me because of the wicked
> who reject your instruction.
> Your statutes are the theme of my song
> during my earthly life.
> LORD, I remember your name in the night,
> and I obey your instruction.
> This is my practice:
> I obey your precepts.

120

ח *Cheth*

The LORD is my portion;
I have promised to keep your words.
130   I have sought your favor with all my heart;
be gracious to me according to your promise.
I thought about my ways
and turned my steps back to your decrees.
I hurried, not hesitating
to keep your commands.
Though the ropes of the wicked
were wrapped around me,
I did not forget your instruction.
I rise at midnight to thank you
140   for your righteous judgments.
I am a friend to all who fear you,
to those who keep your precepts.
LORD, the earth is filled with your faithful love;
teach me your statutes.

ט *Teth*

LORD, you have treated your servant well,
just as you promised.
Teach me good judgment and discernment,
for I rely on your commands.
150   Before I was afflicted I went astray,
but now I keep your word.
You are good, and you do what is good;
teach me your statutes.
The arrogant have smeared me with lies,
but I obey your precepts with all my heart.
Their hearts are hard and insensitive,
but I delight in your instruction.
It was good for me to be afflicted
so that I could learn your statutes.
160   Instruction from your lips is better for me
than thousands of gold and silver pieces.

י *Yod*

Your hands made me and formed me;
give me understanding
so that I can learn your commands.
Those who fear you will see me and rejoice,
for I put my hope in your word.
I know, LORD, that your judgments are just
and that you have afflicted me fairly.
170   May your faithful love comfort me
as you promised your servant.
May your compassion come to me
so that I may live,
for your instruction is my delight.
Let the arrogant be put to shame
for slandering me with lies;
I will meditate on your precepts.
Let those who fear you,
those who know your decrees, turn to me.
180   May my heart be blameless regarding your statutes
so that I will not be put to shame.

כ *Kaph*

I long for your salvation;
I put my hope in your word.
My eyes grow weary
looking for what you have promised;
I ask, "When will you comfort me?"
Though I have become like a wineskin dried by smoke,
I do not forget your statutes.
190   How many days must your servant wait?
When will you execute judgment on my persecutors?
The arrogant have dug pits for me;
they violate your instruction.
All your commands are true;
people persecute me with lies — help me!

They almost ended my life on earth,
but I did not abandon your precepts.
Give me life in accordance with your faithful love,
and I will obey the decree you have spoken.

200 ל *Lamed*

LORD, your word is forever;
it is firmly fixed in heaven.
Your faithfulness is for all generations;
you established the earth, and it stands firm.
Your judgments stand firm today,
for all things are your servants.
If your instruction had not been my delight,
I would have died in my affliction.
I will never forget your precepts,
210 for you have given me life through them.
I am yours; save me,
for I have studied your precepts.
The wicked hope to destroy me,
but I contemplate your decrees.
I have seen a limit to all perfection,
but your command is without limit.

מ *Mem*

How I love your instruction!
It is my meditation all day long.
220 Your command makes me wiser than my enemies,
for it is always with me.
I have more insight than all my teachers
because your decrees are my meditation.
I understand more than the elders
because I obey your precepts.
I have kept my feet from every evil path
to follow your word.
I have not turned from your judgments,
for you yourself have instructed me.

230   How sweet your word is to my taste—
        sweeter than honey in my mouth.
        I gain understanding from your precepts;
        therefore I hate every false way.

ב *Nun*

        Your word is a lamp for my feet
        and a light on my path.
        I have solemnly sworn
        to keep your righteous judgments.
        I am severely afflicted;
240   LORD, give me life according to your word.
        LORD, please accept my freewill offerings of praise,
        and teach me your judgments.
        My life is constantly in danger,
        yet I do not forget your instruction.
        The wicked have set a trap for me,
        but I have not wandered from your precepts.
        I have your decrees as a heritage forever;
        indeed, they are the joy of my heart.
        I am resolved to obey your statutes
250   to the very end.

ס *Samek*

        I hate those who are double-minded,
        but I love your instruction.
        You are my shelter and my shield;
        I put my hope in your word.
        Depart from me, you evil ones,
        so that I may obey my God's commands.
        Sustain me as you promised, and I will live;
        do not let me be ashamed of my hope.
260   Sustain me so that I can be safe
        and always be concerned about your statutes.
        You reject all who stray from your statutes,
        for their deceit is a lie.

You remove all the wicked on earth
as if they were dross from metal;
therefore, I love your decrees.
I tremble in awe of you;
I fear your judgments.

ע *Ayin*

270   I have done what is just and right;
do not leave me to my oppressors.
Guarantee your servant's well-being;
do not let the arrogant oppress me.
My eyes grow weary looking for your salvation
and for your righteous promise.
Deal with your servant based on your faithful love;
teach me your statutes.
I am your servant; give me understanding
so that I may know your decrees.
280   It is time for the Lord to act,
for they have violated your instruction.
Since I love your commands
more than gold, even the purest gold,
I carefully follow all your precepts
and hate every false way.

פ *Pe*

Your decrees are wondrous;
therefore I obey them.
The revelation of your words brings light
290   and gives understanding to the inexperienced.
I open my mouth and pant
because I long for your commands.
Turn to me and be gracious to me,
as is your practice toward those who love your name.
Make my steps steady through your promise;
don't let any sin dominate me.
Redeem me from human oppression,

and I will keep your precepts.
Make your face shine on your servant,
and teach me your statutes.
300   My eyes pour out streams of tears
because people do not follow your instruction.

צ *Tsade*

You are righteous, LORD,
and your judgments are just.
The decrees you issue are righteous
and altogether trustworthy.
My anger overwhelms me
because my foes forget your words.
310   Your word is completely pure,
and your servant loves it.
I am insignificant and despised,
but I do not forget your precepts.
Your righteousness is an everlasting righteousness,
and your instruction is true.
Trouble and distress have overtaken me,
but your commands are my delight.
Your decrees are righteous forever.
Give me understanding, and I will live.

320   ק *Qoph*

I call with all my heart; answer me, LORD.
I will obey your statutes.
I call to you; save me,
and I will keep your decrees.
I rise before dawn and cry out for help;
I put my hope in your word.
I am awake through each watch of the night
to meditate on your promise.
In keeping with your faithful love, hear my voice.
330   LORD, give me life in keeping with your justice.
Those who pursue evil plans come near;

they are far from your instruction.
You are near, Lord,
and all your commands are true.
Long ago I learned from your decrees
that you have established them forever.

ר *Resh*

Consider my affliction and rescue me,
for I have not forgotten your instruction.
340 Champion my cause and redeem me;
give me life as you promised.
Salvation is far from the wicked
because they do not study your statutes.
Your compassions are many, Lord;
give me life according to your judgments.
My persecutors and foes are many.
I have not turned from your decrees.
I have seen the disloyal and feel disgust
because they do not keep your word.
350 Consider how I love your precepts;
Lord, give me life according to your faithful love.
The entirety of your word is truth,
each of your righteous judgments endures forever.

שׂ *Sin*/ שׁ *Shin*

Princes have persecuted me without cause,
but my heart fears only your word.
I rejoice over your promise
like one who finds vast treasure.
I hate and abhor falsehood,
360 but I love your instruction.
I praise you seven times a day
for your righteous judgments.
Abundant peace belongs to those
who love your instruction;
nothing makes them stumble.

LORD, I hope for your salvation
and carry out your commands.
I obey your decrees
and love them greatly.
370   I obey your precepts and decrees,
for all my ways are before you.

ת *Taw*

Let my cry reach you, LORD;
give me understanding according to your word.
Let my plea reach you;
rescue me according to your promise.
My lips pour out praise,
for you teach me your statutes.
My tongue sings about your promise,
380   for all your commands are righteous.
May your hand be ready to help me,
for I have chosen your precepts.
I long for your salvation, LORD,
and your instruction is my delight.
Let me live, and I will praise you;
may your judgments help me.
I wander like a lost sheep;
seek your servant,
for I do not forget your commands.

120   A song of ascents.

In my distress I called to the LORD,
and he answered me.
"LORD, rescue me from lying lips
and a deceitful tongue."

What will he give you,
and what will he do to you,
you deceitful tongue?

A warrior's sharp arrows
10   with burning charcoal!

What misery that I have stayed in Meshech,
that I have lived among the tents of Kedar!
I have dwelt too long
with those who hate peace.
I am for peace; but when I speak,
they are for war.

121   A song of ascents.

I lift my eyes toward the mountains.
Where will my help come from?
My help comes from the Lord,
the Maker of heaven and earth.

He will not allow your foot to slip;
your Protector will not slumber.
Indeed, the Protector of Israel
does not slumber or sleep.

10   The Lord protects you;
the Lord is a shelter right by your side.
The sun will not strike you by day
or the moon by night.

The Lord will protect you from all harm;
he will protect your life.
The Lord will protect your coming and going
both now and forever.

122   A song of ascents. Of David.

I rejoiced with those who said to me,
"Let's go to the house of the Lord."
Our feet were standing
within your gates, Jerusalem—

Jerusalem, built as a city should be,
solidly united,
where the tribes, the LORD's tribes, go up
to give thanks to the name of the LORD.
10   (This is an ordinance for Israel.)
There, thrones for judgment are placed,
thrones of the house of David.

Pray for the well-being of Jerusalem:
"May those who love you be secure;
may there be peace within your walls,
security within your fortresses."
Because of my brothers and friends,
I will say, "May peace be in you."
Because of the house of the LORD our God,
20   I will pursue your prosperity.

123   A song of ascents.

I lift my eyes to you,
the one enthroned in heaven.
Like a servant's eyes on his master's hand,
like a servant girl's eyes on her mistress's hand,
so our eyes are on the LORD our God
until he shows us favor.

Show us favor, LORD, show us favor,
for we've had more than enough contempt.
10   We've had more than enough
scorn from the arrogant
and contempt from the proud.

124   A song of ascents. Of David.

If the LORD had not been on our side—
let Israel say—
If the LORD had not been on our side

when people attacked us,
then they would have swallowed us alive
in their burning anger against us.
Then the water would have engulfed us;
the torrent would have swept over us;
10   the raging water would have swept over us.

Blessed be the LORD,
who has not let us be ripped apart by their teeth.
We have escaped like a bird from the hunter's net;
the net is torn, and we have escaped.
Our help is in the name of the LORD,
the Maker of heaven and earth.

125   A song of ascents.

Those who trust in the LORD are like Mount Zion
It cannot be shaken; it remains forever.
The mountains surround Jerusalem
and the LORD surrounds his people,
both now and forever.

The scepter of the wicked will not remain
over the land allotted to the righteous,
so that the righteous will not apply their hands to injustice.
10   Do what is good, LORD, to the good,
to those whose hearts are upright.
But as for those who turn aside to crooked ways,
the LORD will banish them with the evildoers.

Peace be with Israel.

126   A song of ascents.

When the LORD restored the fortunes of Zion,
we were like those who dream.
Our mouths were filled with laughter then,
and our tongues with shouts of joy.

Then they said among the nations,
"The LORD has done great things for them."
The LORD had done great things for us;
we were joyful.

10   Restore our fortunes, LORD,
like watercourses in the Negev.
Those who sow in tears
will reap with shouts of joy.
Though one goes along weeping,
carrying the bag of seed,
he will surely come back with shouts of joy,
carrying his sheaves.

127   **A song of ascents. Of Solomon.**

Unless the LORD builds a house,
its builders labor over it in vain;
unless the LORD watches over a city,
the watchman stays alert in vain.
In vain you get up early and stay up late,
working hard to have enough food —
yes, he gives sleep to the one he loves.

Sons are indeed a heritage from the LORD,
10   offspring, a reward.
Like arrows in the hand of a warrior
are the sons born in one's youth.
Happy is the man who has filled his quiver with them.
They will never be put to shame
when they speak with their enemies at the city gate.

128   A song of ascents.

How happy is everyone who fears the LORD,
who walks in his ways!
You will surely eat
what your hands have worked for.

You will be happy,
and it will go well for you.
Your wife will be like a fruitful vine
within your house,
10   your children, like young olive trees
around your table.
In this very way
the man who fears the Lord
will be blessed.

May the Lord bless you from Zion,
so that you will see the prosperity of Jerusalem
all the days of your life
and will see your children's children!

20   Peace be with Israel.

129   A song of ascents.

Since my youth they have often attacked me—
let Israel say—
Since my youth they have often attacked me,
but they have not prevailed against me.
Plowmen plowed over my back;
they made their furrows long.
The Lord is righteous;
he has cut the ropes of the wicked.

10   Let all who hate Zion
be driven back in disgrace.
Let them be like grass on the rooftops,
which withers before it grows up
and can't even fill the hands of the reaper
or the arms of the one who binds sheaves.
Then none who pass by will say,
"May the Lord's blessing be on you.
We bless you in the name of the Lord."

130   A song of ascents.

> Out of the depths I call to you, LORD!
> Lord, listen to my voice;
> let your ears be attentive
> to my cry for help.
>
> LORD, if you kept an account of iniquities,
> Lord, who could stand?
> But with you there is forgiveness,
> so that you may be revered.
>
> I wait for the LORD; I wait
> and put my hope in his word.
> I wait for the Lord
> more than watchmen for the morning—
> more than watchmen for the morning.
>
> Israel, put your hope in the LORD.
> For there is faithful love with the LORD,
> and with him is redemption in abundance.
> And he will redeem Israel
> from all its iniquities.

131   A song of ascents. Of David.

> LORD, my heart is not proud;
> my eyes are not haughty.
> I do not get involved with things
> too great or too wondrous for me.
> Instead, I have calmed and quieted my soul
> like a weaned child with its mother;
> my soul is like a weaned child.
>
> Israel, put your hope in the LORD,
> both now and forever.

132   A song of ascents.

LORD, remember David
and all the hardships he endured,
and how he swore an oath to the LORD,
making a vow to the Mighty One of Jacob:
"I will not enter my house
or get into my bed,
I will not allow my eyes to sleep
or my eyelids to slumber
10   until I find a place for the LORD,
a dwelling for the Mighty One of Jacob."

We heard of the ark in Ephrathah;
we found it in the fields of Jaar.
Let's go to his dwelling place;
let's worship at his footstool.
Rise up, LORD, come to your resting place,
you and your powerful ark.
May your priests be clothed with righteousness,
and may your faithful people shout for joy.
20   For the sake of your servant David,
do not reject your anointed one.

The LORD swore an oath to David,
a promise he will not abandon:
"I will set one of your offspring
on your throne.
If your sons keep my covenant
and my decrees that I will teach them,
their sons will also sit on your throne forever."

For the LORD has chosen Zion;
30   he has desired it for his home:
"This is my resting place forever;
I will make my home here
because I have desired it.
I will abundantly bless its food;

I will satisfy its needy with bread.
I will clothe its priests with salvation,
and its faithful people will shout for joy.
There I will make a horn grow for David;
I have prepared a lamp for my anointed one.
40   I will clothe his enemies with shame,
but the crown he wears will be glorious."

133   A song of ascents. Of David.

How delightfully good
when brothers live together in harmony!
It is like fine oil on the head,
running down on the beard,
running down Aaron's beard
onto his robes.
It is like the dew of Hermon
falling on the mountains of Zion.
10   For there the LORD has appointed the blessing—
life forevermore.

134   A song of ascents.

Now bless the LORD,
all you servants of the LORD
who stand in the LORD's house at night!
Lift up your hands in the holy place
and bless the LORD!

May the LORD,
Maker of heaven and earth,
bless you from Zion.

135   Praise the name of the LORD.
Give praise, you servants of the LORD
who stand in the house of the LORD,
in the courts of the house of our God.
Praise the LORD, for the LORD is good;

sing praise to his name, for it is delightful.
For the Lord has chosen Jacob for himself,
Israel as his treasured possession.

For I know that the Lord is great;
our Lord is greater than all gods.
The Lord does whatever he pleases
in heaven and on earth,
in the seas and all the depths.
He causes the clouds to rise from the ends of the earth.
He makes lightning for the rain
and brings the wind from his storehouses.

He struck down the firstborn of Egypt,
both people and animals.
He sent signs and wonders against you, Egypt,
against Pharaoh and all his officials.
He struck down many nations
and slaughtered mighty kings:
Sihon king of the Amorites,
Og king of Bashan,
and all the kings of Canaan.
He gave their land as an inheritance,
an inheritance to his people Israel.

Lord, your name endures forever,
your reputation, Lord,
through all generations.
For the Lord will vindicate his people
and have compassion on his servants.

The idols of the nations are of silver and gold,
made by human hands.
They have mouths but cannot speak,
eyes, but cannot see.
They have ears but cannot hear;
indeed, there is no breath in their mouths.

Those who make them are just like them,
40   as are all who trust in them.

House of Israel, bless the LORD!
House of Aaron, bless the LORD!
House of Levi, bless the LORD!
You who revere the LORD, bless the LORD!
Blessed be the LORD from Zion;
he dwells in Jerusalem.
Hallelujah!

136   Give thanks to the LORD, for he is good.
His faithful love endures forever.
Give thanks to the God of gods.
His faithful love endures forever.
Give thanks to the Lord of lords.
His faithful love endures forever.
He alone does great wonders.
His faithful love endures forever.
He made the heavens skillfully.
10   His faithful love endures forever.
He spread the land on the waters.
His faithful love endures forever.
He made the great lights:
His faithful love endures forever.
the sun to rule by day,
His faithful love endures forever.
the moon and stars to rule by night.
His faithful love endures forever.
He struck the firstborn of the Egyptians
20   His faithful love endures forever.
and brought Israel out from among them
His faithful love endures forever.
with a strong hand and outstretched arm.
His faithful love endures forever.
He divided the Red Sea
His faithful love endures forever.
and led Israel through,

His faithful love endures forever.
but hurled Pharaoh and his army into the Red Sea.
His faithful love endures forever.
30   He led his people in the wilderness.
His faithful love endures forever.
He struck down great kings
His faithful love endures forever.
and slaughtered famous kings—
His faithful love endures forever.
Sihon king of the Amorites
His faithful love endures forever.
and Og king of Bashan—
40   His faithful love endures forever.
and gave their land as an inheritance,
His faithful love endures forever.
an inheritance to Israel his servant.
His faithful love endures forever.
He remembered us in our humiliation
His faithful love endures forever.
and rescued us from our foes.
His faithful love endures forever.
He gives food to every creature.
50   His faithful love endures forever.
Give thanks to the God of heaven!
His faithful love endures forever.

137   By the rivers of Babylon—
there we sat down and wept
when we remembered Zion.
There we hung up our lyres
on the poplar trees,
for our captors there asked us for songs,
and our tormentors, for rejoicing:
"Sing us one of the songs of Zion."

How can we sing the LORD's song
10   on foreign soil?
If I forget you, Jerusalem,

may my right hand forget its skill.
May my tongue stick to the roof of my mouth
if I do not remember you,
if I do not exalt Jerusalem as my greatest joy!

Remember, LORD, what the Edomites said
that day at Jerusalem:
"Destroy it! Destroy it
down to its foundations!"
20   Daughter Babylon, doomed to destruction,
happy is the one who pays you back
what you have done to us.
Happy is he who takes your little ones
and dashes them against the rocks.

138   Of David.

I will give you thanks with all my heart;
I will sing your praise before the heavenly beings.
I will bow down toward your holy temple
and give thanks to your name
for your constant love and truth.
You have exalted your name
and your promise above everything else.
On the day I called, you answered me;
10   you increased strength within me.

All the kings on earth will give you thanks, LORD,
when they hear what you have promised.
They will sing of the LORD's ways,
for the LORD's glory is great.
Though the LORD is exalted,
he takes note of the humble;
but he knows the haughty from a distance.

If I walk into the thick of danger,
you will preserve my life
20   from the anger of my enemies.

You will extend your hand;
your right hand will save me.
The LORD will fulfill his purpose for me.
LORD, your faithful love endures forever;
do not abandon the work of your hands.

139 For the choir director. A psalm of David.

LORD, you have searched me and known me.
You know when I sit down and when I stand up;
you understand my thoughts from far away.
You observe my travels and my rest;
you are aware of all my ways.
Before a word is on my tongue,
you know all about it, LORD.
You have encircled me;
you have placed your hand on me.
This wondrous knowledge is beyond me.
It is lofty; I am unable to reach it.

Where can I go to escape your Spirit?
Where can I flee from your presence?
If I go up to heaven, you are there;
if I make my bed in Sheol, you are there.
If I fly on the wings of the dawn
and settle down on the western horizon,
even there your hand will lead me;
your right hand will hold on to me.
If I say, "Surely the darkness will hide me,
and the light around me will be night"—
even the darkness is not dark to you.
The night shines like the day;
darkness and light are alike to you.

For it was you who created my inward parts;
you knit me together in my mother's womb.
I will praise you
because I have been remarkably and wondrously made.

30   Your works are wondrous,
and I know this very well.
My bones were not hidden from you
when I was made in secret,
when I was formed in the depths of the earth.
Your eyes saw me when I was formless;
all my days were written in your book and planned
before a single one of them began.

God, how precious your thoughts are to me;
how vast their sum is!
40   If I counted them,
they would outnumber the grains of sand;
when I wake up, I am still with you.

God, if only you would kill the wicked—
you bloodthirsty men, stay away from me—
who invoke you deceitfully.
Your enemies swear by you falsely.
Lord, don't I hate those who hate you,
and detest those who rebel against you?
I hate them with extreme hatred;
50   I consider them my enemies.

Search me, God, and know my heart;
test me and know my concerns.
See if there is any offensive way in me;
lead me in the everlasting way.

140   For the choir director. A psalm of David.

Rescue me, Lord, from evil men.
Keep me safe from violent men
who plan evil in their hearts.
They stir up wars all day long.
They make their tongues
as sharp as a snake's bite;
    viper's venom is under their lips.*Selah*

10 Protect me, Lord,
from the power of the wicked.
Keep me safe from violent men
who plan to make me stumble.
The proud hide a trap with ropes for me;
they spread a net along the path
and set snares for me.*Selah*

I say to the Lord, "You are my God."
Listen, Lord, to my cry for help.
Lord, my Lord, my strong Savior,
20 you shield my head on the day of battle.
Lord, do not grant the desires of the wicked;
do not let them achieve their goals.
Otherwise, they will become proud.*Selah*

When those who surround me rise up,
may the trouble their lips cause overwhelm them.
Let hot coals fall on them.
Let them be thrown into the fire,
into the abyss, never again to rise.
Do not let a slanderer stay in the land.
30 Let evil relentlessly hunt down a violent man.

I know that the Lord upholds
the just cause of the poor,
justice for the needy.
Surely the righteous will praise your name;
the upright will live in your presence.

141 A psalm of David.

Lord, I call on you; hurry to help me.
Listen to my voice when I call on you.
May my prayer be set before you as incense,
the raising of my hands as the evening offering.

LORD, set up a guard for my mouth;
keep watch at the door of my lips.
Do not let my heart turn to any evil thing
or perform wicked acts with evildoers.
10 Do not let me feast on their delicacies.
Let the righteous one strike me—
it is an act of faithful love;
let him rebuke me—
it is oil for my head;
let me not refuse it.
Even now my prayer is against
the evil acts of the wicked.
When their rulers will be thrown off
the sides of a cliff,
20 the people will listen to my words,
for they are pleasing.

As when one plows and breaks up the soil,
turning up rocks,
so our bones have been scattered
at the mouth of Sheol.

But my eyes look to you, LORD, my Lord.
I seek refuge in you; do not let me die.
Protect me from the trap they have set for me,
and from the snares of evildoers.
30 Let the wicked fall into their own nets,
while I pass by safely.

142 A *Maskil* of David. When he was in the cave. A prayer.

I cry aloud to the LORD;
I plead aloud to the LORD for mercy.
I pour out my complaint before him;
I reveal my trouble to him.
Although my spirit is weak within me,
you know my way.

Along this path I travel
    they have hidden a trap for me.
10   Look to the right and see:
    no one stands up for me;
    there is no refuge for me;
    no one cares about me.

    I cry to you, LORD;
    I say, "You are my shelter,
    my portion in the land of the living."
    Listen to my cry,
    for I am very weak.
    Rescue me from those who pursue me,
20   for they are too strong for me.
    Free me from prison
    so that I can praise your name.
    The righteous will gather around me
    because you deal generously with me.

143   A psalm of David.

    LORD, hear my prayer.
    In your faithfulness listen to my plea,
    and in your righteousness answer me.
    Do not bring your servant into judgment,
    for no one alive is righteous in your sight.

    For the enemy has pursued me,
    crushing me to the ground,
    making me live in darkness
10   like those long dead.
    My spirit is weak within me;
    my heart is overcome with dismay.

    I remember the days of old;
    I meditate on all you have done;
    I reflect on the work of your hands.

I spread out my hands to you;
    I am like parched land before you.*Selah*

Answer me quickly, LORD;
my spirit fails.
20   Don't hide your face from me,
or I will be like those
going down to the Pit.
Let me experience
your faithful love in the morning,
for I trust in you.
Reveal to me the way I should go
because I appeal to you.
Rescue me from my enemies, LORD;
I come to you for protection.
30   Teach me to do your will,
for you are my God.
May your gracious Spirit
lead me on level ground.

For your name's sake, LORD,
let me live.
In your righteousness deliver me from trouble,
and in your faithful love destroy my enemies.
Wipe out all those who attack me,
for I am your servant.

144   Of David.

Blessed be the LORD, my rock
who trains my hands for battle
and my fingers for warfare.
He is my faithful love and my fortress,
my stronghold and my deliverer.
He is my shield, and I take refuge in him;
he subdues my people under me.

Lord, what is a human that you care for him,
a son of man that you think of him?
A human is like a breath;
his days are like a passing shadow.

Lord, part your heavens and come down.
Touch the mountains, and they will smoke.
Flash your lightning and scatter the foe;
shoot your arrows and rout them.
Reach down from on high;
rescue me from deep water, and set me free
from the grasp of foreigners
whose mouths speak lies,
whose right hands are deceptive.

God, I will sing a new song to you;
I will play on a ten-stringed harp for you
the one who gives victory to kings,
who frees his servant David
from the deadly sword.
Set me free and rescue me
from foreigners
whose mouths speak lies,
whose right hands are deceptive.

Then our sons will be like plants
nurtured in their youth,
our daughters, like corner pillars
that are carved in the palace style.
Our storehouses will be full,
supplying all kinds of produce;
our flocks will increase by thousands
and tens of thousands in our open fields.
Our cattle will be well fed.
There will be no breach in the walls,
no going into captivity,
and no cry of lament in our public squares.

Happy are the people with such blessings.
Happy are the people whose God is the Lord.

145   A hymn of David.

I exalt you, my God the King,
and bless your name forever and ever.
I will bless you every day;
I will praise your name forever and ever.

The Lord is great and is highly praised;
his greatness is unsearchable.
One generation will declare your works to the next
and will proclaim your mighty acts.
10   I will speak of your splendor and glorious majesty
and your wondrous works.
They will proclaim the power of your awe-inspiring acts,
and I will declare your greatness.
They will give a testimony of your great goodness
and will joyfully sing of your righteousness.

The Lord is gracious and compassionate,
slow to anger and great in faithful love.
The Lord is good to everyone;
his compassion rests on all he has made.
20   All you have made will thank you, Lord;
the faithful will bless you.
They will speak of the glory of your kingdom
and will declare your might,
informing all people of your mighty acts
and of the glorious splendor of your kingdom.
Your kingdom is an everlasting kingdom;
your rule is for all generations.
The Lord is faithful in all his words
and gracious in all his actions.

30   The Lord helps all who fall;
he raises up all who are oppressed.

All eyes look to you,
and you give them their food at the proper time.
You open your hand
and satisfy the desire of every living thing.

The LORD is righteous in all his ways
and faithful in all his acts.
The LORD is near all who call out to him,
all who call out to him with integrity.
40   He fulfills the desires of those who fear him;
he hears their cry for help and saves them.
The LORD guards all those who love him,
but he destroys all the wicked.
My mouth will declare the LORD's praise;
let every living thing
bless his holy name forever and ever.

146   Hallelujah!
My soul, praise the LORD.
I will praise the LORD all my life;
I will sing to my God as long as I live.

Do not trust in nobles,
in a son of man, who cannot save.
When his breath leaves him,
he returns to the ground;
on that day his plans die.

10   Happy is the one whose help is the God of Jacob,
whose hope is in the LORD his God,
the Maker of heaven and earth,
the sea and everything in them.
He remains faithful forever,
executing justice for the exploited
and giving food to the hungry.
The LORD frees prisoners.
The LORD opens the eyes of the blind.
The LORD raises up those who are oppressed.

20   The LORD loves the righteous.
The LORD protects resident aliens
and helps the fatherless and the widow,
but he frustrates the ways of the wicked.

The LORD reigns forever;
Zion, your God reigns for all generations.
Hallelujah!

147   Hallelujah!
How good it is to sing to our God,
for praise is pleasant and lovely.

The LORD rebuilds Jerusalem;
he gathers Israel's exiled people.
He heals the brokenhearted
and bandages their wounds.
He counts the number of the stars;
he gives names to all of them.
10   Our Lord is great, vast in power;
his understanding is infinite.
The LORD helps the oppressed
but brings the wicked to the ground.

Sing to the LORD with thanksgiving;
play the lyre to our God,
who covers the sky with clouds,
prepares rain for the earth,
and causes grass to grow on the hills.
He provides the animals with their food,
20   and the young ravens what they cry for.

He is not impressed by the strength of a horse;
he does not value the power of a warrior.
The LORD values those who fear him,
those who put their hope in his faithful love.

Exalt the LORD, Jerusalem;
praise your God, Zion!
For he strengthens the bars of your city gates
and blesses your children within you.
He endows your territory with prosperity;
30   he satisfies you with the finest wheat.

He sends his command throughout the earth;
his word runs swiftly.
He spreads snow like wool;
he scatters frost like ashes;
he throws his hailstones like crumbs.
Who can withstand his cold?
He sends his word and melts them;
he unleashes his winds, and the water flows.

He declares his word to Jacob,
40   his statutes and judgments to Israel.
He has not done this for every nation;
they do not know his judgments.
Hallelujah!

148   Hallelujah!
Praise the LORD from the heavens;
praise him in the heights.
Praise him, all his angels;
praise him, all his heavenly armies.
Praise him, sun and moon;
praise him, all you shining stars.
Praise him, highest heavens,
and you waters above the heavens.
10   Let them praise the name of the LORD,
for he commanded, and they were created.
He set them in position forever and ever;
he gave an order that will never pass away.

Praise the LORD from the earth,
all sea monsters and ocean depths,

lightning and hail, snow and cloud,
stormy wind that executes his command,
mountains and all hills,
fruit trees and all cedars,
20   wild animals and all cattle,
creatures that crawl and flying birds,
kings of the earth and all peoples,
princes and all judges of the earth,
young men as well as young women,
old and young together.
Let them praise the name of the LORD,
for his name alone is exalted.
His majesty covers heaven and earth.
He has raised up a horn for his people,
30   resulting in praise to all his faithful ones,
to the Israelites, the people close to him.
Hallelujah!

149   Hallelujah!
Sing to the LORD a new song,
his praise in the assembly of the faithful.
Let Israel celebrate its Maker;
let the children of Zion rejoice in their King.
Let them praise his name with dancing
and make music to him with tambourine and lyre.
For the LORD takes pleasure in his people;
he adorns the humble with salvation.
10   Let the faithful celebrate in triumphal glory;
let them shout for joy on their beds.

Let the exaltation of God be in their mouths
and a double-edged sword in their hands,
inflicting vengeance on the nations
and punishment on the peoples,
binding their kings with chains
and their dignitaries with iron shackles,
carrying out the judgment decreed against them.

This honor is for all his faithful people.
Hallelujah!

150 Hallelujah!
Praise God in his sanctuary.
Praise him in his mighty expanse.
Praise him for his powerful acts;
praise him for his abundant greatness.

Praise him with the blast of a ram's horn;
praise him with harp and lyre.
Praise him with tambourine and dance;
praise him with strings and flute.
10   Praise him with resounding cymbals;
praise him with clashing cymbals.

Let everything that breathes praise the LORD.
Hallelujah!

Introduction to Job

Ryan Stokes

The book of Job is one of the most intriguing books in the HS. The story of the innocent Job's extreme suffering and his desperate quest to make sense of it has captured the sympathy and imagination of readers for millennia. Unfortunately, the book of Job is also arguably the most challenging of the HS to interpret. The Hebrew in which the book is written is notoriously difficult to translate. Even more perplexing is the way that different portions of the book seem to stand in considerable tension with one another. This tension is perhaps best exemplified by the differing ways that the book portrays the man Job.

The book's prologue (1.1–2.21) introduces the character of Job as one who is blameless, but who nevertheless loses all that he has in a series of tragedies. At first, Job dutifully accepts his suffering from the hand of Yahweh. In the center portion of the work, Job converses with his friends about his situation and attempts to vindicate his own righteousness (3.1–42.12). In this section, in contrast with the earlier portion of the book, Job boldly gives vent to his dissatisfaction with Yahweh's governance of humankind. Job's misguided audacity eventually earns Yahweh's rebuke. In the conclusion (42.13–30), the narrative supposes that Job has spoken accurately about Yahweh, and Job is rewarded for his faithful patience. Differences such as these have led many scholars to hypothesize that the book of Job is not the work of a single author, but was written by multiple individuals who wrote at different times and contributed complementary perspectives to the work.

Whether Job was written all at once by one author or was composed over a lengthy period of time by different writers, interpreters of HS must keep a few things in mind as they read Job. The book of Job, as it is incorporated into the HS, is supposed to be a single, coherent story. Consequently, those who read Job as Scripture should make every effort to comprehend the story as a whole rather than simply observe the tension among its various components. The book of Job, nevertheless, takes the form of conversations that present multiple, complementary perspectives. This complexity is one of the reasons for the book of Job's enduring value.

Another feature of the book of Job that has confounded interpreters is the role that Satan plays in the story. The biblical portrait of Satan is not as simple as is often assumed. The Scriptures actually portray Satan in diverse ways. Many passages, especially in the NT, describe Satan as a rebel who opposes Yahweh's plan. Others, however, speak of Satan as one who takes orders from Yahweh. This latter portrayal is what we find in Job. In fact, the Hebrew of Job calls this figure not by the name "Satan," but by the title "the Satan," which means something akin to "the Attacker" or perhaps even "the Executioner." The book of Job suggests that "the Satan" is Yahweh's attacker, the one who is responsible for punishing sinners on Yahweh's behalf. In this particular story, Yahweh grants Satan special permission to attack Job, despite Job's innocence. Like the book of Job, the biblical figure of the Satan is a complex one, and appreciating this complexity positions one better to understand the message of the book.

When dealing with a multifaceted matter, such as the problem of evil, a simplistic, "one-size-fits-all" solution would be entirely insufficient and misleading. Only a book that deals in a complex manner with the issue, offering a variety of approaches to understanding it, can deal adequately with such a problem. Although the book of Job offers readers a variety of perspectives concerning suffering, Job's story leaves readers with no doubt that even those who "fear the Lord" will at times experience suffering. While righteous living does not guarantee freedom from suffering, the example of Job encourages readers to reflect on the nature of Yahweh and to live wisely as they suffer.

Outline

1. Narrative Introduction (1.1–2.21)
2. Conversations about Job's Suffering (3.1–42.12)
   a. Job's Conversations with His Friends (3.1–31.84)
   b. Elihu Confronts Job (32.1–37.53)
   c. Job's Conversation with Yahweh (38.1–42.12)
3. Narrative Conclusion (42.13–30)

Suggested Resources

Balentine, Samuel E. *Job*. Smyth & Helwys Bible Commentary. Macon, GA: Smyth & Helwys, 2016.

Longman, Tremper, III. *Job*. Baker Commentary on the Old Testament Wisdom and Psalms. Grand Rapids: Baker Academics, 2012.

Seow, C. L. *Job 1–21: Interpretation and Commentary*. Illuminations. Grand Rapids: Eerdmans, 2013.

Walton, John H. *Job*. NIV Application Commentary. Grand Rapids: Zondervan, 2012.

Wilson, Lindsay. *Job*. Two Horizons Old Testament Commentary. Grand Rapids: Eerdmans, 2015.

Job

1 There was a man in the country of Uz named Job. He was a man of complete integrity, who feared God and turned away from evil. He had seven sons and three daughters. His estate included seven thousand sheep and goats, three thousand camels, five hundred yoke of oxen, five hundred female donkeys, and a very large number of servants. Job was the greatest man among all the people of the east.

His sons used to take turns having banquets at their homes. They would send an invitation to their three sisters to eat and drink with them. Whenever a round of banqueting was over, Job would send for his children and purify them, rising early in the morning to offer burnt offerings for all of them. For Job thought, "Perhaps my children have sinned, having cursed God in their hearts." This was Job's regular practice.

10 One day the sons of God came to present themselves before the LORD, and Satan also came with them. The LORD asked Satan, "Where have you come from?"

"From roaming through the earth," Satan answered him, "and walking around on it."

Then the LORD said to Satan, "Have you considered my servant Job? No one else on earth is like him, a man of perfect integrity, who fears God and turns away from evil."

Satan answered the LORD, "Does Job fear God for nothing? Haven't you placed a hedge around him, his household, and everything he owns? You have blessed the work of his hands, and his possessions have increased in the land. But stretch out your hand and strike everything he owns, and he will surely curse you to your face."

"Very well," the LORD told Satan, "everything he owns is in your power. However, do not lay a 20 hand on Job himself." So Satan left the LORD's presence.

One day when Job's sons and daughters were eating and drinking wine in their oldest brother's house, a messenger came to Job and reported, "While the oxen were plowing and the donkeys grazing nearby, the Sabeans swooped down and took them away. They struck down the servants with the sword, and I alone have escaped to tell you!"

He was still speaking when another messenger came and reported, "God's fire fell from heaven. It burned the sheep and the servants and devoured them, and I alone have escaped to tell you!"

That messenger was still speaking when yet another came and reported, "The Chaldeans formed three bands, made a raid on the camels, and took them away. They struck down the servants with the sword, and I alone have escaped to tell you!"

30 He was still speaking when another messenger came and reported, "Your sons and daughters were eating and drinking wine in their oldest brother's house. Suddenly a powerful wind swept in

from the desert and struck the four corners of the house. It collapsed on the young people so that they died, and I alone have escaped to tell you!"

Then Job stood up, tore his robe, and shaved his head. He fell to the ground and worshiped, saying:

> Naked I came from my mother's womb,
> and naked I will leave this life.
> The LORD gives, and the LORD takes away.
> Blessed be the name of the LORD.

40   Throughout all this Job did not sin or blame God for anything.

2 One day the sons of God came again to present themselves before the LORD, and Satan also came with them to present himself before the LORD. The LORD asked Satan, "Where have you come from?"

"From roaming through the earth," Satan answered him, "and walking around on it."

Then the LORD said to Satan, "Have you considered my servant Job? No one else on earth is like him, a man of perfect integrity, who fears God and turns away from evil. He still retains his integrity, even though you incited me against him, to destroy him for no good reason."

"Skin for skin!" Satan answered the LORD. "A man will give up everything he owns in exchange for his life. But stretch out your hand and strike his flesh and bones, and he will surely curse you to your face."

10   "Very well," the LORD told Satan, "he is in your power; only spare his life." So Satan left the LORD's presence and infected Job with terrible boils from the soles of his feet to the top of his head. Then Job took a piece of broken pottery to scrape himself while he sat among the ashes.

His wife said to him, "Are you still holding on to your integrity? Curse God and die!"

"You speak as a foolish woman speaks," he told her. "Should we accept only good from God and not adversity?" Throughout all this Job did not sin in what he said.

Now when Job's three friends—Eliphaz the Temanite, Bildad the Shuhite, and Zophar the Naamathite—heard about all this adversity that had happened to him, each of them came from his home. They met together to go and sympathize with him and comfort him. When they looked from a distance, they could barely recognize him. They wept aloud, and each man tore his robe

20   and threw dust into the air and on his head. Then they sat on the ground with him seven days and nights, but no one spoke a word to him because they saw that his suffering was very intense.

3 After this, Job began to speak and cursed the day he was born. He said:

> May the day I was born perish,
> and the night that said,

"A boy is conceived."
If only that day had turned to darkness!
May God above not care about it,
or light shine on it.
May darkness and gloom reclaim it,
and a cloud settle over it.

10 May what darkens the day terrify it.
If only darkness had taken that night away!
May it not appear among the days of the year
or be listed in the calendar.
Yes, may that night be barren;
may no joyful shout be heard in it.
Let those who curse days
condemn it,
those who are ready to rouse Leviathan.
May its morning stars grow dark.

20 May it wait for daylight but have none;
may it not see the breaking of dawn.
For that night did not shut
the doors of my mother's womb,
and hide sorrow from my eyes.

Why was I not stillborn;
why didn't I die as I came from the womb?
Why did the knees receive me,
and why were there breasts for me to nurse?
Now I would certainly be lying down in peace;

30 I would be asleep.
Then I would be at rest
with the kings and counselors of the earth,
who rebuilt ruined cities for themselves,
or with princes who had gold,
who filled their houses with silver.
Or why was I not hidden like a miscarried child,
like infants who never see daylight?
There the wicked cease to make trouble,
and there the weary find rest.

40 The captives are completely at rest;

they do not hear a taskmaster's voice.
Both small and great are there,
and the slave is set free from his master.

Why is light given to one burdened with grief,
and life to those whose existence is bitter,
who wait for death, but it does not come,
and search for it more than for hidden treasure,
who are filled with much joy
and are glad when they reach the grave?

50 Why is life given to a man whose path is hidden,
whom God has hedged in?
I sigh when food is put before me,
and my groans pour out like water.
For the thing I feared has overtaken me,
and what I dreaded has happened to me.
I cannot relax or be calm;
I have no rest, for turmoil has come.

First Series of Speeches

4 Then Eliphaz the Temanite replied:
Should anyone try to speak with you
when you are exhausted?
Yet who can keep from speaking?
Indeed, you have instructed many
and have strengthened weak hands.
Your words have steadied the one who was stumbling
and braced the knees that were buckling.
But now that this has happened to you,
10 you have become exhausted.
It strikes you, and you are dismayed.
Isn't your piety your confidence,
and the integrity of your life your hope?
Consider: Who has perished when he was innocent?
Where have the honest been destroyed?
In my experience, those who plow injustice
and those who sow trouble reap the same.

They perish at a single blast from God
and come to an end by the breath of his nostrils.

20 The lion may roar and the fierce lion growl,
but the teeth of young lions are broken.
The strong lion dies if it catches no prey,
and the cubs of the lioness are scattered.

A word was brought to me in secret;
my ears caught a whisper of it.
Among unsettling thoughts from visions in the night,
when deep sleep comes over men,
fear and trembling came over me
and made all my bones shake.

30 I felt a draft on my face,
and the hair on my body stood up.
A figure stood there,
but I could not recognize its appearance;
a form loomed before my eyes.
I heard a whispering voice:
"Can a mortal be righteous before God?
Can a man be more pure than his Maker?"
If God puts no trust in his servants
and he charges his angels with foolishness,

40 how much more those who dwell in clay houses,
whose foundation is in the dust,
who are crushed like a moth!
They are smashed to pieces from dawn to dusk;
they perish forever while no one notices.
Are their tent cords not pulled up?
They die without wisdom.

5 Call out! Will anyone answer you?
Which of the holy ones will you turn to?
For anger kills a fool,
and jealousy slays the gullible.
I have seen a fool taking root,
but I immediately pronounced a curse on his home.
His children are far from safety.

They are crushed at the city gate,
with no one to rescue them.
The hungry consume his harvest,
even taking it out of the thorns.
The thirsty pant for his children's wealth.
For distress does not grow out of the soil,
and trouble does not sprout from the ground.
But humans are born for trouble
as surely as sparks fly upward.

However, if I were you, I would appeal to God
and would present my case to him.
He does great and unsearchable things,
wonders without number.
He gives rain to the earth
and sends water to the fields.
He sets the lowly on high,
and mourners are lifted to safety.
He frustrates the schemes of the crafty
so that they achieve no success.
He traps the wise in their craftiness
so that the plans of the deceptive
are quickly brought to an end.
They encounter darkness by day,
and they grope at noon
as if it were night.
He saves the needy from their sharp words
and from the clutches of the powerful.
So the poor have hope,
and injustice shuts its mouth.
See how happy is the person whom God corrects;
so do not reject the discipline of the Almighty.
For he wounds but he also bandages;
he strikes, but his hands also heal.
He will rescue you from six calamities;
no harm will touch you in seven.
In famine he will redeem you from death,
and in battle, from the power of the sword.

You will be safe from slander
and not fear destruction when it comes.
You will laugh at destruction and hunger
and not fear the land's wild creatures.
For you will have a covenant with the stones of the field,
and the wild animals will be at peace with you.
You will know that your tent is secure,
and nothing will be missing when you inspect your home.
You will also know that your offspring will be many
and your descendants like the grass of the earth.
You will approach the grave in full vigor,
as a stack of sheaves is gathered in its season.

We have investigated this, and it is true!
Hear it and understand it for yourself.

6 Then Job answered:
If only my grief could be weighed
and my devastation placed with it on the scales.
For then it would outweigh the sand of the seas!
That is why my words are rash.
Surely the arrows of the Almighty have pierced me;
my spirit drinks their poison.
God's terrors are arrayed against me.
Does a wild donkey bray over fresh grass
or an ox low over its fodder?
Is bland food eaten without salt?
Is there flavor in an egg white?
I refuse to touch them;
they are like contaminated food.

If only my request would be granted
and God would provide what I hope for:
that he would decide to crush me,
to unleash his power and cut me off!
It would still bring me comfort,
and I would leap for joy in unrelenting pain
that I have not denied the words of the Holy One.

What strength do I have, that I should continue to hope?
What is my future, that I should be patient?
Is my strength that of stone,
or my flesh made of bronze?
Since I cannot help myself,
the hope for success has been banished from me.

A despairing man should receive loyalty from his friends,
even if he abandons the fear of the Almighty.
30 My brothers are as treacherous as a wadi,
as seasonal streams that overflow
and become darkened because of ice,
and the snow melts into them.
The wadis evaporate in warm weather;
they disappear from their channels in hot weather.
Caravans turn away from their routes,
go up into the desert, and perish.
The caravans of Tema look for these streams.
The traveling merchants of Sheba hope for them.
40 They are ashamed because they had been confident of finding water.
When they arrive there, they are disappointed.
So this is what you have now become to me.
When you see something dreadful, you are afraid.
Have I ever said, "Give me something"
or "Pay a bribe for me from your wealth"
or "Deliver me from the enemy's hand"
or "Redeem me from the hand of the ruthless"?

Teach me, and I will be silent.
Help me understand what I did wrong.
50 How painful honest words can be!
But what does your rebuke prove?
Do you think that you can disprove my words
or that a despairing man's words are mere wind?
No doubt you would cast lots for a fatherless child
and negotiate a price to sell your friend.

But now, please look at me;
I will not lie to your face.
Reconsider; don't be unjust.
Reconsider; my righteousness is still the issue.
60 Is there injustice on my tongue
or can my palate not taste disaster?

7 Isn't each person consigned to forced labor on earth?
Are not his days like those of a hired worker?
Like a slave he longs for shade;
like a hired worker he waits for his pay.
So I have been made to inherit months of futility,
and troubled nights have been assigned to me.
When I lie down I think,
"When will I get up?"
But the evening drags on endlessly,
10 and I toss and turn until dawn.
My flesh is clothed with maggots and encrusted with dirt.
My skin forms scabs and then oozes.

My days pass more swiftly than a weaver's shuttle;
they come to an end without hope.
Remember that my life is but a breath.
My eye will never again see anything good.
The eye of anyone who looks on me
will no longer see me.
Your eyes will look for me, but I will be gone.
20 As a cloud fades away and vanishes,
so the one who goes down to Sheol will never rise again.
He will never return to his house;
his hometown will no longer remember him.

Therefore I will not restrain my mouth.
I will speak in the anguish of my spirit;
I will complain in the bitterness of my soul.
Am I the sea or a sea monster,
that you keep me under guard?
When I say, "My bed will comfort me,

30 and my couch will ease my complaint,"
then you frighten me with dreams,
and terrify me with visions,
so that I prefer strangling—
death rather than life in this body.
I give up! I will not live forever.
Leave me alone, for my days are a breath.

What is a mere human, that you think so highly of him
and pay so much attention to him?
You inspect him every morning,
40 and put him to the test every moment.
Will you ever look away from me,
or leave me alone long enough to swallow?
If I have sinned, what have I done to you,
Watcher of humanity?
Why have you made me your target,
so that I have become a burden to you?
Why not forgive my sin
and pardon my iniquity?
For soon I will lie down in the grave.
50 You will eagerly seek me, but I will be gone.

8 Then Bildad the Shuhite replied:
How long will you go on saying these things?
Your words are a blast of wind.
Does God pervert justice?
Does the Almighty pervert what is right?
Since your children sinned against him,
he gave them over to their rebellion.
But if you earnestly seek God
and ask the Almighty for mercy,
10 if you are pure and upright,
then he will move even now on your behalf
and restore the home where your righteousness dwells.
Then, even if your beginnings were modest,
your final days will be full of prosperity.

For ask the previous generation,
and pay attention to what their ancestors discovered,
since we were born only yesterday and know nothing.
Our days on earth are but a shadow.
Will they not teach you and tell you
20 and speak from their understanding?
Does papyrus grow where there is no marsh?
Do reeds flourish without water?
While still uncut shoots,
they would dry up quicker than any other plant.
Such is the destiny of all who forget God;
the hope of the godless will perish.
His source of confidence is fragile;
what he trusts in is a spider's web.
He leans on his web, but it doesn't stand firm.
30 He grabs it, but it does not hold up.
He is a well-watered plant in the sunshine;
his shoots spread out over his garden.
His roots are intertwined around a pile of rocks.
He looks for a home among the stones.
If he is uprooted from his place,
it will deny knowing him, saying, "I never saw you."
Surely this is the joy of his way of life;
yet others will sprout from the dust.
Look, God does not reject a person of integrity,
40 and he will not support evildoers.
He will yet fill your mouth with laughter
and your lips with a shout of joy.
Your enemies will be clothed with shame;
the tent of the wicked will no longer exist.

9 Then Job answered:
Yes, I know what you've said is true,
but how can a person be justified before God?
If one wanted to take him to court,
he could not answer God once in a thousand times.
God is wise and all-powerful.
Who has opposed him and come out unharmed?

He removes mountains without their knowledge,
overturning them in his anger.

10 He shakes the earth from its place
so that its pillars tremble.
He commands the sun not to shine
and seals off the stars.
He alone stretches out the heavens
and treads on the waves of the sea.
He makes the stars: the Bear, Orion,
the Pleiades, and the constellations of the southern sky.
He does great and unsearchable things,
wonders without number.

20 If he passed by me, I wouldn't see him;
if he went by, I wouldn't recognize him.
If he snatches something, who can stop him?
Who can ask him, "What are you doing?"
God does not hold back his anger;
Rahab's assistants cringe in fear beneath him!

How then can I answer him
or choose my arguments against him?
Even if I were in the right, I could not answer.
I could only beg my Judge for mercy.

30 If I summoned him and he answered me,
I do not believe he would pay attention to what I said.
He batters me with a whirlwind
and multiplies my wounds without cause.
He doesn't let me catch my breath
but fills me with bitter experiences.
If it is a matter of strength, look, he is the powerful one!
If it is a matter of justice, who can summon him?
Even if I were in the right, my own mouth would condemn me;
if I were blameless, my mouth would declare me guilty.

40 Though I am blameless,
I no longer care about myself;
I renounce my life.
It is all the same. Therefore I say,

"He destroys both the blameless and the wicked."
When catastrophe brings sudden death,
he mocks the despair of the innocent.
The earth is handed over to the wicked;
he blindfolds its judges.
If it isn't he, then who is it?

50 My days fly by faster than a runner;
they flee without seeing any good.
They sweep by like boats made of papyrus,
like an eagle swooping down on its prey.
If I said, "I will forget my complaint,
change my expression, and smile,"
I would still live in terror of all my pains.
I know you will not acquit me.
Since I will be found guilty,
why should I struggle in vain?
60 If I wash myself with snow,
and cleanse my hands with lye,
then you dip me in a pit of mud,
and my own clothes despise me!

For he is not a man like me, that I can answer him,
that we can take each other to court.
There is no mediator between us,
to lay his hand on both of us.
Let him take his rod away from me
so his terror will no longer frighten me.
70 Then I would speak and not fear him.
But that is not the case; I am on my own.

10 I am disgusted with my life.
I will give vent to my complaint
and speak in the bitterness of my soul.
I will say to God,
"Do not declare me guilty!
Let me know why you prosecute me.
Is it good for you to oppress,

to reject the work of your hands,
and favor the plans of the wicked?
10 Do you have eyes of flesh,
or do you see as a human sees?
Are your days like those of a human,
or your years like those of a man,
that you look for my iniquity
and search for my sin,
even though you know that I am not wicked
and that there is no one who can rescue from your power?

"Your hands shaped me and formed me.
Will you now turn and destroy me?
20 Please remember that you formed me like clay.
Will you now return me to dust?
Did you not pour me out like milk
and curdle me like cheese?
You clothed me with skin and flesh,
and wove me together with bones and tendons.
You gave me life and faithful love,
and your care has guarded my life.

"Yet you concealed these thoughts in your heart;
I know that this was your hidden plan:
30 if I sin, you would notice,
and would not acquit me of my iniquity.
If I am wicked, woe to me!
And even if I am righteous, I cannot lift up my head.
I am filled with shame
and have drunk deeply of my affliction.
If I am proud, you hunt me like a lion
and again display your miraculous power against me.
You produce new witnesses against me
and multiply your anger toward me.
40 Hardships assault me, wave after wave.

"Why did you bring me out of the womb?
I should have died and never been seen.

I wish I had never existed
but had been carried from the womb to the grave.
Are my days not few? Stop it!
Leave me alone, so that I can smile a little
before I go to a land of darkness and gloom,
never to return.
It is a land of blackness like the deepest darkness,
50   gloomy and chaotic,
where even the light is like the darkness."

11 Then Zophar the Naamathite replied:
Should this abundance of words go unanswered
and such a talker be acquitted?
Should your babbling put others to silence,
so that you can keep on ridiculing
with no one to humiliate you?
You have said, "My teaching is sound,
and I am pure in your sight."
But if only God would speak
10   and open his lips against you!
He would show you the secrets of wisdom,
for true wisdom has two sides.
Know then that God has chosen to overlook some of your iniquity.

Can you fathom the depths of God
or discover the limits of the Almighty?
They are higher than the heavens—what can you do?
They are deeper than Sheol—what can you know?
Their measure is longer than the earth
and wider than the sea.

20   If he passes by and throws someone in prison
or convenes a court, who can stop him?
Surely he knows which people are worthless.
If he sees iniquity, will he not take note of it?
But a stupid person will gain understanding
as soon as a wild donkey is born a human!

As for you, if you redirect your heart
and spread out your hands to him in prayer—
if there is iniquity in your hand, remove it,
and don't allow injustice to dwell in your tents—
30   then you will hold your head high, free from fault.
You will be firmly established and unafraid.
For you will forget your suffering,
recalling it only as water that has flowed by.
Your life will be brighter than noonday;
its darkness will be like the morning.
You will be confident, because there is hope.
You will look carefully about and lie down in safety.

You will lie down with no one to frighten you,
and many will seek your favor.
40   But the sight of the wicked will fail.
Their way of escape will be cut off,
and their only hope is their last breath.

12 Then Job answered:
No doubt you are the people,
and wisdom will die with you!
But I also have a mind like you;
I am not inferior to you.
Who doesn't know the things you are talking about?

I am a laughingstock to my friends,
by calling on God, who answers me.
The righteous and blameless man is a laughingstock.
10   The one who is at ease holds calamity in contempt
and thinks it is prepared for those whose feet are slipping.
The tents of robbers are safe,
and those who trouble God are secure;
God holds them in his hands.

But ask the animals, and they will instruct you;
ask the birds of the sky, and they will tell you.
Or speak to the earth, and it will instruct you;

let the fish of the sea inform you.
Which of all these does not know
that the hand of the LORD has done this?
The life of every living thing is in his hand,
as well as the breath of all humanity.
Doesn't the ear test words
as the palate tastes food?
Wisdom is found with the elderly,
and understanding comes with long life.

Wisdom and strength belong to God;
counsel and understanding are his.
Whatever he tears down cannot be rebuilt;
whoever he imprisons cannot be released.
When he withholds water, everything dries up,
and when he releases it, it destroys the land.
True wisdom and power belong to him.
The deceived and the deceiver are his.
He leads counselors away barefoot
and makes judges go mad.
He releases the bonds put on by kings
and fastens a belt around their waists.
He leads priests away barefoot
and overthrows established leaders.
He deprives trusted advisers of speech
and takes away the elders' good judgment.
He pours out contempt on nobles
and disarms the strong.
He reveals mysteries from the darkness
and brings the deepest darkness into the light.
He makes nations great, then destroys them;
he enlarges nations, then leads them away.
He deprives the world's leaders of reason,
and makes them wander in a trackless wasteland.
They grope around in darkness without light;
he makes them stagger like a drunkard.

13   Look, my eyes have seen all this;
my ears have heard and understood it.
Everything you know, I also know;
I am not inferior to you.
Yet I prefer to speak to the Almighty
and argue my case before God.
You use lies like plaster;
you are all worthless healers.
If only you would shut up
10   and let that be your wisdom!

Hear now my argument,
and listen to my defense.
Would you testify unjustly on God's behalf
or speak deceitfully for him?
Would you show partiality to him
or argue the case in his defense?
Would it go well if he examined you?
Could you deceive him as you would deceive a man?
Surely he would rebuke you
20   if you secretly showed partiality.
Would God's majesty not terrify you?
Would his dread not fall on you?
Your memorable sayings are proverbs of ash;
your defenses are made of clay.

Be quiet, and I will speak.
Let whatever comes happen to me.
I will put myself at risk
and take my life in my own hands.
Even if he kills me, I will hope in him.
30   I will still defend my ways before him.
Yes, this will result in my deliverance,
for no godless person can appear before him.
Pay close attention to my words;
let my declaration ring in your ears.
Now then, I have prepared my case;
I know that I am right.

Can anyone indict me?
If so, I will be silent and die.

Only grant these two things to me, God,
40   so that I will not have to hide from your presence:
remove your hand from me,
and do not let your terror frighten me.
Then call, and I will answer,
or I will speak, and you can respond to me.
How many iniquities and sins have I committed?
Reveal to me my transgression and sin.
Why do you hide your face
and consider me your enemy?
Will you frighten a wind-driven leaf?
50   Will you chase after dry straw?
For you record bitter accusations against me
and make me inherit the iniquities of my youth.
You put my feet in the stocks
and stand watch over all my paths,
setting a limit for the soles of my feet.

A person wears out like something rotten,
like a moth-eaten garment.

14   Anyone born of woman
is short of days and full of trouble.
He blossoms like a flower, then withers;
he flees like a shadow and does not last.
Do you really take notice of one like this?
Will you bring me into judgment against you?
Who can produce something pure from what is impure?
No one!
Since a person's days are determined
10   and the number of his months depends on you,
and since you have set limits he cannot pass,
look away from him and let him rest
so that he can enjoy his day like a hired worker.

There is hope for a tree:
If it is cut down, it will sprout again,
and its shoots will not die.
If its roots grow old in the ground
and its stump starts to die in the soil,
the scent of water makes it thrive
20   and produce twigs like a sapling.
But a person dies and fades away;
he breathes his last—where is he?
As water disappears from a lake
and a river becomes parched and dry,
so people lie down never to rise again.
They will not wake up until the heavens are no more;
they will not stir from their sleep.

If only you would hide me in Sheol
and conceal me until your anger passes.
30   If only you would appoint a time for me
and then remember me.
When a person dies, will he come back to life?
If so, I would wait all the days of my struggle
until my relief comes.
You would call, and I would answer you.
You would long for the work of your hands.
For then you would count my steps
but would not take note of my sin.
My rebellion would be sealed up in a bag,
40   and you would cover over my iniquity.

But as a mountain collapses and crumbles
and a rock is dislodged from its place,
as water wears away stones
and torrents wash away the soil from the land,
so you destroy a man's hope.
You completely overpower him, and he passes on;
you change his appearance and send him away.
If his sons receive honor, he does not know it;
if they become insignificant, he is unaware of it.

50   He feels only the pain of his own body
     and mourns only for himself.

15   Then Eliphaz the Temanite replied:
         Does a wise man answer with empty counsel
         or fill himself with the hot east wind?
         Should he argue with useless talk
         or with words that serve no good purpose?
         But you even undermine the fear of God
         and hinder meditation before him.
         Your iniquity teaches you what to say,
         and you choose the language of the crafty.
10   Your own mouth condemns you, not I;
         your own lips testify against you.

         Were you the first human ever born,
         or were you brought forth before the hills?
         Do you listen in on the council of God,
         or have a monopoly on wisdom?
         What do you know that we don't?
         What do you understand that is not clear to us?
         Both the gray-haired and the elderly are with us—
         older than your father.
20   Are God's consolations not enough for you,
         even the words that deal gently with you?
         Why has your heart misled you,
         and why do your eyes flash
         as you turn your anger against God
         and allow such words to leave your mouth?

         What is a mere human, that he should be pure,
         or one born of a woman, that he should be righteous?
         If God puts no trust in his holy ones
         and the heavens are not pure in his sight,
30   how much less one who is revolting and corrupt,
         who drinks injustice like water?

Listen to me and I will inform you.
I will describe what I have seen,
what the wise have declared and not concealed,
that came from their ancestors,
to whom alone the land was given
when no foreigner passed among them.
A wicked person writhes in pain all his days,
throughout the number of years reserved for the ruthless.
40 Dreadful sounds fill his ears;
when he is at peace, a robber attacks him.
He doesn't believe he will return from darkness;
he is destined for the sword.
He wanders about for food, asking, "Where is it?"
He knows the day of darkness is at hand.
Trouble and distress terrify him,
overwhelming him like a king prepared for battle.
For he has stretched out his hand against God
and has arrogantly opposed the Almighty.
50 He rushes headlong at him
with his thick, studded shields.
Though his face is covered with fat
and his waistline bulges with it,
he will dwell in ruined cities,
in abandoned houses destined to become piles of rubble.
He will no longer be rich; his wealth will not endure.
His possessions will not increase in the land.
He will not escape from the darkness;
flames will wither his shoots,
60 and by the breath of God's mouth, he will depart.
Let him not put trust in worthless things, being led astray,
for what he gets in exchange will prove worthless.
It will be accomplished before his time,
and his branch will not flourish.
He will be like a vine that drops its unripe grapes
and like an olive tree that sheds its blossoms.
For the company of the godless will have no children,
and fire will consume the tents of those who offer bribes.
They conceive trouble and give birth to evil;

70   their womb prepares deception.

16 Then Job answered:
       I have heard many things like these.
       You are all miserable comforters.
       Is there no end to your empty words?
       What provokes you that you continue testifying?
       If you were in my place I could also talk like you.
       I could string words together against you
       and shake my head at you.
       Instead, I would encourage you with my mouth,
10   and the consolation from my lips would bring relief.

       If I speak, my suffering is not relieved,
       and if I hold back, does any of it leave me?
       Surely he has now exhausted me.
       You have devastated my entire family.
       You have shriveled me up—it has become a witness;
       my frailty rises up against me and testifies to my face.
       His anger tears at me, and he harasses me.
       He gnashes his teeth at me.
       My enemy pierces me with his eyes.
20   They open their mouths against me
       and strike my cheeks with contempt;
       they join themselves together against me.
       God hands me over to the unjust;
       he throws me to the wicked.
       I was at ease, but he shattered me;
       he seized me by the scruff of the neck
       and smashed me to pieces.
       He set me up as his target;
       his archers surround me.
30   He pierces my kidneys without mercy
       and pours my bile on the ground.
       He breaks through my defenses again and again;
       he charges at me like a warrior.

       I have sewn sackcloth over my skin;

I have buried my strength in the dust.
My face has grown red with weeping,
and darkness covers my eyes,
although my hands are free from violence
and my prayer is pure.

40   Earth, do not cover my blood;
may my cry for help find no resting place.
Even now my witness is in heaven,
and my advocate is in the heights!
My friends scoff at me
as I weep before God.
I wish that someone might argue for a man with God
just as anyone would for a friend.
For only a few years will pass
before I go the way of no return.

17   My spirit is broken.
My days are extinguished.
A graveyard awaits me.
Surely mockers surround me,
and my eyes must gaze at their rebellion.

Accept my pledge! Put up security for me.
Who else will be my sponsor?
You have closed their minds to understanding,
therefore you will not honor them.

10   If a man denounces his friends for a price,
the eyes of his children will fail.

He has made me an object of scorn to the people;
I have become a man people spit at.
My eyes have grown dim from grief,
and my whole body has become but a shadow.
The upright are appalled at this,
and the innocent are roused against the godless.
Yet the righteous person will hold to his way,
and the one whose hands are clean will grow stronger.

20 But come back and try again, all of you.
I will not find a wise man among you.

My days have slipped by;
my plans have been ruined,
even the things dear to my heart.
They turned night into day
and made light seem near in the face of darkness.
If I await Sheol as my home,
spread out my bed in darkness,
and say to corruption, "You are my father,"
30 and to the maggot, "My mother" or "My sister,"
where then is my hope?
Who can see any hope for me?
Will it go down to the gates of Sheol,
or will we descend together to the dust?

18 Then Bildad the Shuhite replied:
How long until you stop talking?
Show some sense, and then we can talk.
Why are we regarded as cattle,
as stupid in your sight?
You who tear yourself in anger—
should the earth be abandoned on your account,
or a rock be removed from its place?

Yes, the light of the wicked is extinguished;
10 the flame of his fire does not glow.
The light in his tent grows dark,
and the lamp beside him is put out.
His powerful stride is shortened,
and his own schemes trip him up.
For his own feet lead him into a net,
and he strays into its mesh.
A trap catches him by the heel;
a noose seizes him.
A rope lies hidden for him on the ground,
20 and a snare waits for him along the path.

Terrors frighten him on every side
and harass him at every step.
His strength is depleted;
disaster lies ready for him to stumble.
Parts of his skin are eaten away;
death's firstborn consumes his limbs.
He is ripped from the security of his tent
and marched away to the king of terrors.
Nothing he owned remains in his tent.
30   Burning sulfur is scattered over his home.
His roots below dry up,
and his branches above wither away.
All memory of him perishes from the earth;
he has no name anywhere.
He is driven from light to darkness
and chased from the inhabited world.
He has no children or descendants among his people,
no survivor where he used to live.
Those in the west are appalled at his fate,
40   while those in the east tremble in horror.
Indeed, such is the dwelling of the unjust man,
and this is the place of the one who does not know God.

19 Then Job answered:
How long will you torment me
and crush me with words?
You have humiliated me ten times now,
and you mistreat me without shame.
Even if it is true that I have sinned,
my mistake concerns only me.
If you really want to appear superior to me
and would use my disgrace as evidence against me,
10   then understand that it is God who has wronged me
and caught me in his net.

I cry out, "Violence!" but get no response;
I call for help, but there is no justice.
He has blocked my way so that I cannot pass through;

he has veiled my paths with darkness.
He has stripped me of my honor
and removed the crown from my head.
He tears me down on every side so that I am ruined.
He uproots my hope like a tree.
His anger burns against me,
and he regards me as one of his enemies.
His troops advance together;
they construct a ramp against me
and camp around my tent.

He has removed my brothers from me;
my acquaintances have abandoned me.
My relatives stop coming by,
and my close friends have forgotten me.
My house guests and female servants regard me as a stranger;
I am a foreigner in their sight.
I call for my servant, but he does not answer,
even if I beg him with my own mouth.
My breath is offensive to my wife,
and my own family finds me repulsive.
Even young boys scorn me.
When I stand up, they mock me.
All of my best friends despise me,
and those I love have turned against me.
My skin and my flesh cling to my bones;
I have escaped with only the skin of my teeth.

Have mercy on me, my friends, have mercy,
for God's hand has struck me.
Why do you persecute me as God does?
Will you never get enough of my flesh?

I wish that my words were written down,
that they were recorded on a scroll
or were inscribed in stone forever
by an iron stylus and lead!
But I know that my Redeemer lives,

50   and at the end he will stand on the dust.
        Even after my skin has been destroyed,
        yet I will see God in my flesh.
        I will see him myself;
        my eyes will look at him, and not as a stranger.
        My heart longs within me.

        If you say, "How will we pursue him,
        since the root of the problem lies with him?"
        then be afraid of the sword,
        because wrath brings punishment by the sword,
60   so that you may know there is a judgment.

20 Then Zophar the Naamathite replied:
        This is why my unsettling thoughts compel me to answer,
        because I am upset!
        I have heard a rebuke that insults me,
        and my understanding makes me reply.

        Don't you know that ever since antiquity,
        from the time a human was placed on earth,
        the joy of the wicked has been brief
        and the happiness of the godless has lasted only a moment?
10   Though his arrogance reaches heaven,
        and his head touches the clouds,
        he will vanish forever like his own dung.
        Those who know him will ask, "Where is he?"
        He will fly away like a dream and never be found;
        he will be chased away like a vision in the night.
        The eye that saw him will see him no more,
        and his household will no longer see him.
        His children will beg from the poor,
        for his own hands must give back his wealth.
20   His frame may be full of youthful vigor,
        but it will lie down with him in dust.

        Though evil tastes sweet in his mouth
        and he conceals it under his tongue,

though he cherishes it and will not let it go
but keeps it in his mouth,
yet the food in his stomach turns
into cobras' venom inside him.
He swallows wealth but must vomit it up;
God will force it from his stomach.
He will suck the poison of cobras;
a viper's fangs will kill him.
He will not enjoy the streams,
the rivers flowing with honey and curds.
He must return the fruit of his labor without consuming it;
he doesn't enjoy the profits from his trading.
For he oppressed and abandoned the poor;
he seized a house he did not build.

Because his appetite is never satisfied,
he does not let anything he desires escape.
Nothing is left for him to consume;
therefore, his prosperity will not last.
At the height of his success distress will come to him;
the full weight of misery will crush him.
When he fills his stomach,
God will send his burning anger against him,
raining it down on him while he is eating.
If he flees from an iron weapon,
an arrow from a bronze bow will pierce him.
He pulls it out of his back,
the flashing tip out of his liver.
Terrors come over him.
Total darkness is reserved for his treasures.
A fire unfanned by human hands will consume him;
it will feed on what is left in his tent.
The heavens will expose his iniquity,
and the earth will rise up against him.
The possessions in his house will be removed,
flowing away on the day of God's anger.
This is the wicked person's lot from God,
the inheritance God ordained for him.

21 Then Job answered:

> Pay close attention to my words;
> let this be the consolation you offer.
> Bear with me while I speak;
> then after I have spoken, you may continue mocking.
>
> As for me, is my complaint against a human being?
> Then why shouldn't I be impatient?
> Look at me and shudder;
> put your hand over your mouth.
> When I think about it, I am terrified
> and my body trembles in horror.
> Why do the wicked continue to live,
> growing old and becoming powerful?
> Their children are established while they are still alive,
> and their descendants, before their eyes.
> Their homes are secure and free of fear;
> no rod from God strikes them.
> Their bulls breed without fail;
> their cows calve and do not miscarry.
> They let their little ones run around like lambs;
> their children skip about,
> singing to the tambourine and lyre
> and rejoicing at the sound of the flute.
> They spend their days in prosperity
> and go down to Sheol in peace.
> Yet they say to God, "Leave us alone!
> We don't want to know your ways.
> Who is the Almighty, that we should serve him,
> and what will we gain by pleading with him?"
> But their prosperity is not of their own doing.
> The counsel of the wicked is far from me!
>
> How often is the lamp of the wicked put out?
> Does disaster come on them?
> Does he apportion destruction in his anger?

Are they like straw before the wind,
like chaff a storm sweeps away?
God reserves a person's punishment for his children.
Let God repay the person himself, so that he may know it.
40 Let his own eyes see his demise;
let him drink from the Almighty's wrath!
For what does he care about his family once he is dead,
when the number of his months has run out?

Can anyone teach God knowledge,
since he judges the exalted ones?
One person dies in excellent health,
completely secure and at ease.
His body is well fed,
and his bones are full of marrow.
50 Yet another person dies with a bitter soul,
having never tasted prosperity.
But they both lie in the dust,
and worms cover them.

I know your thoughts very well,
the schemes by which you would wrong me.
For you say, "Where now is the nobleman's house?"
and "Where are the tents the wicked lived in?"
Have you never consulted those who travel the roads?
Don't you accept their reports?
60 Indeed, the evil person is spared from the day of disaster,
rescued from the day of wrath.
Who would denounce his behavior to his face?
Who would repay him for what he has done?
He is carried to the grave,
and someone keeps watch over his tomb.
The dirt on his grave is sweet to him.
Everyone follows behind him,
and those who go before him are without number.

So how can you offer me such futile comfort?
70 Your answers are deceptive.

22   Then Eliphaz the Temanite replied:
                Can a man be of any use to God?
                Can even a wise man be of use to him?
                Does it delight the Almighty if you are righteous?
                Does he profit if you perfect your behavior?

                Does he correct you and take you to court
                because of your piety?
                Isn't your wickedness abundant
                and aren't your iniquities endless?
10   For you took collateral from your brothers without cause,
                stripping off their clothes and leaving them naked.
                You gave no water to the thirsty
                and withheld food from the famished,
                while the land belonged to a powerful man
                and an influential man lived on it.
                You sent widows away empty-handed,
                and the strength of the fatherless was crushed.
                Therefore snares surround you,
                and sudden dread terrifies you,
20   or darkness, so you cannot see,
                and a flood of water covers you.

                Isn't God as high as the heavens?
                And look at the highest stars—how lofty they are!
                Yet you say, "What does God know?
                Can he judge through total darkness?
                Clouds veil him so that he cannot see,
                as he walks on the circle of the sky."
                Will you continue on the ancient path
                that wicked men have walked?
30   They were snatched away before their time,
                and their foundations were washed away by a river.
                They were the ones who said to God, "Leave us alone!"
                and "What can the Almighty do to us?"
                But it was he who filled their houses with good things.
                The counsel of the wicked is far from me!
                The righteous see this and rejoice;

the innocent mock them, saying,
"Surely our opponents are destroyed,
and fire has consumed what they left behind."

40 Come to terms with God and be at peace;
in this way good will come to you.
Receive instruction from his mouth,
and place his sayings in your heart.
If you return to the Almighty, you will be renewed.
If you banish injustice from your tent
and consign your gold to the dust,
the gold of Ophir to the stones in the wadis,
the Almighty will be your gold
and your finest silver.
50 Then you will delight in the Almighty
and lift up your face to God.
You will pray to him, and he will hear you,
and you will fulfill your vows.
When you make a decision, it will be carried out,
and light will shine on your ways.
When others are humiliated and you say, "Lift them up,"
God will save the humble.
He will even rescue the guilty one,
who will be rescued by the purity of your hands.

23 Then Job answered:
Today also my complaint is bitter.
His hand is heavy despite my groaning.
If only I knew how to find him,
so that I could go to his throne.
I would plead my case before him
and fill my mouth with arguments.
I would learn how he would answer me;
and understand what he would say to me.
10 Would he prosecute me forcefully?
No, he would certainly pay attention to me.
Then an upright man could reason with him,
and I would escape from my Judge forever.

If I go east, he is not there,
and if I go west, I cannot perceive him.
When he is at work to the north, I cannot see him;
when he turns south, I cannot find him.
Yet he knows the way I have taken;
when he has tested me, I will emerge as pure gold.
20 My feet have followed in his tracks;
I have kept to his way and not turned aside.
I have not departed from the commands from his lips;
I have treasured the words from his mouth
more than my daily food.

But he is unchangeable; who can oppose him?
He does what he desires.
He will certainly accomplish what he has decreed for me,
and he has many more things like these in mind.
Therefore I am terrified in his presence;
30 when I consider this, I am afraid of him.
God has made my heart faint;
the Almighty has terrified me.
Yet I am not destroyed by the darkness,
by the thick darkness that covers my face.

24 Why does the Almighty not reserve times for judgment?
Why do those who know him never see his days?
The wicked displace boundary markers.
They steal a flock and provide pasture for it.
They drive away the donkeys owned by the fatherless
and take the widow's ox as collateral.
They push the needy off the road;
the poor of the land are forced into hiding.
Like wild donkeys in the wilderness,
10 the poor go out to their task of foraging for food;
the desert provides nourishment for their children.
They gather their fodder in the field
and glean the vineyards of the wicked.
Without clothing, they spend the night naked,

having no covering against the cold.
Drenched by mountain rains,
they huddle against the rocks, shelterless.
The fatherless infant is snatched from the breast;
the nursing child of the poor is seized as collateral.
20 Without clothing, they wander about naked.
They carry sheaves but go hungry.
They crush olives in their presses;
they tread the winepresses, but go thirsty.
From the city, men groan;
the mortally wounded cry for help,
yet God pays no attention to this crime.

The wicked are those who rebel against the light.
They do not recognize its ways
or stay on its paths.
30 The murderer rises at dawn
to kill the poor and needy,
and by night he becomes a thief.
The adulterer's eye watches for twilight,
thinking, "No eye will see me,"
and he covers his face.
In the dark they break into houses;
by day they lock themselves in,
never experiencing the light.
For the morning is like darkness to them.
40 Surely they are familiar with the terrors of darkness!

They float on the surface of the water.
Their section of the land is cursed,
so that they never go to their vineyards.
As dry ground and heat snatch away the melted snow,
so Sheol steals those who have sinned.
The womb forgets them;
worms feed on them;
they are remembered no more.
So injustice is broken like a tree.
50 They prey on the childless woman who is unable to conceive,

and do not deal kindly with the widow.
Yet God drags away the mighty by his power;
when he rises up, they have no assurance of life.
He gives them a sense of security, so they can rely on it,
but his eyes watch over their ways.
They are exalted for a moment, then gone;
they are brought low and shrivel up like everything else.
They wither like heads of grain.

If this is not true, then who can prove me a liar
60   and show that my speech is worthless?

25 Then Bildad the Shuhite replied:
Dominion and dread belong to him,
the one who establishes harmony in his heights.
Can his troops be numbered?
Does his light not shine on everyone?
How can a human be justified before God?
How can one born of woman be pure?
If even the moon does not shine
and the stars are not pure in his sight,
10   how much less a human, who is a maggot,
a son of man, who is a worm!

26 Then Job answered:
How you have helped the powerless
and delivered the arm that is weak!
How you have counseled the unwise
and abundantly provided insight!
With whom did you speak these words?
Whose breath came out of your mouth?

The departed spirits tremble
beneath the waters and all that inhabit them.
Sheol is naked before God,
10   and Abaddon has no covering.
He stretches the northern skies over empty space;
he hangs the earth on nothing.

He wraps up the water in his clouds,
yet the clouds do not burst beneath its weight.
He obscures the view of his throne,
spreading his cloud over it.
He laid out the horizon on the surface of the waters
at the boundary between light and darkness.
The pillars that hold up the sky tremble,
astounded at his rebuke.
By his power he stirred the sea,
and by his understanding he crushed Rahab.
By his breath the heavens gained their beauty;
his hand pierced the fleeing serpent.
These are but the fringes of his ways;
how faint is the word we hear of him!
Who can understand his mighty thunder?

27 Job continued his discourse, saying:

As God lives, who has deprived me of justice,
and the Almighty who has made me bitter,
as long as my breath is still in me
and the breath from God remains in my nostrils,
my lips will not speak unjustly,
and my tongue will not utter deceit.
I will never affirm that you are right.
I will maintain my integrity until I die.
I will cling to my righteousness and never let it go.
My conscience will not accuse me as long as I live!

May my enemy be like the wicked
and my opponent like the unjust.
For what hope does the godless person have when he is cut off,
when God takes away his life?
Will God hear his cry
when distress comes on him?
Will he delight in the Almighty?
Will he call on God at all times?
I will teach you about God's power.
I will not conceal what the Almighty has planned.

All of you have seen this for yourselves,
why do you keep up this empty talk?

This is a wicked man's lot from God,
the inheritance the ruthless receive from the Almighty.
Even if his children increase, they are destined for the sword;
his descendants will never have enough food.
Those who survive him will be buried by the plague,
yet their widows will not weep for them.
30   Though he piles up silver like dust
and heaps up fine clothing like clay—
he may heap it up, but the righteous will wear it,
and the innocent will divide up his silver.
The house he built is like a moth's cocoon
or a shelter set up by a watchman.
He lies down wealthy, but will do so no more;
when he opens his eyes, it is gone.
Terrors overtake him like a flood;
a storm wind sweeps him away at night.
40   An east wind picks him up, and he is gone;
it carries him away from his place.
It blasts at him without mercy,
while he flees desperately from its force.
It claps its hands at him
and scoffs at him from its place.

28   Surely there is a mine for silver
and a place where gold is refined.
Iron is taken from the ground,
and copper is smelted from ore.
A miner puts an end to the darkness;
he probes the deepest recesses
for ore in the gloomy darkness.
He cuts a shaft far from human habitation,
in places unknown to those who walk above ground.
10   Suspended far away from people,
the miners swing back and forth.
Food may come from the earth,

but below the surface the earth is transformed as by fire.
Its rocks are a source of lapis lazuli,
containing flecks of gold.
No bird of prey knows that path;
no falcon's eye has seen it.
Proud beasts have never walked on it;
no lion has ever prowled over it.
The miner uses a flint tool
and turns up ore from the root of the mountains.
He cuts out channels in the rocks,
and his eyes spot every treasure.
He dams up the streams from flowing
so that he may bring to light what is hidden.

But where can wisdom be found,
and where is understanding located?
No one can know its value,
since it cannot be found in the land of the living.
The ocean depths say, "It's not in me,"
while the sea declares, "I don't have it."
Gold cannot be exchanged for it,
and silver cannot be weighed out for its price.
Wisdom cannot be valued in the gold of Ophir,
in precious onyx or lapis lazuli.
Gold and glass do not compare with it,
and articles of fine gold cannot be exchanged for it.
Coral and quartz are not worth mentioning.
The price of wisdom is beyond pearls.
Topaz from Cush cannot compare with it,
and it cannot be valued in pure gold.

Where then does wisdom come from,
and where is understanding located?
It is hidden from the eyes of every living thing
and concealed from the birds of the sky.
Abaddon and Death say,
"We have heard news of it with our ears."
But God understands the way to wisdom,

and he knows its location.
For he looks to the ends of the earth
50 and sees everything under the heavens.
When God fixed the weight of the wind
and distributed the water by measure,
when he established a limit for the rain
and a path for the lightning,
he considered wisdom and evaluated it;
he established it and examined it.
He said to mankind,
"The fear of the LORD—that is wisdom.
And to turn from evil is understanding."

29 Job continued his discourse, saying:
If only I could be as in months gone by,
in the days when God watched over me,
when his lamp shone above my head,
and I walked through darkness by his light!
I would be as I was in the days of my youth
when God's friendship rested on my tent,
when the Almighty was still with me
and my children were around me,
10 when my feet were bathed in curds
and the rock poured out streams of oil for me!

When I went out to the city gate
and took my seat in the town square,
the young men saw me and withdrew,
while older men stood to their feet.
City officials stopped talking
and covered their mouths with their hands.
The noblemen's voices were hushed,
and their tongues stuck to the roof of their mouths.
20 When they heard me, they blessed me,
and when they saw me, they spoke well of me.
For I rescued the poor who cried out for help,
and the fatherless child who had no one to support him.
The dying blessed me,

and I made the widow's heart rejoice.
I clothed myself in righteousness,
and it enveloped me;
my just decisions were like a robe and a turban.
I was eyes to the blind
30   and feet to the lame.
I was a father to the needy,
and I examined the case of the stranger.
I shattered the fangs of the unjust
and snatched the prey from his teeth.

So I thought, "I will die in my own nest
and multiply my days as the sand.
My roots will have access to water,
and the dew will rest on my branches all night.
My whole being will be refreshed within me,
40   and my bow will be renewed in my hand."

Men listened to me with expectation,
waiting silently for my advice.
After a word from me they did not speak again;
my speech settled on them like dew.
They waited for me as for the rain
and opened their mouths as for spring showers.
If I smiled at them, they couldn't believe it;
they were thrilled at the light of my countenance.
I directed their course and presided as chief.
50   I lived as a king among his troops,
like one who comforts those who mourn.

30   But now they mock me,
men younger than I am,
whose fathers I would have refused to put
with my sheep dogs.
What use to me was the strength of their hands?
Their vigor had left them.
Emaciated from poverty and hunger,
they gnawed the dry land,

the desolate wasteland by night.

10   They plucked mallow among the shrubs,
and the roots of the broom tree were their food.
They were banished from human society;
people shouted at them as if they were thieves.
They are living on the slopes of the wadis,
among the rocks and in holes in the ground.
They bray among the shrubs;
they huddle beneath the thistles.
Foolish men, without even a name.
They were forced to leave the land.

20   Now I am mocked by their songs;
I have become an object of scorn to them.
They despise me and keep their distance from me;
they do not hesitate to spit in my face.
Because God has loosened my bowstring and oppressed me,
they have cast off restraint in my presence.
The rabble rise up at my right;
they trap my feet
and construct their siege ramp against me.
They tear up my path;
30   they contribute to my destruction,
without anyone to help them.
They advance as through a gaping breach;
they keep rolling in through the ruins.
Terrors are turned loose against me;
they chase my dignity away like the wind,
and my prosperity has passed by like a cloud.

Now my life is poured out before me,
and days of suffering have seized me.
Night pierces my bones,
40   but my gnawing pains never rest.
My clothing is distorted with great force;
he chokes me by the neck of my garment.
He throws me into the mud,
and I have become like dust and ashes.

I cry out to you for help, but you do not answer me;
when I stand up, you merely look at me.
You have turned against me with cruelty;
you harass me with your strong hand.
You lift me up on the wind and make me ride it;
50   you scatter me in the storm.
Yes, I know that you will lead me to death—
the place appointed for all who live.

Yet no one would stretch out his hand
against a ruined person
when he cries out to him for help
because of his distress.
Have I not wept for those who have fallen on hard times?
Has my soul not grieved for the needy?
But when I hoped for good, evil came;
60   when I looked for light, darkness came.
I am churning within and cannot rest;
days of suffering confront me.
I walk about blackened, but not by the sun.
I stood in the assembly and cried out for help.
I have become a brother to jackals
and a companion of ostriches.
My skin blackens and flakes off,
and my bones burn with fever.
My lyre is used for mourning
70   and my flute for the sound of weeping.

31   I have made a covenant with my eyes.
How then could I look at a young woman?
For what portion would I have from God above,
or what inheritance from the Almighty on high?
Doesn't disaster come to the unjust
and misfortune to evildoers?
Does he not see my ways
and number all my steps?

If I have walked in falsehood
or my foot has rushed to deceit,
let God weigh me on accurate scales,
and he will recognize my integrity.

If my step has turned from the way,
my heart has followed my eyes,
or impurity has stained my hands,
let someone else eat what I have sown,
and let my crops be uprooted.

If my heart has gone astray over a woman
or I have lurked at my neighbor's door,
let my own wife grind grain for another man,
and let other men sleep with her.
For that would be a disgrace;
it would be an iniquity deserving punishment.
For it is a fire that consumes down to Abaddon;
it would destroy my entire harvest.

If I have dismissed the case of my male or female servants
when they made a complaint against me,
what could I do when God stands up to judge?
How should I answer him when he calls me to account?
Did not the one who made me in the womb also make them?
Did not the same God form us both in the womb?

If I have refused the wishes of the poor
or let the widow's eyes go blind,
if I have eaten my few crumbs alone
without letting the fatherless eat any of it—
for from my youth, I raised him as his father,
and since the day I was born I guided the widow—
if I have seen anyone dying for lack of clothing
or a needy person without a cloak,
if he did not bless me
while warming himself with the fleece from my sheep,
if I ever cast my vote against a fatherless child

when I saw that I had support in the city gate,
then let my shoulder blade fall from my back,
and my arm be pulled from its socket.
For disaster from God terrifies me,
and because of his majesty I could not do these things.

If I placed my confidence in gold
or called fine gold my trust,
if I have rejoiced because my wealth is great
or because my own hand has acquired so much,
if I have gazed at the sun when it was shining
or at the moon moving in splendor,
so that my heart was secretly enticed
and I threw them a kiss,
this would also be an iniquity deserving punishment,
for I would have denied God above.

Have I rejoiced over my enemy's distress,
or become excited when trouble came his way?
I have not allowed my mouth to sin
by asking for his life with a curse.
Haven't the members of my household said,
"Who is there who has not had enough to eat at Job's table?"
No stranger had to spend the night on the street,
for I opened my door to the traveler.
Have I covered my transgressions as others do
by hiding my iniquity in my heart
because I greatly feared the crowds
and because the contempt of the clans terrified me,
so I grew silent and would not go outside?

If only I had someone to hear my case!
Here is my signature; let the Almighty answer me.
Let my Opponent compose his indictment.
I would surely carry it on my shoulder
and wear it like a crown.
I would give him an account of all my steps;
I would approach him like a prince.

If my land cries out against me
and its furrows join in weeping,
if I have consumed its produce without payment
80   or shown contempt for its tenants,
then let thorns grow instead of wheat
and stinkweed instead of barley.

The words of Job are concluded.

32 So these three men quit answering Job, because he was righteous in his own eyes. Then Elihu son of Barachel the Buzite from the family of Ram became angry. He was angry at Job because he had justified himself rather than God. He was also angry at Job's three friends because they had failed to refute him and yet had condemned him.

Now Elihu had waited to speak to Job because they were all older than he. But when he saw that the three men could not answer Job, he became angry.

So Elihu son of Barachel the Buzite replied:

I am young in years,
while you are old;
10   therefore I was timid and afraid
to tell you what I know.
I thought that age should speak
and maturity should teach wisdom.
But it is the spirit in a person—
the breath from the Almighty—
that gives anyone understanding.
It is not only the old who are wise
or the elderly who understand how to judge.
Therefore I say, "Listen to me.
20   I too will declare what I know."
Look, I waited for your conclusions;
I listened to your insights
as you sought for words.
I paid close attention to you.
Yet no one proved Job wrong;
not one of you refuted his arguments.
So do not claim, "We have found wisdom;
let God deal with him, not man."

But Job has not directed his argument to me,
and I will not respond to him with your arguments.

Job's friends are dismayed and can no longer answer;
words have left them.
Should I continue to wait now that they are silent,
now that they stand there and no longer answer?
I too will answer;
yes, I will tell what I know.
For I am full of words,
and my spirit compels me to speak.
My heart is like unvented wine;
it is about to burst like new wineskins.
I must speak so that I can find relief;
I must open my lips and respond.
I will be partial to no one,
and I will not give anyone an undeserved title.
For I do not know how to give such titles;
otherwise, my Maker would remove me in an instant.

33 But now, Job, pay attention to my speech,
and listen to all my words.
I am going to open my mouth;
my tongue will form words on my palate.
My words come from my upright heart,
and my lips speak with sincerity what they know.
The Spirit of God has made me,
and the breath of the Almighty gives me life.
Refute me if you can.
Prepare your case against me; take your stand.
I am just like you before God;
I was also pinched off from a piece of clay.
Fear of me should not terrify you;
no pressure from me should weigh you down.

Surely you have spoken in my hearing,
and I have heard these very words:
"I am pure, without transgression;

I am clean and have no iniquity.
But he finds reasons to oppose me;

20   he regards me as his enemy.
He puts my feet in the stocks;
he stands watch over all my paths."

But I tell you that you are wrong in this matter,
since God is greater than man.
Why do you take him to court
for not answering anything a person asks?
For God speaks time and again,
but a person may not notice it.
In a dream, a vision in the night,

30   when deep sleep comes over people
as they slumber on their beds,
he uncovers their ears
and terrifies them with warnings,
in order to turn a person from his actions
and suppress the pride of a person.
God spares his soul from the Pit,
his life from crossing the river of death.
A person may be disciplined on his bed with pain
and constant distress in his bones,

40   so that he detests bread,
and his soul despises his favorite food.
His flesh wastes away to nothing,
and his unseen bones stick out.
He draws near to the Pit,
and his life to the executioners.
If there is an angel on his side,
one mediator out of a thousand,
to tell a person what is right for him
and to be gracious to him and say,

50   "Spare him from going down to the Pit;
I have found a ransom,"
then his flesh will be healthier than in his youth,
and he will return to the days of his youthful vigor.
He will pray to God, and God will delight in him.

That person will see his face with a shout of joy,
and God will restore his righteousness to him.
He will look at men and say,
"I have sinned and perverted what was right;
yet I did not get what I deserved.
He redeemed my soul from going down to the Pit,
and I will continue to see the light."
God certainly does all these things
two or three times to a person
in order to turn him back from the Pit,
so he may shine with the light of life.
Pay attention, Job, and listen to me.
Be quiet, and I will speak.
But if you have something to say, answer me;
speak, for I would like to justify you.
If not, then listen to me;
be quiet, and I will teach you wisdom.

34 Then Elihu continued, saying:

Hear my words, you wise ones,
and listen to me, you knowledgeable ones.
Doesn't the ear test words
as the palate tastes food?
Let us judge for ourselves what is right;
let us decide together what is good.
For Job has declared, "I am righteous,
yet God has deprived me of justice.
Would I lie about my case?
My wound is incurable,
though I am without transgression."
What man is like Job?
He drinks derision like water.
He keeps company with evildoers
and walks with wicked men.
For he has said, "A man gains nothing
when he becomes God's friend."

Therefore listen to me, you men of understanding.

20 It is impossible for God to do wrong,
and for the Almighty to act unjustly.
For he repays a person according to his deeds,
and he gives him what his conduct deserves.
Indeed, it is true that God does not act wickedly
and the Almighty does not pervert justice.
Who gave him authority over the earth?
Who put him in charge of the entire world?
If he put his mind to it
and withdrew the spirit and breath he gave,
30 every living thing would perish together
and mankind would return to the dust.

If you have understanding, hear this;
listen to what I have to say.
Could one who hates justice govern the world?
Will you condemn the mighty Righteous One,
who says to a king, "Worthless man!"
and to nobles, "Wicked men!"?
God is not partial to princes
and does not favor the rich over the poor,
40 for they are all the work of his hands.
They die suddenly in the middle of the night;
people shudder, then pass away.
Even the mighty are removed without effort.

For his eyes watch over a man's ways,
and he observes all his steps.
There is no darkness, no deep darkness,
where evildoers can hide.
God does not need to examine a person further,
that one should approach him in court.
He shatters the mighty without an investigation
50 and sets others in their place.
Therefore, he recognizes their deeds
and overthrows them by night, and they are crushed.
In full view of the public,

he strikes them for their wickedness,
because they turned aside from following him
and did not understand any of his ways
but caused the poor to cry out to him,
and he heard the outcry of the needy.
But when God is silent, who can declare him guilty?
60   When he hides his face, who can see him?
Yet he watches over both individuals and nations,
so that godless men should not rule
or ensnare the people.

Suppose someone says to God,
"I have endured my punishment;
I will no longer act wickedly.
Teach me what I cannot see;
if I have done wrong, I won't do it again."
Should God repay you on your terms
70   when you have rejected his?
You must choose, not I!
So declare what you know.
Reasonable men will say to me,
along with the wise men who hear me,
"Job speaks without knowledge;
his words are without insight."
If only Job were tested to the limit,
because his answers are like those of wicked men.
For he adds rebellion to his sin;
80   he scornfully claps in our presence,
while multiplying his words against God.

35 Then Elihu continued, saying:
Do you think it is just when you say,
"I am righteous before God"?
For you ask, "What does it profit you,
and what benefit comes to me, if I do not sin?"
I will answer you
and your friends with you.
Look at the heavens and see;

gaze at the clouds high above you.
10　If you sin, how does it affect God?
If you multiply your transgressions, what does it do to him?
If you are righteous, what do you give him,
or what does he receive from your hand?
Your wickedness affects a person like yourself,
and your righteousness, a son of man.
People cry out because of severe oppression;
they shout for help because of the power of the mighty.
But no one asks, "Where is God my Maker,
who provides us with songs in the night,
20　who gives us more understanding than the animals of the earth
and makes us wiser than the birds of the sky?"
There they cry out, but he does not answer,
because of the pride of evil people.
Indeed, God does not listen to empty cries,
and the Almighty does not take note of it—
how much less when you complain
that you do not see him,
that your case is before him
and you are waiting for him.
30　But now, because God's anger does not punish
and he does not pay attention to transgression,
Job opens his mouth in vain
and multiplies words without knowledge.

36　Then Elihu continued, saying:
Be patient with me a little longer, and I will inform you,
for there is still more to be said on God's behalf.
I will get my knowledge from a distant place
and ascribe justice to my Maker.
Indeed, my words are not false;
one who has complete knowledge is with you.

Yes, God is mighty, but he despises no one;
he understands all things.
10　He does not keep the wicked alive,
but he gives justice to the oppressed.

He does not withdraw his gaze from the righteous,
but he seats them forever with enthroned kings,
and they are exalted.

If people are bound with chains
and trapped by the cords of affliction,
God tells them what they have done
and how arrogantly they have transgressed.
He opens their ears to correction
20   and tells them to repent from iniquity.
If they listen and serve him,
they will end their days in prosperity
and their years in happiness.
But if they do not listen,
they will cross the river of death
and die without knowledge.

Those who have a godless heart harbor anger;
even when God binds them, they do not cry for help.
They die in their youth;
30   their life ends among male cult prostitutes.
God rescues the afflicted by their affliction;
he instructs them by their torment.

Indeed, he lured you from the jaws of distress
to a spacious and unconfined place.
Your table was spread with choice food.
Yet now you are obsessed with the judgment due the wicked;
judgment and justice have seized you.
Be careful that no one lures you with riches;
do not let a large ransom lead you astray.
40   Can your wealth or all your physical exertion
keep you from distress?
Do not long for the night
when nations will disappear from their places.
Be careful that you do not turn to iniquity,
for that is why you have been tested by affliction.

Look, God shows himself exalted by his power.
Who is a teacher like him?
Who has appointed his way for him,
and who has declared, "You have done wrong"?
50   Remember that you should praise his work,
which people have sung about.
All mankind has seen it;
people have looked at it from a distance.
Yes, God is exalted beyond our knowledge;
the number of his years cannot be counted.
For he makes waterdrops evaporate;
they distill the rain into its mist,
which the clouds pour out
and shower abundantly on mankind.
60   Can anyone understand how the clouds spread out
or how the thunder roars from God's pavilion?
See how he spreads his lightning around him
and covers the depths of the sea.
For he judges the nations with these;
he gives food in abundance.
He covers his hands with lightning
and commands it to hit its mark.
The thunder declares his presence;
the cattle also, the approaching storm.

37   My heart pounds at this
and leaps from my chest.
Just listen to his thunderous voice
and the rumbling that comes from his mouth.
He lets it loose beneath the entire sky;
his lightning to the ends of the earth.

Then there comes a roaring sound;
God thunders with his majestic voice.
He does not restrain the lightning
10   when his rumbling voice is heard.
God thunders wondrously with his voice;
he does great things that we cannot comprehend.

For he says to the snow, "Fall to the earth,"
and the torrential rains, his mighty torrential rains,
serve as his sign to all mankind,
so that all men may know his work.
The wild animals enter their lairs
and stay in their dens.
The windstorm comes from its chamber,
20   and the cold from the driving north winds.
Ice is formed by the breath of God,
and watery expanses are frozen.
He saturates clouds with moisture;
he scatters his lightning through them.
They swirl about,
turning round and round at his direction,
accomplishing everything he commands them
over the surface of the inhabited world.
He causes this to happen for punishment,
30   for his land, or for his faithful love.

Listen to this, Job.
Stop and consider God's wonders.
Do you know how God directs his clouds
or makes their lightning flash?
Do you understand how the clouds float,
those wonderful works of him who has perfect knowledge?
You whose clothes get hot
when the south wind brings calm to the land,
can you help God spread out the skies
40   as hard as a cast metal mirror?
Teach us what we should say to him;
we cannot prepare our case because of our darkness.
Should he be told that I want to speak?
Can a man speak when he is confused?
Now no one can even look at the sun
after a wind has swept through and cleared the sky.
Out of the north he comes, shrouded in a golden glow;
awesome majesty surrounds him.
The Almighty—we cannot reach him—

50   he is exalted in power!
    He will not violate justice and abundant righteousness,
    therefore, men fear him.
    He does not look favorably on any who are wise in heart.

38 Then the LORD answered Job from the whirlwind. He said:
    Who is this who obscures my counsel
    with ignorant words?
    Get ready to answer me like a man;
    when I question you, you will inform me.
    Where were you when I established the earth?
    Tell me, if you have understanding.
    Who fixed its dimensions? Certainly you know!
    Who stretched a measuring line across it?
10   What supports its foundations?
    Or who laid its cornerstone
    while the morning stars sang together
    and all the sons of God shouted for joy?

    Who enclosed the sea behind doors
    when it burst from the womb,
    when I made the clouds its garment
    and total darkness its blanket,
    when I determined its boundaries
    and put its bars and doors in place,
20   when I declared, "You may come this far, but no farther;
    your proud waves stop here"?

    Have you ever in your life commanded the morning
    or assigned the dawn its place,
    so it may seize the edges of the earth
    and shake the wicked out of it?
    The earth is changed as clay is by a seal;
    its hills stand out like the folds of a garment.
    Light is withheld from the wicked,
    and the arm raised in violence is broken.

30   Have you traveled to the sources of the sea

or walked in the depths of the oceans?
Have the gates of death been revealed to you?
Have you seen the gates of deep darkness?
Have you comprehended the extent of the earth?
Tell me, if you know all this.

Where is the road to the home of light?
Do you know where darkness lives,
so you can lead it back to its border?
Are you familiar with the paths to its home?
40   Don't you know? You were already born;
you have lived so long!
Have you entered the place where the snow is stored?
Or have you seen the storehouses of hail,
which I hold in reserve for times of trouble,
for the day of warfare and battle?
What road leads to the place where light is dispersed?
Where is the source of the east wind that spreads across the earth?

Who cuts a channel for the flooding rain
or clears the way for lightning,
50   to bring rain on an uninhabited land,
on a desert with no human life,
to satisfy the parched wasteland
and cause the grass to sprout?
Does the rain have a father?
Who fathered the drops of dew?
Whose womb did the ice come from?
Who gave birth to the frost of heaven
when water becomes as hard as stone,
and the surface of the watery depths is frozen?

60   Can you fasten the chains of the Pleiades
or loosen the belt of Orion?
Can you bring out the constellations in their season
and lead the Bear and her cubs?
Do you know the laws of heaven?
Can you impose its authority on earth?

Can you command the clouds
so that a flood of water covers you?
Can you send out lightning bolts, and they go?
Do they report to you, "Here we are"?

70   Who put wisdom in the heart
or gave the mind understanding?
Who has the wisdom to number the clouds?
Or who can tilt the water jars of heaven
when the dust hardens like cast metal
and the clods of dirt stick together?

Can you hunt prey for a lioness
or satisfy the appetite of young lions
when they crouch in their dens
and lie in wait within their lairs?
80   Who provides the raven's food
when its young cry out to God
and wander about for lack of food?

39   Do you know when mountain goats give birth?
Have you watched the deer in labor?
Can you count the months they are pregnant
so you can know the time they give birth?
They crouch down to give birth to their young;
they deliver their newborn.
Their offspring are healthy and grow up in the open field.
They leave and do not return.

Who set the wild donkey free?
10   Who released the swift donkey from its harness?
I made the desert its home,
and the salty wasteland its dwelling.
It scoffs at the noise of the village
and never hears the shouts of a driver.
It roams the mountains for its pastureland,
searching for anything green.
Would the wild ox be willing to serve you?

Would it spend the night by your feeding trough?
Can you hold the wild ox to a furrow by its harness?
Will it plow the valleys behind you?
Can you depend on it because its strength is great?
Would you leave it to do your hard work?
Can you trust the wild ox to harvest your grain
and bring it to your threshing floor?

The wings of the ostrich flap joyfully,
but are her feathers and plumage like the stork's?
She abandons her eggs on the ground
and lets them be warmed in the sand.
She forgets that a foot may crush them
or that some wild animal may trample them.
She treats her young harshly, as if they were not her own,
with no fear that her labor may have been in vain.
For God has deprived her of wisdom;
he has not endowed her with understanding.
When she proudly spreads her wings,
she laughs at the horse and its rider.

Do you give strength to the horse?
Do you adorn his neck with a mane?
Do you make him leap like a locust?
His proud snorting fills one with terror.
He paws in the valley and rejoices in his strength;
he charges into battle.
He laughs at fear, since he is afraid of nothing;
he does not run from the sword.
A quiver rattles at his side,
along with a flashing spear and a javelin.
He charges ahead with trembling rage;
he cannot stand still at the sound of the ram's horn.
When the ram's horn blasts, he snorts defiantly.
He smells the battle from a distance;
he hears the officers' shouts and the battle cry.

Does the hawk take flight by your understanding

and spread its wings to the south?
Does the eagle soar at your command
and make its nest on high?
It lives on a cliff where it spends the night;
its stronghold is on a rocky crag.
From there it searches for prey;
its eyes penetrate the distance.
60   Its brood gulps down blood,
and where the slain are, it is there.

40 The LORD answered Job:
Will the one who contends with the Almighty correct him?
Let him who argues with God give an answer.

Then Job answered the LORD:
I am so insignificant. How can I answer you?
I place my hand over my mouth.
I have spoken once, and I will not reply;
twice, but now I can add nothing.

Then the LORD answered Job from the whirlwind:
10   Get ready to answer me like a man;
When I question you, you will inform me.
Would you really challenge my justice?
Would you declare me guilty to justify yourself?
Do you have an arm like God's?
Can you thunder with a voice like his?

Adorn yourself with majesty and splendor,
and clothe yourself with honor and glory.
Pour out your raging anger;
look on every proud person and humiliate him.
20   Look on every proud person and humble him;
trample the wicked where they stand.
Hide them together in the dust;
imprison them in the grave.
Then I will confess to you
that your own right hand can deliver you.

Look at Behemoth,
which I made along with you.
He eats grass like cattle.
Look at the strength of his back
and the power in the muscles of his belly.
He stiffens his tail like a cedar tree;
the tendons of his thighs are woven firmly together.
His bones are bronze tubes;
his limbs are like iron rods.
He is the foremost of God's works;
only his Maker can draw the sword against him.
The hills yield food for him,
while all sorts of wild animals play there.
He lies under the lotus plants,
hiding in the protection of marshy reeds.
Lotus plants cover him with their shade;
the willows by the brook surround him.
Though the river rages, Behemoth is unafraid;
he remains confident, even if the Jordan surges up to his mouth.
Can anyone capture him while he looks on,
or pierce his nose with snares?

41

Can you pull in Leviathan with a hook
or tie his tongue down with a rope?
Can you put a cord through his nose
or pierce his jaw with a hook?
Will he beg you for mercy
or speak softly to you?
Will he make a covenant with you
so that you can take him as a slave forever?
Can you play with him like a bird
or put him on a leash for your girls?
Will traders bargain for him
or divide him among the merchants?
Can you fill his hide with harpoons
or his head with fishing spears?
Lay a hand on him.

You will remember the battle
and never repeat it!
Any hope of capturing him proves false.
Does a person not collapse at the very sight of him?
No one is ferocious enough to rouse Leviathan;
who then can stand against me?
Who confronted me, that I should repay him?
Everything under heaven belongs to me.

I cannot be silent about his limbs,
his power, and his graceful proportions.
Who can strip off his outer covering?
Who can penetrate his double layer of armor?
Who can open his jaws,
surrounded by those terrifying teeth?
His pride is in his rows of scales,
closely sealed together.
One scale is so close to another
that no air can pass between them.
They are joined to one another,
so closely connected they cannot be separated.
His snorting flashes with light,
while his eyes are like the rays of dawn.
Flaming torches shoot from his mouth;
fiery sparks fly out!
Smoke billows from his nostrils
as from a boiling pot or burning reeds.
His breath sets coals ablaze,
and flames pour out of his mouth.
Strength resides in his neck,
and dismay dances before him.
The folds of his flesh are joined together,
solid as metal and immovable.
His heart is as hard as a rock,
as hard as a lower millstone!
When Leviathan rises, the mighty are terrified;
they withdraw because of his thrashing.
The sword that reaches him will have no effect,

nor will a spear, dart, or arrow.
He regards iron as straw,
and bronze as rotten wood.
No arrow can make him flee;
slingstones become like stubble to him.
A club is regarded as stubble,
and he laughs at the sound of a javelin.
60 His undersides are jagged potsherds,
spreading the mud like a threshing sledge.
He makes the depths seethe like a cauldron;
he makes the sea like an ointment jar.
He leaves a shining wake behind him;
one would think the deep had gray hair!
He has no equal on earth—
a creature devoid of fear!
He surveys everything that is haughty;
he is king over all the proud beasts.

42 Then Job replied to the LORD:
I know that you can do anything
and no plan of yours can be thwarted.
You asked, "Who is this who conceals my counsel with ignorance?"
Surely I spoke about things I did not understand,
things too wondrous for me to know.
You said, "Listen now, and I will speak.
When I question you, you will inform me."
I had heard reports about you,
10 but now my eyes have seen you.
Therefore, I reject my words and am sorry for them;
I am dust and ashes.

After the LORD had finished speaking to Job, he said to Eliphaz the Temanite, "I am angry with you and your two friends, for you have not spoken the truth about me, as my servant Job has. Now take seven bulls and seven rams, go to my servant Job, and offer a burnt offering for yourselves. Then my servant Job will pray for you. I will surely accept his prayer and not deal with you as your folly deserves. For you have not spoken the truth about me, as my servant Job has." Then Eliphaz the Temanite, Bildad the Shuhite, and Zophar the Naamathite went and did as the LORD had told them, and the LORD accepted Job's prayer.

20 After Job had prayed for his friends, the LORD restored his fortunes and doubled his previous possessions. All his brothers, sisters, and former acquaintances came to him and dined with him in his house. They sympathized with him and comforted him concerning all the adversity the LORD had brought on him. Each one gave him a piece of silver and a gold earring.

So the LORD blessed the last part of Job's life more than the first. He owned fourteen thousand sheep and goats, six thousand camels, one thousand yoke of oxen, and one thousand female donkeys. He also had seven sons and three daughters. He named his first daughter Jemimah, his second Keziah, and his third Keren-happuch. No women as beautiful as Job's daughters could be found in all the land, and their father granted them an inheritance with their brothers.

Job lived 140 years after this and saw his children and their children to the fourth generation.
30 Then Job died, old and full of days.

Introduction to Proverbs

Andrea L. Robinson

Proverbs is the centerpiece of biblical wisdom literature. While other books of biblical wisdom bring their own distinct flavors to the canon of Scripture, Proverbs outlines the foundations and ideals of godly wisdom. Solomon is traditionally regarded as the author of Proverbs, but the book is actually an anthology of wisdom sayings from multiple authors. Although Solomon contributed much of the book's content, another hand is likely responsible for the final form of the collection. Proverbial wisdom is largely timeless, and ascertaining a precise author, setting, or time period is not crucial to interpretation.

As the practicality of many proverbs transcends time and culture, readers learn how to orient their lives according to Yahweh's unchanging order within a world that is constantly changing. Wisdom is the compass by which the ambiguities of life can be successfully navigated. By studying the specific examples provided in Proverbs, readers learn how to exercise wisdom in other areas of life. The contributors of the book teach that continual growth in wisdom can occur through observing the world, living reflectively, and discerning the best course of action for specific circumstances.

Individual proverbs are short, pithy statements that prove generally true but are not universal laws. Proverbs are guidelines that help humans live a fulfilling life by describing the way that the world typically functions. Much like the laws in the Torah, proverbs are intended to shape the worldview of Yahweh's people. Whereas legal stipulations take the form of express commands, wisdom takes the form of advice based on observation and experience. And whereas obedience to legal commands results in the fulfillment of Yahweh's promises, no such promises are attached to wisdom literature, only the increased probability of a good life.

Like real life, proverbs are diverse and random, and even sometimes contradictory. The seemingly random arrangement does not, however, imply that the collection should be studied in a piecemeal fashion. While many proverbs can stand on their own as meaningful bits of godly advice, the book is more than a list of arbitrary guidelines. When read as a whole, Proverbs offers a consistent message that teaches readers how to make wise decisions that are rooted in the very fabric of creation.

Accordingly, wisdom is the key to discovering the inherent order of Yahweh's creation and living benevolently within it. Proverbial wisdom calls humans to steward responsibly and learn from the natural world. Individuals can draw nearer to the creator through observing his creation. The created order is also connected to the social order in Proverbs. One who acts according to wisdom contributes to the well-being of both human and non-human creation.

Moreover, proverbial wisdom bridges the gap between secular and spiritual life by outlining how faith in Yahweh is lived out practically. The sages of Proverbs teach that life can often surpass human comprehension, and thus, reliance on the Lord is necessary. Indeed, the "fear of the Lord" is a central theme throughout Proverbs. Loving the Lord and obeying him enables humans to cultivate a lifelong journey of ever-increasing wisdom.

An atypical feature of Proverbs within the canon of Scripture is that redemption history takes a background role. The collection encourages a broader understanding of the biblical narrative as Yahweh's plan for humanity consists of more than mere salvation from damnation. Rather, Yahweh's redemptive plan entails individual flourishing in the context of harmonious relationships with both human and non-human creation.

Outline

1. Speeches of Solomon: An Introduction to Wisdom (Prov 1–9)
2. Proverbs of Solomon: Collection 1 (Prov 10–22)
3. Words of the Wise (Prov 22–24)
4. Proverbs of Solomon: Collection 2 (Prov 25–29)
5. Proverbs of Agur: Inverted Wisdom (Prov 30)
6. Proverbs of King Lemuel: The Woman of Wisdom (Prov 31)

Suggested Resources

Bartholomew, Craig G., and Ryan P. O'Dowd. *Old Testament Wisdom Literature: A Theological Introduction.* Downers Grove, IL: InterVarsity Press, 2011.

Kidner, Derek. *Proverbs.* Tyndale Old Testament Commentaries. Leicester: InterVarsity Press, 1964.

Longman, Tremper, III. *Proverbs.* Baker Commentary on the Old Testament Wisdom and Psalms. Grand Rapids: Eerdmans, 2006.

Pauw, Amy Plantinga. *Proverbs and Ecclesiastes.* Belief: A Theological Commentary on the Bible. Louisville: Westminster John Knox, 2015.

Waltke, Bruce. *The Book of Proverbs.* New International Commentary on the Old Testament. 2 vols. Grand Rapids: Eerdmans, 2005.

Proverbs

I   The proverbs of Solomon son of David, king of Israel:
For learning wisdom and discipline;
for understanding insightful sayings;
for receiving prudent instruction
in righteousness, justice, and integrity;
for teaching shrewdness to the inexperienced,
knowledge and discretion to a young man—
let a wise person listen and increase learning,
and let a discerning person obtain guidance—
10   for understanding a proverb or a parable,
the words of the wise, and their riddles.

The fear of the Lord
is the beginning of knowledge;
fools despise wisdom and discipline.

Listen, my son, to your father's instruction,
and don't reject your mother's teaching,
for they will be a garland of favor on your head
and pendants around your neck.
My son, if sinners entice you,
20   don't be persuaded.
If they say — "Come with us!
Let's set an ambush and kill someone.
Let's attack some innocent person just for fun!
Let's swallow them alive, like Sheol,
whole, like those who go down to the Pit.
We'll find all kinds of valuable property
and fill our houses with plunder.
Throw in your lot with us,
and we'll all share the loot"—
30   my son, don't travel that road with them

or set foot on their path,
because their feet run toward evil
and they hurry to shed blood.
It is useless to spread a net
where any bird can see it,
but they set an ambush to kill themselves;
they attack their own lives.
Such are the paths of all who make profit dishonestly;
it takes the lives of those who receive it.

40 Wisdom calls out in the street;
she makes her voice heard in the public squares.
She cries out above the commotion;
she speaks at the entrance of the city gates:
"How long, inexperienced ones, will you love ignorance?
How long will you mockers enjoy mocking
and you fools hate knowledge?
If you respond to my warning,
then I will pour out my spirit on you
and teach you my words.
50 Since I called out and you refused,
extended my hand and no one paid attention,
since you neglected all my counsel
and did not accept my correction,
I, in turn, will laugh at your calamity.
I will mock when terror strikes you,
when terror strikes you like a storm
and your calamity comes like a whirlwind,
when trouble and stress overcome you.
Then they will call me, but I won't answer;
60 they will search for me, but won't find me.
Because they hated knowledge,
didn't choose to fear the LORD,
were not interested in my counsel,
and rejected all my correction,
they will eat the fruit of their way
and be glutted with their own schemes.
For the apostasy of the inexperienced will kill them,

and the complacency of fools will destroy them.
But whoever listens to me will live securely
70 and be undisturbed by the dread of danger."

2 My son, if you accept my words
and store up my commands within you,
listening closely to wisdom
and directing your heart to understanding;
furthermore, if you call out to insight
and lift your voice to understanding,
if you seek it like silver
and search for it like hidden treasure,
then you will understand the fear of the LORD
10 and discover the knowledge of God.
For the LORD gives wisdom;
from his mouth come knowledge and understanding.
He stores up success for the upright;
He is a shield for those who live with integrity
so that he may guard the paths of justice
and protect the way of his faithful followers.
Then you will understand righteousness, justice,
and integrity — every good path.
For wisdom will enter your heart,
20 and knowledge will delight you.
Discretion will watch over you,
and understanding will guard you.
It will rescue you from the way of evil—
from anyone who says perverse things,
from those who abandon the right paths
to walk in ways of darkness,
from those who enjoy doing evil
and celebrate perversion,
whose paths are crooked,
30 and whose ways are devious.
It will rescue you from a forbidden woman,
from a wayward woman with her flattering talk,
who abandons the companion of her youth
and forgets the covenant of her God;

for her house sinks down to death
and her ways to the land of the departed spirits.
None return who go to her;
none reach the paths of life.
So follow the way of the good,
40   and keep to the paths of the righteous.
For the upright will inhabit the land,
and those of integrity will remain in it;
but the wicked will be cut off from the land,
and the treacherous ripped out of it.

3   My son, don't forget my teaching,
but let your heart keep my commands;
for they will bring you
many days, a full life, and well-being.
Never let loyalty and faithfulness leave you.
Tie them around your neck;
write them on the tablet of your heart.
Then you will find favor and high regard
with God and people.

10   Trust in the LORD with all your heart,
and do not rely on your own understanding;
in all your ways know him,
and he will make your paths straight.
Don't be wise in your own eyes;
fear the LORD and turn away from evil.
This will be healing for your body
and strengthening for your bones.
Honor the LORD with your possessions
and with the first produce of your entire harvest;
20   then your barns will be completely filled,
and your vats will overflow with new wine.
Do not despise the LORD's instruction, my son,
and do not loathe his discipline;
for the LORD disciplines the one he loves,
just as a father disciplines the son in whom he delights.

Happy is a man who finds wisdom
and who acquires understanding,
for she is more profitable than silver,
and her revenue is better than gold.
30 She is more precious than jewels;
nothing you desire can equal her.
Long life is in her right hand;
in her left, riches and honor.
Her ways are pleasant,
and all her paths, peaceful.
She is a tree of life to those who embrace her,
and those who hold on to her are happy.

The Lord founded the earth by wisdom
and established the heavens by understanding.
40 By his knowledge the watery depths broke open,
and the clouds dripped with dew.

Maintain sound wisdom and discretion.
My son, don't lose sight of them.
They will be life for you
and adornment for your neck.
Then you will go safely on your way;
your foot will not stumble.
When you lie down, you will not be afraid;
you will lie down, and your sleep will be pleasant.
50 Don't fear sudden danger
or the ruin of the wicked when it comes,
for the Lord will be your confidence
and will keep your foot from a snare.

When it is in your power,
don't withhold good from the one to whom it belongs.
Don't say to your neighbor, "Go away! Come back later.
I'll give it tomorrow" — when it is there with you.
Don't plan any harm against your neighbor,
for he trusts you and lives near you.
60 Don't accuse anyone without cause,

when he has done you no harm.
Don't envy a violent man
or choose any of his ways;
for the devious are detestable to the LORD,
but he is a friend to the upright.
The LORD's curse is on the household of the wicked,
but he blesses the home of the righteous;
He mocks those who mock
but gives grace to the humble.
70 The wise will inherit honor,
but he holds up fools to dishonor.

4 Listen, sons, to a father's discipline,
and pay attention so that you may gain understanding,
for I am giving you good instruction.
Don't abandon my teaching.
When I was a son with my father,
tender and precious to my mother,
he taught me and said,
"Your heart must hold on to my words.
Keep my commands and live.
10 Get wisdom, get understanding;
don't forget or turn away from the words from my mouth.
Don't abandon wisdom, and she will watch over you;
love her, and she will guard you.
Wisdom is supreme — so get wisdom.
And whatever else you get, get understanding.
Cherish her, and she will exalt you;
if you embrace her, she will honor you.
She will place a garland of favor on your head;
she will give you a crown of beauty."

20 Listen, my son. Accept my words,
and you will live many years.
I am teaching you the way of wisdom;
I am guiding you on straight paths.
When you walk, your steps will not be hindered;
when you run, you will not stumble.

Hold on to instruction; don't let go.
Guard it, for it is your life.
Keep off the path of the wicked;
don't proceed on the way of evil ones.
30 Avoid it; don't travel on it.
Turn away from it, and pass it by.
For they can't sleep
unless they have done what is evil;
they are robbed of sleep
unless they make someone stumble.
They eat the bread of wickedness
and drink the wine of violence.
The path of the righteous is like the light of dawn,
shining brighter and brighter until midday.
40 But the way of the wicked is like the darkest gloom;
they don't know what makes them stumble.

My son, pay attention to my words;
listen closely to my sayings.
Don't lose sight of them;
keep them within your heart.
For they are life to those who find them,
and health to one's whole body.
Guard your heart above all else,
for it is the source of life.
50 Don't let your mouth speak dishonestly,
and don't let your lips talk deviously.
Let your eyes look forward;
fix your gaze straight ahead.
Carefully consider the path for your feet,
and all your ways will be established.
Don't turn to the right or to the left;
keep your feet away from evil.

5 My son, pay attention to my wisdom;
listen closely to my understanding
so that you may maintain discretion
and your lips safeguard knowledge.

Though the lips of the forbidden woman drip honey
and her words are smoother than oil,
in the end she's as bitter as wormwood
and as sharp as a double-edged sword.
Her feet go down to death;
10   her steps head straight for Sheol.
She doesn't consider the path of life;
she doesn't know that her ways are unstable.

So now, sons, listen to me,
and don't turn away from the words from my mouth.
Keep your way far from her.
Don't go near the door of her house.
Otherwise, you will give up your vitality to others
and your years to someone cruel;
strangers will drain your resources,
20   and your hard-earned pay will end up in a foreigner's house.
At the end of your life, you will lament
when your physical body has been consumed,
and you will say, "How I hated discipline,
and how my heart despised correction.
I didn't obey my teachers
or listen closely to my instructors.
I am on the verge of complete ruin
before the entire community."

Drink water from your own cistern,
30   water flowing from your own well.
Should your springs flow in the streets,
streams in the public squares?
They should be for you alone
and not for you to share with strangers.
Let your fountain be blessed,
and take pleasure in the wife of your youth.
A loving deer, a graceful doe—
let her breasts always satisfy you;
be lost in her love forever.
40   Why, my son, would you lose yourself

with a forbidden woman
or embrace a wayward woman?
For a man's ways are before the LORD's eyes,
and he considers all his paths.
A wicked man's iniquities will trap him;
he will become tangled in the ropes of his own sin.
He will die because there is no discipline,
and be lost because of his great stupidity.

6 My son, if you have put up security for your neighbor
or entered into an agreement with a stranger,
you have been snared by the words of your mouth—
trapped by the words from your mouth.
Do this, then, my son, and free yourself,
for you have put yourself in your neighbor's power:
Go, humble yourself, and plead with your neighbor.
Don't give sleep to your eyes
or slumber to your eyelids.
10 Escape like a gazelle from a hunter,
like a bird from a hunter's trap.

Go to the ant, you slacker!
Observe its ways and become wise.
Without leader, administrator, or ruler,
it prepares its provisions in summer;
it gathers its food during harvest.
How long will you stay in bed, you slacker?
When will you get up from your sleep?
A little sleep, a little slumber,
20 a little folding of the arms to rest,
and your poverty will come like a robber,
your need, like a bandit.

A worthless person, a wicked man
goes around speaking dishonestly,
winking his eyes, signaling with his feet,
and gesturing with his fingers.
He always plots evil with perversity in his heart;

he stirs up trouble.
Therefore calamity will strike him suddenly;
30   he will be shattered instantly, beyond recovery.

The Lord hates six things;
in fact, seven are detestable to him:
arrogant eyes, a lying tongue,
hands that shed innocent blood,
a heart that plots wicked schemes,
feet eager to run to evil,
a lying witness who gives false testimony,
and one who stirs up trouble among brothers.

My son, keep your father's command,
40   and don't reject your mother's teaching.
Always bind them to your heart;
tie them around your neck.
When you walk here and there, they will guide you;
when you lie down, they will watch over you;
when you wake up, they will talk to you.
For a command is a lamp, teaching is a light,
and corrective discipline is the way to life.
They will protect you from an evil woman,
from the flattering tongue of a wayward woman.
50   Don't lust in your heart for her beauty
or let her captivate you with her eyelashes.
For a prostitute's fee is only a loaf of bread,
but the wife of another man goes after a precious life.
Can a man embrace fire
and his clothes not be burned?
Can a man walk on burning coals
without scorching his feet?
So it is with the one who sleeps with
another man's wife;
60   no one who touches her will go unpunished.
People don't despise the thief if he steals
to satisfy himself when he is hungry.
Still, if caught, he must pay seven times as much;

he must give up all the wealth in his house.
The one who commits adultery lacks sense;
whoever does so destroys himself.
He will get a beating and dishonor,
and his disgrace will never be removed.
For jealousy enrages a husband,
70   and he will show no mercy when he takes revenge.
He will not be appeased by anything
or be persuaded by lavish bribes.

7   My son, obey my words,
and treasure my commands.
Keep my commands and live,
and guard my instructions
as you would the pupil of your eye.
Tie them to your fingers;
write them on the tablet of your heart.
Say to wisdom, "You are my sister,"
and call understanding your relative.
10   She will keep you from a forbidden woman,
a wayward woman with her flattering talk.

At the window of my house
I looked through my lattice.
I saw among the inexperienced,
I noticed among the youths,
a young man lacking sense.
Crossing the street near her corner,
he strolled down the road to her house
at twilight, in the evening,
20   in the dark of the night.
A woman came to meet him
dressed like a prostitute,
having a hidden agenda.
She is loud and defiant;
her feet do not stay at home.
Now in the street, now in the squares,
she lurks at every corner.

She grabs him and kisses him;
she brazenly says to him,
30   "I've made fellowship offerings;
today I've fulfilled my vows.
So I came out to meet you,
to search for you, and I've found you.
I've spread coverings on my bed—
richly colored linen from Egypt.
I've perfumed my bed
with myrrh, aloes, and cinnamon.
Come, let's drink deeply of lovemaking until morning.
Let's feast on each other's love!
40   My husband isn't home;
he went on a long journey.
He took a bag of silver with him
and will come home at the time of the full moon."
She seduces him with her persistent pleading;
she lures with her flattering talk.
He follows her impulsively
like an ox going to the slaughter,
like a deer bounding toward a trap
until an arrow pierces its liver,
50   like a bird darting into a snare—
he doesn't know it will cost him his life.

Now, sons, listen to me,
and pay attention to the words from my mouth.
Don't let your heart turn aside to her ways;
don't stray onto her paths.
For she has brought many down to death;
her victims are countless.
Her house is the road to Sheol,
descending to the chambers of death.

8   Doesn't wisdom call out?
Doesn't understanding make her voice heard?
At the heights overlooking the road,
at the crossroads, she takes her stand.

Beside the gates leading into the city,
at the main entrance, she cries out:
"People, I call out to you;
my cry is to the children of Adam.
Learn to be shrewd, you who are inexperienced;
10   develop common sense, you who are foolish.
Listen, for I speak of noble things,
and what my lips say is right.
For my mouth tells the truth,
and wickedness is detestable to my lips.
All the words from my mouth are righteous;
none of them are deceptive or perverse.
All of them are clear to the perceptive,
and right to those who discover knowledge.
Accept my instruction instead of silver,
20   and knowledge rather than pure gold.
For wisdom is better than jewels,
and nothing desirable can equal it.
I, wisdom, share a home with shrewdness
and have knowledge and discretion.
To fear the Lord is to hate evil.
I hate arrogant pride, evil conduct,
and perverse speech.
I possess good advice and sound wisdom;
I have understanding and strength.
30   It is by me that kings reign
and rulers enact just law;
by me, princes lead,
as do nobles and all righteous judges.
I love those who love me,
and those who search for me find me.
With me are riches and honor,
lasting wealth and righteousness.
My fruit is better than solid gold,
and my harvest than pure silver.
40   I walk in the ways of righteousness,
along the paths of justice,

giving wealth as an inheritance to those who love me,
and filling their treasuries.

"The Lord acquired me
at the beginning of his creation,
before his works of long ago.
I was formed before ancient times,
from the beginning, before the earth began.
I was born
50   when there were no watery depths
and no springs filled with water.
Before the mountains were established,
prior to the hills, I was given birth —
before he made the land, the fields,
or the first soil on earth.
I was there when he established the heavens,
when he laid out the horizon on the surface of the ocean,
when he placed the skies above,
when the fountains of the ocean gushed out,
60   when he set a limit for the sea
so that the waters would not violate his command,
when he laid out the foundations of the earth.
I was a skilled craftsman beside him.
I was his delight every day,
always rejoicing before him.
I was rejoicing in his inhabited world,
delighting in the children of Adam.

"And now, sons, listen to me;
those who keep my ways are happy.
70   Listen to instruction and be wise;
don't ignore it.
Anyone who listens to me is happy,
watching at my doors every day,
waiting by the posts of my doorway.
For the one who finds me finds life
and obtains favor from the Lord,

but the one who misses me harms himself;
all who hate me love death."

9 Wisdom has built her house;
she has carved out her seven pillars.
She has prepared her meat; she has mixed her wine;
she has also set her table.
She has sent out her female servants;
she calls out from the highest points of the city:
"Whoever is inexperienced, enter here!"
To the one who lacks sense, she says,
"Come, eat my bread,
10 and drink the wine I have mixed.
Leave inexperience behind, and you will live;
pursue the way of understanding.
The one who corrects a mocker
will bring abuse on himself;
the one who rebukes the wicked will get hurt.
Don't rebuke a mocker, or he will hate you;
rebuke the wise, and he will love you.
Instruct the wise, and he will be wiser still;
teach the righteous, and he will learn more.

20 "The fear of the LORD is the beginning of wisdom,
and the knowledge of the Holy One is understanding.
For by me your days will be many,
and years will be added to your life.
If you are wise, you are wise for your own benefit;
if you mock, you alone will bear the consequences."

Folly is a rowdy woman;
she is gullible and knows nothing.
She sits by the doorway of her house,
on a seat at the highest point of the city,
30 calling to those who pass by,
who go straight ahead on their paths:
"Whoever is inexperienced, enter here!"
To the one who lacks sense, she says,

"Stolen water is sweet,
and bread eaten secretly is tasty!"
But he doesn't know that the departed spirits are there,
that her guests are in the depths of Sheol.

10 Solomon's proverbs:
A wise son brings joy to his father,
but a foolish son, heartache to his mother.

Ill-gotten gains do not profit anyone,
but righteousness rescues from death.

The LORD will not let the righteous go hungry,
but he denies the wicked what they crave.

Idle hands make one poor,
but diligent hands bring riches.

The son who gathers during summer is prudent;
the son who sleeps during harvest is disgraceful.

Blessings are on the head of the righteous,
but the mouth of the wicked conceals violence.

The remembrance of the righteous is a blessing,
but the name of the wicked will rot.

A wise heart accepts commands,
but foolish lips will be destroyed.

The one who lives with integrity lives securely,
but whoever perverts his ways will be found out.

A sly wink of the eye causes grief,
and foolish lips will be destroyed.

The mouth of the righteous is a fountain of life,
but the mouth of the wicked conceals violence.

Hatred stirs up conflicts,
but love covers all offenses.

Wisdom is found on the lips of the discerning,
but a rod is for the back of the one who lacks sense.

The wise store up knowledge,
but the mouth of the fool hastens destruction.

30   The wealth of the rich is his fortified city;
the poverty of the poor is their destruction.

The reward of the righteous is life;
the wages of the wicked is punishment.

The one who follows instruction is on the path to life,
but the one who rejects correction goes astray.

The one who conceals hatred has lying lips,
and whoever spreads slander is a fool.

When there are many words, sin is unavoidable,
but the one who controls his lips is prudent.

40   The tongue of the righteous is pure silver;
the heart of the wicked is of little value.

The lips of the righteous feed many,
but fools die for lack of sense.

The Lord's blessing enriches,
and he adds no painful effort to it.

As shameful conduct is pleasure for a fool,
so wisdom is for a person of understanding.

What the wicked dreads will come to him,
but what the righteous desire will be given to them.

50 When the whirlwind passes,
the wicked are no more,
but the righteous are secure forever.

Like vinegar to the teeth and smoke to the eyes,
so the slacker is to the one who sends him on an errand.

The fear of the LORD prolongs life,
but the years of the wicked are cut short.

The hope of the righteous is joy,
but the expectation of the wicked will perish.

The way of the LORD is a stronghold for the honorable,
60 but destruction awaits evildoers.

The righteous will never be shaken,
but the wicked will not remain on the earth.

The mouth of the righteous produces wisdom,
but a perverse tongue will be cut out.

The lips of the righteous know what is appropriate,
but the mouth of the wicked, only what is perverse.

11 Dishonest scales are detestable to the LORD,
but an accurate weight is his delight.

When arrogance comes, disgrace follows,
but with humility comes wisdom.

The integrity of the upright guides them,
but the perversity of the treacherous destroys them.

Wealth is not profitable on a day of wrath,
but righteousness rescues from death.

The righteousness of the blameless clears his path,
but the wicked person will fall because of his wickedness.

The righteousness of the upright rescues them,
but the treacherous are trapped by their own desires.

When the wicked person dies,
his expectation comes to nothing,
and hope placed in wealth vanishes.

The righteous one is rescued from trouble;
in his place, the wicked one goes in.

With his mouth the ungodly destroys his neighbor,
but through knowledge the righteous are rescued.

When the righteous thrive, a city rejoices;
when the wicked die, there is joyful shouting.

A city is built up by the blessing of the upright,
but it is torn down by the mouth of the wicked.

Whoever shows contempt for his neighbor lacks sense,
but a person with understanding keeps silent.

A gossip goes around revealing a secret,
but a trustworthy person keeps a confidence.

Without guidance, a people will fall,
but with many counselors there is deliverance.

If someone puts up security for a stranger,
he will suffer for it,
but the one who hates such agreements is protected.

A gracious woman gains honor,
but violent people gain only riches.

A kind man benefits himself,
but a cruel person brings ruin on himself.

The wicked person earns an empty wage,
but the one who sows righteousness, a true reward.

Genuine righteousness leads to life,
40 but pursuing evil leads to death.

Those with twisted minds are detestable to the LORD,
but those with blameless conduct are his delight.

Be assured that a wicked person
will not go unpunished,
but the offspring of the righteous will escape.

A beautiful woman who rejects good sense
is like a gold ring in a pig's snout.

The desire of the righteous turns out well,
but the hope of the wicked leads to wrath.

50 One person gives freely,
yet gains more;
another withholds what is right,
only to become poor.

A generous person will be enriched,
and the one who gives a drink of water
will receive water.

People will curse anyone who hoards grain,
but a blessing will come to the one who sells it.

The one who searches for what is good seeks favor,
but if someone looks for trouble, it will come to him.

60

Anyone trusting in his riches will fall,
but the righteous will flourish like foliage.

The one who brings ruin on his household
will inherit the wind,
and a fool will be a slave
to someone whose heart is wise.

The fruit of the righteous is a tree of life,
but a cunning person takes lives.

If the righteous will be repaid on earth,
how much more the wicked and sinful.

70

12   Whoever loves discipline loves knowledge,
but one who hates correction is stupid.

One who is good obtains favor from the LORD,
but he condemns a person who schemes.

No one can be made secure by wickedness,
but the root of the righteous is immovable.

A wifeof noble character is her husband's crown,
but a wife who causes shame
is like rottenness in his bones.

10

The thoughts of the righteous are just,
but guidance from the wicked is deceitful.

The words of the wicked are a deadly ambush,
but the speech of the upright rescues them.

The wicked are overthrown and perish,
but the house of the righteous will stand.

A man is praised for his insight,
but a twisted mind is despised.

Better to be disregarded, yet have a servant,
than to act important but have no food.

20 The righteous cares about his animal's health,
but even the merciful acts of the wicked are cruel.

The one who works his land will have plenty of food,
but whoever chases fantasies lacks sense.

The wicked desire what evil people have caught,
but the root of the righteous is productive.

By rebellious speech an evil person is trapped,
but a righteous person escapes from trouble.

A person will be satisfied with good
by the fruit of his mouth,
30 and the work of a person's hands will reward him.

A fool's way is right in his own eyes,
but whoever listens to counsel is wise.

A fool's displeasure is known at once,
but whoever ignores an insult is sensible.

Whoever speaks the truth declares what is right,
but a false witness speaks deceit.

There is one who speaks rashly,
like a piercing sword;
but the tongue of the wise brings healing.

40 Truthful lips endure forever,
but a lying tongue, only a moment.

Deceit is in the hearts of those who plot evil,
but those who promote peace have joy.

No disaster overcomes the righteous,
but the wicked are full of misery.

Lying lips are detestable to the LORD,
but faithful people are his delight.

A shrewd person conceals knowledge,
but a foolish heart publicizes stupidity.

50 The diligent hand will rule,
but laziness will lead to forced labor.

Anxiety in a person's heart weighs it down,
but a good word cheers it up.

A righteous person is careful in dealing with his neighbor,
but the ways of the wicked lead them astray.

A lazy hunter doesn't roast his game,
but to a diligent person, his wealth is precious.

There is life in the path of righteousness,
and in its path there is no death.

13 A wise son responds to his father's discipline,
but a mocker doesn't listen to rebuke.

From the fruit of his mouth,
a person will enjoy good things,
but treacherous people have an appetite for violence.

The one who guards his mouth protects his life;
the one who opens his lips invites his own ruin.

The slacker craves, yet has nothing,
but the diligent is fully satisfied.

The righteous hate lying,
but the wicked bring disgust and shame.

Righteousness guards people of integrity,
but wickedness undermines the sinner.

One person pretends to be rich but has nothing;
another pretends to be poor but has abundant wealth.

Riches are a ransom for a person's life,
but a poor person hears no threat.

The light of the righteous shines brightly,
but the lamp of the wicked is put out.

Arrogance leads to nothing but strife,
but wisdom is gained by those who take advice.

Wealth obtained by fraud will dwindle,
but whoever earns it through labor will multiply it.

Hope delayed makes the heart sick,
but desire fulfilled is a tree of life.

The one who has contempt for instruction will pay the penalty,
but the one who respects a command will be rewarded.

A wise person's instruction is a fountain of life,
turning people away from the snares of death.

Good sense wins favor,
but the way of the treacherous never changes.

Every sensible person acts knowledgeably,
but a fool displays his stupidity.

A wicked envoy falls into trouble,
but a trustworthy courier brings healing.

Poverty and disgrace come to those
who ignore discipline,
but the one who accepts correction will be honored.

Desire fulfilled is sweet to the taste,
40   but to turn from evil is detestable to fools.

The one who walks with the wise will become wise,
but a companion of fools will suffer harm.

Disaster pursues sinners,
but good rewards the righteous.

A good man leaves an inheritance to his grandchildren,
but the sinner's wealth is stored up for the righteous.

The uncultivated field of the poor yields abundant food,
but without justice, it is swept away.

The one who will not use the rod hates his son,
50   but the one who loves him disciplines him diligently.

A righteous person eats until he is satisfied,
but the stomach of the wicked is empty.

14   Every wise woman builds her house,
but a foolish one tears it down with her own hands.

Whoever lives with integrity fears the LORD,
but the one who is devious in his ways despises him.

The proud speech of a fool brings a rod of discipline,
but the lips of the wise protect them.

Where there are no oxen, the feeding trough is empty,
but an abundant harvest comes through the strength of an ox.

An honest witness does not deceive,
but a dishonest witness utters lies.

A mocker seeks wisdom and doesn't find it,
but knowledge comes easily to the perceptive.

Stay away from a foolish person;
you will gain no knowledge from his speech.

The sensible person's wisdom is to consider his way,
but the stupidity of fools deceives them.

Fools mock at making reparation,
but there is goodwill among the upright.

The heart knows its own bitterness,
and no outsider shares in its joy.

The house of the wicked will be destroyed,
but the tent of the upright will flourish.

There is a way that seems right to a person,
but its end is the way to death.

Even in laughter a heart may be sad,
and joy may end in grief.

The disloyal one will get what his conduct deserves,
and a good one, what his deeds deserve.

The inexperienced one believes anything,
but the sensible one watches his steps.

A wise person is cautious and turns from evil,
but a fool is easily angered and is careless.

A quick-tempered person acts foolishly,
and one who schemes is hated.

The inexperienced inherit foolishness,
but the sensible are crowned with knowledge.

The evil bow before those who are good,
and the wicked, at the gates of the righteous.

A poor person is hated even by his neighbor,
40   but there are many who love the rich.

The one who despises his neighbor sins,
but whoever shows kindness to the poor will be happy.

Don't those who plan evil go astray?
But those who plan good find loyalty and faithfulness.

There is profit in all hard work,
but endless talk leads only to poverty.

The crown of the wise is their wealth,
but the foolishness of fools produces foolishness.

A truthful witness rescues lives,
50   but one who utters lies is deceitful.

In the fear of the Lord one has strong confidence
and his children have a refuge.

The fear of the Lord is a fountain of life,
turning people away from the snares of death.

A large population is a king's splendor,
but a shortage of people is a ruler's devastation.

A patient person shows great understanding,
but a quick-tempered one promotes foolishness.

A tranquil heart is life to the body,
but jealousy is rottenness to the bones.

The one who oppresses the poor person insults his Maker,
but one who is kind to the needy honors him.

The wicked one is thrown down by his own sin,
but the righteous one has a refuge in his death.

Wisdom resides in the heart of the discerning;
she is known even among fools.

Righteousness exalts a nation,
but sin is a disgrace to any people.

A king favors a prudent servant,
but his anger falls on a disgraceful one.

15 A gentle answer turns away anger,
but a harsh word stirs up wrath.

The tongue of the wise makes knowledge attractive,
but the mouth of fools blurts out foolishness.

The eyes of the Lord are everywhere,
observing the wicked and the good.

The tongue that heals is a tree of life,
but a devious tongue breaks the spirit.

A fool despises his father's discipline,
but a person who accepts correction is sensible.

The house of the righteous has great wealth,
but trouble accompanies the income of the wicked.

The lips of the wise broadcast knowledge,
but not so the heart of fools.

The sacrifice of the wicked is detestable to the LORD,
but the prayer of the upright is his delight.

The LORD detests the way of the wicked,
but he loves the one who pursues righteousness.

Discipline is harsh for the one who leaves the path;
the one who hates correction will die.

Sheol and Abaddon lie open before the LORD—
how much more, human hearts.

A mocker doesn't love one who corrects him;
he will not consult the wise.

A joyful heart makes a face cheerful,
but a sad heart produces a broken spirit.

A discerning mind seeks knowledge,
but the mouth of fools feeds on foolishness.

All the days of the oppressed are miserable,
but a cheerful heart has a continual feast.

Better a little with the fear of the LORD
than great treasure with turmoil.

Better a meal of vegetables where there is love
than a fattened ox with hatred.

A hot-tempered person stirs up conflict,
but one slow to anger calms strife.

A slacker's way is like a thorny hedge,
but the path of the upright is a highway.

40 A wise son brings joy to his father,
but a foolish man despises his mother.

Foolishness brings joy to one without sense,
but a person with understanding walks a straight path.

Plans fail when there is no counsel,
but with many advisers they succeed.

A person takes joy in giving an answer;
and a timely word — how good that is!

For the prudent the path of life leads upward,
so that he may avoid going down to Sheol.

50 The LORD tears apart the house of the proud,
but he protects the widow's territory.

The LORD detests the plans of the one who is evil,
but pleasant words are pure.

The one who profits dishonestly troubles his household,
but the one who hates bribes will live.

The mind of the righteous person thinks before answering,
but the mouth of the wicked blurts out evil things.

The LORD is far from the wicked,
but he hears the prayer of the righteous.

Bright eyes cheer the heart;
60 good news strengthens the bones.

One who listens to life-giving rebukes
will be at home among the wise.

Anyone who ignores discipline despises himself,
but whoever listens to correction acquires good sense.

The fear of the LORD is what wisdom teaches,
and humility comes before honor.

16 The reflections of the heart belong to mankind,
but the answer of the tongue is from the LORD.

All a person's ways seem right to him,
but the LORD weighs motives.

Commit your activities to the LORD,
and your plans will be established.

The LORD has prepared everything for his purpose—
even the wicked for the day of disaster.

Everyone with a proud heart is detestable to the LORD;
be assured, he will not go unpunished.

Iniquity is atoned for by loyalty and faithfulness,
and one turns from evil by the fear of the LORD.

When a person's ways please the LORD,
he makes even his enemies to be at peace with him.

Better a little with righteousness
than great income with injustice.

A person's heart plans his way,
but the LORD determines his steps.

God's verdict is on the lips of a king;
his mouth should not give an unfair judgment.

Honest balances and scales are the LORD's;
all the weights in the bag are his concern.

Wicked behavior is detestable to kings,
since a throne is established through righteousness.

Righteous lips are a king's delight,
and he loves one who speaks honestly.

A king's fury is a messenger of death,
but a wise person appeases it.

When a king's face lights up, there is life;
30   his favor is like a cloud with spring rain.

Get wisdom—
how much better it is than gold!
And get understanding—
it is preferable to silver.

The highway of the upright avoids evil;
the one who guards his way protects his life.

Pride comes before destruction,
and an arrogant spirit before a fall.

Better to be lowly of spirit with the humble
40   than to divide plunder with the proud.

The one who understands a matter finds success,
and the one who trusts in the Lord will be happy.

Anyone with a wise heart is called discerning,
and pleasant speech increases learning.

Insight is a fountain of life for its possessor,
but the discipline of fools is folly.

The heart of a wise person instructs his mouth;
it adds learning to his speech.

Pleasant words are a honeycomb:
50   sweet to the taste and health to the body.

There is a way that seems right to a person,
    but its end is the way to death.

A worker's appetite works for him
    because his hunger urges him on.

A worthless person digs up evil,
    and his speech is like a scorching fire.

A contrary person spreads conflict,
    and a gossip separates close friends.

A violent person lures his neighbor,
60   leading him on a path that is not good.

The one who narrows his eyes is planning deceptions;
    the one who compresses his lips brings about evil.

Gray hair is a glorious crown;
    it is found in the ways of righteousness.

Patience is better than power,
    and controlling one's emotions, than capturing a city.

The lot is cast into the lap,
    but its every decision is from the LORD.

17   Better a dry crust with peace
    than a house full of feasting with strife.

A prudent servant will rule over a disgraceful son
    and share an inheritance among brothers.

A crucible for silver, and a smelter for gold,
    and the LORD is the tester of hearts.

A wicked person listens to malicious talk;
a liar pays attention to a destructive tongue.

The one who mocks the poor insults his Maker,
and one who rejoices over calamity
will not go unpunished.

Grandchildren are the crown of the elderly,
and the pride of children is their fathers.

Eloquent words are not appropriate on a fool's lips;
how much worse are lies for a ruler.

A bribe seems like a magic stone to its owner;
wherever he turns, he succeeds.

Whoever conceals an offense promotes love,
but whoever gossips about it separates friends.

A rebuke cuts into a perceptive person
more than a hundred lashes into a fool.

An evil person desires only rebellion;
a cruel messenger will be sent against him.

Better for a person to meet a bear robbed of her cubs
than a fool in his foolishness.

If anyone returns evil for good,
evil will never depart from his house.

To start a conflict is to release a flood;
stop the dispute before it breaks out.

Acquitting the guilty and condemning the just—
both are detestable to the LORD.

Why does a fool have money in his hand
with no intention of buying wisdom?

A friend loves at all times,
and a brother is born for a difficult time.

One without sense enters an agreement
and puts up security for his friend.

One who loves to offend loves strife;
one who builds a high threshold invites injury.

40 One with a twisted mind will not succeed,
and one with deceitful speech will fall into ruin.

A man fathers a fool to his own sorrow;
the father of a fool has no joy.

A joyful heart is good medicine,
but a broken spirit dries up the bones.

A wicked person secretly takes a bribe
to subvert the course of justice.

Wisdom is the focus of the perceptive,
but a fool's eyes roam to the ends of the earth.

50 A foolish son is grief to his father
and bitterness to the one who bore him.

It is certainly not good to fine an innocent person
or to beat a noble for his honesty.

The one who has knowledge restrains his words,
and one who keeps a cool head
is a person of understanding.

Even a fool is considered wise when he keeps silent —
discerning, when he seals his lips.

18 One who isolates himself pursues selfish desires;
he rebels against all sound wisdom.

A fool does not delight in understanding,
but only wants to show off his opinions.

When a wicked person comes, contempt also comes,
and along with dishonor, derision.

The words of a person's mouth are deep waters,
a flowing river, a fountain of wisdom.

It is not good to show partiality to the guilty,
10   denying an innocent person justice.

A fool's lips lead to strife,
and his mouth provokes a beating.

A fool's mouth is his devastation,
and his lips are a trap for his life.

A gossip's words are like choice food
that goes down to one's innermost being.

The one who is lazy in his work
is brother to a vandal.

The name of the LORD is a strong tower;
20   the righteous run to it and are protected.

The wealth of the rich is his fortified city;
in his imagination it is like a high wall.

Before his downfall a person's heart is proud,
but humility comes before honor.

The one who gives an answer before he listens—
this is foolishness and disgrace for him.

A person's spirit can endure sickness,
but who can survive a broken spirit?

The mind of the discerning acquires knowledge,
and the ear of the wise seeks it.

A person's gift opens doors for him
and brings him before the great.

The first to state his case seems right
until another comes and cross-examines him.

Casting the lot ends quarrels
and separates powerful opponents.

An offended brother is harder to reach
than a fortified city,
and quarrels are like the bars of a fortress.

From the fruit of a person's mouth his stomach is satisfied;
he is filled with the product of his lips.

Death and life are in the power of the tongue,
and those who love it will eat its fruit.

A man who finds a wife finds a good thing
and obtains favor from the LORD.

The poor person pleads,
but the rich one answers roughly.

One with many friends may be harmed,
but there is a friend who stays closer than a brother.

19 Better a poor person who lives with integrity
than someone who has deceitful lips and is a fool.

Even zeal is not good without knowledge,
and the one who acts hastily sins.

A person's own foolishness leads him astray,
yet his heart rages against the LORD.

Wealth attracts many friends,
but a poor person is separated from his friend.

A false witness will not go unpunished,
10 and one who utters lies will not escape.

Many seek a ruler's favor,
and everyone is a friend of one who gives gifts.

All the brothers of a poor person hate him;
how much more do his friends
keep their distance from him!
He may pursue them with words,
but they are not there.

The one who acquires good sense loves himself;
one who safeguards understanding finds success.

20 A false witness will not go unpunished,
and one who utters lies perishes.

Luxury is not appropriate for a fool —
how much less for a slave to rule over princes!

A person's insight gives him patience,
and his virtue is to overlook an offense.

A king's rage is like the roaring of a lion,
but his favor is like dew on the grass.

A foolish son is his father's ruin,
and a wife's nagging is an endless dripping.

30 A house and wealth are inherited from fathers,
but a prudent wife is from the Lord.

Laziness induces deep sleep,
and a lazy person will go hungry.

The one who keeps commands preserves himself;
one who disregards his ways will die.

Kindness to the poor is a loan to the Lord,
and he will give a reward to the lender.

Discipline your son while there is hope;
don't set your heart on being the cause of his death.

40 A person with intense anger bears the penalty;
if you rescue him, you'll have to do it again.

Listen to counsel and receive instruction
so that you may be wise later in life.

Many plans are in a person's heart,
but the Lord's decree will prevail.

What is desirable in a person is his fidelity;
better to be a poor person than a liar.

The fear of the Lord leads to life;
one will sleep at night without danger.

50 The slacker buries his hand in the bowl;
he doesn't even bring it back to his mouth!

Strike a mocker, and the inexperienced learn a lesson;
rebuke the discerning, and he gains knowledge.

The one who plunders his father and evicts his mother
is a disgraceful and shameful son.

If you stop listening to correction, my son,
you will stray from the words of knowledge.

A worthless witness mocks justice,
and a wicked mouth swallows iniquity.

60 Judgments are prepared for mockers,
and beatings for the backs of fools.

20 Wine is a mocker, beer is a brawler;
whoever goes astray because of them is not wise.

A king's terrible wrath is like the roaring of a lion;
anyone who provokes him endangers himself.

Honor belongs to the person who ends a dispute,
but any fool can get himself into a quarrel.

The slacker does not plow during planting season;
at harvest time he looks, and there is nothing.

10 Counsel in a person's heart is deep water;
but a person of understanding draws it out.

Many a person proclaims his own loyalty,
but who can find a trustworthy person?

A righteous person acts with integrity;
his children who come after him will be happy.

A king sitting on a throne to judge
separates out all evil with his eyes.

Who can say, "I have kept my heart pure;
I am cleansed from my sin"?

Differing weights and varying measures—
both are detestable to the LORD.

Even a young man is known by his actions—
by whether his behavior is pure and upright.

The hearing ear and the seeing eye—
the LORD made them both.

Don't love sleep, or you will become poor;
open your eyes, and you'll have enough to eat.

"It's worthless, it's worthless!" the buyer says,
but after he is on his way, he gloats.

There is gold and a multitude of jewels,
but knowledgeable lips are a rare treasure.

Take his garment,
for he has put up security for a stranger;
get collateral if it is for foreigners.

Food gained by fraud is sweet to a person,
but afterward his mouth is full of gravel.

Finalize plans with counsel,
and wage war with sound guidance.

The one who reveals secrets is a constant gossip;
avoid someone with a big mouth.

Whoever curses his father or mother —
his lamp will go out in deep darkness.

An inheritance gained prematurely
will not be blessed ultimately.

Don't say, "I will avenge this evil!"
Wait on the LORD, and he will rescue you.

Differing weights are detestable to the LORD,
and dishonest scales are unfair.

Even a courageous person's steps are determined by the LORD,
so how can anyone understand his own way?

50 It is a trap for anyone to dedicate something rashly
and later to reconsider his vows.

A wise king separates out the wicked
and drives the threshing wheel over them.

The LORD's lamp sheds light on a person's life,
searching the innermost parts.

Loyalty and faithfulness guard a king;
through loyalty he maintains his throne.

The glory of young men is their strength,
and the splendor of old men is gray hair.

60 Lashes and wounds purge away evil,
and beatings cleanse the innermost parts.

21 A king's heart is like channeled water in the LORD's hand:
He directs it wherever he chooses.

All a person's ways seem right to him,
but the LORD weighs hearts.

Doing what is righteous and just
is more acceptable to the LORD than sacrifice.

The lamp that guides the wicked—
haughty eyes and an arrogant heart — is sin.

The plans of the diligent certainly lead to profit,
but anyone who is reckless certainly becomes poor.

Making a fortune through a lying tongue
is a vanishing mist, a pursuit of death.

The violence of the wicked sweeps them away
because they refuse to act justly.

A guilty one's conduct is crooked,
but the behavior of the innocent is upright.

Better to live on the corner of a roof
than to share a house with a nagging wife.

A wicked person desires evil;
he has no consideration for his neighbor.

When a mocker is punished,
the inexperienced become wiser;
when one teaches a wise man,
he acquires knowledge.

The Righteous One considers the house of the wicked;
he brings the wicked to ruin.

The one who shuts his ears to the cry of the poor
will himself also call out and not be answered.

A secret gift soothes anger,
and a covert bribe, fierce rage.

Justice executed is a joy to the righteous
but a terror to evildoers.

The person who strays from the way of prudence
will come to rest in the assembly of the departed spirits.

The one who loves pleasure will become poor;
whoever loves wine and oil will not get rich.

The wicked are a ransom for the righteous,
and the treacherous, for the upright.

Better to live in a wilderness
than with a nagging and hot-tempered wife.

Precious treasure and oil are in the dwelling of a wise person,
but a fool consumes them.

The one who pursues righteousness and faithful love
will find life, righteousness, and honor.

A wise person went up against a city of warriors
and brought down its secure fortress.

The one who guards his mouth and tongue
keeps himself out of trouble.

The arrogant and proud person, named "Mocker,"
acts with excessive arrogance.

A slacker's craving will kill him
because his hands refuse to work.
He is filled with craving all day long,
but the righteous give and don't hold back.

The sacrifice of a wicked person is detestable —
how much more so
when he brings it with ulterior motives!

A lying witness will perish,
but the one who listens will speak successfully.

A wicked person puts on a bold face,
but the upright one considers his way.

No wisdom, no understanding, and no counsel
will prevail against the LORD.

A horse is prepared for the day of battle,
but victory comes from the LORD.

22 A good name is to be chosen over great wealth;
favor is better than silver and gold.

Rich and poor have this in common:
the LORD makes them all.

A sensible person sees danger and takes cover,
but the inexperienced keep going and are punished.

Humility, the fear of the LORD,
results in wealth, honor, and life.

There are thorns and snares on the way of the crooked;
the one who guards himself stays far from them.

Start a youth out on his way;
even when he grows old he will not depart from it.

The rich rule over the poor,
and the borrower is a slave to the lender.

The one who sows injustice will reap disaster,
and the rod of his fury will be destroyed.

A generous person will be blessed,
for he shares his food with the poor.

Drive out a mocker, and conflict goes too;
then quarreling and dishonor will cease.

The one who loves a pure heart
and gracious lips — the king is his friend.

The Lord's eyes keep watch over knowledge,
but he overthrows the words of the treacherous.

The slacker says, "There's a lion outside!
I'll be killed in the public square!"

The mouth of the forbidden woman is a deep pit;
a man cursed by the Lord will fall into it.

Foolishness is bound to the heart of a youth;
a rod of discipline will separate it from him.

Oppressing the poor to enrich oneself,
and giving to the rich — both lead only to poverty.

Listen closely, pay attention to the words of the wise,
and apply your mind to my knowledge.
For it is pleasing if you keep them within you
and if they are constantly on your lips.
I have instructed you today — even you—
so that your confidence may be in the Lord.
Haven't I written for you thirty sayings
about counsel and knowledge,
in order to teach you true and reliable words,
so that you may give a dependable report
to those who sent you?

Don't rob a poor person because he is poor,
and don't crush the oppressed at the city gate,
for the Lord will champion their cause
and will plunder those who plunder them.

Don't make friends with an angry person,
and don't be a companion of a hot-tempered one,
or you will learn his ways
and entangle yourself in a snare.

Don't be one of those who enter agreements,
who put up security for loans.
If you have nothing with which to pay,
even your bed will be taken from under you.

Don't move an ancient boundary marker
that your ancestors set up.

Do you see a person skilled in his work?
He will stand in the presence of kings.
60   He will not stand in the presence of the unknown.

23   When you sit down to dine with a ruler,
consider carefully what is before you,
and put a knife to your throat
if you have a big appetite;
don't desire his choice food,
for that food is deceptive.

Don't wear yourself out to get rich;
because you know better, stop!
As soon as your eyes fly to it, it disappears,
10   for it makes wings for itself
and flies like an eagle to the sky.

Don't eat a stingy person's bread,
and don't desire his choice food,
for it's like someone calculating inwardly.
"Eat and drink," he says to you,
but his heart is not with you.
You will vomit the little you've eaten
and waste your pleasant words.

Don't speak to a fool,
20   for he will despise the insight of your words.

Don't move an ancient boundary marker,
and don't encroach on the fields of the fatherless,

for their Redeemer is strong,
and he will champion their cause against you.

Apply yourself to discipline
and listen to words of knowledge.

Don't withhold discipline from a youth;
if you punish him with a rod, he will not die.
Punish him with a rod,
and you will rescue his life from Sheol.

My son, if your heart is wise,
my heart will indeed rejoice.
My innermost being will celebrate
when your lips say what is right.

Don't let your heart envy sinners;
instead, always fear the LORD.
For then you will have a future,
and your hope will not be dashed.

Listen, my son, and be wise;
keep your mind on the right course.
Don't associate with those who drink too much wine
or with those who gorge themselves on meat.
For the drunkard and the glutton will become poor,
and grogginess will clothe them in rags.

Listen to your father who gave you life,
and don't despise your mother when she is old.
Buy — and do not sell — truth,
wisdom, instruction, and understanding.
The father of a righteous son will rejoice greatly,
and one who fathers a wise son will delight in him.
Let your father and mother have joy,
and let her who gave birth to you rejoice.

My son, give me your heart,
and let your eyes observe my ways.
For a prostitute is a deep pit,
and a wayward woman is a narrow well;
indeed, she sets an ambush like a robber
and increases the number of unfaithful people.

Who has woe? Who has sorrow?
60   Who has conflicts? Who has complaints?
Who has wounds for no reason?
Who has red eyes?
Those who linger over wine;
those who go looking for mixed wine.
Don't gaze at wine because it is red,
because it gleams in the cup
and goes down smoothly.
In the end it bites like a snake
and stings like a viper.
70   Your eyes will see strange things,
and you will say absurd things.
You'll be like someone sleeping out at sea
or lying down on the top of a ship's mast.
"They struck me, but I feel no pain!
They beat me, but I didn't know it!
When will I wake up?
I'll look for another drink."

24   Don't envy the evil
or desire to be with them,
for their hearts plan violence,
and their words stir up trouble.

A house is built by wisdom,
and it is established by understanding;
by knowledge the rooms are filled
with every precious and beautiful treasure.

A wise warrior is better than a strong one,
10 and a man of knowledge than one of strength;
for you should wage war with sound guidance—
victory comes with many counselors.

Wisdom is inaccessible to a fool;
he does not open his mouth at the city gate.

The one who plots evil
will be called a schemer.
A foolish scheme is sin,
and a mocker is detestable to people.

If you do nothing in a difficult time,
20 your strength is limited.
Rescue those being taken off to death,
and save those stumbling toward slaughter.
If you say, "But we didn't know about this,"
won't he who weighs hearts consider it?
Won't he who protects your life know?
Won't he repay a person according to his work?

Eat honey, my son, for it is good,
and the honeycomb is sweet to your palate;
realize that wisdom is the same for you.
30 If you find it, you will have a future,
and your hope will never fade.

Don't set an ambush, you wicked one,
at the camp of the righteous man;
don't destroy his dwelling.
Though a righteous person falls seven times,
he will get up,
but the wicked will stumble into ruin.

Don't gloat when your enemy falls,
and don't let your heart rejoice when he stumbles,

40 or the LORD will see, be displeased,
 and turn his wrath away from him.

 Don't be agitated by evildoers,
 and don't envy the wicked.
 For the evil have no future;
 the lamp of the wicked will be put out.

 My son, fear the LORD, as well as the king,
 and don't associate with rebels,
 for destruction will come suddenly from them;
 who knows what distress these two can bring?

50 These sayings also belong to the wise:

It is not good to show partiality in judgment.
 Whoever says to the guilty, "You are innocent"—
 peoples will curse him, and nations will denounce him;
 but it will go well with those who convict the guilty,
 and a generous blessing will come to them.

 He who gives an honest answer
 gives a kiss on the lips.

 Complete your outdoor work, and prepare your field;
 afterward, build your house.

60 Don't testify against your neighbor without cause.
 Don't deceive with your lips.
 Don't say, "I'll do to him what he did to me;
 I'll repay the man for what he has done."

 I went by the field of a slacker
 and by the vineyard of one lacking sense.
 Thistles had come up everywhere,
 weeds covered the ground,
 and the stone wall was ruined.
 I saw, and took it to heart;

70 I looked, and received instruction:
a little sleep, a little slumber,
a little folding of the arms to rest,
and your poverty will come like a robber,
and your need, like a bandit.

25 These too are proverbs of Solomon,
which the men of King Hezekiah of Judah copied.

It is the glory of God to conceal a matter
and the glory of kings to investigate a matter.
As the heavens are high and the earth is deep,
so the hearts of kings cannot be investigated.

Remove impurities from silver,
and material will be produced for a silversmith.
Remove the wicked from the king's presence,
10 and his throne will be established in righteousness.

Don't boast about yourself before the king,
and don't stand in the place of the great;
for it is better for him to say to you, "Come up here!"
than to demote you in plain view of a noble.

Don't take a matter to court hastily.
Otherwise, what will you do afterward
if your opponent humiliates you?
Make your case with your opponent
without revealing another's secret;
20 otherwise, the one who hears will disgrace you,
and you'll never live it down.

A word spoken at the right time
is like gold apples in silver settings.
A wise correction to a receptive ear
is like a gold ring or an ornament of gold.

To those who send him, a trustworthy envoy
is like the coolness of snow on a harvest day;
he refreshes the life of his masters.

The one who boasts about a gift that does not exist
is like clouds and wind without rain.
A ruler can be persuaded through patience,
and a gentle tongue can break a bone.
If you find honey, eat only what you need;
otherwise, you'll get sick from it and vomit.
Seldom set foot in your neighbor's house;
otherwise, he'll get sick of you and hate you.

A person giving false testimony against his neighbor
is like a club, a sword, or a sharp arrow.
Trusting an unreliable person in a difficult time
is like a rotten tooth or a faltering foot.

Singing songs to a troubled heart
is like taking off clothing on a cold day
or like pouring vinegar on soda.

If your enemy is hungry, give him food to eat,
and if he is thirsty, give him water to drink,
for you will heap burning coals on his head,
and the LORD will reward you.

The north wind produces rain,
and a backbiting tongue, angry looks.
Better to live on the corner of a roof
than to share a house with a nagging wife.
Good news from a distant land
is like cold water to a parched throat.
A righteous person who yields to the wicked
is like a muddied spring or a polluted well.
It is not good to eat too much honey
or to seek glory after glory.

A person who does not control his temper
is like a city whose wall is broken down.

26 Like snow in summer and rain at harvest,
honor is inappropriate for a fool.
Like a flitting sparrow or a fluttering swallow,
an undeserved curse goes nowhere.
A whip for the horse, a bridle for the donkey,
and a rod for the backs of fools.
Don't answer a fool according to his foolishness
or you'll be like him yourself.
Answer a fool according to his foolishness
or he'll become wise in his own eyes.
The one who sends a message by a fool's hand
cuts off his own feet and drinks violence.
A proverb in the mouth of a fool
is like lame legs that hang limp.
Giving honor to a fool
is like binding a stone in a sling.
A proverb in the mouth of a fool
is like a stick with thorns,
brandished by the hand of a drunkard.
The one who hires a fool or who hires those passing by
is like an archer who wounds everyone indiscriminately.
As a dog returns to its vomit,
so also a fool repeats his foolishness.
Do you see a person who is wise in his own eyes?
There is more hope for a fool than for him.

The slacker says, "There's a lion in the road—
a lion in the public square!"
A door turns on its hinges,
and a slacker, on his bed.
The slacker buries his hand in the bowl;
he is too weary to bring it to his mouth!
In his own eyes, a slacker is wiser
than seven who can answer sensibly.

A person who is passing by and meddles in a quarrel that's not his
is like one who grabs a dog by the ears.
Like a madman who throws flaming darts and deadly arrows,
so is the person who deceives his neighbor
and says, "I was only joking!"

Without wood, fire goes out;
40   without a gossip, conflict dies down.
As charcoal for embers and wood for fire,
so is a quarrelsome person for kindling strife.
A gossip's words are like choice food
that goes down to one's innermost being.

Smooth lips with an evil heart
are like glaze on an earthen vessel.
A hateful person disguises himself with his speech
and harbors deceit within.
When he speaks graciously, don't believe him,
50   for there are seven detestable things in his heart.
Though his hatred is concealed by deception,
his evil will be revealed in the assembly.
The one who digs a pit will fall into it,
and whoever rolls a stone—
it will come back on him.
A lying tongue hates those it crushes,
and a flattering mouth causes ruin.

27   Don't boast about tomorrow,
for you don't know what a day might bring.

Let another praise you, and not your own mouth—
a stranger, and not your own lips.

A stone is heavy, and sand a burden,
but aggravation from a fool outweighs them both.

Fury is cruel, and anger a flood,
but who can withstand jealousy?

Better an open reprimand
than concealed love.

The wounds of a friend are trustworthy,
but the kisses of an enemy are excessive.

A person who is full tramples on a honeycomb,
but to a hungry person, any bitter thing is sweet.

Anyone wandering from his home
is like a bird wandering from its nest.

Oil and incense bring joy to the heart,
and the sweetness of a friend is better than self-counsel.

Don't abandon your friend or your father's friend,
and don't go to your brother's house
in your time of calamity;
better a neighbor nearby than a brother far away.

Be wise, my son, and bring my heart joy,
so that I can answer anyone who taunts me.

A sensible person sees danger and takes cover;
the inexperienced keep going and are punished.

Take his garment,
for he has put up security for a stranger;
get collateral if it is for foreigners.

If one blesses his neighbor
with a loud voice early in the morning,
it will be counted as a curse to him.

An endless dripping on a rainy day
and a nagging wife are alike;
the one who controls her controls the wind
and grasps oil with his right hand.

Iron sharpens iron,
and one person sharpens another.

Whoever tends a fig tree will eat its fruit,
40   and whoever looks after his master will be honored.

As water reflects the face,
so the heart reflects the person.

Sheol and Abaddon are never satisfied,
and people's eyes are never satisfied.

As a crucible refines silver,
and a smelter refines gold,
so a person should refine his praise.

Though you grind a fool
in a mortar with a pestle along with grain,
50   you will not separate his foolishness from him.

Know well the condition of your flock,
and pay attention to your herds,
for wealth is not forever;
not even a crown lasts for all time.
When hay is removed and new growth appears
and the grain from the hills is gathered in,
lambs will provide your clothing,
and goats, the price of a field;
there will be enough goat's milk for your food—
60   food for your household
and nourishment for your female servants.

28   The wicked flee when no one is pursuing them,
but the righteous are as bold as a lion.

When a land is in rebellion, it has many rulers,
but with a discerning and knowledgeable person, it endures.

A destitute leader who oppresses the poor
is like a driving rain that leaves no food.

Those who reject the law praise the wicked,
but those who keep the law pit themselves against them.

The evil do not understand justice,
but those who seek the LORD understand everything.

Better the poor person who lives with integrity
than the rich one who distorts right and wrong.

A discerning son keeps the law,
but a companion of gluttons humiliates his father.

Whoever increases his wealth through excessive interest
collects it for one who is kind to the poor.

Anyone who turns his ear away from hearing the law—
even his prayer is detestable.

The one who leads the upright into an evil way
will fall into his own pit,
but the blameless will inherit what is good.

A rich person is wise in his own eyes,
but a poor one who has discernment sees through him.

When the righteous triumph,
there is great rejoicing,
but when the wicked come to power,
people hide.

The one who conceals his sins
will not prosper,
but whoever confesses and renounces them
will find mercy.

Happy is the one who is always reverent,
but one who hardens his heart falls into trouble.

A wicked ruler over a helpless people
is like a roaring lion or a charging bear.

A leader who lacks understanding
is very oppressive,
but one who hates dishonest profit
prolongs his life.

40   Someone burdened by bloodguilt
will be a fugitive until death.
Let no one help him.

The one who lives with integrity will be helped,
but one who distorts right and wrong
will suddenly fall.

The one who works his land
will have plenty of food,
but whoever chases fantasies
will have his fill of poverty.

50   A faithful person will have many blessings,
but one in a hurry to get rich
will not go unpunished.

It is not good to show partiality—
yet even a courageous person may sin for a piece of bread.

A greedy one is in a hurry for wealth;
he doesn't know that poverty will come to him.

One who rebukes a person will later find more favor
than one who flatters with his tongue.

The one who robs his father or mother
60   and says, "That's no sin,"
        is a companion to a person who destroys.

        A greedy person stirs up conflict,
        but whoever trusts in the LORD will prosper.

        The one who trusts in himself is a fool,
        but one who walks in wisdom will be safe.

        The one who gives to the poor
        will not be in need,
        but one who turns his eyes away
        will receive many curses.

70   When the wicked come to power,
        people hide,
        but when they are destroyed,
        the righteous flourish.

29   One who becomes stiff-necked,
        after many reprimands
        will be shattered instantly—
        beyond recovery.

        When the righteous flourish, the people rejoice,
        but when the wicked rule, people groan.

        A man who loves wisdom brings joy to his father,
        but one who consorts with prostitutes destroys his wealth.

        By justice a king brings stability to a land,
10   but a person who demands "contributions"
        demolishes it.

        A person who flatters his neighbor
        spreads a net for his feet.

An evil person is caught by sin,
but the righteous one sings and rejoices.

The righteous person knows the rights of the poor,
but the wicked one does not understand these concerns.

Mockers inflame a city,
but the wise turn away anger.

20 If a wise person goes to court with a fool,
there will be ranting and raving but no resolution.

Bloodthirsty men hate an honest person,
but the upright care about him.

A fool gives full vent to his anger,
but a wise person holds it in check.

If a ruler listens to lies,
all his officials will be wicked.

The poor and the oppressor have this in common:
the LORD gives light to the eyes of both.

30 A king who judges the poor with fairness—
his throne will be established forever.

A rod of correction imparts wisdom,
but a youth left to himself
is a disgrace to his mother.

When the wicked increase, rebellion increases,
but the righteous will see their downfall.

Discipline your child, and it will bring you peace of mind
and give you delight.

Without revelation people run wild,
but one who follows divine instruction will be happy.

A servant cannot be disciplined by words;
though he understands, he doesn't respond.

Do you see someone who speaks too soon?
There is more hope for a fool than for him.

A servant pampered from his youth
will become arrogant later on.

An angry person stirs up conflict,
and a hot-tempered one increases rebellion.

A person's pride will humble him,
but a humble spirit will gain honor.

To be a thief's partner is to hate oneself;
he hears the curse but will not testify.

The fear of mankind is a snare,
but the one who trusts in the LORD is protected.

Many desire a ruler's favor,
but a person receives justice from the LORD.

An unjust person is detestable to the righteous,
and one whose way is upright
is detestable to the wicked.

30 The words of Agur son of Jakeh. The pronouncement.

The man's oration to Ithiel, to Ithiel and Ucal:

I am more stupid than any other person,
and I lack a human's ability to understand.
I have not gained wisdom,

and I have no knowledge of the Holy One.
Who has gone up to heaven and come down?
Who has gathered the wind in his hands?
Who has bound up the waters in a cloak?
Who has established all the ends of the earth?
What is his name,
and what is the name of his son—
if you know?
Every word of God is pure;
he is a shield to those who take refuge in him.
Don't add to his words,
or he will rebuke you, and you will be proved a liar.

Two things I ask of you;
don't deny them to me before I die:
Keep falsehood and deceitful words far from me.
Give me neither poverty nor wealth;
feed me with the food I need.
Otherwise, I might have too much
and deny you, saying, "Who is the LORD?"
or I might have nothing and steal,
profaning the name of my God.

Don't slander a servant to his master
or he will curse you, and you will become guilty.

There is a generation that curses its father
and does not bless its mother.
There is a generation that is pure in its own eyes,
yet is not washed from its filth.
There is a generation — how haughty its eyes
and pretentious its looks.
There is a generation whose teeth are swords,
whose fangs are knives,
devouring the oppressed from the land
and the needy from among mankind.

The leech has two daughters: "Give, Give!"
Three things are never satisfied;
four never say, "Enough!":
Sheol; a childless womb;
earth, which is never satisfied with water;
and fire, which never says, "Enough!"

As for the eye that ridicules a father
and despises obedience to a mother,
may ravens of the valley pluck it out
and young vultures eat it.

Three things are too wondrous for me;
four I can't understand:
the way of an eagle in the sky,
the way of a snake on a rock,
the way of a ship at sea,
and the way of a man with a young woman.

This is the way of an adulteress:
she eats and wipes her mouth
and says, "I've done nothing wrong."

The earth trembles under three things;
it cannot bear up under four:
a servant when he becomes king,
a fool when he is stuffed with food,
an unloved woman when she marries,
and a servant girl when she ousts her queen.

Four things on earth are small,
yet they are extremely wise:
ants are not a strong people,
yet they store up their food in the summer;
hyraxes are not a mighty people,
yet they make their homes in the cliffs;
locusts have no king,
yet all of them march in ranks;

a lizard can be caught in your hands,
yet it lives in kings' palaces.

Three things are stately in their stride;
four are stately in their walk:
a lion, which is mightiest among beasts
and doesn't retreat before anything;
a strutting rooster; a goat;
and a king at the head of his army.

80   If you have been foolish by exalting yourself
or if you've been scheming,
put your hand over your mouth.
For the churning of milk produces butter,
and twisting a nose draws blood,
and stirring up anger produces strife.

31   The words of King Lemuel,
a pronouncement that his mother taught him:

What should I say, my son?
What, son of my womb?
What, son of my vows?
Don't spend your energy on women
or your efforts on those who destroy kings.
It is not for kings, Lemuel,
it is not for kings to drink wine
10   or for rulers to desire beer.
Otherwise, he will drink,
forget what is decreed,
and pervert justice for all the oppressed.
Give beer to one who is dying
and wine to one whose life is bitter.
Let him drink so that he can forget his poverty
and remember his trouble no more.
Speak up for those who have no voice,
for the justice of all who are dispossessed.

20 Speak up, judge righteously,
    and defend the cause of the oppressed and needy.

    Who can find a wife of noble character?
    She is far more precious than jewels.
    The heart of her husband trusts in her,
    and he will not lack anything good.
    She rewards him with good, not evil,
    all the days of her life.
    She selects wool and flax
    and works with willing hands.
30 She is like the merchant ships,
    bringing her food from far away.
    She rises while it is still night
    and provides food for her household
    and portions for her female servants.
    She evaluates a field and buys it;
    she plants a vineyard with her earnings.
    She draws on her strength
    and reveals that her arms are strong.
    She sees that her profits are good,
40 and her lamp never goes out at night.
    She extends her hands to the spinning staff,
    and her hands hold the spindle.
    Her hands reach out to the poor,
    and she extends her hands to the needy.
    She is not afraid for her household when it snows,
    for all in her household are doubly clothed.
    She makes her own bed coverings;
    her clothing is fine linen and purple.
    Her husband is known at the city gates,
50 where he sits among the elders of the land.
    She makes and sells linen garments;
    she delivers belts to the merchants.
    Strength and honor are her clothing,
    and she can laugh at the time to come.
    Her mouth speaks wisdom,
    and loving instruction is on her tongue.

She watches over the activities of her household
and is never idle.
Her children rise up and call her blessed;
her husband also praises her:
"Many women have done noble deeds,
but you surpass them all!"
Charm is deceptive and beauty is fleeting,
but a woman who fears the LORD will be praised.
Give her the reward of her labor,
and let her works praise her at the city gates.

Introduction to Ruth

Richard Anthony Purcell

The book of Ruth imaginatively explores and reshapes two biblical concepts: "a valiant warrior" (*ḥayil*) and "covenant loyalty" (*ḥesed*). The narrative does so through a most unlikely cast of characters: Naomi, a bereft Israelite woman, Boaz, an older Israelite bachelor, and most surprisingly Ruth, a widowed Moabite foreigner! The story centers on the actions of the destitute Moabitess Ruth, a member of one of Israel's oldest and most slandered enemy nations (e.g., Gen 19.48–60). The book of Ruth, then, selects an outsider to model *ḥayil* and *ḥesed* for its audience.

Both Ruth and Boaz serve as exemplars of *ḥayil* (2.1–2; 3.17–19). Throughout the HS, the term *ḥayil* refers to warrior prowess and might (e.g., Judg 3.46–47; 1 Sam 2.13). Boaz is introduced in 2.1 as a "prominent man of noble character," which might more literally be rendered, "a valiant warrior." The book of Ruth, though, reimagines what it means to be a person of *ḥayil*. Boaz practices *ḥayil* not through warrior prowess but through compassionate and life-giving application of the Torah (4.1–22). Even more startling, Ruth is marked out as a woman of *ḥayil* (a rare phrase in the HS, see Prov 12.7–9 and 31.22–23) for her practice of *ḥesed* in 3.16–19. The book of Ruth recasts *ḥayil* as the practice of *ḥesed*, empathetic and life-giving love.

The book of Ruth also serves as an exposition of *ḥesed*, the Hebrew concept of covenant loyalty and empathetic care. The book portrays *ḥesed* and its life-giving power in narrative form, as the primary characters model *ḥesed* in their commitments and actions (e.g., 1.13–14, 25–36; 2.15–43; 3.16–17). Ruth displays loving covenant loyalty as she "clings to" Naomi rather than seeking her own best interests (1.22–23). As the narrative unfolds, Ruth stands with Naomi (forsaking her own people and gods, e.g., 1.25–36 and 2.21–23), provides for Naomi (e.g., 2.3–7; 4.28–34), and secures a future for Naomi in the form of family, land, and progeny (chs. 3–4). Boaz enacts *ḥesed* in his dealings with Ruth, a poor and widowed foreigner, often "bending the rules" in the process. With Ruth's own *ḥesed*-acts as his inspiration, Boaz protects Ruth (2.15–18), commands his servants to eschew standard gleaning expectations (2.31–33), agrees to marry Ruth (3.16–22), and reframes separate land redemption and levirate marriage laws from Lev 25 and Deut 25 to provide for the women and maintain their family lineage (4.18–22). In blending these legal statutes, Boaz applies a hermeneutic of *ḥesed* to go beyond the letter of the law. Within the narrative, true strength and love consists of accepting and caring for those on the margins. The narrative's closing genealogy illustrates the transformative result of such life-giving *ḥesed*—the Davidic dynasty (4.35–44) and, according to Matthew's Gospel, the Messiah himself (Matt 1:1–16, esp. vv. 5–6).

Ruth echoes multiple themes within the HS and thus has held various places within the canon. The modern Jewish canon situates Ruth among the Megillot (or "Five Scrolls," including Song of Songs, Ruth,

Lamentations, Ecclesiastes, and Esther), associating it with the liturgical festival of *Shavuot* and the wheat harvest (see Deut 16.13–18 and Ruth 1.43–44; 2.47–49). The Septuagint and later Christian canons place Ruth between Judges and Samuel, following the literary signals of the narrative that opens with "During the time of the judges" and closes with the genealogy of David. Here, the book provides a counterpoint to the vile abuse of women that occurs in the latter half of Judges as the Israelites pursue "whatever seemed right to him" (Judg 17.9–10). The early Jewish canonical arrangement adopted by the HS places Ruth immediately after Proverbs, which ends with a poetic evocation of the ideal wise woman, the woman of *ḥayil* (Prov 31.22–66). In this position, the narrative of Ruth provides a historical exemplar of Proverb's ideal woman of *ḥayil* in the character of Ruth. The book's positive stance towards foreigners might be read in conversation with Deuteronomy and its laws barring Moabites from the people of Israel (Deut 23.3–8) or the xenophobic rhetoric of Ezra-Nehemiah (Ezra 9.1–8; Neh 13.44–52). The book of Ruth ultimately envisions a welcoming Israelite community with space for all willing to practice *ḥesed* and seek Yahweh as their God.

Outline

1. Setting the Scene: Loss in the Land of Moab (1.1–8)

2. Return to Bethlehem: Ruth's Commitment to Naomi and Her God (1.9–44)

3. A Kinsmen Redeemer: Ruth in the Field of Boaz (2.1–49)

4. A Glimpse of Hope: Ruth and Boaz at the Threshing Floor (3.1–31)

5. Applying the Law with *ḥesed*: Boaz Marries Ruth and Redeems Naomi's Land (4.1–27)

6. The Fruits of *ḥesed*: Ruth Gives Birth to Obed and the Davidic Dynasty (4.28–34)

7. The Davidic Genealogy (4.35–44)

Suggested Resources

Block, Daniel. *Judges, Ruth*. New American Commentary. Nashville: Broadman & Holman, 1999.

Eskenazi, Tamara Cohn, and Tikva Frymer-Kensky. *Ruth*. Jewish Publication Society Bible Commentary. Philadelphia: Jewish Publication Society, 2001.

LaCocque, André. *Ruth: A Continental Commentary*. Continental Commentary. Minneapolis: Fortress, 2004.

Linafelt, Tod, and Timothy K. Beal. *Ruth and Esther*. Berit Olam. Collegeville, MN: Liturgical Press, 1999.

Queen-Sutherland, Kandy. *Ruth and Esther*. Smyth & Helwys Bible Commentary. Macon, GA: Smyth & Helwys, 2016.

Ruth

1 During the time of the judges, there was a famine in the land. A man left Bethlehem in Judah with his wife and two sons to stay in the territory of Moab for a while. The man's name was Elimelech, and his wife's name was Naomi. The names of his two sons were Mahlon and Chilion. They were Ephrathites from Bethlehem in Judah. They entered the fields of Moab and settled there. Naomi's husband, Elimelech, died, and she was left with her two sons. Her sons took Moabite women as their wives: one was named Orpah and the second was named Ruth. After they lived in Moab about ten years, both Mahlon and Chilion also died, and the woman was left without her two children and without her husband.

She and her daughters-in-law set out to return from the territory of Moab, because she had heard
10 in Moab that the Lord had paid attention to his people's need by providing them food. She left the place where she had been living, accompanied by her two daughters-in-law, and traveled along the road leading back to the land of Judah.

Naomi said to them, "Each of you go back to your mother's home. May the Lord show kindness to you as you have shown to the dead and to me. May the Lord grant each of you rest in the house of a new husband." She kissed them, and they wept loudly.

They said to her, "We insist on returning with you to your people."

But Naomi replied, "Return home, my daughters. Why do you want to go with me? Am I able to have any more sons who could become your husbands? Return home, my daughters. Go on, for I am too old to have another husband. Even if I thought there was still hope for me to have
20 a husband tonight and to bear sons, would you be willing to wait for them to grow up? Would you restrain yourselves from remarrying? No, my daughters, my life is much too bitter for you to share, because the Lord's hand has turned against me." Again they wept loudly, and Orpah kissed her mother-in-law, but Ruth clung to her. Naomi said, "Look, your sister-in-law has gone back to her people and to her gods. Follow your sister-in-law."

But Ruth replied:

> Don't plead with me to abandon you
> or to return and not follow you.
> For wherever you go, I will go,
> and wherever you live, I will live;
30 > your people will be my people,
> and your God will be my God.

Where you die, I will die,
and there I will be buried.
May the LORD punish me,
and do so severely,
if anything but death separates you and me.

When Naomi saw that Ruth was determined to go with her, she stopped talking to her.

The two of them traveled until they came to Bethlehem. When they entered Bethlehem, the whole town was excited about their arrival and the local women exclaimed, "Can this be Naomi?"

40 "Don't call me Naomi. Call me Mara," she answered, "for the Almighty has made me very bitter. I went away full, but the LORD has brought me back empty. Why do you call me Naomi, since the LORD has opposed me, and the Almighty has afflicted me?"

So Naomi came back from the territory of Moab with her daughter-in-law Ruth the Moabitess. They arrived in Bethlehem at the beginning of the barley harvest.

2 Now Naomi had a relative on her husband's side. He was a prominent man of noble character from Elimelech's family. His name was Boaz.

Ruth the Moabitess asked Naomi, "Will you let me go into the fields and gather fallen grain behind someone with whom I find favor?"

Naomi answered her, "Go ahead, my daughter." So Ruth left and entered the field to gather grain behind the harvesters. She happened to be in the portion of the field belonging to Boaz, who was from Elimelech's family.

Later, when Boaz arrived from Bethlehem, he said to the harvesters, "The LORD be with you."

"The LORD bless you," they replied.

10 Boaz asked his servant who was in charge of the harvesters, "Whose young woman is this?"

The servant answered, "She is the young Moabite woman who returned with Naomi from the territory of Moab. She asked, 'Will you let me gather fallen grain among the bundles behind the harvesters?' She came and has been on her feet since early morning, except that she rested a little in the shelter."

Then Boaz said to Ruth, "Listen, my daughter. Don't go and gather grain in another field, and don't leave this one, but stay here close to my female servants. See which field they are harvesting, and follow them. Haven't I ordered the young men not to touch you? When you are thirsty, go and drink from the jars the young men have filled."

She fell facedown, bowed to the ground, and said to him, "Why have I found favor with you, so 20 that you notice me, although I am a foreigner?"

Boaz answered her, "Everything you have done for your mother-in-law since your husband's death has been fully reported to me: how you left your father and mother and your native land, and how you came to a people you didn't previously know. May the LORD reward you for what you have done, and may you receive a full reward from the LORD God of Israel, under whose wings you have come for refuge."

"My lord," she said, "I have found favor with you, for you have comforted and encouraged your servant, although I am not like one of your female servants."

At mealtime Boaz told her, "Come over here and have some bread and dip it in the vinegar sauce." So she sat beside the harvesters, and he offered her roasted grain. She ate and was satisfied and had some left over.

When she got up to gather grain, Boaz ordered his young men, "Let her even gather grain among the bundles, and don't humiliate her. Pull out some stalks from the bundles for her and leave them for her to gather. Don't rebuke her." So Ruth gathered grain in the field until evening. She beat out what she had gathered, and it was about twenty-six quarts of barley. She picked up the grain and went into the town, where her mother-in-law saw what she had gleaned. She brought out what she had left over from her meal and gave it to her.

Her mother-in-law said to her, "Where did you gather barley today, and where did you work? May the LORD bless the man who noticed you."

Ruth told her mother-in-law whom she had worked with and said, "The name of the man I worked with today is Boaz."

Then Naomi said to her daughter-in-law, "May the LORD bless him because he has not abandoned his kindness to the living or the dead." Naomi continued, "The man is a close relative. He is one of our family redeemers."

Ruth the Moabitess said, "He also told me, 'Stay with my young men until they have finished all of my harvest.'"

So Naomi said to her daughter-in-law Ruth, "My daughter, it is good for you to work with his female servants, so that nothing will happen to you in another field." Ruth stayed close to Boaz's female servants and gathered grain until the barley and the wheat harvests were finished. And she lived with her mother-in-law.

3 Ruth's mother-in-law Naomi said to her, "My daughter, shouldn't I find rest for you, so that you will be taken care of? Now isn't Boaz our relative? Haven't you been working with his female servants? This evening he will be winnowing barley on the threshing floor. Wash, put on perfumed oil, and wear your best clothes. Go down to the threshing floor, but don't let the man know you are there until he has finished eating and drinking. When he lies down, notice the place where he's lying, go in and uncover his feet, and lie down. Then he will explain to you what you should do."

So Ruth said to her, "I will do everything you say." She went down to the threshing floor and did everything her mother-in-law had charged her to do. After Boaz ate, drank, and was in good spirits, he went to lie down at the end of the pile of barley, and she came secretly, uncovered his feet, and lay down.

At midnight, Boaz was startled, turned over, and there lying at his feet was a woman! So he asked, "Who are you?"

"I am Ruth, your servant," she replied. "Take me under your wing, for you are a family redeemer."

Then he said, "May the LORD bless you, my daughter. You have shown more kindness now than before, because you have not pursued younger men, whether rich or poor. Now don't be afraid, my daughter. I will do for you whatever you say, since all the people in my town know that you are a woman of noble character. Yes, it is true that I am a family redeemer, but there is a
20 redeemer closer than I am. Stay here tonight, and in the morning, if he wants to redeem you, that's good. Let him redeem you. But if he doesn't want to redeem you, as the LORD lives, I will. Now lie down until morning."

So she lay down at his feet until morning but got up while it was still dark. Then Boaz said, "Don't let it be known that a woman came to the threshing floor." And he told Ruth, "Bring the shawl you're wearing and hold it out." When she held it out, he shoveled six measures of barley into her shawl, and she went into the town.

She went to her mother-in-law, Naomi, who asked her, "What happened, my daughter?"

Then Ruth told her everything the man had done for her. She said, "He gave me these six measures of barley, because he said, 'Don't go back to your mother-in-law empty-handed.'"
30 Naomi said, "My daughter, wait until you find out how things go, for he won't rest unless he resolves this today."

4 Boaz went to the gate of the town and sat down there. Soon the family redeemer Boaz had spoken about came by. Boaz said, "Come over here and sit down." So he went over and sat down. Then Boaz took ten men of the town's elders and said, "Sit here." And they sat down. He said to the redeemer, "Naomi, who has returned from the territory of Moab, is selling the portion of the field that belonged to our brother Elimelech. I thought I should inform you: Buy it back in the presence of those seated here and in the presence of the elders of my people. If you want to redeem it, do it. But if you do not want to redeem it, tell me so that I will know, because there isn't anyone other than you to redeem it, and I am next after you."

"I want to redeem it," he answered.
10 Then Boaz said, "On the day you buy the field from Naomi, you will acquire Ruth the Moabitess, the wife of the deceased man, to perpetuate the man's name on his property."

The redeemer replied, "I can't redeem it myself, or I will ruin my own inheritance. Take my right of redemption, because I can't redeem it."

At an earlier period in Israel, a man removed his sandal and gave it to the other party in order to make any matter legally binding concerning the right of redemption or the exchange of property. This was the method of legally binding a transaction in Israel.

So the redeemer removed his sandal and said to Boaz, "Buy back the property yourself."

Boaz said to the elders and all the people, "You are witnesses today that I am buying from Naomi everything that belonged to Elimelech, Chilion, and Mahlon. I have also acquired Ruth the
²⁰ Moabitess, Mahlon's widow, as my wife, to perpetuate the deceased man's name on his property, so that his name will not disappear among his relatives or from the gate of his hometown. You are witnesses today."

All the people who were at the city gate, including the elders, said, "We are witnesses. May the LORD make the woman who is entering your house like Rachel and Leah, who together built the house of Israel. May you be powerful in Ephrathah and your name well known in Bethlehem. May your house become like the house of Perez, the son Tamar bore to Judah, because of the offspring the LORD will give you by this young woman."

Boaz took Ruth and she became his wife. He slept with her, and the LORD granted conception to her, and she gave birth to a son. The women said to Naomi, "Blessed be the LORD, who has
³⁰ not left you without a family redeemer today. May his name become well known in Israel. He will renew your life and sustain you in your old age. Indeed, your daughter-in-law, who loves you and is better to you than seven sons, has given birth to him." Naomi took the child, placed him on her lap, and became a mother to him. The neighbor women said, "A son has been born to Naomi," and they named him Obed. He was the father of Jesse, the father of David.

Now these are the family records of Perez:
> Perez fathered Hezron,
> Hezron fathered Ram,
> Ram fathered Amminadab,
> Amminadab fathered Nahshon,
⁴⁰ Nahshon fathered Salmon,
> Salmon fathered Boaz,
> Boaz fathered Obed,
> Obed fathered Jesse,
> and Jesse fathered David.

Introduction to Song of Songs

Tremper Longman III

Song of Songs has an interesting history of interpretation, with the earliest preserved comments coming from around 100 AD. Around this date, Rabbi Aqiba states, with what looks like urgency, "whoever sings the Song of Songs with a tremulous voice in a banquet hall and (so) treats it as a sort of ditty has no share in the world to come" (tractate Sanhedrin 12.10). This quote tells us two things: (1) the Song's erotic language was clear to many who read it, and (2) the religious authorities were trying to give the sexual language a religious meaning. The latter becomes even clearer in a second comment by Aqiba: "for all the Writings are holy, but the Song of Song is the Holy of Holies."

Thus, Aqiba promoted an allegorical interpretation of the Song in which the woman speaker represents Israel and the male voice represents Yahweh. Accordingly, the mutual love expressed between the man and the woman is that between Yahweh and his people. Christian interpreters followed suit, believing that the woman stood for the church, while the man stood for Jesus. In these types of allegorical readings, symbolic meaning was also assigned to the language. Thus, the Targum of the Song (an Aramaic interpretive paraphrase of the Hebrew dated to the 9th century AD) understood the woman's (Israel's) request that the man (Yahweh) take her into his bedroom (1.9) as a reference to the entrance into the promised land after the exodus. Hippolytus, a 2nd century AD Christian commentator, understood the woman's reference to the sachet of myrrh lodged between her breasts (1.3–4) to point to Jesus who spans the OT and NT.

While this type of reading was dominant in church and synagogue up until the nineteenth century, today most interpreters believe an allegorical approach was driven by the erroneous belief that the Bible could not contain such a blatantly sensual book. After all, during much of this time, the church and synagogue under the influence of Platonism believed that one's body (and its sexual desires) and one's soul worked at odds with each other, the former needing to be repressed in the interest of spiritual growth.

Today, most readers of the Song reject the idea that it is an allegory, rather reading it as a love poem or a collection of love poems. Differences exist between those who believe the poetry tells a story either of the growing relationship between a man and a woman sometimes identified as Solomon and a woman identified as the Shulammite (6.48) or of a love triangle, the love of a woman for her shepherd boyfriend threatened by the king, again sometimes identified as Solomon.

The difficulties of identifying a clear plot or even the exact number of primary characters (two or three) lead many to see the Song as a collection of love poems whose major emphasis celebrates the physical intimacy between a man and a woman with a minor theme on the difficulties of achieving romantic bliss (e.g. the poem in 5.9–6.12). Reading the Song in this way, readers can identify themselves with the unnamed man and woman while the daughters of Jerusalem serve to represent both those who encourage this intimate and passionate relationship.

While not an allegory, the Song does have theological meaning when read in the context of the broader canon of Scripture. Elsewhere in the HS, Yahweh's relationship with his people is likened to a marriage (positively in Jer 2.1–11; Hos 2.54–66, and negative in many places including Hosea 1; Ezekiel 16; 23). Thus, the picture of passionate, intimate, and exclusive love between the man and the woman can inform the use of the marriage metaphor for Yahweh and his people, reminding us that that relationship too should be intimate, passionate, and exclusive.

The marriage metaphor in the New Testament is used for the relationship between the church and Jesus (Eph 5.21–33). Thus, Christian readers can read the Song as calling for an intimate, passionate, exclusive relationship with Jesus.

Outline

1. Superscription (1.1)
2. Poem One: The Woman's Pursuit (1.2–14)
3. Poem Two: Dark, but Beautiful (1.15–22)
4. Poem Three: An Invitation to a Tryst (1.23–33)
5. Poem Four: A Beautiful Mare (1.34–39)
6. Poem Five: Intimate Fragrances (1.40–46)
7. Poem Six: Outdoor Love (1.47–56)
8. Poem Seven: Flowers and Trees (2.1–22)
9. Poem Eight: A Poem of Spring (2.23–61)
10. Poem Nine: Seeking and (Not) Finding (3.1–18)
11. Poem Ten: A Royal Wedding Procession (3.19–42)
12. Poem Eleven: From Head to Breasts (4.1–27)
13. Poem Twelve: The Invitation (4.28–36)
14. Poem Thirteen: Eating in the Garden of Love (4.37–5.8)
15. Poem Fourteen: To Search and (Not) Find, Once Again (5.9–12)
16. Poem Fifteen: Awesome As an Army under Banners (6.13–38)
17. Poem Sixteen: A Surprise in the Nut Grove (6.39–46)
18. Poem Seventeen: The Dancing Shulammite (6.47–7.31)
19. Poem Eighteen: I Will Give You My Love (7.32–43)
20. Poem Nineteen: Yearning for Love (8.1–13)
21. Poem Twenty: Like a Seal (8.14–30)
22. Poem Twenty-One: Protecting the Sister (8.31–44)
23. Poem Twenty-Two: Who Owns the Vineyard? (8.45–51)
24. Poem Twenty-Three: Be Like a Gazelle (8.52–60)

Suggested Resources

Athas, George. *Ecclesiastes, Song of Songs*. The Story of God Bible Commentary. Grand Rapids: Zondervan, 2020.

Duguid, Iain M. *The Song of Songs*. Tyndale Old Testament Commentaries. Downers Grove, IL: InterVarsity Press, 2015.

Longman, Tremper, III. *Song of Songs*. New International Commentary on the Old Testament. Grand Rapids: Eerdmans, 2001.

Provan, Iain. *Ecclesiastes, Song of Songs*. NIV Application Commentary. Grand Rapids: Zondervan, 2001.

Song of Songs

I The Song of Songs, which is Solomon's.

Woman
Oh, that he would kiss me with the kisses of his mouth!
For your caresses are more delightful than wine.
The fragrance of your perfume is intoxicating;
your name is perfume poured out.
No wonder young women adore you.
Take me with you—let's hurry.
Oh, that the king would bring me to his chambers.

10 Young Women
We will rejoice and be glad in you;
we will celebrate your caresses more than wine.

Woman
It is only right that they adore you.

Daughters of Jerusalem,
I am dark like the tents of Kedar,
yet lovely like the curtains of Solomon.
Do not stare at me because I am dark,
for the sun has gazed on me.
20 My mother's sons were angry with me;
they made me take care of the vineyards.
I have not taken care of my own vineyard.

Tell me, you whom I love:
Where do you pasture your sheep?
Where do you let them rest at noon?
Why should I be like one who veils herself
beside the flocks of your companions?

Man
If you do not know,
30   most beautiful of women,
follow the tracks of the flock,
and pasture your young goats
near the shepherds' tents.

I compare you, my darling,
to a mare among Pharaoh's chariots.
Your cheeks are beautiful with jewelry,
your neck with its necklace.
We will make gold jewelry for you,
accented with silver.

40   Woman
While the king is on his couch,
my perfume releases its fragrance.
The one I love is a sachet of myrrh to me,
spending the night between my breasts.
The one I love is a cluster of henna blossoms to me,
in the vineyards of En-gedi.

Man
How beautiful you are, my darling.
How very beautiful!
50   Your eyes are doves.

Woman
How handsome you are, my love.
How delightful!
Our bed is verdant;
the beams of our house are cedars,
and our rafters are cypresses.

2   I am a wildflower of Sharon,
a lily of the valleys.

Man
Like a lily among thorns,
so is my darling among the young women.

Woman
Like an apricot tree among the trees of the forest,
so is my love among the young men.
I delight to sit in his shade,
and his fruit is sweet to my taste.
He brought me to the banquet hall,
and he looked on me with love.
Sustain me with raisins;
refresh me with apricots,
for I am lovesick.
May his left hand be under my head,
and his right arm embrace me.
Young women of Jerusalem, I charge you
by the gazelles and the wild does of the field,
do not stir up or awaken love
until the appropriate time.

Listen! My love is approaching.
Look! Here he comes,
leaping over the mountains,
bounding over the hills.
My love is like a gazelle
or a young stag.
See, he is standing behind our wall,
gazing through the windows,
peering through the lattice.
My love calls to me:

Man
Arise, my darling.
Come away, my beautiful one.
For now the winter is past;
the rain has ended and gone away.
The blossoms appear in the countryside.

The time of singing has come,
40   and the turtledove's cooing is heard in our land.
The fig tree ripens its figs;
the blossoming vines give off their fragrance.
Arise, my darling.
Come away, my beautiful one.

My dove, in the clefts of the rock,
in the crevices of the cliff,
let me see your face,
let me hear your voice;
for your voice is sweet,
50   and your face is lovely.

Woman
Catch the foxes for us—
the little foxes that ruin the vineyards—
for our vineyards are in bloom.

Woman
My love is mine and I am his;
he feeds among the lilies.
Until the day breaks
and the shadows flee,
60   turn around, my love, and be like a gazelle
or a young stag on the divided mountains.

3   In my bed at night
I sought the one I love;
I sought him, but did not find him.
I will arise now and go about the city,
through the streets and the plazas.
I will seek the one I love.
I sought him, but did not find him.
The guards who go about the city found me.
I asked them, "Have you seen the one I love?"
10   I had just passed them
when I found the one I love.

I held on to him and would not let him go
until I brought him to my mother's house—
to the chamber of the one who conceived me.
Young women of Jerusalem, I charge you
by the gazelles and the wild does of the field,
do not stir up or awaken love
until the appropriate time.

Narrator
20 Who is this coming up from the wilderness
like columns of smoke,
scented with myrrh and frankincense
from every fragrant powder of the merchant?

Look! Solomon's bed
surrounded by sixty warriors
from the mighty men of Israel.
All of them are skilled with swords
and trained in warfare.
Each has his sword at his side
30 to guard against the terror of the night.

King Solomon made a carriage for himself
with wood from Lebanon.
He made its posts of silver,
its back of gold,
and its seat of purple.
Its interior is inlaid with love
by the young women of Jerusalem.
Go out, young women of Zion,
and gaze at King Solomon,
40 wearing the crown his mother placed on him
on the day of his wedding—
the day of his heart's rejoicing.

4 Man
How beautiful you are, my darling.
How very beautiful!

Behind your veil,
your eyes are doves.
Your hair is like a flock of goats
streaming down Mount Gilead.
Your teeth are like a flock of newly shorn sheep
coming up from washing,
10   each one bearing twins,
and none has lost its young.
Your lips are like a scarlet cord,
and your mouth is lovely.
Behind your veil,
your brow is like a slice of pomegranate.
Your neck is like the tower of David,
constructed in layers.
A thousand shields are hung on it—
all of them shields of warriors.
20   Your breasts are like two fawns,
twins of a gazelle, that feed among the lilies.
Until the day breaks
and the shadows flee,
I will make my way to the mountain of myrrh
and the hill of frankincense.
You are absolutely beautiful, my darling;
there is no imperfection in you.

Come with me from Lebanon, my bride;
come with me from Lebanon!
30   Descend from the peak of Amana,
from the summit of Senir and Hermon,
from the dens of the lions,
from the mountains of the leopards.
You have captured my heart, my sister, my bride.
You have captured my heart with one glance of your eyes,
with one jewel of your necklace.
How delightful your caresses are, my sister, my bride.
Your caresses are much better than wine,
and the fragrance of your perfume than any balsam.
40   Your lips drip sweetness like the honeycomb, my bride.

Honey and milk are under your tongue.
The fragrance of your garments is like the fragrance of Lebanon.

My sister, my bride, you are a locked garden—
a locked garden and a sealed spring.
Your branches are a paradise of pomegranates
with choicest fruits;
henna with nard,
nard and saffron, calamus and cinnamon,
with all the trees of frankincense,
myrrh and aloes,
with all the best spices.
You are a garden spring,
a well of flowing water
streaming from Lebanon.

Woman
Awaken, north wind;
come, south wind.
Blow on my garden,
and spread the fragrance of its spices.
Let my love come to his garden
and eat its choicest fruits.

Man
I have come to my garden—my sister, my bride.
I gather my myrrh with my spices.
I eat my honeycomb with my honey.
I drink my wine with my milk.

Narrator
Eat, friends!
Drink, be intoxicated with caresses!

Woman
I was sleeping, but my heart was awake.
A sound! My love was knocking!

Man
Open to me, my sister, my darling,
my dove, my perfect one.
For my head is drenched with dew,
my hair with droplets of the night.

Woman
I have taken off my clothing.
How can I put it back on?
20 I have washed my feet.
How can I get them dirty?
My love thrust his hand through the opening,
and my feelings were stirred for him.
I rose to open for my love.
My hands dripped with myrrh,
my fingers with flowing myrrh
on the handles of the bolt.
I opened to my love,
but my love had turned and gone away.
30 My heart sank because he had left.
I sought him, but did not find him.
I called him, but he did not answer.
The guards who go about the city found me.
They beat and wounded me;
they took my cloak from me—
the guardians of the walls.
Young women of Jerusalem, I charge you,
if you find my love,
tell him that I am lovesick.

40 Young Women
What makes the one you love better than another,
most beautiful of women?
What makes him better than another,
that you would give us this charge?

Woman
My love is fit and strong,

notable among ten thousand.
His head is purest gold.
His hair is wavy
and black as a raven.
His eyes are like doves
beside flowing streams,
washed in milk
and set like jewels.
His cheeks are like beds of spice,
mounds of perfume.
His lips are lilies,
dripping with flowing myrrh.
His arms are rods of gold
set with beryl.
His body is an ivory panel
covered with lapis lazuli.
His legs are alabaster pillars
set on pedestals of pure gold.
His presence is like Lebanon,
as majestic as the cedars.
His mouth is sweetness.
He is absolutely desirable.
This is my love, and this is my friend,
young women of Jerusalem.

6

Young Women
Where has your love gone,
most beautiful of women?
Which way has he turned?
We will seek him with you.

Woman
My love has gone down to his garden,
to beds of spice,
to feed in the gardens
and gather lilies.
I am my love's and my love is mine;
he feeds among the lilies.

Man
You are as beautiful as Tirzah, my darling,
lovely as Jerusalem,
awe-inspiring as an army with banners.
Turn your eyes away from me,
for they captivate me.
Your hair is like a flock of goats
20 streaming down from Gilead.
Your teeth are like a flock of ewes
coming up from washing,
each one having a twin,
and not one missing.
Behind your veil,
your brow is like a slice of pomegranate.
There are sixty queens
and eighty concubines
and young women without number.
30 But my dove, my virtuous one, is unique;
she is the favorite of her mother,
perfect to the one who gave her birth.
Women see her and declare her fortunate;
queens and concubines also, and they sing her praises:

Who is this who shines like the dawn,
as beautiful as the moon,
bright as the sun,
awe-inspiring as an army with banners?

Woman
40 I came down to the walnut grove
to see the blossoms of the valley,
to see if the vines were budding
and the pomegranates blooming.
I didn't know what was happening to me.
I felt like I was
in a chariot with a nobleman.

Young Women
Come back, come back, Shulammite!
Come back, come back, that we may look at you!

50 Man
How you gaze at the Shulammite,
as you look at the dance of the two camps!

7 How beautiful are your sandaled feet, princess!
The curves of your thighs are like jewelry,
the handiwork of a master.
Your navel is a rounded bowl;
it never lacks mixed wine.
Your belly is a mound of wheat
surrounded by lilies.
Your breasts are like two fawns,
twins of a gazelle.
10 Your neck is like a tower of ivory,
your eyes like pools in Heshbon
by Bath-rabbim's gate.
Your nose is like the tower of Lebanon
looking toward Damascus.
Your head crowns you like Mount Carmel,
the hair of your head like purple cloth—
a king could be held captive in your tresses.
How beautiful you are and how pleasant,
my love, with such delights!
20 Your stature is like a palm tree;
your breasts are clusters of fruit.
I said, "I will climb the palm tree
and take hold of its fruit."
May your breasts be like clusters of grapes,
and the fragrance of your breath like apricots.
Your mouth is like fine wine—

Woman
flowing smoothly for my love,
gliding past my lips and teeth!

30   I am my love's,
    and his desire is for me.

    Come, my love,
    let's go to the field;
    let's spend the night among the henna blossoms.
    Let's go early to the vineyards;
    let's see if the vine has budded,
    if the blossom has opened,
    if the pomegranates are in bloom.
    There I will give you my caresses.
40   The mandrakes give off a fragrance,
    and at our doors is every delicacy,
    both new and old.
    I have treasured them up for you, my love.

8   If only I could treat you like my brother,
    one who nursed at my mother's breasts,
    I would find you in public and kiss you,
    and no one would scorn me.
    I would lead you, I would take you,
    to the house of my mother who taught me.
    I would give you spiced wine to drink
    from the juice of my pomegranate.
    May his left hand be under my head,
10   and his right arm embrace me.
    Young women of Jerusalem, I charge you,
    do not stir up or awaken love
    until the appropriate time.

    Young Women
    Who is this coming up from the wilderness,
    leaning on the one she loves?

    Woman
    I awakened you under the apricot tree.
    There your mother conceived you;
20   there she conceived and gave you birth.

Set me as a seal on your heart,
as a seal on your arm.
For love is as strong as death;
jealousy is as unrelenting as Sheol.
Love's flames are fiery flames—
an almighty flame!
A huge torrent cannot extinguish love;
rivers cannot sweep it away.
If a man were to give all his wealth for love,
30 it would be utterly scorned.

Brothers
Our sister is young;
she has no breasts.
What will we do for our sister
on the day she is spoken for?
If she is a wall,
we will build a silver barricade on her.
If she is a door,
we will enclose her with cedar planks.

40 Woman
I am a wall
and my breasts like towers.
So to him I have become
like one who finds peace.

Solomon owned a vineyard in Baal-hamon.
He leased the vineyard to tenants.
Each was to bring for his fruit
one thousand pieces of silver.
I have my own vineyard.
50 The one thousand are for you, Solomon,
but two hundred for those who take care of its fruits.

Man
You who dwell in the gardens,

companions are listening for your voice;
let me hear you!

Woman
Run away with me, my love,
and be like a gazelle
or a young stag
on the mountains of spices.

Introduction to Ecclesiastes

Russell L. Meek

Readers often avoid this small book tucked into the Writings section of the HS because it seems pessimistic and devoid of hope. And when readers do engage the book—named "Qohelet" after the title of its main speaker—they often interpret its meaning to be something along the lines of, "Everything is meaningless without God." Ecclesiastes is no pessimistic book, though, and while it is true that everything *is* meaningless without Yahweh, that is not the book's primary message to either its ancient or modern readers. Instead, Ecclesiastes offers the reflections of an Israelite wise man who is struggling to reconcile what he knows of Yahweh with what he sees in the world around him. In the process, he offers readers advice for how to navigate this world marred by sin.

The primary key to understanding the message of Ecclesiastes is to see that the book is built upon the theological foundation of the book of Genesis. Through repeated vocabulary and thematic elements, Ecclesiastes alludes to Genesis in its view of 1) enjoying Yahweh's gifts; 2) Yahweh's sovereignty; 3) sin and death; and 4) the role of humans in this life "under the sun." Further, Ecclesiastes explores life in the post-fall world by using the key word *hebel* (translated "futility" by the CSB) to point readers back to the story of Cain and Abel (*hebel* in Hebrew). In Gen 4, readers see that life does not always work out as it should—the righteous Abel receives the fruits of wickedness, while the wicked Cain receives the fruits of righteousness (descendants, land, wealth, and even a mark of protection from Yahweh). The author of Ecclesiastes recognizes that the same breakdown between actions and their expected consequences happens in his world—and ours today—and using a literary device known as allusion, he labels those things *hebel*, or Abel.

In light of the "Abelness" of the world—that sin has turned it upside down—Ecclesiastes offers readers two ways to navigate this life "under the sun." The first is through fearing Yahweh, or living in obedience to him because of the covenant he established with his people at Mount Sinai—and later on the cross. Ecclesiastes's concern with fearing Yahweh is scattered throughout the book, but the clearest statement comes in the book's concluding verses. The second means for navigating the post-fall world is through enjoying Yahweh's gifts when he allows it. These gifts—food, work, wine, and a spouse—are the very gifts Yahweh gave Adam and Eve, and by enjoying them readers reclaim, in a small yet real sense, what was lost in Eden and anticipate what will be gained in the new heavens and new earth.

Ecclesiastes, then, does not represent the musings of a cynical, world-hardened man. Rather, it contains the reflections of a person who is attempting to reconcile what he sees "under the sun" with what he knows of Yahweh, the book beckons readers today to do the same through honest acknowledgment of the upside-down nature of the world, humble submission to the God of the universe, and eager enjoyment of the gifts he has given. Ecclesiastes, like its counterparts Daniel and Esther in the Writings, shows readers what it means to live in covenant relationship with Yahweh.

Outline

1. Introduction (1.1)
2. Brief poem regarding the cyclic nature of life (1.2–32)
3. The "Teacher" applies his heart to wisdom (1.33–43)
4. The Teacher investigates pleasure, kingdom building, wisdom, and work, struggling to understand their "Abelness" (2.1–42)
5. Appropriate times for various activities (3.1–16)
6. Yahweh is sovereign, though death overtakes everyone (3.17–4.5)
7. Work and the benefits of companionship (4.6–24)
8. Fear Yahweh (5.1–9)
9. Wealth and enjoyment, Yahweh's sovereignty, and the "Abelness" of life (5.10–6.19)
10. Series of proverbs (7.1–33)
11. The righteous perish and the wicked live, but fear Yahweh (7.34–52)
12. Wisdom and folly, wickedness and righteousness (8.1–27)
13. Despite life's uncertainties, enjoy! (9.1–18)
14. Everything is marked by "Abelness" (9.19–31)
15. Another series of proverbs (10.1–45)
16. Be wise and enjoy life as much as Yahweh allows it (11.1–31)
17. Death and dying (12.1–27)
18. "Fear God and keep his commands" (12.28–36)

Suggested Resources

Bartholomew, Craig G. *Ecclesiastes.* Baker Commentary on the Old Testament Wisdom and Psalms. Grand Rapids: Baker Academic, 2009.

Fox, Michael V. *A Time to Tear Down and a Time to Build Up: A Rereading of Ecclesiastes.* Grand Rapids: Eerdmans, 1999.

Fredericks, Daniel C., and Daniel J. Estes. *Ecclesiastes and the Song of Songs.* Downers Grove, IL: InterVarsity Press, 2010.

Longman, Tremper, III. *The Book of Ecclesiastes.* New International Commentary on the Old Testament. Grand Rapids: Eerdmans, 1998.

Provan, Iain. *Ecclesiastes, Song of Songs.* NIV Application Commentary. Grand Rapids: Zondervan, 2001.

Ecclesiastes

1 The words of the Teacher, son of David, king in Jerusalem.
     "Absolute futility," says the Teacher.
     "Absolute futility. Everything is futile."
     What does a person gain for all his efforts
     that he labors at under the sun?
     A generation goes and a generation comes,
     but the earth remains forever.
     The sun rises and the sun sets;
     panting, it hurries back to the place
10   where it rises.
     Gusting to the south,
     turning to the north,
     turning, turning, goes the wind,
     and the wind returns in its cycles.
     All the streams flow to the sea,
     yet the sea is never full;
     to the place where the streams flow,
     there they flow again.
     All things are wearisome,
20   more than anyone can say.
     The eye is not satisfied by seeing
     or the ear filled with hearing.
     What has been is what will be,
     and what has been done is what will be done;
     there is nothing new under the sun.
     Can one say about anything,
     "Look, this is new"?
     It has already existed in the ages before us.
     There is no remembrance of those who came before;
30   and of those who will come after
     there will also be no remembrance
     by those who follow them.

I, the Teacher, have been king over Israel in Jerusalem. I applied my mind to examine and explore through wisdom all that is done under heaven. God has given people this miserable task to keep them occupied. I have seen all the things that are done under the sun and have found everything to be futile, a pursuit of the wind.

> What is crooked cannot be straightened;
> what is lacking cannot be counted.

I said to myself, "See, I have amassed wisdom far beyond all those who were over Jerusalem
40 before me, and my mind has thoroughly grasped wisdom and knowledge." I applied my mind to know wisdom and knowledge, madness and folly; I learned that this too is a pursuit of the wind.

> For with much wisdom is much sorrow;
> as knowledge increases, grief increases.

2 I said to myself, "Go ahead, I will test you with pleasure; enjoy what is good." But it turned out to be futile. I said about laughter, "It is madness," and about pleasure, "What does this accomplish?" I explored with my mind the pull of wine on my body — my mind still guiding me with wisdom— and how to grasp folly, until I could see what is good for people to do under heaven during the few days of their lives.

I increased my achievements. I built houses and planted vineyards for myself. I made gardens and parks for myself and planted every kind of fruit tree in them. I constructed reservoirs for myself from which to irrigate a grove of flourishing trees. I acquired male and female servants and had slaves who were born in my house. I also owned livestock — large herds and flocks —
10 more than all who were before me in Jerusalem. I also amassed silver and gold for myself, and the treasure of kings and provinces. I gathered male and female singers for myself, and many concubines, the delights of men. So I became great and surpassed all who were before me in Jerusalem; my wisdom also remained with me. All that my eyes desired, I did not deny them. I did not refuse myself any pleasure, for I took pleasure in all my struggles. This was my reward for all my struggles. When I considered all that I had accomplished and what I had labored to achieve, I found everything to be futile and a pursuit of the wind. There was nothing to be gained under the sun.

Then I turned to consider wisdom, madness, and folly, for what will the king's successor be like? He will do what has already been done. And I realized that there is an advantage to wisdom over
20 folly, like the advantage of light over darkness.

The wise person has eyes in his head,
but the fool walks in darkness.

Yet I also knew that one fate comes to them both. So I said to myself, "What happens to the fool will also happen to me. Why then have I been overly wise?" And I said to myself that this is also futile. For, just like the fool, there is no lasting remembrance of the wise, since in the days to come both will be forgotten. How is it that the wise person dies just like the fool? Therefore, I hated life because the work that was done under the sun was distressing to me. For everything is futile and a pursuit of the wind.

I hated all my work that I labored at under the sun because I must leave it to the one who comes after me. And who knows whether he will be wise or a fool? Yet he will take over all my work that I labored at skillfully under the sun. This too is futile. So I began to give myself over to despair concerning all my work that I had labored at under the sun. When there is a person whose work was done with wisdom, knowledge, and skill, and he must give his portion to a person who has not worked for it, this too is futile and a great wrong. For what does a person get with all his work and all his efforts that he labors at under the sun? For all his days are filled with grief, and his occupation is sorrowful; even at night, his mind does not rest. This too is futile.

There is nothing better for a person than to eat, drink, and enjoy his work. I have seen that even this is from God's hand, because who can eat and who can enjoy life apart from him? For to the person who is pleasing in his sight, he gives wisdom, knowledge, and joy; but to the sinner he gives the task of gathering and accumulating in order to give to the one who is pleasing in God's sight. This too is futile and a pursuit of the wind.

3   There is an occasion for everything,
and a time for every activity under heaven:
a time to give birth and a time to die;
a time to plant and a time to uproot;
a time to kill and a time to heal;
a time to tear down and a time to build;
a time to weep and a time to laugh;
a time to mourn and a time to dance;
a time to throw stones and a time to gather stones;
a time to embrace and a time to avoid embracing;
a time to search and a time to count as lost;
a time to keep and a time to throw away;
a time to tear and a time to sew;

> a time to be silent and a time to speak;
> a time to love and a time to hate;
> a time for war and a time for peace.

What does the worker gain from his struggles? I have seen the task that God has given the children of Adam to keep them occupied. He has made everything appropriate in its time. He has also put eternity in their hearts, but no one can discover the work God has done from beginning to end. I know that there is nothing better for them than to rejoice and enjoy the good life. It is also the gift of God whenever anyone eats, drinks, and enjoys all his efforts. I know that everything God does will last forever; there is no adding to it or taking from it. God works so that people will be in awe of him. Whatever is, has already been, and whatever will be, already is. However, God seeks justice for the persecuted.

I also observed under the sun: there is wickedness at the place of judgment and there is wickedness at the place of righteousness. I said to myself, "God will judge the righteous and the wicked, since there is a time for every activity and every work." I said to myself, "This happens so that God may test the children of Adam and they may see for themselves that they are like animals." For the fate of the children of Adam and the fate of animals is the same. As one dies, so dies the other; they all have the same breath. People have no advantage over animals since everything is futile. All are going to the same place; all come from dust, and all return to dust. Who knows if the spirits of the children of Adam go upward and the spirits of animals go downward to the earth? I have seen that there is nothing better than for a person to enjoy his activities because that is his reward. For who can enable him to see what will happen after he dies?

4 Again, I observed all the acts of oppression being done under the sun. Look at the tears of those who are oppressed; they have no one to comfort them. Power is with those who oppress them; they have no one to comfort them. So I commended the dead, who have already died, more than the living, who are still alive. But better than either of them is the one who has not yet existed, who has not seen the evil activity that is done under the sun.

I saw that all labor and all skillful work is due to one person's jealousy of another. This too is futile and a pursuit of the wind.

> The fool folds his arms
> and consumes his own flesh.
> Better one handful with rest
> than two handfuls with effort and a pursuit of the wind.

Again, I saw futility under the sun: There is a person without a companion, without even a son or brother, and though there is no end to all his struggles, his eyes are still not content with riches. "Who am I struggling for," he asks, "and depriving myself of good things?" This too is futile and a miserable task.

Two are better than one because they have a good reward for their efforts. For if either falls, his companion can lift him up; but pity the one who falls without another to lift him up. Also, if two lie down together, they can keep warm; but how can one person alone keep warm? And if someone overpowers one person, two can resist him. A cord of three strands is not easily broken.

20   Better is a poor but wise youth than an old but foolish king who no longer pays attention to warnings. For he came from prison to be king, even though he was born poor in his kingdom. I saw all the living, who move about under the sun, follow a second youth who succeeds him. There is no limit to all the people who were before them, yet those who come later will not rejoice in him. This too is futile and a pursuit of the wind.

5 Guard your steps when you go to the house of God. Better to approach in obedience than to offer the sacrifice as fools do, for they ignorantly do wrong. Do not be hasty to speak, and do not be impulsive to make a speech before God. God is in heaven and you are on earth, so let your words be few. Just as dreams accompany much labor, so also a fool's voice comes with many words. When you make a vow to God, don't delay fulfilling it, because he does not delight in fools. Fulfill what you vow. Better that you do not vow than that you vow and not fulfill it. Do not let your mouth bring guilt on you, and do not say in the presence of the messenger that it was a mistake. Why should God be angry with your words and destroy the work of your hands? For many dreams bring futility; so do many words. Therefore, fear God.

10 If you see oppression of the poor and perversion of justice and righteousness in the province, don't be astonished at the situation, because one official protects another official, and higher officials protect them. The profit from the land is taken by all; the king is served by the field.

The one who loves silver is never satisfied with silver, and whoever loves wealth is never satisfied with income. This too is futile. When good things increase, the ones who consume them multiply; what, then, is the profit to the owner, except to gaze at them with his eyes? The sleep of the worker is sweet, whether he eats little or much, but the abundance of the rich permits him no sleep.

There is a sickening tragedy I have seen under the sun: wealth kept by its owner to his harm. That wealth was lost in a bad venture, so when he fathered a son, he was empty-handed. As he

20 came from his mother's womb, so he will go again, naked as he came; he will take nothing for his efforts that he can carry in his hands. This too is a sickening tragedy: exactly as he comes, so he will go. What does the one gain who struggles for the wind? What is more, he eats in darkness all his days, with much frustration, sickness, and anger.

Here is what I have seen to be good: It is appropriate to eat, drink, and experience good in all the labor one does under the sun during the few days of his life God has given him, because that is his reward. Furthermore, everyone to whom God has given riches and wealth, he has also allowed him to enjoy them, take his reward, and rejoice in his labor. This is a gift of God, for he does not often consider the days of his life because God keeps him occupied with the joy of his heart.

6 Here is a tragedy I have observed under the sun, and it weighs heavily on humanity: God gives a person riches, wealth, and honor so that he lacks nothing of all he desires for himself, but God does not allow him to enjoy them. Instead, a stranger will enjoy them. This is futile and a sickening tragedy. A man may father a hundred children and live many years. No matter how long he lives, if he is not satisfied by good things and does not even have a proper burial, I say that a stillborn child is better off than he. For he comes in futility and he goes in darkness, and his name is shrouded in darkness. Though a stillborn child does not see the sun and is not conscious, it has more rest than he. And if a person lives a thousand years twice, but does not experience happiness, do not both go to the same place?

10   All of a person's labor is for his stomach,
          yet the appetite is never satisfied.

What advantage then does the wise person have over the fool? What advantage is there for the poor person who knows how to conduct himself before others? Better what the eyes see than wandering desire. This too is futile and a pursuit of the wind.

Whatever exists was given its name long ago, and it is known what mankind is. But he is not able to contend with the one stronger than he. For when there are many words, they increase futility. What is the advantage for mankind? For who knows what is good for anyone in life, in the few days of his futile life that he spends like a shadow? Who can tell anyone what will happen after him under the sun?

7   A good name is better than fine perfume,
          and the day of one's death is better than the day of one's birth.
       It is better to go to a house of mourning
          than to go to a house of feasting,
          since that is the end of all mankind,
          and the living should take it to heart.
       Grief is better than laughter,
          for when a face is sad, a heart may be glad.
       The heart of the wise is in a house of mourning,
10   but the heart of fools is in a house of pleasure.

It is better to listen to rebuke from a wise person
than to listen to the song of fools,
for like the crackling of burning thorns under the pot,
so is the laughter of the fool.
This too is futile.
Surely, the practice of extortion turns a wise person into a fool,
and a bribe corrupts the mind.
The end of a matter is better than its beginning;
a patient spirit is better than a proud spirit.
20 Don't let your spirit rush to be angry,
for anger abides in the heart of fools.
Don't say, "Why were the former days better than these?"
since it is not wise of you to ask this.
Wisdom is as good as an inheritance
and an advantage to those who see the sun,
because wisdom is protection as silver is protection;
but the advantage of knowledge
is that wisdom preserves the life of its owner.
Consider the work of God,
30 for who can straighten out
what he has made crooked?

In the day of prosperity be joyful, but in the day of adversity, consider: God has made the one as well as the other, so that no one can discover anything that will come after him.

In my futile life I have seen everything: someone righteous perishes in spite of his righteousness, and someone wicked lives long in spite of his evil. Don't be excessively righteous, and don't be overly wise. Why should you destroy yourself? Don't be excessively wicked, and don't be foolish. Why should you die before your time? It is good that you grasp the one and do not let the other slip from your hand. For the one who fears God will end up with both of them.

Wisdom makes the wise person stronger
40 than ten rulers of a city.
There is certainly no one righteous on the earth
who does good and never sins.

Don't pay attention to everything people say, or you may hear your servant cursing you, for in your heart you know that many times you yourself have cursed others.

I have tested all this by wisdom. I resolved, "I will be wise," but it was beyond me. What exists is beyond reach and very deep. Who can discover it? I turned my thoughts to know, explore, and examine wisdom and an explanation for things, and to know that wickedness is stupidity and folly is madness. And I find more bitter than death the woman who is a trap: her heart a net and her hands chains. The one who pleases God will escape her, but the sinner will be captured by her. "Look," says the Teacher, "I have

50 discovered this by adding one thing to another to find out the explanation, which my soul continually searches for but does not find: I found one person in a thousand, but none of those was a woman. Only see this: I have discovered that God made people upright, but they pursued many schemes."

8 Who is like the wise person, and who knows the interpretation of a matter? A person's wisdom brightens his face, and the sternness of his face is changed.

Keep the king's command because of your oath made before God. Do not be in a hurry; leave his presence, and don't persist in a bad cause, since he will do whatever he wants. For the king's word is authoritative, and who can say to him, "What are you doing?" The one who keeps a command will not experience anything harmful, and a wise heart knows the right time and procedure. For every activity there is a right time and procedure, even though a person's troubles are heavy on him. Yet no one knows what will happen because who can tell him what will happen? No one has authority over the wind to restrain it, and there is no authority over the day of death;

10 no one is discharged during battle, and wickedness will not allow those who practice it to escape. All this I have seen, applying my mind to all the work that is done under the sun, at a time when one person has authority over another to his harm.

In such circumstances, I saw the wicked buried. They came and went from the holy place, and they were praised in the city where they did those things. This too is futile. Because the sentence against an evil act is not carried out quickly, the heart of people is filled with the desire to commit evil. Although a sinner does evil a hundred times and prolongs his life, I also know that it will go well with God-fearing people, for they are reverent before him. However, it will not go well with the wicked, and they will not lengthen their days like a shadow, for they are not reverent before God.

There is a futility that is done on the earth: there are righteous people who get what the actions

20 of the wicked deserve, and there are wicked people who get what the actions of the righteous deserve. I say that this too is futile. So I commended enjoyment because there is nothing better for a person under the sun than to eat, drink, and enjoy himself, for this will accompany him in his labor during the days of his life that God gives him under the sun.

When I applied my mind to know wisdom and to observe the activity that is done on the earth (even though one's eyes do not close in sleep day or night), I observed all the work of God and concluded that a person is unable to discover the work that is done under the sun. Even though a person labors hard to explore it, he cannot find it; even if a wise person claims to know it, he is unable to discover it.

9 Indeed, I took all this to heart and explained it all: The righteous, the wise, and their works are in God's hands. People don't know whether to expect love or hate. Everything lies ahead of them. Everything is the same for everyone: There is one fate for the righteous and the wicked, for the good and the bad, for the clean and the unclean, for the one who sacrifices and the one who does not sacrifice. As it is for the good, so also it is for the sinner; as it is for the one who takes an oath, so also for the one who fears an oath. This is an evil in all that is done under the sun: there is one fate for everyone. In addition, the hearts of people are full of evil, and madness is in their hearts while they live; after that they go to the dead. But there is hope for whoever is joined with all the living, since a live dog is better than a dead lion. For the living know that they will die, but the

10 dead don't know anything. There is no longer a reward for them because the memory of them is forgotten. Their love, their hate, and their envy have already disappeared, and there is no longer a portion for them in all that is done under the sun.

Go, eat your bread with pleasure, and drink your wine with a cheerful heart, for God has already accepted your works. Let your clothes be white all the time, and never let oil be lacking on your head. Enjoy life with the wife you love all the days of your fleeting life, which has been given to you under the sun, all your fleeting days. For that is your portion in life and in your struggle under the sun. Whatever your hands find to do, do with all your strength, because there is no work, planning, knowledge, or wisdom in Sheol where you are going.

Again I saw under the sun that the race is not to the swift, or the battle to the strong, or bread to

20 the wise, or riches to the discerning, or favor to the skillful; rather, time and chance happen to all of them. For certainly no one knows his time: like fish caught in a cruel net or like birds caught in a trap, so people are trapped in an evil time as it suddenly falls on them.

I have observed that this also is wisdom under the sun, and it is significant to me: There was a small city with few men in it. A great king came against it, surrounded it, and built large siege works against it. Now a poor wise man was found in the city, and he delivered the city by his wisdom. Yet no one remembered that poor man. And I said, "Wisdom is better than strength, but the wisdom of the poor man is despised, and his words are not heeded."

> The calm words of the wise are heeded
> more than the shouts of a ruler over fools.
30 Wisdom is better than weapons of war,
> but one sinner can destroy much good.

10
> Dead flies make a perfumer's oil ferment and stink;
> so a little folly outweighs wisdom and honor.
> A wise person's heart goes to the right,
> but a fool's heart to the left.

Even when the fool walks along the road, his heart lacks sense,
and he shows everyone he is a fool.
If the ruler's anger rises against you, don't leave your post,
for calmness puts great offenses to rest.

There is an evil I have seen under the sun, an error proceeding from the presence of the ruler:
10   The fool is appointed to great heights,
but the rich remain in lowly positions.
I have seen slaves on horses,
but princes walking on the ground like slaves.

The one who digs a pit may fall into it,
and the one who breaks through a wall may be bitten by a snake.
The one who quarries stones may be hurt by them;
the one who splits logs may be endangered by them.
If the ax is dull, and one does not sharpen its edge,
then one must exert more strength;
20   however, the advantage of wisdom is that it brings success.
If the snake bites before it is charmed,
then there is no advantage for the charmer.
The words from the mouth of a wise person are gracious,
but the lips of a fool consume him.
The beginning of the words from his mouth is folly,
but the end of his speaking is evil madness;
yet the fool multiplies words.
No one knows what will happen,
and who can tell anyone what will happen after him?
30   The struggles of fools weary them,
for they don't know how to go to the city.
Woe to you, land, when your king is a youth
and your princes feast in the morning.
Blessed are you, land, when your king is a son of nobles
and your princes feast at the proper time—
for strength and not for drunkenness.
Because of laziness the roof caves in,
and because of negligent hands the house leaks.
A feast is prepared for laughter,
40   and wine makes life happy,

and money is the answer for everything.
Do not curse the king even in your thoughts,
and do not curse a rich person even in your bedroom,
for a bird of the sky may carry the message,
and a winged creature may report the matter.

11   Send your bread on the surface of the water,
for after many days you may find it.
Give a portion to seven or even to eight,
for you don't know what disaster may happen on earth.
If the clouds are full, they will pour out rain on the earth;
whether a tree falls to the south or the north,
the place where the tree falls, there it will lie.
One who watches the wind will not sow,
and the one who looks at the clouds will not reap.
10 Just as you don't know the path of the wind,
or how bones develop in the womb of a pregnant woman,
so also you don't know the work of God who makes everything.
In the morning sow your seed,
and at evening do not let your hand rest,
because you don't know which will succeed,
whether one or the other,
or if both of them will be equally good.
Light is sweet,
and it is pleasing for the eyes to see the sun.
20 Indeed, if someone lives many years,
let him rejoice in them all,
and let him remember the days of darkness, since they will be many.
All that comes is futile.
Rejoice, young person, while you are young,
and let your heart be glad in the days of your youth.
And walk in the ways of your heart
and in the desire of your eyes;
but know that for all of these things God will bring you to judgment.
Remove sorrow from your heart,
30 and put away pain from your flesh,
because youth and the prime of life are fleeting.

12 So remember your Creator in the days of your youth:

> Before the days of adversity come,
> and the years approach when you will say,
> "I have no delight in them";
> before the sun and the light are darkened,
> and the moon and the stars,
> and the clouds return after the rain;
> on the day when the guardians of the house tremble,
> and the strong men stoop,
> the women who grind grain cease because they are few,
> and the ones who watch through the windows see dimly,
> the doors at the street are shut
> while the sound of the mill fades;
> when one rises at the sound of a bird,
> and all the daughters of song grow faint.
> Also, they are afraid of heights and dangers on the road;
> the almond tree blossoms,
> the grasshopper loses its spring,
> and the caper berry has no effect;
> for the mere mortal is headed to his eternal home,
> and mourners will walk around in the street;
> before the silver cord is snapped,
> and the gold bowl is broken,
> and the jar is shattered at the spring,
> and the wheel is broken into the well;
> and the dust returns to the earth as it once was,
> and the spirit returns to God who gave it.

"Absolute futility," says the Teacher. "Everything is futile."

In addition to the Teacher being a wise man, he constantly taught the people knowledge; he weighed, explored, and arranged many proverbs. The Teacher sought to find delightful sayings and write words of truth accurately. The sayings of the wise are like cattle prods, and those from masters of collections are like firmly embedded nails. The sayings are given by one Shepherd.

But beyond these, my son, be warned: there is no end to the making of many books, and much study wearies the body. When all has been heard, the conclusion of the matter is this: fear God and keep his commands, because this is for all humanity. For God will bring every act to judgment, including every hidden thing, whether good or evil.

Introduction to Lamentations

John Hobbins

The book of Lamentations is part of a subcollection in the HS referred to as the Five Scrolls (Megillot). Lamentations is read on the ninth of Av, a day of mourning for the destruction of Jerusalem. Lamentations is placed after Jeremiah in other ancient arrangements. Historically, tradition claimed Jeremiah as the book's author.

In the ninth year of King Zedekiah, in the tenth month, on the tenth day of the month (in 586 BC), Nebuchadnezzar, king of Babylon, marched against Jerusalem and laid siege to it. The siege lasted eighteen months. As time went on, the suffering grew ever more terrible. In the eleventh year of King Zedekiah, in the fourth month, on the ninth day of the month, the hunger became unbearable, and the city was breached (Jer 52.10–11; 2 Kgs 24.33–25.8).

The famine and slaughter at the hands of the Babylonians are graphically described in the book of Lamentations. The first two chapters contain a lament on behalf of Zion (1.1–77; 2.1–136) as well as a lament by Zion (1.78–154; 2.137–157). Zion is portrayed as the fierce and fearless mother of her people. She is a mother deprived of her children. She reproves her Lord and judge with unmatched bitterness of soul (2.137–150). Zion's prayer is that Yahweh sees her infinite forlornness. She is penitent, angry, and yet inconsolable at the same time. Four times she shouts, "Yahweh!" (1.63, 76, 135; 2.138). In the economy of the book, her prayer *goes unanswered*. Zion confesses that Yahweh is righteous and that she is guilty (1.20–26).

Never *once* in Scripture does Yahweh or someone on Yahweh's behalf suggest that it is inappropriate to cry out in anger to Yahweh when one's life and health are compromised. On the contrary, the task of the believer is to advocate on one's own behalf and for others to Yahweh's face in the teeth of distress. The chief substance of the book of Lamentations is in fact a questioning of God's failure to save in a crisis of enormous proportions.

It is right and proper to cry out for deliverance regardless of the degree to which one's distress is one's own fault or the fault of the person on whose behalf one intercedes. Zion is *not out of line* in her protest. She is doing what she knew Yahweh expected her to do.

The peerless achievement of Lamentations is that it does not report a divine answer to the questions asked. Silence is all we hear. Lamentations 3 is a monologue and prayer of a lamenting woman caught up in grief "because of all the women in my city" (3.21–22). She speaks on behalf of the women (e.g. "we") in Lam 3.95–115. A pinnacle of hope is reached in her prayer: Yahweh's mercies are new every morning; great is his faithfulness (Lam 3.50–57). Lamentations 4 is also a lament of an individual. The themes from chs. 1–2 are taken up again. In 4.81–100, voice is given to the "we" of the entire people. Lamentations 5 is a "we" lament from start to finish. The prayer does not end on a note of hope, but contemplates the possibility, in a spasm of boundless grief, that Yahweh has utterly rejected his people (5.41–44). It is a fitting end to a most powerful expression of despair in the face of unimaginable suffering.

Since Zion was rebuilt only to be destroyed again, those who await her salvation, the fulfillment of the promises which regard her, weep *for* and *with* Zion to this day. Jesus wept over her, for he loved her and dreaded her destruction (Luke 19:41-44). Paul expected that the deliverer would come from her (Rom 11:26–27). Believers wait for the fulfillment of God's promises to Zion to this day. Her restoration and ours will be accomplished together.

Outline

1. How she sits alone (1.1–154)

2. He has thrown down Israel's glory (2.1–157)

3. Under the rod of Yahweh's wrath (3.1–157)

4. How the gold has become tarnished (4.1–110)

5. Bring us back to yourself, Yahweh (5.1–44)

Suggested Resources

Berlin, Adele. *Lamentations*. Old Testament Library. Louisville: Westminster John Knox, 2002.

Dobbs-Allsopp, F. W. *Lamentations*. Interpretation. Louisville: John Knox, 2002.

Hillers, Delbert R. *Lamentations*. Anchor Bible Commentary. 2nd ed. New York: Doubleday, 1992.

Wright, Christopher J. H. *The Message of Lamentations*. The Bible Speaks Today Series. Downers Grove, IL: InterVarsity, 2015.

Lamentations

I   א *Aleph*
How she sits alone,
the city once crowded with people!
She who was great among the nations
has become like a widow.
The princess among the provinces
has been put to forced labor.

ב *Beth*
She weeps bitterly during the night,
with tears on her cheeks.
There is no one to offer her comfort,
not one from all her lovers.
All her friends have betrayed her;
they have become her enemies.

ג *Gimel*
Judah has gone into exile
following affliction and harsh slavery;
she lives among the nations
but finds no place to rest.
All her pursuers have overtaken her
in narrow places.

ד *Daleth*
The roads to Zion mourn,
for no one comes to the appointed festivals.
All her gates are deserted;
her priests groan,
her young women grieve,
and she herself is bitter.

ה *He*

30 Her adversaries have become her masters;
her enemies are at ease,
for the Lord has made her suffer
because of her many transgressions.
Her children have gone away
as captives before the adversary.

ו *Waw*

All the splendor has vanished
from Daughter Zion.
Her leaders are like stags
40 that find no pasture;
they stumble away exhausted
before the hunter.

ז *Zayin*

During the days of her affliction and homelessness
Jerusalem remembers all her precious belongings
that were hers in days of old.
When her people fell into the adversary's hand,
she had no one to help.
The adversaries looked at her,
50 laughing over her downfall.

ח *Cheth*

Jerusalem has sinned grievously;
therefore, she has become an object of scorn.
All who honored her now despise her,
for they have seen her nakedness.
She herself groans and turns away.

ט *Teth*

Her uncleanness stains her skirts.
She never considered her end.
60 Her downfall was astonishing;
there was no one to comfort her.

LORD, look on my affliction,
for the enemy boasts.

י *Yod*
The adversary has seized
all her precious belongings.
She has even seen the nations
enter her sanctuary—
those you had forbidden
to enter your assembly.

כ *Kaph*
All her people groan
while they search for bread.
They have traded their precious belongings for food
in order to stay alive.
LORD, look and see
how I have become despised.

ל *Lamed*
Is this nothing to you, all you who pass by?
Look and see!
Is there any pain like mine,
which was dealt out to me,
which the LORD made me suffer
on the day of his burning anger?

מ *Mem*
He sent fire from on high into my bones;
he made it descend.
He spread a net for my feet
and turned me back.
He made me desolate,
sick all day long.

נ *Nun*
My transgressions have been formed into a yoke,
fastened together by his hand;

they have been placed on my neck,
and the Lord has broken my strength.
He has handed me over
to those I cannot withstand.

ס *Samek*
100 The Lord has rejected
all the mighty men within me.
He has summoned an army against me
to crush my young warriors.
The Lord has trampled Virgin Daughter Judah
like grapes in a winepress.

ע *Ayin*
I weep because of these things;
my eyes flow with tears.
For there is no one nearby to comfort me,
110 no one to keep me alive.
My children are desolate
because the enemy has prevailed.

פ *Pe*
Zion stretches out her hands;
there is no one to comfort her.
The Lord has issued a decree against Jacob
that his neighbors should be his adversaries.
Jerusalem has become
something impure among them.

120 צ *Tsade*
The Lord is just,
for I have rebelled against his command.
Listen, all you people;
look at my pain.
My young women and young men
have gone into captivity.

ק *Qoph*
I called to my lovers,
but they betrayed me.
130 My priests and elders
perished in the city
while searching for food
to keep themselves alive.

ר *Resh*
Lord, see how I am in distress.
I am churning within;
my heart is broken,
for I have been very rebellious.
Outside, the sword takes the children;
140 inside, there is death.

ש *Shin*
People have heard me groaning,
but there is no one to comfort me.
All my enemies have heard of my misfortune;
they are glad that you have caused it.
Bring on the day you have announced,
so that they may become like me.

ת *Taw*
Let all their wickedness come before you,
150 and deal with them
as you have dealt with me
because of all my transgressions.
For my groans are many,
and I am sick at heart.

2   א *Aleph*
How the Lord has overshadowed
Daughter Zion with his anger!
He has thrown down Israel's glory
from heaven to earth.

He did not acknowledge his footstool
in the day of his anger.

ב *Beth*
Without compassion the Lord has swallowed up
all the dwellings of Jacob.
In his wrath he has demolished
the fortified cities of Daughter Judah.
He brought them to the ground
and defiled the kingdom and its leaders.

ג *Gimel*
He has cut off every horn of Israel
in his burning anger
and withdrawn his right hand
in the presence of the enemy.
He has blazed against Jacob like a flaming fire
that consumes everything.

ד *Daleth*
He has strung his bow like an enemy;
his right hand is positioned like an adversary.
He has killed everyone who was the delight to the eye,
pouring out his wrath like fire
on the tent of Daughter Zion.

ה *He*
The Lord is like an enemy;
he has swallowed up Israel.
He swallowed up all its palaces
and destroyed its fortified cities.
He has multiplied mourning and lamentation
within Daughter Judah.

ו *Waw*
He has wrecked his temple
as if it were merely a shack in a field,
destroying his place of meeting.

The LORD has abolished
40 appointed festivals and Sabbaths in Zion.
He has despised king and priest
in his fierce anger.

ז *Zayin*
The Lord has rejected his altar,
repudiated his sanctuary;
he has handed the walls of her palaces
over to the enemy.
They have raised a shout in the house of the LORD
as on the day of an appointed festival.

50 ח *Cheth*
The LORD determined to destroy
the wall of Daughter Zion.
He stretched out a measuring line
and did not restrain himself from destroying.
He made the ramparts and walls grieve;
together they waste away.

ט *Teth*
Zion's gates have fallen to the ground;
he has destroyed and shattered the bars on her gates.
60 Her king and her leaders live among the nations,
instruction is no more,
and even her prophets receive
no vision from the LORD.

י *Yod*
The elders of Daughter Zion
sit on the ground in silence.
They have thrown dust on their heads
and put on sackcloth.
The young women of Jerusalem
70 have bowed their heads to the ground.

כ *Kaph*
My eyes are worn out from weeping;
I am churning within.
My heart is poured out in grief
because of the destruction of my dear people,
because infants and nursing babies faint
in the streets of the city.

ל *Lamed*
They cry out to their mothers,
"Where is the grain and wine?"
as they faint like the wounded
in the streets of the city,
as their life pours out
in the arms of their mothers.

מ *Mem*
What can I say on your behalf?
What can I compare you to, Daughter Jerusalem?
What can I liken you to,
so that I may console you, Virgin Daughter Zion?
For your ruin is as vast as the sea.
Who can heal you?

נ *Nun*
Your prophets saw visions for you
that were empty and deceptive;
they did not reveal your iniquity
and so restore your fortunes.
They saw pronouncements for you
that were empty and misleading.

ס *Samek*
All who pass by
scornfully clap their hands at you.
They hiss and shake their heads
at Daughter Jerusalem:
Is this the city that was called

the perfection of beauty,
the joy of the whole earth?

פ *Pe*
All your enemies
open their mouths against you.
They hiss and gnash their teeth,
saying, "We have swallowed her up.
This is the day we have waited for!
We have lived to see it."

ע *Ayin*
The LORD has done what he planned;
he has accomplished his decree,
which he ordained in days of old.
He has demolished without compassion,
letting the enemy gloat over you
and exalting the horn of your adversaries.

צ *Tsade*
The hearts of the people cry out to the Lord.
Wall of Daughter Zion,
let your tears run down like a river
day and night.
Give yourself no relief
and your eyes no rest.

ק *Qoph*
Arise, cry out in the night
from the first watch of the night.
Pour out your heart like water
before the Lord's presence.
Lift up your hands to him
for the lives of your children
who are fainting from hunger
at the head of every street.

ר *Resh*

Lord, look and consider
to whom you have done this.
Should women eat their own children,
the infants they have nurtured?
Should priests and prophets
be killed in the Lord's sanctuary?

ש *Shin*

Both young and old
are lying on the ground in the streets.
My young women and young men
have fallen by the sword.
You have killed them in the day of your anger,
slaughtering without compassion.

ת *Taw*

You summon those who terrorize me on every side,
as if for an appointed festival day;
on the day of the Lord's anger
no one escaped or survived.
My enemy has destroyed
those I nurtured and reared.

3

א *Aleph*

I am the man who has seen affliction
under the rod of God's wrath.
He has driven me away and forced me to walk
in darkness instead of light.
Yes, he repeatedly turns his hand
against me all day long.

ב *Beth*

He has worn away my flesh and skin;
he has broken my bones.
He has laid siege against me,
encircling me with bitterness and hardship.

He has made me dwell in darkness
like those who have been dead for ages.

ג *Gimel*
He has walled me in so I cannot get out;
he has weighed me down with chains.
Even when I cry out and plead for help,
he blocks out my prayer.
He has walled in my ways with blocks of stone;
he has made my paths crooked.

ד *Daleth*
He is a bear waiting in ambush,
a lion in hiding.
He forced me off my way and tore me to pieces;
he left me desolate.
He strung his bow
and set me as the target for his arrow.

ה *He*
He pierced my kidneys
with shafts from his quiver.
I am a laughingstock to all my people,
mocked by their songs all day long.
He filled me with bitterness,
satiated me with wormwood.

ו *Waw*
He ground my teeth with gravel
and made me cower in the dust.
I have been deprived of peace;
I have forgotten what prosperity is.
Then I thought, "My future is lost,
as well as my hope from the LORD."

ז *Zayin*
Remember my affliction and my homelessness,
the wormwood and the poison.

I continually remember them
and have become depressed.
Yet I call this to mind,
and therefore I have hope:

50 ח *Cheth*
Because of the LORD's faithful love
we do not perish,
for his mercies never end.
They are new every morning;
great is your faithfulness!
I say, "The LORD is my portion,
therefore I will put my hope in him."

ט *Teth*
The LORD is good to those who wait for him,
60 to the person who seeks him.
It is good to wait quietly
for salvation from the LORD.
It is good for a man to bear the yoke
while he is still young.

י *Yod*
Let him sit alone and be silent,
for God has disciplined him.
Let him put his mouth in the dust—
perhaps there is still hope.
70 Let him offer his cheek
to the one who would strike him;
let him be filled with disgrace.

כ *Kaph*
For the Lord
will not reject us forever.
Even if he causes suffering,
he will show compassion
according to the abundance of his faithful love.

For he does not enjoy bringing affliction
or suffering on mankind.

ל *Lamed*
Crushing all the prisoners of the land
beneath one's feet,
denying justice to a man
in the presence of the Most High,
or subverting a person in his lawsuit—
the Lord does not approve of these things.

מ *Mem*
Who is there who speaks and it happens,
unless the Lord has ordained it?
Do not both adversity and good
come from the mouth of the Most High?
Why should any living person complain,
any man, because of the punishment for his sins?

נ *Nun*
Let's examine and probe our ways,
and turn back to the LORD.
Let's lift up our hearts and our hands
to God in heaven:
"We have sinned and rebelled;
you have not forgiven.

ס *Samek*
"You have covered yourself in anger and pursued us;
you have killed without compassion.
You have covered yourself with a cloud
so that no prayer can get through.
You have made us disgusting filth
among the peoples.

פ *Pe*
"All our enemies
open their mouths against us.

We have experienced panic and pitfall,
devastation and destruction."
My eyes flow with streams of tears
because of the destruction of my dear people.

ע *Ayin*
My eyes overflow unceasingly,
without end,
until the LORD looks down
from heaven and sees.
My eyes bring me grief
because of the fate of all the women in my city.

צ *Tsade*
For no reason, my enemies
hunted me like a bird.
They smothered my life in a pit
and threw stones on me.
Water flooded over my head,
and I thought, "I'm going to die!"

ק *Qoph*
I called on your name, LORD,
from the depths of the pit.
You heard my plea:
Do not ignore my cry for relief.
You came near whenever I called you;
you said, "Do not be afraid."

ר *Resh*
You championed my cause, Lord;
you redeemed my life.
LORD, you saw the wrong done to me;
judge my case.
You saw all their vengefulness,
all their plots against me.

�406 *Sin/ ﬖ Shin*
LORD, you heard their insults,
all their plots against me.
The slander and murmuring of my opponents
attack me all day long.
When they sit and when they rise, look,
150   I am mocked by their songs.

ﬡ *Taw*
You will pay them back what they deserve, LORD,
according to the work of their hands.
You will give them a heart filled with anguish.
May your curse be on them!
You will pursue them in anger and destroy them
under your heavens.

4   ﬡ *Aleph*
How the gold has become tarnished,
the fine gold become dull!
The stones of the temple lie scattered
at the head of every street.

ﬢ *Beth*
Zion's precious children—
once worth their weight in pure gold—
how they are regarded as clay jars,
10   the work of a potter's hands!

﬙ *Gimel*
Even jackals offer their breasts
to nurse their young,
but my dear people have become cruel
like ostriches in the wilderness.

ﬧ *Daleth*
The nursing baby's tongue
clings to the roof of his mouth from thirst.

Infants beg for food,
but no one gives them any.

ה *He*
Those who used to eat delicacies
are destitute in the streets;
those who were reared in purple garments
huddle in trash heaps.

ו *Waw*
The punishment of my dear people
is greater than that of Sodom,
which was overthrown in an instant
without a hand laid on it.

ז *Zayin*
Her dignitaries were brighter than snow,
whiter than milk;
their bodies were more ruddy than coral,
their appearance like lapis lazuli.

ח *Cheth*
Now they appear darker than soot;
they are not recognized in the streets.
Their skin has shriveled on their bones;
it has become dry like wood.

ט *Teth*
Those slain by the sword are better off
than those slain by hunger,
who waste away, pierced with pain
because the fields lack produce.

י *Yod*
The hands of compassionate women
have cooked their own children;
they became their food
during the destruction of my dear people.

כ *Kaph*
The Lord has exhausted his wrath,
poured out his burning anger;
he has ignited a fire in Zion,
and it has consumed her foundations.

ל *Lamed*
The kings of the earth
and all the world's inhabitants did not believe
that an enemy or adversary
60   could enter Jerusalem's gates.

מ *Mem*
Yet it happened because of the sins of her prophets
and the iniquities of her priests,
who shed the blood of the righteous within her.

נ *Nun*
Blind, they stumbled in the streets,
defiled by this blood,
so that no one dared
to touch their garments.

70   ס *Samek*
"Stay away! Unclean!" people shouted at them.
"Away, away! Don't touch us!"
So they wandered aimlessly.
It was said among the nations,
"They can stay here no longer."

פ *Pe*
The Lord himself has scattered them;
he no longer watches over them.
The priests are not respected;
80   the elders find no favor.

ע *Ayin*
All the while our eyes were failing
as we looked in vain for help;
we watched from our towers
for a nation that would not save us.

צ *Tsade*
Our steps were closely followed
so that we could not walk in our streets.
Our end approached; our time ran out.
90 Our end had come!

ק *Qoph*
Those who chased us were swifter
than eagles in the sky;
they relentlessly pursued us over the mountains
and ambushed us in the wilderness.

ר *Resh*
The Lord's anointed, the breath of our life,
was captured in their traps.
We had said about him,
100 "We will live under his protection among the nations."

ש *Sin*
So rejoice and be glad, Daughter Edom,
you resident of the land of Uz!
Yet the cup will pass to you as well;
you will get drunk and expose yourself.

ת *Taw*
Daughter Zion, your punishment is complete;
he will not lengthen your exile.
But he will punish your iniquity, Daughter Edom,
110 and will expose your sins.

5 Lord, remember what has happened to us.
Look, and see our disgrace!

Our inheritance has been turned over to strangers,
our houses to foreigners.
We have become orphans, fatherless;
our mothers are widows.
We must pay for the water we drink;
our wood comes at a price.
We are closely pursued;
we are tired, and no one offers us rest.
We made a treaty with Egypt
and with Assyria, to get enough food.
Our ancestors sinned; they no longer exist,
but we bear their punishment.
Slaves rule over us;
no one rescues us from them.
We secure our food at the risk of our lives
because of the sword in the wilderness.
Our skin is as hot as an oven
from the ravages of hunger.
Women have been raped in Zion,
virgins in the cities of Judah.
Princes have been hung up by their hands;
elders are shown no respect.
Young men labor at millstones;
boys stumble under loads of wood.
The elders have left the city gate,
the young men, their music.
Joy has left our hearts;
our dancing has turned to mourning.
The crown has fallen from our head.
Woe to us, for we have sinned.
Because of this, our heart is sick;
because of these, our eyes grow dim:
because of Mount Zion, which lies desolate
and has jackals prowling in it.
You, LORD, are enthroned forever;
your throne endures from generation to generation.
Why do you continually forget us,
abandon us for our entire lives?

Lord, bring us back to yourself, so we may return;
renew our days as in former times,
unless you have completely rejected us
and are intensely angry with us.

Introduction to Esther

Ron Lindo

The book of Esther is unique among the HS: it does not explicitly mention Yahweh or any Israelite religious content. Thus, some argue that Esther was either added to the canon late or written initially without the canon in mind. However, Esther's placement after Lamentations and before Daniel illuminates certain implicit elements of Esther's plot and theology.

Two Israelites, Mordecai and Esther, are the main protagonists. They find themselves mixed into the affairs of the Persian court. Separately, they transition from being identified as regular Persian citizens to Esther becoming queen and Mordecai becoming the king's primary advisor. More so, each section's structure revolves around individuals who provide the king with advice, leading him to issue a royal proclamation.

During the prologue (Esth 1), this advice comes from Memucan, one of the king's wise men. The main plot (Esth 2–9) consists of three episodes. In episode one, the king listens to his male attendants (Esth 2). In episode two (Esth 3–7), Haman deceives the king with bad advice. However, by the end of this episode, the king gains better advice through listening to one of his eunuchs, Harbona. Mordecai and Esther finally have the king's ear in episode three (Esth 8–9). The book's epilogue (Esth 10) suggests that once Mordecai is second in command, the kingdom is also in good hands; both the Israelites and other ethnic groups can now prosper within the Persian empire.

The authorial purpose behind the book's current structure is related to the reference to Jeremiah's letter found in Mordecai's introduction (see Esth 2.9–10 and Jer 29.1–9). Jeremiah commands the exiles to "pray to the Lord" on behalf of their new exilic home, "for when it thrives, you will thrive" (Jer 29.12–13). The Hebrew word "thrive" (*shâlôm*) is used strategically within Esther to demonstrate how Mordecai transitioned from seeking Esther's "well-being" (*shâlôm*; Esth 2.20–21) to sending letters of "well-being" (*shâlôm*) throughout the Persian empire.

Jeremiah's letter also stated that Yahweh plans to give his people "a future and a hope" (Jer 29.20–21). However, this was not the experience of many Israelites directly after the fall of Jerusalem. Instead, Lamentations describes the horrors of exile. As exiles, the Israelites were rejected by the nations (Lam 1), wore sackcloth (Lam 2.64–70), had their enemies exalted over them (Lam 2.114–120), lacked "well-being" (*shâlôm*; Lam 3.39–40), faced annihilation (Lam 4.81–85), and became orphans (Lam 5.3–4). In response, Esther's author explains how the Israelites were saved by an orphan raised in exile (Esth 2.10–11). Though their enemies had been exalted over them—causing them to wear sackcloth while facing annihilation (Esth 3–4)—they still prospered. While Lamentations' conclusion is unsure whether Yahweh will reject Israel forever (Lam 5.39–44), Esther's epilogue affirms that Yahweh's people will not be dismissed permanently.

Like Esther, Daniel 9 also refers to Jeremiah's letter. The angel Gabriel clarifies that the meaning of the "seventy years" mentioned in this letter refers to the Messiah's coming (Dan 9.44–74). Given that Daniel's events occur years before Esther's events, the reader can infer something important from this canonical arrangement. Long before Mordecai and Esther influenced Persia's kingdom, Yahweh intended for a remnant of his people to be exiled among the nations so the nations could prosper.

Outline

1. Prologue (1.1–42)
   a. The King Performs an Action (1.1–14)
   b. Situational Complication (1.15–20)
   c. The King is Advised (1.21–38)
   d. The King Implements the Advice (1.39)
   e. A Solution is provided (1.40–42)

2. Plot (2.1–9.55)
   a. Episode 1 (2.1–46)
      i. The King Performs an Action (2.1–2)
      ii. Situational Complication (2.5–20)
      iii. The King is Advised (2.2–7)
      iv. The King Implements the Advice (2.7)
      v. A Solution is provided (2.8–46)
   b. Episode 2 (3.1–7.21)
      i. The King Performs an Action (3.1–4)
      ii. Situational Complication (3.4–14)
      iii. The King is Advised (3.14–21)
      iv. The King Implements the Advice (3.22–33)
      v. A Solution is provided (4.1–7.21)
   c. Episode 3 (8.1–9.55)
      i. The King Performs an Action (8.1–4)
      ii. Situational Complication (8.5–12)
      iii. The King is Advised (9.14–21)
      iv. The King Implements the Advice (8.13–38)
      v. A Solution is provided (9.1–13, 21–37)

3. Postscript (10.1–6)
   a. The King Performs an Action (10.1)
   b. A Consistent Solution is provided (10.1–6)

Suggested Resources

Queen-Sutherland, Kandy. *Ruth & Esther*. Smyth & Helwys Bible Commentary. Macon, GA: Smyth & Helwys, 2016.

Reid, Debra. *Esther*. Tyndale Old Testament Commentaries. Downers Grove, IL: InterVarsity Press, 2008.

Taylor, Marion. *Ruth, Esther*. The Story of God Bible Commentary. Grand Rapids: Zondervan, 2020.

Tomasino, Anthony. *Esther*. Evangelical Exegetical Commentary. Bellingham, WA: Lexham Press, 2016.

Webb, Barry G. *Five Festal Garments: Christian Reflections on the Song of Songs, Ruth, Lamentations, Ecclesiastes and Esther*. New Studies in Biblical Theology. Downers Grove, IL: InterVarsity Press, 2000.

Esther

I These events took place during the days of Ahasuerus, who ruled 127 provinces from India to Cush. In those days King Ahasuerus reigned from his royal throne in the fortress at Susa. He held a feast in the third year of his reign for all his officials and staff, the army of Persia and Media, the nobles, and the officials from the provinces. He displayed the glorious wealth of his kingdom and the magnificent splendor of his greatness for a total of 180 days.

At the end of this time, the king held a week-long banquet in the garden courtyard of the royal palace for all the people, from the greatest to the least, who were present in the fortress of Susa. White and blue linen hangings were fastened with fine white and purple linen cords to silver rods on marble columns. Gold and silver couches were arranged on a mosaic pavement of red feldspar, 10 marble, mother-of-pearl, and precious stones.

Drinks were served in an array of gold goblets, each with a different design. Royal wine flowed freely, according to the king's bounty. The drinking was according to royal decree: "There are no restrictions." The king had ordered every wine steward in his household to serve whatever each person wanted. Queen Vashti also gave a feast for the women of King Ahasuerus's palace.

On the seventh day, when the king was feeling good from the wine, Ahasuerus commanded Mehuman, Biztha, Harbona, Bigtha, Abagtha, Zethar, and Carkas—the seven eunuchs who personally served him—to bring Queen Vashti before him with her royal crown. He wanted to show off her beauty to the people and the officials, because she was very beautiful. But Queen Vashti refused to come at the king's command that was delivered by his eunuchs. The king 20 became furious and his anger burned within him.

The king consulted the wise men who understood the times, for it was his normal procedure to confer with experts in law and justice. The most trusted ones were Carshena, Shethar, Admatha, Tarshish, Meres, Marsena, and Memucan. They were the seven officials of Persia and Media who had personal access to the king and occupied the highest positions in the kingdom. The king asked, "According to the law, what should be done with Queen Vashti, since she refused to obey King Ahasuerus's command that was delivered by the eunuchs?"

Memucan said in the presence of the king and his officials, "Queen Vashti has wronged not only the king, but all the officials and the peoples who are in every one of King Ahasuerus's provinces. For the queen's action will become public knowledge to all the women and cause them 30 to despise their husbands and say, 'King Ahasuerus ordered Queen Vashti brought before him, but she did not come.' Before this day is over, the noble women of Persia and Media who hear about the queen's act will say the same thing to all the king's officials, resulting in more contempt and fury.

"If it meets the king's approval, he should personally issue a royal decree. Let it be recorded in the laws of the Persians and the Medes, so that it cannot be revoked: Vashti is not to enter King Ahasuerus's presence, and her royal position is to be given to another woman who is more worthy than she. The decree the king issues will be heard throughout his vast kingdom, so all women will honor their husbands, from the greatest to the least."

The king and his counselors approved the proposal, and he followed Memucan's advice. He
40 sent letters to all the royal provinces, to each province in its own script and to each ethnic group in its own language, that every man should be master of his own house and speak in the language of his own people.

2 Some time later, when King Ahasuerus's rage had cooled down, he remembered Vashti, what she had done, and what was decided against her. The king's personal attendants suggested, "Let a search be made for beautiful young virgins for the king. Let the king appoint commissioners in each province of his kingdom, so that they may gather all the beautiful young virgins to the harem at the fortress of Susa. Put them under the supervision of Hegai, the king's eunuch, keeper of the women, and give them the required beauty treatments. Then the young woman who pleases the king will become queen instead of Vashti." This suggestion pleased the king, and he did accordingly.

In the fortress of Susa, there was a Jewish man named Mordecai son of Jair, son of Shimei, son of Kish, a Benjaminite. Kish had been taken into exile from Jerusalem with the other captives
10 when King Nebuchadnezzar of Babylon took King Jeconiah of Judah into exile. Mordecai was the legal guardian of his cousin Hadassah (that is, Esther), because she had no father or mother. The young woman had a beautiful figure and was extremely good-looking. When her father and mother died, Mordecai had adopted her as his own daughter.

When the king's command and edict became public knowledge and when many young women were gathered at the fortress of Susa under Hegai's supervision, Esther was taken to the palace, into the supervision of Hegai, keeper of the women. The young woman pleased him and gained his favor so that he accelerated the process of the beauty treatments and the special diet that she received. He assigned seven hand-picked female servants to her from the palace and transferred her and her servants to the harem's best quarters.

20 Esther did not reveal her ethnicity or her family background, because Mordecai had ordered her not to make them known. Every day Mordecai took a walk in front of the harem's courtyard to learn how Esther was doing and to see what was happening to her.

During the year before each young woman's turn to go to King Ahasuerus, the harem regulation required her to receive beauty treatments with oil of myrrh for six months and then with perfumes and cosmetics for another six months. When the young woman would go to the king, she was given whatever she requested to take with her from the harem to the palace. She would go in the evening, and in the morning she would return to a second harem under the supervision of the king's eunuch Shaashgaz, keeper of the concubines. She never went to the king again, unless he desired her and summoned her by name.

30 Esther was the daughter of Abihail, the uncle of Mordecai who had adopted her as his own daughter. When her turn came to go to the king, she did not ask for anything except what Hegai, the king's eunuch, keeper of the women, suggested. Esther gained favor in the eyes of everyone who saw her.

She was taken to King Ahasuerus in the palace in the tenth month, the month Tebeth, in the seventh year of his reign. The king loved Esther more than all the other women. She won more favor and approval from him than did any of the other virgins. He placed the royal crown on her head and made her queen in place of Vashti. The king held a great banquet for all his officials and staff. It was Esther's banquet. He freed his provinces from tax payments and gave gifts worthy of the king's bounty.

When the virgins were gathered a second time, Mordecai was sitting at the King's Gate. Esther 40 still did not reveal her family background or her ethnicity, as Mordecai had directed. She obeyed Mordecai's orders, as she always had while he raised her.

During those days while Mordecai was sitting at the King's Gate, Bigthan and Teresh, two of the king's eunuchs who guarded the entrance, became infuriated and planned to assassinate King Ahasuerus. When Mordecai learned of the plot, he reported it to Queen Esther, and she told the king on Mordecai's behalf. When the report was investigated and verified, both men were hanged on the gallows. This event was recorded in the Historical Record in the king's presence.

3 After all this took place, King Ahasuerus honored Haman, son of Hammedatha the Agagite. He promoted him in rank and gave him a higher position than all the other officials. The entire royal staff at the King's Gate bowed down and paid homage to Haman, because the king had commanded this to be done for him. But Mordecai would not bow down or pay homage. The members of the royal staff at the King's Gate asked Mordecai, "Why are you disobeying the king's command?" When they had warned him day after day and he still would not listen to them, they told Haman in order to see if Mordecai's actions would be tolerated, since he had told them he was a Jew.

When Haman saw that Mordecai was not bowing down or paying him homage, he was filled with rage. And when he learned of Mordecai's ethnic identity, it seemed repugnant to Haman 10 to do away with Mordecai alone. He planned to destroy all of Mordecai's people, the Jews, throughout Ahasuerus's kingdom.

In the first month, the month of Nisan, in King Ahasuerus's twelfth year, the *pur*—that is, the lot—was cast before Haman for each day in each month, and it fell on the twelfth month, the month Adar. Then Haman informed King Ahasuerus, "There is one ethnic group, scattered throughout the peoples in every province of your kingdom, keeping themselves separate. Their laws are different from everyone else's and they do not obey the king's laws. It is not in the king's best interest to tolerate them. If the king approves, let an order be drawn up authorizing their destruction, and I will pay 375 tons of silver to the officials for deposit in the royal treasury."

The king removed his signet ring from his hand and gave it to Haman son of Hammedatha the Agagite, the enemy of the Jews. Then the king told Haman, "The money and people are given to you to do with as you see fit."

The royal scribes were summoned on the thirteenth day of the first month, and the order was written exactly as Haman commanded. It was intended for the royal satraps, the governors of each of the provinces, and the officials of each ethnic group and written for each province in its own script and to each ethnic group in its own language. It was written in the name of King Ahasuerus and sealed with the royal signet ring. Letters were sent by couriers to each of the royal provinces telling the officials to destroy, kill, and annihilate all the Jewish people—young and old, women and children—and plunder their possessions on a single day, the thirteenth day of Adar, the twelfth month.

A copy of the text, issued as law throughout every province, was distributed to all the peoples so that they might get ready for that day. The couriers left, spurred on by royal command, and the law was issued in the fortress of Susa. The king and Haman sat down to drink, while the city of Susa was in confusion.

4 When Mordecai learned all that had occurred, he tore his clothes, put on sackcloth and ashes, went into the middle of the city, and cried loudly and bitterly. He went only as far as the King's Gate, since the law prohibited anyone wearing sackcloth from entering the King's Gate. There was great mourning among the Jewish people in every province where the king's command and edict reached. They fasted, wept, and lamented, and many lay in sackcloth and ashes.

Esther's female servants and her eunuchs came and reported the news to her, and the queen was overcome with fear. She sent clothes for Mordecai to wear so that he would take off his sackcloth, but he did not accept them. Esther summoned Hathach, one of the king's eunuchs who attended her, and dispatched him to Mordecai to learn what he was doing and why. So Hathach went out to Mordecai in the city square in front of the King's Gate. Mordecai told him everything that had happened as well as the exact amount of money Haman had promised to pay the royal treasury for the slaughter of the Jews.

Mordecai also gave him a copy of the written decree issued in Susa ordering their destruction, so that Hathach might show it to Esther, explain it to her, and command her to approach the king, implore his favor, and plead with him personally for her people. Hathach came and repeated Mordecai's response to Esther.

Esther spoke to Hathach and commanded him to tell Mordecai, "All the royal officials and the people of the royal provinces know that one law applies to every man or woman who approaches the king in the inner courtyard and who has not been summoned—the death penalty—unless the

20 king extends the gold scepter, allowing that person to live. I have not been summoned to appear
before the king for the last thirty days." Esther's response was reported to Mordecai.

Mordecai told the messenger to reply to Esther, "Don't think that you will escape the fate of all
the Jews because you are in the king's palace. If you keep silent at this time, relief and deliverance
will come to the Jewish people from another place, but you and your father's family will be
destroyed. Who knows, perhaps you have come to your royal position for such a time as this."

Esther sent this reply to Mordecai: "Go and assemble all the Jews who can be found in Susa
and fast for me. Don't eat or drink for three days, night or day. I and my female servants will
also fast in the same way. After that, I will go to the king even if it is against the law. If I perish, I
perish." So Mordecai went and did everything Esther had commanded him.

5 On the third day, Esther dressed in her royal clothing and stood in the inner courtyard of
the palace facing it. The king was sitting on his royal throne in the royal courtroom, facing its
entrance. As soon as the king saw Queen Esther standing in the courtyard, she gained favor with
him. The king extended the gold scepter in his hand toward Esther, and she approached and
touched the tip of the scepter.

"What is it, Queen Esther?" the king asked her. "Whatever you want, even to half the kingdom,
will be given to you."

"If it pleases the king," Esther replied, "may the king and Haman come today to the banquet I
have prepared for them."

10 The king said, "Hurry, and get Haman so we can do as Esther has requested." So the king and
Haman went to the banquet Esther had prepared.

While drinking the wine, the king asked Esther, "Whatever you ask will be given to you.
Whatever you want, even to half the kingdom, will be done."

Esther answered, "This is my petition and my request: If I have found favor in the eyes of the
king, and if it pleases the king to grant my petition and perform my request, may the king and
Haman come to the banquet I will prepare for them. Tomorrow I will do what the king has asked."

That day Haman left full of joy and in good spirits. But when Haman saw Mordecai at the
King's Gate, and Mordecai didn't rise or tremble in fear at his presence, Haman was filled with rage
toward Mordecai. Yet Haman controlled himself and went home. He sent for his friends and his
20 wife Zeresh to join him. Then Haman described for them his glorious wealth and his many sons.
He told them all how the king had honored him and promoted him in rank over the other officials
and the royal staff. "What's more," Haman added, "Queen Esther invited no one but me to join the
king at the banquet she had prepared. I am invited again tomorrow to join her with the king. Still,
none of this satisfies me since I see Mordecai the Jew sitting at the King's Gate all the time."

His wife Zeresh and all his friends told him, "Have them build a gallows seventy-five feet tall.
Ask the king in the morning to hang Mordecai on it. Then go to the banquet with the king and
enjoy yourself." The advice pleased Haman, so he had the gallows constructed.

That night sleep escaped the king, so he ordered the book recording daily events to be brought and read to the king. They found the written report of how Mordecai had informed on Bigthana and Teresh, two of the king's eunuchs who guarded the entrance, when they planned to assassinate King Ahasuerus. The king inquired, "What honor and special recognition have been given to Mordecai for this act?"

The king's personal attendants replied, "Nothing has been done for him."

The king asked, "Who is in the court?" Now Haman was just entering the outer court of the palace to ask the king to hang Mordecai on the gallows he had prepared for him.

The king's attendants answered him, "Haman is there, standing in the court."

"Have him enter," the king ordered. Haman entered, and the king asked him, "What should be done for the man the king wants to honor?"

Haman thought to himself, "Who is it the king would want to honor more than me?" Haman told the king, "For the man the king wants to honor: Have them bring a royal garment that the king himself has worn and a horse the king himself has ridden, which has a royal crown on its head. Put the garment and the horse under the charge of one of the king's most noble officials. Have them clothe the man the king wants to honor, parade him on the horse through the city square, and call out before him, 'This is what is done for the man the king wants to honor.'"

The king told Haman, "Hurry, and do just as you proposed. Take a garment and a horse for Mordecai the Jew, who is sitting at the King's Gate. Do not leave out anything you have suggested."

So Haman took the garment and the horse. He clothed Mordecai and paraded him through the city square, calling out before him, "This is what is done for the man the king wants to honor."

Then Mordecai returned to the King's Gate, but Haman hurried off for home, mournful and with his head covered. Haman told his wife Zeresh and all his friends everything that had happened. His advisers and his wife Zeresh said to him, "Since Mordecai is Jewish, and you have begun to fall before him, you won't overcome him, because your downfall is certain." While they were still speaking with him, the king's eunuchs arrived and rushed Haman to the banquet Esther had prepared.

7 The king and Haman came to feast with Esther the queen. Once again, on the second day while drinking wine, the king asked Esther, "Queen Esther, whatever you ask will be given to you. Whatever you seek, even to half the kingdom, will be done."

Queen Esther answered, "If I have found favor with you, Your Majesty, and if the king is pleased, spare my life; this is my request. And spare my people; this is my desire. For my people and I have been sold to destruction, death, and annihilation. If we had merely been sold as male and female slaves, I would have kept silent. Indeed, the trouble wouldn't be worth burdening the king."

King Ahasuerus spoke up and asked Queen Esther, "Who is this, and where is the one who would devise such a scheme?"

10   Esther answered, "The adversary and enemy is this evil Haman."

Haman stood terrified before the king and queen. The king arose in anger and went from where they were drinking wine to the palace garden. Haman remained to beg Queen Esther for his life because he realized the king was planning something terrible for him. Just as the king returned from the palace garden to the banquet hall, Haman was falling on the couch where Esther was reclining. The king exclaimed, "Would he actually violate the queen while I am in the house?" As soon as the statement left the king's mouth, they covered Haman's face.

Harbona, one of the king's eunuchs, said, "There is a gallows seventy-five feet tall at Haman's house that he made for Mordecai, who gave the report that saved the king."

The king said, "Hang him on it."

20   They hanged Haman on the gallows he had prepared for Mordecai. Then the king's anger subsided.

8 That same day King Ahasuerus awarded Queen Esther the estate of Haman, the enemy of the Jews. Mordecai entered the king's presence because Esther had revealed her relationship to Mordecai. The king removed his signet ring he had recovered from Haman and gave it to Mordecai, and Esther put him in charge of Haman's estate.

Then Esther addressed the king again. She fell at his feet, wept, and begged him to revoke the evil of Haman the Agagite and his plot he had devised against the Jews. The king extended the gold scepter toward Esther, so she got up and stood before the king.

She said, "If it pleases the king and I have found favor with him, if the matter seems right to the king and I am pleasing in his eyes, let a royal edict be written. Let it revoke the documents the
10   scheming Haman son of Hammedatha the Agagite wrote to destroy the Jews who are in all the king's provinces. For how could I bear to see the disaster that would come on my people? How could I bear to see the destruction of my relatives?"

King Ahasuerus said to Esther the queen and to Mordecai the Jew, "Look, I have given Haman's estate to Esther, and he was hanged on the gallows because he attacked the Jews. Write in the king's name whatever pleases you concerning the Jews, and seal it with the royal signet ring. A document written in the king's name and sealed with the royal signet ring cannot be revoked."

On the twenty-third day of the third month—that is, the month Sivan—the royal scribes were summoned. Everything was written exactly as Mordecai commanded for the Jews, to the satraps, the governors, and the officials of the 127 provinces from India to Cush. The edict was written for
20   each province in its own script, for each ethnic group in its own language, and to the Jews in their own script and language.

Mordecai wrote in King Ahasuerus's name and sealed the edicts with the royal signet ring. He sent the documents by mounted couriers, who rode fast horses bred in the royal stables.

The king's edict gave the Jews in each and every city the right to assemble and defend themselves, to destroy, kill, and annihilate every ethnic and provincial army hostile to them, including women and children, and to take their possessions as spoils of war. This would take place on a single day throughout all the provinces of King Ahasuerus, on the thirteenth day of the twelfth month, the month Adar.

A copy of the text, issued as law throughout every province, was distributed to all the peoples
30 so the Jews could be ready to avenge themselves against their enemies on that day. The couriers rode out in haste on their royal horses at the king's urgent command. The law was also issued in the fortress of Susa.

Mordecai went from the king's presence clothed in royal blue and white, with a great gold crown and a purple robe of fine linen. The city of Susa shouted and rejoiced, and the Jews celebrated with gladness, joy, and honor. In every province and every city where the king's command and edict reached, gladness and joy took place among the Jews. There was a celebration and a holiday. And many of the ethnic groups of the land professed themselves to be Jews because fear of the Jews had overcome them.

9 The king's command and law went into effect on the thirteenth day of the twelfth month, the month Adar. On the day when the Jews' enemies had hoped to overpower them, just the opposite happened. The Jews overpowered those who hated them. In each of King Ahasuerus's provinces the Jews assembled in their cities to attack those who intended to harm them. Not a single person could withstand them; fear of them fell on every nationality.

All the officials of the provinces, the satraps, the governors, and the royal civil administrators aided the Jews because they feared Mordecai. For Mordecai exercised great power in the palace, and his fame spread throughout the provinces as he became more and more powerful.

The Jews put all their enemies to the sword, killing and destroying them. They did what
10 they pleased to those who hated them. In the fortress of Susa the Jews killed and destroyed five hundred men, including Parshandatha, Dalphon, Aspatha, Poratha, Adalia, Aridatha, Parmashta, Arisai, Aridai, and Vaizatha. They killed these ten sons of Haman son of Hammedatha, the enemy of the Jews. However, they did not seize any plunder.

On that day the number of people killed in the fortress of Susa was reported to the king. The king said to Queen Esther, "In the fortress of Susa the Jews have killed and destroyed five hundred men, including Haman's ten sons. What have they done in the rest of the royal provinces? Whatever you ask will be given to you. Whatever you seek will also be done."

Esther answered, "If it pleases the king, may the Jews who are in Susa also have tomorrow to carry out today's law, and may the bodies of Haman's ten sons be hung on the gallows." The king
20 gave the orders for this to be done, so a law was announced in Susa, and they hung the bodies of Haman's ten sons. The Jews in Susa assembled again on the fourteenth day of the month of Adar and killed three hundred men in Susa, but they did not seize any plunder.

The rest of the Jews in the royal provinces assembled, defended themselves, and gained relief from their enemies. They killed seventy-five thousand of those who hated them, but they did not seize any plunder. They fought on the thirteenth day of the month of Adar and rested on the fourteenth, and it became a day of feasting and rejoicing.

But the Jews in Susa had assembled on the thirteenth and the fourteenth days of the month. They rested on the fifteenth day of the month, and it became a day of feasting and rejoicing. This explains why the rural Jews who live in villages observe the fourteenth day of the month of Adar as a time of rejoicing and feasting. It is a holiday when they send gifts to one another.

Mordecai recorded these events and sent letters to all the Jews in all of King Ahasuerus's provinces, both near and far. He ordered them to celebrate the fourteenth and fifteenth days of the month of Adar every year because during those days the Jews gained relief from their enemies. That was the month when their sorrow was turned into rejoicing and their mourning into a holiday. They were to be days of feasting, rejoicing, and of sending gifts to one another and to the poor.

So the Jews agreed to continue the practice they had begun, as Mordecai had written them to do. For Haman son of Hammedatha the Agagite, the enemy of all the Jews, had plotted against the Jews to destroy them. He cast the *pur*—that is, the lot—to crush and destroy them. But when the matter was brought before the king, he commanded by letter that the evil plan Haman had devised against the Jews return on his own head and that he should be hanged with his sons on the gallows. For this reason these days are called Purim, from the word *pur*. Because of all the instructions in this letter as well as what they had witnessed and what had happened to them, the Jews bound themselves, their descendants, and all who joined with them to a commitment that they would not fail to celebrate these two days each and every year according to the written instructions and according to the time appointed. These days are remembered and celebrated by every generation, family, province, and city, so that these days of Purim will not lose their significance in Jewish life and their memory will not fade from their descendants.

Queen Esther, daughter of Abihail, along with Mordecai the Jew, wrote this second letter with full authority to confirm the letter about Purim. He sent letters with assurances of peace and security to all the Jews who were in the 127 provinces of the kingdom of Ahasuerus, in order to confirm these days of Purim at their proper time just as Mordecai the Jew and Esther the queen had established them and just as they had committed themselves and their descendants to the practices of fasting and lamentation. So Esther's command confirmed these customs of Purim, which were then written into the record.

10 King Ahasuerus imposed a tax throughout the land even to the farthest shores. All of his powerful and magnificent accomplishments and the detailed account of Mordecai's great rank with which the king had honored him, have they not been written in the Book of the Historical Events of the Kings of Media and Persia? Mordecai the Jew was second only to King Ahasuerus. He was famous among the Jews and highly esteemed by many of his relatives. He continued to pursue prosperity for his people and to speak for the well-being of all his descendants.

Introduction to Daniel

John Goldingay

The book of Daniel relates a series of stories about Daniel and his three friends, and a series of visions about events to come. Daniel and his friends were taken to Babylon as forced migrants just before the fall of Jerusalem in 587 BC, and the first half of the book relates the series of stories about them that tell of challenges they face in this alien context, of their faithfulness to Yahweh, and of Yahweh's faithfulness to them as he miraculously rescues them from danger and enables them to flourish. The stories would act as encouragement to people forced to live in foreign countries under imperial pressure, encouraging them to be faithful to Yahweh even though they might not experience the miraculous protection and recognition that came to Daniel and his friends.

The stories include a vision that describes four reigns that are to follow that of the Babylonian king, Nebuchadnezzar. The further visions in the second half of the book take up the themes of this first vision and relate the history that is to unfold after Daniel's day. They focus on a great crisis that comes to Jerusalem four centuries later, in the 160s BC, when the Hellenistic king Antiochus Epiphanes bans people from serving Yahweh in accordance with the Torah and introduces pagan worship into the temple in Jerusalem. Whereas the visions in chs. 7–12 are irrelevant to Daniel and his friends, they bring Yahweh's message to Jews living in the crisis in the 160s and encourage people to be faithful to Yahweh in this context as the stories do so in that other context.

In the ancient Near East it was sometimes a convention to present accounts of past events as if they were prophecies, and Daniel's visions are an example of that within the Scriptures. The visions that are inspired by the Holy Spirit are in another sense inspired by Daniel: that is, the vision in Dan 2 is the fountainhead of the other visions, which assure people that Yahweh has been in control of events in between. The climax of each vision relates an act whereby Yahweh puts down oppressors and restores his people, and these promises found some fulfilment in the deliverance of Jerusalem from Antiochus. This deliverance would thus be evidence that the visions really did come from Yahweh. One may guess that this awareness led to the inclusion of the book of Daniel in Scripture by the community. The visions also envisage a more final putting down of oppression and a more final restoration of Yahweh's people, and thus inspire readers to continue to look to his future with confidence.

The opening and closing chapters of the book are in Hebrew but the central chapters are in a sister language, Aramaic. We do not know why it should be so, but it compares with the way many people in the United States can move easily between English and Spanish.

Outline

1. Introduction to the stories and the visions (1.1–32)

2. Daniel interprets Nebuchadnezzar's dream of a statue symbolizing the four reigns (2.1–99)

3. Daniel's three friends insist on not bowing down to an image, and Yahweh rescues them (3.1–58)

4. Daniel interprets another dream for Nebuchadnezzar, which comes true (4.1–100)

5. Daniel interprets an inscription on a wall for Belshazzar, which comes true (5.1–59)

6. Daniel insists on being faithful in prayer, and Yahweh rescues him (6.1–57)

7. Daniel has a dream of four monsters symbolizing four reigns that are followed by God's reign (7.1–71)

8. Daniel has a vision of two strange animals symbolizing Medo-Persia and Greece (8.1–59)

9. Daniel asks about how long the devastation of Jerusalem will last, and Gabriel explains (9.1–74)

10. Daniel has a vision of Persian and Greek kings fighting and of the deliverance of Yahweh's people (10.1–12.32)

Suggested Resources

Goldingay, John. *Daniel*. Word Biblical Commentary. Rev. ed. Grand Rapids: Zondervan, 2019.

———. *Daniel and the Twelve Prophets for Everyone*. Louisville: Westminster John Knox, 2016.

Newsom, Carol A., with Brennan W. Breed. *Daniel*. Old Testament Library. Louisville: Westminster John Knox, 2014.

Russell, David S. *Daniel*. The Daily Bible Study Series. Louisville: Westminster John Knox, 1981.

Wright, Christopher J. H. *Hearing the Message of Daniel*. Grand Rapids: Zondervan, 2017.

Daniel

1 In the third year of the reign of King Jehoiakim of Judah, King Nebuchadnezzar of Babylon came to Jerusalem and laid siege to it. The Lord handed King Jehoiakim of Judah over to him, along with some of the vessels from the house of God. Nebuchadnezzar carried them to the land of Babylon, to the house of his god, and put the vessels in the treasury of his god.

The king ordered Ashpenaz, his chief eunuch, to bring some of the Israelites from the royal family and from the nobility— young men without any physical defect, good-looking, suitable for instruction in all wisdom, knowledgeable, perceptive, and capable of serving in the king's palace. He was to teach them the Chaldean language and literature. The king assigned them daily provisions from the royal food and from the wine that he drank. They were to be trained for three years, and at the end of that time they were to attend the king. Among them, from the Judahites, were Daniel, Hananiah, Mishael, and Azariah. The chief eunuch gave them names; he gave the name Belteshazzar to Daniel, Shadrach to Hananiah, Meshach to Mishael, and Abednego to Azariah.

Daniel determined that he would not defile himself with the king's food or with the wine he drank. So he asked permission from the chief eunuch not to defile himself. God had granted Daniel kindness and compassion from the chief eunuch, yet he said to Daniel, "I fear my lord the king, who assigned your food and drink. What if he sees your faces looking thinner than the other young men your age? You would endanger my life with the king."

So Daniel said to the guard whom the chief eunuch had assigned to Daniel, Hananiah, Mishael, and Azariah, "Please test your servants for ten days. Let us be given vegetables to eat and water to drink. Then examine our appearance and the appearance of the young men who are eating the king's food, and deal with your servants based on what you see." He agreed with them about this and tested them for ten days. At the end of ten days they looked better and healthier than all the young men who were eating the king's food. So the guard continued to remove their food and the wine they were to drink and gave them vegetables.

God gave these four young men knowledge and understanding in every kind of literature and wisdom. Daniel also understood visions and dreams of every kind. At the end of the time that the king had said to present them, the chief eunuch presented them to Nebuchadnezzar. The king interviewed them, and among all of them, no one was found equal to Daniel, Hananiah, Mishael, and Azariah. So they began to attend the king. In every matter of wisdom and understanding that the king consulted them about, he found them ten times better than all the magicians and mediums in his entire kingdom. Daniel remained there until the first year of King Cyrus.

2 In the second year of his reign, Nebuchadnezzar had dreams that troubled him, and sleep deserted him. So the king gave orders to summon the magicians, mediums, sorcerers, and Chaldeans to tell the king his dreams. When they came and stood before the king, he said to them, "I have had a dream and am anxious to understand it."

The Chaldeans spoke to the king (Aramaic begins here): "May the king live forever. Tell your servants the dream, and we will give the interpretation."

The king replied to the Chaldeans, "My word is final: If you don't tell me the dream and its interpretation, you will be torn limb from limb, and your houses will be made a garbage dump. But if you make the dream and its interpretation known to me, you'll receive gifts, a reward, and great
10 honor from me. So make the dream and its interpretation known to me."

They answered a second time, "May the king tell the dream to his servants, and we will make known the interpretation."

The king replied, "I know for certain you are trying to gain some time, because you see that my word is final. If you don't tell me the dream, there is one decree for you. You have conspired to tell me something false or fraudulent until the situation changes. So tell me the dream and I will know you can give me its interpretation."

The Chaldeans answered the king, "No one on earth can make known what the king requests. Consequently, no king, however great and powerful, has ever asked anything like this of any magician, medium, or Chaldean. What the king is asking is so difficult that no one can make
20 it known to him except the gods, whose dwelling is not with mortals." Because of this, the king became violently angry and gave orders to destroy all the wise men of Babylon. The decree was issued that the wise men were to be executed, and they searched for Daniel and his friends, to execute them.

Then Daniel responded with tact and discretion to Arioch, the captain of the king's guard, who had gone out to execute the wise men of Babylon. He asked Arioch, the king's officer, "Why is the decree from the king so harsh?" Then Arioch explained the situation to Daniel. So Daniel went and asked the king to give him some time, so that he could give the king the interpretation.

Then Daniel went to his house and told his friends Hananiah, Mishael, and Azariah about the matter, urging them to ask the God of the heavens for mercy concerning this mystery, so Daniel
30 and his friends would not be destroyed with the rest of Babylon's wise men. The mystery was then revealed to Daniel in a vision at night, and Daniel praised the God of the heavens and declared:

> May the name of God
> be praised forever and ever,
> for wisdom and power belong to him.

He changes the times and seasons;
he removes kings and establishes kings.
He gives wisdom to the wise
and knowledge to those
who have understanding.
He reveals the deep and hidden things;
he knows what is in the darkness,
and light dwells with him.
I offer thanks and praise to you,
God of my ancestors,
because you have given me
wisdom and power.
And now you have let me know
what we asked of you,
for you have let us know
the king's mystery.

Therefore Daniel went to Arioch, whom the king had assigned to destroy the wise men of Babylon. He came and said to him, "Don't destroy the wise men of Babylon! Bring me before the king, and I will give him the interpretation."

Then Arioch quickly brought Daniel before the king and said to him, "I have found a man among the Judean exiles who can let the king know the interpretation."

The king said in reply to Daniel, whose name was Belteshazzar, "Are you able to tell me the dream I had and its interpretation?"

Daniel answered the king, "No wise man, medium, magician, or diviner is able to make known to the king the mystery he asked about. But there is a God in heaven who reveals mysteries, and he has let King Nebuchadnezzar know what will happen in the last days. Your dream and the visions that came into your mind as you lay in bed were these: Your Majesty, while you were in your bed, thoughts came to your mind about what will happen in the future. The revealer of mysteries has let you know what will happen. As for me, this mystery has been revealed to me, not because I have more wisdom than anyone living, but in order that the interpretation might be made known to the king, and that you may understand the thoughts of your mind.

"Your Majesty, as you were watching, suddenly a colossal statue appeared. That statue, tall and dazzling, was standing in front of you, and its appearance was terrifying. The head of the statue was pure gold, its chest and arms were silver, its stomach and thighs were bronze, its legs were iron, and its feet were partly iron and partly fired clay. As you were watching, a stone broke off without a hand touching it, struck the statue on its feet of iron and fired clay, and crushed them.

Then the iron, the fired clay, the bronze, the silver, and the gold were shattered and became like chaff from the summer threshing floors. The wind carried them away, and not a trace of them could be found. But the stone that struck the statue became a great mountain and filled the whole earth.

"This was the dream; now we will tell the king its interpretation. Your Majesty, you are king of kings. The God of the heavens has given you sovereignty, power, strength, and glory. Wherever people live — or wild animals, or birds of the sky — he has handed them over to you and made you ruler over them all. You are the head of gold.

"After you, there will arise another kingdom, inferior to yours, and then another, a third
80 kingdom, of bronze, which will rule the whole earth. A fourth kingdom will be as strong as iron; for iron crushes and shatters everything, and like iron that smashes, it will crush and smash all the others. You saw the feet and toes, partly of a potter's fired clay and partly of iron — it will be a divided kingdom, though some of the strength of iron will be in it. You saw the iron mixed with clay, and that the toes of the feet were partly iron and partly fired clay — part of the kingdom will be strong, and part will be brittle. You saw the iron mixed with clay — the peoples will mix with one another but will not hold together, just as iron does not mix with fired clay.

"In the days of those kings, the God of the heavens will set up a kingdom that will never be destroyed, and this kingdom will not be left to another people. It will crush all these kingdoms and bring them to an end, but will itself endure forever. You saw a stone break off from the mountain
90 without a hand touching it, and it crushed the iron, bronze, fired clay, silver, and gold. The great God has told the king what will happen in the future. The dream is certain, and its interpretation reliable."

Then King Nebuchadnezzar fell facedown, worshiped Daniel, and gave orders to present an offering and incense to him. The king said to Daniel, "Your God is indeed God of gods, Lord of kings, and a revealer of mysteries, since you were able to reveal this mystery." Then the king promoted Daniel and gave him many generous gifts. He made him ruler over the entire province of Babylon and chief governor over all the wise men of Babylon. At Daniel's request, the king appointed Shadrach, Meshach, and Abednego to manage the province of Babylon. But Daniel remained at the king's court.

3 King Nebuchadnezzar made a gold statue, ninety feet high and nine feet wide. He set it up on the plain of Dura in the province of Babylon. King Nebuchadnezzar sent word to assemble the satraps, prefects, governors, advisers, treasurers, judges, magistrates, and all the rulers of the provinces to attend the dedication of the statue King Nebuchadnezzar had set up. So the satraps, prefects, governors, advisers, treasurers, judges, magistrates, and all the rulers of the provinces assembled for the dedication of the statue the king had set up. Then they stood before the statue Nebuchadnezzar had set up.

A herald loudly proclaimed, "People of every nation and language, you are commanded: When you hear the sound of the horn, flute, zither, lyre, harp, drum, and every kind of music, you are to fall facedown and worship the gold statue that King Nebuchadnezzar has set up. But whoever does not fall down and worship will immediately be thrown into a furnace of blazing fire."

Therefore, when all the people heard the sound of the horn, flute, zither, lyre, harp, and every kind of music, people of every nation and language fell down and worshiped the gold statue that King Nebuchadnezzar had set up.

Some Chaldeans took this occasion to come forward and maliciously accuse the Jews. They said to King Nebuchadnezzar, "May the king live forever. You as king have issued a decree that everyone who hears the sound of the horn, flute, zither, lyre, harp, drum, and every kind of music must fall down and worship the gold statue. Whoever does not fall down and worship will be thrown into a furnace of blazing fire. There are some Jews you have appointed to manage the province of Babylon: Shadrach, Meshach, and Abednego. These men have ignored you, the king; they do not serve your gods or worship the gold statue you have set up."

Then in a furious rage Nebuchadnezzar gave orders to bring in Shadrach, Meshach, and Abednego. So these men were brought before the king. Nebuchadnezzar asked them, "Shadrach, Meshach, and Abednego, is it true that you don't serve my gods or worship the gold statue I have set up? Now if you're ready, when you hear the sound of the horn, flute, zither, lyre, harp, drum, and every kind of music, fall down and worship the statue I made. But if you don't worship it, you will immediately be thrown into a furnace of blazing fire — and who is the god who can rescue you from my power?"

Shadrach, Meshach, and Abednego replied to the king, "Nebuchadnezzar, we don't need to give you an answer to this question. If the God we serve exists, then he can rescue us from the furnace of blazing fire, and he can rescue us from the power of you, the king. But even if he does not rescue us, we want you as king to know that we will not serve your gods or worship the gold statue you set up."

Then Nebuchadnezzar was filled with rage, and the expression on his face changed toward Shadrach, Meshach, and Abednego. He gave orders to heat the furnace seven times more than was customary, and he commanded some of the best soldiers in his army to tie up Shadrach, Meshach, and Abednego and throw them into the furnace of blazing fire. So these men, in their trousers, robes, head coverings, and other clothes, were tied up and thrown into the furnace of blazing fire. Since the king's command was so urgent and the furnace extremely hot, the raging flames killed those men who carried up Shadrach, Meshach, and Abednego. And these three men, Shadrach, Meshach, and Abednego fell, bound, into the furnace of blazing fire.

Then King Nebuchadnezzar jumped up in alarm. He said to his advisers, "Didn't we throw three men, bound, into the fire?"

"Yes, of course, Your Majesty," they replied to the king.

He exclaimed, "Look! I see four men, not tied, walking around in the fire unharmed; and the fourth looks like a son of the gods."

Nebuchadnezzar then approached the door of the furnace of blazing fire and called, "Shadrach, Meshach, and Abednego, you servants of the Most High God — come out!" So Shadrach, Meshach, and Abednego came out of the fire. When the satraps, prefects, governors, and the
50 king's advisers gathered around, they saw that the fire had no effect on the bodies of these men: not a hair of their heads was singed, their robes were unaffected, and there was no smell of fire on them. Nebuchadnezzar exclaimed, "Praise to the God of Shadrach, Meshach, and Abednego! He sent his angel and rescued his servants who trusted in him. They violated the king's command and risked their lives rather than serve or worship any god except their own God. Therefore I issue a decree that anyone of any people, nation, or language who says anything offensive against the God of Shadrach, Meshach, and Abednego will be torn limb from limb and his house made a garbage dump. For there is no other god who is able to deliver like this." Then the king rewarded Shadrach, Meshach, and Abednego in the province of Babylon.

4   King Nebuchadnezzar,

To those of every people, nation, and language, who live on the whole earth:

May your prosperity increase. I am pleased to tell you about the miracles and wonders the Most High God has done for me.

How great are his miracles,
    and how mighty his wonders!
His kingdom is an eternal kingdom,
    and his dominion is from generation to generation.

I, Nebuchadnezzar, was at ease in my house and flourishing in my palace. I had a dream, and
10 it frightened me; while in my bed, the images and visions in my mind alarmed me. So I issued a decree to bring all the wise men of Babylon to me in order that they might make the dream's interpretation known to me. When the magicians, mediums, Chaldeans, and diviners came in, I told them the dream, but they could not make its interpretation known to me.

Finally Daniel, named Belteshazzar after the name of my god — and a spirit of the holy gods is in him — came before me. I told him the dream: "Belteshazzar, head of the magicians, because I know that you have the spirit of the holy gods and that no mystery puzzles you, explain to me the visions of my dream that I saw, and its interpretation. In the visions of my mind as I was lying in bed, I saw this:

> There was a tree in the middle of the earth,
> and it was very tall.
> The tree grew large and strong;
> its top reached to the sky,
> and it was visible to the ends of the earth.
> Its leaves were beautiful, its fruit was abundant,
> and on it was food for all.
> Wild animals found shelter under it,
> the birds of the sky lived in its branches,
> and every creature was fed from it.

20

"As I was lying in my bed, I also saw in the visions of my mind a watcher, a holy one, coming down from heaven. He called out loudly:

30

> Cut down the tree and chop off its branches;
> strip off its leaves and scatter its fruit.
> Let the animals flee from under it,
> and the birds from its branches.
> But leave the stump with its roots in the ground
> and with a band of iron and bronze around it
> in the tender grass of the field.
> Let him be drenched with dew from the sky
> and share the plants of the earth
> with the animals.
> Let his mind be changed from that of a human,
> and let him be given the mind of an animal
> for seven periods of time.
> This word is by decree of the watchers,
> and the decision is by command from the holy ones.
> This is so that the living will know
> that the Most High is ruler
> over human kingdoms.
> He gives them to anyone he wants
> and sets the lowliest of people over them.

40

50

This is the dream that I, King Nebuchadnezzar, had. Now, Belteshazzar, tell me the interpretation, because none of the wise men of my kingdom can make the interpretation known to me. But you can, because you have a spirit of the holy gods."

Then Daniel, whose name is Belteshazzar, was stunned for a moment, and his thoughts alarmed him. The king said, "Belteshazzar, don't let the dream or its interpretation alarm you."

Belteshazzar answered, "My lord, may the dream apply to those who hate you, and its interpretation to your enemies! The tree you saw, which grew large and strong, whose top reached to the sky and was visible to the whole earth, and whose leaves were beautiful and its fruit abundant — and on it was food for all, under it the wild animals lived, and in its branches
60 the birds of the sky lived— that tree is you, Your Majesty. For you have become great and strong: your greatness has grown and even reaches the sky, and your dominion extends to the ends of the earth.

"The king saw a watcher, a holy one, coming down from heaven and saying, 'Cut down the tree and destroy it, but leave the stump with its roots in the ground and with a band of iron and bronze around it in the tender grass of the field. Let him be drenched with dew from the sky and share food with the wild animals for seven periods of time.' This is the interpretation, Your Majesty, and this is the decree of the Most High that has been issued against my lord the king: You will be driven away from people to live with the wild animals. You will feed on grass like cattle and be drenched with dew from the sky for seven periods of time, until
70 you acknowledge that the Most High is ruler over human kingdoms, and he gives them to anyone he wants. As for the command to leave the tree's stump with its roots, your kingdom will be restored to you as soon as you acknowledge that Heaven rules. Therefore, may my advice seem good to you my king. Separate yourself from your sins by doing what is right, and from your injustices by showing mercy to the needy. Perhaps there will be an extension of your prosperity."

All this happened to King Nebuchadnezzar. At the end of twelve months, as he was walking on the roof of the royal palace in Babylon, the king exclaimed, "Is this not Babylon the Great that I have built to be a royal residence by my vast power and for my majestic glory?"

While the words were still in the king's mouth, a voice came from heaven: "King
80 Nebuchadnezzar, to you it is declared that the kingdom has departed from you. You will be driven away from people to live with the wild animals, and you will feed on grass like cattle for seven periods of time, until you acknowledge that the Most High is ruler over human kingdoms, and he gives them to anyone he wants."

At that moment the message against Nebuchadnezzar was fulfilled. He was driven away from people. He ate grass like cattle, and his body was drenched with dew from the sky, until his hair grew like eagles' feathers and his nails like birds' claws.

But at the end of those days, I, Nebuchadnezzar, looked up to heaven, and my sanity returned to me. Then I praised the Most High and honored and glorified him who lives forever:

For his dominion is an everlasting dominion,
90   and his kingdom is from generation to generation.
All the inhabitants of the earth are counted as nothing,
   and he does what he wants with the army of heaven
   and the inhabitants of the earth.
There is no one who can block his hand
   or say to him, "What have you done?"

At that time my sanity returned to me, and my majesty and splendor returned to me for the glory of my kingdom. My advisers and my nobles sought me out, I was reestablished over my kingdom, and even more greatness came to me. Now I, Nebuchadnezzar, praise, exalt, and glorify the King of the heavens, because all his works are true and his ways are just. He is able to humble 100 those who walk in pride.

5 King Belshazzar held a great feast for a thousand of his nobles and drank wine in their presence. Under the influence of the wine, Belshazzar gave orders to bring in the gold and silver vessels that his predecessor Nebuchadnezzar had taken from the temple in Jerusalem, so that the king and his nobles, wives, and concubines could drink from them. So they brought in the gold vessels that had been taken from the temple, the house of God in Jerusalem, and the king and his nobles, wives, and concubines drank from them. They drank the wine and praised their gods made of gold and silver, bronze, iron, wood, and stone.

At that moment the fingers of a man's hand appeared and began writing on the plaster of the king's palace wall next to the lampstand. As the king watched the hand that was writing, his 10 face turned pale, and his thoughts so terrified him that he soiled himself and his knees knocked together. The king shouted to bring in the mediums, Chaldeans, and diviners. He said to these wise men of Babylon, "Whoever reads this inscription and gives me its interpretation will be clothed in purple, have a gold chain around his neck, and have the third highest position in the kingdom." So all the king's wise men came in, but none could read the inscription or make its interpretation known to him. Then King Belshazzar became even more terrified, his face turned pale, and his nobles were bewildered.

Because of the outcry of the king and his nobles, the queen came to the banquet hall. "May the king live forever," she said. "Don't let your thoughts terrify you or your face be pale. There is a man in your kingdom who has a spirit of the holy gods in him. In the days of your predecessor he 20 was found to have insight, intelligence, and wisdom like the wisdom of the gods. Your predecessor, King Nebuchadnezzar, appointed him chief of the magicians, mediums, Chaldeans, and diviners. Your own predecessor, the king, did this because Daniel, the one the king named Belteshazzar, was found to have an extraordinary spirit, knowledge and intelligence, and the ability to interpret dreams, explain riddles, and solve problems. Therefore, summon Daniel, and he will give the interpretation."

Then Daniel was brought before the king. The king said to him, "Are you Daniel, one of the Judean exiles that my predecessor the king brought from Judah? I've heard that you have a spirit of the gods in you, and that insight, intelligence, and extraordinary wisdom are found in you. Now the wise men and mediums were brought before me to read this inscription and make its
30 interpretation known to me, but they could not give its interpretation. However, I have heard about you that you can give interpretations and solve problems. Therefore, if you can read this inscription and give me its interpretation, you will be clothed in purple, have a gold chain around your neck, and have the third highest position in the kingdom."

Then Daniel answered the king, "You may keep your gifts and give your rewards to someone else; however, I will read the inscription for the king and make the interpretation known to him. Your Majesty, the Most High God gave sovereignty, greatness, glory, and majesty to your predecessor Nebuchadnezzar. Because of the greatness he gave him, all peoples, nations, and languages were terrified and fearful of him. He killed anyone he wanted and kept alive anyone he wanted; he exalted anyone he wanted and humbled anyone he wanted. But when his heart was exalted and his spirit
40 became arrogant, he was deposed from his royal throne and his glory was taken from him. He was driven away from people, his mind was like an animal's, he lived with the wild donkeys, he was fed grass like cattle, and his body was drenched with dew from the sky until he acknowledged that the Most High God is ruler over human kingdoms and sets anyone he wants over them.

"But you his successor, Belshazzar, have not humbled your heart, even though you knew all this. Instead, you have exalted yourself against the Lord of the heavens. The vessels from his house were brought to you, and as you and your nobles, wives, and concubines drank wine from them, you praised the gods made of silver and gold, bronze, iron, wood, and stone, which do not see or hear or understand. But you have not glorified the God who holds your life-breath in his hand and who controls the whole course of your life. Therefore, he sent the hand, and this writing was inscribed.

50 "This is the writing that was inscribed: MENE, MENE, TEKEL, and PARSIN. This is the interpretation of the message:

'Mene' means that God has numbered the days of your kingdom and brought it to an end.
'Tekel' means that you have been weighed on the balance and found deficient.
'Peres' means that your kingdom has been divided and given to the Medes and Persians."

Then Belshazzar gave an order, and they clothed Daniel in purple, placed a gold chain around his neck, and issued a proclamation concerning him that he should be the third ruler in the kingdom.

That very night Belshazzar the king of the Chaldeans was killed, and Darius the Mede received the kingdom at the age of sixty-two.

6 Darius decided to appoint 120 satraps over the kingdom, stationed throughout the realm, and over them three administrators, including Daniel. These satraps would be accountable to them so that the king would not be defrauded. Daniel distinguished himself above the administrators and satraps because he had an extraordinary spirit, so the king planned to set him over the whole realm. The administrators and satraps, therefore, kept trying to find a charge against Daniel regarding the kingdom. But they could find no charge or corruption, for he was trustworthy, and no negligence or corruption was found in him. Then these men said, "We will never find any charge against this Daniel unless we find something against him concerning the law of his God."

So the administrators and satraps went together to the king and said to him, "May King
10 Darius live forever. All the administrators of the kingdom—the prefects, satraps, advisers, and governors—have agreed that the king should establish an ordinance and enforce an edict that, for thirty days, anyone who petitions any god or man except you, the king, will be thrown into the lions' den. Therefore, Your Majesty, establish the edict and sign the document so that, as a law of the Medes and Persians, it is irrevocable and cannot be changed." So King Darius signed the written edict.

When Daniel learned that the document had been signed, he went into his house. The windows in its upstairs room opened toward Jerusalem, and three times a day he got down on his knees, prayed, and gave thanks to his God, just as he had done before. Then these men went as a group and found Daniel petitioning and imploring his God. So they approached the king and asked
20 about his edict: "Didn't you sign an edict that for thirty days any person who petitions any god or man except you, the king, will be thrown into the lions' den?"

The king answered, "As a law of the Medes and Persians, the order stands and is irrevocable."

Then they replied to the king, "Daniel, one of the Judean exiles, has ignored you, the king, and the edict you signed, for he prays three times a day." As soon as the king heard this, he was very displeased; he set his mind on rescuing Daniel and made every effort until sundown to deliver him.

Then these men went together to the king and said to him, "You know, Your Majesty, that it is a law of the Medes and Persians that no edict or ordinance the king establishes can be changed."

So the king gave the order, and they brought Daniel and threw him into the lions' den. The king said to Daniel, "May your God, whom you continually serve, rescue you!" A stone was
30 brought and placed over the mouth of the den. The king sealed it with his own signet ring and with the signet rings of his nobles, so that nothing in regard to Daniel could be changed. Then the king went to his palace and spent the night fasting. No diversions were brought to him, and he could not sleep.

At the first light of dawn the king got up and hurried to the lions' den. When he reached the den, he cried out in anguish to Daniel. "Daniel, servant of the living God," the king said, "has your God, whom you continually serve, been able to rescue you from the lions?"

Then Daniel spoke with the king: "May the king live forever. My God sent his angel and shut the lions' mouths; and they haven't harmed me, for I was found innocent before him. And also before you, Your Majesty, I have not done harm."

40 The king was overjoyed and gave orders to take Daniel out of the den. When Daniel was brought up from the den, he was found to be unharmed, for he trusted in his God. The king then gave the command, and those men who had maliciously accused Daniel were brought and thrown into the lions' den — they, their children, and their wives. They had not reached the bottom of the den before the lions overpowered them and crushed all their bones.

Then King Darius wrote to those of every people, nation, and language who live on the whole earth: "May your prosperity abound. I issue a decree that in all my royal dominion, people must tremble in fear before the God of Daniel:

> For he is the living God,
> and he endures forever;
50 > his kingdom will never be destroyed,
> and his dominion has no end.
> He rescues and delivers;
> he performs signs and wonders
> in the heavens and on the earth,
> for he has rescued Daniel
> from the power of the lions."

So Daniel prospered during the reign of Darius and the reign of Cyrus the Persian.

7 In the first year of King Belshazzar of Babylon, Daniel had a dream with visions in his mind as he was lying in his bed. He wrote down the dream, and here is the summary of his account. Daniel said, "In my vision at night I was watching, and suddenly the four winds of heaven stirred up the great sea. Four huge beasts came up from the sea, each different from the other.

"The first was like a lion but had eagle's wings. I continued watching until its wings were torn off. It was lifted up from the ground, set on its feet like a man, and given a human mind.

"Suddenly, another beast appeared, a second one, that looked like a bear. It was raised up on one side, with three ribs in its mouth between its teeth. It was told, 'Get up! Gorge yourself on flesh.'

"After this, while I was watching, suddenly another beast appeared. It was like a leopard with 10 four wings of a bird on its back. It had four heads, and it was given dominion.

"After this, while I was watching in the night visions, suddenly a fourth beast appeared, frightening and dreadful, and incredibly strong, with large iron teeth. It devoured and crushed, and it trampled with its feet whatever was left. It was different from all the beasts before it, and it had ten horns.

"While I was considering the horns, suddenly another horn, a little one, came up among them, and three of the first horns were uprooted before it. And suddenly in this horn there were eyes like the eyes of a human and a mouth that was speaking arrogantly.

"As I kept watching,
    thrones were set in place,
    and the Ancient of Days took his seat.
20   His clothing was white like snow,
    and the hair of his head like whitest wool.
    His throne was flaming fire;
    its wheels were blazing fire.
    A river of fire was flowing,
    coming out from his presence.
    Thousands upon thousands served him;
    ten thousand times ten thousand stood before him.
    The court was convened,
    and the books were opened.

30 "I watched, then, because of the sound of the arrogant words the horn was speaking. As I continued watching, the beast was killed and its body destroyed and given over to the burning fire. As for the rest of the beasts, their dominion was removed, but an extension of life was granted to them for a certain period of time. I continued watching in the night visions,
    and suddenly one like a son of man
    was coming with the clouds of heaven.
    He approached the Ancient of Days
    and was escorted before him.
    He was given dominion
    and glory and a kingdom,
40   so that those of every people,
    nation, and language
    should serve him.
    His dominion is an everlasting dominion
    that will not pass away,
    and his kingdom is one
    that will not be destroyed.

"As for me, Daniel, my spirit was deeply distressed within me, and the visions in my mind terrified me. I approached one of those who were standing by and asked him to clarify all this. So he let me know the interpretation of these things: 'These huge beasts, four in number, are four kings who will rise from the earth. But the holy ones of the Most High will receive the kingdom and possess it forever, yes, forever and ever.'

"Then I wanted to be clear about the fourth beast, the one different from all the others, extremely terrifying, with iron teeth and bronze claws, devouring, crushing, and trampling with its feet whatever was left. I also wanted to know about the ten horns on its head and about the other horn that came up, before which three fell — the horn that had eyes, and a mouth that spoke arrogantly, and that looked bigger than the others. As I was watching, this horn waged war against the holy ones and was prevailing over them until the Ancient of Days arrived and a judgment was given in favor of the holy ones of the Most High, for the time had come, and the holy ones took possession of the kingdom.

"This is what he said: 'The fourth beast will be a fourth kingdom on the earth, different from all the other kingdoms. It will devour the whole earth, trample it down, and crush it. The ten horns are ten kings who will rise from this kingdom. Another king, different from the previous ones, will rise after them and subdue three kings. He will speak words against the Most High and oppress the holy ones of the Most High. He will intend to change religious festivals and laws, and the holy ones will be handed over to him for a time, times, and half a time. But the court will convene, and his dominion will be taken away, to be completely destroyed forever. The kingdom, dominion, and greatness of the kingdoms under all of heaven will be given to the people, the holy ones of the Most High. His kingdom will be an everlasting kingdom, and all rulers will serve and obey him.'

"This is the end of the account. As for me, Daniel, my thoughts terrified me greatly, and my face turned pale, but I kept the matter to myself."

8 In the third year of King Belshazzar's reign, a vision appeared to me, Daniel, after the one that had appeared to me earlier. I saw the vision, and as I watched, I was in the fortress city of Susa, in the province of Elam. I saw in the vision that I was beside the Ulai Canal. I looked up, and there was a ram standing beside the canal. He had two horns. The two horns were long, but one was longer than the other, and the longer one came up last. I saw the ram charging to the west, the north, and the south. No animal could stand against him, and there was no rescue from his power. He did whatever he wanted and became great.

As I was observing, a male goat appeared, coming from the west across the surface of the entire earth without touching the ground. The goat had a conspicuous horn between his eyes. He came toward the two-horned ram I had seen standing beside the canal and rushed at him with savage fury. I saw him approaching the ram, and infuriated with him, he struck the ram, breaking his two horns, and the ram was not strong enough to stand against him. The goat threw him to the ground and trampled him, and there was no one to rescue the ram from his power. Then the male goat acted even more arrogantly, but when he became powerful, the large horn was broken. Four conspicuous horns came up in its place, pointing toward the four winds of heaven.

From one of them a little horn emerged and grew extensively toward the south and the east and toward the beautiful land. It grew as high as the heavenly army, made some of the army and some of the stars fall to the earth, and trampled them. It acted arrogantly even against the Prince of the heavenly army; it revoked his regular sacrifice and overthrew the place of his sanctuary. In the rebellion, the army was given up, together with the regular sacrifice. The horn threw truth to the ground and was successful in what it did.

Then I heard a holy one speaking, and another holy one said to the speaker, "How long will the events of this vision last — the regular sacrifice, the rebellion that makes desolate, and the giving over of the sanctuary and of the army to be trampled?"

He said to me, "For 2,300 evenings and mornings; then the sanctuary will be restored."

While I, Daniel, was watching the vision and trying to understand it, there stood before me someone who appeared to be a man. I heard a human voice calling from the middle of the Ulai: "Gabriel, explain the vision to this man."

So he approached where I was standing; when he came near, I was terrified and fell facedown. "Son of man," he said to me, "understand that the vision refers to the time of the end." While he was speaking to me, I fell into a deep sleep, with my face to the ground. Then he touched me, made me stand up, and said, "I am here to tell you what will happen at the conclusion of the time of wrath, because it refers to the appointed time of the end. The two-horned ram that you saw represents the kings of Media and Persia. The shaggy goat represents the king of Greece, and the large horn between his eyes represents the first king. The four horns that took the place of the broken horn represent four kingdoms. They will rise from that nation, but without its power.

> Near the end of their kingdoms,
> when the rebels have reached
> the full measure of their sin,
> a ruthless king, skilled in intrigue,
> will come to the throne.
> His power will be great,
> but it will not be his own.
> He will cause outrageous destruction
> and succeed in whatever he does.
> He will destroy the powerful
> along with the holy people.

He will cause deceit to prosper
through his cunning and by his influence,
and in his own mind he will exalt himself.
He will destroy many in a time of peace;
he will even stand against the Prince of princes.
Yet he will be broken — not by human hands.
The vision of the evenings and the mornings
that has been told is true.
Now you are to seal up the vision
because it refers to many days in the future."

I, Daniel, was overcome and lay sick for days. Then I got up and went about the king's business. I was greatly disturbed by the vision and could not understand it.

9 In the first year of Darius, the son of Ahasuerus, a Mede by birth, who was made king over the Chaldean kingdom — in the first year of his reign, I, Daniel, understood from the books according to the word of the LORD to the prophet Jeremiah that the number of years for the desolation of Jerusalem would be seventy. So I turned my attention to the Lord God to seek him by prayer and petitions, with fasting, sackcloth, and ashes.

I prayed to the LORD my God and confessed:

Ah, Lord — the great and awe-inspiring God who keeps his gracious covenant with those who love him and keep his commands— we have sinned, done wrong, acted wickedly, rebelled, and turned away from your commands and ordinances. We have not listened to your servants the prophets, who spoke in your name to our kings, leaders, ancestors, and all the people of the land.

Lord, righteousness belongs to you, but this day public shame belongs to us: the men of Judah, the residents of Jerusalem, and all Israel — those who are near and those who are far, in all the countries where you have banished them because of the disloyalty they have shown toward you. LORD, public shame belongs to us, our kings, our leaders, and our ancestors, because we have sinned against you. Compassion and forgiveness belong to the Lord our God, though we have rebelled against him and have not obeyed the LORD our God by following his instructions that he set before us through his servants the prophets.

All Israel has broken your law and turned away, refusing to obey you. The promised curse written in the law of Moses, the servant of God, has been poured out on us because we have sinned against him. He has carried out his words that he spoke against us and against our rulers by bringing on us a disaster that is so great that nothing like what has been done to

Jerusalem has ever been done under all of heaven. Just as it is written in the law of Moses, all this disaster has come on us, yet we have not sought the favor of the LORD our God by turning from our iniquities and paying attention to your truth. So the LORD kept the disaster in mind and brought it on us, for the LORD our God is righteous in all he has done. But we have not obeyed him.

Now, Lord our God—who brought your people out of the land of Egypt with a strong hand and made your name renowned as it is this day—we have sinned, we have acted wickedly. Lord, in keeping with all your righteous acts, may your anger and wrath turn away from your city Jerusalem, your holy mountain; for because of our sins and the iniquities of our ancestors, Jerusalem and your people have become an object of ridicule to all those around us.

Therefore, our God, hear the prayer and the petitions of your servant. Make your face shine on your desolate sanctuary for the Lord's sake. Listen closely, my God, and hear. Open your eyes and see our desolations and the city that bears your name. For we are not presenting our petitions before you based on our righteous acts, but based on your abundant compassion. Lord, hear! Lord, forgive! Lord, listen and act! My God, for your own sake, do not delay, because your city and your people bear your name.

While I was speaking, praying, confessing my sin and the sin of my people Israel, and presenting my petition before the LORD my God concerning the holy mountain of my God— while I was praying, Gabriel, the man I had seen in the first vision, reached me in my extreme weariness, about the time of the evening offering. He gave me this explanation: "Daniel, I've come now to give you understanding. At the beginning of your petitions an answer went out, and I have come to give it, for you are treasured by God. So consider the message and understand the vision:

> Seventy weeks are decreed
> about your people and your holy city—
> to bring the rebellion to an end,
> to put a stop to sin,
> to atone for iniquity,
> to bring in everlasting righteousness,
> to seal up vision and prophecy,
> and to anoint the most holy place.
> Know and understand this:
> From the issuing of the decree
> to restore and rebuild Jerusalem
> until an Anointed One, the ruler,

will be seven weeks and sixty-two weeks.
It will be rebuilt with a plaza and a moat,
but in difficult times.
After those sixty-two weeks
60   the Anointed One will be cut off
and will have nothing.
The people of the coming ruler
will destroy the city and the sanctuary.
The end will come with a flood,
and until the end there will be war;
desolations are decreed.
He will make a firm covenant
with many for one week,
but in the middle of the week
70   he will put a stop to sacrifice and offering.
And the abomination of desolation
will be on a wing of the temple
until the decreed destruction
is poured out on the desolator."

10 In the third year of King Cyrus of Persia, a message was revealed to Daniel, who was named Belteshazzar. The message was true and was about a great conflict. He understood the message and had understanding of the vision.

In those days I, Daniel, was mourning for three full weeks. I didn't eat any rich food, no meat or wine entered my mouth, and I didn't put any oil on my body until the three weeks were over. On the twenty-fourth day of the first month, as I was standing on the bank of the great river, the Tigris, I looked up, and there was a man dressed in linen, with a belt of gold from Uphaz around his waist. His body was like beryl, his face like the brilliance of lightning, his eyes like flaming torches, his arms and feet like the gleam of polished bronze, and the sound of his words like the
10   sound of a multitude.

Only I, Daniel, saw the vision. The men who were with me did not see it, but a great terror fell on them, and they ran and hid. I was left alone, looking at this great vision. No strength was left in me; my face grew deathly pale, and I was powerless. I heard the words he said, and when I heard them I fell into a deep sleep, with my face to the ground.

Suddenly, a hand touched me and set me shaking on my hands and knees. He said to me, "Daniel, you are a man treasured by God. Understand the words that I'm saying to you. Stand on your feet, for I have now been sent to you." After he said this to me, I stood trembling.

"Don't be afraid, Daniel," he said to me, "for from the first day that you purposed to understand and to humble yourself before your God, your prayers were heard. I have come because of your prayers. But the prince of the kingdom of Persia opposed me for twenty-one days. Then Michael, one of the chief princes, came to help me after I had been left there with the kings of Persia. Now I have come to help you understand what will happen to your people in the last days, for the vision refers to those days."

While he was saying these words to me, I turned my face toward the ground and was speechless. Suddenly one with human likeness touched my lips. I opened my mouth and said to the one standing in front of me, "My lord, because of the vision, anguish overwhelms me and I am powerless. How can someone like me, your servant, speak with someone like you, my lord? Now I have no strength, and there is no breath in me."

Then the one with a human appearance touched me again and strengthened me. He said, "Don't be afraid, you who are treasured by God. Peace to you; be very strong!"

As he spoke to me, I was strengthened and said, "Let my lord speak, for you have strengthened me."

He said, "Do you know why I've come to you? I must return at once to fight against the prince of Persia, and when I leave, the prince of Greece will come. However, I will tell you what is recorded in the book of truth. (No one has the courage to support me against those princes except Michael, your prince. In the first year of Darius the Mede, I stood up to strengthen and protect him.) Now I will tell you the truth.

"Three more kings will arise in Persia, and the fourth will be far richer than the others. By the power he gains through his riches, he will stir up everyone against the kingdom of Greece. Then a warrior king will arise; he will rule a vast realm and do whatever he wants. But as soon as he is established, his kingdom will be broken up and divided to the four winds of heaven, but not to his descendants; it will not be the same kingdom that he ruled, because his kingdom will be uprooted and will go to others besides them.

"The king of the South will grow powerful, but one of his commanders will grow more powerful and will rule a kingdom greater than his. After some years they will form an alliance, and the daughter of the king of the South will go to the king of the North to seal the agreement. She will not retain power, and his strength will not endure. She will be given up, together with her entourage, her father, and the one who supported her during those times. In the place of the king of the South, one from her family will rise up, come against the army, and enter the fortress of the king of the North. He will take action against them and triumph. He will take even their gods captive to Egypt, with their metal images and their precious articles of silver and gold. For some years he will stay away from the king of the North, who will enter the kingdom of the king of the South and then return to his own land.

20   "His sons will mobilize for war and assemble a large number of armed forces. They will advance, sweeping through like a flood, and will again wage war as far as his fortress. Infuriated, the king of the South will march out to fight with the king of the North, who will raise a large army, but they will be handed over to his enemy. When the army is carried off, he will become arrogant and cause tens of thousands to fall, but he will not triumph. The king of the North will again raise a multitude larger than the first. After some years he will advance with a great army and many supplies.

"In those times many will rise up against the king of the South. Violent ones among your own people will assert themselves to fulfill a vision, but they will fail. Then the king of the North will come, build up a siege ramp, and capture a well-fortified city. The forces of the South will

30   not stand; even their select troops will not be able to resist. The king of the North who comes against him will do whatever he wants, and no one can oppose him. He will establish himself in the beautiful land with total destruction in his hand. He will resolve to come with the force of his whole kingdom and will reach an agreement with him. He will give him a daughter in marriage to destroy it, but she will not stand with him or support him. Then he will turn his attention to the coasts and islands and capture many. But a commander will put an end to his taunting; instead, he will turn his taunts against him. He will turn his attention back to the fortresses of his own land, but he will stumble, fall, and be no more.

"In his place one will arise who will send out a tax collector for the glory of the kingdom; but within a few days he will be broken, though not in anger or in battle.

40   "In his place a despised person will arise; royal honors will not be given to him, but he will come during a time of peace and seize the kingdom by intrigue. A flood of forces will be swept away before him; they will be broken, as well as the covenant prince. After an alliance is made with him, he will act deceitfully. He will rise to power with a small nation. During a time of peace, he will come into the richest parts of the province and do what his fathers and predecessors never did. He will lavish plunder, loot, and wealth on his followers, and he will make plans against fortified cities, but only for a time.

"With a large army he will stir up his power and his courage against the king of the South. The king of the South will prepare for battle with an extremely large and powerful army, but he will not succeed, because plots will be made against him. Those who eat his provisions will destroy him; his

50   army will be swept away, and many will fall slain. The two kings, whose hearts are bent on evil, will speak lies at the same table but to no avail, for still the end will come at the appointed time. The king of the North will return to his land with great wealth, but his heart will be set against the holy covenant; he will take action, then return to his own land.

"At the appointed time he will come again to the South, but this time will not be like the first. Ships of Kittim will come against him, and being intimidated, he will withdraw. Then he will rage against the holy covenant and take action. On his return, he will favor those who abandon the holy covenant. His forces will rise up and desecrate the temple fortress. They will abolish the regular sacrifice and set up the abomination of desolation. With flattery he will corrupt those who act wickedly toward the covenant, but the people who know their God will be strong and take action. Those who have insight among the people will give understanding to many, yet they will fall by the sword and flame, and they will be captured and plundered for a time. When they fall, they will be helped by some, but many others will join them insincerely. Some of those who have insight will fall so that they may be refined, purified, and cleansed until the time of the end, for it will still come at the appointed time.

"Then the king will do whatever he wants. He will exalt and magnify himself above every god, and he will say outrageous things against the God of gods. He will be successful until the time of wrath is completed, because what has been decreed will be accomplished. He will not show regard for the gods of his ancestors, the god desired by women, or for any other god, because he will magnify himself above all. Instead, he will honor a god of fortresses — a god his ancestors did not know — with gold, silver, precious stones, and riches. He will deal with the strongest fortresses with the help of a foreign god. He will greatly honor those who acknowledge him, making them rulers over many and distributing land as a reward.

"At the time of the end, the king of the South will engage him in battle, but the king of the North will storm against him with chariots, horsemen, and many ships. He will invade countries and sweep through them like a flood. He will also invade the beautiful land, and many will fall. But these will escape from his power: Edom, Moab, and the prominent people of the Ammonites. He will extend his power against the countries, and not even the land of Egypt will escape. He will get control over the hidden treasures of gold and silver and over all the riches of Egypt. The Libyans and Cushites will also be in submission. But reports from the east and the north will terrify him, and he will go out with great fury to annihilate and completely destroy many. He will pitch his royal tents between the sea and the beautiful holy mountain, but he will meet his end with no one to help him.

I2
At that time
Michael, the great prince
who stands watch over your people, will rise up.
There will be a time of distress
such as never has occurred
since nations came into being until that time.
But at that time all your people
who are found written in the book will escape.
Many who sleep in the dust
of the earth will awake,
some to eternal life,
and some to disgrace and eternal contempt.

> Those who have insight will shine
> like the bright expanse of the heavens,
> and those who lead many to righteousness,
> like the stars forever and ever.

"But you, Daniel, keep these words secret and seal the book until the time of the end. Many will roam about, and knowledge will increase."

Then I, Daniel, looked, and two others were standing there, one on this bank of the river and one on the other. One of them said to the man dressed in linen, who was above the water of the river, "How long until the end of these wondrous things?" Then I heard the man dressed in linen, who was above the water of the river. He raised both his hands toward heaven and swore by him who lives eternally that it would be for a time, times, and half a time. When the power of the holy people is shattered, all these things will be completed.

I heard but did not understand. So I asked, "My lord, what will be the outcome of these things?"

He said, "Go on your way, Daniel, for the words are secret and sealed until the time of the end. Many will be purified, cleansed, and refined, but the wicked will act wickedly; none of the wicked will understand, but those who have insight will understand. From the time the daily sacrifice is abolished and the abomination of desolation is set up, there will be 1,290 days. Happy is the one who waits for and reaches 1,335 days. But as for you, go on your way to the end; you will rest, and then you will stand to receive your allotted inheritance at the end of the days."

Introduction to Ezra-Nehemiah

Jean P. Musavuli

The English Bible presents Ezra-Nehemiah as two separate books; however, from their earliest appearance in the HS, they were a single volume, a collection of pieces by multiple authors. The authors occasionally use third person narration style, but more often use the first person style to report events for which they were either actors or witnesses.

Although Ezra-Nehemiah comes before Chronicles in the HS, chronologically it is the opposite. Ezra-Nehemiah naturally continues the Chronicles Corpus. The Chronicles Corpus ends with the demise of Judah, when Nebuchadnezzar destroyed the city of Jerusalem, including the temple. The inhabitants of Jerusalem were taken into exile and the temple articles looted. Exile was Yahweh's punishment for his people's sins and for not repenting upon the prophets' warnings. However, Yahweh promised that he would one day restore the remnant of his people from captivity (Jer 29.19–25).

Yahweh restored his people to the promised land so that they may serve him again, first and foremost by rebuilding the temple. The return from exile reminds Israel of their deliverance from Egypt for a similar purpose of serving Yahweh in the desert where they built him the tabernacle as they headed to Canaan (Exodus). Ezra-Nehemiah is concerned not only about the restoration of the people to their land, but also the restoration of the people's religion, their social well-being, and security. The restoration reversed the judgment: just as Yahweh used an eastern king (Babylonian Nebuchadnezzar) to bring punishment and desolation against Judah (2 Kgs 25; 2 Chr 36), he also used eastern kings to support the restoration, in three major rounds, as seen in Ezra-Nehemiah.

First, the Persian king Cyrus published a decree, under Yahweh's command, liberating and allowing the Jewish people to return to their land and rebuild the temple. Cyrus gave provisions for the rebuilding and returned the temple's articles formerly looted by Nebuchadnezzar. The returnees reached Jerusalem under the leadership of Joshua the priest and Zerubbabel or Sheshbazzar, who was appointed governor and led the construction work. This was very great, shocking, and even unbelievable news—it was like a dream (Ps 126). However, serving Yahweh was not as easy as they might have expected. After the foundation of the temple was laid, opposition to the work rose from their enemies using all possible means, thus stopping the work for many years. It took the ministry of prophets Zechariah and Haggai to revive the people for the work again, as well as an official permission from Darius.

Secondly, while the physical temple was built, the spiritual temple, that is true religion rooted in the heart, needed to be reconstructed. Ezra pursued this through teaching torah, after he came from the east, and was commissioned by the Persian King Artaxerxes. Ezra taught the Torah, contextualizing it to the current realities of the returnees. The results of Ezra's ministry seemed to be great as the people decisively repented from their sins and pledged to obey Yahweh's commands. However, Ezra-Nehemiah shows that the repentance was ephemeral, and so the need for a continuous ministry. To no surprise, Ezra is seen teaching the torah in Jerusalem again roughly fourteen years later.

Third, the people's concerns for spiritual renewal did not preclude their need for physical security. In fact, they were under continuous threats as the city walls were still in ashes. The rebuilding of the walls required another movement from the east through Nehemiah, commissioned and appointed governor of Judah by Artaxerxes. Although the gracious hand of Yahweh was upon him, Nehemiah's mission still encountered opposition both from without and from within. It took trust in Yahweh expressed through prayer, hard work toward unity, and determination to conquer opposition and complete the work of the walls.

Nevertheless, Nehemiah also kept noticing that the people continually abandoned the torah of Yahweh, so one needed to remind them and require them to observe it. Ezra is seen again helping with this task which fit his position better as scribe and priest. Even after the people pledged once more to abide by torah, Ezra-Nehemiah concludes with depicting an unsatisfying spiritual restoration of the people. They still needed a deeper transformation, that they may love Yahweh with all their heart, soul, mind, and strength; expressing reason to keep longing for the promised "new heart" (Ezek 36.45–46).

Finally, however, while the East kept supporting Jerusalem's restoration wave after wave, the Jews in Jerusalem kept excluding foreigners. This can be excused only when one understands the context of the post-exilic Jewish people: as a remnant of Israel, they needed to reconstruct their identity which had been continuously obliterated for decades. Once again, their identity formed and shaped by the Torah, was inherent to the fulfillment of their Yahweh-given mission as a people.

Outline

1. Return under Cyrus' decree and rebuilding of the temple (Ezra 1.1–6.46)
   a. Cyrus' decree (Ezra 1.1–10)
   b. Return and settlement in Judah (Ezra 1.11–2.101)
   c. Rebuilding of the temple amid opposition (Ezra 3.1–6.46)

2. Return and ministry of Ezra (Ezra 7.1–10.64)
   a. Ezra's commission by Artaxerxes and arrival in Jerusalem (Ezra 7.1–8.81)
   b. Ezra's arrival and ministry in Jerusalem (Ezra 9.1–10.64)

3. Return and work of Nehemiah (Nehemiah 1.1–13.58)
   a. The bad news, the prayer, the commission and Nehemiah's return (Neh 1.1–2.40)
   b. The rebuilding of the wall amid opposition (Neh 3.1–6.38)
   c. Religious reforms and covenant renewal (Neh 7.1–13.58)

Suggested Resources

Fencham, Charles. *Ezra and Nehemiah*. New International Commentary on the Old Testament. Grand Rapids: Eerdmans, 1983.

Goldingay, John. *Ezra, Nehemiah and Esther for Everyone*. Old Testament for Everyone. London: SPCK Publishers, 2013.

Redditt, Paul. *Ezra-Nehemiah*. Smith & Helwys Bible Commentary. Macon, GA: Smyth & Helwys, 2018.

Throntveit, Mark. *Ezra-Nehemiah*. Interpretation. Louisville: Westminster John Knox, 1992.

Williamson, Hugh. *Ezra and Nehemiah*. Word Biblical Commentary. Sheffield: Sheffield Academic Press, 1987.

Ezra

1 In the first year of King Cyrus of Persia, in order to fulfill the word of the LORD spoken through Jeremiah, the LORD roused the spirit of King Cyrus to issue a proclamation throughout his entire kingdom and to put it in writing:

> This is what King Cyrus of Persia says: "The LORD, the God of the heavens, has given me all the kingdoms of the earth and has appointed me to build him a house at Jerusalem in Judah. Any of his people among you, may his God be with him, and may he go to Jerusalem in Judah and build the house of the LORD, the God of Israel, the God who is in Jerusalem. Let every survivor, wherever he resides, be assisted by the men of that region with silver, gold, goods, and livestock, along with a freewill offering for the house of God in Jerusalem."

So the family heads of Judah and Benjamin, along with the priests and Levites—everyone whose spirit God had roused—prepared to go up and rebuild the LORD's house in Jerusalem. All their neighbors supported them with silver articles, gold, goods, livestock, and valuables, in addition to all that was given as a freewill offering. King Cyrus also brought out the articles of the LORD's house that Nebuchadnezzar had taken from Jerusalem and had placed in the house of his gods. King Cyrus of Persia had them brought out under the supervision of Mithredath the treasurer, who counted them out to Sheshbazzar the prince of Judah. This was the inventory:

> 30 gold basins, 1,000 silver basins,
> 29 silver knives, 30 gold bowls,
> 410 various silver bowls, and 1,000 other articles.

The gold and silver articles totaled 5,400. Sheshbazzar brought all of them when the exiles went up from Babylon to Jerusalem.

2 These now are the people of the province who came from those captive exiles King Nebuchadnezzar of Babylon had deported to Babylon. They returned to Jerusalem and Judah, each to his own town. They came with Zerubbabel, Jeshua, Nehemiah, Seraiah, Reelaiah, Mordecai, Bilshan, Mispar, Bigvai, Rehum, and Baanah.

The number of the Israelite men included

Parosh's descendants	2,172
Shephatiah's descendants	372
Arah's descendants	775
Pahath-moab's descendants:	
Jeshua's and Joab's descendants	2,812
Elam's descendants	1,254
Zattu's descendants	945
Zaccai's descendants	760
Bani's descendants	642
Bebai's descendants	623
Azgad's descendants	1,222
Adonikam's descendants	666
Bigvai's descendants	2,056
Adin's descendants	454
Ater's descendants: of Hezekiah	98
Bezai's descendants	323
Jorah's descendants	112
Hashum's descendants	223
Gibbar's descendants	95
Bethlehem's people	123
Netophah's men	56
Anathoth's men	128
Azmaveth's people	42
Kiriatharim's, Chephirah's, and Beeroth's people	743
Ramah's and Geba's people	621
Michmas's men	122
Bethel's and Ai's men	223
Nebo's people	52
Magbish's people	156
the other Elam's people	1,254
Harim's people	320
Lod's, Hadid's, and Ono's people	725
Jericho's people	345
Senaah's people	3,630

The priests included

Jedaiah's descendants of the house of Jeshua	973
Immer's descendants	1,052

Pashhur's descendants	1,247
and Harim's descendants	1,017

The Levites included
Jeshua's and Kadmiel's descendants
from Hodaviah's descendants   74

The singers included
Asaph's descendants   128

50 The gatekeepers' descendants included
Shallum's descendants, Ater's descendants,
Talmon's descendants, Akkub's descendants,
Hatita's descendants, Shobai's descendants, in all   139

The temple servants included
Ziha's descendants, Hasupha's descendants,
Tabbaoth's descendants, Keros's descendants,
Siaha's descendants, Padon's descendants,
Lebanah's descendants, Hagabah's descendants,
Akkub's descendants, Hagab's descendants,
60 Shalmai's descendants, Hanan's descendants,
Giddel's descendants, Gahar's descendants,
Reaiah's descendants, Rezin's descendants,
Nekoda's descendants, Gazzam's descendants,
Uzza's descendants, Paseah's descendants,
Besai's descendants, Asnah's descendants,
Meunim's descendants, Nephusim's descendants,
Bakbuk's descendants, Hakupha's descendants,
Harhur's descendants, Bazluth's descendants,
Mehida's descendants, Harsha's descendants,
70 Barkos's descendants, Sisera's descendants,
Temah's descendants, Neziah's descendants,
and Hatipha's descendants.

The descendants of Solomon's servants included
Sotai's descendants, Hassophereth's descendants,
Peruda's descendants, Jaalah's descendants,

Darkon's descendants, Giddel's descendants,
Shephatiah's descendants, Hattil's descendants,
Pochereth-hazzebaim's descendants, and Ami's descendants.
    All the temple servants

80 and the descendants of Solomon's servants   392.

The following are those who came from Tel-melah, Tel-harsha, Cherub, Addan, and Immer but were unable to prove that their ancestral families and their lineage were Israelite:

Delaiah's descendants,
Tobiah's descendants,
Nekoda's descendants   652

and from the descendants of the priests: the descendants of Hobaiah, the descendants of Hakkoz, the descendants of Barzillai—who had taken a wife from the daughters of Barzillai the Gileadite and who bore their name. These searched for their entries in the genealogical records, but they could not be found, so they were disqualified from the priesthood. The governor ordered 90 them not to eat the most holy things until there was a priest who could consult the Urim and Thummim.

    The whole combined assembly numbered   42,360
not including their 7,337 male and female servants,
and their 200 male and female singers.
    They had 736 horses, 245 mules,
    435 camels, and 6,720 donkeys.

After they arrived at the LORD's house in Jerusalem, some of the family heads gave freewill offerings for the house of God in order to have it rebuilt on its original site. Based on what they could give, they gave 61,000 gold coins, 6,250 pounds of silver, and 100 priestly garments to the 100 treasury for the project. The priests, Levites, singers, gatekeepers, temple servants, and some of the people settled in their towns, and the rest of Israel settled in their towns.

3 When the seventh month arrived, and the Israelites were in their towns, the people gathered as one in Jerusalem. Jeshua son of Jozadak and his brothers the priests along with Zerubbabel son of Shealtiel and his brothers began to build the altar of Israel's God in order to offer burnt offerings on it, as it is written in the law of Moses, the man of God. They set up the altar on its foundation and offered burnt offerings for the morning and evening on it to the LORD even though they feared the surrounding peoples. They celebrated the Festival of Shelters as prescribed, and offered burnt offerings each day, based on the number specified by ordinance for each festival day. After that, they offered the regular burnt offering and the offerings for the beginning of each month and for all the LORD's appointed holy occasions, as well as the freewill offerings brought to the LORD.

10   On the first day of the seventh month they began to offer burnt offerings to the LORD, even though the foundation of the LORD's temple had not yet been laid. They gave money to the stonecutters and artisans, and gave food, drink, and oil to the people of Sidon and Tyre, so they would bring cedar wood from Lebanon to Joppa by sea, according to the authorization given them by King Cyrus of Persia.

In the second month of the second year after they arrived at God's house in Jerusalem, Zerubbabel son of Shealtiel, Jeshua son of Jozadak, and the rest of their brothers, including the priests, the Levites, and all who had returned to Jerusalem from the captivity, began to build. They appointed the Levites who were twenty years old or more to supervise the work on the LORD's house. Jeshua with his sons and brothers, Kadmiel with his sons, and the sons of Judah and of Henadad, with 20 their sons and brothers, the Levites, joined together to supervise those working on the house of God.

When the builders had laid the foundation of the LORD's temple, the priests, dressed in their robes and holding trumpets, and the Levites descended from Asaph, holding cymbals, took their positions to praise the LORD, as King David of Israel had instructed. They sang with praise and thanksgiving to the LORD: "For he is good; his faithful love to Israel endures forever." Then all the people gave a great shout of praise to the LORD because the foundation of the LORD's house had been laid.

But many of the older priests, Levites, and family heads, who had seen the first temple, wept loudly when they saw the foundation of this temple, but many others shouted joyfully. The people 30 could not distinguish the sound of the joyful shouting from that of the weeping, because the people were shouting so loudly. And the sound was heard far away.

4 When the enemies of Judah and Benjamin heard that the returned exiles were building a temple for the LORD, the God of Israel, they approached Zerubbabel and the family heads and said to them, "Let us build with you, for we also worship your God and have been sacrificing to him since the time King Esar-haddon of Assyria brought us here."

    But Zerubbabel, Jeshua, and the other heads of Israel's families answered them, "You may have no part with us in building a house for our God, since we alone will build it for the LORD, the God of Israel, as King Cyrus, the king of Persia has commanded us." Then the people who were already in the land discouraged the people of Judah and made them afraid to build. They also bribed officials to act against them to frustrate their plans throughout the reign of King Cyrus of Persia 10 and until the reign of King Darius of Persia.

At the beginning of the reign of Ahasuerus, the people who were already in the land wrote an accusation against the residents of Judah and Jerusalem. During the time of King Artaxerxes of Persia, Bishlam, Mithredath, Tabeel and the rest of his colleagues wrote to King Artaxerxes. The letter was written in Aramaic and translated.

Rehum the chief deputy and Shimshai the scribe wrote a letter to King Artaxerxes concerning Jerusalem as follows:

From Rehum the chief deputy, Shimshai the scribe, and the rest of their colleagues—the judges and magistrates from Tripolis, Persia, Erech, Babylon, Susa (that is, the people of Elam), and the rest of the peoples whom the great and illustrious Ashurbanipal deported and settled in the cities of Samaria and the region west of the Euphrates River.

This is the text of the letter they sent to him:

To King Artaxerxes from your servants, the men from the region west of the Euphrates River:

Let it be known to the king that the Jews who came from you have returned to us at Jerusalem. They are rebuilding that rebellious and evil city, finishing its walls, and repairing its foundations. Let it now be known to the king that if that city is rebuilt and its walls are finished, they will not pay tribute, duty, or land tax, and the royal revenue will suffer. Since we have taken an oath of loyalty to the king, and it is not right for us to witness his dishonor, we have sent to inform the king that a search should be made in your predecessors' record books. In these record books you will discover and verify that the city is a rebellious city, harmful to kings and provinces. There have been revolts in it since ancient times. That is why this city was destroyed. We advise the king that if this city is rebuilt and its walls are finished, you will not have any possession west of the Euphrates.

The king sent a reply to his chief deputy Rehum, Shimshai the scribe, and the rest of their colleagues living in Samaria and elsewhere in the region west of the Euphrates River:

Greetings.

The letter you sent us has been translated and read in my presence. I issued a decree and a search was conducted. It was discovered that this city has had uprisings against kings since ancient times, and there have been rebellions and revolts in it. Powerful kings have also ruled over Jerusalem and exercised authority over the whole region west of the Euphrates River, and tribute, duty, and land tax were paid to them. Therefore, issue an order for these men to stop, so that this city will not be rebuilt until a further decree has been pronounced by me. See that you not neglect this matter. Otherwise, the damage will increase and the royal interests will suffer.

As soon as the text of King Artaxerxes's letter was read to Rehum, Shimshai the scribe, and their colleagues, they immediately went to the Jews in Jerusalem and forcibly stopped them.

5 Now the construction of God's house in Jerusalem had stopped and remained at a standstill until the second year of the reign of King Darius of Persia. But when the prophets Haggai and Zechariah son of Iddo prophesied to the Jews who were in Judah and Jerusalem, in the name of the God of Israel who was over them, Zerubbabel son of Shealtiel and Jeshua son of Jozadak began to rebuild God's house in Jerusalem. The prophets of God were with them, helping them.

At that time Tattenai the governor of the region west of the Euphrates River, Shethar-bozenai, and their colleagues came to the Jews and asked, "Who gave you the order to rebuild this temple and finish this structure?" They also asked them, "What are the names of the workers who are constructing this building?" But God was watching over the Jewish elders. These men wouldn't stop them until a report was sent to Darius, so that they could receive written instructions about
10 this matter.

This is the text of the letter that Tattenai the governor of the region west of the Euphrates River, Shethar-bozenai, and their colleagues, the officials in the region, sent to King Darius. They sent him a report, written as follows:

To King Darius:

All greetings.

Let it be known to the king that we went to the house of the great God in the province of Judah. It is being built with cut stones, and its beams are being set in the walls. This work is being done diligently and succeeding through the people's efforts. So we questioned the elders and asked, "Who gave you the order to rebuild this temple and finish this structure?" We also
20 asked them for their names, so that we could write down the names of their leaders for your information.

This is the reply they gave us:

We are the servants of the God of the heavens and earth, and we are rebuilding the temple that was built many years ago, which a great king of Israel built and finished. But since our ancestors angered the God of the heavens, he handed them over to King Nebuchadnezzar of Babylon, the Chaldean, who destroyed this temple and deported the people to Babylon. However, in the first year of King Cyrus of Babylon, he issued a decree to rebuild the house of God. He also took from the temple in Babylon the gold and silver articles of God's house that Nebuchadnezzar had taken from the temple in Jerusalem and carried them to the temple in Babylon. He released them from the temple in Babylon to a man named Sheshbazzar, the governor by the appointment of King Cyrus. Cyrus told him, "Take these articles, put them in the temple in Jerusalem, and let the house of God be rebuilt on its original site." Then this same Sheshbazzar came and laid the foundation of God's house in Jerusalem. It has been under construction from that time until now, but it has not been completed.

So if it pleases the king, let a search of the royal archives in Babylon be conducted to see if it is true that a decree was issued by King Cyrus to rebuild the house of God in Jerusalem. Let the king's decision regarding this matter be sent to us.

6 King Darius gave the order, and they searched in the library of Babylon in the archives. But it was in the fortress of Ecbatana in the province of Media that a scroll was found with this record written on it:

In the first year of King Cyrus, he issued a decree concerning the house of God in Jerusalem:

Let the house be rebuilt as a place for offering sacrifices, and let its original foundations be retained. Its height is to be ninety feet and its width ninety feet, with three layers of cut stones and one of timber. The cost is to be paid from the royal treasury. The gold and silver articles of God's house that Nebuchadnezzar took from the temple in Jerusalem and carried to Babylon must also be returned. They are to be brought to the temple in Jerusalem where they belong and put into the house of God.

Therefore, you must stay away from that place, Tattenai governor of the region west of the Euphrates River, Shethar-bozenai, and your colleagues, the officials in the region. Leave the construction of the house of God alone. Let the governor and elders of the Jews rebuild this house of God on its original site.

I hereby issue a decree concerning what you are to do, so that the elders of the Jews can rebuild the house of God:

The cost is to be paid in full to these men out of the royal revenues from the taxes of the region west of the Euphrates River, so that the work will not stop. Whatever is needed—young bulls, rams, and lambs for burnt offerings to the God of the heavens, or wheat, salt, wine, and oil, as requested by the

20 priests in Jerusalem—let it be given to them every day without fail, so that they can offer sacrifices of pleasing aroma to the God of the heavens and pray for the life of the king and his sons.

I also issue a decree concerning any man who interferes with this directive:

Let a beam be torn from his house and raised up; he will be impaled on it, and his house will be made into a garbage dump because of this offense. May the God who caused his name to dwell there overthrow any king or people who dares to harm or interfere with this house of God in Jerusalem. I, Darius, have issued the decree. Let it be carried out diligently.

Then Tattenai governor of the region west of the Euphrates River, Shethar-bozenai, and their colleagues diligently carried out what King Darius had decreed. So the Jewish elders continued successfully with the building under the prophesying of Haggai the prophet and Zechariah son of 30 Iddo. They finished the building according to the command of the God of Israel and the decrees of Cyrus, Darius, and King Artaxerxes of Persia. This house was completed on the third day of the month of Adar in the sixth year of the reign of King Darius.

Then the Israelites, including the priests, the Levites, and the rest of the exiles, celebrated the dedication of the house of God with joy. For the dedication of God's house they offered one hundred bulls, two hundred rams, and four hundred lambs, as well as twelve male goats as a sin offering for all Israel—one for each Israelite tribe. They also appointed the priests by their divisions and the Levites by their groups to the service of God in Jerusalem, according to what is written in the book of Moses.

The exiles observed the Passover on the fourteenth day of the first month. All of the priests 40 and Levites were ceremonially clean, because they had purified themselves. They killed the Passover lamb for themselves, their priestly brothers, and all the exiles. The Israelites who had returned from exile ate it, together with all who had separated themselves from the uncleanness of the Gentiles of the land in order to worship the Lord, the God of Israel. They observed the Festival of Unleavened Bread for seven days with joy, because the Lord had made them joyful, having changed the Assyrian king's attitude toward them, so that he supported them in the work on the house of the God of Israel.

7 After these events, during the reign of King Artaxerxes of Persia, Ezra—
Seraiah's son, Azariah's son,
Hilkiah's son, Shallum's son,
Zadok's son, Ahitub's son,
Amariah's son, Azariah's son,
Meraioth's son, Zerahiah's son,

Uzzi's son, Bukki's son,

Abishua's son, Phinehas's son,

Eleazar's son, the chief priest Aaron's son

—came up from Babylon. He was a scribe skilled in the law of Moses, which the LORD, the God of Israel, had given. The king had granted him everything he requested because the hand of the LORD his God was on him. Some of the Israelites, priests, Levites, singers, gatekeepers, and temple servants accompanied him to Jerusalem in the seventh year of King Artaxerxes.

Ezra came to Jerusalem in the fifth month, during the seventh year of the king. He began the journey from Babylon on the first day of the first month and arrived in Jerusalem on the first day of the fifth month since the gracious hand of his God was on him. Now Ezra had determined in his heart to study the law of the LORD, obey it, and teach its statutes and ordinances in Israel.

This is the text of the letter King Artaxerxes gave to Ezra the priest and scribe, an expert in matters of the LORD's commands and statutes for Israel:

Artaxerxes, king of kings, to Ezra the priest, an expert in the law of the God of the heavens:

Greetings.

I issue a decree that any of the Israelites in my kingdom, including their priests and Levites, who want to go to Jerusalem, may go with you. You are sent by the king and his seven counselors to evaluate Judah and Jerusalem according to the law of your God, which is in your possession. You are also to bring the silver and gold the king and his counselors have willingly given to the God of Israel, whose dwelling is in Jerusalem, and all the silver and gold you receive throughout the province of Babylon, together with the freewill offerings given by the people and the priests to the house of their God in Jerusalem. Then you are to be diligent to buy with this money bulls, rams, and lambs, along with their grain and drink offerings, and offer them on the altar at the house of your God in Jerusalem. You may do whatever seems best to you and your brothers with the rest of the silver and gold, according to the will of your God. Deliver to the God of Jerusalem all the articles given to you for the service of the house of your God. You may use the royal treasury to pay for anything else needed for the house of your God.

I, King Artaxerxes, issue a decree to all the treasurers in the region west of the Euphrates River:

Whatever Ezra the priest, an expert in the law of the God of the heavens, asks of you must be provided in full, up to 7,500 pounds of silver, 500 bushels of wheat, 550 gallons of wine, 550 gallons of oil, and salt without limit. Whatever is commanded by the God of the heavens must be done diligently for the house of the God of the heavens, so that wrath will not fall on the realm of the king and his sons. Be advised that you do not have authority to impose tribute, duty, and land tax on any priests, Levites, singers, doorkeepers, temple servants, or other servants of this house of God.

And you, Ezra, according to God's wisdom that you possess, appoint magistrates and judges to judge all the people in the region west of the Euphrates who know the laws of your God and to teach anyone who does not know them. Anyone who does not keep the law of your God and the law of the king, let the appropriate judgment be executed against him, whether death, banishment, confiscation of property, or imprisonment.

Blessed be the LORD, the God of our ancestors, who has put it into the king's mind to glorify the house of the LORD in Jerusalem, and who has shown favor to me before the king, his counselors, and all his powerful officers. So I took courage because I was strengthened by the hand of the LORD my God, and I gathered Israelite leaders to return with me.

8 These are the family heads and the genealogical records of those who returned with me from Babylon during the reign of King Artaxerxes:

> Gershom, from Phinehas's descendants;
> Daniel, from Ithamar's descendants;
> Hattush, from David's descendants,
> who was of Shecaniah's descendants;
> Zechariah, from Parosh's descendants,
> and 150 men with him who were registered by genealogy;
> Eliehoenai son of Zerahiah
> from Pahath-moab's descendants,
> and 200 men with him;
> Shecaniah son of Jahaziel
> from Zattu's descendants,
> and 300 men with him;
> Ebed son of Jonathan
> from Adin's descendants,
> and 50 men with him;
> Jeshaiah son of Athaliah
> from Elam's descendants,
> and 70 men with him;
> Zebadiah son of Michael
> from Shephatiah's descendants,

and 80 men with him;
Obadiah son of Jehiel
from Joab's descendants,
and 218 men with him;
Shelomith son of Josiphiah
from Bani's descendants,
and 160 men with him;
30   Zechariah son of Bebai
from Bebai's descendants,
and 28 men with him;
Johanan son of Hakkatan
from Azgad's descendants,
and 110 men with him;
these are the last ones, from Adonikam's descendants,
and their names are
Eliphelet, Jeuel, and Shemaiah,
and 60 men with them;
40   Uthai and Zaccur
from Bigvai's descendants,
and 70 men with them.

I gathered them at the river that flows to Ahava, and we camped there for three days. I searched among the people and priests, but found no Levites there. Then I summoned the leaders: Eliezer, Ariel, Shemaiah, Elnathan, Jarib, Elnathan, Nathan, Zechariah, and Meshullam, as well as the teachers Joiarib and Elnathan. I sent them to Iddo, the leader at Casiphia, with a message for him and his brothers, the temple servants at Casiphia, that they should bring us ministers for the house of our God. Since the gracious hand of our God was on us, they brought us Sherebiah—a man of insight from the descendants of Mahli, a descendant of Levi son of Israel—along with his sons 50   and brothers, 18 men, plus Hashabiah, along with Jeshaiah, from the descendants of Merari, and his brothers and their sons, 20 men. There were also 220 of the temple servants, who had been appointed by David and the leaders for the work of the Levites. All were identified by name.

I proclaimed a fast by the Ahava River, so that we might humble ourselves before our God and ask him for a safe journey for us, our dependents, and all our possessions. I did this because I was ashamed to ask the king for infantry and cavalry to protect us from enemies during the journey, since we had told him, "The hand of our God is gracious to all who seek him, but his fierce anger is against all who abandon him." So we fasted and pleaded with our God about this, and he was receptive to our prayer.

I selected twelve of the leading priests, along with Sherebiah, Hashabiah, and ten of their
brothers. I weighed out to them the silver, the gold, and the articles—the contribution for the
house of our God that the king, his counselors, his leaders, and all the Israelites who were present
had offered. I weighed out to them 24 tons of silver, silver articles weighing 7,500 pounds,
7,500 pounds of gold, twenty gold bowls worth a thousand gold coins, and two articles of fine
gleaming bronze, as valuable as gold. Then I said to them, "You are holy to the LORD, and the
articles are holy. The silver and gold are a freewill offering to the LORD God of your ancestors.
Guard them carefully until you weigh them out in the chambers of the LORD's house before the
leading priests, Levites, and heads of the Israelite families in Jerusalem." So the priests and Levites
took charge of the silver, the gold, and the articles that had been weighed out, to bring them to the
house of our God in Jerusalem.

We set out from the Ahava River on the twelfth day of the first month to go to Jerusalem. We
were strengthened by our God, and he kept us from the grasp of the enemy and from ambush
along the way. So we arrived at Jerusalem and rested there for three days. On the fourth day the
silver, the gold, and the articles were weighed out in the house of our God into the care of the
priest Meremoth son of Uriah. Eleazar son of Phinehas was with him. The Levites Jozabad son of
Jeshua and Noadiah son of Binnui were also with them. Everything was verified by number and
weight, and the total weight was recorded at that time.

The exiles who had returned from the captivity offered burnt offerings to the God of Israel:
twelve bulls for all Israel, ninety-six rams, and seventy-seven lambs, along with twelve male goats
as a sin offering. All this was a burnt offering for the LORD. They also delivered the king's edicts
to the royal satraps and governors of the region west of the Euphrates, so that they would support
the people and the house of God.

9 After these things had been done, the leaders approached me and said, "The people of Israel,
the priests, and the Levites have not separated themselves from the surrounding peoples whose
detestable practices are like those of the Canaanites, Hethites, Perizzites, Jebusites, Ammonites,
Moabites, Egyptians, and Amorites. Indeed, the Israelite men have taken some of their daughters
as wives for themselves and their sons, so that the holy seed has become mixed with the
surrounding peoples. The leaders and officials have taken the lead in this unfaithfulness!" When I
heard this report, I tore my tunic and robe, pulled out some of the hair from my head and beard,
and sat down devastated.

Everyone who trembled at the words of the God of Israel gathered around me, because of the
unfaithfulness of the exiles, while I sat devastated until the evening offering. At the evening
offering, I got up from my time of humiliation, with my tunic and robe torn. Then I fell on my
knees and spread out my hands to the LORD my God. And I said:

My God, I am ashamed and embarrassed to lift my face toward you, my God, because our iniquities are higher than our heads and our guilt is as high as the heavens. Our guilt has been terrible from the days of our ancestors until the present. Because of our iniquities we have been handed over, along with our kings and priests, to the surrounding kings, and to the sword, captivity, plundering, and open shame, as it is today. But now, for a brief moment, grace has come from the LORD our God to preserve a remnant for us and give us a stake in his holy place. Even in our slavery, God has given us a little relief and light to our eyes. Though we are slaves,
20 our God has not abandoned us in our slavery. He has extended grace to us in the presence of the Persian kings, giving us relief, so that we can rebuild the house of our God and repair its ruins, to give us a wall in Judah and Jerusalem.

Now, our God, what can we say in light of this? For we have abandoned the commands you gave through your servants the prophets, saying, "The land you are entering to possess is an impure land. The surrounding peoples have filled it from end to end with their uncleanness by their impurity and detestable practices. So do not give your daughters to their sons in marriage or take their daughters for your sons. Never pursue their welfare or prosperity, so that you will be strong, eat the good things of the land, and leave it as an inheritance to your sons forever." After all that has happened to us because of our evil deeds and terrible guilt—though you, our
30 God, have punished us less than our iniquities deserve and have allowed us to survive—should we break your commands again and intermarry with the peoples who commit these detestable practices? Wouldn't you become so angry with us that you would destroy us, leaving neither remnant nor survivor? LORD God of Israel, you are righteous, for we survive as a remnant today. Here we are before you with our guilt, though no one can stand in your presence because of this.

10 While Ezra prayed and confessed, weeping and falling facedown before the house of God, an extremely large assembly of Israelite men, women, and children gathered around him. The people also wept bitterly. Then Shecaniah son of Jehiel, an Elamite, responded to Ezra, "We have been unfaithful to our God by marrying foreign women from the surrounding peoples, but there is still hope for Israel in spite of this. Therefore, let's make a covenant before our God to send away all the foreign wives and their children, according to the counsel of my lord and of those who tremble at the command of our God. Let it be done according to the law. Get up, for this matter is your responsibility, and we support you. Be strong and take action!"

Then Ezra got up and made the leading priests, Levites, and all Israel take an oath to do what
10 had been said; so they took the oath. Ezra then went from the house of God and walked to the chamber of Jehohanan son of Eliashib, where he spent the night. He did not eat food or drink water, because he was mourning over the unfaithfulness of the exiles.

They circulated a proclamation throughout Judah and Jerusalem that all the exiles should gather at Jerusalem. Whoever did not come within three days would forfeit all his possessions, according to the decision of the leaders and elders, and would be excluded from the assembly of the exiles.

So all the men of Judah and Benjamin gathered in Jerusalem within the three days. On the twentieth day of the ninth month, all the people sat in the square at the house of God, trembling because of this matter and because of the heavy rain. Then the priest Ezra stood up and said to them, "You have been unfaithful by marrying foreign women, adding to Israel's guilt. Therefore, make a confession to the LORD, the God of your ancestors, and do his will. Separate yourselves from the surrounding peoples and your foreign wives."

Then all the assembly responded loudly, "Yes, we will do as you say! But there are many people, and it is the rainy season. We don't have the stamina to stay out in the open. This isn't something that can be done in a day or two, for we have rebelled terribly in this matter. Let our leaders represent the entire assembly. Then let all those in our towns who have married foreign women come at appointed times, together with the elders and judges of each town, in order to avert the fierce anger of our God concerning this matter." Only Jonathan son of Asahel and Jahzeiah son of Tikvah opposed this, with Meshullam and Shabbethai the Levite supporting them.

The exiles did what had been proposed. The priest Ezra selected men who were family heads, all identified by name, to represent their ancestral families. They convened on the first day of the tenth month to investigate the matter, and by the first day of the first month they had dealt with all the men who had married foreign women.

The following were found to have married foreign women from the descendants of the priests:

from the descendants of Jeshua son of Jozadak and his brothers: Maaseiah, Eliezer, Jarib, and Gedaliah. They pledged to send their wives away, and being guilty, they offered a ram from the flock for their guilt;

Hanani and Zebadiah from Immer's descendants;
Maaseiah, Elijah, Shemaiah, Jehiel, and Uzziah from Harim's descendants;
Elioenai, Maaseiah, Ishmael, Nethanel, Jozabad, and Elasah from Pashhur's descendants.

The Levites:
Jozabad, Shimei, Kelaiah (that is Kelita), Pethahiah, Judah, and Eliezer.

The singers:
Eliashib.

The gatekeepers:
Shallum, Telem, and Uri.

The Israelites:

Parosh's descendants: Ramiah, Izziah, Malchijah, Mijamin, Eleazar, Malchijah, and Benaiah;

50 Elam's descendants: Mattaniah, Zechariah, Jehiel, Abdi, Jeremoth, and Elijah;

Zattu's descendants: Elioenai, Eliashib, Mattaniah, Jeremoth, Zabad, and Aziza;

Bebai's descendants: Jehohanan, Hananiah, Zabbai, and Athlai;

Bani's descendants: Meshullam, Malluch, Adaiah, Jashub, Sheal, and Jeremoth;

Pahath-moab's descendants: Adna, Chelal, Benaiah, Maaseiah, Mattaniah, Bezalel, Binnui, and Manasseh;

Harim's descendants: Eliezer, Isshijah, Malchijah, Shemaiah, Shimeon, Benjamin, Malluch, and Shemariah;

Hashum's descendants: Mattenai, Mattattah, Zabad, Eliphelet, Jeremai, Manasseh, and Shimei;

60 Bani's descendants: Maadai, Amram, Uel, Benaiah, Bedeiah, Cheluhi, Vaniah, Meremoth, Eliashib, Mattaniah, Mattenai, Jaasu, Bani, Binnui, Shimei, Shelemiah, Nathan, Adaiah, Machnadebai, Shashai, Sharai, Azarel, Shelemiah, Shemariah, Shallum, Amariah, and Joseph;

Nebo's descendants: Jeiel, Mattithiah, Zabad, Zebina, Jaddai, Joel, and Benaiah.

All of these had married foreign women, and some of the wives had given birth to children.

Nehemiah

1 The words of Nehemiah son of Hacaliah:

During the month of Chislev in the twentieth year, when I was in the fortress city of Susa, Hanani, one of my brothers, arrived with men from Judah, and I questioned them about Jerusalem and the Jewish remnant that had survived the exile. They said to me, "The remnant in the province, who survived the exile, are in great trouble and disgrace. Jerusalem's wall has been broken down, and its gates have been burned."

When I heard these words, I sat down and wept. I mourned for a number of days, fasting and praying before the God of the heavens. I said,

LORD, the God of the heavens, the great and awe-inspiring God who keeps his gracious covenant
10 with those who love him and keep his commands, let your eyes be open and your ears be attentive to hear your servant's prayer that I now pray to you day and night for your servants, the Israelites. I confess the sins we have committed against you. Both I and my father's family have sinned. We have acted corruptly toward you and have not kept the commands, statutes, and ordinances you gave your servant Moses. Please remember what you commanded your servant Moses: "If you are unfaithful, I will scatter you among the peoples. But if you return to me and carefully observe my commands, even though your exiles were banished to the farthest horizon, I will gather them from there and bring them to the place where I chose to have my name dwell." They are your servants and your people. You redeemed them by your great power and strong hand. Please, Lord, let your ear be attentive to the prayer of your servant and to that of your servants who delight to revere your
20 name. Give your servant success today, and grant him compassion in the presence of this man.

At the time, I was the king's cupbearer.

2 During the month of Nisan in the twentieth year of King Artaxerxes, when wine was set before him, I took the wine and gave it to the king. I had never been sad in his presence, so the king said to me, "Why do you look so sad, when you aren't sick? This is nothing but sadness of heart."
I was overwhelmed with fear and replied to the king, "May the king live forever! Why should I not be sad when the city where my ancestors are buried lies in ruins and its gates have been destroyed by fire?"

Then the king asked me, "What is your request?"

So I prayed to the God of the heavens and answered the king, "If it pleases the king, and if your servant has found favor with you, send me to Judah and to the city where my ancestors are buried,
so that I may rebuild it."

The king, with the queen seated beside him, asked me, "How long will your journey take, and when will you return?" So I gave him a definite time, and it pleased the king to send me.

I also said to the king, "If it pleases the king, let me have letters written to the governors of the region west of the Euphrates River, so that they will grant me safe passage until I reach Judah. And let me have a letter written to Asaph, keeper of the king's forest, so that he will give me timber to rebuild the gates of the temple's fortress, the city wall, and the home where I will live." The king granted my requests, for the gracious hand of my God was on me.

I went to the governors of the region west of the Euphrates and gave them the king's letters. The king had also sent officers of the infantry and cavalry with me. When Sanballat the Horonite and Tobiah the Ammonite official heard that someone had come to pursue the prosperity of the Israelites, they were greatly displeased.

After I arrived in Jerusalem and had been there three days, I got up at night and took a few men with me. I didn't tell anyone what my God had laid on my heart to do for Jerusalem. The only animal I took was the one I was riding. I went out at night through the Valley Gate toward the Serpent's Well and the Dung Gate, and I inspected the walls of Jerusalem that had been broken down and its gates that had been destroyed by fire. I went on to the Fountain Gate and the King's Pool, but farther down it became too narrow for my animal to go through. So I went up at night by way of the valley and inspected the wall. Then heading back, I entered through the Valley Gate and returned. The officials did not know where I had gone or what I was doing, for I had not yet told the Jews, priests, nobles, officials, or the rest of those who would be doing the work. So I said to them, "You see the trouble we are in. Jerusalem lies in ruins and its gates have been burned. Come, let's rebuild Jerusalem's wall, so that we will no longer be a disgrace." I told them how the gracious hand of my God had been on me, and what the king had said to me.

They said, "Let's start rebuilding," and their hands were strengthened to do this good work.

When Sanballat the Horonite, Tobiah the Ammonite official, and Geshem the Arab heard about this, they mocked and despised us, and said, "What is this you're doing? Are you rebelling against the king?"

I gave them this reply, "The God of the heavens is the one who will grant us success. We, his servants, will start building, but you have no share, right, or historic claim in Jerusalem."

3 The high priest Eliashib and his fellow priests began rebuilding the Sheep Gate. They dedicated it and installed its doors. After building the wall to the Tower of the Hundred and the Tower of

Hananel, they dedicated it. The men of Jericho built next to Eliashib, and next to them Zaccur son of Imri built.

The sons of Hassenaah built the Fish Gate. They built it with beams and installed its doors, bolts, and bars. Next to them Meremoth son of Uriah, son of Hakkoz, made repairs. Beside them Meshullam son of Berechiah, son of Meshezabel, made repairs. Next to them Zadok son of Baana made repairs. Beside them the Tekoites made repairs, but their nobles did not lift a finger to help their supervisors.

10 Joiada son of Paseah and Meshullam son of Besodeiah repaired the Old Gate. They built it with beams and installed its doors, bolts, and bars. Next to them the repairs were done by Melatiah the Gibeonite, Jadon the Meronothite, and the men of Gibeon and Mizpah, who were under the authority of the governor of the region west of the Euphrates River. After him Uzziel son of Harhaiah, the goldsmith, made repairs, and next to him Hananiah son of the perfumer made repairs. They restored Jerusalem as far as the Broad Wall.

Next to them Rephaiah son of Hur, ruler of half the district of Jerusalem, made repairs. After them Jedaiah son of Harumaph made repairs across from his house. Next to him Hattush the son of Hashabneiah made repairs. Malchijah son of Harim and Hasshub son of Pahath-moab made repairs to another section, as well as to the Tower of the Ovens. Beside him Shallum son of

20 Hallohesh, ruler of half the district of Jerusalem, made repairs—he and his daughters.

Hanun and the inhabitants of Zanoah repaired the Valley Gate. They rebuilt it and installed its doors, bolts, and bars, and repaired five hundred yards of the wall to the Dung Gate. Malchijah son of Rechab, ruler of the district of Beth-haccherem, repaired the Dung Gate. He rebuilt it and installed its doors, bolts, and bars.

Shallun son of Col-hozeh, ruler of the district of Mizpah, repaired the Fountain Gate. He rebuilt it and roofed it. Then he installed its doors, bolts, and bars. He also made repairs to the wall of the Pool of Shelah near the king's garden, as far as the stairs that descend from the city of David.

After him Nehemiah son of Azbuk, ruler of half the district of Beth-zur, made repairs up to

30 a point opposite the tombs of David, as far as the artificial pool and the House of the Warriors. Next to him the Levites made repairs under Rehum son of Bani. Beside him Hashabiah, ruler of half the district of Keilah, made repairs for his district. After him their fellow Levites made repairs under Binnui son of Henadad, ruler of half the district of Keilah. Next to him Ezer son of Jeshua, ruler of Mizpah, made repairs to another section opposite the ascent to the armory at the Angle.

After him Baruch son of Zabbai diligently repaired another section, from the Angle to the door of the house of the high priest Eliashib. Beside him Meremoth son of Uriah, son of Hakkoz, made repairs to another section, from the door of Eliashib's house to the end of his house. And next to him the priests from the surrounding area made repairs.

After them Benjamin and Hasshub made repairs opposite their house. Beside them Azariah
son of Maaseiah, son of Ananiah, made repairs beside his house. After him Binnui son of Henadad made repairs to another section, from the house of Azariah to the Angle and the corner. Palal son of Uzai made repairs opposite the Angle and tower that juts out from the king's upper palace, by the courtyard of the guard. Beside him Pedaiah son of Parosh and the temple servants living on Ophel made repairs opposite the Water Gate toward the east and the tower that juts out. Next to him the Tekoites made repairs to another section from a point opposite the great tower that juts out, as far as the wall of Ophel.

Each of the priests made repairs above the Horse Gate, each opposite his own house. After them Zadok son of Immer made repairs opposite his house. And beside him Shemaiah son of Shecaniah, guard of the East Gate, made repairs. Next to him Hananiah son of Shelemiah and
Hanun the sixth son of Zalaph made repairs to another section.

After them Meshullam son of Berechiah made repairs opposite his room. Next to him Malchijah, one of the goldsmiths, made repairs to the house of the temple servants and the merchants, opposite the Inspection Gate, and as far as the upstairs room on the corner. The goldsmiths and merchants made repairs between the upstairs room on the corner and the Sheep Gate.

4 When Sanballat heard that we were rebuilding the wall, he became furious. He mocked the Jews before his colleagues and the powerful men of Samaria and said, "What are these pathetic Jews doing? Can they restore it by themselves? Will they offer sacrifices? Will they ever finish it? Can they bring these burnt stones back to life from the mounds of rubble?" Then Tobiah the Ammonite, who was beside him, said, "Indeed, even if a fox climbed up what they are building, he would break down their stone wall!"

Listen, our God, for we are despised. Make their insults return on their own heads and let them be taken as plunder to a land of captivity. Do not cover their guilt or let their sin be erased from your sight, because they have angered the builders.

So we rebuilt the wall until the entire wall was joined together up to half its height, for the people had the will to keep working.

When Sanballat, Tobiah, and the Arabs, Ammonites, and Ashdodites heard that the repair to the walls of Jerusalem was progressing and that the gaps were being closed, they became furious. They all plotted together to come and fight against Jerusalem and throw it into confusion. So we prayed to our God and stationed a guard because of them day and night.

In Judah, it was said:

The strength of the laborer fails,
since there is so much rubble.

20   We will never be able
              to rebuild the wall.

And our enemies said, "They won't realize it until we're among them and can kill them and stop the work." When the Jews who lived nearby arrived, they said to us time and again, "Everywhere you turn, they attack us." So I stationed people behind the lowest sections of the wall, at the vulnerable areas. I stationed them by families with their swords, spears, and bows. After I made an inspection, I stood up and said to the nobles, the officials, and the rest of the people, "Don't be afraid of them. Remember the great and awe-inspiring Lord, and fight for your countrymen, your sons and daughters, your wives and homes."

When our enemies heard that we knew their scheme and that God had frustrated it, every one of us returned to his own work on the wall. From that day on, half of my men did the work while 30 the other half held spears, shields, bows, and armor. The officers supported all the people of Judah, who were rebuilding the wall. The laborers who carried the loads worked with one hand and held a weapon with the other. Each of the builders had his sword strapped around his waist while he was building, and the one who sounded the ram's horn was beside me. Then I said to the nobles, the officials, and the rest of the people, "The work is enormous and spread out, and we are separated far from one another along the wall. Wherever you hear the sound of the ram's horn, rally to us there. Our God will fight for us!" So we continued the work, while half of the men were holding spears from daybreak until the stars came out. At that time, I also said to the people, "Let everyone and his servant spend the night inside Jerusalem, so that they can stand guard by night and work by day." And I, my brothers, my servants, and the men of the guard with me never took 40 off our clothes. Each carried his weapon, even when washing.

5 There was a widespread outcry from the people and their wives against their Jewish countrymen. Some were saying, "We, our sons, and our daughters are numerous. Let us get grain so that we can eat and live." Others were saying, "We are mortgaging our fields, vineyards, and homes to get grain during the famine." Still others were saying, "We have borrowed money to pay the king's tax on our fields and vineyards. We and our children are just like our countrymen and their children, yet we are subjecting our sons and daughters to slavery. Some of our daughters are already enslaved, but we are powerless because our fields and vineyards belong to others."

I became extremely angry when I heard their outcry and these complaints. After seriously considering the matter, I accused the nobles and officials, saying to them, "Each of you is 10 charging his countrymen interest." So I called a large assembly against them and said, "We have done our best to buy back our Jewish countrymen who were sold to foreigners, but now you sell your own countrymen, and we have to buy them back." They remained silent and could not say a word. Then I said, "What you are doing isn't right. Shouldn't you walk in the fear of our God and not invite the reproach of our foreign enemies? Even I, as well as my brothers and my servants, have been lending them money and grain. Please, let's stop charging this interest. Return their fields, vineyards, olive groves, and houses to them immediately, along with the percentage of the money, grain, new wine, and fresh oil that you have been assessing them."

They responded, "We will return these things and require nothing more from them. We will
20 do as you say."

So I summoned the priests and made everyone take an oath to do this. I also shook the folds of my robe and said, "May God likewise shake from his house and property everyone who doesn't keep this promise. May he be shaken out and have nothing!"

The whole assembly said, "Amen," and they praised the Lord. Then the people did as they had promised.

Furthermore, from the day King Artaxerxes appointed me to be their governor in the land of Judah—from the twentieth year until his thirty-second year, twelve years—I and my associates never ate from the food allotted to the governor. The governors who preceded me had heavily burdened the people, taking from them food and wine as well as a pound of silver. Their
20 subordinates also oppressed the people, but because of the fear of God, I didn't do this. Instead, I devoted myself to the construction of this wall, and all my subordinates were gathered there for the work. We didn't buy any land.

There were 150 Jews and officials, as well as guests from the surrounding nations at my table. Each day, one ox, six choice sheep, and some fowl were prepared for me. An abundance of all kinds of wine was provided every ten days. But I didn't demand the food allotted to the governor, because the burden on the people was so heavy.

Remember me favorably, my God, for all that I have done for this people.

6 When Sanballat, Tobiah, Geshem the Arab, and the rest of our enemies heard that I had rebuilt the wall and that no gap was left in it—though at that time I had not installed the doors in the city gates—Sanballat and Geshem sent me a message: "Come, let's meet together in the villages of the Ono Valley." They were planning to harm me.

So I sent messengers to them, saying, "I am doing important work and cannot come down. Why should the work cease while I leave it and go down to you?" Four times they sent me the same proposal, and I gave them the same reply.

Sanballat sent me this same message a fifth time by his aide, who had an open letter in his hand. In it was written:

10 It is reported among the nations—and Geshem agrees—that you and the Jews plan to rebel. This is the reason you are building the wall. According to these reports, you are to become their

king and have even set up the prophets in Jerusalem to proclaim on your behalf, "There is a king in Judah." These rumors will be heard by the king. So come, let's confer together.

Then I replied to him, "There is nothing to these rumors you are spreading; you are inventing them in your own mind." For they were all trying to intimidate us, saying, "They will drop their hands from the work, and it will never be finished."

But now, my God, strengthen my hands.

I went to the house of Shemaiah son of Delaiah, son of Mehetabel, who was restricted to his house. He said:

20   Let's meet at the house of God,
         inside the temple.
         Let's shut the temple doors
         because they're coming to kill you.
         They're coming to kill you tonight!

But I said, "Should a man like me run away? How can someone like me enter the temple and live? I will not go." I realized that God had not sent him, because of the prophecy he spoke against me. Tobiah and Sanballat had hired him. He was hired, so that I would be intimidated, do as he suggested, sin, and get a bad reputation, in order that they could discredit me.

My God, remember Tobiah and Sanballat for what they have done, and also the prophetess
30 Noadiah and the other prophets who wanted to intimidate me.

The wall was completed in fifty-two days, on the twenty-fifth day of the month Elul. When all our enemies heard this, all the surrounding nations were intimidated and lost their confidence, for they realized that this task had been accomplished by our God.

During those days, the nobles of Judah sent many letters to Tobiah, and Tobiah's letters came to them. For many in Judah were bound by oath to him, since he was a son-in-law of Shecaniah son of Arah, and his son Jehohanan had married the daughter of Meshullam son of Berechiah. These nobles kept mentioning Tobiah's good deeds to me, and they reported my words to him. And Tobiah sent letters to intimidate me.

7 When the wall had been rebuilt and I had the doors installed, the gatekeepers, singers, and Levites were appointed. Then I put my brother Hanani in charge of Jerusalem, along with Hananiah, commander of the fortress, because he was a faithful man who feared God more than most. I said to them, "Do not open the gates of Jerusalem until the sun is hot, and let the doors be shut and securely fastened while the guards are on duty. Station the citizens of Jerusalem as guards, some at their posts and some at their homes."

The city was large and spacious, but there were few people in it, and no houses had been built yet. Then my God put it into my mind to assemble the nobles, the officials, and the people to be registered by genealogy. I found the genealogical record of those who came back first, and I found the following written in it:

These are the people of the province who went up among the captive exiles deported by King Nebuchadnezzar of Babylon. Each of them returned to Jerusalem and Judah, to his own town. They came with Zerubbabel, Jeshua, Nehemiah, Azariah, Raamiah, Nahamani, Mordecai, Bilshan, Mispereth, Bigvai, Nehum, and Baanah.

The number of the Israelite men included

Parosh's descendants	2,172
Shephatiah's descendants	372
Arah's descendants	652
Pahath-moab's descendants:	
Jeshua's and Joab's descendants	2,818
Elam's descendants	1,254
Zattu's descendants	845
Zaccai's descendants	760
Binnui's descendants	648
Bebai's descendants	628
Azgad's descendants	2,322
Adonikam's descendants	667
Bigvai's descendants	2,067
Adin's descendants	655
Ater's descendants: of Hezekiah	98
Hashum's descendants	328
Bezai's descendants	324
Hariph's descendants	112
Gibeon's descendants	95
Bethlehem's and Netophah's men	188
Anathoth's men	128
Beth-azmaveth's men	42
Kiriath-jearim's, Chephirah's, and Beeroth's men	743
Ramah's and Geba's men	621
Michmas's men	122
Bethel's and Ai's men	123
the other Nebo's men	52
the other Elam's people	1,254

Harim's people	320
Jericho's people	345
Lod's, Hadid's, and Ono's people	721
Senaah's people	3,930.

The priests included

Jedaiah's descendants of the house of Jeshua	973
Immer's descendants	1,052
Pashhur's descendants	1,247
Harim's descendants	1,017.

The Levites included

Jeshua's descendants: of Kadmiel	
Hodevah's descendants	74.

The singers included

Asaph's descendants	148.

The gatekeepers included

Shallum's descendants, Ater's descendants,	
Talmon's descendants, Akkub's descendants,	
Hatita's descendants, Shobai's descendants	138.

The temple servants included

Ziha's descendants, Hasupha's descendants,
Tabbaoth's descendants, Keros's descendants,
Sia's descendants, Padon's descendants,
Lebanah's descendants, Hagabah's descendants,
Shalmai's descendants, Hanan's descendants,
Giddel's descendants, Gahar's descendants,
Reaiah's descendants, Rezin's descendants,
Nekoda's descendants, Gazzam's descendants,
Uzza's descendants, Paseah's descendants,
Besai's descendants, Meunim's descendants,
Nephishesim's descendants, Bakbuk's descendants,
Hakupha's descendants, Harhur's descendants,
Bazlith's descendants, Mehida's descendants,
Harsha's descendants, Barkos's descendants,

Sisera's descendants, Temah's descendants,
Neziah's descendants, Hatipha's descendants.

The descendants of Solomon's servants included

80   Sotai's descendants, Sophereth's descendants,
Perida's descendants, Jaala's descendants,
Darkon's descendants, Giddel's descendants,
Shephatiah's descendants, Hattil's descendants,
Pochereth-hazzebaim's descendants, Amon's descendants.

All the temple servants
and the descendants of Solomon's servants   392.

The following are those who came from Tel-melah, Tel-harsha, Cherub, Addon, and Immer,
but were unable to prove that their ancestral families and their lineage were Israelite:
Delaiah's descendants,
90   Tobiah's descendants,
and Nekoda's descendants   642

and from the priests: the descendants of Hobaiah, the descendants of Hakkoz, and the
descendants of Barzillai—who had taken a wife from the daughters of Barzillai the Gileadite
and who bore their name. These searched for their entries in the genealogical records, but
they could not be found, so they were disqualified from the priesthood. The governor ordered
them not to eat the most holy things until there was a priest who could consult the Urim and
Thummim.

The whole combined assembly numbered   42,360
not including their 7,337 male and female servants,
100   as well as their 245 male and female singers.
They had 736 horses, 245 mules,
435 camels, and 6,720 donkeys.

Some of the family heads contributed to the project. The governor gave 1,000 gold coins,
50 bowls, and 530 priestly garments to the treasury. Some of the family heads gave 20,000 gold
coins and 2,200 silver minas to the treasury for the project. The rest of the people gave
20,000 gold coins, 2,000 silver minas, and 67 priestly garments. The priests, Levites, gatekeepers,
temple singers, some of the people, temple servants, and all Israel settled in their towns.

8 When the seventh month came and the Israelites had settled in their towns, all the people gathered together at the square in front of the Water Gate. They asked the scribe Ezra to bring the book of the law of Moses that the LORD had given Israel. On the first day of the seventh month, the priest Ezra brought the law before the assembly of men, women, and all who could listen with understanding. While he was facing the square in front of the Water Gate, he read out of it from daybreak until noon before the men, the women, and those who could understand. All the people listened attentively to the book of the law. The scribe Ezra stood on a high wooden platform made for this purpose. Mattithiah, Shema, Anaiah, Uriah, Hilkiah, and Maaseiah stood beside him on his right; to his left were Pedaiah, Mishael, Malchijah, Hashum, Hash-baddanah,
10 Zechariah, and Meshullam. Ezra opened the book in full view of all the people, since he was elevated above everyone. As he opened it, all the people stood up. Ezra blessed the LORD, the great God, and with their hands uplifted all the people said, "Amen, Amen!" Then they knelt low and worshiped the LORD with their faces to the ground.

Jeshua, Bani, Sherebiah, Jamin, Akkub, Shabbethai, Hodiah, Maaseiah, Kelita, Azariah, Jozabad, Hanan, and Pelaiah, who were Levites, explained the law to the people as they stood in their places. They read out of the book of the law of God, translating and giving the meaning so that the people could understand what was read. Nehemiah the governor, Ezra the priest and scribe, and the Levites who were instructing the people said to all of them, "This day is holy to the LORD your God. Do not mourn or weep." For all the people were weeping as they heard the words
20 of the law. Then he said to them, "Go and eat what is rich, drink what is sweet, and send portions to those who have nothing prepared, since today is holy to our Lord. Do not grieve, because the joy of the LORD is your strength." And the Levites quieted all the people, saying, "Be still, since today is holy. Don't grieve." Then all the people began to eat and drink, send portions, and have a great celebration, because they had understood the words that were explained to them.

On the second day, the family heads of all the people, along with the priests and Levites, assembled before the scribe Ezra to study the words of the law. They found written in the law how the LORD had commanded through Moses that the Israelites should dwell in shelters during the festival of the seventh month. So they proclaimed and spread this news throughout their towns and in Jerusalem, saying, "Go out to the hill country and bring back branches of
30 olive, wild olive, myrtle, palm, and other leafy trees to make shelters, just as it is written." The people went out, brought back branches, and made shelters for themselves on each of their rooftops and courtyards, the court of the house of God, the square by the Water Gate, and the square by the Ephraim Gate. The whole community that had returned from exile made shelters and lived in them. The Israelites had not celebrated like this from the days of Joshua son of Nun until that day. And there was tremendous joy. Ezra read out of the book of the law of God every day, from the first day to the last. The Israelites celebrated the festival for seven days, and on the eighth day there was a solemn assembly, according to the ordinance.

9 On the twenty-fourth day of this month the Israelites assembled; they were fasting, wearing sackcloth, and had put dust on their heads. Those of Israelite descent separated themselves from all foreigners, and they stood and confessed their sins and the iniquities of their ancestors. While they stood in their places, they read from the book of the law of the LORD their God for a fourth of the day and spent another fourth of the day in confession and worship of the LORD their God. Jeshua, Bani, Kadmiel, Shebaniah, Bunni, Sherebiah, Bani, and Chenani stood on the raised platform built for the Levites and cried out loudly to the LORD their God. Then the Levites— Jeshua, Kadmiel, Bani, Hashabneiah, Sherebiah, Hodiah, Shebaniah, and Pethahiah—said, "Stand up. Blessed be the LORD your God from everlasting to everlasting."

10   Blessed be your glorious name,
     and may it be exalted above all blessing and praise.
    You, LORD, are the only God.
    You created the heavens,
     the highest heavens with all their stars,
     the earth and all that is on it,
     the seas and all that is in them.
    You give life to all of them,
     and all the stars of heaven worship you.
    You, the LORD,
20   are the God who chose Abram
    and brought him out of Ur of the Chaldeans,
    and changed his name to Abraham.
    You found his heart faithful in your sight,
     and made a covenant with him
    to give the land of the Canaanites,
    Hethites, Amorites, Perizzites,
    Jebusites, and Girgashites—
    to give it to his descendants.
    You have fulfilled your promise,
30   for you are righteous.

    You saw the oppression of our ancestors in Egypt
    and heard their cry at the Red Sea.
    You performed signs and wonders against Pharaoh,
    all his officials, and all the people of his land,
    for you knew how arrogantly they treated our ancestors.
    You made a name for yourself
    that endures to this day.

You divided the sea before them,
and they crossed through it on dry ground.
40 You hurled their pursuers into the depths
like a stone into raging water.
You led them with a pillar of cloud by day,
and with a pillar of fire by night,
to illuminate the way they should go.
You came down on Mount Sinai,
and spoke to them from heaven.
You gave them impartial ordinances, reliable instructions,
and good statutes and commands.
You revealed your holy Sabbath to them,
50 and gave them commands, statutes, and instruction
through your servant Moses.
You provided bread from heaven for their hunger;
you brought them water from the rock for their thirst.
You told them to go in and possess the land
you had sworn to give them.

But our ancestors acted arrogantly;
they became stiff-necked and did not listen to your commands.
They refused to listen
and did not remember your wonders
60 you performed among them.
They became stiff-necked and appointed a leader
to return to their slavery in Egypt.
But you are a forgiving God,
gracious and compassionate,
slow to anger and abounding in faithful love,
and you did not abandon them.
Even after they had cast an image of a calf
for themselves and said,
"This is your god who brought you out of Egypt,"
70 and they had committed terrible blasphemies,
you did not abandon them in the wilderness
because of your great compassion.
During the day the pillar of cloud
never turned away from them,

guiding them on their journey.
And during the night the pillar of fire
illuminated the way they should go.
You sent your good Spirit to instruct them.
You did not withhold your manna from their mouths,
80 and you gave them water for their thirst.
You provided for them in the wilderness forty years,
and they lacked nothing.
Their clothes did not wear out,
and their feet did not swell.

You gave them kingdoms and peoples
and established boundaries for them.
They took possession
of the land of King Sihon of Heshbon
and of the land of King Og of Bashan.
90 You multiplied their descendants
like the stars of the sky
and brought them to the land
you told their ancestors to go in and possess.
So their descendants went in and possessed the land:
You subdued the Canaanites who inhabited the land before them
and handed their kings and the surrounding peoples over to them,
to do as they pleased with them.
They captured fortified cities and fertile land
and took possession of well-supplied houses,
100 cisterns cut out of rock, vineyards,
olive groves, and fruit trees in abundance.
They ate, were filled,
became prosperous, and delighted in your great goodness.

But they were disobedient and rebelled against you.
They flung your law behind their backs
and killed your prophets
who warned them
in order to turn them back to you.
They committed terrible blasphemies.
110 So you handed them over to their enemies,

who oppressed them.
In their time of distress, they cried out to you,
and you heard from heaven.
In your abundant compassion
you gave them deliverers, who rescued them
from the power of their enemies.
But as soon as they had relief,
they again did what was evil in your sight.
So you abandoned them to the power of their enemies,
120 who dominated them.
When they cried out to you again,
you heard from heaven and rescued them
many times in your compassion.
You warned them to turn back to your law,
but they acted arrogantly
and would not obey your commands.
They sinned against your ordinances,
which a person will live by if he does them.
They stubbornly resisted,
130 stiffened their necks, and would not obey.
You were patient with them for many years,
and your Spirit warned them through your prophets,
but they would not listen.
Therefore, you handed them over to the surrounding peoples.
However, in your abundant compassion,
you did not destroy them or abandon them,
for you are a gracious and compassionate God.

So now, our God—the great, mighty,
and awe-inspiring God who keeps his gracious covenant—
140 do not view lightly all the hardships that have afflicted us,
our kings and leaders,
our priests and prophets,
our ancestors and all your people,
from the days of the Assyrian kings until today.
You are righteous concerning all that has happened to us,
because you have acted faithfully,
while we have acted wickedly.

Our kings, leaders, priests, and ancestors
did not obey your law
150   or listen to your commands
and warnings you gave them.
When they were in their kingdom,
with your abundant goodness that you gave them,
and in the spacious and fertile land you set before them,
they would not serve you or turn from their wicked ways.

Here we are today,
slaves in the land you gave our ancestors
so that they could enjoy its fruit and its goodness.
Here we are—slaves in it!
160   Its abundant harvest goes to the kings
you have set over us,
because of our sins.
They rule over our bodies
and our livestock as they please.
We are in great distress.

In view of all this, we are making a binding agreement in writing on a sealed document containing the names of our leaders, Levites, and priests.

10   Those whose seals were on the document were
the governor Nehemiah son of Hacaliah, and Zedekiah,
Seraiah, Azariah, Jeremiah,
Pashhur, Amariah, Malchijah,
Hattush, Shebaniah, Malluch,
Harim, Meremoth, Obadiah,
Daniel, Ginnethon, Baruch,
Meshullam, Abijah, Mijamin,
Maaziah, Bilgai, and Shemaiah.
10   These were the priests.

The Levites were
Jeshua son of Azaniah,
Binnui of the sons of Henadad, Kadmiel,
and their brothers

Shebaniah, Hodiah, Kelita, Pelaiah, Hanan,
Mica, Rehob, Hashabiah,
Zaccur, Sherebiah, Shebaniah,
Hodiah, Bani, and Beninu.

The heads of the people were
20 Parosh, Pahath-moab, Elam, Zattu, Bani,
Bunni, Azgad, Bebai,
Adonijah, Bigvai, Adin,
Ater, Hezekiah, Azzur,
Hodiah, Hashum, Bezai,
Hariph, Anathoth, Nebai,
Magpiash, Meshullam, Hezir,
Meshezabel, Zadok, Jaddua,
Pelatiah, Hanan, Anaiah,
Hoshea, Hananiah, Hasshub,
30 Hallohesh, Pilha, Shobek,
Rehum, Hashabnah, Maaseiah,
Ahijah, Hanan, Anan,
Malluch, Harim, Baanah.

The rest of the people—the priests, Levites, gatekeepers, singers, and temple servants, along with their wives, sons, and daughters, everyone who is able to understand and who has separated themselves from the surrounding peoples to obey the law of God—join with their noble brothers and commit themselves with a sworn oath to follow the law of God given through God's servant Moses and to obey carefully all the commands, ordinances, and statutes of the LORD our Lord.

We will not give our daughters in marriage to the surrounding peoples and will not take their
40 daughters as wives for our sons.

When the surrounding peoples bring merchandise or any kind of grain to sell on the Sabbath day, we will not buy from them on the Sabbath or a holy day. We will also leave the land uncultivated in the seventh year and will cancel every debt.

We will impose the following commands on ourselves:

To give an eighth of an ounce of silver yearly for the service of the house of our God: the bread displayed before the LORD, the daily grain offering, the regular burnt offering, the Sabbath and New Moon offerings, the appointed festivals, the holy things, the sin offerings to atone for Israel, and for all the work of the house of our God.

We have cast lots among the priests, Levites, and people for the donation of wood by our ancestral families at the appointed times each year. They are to bring the wood to our God's house to burn on the altar of the LORD our God, as it is written in the law.

We will bring the firstfruits of our land and of every fruit tree to the LORD's house year by year. We will also bring the firstborn of our sons and our livestock, as prescribed by the law, and will bring the firstborn of our herds and flocks to the house of our God, to the priests who serve in our God's house. We will bring a loaf from our first batch of dough to the priests at the storerooms of the house of our God. We will also bring the firstfruits of our grain offerings, of every fruit tree, and of the new wine and fresh oil. A tenth of our land's produce belongs to the Levites, for the Levites are to collect the one-tenth offering in all our agricultural towns. A priest from Aaron's descendants is to accompany the Levites when they collect the tenth, and the Levites are to take a tenth of this offering to the storerooms of the treasury in the house of our God. For the Israelites and the Levites are to bring the contributions of grain, new wine, and fresh oil to the storerooms where the articles of the sanctuary are kept and where the priests who minister are, along with the gatekeepers and singers. We will not neglect the house of our God.

11 Now the leaders of the people stayed in Jerusalem, and the rest of the people cast lots for one out of ten to come and live in Jerusalem, the holy city, while the other nine-tenths remained in their towns. The people blessed all the men who volunteered to live in Jerusalem.

These are the heads of the province who stayed in Jerusalem (but in the villages of Judah each lived on his own property in their towns—the Israelites, priests, Levites, temple servants, and descendants of Solomon's servants—while some of the descendants of Judah and Benjamin settled in Jerusalem):

Judah's descendants:

Athaiah son of Uzziah, son of Zechariah, son of Amariah, son of Shephatiah, son of Mahalalel, of Perez's descendants; and Maaseiah son of Baruch, son of Col-hozeh, son of Hazaiah, son of Adaiah, son of Joiarib, son of Zechariah, a descendant of the Shilonite. The total number of Perez's descendants, who settled in Jerusalem, was 468 capable men.

These were Benjamin's descendants:

Sallu son of Meshullam, son of Joed, son of Pedaiah, son of Kolaiah, son of Maaseiah, son of Ithiel, son of Jeshaiah, and after him Gabbai and Sallai: 928. Joel son of Zichri was the officer over them, and Judah son of Hassenuah was second in command over the city.

The priests:

Jedaiah son of Joiarib, Jachin, and Seraiah son of Hilkiah, son of Meshullam, son of Zadok, son of Meraioth, son of Ahitub, the chief official of God's temple, and their relatives who did the work at the temple: 822. Adaiah son of Jeroham, son of Pelaliah, son of Amzi, son of Zechariah, son of Pashhur, son of Malchijah and his relatives, the heads of families: 242. Amashsai son of Azarel, son of Ahzai, son of Meshillemoth, son of Immer, and their relatives, capable men: 128. Zabdiel son of Haggedolim, was their chief.

The Levites:

Shemaiah son of Hasshub, son of Azrikam, son of Hashabiah, son of Bunni; and Shabbethai and Jozabad, from the heads of the Levites, who supervised the work outside the house of God; Mattaniah son of Mica, son of Zabdi, son of Asaph, the one who began the thanksgiving in prayer; Bakbukiah, second among his relatives; and Abda son of Shammua, son of Galal, son of Jeduthun. All the Levites in the holy city: 284.

The gatekeepers:

Akkub, Talmon, and their relatives, who guarded the city gates: 172.

The rest of Israel, the priests, and the Levites were in all the villages of Judah, each on his own inherited property. The temple servants lived on Ophel; Ziha and Gishpa supervised the temple servants.

The leader of the Levites in Jerusalem was Uzzi son of Bani, son of Hashabiah, son of Mattaniah, son of Mica, of the descendants of Asaph, who were singers for the service of God's house. There was, in fact, a command of the king regarding them, and an ordinance regulating the singers' daily tasks. Pethahiah son of Meshezabel, of the descendants of Zerah son of Judah, was the king's agent in every matter concerning the people.

As for the farming settlements with their fields:
> Some of Judah's descendants lived in Kiriath-arba
> and Dibon and their surrounding villages, and Jekabzeel and its settlements;
> in Jeshua, Moladah, Beth-pelet,

Hazar-shual, and Beer-sheba and its surrounding villages;
in Ziklag and Meconah and its surrounding villages;
in En-rimmon, Zorah, Jarmuth, and
Zanoah and Adullam with their settlements;
in Lachish with its fields and Azekah and its surrounding villages.
So they settled from Beer-sheba to Hinnom Valley.

50 Benjamin's descendants:
from Geba, Michmash, Aija,
and Bethel and its surrounding villages,
Anathoth, Nob, Ananiah,
Hazor, Ramah, Gittaim,
Hadid, Zeboim, Neballat,
Lod, and Ono, in Craftsmen's Valley.
Some of the Judean divisions of Levites were in Benjamin.

12 These are the priests and Levites who went up with Zerubbabel son of Shealtiel and with Jeshua:
Seraiah, Jeremiah, Ezra,
Amariah, Malluch, Hattush,
Shecaniah, Rehum, Meremoth,
Iddo, Ginnethoi, Abijah,
Mijamin, Maadiah, Bilgah,
Shemaiah, Joiarib, Jedaiah,
Sallu, Amok, Hilkiah, Jedaiah.

These were the heads of the priests and their relatives in the days of Jeshua.

10 The Levites:
Jeshua, Binnui, Kadmiel,
Sherebiah, Judah, and Mattaniah—
he and his relatives were in charge of the songs of praise.
Bakbukiah, Unni, and their relatives stood opposite them in the services.
Jeshua fathered Joiakim,
Joiakim fathered Eliashib,
Eliashib fathered Joiada,
Joiada fathered Jonathan,
and Jonathan fathered Jaddua.

20 In the days of Joiakim, the heads of the priestly families were

Meraiah	of Seraiah,
Hananiah	of Jeremiah,
Meshullam	of Ezra,
Jehohanan	of Amariah,
Jonathan	of Malluchi,
Joseph	of Shebaniah,
Adna	of Harim,
Helkai	of Meraioth,
Zechariah	of Iddo,
Meshullam	of Ginnethon,
Zichri	of Abijah,
Piltai	of Moadiah, of Miniamin,
Shammua	of Bilgah,
Jehonathan	of Shemaiah,
Mattenai	of Joiarib,
Uzzi	of Jedaiah,
Kallai	of Sallai,
Eber	of Amok,
Hashabiah	of Hilkiah,
and Nethanel	of Jedaiah.

In the days of Eliashib, Joiada, Johanan, and Jaddua, the heads of the families of the Levites and priests were recorded while Darius the Persian ruled. Levi's descendants, the family heads, were recorded in the Book of the Historical Events during the days of Johanan son of Eliashib. The heads of the Levites—Hashabiah, Sherebiah, and Jeshua son of Kadmiel, along with their relatives opposite them—gave praise and thanks, division by division, as David the man of God had prescribed. This included Mattaniah, Bakbukiah, and Obadiah. Meshullam, Talmon, and Akkub were gatekeepers who guarded the storerooms at the city gates. These served in the days of Joiakim son of Jeshua, son of Jozadak, and in the days of Nehemiah the governor and Ezra the priest and scribe.

50 At the dedication of the wall of Jerusalem, they sent for the Levites wherever they lived and brought them to Jerusalem to celebrate the joyous dedication with thanksgiving and singing accompanied by cymbals, harps, and lyres. The singers gathered from the region around Jerusalem, from the settlements of the Netophathites, from Beth-gilgal, and from the fields of Geba and Azmaveth, for they had built settlements for themselves around Jerusalem. After the priests and Levites had purified themselves, they purified the people, the city gates, and the wall.

Then I brought the leaders of Judah up on top of the wall, and I appointed two large processions that gave thanks. One went to the right on the wall, toward the Dung Gate. Hoshaiah and half the leaders of Judah followed, along with Azariah, Ezra, Meshullam, Judah, Benjamin, Shemaiah, Jeremiah, and some of the priests' sons with trumpets, and Zechariah son of Jonathan, son of Shemaiah, son of Mattaniah, son of Micaiah, son of Zaccur, son of Asaph followed as well as his relatives—Shemaiah, Azarel, Milalai, Gilalai, Maai, Nethanel, Judah, and Hanani, with the musical instruments of David, the man of God. Ezra the scribe went in front of them. At the Fountain Gate they climbed the steps of the city of David on the ascent of the wall and went above the house of David to the Water Gate on the east.

The second thanksgiving procession went to the left, and I followed it with half the people along the top of the wall, past the Tower of the Ovens to the Broad Wall, above the Ephraim Gate, and by the Old Gate, the Fish Gate, the Tower of Hananel, and the Tower of the Hundred, to the Sheep Gate. They stopped at the Gate of the Guard. The two thanksgiving processions stood in the house of God. So did I and half of the officials accompanying me, as well as the priests:

> Eliakim, Maaseiah, Miniamin,
> Micaiah, Elioenai, Zechariah,
> and Hananiah, with trumpets;
> and Maaseiah, Shemaiah, Eleazar,
> Uzzi, Jehohanan, Malchijah, Elam, and Ezer.

Then the singers sang, with Jezrahiah as the leader. On that day they offered great sacrifices and rejoiced because God had given them great joy. The women and children also celebrated, and Jerusalem's rejoicing was heard far away.

On that same day men were placed in charge of the rooms that housed the supplies, contributions, firstfruits, and tenths. The legally required portions for the priests and Levites were gathered from the village fields, because Judah was grateful to the priests and Levites who were serving. They performed the service of their God and the service of purification, along with the singers and gatekeepers, as David and his son Solomon had prescribed. For long ago, in the days of David and Asaph, there were heads of the singers and songs of praise and thanksgiving to God. So in the days of Zerubbabel and Nehemiah, all Israel contributed the daily portions for the singers and gatekeepers. They also set aside daily portions for the Levites, and the Levites set aside daily portions for Aaron's descendants.

13 At that time the book of Moses was read publicly to the people. The command was found written in it that no Ammonite or Moabite should ever enter the assembly of God, because they did not meet the Israelites with food and water. Instead, they hired Balaam against them to curse them, but our God turned the curse into a blessing. When they heard the law, they separated all those of mixed descent from Israel.

Now before this, the priest Eliashib had been put in charge of the storerooms of the house of our God. He was a relative of Tobiah and had prepared a large room for him where they had previously stored the grain offerings, the frankincense, the articles, and the tenths of grain, new wine, and fresh oil prescribed for the Levites, singers, and gatekeepers, along with the contributions for the priests.

While all this was happening, I was not in Jerusalem, because I had returned to King Artaxerxes of Babylon in the thirty-second year of his reign. It was only later that I asked the king for a leave of absence so I could return to Jerusalem. Then I discovered the evil that Eliashib had done on behalf of Tobiah by providing him a room in the courts of God's house. I was greatly displeased and threw all of Tobiah's household possessions out of the room. I ordered that the rooms be purified, and I had the articles of the house of God restored there, along with the grain offering and frankincense. I also found out that because the portions for the Levites had not been given, each of the Levites and the singers performing the service had gone back to his own field. Therefore, I rebuked the officials, asking, "Why has the house of God been neglected?" I gathered the Levites and singers together and stationed them at their posts. Then all Judah brought a tenth of the grain, new wine, and fresh oil into the storehouses. I appointed as treasurers over the storehouses the priest Shelemiah, the scribe Zadok, and Pedaiah of the Levites, with Hanan son of Zaccur, son of Mattaniah to assist them, because they were considered trustworthy. They were responsible for the distribution to their colleagues.

Remember me for this, my God, and don't erase the deeds of faithful love I have done for the house of my God and for its services.

At that time I saw people in Judah treading winepresses on the Sabbath. They were also bringing in stores of grain and loading them on donkeys, along with wine, grapes, and figs. All kinds of goods were being brought to Jerusalem on the Sabbath day. So I warned them against selling food on that day. The Tyrians living there were importing fish and all kinds of merchandise and selling them on the Sabbath to the people of Judah in Jerusalem.

I rebuked the nobles of Judah and said to them, "What is this evil you are doing—profaning the Sabbath day? Didn't your ancestors do the same, so that our God brought all this disaster on us and on this city? And now you are rekindling his anger against Israel by profaning the Sabbath!"

When shadows began to fall on the city gates of Jerusalem just before the Sabbath, I gave orders that the city gates be closed and not opened until after the Sabbath. I posted some of my men at the gates, so that no goods could enter during the Sabbath day. Once or twice the merchants and those who sell all kinds of goods camped outside Jerusalem, but I warned them, "Why are you camping in front of the wall? If you do it again, I'll use force against you." After that they did not come again on the Sabbath. Then I instructed the Levites to purify themselves and guard the city gates in order to keep the Sabbath day holy.

Remember me for this also, my God, and look on me with compassion according to the abundance of your faithful love.

In those days I also saw Jews who had married women from Ashdod, Ammon, and Moab. Half of their children spoke the language of Ashdod or the language of one of the other peoples but could not speak Hebrew. I rebuked them, cursed them, beat some of their men, and pulled out their hair. I forced them to take an oath before God and said, "You must not give your daughters in marriage to their sons or take their daughters as wives for your sons or yourselves! Didn't King Solomon of Israel sin in matters like this? There was not a king like him among many nations. He was loved by his God, and God made him king over all Israel, yet foreign women drew him into sin. Why then should we hear about you doing all this terrible evil and acting unfaithfully against our God by marrying foreign women?" Even one of the sons of Jehoiada, son of the high priest Eliashib, had become a son-in-law to Sanballat the Horonite. So I drove him away from me.

Remember them, my God, for defiling the priesthood as well as the covenant of the priesthood and the Levites.

So I purified them from everything foreign and assigned specific duties to each of the priests and Levites. I also arranged for the donation of wood at the appointed times and for the firstfruits.

Remember me, my God, with favor.

Introduction to Chronicles

David S. Casas

The Chronicles Corpus is often overlooked as mere repetition of the sagas of Samuel and Kings by a later historian. The taxing genealogies and the exclusive emphasis on the kingdom of Judah and David's line, as well as the absence of some of the more captivating stories of the monarchical period, tempts the average reader to gloss over the details of the books. Nevertheless, the reader of Chronicles is standing at the threshold of the words of the probable last writer of the HS. No human king is on the throne of Israel at the time of composition; in fact, there is no physical kingdom. Jerusalem, the capital of Judah, was destroyed and now being rebuilt as a vassal of the Persian empire. The rebuilt temple was a mere semblance of what it once was. This is the reality in which the Chronicler writes.

Some suggest that the Chronicler is providing a historical revision of ancient Israel in an attempt to idealize the Judean kings, especially David and Solomon. However, the various references to a host of prophets, including the messages of the well-known seers Samuel (1 Chr 11), Elijah (2 Chr 21), and Jeremiah (2 Chr 36), as well as lesser-known prophets, such as Ahijah (2 Chr 10), Shemaiah (2 Chr 12), and Azariah (2 Chr 15), suggest no such attempt by the Chronicler to whitewash history. Rather, Chronicles is a deliberate and independent interpretation of Israel's history with a theology dependent on Deuteronomy—a theology that envisions Yahweh's eschatological redemptive plan for a new Israel and a greater son of David.

Chronicles begins with "Adam, Seth, Enoch" and continues with nine chapters of uninterrupted genealogies mirroring portions of Genesis. The genealogies are followed by five more literary sections providing a detailed narrative on David, Solomon, Jehoshaphat, Hezekiah, and Josiah. Four themes best reflect the Chronicler's theology: legitimacy, providence, covenant, and the Davidic Messiah. First, in order for Yahweh's covenantal promises to be attested, the people to whom the covenant was directed must be legitimate and ascribed such legitimacy through genealogical record (1 Chr 9.1–3). Second, Yahweh's providence (his particular purposes and plans for his people) are made known through real-life human action and dialogue (e.g., 2 Chr 10.24–26; 18.47–48; 32.56–58). Third, the covenant is the primary element that most clearly expresses the meaning of Israel's continuity and their future as Yahweh's people, in spite of their rebellion. The emphasis on the covenant is demonstrated by the covenant-centered worship in the temple (1 Chr 28; 2 Chr 24; 29–31) and reiterated to and ratified by new generations (2 Chr 15.18–19; 17.12–14; 34.66–67). The habitual violation of the covenant is the reason for exile (2 Chr 36.28–29), and the covenant promises are the source for hope of future restoration (2 Chr 36.40–45). Last, the permanence of the Davidic covenant provides hope for a future deliverer and the reign of David's greater son (1 Chr 17). The promise to David and his line is explicitly mentioned in 2 Chr 7.33–35; 13.6–8; 21.10–12. In spite of the failures of the various kings, Yahweh's promise to establish David's throne is seen, for example, in the Chronicler's exclusive attention to his line, providing detail of King Manasseh's repentance and restoration—a detail left out of 2 Kings (2 Chr 33.19–20)—and ascribing King Josiah's commands for temple worship to David's writings as on par with the Torah (2 Chr 35.6–7, 28–30).

Chronicles, as the final voice of the HS, gives the reader a historical retelling of the people of Israel with a message of warning and hope in a renewed covenant. Continual violation of his covenant had consequences—even disastrous results. Nevertheless, as the prophet Azariah exhorted King Asa, "For many years Israel has been without the true God, without a teaching priest, and without instruction, but when they turned to the Lord God of Israel in their distress and sought him, he was found by them" (2 Chr 15.3–5). Because of Yahweh's eternal promise of blessing and a future king, there is always hope for redemption and restoration for a repentant people.

Outline
1 Chronicles
1. The genealogies of the nation and its neighbors (1 Chr 1.1–9.53)
2. The line of Saul and its demise (1 Chr 9.54–10.21)
3. David's early reign as king over "all Israel" (1 Chr 11.1–29.55)

2 Chronicles
1. Solomon ascends to the throne and exceeds in worship, wisdom and wealth (2 Chr 1–9)
2. The kingdom divides (2 Chr 10)
3. The reign of Rehoboam, the prophecy of Shemaiah, the migration of the priests and Levites, and Shisak's invasion (2 Chr 11–12)
4. The reign of Abijah (2 Chr 13.1–14.1)
5. The reign of Asa and his reforms (2 Chr 14–16)
6. The reign of Jehoshaphat, the alliance with the Northern Kingdom, and his reforms (2 Chr 17.1–21.1)
7. The reign of Jehoram (2 Chr 21.1–37)
8. The reign of Ahaziah and interregnum of Athaliah, his mother (2 Chr 22)
9. The coup of Joash, his reign and reformation (2 Chr 23–24)
10. The reign of Amaziah (2 Chr 25)
11. The reign of Uzziah (2 Chr 26)
12. The reign of Jotham (2 Chr 27)
13. The reign of Ahaz and the Syro-Ephraimitic War (2 Chr 28)
14. The reign of Hezekiah and his reforms (2 Chr 29–32)
15. The reign of Manasseh (2 Chr 33.1–36)
16. The reign of Amon (2 Chr 33.36–43)
17. The reign of Josiah and his reforms (2 Chr 34–35)

18. Judah in exile, and the vassal reigns of Jehoahaz, Jehoiakim, Jehoiachin, and Zedekiah (2 Chr 36.1–39)

19. Epilogue: The reasons for exile and decree of Cyrus, king of Persia (2 Chr 36.40–45)

Suggested Resources

Boda, Mark. *1–2 Chronicles*. Cornerstone Biblical Commentary. Carol Stream, IL: Tyndale House, 2010.

Goldingay, John. *1 and 2 Chronicles for Everyone*. Louisville: Westminster John Knox, 2012.

Hahn, Scott W. *The Kingdom of God as Liturgical Empire: A Theological Commentary on 1–2 Chronicles*. Grand Rapids: Baker Academic, 2012.

Hill, Andrew E. *1 and 2 Chronicles*. NIV Application Commentary. Grand Rapids: Zondervan, 2010.

Merrill, Eugene H. *A Commentary on 1 & 2 Chronicles*. Kregel Exegetical Library. Grand Rapids: Kregel, 2015.

1 Chronicles

1 Adam, Seth, Enosh,
Kenan, Mahalalel, Jared,
Enoch, Methuselah, Lamech,
Noah, Noah's sons:
Shem, Ham, and Japheth.

Japheth's sons: Gomer, Magog, Madai, Javan, Tubal, Meshech, and Tiras.
Gomer's sons: Ashkenaz, Riphath, and Togarmah.
Javan's sons: Elishah, Tarshish, Kittim, and Rodanim.

Ham's sons: Cush, Mizraim, Put, and Canaan.
10 Cush's sons: Seba, Havilah, Sabta, Raama, and Sabteca.
Raama's sons: Sheba and Dedan.
Cush fathered Nimrod, who was the first to become a great warrior on earth.
Mizraim fathered the people of Lud, Anam, Lehab, Naphtuh, Pathrus, Casluh (the Philistines came from them), and Caphtor.
Canaan fathered Sidon as his firstborn and Heth, as well as the Jebusites, Amorites, Girgashites, Hivites, Arkites, Sinites, Arvadites, Zemarites, and Hamathites.

Shem's sons: Elam, Asshur, Arpachshad, Lud, Aram, Uz, Hul, Gether, and Meshech.
Arpachshad fathered Shelah, and Shelah fathered Eber. Two sons were born to Eber.
One of them was named Peleg because the earth was divided during his lifetime, and the
20 name of his brother was Joktan. Joktan fathered Almodad, Sheleph, Hazarmaveth, Jerah, Hadoram, Uzal, Diklah, Ebal, Abimael, Sheba, Ophir, Havilah, and Jobab. All of these were Joktan's sons.

Shem, Arpachshad, Shelah,
Eber, Peleg, Reu,
Serug, Nahor, Terah,
and Abram (that is, Abraham).

Abraham's sons: Isaac and Ishmael.

These are their family records: Nebaioth, Ishmael's firstborn, Kedar, Adbeel, Mibsam, Mishma, Dumah, Massa, Hadad, Tema, Jetur, Naphish, and Kedemah.

30 These were Ishmael's sons.

The sons born to Keturah, Abraham's concubine: Zimran, Jokshan, Medan, Midian, Ishbak, and Shuah.
Jokshan's sons: Sheba and Dedan.
Midian's sons: Ephah, Epher, Hanoch, Abida, and Eldaah.
All of these were Keturah's descendants.

Abraham fathered Isaac.
Isaac's sons: Esau and Israel.
Esau's sons: Eliphaz, Reuel, Jeush, Jalam, and Korah.
Eliphaz's sons: Teman, Omar, Zephi, Gatam, and Kenaz; and by Timna, Amalek.
40 Reuel's sons: Nahath, Zerah, Shammah, and Mizzah.

Seir's sons: Lotan, Shobal, Zibeon, Anah, Dishon, Ezer, and Dishan.
Lotan's sons: Hori and Homam. Timna was Lotan's sister.
Shobal's sons: Alian, Manahath, Ebal, Shephi, and Onam.
Zibeon's sons: Aiah and Anah.
Anah's son: Dishon.
Dishon's sons: Hamran, Eshban, Ithran, and Cheran.
Ezer's sons: Bilhan, Zaavan, and Jaakan.
Dishan's sons: Uz and Aran.

These were the kings who reigned in the land of Edom
50 before any king reigned over the Israelites:
Bela son of Beor.
Bela's town was named Dinhabah.
When Bela died, Jobab son of Zerah from Bozrah reigned in his place.
When Jobab died, Husham from the land of the Temanites reigned in his place.
When Husham died, Hadad son of Bedad, who defeated Midian in the territory
of Moab, reigned in his place.
Hadad's town was named Avith.
When Hadad died, Samlah from Masrekah reigned in his place.
When Samlah died, Shaul from Rehoboth on the Euphrates River reigned in his place.
60 When Shaul died, Baal-hanan son of Achbor reigned in his place.
When Baal-hanan died, Hadad reigned in his place.

Hadad's city was named Pai, and his wife's name was Mehetabel
daughter of Matred, daughter of Me-zahab.
Then Hadad died.

Edom's chiefs: Timna, Alvah, Jetheth, Oholibamah, Elah, Pinon, Kenaz, Teman, Mibzar,
Magdiel, and Iram.
These were Edom's chiefs.

2   These were Israel's sons:
Reuben, Simeon, Levi,
Judah, Issachar, Zebulun,
Dan, Joseph, Benjamin,
Naphtali, Gad, and Asher.

Judah's sons: Er, Onan, and Shelah. These three were born to him by Bath-shua the Canaanite
woman. Er, Judah's firstborn, was evil in the LORD's sight, so he put him to death. Judah's
daughter-in-law Tamar bore Perez and Zerah to him. Judah had five sons in all.

Perez's sons: Hezron and Hamul.
10   Zerah's sons: Zimri, Ethan, Heman, Calcol, and Dara—five in all.
Carmi's son: Achar, who brought trouble on Israel when he was unfaithful by taking the things
set apart for destruction.
Ethan's son: Azariah.
Hezron's sons, who were born to him: Jerahmeel, Ram, and Chelubai.

Ram fathered Amminadab, and Amminadab fathered Nahshon, a leader of Judah's
descendants.
Nahshon fathered Salma, and Salma fathered Boaz.
Boaz fathered Obed, and Obed fathered Jesse.
Jesse fathered Eliab, his firstborn; Abinadab was born second, Shimea third, Nethanel fourth,
20   Raddai fifth, Ozem sixth, and David seventh. Their sisters were Zeruiah and Abigail. Zeruiah's
three sons: Abishai, Joab, and Asahel. Amasa's mother was Abigail, and his father was Jether
the Ishmaelite.

Caleb son of Hezron had children by his wife Azubah and by Jerioth. These were Azubah's
sons: Jesher, Shobab, and Ardon. When Azubah died, Caleb married Ephrath, and she bore
Hur to him. Hur fathered Uri, and Uri fathered Bezalel. After this, Hezron slept with the
daughter of Machir the father of Gilead. Hezron had married her when he was sixty years old,

and she bore Segub to him. Segub fathered Jair, who possessed twenty-three towns in the land of Gilead. But Geshur and Aram captured Jair's Villages along with Kenath and its surrounding villages—sixty towns. All these were the descendants of Machir father of Gilead. After Hezron's death in Caleb-ephrathah, his wife Abijah bore Ashhur to him. He was the father of Tekoa.

The sons of Jerahmeel, Hezron's firstborn: Ram, his firstborn, Bunah, Oren, Ozem, and Ahijah. Jerahmeel had another wife named Atarah, who was the mother of Onam.
The sons of Ram, Jerahmeel's firstborn: Maaz, Jamin, and Eker.
Onam's sons: Shammai and Jada.
Shammai's sons: Nadab and Abishur. Abishur's wife was named Abihail, who bore Ahban and Molid to him.
Nadab's sons: Seled and Appaim. Seled died without children.
Appaim's son: Ishi.
Ishi's son: Sheshan.
Sheshan's descendant: Ahlai.
The sons of Jada, brother of Shammai: Jether and Jonathan. Jether died without children.
Jonathan's sons: Peleth and Zaza. These were the descendants of Jerahmeel.
Sheshan had no sons, only daughters, but he did have an Egyptian servant whose name was Jarha. Sheshan gave his daughter in marriage to his servant Jarha, and she bore Attai to him.

Attai fathered Nathan, and Nathan fathered Zabad.
Zabad fathered Ephlal, and Ephlal fathered Obed.
Obed fathered Jehu, and Jehu fathered Azariah.
Azariah fathered Helez, and Helez fathered Elasah.
Elasah fathered Sismai, and Sismai fathered Shallum.
Shallum fathered Jekamiah, and Jekamiah fathered Elishama.

The sons of Caleb brother of Jerahmeel: Mesha, his firstborn, fathered Ziph, and Mareshah, his second son, fathered Hebron.
Hebron's sons: Korah, Tappuah, Rekem, and Shema.
Shema fathered Raham, who fathered Jorkeam, and Rekem fathered Shammai.
Shammai's son was Maon, and Maon fathered Beth-zur.
Caleb's concubine Ephah was the mother of Haran, Moza, and Gazez. Haran fathered Gazez.
Jahdai's sons: Regem, Jotham, Geshan, Pelet, Ephah, and Shaaph.
Caleb's concubine Maacah was the mother of Sheber and Tirhanah. She was also the mother of Shaaph, Madmannah's father, and of Sheva, the father of Machbenah and Gibea. Caleb's daughter was Achsah.
These were Caleb's descendants.

The sons of Hur, Ephrathah's firstborn:
Shobal fathered Kiriath-jearim;
Salma fathered Bethlehem,
and Hareph fathered Beth-gader.

These were the descendants of Shobal the father of Kiriath-jearim: Haroeh, half of the
Manahathites, and the families of Kiriath-jearim—the Ithrites, Puthites, Shumathites, and
Mishraites. The Zorathites and Eshtaolites descended from these.

Salma's descendants: Bethlehem, the Netophathites, Atroth-beth-joab, and half of the
70 Manahathites, the Zorites, and the families of scribes who lived in Jabez—the Tirathites,
Shimeathites, and Sucathites. These are the Kenites who came from Hammath, the father of
Rechab's family.

3 These were David's sons who were born to him in Hebron:
Amnon was the firstborn, by Ahinoam of Jezreel;
Daniel was born second, by Abigail of Carmel;
Absalom son of Maacah, daughter of King Talmai of Geshur, was third;
Adonijah son of Haggith was fourth;
Shephatiah, by Abital, was fifth;
and Ithream, by David's wife Eglah, was sixth.
Six sons were born to David in Hebron, where he reigned seven years and six months, and he
reigned in Jerusalem thirty-three years.
10 These sons were born to him in Jerusalem:
Shimea, Shobab, Nathan, and Solomon. These four were born to him by Bath-shua daughter
of Ammiel.
David's other sons: Ibhar, Elishua, Eliphelet, Nogah, Nepheg, Japhia, Elishama, Eliada, and
Eliphelet—nine sons.
These were all David's sons, with their sister Tamar, in addition to the sons by his concubines.

Solomon's son was Rehoboam;
his son was Abijah, his son Asa,
his son Jehoshaphat, his son Jehoram,
his son Ahaziah, his son Joash,
20 his son Amaziah, his son Azariah,
his son Jotham, his son Ahaz,
his son Hezekiah, his son Manasseh,

his son Amon, and his son Josiah.

Josiah's sons:

Johanan was the firstborn, Jehoiakim second,

Zedekiah third, and Shallum fourth.

Jehoiakim's sons:

his sons Jeconiah and Zedekiah.

The sons of Jeconiah the captive:

30 his sons Shealtiel, Malchiram, Pedaiah, Shenazzar, Jekamiah, Hoshama, and Nedabiah.

Pedaiah's sons: Zerubbabel and Shimei.

Zerubbabel's sons: Meshullam and Hananiah, with their sister Shelomith; and five others—

Hashubah, Ohel, Berechiah, Hasadiah, and Jushab-hesed.

Hananiah's descendants: Pelatiah, Jeshaiah, and the sons of Rephaiah, Arnan, Obadiah, and

Shecaniah.

The son of Shecaniah: Shemaiah.

Shemaiah's sons: Hattush, Igal, Bariah, Neariah, and Shaphat—six.

Neariah's sons: Elioenai, Hizkiah, and Azrikam—three.

Elioenai's sons: Hodaviah, Eliashib, Pelaiah, Akkub, Johanan, Delaiah, and Anani—seven.

4 Judah's sons: Perez, Hezron, Carmi, Hur, and Shobal.

Reaiah son of Shobal fathered Jahath, and Jahath fathered Ahumai and Lahad.

These were the families of the Zorathites.

These were Etam's sons: Jezreel, Ishma, and Idbash, and their sister was named Hazzelelponi.

Penuel fathered Gedor, and Ezer fathered Hushah.

These were the sons of Hur, Ephrathah's firstborn and the father of Bethlehem:

Ashhur fathered Tekoa and had two wives, Helah and Naarah.

Naarah bore Ahuzzam, Hepher, Temeni, and Haahashtari to him. These were Naarah's sons.

Helah's sons: Zereth, Zohar, and Ethnan. Koz fathered Anub, Zobebah, and the families of

10 Aharhel son of Harum.

Jabez was more honored than his brothers. His mother named him Jabez and said, "I gave birth to him in pain."

Jabez called out to the God of Israel, "If only you would bless me, extend my border, let your hand be with me, and keep me from harm, so that I will not experience pain." And God granted his request.

Chelub brother of Shuhah fathered Mehir, who was the father of Eshton. Eshton fathered Beth-rapha, Paseah, and Tehinnah the father of Irnahash. These were the men of Recah.

Kenaz's sons: Othniel and Seraiah.

Othniel's sons: Hathath and Meonothai.
20   Meonothai fathered Ophrah,
and Seraiah fathered Joab, the ancestor of those in the Craftsmen's Valley, for they were
craftsmen.
The sons of Caleb son of Jephunneh: Iru, Elah, and Naam.
Elah's son: Kenaz.
Jehallelel's sons: Ziph, Ziphah, Tiria, and Asarel.
Ezrah's sons: Jether, Mered, Epher, and Jalon. Mered's wife Bithiah gave birth to Miriam,
Shammai, and Ishbah the father of Eshtemoa. These were the sons of Pharaoh's daughter
Bithiah; Mered had married her. His Judean wife gave birth to Jered the father of Gedor,
Heber the father of Soco, and Jekuthiel the father of Zanoah. The sons of Hodiah's wife, the
30   sister of Naham: the father of Keilah the Garmite and the father of Eshtemoa the Maacathite.
Shimon's sons: Amnon, Rinnah, Ben-hanan, and Tilon.
Ishi's sons: Zoheth and Ben-zoheth.

The sons of Shelah son of Judah: Er the father of Lecah, Laadah the father of Mareshah, the
families of the guild of linen workers at Beth-ashbea, Jokim, the men of Cozeba; and Joash and
Saraph, who married Moabites and returned to Lehem. These names are from ancient records.
They were the potters and residents of Netaim and Gederah. They lived there in the service of
the king.

Simeon's sons: Nemuel, Jamin, Jarib, Zerah, and Shaul;
Shaul's sons: his son Shallum, his son Mibsam, and his son Mishma.
40   Mishma's sons: his son Hammuel, his son Zaccur, and his son Shimei.

Shimei had sixteen sons and six daughters, but his brothers did not have many children, so
their whole family did not become as numerous as the Judeans. They lived in Beer-sheba,
Moladah, Hazar-shual, Bilhah, Ezem, Tolad, Bethuel, Hormah, Ziklag, Beth-marcaboth,
Hazar-susim, Beth-biri, and Shaaraim. These were their cities until David became king. Their
villages were Etam, Ain, Rimmon, Tochen, and Ashan—five cities, and all their surrounding
villages as far as Baal. These were their settlements, and they kept a genealogical record for
themselves.

Meshobab, Jamlech, Joshah son of Amaziah,
Joel, Jehu son of Joshibiah, son of Seraiah, son of Asiel,
50   Elioenai, Jaakobah, Jeshohaiah, Asaiah, Adiel, Jesimiel, Benaiah, and Ziza son of Shiphi, son of
Allon, son of Jedaiah, son of Shimri, son of Shemaiah—

these mentioned by name were leaders in their families. Their ancestral houses increased greatly. They went to the entrance of Gedor, to the east side of the valley to seek pasture for their flocks. They found rich, good pasture, and the land was broad, peaceful, and quiet, for some Hamites had lived there previously.

These who were recorded by name came in the days of King Hezekiah of Judah, attacked the Hamites' tents and the Meunites who were found there, and set them apart for destruction, as they are today. Then they settled in their place because there was pasture for their flocks. Now five hundred men from these sons of Simeon went with Pelatiah, Neariah, Rephaiah, and Uzziel, the descendants of Ishi, as their leaders to Mount Seir. They struck down the remnant of the Amalekites who had escaped, and they still live there today.

5 These were the sons of Reuben the firstborn of Israel. He was the firstborn, but his birthright was given to the sons of Joseph son of Israel, because Reuben defiled his father's bed. He is not listed in the genealogy according to birthright. Although Judah became strong among his brothers and a ruler came from him, the birthright was given to Joseph.

The sons of Reuben, Israel's firstborn:

Hanoch, Pallu, Hezron, and Carmi.

Joel's sons: his son Shemaiah,

his son Gog, his son Shimei,

his son Micah, his son Reaiah,

his son Baal, and his son Beerah.

Beerah was a leader of the Reubenites, and King Tiglath-pileser of Assyria took him into exile. His relatives by their families as they are recorded in their family records:

Jeiel the chief, Zechariah,

and Bela son of Azaz,

son of Shema, son of Joel.

They settled in Aroer as far as Nebo and Baal-meon. They also settled in the east as far as the edge of the desert that extends to the Euphrates River, because their herds had increased in the land of Gilead. During Saul's reign they waged war against the Hagrites, who were defeated by their power. And they lived in their tents throughout the region east of Gilead.

The sons of Gad lived next to them in the land of Bashan as far as Salecah:

Joel the chief, Shapham the second in command, Janai, and Shaphat in Bashan.

Their relatives according to their ancestral houses: Michael, Meshullam, Sheba, Jorai, Jacan, Zia, and Eber—seven.

These were the sons of Abihail son of Huri,

son of Jaroah, son of Gilead,
son of Michael, son of Jeshishai,
son of Jahdo, son of Buz.
Ahi son of Abdiel, son of Guni, was head of their ancestral family. They lived in Gilead, in
Bashan and its surrounding villages, and throughout the pasturelands of Sharon. All of them
30 were registered in the genealogies during the reigns of Judah's King Jotham and Israel's King
Jeroboam.

The descendants of Reuben and Gad and half the tribe of Manasseh had 44,760 warriors who
could serve in the army—men who carried shield and sword, drew the bow, and were trained for
war. They waged war against the Hagrites, Jetur, Naphish, and Nodab. They received help against
these enemies because they cried out to God in battle, and the Hagrites and all their allies were
handed over to them. He was receptive to their prayer because they trusted in him. They captured
the Hagrites' livestock—fifty thousand of their camels, two hundred fifty thousand sheep, and two
thousand donkeys—as well as one hundred thousand people. Many of the Hagrites were killed
because it was God's battle. And they lived there in the Hagrites' place until the exile.

40 The descendants of half the tribe of Manasseh settled in the land from Bashan to Baal-hermon
(that is, Senir or Mount Hermon); they were numerous. These were the heads of their ancestral
families: Epher, Ishi, Eliel, Azriel, Jeremiah, Hodaviah, and Jahdiel. They were valiant warriors,
famous men, and heads of their ancestral houses. But they were unfaithful to the God of their
ancestors. They prostituted themselves with the gods of the nations God had destroyed before
them. So the God of Israel roused the spirit of King Pul (that is, Tiglath-pileser) of Assyria,
and he took the Reubenites, Gadites, and half the tribe of Manasseh into exile. He took them to
Halah, Habor, Hara, and Gozan's river, where they are until today.

6 Levi's sons: Gershom, Kohath, and Merari.
Kohath's sons: Amram, Izhar, Hebron, and Uzziel.
Amram's children: Aaron, Moses, and Miriam.
Aaron's sons: Nadab, Abihu, Eleazar, and Ithamar.
Eleazar fathered Phinehas;
Phinehas fathered Abishua;
Abishua fathered Bukki;
Bukki fathered Uzzi;
Uzzi fathered Zerahiah;
10 Zerahiah fathered Meraioth;
Meraioth fathered Amariah;
Amariah fathered Ahitub;

Ahitub fathered Zadok;

Zadok fathered Ahimaaz;

Ahimaaz fathered Azariah;

Azariah fathered Johanan;

Johanan fathered Azariah, who served as priest in the temple that Solomon built in Jerusalem;

Azariah fathered Amariah;

20 Amariah fathered Ahitub;

Ahitub fathered Zadok;

Zadok fathered Shallum;

Shallum fathered Hilkiah;

Hilkiah fathered Azariah;

Azariah fathered Seraiah;

and Seraiah fathered Jehozadak.

Jehozadak went into exile when the LORD sent Judah and Jerusalem into exile at the hands of Nebuchadnezzar.

Levi's sons: Gershom, Kohath, and Merari.

30 These are the names of Gershom's sons: Libni and Shimei.

Kohath's sons: Amram, Izhar, Hebron and Uzziel.

Merari's sons: Mahli and Mushi.

These are the Levites' families according to their fathers:

Of Gershom: his son Libni,

his son Jahath, his son Zimmah,

his son Joah, his son Iddo,

his son Zerah, and his son Jeatherai.

Kohath's sons: his son Amminadab,

his son Korah, his son Assir,

40 his son Elkanah, his son Ebiasaph,

his son Assir, his son Tahath,

his son Uriel, his son Uzziah,

and his son Shaul.

Elkanah's sons: Amasai and Ahimoth,

his son Elkanah, his son Zophai,

his son Nahath, his son Eliab,

his son Jeroham, and his son Elkanah.

Samuel's sons: his firstborn Joel,

and his second son Abijah.

50   Merari's sons: Mahli, his son Libni,
    his son Shimei, his son Uzzah,
    his son Shimea, his son Haggiah,
    and his son Asaiah.

These are the men David put in charge of the music in the LORD's temple after the ark came to rest there. They ministered with song in front of the tabernacle, the tent of meeting, until Solomon built the LORD's temple in Jerusalem, and they performed their task according to the regulations given to them. These are the men who served with their sons.

    From the Kohathites: Heman the singer,
    son of Joel, son of Samuel,
60   son of Elkanah, son of Jeroham,
    son of Eliel, son of Toah,
    son of Zuph, son of Elkanah,
    son of Mahath, son of Amasai,
    son of Elkanah, son of Joel,
    son of Azariah, son of Zephaniah,
    son of Tahath, son of Assir,
    son of Ebiasaph, son of Korah,
    son of Izhar, son of Kohath,
    son of Levi, son of Israel.

70   Heman's relative was Asaph, who stood at his right hand:
    Asaph son of Berechiah, son of Shimea,
    son of Michael, son of Baaseiah,
    son of Malchijah, son of Ethni,
    son of Zerah, son of Adaiah,
    son of Ethan, son of Zimmah,
    son of Shimei, son of Jahath,
    son of Gershom, son of Levi.

    On the left, their relatives were Merari's sons:
    Ethan son of Kishi, son of Abdi,
80   son of Malluch, son of Hashabiah,
    son of Amaziah, son of Hilkiah,
    son of Amzi, son of Bani,
    son of Shemer, son of Mahli,

son of Mushi, son of Merari,
son of Levi.

Their relatives, the Levites, were assigned to all the service of the tabernacle, God's temple. But Aaron and his sons did all the work of the most holy place. They presented the offerings on the altar of burnt offerings and on the altar of incense to make atonement for Israel according to all that Moses the servant of God had commanded.

90   These are Aaron's sons: his son Eleazar,
his son Phinehas, his son Abishua,
his son Bukki, his son Uzzi,
his son Zerahiah, his son Meraioth,
his son Amariah, his son Ahitub,
his son Zadok, and his son Ahimaaz.

These were the places assigned to Aaron's descendants from the Kohathite family for their settlements in their territory, because the first lot was for them. They were given Hebron in the land of Judah and its surrounding pasturelands, but the fields and settlements around the city were given to Caleb son of Jephunneh. Aaron's descendants were given:

100   Hebron (a city of refuge), Libnah and its pasturelands, Jattir, Eshtemoa and its pasturelands, Hilen and its pasturelands, Debir and its pasturelands, Ashan and its pasturelands, and Beth-shemesh and its pasturelands. From the tribe of Benjamin they were given Geba and its pasturelands, Alemeth and its pasturelands, and Anathoth and its pasturelands. They had thirteen towns in all among their families.

To the rest of the Kohathites, ten towns from half the tribe of Manasseh were assigned by lot.

The Gershomites were assigned thirteen towns from the tribes of Issachar, Asher, Naphtali, and Manasseh in Bashan according to their families.

The Merarites were assigned by lot twelve towns from the tribes of Reuben, Gad, and Zebulun 110 according to their families. So the Israelites gave these towns and their pasturelands to the Levites. They assigned by lot the towns named above from the tribes of the descendants of Judah, Simeon, and Benjamin.

Some of the families of the Kohathites were given towns from the tribe of Ephraim for their territory:

Shechem (a city of refuge) with its pasturelands in the hill country of Ephraim, Gezer and its pasturelands, Jokmeam and its pasturelands, Beth-horon and its pasturelands, Aijalon and its pasturelands, and Gath-rimmon and its pasturelands. From half the tribe of Manasseh, Aner and its pasturelands, and Bileam and its pasturelands were given to the rest of the families of the Kohathites.

120 The Gershomites received:
Golan in Bashan and its pasturelands, and Ashtaroth and its pasturelands from the families of half the tribe of Manasseh. From the tribe of Issachar they received Kedesh and its pasturelands, Daberath and its pasturelands, Ramoth and its pasturelands, and Anem and its pasturelands. From the tribe of Asher they received Mashal and its pasturelands, Abdon and its pasturelands, Hukok and its pasturelands, and Rehob and its pasturelands. From the tribe of Naphtali they received Kedesh in Galilee and its pasturelands, Hammon and its pasturelands, and Kiriathaim and its pasturelands.

The rest of the Merarites received:
From the tribe of Zebulun they received Rimmono and its pasturelands and Tabor and its
130 pasturelands. From the tribe of Reuben across the Jordan at Jericho, to the east of the Jordan, they received Bezer in the desert and its pasturelands, Jahzah and its pasturelands, Kedemoth and its pasturelands, and Mephaath and its pasturelands. From the tribe of Gad they received Ramoth in Gilead and its pasturelands, Mahanaim and its pasturelands, Heshbon and its pasturelands, and Jazer and its pasturelands.

7 Issachar's sons: Tola, Puah, Jashub, and Shimron—four.
Tola's sons: Uzzi, Rephaiah, Jeriel, Jahmai, Ibsam, and Shemuel, the heads of their ancestral families. During David's reign, 22,600 descendants of Tola were recorded as valiant warriors in their family records.
Uzzi's son: Izrahiah.
Izrahiah's sons: Michael, Obadiah, Joel, Isshiah. All five of them were chiefs. Along with them, they had 36,000 troops for battle according to the family records of their ancestral families, for they had many wives and children. Their tribesmen who were valiant warriors belonging to all the families of Issachar totaled 87,000 in their genealogies.

10 Three of Benjamin's sons: Bela, Becher, and Jediael.
Bela's sons: Ezbon, Uzzi, Uzziel, Jerimoth, and Iri—five. They were valiant warriors and heads of their ancestral families; 22,034 were listed in their genealogies.
Becher's sons: Zemirah, Joash, Eliezer, Elioenai, Omri, Jeremoth, Abijah, Anathoth, and Alemeth; all these were Becher's sons. Their family records were recorded according to the heads of their ancestral families—20,200 valiant warriors.
Jediael's son: Bilhan.

Bilhan's sons: Jeush, Benjamin, Ehud, Chenaanah, Zethan, Tarshish, and Ahishahar. All these sons of Jediael listed by family heads were valiant warriors; there were 17,200 who could serve in the army. Shuppim and Huppim were sons of Ir, and the Hushim were the sons of Aher.

20 Naphtali's sons: Jahziel, Guni, Jezer, and Shallum—Bilhah's sons.

Manasseh's sons through his Aramean concubine: Asriel and Machir the father of Gilead.
Machir took wives from Huppim and Shuppim. The name of his sister was Maacah. Another descendant was named Zelophehad, but he had only daughters.
Machir's wife Maacah gave birth to a son, and she named him Peresh. His brother was named Sheresh, and his sons were Ulam and Rekem.
Ulam's son: Bedan. These were the sons of Gilead son of Machir, son of Manasseh. His sister Hammolecheth gave birth to Ishhod, Abiezer, and Mahlah.
Shemida's sons: Ahian, Shechem, Likhi, and Aniam.

> Ephraim's sons: Shuthelah, and his son Bered,
30 > his son Tahath, his son Eleadah,
> his son Tahath, his son Zabad,
> his son Shuthelah, also Ezer, and Elead.

The men of Gath, born in the land, killed them because they went down to raid their cattle. Their father Ephraim mourned a long time, and his relatives came to comfort him. He slept with his wife, and she conceived and gave birth to a son. So he named him Beriah, because there had been misfortune in his home. His daughter was Sheerah, who built Lower and Upper Beth-horon and Uzzen-sheerah,

> his son Rephah, his son Resheph,
> his son Telah, his son Tahan,
40 > his son Ladan, his son Ammihud,
> his son Elishama, his son Nun,
> and his son Joshua.

Their holdings and settlements were Bethel and its surrounding villages; Naaran to the east, Gezer and its villages to the west, and Shechem and its villages as far as Ayyah and its villages, and along the borders of the descendants of Manasseh, Beth-shean, Taanach, Megiddo, and Dor with their surrounding villages. The sons of Joseph son of Israel lived in these towns.

Asher's sons: Imnah, Ishvah, Ishvi, and Beriah, with their sister Serah.

Beriah's sons: Heber, and Malchiel, who fathered Birzaith.

50 Heber fathered Japhlet, Shomer, and Hotham, with their sister Shua.

Japhlet's sons: Pasach, Bimhal, and Ashvath. These were Japhlet's sons.

Shemer's sons: Ahi, Rohgah, Hubbah, and Aram.

His brother Helem's sons: Zophah, Imna, Shelesh, and Amal.

Zophah's sons: Suah, Harnepher, Shual, Beri, Imrah, Bezer, Hod, Shamma, Shilshah, Ithran, and Beera.

Jether's sons: Jephunneh, Pispa, and Ara.

Ulla's sons: Arah, Hanniel, and Rizia.

All these were Asher's descendants. They were the heads of their ancestral families, chosen men, valiant warriors, and chiefs among the leaders. The number of men listed in their

60 genealogies for military service was 26,000.

8 Benjamin fathered Bela, his firstborn; Ashbel was born second, Aharah third, Nohah fourth, and Rapha fifth.

Bela's sons: Addar, Gera, Abihud, Abishua, Naaman, Ahoah, Gera, Shephuphan, and Huram. These were Ehud's sons, who were the heads of the families living in Geba and who were deported to Manahath: Naaman, Ahijah, and Gera. Gera deported them and was the father of Uzza and Ahihud.

Shaharaim had sons in the territory of Moab after he had divorced his wives Hushim and Baara. His sons by his wife Hodesh: Jobab, Zibia, Mesha, Malcam, Jeuz, Sachia, and Mirmah. These were his sons, family heads. He also had sons by Hushim: Abitub and Elpaal.

10 Elpaal's sons: Eber, Misham, and Shemed who built Ono and Lod and its surrounding villages, Beriah and Shema, who were the family heads of Aijalon's residents and who drove out the residents of Gath, Ahio, Shashak, and Jeremoth.

Zebadiah, Arad, Eder, Michael, Ishpah, and Joha were Beriah's sons.

Zebadiah, Meshullam, Hizki, Heber, Ishmerai, Izliah, and Jobab were Elpaal's sons.

Jakim, Zichri, Zabdi, Elienai, Zillethai, Eliel, Adaiah, Beraiah, and Shimrath were Shimei's sons.

Ishpan, Eber, Eliel, Abdon, Zichri, Hanan, Hananiah, Elam, Anthothijah, Iphdeiah, and Penuel were Shashak's sons.

Shamsherai, Shehariah, Athaliah, Jaareshiah, Elijah, and Zichri were Jeroham's sons.

20 These were family heads, chiefs according to their family records; they lived in Jerusalem.

Jeiel fathered Gibeon and lived in Gibeon. His wife's name was Maacah. Abdon was his firstborn son, then Zur, Kish, Baal, Nadab, Gedor, Ahio, Zecher, and Mikloth who fathered Shimeah. These also lived opposite their relatives in Jerusalem, with their other relatives.

Ner fathered Kish, Kish fathered Saul, and Saul fathered Jonathan, Malchishua, Abinadab, and Esh-baal.

Jonathan's son was Merib-baal, and Merib-baal fathered Micah.

Micah's sons: Pithon, Melech, Tarea, and Ahaz.

Ahaz fathered Jehoaddah, Jehoaddah fathered Alemeth, Azmaveth, and Zimri, and Zimri fathered Moza.

30 Moza fathered Binea. His son was Raphah, his son Elasah, and his son Azel.

Azel had six sons, and these were their names: Azrikam, Bocheru, Ishmael, Sheariah, Obadiah, and Hanan. All these were Azel's sons.

His brother Eshek's sons: Ulam was his firstborn, Jeush second, and Eliphelet third.

Ulam's sons were valiant warriors and archers. They had many sons and grandsons—150 of them.

All these were among Benjamin's sons.

9 All Israel was registered in the genealogies that are written in the Book of the Kings of Israel. But Judah was exiled to Babylon because of their unfaithfulness. The first to live in their towns on their own property again were Israelites, priests, Levites, and temple servants.

These people from the descendants of Judah, Benjamin, Ephraim, and Manasseh settled in Jerusalem:

Uthai son of Ammihud, son of Omri, son of Imri, son of Bani, a descendant of Perez son of Judah;

from the Shilonites:

Asaiah the firstborn and his sons;

10 and from the descendants of Zerah:

Jeuel and their relatives—690 in all.

The Benjaminites: Sallu son of Meshullam, son of Hodaviah, son of Hassenuah;

Ibneiah son of Jeroham;

Elah son of Uzzi, son of Michri;

Meshullam son of Shephatiah, son of Reuel, son of Ibnijah;

and their relatives according to their family records—956 in all. All these men were heads of their ancestral families.

The priests: Jedaiah; Jehoiarib; Jachin;

Azariah son of Hilkiah, son of Meshullam, son of Zadok, son of Meraioth, son of Ahitub, the

20 chief official of God's temple;

Adaiah son of Jeroham, son of Pashhur, son of Malchijah;

Maasai son of Adiel, son of Jahzerah, son of Meshullam, son of Meshillemith, son of Immer;

and their relatives, the heads of their ancestral families—1,760 in all. They were capable men employed in the ministry of God's temple.

The Levites: Shemaiah son of Hasshub, son of Azrikam, son of Hashabiah of the Merarites; Bakbakkar, Heresh, Galal, and Mattaniah, son of Mica, son of Zichri, son of Asaph; Obadiah son of Shemaiah, son of Galal, son of Jeduthun; and Berechiah son of Asa, son of Elkanah who lived in the settlements of the Netophathites.

The gatekeepers: Shallum, Akkub, Talmon, Ahiman, and their relatives.
30 Shallum was their chief; he was previously stationed at the King's Gate on the east side. These were the gatekeepers from the camp of the Levites.
Shallum son of Kore, son of Ebiasaph, son of Korah and his relatives from his ancestral family, the Korahites, were assigned to guard the thresholds of the tent. Their ancestors had been assigned to the LORD's camp as guardians of the entrance. In earlier times Phinehas son of Eleazar had been their leader, and the LORD was with him. Zechariah son of Meshelemiah was the gatekeeper at the entrance to the tent of meeting.

The total number of those chosen to be gatekeepers at the thresholds was 212. They were registered by genealogy in their settlements. David and the seer Samuel had appointed them to their trusted positions. So they and their sons were assigned as guards to the gates of the LORD's
40 temple, which had been the tent-temple. The gatekeepers were on the four sides: east, west, north, and south. Their relatives came from their settlements at fixed times to be with them seven days, but the four chief gatekeepers, who were Levites, were entrusted with the rooms and the treasuries of God's temple. They spent the night in the vicinity of God's temple, because they had guard duty and were in charge of opening it every morning.
Some of them were in charge of the utensils used in worship. They would count them when they brought them in and when they took them out. Others were put in charge of the furnishings and all the utensils of the sanctuary, as well as the fine flour, wine, oil, incense, and spices. Some of the priests' sons mixed the spices. A Levite called Mattithiah, the firstborn of Shallum the Korahite, was entrusted with baking the bread. Some of the Kohathites' relatives were responsible
50 for preparing the rows of the Bread of the Presence every Sabbath.
The singers, the heads of the Levite families, stayed in the temple chambers and were exempt from other tasks because they were on duty day and night. These were the heads of the Levite families, chiefs according to their family records; they lived in Jerusalem.

Jeiel fathered Gibeon and lived in Gibeon. His wife's name was Maacah. Abdon was his firstborn son, then Zur, Kish, Baal, Ner, Nadab, Gedor, Ahio, Zechariah, and Mikloth. Mikloth fathered Shimeam. These also lived opposite their relatives in Jerusalem with their other relatives.

Ner fathered Kish, Kish fathered Saul, and Saul fathered Jonathan, Malchishua, Abinadab, and Esh-baal.

Jonathan's son was Merib-baal, and Merib-baal fathered Micah.

60 Micah's sons: Pithon, Melech, Tahrea, and Ahaz.

Ahaz fathered Jarah;

Jarah fathered Alemeth, Azmaveth, and Zimri;

Zimri fathered Moza.

Moza fathered Binea.

His son was Rephaiah, his son Elasah, and his son Azel.

Azel had six sons, and these were their names: Azrikam, Bocheru, Ishmael, Sheariah, Obadiah, and Hanan. These were Azel's sons.

10 The Philistines fought against Israel, and Israel's men fled from them. Many were killed on Mount Gilboa. The Philistines pursued Saul and his sons and killed his sons Jonathan, Abinadab, and Malchishua. When the battle intensified against Saul, the archers spotted him and severely wounded him. Then Saul said to his armor-bearer, "Draw your sword and run me through with it, or these uncircumcised men will come and torture me." But his armor-bearer would not do it because he was terrified. Then Saul took his sword and fell on it. When his armor-bearer saw that Saul was dead, he also fell on his own sword and died. So Saul and his three sons died—his whole house died together.

When all the men of Israel in the valley saw that the army had fled and that Saul and his sons 10 were dead, they abandoned their cities and fled. So the Philistines came and settled in them.

The next day when the Philistines came to strip the slain, they found Saul and his sons dead on Mount Gilboa. They stripped Saul, cut off his head, took his armor, and sent messengers throughout the land of the Philistines to spread the good news to their idols and the people. Then they put his armor in the temple of their gods and hung his skull in the temple of Dagon.

When all Jabesh-gilead heard of everything the Philistines had done to Saul, all their brave men set out and retrieved the body of Saul and the bodies of his sons and brought them to Jabesh. They buried their bones under the oak in Jabesh and fasted seven days.

Saul died for his unfaithfulness to the LORD because he did not keep the LORD's word. He even 20 consulted a medium for guidance, but he did not inquire of the LORD. So the LORD put him to death and turned the kingdom over to David son of Jesse.

11 All Israel came together to David at Hebron and said, "Here we are, your own flesh and blood. Even previously when Saul was king, you were leading Israel out to battle and bringing us back. The LORD your God also said to you, 'You will shepherd my people Israel, and you will be ruler over my people Israel.'"

So all the elders of Israel came to the king at Hebron. David made a covenant with them at Hebron in the LORD's presence, and they anointed David king over Israel, in keeping with the LORD's word through Samuel.

David and all Israel marched to Jerusalem (that is, Jebus); the Jebusites who inhabited the land were there. The inhabitants of Jebus said to David, "You will never get in here." Yet David did capture the stronghold of Zion, that is, the city of David.

David said, "Whoever is the first to kill a Jebusite will become chief commander." Joab son of Zeruiah went up first, so he became the chief.

Then David took up residence in the stronghold; therefore, it was called the city of David. He built up the city all the way around, from the supporting terraces to the surrounding parts, and Joab restored the rest of the city. David steadily grew more powerful, and the LORD of Armies was with him.

The following were the chiefs of David's warriors who, together with all Israel, strongly supported him in his reign to make him king according to the LORD's word about Israel. This is the list of David's warriors:

Jashobeam son of Hachmoni was chief of the Thirty; he wielded his spear against three hundred and killed them at one time.

After him, Eleazar son of Dodo the Ahohite was one of the three warriors. He was with David at Pas-dammim when the Philistines had gathered there for battle. There was a portion of a field full of barley, where the troops had fled from the Philistines. But Eleazar and David took their stand in the middle of the field and defended it. They killed the Philistines, and the LORD gave them a great victory.

Three of the thirty chief men went down to David, to the rock at the cave of Adullam, while the Philistine army was encamped in Rephaim Valley. At that time David was in the stronghold, and a Philistine garrison was at Bethlehem. David was extremely thirsty and said, "If only someone would bring me water to drink from the well at the city gate of Bethlehem!" So the Three broke through the Philistine camp and drew water from the well at the gate of Bethlehem. They brought it back to David, but he refused to drink it. Instead, he poured it out to the LORD. David said, "I would never do such a thing in the presence of my God! How can I drink the blood of these men who risked their lives?" For they brought it at the risk of their lives. So he would not drink it. Such were the exploits of the three warriors.

Abishai, Joab's brother, was the leader of the Three. He raised his spear against three hundred men and killed them, gaining a reputation among the Three. He was more honored than the Three and became their commander even though he did not become one of the Three.

Benaiah son of Jehoiada was the son of a brave man from Kabzeel, a man of many exploits. Benaiah killed two sons of Ariel of Moab, and he went down into a pit on a snowy day and killed a lion. He also killed an Egyptian who was seven and a half feet tall. Even though the Egyptian had a spear in his hand like a weaver's beam, Benaiah went down to him with a staff, snatched the spear out of the Egyptian's hand, and then killed him with his own spear. These were the exploits of Benaiah son of Jehoiada, who had a reputation among the three warriors. He was the most honored of the Thirty, but he did not become one of the Three. David put him in charge of his bodyguard.

The best soldiers were

Joab's brother Asahel,

Elhanan son of Dodo of Bethlehem,

Shammoth the Harorite,

Helez the Pelonite,

Ira son of Ikkesh the Tekoite,

Abiezer the Anathothite,

Sibbecai the Hushathite,

Ilai the Ahohite,

Maharai the Netophathite,

Heled son of Baanah the Netophathite,

Ithai son of Ribai from Gibeah of the Benjaminites,

Benaiah the Pirathonite,

Hurai from the wadis of Gaash,

Abiel the Arbathite,

Azmaveth the Baharumite,

Eliahba the Shaalbonite,

the sons of Hashem the Gizonite,

Jonathan son of Shagee the Hararite,

Ahiam son of Sachar the Hararite,

Eliphal son of Ur,

Hepher the Mecherathite,

Ahijah the Pelonite,

Hezro the Carmelite,

Naarai son of Ezbai,

Joel the brother of Nathan,

Mibhar son of Hagri,

Zelek the Ammonite,

Naharai the Beerothite, the armor-bearer for Joab son of Zeruiah,

Ira the Ithrite,

Gareb the Ithrite,

Uriah the Hethite,

Zabad son of Ahlai,
80   Adina son of Shiza the Reubenite, chief of the Reubenites, and thirty with him,
Hanan son of Maacah,
Joshaphat the Mithnite,
Uzzia the Ashterathite,
Shama and Jeiel the sons of Hotham the Aroerite,
Jediael son of Shimri and his brother Joha the Tizite,
Eliel the Mahavite,
Jeribai and Joshaviah, the sons of Elnaam,
Ithmah the Moabite,
Eliel, Obed, and Jaasiel the Mezobaite.

12 The following were the men who came to David at Ziklag while he was still banned from the presence of Saul son of Kish. They were among the warriors who helped him in battle. They were archers who could use either the right or left hand, both to sling stones and shoot arrows from a bow. They were Saul's relatives from Benjamin:

Their chief was Ahiezer son of Shemaah the Gibeathite.
Then there was his brother Joash;
Jeziel and Pelet sons of Azmaveth;
Beracah, Jehu the Anathothite;
Ishmaiah the Gibeonite, a warrior among the Thirty and a leader over the Thirty;
10   Jeremiah, Jahaziel, Johanan, Jozabad the Gederathite;
Eluzai, Jerimoth, Bealiah, Shemariah, Shephatiah the Haruphite;
Elkanah, Isshiah, Azarel, Joezer, and Jashobeam, the Korahites;
and Joelah and Zebadiah, the sons of Jeroham from Gedor.

Some Gadites defected to David at his stronghold in the desert. They were valiant warriors, trained for battle, expert with shield and spear. Their faces were like the faces of lions, and they were as swift as gazelles on the mountains.

Ezer was the chief, Obadiah second, Eliab third,
Mishmannah fourth, Jeremiah fifth,
Attai sixth, Eliel seventh,
20   Johanan eighth, Elzabad ninth,
Jeremiah tenth, and Machbannai eleventh.

These Gadites were army commanders; the least of them was a match for a hundred, and the greatest of them for a thousand. These are the men who crossed the Jordan in the first month when it was overflowing all its banks, and put to flight all those in the valleys to the east and to the west.

Other Benjaminites and men from Judah also went to David at the stronghold. David went out to meet them and said to them, "If you have come in peace to help me, my heart will be united with you, but if you have come to betray me to my enemies even though my hands have done no wrong, may the God of our ancestors look on it and judge."

Then the Spirit enveloped Amasai, chief of the Thirty, and he said:

30
> We are yours, David,
> we are with you, son of Jesse!
> Peace, peace to you,
> and peace to him who helps you,
> for your God helps you.

So David received them and made them leaders of his troops.

Some Manassites defected to David when he went with the Philistines to fight against Saul. However, they did not help the Philistines because the Philistine rulers sent David away after a discussion. They said, "It will be our heads if he defects to his master Saul." When David went to Ziklag, some men from Manasseh defected to him: Adnah, Jozabad, Jediael, Michael, Jozabad,
40 Elihu, and Zillethai, chiefs of thousands in Manasseh. They helped David against the raiders, for they were all valiant warriors and commanders in the army. At that time, men came day after day to help David until there was a great army, like an army of God.

The numbers of the armed troops who came to David at Hebron to turn Saul's kingdom over to him, according to the LORD's word, were as follows:

> From the Judahites: 6,800 armed troops bearing shields and spears.
> From the Simeonites: 7,100 valiant warriors ready for war.
> From the Levites: 4,600 in addition to Jehoiada, leader of the house of Aaron, with
> 3,700 men; and Zadok, a young valiant warrior, with 22 commanders from his ancestral
> family.
50
> From the Benjaminites, the relatives of Saul: 3,000 (up to that time the majority of the
> Benjaminites maintained their allegiance to the house of Saul).
> From the Ephraimites: 20,800 valiant warriors who were famous men in their
> ancestral families.
> From half the tribe of Manasseh: 18,000 designated by name to come and make
> David king.
> From the Issacharites, who understood the times and knew what Israel should do:
> 200 chiefs with all their relatives under their command.
> From Zebulun: 50,000 who could serve in the army, trained for battle with all kinds of
> weapons of war, with one purpose to help David.
60
> From Naphtali: 1,000 commanders accompanied by 37,000 men with shield and spear.
> From the Danites: 28,600 trained for battle.

From Asher: 40,000 who could serve in the army, trained for battle.

From across the Jordan—from the Reubenites, Gadites, and half the tribe of Manasseh: 120,000 men equipped with all the military weapons of war.

All these warriors, lined up in battle formation, came to Hebron wholeheartedly determined to make David king over all Israel. All the rest of Israel was also of one mind to make David king. They spent three days there eating and drinking with David, for their relatives had provided for them. In addition, their neighbors from as far away as Issachar, Zebulun, and Naphtali came and brought food on donkeys, camels, mules, and oxen—abundant provisions of flour, fig cakes, raisins, wine and oil, herds, and flocks. Indeed, there was joy in Israel.

70

13 David consulted with all his leaders, the commanders of hundreds and of thousands. Then he said to the whole assembly of Israel, "If it seems good to you, and if this is from the LORD our God, let's spread out and send the message to the rest of our relatives in all the districts of Israel, including the priests and Levites in their cities with pasturelands, that they should gather together with us. Then let's bring back the ark of our God, for we did not inquire of him in Saul's days." Since the proposal seemed right to all the people, the whole assembly agreed to do it.

So David assembled all Israel, from the Shihor of Egypt to the entrance of Hamath, to bring the ark of God from Kiriath-jearim. David and all Israel went to Baalah (that is, Kiriath-jearim that belongs to Judah) to take from there the ark of God, which bears the name of the LORD who is enthroned between the cherubim. At Abinadab's house they set the ark of God on a new cart. Uzzah and Ahio were guiding the cart.

10

David and all Israel were dancing with all their might before God with songs and with lyres, harps, tambourines, cymbals, and trumpets. When they came to Chidon's threshing floor, Uzzah reached out to hold the ark because the oxen had stumbled. Then the LORD's anger burned against Uzzah, and he struck him dead because he had reached out to the ark. So he died there in the presence of God.

David was angry because of the LORD's outburst against Uzzah, so he named that place Outburst Against Uzzah, as it is still named today. David feared God that day and said, "How can I ever bring the ark of God to me?" So David did not bring the ark of God home to the city of David; instead, he diverted it to the house of Obed-edom of Gath. The ark of God remained with Obed-edom's family in his house for three months, and the LORD blessed his family and all that he had.

14 King Hiram of Tyre sent envoys to David, along with cedar logs, stonemasons, and carpenters to build a palace for him. Then David knew that the LORD had established him as king over Israel and that his kingdom had been exalted for the sake of his people Israel.

David took more wives in Jerusalem, and he became the father of more sons and daughters. These are the names of the children born to him in Jerusalem: Shammua, Shobab,

Nathan, Solomon, Ibhar, Elishua, Elpelet, Nogah, Nepheg, Japhia, Elishama, Beeliada, and Eliphelet.

When the Philistines heard that David had been anointed king over all Israel, they all went in search of David; when David heard of this, he went out to face them. Now the Philistines had come and raided in Rephaim Valley, so David inquired of God, "Should I attack the Philistines? Will you hand them over to me?"

The LORD replied, "Attack, and I will hand them over to you."

So the Israelites went up to Baal-perazim, and David defeated the Philistines there. Then David said, "Like a bursting flood, God has used me to burst out against my enemies." Therefore, they named that place The Lord Bursts Out. The Philistines abandoned their idols there, and David ordered that they be burned in the fire.

Once again the Philistines raided in the valley. So David again inquired of God, and God answered him, "Do not pursue them directly. Circle around them and attack them opposite the balsam trees. When you hear the sound of marching in the tops of the balsam trees, then go out to battle, for God will have gone out ahead of you to strike down the army of the Philistines." So David did as God commanded him, and they struck down the Philistine army from Gibeon to Gezer. Then David's fame spread throughout the lands, and the LORD caused all the nations to be terrified of him.

15 David built houses for himself in the city of David, and he prepared a place for the ark of God and pitched a tent for it. Then David said, "No one but the Levites may carry the ark of God, because the LORD has chosen them to carry the ark of the LORD and to minister before him forever."

David assembled all Israel at Jerusalem to bring the ark of the LORD to the place he had prepared for it. Then he gathered together the descendants of Aaron and the Levites:

From the Kohathites, Uriel the leader and 120 of his relatives; from the Merarites, Asaiah the leader and 220 of his relatives; from the Gershomites, Joel the leader and 130 of his relatives; from the Elizaphanites, Shemaiah the leader and 200 of his relatives; from the Hebronites, Eliel the leader and 80 of his relatives; from the Uzzielites, Amminadab the leader and 112 of his relatives.

David summoned the priests Zadok and Abiathar and the Levites Uriel, Asaiah, Joel, Shemaiah, Eliel, and Amminadab. He said to them, "You are the heads of the Levite families. You and your relatives must consecrate yourselves so that you may bring the ark of the LORD God of Israel to the place I have prepared for it. For the LORD our God burst out in anger against us because you Levites were not with us the first time, for we didn't inquire of him about the proper procedures." So the priests and the Levites consecrated themselves to bring up the ark of the LORD God of Israel. Then the Levites carried the ark of God the way Moses had commanded according to the word of the LORD: on their shoulders with the poles.

Then David told the leaders of the Levites to appoint their relatives as singers and to have them raise their voices with joy accompanied by musical instruments—harps, lyres, and cymbals. So the Levites appointed Heman son of Joel; from his relatives, Asaph son of Berechiah; and from their

relatives the Merarites, Ethan son of Kushaiah. With them were their relatives second in rank: Zechariah, Jaaziel, Shemiramoth, Jehiel, Unni, Eliab, Benaiah, Maaseiah, Mattithiah, Eliphelehu, Mikneiah, and the gatekeepers Obed-edom and Jeiel. The singers Heman, Asaph, and Ethan were to sound the bronze cymbals; Zechariah, Aziel, Shemiramoth, Jehiel, Unni, Eliab, Maaseiah, and Benaiah were to play harps according to *Alamoth* and Mattithiah, Eliphelehu, Mikneiah, Obed-edom, Jeiel, and Azaziah were to lead the music with lyres according to the *Sheminith*. Chenaniah, the leader of the Levites in music, was to direct the music because he was skillful. Berechiah and Elkanah were to be gatekeepers for the ark. The priests, Shebaniah, Joshaphat, Nethanel, Amasai, Zechariah, Benaiah, and Eliezer, were to blow trumpets before the ark of God. Obed-edom and
30 Jehiah were also to be gatekeepers for the ark.

David, the elders of Israel, and the commanders of thousands went with rejoicing to bring the ark of the covenant of the LORD from the house of Obed-edom. Because God helped the Levites who were carrying the ark of the covenant of the LORD, with God's help, they sacrificed seven bulls and seven rams.

Now David was dressed in a robe of fine linen, as were all the Levites who were carrying the ark, as well as the singers and Chenaniah, the music leader of the singers. David also wore a linen ephod. So all Israel brought up the ark of the covenant of the LORD with shouts, the sound of the ram's horn, trumpets, and cymbals, and the playing of harps and lyres. As the ark of the covenant of the LORD was entering the city of David, Saul's daughter Michal looked down from the window
40 and saw King David leaping and dancing, and she despised him in her heart.

16 They brought the ark of God and placed it inside the tent David had pitched for it. Then they offered burnt offerings and fellowship offerings in God's presence. When David had finished offering the burnt offerings and the fellowship offerings, he blessed the people in the name of the LORD. Then he distributed to each and every Israelite, both men and women, a loaf of bread, a date cake, and a raisin cake.

David appointed some of the Levites to be ministers before the ark of the LORD, to celebrate the LORD God of Israel, and to give thanks and praise to him. Asaph was the chief and Zechariah was second to him. Jeiel, Shemiramoth, Jehiel, Mattithiah, Eliab, Benaiah, Obed-edom, and Jeiel played the harps and lyres, while Asaph sounded the cymbals and the priests Benaiah and Jahaziel
10 blew the trumpets regularly before the ark of the covenant of God.

On that day David decreed for the first time that thanks be given to the LORD by Asaph and his relatives:

> Give thanks to the LORD; call on his name;
> proclaim his deeds among the peoples.
> Sing to him; sing praise to him;
> tell about all his wondrous works!

Boast in his holy name;
let the hearts of those who seek the Lord rejoice.
Seek the Lord and his strength;
20 seek his face always.
Remember the wondrous works he has done,
his wonders, and the judgments he has pronounced,
you offspring of Israel his servant,
Jacob's descendants—his chosen ones.

He is the Lord our God;
his judgments govern the whole earth.
Remember his covenant forever—
the promise he ordained for a thousand generations,
the covenant he made with Abraham,
30 swore to Isaac,
and confirmed to Jacob as a decree,
and to Israel as a permanent covenant:
"I will give the land of Canaan to you
as your inherited portion."

When they were few in number,
very few indeed, and resident aliens in Canaan
wandering from nation to nation
and from one kingdom to another,
he allowed no one to oppress them;
40 he rebuked kings on their behalf:
"Do not touch my anointed ones
or harm my prophets."

Let the whole earth sing to the Lord.
Proclaim his salvation from day to day.
Declare his glory among the nations,
his wondrous works among all peoples.

For the Lord is great and highly praised;
he is feared above all gods.
For all the gods of the peoples are worthless idols,
50 but the Lord made the heavens.

Splendor and majesty are before him;
strength and joy are in his place.
Ascribe to the LORD, families of the peoples,
ascribe to the LORD glory and strength.
Ascribe to the LORD the glory of his name;
bring an offering and come before him.
Worship the LORD in the splendor of his holiness;
let the whole earth tremble before him.

The world is firmly established;
60   it cannot be shaken.
Let the heavens be glad and the earth rejoice,
and let them say among the nations, "The LORD reigns!"
Let the sea and all that fills it resound;
let the fields and everything in them exult.
Then the trees of the forest will shout for joy before the LORD,
for he is coming to judge the earth.

Give thanks to the LORD, for he is good;
his faithful love endures forever.
And say, "Save us, God of our salvation;
70   gather us and rescue us from the nations
so that we may give thanks to your holy name
and rejoice in your praise.
Blessed be the LORD God of Israel
from everlasting to everlasting."

Then all the people said, "Amen" and "Praise the LORD."

So David left Asaph and his relatives there before the ark of the LORD's covenant to minister regularly before the ark according to the daily requirements. He assigned Obed-edom and his sixty-eight relatives. Obed-edom son of Jeduthun and Hosah were to be gatekeepers. David left the priest Zadok and his fellow priests before the tabernacle of the LORD at the high place in Gibeon to offer
80   burnt offerings regularly, morning and evening, to the LORD on the altar of burnt offerings and to do everything that was written in the law of the LORD, which he had commanded Israel to keep. With them were Heman, Jeduthun, and the rest who were chosen and designated by name to give thanks to the LORD—for his faithful love endures forever. Heman and Jeduthun had with them trumpets and cymbals to play and musical instruments of God. Jeduthun's sons were at the city gate.

Then all the people went home, and David returned home to bless his household.

17 When David had settled into his palace, he said to the prophet Nathan, "Look! I am living in a cedar house while the ark of the LORD's covenant is under tent curtains."

So Nathan told David, "Do all that is on your mind, for God is with you."

But that night the word of God came to Nathan: "Go to David my servant and say, 'This is what the LORD says: You are not the one to build me a house to dwell in. From the time I brought Israel out of Egypt until today I have not dwelt in a house; instead, I have moved from one tent site to another, and from one tabernacle location to another. In all my journeys throughout Israel, have I ever spoken a word to even one of the judges of Israel, whom I commanded to shepherd my people, asking: Why haven't you built me a house of cedar?'

10 "So now this is what you are to say to my servant David: 'This is what the LORD of Armies says: I took you from the pasture, from tending the flock, to be ruler over my people Israel. I have been with you wherever you have gone, and I have destroyed all your enemies before you. I will make a name for you like that of the greatest on the earth. I will designate a place for my people Israel and plant them, so that they may live there and not be disturbed again. Evildoers will not continue to oppress them as they have done ever since the day I ordered judges to be over my people Israel. I will also subdue all your enemies.

"'Furthermore, I declare to you that the LORD himself will build a house for you. When your time comes to be with your ancestors, I will raise up after you your descendant, who is one of your own sons, and I will establish his kingdom. He is the one who will build a house

20 for me, and I will establish his throne forever. I will be his father, and he will be my son. I will not remove my faithful love from him as I removed it from the one who was before you. I will appoint him over my house and my kingdom forever, and his throne will be established forever.'"

Nathan reported all these words and this entire vision to David.

Then King David went in, sat in the LORD's presence, and said,

Who am I, LORD God, and what is my house that you have brought me this far? This was a little thing to you, God, for you have spoken about your servant's house in the distant future. You regard me as a man of distinction, LORD God. What more can David say to you for honoring your servant? You know your servant. LORD, you have done this whole great thing,

30 making known all these great promises for the sake of your servant and according to your will. LORD, there is no one like you, and there is no God besides you, as all we have heard confirms. And who is like your people Israel? God, you came to one nation on earth to redeem a people for yourself, to make a name for yourself through great and awesome works by driving out nations before your people you redeemed from Egypt. You made your people Israel your own people forever, and you, LORD, have become their God.

Now, Lord, let the word that you have spoken concerning your servant and his house be confirmed forever, and do as you have promised. Let your name be confirmed and magnified forever in the saying, "The Lord of Armies, the God of Israel, is God over Israel." May the house of your servant David be established before you. Since you, my God, have revealed to your servant that you will build him a house, your servant has found courage to pray in your presence. Lord, you indeed are God, and you have promised this good thing to your servant. So now, you have been pleased to bless your servant's house that it may continue before you forever. For you, Lord, have blessed it, and it is blessed forever.

18 After this, David defeated the Philistines, subdued them, and took Gath and its surrounding villages from Philistine control. He also defeated the Moabites, and they became David's subjects and brought tribute.

David also defeated King Hadadezer of Zobah at Hamath when he went to establish his control at the Euphrates River. David captured one thousand chariots, seven thousand horsemen, and twenty thousand foot soldiers from him, hamstrung all the horses, and kept a hundred chariots.

When the Arameans of Damascus came to assist King Hadadezer of Zobah, David struck down twenty-two thousand Aramean men. Then he placed garrisons in Aram of Damascus, and the Arameans became David's subjects and brought tribute. The Lord made David victorious wherever he went.

David took the gold shields carried by Hadadezer's officers and brought them to Jerusalem. From Tibhath and Cun, Hadadezer's cities, David also took huge quantities of bronze, from which Solomon made the bronze basin, the pillars, and the bronze articles.

When King Tou of Hamath heard that David had defeated the entire army of King Hadadezer of Zobah, he sent his son Hadoram to King David to greet him and to congratulate him because David had fought against Hadadezer and defeated him, for Tou and Hadadezer had fought many wars. Hadoram brought all kinds of gold, silver, and bronze items. King David also dedicated these to the Lord, along with the silver and gold he had carried off from all the nations—from Edom, Moab, the Ammonites, the Philistines, and the Amalekites.

Abishai son of Zeruiah struck down eighteen thousand Edomites in the Salt Valley. He put garrisons in Edom, and all the Edomites were subject to David. The Lord made David victorious wherever he went.

So David reigned over all Israel, administering justice and righteousness for all his people.

> Joab son of Zeruiah was over the army;
> Jehoshaphat son of Ahilud was court historian;
> Zadok son of Ahitub and Ahimelech son of Abiathar were priests;
> Shavsha was court secretary;
> Benaiah son of Jehoiada was over the Cherethites and the Pelethites;
> and David's sons were the chief officials at the king's side.

19 Some time later, King Nahash of the Ammonites died, and his son became king in his place. Then David said, "I'll show kindness to Hanun son of Nahash, because his father showed kindness to me."

So David sent messengers to console him concerning his father. However, when David's emissaries arrived in the land of the Ammonites to console him, the Ammonite leaders said to Hanun, "Just because David has sent men with condolences for you, do you really believe he's showing respect for your father? Instead, haven't his emissaries come in order to scout out, overthrow, and spy on the land?" So Hanun took David's emissaries, shaved them, cut their clothes in half at the hips, and sent them away.

It was reported to David about his men, so he sent messengers to meet them, since the men 10 were deeply humiliated. The king said, "Stay in Jericho until your beards grow back; then return."

When the Ammonites realized they had made themselves repulsive to David, Hanun and the Ammonites sent thirty-eight tons of silver to hire chariots and horsemen from Aram-naharaim, Aram-maacah, and Zobah. They hired thirty-two thousand chariots and the king of Maacah with his army, who came and camped near Medeba. The Ammonites also came together from their cities for the battle.

David heard about this and sent Joab and all the elite troops. The Ammonites marched out and lined up in battle formation at the entrance of the city while the kings who had come were in the field by themselves. When Joab saw that there was a battle line in front of him and another behind him, he chose some of Israel's finest young men and lined up in formation to engage the 20 Arameans. He placed the rest of the forces under the command of his brother Abishai. They lined up in formation to engage the Ammonites.

"If the Arameans are too strong for me," Joab said, "then you'll be my help. However, if the Ammonites are too strong for you, I'll help you. Be strong! Let's prove ourselves strong for our people and for the cities of our God. May the Lord's will be done."

Joab and the people with him approached the Arameans for battle, and they fled before him. When the Ammonites saw that the Arameans had fled, they likewise fled before Joab's brother Abishai and entered the city. Then Joab went to Jerusalem.

When the Arameans realized that they had been defeated by Israel, they sent messengers to summon the Arameans who were beyond the Euphrates River. They were led by Shophach, the 30 commander of Hadadezer's army.

When this was reported to David, he gathered all Israel and crossed the Jordan. He came up to the Arameans and lined up against them. When David lined up to engage them, they fought against him. But the Arameans fled before Israel, and David killed seven thousand of their charioteers and forty thousand foot soldiers. He also killed Shophach, commander of the army. When Hadadezer's subjects saw that they had been defeated by Israel, they made peace with David and became his subjects. After this, the Arameans were never willing to help the Ammonites again.

20 In the spring when kings march out to war, Joab led the army and destroyed the Ammonites' land. He came to Rabbah and besieged it, but David remained in Jerusalem. Joab attacked Rabbah and demolished it. Then David took the crown from the head of their king, and it was placed on David's head. He found that the crown weighed seventy-five pounds of gold, and there was a precious stone in it. In addition, David took away a large quantity of plunder from the city. He brought out the people who were in it and put them to work with saws, iron picks, and axes. David did the same to all the Ammonite cities. Then he and all his troops returned to Jerusalem.

After this, a war broke out with the Philistines at Gezer. At that time Sibbecai the Hushathite killed Sippai, a descendant of the Rephaim, and the Philistines were subdued.

10   Once again there was a battle with the Philistines, and Elhanan son of Jair killed Lahmi the brother of Goliath of Gath. The shaft of his spear was like a weaver's beam.

There was still another battle at Gath where there was a man of extraordinary stature with six fingers on each hand and six toes on each foot—twenty-four in all. He, too, was descended from the giant. When he taunted Israel, Jonathan son of David's brother Shimei killed him.

These were the descendants of the giant in Gath killed by David and his soldiers.

21 Satan rose up against Israel and incited David to count the people of Israel. So David said to Joab and the commanders of the troops, "Go and count Israel from Beer-sheba to Dan and bring a report to me so I can know their number."

Joab replied, "May the LORD multiply the number of his people a hundred times over! My lord the king, aren't they all my lord's servants? Why does my lord want to do this? Why should he bring guilt on Israel?"

Yet the king's order prevailed over Joab. So Joab left and traveled throughout Israel and then returned to Jerusalem. Joab gave the total troop registration to David. In all Israel there were one million one hundred thousand armed men and in Judah itself four hundred seventy thousand

10   armed men. But he did not include Levi and Benjamin in the count because the king's command was detestable to him. This command was also evil in God's sight, so he afflicted Israel.

David said to God, "I have sinned greatly because I have done this thing. Now, please take away your servant's guilt, for I've been very foolish."

Then the LORD instructed Gad, David's seer, "Go and say to David, 'This is what the LORD says: I am offering you three choices. Choose one of them for yourself, and I will do it to you.'"

So Gad went to David and said to him, "This is what the LORD says: 'Take your choice: three years of famine, or three months of devastation by your foes with the sword of your enemy overtaking you, or three days of the sword of the LORD—a plague on the land, the angel of the LORD bringing destruction to the whole territory of Israel.' Now decide what answer I should take

20   back to the one who sent me."

David answered Gad, "I'm in anguish. Please, let me fall into the LORD's hands because his mercies are very great, but don't let me fall into human hands."

So the LORD sent a plague on Israel, and seventy thousand Israelite men died. Then God sent an angel to Jerusalem to destroy it, but when the angel was about to destroy the city, the LORD looked, relented concerning the destruction, and said to the angel who was destroying the people, "Enough, withdraw your hand now!" The angel of the LORD was then standing at the threshing floor of Ornan the Jebusite.

When David looked up and saw the angel of the LORD standing between earth and heaven, with his drawn sword in his hand stretched out over Jerusalem, David and the elders, covered in 30 sackcloth, fell facedown. David said to God, "Wasn't I the one who gave the order to count the people? I am the one who has sinned and acted very wickedly. But these sheep, what have they done? LORD my God, please let your hand be against me and against my father's family, but don't let the plague be against your people."

So the angel of the LORD ordered Gad to tell David to go and set up an altar to the LORD on the threshing floor of Ornan the Jebusite. David went up at Gad's command spoken in the name of the LORD.

Ornan was threshing wheat when he turned and saw the angel. His four sons, who were with him, hid. David came to Ornan, and when Ornan looked and saw David, he left the threshing floor and bowed to David with his face to the ground.

40 Then David said to Ornan, "Give me this threshing-floor plot so that I may build an altar to the LORD on it. Give it to me for the full price, so the plague on the people may be stopped."

Ornan said to David, "Take it! My lord the king may do whatever he wants. See, I give the oxen for the burnt offerings, the threshing sledges for the wood, and the wheat for the grain offering—I give it all."

King David answered Ornan, "No, I insist on paying the full price, for I will not take for the LORD what belongs to you or offer burnt offerings that cost me nothing."

So David gave Ornan fifteen pounds of gold for the plot. He built an altar to the LORD there and offered burnt offerings and fellowship offerings. He called on the LORD, and he answered him with fire from heaven on the altar of burnt offering.

Then the LORD spoke to the angel, and he put his sword back into its sheath. At that time, 50 David offered sacrifices there when he saw that the LORD answered him at the threshing floor of Ornan the Jebusite. The tabernacle of the LORD, which Moses made in the wilderness, and the altar of burnt offering were at the high place in Gibeon, but David could not go before it to inquire **22** of God, because he was terrified of the sword of the LORD's angel. Then David said, "This is the house of the LORD God, and this is the altar of burnt offering for Israel."

So David gave orders to gather the resident aliens that were in the land of Israel, and he appointed stonecutters to cut finished stones for building God's house. David supplied a great deal of iron to make the nails for the doors of the gates and for the fittings, together with an immeasurable quantity of bronze, and innumerable cedar logs because the Sidonians and Tyrians had brought a large quantity of cedar logs to David. David said, "My son Solomon is young and inexperienced, and the house that is to be built for the LORD must be exceedingly great and famous and glorious in all the lands. Therefore, I will make provision for it." So David made lavish preparations for it before his death.

Then he summoned his son Solomon and charged him to build a house for the LORD God of Israel. "My son," David said to Solomon, "It was in my heart to build a house for the name of the LORD my God, but the word of the LORD came to me: 'You have shed much blood and waged great wars. You are not to build a house for my name because you have shed so much blood on the ground before me. But a son will be born to you; he will be a man of rest. I will give him rest from all his surrounding enemies, for his name will be Solomon, and I will give peace and quiet to Israel during his reign. He is the one who will build a house for my name. He will be my son, and I will be his father. I will establish the throne of his kingdom over Israel forever.'

"Now, my son, may the LORD be with you, and may you succeed in building the house of the LORD your God, as he said about you. Above all, may the LORD give you insight and understanding when he puts you in charge of Israel so that you may keep the law of the LORD your God. Then you will succeed if you carefully follow the statutes and ordinances the LORD commanded Moses for Israel. Be strong and courageous. Don't be afraid or discouraged.

"Notice I have taken great pains to provide for the house of the LORD—3,775 tons of gold, 37,750 tons of silver, and bronze and iron that can't be weighed because there is so much of it. I have also provided timber and stone, but you will need to add more to them. You also have many workers: stonecutters, masons, carpenters, and people skilled in every kind of work in gold, silver, bronze, and iron—beyond number. Now begin the work, and may the LORD be with you."

Then David ordered all the leaders of Israel to help his son Solomon: "The LORD your God is with you, isn't he? And hasn't he given you rest on every side? For he has handed the land's inhabitants over to me, and the land has been subdued before the LORD and his people. Now determine in your mind and heart to seek the LORD your God. Get started building the LORD God's sanctuary so that you may bring the ark of the LORD's covenant and the holy articles of God to the temple that is to be built for the name of the LORD."

23 When David was old and full of days, he installed his son Solomon as king over Israel. Then he gathered all the leaders of Israel, the priests, and the Levites. The Levites thirty years old or more were counted; the total number of men was thirty-eight thousand by headcount. "Of these," David said, "twenty-four thousand are to be in charge of the work on the LORD's temple, six thousand are to be officers and judges, four thousand are to be gatekeepers, and four thousand are to praise the LORD with the instruments that I have made for worship."

Then David divided them into divisions according to Levi's sons: Gershom, Kohath, and Merari.

The Gershonites: Ladan and Shimei.

10 Ladan's sons: Jehiel was the first, then Zetham, and Joel—three.

Shimei's sons: Shelomoth, Haziel, and Haran—three. Those were the heads of the families of Ladan.

Shimei's sons: Jahath, Zizah, Jeush, and Beriah. Those were Shimei's sons—four. Jahath was the first and Zizah was the second; however, Jeush and Beriah did not have many sons, so they became one family and received a single assignment.

Kohath's sons: Amram, Izhar, Hebron, and Uzziel—four.

Amram's sons: Aaron and Moses.

Aaron, along with his descendants, was set apart forever to consecrate the most holy things, to burn incense in the presence of the Lord, to minister to him, and to pronounce blessings in his 20 name forever. As for Moses the man of God, his sons were named among the tribe of Levi.

Moses's sons: Gershom and Eliezer.

Gershom's sons: Shebuel was first.

Eliezer's sons were Rehabiah, first; Eliezer did not have any other sons, but Rehabiah's sons were very numerous.

Izhar's sons: Shelomith was first.

Hebron's sons: Jeriah was first, Amariah second, Jahaziel third, and Jekameam fourth.

Uzziel's sons: Micah was first, and Isshiah second.

Merari's sons: Mahli and Mushi.

Mahli's sons: Eleazar and Kish.

30 Eleazar died having no sons, only daughters. Their cousins, the sons of Kish, married them.

Mushi's sons: Mahli, Eder, and Jeremoth—three.

These were the descendants of Levi by their ancestral families—the family heads, according to their registration by name in the headcount—twenty years old or more, who worked in the service of the Lord's temple. For David said, "The Lord God of Israel has given rest to his people, and he has come to stay in Jerusalem forever. Also, the Levites no longer need to carry the tabernacle or any of the equipment for its service"—for according to the last words of David, the Levites twenty years old or more were to be counted—"but their duty will be to assist the descendants of Aaron with the service of the Lord's temple, being responsible for the courts and the chambers, the purification of all the holy things, and the work of the service of God's temple—as well as the 40 rows of the Bread of the Presence, the fine flour for the grain offering, the wafers of unleavened bread, the baking, the mixing, and all measurements of volume and length. They are also to stand every morning to give thanks and praise to the Lord, and likewise in the evening. Whenever burnt offerings are offered to the LORD on the Sabbaths, New Moons, and appointed festivals, they are to offer them regularly in the LORD's presence according to the number prescribed for them. They are to carry out their responsibilities for the tent of meeting, for the holy place, and for their relatives, the descendants of Aaron, in the service of the LORD's temple."

24 The divisions of the descendants of Aaron were as follows: Aaron's sons were Nadab, Abihu, Eleazar, and Ithamar. But Nadab and Abihu died before their father, and they had no sons, so Eleazar and Ithamar served as priests. Together with Zadok from the descendants of Eleazar and Ahimelech from the descendants of Ithamar, David divided them according to the assigned duties of their service. Since more leaders were found among Eleazar's descendants than Ithamar's, they were divided accordingly: sixteen heads of ancestral families were from Eleazar's descendants, and eight heads of ancestral families were from Ithamar's. They were assigned by lot, for there were officers of the sanctuary and officers of God among both Eleazar's and Ithamar's descendants.

The secretary, Shemaiah son of Nethanel, a Levite, recorded them in the presence of the king and the officers, the priest Zadok, Ahimelech son of Abiathar, and the heads of families of the priests and the Levites. One ancestral family was taken for Eleazar, and then one for Ithamar.

The first lot fell to Jehoiarib, the second to Jedaiah,
the third to Harim, the fourth to Seorim,
the fifth to Malchijah, the sixth to Mijamin,
the seventh to Hakkoz, the eighth to Abijah,
the ninth to Jeshua, the tenth to Shecaniah,
the eleventh to Eliashib, the twelfth to Jakim,
the thirteenth to Huppah, the fourteenth to Jeshebeab,
the fifteenth to Bilgah, the sixteenth to Immer,
the seventeenth to Hezir, the eighteenth to Happizzez,
the nineteenth to Pethahiah, the twentieth to Jehezkel,
the twenty-first to Jachin, the twenty-second to Gamul,
the twenty-third to Delaiah, and the twenty-fourth to Maaziah.

These had their assigned duties for service when they entered the LORD's temple, according to their regulations, which they received from their ancestor Aaron, as the LORD God of Israel had commanded him.

As for the rest of Levi's sons:
from Amram's sons: Shubael;
from Shubael's sons: Jehdeiah.
From Rehabiah:
from Rehabiah's sons: Isshiah was the first.

From the Izharites: Shelomoth;
from Shelomoth's sons: Jahath.
Hebron's sons:
Jeriah the first, Amariah the second,
Jahaziel the third, and Jekameam the fourth.
From Uzziel's sons: Micah;
from Micah's sons: Shamir.
Micah's brother: Isshiah;
40   from Isshiah's sons: Zechariah.
Merari's sons: Mahli and Mushi,
and from his sons, Jaaziah his son.
Merari's sons, by his son Jaaziah:
Shoham, Zaccur, and Ibri.
From Mahli: Eleazar, who had no sons.
From Kish, from Kish's sons: Jerahmeel.
Mushi's sons: Mahli, Eder, and Jerimoth.

Those were the descendants of the Levites according to their ancestral families. They also cast lots the same way as their relatives the descendants of Aaron did in the presence of King David,
50 Zadok, Ahimelech, and the heads of the families of the priests and Levites—the family heads and their younger brothers alike.

25 David and the officers of the army also set apart some of the sons of Asaph, Heman, and Jeduthun, who were to prophesy accompanied by lyres, harps, and cymbals. This is the list of the men who performed their service:
From Asaph's sons:
Zaccur, Joseph, Nethaniah, and Asarelah, sons of Asaph, under Asaph's authority, who prophesied under the authority of the king.
From Jeduthun: Jeduthun's sons:
Gedaliah, Zeri, Jeshaiah, Shimei, Hashabiah, and Mattithiah—six—under the authority of their father Jeduthun, prophesying to the accompaniment of lyres, giving thanks and praise to
10 the LORD.
From Heman: Heman's sons:
Bukkiah, Mattaniah, Uzziel, Shebuel, Jerimoth, Hananiah, Hanani, Eliathah, Giddalti, Romamti-ezer, Joshbekashah, Mallothi, Hothir, and Mahazioth. All these sons of Heman, the king's seer, were given by the promises of God to exalt him, for God had given Heman fourteen sons and three daughters.

All these men were under their own fathers' authority for the music in the Lord's temple, with cymbals, harps, and lyres for the service of God's temple. Asaph, Jeduthun, and Heman were under the king's authority. They numbered 288 together with their relatives who were all trained and skillful in music for the Lord. They cast lots for their duties, young and old alike, teacher as well as pupil.

The first lot for Asaph fell to Joseph, his sons, and his relatives— 12
to Gedaliah the second: him, his relatives, and his sons— 12
the third to Zaccur, his sons, and his relatives— 12
the fourth to Izri, his sons, and his relatives— 12
the fifth to Nethaniah, his sons, and his relatives— 12
the sixth to Bukkiah, his sons, and his relatives— 12
the seventh to Jesarelah, his sons, and his relatives— 12
the eighth to Jeshaiah, his sons, and his relatives— 12
the ninth to Mattaniah, his sons, and his relatives— 12
the tenth to Shimei, his sons, and his relatives— 12
the eleventh to Azarel, his sons, and his relatives— 12
the twelfth to Hashabiah, his sons, and his relatives— 12
the thirteenth to Shubael, his sons, and his relatives— 12
the fourteenth to Mattithiah, his sons, and his relatives— 12
the fifteenth to Jeremoth, his sons, and his relatives— 12
the sixteenth to Hananiah, his sons, and his relatives— 12
the seventeenth to Joshbekashah, his sons, and his relatives— 12
the eighteenth to Hanani, his sons, and his relatives— 12
the nineteenth to Mallothi, his sons, and his relatives— 12
the twentieth to Eliathah, his sons, and his relatives— 12
the twenty-first to Hothir, his sons, and his relatives— 12
the twenty-second to Giddalti, his sons, and his relatives— 12
the twenty-third to Mahazioth, his sons, and his relatives— 12
and the twenty-fourth to Romamti-ezer, his sons, and his relatives— 12.

26 The following were the divisions of the gatekeepers:

From the Korahites: Meshelemiah son of Kore, one of the sons of Asaph.
Meshelemiah had sons:
Zechariah the firstborn, Jediael the second,
Zebadiah the third, Jathniel the fourth,
Elam the fifth, Jehohanan the sixth,

and Eliehoenai the seventh.

Obed-edom also had sons:

Shemaiah the firstborn, Jehozabad the second,

10 Joah the third, Sachar the fourth,

Nethanel the fifth, Ammiel the sixth,

Issachar the seventh, and Peullethai the eighth,

for God blessed him.

Also, to his son Shemaiah were born sons who ruled their ancestral families because they were strong, capable men.

Shemaiah's sons: Othni, Rephael, Obed, and Elzabad; his relatives Elihu and Semachiah were also capable men. All of these were among the sons of Obed-edom with their sons and relatives; they were capable men with strength for the work—sixty-two from Obed-edom. Meshelemiah also had sons and relatives who were capable men—eighteen.

20 Hosah, from the Merarites, also had sons: Shimri the first (although he was not the firstborn, his father had appointed him as the first), Hilkiah the second, Tebaliah the third, and Zechariah the fourth. The sons and relatives of Hosah were thirteen in all.

These divisions of the gatekeepers, under their leading men, had duties for ministering in the LORD's temple, just as their relatives did. They cast lots for each temple gate according to their ancestral families, young and old alike.

The lot for the east gate fell to Shelemiah. They also cast lots for his son Zechariah, an insightful counselor, and his lot came out for the north gate. Obed-edom's was the south gate, and his sons' lot was for the storehouses; it was the west gate and the gate of Shallecheth on the ascending highway for Shuppim and Hosah.

30 There were guards stationed at every watch. There were six Levites each day on the east, four each day on the north, four each day on the south, and two pair at the storehouses. As for the court on the west, there were four at the highway and two at the court. Those were the divisions of the gatekeepers from the descendants of the Korahites and Merarites.

From the Levites, Ahijah was in charge of the treasuries of God's temple and the treasuries of what had been dedicated. From the sons of Ladan, who were the descendants of the Gershonites through Ladan and were the family heads belonging to Ladan the Gershonite: Jehieli. The sons of Jehieli, Zetham and his brother Joel, were in charge of the treasuries of the LORD's temple.

From the Amramites, the Izharites, the Hebronites, and the Uzzielites: Shebuel, a descendant of Moses's son Gershom, was the officer in charge of the treasuries. His relatives through Eliezer:

40 his son Rehabiah, his son Jeshaiah, his son Joram, his son Zichri, and his son Shelomith. This Shelomith and his relatives were in charge of all the treasuries of what had been dedicated by King David, by the family heads who were the commanders of thousands and of hundreds, and

by the army commanders. They dedicated part of the plunder from their battles for the repair of the LORD's temple. All that the seer Samuel, Saul son of Kish, Abner son of Ner, and Joab son of Zeruiah had dedicated, along with everything else that had been dedicated, were in the care of Shelomith and his relatives.

From the Izrahites: Chenaniah and his sons had duties outside the temple as officers and judges over Israel. From the Hebronites: Hashabiah and his relatives, 1,700 capable men, had assigned duties in Israel west of the Jordan for all the work of the LORD and for the service of
50 the king. From the Hebronites: Jerijah was the head of the Hebronites, according to the family records of his ancestors. A search was made in the fortieth year of David's reign and strong, capable men were found among them at Jazer in Gilead. There were among Jerijah's relatives 2,700 capable men who were family heads. King David appointed them over the Reubenites, the Gadites, and half the tribe of Manasseh as overseers in every matter relating to God and the king.

27 This is the list of the Israelites, the family heads, the commanders of thousands and the commanders of hundreds, and their officers who served the king in every matter to do with the divisions that were on rotated military duty each month throughout the year. There were 24,000 in each division:

Jashobeam son of Zabdiel was in charge of the first division, for the first month; 24,000 were in his division. He was a descendant of Perez and chief of all the army commanders for the first month.

Dodai the Ahohite was in charge of the division for the second month, and Mikloth was the leader; 24,000 were in his division.

The third army commander, as chief for the third month, was Benaiah son of the priest
10 Jehoiada; 24,000 were in his division. This Benaiah was a mighty man among the Thirty and over the Thirty, and his son Ammizabad was in charge of his division.

The fourth commander, for the fourth month, was Joab's brother Asahel, and his son Zebadiah was commander after him; 24,000 were in his division.

The fifth, for the fifth month, was the commander Shamhuth the Izrahite; 24,000 were in his division.

The sixth, for the sixth month, was Ira son of Ikkesh the Tekoite; 24,000 were in his division.

The seventh, for the seventh month, was Helez the Pelonite from the descendants of Ephraim; 24,000 were in his division.

The eighth, for the eighth month, was Sibbecai the Hushathite, a Zerahite; 24,000 were in his
20 division.

The ninth, for the ninth month, was Abiezer the Anathothite, a Benjaminite; 24,000 were in his division.

The tenth, for the tenth month, was Maharai the Netophathite, a Zerahite; 24,000 were in his division.

The eleventh, for the eleventh month, was Benaiah the Pirathonite from the descendants of Ephraim; 24,000 were in his division.

The twelfth, for the twelfth month, was Heldai the Netophathite, of Othniel's family; 24,000 were in his division.

The following were in charge of the tribes of Israel:

30 For the Reubenites, Eliezer son of Zichri was the chief official;

for the Simeonites, Shephatiah son of Maacah;

for the Levites, Hashabiah son of Kemuel; for Aaron, Zadok;

for Judah, Elihu, one of David's brothers; for Issachar, Omri son of Michael;

for Zebulun, Ishmaiah son of Obadiah;

for Naphtali, Jerimoth son of Azriel;

for the Ephraimites, Hoshea son of Azaziah;

for half the tribe of Manasseh, Joel son of Pedaiah;

for half the tribe of Manasseh in Gilead, Iddo son of Zechariah;

for Benjamin, Jaasiel son of Abner;

40 for Dan, Azarel son of Jeroham.

Those were the leaders of the tribes of Israel.

David didn't count the men aged twenty or under, for the Lord had said he would make Israel as numerous as the stars of the sky. Joab son of Zeruiah began to count them, but he didn't complete it. There was wrath against Israel because of this census, and the number was not entered in the Historical Record of King David.

Azmaveth son of Adiel was in charge of the king's storehouses.

Jonathan son of Uzziah was in charge of the storehouses in the country, in the cities, in the villages, and in the fortresses.

Ezri son of Chelub was in charge of those who worked in the fields tilling the soil.

50 Shimei the Ramathite was in charge of the vineyards.

Zabdi the Shiphmite was in charge of the produce of the vineyards for the wine cellars.

Baal-hanan the Gederite was in charge of the olive and sycamore trees in the Judean foothills.

Joash was in charge of the stores of olive oil.

Shitrai the Sharonite was in charge of the herds that grazed in Sharon, while Shaphat son of Adlai was in charge of the herds in the valleys.

Obil the Ishmaelite was in charge of the camels.

Jehdeiah the Meronothite was in charge of the donkeys.

Jaziz the Hagrite was in charge of the flocks.

All these were officials in charge of King David's property.

60   David's uncle Jonathan was a counselor; he was a man of understanding and a scribe. Jehiel son of Hachmoni attended the king's sons. Ahithophel was the king's counselor. Hushai the Archite was the king's friend. After Ahithophel came Jehoiada son of Benaiah, then Abiathar. Joab was the commander of the king's army.

28 David assembled all the leaders of Israel in Jerusalem: the leaders of the tribes, the leaders of the divisions in the king's service, the commanders of thousands and the commanders of hundreds, and the officials in charge of all the property and cattle of the king and his sons, along with the court officials, the fighting men, and all the best soldiers. Then King David rose to his feet and said, "Listen to me, my brothers and my people. It was in my heart to build a house as a resting place for the ark of the LORD's covenant and as a footstool for our God. I had made preparations to build, but God said to me, 'You are not to build a house for my name because you are a man of war and have shed blood.'

    "Yet the LORD God of Israel chose me out of all my father's family to be king over Israel forever. For he chose Judah as leader, and from the house of Judah, my father's family, and from
10 my father's sons, he was pleased to make me king over all Israel. And out of all my sons—for the LORD has given me many sons—he has chosen my son Solomon to sit on the throne of the LORD's kingdom over Israel. He said to me, 'Your son Solomon is the one who is to build my house and my courts, for I have chosen him to be my son, and I will be his father. I will establish his kingdom forever if he perseveres in keeping my commands and my ordinances as he is doing today.'

    "So now in the sight of all Israel, the assembly of the LORD, and in the hearing of our God, observe and follow all the commands of the LORD your God so that you may possess this good land and leave it as an inheritance to your descendants forever.

    "As for you, Solomon my son, know the God of your father, and serve him wholeheartedly and with a willing mind, for the LORD searches every heart and understands the intention of
20 every thought. If you seek him, he will be found by you, but if you abandon him, he will reject you forever. Realize now that the LORD has chosen you to build a house for the sanctuary. Be strong, and do it."

    Then David gave his son Solomon the plans for the portico of the temple and its buildings, treasuries, upstairs rooms, inner rooms, and a room for the mercy seat. The plans contained everything he had in mind for the courts of the LORD's house, all the surrounding chambers, the treasuries of God's house, and the treasuries for what is dedicated. Also included were plans for the divisions of the priests and the Levites; all the work of service in the LORD's house; all the articles of service of the LORD's house; the weight of gold for all the articles for every kind of service; the weight of all the silver articles for every kind of service; the weight of the gold
30 lampstands and their gold lamps, including the weight of each lampstand and its lamps; the weight of each silver lampstand and its lamps, according to the service of each lampstand; the weight of gold for each table for the rows of the Bread of the Presence and the silver for the silver tables; the pure gold for the forks, sprinkling basins, and pitchers; the weight of each gold dish; the weight of

each silver bowl; the weight of refined gold for the altar of incense; and the plans for the chariot of the gold cherubim that spread out their wings and cover the ark of the LORD's covenant.

David concluded, "By the LORD's hand on me, he enabled me to understand everything in writing, all the details of the plan."

Then David said to his son Solomon, "Be strong and courageous, and do the work. Don't be afraid or discouraged, for the LORD God, my God, is with you. He won't leave you or abandon you until all the work for the service of the LORD's house is finished. Here are the divisions of the priests and the Levites for all the service of God's house. Every willing person of any skill will be at your disposal for the work, and the leaders and all the people are at your every command."

29 Then King David said to all the assembly, "My son Solomon—God has chosen him alone—is young and inexperienced. The task is great because the building will not be built for a human but for the LORD God. So to the best of my ability I've made provision for the house of my God: gold for the gold articles, silver for the silver, bronze for the bronze, iron for the iron, and wood for the wood, as well as onyx, stones for mounting, antimony, stones of various colors, all kinds of precious stones, and a great quantity of marble. Moreover, because of my delight in the house of my God, I now give my personal treasures of gold and silver for the house of my God over and above all that I've provided for the holy house: 100 tons of gold (gold of Ophir) and 250 tons of refined silver for overlaying the walls of the buildings, the gold for the gold work and the silver for the silver, for all the work to be done by the craftsmen. Now who will volunteer to consecrate himself to the LORD today?"

Then the leaders of the households, the leaders of the tribes of Israel, the commanders of thousands and of hundreds, and the officials in charge of the king's work gave willingly. For the service of God's house they gave 185 tons of gold and 10,000 gold coins, 375 tons of silver, 675 tons of bronze, and 4,000 tons of iron. Whoever had precious stones gave them to the treasury of the LORD's house under the care of Jehiel the Gershonite. Then the people rejoiced because of their leaders' willingness to give, for they had given to the LORD wholeheartedly. King David also rejoiced greatly.

Then David blessed the LORD in the sight of all the assembly. David said,
May you be blessed, LORD God of our father Israel, from eternity to eternity. Yours, LORD, is the greatness and the power and the glory and the splendor and the majesty, for everything in the heavens and on earth belongs to you. Yours, LORD, is the kingdom, and you are exalted as head over all. Riches and honor come from you, and you are the ruler of everything. Power and might are in your hand, and it is in your hand to make great and to give strength to all. Now therefore, our God, we give you thanks and praise your glorious name.

But who am I, and who are my people, that we should be able to give as generously as this? For everything comes from you, and we have given you only what comes from your own hand. For we are aliens and temporary residents in your presence as were all our ancestors. Our days on earth are like a shadow, without hope. Lord our God, all this wealth that we've provided for building you a house for your holy name comes from your hand; everything belongs to you.

30   I know, my God, that you test the heart and that you are pleased with what is right. I have willingly given all these things with an upright heart, and now I have seen your people who are present here giving joyfully and willingly to you. Lord God of Abraham, Isaac, and Israel, our ancestors, keep this desire forever in the thoughts of the hearts of your people, and confirm their hearts toward you. Give my son Solomon an undivided heart to keep and to carry out all your commands, your decrees, and your statutes, and to build the building for which I have made provision.

    Then David said to the whole assembly, "Blessed be the Lord your God." So the whole assembly praised the Lord God of their ancestors. They knelt low and paid homage to the Lord and the king.

40   The following day they offered sacrifices to the Lord and burnt offerings to the Lord: a thousand bulls, a thousand rams, and a thousand lambs, along with their drink offerings, and sacrifices in abundance for all Israel. They ate and drank with great joy in the Lord's presence that day.

    Then, for a second time, they made David's son Solomon king; they anointed him as the Lord's ruler, and Zadok as the priest. Solomon sat on the Lord's throne as king in place of his father David. He prospered, and all Israel obeyed him. All the leaders and the mighty men, and all of King David's sons as well, pledged their allegiance to King Solomon. The Lord highly exalted Solomon in the sight of all Israel and bestowed on him such royal majesty as had not been bestowed on any king over Israel before him.

50   David son of Jesse was king over all Israel. The length of his reign over Israel was forty years; he reigned in Hebron for seven years and in Jerusalem for thirty-three. He died at a good old age, full of days, riches, and honor, and his son Solomon became king in his place. As for the events of King David's reign, from beginning to end, note that they are written in the Events of the Seer Samuel, the Events of the Prophet Nathan, and the Events of the Seer Gad, along with all his reign, his might, and the incidents that affected him and Israel and all the kingdoms of the surrounding lands.

2 Chronicles

1 Solomon son of David strengthened his hold on his kingdom. The LORD his God was with him and highly exalted him. Then Solomon spoke to all Israel, to the commanders of thousands and of hundreds, to the judges, and to every leader in all Israel—the family heads. Solomon and the whole assembly with him went to the high place that was in Gibeon because God's tent of meeting, which the LORD's servant Moses had made in the wilderness, was there. Now David had brought the ark of God from Kiriath-jearim to the place he had set up for it, because he had pitched a tent for it in Jerusalem, but he put the bronze altar, which Bezalel son of Uri, son of Hur, had made, in front of the LORD's tabernacle. Solomon and the assembly inquired of him there. Solomon offered sacrifices there in the LORD's presence on the bronze altar at the tent of meeting; he offered a thousand burnt offerings on it.

That night God appeared to Solomon and said to him, "Ask. What should I give you?"

And Solomon said to God, "You have shown great and faithful love to my father David, and you have made me king in his place. LORD God, let your promise to my father David now come true. For you have made me king over a people as numerous as the dust of the earth. Now grant me wisdom and knowledge so that I may lead these people, for who can judge this great people of yours?"

God said to Solomon, "Since this was in your heart, and you have not requested riches, wealth, or glory, or for the life of those who hate you, and you have not even requested long life, but you have requested for yourself wisdom and knowledge that you may judge my people over whom I have made you king, wisdom and knowledge are given to you. I will also give you riches, wealth, and glory, unlike what was given to the kings who were before you, or will be given to those after you." So Solomon went to Jerusalem from the high place that was in Gibeon in front of the tent of meeting, and he reigned over Israel.

Solomon accumulated 1,400 chariots and 12,000 horsemen, which he stationed in the chariot cities and with the king in Jerusalem. The king made silver and gold as common in Jerusalem as stones, and he made cedar as abundant as sycamore in the Judean foothills. Solomon's horses came from Egypt and Kue. The king's traders would get them from Kue at the going price. A chariot could be imported from Egypt for fifteen pounds of silver and a horse for nearly four pounds. In the same way, they exported them to all the kings of the Hittites and to the kings of Aram through their agents.

Solomon decided to build a temple for the name of the LORD and a royal palace for himself, so he assigned 70,000 men as porters, 80,000 men as stonecutters in the mountains, and 3,600 as supervisors over them.

Then Solomon sent word to King Hiram of Tyre:

Do for me what you did for my father David. You sent him cedars to build him a house to live in. Now I am building a temple for the name of the LORD my God in order to dedicate it to him for burning fragrant incense before him, for displaying the rows of the Bread of the Presence continuously, and for sacrificing burnt offerings for the morning and the evening, the Sabbaths and the New Moons, and the appointed festivals of the LORD our God. This is ordained for Israel permanently. The temple that I am building will be great, for our God is greater than any of the gods. But who is able to build a temple for him, since even heaven and the highest heaven cannot contain him? Who am I then that I should build a temple for him except as a place to burn incense before him? Therefore, send me an artisan who is skilled in engraving to work with gold, silver, bronze, and iron, and with purple, crimson, and blue yarn. He will work with the artisans who are with me in Judah and Jerusalem, appointed by my father David. Also, send me cedar, cypress, and algum logs from Lebanon, for I know that your servants know how to cut the trees of Lebanon. Note that my servants will be with your servants to prepare logs for me in abundance because the temple I am building will be great and wondrous. I will give your servants, the woodcutters who cut the trees, one hundred twenty thousand bushels of wheat flour, one hundred twenty thousand bushels of barley, one hundred twenty thousand gallons of wine, and one hundred twenty thousand gallons of oil.

Then King Hiram of Tyre wrote a letter and sent it to Solomon:

Because the LORD loves his people, he set you over them as king.

Hiram also said:

Blessed be the LORD God of Israel, who made the heavens and the earth! He gave King David a wise son with insight and understanding, who will build a temple for the LORD and a royal palace for himself. I have now sent Huram-abi, a skillful man who has understanding. He is the son of a woman from the daughters of Dan. His father is a man of Tyre. He knows how to work with gold, silver, bronze, iron, stone, and wood, with purple, blue, crimson yarn, and fine linen. He knows how to do all kinds of engraving and to execute any design that may be given him. I have sent him to be with your artisans and the artisans of my lord, your father David. Now, let my lord send the wheat, barley, oil, and wine to his servants as promised. We will cut logs from Lebanon, as many as you need, and bring them to you as rafts by sea to Joppa. You can then take them up to Jerusalem.

Solomon took a census of all the resident alien men in the land of Israel, after the census that his father David had conducted, and the total was 153,600. Solomon made 70,000 of them porters, 80,000 stonecutters in the mountains, and 3,600 supervisors to make the people work.

3 Then Solomon began to build the LORD's temple in Jerusalem on Mount Moriah where the LORD had appeared to his father David, at the site David had prepared on the threshing floor of Ornan the Jebusite. He began to build on the second day of the second month in the fourth year of his reign. These are Solomon's foundations for building God's temple: the length was ninety feet, and the width thirty feet. The portico, which was across the front extending across the width of the temple, was thirty feet wide; its height was thirty feet; he overlaid its inner surface with pure gold. The larger room he paneled with cypress wood, overlaid with fine gold, and decorated with palm trees and chains. He adorned the temple with precious stones for beauty, and the gold was the gold of Parvaim. He overlaid the temple— the beams, the thresholds, its walls and doors—with gold, and he carved cherubim on the walls.

10 Then he made the most holy place; its length corresponded to the width of the temple, 30 feet, and its width was 30 feet. He overlaid it with forty-five thousand pounds of fine gold. The weight of the nails was twenty ounces of gold, and he overlaid the ceiling with gold.

He made two cherubim of sculptured work, for the most holy place, and he overlaid them with gold. The overall length of the wings of the cherubim was 30 feet: the wing of one was 7 ½ feet, touching the wall of the room; its other wing was 7 ½ feet, touching the wing of the other cherub. The wing of the other cherub was 7 ½ feet, touching the wall of the room; its other wing was 7 ½ feet, reaching the wing of the other cherub. The wingspan of these cherubim was 30 feet. They stood on their feet and faced the larger room.

He made the curtain of blue, purple, and crimson yarn and fine linen, and he wove cherubim 20 into it.

In front of the temple he made two pillars, each 27 feet high. The capital on top of each was 7 ½ feet high. He had made chainwork in the inner sanctuary and also put it on top of the pillars. He made a hundred pomegranates and fastened them into the chainwork. Then he set up the pillars in front of the sanctuary, one on the right and one on the left. He named the one on the right Jachin and the one on the left Boaz.

4 He made a bronze altar 30 feet long, 30 feet wide, and 15 feet high.

Then he made the cast metal basin, 15 feet from brim to brim, perfectly round. It was 7 ½ feet high and 45 feet in circumference. The likeness of oxen was below it, completely encircling it, ten every half yard, completely surrounding the basin. The oxen were cast in two rows when the basin was cast. It stood on twelve oxen, three facing north, three facing west, three facing south, and three facing east. The basin was on top of them and all their hindquarters were toward the center. The basin was three inches thick, and its rim was fashioned like the brim of a cup or a lily blossom. It could hold eleven thousand gallons.

He made ten basins for washing and he put five on the right and five on the left. The parts of the burnt offering were rinsed in them, but the basin was used by the priests for washing.

He made the ten gold lampstands according to their specifications and put them in the sanctuary, five on the right and five on the left. He made ten tables and placed them in the sanctuary, five on the right and five on the left. He also made a hundred gold bowls.

He made the courtyard of the priests and the large court, and doors for the court. He overlaid the doors with bronze. He put the basin on the right side, toward the southeast. Then Huram made the pots, the shovels, and the bowls.

So Huram finished doing the work that he was doing for King Solomon in God's temple: two pillars; the bowls and the capitals on top of the two pillars; the two gratings for covering both bowls of the capitals that were on top of the pillars; the four hundred pomegranates for the two gratings (two rows of pomegranates for each grating covering both capitals' bowls on top of the pillars). He also made the water carts and the basins on the water carts. The one basin and the twelve oxen underneath it, the pots, the shovels, the forks, and all their utensils—Huram-abi made them for King Solomon for the LORD's temple. All these were made of polished bronze. The king had them cast in clay molds in the Jordan Valley between Succoth and Zeredah. Solomon made all these utensils in such great abundance that the weight of the bronze was not determined.

Solomon also made all the equipment in God's temple: the gold altar; the tables on which to put the Bread of the Presence; the lampstands and their lamps of pure gold to burn in front of the inner sanctuary according to specifications; the flowers, lamps, and gold tongs—of purest gold; the wick trimmers, sprinkling basins, ladles, and firepans—of purest gold; and the entryway to the temple, its inner doors to the most holy place, and the doors of the temple sanctuary—of gold.

5 So all the work Solomon did for the LORD's temple was completed. Then Solomon brought the consecrated things of his father David—the silver, the gold, and all the utensils—and put them in the treasuries of God's temple.

At that time Solomon assembled at Jerusalem the elders of Israel—all the tribal heads, the ancestral chiefs of the Israelites—in order to bring the ark of the covenant of the LORD up from the city of David, that is, Zion. So all the men of Israel were assembled in the king's presence at the festival; this was in the seventh month.

All the elders of Israel came, and the Levites picked up the ark. They brought up the ark, the tent of meeting, and the holy utensils that were in the tent. The priests and the Levites brought them up. King Solomon and the entire congregation of Israel who had gathered around him were in front of the ark sacrificing sheep, goats, and cattle that could not be counted or numbered because there were so many. The priests brought the ark of the LORD's covenant to its place, into the inner sanctuary of the temple, to the most holy place, beneath the wings of the cherubim. And the cherubim spread their wings over the place of the ark so that the cherubim formed a cover above the ark and its poles. The poles were so long that their ends were seen from the holy place in front of the inner sanctuary, but they were not seen from outside; they are still there today. Nothing was in the ark except the two tablets that Moses had put in it at Horeb, where the LORD had made a covenant with the Israelites when they came out of Egypt.

Now all the priests who were present had consecrated themselves regardless of their divisions. When the priests came out of the holy place, the Levitical singers dressed in fine linen and carrying cymbals, harps, and lyres were standing east of the altar, and with them were 120 priests blowing trumpets. The Levitical singers were descendants of Asaph, Heman, and Jeduthun and their sons and relatives. The trumpeters and singers joined together to praise and thank the LORD with one voice. They raised their voices, accompanied by trumpets, cymbals, and musical instruments, in praise to the LORD:

> For he is good;
> his faithful love endures forever.

The temple, the LORD's temple, was filled with a cloud. And because of the cloud, the priests were not able to continue ministering, for the glory of the LORD filled God's temple.

6 Then Solomon said:
> The LORD said he would dwell in total darkness,
> but I have built an exalted temple for you,
> a place for your dwelling forever.

Then the king turned and blessed the entire congregation of Israel while they were standing. He said:
> Blessed be the LORD God of Israel!
> He spoke directly to my father David,
> and he has fulfilled the promise
> by his power.

He said,
"Since the day I brought my people Israel
out of the land of Egypt,
I have not chosen a city to build a temple in
among any of the tribes of Israel,
so that my name would be there,
and I have not chosen a man
to be ruler over my people Israel.
But I have chosen Jerusalem
20   so that my name will be there,
and I have chosen David
to be over my people Israel."

My father David had his heart set
on building a temple for the name of the Lord, the God of Israel.
However, the Lord said to my father David,
"Since it was your desire to build a temple for my name,
you have done well to have this desire.
Yet, you are not the one to build the temple,
but your son, your own offspring,
30   will build the temple for my name."
So the Lord has fulfilled what he promised.
I have taken the place of my father David
and I sit on the throne of Israel, as the Lord promised.
I have built the temple for the name of the Lord, the God of Israel.
I have put the ark there,
where the Lord's covenant is
that he made with the Israelites.

Then Solomon stood before the altar of the Lord in front of the entire congregation of Israel
and spread out his hands. For Solomon had made a bronze platform 7 ½ feet long, 7 ½ feet
40   wide, and 4 ½ feet high and put it in the court. He stood on it, knelt down in front of the entire
congregation of Israel, and spread out his hands toward heaven. He said:
Lord God of Israel,
there is no God like you
in heaven or on earth,
who keeps his gracious covenant
with your servants who walk before you

with all their heart.
You have kept what you promised
to your servant, my father David.
50 You spoke directly to him,
and you fulfilled your promise by your power,
as it is today.
Therefore, Lord God of Israel,
keep what you promised
to your servant, my father David:
"You will never fail to have a man
to sit before me on the throne of Israel,
if only your sons take care to walk in my Law
as you have walked before me."
60 Now, Lord God of Israel, please confirm
what you promised to your servant David.

But will God indeed live on earth with humans?
Even heaven, the highest heaven, cannot contain you,
much less this temple I have built.
Listen to your servant's prayer and his petition,
Lord my God,
so that you may hear the cry and the prayer
that your servant prays before you,
so that your eyes watch over this temple
70 day and night,
toward the place where you said
you would put your name;
and so that you may hear the prayer
your servant prays toward this place.
Hear the petitions of your servant
and your people Israel,
which they pray toward this place.
May you hear in your dwelling place in heaven.
May you hear and forgive.

80 If a man sins against his neighbor
and is forced to take an oath
and he comes to take an oath

before your altar in this temple,
may you hear in heaven and act.
May you judge your servants,
condemning the wicked man by bringing
what he has done on his own head
and providing justice for the righteous
by rewarding him according to his righteousness.

90 If your people Israel are defeated before an enemy,
because they have sinned against you,
and they return to you and praise your name,
and they pray and plead for mercy
before you in this temple,
may you hear in heaven
and forgive the sin of your people Israel.
May you restore them to the land
you gave them and their ancestors.

When the skies are shut and there is no rain
100 because they have sinned against you,
and they pray toward this place
and praise your name,
and they turn from their sins
because you are afflicting them,
may you hear in heaven
and forgive the sin of your servants
and your people Israel,
so that you may teach them the good way
they should walk in.
110 May you send rain on your land
that you gave your people for an inheritance.

When there is famine in the land,
when there is pestilence,
when there is blight or mildew, locust or grasshopper,
when their enemies besiege them
in the land and its cities,
when there is any plague or illness,

every prayer or petition
that any person or that all your people Israel may have—
they each know their own affliction and suffering—
as they spread out their hands toward this temple,
may you hear in heaven, your dwelling place,
and may you forgive and give to everyone
according to all their ways, since you know each heart,
for you alone know the human heart,
so that they may fear you
and walk in your ways
all the days they live on the land
you gave our ancestors.

Even for the foreigner who is not of your people Israel
but has come from a distant land
because of your great name
and your strong hand and outstretched arm:
when he comes and prays toward this temple,
may you hear in heaven in your dwelling place,
and do all the foreigner asks you.
Then all the peoples of the earth will know your name,
to fear you as your people Israel do
and know that this temple I have built
bears your name.

When your people go out to fight against their enemies,
wherever you send them,
and they pray to you
in the direction of this city you have chosen
and the temple that I have built for your name,
may you hear their prayer and petition in heaven
and uphold their cause.

When they sin against you—
for there is no one who does not sin—
and you are angry with them
and hand them over to the enemy,
and their captors deport them

to a distant or nearby country,
and when they come to their senses
in the land where they were deported
and repent and petition you in their captors' land,
saying, "We have sinned and done wrong;
we have been wicked,"
and when they return to you with all their mind and all their heart
160   in the land of their captivity where they were taken captive,
and when they pray in the direction of their land
that you gave their ancestors,
and the city you have chosen,
and toward the temple I have built for your name,
may you hear their prayer and petitions in heaven,
your dwelling place,
and uphold their cause.
May you forgive your people
who sinned against you.

170   Now, my God,
please let your eyes be open
and your ears attentive
to the prayer of this place.
Now therefore:

Arise, Lord God, come to your resting place,
you and your powerful ark.
May your priests, Lord God, be clothed with salvation,
and may your faithful people rejoice in goodness.
Lord God, do not reject your anointed one;
180   remember your servant David's acts of faithful love.

7 When Solomon finished praying, fire descended from heaven and consumed the burnt offering and the sacrifices, and the glory of the Lord filled the temple. The priests were not able to enter the Lord's temple because the glory of the Lord filled the temple of the Lord. All the Israelites were watching when the fire descended and the glory of the Lord came on the temple. They bowed down on the pavement with their faces to the ground. They worshiped and praised the Lord:
    For he is good,
    for his faithful love endures forever.

The king and all the people were offering sacrifices in the LORD's presence. King Solomon offered a sacrifice of twenty-two thousand cattle and one hundred twenty thousand sheep and goats. In this manner the king and all the people dedicated God's temple. The priests and the Levites were standing at their stations. The Levites had the musical instruments of the LORD, which King David had made to give thanks to the LORD—"for his faithful love endures forever"—when he offered praise with them. Across from the Levites, the priests were blowing trumpets, and all the people were standing. Since the bronze altar that Solomon had made could not accommodate the burnt offering, the grain offering, and the fat of the fellowship offerings, Solomon first consecrated the middle of the courtyard that was in front of the LORD's temple and then offered the burnt offerings and the fat of the fellowship offerings there.

So Solomon and all Israel with him—a very great assembly, from the entrance to Hamath to the Brook of Egypt—observed the festival at that time for seven days. On the eighth day they held a solemn assembly, for the dedication of the altar lasted seven days and the festival seven days. On the twenty-third day of the seventh month he sent the people home, rejoicing and with happy hearts for the goodness the LORD had done for David, for Solomon, and for his people Israel.

So Solomon finished the LORD's temple and the royal palace. Everything that had entered Solomon's heart to do for the LORD's temple and for his own palace succeeded.

Then the LORD appeared to Solomon at night and said to him:

I have heard your prayer and have chosen this place for myself as a temple of sacrifice. If I shut the sky so there is no rain, or if I command the grasshopper to consume the land, or if I send pestilence on my people, and my people, who bear my name, humble themselves, pray and seek my face, and turn from their evil ways, then I will hear from heaven, forgive their sin, and heal their land. My eyes will now be open and my ears attentive to prayer from this place. And I have now chosen and consecrated this temple so that my name may be there forever; my eyes and my heart will be there at all times.

As for you, if you walk before me as your father David walked, doing everything I have commanded you, and if you keep my statutes and ordinances, I will establish your royal throne, as I promised your father David: You will never fail to have a man ruling in Israel.

However, if you turn away and abandon my statutes and my commands that I have set before you and if you go and serve other gods and bow in worship to them, then I will uproot Israel from the soil that I gave them, and this temple that I have sanctified for my name I will banish from my presence; I will make it an object of scorn and ridicule among all the peoples. As for this temple, which was exalted, everyone who passes by will be appalled and will say, "Why did the Lord do this to this land and this temple?" Then they will say, "Because they abandoned the Lord God of their ancestors who brought them out of the land of Egypt. They clung to other gods and bowed in worship to them and served them. Because of this, he brought all this ruin on them."

8 At the end of twenty years during which Solomon had built the Lord's temple and his own palace—Solomon had rebuilt the cities Hiram gave him and settled Israelites there—Solomon went to Hamath-zobah and seized it. He built Tadmor in the wilderness along with all the storage cities that he built in Hamath. He built Upper Beth-horon and Lower Beth-horon—fortified cities with walls, gates, and bars—Baalath, all the storage cities that belonged to Solomon, all the chariot cities, the cavalry cities, and everything Solomon desired to build in Jerusalem, Lebanon, or anywhere else in the land of his dominion.

As for all the peoples who remained of the Hethites, Amorites, Perizzites, Hivites, and Jebusites, who were not from Israel—their descendants who remained in the land after them, those the Israelites had not completely destroyed—Solomon imposed forced labor on them; it is this way today. But Solomon did not consign the Israelites to be slaves for his work; they were soldiers, commanders of his captains, and commanders of his chariots and his cavalry. These were King Solomon's deputies: 250 who supervised the people.

Solomon brought the daughter of Pharaoh from the city of David to the house he had built for her, for he said, "My wife must not live in the house of King David of Israel because the places the ark of the Lord has come into are holy."

At that time Solomon offered burnt offerings to the Lord on the Lord's altar he had made in front of the portico. He followed the daily requirement for offerings according to the commandment of Moses for Sabbaths, New Moons, and the three annual appointed festivals: the Festival of Unleavened Bread, the Festival of Weeks, and the Festival of Shelters. According to the ordinances of his father David, he appointed the divisions of the priests over their service, of the Levites over their responsibilities to offer praise and to minister before the priests following the daily requirement, and of the gatekeepers by their divisions with respect to each temple gate, for this had been the command of David, the man of God. They did not turn aside from the king's command regarding the priests and the Levites concerning any matter or concerning the treasuries. All of Solomon's work was carried out from the day the foundation was laid for the Lord's temple until it was finished. So the Lord's temple was completed.

At that time Solomon went to Ezion-geber and to Eloth on the seashore in the land of Edom. So Hiram sent ships to him by his servants along with crews of experienced seamen. They went with Solomon's servants to Ophir, took from there seventeen tons of gold, and delivered it to King Solomon.

9 The queen of Sheba heard of Solomon's fame, so she came to test Solomon with difficult questions at Jerusalem with a very large entourage, with camels bearing spices, gold in abundance, and precious stones. She came to Solomon and spoke with him about everything that was on her mind. So Solomon answered all her questions; nothing was too difficult for Solomon to explain to her. When the queen of Sheba observed Solomon's wisdom, the palace he had built, the food at his table, his servants' residence, his attendants' service and their attire, his cupbearers and their attire, and the burnt offerings he offered at the LORD's temple, it took her breath away.

She said to the king, "The report I heard in my own country about your words and about your wisdom is true. But I didn't believe their reports until I came and saw with my own eyes. Indeed, I was not even told half of your great wisdom! You far exceed the report I heard. How happy are your men. How happy are these servants of yours, who always stand in your presence hearing your wisdom. Blessed be the LORD your God! He delighted in you and put you on his throne as king for the LORD your God. Because your God loved Israel enough to establish them forever, he has set you over them as king to carry out justice and righteousness."

Then she gave the king four and a half tons of gold, a great quantity of spices, and precious stones. There never were such spices as those the queen of Sheba gave to King Solomon. In addition, Hiram's servants and Solomon's servants who brought gold from Ophir also brought algum wood and precious stones. The king made the algum wood into walkways for the LORD's temple and for the king's palace and into lyres and harps for the singers. Never before had anything like them been seen in the land of Judah.

King Solomon gave the queen of Sheba her every desire, whatever she asked—far more than she had brought the king. Then she, along with her servants, returned to her own country.

The weight of gold that came to Solomon annually was twenty-five tons, besides what was brought by the merchants and traders. All the Arabian kings and governors of the land also brought gold and silver to Solomon.

King Solomon made two hundred large shields of hammered gold; 15 pounds of hammered gold went into each shield. He made three hundred small shields of hammered gold; 7 ½ pounds of gold went into each shield. The king put them in the House of the Forest of Lebanon.

The king also made a large ivory throne and overlaid it with pure gold. The throne had six steps; there was a footstool covered in gold for the throne, armrests on either side of the seat, and two lions standing beside the armrests. Twelve lions were standing there on the six steps, one at each end. Nothing like it had ever been made in any other kingdom.

All of King Solomon's drinking cups were gold, and all the utensils of the House of the Forest of Lebanon were pure gold. There was no silver, since it was considered as nothing in Solomon's time, for the king's ships kept going to Tarshish with Hiram's servants, and once every three years the ships of Tarshish would arrive bearing gold, silver, ivory, apes, and peacocks.

King Solomon surpassed all the kings of the world in riches and wisdom. All the kings of the world wanted an audience with Solomon to hear the wisdom God had put in his heart. Each of them would bring his own gift—items of silver and gold, clothing, weapons, spices, and horses and mules—as an annual tribute.

Solomon had four thousand stalls for horses and chariots, and twelve thousand horsemen. He stationed them in the chariot cities and with the king in Jerusalem. He ruled over all the kings from the Euphrates River to the land of the Philistines and as far as the border of Egypt. The king made silver as common in Jerusalem as stones, and he made cedar as abundant as sycamore in the Judean foothills. They were bringing horses for Solomon from Egypt and from all the countries.

The remaining events of Solomon's reign, from beginning to end, are written in the Events of the Prophet Nathan, the Prophecy of Ahijah the Shilonite, and the Visions of the Seer Iddo concerning Jeroboam son of Nebat. Solomon reigned in Jerusalem over all Israel for forty years. Solomon rested with his ancestors and was buried in the city of his father David. His son Rehoboam became king in his place.

10 Then Rehoboam went to Shechem, for all Israel had gone to Shechem to make him king. When Jeroboam son of Nebat heard about it—for he was in Egypt where he had fled from King Solomon's presence—Jeroboam returned from Egypt. So they summoned him. Then Jeroboam and all Israel came and spoke to Rehoboam: "Your father made our yoke harsh. Therefore, lighten your father's harsh service and the heavy yoke he put on us, and we will serve you."

Rehoboam replied, "Return to me in three days." So the people left.

Then King Rehoboam consulted with the elders who had attended his father Solomon when he was alive, asking, "How do you advise me to respond to this people?"

They replied, "If you will be kind to this people and please them by speaking kind words to them, they will be your servants forever."

But he rejected the advice of the elders who had advised him, and he consulted with the young men who had grown up with him, the ones attending him. He asked them, "What message do you advise we send back to this people who said to me, 'Lighten the yoke your father put on us'?"

Then the young men who had grown up with him told him, "This is what you should say to the people who said to you, 'Your father made our yoke heavy, but you, make it lighter on us!' This is what you should say to them: 'My little finger is thicker than my father's waist! Now therefore, my father burdened you with a heavy yoke, but I will add to your yoke; my father disciplined you with whips, but I, with barbed whips.'"

So Jeroboam and all the people came to Rehoboam on the third day, just as the king had ordered, saying, "Return to me on the third day." Then the king answered them harshly. King Rehoboam rejected the elders' advice and spoke to them according to the young men's advice, saying, "My father made your yoke heavy, but I will add to it; my father disciplined you with whips, but I, with barbed whips."

The king did not listen to the people because the turn of events came from God, in order that the LORD might carry out his word that he had spoken through Ahijah the Shilonite to Jeroboam son of Nebat.

When all Israel saw that the king had not listened to them, the people answered the king:

> What portion do we have in David?
> We have no inheritance in the son of Jesse.
> Israel, each to your tent;
> David, look after your own house now!

So all Israel went to their tents. But as for the Israelites living in the cities of Judah, Rehoboam reigned over them.

Then King Rehoboam sent Hadoram, who was in charge of the forced labor, but the Israelites stoned him to death. However, King Rehoboam managed to get into his chariot to flee to Jerusalem. Israel is in rebellion against the house of David until today.

11 When Rehoboam arrived in Jerusalem, he mobilized the house of Judah and Benjamin—one hundred eighty thousand fit young soldiers—to fight against Israel to restore the reign to Rehoboam. But the word of the LORD came to Shemaiah, the man of God: "Say to Rehoboam son of Solomon, king of Judah, to all Israel in Judah and Benjamin, and to the rest of the people, 'This is what the LORD says: You are not to march up and fight against your brothers. Each of you return home, for this incident has come from me.'"

So they listened to what the LORD said and turned back from going against Jeroboam.

Rehoboam stayed in Jerusalem, and he fortified cities in Judah. He built up Bethlehem, Etam, Tekoa, Beth-zur, Soco, Adullam, Gath, Mareshah, Ziph, Adoraim, Lachish, Azekah, Zorah, Aijalon, and Hebron, which are fortified cities in Judah and in Benjamin. He strengthened their fortifications and put leaders in them with supplies of food, oil, and wine. He also put large shields and spears in each and every city to make them very strong. So Judah and Benjamin were his.

The priests and Levites from all their regions throughout Israel took their stand with Rehoboam, for the Levites left their pasturelands and their possessions and went to Judah and Jerusalem, because Jeroboam and his sons refused to let them serve as priests of the LORD. Jeroboam appointed his own priests for the high places, the goat-demons, and the golden calves he had made. Those from every tribe of Israel who had determined in their hearts to seek the LORD their God followed the Levites to Jerusalem to sacrifice to the LORD, the God of their ancestors. So they strengthened the kingdom of Judah and supported Rehoboam son of Solomon for three years, because they walked in the ways of David and Solomon for three years.

Rehoboam married Mahalath, daughter of David's son Jerimoth and of Abihail daughter of Jesse's son Eliab. She bore sons to him: Jeush, Shemariah, and Zaham. After her, he married Maacah daughter of Absalom. She bore Abijah, Attai, Ziza, and Shelomith to him. Rehoboam loved Maacah daughter of Absalom more than all his wives and concubines. He acquired eighteen wives and sixty concubines and was the father of twenty-eight sons and sixty daughters.

Rehoboam appointed Abijah son of Maacah as chief, leader among his brothers, intending to make him king. Rehoboam also showed discernment by dispersing some of his sons to all the regions of Judah and Benjamin and to all the fortified cities. He gave them plenty of provisions and
30 sought many wives for them.

12 When Rehoboam had established his sovereignty and royal power, he abandoned the law of the LORD—he and all Israel with him. Because they were unfaithful to the LORD, in the fifth year of King Rehoboam, King Shishak of Egypt went to war against Jerusalem with 1,200 chariots, 60,000 cavalrymen, and countless people who came with him from Egypt—Libyans, Sukkiim, and Cushites. He captured the fortified cities of Judah and came as far as Jerusalem.

Then the prophet Shemaiah went to Rehoboam and the leaders of Judah who were gathered at Jerusalem because of Shishak. He said to them, "This is what the LORD says: You have abandoned me; therefore, I have abandoned you to Shishak."

So the leaders of Israel and the king humbled themselves and said, "The LORD is righteous."
10 When the LORD saw that they had humbled themselves, the LORD's message came to Shemaiah: "They have humbled themselves; I will not destroy them but will grant them a little deliverance. My wrath will not be poured out on Jerusalem through Shishak. However, they will become his servants so that they may recognize the difference between serving me and serving the kingdoms of other lands."

So King Shishak of Egypt went to war against Jerusalem. He seized the treasuries of the LORD's temple and the treasuries of the royal palace. He took everything. He took the gold shields that Solomon had made. King Rehoboam made bronze shields to replace them and committed them into the care of the captains of the guards who protected the entrance to the king's palace. Whenever the king entered the LORD's temple, the guards would carry the shields and take them
20 back to the armory. When Rehoboam humbled himself, the LORD's anger turned away from him, and he did not destroy him completely. Besides that, conditions were good in Judah.

King Rehoboam established his royal power in Jerusalem. Rehoboam was forty-one years old when he became king, and he reigned seventeen years in Jerusalem, the city the LORD had chosen from all the tribes of Israel to put his name. Rehoboam's mother's name was Naamah the Ammonite. Rehoboam did what was evil, because he did not determine in his heart to seek the LORD.

The events of Rehoboam's reign, from beginning to end, are written in the Events of the Prophet Shemaiah and of the Seer Iddo concerning genealogies. There was war between

Rehoboam and Jeroboam throughout their reigns. Rehoboam rested with his ancestors and was buried in the city of David. His son Abijah became king in his place.

13 In the eighteenth year of Israel's King Jeroboam, Abijah became king over Judah, and he reigned three years in Jerusalem. His mother's name was Micaiah daughter of Uriel; she was from Gibeah.

There was war between Abijah and Jeroboam. Abijah set his army of warriors in order with four hundred thousand fit young men. Jeroboam arranged his mighty army of eight hundred thousand fit young men in battle formation against him. Then Abijah stood on Mount Zemaraim, which is in the hill country of Ephraim, and said, "Jeroboam and all Israel, hear me. Don't you know that the Lord God of Israel gave the kingship over Israel to David and his descendants forever by a covenant of salt? But Jeroboam son of Nebat, a servant of Solomon son of David, rose up and rebelled against his lord. Then worthless and wicked men gathered around him to

10 resist Rehoboam son of Solomon when Rehoboam was young, inexperienced, and unable to assert himself against them.

"And now you are saying you can assert yourselves against the Lord's kingdom, which is in the hand of one of David's sons. You are a vast number and have with you the golden calves that Jeroboam made for you as gods. Didn't you banish the priests of the Lord, the descendants of Aaron and the Levites, and make your own priests like the peoples of other lands do? Whoever comes to ordain himself with a young bull and seven rams may become a priest of what are not gods.

"But as for us, the Lord is our God. We have not abandoned him; the priests ministering to the Lord are descendants of Aaron, and the Levites serve at their tasks. They offer a burnt offering and fragrant incense to the Lord every morning and every evening, and they set the rows

20 of the Bread of the Presence on the ceremonially clean table. They light the lamps of the gold lampstand every evening. We are carrying out the requirements of the Lord our God, while you have abandoned him. Look, God and his priests are with us at our head. The trumpets are ready to sound the charge against you. Israelites, don't fight against the Lord God of your ancestors, for you will not succeed."

Now Jeroboam had sent an ambush around to advance from behind them. So they were in front of Judah, and the ambush was behind them. Judah turned and discovered that the battle was in front of them and behind them, so they cried out to the Lord. Then the priests blew the trumpets, and the men of Judah raised the battle cry. When the men of Judah raised the battle cry, God routed Jeroboam and all Israel before Abijah and Judah. So the Israelites fled before Judah,

30 and God handed them over to them. Then Abijah and his people struck them with a mighty blow, and five hundred thousand fit young men of Israel were killed. The Israelites were subdued at that time. The Judahites succeeded because they depended on the Lord, the God of their ancestors.

Abijah pursued Jeroboam and captured some cities from him: Bethel, Jeshanah, and Ephron, along with their surrounding villages. Jeroboam no longer retained his power during Abijah's reign; ultimately, the Lord struck him and he died.

However, Abijah grew strong, acquired fourteen wives, and fathered twenty-two sons and sixteen daughters. The rest of the events of Abijah's reign, along with his ways and his sayings, are written in the Writing of the Prophet Iddo.

14 Abijah rested with his ancestors and was buried in the city of David. His son Asa became king in his place. During his reign the land experienced peace for ten years.

Asa did what was good and right in the sight of the LORD his God. He removed the pagan altars and the high places. He shattered their sacred pillars and chopped down their Asherah poles. He told the people of Judah to seek the LORD God of their ancestors and to carry out the instruction and the commands. He also removed the high places and the shrines from all the cities of Judah, and the kingdom experienced peace under him.

Because the land experienced peace, Asa built fortified cities in Judah. No one made war with him in those days because the LORD gave him rest. So he said to the people of Judah, "Let's build these cities and surround them with walls and towers, with doors and bars. The land is still ours because we sought the LORD our God. We sought him and he gave us rest on every side." So they built and succeeded.

Asa had an army of three hundred thousand from Judah bearing large shields and spears, and two hundred eighty thousand from Benjamin bearing regular shields and drawing the bow. All these were valiant warriors. Then Zerah the Cushite came against them with an army of one million men and three hundred chariots. They came as far as Mareshah. So Asa marched out against him and lined up in battle formation in Zephathah Valley at Mareshah.

Then Asa cried out to the LORD his God, "LORD, there is no one besides you to help the mighty and those without strength. Help us, LORD our God, for we depend on you, and in your name we have come against this large army. LORD, you are our God. Do not let a mere mortal hinder you."

So the LORD routed the Cushites before Asa and before Judah, and the Cushites fled. Then Asa and the people who were with him pursued them as far as Gerar. The Cushites fell until they had no survivors, for they were crushed before the LORD and his army. So the people of Judah carried off a great supply of loot. Then they attacked all the cities around Gerar because the terror of the LORD was on them. They also plundered all the cities, since there was a great deal of plunder in them. They also attacked the tents of the herdsmen and captured many sheep and camels. Then they returned to Jerusalem.

15 The Spirit of God came on Azariah son of Oded. So he went out to meet Asa and said to him, "Asa and all Judah and Benjamin, hear me. The LORD is with you when you are with him. If you seek him, he will be found by you, but if you abandon him, he will abandon you. For many years Israel has been without the true God, without a teaching priest, and without instruction, but when they turned to the LORD God of Israel in their distress and sought him, he was found by them. In those times there was no peace for those who went about their daily activities because the residents of the lands had many conflicts. Nation was crushed by nation and city by city, for God troubled them with every possible distress. But as for you, be strong; don't give up, for your work has a reward."

When Asa heard these words and the prophecy of Azariah son of Oded the prophet, he took courage and removed the abhorrent idols from the whole land of Judah and Benjamin and from the cities he had captured in the hill country of Ephraim. He renovated the altar of the LORD that was in front of the portico of the LORD's temple. Then he gathered all Judah and Benjamin, as well as those from the tribes of Ephraim, Manasseh, and Simeon who were residing among them, for they had defected to him from Israel in great numbers when they saw that the LORD his God was with him.

They were gathered in Jerusalem in the third month of the fifteenth year of Asa's reign. At that time they sacrificed to the LORD seven hundred cattle and seven thousand sheep and goats from all the plunder they had brought. Then they entered into a covenant to seek the LORD God of their ancestors with all their heart and all their soul. Whoever would not seek the LORD God of Israel would be put to death, young or old, man or woman. They took an oath to the LORD in a loud voice, with shouting, with trumpets, and with rams' horns. All Judah rejoiced over the oath, for they had sworn it wholeheartedly. They had sought him with all sincerity, and he was found by them. So the LORD gave them rest on every side.

King Asa also removed Maacah, his grandmother, from being queen mother because she had made an obscene image of Asherah. Asa chopped down her obscene image, then crushed it and burned it in the Kidron Valley. The high places were not taken away from Israel; nevertheless, Asa was wholeheartedly devoted his entire life. He brought his father's consecrated gifts and his own consecrated gifts into God's temple: silver, gold, and utensils.

There was no war until the thirty-fifth year of Asa's reign.

16 In the thirty-sixth year of Asa, Israel's King Baasha went to war against Judah. He built Ramah in order to keep anyone from leaving or coming to King Asa of Judah. So Asa brought out the silver and gold from the treasuries of the LORD's temple and the royal palace and sent it to Aram's King Ben-hadad, who lived in Damascus, saying, "There's a treaty between me and you, between my father and your father. Look, I have sent you silver and gold. Go break your treaty with Israel's King Baasha so that he will withdraw from me."

Ben-hadad listened to King Asa and sent the commanders of his armies to the cities of Israel. They attacked Ijon, Dan, Abel-maim, and all the storage cities of Naphtali. When Baasha heard about it, he quit building Ramah and stopped his work. Then King Asa brought all Judah, and they carried away the stones of Ramah and the timbers Baasha had built it with. Then he built Geba and Mizpah with them.

At that time, the seer Hanani came to King Asa of Judah and said to him, "Because you depended on the king of Aram and have not depended on the LORD your God, the army of the king of Aram has escaped from you. Were not the Cushites and Libyans a vast army with many chariots and horsemen? When you depended on the LORD, he handed them over to you. For the eyes of the LORD roam throughout the earth to show himself strong for those who are wholeheartedly devoted to him. You have been foolish in this matter. Therefore, you will have wars from now on." Asa was enraged with the seer and put him in prison because of his anger over this. And Asa mistreated some of the people at that time.

20 Note that the events of Asa's reign, from beginning to end, are written in the Book of the Kings of Judah and Israel. In the thirty-ninth year of his reign, Asa developed a disease in his feet, and his disease became increasingly severe. Yet even in his disease he didn't seek the LORD but only the physicians. Asa rested with his ancestors; he died in the forty-first year of his reign. He was buried in his own tomb that he had made for himself in the city of David. They laid him out in a coffin that was full of spices and various mixtures of prepared ointments; then they made a great fire in his honor.

17 His son Jehoshaphat became king in his place and strengthened himself against Israel. He stationed troops in every fortified city of Judah and set garrisons in the land of Judah and in the cities of Ephraim that his father Asa had captured.

Now the LORD was with Jehoshaphat because he walked in the former ways of his ancestor David. He did not seek the Baals but sought the God of his father and walked by his commands, not according to the practices of Israel. So the LORD established the kingdom in his hand. Then all Judah brought him tribute, and he had riches and honor in abundance. He took great pride in the LORD's ways, and he again removed the high places and Asherah poles from Judah.

In the third year of his reign, Jehoshaphat sent his officials—Ben-hail, Obadiah, Zechariah, 10 Nethanel, and Micaiah—to teach in the cities of Judah. The Levites with them were Shemaiah, Nethaniah, Zebadiah, Asahel, Shemiramoth, Jehonathan, Adonijah, Tobijah, and Tob-adonijah; the priests, Elishama and Jehoram, were with these Levites. They taught throughout Judah, having the book of the LORD's instruction with them. They went throughout the towns of Judah and taught the people.

The terror of the LORD was on all the kingdoms of the lands that surrounded Judah, so they didn't fight against Jehoshaphat. Some of the Philistines also brought gifts and silver as tribute to Jehoshaphat, and the Arabs brought him flocks: 7,700 rams and 7,700 male goats.

Jehoshaphat grew stronger and stronger. He built fortresses and storage cities in Judah and carried out great works in the towns of Judah. He had fighting men, valiant warriors, in Jerusalem. These 20 are their numbers according to their ancestral families. For Judah, the commanders of thousands:

Adnah the commander and three hundred thousand valiant warriors with him;

next to him, Jehohanan the commander and two hundred eighty thousand with him;

next to him, Amasiah son of Zichri, the volunteer of the LORD, and two hundred thousand valiant warriors with him;

from Benjamin, Eliada, a valiant warrior, and two hundred thousand with him armed with bow and shield;

next to him, Jehozabad and one hundred eighty thousand with him equipped for war. These were the ones who served the king, besides those he stationed in the fortified cities throughout all Judah.

18 Now Jehoshaphat had riches and honor in abundance, and he made an alliance with Ahab through marriage. Then after some years, he went down to visit Ahab in Samaria. Ahab slaughtered many sheep, goats, and cattle for him and for the people who were with him, and he persuaded him to attack Ramoth-gilead, for Israel's King Ahab asked Judah's King Jehoshaphat, "Will you go with me to Ramoth-gilead?"

He replied to him, "I am as you are, my people as your people; we will be with you in the battle." But Jehoshaphat said to the king of Israel, "First, please ask what the LORD's will is."

So the king of Israel gathered the prophets, four hundred men, and asked them, "Should we go to Ramoth-gilead for war or should I refrain?"

10   They replied, "March up, and God will hand it over to the king."

But Jehoshaphat asked, "Isn't there a prophet of the LORD here anymore? Let's ask him."

The king of Israel said to Jehoshaphat, "There is still one man who can inquire of the LORD, but I hate him because he never prophesies good about me, but only disaster. He is Micaiah son of Imlah."

"The king shouldn't say that," Jehoshaphat replied.

So the king of Israel called an officer and said, "Hurry and get Micaiah son of Imlah!"

Now the king of Israel and King Jehoshaphat of Judah, clothed in royal attire, were each sitting on his own throne. They were sitting on the threshing floor at the entrance to Samaria's gate, and all the prophets were prophesying in front of them. Then Zedekiah son of Chenaanah made iron 20   horns and said, "This is what the LORD says: You will gore the Arameans with these until they are finished off." And all the prophets were prophesying the same, saying, "March up to Ramoth-gilead and succeed, for the LORD will hand it over to the king."

The messenger who went to call Micaiah instructed him, "Look, the words of the prophets are unanimously favorable for the king. So let your words be like theirs, and speak favorably."

But Micaiah said, "As the LORD lives, I will say whatever my God says."

So he went to the king, and the king asked him, "Micaiah, should we go to Ramoth-gilead for war, or should I refrain?"

Micaiah said, "March up and succeed, for they will be handed over to you."

But the king said to him, "How many times must I make you swear not to tell me anything but
30 the truth in the name of the LORD?"

So Micaiah said:

> I saw all Israel scattered on the hills
> like sheep without a shepherd.
> And the LORD said,
> "They have no master;
> let each return home in peace."

So the king of Israel said to Jehoshaphat, "Didn't I tell you he never prophesies good about me,
but only disaster?"

Then Micaiah said, "Therefore, hear the word of the LORD. I saw the LORD sitting on his
40 throne, and the whole heavenly army was standing at his right hand and at his left hand. And the
LORD said, 'Who will entice King Ahab of Israel to march up and fall at Ramoth-gilead?' So one
was saying this and another was saying that.

"Then a spirit came forward, stood before the LORD, and said, 'I will entice him.'

"The LORD asked him, 'How?'

"So he said, 'I will go and become a lying spirit in the mouth of all his prophets.'

"Then he said, 'You will entice him and also prevail. Go and do that.'

"Now, you see, the LORD has put a lying spirit into the mouth of these prophets of yours, and
the LORD has pronounced disaster against you."

Then Zedekiah son of Chenaanah came up, hit Micaiah on the cheek, and demanded, "Which
50 way did the spirit from the LORD leave me to speak to you?"

Micaiah replied, "You will soon see when you go to hide in an inner chamber on that day."

Then the king of Israel ordered, "Take Micaiah and return him to Amon, the governor of the
city, and to Joash, the king's son, and say, 'This is what the king says: Put this guy in prison and
feed him only a little bread and water until I come back safely.'"

But Micaiah said, "If you ever return safely, the LORD has not spoken through me." Then he
said, "Listen, all you people!"

Then the king of Israel and Judah's King Jehoshaphat went up to Ramoth-gilead. But the king
of Israel said to Jehoshaphat, "I will disguise myself and go into battle, but you wear your royal
attire." So the king of Israel disguised himself, and they went into battle.

60 Now the king of Aram had ordered his chariot commanders, "Do not fight with anyone at all
except the king of Israel."

When the chariot commanders saw Jehoshaphat, they shouted, "He must be the king of
Israel!" So they turned to attack him, but Jehoshaphat cried out and the LORD helped him. God

drew them away from him. When the chariot commanders saw that he was not the king of Israel, they turned back from pursuing him.

But a man drew his bow without taking special aim and struck the king of Israel through the joints of his armor. So he said to the charioteer, "Turn around and take me out of the battle, for I am badly wounded!" The battle raged throughout that day, and the king of Israel propped himself up in his chariot facing the Arameans until evening. Then he died at sunset.

19 King Jehoshaphat of Judah returned to his home in Jerusalem in peace. Then Jehu son of the seer Hanani went out to confront him and said to King Jehoshaphat, "Do you help the wicked and love those who hate the LORD? Because of this, the LORD's wrath is on you. However, some good is found in you, for you have eradicated the Asherah poles from the land and have determined in your heart to seek God."

Jehoshaphat lived in Jerusalem, and once again he went out among the people from Beer-sheba to the hill country of Ephraim and brought them back to the LORD, the God of their ancestors. He appointed judges in all the fortified cities of the land of Judah, city by city. Then he said to the judges, "Consider what you are doing, for you do not judge for a man, but for the LORD, who is 10 with you in the matter of judgment. And now, may the terror of the LORD be on you. Watch what you do, for there is no injustice or partiality or taking bribes with the LORD our God."

Jehoshaphat also appointed in Jerusalem some of the Levites and priests and some of the Israelite family heads for deciding the LORD's will and for settling disputes of the residents of Jerusalem. He commanded them, saying, "In the fear of the LORD, with integrity, and wholeheartedly, you are to do the following: For every dispute that comes to you from your brothers who dwell in their cities—whether it regards differences of bloodguilt, law, commandment, statutes, or judgments—you are to warn them, so they will not incur guilt before the LORD and wrath will not come on you and your brothers. Do this, and you will not incur guilt.

"Note that Amariah, the chief priest, is over you in all matters related to the LORD, and 20 Zebadiah son of Ishmael, the ruler of the house of Judah, in all matters related to the king, and the Levites are officers in your presence. Be strong; may the LORD be with those who do what is good."

20 After this, the Moabites and Ammonites, together with some of the Meunites, came to fight against Jehoshaphat. People came and told Jehoshaphat, "A vast number from beyond the Dead Sea and from Edom has come to fight against you; they are already in Hazazon-tamar" (that is, En-gedi). Jehoshaphat was afraid, and he resolved to seek the LORD. Then he proclaimed a fast for all Judah, who gathered to seek the LORD. They even came from all the cities of Judah to seek him.

Then Jehoshaphat stood in the assembly of Judah and Jerusalem in the LORD's temple before the new courtyard. He said:

LORD, God of our ancestors, are you not the God who is in heaven, and do you not rule over all the kingdoms of the nations? Power and might are in your hand, and no one can stand against

10 you. Are you not our God who drove out the inhabitants of this land before your people Israel and who gave it forever to the descendants of Abraham your friend? They have lived in the land and have built you a sanctuary in it for your name and have said, "If disaster comes on us— sword or judgment, pestilence or famine—we will stand before this temple and before you, for your name is in this temple. We will cry out to you because of our distress, and you will hear and deliver."

Now here are the Ammonites, Moabites, and the inhabitants of Mount Seir. You did not let Israel invade them when Israel came out of the land of Egypt, but Israel turned away from them and did not destroy them. Look how they repay us by coming to drive us out of your possession that you gave us as an inheritance. Our God, will you not judge them? For we are powerless

20 before this vast number that comes to fight against us. We do not know what to do, but we look to you.

All Judah was standing before the LORD with their dependents, their wives, and their children. In the middle of the congregation, the Spirit of the LORD came on Jahaziel (son of Zechariah, son of Benaiah, son of Jeiel, son of Mattaniah, a Levite from Asaph's descendants), and he said, "Listen carefully, all Judah and you inhabitants of Jerusalem, and King Jehoshaphat. This is what the LORD says: 'Do not be afraid or discouraged because of this vast number, for the battle is not yours, but God's. Tomorrow, go down against them. You will see them coming up the Ascent of Ziz, and you will find them at the end of the valley facing the Wilderness of Jeruel. You do not have to fight this battle. Position yourselves, stand still, and see the salvation of the LORD. He is

30 with you, Judah and Jerusalem. Do not be afraid or discouraged. Tomorrow, go out to face them, for the LORD is with you.'"

Then Jehoshaphat knelt low with his face to the ground, and all Judah and the inhabitants of Jerusalem fell down before the LORD to worship him. Then the Levites from the sons of the Kohathites and the Korahites stood up to praise the LORD God of Israel shouting loudly.

In the morning they got up early and went out to the wilderness of Tekoa. As they were about to go out, Jehoshaphat stood and said, "Hear me, Judah and you inhabitants of Jerusalem. Believe in the LORD your God, and you will be established; believe in his prophets, and you will succeed." Then he consulted with the people and appointed some to sing for the LORD and some to praise the splendor of his holiness. When they went out in front of the armed forces, they kept singing:

40   Give thanks to the LORD,
       for his faithful love endures forever.

The moment they began their shouts and praises, the LORD set an ambush against the Ammonites, Moabites, and the inhabitants of Mount Seir who came to fight against Judah, and they were defeated. The Ammonites and Moabites turned against the inhabitants of Mount Seir and completely annihilated them. When they had finished with the inhabitants of Seir, they helped destroy each other.

When Judah came to a place overlooking the wilderness, they looked for the large army, but there were only corpses lying on the ground; nobody had escaped. Then Jehoshaphat and his people went to gather the plunder. They found among them an abundance of goods on the bodies and valuable items. So they stripped them until nobody could carry any more. They were gathering the plunder for three days because there was so much. They assembled in the Valley of Beracah on the fourth day, for there they blessed the LORD. Therefore, that place is still called the Valley of Beracah today.

Then all the men of Judah and Jerusalem turned back with Jehoshaphat their leader, returning joyfully to Jerusalem, for the LORD enabled them to rejoice over their enemies. So they came into Jerusalem to the LORD's temple with harps, lyres, and trumpets.

The terror of God was on all the kingdoms of the lands when they heard that the LORD had fought against the enemies of Israel. Then Jehoshaphat's kingdom was quiet, for his God gave him rest on every side.

Jehoshaphat became king over Judah. He was thirty-five years old when he became king, and he reigned twenty-five years in Jerusalem. His mother's name was Azubah daughter of Shilhi. He walked in the ways of Asa his father; he did not turn away from it but did what was right in the LORD's sight. However, the high places were not taken away; the people had not yet set their hearts on the God of their ancestors.

The rest of the events of Jehoshaphat's reign from beginning to end are written in the Events of Jehu son of Hanani, which is recorded in the Book of Israel's Kings.

After this, Judah's King Jehoshaphat made an alliance with Israel's King Ahaziah, who was guilty of wrongdoing. Jehoshaphat formed an alliance with him to make ships to go to Tarshish, and they made the ships in Ezion-geber. Then Eliezer son of Dodavahu of Mareshah prophesied against Jehoshaphat, saying, "Because you formed an alliance with Ahaziah, the LORD has broken up what you have made." So the ships were wrecked and were not able to go to Tarshish.

21 Jehoshaphat rested with his ancestors and was buried with his ancestors in the city of David. His son Jehoram became king in his place. He had brothers, sons of Jehoshaphat: Azariah, Jehiel, Zechariah, Azariah, Michael, and Shephatiah; all these were the sons of King Jehoshaphat of Judah. Their father had given them many gifts of silver, gold, and valuable things, along with fortified cities in Judah, but he gave the kingdom to Jehoram because he was the firstborn. When

Jehoram had established himself over his father's kingdom, he strengthened his position by killing with the sword all his brothers as well as some of the princes of Israel.

Jehoram was thirty-two years old when he became king, and he reigned eight years in Jerusalem. He walked in the ways of the kings of Israel, as the house of Ahab had done, for Ahab's daughter was his wife. He did what was evil in the Lord's sight, but for the sake of the covenant the Lord had made with David, he was unwilling to destroy the house of David since the Lord had promised to give a lamp to David and to his sons forever.

During Jehoram's reign, Edom rebelled against Judah's control and appointed their own king. So Jehoram crossed into Edom with his commanders and all his chariots. Then at night he set out to attack the Edomites who had surrounded him and the chariot commanders. And now Edom is still in rebellion against Judah's control today. Libnah also rebelled at that time against his control because he had abandoned the Lord, the God of his ancestors. Jehoram also built high places in the hills of Judah, and he caused the inhabitants of Jerusalem to prostitute themselves, and he led Judah astray.

Then a letter came to Jehoram from the prophet Elijah, saying:

This is what the Lord, the God of your ancestor David says: "Because you have not walked in the ways of your father Jehoshaphat or in the ways of King Asa of Judah but have walked in the ways of the kings of Israel, have caused Judah and the inhabitants of Jerusalem to prostitute themselves like the house of Ahab prostituted itself, and also have killed your brothers, your father's family, who were better than you, the Lord is now about to strike your people, your sons, your wives, and all your possessions with a horrible affliction. You yourself will be struck with many illnesses, including a disease of the intestines, until your intestines come out day after day because of the disease."

The Lord roused the spirit of the Philistines and the Arabs who lived near the Cushites to attack Jehoram. So they went to war against Judah and invaded it. They carried off all the possessions found in the king's palace and also his sons and wives; not a son was left to him except Jehoahaz, his youngest son.

After all these things, the Lord afflicted him in his intestines with an incurable disease. This continued day after day until two full years passed. Then his intestines came out because of his disease, and he died from severe illnesses. But his people did not hold a fire in his honor like the fire in honor of his predecessors.

Jehoram was thirty-two years old when he became king; he reigned eight years in Jerusalem. He died to no one's regret and was buried in the city of David but not in the tombs of the kings.

22 Then the inhabitants of Jerusalem made Ahaziah, his youngest son, king in his place, because the troops that had come with the Arabs to the camp had killed all the older sons. So Ahaziah son of Jehoram became king of Judah. Ahaziah was twenty-two years old when he became king, and he reigned one year in Jerusalem. His mother's name was Athaliah, granddaughter of Omri.

He walked in the ways of the house of Ahab, for his mother gave him evil advice. So he did what was evil in the LORD's sight like the house of Ahab, for they were his advisers after the death of his father, to his destruction. He also followed their advice and went with Joram son of Israel's King Ahab to fight against King Hazael of Aram, in Ramoth-gilead. The Arameans wounded Joram, so he returned to Jezreel to recover from the wounds they inflicted on him in Ramoth-gilead when he fought against King Hazael of Aram. Then Judah's King Ahaziah son of Jehoram went down to Jezreel to visit Joram son of Ahab since Joram was ill.

Ahaziah's downfall came from God when he went to Joram. When Ahaziah arrived, he went out with Joram to meet Jehu son of Nimshi, whom the LORD had anointed to destroy the house of Ahab. So when Jehu executed judgment on the house of Ahab, he found the rulers of Judah and the sons of Ahaziah's brothers who were serving Ahaziah, and he killed them. Then Jehu looked for Ahaziah, and Jehu's soldiers captured him (he was hiding in Samaria). So they brought Ahaziah to Jehu, and they killed him. The soldiers buried him, for they said, "He is the grandson of Jehoshaphat who sought the LORD with all his heart." So no one from the house of Ahaziah had the strength to rule the kingdom.

When Athaliah, Ahaziah's mother, saw that her son was dead, she proceeded to annihilate all the royal heirs of the house of Judah. Jehoshabeath, the king's daughter, rescued Joash son of Ahaziah from the king's sons who were being killed and put him and the one who nursed him in a bedroom. Now Jehoshabeath was the daughter of King Jehoram and the wife of the priest Jehoiada. Since she was Ahaziah's sister, she hid Joash from Athaliah so that she did not kill him. He was hiding with them in God's temple for six years while Athaliah reigned over the land.

23 Then, in the seventh year, Jehoiada summoned his courage and took the commanders of hundreds into a covenant with him: Azariah son of Jeroham, Ishmael son of Jehohanan, Azariah son of Obed, Maaseiah son of Adaiah, and Elishaphat son of Zichri. They made a circuit throughout Judah. They gathered the Levites from all the cities of Judah and the family heads of Israel, and they came to Jerusalem.

Then the whole assembly made a covenant with the king in God's temple. Jehoiada said to them, "Here is the king's son! He will reign, just as the LORD promised concerning David's sons. This is what you are to do: a third of you, priests and Levites who are coming on duty on the Sabbath, are to be gatekeepers. A third are to be at the king's palace, and a third are to be at the Foundation Gate, and all the troops will be in the courtyards of the LORD's temple. No one is to enter the LORD's temple but the priests and those Levites who serve; they may enter because they are holy, but all the people are to obey the requirement of the LORD. The Levites are to completely surround the king with weapons in hand. Anyone who enters the temple is to be put to death. Accompany the king in all his daily tasks."

So the commanders of hundreds did everything the priest Jehoiada commanded. They each brought their men—those coming on duty on the Sabbath and those going off duty on the Sabbath—for the priest Jehoiada did not release the divisions. The priest Jehoiada gave to the commanders of hundreds King David's spears, shields, and quivers that were in God's temple. Then he stationed all the troops with their weapons in hand surrounding the king—from the

20 right side of the temple to the left side, by the altar and by the temple.

They brought out the king's son, put the crown on him, gave him the testimony, and made him king. Jehoiada and his sons anointed him and cried, "Long live the king!"

When Athaliah heard the noise from the troops, the guards, and those praising the king, she went to the troops in the LORD's temple. As she looked, there was the king standing by his pillar at the entrance. The commanders and the trumpeters were by the king, and all the people of the land were rejoicing and blowing trumpets while the singers with musical instruments were leading the praise. Athaliah tore her clothes and screamed, "Treason! Treason!"

Then the priest Jehoiada sent out the commanders of hundreds, those in charge of the army, saying, "Take her out between the ranks, and put anyone who follows her to death by the sword,"

30 for the priest had said, "Don't put her to death in the LORD's temple." So they arrested her, and she went by the entrance of the Horse Gate to the king's palace, where they put her to death.

Then Jehoiada made a covenant between himself, the king, and the people that they would be the LORD's people. So all the people went to the temple of Baal and tore it down. They smashed its altars and images and killed Mattan, the priest of Baal, at the altars.

Then Jehoiada put the oversight of the LORD's temple into the hands of the Levitical priests, whom David had appointed over the LORD's temple, to offer burnt offerings to the LORD as it is written in the law of Moses, with rejoicing and song ordained by David. He stationed gatekeepers at the gates of the LORD's temple so that nothing unclean could enter for any reason. Then he took with him the commanders of hundreds, the nobles, the governors of the people, and all the people

40 of the land and brought the king down from the LORD's temple. They entered the king's palace through the Upper Gate and seated the king on the throne of the kingdom. All the people of the land rejoiced, and the city was quiet, for they had put Athaliah to death by the sword.

24 Joash was seven years old when he became king, and he reigned forty years in Jerusalem. His mother's name was Zibiah; she was from Beer-sheba. Throughout the time of the priest Jehoiada, Joash did what was right in the LORD's sight. Jehoiada acquired two wives for him, and he was the father of sons and daughters.

Afterward, Joash took it to heart to renovate the Lord's temple. So he gathered the priests and Levites and said, "Go out to the cities of Judah and collect silver from all Israel to repair the temple of your God as needed year by year, and do it quickly."

However, the Levites did not hurry. So the king called Jehoiada the high priest and said, "Why haven't you required the Levites to bring from Judah and Jerusalem the tax imposed by the Lord's servant Moses and the assembly of Israel for the tent of the testimony? For the sons of that wicked Athaliah broke into the Lord's temple and even used the sacred things of the Lord's temple for the Baals."

At the king's command a chest was made and placed outside the gate of the Lord's temple. Then a proclamation was issued in Judah and Jerusalem that the tax God's servant Moses imposed on Israel in the wilderness be brought to the Lord. All the leaders and all the people rejoiced, brought the tax, and put it in the chest until it was full. Whenever the chest was brought by the Levites to the king's overseers, and when they saw that there was a large amount of silver, the king's secretary and the high priest's deputy came and emptied the chest, picked it up, and returned it to its place. They did this daily and gathered the silver in abundance. Then the king and Jehoiada gave it to those in charge of the labor on the Lord's temple, who were hiring stonecutters and carpenters to renovate the Lord's temple, also blacksmiths and coppersmiths to repair the Lord's temple.

The workmen did their work, and through them the repairs progressed. They restored God's temple to its specifications and reinforced it. When they finished, they presented the rest of the silver to the king and Jehoiada, who made articles for the Lord's temple with it—articles for ministry and for making burnt offerings, and ladles and articles of gold and silver. They regularly offered burnt offerings in the Lord's temple throughout Jehoiada's life.

Jehoiada died when he was old and full of days; he was 130 years old at his death. He was buried in the city of David with the kings because he had done what was good in Israel with respect to God and his temple.

However, after Jehoiada died, the rulers of Judah came and paid homage to the king. Then the king listened to them, and they abandoned the temple of the Lord, the God of their ancestors, and served the Asherah poles and the idols. So there was wrath against Judah and Jerusalem for this guilt of theirs. Nevertheless, he sent them prophets to bring them back to the Lord; they admonished them, but the people would not listen.

The Spirit of God enveloped Zechariah son of Jehoiada the priest. He stood above the people and said to them, "This is what God says, 'Why are you transgressing the Lord's commands so that you do not prosper? Because you have abandoned the Lord, he has abandoned you.'" But they conspired against him and stoned him at the king's command in the courtyard of the Lord's temple. King Joash didn't remember the kindness that Zechariah's father Jehoiada had extended to him, but killed his son. While he was dying, he said, "May the Lord see and demand an account."

At the turn of the year, an Aramean army attacked Joash. They entered Judah and Jerusalem and destroyed all the leaders of the people among them and sent all the plunder to the king of Damascus. Although the Aramean army came with only a few men, the LORD handed over a vast army to them because the people of Judah had abandoned the LORD, the God of their ancestors. So they executed judgment on Joash.

When the Arameans saw that Joash had many wounds, they left him. His servants conspired against him, and killed him on his bed, because he had shed the blood of the sons of the priest Jehoiada. So he died, and they buried him in the city of David, but they did not bury him in the 50 tombs of the kings.

Those who conspired against him were Zabad, son of the Ammonite woman Shimeath, and Jehozabad, son of the Moabite woman Shimrith. The accounts concerning his sons, the many divine pronouncements about him, and the restoration of God's temple are recorded in the Writing of the Book of the Kings. His son Amaziah became king in his place.

25 Amaziah became king when he was twenty-five years old, and he reigned twenty-nine years in Jerusalem. His mother's name was Jehoaddan; she was from Jerusalem. He did what was right in the LORD's sight but not wholeheartedly.

As soon as the kingdom was firmly in his grasp, he executed his servants who had killed his father the king. However, he did not put their children to death, because—as it is written in the Law, in the book of Moses, where the LORD commanded—"Fathers are not to die because of children, and children are not to die because of fathers, but each one will die for his own sin."

Then Amaziah gathered Judah and assembled them according to ancestral families, according to commanders of thousands, and according to commanders of hundreds. He numbered those 10 twenty years old or more for all Judah and Benjamin. He found there to be three hundred thousand fit young men who could serve in the army, bearing spear and shield. Then for 7,500 pounds of silver he hired one hundred thousand valiant warriors from Israel.

However, a man of God came to him and said, "King, do not let Israel's army go with you, for the LORD is not with Israel—all the Ephraimites. But if you go with them, do it! Be strong for battle! But God will make you stumble before the enemy, for God has the power to help or to make one stumble."

Then Amaziah said to the man of God, "What should I do about the 7,500 pounds of silver I gave to Israel's division?"

The man of God replied, "The LORD is able to give you much more than this."

20 So Amaziah released the division that came to him from Ephraim to go home. But they got very angry with Judah and returned home in a fierce rage.

Amaziah strengthened his position and led his people to the Salt Valley. He struck down ten thousand Seirites, and the Judahites captured ten thousand alive. They took them to the top of a cliff where they threw them off, and all of them were dashed to pieces.

As for the men of the division that Amaziah sent back so they would not go with him into battle, they raided the cities of Judah from Samaria to Beth-horon, struck down three thousand of their people, and took a great deal of plunder.

After Amaziah came from the attack on the Edomites, he brought the gods of the Seirites and set them up as his gods. He worshiped before them and burned incense to them. So the LORD's anger was against Amaziah, and he sent a prophet to him, who said, "Why have you sought a people's gods that could not rescue their own people from you?"

While he was still speaking to him, the king asked, "Have we made you the king's counselor? Stop, why should you lose your life?"

So the prophet stopped, but he said, "I know that God intends to destroy you, because you have done this and have not listened to my advice."

King Amaziah of Judah took counsel and sent word to Jehoash son of Jehoahaz, son of Jehu, king of Israel, and challenged him: "Come, let's meet face to face."

King Jehoash of Israel sent word to King Amaziah of Judah, saying, "The thistle in Lebanon sent a message to the cedar in Lebanon, saying, 'Give your daughter to my son as a wife.' Then a wild animal in Lebanon passed by and trampled the thistle. You have said, 'Look, I have defeated Edom,' and you have become overconfident that you will get glory. Now stay at home. Why stir up such trouble so that you fall and Judah with you?"

But Amaziah would not listen, for this turn of events was from God in order to hand them over to their enemies because they went after the gods of Edom. So King Jehoash of Israel advanced. He and King Amaziah of Judah met face to face at Beth-shemesh that belonged to Judah. Judah was routed before Israel, and each man fled to his own tent. King Jehoash of Israel captured Judah's King Amaziah son of Joash, son of Jehoahaz, at Beth-shemesh. Then Jehoash took him to Jerusalem and broke down two hundred yards of Jerusalem's wall from the Ephraim Gate to the Corner Gate. He took all the gold, silver, all the utensils that were found with Obed-edom in God's temple, the treasures of the king's palace, and the hostages. Then he returned to Samaria.

Judah's King Amaziah son of Joash lived fifteen years after the death of Israel's King Jehoash son of Jehoahaz. The rest of the events of Amaziah's reign, from beginning to end, are written in the Book of the Kings of Judah and Israel.

From the time Amaziah turned from following the LORD, a conspiracy was formed against him in Jerusalem, and he fled to Lachish. However, men were sent after him to Lachish, and they put him to death there. They carried him back on horses and buried him with his ancestors in the city of Judah.

26 All the people of Judah took Uzziah, who was sixteen years old, and made him king in place of his father Amaziah. After Amaziah the king rested with his ancestors, Uzziah rebuilt Eloth and restored it to Judah.

Uzziah was sixteen years old when he became king, and he reigned fifty-two years in Jerusalem. His mother's name was Jecoliah; she was from Jerusalem. He did what was right in the LORD's sight just as his father Amaziah had done. He sought God throughout the lifetime of Zechariah, the teacher of the fear of God. During the time that he sought the LORD, God gave him success.

Uzziah went out to wage war against the Philistines, and he tore down the wall of Gath, the wall of Jabneh, and the wall of Ashdod. Then he built cities in the vicinity of Ashdod and among the Philistines. God helped him against the Philistines, the Arabs that live in Gur-baal, and the Meunites. The Ammonites paid tribute to Uzziah, and his fame spread as far as the entrance of Egypt, for God made him very powerful. Uzziah built towers in Jerusalem at the Corner Gate, the Valley Gate, and the corner buttress, and he fortified them. Since he had many cattle both in the Judean foothills and the plain, he built towers in the desert and dug many wells. And since he was a lover of the soil, he had farmers and vinedressers in the hills and in the fertile lands.

Uzziah had an army equipped for combat that went out to war by division according to their assignments, as recorded by Jeiel the court secretary and Maaseiah the officer under the authority of Hananiah, one of the king's commanders. The total number of family heads was 2,600 valiant warriors. Under their authority was an army of 307,500 equipped for combat, a powerful force to help the king against the enemy. Uzziah provided the entire army with shields, spears, helmets, armor, bows, and slingstones. He made skillfully designed devices in Jerusalem to shoot arrows and catapult large stones for use on the towers and on the corners. So his fame spread even to distant places, for he was wondrously helped until he became strong.

But when he became strong, he grew arrogant, and it led to his own destruction. He acted unfaithfully against the LORD his God by going into the LORD's sanctuary to burn incense on the incense altar. The priest Azariah, along with eighty brave priests of the LORD, went in after him. They took their stand against King Uzziah and said, "Uzziah, you have no right to offer incense to the LORD—only the consecrated priests, the descendants of Aaron, have the right to offer incense. Leave the sanctuary, for you have acted unfaithfully! You will not receive honor from the LORD God."

Uzziah, with a firepan in his hand to offer incense, was enraged. But when he became enraged with the priests, in the presence of the priests in the LORD's temple beside the altar of incense, a skin disease broke out on his forehead. Then Azariah the chief priest and all the priests turned to him and saw that he was diseased on his forehead. They rushed him out of there. He himself also hurried to get out because the LORD had afflicted him. So King Uzziah was diseased to the time of his death. He lived in quarantine with a serious skin disease and was excluded from access to the LORD's temple, while his son Jotham was over the king's household governing the people of the land.

Now the prophet Isaiah son of Amoz wrote about the rest of the events of Uzziah's reign, from beginning to end. Uzziah rested with his ancestors, and he was buried with his ancestors in the burial ground of the kings' cemetery, for they said, "He has a skin disease." His son Jotham became
40 king in his place.

27 Jotham was twenty-five years old when he became king, and he reigned sixteen years in Jerusalem. His mother's name was Jerushah daughter of Zadok. He did what was right in the LORD's sight just as his father Uzziah had done. In addition, he didn't enter the LORD's sanctuary, but the people still behaved corruptly.

Jotham built the Upper Gate of the LORD's temple, and he built extensively on the wall of Ophel. He also built cities in the hill country of Judah and fortresses and towers in the forests. He waged war against the king of the Ammonites. He overpowered the Ammonites, and that year they gave him 7,500 pounds of silver, 60,000 bushels of wheat, and 60,000 bushels of barley. They paid him the same in the second and third years. So Jotham strengthened his position because he
10 did not waver in obeying the LORD his God.

As for the rest of the events of Jotham's reign, along with all his wars and his ways, note that they are written in the Book of the Kings of Israel and Judah. He was twenty-five years old when he became king, and he reigned sixteen years in Jerusalem. Jotham rested with his ancestors and was buried in the city of David. His son Ahaz became king in his place.

28 Ahaz was twenty years old when he became king, and he reigned sixteen years in Jerusalem. He did not do what was right in the LORD's sight like his ancestor David, for he walked in the ways of the kings of Israel and made cast images of the Baals. He burned incense in Ben Hinnom Valley and burned his children in the fire, imitating the detestable practices of the nations the LORD had dispossessed before the Israelites. He sacrificed and burned incense on the high places, on the hills, and under every green tree.

So the LORD his God handed Ahaz over to the king of Aram. He attacked him and took many captives to Damascus.

Ahaz was also handed over to the king of Israel, who struck him with great force: Pekah son
10 of Remaliah killed one hundred twenty thousand in Judah in one day—all brave men—because they had abandoned the LORD God of their ancestors. An Ephraimite warrior named Zichri killed the king's son Maaseiah, Azrikam governor of the palace, and Elkanah who was second to the king. Then the Israelites took two hundred thousand captives from their brothers—women, sons, and daughters. They also took a great deal of plunder from them and brought it to Samaria.

A prophet of the LORD named Oded was there. He went out to meet the army that came to Samaria and said to them, "Look, the LORD God of your ancestors handed them over to you because of his wrath against Judah, but you slaughtered them in a rage that has reached heaven.

Now you plan to reduce the people of Judah and Jerusalem, male and female, to slavery. Are you
20 not also guilty before the LORD your God? Listen to me and return the captives you took from
your brothers, for the LORD's burning anger is on you."

So some men who were leaders of the Ephraimites—Azariah son of Jehohanan, Berechiah
son of Meshillemoth, Jehizkiah son of Shallum, and Amasa son of Hadlai—stood in opposition
to those coming from the war. They said to them, "You must not bring the captives here, for you
plan to bring guilt on us from the LORD to add to our sins and our guilt. For we have much guilt,
and burning anger is on Israel."

The army left the captives and the plunder in the presence of the officers and the congregation.
Then the men who were designated by name took charge of the captives and provided clothes for
their naked ones from the plunder. They clothed them, gave them sandals, food and drink, dressed
their wounds, and provided donkeys for all the feeble. The Israelites brought them to Jericho, the
30 City of Palms, among their brothers. Then they returned to Samaria.

At that time King Ahaz asked the king of Assyria for help. The Edomites came again, attacked
Judah, and took captives. The Philistines also raided the cities of the Judean foothills and the
Negev of Judah. They captured and occupied Beth-shemesh, Aijalon, and Gederoth, as well as
Soco, Timnah, and Gimzo with their surrounding villages. For the LORD humbled Judah because
of King Ahaz of Judah, who threw off restraint in Judah and was unfaithful to the LORD. Then
King Tiglath-pileser of Assyria came against Ahaz; he oppressed him and did not give him
support. Although Ahaz plundered the LORD's temple and the palace of the king and of the rulers
and gave the plunder to the king of Assyria, it did not help him.

40 At the time of his distress, King Ahaz himself became more unfaithful to the LORD. He
sacrificed to the gods of Damascus which had defeated him; he said, "Since the gods of the kings
of Aram are helping them, I will sacrifice to them so that they will help me." But they were the
downfall of him and of all Israel.

Then Ahaz gathered up the utensils of God's temple, cut them into pieces, shut the doors of
the LORD's temple, and made himself altars on every street corner in Jerusalem. He made high
places in every city of Judah to offer incense to other gods, and he angered the LORD, the God of
his ancestors.

As for the rest of his deeds and all his ways, from beginning to end, they are written in the Book
of the Kings of Judah and Israel. Ahaz rested with his ancestors and was buried in the city, in
50 Jerusalem, but they did not bring him into the tombs of the kings of Israel. His son Hezekiah
became king in his place.

29 Hezekiah was twenty-five years old when he became king, and he reigned twenty-nine years in
Jerusalem. His mother's name was Abijah daughter of Zechariah. He did what was right in the
LORD's sight just as his ancestor David had done.

In the first year of his reign, in the first month, he opened the doors of the LORD's temple and repaired them. Then he brought in the priests and Levites and gathered them in the eastern public square. He said to them, "Hear me, Levites. Consecrate yourselves now and consecrate the temple of the LORD, the God of your ancestors. Remove everything impure from the holy place. For our ancestors were unfaithful and did what is evil in the sight of the LORD our God. They abandoned him, turned their faces away from the LORD's dwelling place, and turned their backs on him. They also closed the doors of the portico, extinguished the lamps, did not burn incense, and did not offer burnt offerings in the holy place of the God of Israel. Therefore, the wrath of the LORD was on Judah and Jerusalem, and he made them an object of terror, horror, and mockery, as you see with your own eyes. Our fathers fell by the sword, and our sons, our daughters, and our wives are in captivity because of this. It is in my heart now to make a covenant with the LORD, the God of Israel so that his burning anger may turn away from us. My sons, don't be negligent now, for the LORD has chosen you to stand in his presence, to serve him, and to be his ministers and burners of incense."

Then the Levites stood up:
>   Mahath son of Amasai and Joel son of Azariah from the Kohathites;
>   Kish son of Abdi and Azariah son of Jehallelel from the Merarites;
>   Joah son of Zimmah and Eden son of Joah from the Gershonites;
>   Shimri and Jeuel from the Elizaphanites;
>   Zechariah and Mattaniah from the Asaphites;
>   Jehiel and Shimei from the Hemanites;
>   Shemaiah and Uzziel from the Jeduthunites.

They gathered their brothers together, consecrated themselves, and went according to the king's command by the words of the LORD to cleanse the LORD's temple.

The priests went to the entrance of the LORD's temple to cleanse it. They took all the unclean things they found in the LORD's sanctuary to the courtyard of the LORD's temple. Then the Levites received them and took them outside to the Kidron Valley. They began the consecration on the first day of the first month, and on the eighth day of the month they came to the portico of the LORD's temple. They consecrated the LORD's temple for eight days, and on the sixteenth day of the first month they finished.

Then they went inside to King Hezekiah and said, "We have cleansed the whole temple of the LORD, the altar of burnt offering and all its utensils, and the table for the rows of the Bread of the Presence and all its utensils. We have set up and consecrated all the utensils that King Ahaz rejected during his reign when he became unfaithful. They are in front of the altar of the LORD."

King Hezekiah got up early, gathered the city officials, and went to the LORD's temple. They
40 brought seven bulls, seven rams, seven lambs, and seven male goats as a sin offering for the kingdom,
for the sanctuary, and for Judah. Then he told the descendants of Aaron, the priests, to offer them
on the altar of the LORD. So they slaughtered the bulls, and the priests received the blood and
splattered it on the altar. They slaughtered the rams and splattered the blood on the altar. They
slaughtered the lambs and splattered the blood on the altar. Then they brought the goats for the sin
offering right into the presence of the king and the congregation, who laid their hands on them. The
priests slaughtered the goats and put their blood on the altar for a sin offering, to make atonement
for all Israel, for the king said that the burnt offering and sin offering were for all Israel.

Hezekiah stationed the Levites in the LORD's temple with cymbals, harps, and lyres according
to the command of David, Gad the king's seer, and the prophet Nathan. For the command was
50 from the LORD through his prophets. The Levites stood with the instruments of David, and the
priests with the trumpets.

Then Hezekiah ordered that the burnt offering be offered on the altar. When the burnt
offerings began, the song of the LORD and the trumpets began, accompanied by the instruments
of King David of Israel. The whole assembly was worshiping, singing the song, and blowing the
trumpets—all this continued until the burnt offering was completed. When the burnt offerings
were completed, the king and all those present with him bowed down and worshiped. Then King
Hezekiah and the officials told the Levites to sing praise to the LORD in the words of David and of
the seer Asaph. So they sang praises with rejoicing and knelt low and worshiped.

Hezekiah concluded, "Now you are consecrated to the LORD. Come near and bring sacrifices
60 and thanksgiving offerings to the LORD's temple." So the congregation brought sacrifices and
thanksgiving offerings, and all those with willing hearts brought burnt offerings. The number of
burnt offerings the congregation brought was seventy bulls, one hundred rams, and two hundred
lambs; all these were for a burnt offering to the LORD. Six hundred bulls and three thousand sheep
and goats were consecrated.

However, since there were not enough priests, they weren't able to skin all the burnt offerings,
so their Levite brothers helped them until the work was finished and until the priests consecrated
themselves. For the Levites were more conscientious to consecrate themselves than the priests
were. Furthermore, the burnt offerings were abundant, along with the fat of the fellowship
offerings and with the drink offerings for the burnt offering.

70 So the service of the LORD's temple was established. Then Hezekiah and all the people rejoiced
over how God had prepared the people, for it had come about suddenly.

30 Then Hezekiah sent word throughout all Israel and Judah, and he also wrote letters to Ephraim
and Manasseh to come to the LORD's temple in Jerusalem to observe the Passover of the LORD,
the God of Israel. For the king and his officials and the entire congregation in Jerusalem decided to
observe the Passover of the LORD in the second month, because they were not able to observe it at

the appropriate time. Not enough of the priests had consecrated themselves, and the people hadn't been gathered together in Jerusalem. The proposal pleased the king and the congregation, so they affirmed the proposal and spread the message throughout all Israel, from Beer-sheba to Dan, to come to observe the Passover of the LORD, the God of Israel in Jerusalem, for they hadn't observed it often, as prescribed.

10 So the couriers went throughout Israel and Judah with letters from the hand of the king and his officials, and according to the king's command, saying, "Israelites, return to the LORD, the God of Abraham, Isaac, and Israel so that he may return to those of you who remain, who have escaped the grasp of the kings of Assyria. Don't be like your ancestors and your brothers who were unfaithful to the LORD, the God of their ancestors so that he made them an object of horror as you yourselves see. Don't become obstinate now like your ancestors did. Give your allegiance to the LORD, and come to his sanctuary that he has consecrated forever. Serve the LORD your God so that he may turn his burning anger away from you, for when you return to the LORD, your brothers and your sons will receive mercy in the presence of their captors and will return to this land. For the LORD your God is gracious and merciful; he will not turn his face away from you if

20 you return to him."

The couriers traveled from city to city in the land of Ephraim and Manasseh as far as Zebulun, but the inhabitants laughed at them and mocked them. But some from Asher, Manasseh, and Zebulun humbled themselves and came to Jerusalem. Also, the power of God was at work in Judah to unite them to carry out the command of the king and his officials by the word of the LORD.

A very large assembly of people was gathered in Jerusalem to observe the Festival of Unleavened Bread in the second month. They proceeded to take away the altars that were in Jerusalem, and they took away the incense altars and threw them into the Kidron Valley. They slaughtered the Passover lamb on the fourteenth day of the second month. The priests and Levites

30 were ashamed, and they consecrated themselves and brought burnt offerings to the LORD's temple. They stood at their prescribed posts, according to the law of Moses, the man of God. The priests splattered the blood received from the Levites, for there were many in the assembly who had not consecrated themselves, and so the Levites were in charge of slaughtering the Passover lambs for every unclean person to consecrate the lambs to the LORD. A large number of the people—many from Ephraim, Manasseh, Issachar, and Zebulun—were ritually unclean, yet they had eaten the Passover contrary to what was written. But Hezekiah had interceded for them, saying, "May the good LORD provide atonement on behalf of whoever sets his whole heart on seeking God, the LORD, the God of his ancestors, even though not according to the purification rules of the sanctuary." So the LORD heard Hezekiah and healed the people. The Israelites who were present

40 in Jerusalem observed the Festival of Unleavened Bread seven days with great joy, and the Levites and the priests praised the LORD day after day with loud instruments. Then Hezekiah encouraged all the Levites who performed skillfully before the LORD. They ate at the appointed festival

for seven days, sacrificing fellowship offerings and giving thanks to the LORD, the God of their ancestors.

The whole congregation decided to observe seven more days, so they observed seven days with joy, for King Hezekiah of Judah contributed one thousand bulls and seven thousand sheep for the congregation. Also, the officials contributed one thousand bulls and ten thousand sheep for the congregation, and many priests consecrated themselves. Then the whole assembly of Judah with the priests and Levites, the whole assembly that came from Israel, the resident aliens who came from the land of Israel, and those who were living in Judah, rejoiced. There was great rejoicing in Jerusalem, for nothing like this was known since the days of Solomon son of David, the king of Israel.

Then the priests and the Levites stood to bless the people, and God heard them, and their prayer came into his holy dwelling place in heaven.

31 When all this was completed, all Israel who had attended went out to the cities of Judah and broke up the sacred pillars, chopped down the Asherah poles, and tore down the high places and altars throughout Judah and Benjamin, as well as in Ephraim and Manasseh, to the last one. Then all the Israelites returned to their cities, each to his own possession.

Hezekiah reestablished the divisions of the priests and Levites for the burnt offerings and fellowship offerings, for ministry, for giving thanks, and for praise in the gates of the camp of the LORD, each division corresponding to his service among the priests and Levites. The king contributed from his own possessions for the regular morning and evening burnt offerings, the burnt offerings of the Sabbaths, of the New Moons, and of the appointed feasts, as written in the law of the LORD. He told the people who lived in Jerusalem to give a contribution for the priests and Levites so that they could devote their energy to the law of the LORD. When the word spread, the Israelites gave liberally of the best of the grain, new wine, fresh oil, honey, and of all the produce of the field, and they brought in an abundance, a tenth of everything. As for the Israelites and Judahites who lived in the cities of Judah, they also brought a tenth of the herds and flocks, and a tenth of the dedicated things that were consecrated to the LORD their God. They gathered them into large piles. In the third month they began building up the piles, and they finished in the seventh month. When Hezekiah and his officials came and viewed the piles, they blessed the LORD and his people Israel.

Hezekiah asked the priests and Levites about the piles. The chief priest Azariah, of the household of Zadok, answered him, "Since they began bringing the offering to the LORD's temple, we have been eating and are satisfied and there is plenty left over because the LORD has blessed his people; this abundance is what is left over."

Hezekiah told them to prepare chambers in the LORD's temple, and they prepared them. The offering, the tenth, and the dedicated things were brought faithfully. Conaniah the Levite was the officer in charge of them, and his brother Shimei was second. Jehiel, Azaziah, Nahath, Asahel, Jerimoth, Jozabad, Eliel, Ismachiah, Mahath, and Benaiah were deputies under the authority of

Conaniah and his brother Shimei by appointment of King Hezekiah and of Azariah the chief official of God's temple.

Kore son of Imnah the Levite, the keeper of the East Gate, was over the freewill offerings to God to distribute the contribution to the LORD and the consecrated things. Eden, Miniamin,
30 Jeshua, Shemaiah, Amariah, and Shecaniah in the cities of the priests were to distribute it faithfully under his authority to their brothers by divisions, whether large or small. In addition, they distributed it to males registered by genealogy three years old and above; to all who would enter the LORD's temple for their daily duty, for their service in their responsibilities according to their divisions. They distributed also to those recorded by genealogy of the priests by their ancestral families and the Levites twenty years old and above, by their responsibilities in their divisions; to those registered by genealogy—with all their dependents, wives, sons, and daughters—of the whole assembly (for they had faithfully consecrated themselves as holy); and to the descendants of Aaron, the priests, in the common fields of their cities, in each and every city. There were men who were registered by name to distribute a portion to every male among the
40 priests and to every Levite recorded by genealogy.

Hezekiah did this throughout all Judah. He did what was good and upright and true before the LORD his God. He was diligent in every deed that he began in the service of God's temple, in the instruction and the commands, in order to seek his God, and he prospered.

32 After Hezekiah's faithful deeds, King Sennacherib of Assyria came and entered Judah. He laid siege to the fortified cities and intended to break into them. Hezekiah saw that Sennacherib had come and that he planned war on Jerusalem, so he consulted with his officials and his warriors about stopping up the water of the springs that were outside the city, and they helped him. Many people gathered and stopped up all the springs and the stream that flowed through the land; they said, "Why should the kings of Assyria come and find abundant water?" Then Hezekiah strengthened his position by rebuilding the entire broken-down wall and heightening the towers and the other outside wall. He repaired the supporting terraces of the city of David, and made an abundance of weapons and shields.
10 He set military commanders over the people and gathered the people in the square of the city gate. Then he encouraged them, saying, "Be strong and courageous! Don't be afraid or discouraged before the king of Assyria or before the large army that is with him, for there are more with us than with him. He has only human strength, but we have the LORD our God to help us and to fight our battles." So the people relied on the words of King Hezekiah of Judah.

After this, while King Sennacherib of Assyria with all his armed forces besieged Lachish, he sent his servants to Jerusalem against King Hezekiah of Judah and against all those of Judah who were in Jerusalem, saying, "This is what King Sennacherib of Assyria says: 'What are you relying on that you remain in Jerusalem under siege? Isn't Hezekiah misleading you to give you over to death

by famine and thirst when he says, "The LORD our God will keep us from the grasp of the king
20   of Assyria"? Didn't Hezekiah himself remove his high places and his altars and say to Judah and
Jerusalem, "You must worship before one altar, and you must burn incense on it"?

"Don't you know what I and my predecessors have done to all the peoples of the lands? Have
any of the national gods of the lands been able to rescue their land from my power? Who among
all the gods of these nations that my predecessors completely destroyed was able to rescue his
people from my power, that your God should be able to deliver you from my power? So now,
don't let Hezekiah deceive you, and don't let him mislead you like this. Don't believe him, for no
god of any nation or kingdom has been able to rescue his people from my power or the power of
my predecessors. How much less will your God rescue you from my power!'"

His servants said more against the LORD God and against his servant Hezekiah. He also wrote
letters to mock the LORD, the God of Israel, saying against him:

30

> Just like the national gods of the lands that did not rescue their people from my power, so
> Hezekiah's God will not rescue his people from my power.

Then they called out loudly in Hebrew to the people of Jerusalem, who were on the wall, to
frighten and discourage them in order that he might capture the city. They spoke against the God
of Jerusalem like they had spoken against the gods of the peoples of the earth, which were made by
human hands.

King Hezekiah and the prophet Isaiah son of Amoz prayed about this and cried out to heaven,
and the LORD sent an angel who annihilated every valiant warrior, leader, and commander in the
camp of the king of Assyria. So the king of Assyria returned in disgrace to his land. He went to the
40   temple of his god, and there some of his own children struck him down with the sword.

So the LORD saved Hezekiah and the inhabitants of Jerusalem from the power of King
Sennacherib of Assyria and from the power of all others. He gave them rest on every side. Many
were bringing an offering to the LORD to Jerusalem and valuable gifts to King Hezekiah of Judah,
and he was exalted in the eyes of all the nations after that.

In those days Hezekiah became sick to the point of death, so he prayed to the LORD, who spoke
to him and gave him a miraculous sign. However, because his heart was proud, Hezekiah didn't
respond according to the benefit that had come to him. So there was wrath on him, Judah, and
Jerusalem. Then Hezekiah humbled himself for the pride of his heart—he and the inhabitants of
Jerusalem—so the LORD's wrath didn't come on them during Hezekiah's lifetime.

50   Hezekiah had abundant riches and glory, and he made himself treasuries for silver, gold,
precious stones, spices, shields, and every desirable item. He made warehouses for the harvest

of grain, new wine, and fresh oil, and stalls for all kinds of cattle, and pens for flocks. He made cities for himself, and he acquired vast numbers of flocks and herds, for God gave him abundant possessions.

This same Hezekiah blocked the upper outlet of the water from the Gihon Spring and channeled it smoothly downward and westward to the city of David. Hezekiah succeeded in everything he did. When the ambassadors of Babylon's rulers were sent to him to inquire about the miraculous sign that happened in the land, God left him to test him and discover what was in his heart.

60 As for the rest of the events of Hezekiah's reign and his deeds of faithful love, note that they are written in the Visions of the Prophet Isaiah son of Amoz, and in the Book of the Kings of Judah and Israel. Hezekiah rested with his ancestors and was buried on the ascent to the tombs of David's descendants. All Judah and the inhabitants of Jerusalem paid him honor at his death. His son Manasseh became king in his place.

33 Manasseh was twelve years old when he became king, and he reigned fifty-five years in Jerusalem. He did what was evil in the Lord's sight, imitating the detestable practices of the nations that the Lord had dispossessed before the Israelites. He rebuilt the high places that his father Hezekiah had torn down and reestablished the altars for the Baals. He made Asherah poles, and he bowed in worship to all the stars in the sky and served them. He built altars in the Lord's temple, where the Lord had said, "Jerusalem is where my name will remain forever." He built altars to all the stars in the sky in both courtyards of the Lord's temple. He passed his sons through the fire in Ben Hinnom Valley. He practiced witchcraft, divination, and sorcery, and consulted mediums and spiritists. He did a huge amount of evil in the Lord's sight, angering him.

10 Manasseh set up a carved image of the idol, which he had made, in God's temple that God had spoken about to David and his son Solomon: "I will establish my name forever in this temple and in Jerusalem, which I have chosen out of all the tribes of Israel. I will never again remove the feet of the Israelites from the land where I stationed your ancestors, if only they will be careful to do all I have commanded them through Moses—all the law, statutes, and judgments." So Manasseh caused Judah and the inhabitants of Jerusalem to stray so that they did worse evil than the nations the Lord had destroyed before the Israelites.

The Lord spoke to Manasseh and his people, but they didn't listen. So he brought against them the military commanders of the king of Assyria. They captured Manasseh with hooks, bound him with bronze shackles, and took him to Babylon. When he was in distress, he sought the favor of 20 the Lord his God and earnestly humbled himself before the God of his ancestors. He prayed to him, and the Lord was receptive to his prayer. He granted his request and brought him back to Jerusalem, to his kingdom. So Manasseh came to know that the Lord is God.

After this, he built the outer wall of the city of David from west of Gihon in the valley to the entrance of the Fish Gate; he brought it around Ophel, and he heightened it considerably. He also placed military commanders in all the fortified cities of Judah.

He removed the foreign gods and the idol from the LORD's temple, along with all the altars that he had built on the mountain of the LORD's temple and in Jerusalem, and he threw them outside the city. He built the altar of the LORD and offered fellowship and thanksgiving sacrifices on it. Then he told Judah to serve the LORD, the God of Israel. However, the people still sacrificed at 30 the high places, but only to the LORD their God.

The rest of the events of Manasseh's reign, along with his prayer to his God and the words of the seers who spoke to him in the name of the LORD, the God of Israel, are written in the Events of Israel's Kings. His prayer and how God was receptive to his prayer, and all his sin and unfaithfulness and the sites where he built high places and set up Asherah poles and carved images before he humbled himself, they are written in the Events of Hozai. Manasseh rested with his ancestors, and he was buried in his own house. His son Amon became king in his place.

Amon was twenty-two years old when he became king, and he reigned two years in Jerusalem. He did what was evil in the LORD's sight, just as his father Manasseh had done. Amon sacrificed to all the carved images that his father Manasseh had made, and he served them. But he did not humble himself 40 before the LORD like his father Manasseh humbled himself; instead, Amon increased his guilt.

So his servants conspired against him and put him to death in his own house. The common people killed all who had conspired against King Amon, and they made his son Josiah king in his place.

34 Josiah was eight years old when he became king, and he reigned thirty-one years in Jerusalem. He did what was right in the LORD's sight and walked in the ways of his ancestor David; he did not turn aside to the right or the left.

In the eighth year of his reign, while he was still a youth, Josiah began to seek the God of his ancestor David, and in the twelfth year he began to cleanse Judah and Jerusalem of the high places, the Asherah poles, the carved images, and the cast images. Then in his presence the altars of the Baals were torn down, and he chopped down the shrines that were above them. He shattered the Asherah poles, the carved images, and the cast images, crushed them to dust, and scattered them over the graves of those who had sacrificed to them. He burned the bones of the priests on their 10 altars. So he cleansed Judah and Jerusalem. He did the same in the cities of Manasseh, Ephraim, and Simeon, and as far as Naphtali and on their surrounding mountain shrines. He tore down the altars, and he smashed the Asherah poles and the carved images to powder. He chopped down all the shrines throughout the land of Israel and returned to Jerusalem.

In the eighteenth year of his reign, in order to cleanse the land and the temple, Josiah sent Shaphan son of Azaliah, along with Maaseiah the governor of the city and the court historian Joah son of Joahaz, to repair the temple of the Lord his God.

So they went to the high priest Hilkiah and gave him the silver brought into God's temple. The Levites and the doorkeepers had collected it from Manasseh, Ephraim, and from the entire remnant of Israel, and from all Judah, Benjamin, and the inhabitants of Jerusalem. They gave it to 20 those doing the work—those who oversaw the Lord's temple. They gave it to the workmen who were working in the Lord's temple, to repair and restore the temple; they gave it to the carpenters and builders and also used it to buy quarried stone and timbers—for joining and making beams—for the buildings that Judah's kings had destroyed.

The men were doing the work with integrity. Their overseers were Jahath and Obadiah, Levites from the Merarites, and Zechariah and Meshullam from the Kohathites as supervisors. The Levites were all skilled with musical instruments. They were also over the porters and were supervising all those doing the work task by task. Some of the Levites were secretaries, officers, and gatekeepers.

When they brought out the silver that had been deposited in the Lord's temple, the priest 30 Hilkiah found the book of the law of the Lord written by the hand of Moses. Consequently, Hilkiah told the court secretary Shaphan, "I have found the book of the law in the Lord's temple," and he gave the book to Shaphan.

Shaphan took the book to the king, and also reported, "Your servants are doing all that was placed in their hands. They have emptied out the silver that was found in the Lord's temple and have given it to the overseers and to those doing the work." Then the court secretary Shaphan told the king, "The priest Hilkiah gave me a book," and Shaphan read from it in the presence of the king.

When the king heard the words of the law, he tore his clothes. Then he commanded Hilkiah, Ahikam son of Shaphan, Abdon son of Micah, the court secretary Shaphan, and the king's servant Asaiah, "Go and inquire of the Lord for me and for those remaining in Israel and Judah, 40 concerning the words of the book that was found. For great is the Lord's wrath that is poured out on us because our ancestors have not kept the word of the Lord in order to do everything written in this book."

So Hilkiah and those the king had designated went to the prophetess Huldah, the wife of Shallum son of Tokhath, son of Hasrah, keeper of the wardrobe. She lived in Jerusalem in the Second District. They spoke with her about this.

She said to them, "This is what the Lord God of Israel says: Say to the man who sent you to me, 'This is what the Lord says: I am about to bring disaster on this place and on its inhabitants, fulfilling all the curses written in the book that they read in the presence of the king of Judah, because they have abandoned me and burned incense to other gods so as to anger me with all the

50 works of their hands. My wrath will be poured out on this place, and it will not be quenched.'
Say this to the king of Judah who sent you to inquire of the LORD: 'This is what the LORD God
of Israel says: As for the words that you heard, because your heart was tender and you humbled
yourself before God when you heard his words against this place and against its inhabitants, and
because you humbled yourself before me, and you tore your clothes and wept before me, I myself
have heard'—this is the LORD's declaration. 'I will indeed gather you to your ancestors, and you
will be gathered to your grave in peace. Your eyes will not see all the disaster that I am bringing on
this place and on its inhabitants.'"

Then they reported to the king.

So the king sent messengers and gathered all the elders of Judah and Jerusalem. The king went
60 up to the LORD's temple with all the men of Judah and the inhabitants of Jerusalem, as well as the
priests and the Levites—all the people from the oldest to the youngest. He read in their hearing all
the words of the book of the covenant that had been found in the LORD's temple. Then the king
stood at his post and made a covenant in the LORD's presence to follow the LORD and to keep his
commands, his decrees, and his statutes with all his heart and with all his soul in order to carry out
the words of the covenant written in this book.

He had all those present in Jerusalem and Benjamin agree to it. So all the inhabitants of
Jerusalem carried out the covenant of God, the God of their ancestors.

So Josiah removed everything that was detestable from all the lands belonging to the Israelites,
and he required all who were present in Israel to serve the LORD their God. Throughout his reign
70 they did not turn aside from following the LORD, the God of their ancestors.

35 Josiah observed the LORD's Passover and slaughtered the Passover lambs on the fourteenth day of
the first month. He appointed the priests to their responsibilities and encouraged them to serve in
the LORD's temple. He said to the Levites who taught all Israel the holy things of the LORD, "Put
the holy ark in the temple built by Solomon son of David king of Israel. Since you do not have to
carry it on your shoulders, now serve the LORD your God and his people Israel.

"Organize your ancestral families by your divisions according to the written instruction of
King David of Israel and that of his son Solomon. Serve in the holy place by the groupings of the
ancestral families for your brothers, the lay people, and according to the division of the Levites
by family. Slaughter the Passover lambs, consecrate yourselves, and make preparations for your
10 brothers to carry out the word of the LORD through Moses."

Then Josiah donated thirty thousand sheep, lambs, and young goats, plus three thousand cattle
from his own possessions, for the Passover sacrifices for all the lay people who were present.
His officials also donated willingly for the people, the priests, and the Levites. Hilkiah, Zechariah,
and Jehiel, chief officials of God's temple, gave twenty-six hundred Passover sacrifices and
three hundred cattle for the priests. Conaniah and his brothers Shemaiah and Nethanel, and

Hashabiah, Jeiel, and Jozabad, officers of the Levites, donated five thousand Passover sacrifices for the Levites, plus five hundred cattle.

So the service was established; the priests stood at their posts and the Levites in their divisions according to the king's command. Then they slaughtered the Passover lambs, and while the Levites were skinning the animals, the priests splattered the blood they had been given. They removed the burnt offerings so that they might be given to the groupings of the ancestral families of the lay people to offer to the LORD, according to what is written in the book of Moses; they did the same with the cattle. They roasted the Passover lambs with fire according to regulation. They boiled the holy sacrifices in pots, kettles, and bowls; and they quickly brought them to the lay people. Afterward, they made preparations for themselves and for the priests, since the priests, the descendants of Aaron, were busy offering up burnt offerings and fat until night. So the Levites made preparations for themselves and for the priests, the descendants of Aaron.

The singers, the descendants of Asaph, were at their stations according to the command of David, Asaph, Heman, and Jeduthun the king's seer. Also, the gatekeepers were at each temple gate. None of them left their tasks because their Levite brothers had made preparations for them.

So all the service of the LORD was established that day for observing the Passover and for offering burnt offerings on the altar of the LORD, according to the command of King Josiah. The Israelites who were present in Judah also observed the Passover at that time and the Festival of Unleavened Bread for seven days. No Passover had been observed like it in Israel since the days of the prophet Samuel. None of the kings of Israel ever observed a Passover like the one that Josiah observed with the priests, the Levites, all Judah, the Israelites who were present in Judah, and the inhabitants of Jerusalem. In the eighteenth year of Josiah's reign, this Passover was observed.

After all this that Josiah had prepared for the temple, King Neco of Egypt marched up to fight at Carchemish by the Euphrates, and Josiah went out to confront him. But Neco sent messengers to him, saying, "What is the issue between you and me, king of Judah? I have not come against you today but I am fighting another dynasty. God told me to hurry. Stop opposing God who is with me; don't make him destroy you!"

But Josiah did not turn away from him; instead, in order to fight with him he disguised himself. He did not listen to Neco's words from the mouth of God, but went to the Valley of Megiddo to fight. The archers shot King Josiah, and he said to his servants, "Take me away, for I am severely wounded!" So his servants took him out of the war chariot, carried him in his second chariot, and brought him to Jerusalem. Then he died, and they buried him in the tomb of his ancestors. All Judah and Jerusalem mourned for Josiah. Jeremiah chanted a dirge over Josiah, and all the male and female singers still speak of Josiah in their dirges today. They established them as a statute for Israel, and indeed they are written in the Dirges.

The rest of the events of Josiah's reign, along with his deeds of faithful love according to what is written in the law of the LORD, and his words, from beginning to end, are written in the Book of the Kings of Israel and Judah.

36 Then the common people took Jehoahaz son of Josiah and made him king in Jerusalem in place of his father.

Jehoahaz was twenty-three years old when he became king, and he reigned three months in Jerusalem. The king of Egypt deposed him in Jerusalem and fined the land seventy-five hundred pounds of silver and seventy-five pounds of gold.

Then King Neco of Egypt made Jehoahaz's brother Eliakim king over Judah and Jerusalem and changed Eliakim's name to Jehoiakim. But Neco took his brother Jehoahaz and brought him to Egypt.

Jehoiakim was twenty-five years old when he became king, and he reigned eleven years in
10 Jerusalem. He did what was evil in the sight of the LORD his God. Now King Nebuchadnezzar of Babylon attacked him and bound him in bronze shackles to take him to Babylon. Also Nebuchadnezzar took some of the articles of the LORD's temple to Babylon and put them in his temple in Babylon.

The rest of the deeds of Jehoiakim, the detestable actions he committed, and what was found against him, are written in the Book of Israel's Kings. His son Jehoiachin became king in his place.

Jehoiachin was eighteen years old when he became king, and he reigned three months and ten days in Jerusalem. He did what was evil in the LORD's sight. In the spring Nebuchadnezzar sent for him and brought him to Babylon along with the valuable articles of the LORD's temple. Then he made Jehoiachin's brother Zedekiah king over Judah and Jerusalem.

20 Zedekiah was twenty-one years old when he became king, and he reigned eleven years in Jerusalem. He did what was evil in the sight of the LORD his God and did not humble himself before the prophet Jeremiah at the LORD's command. He also rebelled against King Nebuchadnezzar who had made him swear allegiance by God. He became obstinate and hardened his heart against returning to the LORD, the God of Israel. All the leaders of the priests and the people multiplied their unfaithful deeds, imitating all the detestable practices of the nations, and they defiled the LORD's temple that he had consecrated in Jerusalem.

But the LORD, the God of their ancestors sent word against them by the hand of his messengers, sending them time and time again, for he had compassion on his people and on his dwelling place. But they kept ridiculing God's messengers, despising his words, and scoffing at his prophets, until
30 the LORD's wrath was so stirred up against his people that there was no remedy. So he brought

up against them the king of the Chaldeans, who killed their fit young men with the sword in the house of their sanctuary. He had no pity on young men or young women, elderly or aged; he handed them all over to him. He took everything to Babylon—all the articles of God's temple, large and small, the treasures of the LORD's temple, and the treasures of the king and his officials. Then the Chaldeans burned God's temple. They tore down Jerusalem's wall, burned all its palaces, and destroyed all its valuable articles.

He deported those who escaped from the sword to Babylon, and they became servants to him and his sons until the rise of the Persian kingdom. This fulfilled the word of the LORD through Jeremiah, and the land enjoyed its Sabbath rest all the days of the desolation until seventy years

40 were fulfilled.

In the first year of King Cyrus of Persia, in order to fulfill the word of the LORD spoken through Jeremiah, the LORD roused the spirit of King Cyrus of Persia to issue a proclamation throughout his entire kingdom and also to put it in writing:

> This is what King Cyrus of Persia says: The LORD, the God of the heavens, has given me all the kingdoms of the earth and has appointed me to build him a temple at Jerusalem in Judah. Any of his people among you may go up, and may the LORD his God be with him.

Acknowledgments

McGahan Publishing House CEO, Caleb Poston, and CCO, Duane Cross, would like to extend a special thanks to those who contributed to the successful completion of this project. First, we thank Joshua Stewart for stepping into the role of general editor, finding our group of excellent contributors, and seeing this project come to fruition. We also thank our associate editors, A. Lauren Brown and Jeffrey Audirsch, for their dedication and keen eye. We are indebted to the friendly, helpful people at Lifeway Christian Resources for always being ready to answer questions and guide us in the right direction. We thank Moore County High School students—Raylee Bateman, Reily Cross, and Ruby Jimenez—for their help in various areas of pre-publication. The helpful people at Core Publishing Solutions and Nord Compo helped us take this project to the next level. Finally, we thank Andrew Waters for cover design and David Brown for editing. Without all of these people, this ambitious project would not have been able to reach completion at the level of quality we believe it possesses. We know their work and support will help many Christians experience Scripture in a profound way for years to come.